Fortran 90/95
for Scientists and Engineers

First Edition

Stephen J. Chapman

British Aerospace Australia

WCB McGraw-Hill

**Boston, Massachusetts   Burr Ridge, Illinois
Dubuque, Iowa   Madison, Wisconsin   New York, New York
San Francisco, California   St. Louis, Missouri**

This book is dedicated to my wife Rosa, the great love of my life and the mother of our seven wonderful children.

WCB/McGraw-Hill

A Division of The McGraw·Hill Companies

FORTRAN 90/95 FOR SCIENTISTS AND ENGINEERS

This book is printed on acid-free paper.

4 5 6 7 8 9 0 DOC/DOC 9 0 9

ISBN 0-07-011938-4

Vice president and editorial director: *Kevin Kane*
Publisher: *Tom Casson*
Executive editor: *Eric Munson*
Marketing manager: *John Wannemacher*
Project manager: *Kari Geltemeyer*
Production supervisor: *Heather D. Burbridge*
Designer: *Kiera Cunningham*
Compositor: *York Graphic Services, Inc.*
Typeface: *10/12 Times Roman*
Printer: *R. R. Donnelley & Sons Company*

Library of Congress Cataloging-in-Publication Data

Chapman, Stephen J.
    Fortran 90/95 for scientists and engineers / Stephen J. Chapman.
        p.   cm.
    Includes index.
    ISBN 0-07-011938-4
    1. FORTRAN 90 (Computer program language)   2. FORTRAN 95 (Computer program language)   I. Title.
    QA76.73.F25C425   1998
    005.13′3–dc21   97–15699

http://www.mhhe.com

Stephen J. Chapman received a BS in Electrical Engineering from Louisiana State University (1975) and an MSE in Electrical Engineering from the University of Central Florida (1979), and pursued further graduate studies at Rice University.

From 1975 to 1980, he served as an officer in the U. S. Navy, assigned to teach Electrical Engineering at the U. S. Naval Nuclear Power School in Orlando, Florida. From 1980 to 1982, he was affiliated with the University of Houston, where he ran the power systems program in the College of Technology.

From 1982 to 1988 and from 1991 to 1995, he served as a Member of the Technical Staff of the Massachusetts Institute of Technology's Lincoln Laboratory, both at the main facility in Lexington, Massachusetts, and at the field site on Kwajalein Atoll in the Republic of the Marshall Islands. While there, he did research in radar signal processing systems. He ultimately became the leader of four large operational range instrumentation radars at the Kwajalein field site (TRADEX, ALTAIR, ALCOR, and MMW). Each of the four radars was controlled by large (100,000+ lines) real-time programs written largely in Fortran; the trials and tribulations associated with modifying those radar systems strongly influenced his views about proper design of Fortran programs.

From 1988 to 1991, Mr. Chapman was a research engineer in Shell Development Company in Houston, Texas, where he did seismic signal processing research. The research culminated in a number of large Fortran programs used to process seismic data. He was also affiliated with the University of Houston, where he continued to teach on a part-time basis.

Mr. Chapman is currently Manager of Technical Systems for British Aerospace Australia, in Melbourne, Australia. In this position, he provides technical direction for the work of younger engineers within the company. He is also continuing to teach at local universities on a part-time basis.

Mr. Chapman is a Senior Member of the Institute of Electrical and Electronic Engineers (and several of its component societies). He is also a member of the Association for Computing Machinery and the Institution of Engineers (Australia).

The book was conceived as a result of my experience writing and maintaining large Fortran programs in both the defense and geophysical fields and as a follow-up to my FORTRAN 77 book published by HarperCollins. During my time in industry, it became obvious that the strategies and techniques required to write large, *maintainable* Fortran programs were quite different from those that new engineers were learning in their Fortran programming classes at school. The incredible cost of maintaining and modifying large programs once they are placed into service absolutely demands that they be written to be easily understood and modified by people other than their original programmers. My goal for this book is to teach simultaneously both the fundamentals of the Fortran language and a programming style that results in good, maintainable programs. In addition, it is intended to serve as a reference for graduates working in industry.

It is quite difficult to teach undergraduates the importance of taking extra effort during the early stages of the program design process in order to make their programs more maintainable. Class programming assignments must by their very nature be simple enough for one person to complete in a short period of time, and the programs do not have to be maintained for years. Because the projects are simple, a student can often "wing it" and still produce working code. A student can take a course, perform all of the programming assignments, pass all of the tests, and still not learn the habits that are really needed when working on large projects in industry.

From the very beginning this book teaches Fortran in a style suitable for use on large projects. It emphasizes the importance of going through a detailed design process before any code is written, using a top-down design technique to break the program into logical portions that can be implemented separately. It stresses the use of procedures to implement those individual portions and the importance of unit testing before combining the procedures into a finished product. Finally, it emphasizes the importance of exhaustively testing the finished program with many different input data sets before releasing it for use.

In addition, this book teaches Fortran as it is actually encountered by engineers and scientists working in industry and in laboratories. Two facts of life are common in all programming environments: large amounts of old legacy code that have to be maintained and the existence of subroutine libraries to make some programming tasks easier. The legacy code at a particular site may have been originally written in

FORTRAN IV (or an even earlier version!), and it may use programming constructs that are no longer common today. For example, such code may use arithmetic IF statements, or computed or assigned GO TO statements. Chapter 14 is devoted to the older features of the language that are no longer in common use, but are encountered in legacy code. The chapter emphasizes that these features should *never* be used in a new program but also prepares the student to handle them when he or she encounters them.

Similarly, Chapter 13 prepares the student to use Fortran libraries. It teaches the student about the types of libraries available and about how to select and interface with a particular procedure from a library. It introduces commonly used mathematical libraries such as the NAG Library, the IMSL Library, and the LAPACK Library. Both a small subset of the LAPACK Library and a small library called BOOKLIB are supplied for use with this book. These libraries are used in Chapter 13 to teach the student to use library indexes, to read manual pages, and to interface with library procedures.

FEATURES OF THIS BOOK

Many features of this book are designed to emphasize the proper way to write reliable Fortran programs. These features should serve a student well as he or she is first learning Fortran and should also be useful to the practitioner on the job.

Emphasis on Modern Fortran 90/95

The book consistently teaches the best current practice in all of its examples. Many Fortran 90/95 features duplicate and supersede older features of the Fortran language. In those cases the proper usage of the modern language is presented. Examples of older usage are largely relegated to Chapter 14 where their old/undesirable nature is emphasized. Examples of Fortran 90/95 features that supersede older features are the use of modules to share data instead of COMMON blocks, the use of DO ... END DO loops instead of DO ... CONTINUE loops, the use of internal procedures instead of statement functions, and the use of CASE constructs instead of computed GO TOs.

Emphasis on Strong Typing

The IMPLICIT NONE statement is used consistently throughout the book to force the explicit typing of every variable used in every program and to catch common typographical errors at compilation time. In conjunction with the explicit declaration of every variable in a program, the book emphasizes the importance of creating a data dictionary that describes the purpose of each variable in a program unit.

Emphasis on Top-Down Design Methodology

The book introduces a top-down design methodology in Chapter 3 and then uses it consistently throughout the rest of the book. This methodology encourages a student to think about the proper design of a program *before* beginning to code. It emphasizes the importance of clearly defining the problem to be solved and the required inputs and outputs before beginning any other work. Once the problem is properly defined, the book teaches the student to employ stepwise refinement to break the task down into successively smaller subtasks and to implement the subtasks as separate subroutines or functions. Finally, it teaches the importance of testing at all stages of the process, both unit testing of the component routines and exhaustive testing of the final product. Several examples are given of programs that work properly for some data sets and then fail for others.

The formal design process taught by the book may be summarized as follows:

1. *Clearly state the problem that you are trying to solve.*
2. *Define the inputs required by the program and the outputs to be produced by the program.*
3. *Describe the algorithm that you intend to implement in the program.* This step involves top-down design and stepwise decomposition, using pseudocode or flow charts.
4. *Turn the algorithm into Fortran statements.*
5. *Test the Fortran program.* This step includes unit testing of specific subprograms and also exhaustive testing of the final program with many different data sets.

Emphasis on Procedures

The book emphasizes the use of subroutines and functions to logically decompose tasks into smaller subtasks. It teaches the advantages of procedures for data hiding. It also emphasizes the importance of unit testing procedures before they are combined into the final program. In addition, the book explains how to avoid the common mistakes made with procedures (argument type mismatches, array length mismatches, etc.). It emphasizes the advantages associated with explicit interfaces to procedures, which allow the Fortran compiler to catch most common programming errors at compilation time.

Libraries

The book introduces the concept of Fortran libraries to the student. It teaches the student about the types of libraries available and about how to select and interface with a particular procedure from a library. It introduces commonly used mathematical libraries such as the NAG Library, the IMSL Library, and the LAPACK Library. Both a small subset of the LAPACK Library and a small library called BOOKLIB are included with the instructor's manual that accompanies this book and are available for downloading at the book's World Wide Web site. Documentation for the libraries is available from the same sources. These sample libraries are used in Chapter 13 to teach the student how to use library indexes, to read manual pages, and to interface with library procedures.

Emphasis on Portability and Standard Fortran 90/95

The book stresses the importance of writing portable Fortran code so that a program can easily be moved from one type of computer to another one. It teaches students to use only standard Fortran 90/95 statements in their programs so that they will be as portable as possible. In addition, it teaches the use of features such as the SELECTED_REAL_KIND function to avoid precision and kind differences when moving from computer to computer and the ACHAR and IACHAR functions to avoid problems when moving from ASCII to EBCDIC computers.

The book also teaches students to isolate machine-dependent code (such as code that calls machine-dependent system libraries) into a few specific procedures so that only those procedures will have to be rewritten when a program is ported between computers.

Good Programming Practice Boxes

These boxes highlight good programming practices when they are introduced. In addition, the good programming practices introduced in a chapter are summarized at the end of the chapter. A sample Good Programming Practice box is shown below.

> ***Good Programming Practice***
> Always indent the body of an IF structure by two or more spaces to improve the readability of the code.

Programming Pitfalls Boxes

These boxes highlight common errors so that they can be avoided. A sample Programming Pitfalls box is shown below.

> ***Programming Pitfalls***
> Beware of integer arithmetic. Integer division often gives unexpected results.

Fortran 95-only Features

Fortran 95-only features are distinguished by a special background. An example of a Fortran 95-only feature is shown below.

> Fortran 95 provides an intrinsic function NULL() that can be used to nullify a pointer at the time it is declared (or at any time during the execution of a program). In Fortran 95, pointers can be declared and nullified as follows:
>
> ```
> REAL, POINTER :: p1 = NULL(), p2 = NULL()
> INTEGER, POINTER :: i1 = NULL()
> ...
> (additional specification statements)
> ```
>
> The details of the NULL() function are described in Appendix B.

Emphasis on the Limits of Computer Mathematics

Chapters 8 and 12 introduce problems associated with the limited precision of computer mathematics and discuss ways to avoid them. In the discussion of double-precision real data in Chapter 8, the book introduces ill-conditioned systems of equations and shows how the limited precision of computer mathematics can lead to incorrect answers even though the algorithm being used is correct. It then provides guidelines for using the double-precision real data type to avoid these problems.

Chapter 12 is an introduction to numerical methods. It expands on the material in Chapter 8 to discuss truncation and rounding errors, errors caused by the subtraction of nearly equal numbers, cascading errors, and errors associated with incorrect models. The examples in the chapter include higher-order least-squares fits, numerical integration, and finding the roots of equations. Examples of numerical methods from other chapters include random number generators, statistical subroutines, sorting, solving simultaneous equations, and taking derivatives.

Emphasis on Pointers and Dynamic Data Structures

Chapter 11 contains a detailed discussion of Fortran pointers, including possible problems resulting from the incorrect use of pointers, such as memory leaks and pointers to deallocated memory. Examples of dynamic data structures in the chapter include linked lists and binary trees.

Sidebars

Sidebars scattered throughout the book provide additional information of potential interest to the student. Some sidebars are historical in nature. For example, one sidebar in Chapter 1 describes the IBM Model 704, the first computer to ever run Fortran. Other sidebars reinforce lessons from the main text. For example, Chapter 6 contains a sidebar reviewing and summarizing the many different types of arrays found in Fortran 90/95.

Completeness

Finally, the book endeavors to be a complete reference to the Fortran 90/95 language so that a practitioner can locate any required information quickly. Special attention has been paid to the index to make features easy to find. A special effort has also been made to cover such obscure and little-understood features as passing subprogram names by reference and defaulting values in list-directed input statements.

PEDAGOGICAL FEATURES

The book includes several features designed to aid student comprehension. A total of 20 quizzes are scattered throughout the chapters; answers to all questions appear in Appendix E. These quizzes can serve as useful self-tests of comprehension. In addition, there are approximately 310 end-of-chapter exercises. Answers to selected exercises are available at the book's Web site, and of course, answers to all exercises are included in the instructor's manual. Good programming practices are highlighted in all chapters with special Good Programming Practice boxes, and common errors are highlighted in Programming Pitfalls boxes. End-of-chapter materials include summaries of the Good Programming Practice boxes and summaries of Fortran statements and structures. Finally, a detailed description of every Fortran 90/95 intrinsic procedure is included in Appendix B, and an extensive glossary appears as Appendix D.

A very important pedagogical feature of the book is the LAPACK subset library and the `BOOKLIB` library, which are supplied on a diskette that accompanies the instructor's manual and are available for download at the book's Web site http://www.mhhe.com/engineering/chapman. The instructor can compile and install these libraries on whatever computer is being used to teach Fortran, and the students can use them to learn how to choose and link to library subroutines.

The book is accompanied by an instructor's manual, containing the solutions to all end-of-chapter exercises and the descriptions of the LAPACK subset and `BOOKLIB` libraries. The instructor's manual comes with a floppy disk containing the source code for all examples in the book, all end-of-chapter exercises, the LAPACK subset library and `BOOKLIB` library, and a few useful utilities such as one to convert a fixed-source form program to free form.

A BRIEF NOTE ABOUT FORTRAN COMPILERS

Three Fortran 90 compilers were used during the preparation of this book: the Lahey Fortran 90 compiler, the Microsoft Fortran Powerstation version 4.0, and NAGWare Fortran 90 compiler. After this book was in production, Microsoft dropped all of its Fortran products, and all future development of the product was taken over by Digital Equipment Corporation (DEC). Therefore, any reference to Microsoft Fortran in this book may be considered a reference to DEC Fortran.

References to all three compiler vendors may be found at this book's World Wide Web site.

A FINAL NOTE TO THE USER

No matter how hard I try to proofread a document like this book, it is inevitable that some typographical errors will slip through and appear in print. If you should spot any such errors, please drop me a note via the publisher, and I will do my best to get them eliminated from subsequent printings and editions. Thank you very much for your help in this matter.

I will maintain a complete list of errata and corrections at the book's World Wide Web site, which is http://www.mhhe.com/engineering/chapman. Please check that site for any updates and/or corrections.

ACKNOWLEDGMENTS

I would like to thank Mr. Bob Runyan of Lahey Computer Systems, Inc., for providing me with copies of Lahey's Fortran 90 compiler to use while developing this book. Lahey was also kind enough to allow the readers of this book to purchase its ELF90 compiler at a discount. I would like to thank Mr. Sunil Alagade of Microsoft Corporation for providing me with a copy of Microsoft Fortran Powerstation 4.0 Professional, and Ms. Margaret Day of NAG, Ltd., for providing me with a copy of the NAGWare Fortran 90 compiler. I have been able to ensure that every example is compatible with all three compilers.

I would especially like to thank Eric Munson and the staff at McGraw-Hill for publishing this book after the project was dropped when my previous publisher was purchased by Addison-Wesley.

Finally, I would like to thank my wife Rosa and our children Avi, David, Rachel, Aaron, Sarah, Naomi, and Shira for putting up with me during the two years it took me to finish this book. Sometimes it seemed that it would never end. Maybe we'll see more of each other now!

Stephen J. Chapman
Adelaide, South Australia
September 24, 1996

Introduction to Computers and the Fortran Language

The computer is the most important invention of the 20th century. It affects our lives profoundly in very many ways. When we go to the grocery store, computers run the scanners that check out our groceries. Computers maintain our bank balances and run the automatic teller machines that allow us to make banking transactions at any time of the day or night. Computers control our telephone and electric power systems, run our microwave ovens and other appliances, and even control the engines in our cars. Almost any business in the developed world would collapse overnight if it were suddenly deprived of its computers. Considering their importance in our lives, it is almost impossible to believe that the first electronic computers were invented just over 50 years ago.

Just what is this device that has had such an impact on all of our lives? A **computer** is a special type of machine that stores information and performs mathematical calculations on that information at speeds much faster than human beings can think. A **program,** which is stored in the computer's memory, tells the computer what sequence of calculations are required and which information to perform the calculations on. Most computers are very flexible. For example, the computer on which I wrote these words can also balance my checkbook if I load a different program.

Computers can store huge amounts of information, and with proper programming they can make that information instantly available when it is needed. For example, a bank's computer can hold the complete list of all the checks and deposits made by every one of its customers. On a larger scale, credit companies use their computers to hold the credit histories of every person in the United States—literally billions of pieces of information. When requested, they can search through those billions of pieces of information to recover the credit records of any single person and present those records to the user in a matter of seconds.

It is important to realize that *computers do not think as we understand thinking;* they merely follow the steps contained in their programs. When a computer appears to be doing something clever, it is because a clever person has written the program that it is executing. The collective creativity of humans allows the computer to perform its "miracles." This book will help you learn how to write programs of your own so that the computer will do what *you* want it to do.

■ 1.1

THE COMPUTER

A block diagram of a typical computer is shown in Figure 1–1, and a photograph of a typical personal computer is shown in Figure 1–2. The major components of the computer are the **central processing unit (CPU), main memory, secondary memory,** and **input** and **output devices.** These components are described in the following paragraphs.

1.1.1 The CPU

The central processing unit is the heart of any computer. It is divided into a *control unit,* an *arithmetic-logic unit* (ALU), and internal memory. The control unit within the CPU controls all the other parts of the computer, and the ALU performs the actual mathematical calculations. The internal memory within a CPU consists of a series of *memory registers* used for the temporary storage of intermediate results during calculations.

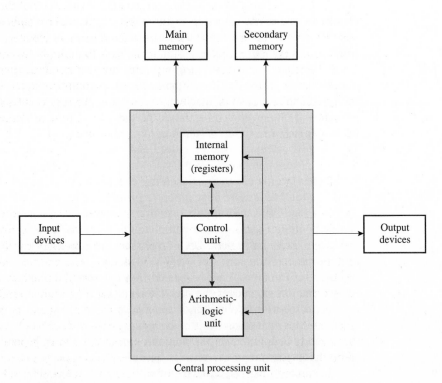

FIGURE 1–1
A block diagram of a typical computer.

FIGURE 1–2
A typical personal computer. *(Courtesy of Gateway 2000.*
Copyright © 1996, Gateway 2000, Inc. All rights reserved.)

The control unit of the CPU interprets the instructions of the computer program. It also fetches data values from input devices or main memory, stores them in the memory registers, and sends data values from memory registers to output devices or main memory. For example, if a program says to multiply two numbers together and save the result, the control unit will fetch the two numbers from main memory and store them in registers. Then it will present the numbers in the registers to the ALU along with directions to multiply them and store the results in another register. Finally, after the ALU multiplies the numbers, the control unit will take the result from the destination register and store it back into main memory.

1.1.2 Main and Secondary Memory

A computer has two major types of memory: *main* or *primary memory,* and *secondary memory.* Main memory usually consists of semiconductor chips. It is very fast and relatively expensive. Data that is stored in main memory can be fetched for use in 100 nanoseconds or less (sometimes *much* less) on a modern computer. Because it is so fast, main memory is used to temporarily store the program currently being executed by the computer, as well as the data that the program requires.

Main memory is not used for the permanent storage of programs or data. Most main memory is *volatile,* meaning that it is erased whenever the computer's power is turned off. Besides, main memory is expensive, so most people buy only enough to hold the largest programs actually being executed at any given time.

Secondary memory consists of devices that are slower and less expensive than main memory. They can store much more information for much less money than main memory can. In addition, most secondary memory devices are *nonvolatile,* meaning that they retain the programs and data stored in them whenever the computer's power is turned off. Typical secondary memory devices are *hard disks, floppy disks,* and tape drives. Secondary storage devices are normally used to store programs and data that are not needed at the moment, but which may be needed some time in the future.

1.1.3 Input and Output Devices

Data is entered into a computer through an input device and is output through an output device. The most common input device on a modern computer is a keyboard. Using a keyboard, we can type programs or data into a computer. Other types of input devices are scanners and microphones.

Output devices permit us to use the data stored in a computer. The most common output devices on today's computers are CRT screens and printers. Other types of output devices include plotters and speakers.

1.2
DATA REPRESENTATION IN A COMPUTER

Computer memories are composed of millions of individual switches, each of which can be ON or OFF, but not at a state in between. Each switch represents one **binary digit** (also called a **bit**); the ON state is interpreted as a binary 1, and the OFF state is interpreted as a binary 0. Taken by itself, a single switch can represent only the numbers 0 and 1. Since we obviously need to work with numbers other than 0 and 1, a number of bits are grouped together to represent each number used in a computer. When several bits are grouped together, they can be used to represent numbers in the *binary* (base 2) *number system.*

The smallest common grouping of bits is called a **byte.** A *byte* is a group of 8 bits that are used together to represent a binary number. The byte is the fundamental unit used to measure the capacity of a computer's memory. For example, my personal computer has a main memory of 28 megabytes (28,000,000 bytes) and a secondary memory (disk drive) with a storage capacity of 825 megabytes.

The next larger grouping of bits in a computer is a **word.** A word consists of 2, 4, or more consecutive bytes that are used to represent a single number in memory. The size of a word varies from computer to computer, so words are not a particularly good way to judge the size of computer memories.

1.2.1 The Binary Number System

In the familiar base 10 number system, the smallest (right most) digit of a number is the one's place (10^0). The next digit is in the ten's place (10^1), and the next one is in the hundred's place (10^2), etc. Thus the number 122_{10} is really $(1 \times 10^2) + (2 \times 10^1) + (2 \times 10^0)$. Each digit is worth a power of 10 more than the digit to the right of it in the base 10 system (see Figure 1–3*a*).

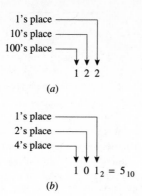

1's place ————
10's place ————
100's place ————

1 2 2

(a)

FIGURE 1–3
(a) The base 10 number 122 is really $(1 \times 10^2) + (2 \times 10^1) + (2 \times 10^0)$. (b) Similarly, the base 2 number 101_2 is really $(1 \times 2^2) + (0 \times 2^1) + (1 \times 2^0)$.

1's place ————
2's place ————
4's place ————

$1\ 0\ 1_2 = 5_{10}$

(b)

Similarly, in the binary number system, the smallest (right most) digit is the one's place (2^0). The next digit is in the two's place (2^1), and the next one is in the four's place (2^2), etc. Each digit is worth a power of two more than the digit to the right of it in the base 2 system. For example, the binary number 101_2 is really $(1 \times 2^2) + (0 \times 2^1) + (1 \times 2^0) = 5$, and the binary number $111_2 = 7$ (see Figure 1–3b).

Note that three binary digits can be used to represent eight possible values: 0 $(= 000_2)$ to 7 $(= 111_2)$. In general, if n bits are grouped together to form a binary number, then they can represent 2^n possible values. Thus a group of 8 bits (1 byte) can represent 256 possible values, a group of 16 bits (2 bytes) can be used to represent 65,536 possible values, and a group of 32 bits (4 bytes) can be used to represent 4,294,967,296 possible values.

In a typical implementation, half of all possible values are reserved for representing negative numbers, and half of the values are reserved for representing positive numbers. Thus a group of 8 bits (1 byte) is usually used to represent numbers between -128 and $+127$, inclusive, and a group of 16 bits (2 bytes) is usually used to represent numbers between $-32,768$ and $+32,767$, inclusive.[1]

1.2.2 Octal and Hexadecimal Representations of Binary Numbers

Computers work in the binary number system, but people think in the decimal number system. Fortunately, we can program the computer to accept inputs and give its outputs in the decimal system, converting them internally to binary form for processing. Most of the time, the fact that computers work with binary numbers is irrelevant to the programmer.

However, there are some cases in which a scientist or engineer has to work directly with the binary representations coded into the computer. For example, individual bits or groups of bits within a word might contain status information about the

---

[1]There are several different schemes for representing negative numbers in a computer's memory. They are described in any good computer engineering textbook. The most common scheme is the so-called *two's-complement* representation, which is described in the sidebar.

1

Two's-Complement Arithmetic

The most common way to represent negative numbers in the binary number system is the two's-complement representation. What is two's complement, and what is so special about it? Let's find out.

The Two's-Complement Representation of Negative Numbers

In the two's-complement representation, the leftmost bit of a number is the *sign bit*. If that bit is 0, then the number is positive; if it is 1, then the number is negative. To change a positive number into the corresponding negative number in the two's-complement system, we perform two steps:

1. Complement the number (change all 1s to 0 and all 0s to 1).
2. Add 1 to the complemented number.

Let's illustrate the process using simple 8-bit integers. As you already know, the 8-bit binary representation of the number 3 would be 00000011. The two's-complement representation of the number −3 would be found as follows:

1. Complement the positive number: 11111100
2. Add 1 to the complemented number: 11111100 + 1 = 11111101

Exactly the same process is used to convert negative numbers back to positive numbers. To convert the number −3 (11111101) back to a positive 3, perform the following steps:

1. Complement the negative number: 00000010
2. Add 1 to the complemented number: 00000010 + 1 = 00000011

Two's-Complement Arithmetic

Now you know how to represent numbers in two's-complement representation and how to convert between positive and two's-complement negative numbers. The special advantage of two's-complement arithmetic is that positive and negative numbers may be added together according to the rules of ordinary addition without regard to the sign, and the resulting answer will be correct, including the proper sign. Consequently, a computer may add any two integers together without checking their signs. This process simplifies the design of computer circuits.

The following examples illustrate this point:

1. Add 3 + 4 in two's-complement arithmetic.

$$
\begin{array}{rl}
3 & \quad 00000011 \\
+\,4 & \quad 00000100 \\
\hline
7 & \quad 00000111
\end{array}
$$

2. Add (−3) + (−4) in two's-complement arithmetic.

$$
\begin{array}{rl}
-3 & \quad 11111101 \\
+\,-4 & \quad 11111100 \\
\hline
-7 & \quad 111111001
\end{array}
$$

In a case like this, we ignore the extra 9th bit resulting from the sum, and the answer is 11111001. The two's complement of 11111001 is 00000111 or 7, so the result of the addition was −7!

3. Add 3 + (−4) in two's-complement arithmetic.

$$
\begin{array}{rl}
3 & \quad 00000011 \\
+\,-4 & \quad 11111100 \\
\hline
-1 & \quad 11111111
\end{array}
$$

The answer is 11111111. The two's complement of 11111111 is 00000001 or 1, so the result of the addition was −1!

With two's-complement numbers, binary addition comes up with the correct answer regardless of whether the numbers being added are both positive, both negative, or mixed.

operation of some machine. If so, the programmer will have to consider the individual bits of the word, and work in the binary number system.

A scientist or engineer who has to work in the binary number system immediately faces the problem that binary numbers are unwieldy. For example, a number like 1100_{10} in the decimal system is 010001001100_2 in the binary system. It is easy to get lost working with such a number! To avoid this problem, we customarily break binary numbers down into groups of 3 or 4 bits and represent those bits by a single base 8 (octal) or base 16 (hexadecimal) number.

To understand this idea, note that a group of 3 bits can represent any number between 0 ($= 000_2$) and 7 ($= 111_2$). These are the numbers found in an **octal** or base 8 arithmetic system. An octal number system has seven digits: 0 through 7. We can break a binary number up into groups of 3 bits, and substitute the appropriate octal digit for each group. Let's use the number 010001001100_2 as an example. Breaking the number into groups of three digits yields $010|001|001|100_2$. If each group of 3 bits is replaced by the appropriate octal number, the value can be written as 2114_8. The octal number represents exactly the same pattern of bits as the binary number, but it is more compact.

Similarly, a group of 4 bits can represent any number between 0 ($= 0000_2$) and 15 ($= 1111_2$). These are the numbers found in a **hexadecimal** or base 16 arithmetic system. A hexadecimal number system has 16 digits: 0 through 9 and A through F. Since the hexadecimal system needs 16 digits, we use digits 0 through 9 for the first 10 of them and then letters A through F for the remaining 6. Thus, $9_{16} = 9_{10}$; $A_{16} = 10_{10}$; $B_{16} = 11_{10}$; and so forth. We can break a binary number up into groups of 4 bits and substitute the appropriate hexadecimal digit for each group. Let's use the number 010001001100_2 again as an example. Breaking the number into groups of four digits yields $0100|0100|1100_2$. If each group of 4 bits is replaced by the appropriate hexadecimal number, the value can be written as $44C_{16}$. The hexadecimal number represents exactly the same pattern of bits as the binary number but does so more compactly.

Some computer vendors prefer to use octal numbers to represent bit patterns, while other computer vendors prefer to use hexadecimal numbers to represent bit patterns. Both representations are equivalent in that they represent the pattern of bits in a compact form. A Fortran language program can input or output numbers in any of the four formats (decimal, binary, octal, or hexadecimal). Table 1–1 lists the decimal, binary, octal, and hexadecimal forms of the numbers from 1 to 16.

1.2.3 Types of Data Stored in Memory

Three common types of data are stored in a computer's memory: *character data, integer data,* and *real data* (numbers with a decimal point). Each type of data has different characteristics and takes up a different amount of memory in the computer.

Character data

The **character data** type consists of characters and symbols. A typical system for representing character data in a non-Oriental language must include the following symbols:

• The 26 uppercase letters 'A' through 'Z'.
• The 26 lowercase letters 'a' through 'z'.
• The 10 digits '0' through '9'.
• Miscellaneous common symbols, such as ",(){}[]!~@#$%^&*.
• Any special letters or symbols required by the language, such as à ç ë £.

1

TABLE 1–1
Table of decimal, binary, octal, and hexadecimal numbers

Decimal	Binary	Octal	Hexadecimal
0	0000	0	0
1	0001	1	1
2	0010	2	2
3	0011	3	3
4	0100	4	4
5	0101	5	5
6	0110	6	6
7	0111	7	7
8	1000	10	8
9	1001	11	9
10	1010	12	A
11	1011	13	B
12	1100	14	C
13	1101	15	D
14	1110	16	E
15	1111	17	F

Since the total number of characters and symbols required to write non-Oriental languages is less than 256, it is customary to use 1 byte of memory to store each character. Therefore, 10,000 characters would occupy 10,000 bytes of the computer's memory.

The particular bit values corresponding to each letter or symbol may vary from computer to computer, depending upon the coding system used for the characters. Two systems are commonly used. The most important coding system is ASCII, which stands for the American Standard Code for Information Interchange (ANSI X3.4 1977). Most computer manufacturers use the ASCII coding system. The other popular system is EBCDIC, which stands for Extended Binary Coded Decimal Interchange Code. IBM uses EBCDIC on its mainframe computers. You can find the 8-bit codes corresponding to each letter and number in these coding systems in Appendix A.

Many countries outside the United States use an international version of the ASCII character set, known as the ISO 646 standard. It is the same as ASCII except that 10 specific characters may be replaced with the extra symbols needed in a particular country, such as £, å, ñ, and ø. This character set can create problems when a program is moved from one country to another, because some symbols will change, and printed information might become corrupted.

Some Oriental languages such as Chinese and Japanese contain more than 256 characters. (In fact, each of these languages requires about 4000 characters.) To accommodate these languages and all of the other languages in the world, a new coding system called *Unicode* has been developed. In the Unicode coding system, each character is stored in 2 bytes of memory, so the Unicode system supports 65,536 possible different characters. The first 128 Unicode characters are identical to the ASCII character set, and other blocks of characters are devoted to various languages such as Chinese, Japanese, Hebrew, Arabic, and Hindi. When the Unicode coding system is used, character data can be represented in any language.

Integer data

The **integer data** type consists of the positive integers, the negative integers, and zero. The amount of memory devoted to storing an integer will vary from computer to computer, but it will usually be 1, 2, 4, or 8 bytes. The most common type of integers in modern computers are 4-byte integers.

Since a finite number of bits are used to store each value, only integers that fall within a certain range can be represented on a computer. Usually, the smallest number that can be stored in an n-bit integer is

$$\text{Smallest Integer Value} = -2^{n-1} \qquad (1-1)$$

and the largest number that can be stored in an n-bit integer is

$$\text{Largest Integer Value} = 2^{n-1} - 1 \qquad (1-2)$$

For a 4-byte integer, the smallest and largest possible values are $-2{,}147{,}483{,}648$ and $2{,}147{,}483{,}647$, respectively. Attempts to use an integer larger than the largest possible value or smaller than the smallest possible value result in an error called an *overflow condition.*[2]

Real data

The integer data type has two fundamental limitations:

1. It is not possible to represent numbers with fractional parts (0.25, 1.5, 3.14159, etc.) as integer data.
2. There are not enough bits available to represent very large positive integers or very small negative integers. The largest and smallest possible integers that can be stored in a given memory location are given by Equations (1–1) and (1–2).

To get around these limitations, computers include a **real** or **floating-point** data type.

The real data type stores numbers in a type of scientific notation. We all know that very large or very small numbers can be most conveniently written in scientific notation. For example, the speed of light in a vacuum is about 299,800,000 meters per second. This number is easier to work with in scientific notation: 2.998×10^8 m/s. The two parts of a number expressed in scientific notation are called the **mantissa** and the **exponent.** The mantissa of the number above is 2.998, and the exponent (in the base 10 system) is 8.

---

[2]When an overflow condition occurs, most processors will abort the program causing the overflow condition. However, this behavior varies among different types of computers.

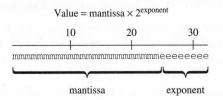

$$\text{Value} = \text{mantissa} \times 2^{\text{exponent}}$$

mantissa

exponent

FIGURE 1–4
This floating-point number includes a 24-bit mantissa and an 8-bit exponent.

The real numbers in a computer are similar to the scientific notation above except that a computer works in the base 2 system instead of in the base 10 system. Real numbers usually occupy 32 bits (4 bytes) of computer memory, divided into two components: a 24-bit mantissa and an 8-bit exponent (see Figure 1–4).[3] The mantissa contains a number between -1.0 and 1.0, and the exponent contains the power of 2 required to scale the number to its actual value.

Real numbers are characterized by two quantities: **precision** and **range**. *Precision* is the number of significant digits that can be preserved in a number, and *range* is the difference between the largest and smallest numbers that can be represented. The precision of a real number depends on the number of bits in its mantissa, while the range of the number depends on the number of bits in its exponent. A 24-bit mantissa can represent approximately $\pm 2^{23}$ numbers, or about seven significant decimal digits, so the precision of real numbers is about seven significant digits. An 8-bit exponent can represent multipliers between 2^{-128} and 2^{127}, so the range of real numbers is from about 10^{-38} to 10^{38}. Note that the real data type can represent numbers much larger or much smaller than integers can, but only with seven significant digits of precision.

When a value with more than seven digits of precision is stored in a real variable, only the most significant 7 bits of the number will be preserved. The remaining information will be lost forever. For example, if the value 12345678.9 is stored in a real variable on an IBM PC, it will be rounded off to 12345680.0. The difference between the original value and the number stored in the computer is known as **round-off error.**

You will use the real data type in many places throughout this book and in your programs after you finish this course. It is quite useful, but you must always remember the limitations associated with round-off error, or your programs might give you an unpleasant surprise. For example, if your program must be able to distinguish between the numbers 1,000,000.0 and 1,000,000.1, then you cannot use the standard real data type.[4] It simply does not have enough precision to tell the difference between these two numbers!

---

[3]This discussion is based on the IEEE Standard 754 for floating-point numbers, which is representative of most modern computers. Some computers use a slightly different division of bits (e.g., a 23-bit mantissa and a 9-bit exponent), but the basic principles are the same in any case.
[4]You will learn how to use high-precision floating-point numbers in Chapter 8.

Programming Pitfalls
Always remember the precision and range of the data types that you are working with. Failure to do so can result in subtle programming errors that are very hard to find.

1

Quiz 1–1
This quiz provides a quick check to see if you understand the concepts introduced in section 1.2. If you have trouble with the quiz, reread the section, ask your instructor, or discuss the material with a fellow student. The answers to this quiz are found in the back of the book.

1. Express the following decimal numbers as their binary equivalents:
   a. 27_{10}
   b. 11_{10}
   c. 35_{10}
   d. 127_{10}

2. Express the following binary numbers as their decimal equivalents:
   a. 1110_2
   b. 01010101_2
   c. 1001_2

3. Express the following binary numbers as octal and hexadecimal numbers:
   a. 1110010110101101_2
   b. 1110111101_2
   c. 1001011100111111_2

4. Is the 4th bit of the number 131_{10} a 1 or a 0?

5. Assume that the following numbers are the contents of a character variable. Find the character corresponding to each number according to the ASCII and EBCDIC encoding schemes.
   a. 77_{10}
   b. 01111011_2
   c. 249_{10}

6. Find the maximum and minimum values that can be stored in a 2-byte integer variable.

7. Can a 4-byte variable of the real data type store larger numbers than a 4-byte variable of the integer data type can store? Why or why not? If it can, what does the real variable give up to make this possible?

1

■ 1.3

COMPUTER LANGUAGES

When a computer executes a program, it executes a string of very simple operations such as load, store, add, subtract, and multiply. Each operation has a unique binary pattern called an *operation code (op code)* to specify it. The program that a computer executes is just a string of op codes (and the data associated with the op codes[5]) in the order necessary to achieve a purpose. Op codes are collectively called **machine language,** since they are the actual language that a computer recognizes and executes.

Unfortunately, we humans find machine language very hard to work with. We prefer to work with English-like statements and algebraic equations that are expressed in forms familiar to us, instead of arbitrary patterns of zeros and ones. We like to program computers with *high-level languages*. We write out our instructions in a high-level language and then use special programs called **compilers** and **linkers** to convert the instructions into the machine language that the computer understands.

Programmers use many different high-level languages, with different characteristics. Some of them are designed to work well for business problems, while others are designed for general scientific use. Still others are especially suited for applications like operating-systems programming. It is important to pick a proper language to match the problem that you are trying to solve.

Some of the common high-level computer languages in use today are Ada, Basic, C, COBOL, Fortran, and Pascal. Of these languages, Fortran is the preeminent language for general scientific computations. It has been around in one form or another for more than 50 years and has been used to implement everything from computer models of nuclear power plants to aircraft design programs to seismic-signal-processing systems, including some projects requiring literally millions of lines of code. The language is especially useful for numerical analysis and technical calculations. In addition, Fortran is the dominant language in the world of supercomputers and massively parallel computers.

■ 1.4

THE HISTORY OF Fortran

Fortran is the grandfather of all scientific computer languages. The name Fortran is derived from FORmula TRANslation, indicating that the language was intended from the start to translate scientific equations into computer code. IBM developed the first version of the FORTRAN[6] language between 1954 and 1957 for use with its Type 704 computer (see Figure 1–5). Before that time, essentially all computer programs

---

[5]The data associated with op codes are called *operands*.
[6]Versions of the language before Fortran 90 were known as FORTRAN (written with all capital letters), while Fortran 90 and later versions are known as Fortran (with only the first letter capitalized).

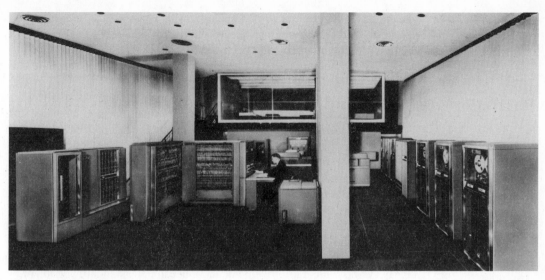

FIGURE 1–5
The IBM Type 704 computer. *(Courtesy of IBM Corporation)*

The IBM Type 704 Computer

The IBM Type 704 computer was the first computer ever to use the FORTRAN language. The 704 was released in 1954 and was widely used from then until about 1960 when the Model 709 replaced it. As you can see from Figure 1–5, the 704 computer occupied a whole room.

What could a computer like that do in 1954? Not much by today's standards. Any PC sitting on a desktop can run rings around it. The 704 could perform about 4000 integer multiplications and divisions per second and an average of about 8000 floating point operations per second. It could read data from magnetic drums (the equivalent of a disk drive) into memory at a rate of about 50,000 bytes per second. The amount of data storage available on a magnetic drum was also very small, so most programs that were not currently in use were stored as decks of punched cards.

By comparison, a typical modern personal computer (circa 1996) performs more than 20,000,000 integer multiplications and divisions per second and millions of floating-point operations per second. Some of today's workstations that are small enough to sit on a desktop can perform more than 100,000,000 floating-point operations per second! Reads from disk into memory occur at rates greater than 10,000,000 bytes per second, and a typical PC disk drive can store more than 800,000,000 bytes of data.

The limited resources available in the 704 and other machines of that generation placed a great premium on efficient programming. The structured programming techniques that we use today were simply not possible, because there was not enough speed or memory to support them. The earliest versions of FORTRAN were designed with those limitations in mind, which is why many archaic features are preserved as living fossils in modern versions of Fortran.

were generated by hand in machine language, which was a slow, tedious, and error-prone process. FORTRAN was a truly revolutionary product. For the first time, a programmer could write a desired algorithm as a series of standard algebraic equations, and the FORTRAN compiler would convert the statements into the machine language that the computer could recognize and execute.

FORTRAN was a wonderful idea! People began using it as soon as it was available, because it made programming so much easier than machine language did. The language was officially released in April 1957, and by the fall of 1958, more than half of all IBM 704 computer programs were being written in FORTRAN.

The first version of FORTRAN was very small compared to our modern versions of Fortran. It contained only a limited number of statement types, supported only the integer and real data types, and had no subroutines. It was a first effort at writing a high-level computer language, and naturally many deficiencies became evident as people started using the language regularly. IBM addressed those problems, releasing FORTRAN II in the spring of 1958.

Further developments continued through 1962 when FORTRAN IV was released. FORTRAN IV was a great improvement, and it became the standard version of Fortran for the next 15 years. In 1966 FORTRAN IV was adopted as an ANSI standard, and it came to be known as FORTRAN 66.

The Fortran language received another major update in 1977. FORTRAN 77 included many new features designed to make structured programs easier to write and maintain, and it quickly became "the" Fortran. FORTRAN 77 introduced structures such as the block IF and was the first version of Fortran in which character variables were truly easy to manipulate.

The next major update of Fortran was Fortran 90.[7] Fortran 90 includes all of FORTRAN 77 as a subset and extends the language in many important new directions. Among the major improvements introduced to the language in Fortran 90 are a new free-source format, array sections, whole-array operations, parameterized data types, derived data types, and explicit interfaces. Fortran 90 is a dramatic improvement over earlier versions of the language.

Fortran 90 was followed in 1997 by a minor update called Fortran 95. Fortran 95 adds a number of new features to the language such as the FORALL construct, pure functions, and some new intrinsic procedures. In addition, it clarifies numerous ambiguities in the Fortran 90 standard.

The subjects of this book are the Fortran 90 and Fortran 95 languages. Most of the book applies to both Fortran 90 and Fortran 95, and we will usually refer to them together as Fortran 90/95. Features that appear only in Fortran 95 are distinguished by a special background. For example:

> The fixed source form has been declared obsolescent in Fortran 95, which means that it is a candidate for deletion in future versions of Fortran.

is a Fortran 95–specific comment.

---

[7]American National Standard Programming Language Fortran, ANSI X3.198-1992; and International Standards Organization ISO/IEC 1539: 1991, Information Technology—Programming Languages—Fortran.

(a)

(b)

FIGURE 1–6
Two pictures illustrating the wide range of computers that run Fortran: *(a)* The original IBM PC *(Courtesy of IBM Corporation)* and *(b)* The Cray T-90 supercomputer *(Courtesy of CRAY Research, Inc.).*

The designers of Fortran 90 and Fortran 95 were careful to make the new versions backward compatible with FORTRAN 77 and earlier versions. Because of this backward compatibility, most of the millions of programs written in FORTRAN 77 also work with Fortran 90/95. Unfortunately, being backward compatible with earlier versions of Fortran required that Fortran 90/95 retain some archaic features that should never be used in any modern program. In this book, you will learn to program in Fortran 90/95 using only its modern features. The older features that are retained for backward compatibility are relegated to Chapter 14, where they are described in case you run into them in older programs. However, you should never use these features in any new program!

1.5

THE EVOLUTION OF Fortran

The Fortran language is a dynamic language that is constantly evolving to keep up with advances in programming practice and computing technology. A major new version appears about once per decade.

The responsibility for developing new versions of the Fortran language lies with the International Organization for Standardization's (ISO) Fortran Working Group, WG5. That organization has delegated authority to the X3J3 Committee of the American National Standards Institute (ANSI) to actually prepare new versions of the language. The preparation of each new version is an extended process. It involves asking for suggestions for inclusion in the language, deciding which suggestions are feasible to implement, writing drafts, circulating them to all interested parties throughout the world, correcting the drafts, and trying again until general agreement is reached. Eventually, a worldwide vote is held and the standard is adopted.

The designers of new versions of the Fortran language must strike a delicate balance between backward compatibility with the existing base of Fortran programs and the introduction of desirable new features. Although modern structured-programming features and approaches have been introduced into the language, many undesirable features from earlier versions of Fortran have been retained for backward compatibility.

The designers have developed a mechanism for identifying undesirable and obsolete features of the Fortran language and for eventually eliminating them from the language. Those parts of the language that have been superseded by new and better methods are declared to be **obsolescent features.** Features that have been declared obsolescent should never be used in any new programs. As the use of these features declines in the existing Fortran code base, they will then be considered for deletion from the language. No feature will ever be deleted from a version of the language unless it was on the obsolescent list in at least one previous version and unless the usage of the feature has dropped off to negligible levels. In this fashion, the language can evolve without threatening the existing Fortran code base.

The redundant, obsolescent, and deleted features of Fortran 90 and Fortran 95 are described in Chapter 14 in case a programmer runs into them in existing programs, but they should never be used in any new programs.

You can get a feeling for just how much the Fortran language has evolved over the years by examining Figures 1–7, 1–8, and 1–9. The code in these figures calculates the solution to the quadratic equation $ax^2 + bx + c = 0$ in the styles of the original FORTRAN I, of FORTRAN 77, and of Fortran 90. It is obvious that the language has become more readable and structured over the years. Amazingly, though, Fortran 90 compilers will still compile the FORTRAN I program with just a few minor changes![8]

FIGURE 1–7
A FORTRAN I program to solve for the roots of the quadratic equation $ax^2 + bx + c = 0$.

```
C    SOLVE QUADRATIC EQUATION IN FORTRAN I
     READ 100,A,B,C
100  FORMAT(3F12.4)
     DISCR = B**2-4*A*C
     IF (DISCR) 10,20,30
```

(continued)

---

[8]Change SQRTF to SQRT, ABSF to ABS, and add an END statement.

(concluded)

```
10    X1=(-B)/2.*A
      X2=SQRTF(ABSF(DISCR))/2.*A
      PRINT 110,X1,X2
110   FORMAT(5H X = ,F12.3,4H +i ,F12.3)
      PRINT 120,X1,X2
120   FORMAT(5H X = ,F12.3,4H -i ,F12.3)
      GOTO 40
20    X1=(-B)/2.*A
      PRINT 130,X1
130   FORMAT(11H X1 = X2 = ,F12.3)
      GOTO 40
30    X1=((-B)+SQRTF(ABSF(DISCR)))/(2.*A)
      X2=((-B)-SQRTF(ABSF(DISCR)))/(2.*A)
      PRINT 140,X1
140   FORMAT(6H X1 = ,F12.3)
      PRINT 150,X2
150   FORMAT(6H X2 = ,F12.3)
40    CONTINUE
      STOP 25252
```

FIGURE 1–8

A FORTRAN 77 program to solve for the roots of the quadratic equation $ax^2 + bx + c = 0$.

```
      PROGRAM QUAD4
C
C     This program reads the coefficients of a quadratic equation of
C     the form
C           A * X**2 + B * X + C = 0,
C     and solves for the roots of the equation (FORTRAN 77 style).
C
C     Get the coefficients of the quadratic equation.
C
      WRITE (*,*) 'Enter the coefficients A, B and C: '
      READ (*,*) A, B, C
C
C     Echo the coefficients to make sure they are entered correctly.
C
      WRITE (*,100) 'The coefficients are : ', A, B, C
100   FORMAT (1X,A,3F10.4)
C
C     Check the discriminant and calculate its roots.
C
      DISCR = B**2 - 4*A*C
      IF ( DISCR .LT. 0) THEN
         WRITE (*,*) ' This equation has complex roots:'
         WRITE (*,*) ' X = ', -B/2*A, ' +i ', SQRT(ABS(DISCR))/2*A
         WRITE (*,*) ' X = ', -B/2*A, ' -i ', SQRT(ABS(DISCR))/2*A
      ELSE IF ( (B**2 - 4.*A*C) .EQ. 0) THEN
         WRITE (*,*) ' This equation has a single repeated real root:'
         WRITE (*,*) ' X = ', -B/2*A
      ELSE
         WRITE (*,*) ' This equation has two distinct real roots:'
         WRITE (*,*) ' X = ', (-B + SQRT(ABS(DISCR)))/2*A
         WRITE (*,*) ' X = ', (-B - SQRT(ABS(DISCR)))/2*A
      END IF
C
      END
```

FIGURE 1–9

A Fortran 90 program to solve for the roots of the quadratic equation $ax^2 + bx + c = 0$.

```fortran
PROGRAM roots
!  Purpose:
!    This program solves for the roots of a quadratic equation of the form
!    A * X**2 + B * X + C = 0. It calculates the answers regardless of the
!    type of roots that the equation possesses (Fortran 90 style).
!
IMPLICIT NONE

!  Declare the variables used in this program

REAL :: a              ! Coefficient of X**2 term of equation
REAL :: b              ! Coefficient of X term of equation
REAL :: c              ! Constant term of equation
REAL :: discriminant   ! Discriminant of the equation
REAL :: imag_part      ! Imaginary part of equation (for complex roots)
REAL :: real_part      ! Real part of equation (for complex roots)
REAL :: x1             ! First solution of equation (for real roots)
REAL :: x2             ! First solution of equation (for real roots)

!  Prompt the user for the coefficients of the equation
WRITE (*,*) 'This program solves for the roots of a quadratic '
WRITE (*,*) 'equation of the form A * X**2 + B * X + C = 0. '
WRITE (*,*) 'Enter the coefficients A, B, and C:'
READ  (*,*) a, b, c

!  Echo back coefficients
WRITE (*,*) 'The coefficients A, B, and C are: ', a, b, c

!  Calculate discriminant
discriminant = b**2 - 4. * a * c

!  Solve for the roots, depending upon the value of the discriminant

IF ( discriminant > 0. ) THEN ! there are two real roots, so...

   X1 = ( -b + sqrt(discriminant) ) / ( 2. * a )
   X2 = ( -b - sqrt(discriminant) ) / ( 2. * a )
   WRITE (*,*) 'This equation has two real roots:'
   WRITE (*,*) 'X1 = ', x1
   WRITE (*,*) 'X2 = ', x2

ELSE IF ( discriminant == 0. ) THEN ! there is one repeated root, so...

   x1 = ( -b ) / ( 2. * a )
   WRITE (*,*) 'This equation has two identical real roots:'
   WRITE (*,*) 'X1 = X2 = ', x1

ELSE ! there are complex roots, so ...

   real_part = ( -b ) / ( 2. * a )
   imag_part = sqrt ( abs ( discriminant ) ) / ( 2. * a )
   WRITE (*,*) 'This equation has complex roots:'
   WRITE (*,*) 'X1 = ', real_part, ' +i ', imag_part
   WRITE (*,*) 'X2 = ', real_part, ' -i ', imag_part

END IF

END PROGRAM
```

1.6

SUMMARY

A computer is a special type of machine that stores information and performs mathematical calculations on that information at speeds much faster than human beings can think. A program, which is stored in the computer's memory, tells the computer what sequence of calculations are required and which information to perform the calculations on.

The major components of a computer are the central processing unit (CPU), main memory, secondary memory, and input and output devices. The CPU performs the control and calculation functions of the computer. Main memory is fast, relatively expensive memory that stores the program being executed and its associated data. Main memory is volatile, meaning that its contents are lost whenever power is turned off. Secondary memory is slower and less expensive than main memory. It is nonvolatile. Hard disks are popular secondary memory devices. Input and output devices are used to read data into the computer and to output data from the computer. The most common input device is a keyboard, and the most common output device is a printer.

Computer memories are composed of millions of individual switches, each of which can be either ON or OFF, but not at a state in between. These individual switches are binary devices called bits. Eight bits are grouped together to form a *byte* of memory, and 2 or more bytes (depending on the computer) are grouped together to form a *word* of memory.

Computer memories can be used to store *character, integer,* or *real* data. Each character in most character data sets occupies 1 byte of memory. The 256 possible values in the byte allow for 256 possible character codes. (Characters in the Unicode character set occupy 2 bytes, allowing for 65,536 possible character codes.) Integer values occupy 1, 2, 4, or 8 bytes of memory, and they store integer quantities. Real values store numbers in a kind of scientific notation. They usually occupy 4 bytes of memory. The bits are divided into a separate mantissa and exponent. The *precision* of the number depends on the number of bits in the mantissa, and the *range* of the number depends on the number of bits in the exponent.

The earliest computers were programmed in *machine language*. This process was slow, cumbersome, and error prone. High-level languages began to appear in about 1954, and they quickly replaced machine-language coding for most uses. FORTRAN was one of the first high-level languages ever created.

The original FORTRAN I computer language and compiler were developed between 1954 and 1957. The language has since gone through many revisions, and a standard mechanism has been created to evolve the language. This book teaches good programming practices using the Fortran 90/95 version of the language.

1.7

EXERCISES

1–1 Express the following decimal numbers as their binary equivalents:

    a. 10_{10} *b.* 32_{10}

    c. 77_{10} *d.* 63_{10}

1–2 Express the following binary numbers as their decimal equivalents:
   a. 01001000_2
   b. 10001001_2
   c. 11111111_2
   d. 0101_2

1–3 Express the following numbers in both octal and hexadecimal forms:
   a. 0101011101110001_2
   b. 330_{10}
   c. 111_{10}
   d. 11111101101_2

1–4 Express the following numbers in binary and decimal forms:
   a. 377_8
   b. $1A8_{16}$
   c. 111_8
   d. $1FF_{16}$

1–5 Some computers (such as IBM mainframes) implement the real data using a 23-bit mantissa and a 9-bit exponent. What precision and range can we expect from real data on these machines?

1–6 Some Cray supercomputers support 46-bit and 64-bit integer data types. What are the maximum and minimum values that we could express in a 46-bit integer? in a 64-bit integer?

1–7 Find the 16-bit two's-complement representation of the following decimal numbers:
   a. 55_{10}
   b. -5_{10}
   c. 1024_{10}
   d. -1024_{10}

1–8 Add the two's-complement numbers 0010010010010010_2 and 1111110011111100_2 using binary arithmetic. Convert the two numbers to decimal form and add them as decimals. Do the two answers agree?

1–9 The largest possible 8-bit two's-complement number is 01111111_2, and the smallest possible 8-bit two's-complement number is 10000000_2. Convert these numbers to decimal form. How do they compare to the results of Equations (1–1) and (1–2)?

1–10 The Fortran language includes a second type of floating-point data known as double precision. A double-precision number usually occupies 8 bytes (64 bits), instead of the 4 bytes occupied by a real number. In the most common implementation, 53 bits are used for the mantissa, and 11 bits are used for the exponent. How many significant digits does a double-precision value have? What is the range of double-precision numbers?

Basic Elements of Fortran

Engineers and scientists design and execute computer programs to accomplish a goal. The goal typically involves technical calculations that would be too difficult or take too long to be performed by hand. Fortran is one of the computer languages commonly used for these technical calculations.

This chapter introduces the basic elements of the Fortran language. By the end of the chapter, you will be able to write simple but functional Fortran programs.

2.1
THE Fortran CHARACTER SET

Every language, whether it is a natural language, such as English, or a computer language, such as Fortran, Pascal, or C, has its own special alphabet. Only the characters in this alphabet may be used with the language.

The special alphabet used with the Fortran 90/95 language is known as the **Fortran character set.** It consists of the 86 symbols shown in Table 2–1.

TABLE 2–1
The Fortran 90/95 character set

Number of Symbols	Type	Values
26	Uppercase letters	A–Z
26	Lowercase letters	a–z
10	Digits	0–9
1	Underscore character	_
5	Arithmetic symbols	+ – * / **
17	Miscellaneous symbols	( ) . = , ' $: ! " % & ; < > ? and blank

Note that uppercase and lowercase letters of the alphabet are equivalent in the Fortran character set. (For example, the uppercase letter A is equivalent to the lowercase letter a.) In other words, Fortran is *case insensitive.* This behavior is in contrast with case-sensitive languages, such as C, in which A and a are two totally different characters.

■ 2.2
THE STRUCTURE OF A Fortran STATEMENT

A Fortran program consists of a series of *statements* designed to accomplish the goal of the programmer. The two basic types of statements in Fortran are **executable statements** and **nonexecutable statements.** Executable statements describe the actions the program takes when it is executed (additions, subtractions, multiplications, divisions, etc.), while nonexecutable statements provide information necessary for the proper operation of the program. This book contains many examples of each type of statement.

As I mentioned in Chapter 1, Fortran was one of the first major computer languages to be developed. It originated in the days before terminals and keyboards when the punched card was the major form of input to the computer. Each punched card had a fixed length of 80 columns, and one character, number, or symbol could be typed in each column. The structure of statements in earlier versions of Fortran reflected this fixed limitation of 80 characters per line. By contrast, Fortran 90 and Fortran 95 were developed in the age of the terminal and keyboard, so they allow free entry of statements in any column. For backward compatibility, Fortran 90/95 also supports the old fixed form.

2.2.1 Free-Source Form

In the modern free-source form, Fortran statements may be entered anywhere on a line, and each line may be up to 132 characters long. If a statement is too long to fit on a single line, then you may continue it on the next line by ending the current line (and optionally starting the next line) with an ampersand (&). For example, the following three Fortran statements are identical:

```
100 output = input1 + input2   ! Sum the inputs

33  output = input1 &
            + input2            ! Sum the inputs

999 output = input1 &          ! Sum the inputs
            & + input2
```

Each statement specifies that the computer should add together the quantities stored in input1 and input2 and save the result in output. A statement can be continued over as many as 40 lines.

In the preceding statements, the numbers at the beginning of the line are called **statement labels.** A statement label is a number between 1 and 99999. It is the "name" of a Fortran statement and may be used to refer to the statement in other parts of the program. Note that a statement label has no significance other than as a "name" for the statement. It is not a line number, and it tells nothing about the order in which statements are executed. For example, one line of a program could be labeled 9999, and the very next line of the program could be labeled 1. The two lines would be executed in the same order regardless of the specific label assigned to each statement. Statement labels are optional, and most Fortran 90/95 statements will not have any. If a statement label is used, it must be unique within a given program unit.[1] For example, if 100 is used as a statement label on a line, it cannot be used again as a statement label on any other line in the same program unit.

Any characters following an exclamation point are **comments** and are ignored by the Fortran compiler. All text from the exclamation point to the end of the line will be ignored, so comments may appear on the same line as an executable statement. In the third statement above, the comment is ignored, so the compiler treats the ampersand as the last character on the line. Comments help document the proper operation of a program.

New Fortran 90/95 programs should always be written in free-source form. All of the examples in this book are written in free-source form.

Good Programming Practice

Always use free-source form when writing new Fortran 90/95 programs.

2.2.2 Fixed-Source Form

A fixed-source form Fortran statement still reflects the structure of the punched computer card. Each card has 80 columns. Figure 2–1 shows the use of these 80 columns in a fixed-source form Fortran statement.

Columns 1 through 5 are reserved for statement labels. A statement label may be located anywhere within columns 1 through 5 with either leading or trailing blanks. For example, the label 100 could be placed in columns 1 to 3, 2 to 4, or 3 to 5, and it would still be the same label.

A letter C or an asterisk (*) placed in column 1 indicates that the statement is a comment. The Fortran compiler completely ignores any statement beginning with these characters.

Column 6 is normally blank. If any character other than a blank or a zero is placed in that column, then the statement is interpreted as a continuation of the statement immediately preceding it. A Fortran statement may be up to 40 lines long.

Columns 7 to 72 contain the Fortran instructions that are interpreted by the compiler. The instructions may be freely placed anywhere within this area. Programmers

---

[1]A *program unit* is a separately compiled piece of Fortran code.

24   CHAPTER 2

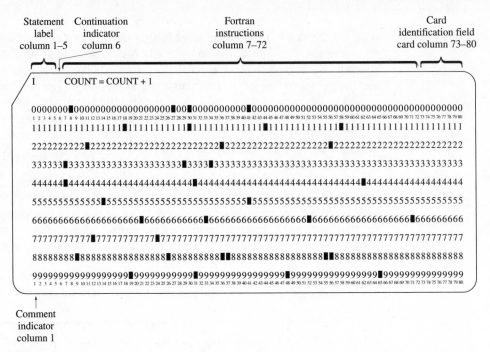

FIGURE 2–1
The structure of a fixed-source form Fortran statement.

typically take advantage of this freedom to indent certain instructions (loops and branches) to make their code more readable.

Columns 73 to 80 are sometimes called the **card identification field.** The compiler totally ignores this field, and the programmer may use it for any desired purpose. In the days when programs were saved on decks of punched cards, this field was used to number the cards in consecutive order. If someone accidentally dropped a numbered card deck, it was possible to reconstruct the order of the statements in the program from the numbers on the cards. Today, these columns are usually blank.

Figure 1–8 shows a sample Fortran program using the fixed-source form. Note that the statement label 100 falls in columns 1 to 5, and the Fortran instructions begin in column 7.

The fixed-source form has been declared obsolescent in Fortran 95, which means that it is a candidate for deletion in future versions of Fortran. You should never use a fixed-source form in any new Fortran program.

2.3

THE STRUCTURE OF A Fortran PROGRAM

Each Fortran program consists of a mixture of executable and nonexecutable statements, which must occur in a specific order. A sample Fortran program appears as

Figure 2–2. This program reads in two numbers, multiplies them together, and prints out the result. Let's examine the significant features of this program.

This Fortran program, like all Fortran program units, is divided into three sections:

1. The *declaration section* consists of a group of nonexecutable statements at the beginning of the program that define the name of the program and the number and types of variables referenced in the program.
2. The *execution section* consists of one or more statements describing the actions to be performed by the program.
3. The *termination section* consists of a statement or statements stopping the execution of the program and telling the compiler that the program is complete.

Note that comments may be inserted freely anywhere within, before, or after the program.

2.3.1 The Declaration Section

The declaration section consists of the nonexecutable statements at the beginning of the program that define the name of the program and the number and types of variables referenced in the program.

The first statement in this section is the PROGRAM statement. It is a nonexecutable statement that specifies the name of the program to the Fortran compiler. Fortran program names may be up to 31 characters long and contain any combination of alphabetic characters, digits, and the underscore (_) character. However, the first character in a program name must always be alphabetic. If present, the PROGRAM statement must be the first line of the program. In Figure 2–2 the name of the program is my_first_program.

FIGURE 2–2
A simple Fortran program.

```
PROGRAM my_first_program

! Purpose:
!   To illustrate some of the basic features of a Fortran program.
!

! Declare the variables used in this program.
INTEGER :: i, j, k                ! All variables are integers

! Get the variables to multiply together.
WRITE (*,*) 'Enter the numbers to multiply: '
READ  (*,*) i, j

! Multiply the numbers together
k = i * j

!  Write out the result.
WRITE (*,*) 'Result = ', k

!  Finish up.
STOP
END PROGRAM
```

The next several lines in the program are comments that describe the purpose of the program. Next comes the INTEGER type declaration statement. This nonexecutable statement is described later in this chapter. Here it declares that this program will use three integer variables called i, j, and k.

2.3.2 The Execution Section

The execution section consists of one or more executable statements describing the actions to be performed by the program.

The first executable statement in this program is the WRITE statement, which writes out a message prompting the user to enter the two numbers to be multiplied together. The next executable statement is a READ statement, which reads in the two integers supplied by the user. The third executable statement instructs the computer to multiply the two numbers i and j together and to store the result in variable k. The final WRITE statement prints out the result for the user to see. Comments may be embedded anywhere throughout the execution section. These statements are explained in detail later in this chapter.

2.3.3 The Termination Section

The termination section consists of the STOP and END PROGRAM statements. The STOP statement tells the computer to stop running the program. The END PROGRAM statement tells the compiler that there are no more statements to be compiled in the program.

When the STOP statement immediately precedes the END PROGRAM statement, as in Figure 2–2, it is optional. The compiler will automatically generate a STOP command when the END PROGRAM statement is reached. The STOP statement is therefore rarely used.

2.3.4 Program Style

The program in Figure 2–2 follows the widely used Fortran convention of capitalizing keywords such as PROGRAM, READ, and WRITE and using lowercase for the program variables. This convention is *not* a Fortran requirement; the program would work just as well if all capital letters or all lowercase letters are used. Since uppercase and lowercase letters are equivalent in Fortran, the program functions identically in either case.

This book follows the convention of capitalizing Fortran keywords and using lowercase for variables, parameters, etc. You do not have to follow this convention, but you should always be consistent in the way you write your programs. Establish a standard practice, or adopt the standard practice of the organization in which you work, and then follow it consistently in all of your programs.

Good Programming Practice
Adopt a programming style and then follow it consistently in all of your programs.

2.3.5 Compiling, Linking, and Executing the Fortran Program

Before the sample program can be run, it must be compiled into object code with a Fortran compiler and then linked with a computer's system libraries to produce an executable program (Figure 2–3). These two steps are usually done together in response to a single programmer command. The details of compiling and linking are different for every compiler and operating system. You should ask your instructor or consult the appropriate manuals to determine the proper procedure for your system.

Depending on the computer and operating system being used, Fortran programs may be compiled, linked, and run in either **batch mode** or **interactive mode.** In batch mode, the commands required to compile, link, and run the program are written into a file together with any data required by the program. This file is submitted to the *batch processor,* which compiles, links, and executes the program without user intervention. In interactive mode, the program is compiled, linked, and executed by commands entered by a user at a terminal or keyboard. A program that is executed in interactive mode can prompt the user for input while it is running. A program under development is usually run in interactive mode so that the programmer can immediately see whether or not it is working properly.

2.4
CONSTANTS AND VARIABLES

A Fortran **constant** is a data object that is defined before a program is executed and that does not change value during the execution of the program. When a Fortran compiler encounters a constant, it places the value of the constant in a known location in memory and then references that memory location whenever the program uses the constant.

A Fortran **variable** is a data object that can change value during the execution of a program. (The value of a Fortran variable may or may not be initialized before a program is executed.) When a Fortran compiler encounters a variable, it reserves a

FIGURE 2–3
Creating an executable Fortran program involves two steps: compiling and linking.

known location in memory for the variable and then references that memory location whenever the program uses the variable.

Each Fortran variable in a program unit must have a unique name. Fortran names may be up to 31 characters long and may contain any combination of alphabetic characters, digits, and the underscore (_) character. However, the first character in a name must always be alphabetic. The following examples are valid variable names:

```
time
distance
z123456789
I_want_to_go_home
```

The following examples are not valid variable names:

```
this_is_a_very_long_variable_name    (Name is too long)
3_days                               (First character is a number)
A$                                   ($ is an illegal character)
```

When writing a program, you should always pick meaningful names for the variables. Meaningful names make a program much easier to read and to maintain. Names such as day, month, and year are quite clear even to a person seeing a program for the first time. You cannot use spaces in Fortran variable names, but you can use underscore characters to create meaningful names. For example, *exchange rate* might become exchange_rate.

> **Good Programming Practice**
> Use meaningful variable names whenever possible.

You should also include a **data dictionary** in the header of any program that you write. A data dictionary lists the definition of each variable used in a program. The definition should include both a description of the contents of the item and the units in which it is measured. A data dictionary may seem unnecessary while the program is being written, but it is invaluable when you or another person has to modify the program at a later time.

> **Good Programming Practice**
> Create a data dictionary for each program to facilitate program maintenance.

Fortran has five intrinsic or "built in" types of constants and variables. Three of them are numeric (types INTEGER, REAL, and COMPLEX), one is logical (type LOGICAL), and one consists of strings of characters (type CHARACTER). The simplest forms of the INTEGER, REAL, CHARACTER, and LOGICAL data types are discussed next. Discussions of their more advanced forms and of the COMPLEX data type appear in Chapter 8.

In addition to the intrinsic data types, Fortran permits a programmer to define **derived data types,** which are special data types intended to solve particular problems. Derived data types are also discussed in Chapter 8.

2.4.1 Integer Constants and Variables

The integer data type consists of integer constants and variables. This data type can store only integer values—it cannot represent numbers with fractional parts.

An integer constant is any number that does not contain a decimal point. If a constant is positive, it may be written either with or without a plus sign. No commas may be embedded within an integer constant. The following examples are valid integer constants.

```
        0
     -999
123456789
      +17
```

The following examples are not valid integer constants:

```
1,000,000     (Embedded commas are illegal.)
    -100.     (If it has a decimal point, it is not an integer constant!)
```

An integer variable is a variable containing a value of the integer data type.

Constants and variables of the integer data type are usually stored in a single word on a computer. Since the length of a word varies from 16 to 64 bits on different computers, the largest integer that can be stored in a computer also varies. The largest and smallest integers that can be stored in a particular computer can be determined from the word size by applying Equations (1–1) and (1–2).

Many Fortran 90/95 compilers support integers with more than one length. For example, most PC compilers support both 16-bit and 32-bit integers. These different lengths of integers are known as different **kinds** of integers. Fortran 90/95 has an explicit mechanism for choosing which kind of integer is used for a given value. This mechanism is explained in Chapter 8.

2.4.2 Real Constants and Variables

The real data type consists of numbers stored in real or floating-point format. Unlike integers, the real data type can represent numbers with fractional components.

A real constant is a constant written with a decimal point. If the constant is positive, it may be written either with or without a plus sign. No commas may be embedded within a real constant.

Real constants may be written with or without an exponent. If used, the exponent consists of the letter E followed by a positive or negative integer that corresponds to the power of 10 used when the number is written in scientific notation. If the exponent is positive, the plus sign may be omitted. The mantissa of the number should contain a decimal point. The following examples are valid real constants:

```
       10.
     -999.9
     +1.0E-3          (= 1.0 × 10⁻³, or 0.001)
   123.45E20          (= 123.45 × 10²⁰, or 1.2345 × 10²²)
     0.12E+1          (= 0.12 × 10¹, or 1.2)
```

The following examples are not valid real constants:

```
   1,000,000.         (Embedded commas are illegal.)
       111E3          (A decimal point is required in the mantissa.)
    -12.0E1.5         (Decimal points are not allowed in exponents.)
```

A real variable is a variable containing a value of the real data type.

A real value is stored in two parts: the **mantissa** and the **exponent.** The number of bits allocated to the mantissa determines the *precision* of the constant (that is, the number of significant digits to which the constant is known), while the number of bits allocated to the exponent determines the *range* of the constant (that is, the largest and the smallest values that can be represented). For a given word size, the more precise a real number is, the smaller its range is, and vice versa, as described in Chapter 1.

Table 2–2 shows the precision and the range of typical real constants and variables on several different computers.

All Fortran 90/95 compilers support real numbers with more than one length. For example, PC compilers support both 32-bit and 64-bit real numbers. These different lengths of real numbers are known as different **kinds.** By selecting the proper kind, it is possible to increase the precision and range of a real constant or variable. Fortran 90/95 has an explicit mechanism for choosing which kind of real is used for a given value. This mechanism is explained in detail in Chapter 8.

2.4.3 Character Constants and Variables

The character data type consists of strings of alphanumeric characters. A character constant is a string of characters enclosed in single (') or double (") quotes. The min-

TABLE 2–2

Precision and range of real numbers on several computers

Computer	Total number of bits	Number of bits in mantissa	Precision in decimal digits	Number of bits in exponent	Exponent range
VAX	32	24	7	8	10^{-38} to 10^{38}
	64*	56	15	8	10^{-38} to 10^{38}
IBM PC	32	24	7	8	10^{-38} to 10^{38}
	64*	53	15	11	10^{-308} to 10^{308}
Sun Sparc	32	24	7	8	10^{-38} to 10^{38}
	64*	53	15	11	10^{-308} to 10^{308}
Cray	64	49	14	15	10^{-2465} to 10^{2465}

*Indicates optional length

imum number of characters in a string is one, while the maximum number of characters in a string varies from compiler to compiler.

The characters between the two single or double quotes are in a **character context.** Any characters representable on a computer are legal in a character context, not just the 86 characters forming the Fortran character set.

The following are valid character constants:

```
'This is a test!'
' '              (A single blank)
'{^}'            (These characters are legal in a character context, even
                 though they are not a part of the Fortran character set.)
"3.141593"       (A character string, not a number.)
```

The following are not valid character constants:

```
This is a test!     (No single or double quotes.)
'This is a test!"   (Mismatched quotes.)
''Try this one.'    (Unbalanced single quotes.)
```

If a character string must include an apostrophe, then that apostrophe may be represented by two consecutive single quotes. For example, the string "Man's best friend" would be written in a character constant as

```
'Man''s best friend'
```

Alternatively, the character string containing a single quote can be surrounded by double quotes. For example, the string "Man's best friend" could be written as

```
"Man's best friend"
```

Similarly, a character string containing double quotes can be surrounded by single quotes. The character string "Who cares?" could be written in a character constant as

```
'"Who cares?"'
```

Character constants are most often used to print descriptive information using the WRITE statement. For example, the string 'Result = ' in Figure 2–2 is a valid character constant:

```
WRITE (*,*) 'Result = ', k
```

A **character variable** is a variable containing a value of the character data type.

2.4.4 Logical Constants and Variables

The logical data type contains one of only two possible values: TRUE or FALSE. A **logical constant** can have one of the following values: .TRUE. or .FALSE.. (The periods are required on either side of the values to distinguish them from variable names.) Thus the following are valid logical constants.

```
.TRUE.
.FALSE.
```

2

The following are not valid logical constants:

TRUE   (No periods—this is a variable name.)
.FALSE   (Unbalanced periods.)

Logical constants are rarely used, but logical expressions and variables are commonly used to control program execution, as you will see in Chapter 3.

A **logical variable** is a variable containing a value of the logical data type.

2.4.5 Default and Explicit Variable Typing

When we look at a constant, it is easy to see whether it is of type integer, real, character, or logical. If a number does not have a decimal point, it is of type integer; if it has a decimal point, it is of type real. If the constant is enclosed in single or double quotes, it is of type character. If it is .TRUE. or .FALSE., it is of type logical. With variables, the situation is not so clear. How do we (or the compiler) know if the variable junk contains an integer, real character, or logical value?

The two ways in which the type of a variable can be defined are **default typing** and **explicit typing.** If the type of a variable is not explicitly specified in the program, then default typing is used. By default:

Variable names beginning with the letters I, J, K, L, M, or N are assumed to be of type integer. Variable names starting with any other letter are assumed to be of type real.

Therefore, a variable called incr is assumed to be of type integer by default, while a variable called big is assumed to be of type real by default. This default typing convention started with the original Fortran I in 1954. Note that no variable names are of types character or logical by default, because these data types didn't exist in Fortran I!

The type of a variable may also be explicitly defined in the declaration section at the beginning of a program. The following Fortran statements can be used to specify the type of variables:[2]

```
INTEGER :: var1, var2, var3, ...
REAL ::    var1, var2, var3, ...
LOGICAL :: var1, var2, var3, ...
```

These nonexecutable statements are called **type declaration statements.** They should be placed after the PROGRAM statement and before the first executable statement in the program, as shown in the next example.

---

[2]The double colon :: is optional in the above statements for backward compatibility with earlier versions of Fortran. Thus the following two statements are equivalent:

```
INTEGER count
INTEGER :: count
```

The form with the double colon is preferred, because the double colons are not optional in more advanced forms of the type specification statement.

```
PROGRAM example
INTEGER :: day, month, year
REAL :: second
LOGICAL :: test1, test2
(Executable statements)
```

No default names are associated with the character data type, so all character variables must be explicitly typed using the CHARACTER type declaration statement. This statement is a bit more complicated than the previous ones, since character variables may have different lengths. Its form is

```
CHARACTER(len=<len>) :: var1, var2, var3, ...
```

where <len> is the number of characters in the variables. The (len=<len>) portion of the statement is optional. If only a number appears in the parentheses, then the character variables declared by the statement are of that length. If the parentheses are entirely absent, then the character variables declared by the statement have length 1. For example, the type declaration statements

```
CHARACTER(len=10) :: first, last
CHARACTER :: initial
CHARACTER(15) :: id
```

define two 10-character variables called first and last, a 1-character variable called initial, and a 15-character variable called id.[3]

2.4.6 Keeping Constants Consistent in a Program

You should always keep your physical constants consistent throughout a program. For example, do not use the value 3.14 for π at one point in a program and then use 3.141593 at another point in the program. Also, you should always write your constants with at least as much precision as your computer will accept. If the real data type on your computer has seven significant digits of precision, then you should write π as 3.141593, not as 3.14!

The best way to achieve consistency and precision throughout a program is to *assign a name to a constant and then to use that name to refer to the constant throughout the program.* If we assign the name pi to the constant 3.141593, then we can refer to pi by name throughout the program and be certain that we are getting the same value everywhere. Furthermore assigning meaningful names to constants improves

---

[3]Character variables may also be declared using the older FORTRAN 77 syntax:

```
CHARACTER*<len> var1, var2, var3, ...
```

where <len> is the length of the character variables being declared. An example of this type of declaration is

```
CHARACTER*10 first
```

This form of type declaration statement has been declared obsolescent in Fortran 95 and should never be used in any new programs.

the overall readability of programs because a programmer can tell at a glance just what the constant represents.

Named constants are created using the PARAMETER attribute of a type declaration statement. The form of a type declaration statement with a PARAMETER attribute is

```
type, PARAMETER :: name = value [, name2 = value2, ...]
```

where type is the type of the constant (integer, real, logical, or character) and name is the name assigned to constant value. Multiple parameters may be declared on a single line if they are separated by commas. For example, the following statement assigns the name pi to the constant 3.141593:

```
REAL, PARAMETER :: pi = 3.141593
```

If the named constant is of type character, then it is not necessary to declare the length of the character string. Since the named constant is being defined on the same line as its type declaration, the Fortran compiler can directly count the number of characters in the string. For example, the following statements declare a named constant error_message to be the 14-character string 'Unknown error!'.

```
CHARACTER, PARAMETER :: error_message = 'Unknown error!'
```

 Good Programming Practice

Keep your physical constants consistent and precise throughout a program. To improve the consistency and understandability of your code, assign a name to every important constant and refer to those constants by name in the program.

Quiz 2–1

This quiz provides a quick check to see if you understand the concepts introduced in section 2.4. If you have trouble with the quiz, reread the section, ask your instructor, or discuss the material with a fellow student. The answers to this quiz are found in the back of the book.

Questions 1 to 14 contain a list of valid and invalid constants. State whether or not each constant is valid. If the constant is valid, specify its type. If it is invalid, explain why it is invalid.

1. 10.0
2. -100,000
3. 123E-5
4. 'That's ok!'
5. -32768
6. 3.14159

(continued)

2

(concluded)

7. `"Who are you?"`

8. `.TRUE.`

9. `'3.14159'`

10. `'Distance =`

11. `"That's ok!"`

12. `17.877E+6`

13. `FALSE.`

14. `13.0^2`

Questions 15 to 18 contain two real constants each. Tell whether or not the two constants represent the same value within the computer:

15. `4650.;  4.65E+3`

16. `-12.71;  -1.27E1`

17. `0.0001;  1.0E4`

18. `3.14159E0;  314.159E-3`

Questions 19 and 20 contain a list of valid and invalid Fortran 90/95 program names. State whether or not each program name is valid. If it is invalid, explain why it is invalid.

19. `PROGRAM new_program`

20. `PROGRAM 3rd`

Questions 21 to 25 contain a list of valid and invalid Fortran 90/95 variable names. State whether or not each variable name is valid. If the variable name is valid, specify its type (assume default typing). If it is invalid, explain why it is invalid.

21. `length`

22. `distance`

23. `1problem`

24. `when_does_school_end`

25. `_ok`

Are the following `PARAMETER` declarations correct or incorrect? If a statement is incorrect, explain why it is invalid.

26. `REAL, PARAMETER begin = -30`

27. `CHARACTER, PARAMETER :: name = 'Steve'`

■ **2.5**

ASSIGNMENT STATEMENTS AND ARITHMETIC CALCULATIONS

Calculations are specified in Fortran with an **assignment statement,** whose general form is

```
variable_name = expression
```

The assignment statement calculates the value of the expression to the right of the equal sign and *assigns* that value to the variable named on the left of the equal sign. Note that the equal sign does not mean *equality* in the usual sense of the word. Instead, it means "store the value of `expression` into location `variable_name`." For this reason, the equal sign is called the **assignment operator.** A statement like

```
i = i + 1
```

is complete nonsense in ordinary algebra, but it makes perfect sense in Fortran. In Fortran the statement means: Take the current value stored in variable `i`, add one to it, and store the result back into variable `i`.

The expression to the right of the assignment operator can be any valid combination of constants, variables, parentheses, and arithmetic or logical operators. The standard arithmetic operators included in Fortran are

+	Addition
–	Subtraction
*	Multiplication
/	Division
**	Exponentiation

Note that the symbols for multiplication (`*`), division (`/`), and exponentiation (`**`) are not the ones used in ordinary mathematical expressions. These special symbols were chosen because they were available in 1950s-era computer character sets and because they were different from the characters being used in variable names.

The five arithmetic operators described above are **binary operators,** which means that they should occur between and apply to two variables or constants, as shown:

```
a + b
a - b
a * b
a / b
a ** b
```

In addition, the + and – symbols can occur as **unary operators,** which means that they apply to one variable or constant, as shown:

```
+23
-a
```

The following rules apply when using Fortran arithmetic operators:

1. No two operators may occur side by side. Thus the expression a * -b is illegal. In Fortran it must be written as a * (-b). Similarly, a ** -2 is illegal and should be written as a ** (-2).
2. Implied multiplication is illegal in Fortran. An expression like $x(y + z)$ means that we should add y and z and then multiply the result by x. The implied multiplication must be written explicitly in Fortran as x * (y + z).
3. Parentheses may be used to group terms whenever desired. When parentheses are used, the expressions inside the parentheses are evaluated before the expressions outside the parentheses. For example, the expression 2 ** ((8 + 2)/5) is evaluated as shown:

```
2 ** ((8 + 2)/5) = 2 ** (10/5)
                 = 2 ** 2
                 = 4
```

2.5.1 Integer Arithmetic

Integer arithmetic is arithmetic involving only integer data. Integer arithmetic always produces an integer result. This rule is especially important to remember when an expression involves division, since there can be no fractional part in the answer. If the division of two integers is not itself an integer, the computer automatically truncates the fractional part of the answer. This behavior can lead to surprising and unexpected answers. For example, integer arithmetic produces the following strange results:

$$\frac{3}{4} = 0 \qquad \frac{4}{4} = 1 \qquad \frac{5}{4} = 1 \qquad \frac{6}{4} = 1$$

$$\frac{7}{4} = 1 \qquad \frac{8}{4} = 2 \qquad \frac{9}{4} = 2$$

Because of this behavior, you should never use integers to calculate real-world quantities that vary continuously, such as distance, speed, or time. Use integers only for things that are intrinsically integer in nature, such as counters and indices.

Programming Pitfalls
Beware of integer arithmetic. Integer division often gives unexpected results.

2.5.2 Real Arithmetic

Real arithmetic (or **floating-point arithmetic**) is arithmetic involving real constants and variables. Real arithmetic always produces a real result that is essentially what you expect. For example, real arithmetic produces the following results:

$$\frac{3.}{4.} = 0.75 \qquad \frac{4.}{4.} = 1. \qquad \frac{5.}{4.} = 1.25 \qquad \frac{6.}{4.} = 1.50$$

$$\frac{7.}{4.} = 1.75 \qquad \frac{8.}{4.} = 2. \qquad \frac{9.}{4.} = 2.25 \qquad \frac{1.}{3.} = 0.3333333$$

However, real numbers do have peculiarities. Because of the finite word length of a computer, some real numbers cannot be represented exactly. For example, the number 1/3 is equal to 0.33333333333... , but since the numbers stored in the computer have limited precision, the representation of 1/3 in the computer might be 0.3333333. As a result of this limitation in precision, some quantities that are theoretically equal will not be equal when the computer evaluates them. For example, on some computers

$$3. * (1. / 3.) \neq 1.$$

but

$$2. * (1. / 2.) = 1$$

Tests for equality must be performed very cautiously when working with real numbers.

Programming Pitfalls
Beware of real arithmetic. Because of limited precision, two theoretically identical expressions often give slightly different results.

2.5.3 Hierarchy of Operations

Often, many arithmetic operations are combined into a single expression. For example, consider the equation for the distance traveled by an object starting from rest and subjected to a constant acceleration:

```
distance = 0.5 * accel * time ** 2
```

This expression contains two multiplications and an exponentiation. In such an expression, it is important to know the order in which the operations are evaluated. If exponentiation is evaluated before multiplication, this expression is equivalent to

```
distance = 0.5 * accel * (time ** 2)
```

But if multiplication is evaluated before exponentiation, this expression is equivalent to

```
distance = (0.5 * accel * time) ** 2
```

These two equations have different results, and you must be able to distinguish between them.

To make the evaluation of expressions unambiguous, Fortran has established a series of rules governing the hierarchy or order in which operations are evaluated within an expression. The Fortran rules generally follow the normal rules of algebra. The order in which the arithmetic operations are evaluated follows.

1. The contents of all parentheses are evaluated first, starting from the innermost parentheses and working outward.
2. All exponentials are evaluated, working from right to left.
3. All multiplications and divisions are evaluated, working from left to right.
4. All additions and subtractions are evaluated, working from left to right.

Following these rules, we see that the first of our two possible interpretations is correct—time is squared before the multiplications are performed.

EXAMPLE 2–1 Variables a, b, c, d, e, f, and g have been initialized to the following values:

$$a = 3. \qquad b = 2. \qquad c = 5. \qquad d = 4.$$
$$e = 10. \qquad f = 2. \qquad g = 3.$$

Evaluate the following Fortran assignment statements:

a. output = a*b+c*d+e/f**g
b. output = a*(b+c)*d+(e/f)**g
c. output = a*(b+c)*(d+e)/f**g

SOLUTION

a. Expression to evaluate   output = a*b+c*d+e/f**g
   Fill in numbers   output = 3.*2.+5.*4.+10./2.**3.
   Evaluate 2.**3.   output = 3.*2.+5.*4.+10./8.
   Evaluate multiplications and
   divisions from left to right   output = 6.   +5.*4.+10./8.
                                   output = 6.   +20. +10./8.
                                   output = 6.   +20. + 1.25
   Evaluate additions   output = 27.25
b. Expression to evaluate   output = a*(b+c)*d+(e/f)**g
   Fill in numbers   output = 3.*(2.+5.)*4.+(10./2.)**3.
   Evaluate parentheses   output = 3.*7.*4.+5.**3.
   Evaluate exponents   output = 3.*7.*4.+125.
   Evaluate multiplications and
   divisions from left to right   output = 21.*4.+125.
                                   output = 84. + 125.
   Evaluate additions   output = 209.
c. Expression to evaluate   output = a*(b+c)*(d+e)/f**g
   Fill in numbers   output = 3.*(2.+5.)*(4.+10.)/2.**3.
   Evaluate parentheses   output = 3.*7.*14./2.**3.
   Evaluate exponents   output = 3.*7.*14./8.
   Evaluate multiplications and
   divisions from left to right   output = 21.*14./8.
                                   output = 294./8.
                                   output = 36.75

2

The preceding examples clearly show how the order in which operations are performed has a major effect on the final result of an algebraic expression.

EXAMPLE 2–2 Variables a, b, and c have been initialized to the following values:

$$a = 3. \quad b = 2. \quad c = 3.$$

Evaluate the following Fortran assignment statements:

a. output = a**(b**c)
b. output = (a**b)**c
c. output = a**b**c

SOLUTION

a. Expression to evaluate   output = a**(b**c)
    Fill in numbers   output = 3.**(2.**3.)
    Evaluate expression in parentheses   output = 3.**8.
    Evaluate remaining expression   output = 6561.
b. Expression to evaluate   output = (a**b)**c
    Fill in numbers   output = (3.**2.)**3.
    Evaluate expression in parentheses   output = 9.**3.
    Evaluate remaining expression   output = 729.
c. Expression to evaluate   output = a**b**c
    Fill in numbers   output = 3.**2.**3.
    Evaluate right-most exponent   output = 3.**8.
    Evaluate remaining exponent   output = 6561.

The results of *a* and *c* are identical, but the expression in *a* is easier to understand and less ambiguous than the expression in *c*.

Every expression in a program should be as clear as possible because any program of value must be maintained and modified during its life. You should always ask yourself, Will I easily understand this expression if I come back to it in six months? Can another programmer look at my code and easily understand what I am doing? If there is any doubt in your mind, use extra parentheses in the expression to make it as clear as possible.

Good Programming Practice
Use parentheses as necessary to make your equations clear and easy to understand.

If parentheses are used within an expression, then the parentheses must be balanced. That is, the expression must contain an equal number of open parentheses and close parentheses. It is an error to have more of one type than the other. Errors of this sort are usually typographical, and they are caught by the Fortran compiler. For example, this expression

$$(2. + 4.) / 2.)$$

produces an error during compilation because of the mismatched parentheses.

2.5.4 Mixed-Mode Arithmetic

When an arithmetic operation is performed using two real numbers, its immediate result is of type real. Similarly, when an arithmetic operation is performed using two integers, the result is of type integer. In general, arithmetic operations are defined only between numbers of the same type. For example, the addition of two real numbers is a valid operation, and the addition of two integers is a valid operation, but the addition of a real number and an integer is not a valid operation. This is true because real numbers and integers are stored in completely different forms in the computer.

What happens if an operation is between a real number and an integer? Expressions containing both real numbers and integers are called **mixed-mode expressions,** and arithmetic involving both real numbers and integers is called *mixed-mode arithmetic*. In the case of an operation between a real number and an integer, the computer converts the integer into a real number, and real arithmetic is used on the numbers. The result is of type real. For example, consider the following equations:

Integer expression	$\dfrac{3}{2}$	is evaluated to be 1	(integer result)
Real expression	$\dfrac{3.}{2.}$	is evaluated to be 1.5	(real result)
Mixed-mode expression	$\dfrac{3.}{2}$	is evaluated to be 1.5	(real result)

The rules governing mixed-mode arithmetic can be confusing to beginning programmers. Even experienced programmers may trip up on them from time to time, especially when the mixed-mode expression involves division. Consider the following expressions:

Expression	Result
1. 1 + 1/4	1
2. 1. + 1/4	1.
3. 1 + 1./4	1.25

Expression 1 contains only integers, so it is evaluated by integer arithmetic. In integer arithmetic 1 / 4 = 0 and 1 + 0 = 1, so the final result is 1 (an integer). Expression 2 is a mixed-mode expression containing both real numbers and integers. However, the first operation to be performed is a division, since division comes before addition in the hierarchy of operations. The division is between integers, so the result is 1 / 4 = 0. Next comes an addition between a real 1. and an integer 0, so the compiler converts the integer 0 into a real number and then performs the addition. The resulting number is 1. (a real number). Expression 3 is also a mixed-mode expression containing both real numbers and integers. The first operation to be performed is a division between a real number and an integer, so the compiler converts the integer 4 into a real number and then performs the division. The result is a real 0.25. The next operation to be performed is an addition between an integer 1 and a real 0.25, so the compiler converts the integer 1 into a real number and then performs the addition. The resulting number is 1.25 (a real number).

To summarize:

1. An operation between an integer and a real number is called a mixed-mode operation, and an expression containing one or more such operations is called a mixed-mode expression.
2. When a mixed-mode operation is encountered, Fortran converts the integer into a real number and then performs the operation to get a real result.
3. The automatic mode conversion does not occur until a real number and an integer both appear in the same operation. Therefore, it is possible for a portion of an expression to be evaluated in integer arithmetic, followed by another portion evaluated in real arithmetic.

Automatic type conversion also occurs when the variable to which the expression is assigned is of a different type than the result of the expression. For example, consider the following assignment statement:

```
nres = 1.25 + 9 / 4
```

where `nres` is an integer. The expression to the right of the equal sign evaluates to `3.25`, which is a real number. Since `nres` is an integer, the `3.25` is automatically converted into the integer number 3 before being stored in `nres`.

Programming Pitfalls
Mixed-mode expressions are dangerous because they are hard to understand and may produce misleading results. Avoid them whenever possible.

Later in this chapter, you will learn about type conversion functions, which can be used to force a variable of one type to be converted into a variable of the other type. We will use them to make our equations clearer.

2.5.5 Mixed-Mode Arithmetic and Exponentiation

As a general rule, mixed-mode arithmetic operations are undesirable because they are hard to understand and can sometimes lead to unexpected results. However, there is one exception to this rule: exponentiation. For exponentiation, mixed-mode operation is actually desirable.

To understand why this is so, consider the assignment statement

```
result = y ** n
```

where `result` and `y` are real and `n` is an integer. The expression `y ** n` is shorthand for "use `y` as a factor `n` times," and that is exactly what the computer does when it encounters this expression. Since `y` is a real number and the computer is multiplying `y` by itself, the computer is really doing real arithmetic and not mixed-mode arithmetic!

Now consider the assignment statement

```
result = y ** x
```

where `result`, `y`, and `x` are real. The expression `y ** x` is shorthand for "use `y` as a factor `x` times," but this time `x` is not an integer. Instead, `x` might be a number like 2.5. It is not physically possible to multiply a number by itself 2.5 times, so we have to rely on indirect methods to calculate `y ** x` in this case. The most common approach is to use the standard algebraic formula, which says

$$y^x = e^{x \ln y} \tag{2-1}$$

Using Equation 2–1 we can evaluate `y ** x` by taking the natural logarithm of `y`, multiplying by `x`, and then calculating e to the resulting power. While this technique certainly works, it takes longer to perform and is less accurate than an ordinary series of multiplications. Therefore, if given a choice, we should try to raise real numbers to integer powers instead of to real powers.

Good Programming Practice
Use integer exponents instead of real exponents whenever possible.

Also, note that it is not possible to raise a negative number to a negative real power. Raising a negative number to an integer power is a perfectly legal operation. For example, `(-2.0)**2 = 4`. However, raising a negative number to a real power will not work, since the natural logarithm of a negative number is undefined. Therefore, the expression `(-2.0)**2.0` will produce a run-time error.

Programming Pitfalls
Never raise a negative number to a real power.

Quiz 2–2

This quiz provides a quick check to see if you understand the concepts introduced in section 2.5. If you have trouble with the quiz, reread the section, ask your instructor, or discuss the material with a fellow student. The answers to this quiz are found in the back of the book.

1. In what order are the arithmetic and logical operations evaluated if they appear within an arithmetic expression? How do parentheses modify this order?

(continued)

(concluded)

2. Are the following expressions legal or illegal? If they are legal, what is their result? If they are illegal, what is wrong with them?
   a. 37 / 3
   b. 37 + 17 / 3
   c. 28 / 3 / 4
   d. (28 / 3) / 4
   e. 28 / (3 / 4)
   f. -3. ** 4. / 2.
   g. 3. ** (-4. / 2.)
   h. 4. ** -3

3. Evaluate the following expressions:
   a. 2 + 5 * 2 - 5
   b. (2 + 5) * (2 - 5)
   c. 2 + (5 * 2) - 5
   d. (2 + 5) * 2 - 5

4. Are the following expressions legal or illegal? If they are legal, what is their result? If they are illegal, what is wrong with them?
   a. 2. ** 2. ** 3.
   b. 2. ** (-2.)
   c. (-2) ** 2
   d. (-2.) ** (-2.2)

5. Are the following statements legal or illegal? If they are legal, what is their result? If they are illegal, what is wrong with them?

   ```
   INTEGER :: i, j
   INTEGER, PARAMETER :: k = 4
   i = k ** 2
   j = i / k
   k = i + j
   ```

6. What value is stored in result after the following statements are executed?

   ```
   REAL :: a, b, c, result
   a = 10.
   b = 1.5
   c = 5.
   result = a / b + b * c ** 2
   ```

7. What values are stored in a and n after the following statements are executed?

   ```
   REAL :: a
   INTEGER :: n, i, j
   i = 10.
   j = 3
   n = i / j
   a = i / j
   ```

◼ 2.6

ASSIGNMENT STATEMENTS AND LOGICAL CALCULATIONS

Like arithmetic calculations, logical calculations are performed with an assignment statement, whose form is

```
logical_variable_name = logical expression
```

The expression to the right of the equal sign can be any combination of valid logical constants, logical variables, and logical operators. A **logical operator** is an operator on numeric, character, or logical data that yields a logical result. The two basic types of logical operators are **relational operators** and **combinational operators.**

2.6.1 Relational Operators

Relational logic operators are operators with two numerical or character operands that yield a logical result. The result depends on the *relationship* between the two values being compared, so these operators are called relational. The general form of a relational operator is

$$a_1 \ op \ a_2$$

where a_1 and a_2 are arithmetic expressions, variables, constants, or character strings and op is one of the relational logical operators in Table 2–3.

Each relational operator has two forms. The first form is composed of symbols, and the second is composed of characters surrounded by periods. In the second form, the periods are a part of the operator and must always be present. The first form of the operators was introduced in Fortran 90, while the second form is a holdover from earlier versions of Fortran. You may use either form of the operators in your program, but the first form is preferred in new programs.

If the relationship between a_1 and a_2 expressed by the operator is true, then the operation returns a value of .TRUE.; otherwise, the operation returns a value of .FALSE..

◼ **TABLE 2–3**
Relational logic operators

Operation		Meaning
New style	Older style	
==	.EQ.	Equal to
/=	.NE.	Not equal to
>	.GT.	Greater than
>=	.GE.	Greater than or equal to
<	.LT.	Less than
<=	.LE.	Less than or equal to

Some relational operations and their results follow:

Operation	Result
3 < 4	.TRUE.
3 <= 4	.TRUE.
3 == 4	.FALSE.
3 > 4	.FALSE.
4 <= 4	.TRUE.
'A' < 'B'	.TRUE.

The last logical expression is .TRUE. because characters are evaluated in alphabetical order.

The equivalence relational operator is written with two equal signs, while the assignment operator is written with a single equal sign. These are very different operators which beginning programmers often confuse. The == symbol is a *comparison* operation that returns a logical result, whereas the = symbol *assigns* the value of the expression to the right of the equal sign to the variable on the left of the equal sign. It is a very common mistake for beginning programmers to use a single equal sign when trying to perform a comparison.

Programming Pitfalls
Be careful not to confuse the equivalence relational operator (==) with the assignment operator (=).

In the hierarchy of operations, relational operators are evaluated after all arithmetic operators have been evaluated. Therefore, the following two expressions are equivalent (both are .TRUE.):

```
7 + 3 < 2 + 11

(7 + 3) < (2 + 11)
```

If the comparison is between real and integer values, then the integer value is converted to a real value before the comparison is performed. Comparisons between numerical data and character data are illegal and will cause a compile-time error.

```
4 == 4.      .TRUE. (Integer is converted to real and comparison is made.)
4 <= 'A'     Illegal—produces a compile-time error.
```

2.6.2 Combinational Logic Operators

Combinational logic operators are operators with one or two logical operands that yield a logical result. There are four binary operators, .AND., .OR., .EQV., and .NEQV., and one unary operator, .NOT.. The general form of a binary combinational logic operation is

$$l_1 \ .op. \ l_2$$

■ **TABLE 2–4**
Combinational logic operators

Operator	Function	Definition
l_1 .AND. l_2	Logical AND	Result is TRUE if both l_1 and l_2 are TRUE.
l_1 .OR. l_2	Logical OR	Result is TRUE if either or both of l_1 and l_2 are TRUE.
l_1 .EQV. l_2	Logical equivalence	Result is TRUE if l_1 is the same as l_2 (either both TRUE or both FALSE).
l_1 .NEQV. l_2	Logical nonequivalence	Result is TRUE if one of l_1 and l_2 is TRUE and the other one is FALSE.
.NOT. l_1	Logical NOT	Result is TRUE if l_1 is FALSE, and FALSE if l_1 is TRUE.

where l_1 and l_2 are logical expressions, variables, or constants, and .op. is one of the combinational operators in Table 2–4.

The periods are a part of the operator and must always be present. If the relationship between l_1 and l_2 expressed by the operator is true, then the operation returns a value of .TRUE.; otherwise, the operation returns a value of .FALSE..

The results of the operators are summarized in the **truth tables** in Table 2–5, which show the result of each operation for all possible combinations of l_1 and l_2.

In the hierarchy of operations, combinational logic operators are evaluated after all arithmetic operations and all relational operators have been evaluated. The order in which the operators in an expression are evaluated follows.

1. All arithmetic operators are evaluated first in the order previously described.
2. All relational operators (==, /=, >, >=, <, <=) are evaluated, working from left to right.

■ **TABLE 2–5(a)**
Truth tables for binary combinational logic operators

l_1	l_2	l_1 .AND. l_2	l_1 .OR. l_2	l_1 .EQV. l_2	l_1 .NEQV. l_2
.FALSE.	.FALSE.	.FALSE.	.FALSE.	.TRUE.	.FALSE.
.FALSE.	.TRUE.	.FALSE.	.TRUE.	.FALSE.	.TRUE.
.TRUE.	.FALSE.	.FALSE.	.TRUE.	.FALSE.	.TRUE.
.TRUE.	.TRUE.	.TRUE.	.TRUE.	.TRUE.	.FALSE.

■ **TABLE 2–5(b)**
Truth table for .NOT. operator

l_1	.NOT. l_1
.FALSE.	.TRUE.
.TRUE.	.FALSE.

3. All `.NOT.` operators are evaluated.
4. All `.AND.` operators are evaluated, working from left to right.
5. All `.OR.` operators are evaluated, working from left to right.
6. All `.EQV.` and `.NEQV.` operators are evaluated, working from left to right.

As with arithmetic operations, parentheses can be used to change the default order of evaluation. Examples of some combinational logic operators and their results are given in Example 2–3.

EXAMPLE 2–3 Assume that the following variables are initialized with the values shown, and calculate the result of the specified expressions:

```
L1 = .TRUE.
L2 = .TRUE.
L3 = .FALSE.
```

Logical Expression	Result
a. `.NOT. L1`	`.FALSE.`
b. `L1 .OR. L3`	`.TRUE.`
c. `L1 .AND. L3`	`.FALSE.`
d. `L2 .NEQV. L3`	`.TRUE.`
e. `L1 .AND. L2 .OR. L3`	`.TRUE.`
f. `L1 .OR. L2 .AND. L3`	`.FALSE.`
g. `.NOT. (L1 .EQV. L2)`	`.FALSE.`

The `.NOT.` operator is evaluated before other combinational logic operators. Therefore, the parentheses in part *g* of Example 2–3 were required. If they had been absent, the expression would have been evaluated in the order (`.NOT. L1`) `.EQV. L2`.

In the Fortran 90 and Fortran 95 standards, combinational logic operations involving numerical or character data are illegal and will cause a compile-time error. For example:

```
4 .AND. 3    Error
```

2.6.3 The Significance of Logical Variables and Expressions

Logical variables and expressions are rarely the final product of a Fortran program. Nevertheless, they are absolutely essential to the proper operation of most programs. As you will see in Chapter 3, logical values control most of the major branching and looping structures of Fortran, so you must be able to read and write logical expressions to understand and use Fortran control statements.

■ 2.7
ASSIGNMENT STATEMENTS AND CHARACTER VARIABLES

Character manipulations are performed with an assignment statement of the form

```
character_variable_name = character expression
```

The assignment statement calculates the value of the character expression to the right of the equal sign and assigns that value to the variable named on the left of the equal sign.

The expression to the right of the equal sign can be any combination of valid character constants, character variables, and character operators. A **character operator** is an operator on character data that yields a character result. The two basic types of character operators are substring specifications and concatenation.

A character expression may be assigned to a character variable with an assignment statement. If the character expression is *shorter* than the length of the character variable to which it is assigned, then the rest of the variable is padded with blanks. For example, the statements

```
CHARACTER(len=3) :: file_ext
file_ext = 'f'
```

store the value 'fƀƀ' into variable `file_ext` (ƀ denotes a blank character). If the character expression is *longer* than the length of the character variable to which it is assigned, then the excess portion of the character variable is discarded. For example, the statements

```
CHARACTER(len=3) :: file_ext_2
file_ext_2 = 'FILE01'
```

store the value 'FIL' into variable `file_ext_2`, and the characters 'E01' are discarded.

2.7.1 Substring Specifications

A **substring specification** selects a portion of a character variable and treats that portion as if it were an independent character variable. For example, if the variable `str1` is a six-character variable containing the string '123456', then the substring `str1(2:4)` would be a three-character variable containing the string '234'. The substring `str1(2:4)` really refers to the same memory locations as characters 2 through 4 of `str1`, so if the contents of `str1(2:4)` are changed, the characters in the middle of variable `str1` will also be changed.

A character substring is denoted by placing integer values representing the starting and ending character numbers separated by a colon in parentheses following the variable name. If the ending character number is less than the starting number, a zero-length character string will be produced.

Example 2–4 illustrates the use of substrings.

EXAMPLE 2–4 What will the contents of variables a, b, and c be at the end of the following program?

```
PROGRAM test
CHARACTER (len=8) :: a, b, c
a = 'ABCDEFGHIJ'
b = '12345678'
c = a(5:7)
b(7:8) = a(2:6)
END PROGRAM
```

SOLUTION The character manipulations in this program are

1. Line 3 assigns the string 'ABCDEFGHIJ' to a, but only the first eight characters are saved because a is only eight characters long. Therefore, a will contain 'ABCDEFGH'.
2. Line 4 assigns the string '12345678' to b.
3. Line 5 assigns the character substring a(5:7) to c. Because c is eight characters long, five blanks will be padded onto variable c and c will contain 'EFGbbbbb'.
4. Line 6 assigns substring a(2:6) to substring b(7:8). Because b(7:8) is only two characters long, only the first two characters of a(2:6) will be used. Therefore, variable b will contain '123456BC'.

2.7.2 The Concatenation (//) Operator

It is possible to combine two or more strings or substrings into a single large string. This operation is known as **concatenation.** The concatenation operator in Fortran is a double slash with no space between the slashes (//). For example, after the following lines are executed

```
PROGRAM test
CHARACTER(len=10) :: a
CHARACTER(len=8) :: b, c
a = 'ABCDEFGHIJ'
b = '12345678'
c = a(1:3) // b(4:5) // a(6:8)
END PROGRAM
```

variable c will contain the string 'ABC45FGH'.

2.7.3 Relational Operators with Character Data

Character strings can be compared in logical expressions using the relational operators ==, /-, <, <=, >, and >=. The result of the comparison is a logical value that is either true or false. For instance, the expression '123' == '123' is true, while the expression '123' == '1234' is false. In standard Fortran, character strings may be compared with character strings, and numbers may be compared with numbers, but character strings may not be compared to numbers.

How are two characters compared to determine if one is greater than the other? The comparison is based on the **collating sequence** of the characters on the computer on which the program is being executed. The collating sequence of the characters is the order in which they occur within a specific character set. For example, the character 'A' is character number 65 in the ASCII character set, while the character 'B' is character number 66 in the set (see Appendix A). Therefore, the logical expression 'A' < 'B' is true in the ASCII character set. On the other hand, the character 'a' is character number 97 in the ASCII set, so 'a' < 'A' is false in the ASCII character set. Note that during character comparisons, a lowercase letter is different from the corresponding uppercase letter.

How are two strings compared to determine if one is greater than the other? The comparison begins with the first character in each string. If they are the same, then the second two characters are compared. This process continues until the first difference is found between the strings. For example, `'AAAAAB' > 'AAAAAA'`.

What happens if the strings are different lengths? The comparison begins with the first letter in each string and progresses through each letter until a difference is found. If the two strings are the same all the way to the end of one of them, then the other string is considered the larger of the two. For example, `'AB' > 'AAAA'` and `'AAAAA' > 'AAAA'`.

2.8

INTRINSIC FUNCTIONS

In mathematics a **function** is an expression that accepts one or more input values and calculates a single result from them. Scientific and technical calculations usually require functions that are more complex than the simple addition, subtraction, multiplication, division, and exponentiation operations that we have discussed so far. Some of these functions are very common and are used in many different technical disciplines. Others are specific to a single problem or a small number of problems. Examples of very common functions are the trigonometric functions, logarithms, and square roots. Examples of rarer functions are the hyperbolic functions and Bessel functions.

The Fortran 90/95 language has mechanisms to support both the very common functions and the less common functions. Many of the most common ones are built directly into the Fortran language. They are called **intrinsic functions.** Less common functions are not included in the Fortran language, but the user can supply any function needed to solve a particular problem as either an **external function** or an **internal function.** External functions will be described in Chapter 6, and internal functions will be described in Chapter 9.

A Fortran function calculates a single output value from one or more input values. The input values to the function are known as **arguments;** they appear in parentheses immediately after the function name. The output of a function is a single number,

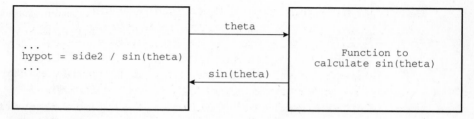

FIGURE 2–4
When a function is included in a Fortran statement, the argument(s) of the function are passed to a separate routine that computes the result of the function. Then the result is used in place of the function in the original calculation.

logical value, or character string, which can be used with other functions, constants, and variables in Fortran expressions. When a function appears in a Fortran statement, the arguments of the function are passed to a separate routine that computes the result of the function, and then the result is used in place of the function in the original calculation. Intrinsic functions are supplied with the Fortran compiler. For external and internal functions, the user must supply the routine.

A list of some common intrinsic functions is given in Table 2–6. A complete list of Fortran 90 and Fortran 95 intrinsic functions is given in Appendix B, along with a brief description of each one.

TABLE 2–6
Some common intrinsic functions

Function name and arguments	Function value	Argument type	Result type	Comments
SQRT(X)	$\sqrt{x}$	R	R	Square root of x for $x \geq 0$.
ABS(X)		R/I	*	Absolute value of x.
ACHAR(I)		I	CHAR(1)	Returns the character at position I in the ASCII collating sequence.
SIN(X)	$\sin(x)$	R	R	Sine of x (x must be in *radians*).
COS(X)	$\cos(x)$	R	R	Cosine of x (x must be in *radians*).
TAN(X)	$\tan(x)$	R	R	Tangent of x (x must be in *radians*).
EXP(X)	e^x	R	R	e is raised to the xth power.
LOG(X)	$\log_e(x)$	R	R	Natural logarithm of x for $x > 0$.
LOG10(X)	$\log_{10}(x)$	R	R	Base-10 logarithm of x for $x > 0$.
IACHAR(C)		CHAR(1)	I	Returns the position of the character C in the ASCII collating sequence.
INT(X)		R	I	Integer part of x (x is truncated).
NINT(X)		R	I	Nearest integer to x (x is rounded).
REAL(I)		I	R	Converts integer value to real.
MOD(A,B)		R/I	*	Remainder or modulo function.
MAX(A,B)		R/I	*	Picks the larger of a and b.
MIN(A,B)		R/I	*	Picks the smaller of a and b.
ASIN(X)	$\sin^{-1}(x)$	R	R	Inverse sine of x for $-1 \leq x \leq 1$ (results in *radians*).
ACOS(X)	$\cos^{-1}(x)$	R	R	Inverse cosine for x for $-1 \leq x \leq 1$ (results in *radians*).
ATAN(X)	$\tan^{-1}(x)$	R	R	Inverse tangent of x (results in *radians*).

Notes: * = Result is of the same type as the input argument(s).
R = REAL, I = INTEGER, CHAR(1) = CHARACTER(len=1)

Fortran functions are used by including them in an expression. For example, the intrinsic function SIN can be used to calculate the sine of a number as follows:

```
y = SIN(theta)
```

where theta is the argument of the function SIN. After this statement is executed, the variable y contains the sine of the value stored in variable theta. Note from Table 2–6 that the trigonometric functions expect their arguments to be in radians. If the variable theta is in degrees, then we must convert degrees to radians ($180° = \pi$ radians) before computing the sine. This conversion can be done in the same statement as the sine calculation:

```
y = SIN (theta*(3.141593/180.))
```

Alternatively, we could create a named constant containing the conversion factor and refer to that constant when the function is executed:

```
INTEGER, PARAMETER :: deg_to_rad = 3.141593 / 180.
y = SIN (theta * deg_to_rad)
```

The REAL, INT, and NINT functions may be used to avoid undesirable mixed-mode expressions by explicitly converting data types from one form to another. The REAL function converts an integer into a real number, and the INT and NINT functions convert real numbers into integers. The INT function truncates the real number, while the NINT function rounds it. To understand the distinction between these two operations, consider the real number 2.9995. The result of INT(2.9995) is 2, while the result of NINT(2.9995) is 3. The NINT function is very useful when converting back from real to integer form, since the small round-off errors occurring in real calculations will not affect the resulting integer value.

The argument of a function can be a constant, a variable, an expression, or even the result of another function. All of the following statements are legal:

```
y  =  SIN(3.141593)      (argument is a constant)
y  =  SIN(x)             (argument is a variable)
y  =  SIN(pi*x)          (argument is an expression)
y  =  SIN(SQRT(x))       (argument is the result of another function)
```

Functions may be used in expressions anywhere that a constant or variable may be used. However, functions may never appear on the left side of the assignment operator (equal sign), since they are not memory locations and nothing can be stored in them.

The type of argument required by a function and the type of value returned by it are specified in Table 2–6 for the intrinsic functions listed there. Some of these intrinsic functions are **generic functions,** which means that they can use more than one type of input data. The absolute value function ABS is a generic function. If X is a real number, then the type of ABS(X) is real. If X is an integer, then the type of ABS(X) is integer. Some functions are called **specific functions;** they can use only one specific type of input data and produce only one specific type of output value. For example, the function IABS requires an integer argument and returns an integer result. A complete list of all intrinsic functions (both generic and specific) appears in Appendix B.

2.9

LIST-DIRECTED INPUT AND OUTPUT STATEMENTS

An **input statement** reads one or more values from an input device and stores them into variables specified by the programmer. The input device could be a keyboard in an interactive environment or an input disk file in a batch environment. An **output statement** writes one or more values to an output device. The output device could be a CRT screen in an interactive environment or an output listing file in a batch environment.

We have already seen input and output statements in `my_first_program`, which is shown in Figure 2–2. The input statement in the figure was of the form

```
READ (*,*) input_list
```

where *input_list* is the list of variables into which the values being read are placed. If there is more than one variable in the list, they should be separated by commas. The parentheses `(*,*)` in the statement contain control information for the read. The first field in the parentheses specifies the *input/output unit* (or io unit) from which the data is to be read. (The concept of an input/output unit is explained in Chapter 4.) An asterisk in this field means that the data is to be read from the standard input device for the computer—usually the keyboard when running in interactive mode and an input file when running in batch mode. The second field in the parentheses specifies the format in which the data is to be read. (Formats are also explained in Chapter 4.) An asterisk in this field means that list-directed input (sometimes called *free-format input*) is to be used.

The term **list-directed input** means that the types of the variables in the variable list determine the required format of the input data. For example, consider the following statements:

```
PROGRAM input_example
INTEGER :: i, j
REAL :: a
CHARACTER(len=12) :: chars
READ (*,*) i, j, a, chars
END PROGRAM
```

The input data supplied to the program must consist of two integers, a real number, and a character string. Furthermore, they must be in that order. The values may be all on one line separated by commas or blanks, or they may be on separate lines. The list-directed READ statement will continue to read input data until values have been found for all of the variables in the list. If the input data supplied to the program at execution time is

```
1, 2, 3., 'This one.'
```

then the variable i will be filled with a 1, j will be filled with a 2, a will be filled with a 3.0, and chars will be filled with 'This one.', as shown in Figure 2–5. Since the input character string is only 9 characters long, whereas the variable chars has room for 12 characters, the string is *left justified* in the character variable and three blanks are automatically added at the end of it to fill out the remaining space. Also

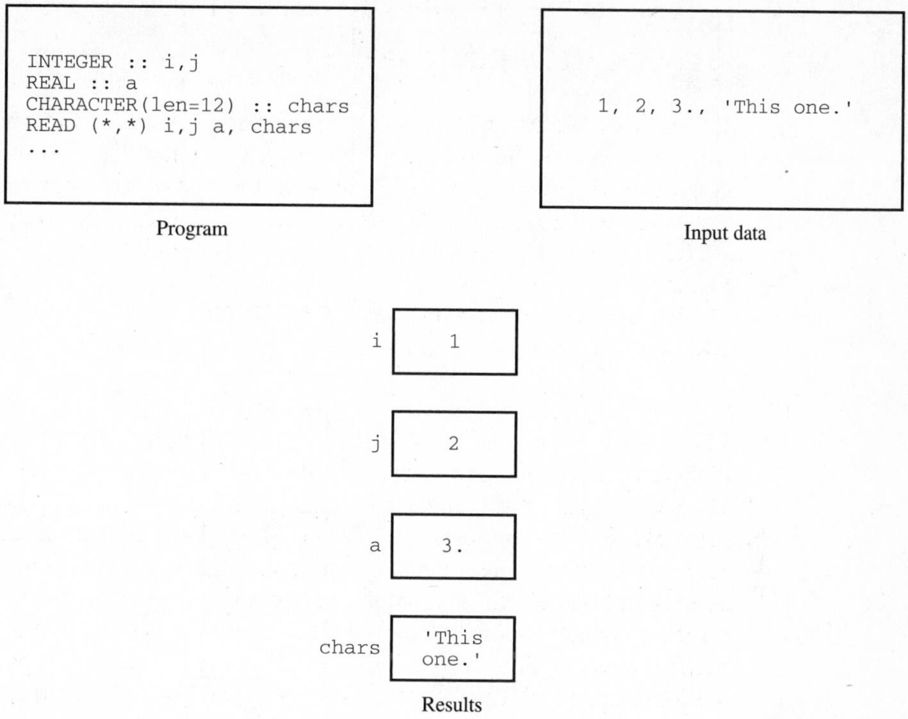

```
INTEGER :: i,j
REAL :: a
CHARACTER(len=12) :: chars
READ (*,*) i,j a, chars
...
```

Program

```
1, 2, 3., 'This one.'
```

Input data

2

i | 1

j | 2

a | 3.

chars | 'This one.'

Results

FIGURE 2–5
For list-directed input, the type and order of the input data values must match the type and order of the supplied input data.

note that for list-directed reads, input character strings must be enclosed in single or double quotes if they contain spaces.

When using list-directed input, the values to be read must match the variables in the input list both in order and type. If the input data had been

```
1, 2, 'This one.' , 3.
```

then a run-time error would have occurred when the program tried to read the data.

Each READ statement in a program begins reading from a new line of input data. If any data is left over on the previous input line, that data is discarded. For example, consider the following program:

```
PROGRAM input_example_2
INTEGER :: i, j, k, l
READ (*,*) i, j
READ (*,*) k, l
END PROGRAM
```

If the input data to this program is

```
1, 2, 3, 4
5, 6, 7, 8
```

```
INTEGER :: i,j,k,l
REAL (*,*) i,j
REAL (*,*) k,l
...
```

Program

```
1, 2, 3, 4
5, 6, 7, 8
```

Input data

i | 1

j | 2

k | 5

l | 6

Results

FIGURE 2–6
Each list-directed READ statement begins reading from a new line of input data, and any
unused data left on the previous line is discarded. Here the values 3 and 4 on the first
line of input data are never used.

then after the READ statements, i will contain a 1, j will contain a 2, k will contain
a 5, and l will contain a 6, as shown in Figure 2–6.

It is a good idea to always *echo* any value that you read into a program from a
keyboard. **Echoing** a value means displaying the value with a WRITE statement after
it has been read. If you do not do so, a typing error in the input data might cause a
wrong answer, and the user of the program would never know that anything was
wrong. You may echo the data either immediately after it is read or somewhere further down in the program output, but every input variable should be echoed somewhere in the program's output.

Good Programming Practice
Echo any variables that a user enters into a program from a keyboard so
that the user can be certain that they were typed and processed correctly.

The *list-directed output statement* is of the form

WRITE (*,*) output_list

where *output_list* is the list of data items (variables, constants, or expressions) that are to be written. If more than one item appears in the list, then the items should be separated by commas. The parentheses (*,*) in the statement contain control information for the write, where the two asterisks have the same meaning as they do in a list-directed read statement.

The term **list-directed output** means that the types of the values in the output list of the write statement determine the format of the output data. For example, consider the following statements:

```
PROGRAM output_example
INTEGER :: ix
LOGICAL :: test
REAL :: theta
ix = 1
test = .TRUE.
theta = 3.141593
WRITE (*,*) ' IX =                    ', ix
WRITE (*,*) ' THETA =                 ', theta
WRITE (*,*) ' COS(THETA) =            ', COS(theta)
WRITE (*,*) ' TEST =                  ', test
WRITE (*,*) REAL(ix), NINT(theta)
END PROGRAM
```

The output resulting from these statements is

```
 IX =                    1
 THETA =                 3.141593
 COS(THETA) =           -1.000000
 TEST =                  T
          1.000000       3
```

This example illustrates several points about the list-directed write statement:

1. The output list may contain constants (' IX = ' is a constant), variables, functions, and expressions. In each case, the value of the constant, variable, function, or expression is output to the standard output device.
2. The format of the output data matches the type of the value being output. For example, even though theta is of type real, NINT(theta) is of type integer. Therefore, the sixth write statement produces an output of 3 (the nearest integer to 3.141593). Also note that when a logical value is included in a WRITE statement, a single T or F (as appropriate) is written out.
3. The output of list-directed write statements is not very pretty. The values printed out do not line up in neat columns, and there is no way to control the number of significant digits displayed for real numbers. You will learn how to produce neatly formatted output in Chapter 4.

Quiz 2–3

This quiz provides a quick check to see if you understand the concepts introduced in sections 2.6 through 2.9. If you have trouble with the quiz, reread the sections, ask your instructor, or discuss the material with a fellow student. The answers to this quiz are found in the back of the book.

(continued)

2

(continued)

Convert the following algebraic equations into Fortran assignment statements:

1. The equivalent resistance R_{eq} of four resistors R_1, R_2, R_3, and R_4 connected in series:

$$R_{eq} = R_1 + R_2 + R_3 + R_4$$

2. The equivalent resistance R_{eq} of four resistors R_1, R_2, R_3, and R_4 connected in parallel:

$$R_{eq} = \cfrac{1}{\cfrac{1}{R_1} + \cfrac{1}{R_2} + \cfrac{1}{R_3} + \cfrac{1}{R_4}}$$

3. The period T of an oscillating pendulum:

$$T = 2\pi\sqrt{\frac{L}{g}}$$

where L is the length of the pendulum and g is the acceleration due to gravity.

4. The equation for damped sinusoidal oscillation:

$$v(t) = V_M e^{-\alpha t} \cos \omega t$$

where V_M is the maximum value of the oscillation, α is the exponential damping factor, and ω is the angular velocity of the oscillation.

Convert the following Fortran assignment statements into algebraic equations:

5. The motion of an object in a constant gravitational field:

```
distance = 0.5 * accel * t**2 + vel_0 * t + pos_0
```

6. The oscillating frequency of a damped RLC circuit:

```
freq = 1. / (2. * pi * sqrt(1 * c))
```

where `pi` is π (3.141592...).

7. Energy storage in an inductor:

```
energy = 1.0 / 2.0 * inductance * current**2
```

8. What values will be printed out when the following statements are executed?

```
PROGRAM quiz_1
INTEGER :: i
LOGICAL :: 1
REAL :: a
a = 0.05
i = nint ( 2. * 3.141593 / a)
1 = i > 100
a = a * (5 / 3)
WRITE (*,*) i, a, 1
END PROGRAM
```

(continued)

2

(concluded)

9. Suppose that the real variables a, b, and c contain the values −10., 0.1, and 2.1, respectively, and that the logical variables 11, 12, and 13 contain the values .TRUE., .FALSE., and .FALSE., respectively. Is each of the following expressions legal or illegal? If an expression is legal, what will its result be?

a. a > b .OR. b > c
b. (.NOT. a) .OR. 11
c. 11 .AND. .NOT. 12
d. a < b .EQV. b < c
e. 11 .OR. 12 .AND. 13
f. 11 .OR. (12 .AND. 13)
g. (11 .OR. 12) .AND. 13
h. a .OR. b .AND. 11

10. Suppose that character variables str1, str2, and str3 contain the values 'abc', 'abcd', and 'ABC', respectively, and that a computer uses the ASCII character set. Is each of the following expressions legal or illegal? If an expression is legal, what will its result be?

a. str2(2:4)
b. str3 // str2(4:4)
c. str1 > str2
d. str1 > str3
e. str2 > 0
f. IACHAR('C') == 67
g. 'Z' >= ACHAR(100)

11. If the input data is as shown, what will be printed out by the following program?

```
PROGRAM quiz_2
INTEGER :: i, j, k
REAL :: a, b, c
READ (*,*) i, j, a
READ (*,*) b, k
c = SIN ((3.141593 / 180) * a)
WRITE (*,*) i, j, k, a, b, c
END PROGRAM
```

The input data is

```
1, 3
2., 45., 17.
30., 180, 6.
```

2.10

INITIALIZATION OF VARIABLES

Consider the following program:

```
PROGRAM init
INTEGER :: i
WRITE (*,*) i
END PROGRAM
```

What value is stored in the variable i? What will be printed out by the WRITE statement? The answer is: We don't know!

The variable i is an example of an **uninitialized variable.** It has been defined by the INTEGER :: i statement, but no value has been placed into it yet. The value of an uninitialized variable is not defined by the Fortran 90/95 standard. Some compilers automatically set uninitialized variables to zero, and some set them to different arbitrary patterns. Some compilers for older versions of Fortran leave whatever values previously existed at the memory location of the variables. Some compilers even produce a run-time error if a variable is used without first being initialized.

Uninitialized variables can present a serious problem. Since they are handled differently on different machines, a program that works fine on one computer may fail when transported to another machine. On some machines, the same program could work sometimes and fail sometimes, depending on the data left behind by the previous program occupying the same memory. Such a situation is totally unacceptable, and we must avoid it by always initializing all of the variables in our programs.

Good Programming Practice
Always initialize all variables in a program before using them.

The three techniques available to initialize variables in a Fortran program are assignment statements, READ statements, and initialization in type declaration statements.[4] An assignment statement assigns the value of the expression to the right of the equal sign to the variable on the left of the equal sign. In the following code the variable i is initialized to 1, and we know that a 1 will be printed out by the WRITE statement.

```
PROGRAM init_1
INTEGER :: i
i = 1
WRITE (*,*) i
END PROGRAM
```

---

[4]A fourth, older technique uses the DATA statement. This statement is kept for backward compatibility with earlier versions of Fortran, but it been superseded by initialization in type declaration statements. DATA statements should not be used in new programs. The DATA statement is described in Chapter 14.

A READ statement may be used to initialize variables with values input by the user. In the following code the variable i is initialized by the READ statement, and we know that whatever value was read by the READ statement will be printed out by the WRITE statement.

```
PROGRAM init_2
INTEGER :: i
READ (*,*) i
WRITE (*,*) i
END PROGRAM
```

The third technique available to initialize variables in a Fortran program is to specify their initial values in the type declaration statement that defines them. This declaration specifies that a value should be preloaded into a variable during the compilation and linking process. Note the fundamental difference between initialization in a type declaration statement and initialization in an assignment statement: A type declaration statement initializes the variable before the program begins to run, while an assignment statement initializes the variable during execution.

The form of a type declaration statement used to initialize variables is

```
type :: var1 = value, [var2 = value, . . . ]
```

Any number of variables may be declared and initialized in a single type declaration statement provided that they are separated by commas. An example of type declaration statements used to initialize a series of variables is

```
REAL :: time = 0.0, distance = 5128.
INTEGER :: loop = 10
LOGICAL :: done = .FALSE.
```

Before program execution, time is initialized to 0.0, distance is initialized to 5128., loop is initialized to 10, and done is initialized to .FALSE..

In the following code, the variable i is initialized by the type declaration statement, so we know that when execution starts, the variable i will contain the value 1. Therefore, the WRITE statement will print out a 1.

```
PROGRAM init_3
INTEGER :: i = 1
WRITE (*,*) i
END PROGRAM
```

2.11

THE IMPLICIT NONE STATEMENT

Another very important nonexecutable statement is the IMPLICIT NONE statement. When it is used, the IMPLICIT NONE statement disables the default typing provisions of Fortran. When the IMPLICIT NONE statement is included in a program, any variable that does not appear in an explicit type declaration statement is considered an error. The IMPLICIT NONE statement should appear after the PROGRAM statement and before any type declaration statements.

2

When the IMPLICIT NONE statement is included in a program, the programmer must explicitly declare the type of every variable in the program. On first thought, this requirement might seem to be a disadvantage, since the programmer must do more work when he or she first writes a program. This initial impression couldn't be more wrong. In fact, there are several advantages to using this statement.

Most programming errors are simple typographical errors. The IMPLICIT NONE statement catches these errors at compilation time—before they can produce subtle errors during execution. For example, consider the following simple program:

```
PROGRAM test_1
REAL :: time = 10.0
WRITE (*,*) 'Time = ', tmie
END PROGRAM
```

In this program the variable time is misspelled tmie at one point. When this program is compiled with the Digital Visual Fortran 5.0 compiler and executed, the output is "Time = 0.000000E+00", which is the wrong answer!

Consider the same program with the IMPLICIT NONE statement present:

```
PROGRAM test_1
IMPLICIT NONE
REAL :: time = 10.0
WRITE (*,*) 'Time = ', tmie
END PROGRAM
```

When compiled with the same compiler, this program produces the following compile-time error:

```
Source Listing    10-May-1997 11:41:18   DIGITAL Visual Fortran V5.0-408    Page 1
                  10-May-1997 11:41:12   test_1.f90
        1 PROGRAM test_1
        2 IMPLICIT NONE
        3 REAL :: time = 10.0
        4 WRITE (*,*) 'Time = ', tmie
        .......................^
(1) Error: This name does not have a type, and must have an explicit type.  [TMIE]

        5 END PROGRAM
```

Instead of having a wrong answer in an otherwise-working program, we have an explicit error message flagging the problem at compilation time. This feature is an enormous advantage when working with longer programs containing many variables.

Another advantage of the IMPLICIT NONE statement is that it makes the code more maintainable. A complete list of all variables must appear in the declaration section of any program using the statement. If the program must be modified, a programmer can easily check the list to avoid using variable names that are already defined in the program. This checking helps to eliminate a very common error in which the modifications to the program inadvertently change the values of some variables used elsewhere in the program.

In general, the use of the IMPLICIT NONE statement becomes more and more advantageous as the size of a programming project increases. The use of IMPLICIT

NONE is so important to the designing of good programs that we will use it consistently everywhere throughout this book.

 Good Programming Practice
Always explicitly define every variable in your programs and use the IMPLICIT NONE statement to help you spot and correct typographical errors before they become program execution errors.

■ **2.12**

PROGRAM EXAMPLES

This chapter has presented the fundamental concepts required to write simple but functional Fortran programs. The following problems use these concepts.

EXAMPLE 2–5 Temperature Conversion: Design a Fortran program that reads an input temperature in degrees Fahrenheit, converts it to an absolute temperature in kelvins, and writes out the result.

SOLUTION The relationship between temperature in degrees Fahrenheit (°F) and temperature in kelvins (K) can be found in any physics textbook. It is

$$T \text{ (in kelvins)} = \left[\frac{5}{9} T \text{ (in °F)} - 32.0 \right] + 273.15 \qquad (2\text{–}2)$$

The physics books also give us sample values on both temperature scales, which we can use to check the operation of our program. Two such values are

The boiling point of water	212°F	373.15 K
The sublimation point of dry ice	−110°F	194.26 K

Our program must perform the following steps:

1. Prompt the user to enter an input temperature in °F.
2. Read the input temperature.
3. Calculate the temperature in kelvins from Equation (2–2).
4. Write out the result and stop.

The resulting program is shown in Figure 2–7.

FIGURE 2–7
Program to convert degrees Fahrenheit into kelvins.

```
PROGRAM temp_conversion

!  Purpose:
!     To convert an input temperature from degrees Fahrenheit to
!     an output temperature in kelvins.
!
```

(continued)

(concluded)

```
!  Record of revisions:
!     Date       Programmer          Description of change
!     ====       ==========          =====================
!   09/03/95 -- S. J. Chapman        Original code
!

IMPLICIT NONE            ! Force explicit declaration of variables

! Declare variables, and define each variable when it is declared
REAL :: temp_f          ! Temperature in degrees Fahrenheit
REAL :: temp_k          ! Temperature in kelvins

! Prompt the user for the input temperature.
WRITE (*,*) 'Enter the temperature in degrees Fahrenheit: '
READ  (*,*) temp_f

! Convert to kelvins.
temp_k = (5. / 9.) * (temp_f - 32.) + 273.15

! Write out the result.
WRITE (*,*) temp_f , ' degrees Fahrenheit = ', temp_k, ' kelvins'

! Finish up.
END PROGRAM
```

To test the completed program, we will run it with the known input values given above. Note that user inputs appear in boldface below.

```
C>temp_conversion
Enter the temperature in degrees Fahrenheit:
212
      212.000000 degrees Fahrenheit =        373.150000 kelvins

C>temp_conversion
Enter the temperature in degrees Fahrenheit:
-110
     -110.000000 degrees Fahrenheit =        194.261100 kelvins
```

The results of the program match the values from the physics book.

In the preceding program, we echoed the input values and printed the output values together with their units. The results of this program make sense only if the units (degrees Fahrenheit and kelvins) are included together with their values. As a general rule, the units associated with any input value should always be printed along with the prompt that requests the value, and the units associated with any output value should always be printed along with that value.

Good Programming Practice
Always include the appropriate units with any values that you read or write in a program.

The program in Example 2–5 exhibits many of the good programming practices that are described in this chapter. It uses the IMPLICIT NONE statement to force the explicit typing of all variables in the program. It includes a data dictionary defining the meanings of all of the variables in the program. It also uses descriptive variable names. The variable `temp_f` is initialized by a READ statement before it is used. All input values are echoed, and appropriate units are attached to all printed values.

EXAMPLE 2–6 Electrical Engineering: Calculating Real, Reactive, and Apparent Power: Figure 2–8 shows a sinusoidal ac voltage source with voltage V supplying a load of impedance $Z\angle\theta$ Ω. From simple circuit theory, the rms current I, the real power P, reactive power Q, apparent power S, and power factor PF supplied to the load are given by the following equations:

$$I = \frac{V}{Z} \tag{2–3}$$

$$P = VI \cos\theta \tag{2–4}$$

$$Q = VI \sin\theta \tag{2–5}$$

$$S = VI \tag{2–6}$$

$$PF = \cos\theta \tag{2–7}$$

V is the rms voltage of the power source in units of volts (V). The units of current are amperes (A), of real power are watts (W), of reactive power are volt-amperes-reactive (VAR), and of apparent power are volt-amperes (VA). The power factor has no units associated with it.

Given the rms voltage of the power source and the magnitude and angle of the impedance Z, write a program that calculates the rms current I, the real power P, reactive power Q, apparent power S, and power factor PF of the load.

SOLUTION In this program we need to read in the rms voltage V of the voltage source and the magnitude Z and angle θ of the impedance. The input voltage source will be measured in volts, the magnitude of the impedance Z in ohms, and the angle of the impedance θ in degrees. Once the data is read, we must convert the angle θ into radians for use with the Fortran trigonometric functions. Next the desired values must be calculated, and the results must be printed out.

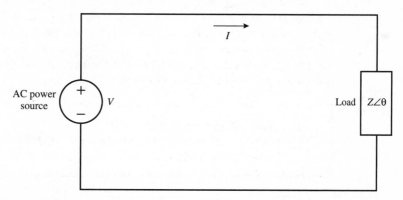

FIGURE 2–8
A sinusoidal ac voltage source with voltage V supplying a load of impedance $Z\angle\theta$ Ω.

The program must perform the following steps:

1. Prompt the user to enter the source voltage in volts.
2. Read the source voltage.
3. Prompt the user to enter the magnitude and angle of the impedance in ohms and degrees.
4. Read the magnitude and angle of the impedance.
5. Calculate the current I from Equation (2–3).
6. Calculate the real power P from Equation (2–4).
7. Calculate the reactive power Q from Equation (2–5).
8. Calculate the apparent power S from Equation (2–6).
9. Calculate the power factor PF from Equation (2–7).
10. Write out the results and stop.

The final Fortran program is shown in Figure 2–9.

FIGURE 2–9
Program to calculate the real power, reactive power, apparent power, and power factor supplied to a load.

```
PROGRAM power
!
!  Purpose:
!    To calculate the current, real, reactive, and apparent power,
!    and the power factor supplied to a load.
!
!  Record of revisions:
!     Date       Programmer        Description of change
!     ====       ==========        =====================
!   09/03/95    S. J. Chapman      Original code
!
IMPLICIT NONE

!  Declare the constants used in this program.
REAL, PARAMETER :: conv = 0.01745329 ! Degrees to radians cnv factor

!  Declare the variables used in this program.
REAL :: amps          ! Current in the load
REAL :: p             ! Real power of load
REAL :: pf            ! Power factor of load
REAL :: q             ! Reactive power of the load
REAL :: s             ! Apparent power of the load
REAL :: theta         ! Impedance angle of the load
REAL :: volts         ! Rms voltage of the power source
REAL :: z             ! Magnitude of the impedance of the load

!  Prompt the user for the rms voltage.
WRITE (*,*) 'Enter the rms voltage of the source: '
READ  (*,*) volts

!  Prompt the user for the magnitude and angle of the impedance.
WRITE (*,*) 'Enter the magnitude and angle of the impedance '
WRITE (*,*) 'in ohms and degrees: '
READ  (*,*) z, theta
```

(continued)

(concluded)

```
! Perform calculations
amps = volts / z                          ! Rms current
p = volts * amps * cos (theta * conv)     ! Real power
q = volts * amps * sin (theta * conv)     ! Reactive power
s = volts * amps                          ! Apparent power
pf = cos (theta * conv)                   ! Power factor

! Write out the results.
WRITE (*,*) 'Voltage         = ', volts, ' volts'
WRITE (*,*) 'Impedance       = ', z, ' ohms at ' , theta,' degrees'
WRITE (*,*) 'Current         = ', amps, ' amps'
WRITE (*,*) 'Real Power      = ', p, ' watts'
WRITE (*,*) 'Reactive Power  = ', q, ' VAR'
WRITE (*,*) 'Apparent Power  = ', s, ' VA'
WRITE (*,*) 'Power Factor    = ', pf

! Finish up.
END PROGRAM
```

This program also exhibits many of the good programming practices that we have described. It uses the IMPLICIT NONE statement to force the explicit typing of all variables in the program. It includes a variable dictionary defining the uses of all of the variables in the program. It also uses descriptive variable names. (Although the variable names are short, P, Q, S, and PF are the standard accepted abbreviations for the corresponding quantities.) All variables are initialized before they are used. The program defines a named constant for the degrees-to-radians conversion factor and then uses that name everywhere throughout the program when the conversion factor is required. All input values are echoed, and appropriate units are attached to all printed values.

To verify the operation of program power, we will do a sample calculation by hand and compare the results with the output of the program. If the rms voltage V is 120 V, the magnitude of the impedance Z is 5 Ω, and the angle θ is 30°, then the values are

$$I = \frac{V}{Z} = \frac{120 \text{ V}}{5 \text{ }\Omega} = 24 \text{ A} \tag{2-3}$$

$$P = VI \cos \theta = (120 \text{ V})(24 \text{ A}) \cos 30° = 2494 \text{ W} \tag{2-4}$$

$$Q = VI \sin \theta = (120 \text{ V})(24 \text{ A}) \sin 30° = 1440 \text{ VAR} \tag{2-5}$$

$$S = VI = (120 \text{ V})(24 \text{ A}) = 2880 \text{ VA} \tag{2-6}$$

$$\text{PF} = \cos \theta = \cos 30° = 0.86603 \tag{2-7}$$

When we run program power with the specified input data, the results are identical with our hand calculations.

```
C>power
Enter the rms voltage of the source:
120
Enter the magnitude and angle of the impedance
in ohms and degrees:
5., 30.
Voltage      =    120.000000 volts
Impedance    =      5.000000 ohms at    30.000000 degrees
Current      =     24.000000 amps
```

```
Real Power     =    2494.153000 watts
Reactive Power =    1440.000000 VAR
Apparent Power =    2880.000000 VA
Power Factor   =    8.660254E-01
```

EXAMPLE 2–7 Carbon 14 Dating: A radioactive isotope of an element is a form of the element that is not stable. Instead, it spontaneously decays into another element over a period of time. Radioactive decay is an exponential process. If Q_0 is the initial quantity of a radioactive substance at time $t = 0$, then the amount of the substance that will be present at any time t in the future is given by

$$Q(t) = Q_o e^{-\lambda t} \tag{2–8}$$

where λ is the radioactive decay constant.

Because radioactive decay occurs at a known rate, it can be used as a clock to measure the time since the decay started. If we know the initial amount of the radioactive material Q_0 present in a sample and the amount of the material Q left at the current time, we can solve for t in Equation (2–8) to determine how long the decay has been going on. The resulting equation is

$$t_{\text{decay}} = -\frac{1}{\lambda} \log \frac{Q}{Q_0} \tag{2–9}$$

Equation (2–9) has practical applications in many areas of science. For example, archaeologists use a radioactive clock based on carbon 14 to determine the time that has passed since a once-living thing died. Carbon 14 is continually taken into the body while a plant or animal is living, so the amount of it present in the body at the time of death is assumed to be known. The decay constant λ of carbon 14 is well-known to be 0.00012097/year, so if the amount of carbon 14 remaining now can be accurately measured, then Equation (2–9) can be used to determine how long ago the living thing died. The amount of carbon 14 remaining as a function of time is shown in Figure 2–10.

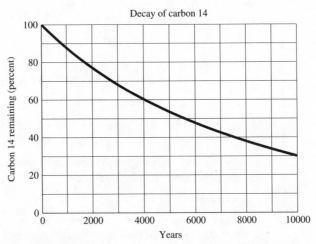

FIGURE 2–10
The radioactive decay of carbon 14 as a function of time. Notice that 50 percent of the original carbon 14 is left after about 5730 years have elapsed.

Write a program that reads the percentage of carbon 14 remaining in a sample, calculates the age of the sample from it, and prints out the result with proper units.

SOLUTION Our program must perform the following steps:

1. Prompt the user to enter the percentage of carbon 14 remaining in the sample.
2. Read in the percentage.
3. Convert the percentage into the fraction $\dfrac{Q}{Q_0}$.
4. Calculate the age of the sample in years using Equation (2–9).
5. Write out the result and stop.

The resulting code is shown in Figure 2–11.

FIGURE 2–11
Program to calculate the age of a sample from the percentage of carbon 14 remaining in it.

```
PROGRAM c14_date
!
!  Purpose:
!    To calculate the age of an organic sample from the percentage
!    of the original carbon 14 remaining in the sample.
!
!  Record of revisions:
!      Date       Programmer          Description of change
!      ====       ==========          =====================
!    09/04/95    S. J. Chapman        Original code
!
IMPLICIT NONE

! Declare the constants used in this program.
REAL, PARAMETER :: lamda = 0.00012097 ! The radioactive decay
                                      ! constant of carbon 14,
                                      ! in units of 1/years.

! Declare the variables used in this program.
REAL :: age      ! The age of the sample in years
REAL :: percent  ! The percentage of carbon 14 remaining at the time
                 ! of the measurement
REAL :: ratio    ! The ratio of the carbon 14 remaining at the time
                 ! of the measurement to the original amount of
                 ! carbon 14.

! Prompt the user for the percentage of C-14 remaining.
WRITE (*,*) 'Enter the percentage of carbon 14 remaining:'
READ  (*,*) percent

! Echo the user's input value.
WRITE (*,*) 'The remaining carbon 14 = ', percent, ' %.'

! Perform calculations
ratio = percent / 100.          ! Convert to fractional ratio
age = (-1.0 / lamda) * log(ratio)  ! Get age in years

! Tell the user about the age of the sample.
WRITE (*,*) 'The age of the sample is  ', age, ' years.'

! Finish up.
END PROGRAM
```

To test the completed program, we will calculate the time it takes for half of the carbon 14 to disappear. This time is known as the *half-life* of carbon 14.

```
C>c14_date
Enter the percentage of carbon 14 remaining:
50.
The remaining carbon 14 =      50.000000 %.
The age of the sample is     5729.910000 years.
```

The *CRC Handbook of Chemistry and Physics* states that the half-life of carbon 14 is 5730 years, so output of the program agrees with the reference book.

2.13
DEBUGGING Fortran PROGRAMS

There is an old saying that the only sure things in life are death and taxes. We can add one more certainty to that list: If you write a program of any significant size, it won't work the first time you try it! Errors in programs are known as **bugs,** and the process of locating and eliminating them is known as **debugging.** Given that we have written a program and it is not working, how do we debug it?

Three types of errors are found in Fortran programs. The first type of error is a **syntax error.** Syntax errors are errors in the Fortran statement itself, such as spelling errors or punctuation errors. These errors are detected by the compiler during compilation. The second type of error is the **run-time error.** A run-time error occurs when an illegal mathematical operation is attempted during program execution (for example, attempting to divide by zero). These errors cause the program to abort during execution. The third type of error is a **logical error.** Logical errors occur when the program compiles and runs successfully but produces the wrong answer.

The most common mistakes made during programming are *typographical errors.* Some typographical errors create invalid Fortran statements. These errors produce syntax errors that the compiler detects. Other typographical errors occur in variable names. For example, the letters in some variable names might have been transposed. If you use the IMPLICIT NONE statement, then the compiler will also catch most of these errors. However, if you inadvertently substitute one legal variable name for another legal variable name, the compiler cannot detect the error. This sort of substitution might occur if you have two similar variable names; for example, if variables vel1 and vel2 are both used for velocities in the program, then one of them might be inadvertently used instead of the other one at some point. This sort of typographical error will produce a logical error. You must check for that sort of error by manually inspecting the code, since the compiler cannot catch it.

Sometimes you can compile and link the program successfully, but run-time errors or logical errors appear when the program is executed. In this case either something is wrong with the input data or something is wrong with the logical structure of the program. The first step in locating this sort of bug should be to check the input data to the program. Your program should have been designed to echo its input data. If not, go back and add WRITE statements to verify that the input values are what you expect them to be.

If the variable names seem to be correct and the input data is correct, then you are probably dealing with a logical error. You should check each of your assignment statements:

1. Break very long assignment statements into several smaller assignment statements. Smaller statements are easier to verify.
2. Check the placement of parentheses in your assignment statements. It is a very common error to have the operations in an assignment statement evaluated in the wrong order. If you have any doubts as to the order in which the variables are being evaluated, add extra sets of parentheses to make your intentions clear.
3. Make sure that you have initialized all of your variables properly.
4. Be sure that any functions you use are in the correct units. For example, the input to trigonometric functions must be in units of radians, not degrees.
5. Check for possible errors due to integer or mixed-mode arithmetic.

If you are still getting the wrong answer, add WRITE statements at various points in your program to see the results of intermediate calculations. If you can locate the point where the calculations go bad, then you know just where to look for the problem, which is 95 percent of the battle.

If you still cannot find the problem after following all the preceding steps, ask another student or your instructor to look at the code. It is very common to see just what you expect to see when you look at your own code. Another person can often quickly spot an error that you have overlooked time after time.

Good Programming Practice

To reduce your debugging effort, follow these practices:

- Use the IMPLICIT NONE statement.
- Echo all input values.
- Initialize all variables.
- Use parentheses to make the functions of assignment statements clear.

All modern compilers have special debugging tools called *symbolic debuggers*. A symbolic debugger is a tool that allows you to walk through the execution of your program one statement at a time and to examine the values of any variables at each step along the way. Symbolic debuggers allow you to see all of the intermediate results without having to insert a lot of WRITE statements into your code. Symbolic debuggers are powerful and flexible, but unfortunately they are different for every type of compiler. If you will be using a symbolic debugger in your class, your instructor will introduce you to the debugger appropriate for your compiler and computer.

■ 2.14

SUMMARY

Chapter 2 presents many of the fundamental concepts required to write functional Fortran programs, describes the basic structure of Fortran programs, and introduces four data types: integer, real, logical, and character. It introduces the assignment statement, arithmetic calculations, intrinsic functions, and list-directed input/output statements. Throughout the chapter, we emphasize features of the language that are important for writing understandable and maintainable Fortran code.

The Fortran statements introduced in this chapter must appear in a specific order in a Fortran program. The proper order is summarized in Table 2–7.

The order in which Fortran expressions are evaluated follows a fixed hierarchy, with operations at a higher level evaluated before operations at lower levels. The hierarchy of operations is summarized in Table 2–8.

The Fortran language includes a number of built-in functions to help us solve problems. These functions are called intrinsic functions, since they are intrinsic to the Fortran language itself. Table 2–6 summarizes some common intrinsic functions and a complete listing of intrinsic functions appears in Appendix B.

The two varieties of intrinsic functions are specific functions and generic functions. Specific functions require that their input data be of a specific type; if data of the wrong type is supplied to a specific function, the result will be meaningless. In contrast, generic functions can accept input data of more than one type and produce correct results.

2.14.1 Summary of Good Programming Practice

Every Fortran program should be designed so that another person who is familiar with Fortran can easily understand it. This principle is very important, since a good pro-

---

■ **TABLE 2–7**
The order of Fortran statements in a program

1. PROGRAM statement

2. IMPLICIT NONE statement

3. Type declaration statements
   REAL statement(s)
   INTEGER statement(s)   } Any number in any order
   LOGICAL statement(s)
   CHARACTER statement(s)

4. Executable statements
   Assignment statement(s)
   READ statement(s)   } Any number in the order required to accomplish the desired task
   WRITE statement(s)
   STOP statement(s)

5. END PROGRAM statement

TABLE 2–8
Fortran hierarchy of operations

1. Operations within parentheses are evaluated, starting with the innermost parentheses and working outward.

2. All exponential operations are evaluated, working from *right* to *left*.

3. All multiplications and divisions are evaluated, working from left to right.

4. All additions and subtractions are evaluated, working from left to right.

5. All relational operators (==, /=, >, >=, <, <=) are evaluated, working from left to right.

6. All .NOT. operators are evaluated.

7. All .AND. operators are evaluated, working from left to right.

8. All .OR. operators are evaluated, working from left to right.

9. All .EQV. and .NEQV. operators are evaluated, working from left to right.

gram may be used for a long period of time. Over that time, conditions will change, and the program will need to be modified to reflect the changes. The program modifications may be done by someone other than the original programmer. The programmer making the modifications must understand the original program well before attempting to change it.

Designing clear, understandable, and maintainable programs is much harder than simply writing code. A programmer must not only develop the discipline to properly document his or her work but also know how to avoid pitfalls along the path to good programs. The following guidelines will help you to develop good programs:

1. Use the free-source format for all new Fortran programs.

2. Use meaningful variable names whenever possible. Use names that can be understood at a glance, like day, month, and year.

3. Always use the IMPLICIT NONE statement to catch typographical errors in your program at compilation time.

4. Create a data dictionary in each program that you write. The data dictionary should explicitly declare and define each variable in the program. Be sure to include the physical units associated with each variable, if applicable.

5. Use a consistent number of significant digits in constants. For example, do not use 3.14 for π in one part of your program and 3.141593 in another part of the program. To ensure consistency, a constant may be named, and the constant may be referenced by name wherever it is needed.

6. Be sure to specify all constants with as much precision as your computer will support. For example, specify π as 3.141593, not as 3.14.

7. Do not use integer arithmetic to calculate continuously varying real-world quantities, such as distance and time. Use integer arithmetic only for things that are intrinsically integral, such as counters.

8. Avoid mixed-mode arithmetic except for exponentiation. If it is necessary to mix integer and real variables in a single expression, use the intrinsic functions REAL, INT, and NINT to make the type conversions explicit.

9. Use extra parentheses whenever necessary to improve the readability of your expressions.

10. Always echo any variables that you enter into a program from a keyboard to make sure that they were typed and processed correctly.

11. Initialize all variables in a program before using them. The variables may be initialized with assignment statements, with READ statements, or directly in type declaration statements.

12. Always print the physical units associated with any value being written out. The units are important for the proper interpretation of a program's results.

2.14.2 Summary of Fortran Statements

The following summary describes the Fortran statements introduced in this chapter.

Assignment Statement

```
variable = expression
```

Examples:

```
pi = 3.141593
distance = 0.5 * acceleration * time ** 2
side = hypot * cos(theta)
```

Description:
   The left side of the assignment statement must be a variable name. The right side of the assignment statement can be any constant, variable, function, or expression. The value of the quantity on the right side of the equal sign is stored into the variable named on the left side of the equal sign.

CHARACTER Statement

```
CHARACTER(len=<len>) :: variable name[, variable name]
CHARACTER(<len>) :: variable name[, variable name]
CHARACTER :: variable name[, variable name]

CHARACTER*<len> :: variable name
CHARACTER variable name*<len>
```

Examples:

```
CHARACTER(len=10) :: first, last, middle
CHARACTER(10) :: first = 'My Name'
CHARACTER :: middle_initial
```

Description:

The CHARACTER statement is a type declaration statement that declares variables of the character data type. The length in characters of each variable is specified by the (len=<len>) or by <len>. If the length is absent, then the length of the variables defaults to 1.

The shaded forms of the CHARACTER statement are holdovers from FORTRAN 77. They have been declared obsolescent in Fortran 95 and should never be used in new programs.

The value of a CHARACTER variable may be initialized with a string when it is declared, as shown in the second example above.

END PROGRAM Statement

```
END PROGRAM [name]
```

Description:

The END PROGRAM statement must be the last statement in a Fortran program segment. It tells the compiler that there are no further statements to process. Program execution stops when the END PROGRAM statement is reached. The name of the program may optionally be included in the END PROGRAM statement.

IMPLICIT NONE Statement

```
IMPLICIT NONE
```

Description:

The IMPLICIT NONE statement turns off default typing in Fortran. When it is used in a program, every variable in the program must be explicitly declared in a type declaration statement.

INTEGER Statement

```
INTEGER :: variable name[, variable name, etc.]
```

Examples:

```
INTEGER :: i, j, count
INTEGER :: day = 4
```

Description:

The INTEGER statement is a type declaration statement that declares variables of the integer data type. This statement overrides the default typing specified in Fortran. The value of an INTEGER variable may be initialized when it is declared, as shown in the second example above.

2

LOGICAL Statement

```
LOGICAL :: variable name[, variable name, etc.]
```

Examples:

```
LOGICAL :: initialize, debug
LOGICAL :: debug = .false.
```

Description:

The LOGICAL statement is a type declaration statement that declares variables of the logical data type. The value of a LOGICAL variable may be initialized when it is declared, as shown in the second example above.

PROGRAM Statement

```
PROGRAM program_name
```

Example:

```
PROGRAM my_program
```

Description:

The PROGRAM statement specifies the name of a Fortran program. It must be the first statement in the program. The name must be unique and cannot be used as a variable name within the program. A program name may consist of 1 to 31 alphabetic, numeric, and underscore characters, but the first character in the program name must be alphabetic.

READ Statement (List-Directed READ)

```
READ (*,*) variable name [, variable name, etc.]
```

Examples:

```
READ (*,*) stress
READ (*,*) distance, time
```

Description:

The list-directed READ statement reads one or more values from the standard input device and loads them into the variables in the list. The values are stored in the order in which the variables are listed. Data values must be separated by blanks or by commas. As many lines as necessary will be read. Each READ statement begins searching for values with a new line.

REAL Statement

```
REAL :: variable name[, variable name, etc.]
REAL :: variable name = value
```

Examples:

```
REAL :: distance, time
REAL :: distance = 100
```

Description:

The REAL statement is a type declaration statement that declares variables of the real data type. This statement overrides the default typing specified in Fortran. The value of a REAL variable may be initialized when it is declared, as shown in the second example above.

STOP Statement

```
STOP
```

Description:

The STOP statement stops the execution of a Fortran program. A program can have more than one STOP statement. A STOP statement that immediately precedes an END PROGRAM statement may be omitted, since execution stops when the END PROGRAM statement is reached.

WRITE Statement (List-Directed WRITE)

```
WRITE (*,*) expression [, expression, etc.]
```

Examples:

```
WRITE (*,*) stress
WRITE (*,*) distance, time
WRITE (*,*) 'SIN(theta) = ', SIN(theta)
```

Description:

The list-directed WRITE statement writes the values of one or more expressions to the standard output device. The values are written in the order in which the expressions are listed.

■ 2.15

EXERCISES

2–1 State whether or not each of the following Fortran 90/95 constants is valid. If valid, state what type of constant it is. If not, state why it is invalid.
   a. `3.14159`
   b. `'.TRUE.'`
   c. `-123,456.789`
   d. `+1E-12`
   e. `'Who's coming for dinner?'`
   f. `.FALSE`
   g. `"Pass / Fail'`
   h. `"Enter name:"`

2–2 For each of the following pairs of numbers, state whether they represent the same value or different values within the computer.
   a. `123.E+0; 123`
   b. `1234.E-3; 1.234E3`
   c. `1.41421, 1.41421E0`
   d. `0.000005E+6; 5.`

2–3 State whether each of the following program names is valid or not. If not, state why the name is invalid.
   a. `junk`
   b. `3rd`
   c. `Who_are_you?`
   d. `time_to_intercept`

2–4 Which of the following expressions are legal in Fortran? If an expression is legal, evaluate it.
   a. `2.**3 / 3**2`
   b. `2 * 6 + 6 ** 2 / 2`
   c. `2 * (-10.) **-3.`
   d. `2 / (-10.) ** 3.`
   e. `23 / (4 / 8)`

2–5 Which of the following expressions are legal in Fortran? If an expression is legal, evaluate it.
   a. `((58/4)*(4/58))`
   b. `((58/4)*(4/58.))`
   c. `((58./4)*(4/58.))`
   d. `((58./4*(4/58.))`

2–6 Evaluate each of the following expressions.
   a. `13 / 5 * 6`
   b. `(13 / 5) * 6`
   c. `13 / (5 * 6)`
   d. `13. / 5 * 6`
   e. `13 / 5 * 6.`
   f. `INT(13. / 5) * 6`
   g. `NINT(13. / 5) * 6`

2–7 Evaluate each of the following expressions.

a. `3 ** 3 ** 2`
b. `(3 ** 3) ** 2`
c. `3 ** (3 ** 2)`

2–8 What values will be output from the following program?

```
PROGRAM sample_1
INTEGER :: i1, i2, i3
REAL :: a1 = 2.4, a2
i1 = a1
i2 = INT (a1 * i1)
i3 = NINT (a1 * i1 )
a2 = a1**i1
WRITE (*,*) i1, i2, i3, a1, a2
END PROGRAM
```

2–9 Which of the following expressions are legal in Fortran? If an expression is legal, evaluate it.

a. `5.5 >= 5`
b. `20 > 20`
c. `.NOT. 6 > 5`
d. `15 <= 'A'`
e. `.TRUE. > .FALSE.`
f. `35 / 17. > 35 / 17`
g. `7 <= 8 .EQV. 3 / 2 == 1`
h. `17.5 .AND. (3.3 > 2.)`

2–10 Which of the following expressions are legal in Fortran? If an expression is legal, evaluate it. Assume the ASCII collating sequence.

a. `'123' > 'abc'`
b. `'9478' == 9478`
c. `ACHAR(65) // ACHAR(95) // ACHAR(72)`
d. `ACHAR(IACHAR('j') + 5)`

2–11 Figure 2–12 shows a right triangle with a hypotenuse of length C and angle θ. From elementary trigonometry, the lengths of sides A and B are given by

$$A = C \cos \theta$$
$$B = C \sin \theta$$

The following program is intended to calculate the lengths of sides A and B given the hypotenuse C and angle θ. Will this program run? Will it produce the correct result? Why or why not?

FIGURE 2–12

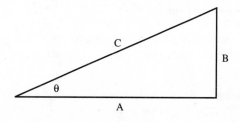

```
PROGRAM triangle
REAL :: a, b, c, theta
WRITE (*,*) 'Enter the length of the hypotenuse C:'
READ (*,*) c
WRITE (*,*) 'Enter the angle THETA in degrees:'
READ (*,*) theta
a = c * COS ( theta )
b = c * SIN ( theta )
WRITE (*,*) 'The length of the adjacent side is ', a
WRITE (*,*) 'The length of the opposite side is ', b
END PROGRAM
```

2–12 What output will be produced by the following program?

```
PROGRAM example
REAL :: a, b, c
INTEGER :: k, l, m
READ (*,*) a, b, c, k
READ (*,*) l, m
WRITE (*,*) a, b, c, k, l, m
END PROGRAM
```

The input data to the program is

```
-3.141592
100, 200., 300, 400
-100, -200, -300
-400
```

2–13 Write a Fortran program that calculates an hourly employee's weekly pay. The program should ask the user for the person's pay rate and the number of hours worked during the week. It should then calculate the total pay from the formula

$$\text{Total Pay} = \text{Hourly Pay Rate} \times \text{Hours Worked}$$

Finally, it should display the total weekly pay. Check your program by computing the weekly pay for a person earning $7.50 per hour and working for 39 hours.

2–14 The potential energy of an object due to its height above the surface of the Earth is given by the equation

$$\text{PE} = mgh \qquad (2\text{–}10)$$

where m is the mass of the object, g is the acceleration due to gravity, and h is the height above the surface of the Earth. The kinetic energy of a moving object is given by the equation

$$\text{KE} = \frac{1}{2}mv^2 \qquad (2\text{–}11)$$

where m is the mass of the object and v is the velocity of the object. Write a Fortran statement for the total energy (potential plus kinetic) possessed by an object in the earth's gravitational field.

2–15 If a stationary ball is released at a height h above the surface of the Earth, the velocity of the ball v when it hits the earth is given by the equation

$$v = \sqrt{2gh} \qquad (2\text{–}12)$$

where g is the acceleration due to gravity and h is the height above the surface of the Earth (assuming no air friction). Write a Fortran equation for the velocity of the ball when it hits the Earth.

2–16 Period of a Pendulum The period of an oscillating pendulum T (in seconds) is given by the equation

$$T = 2\pi \sqrt{\frac{L}{g}} \qquad (2\text{--}13)$$

where L is the length of the pendulum in meters and g is the acceleration due to gravity in meters per second squared. Write a Fortran program to calculate the period of a pendulum of length L. The length of the pendulum will be specified by the user when the program is run. Use good programming practices in your program. (The acceleration due to gravity at the Earth's surface is 9.81 m/sec².)

2–17 Write a program to calculate the hypotenuse of a right triangle given the lengths of its two sides. Use good programming practices in your program.

2–18 Write a program using the IMPLICIT NONE statement and do not declare one of the variables in the program. What sort of error message is generated by your compiler?

2–19 The distance between two points $(x1, y1)$ and $(x2, y2)$ on a Cartesian coordinate plane is given by the equation

$$d = \sqrt{(x1 - x2)^2 + (y1 - y2)^2} \qquad (2\text{--}14)$$

Write a Fortran program to calculate the distance between any two points $(x1, y1)$ and $(x2, y2)$ specified by the user (see Figure 2–13). Use good programming practices in your program. Use the program to calculate the distance between the points (2,3) and (8,−5).

2–20 Decibels Engineers often measure the ratio of two power measurements in *decibels,* or dB. The equation for the ratio of two power measurements in decibels is

$$dB = 10 \log_{10} \frac{P_2}{P_1}$$

where P_2 is the power level being measured and P_1 is some reference power level. Assume that the reference power level P_1 is 1 milliwatt; write a program that accepts an input power P_2 and converts it into dB with respect to the 1 mW reference level.

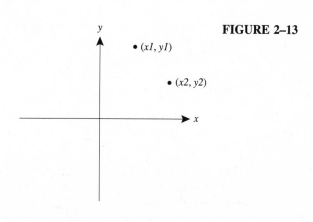

FIGURE 2–13

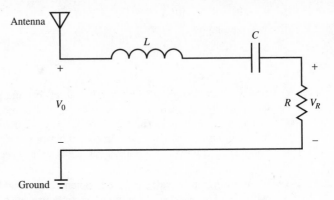

FIGURE 2–14
A simplified representation of an AM radio set.

2–21 Hyperbolic Cosine   The hyperbolic cosine function is defined by the equation

$$\cosh x = \frac{e^x + e^{-x}}{2}$$

Write a Fortran program to calculate the hyperbolic cosine of a user-supplied value x. Use the program to calculate the hyperbolic cosine of 3.0. Compare the answer that your program produces to the answer produced by the Fortran intrinsic function COSH(x).

2–22 Radio Receiver   A simplified version of the front end of an AM radio receiver is shown in Figure 2–14. This receiver consists of an *RLC* tuned circuit containing a resistor, capacitor, and an inductor connected in series. The *RLC* circuit is connected to an external antenna and ground as shown in the picture.

The tuned circuit allows the radio to select a specific station from all the stations transmitting on the AM band. At the resonant frequency of the circuit, essentially all the signal V_0 appearing at the antenna appear across the resistor, which represents the rest of the radio. In other words, the radio receives its strongest signal at the resonant frequency. The resonant frequency of the *LC* circuit is given by the equation

$$f_0 = \frac{1}{2\pi\sqrt{LC}} \tag{2-15}$$

where L is inductance in henrys (H) and C is capacitance in farads (F). Write a program that calculates the resonant frequency of this radio set given specific values of L and C. Test your program by calculating the frequency of the radio when $L = 0.1$ mH and $C = 0.25$ nF.

Control Structures and Program Design

In the previous chapter, we developed several complete working Fortran programs. However, all of the programs were very simple, consisting of a series of Fortran statements that were executed one after another in a fixed order. Such programs are called *sequential* programs. They read input data, process it to produce a desired answer, print out the answer, and quit. There is no way to repeat sections of the program more than once, and there is no way to selectively execute only certain portions of the program depending on values of the input data.

This chapter introduces a number of Fortran statements that allow us to control the order in which statements are executed in a program. The two broad categories of control statements are **branches,** which select specific sections of the code to execute, and **loops,** which cause specific sections of the code to be repeated.

With the introduction of branches and loops, our programs are going to become more complex, and it will be easier to make mistakes. To help avoid programming errors, we will introduce a formal program design procedure based on the technique known as top-down design. We will also introduce two common algorithm-development tools: flowcharts and pseudocode.

3.1

INTRODUCTION TO TOP-DOWN DESIGN TECHNIQUES

Suppose that you are an engineer working in industry, and that you need to write a Fortran program to solve some problem. How do you begin?

When given a new problem, there is a natural tendency to sit down at a terminal and start programming without "wasting" a lot of time thinking about it first. It is often possible to get away with this "on the fly" approach to programming for very small problems, such as many of the examples in this book. In the real world, however, problems are larger, and a programmer attempting this approach will become hopelessly bogged down. For larger problems, it pays to completely think out the problem and the approach you are going to take to it before writing a single line of code.

We will introduce a formal program design in this section and then apply that process to every major application developed in the remainder of the book. For some of the simple examples, the design process will seem like overkill. However, as the problems get larger and larger, the process becomes more and more essential to successful programming.

When I was an undergraduate, one of my professors was fond of saying, "Programming is easy. It's knowing what to program that's hard." His point was forcefully driven home to me after I left the university and began working in industry on larger-scale software projects. I found that the most difficult part of my job was to *understand the problem* I was trying to solve. Once I really understood the problem, it became easy to break the problem apart into smaller, more easily manageable pieces with well-defined functions and then to tackle those pieces one at a time.

Top-down design is the process of starting with a large task and breaking it down into smaller, more easily understandable pieces (subtasks), which perform a portion of the desired task. Each subtask may in turn be subdivided into smaller subtasks if necessary. Once the program is divided into small pieces, we can code and test each piece independently. We do not attempt to combine the subtasks into a complete task until we know that each subtask works properly by itself.

The concept of top-down design is the basis of our formal program design process. The details of the process are shown in Figure 3–1.

1. **Clearly state the problem that you are trying to solve.**

   Programs are usually written to fill some perceived need, but that need may not be articulated clearly by the person requesting the program. For example, a user may ask for a program to solve a system of simultaneous linear equations. This request is not clear enough to allow a programmer to design a program to meet the need; he or she must first know much more about the problem to be solved. Is the system of equations to be solved real or complex? What is the maximum number of equations and unknowns that the program must handle? Are there any symmetries in the equations that might be exploited to make the task easier? The program designer will have to talk with the user requesting the program, and the two of them will have to come up with a clear statement of exactly what they are trying to accomplish. A clear statement of the problem will prevent misunderstandings, and it will also help the program designer to properly organize his or her thoughts. In this example a proper statement of the problem might have been:

   Design and write a program to solve a system of simultaneous linear equations having real coefficients and with up to 20 equations in 20 unknowns.

2. **Define the inputs required by the program and the outputs to be produced by the program.**

   The inputs to the program and the outputs produced by the program must be specified so that the new program will properly fit into the overall processing scheme. In the simultaneous equation example, the coefficients of the equations to be solved are probably in some preexisting order, and the new program needs to be able to read them in that order. Similarly, the program needs to produce the answers required by

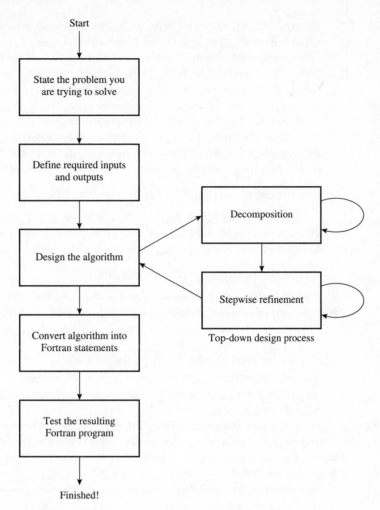

FIGURE 3–1
The program design process used in this book.

the programs that may follow it in the overall processing scheme and to write out those answers in the format needed by the programs following it.

3. **Design the algorithm that you intend to implement in the program.**

An **algorithm** is a step-by-step procedure for finding the solution to a problem. It is at this stage in the process that top-down design techniques come into play. The designer looks for logical divisions within the problem and divides it into subtasks along those lines. This process is called *decomposition*. If the subtasks are themselves large, the designer can break them up into even smaller sub-subtasks. This process continues until the problem has been divided into many small pieces, each of which does a simple, clearly understandable job.

After the problem has been decomposed into small pieces, each piece is further refined through a process called *stepwise refinement.* In stepwise refinement, a designer starts with a general description of what the piece of code should do and then defines the functions of the piece in greater and greater detail until they are specific enough to be turned into Fortran statements. Stepwise refinement is usually done with **pseudocode,** which is described in the next section.

It is often helpful to solve a simple example of the problem by hand during the algorithm development process. If the designer understands the steps that he or she went through in solving the problem by hand, then he or she will be better able to apply decomposition and stepwise refinement to the problem.

4. **Turn the algorithm into Fortran statements.**

If the decomposition and refinement process was carried out properly, this step will be very simple. All the programmer will have to do is to replace pseudocode with the corresponding Fortran statements on a one-for-one basis.

5. **Test the resulting Fortran program.**

This step is the real killer. We must first test the components of the program individually, if possible, and then test the program as a whole. When testing a program, we must verify that it works correctly for *all legal input data sets.* It is very common for a program to be written, tested with some standard data set, and released for use, only to find that it produces the wrong answers (or crashes) with a different input data set. If the algorithm implemented in a program includes different branches, we must test all the branches to confirm that the program operates correctly under every possible circumstance.

Large problems typically go through a series of tests before they are released for general use (see Figure 3–2). The first stage of testing is sometimes called **unit testing.** During unit testing, the individual subtasks of the program are tested separately to confirm that they work correctly. Then the program goes through a series of *builds* during which the individual subtasks are combined to produce the final program. The first build of the program typically includes only a few of the subtasks. It is used to check the interactions among those subtasks and the functions performed by the combinations of the subtasks. Successive builds incorporate more and more subtasks until the entire program is complete. Testing is performed on each build, and any errors (bugs) that are detected are corrected before moving on to the next build.

Testing continues even after the program is complete. The first complete version of the program is usually called the **alpha release.** It is exercised by the programmers and others very close to them in as many different ways as possible, and the bugs discovered during the testing are corrected. When the most serious bugs have been removed from the program, a new version called the **beta release** is prepared. The beta release is normally given to "friendly" outside users who have a need for the program in their normal day-to-day jobs. These users put the program through its paces under many different conditions and with many different input data sets, and they report any bugs that they find to the programmers. When those bugs have been corrected, the program is ready to be released for general use.

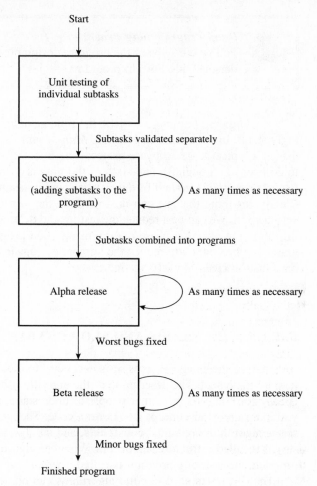

FIGURE 3–2
A typical testing process for a large program.

Because the programs in this book are fairly small, we will not go through the sort of extensive testing described above. However, we will follow the basic principles in testing all of our programs.

The program design process may be summarized as follows:

1. Clearly state the problem that you are trying to solve.
2. Define the inputs required by the program and the outputs to be produced by the program.
3. Design the algorithm that you intend to implement in the program.
4. Turn the algorithm into Fortran statements.
5. Test the Fortran program.

> **Good Programming Practice**
> Follow the steps of the program design process to produce reliable, understandable Fortran programs.

In a large programming project, the time actually spent programming is surprisingly small. In his book *The Mythical Man-Month,*[1] Frederick P. Brooks Jr. suggests that in a typical large software project, one-third of the time is spent planning what to do (steps 1 through 3), one-sixth of the time is spent actually writing the program (step 4), and fully one-half of the time is spent in testing and debugging the program! Clearly, anything that we can do to reduce the testing and debugging time will be very helpful. We can best reduce the testing and debugging time by doing a very careful job in the planning phase and by using good programming practices. Good programming practices will reduce the number of bugs in the program and will make the ones that do creep in easier to find.

■ 3.2
USE OF PSEUDOCODE AND FLOWCHARTS

As a part of the design process, it is necessary to describe the algorithm that you intend to implement. The description of the algorithm should be in a standard form that is easy for both you and other people to understand, and the description should aid you in turning your concept into Fortran code. The standard forms that we use to describe algorithms are called **constructs,** and an algorithm described using these constructs is called a structured algorithm. When the algorithm is implemented in a Fortran program, the resulting program is called a *structured program.*

The constructs used to build algorithms can be described in two different ways: pseudocode and flowcharts. **Pseudocode** is a hybrid mixture of Fortran and English. It is structured like Fortran, with a separate line for each distinct idea or segment of code, but the descriptions on each line are in English. Each line of the pseudocode should describe its idea in plain, easily understandable English. Pseudocode is very useful for developing algorithms, since it is flexible and easy to modify. It is especially useful since pseudocode can be written and modified on the same computer terminal used to write the Fortran program—no special graphical capabilities are required.

For example, the pseudocode for the algorithm in Example 2–5 is

```
Prompt user to enter temperature in degrees Fahrenheit
Read temperature in degrees Fahrenheit (temp_f)
temp_k in kelvins ← (5./9.) * (temp_f - 32) + 273.15
Write temperature in kelvins
```

---

[1]F. P. Brooks Jr., *The Mythical Man-Month* (Addison-Wesley, 1974).

Notice that a left arrow ($\leftarrow$) is used instead of an equal sign ($=$) to indicate that a value is stored in a variable; this convention avoids any confusion between assignment and equality. Pseudocode is intended to aid you in organizing your thoughts before converting them into Fortran code.

Flowcharts are a way to describe algorithms graphically. In a flowchart different graphical symbols represent the different operations in the algorithm, and our standard constructs are made up of collections of one or more of these symbols. Flowcharts are very useful for describing the algorithm implemented in a program after it is completed. However, since they are graphical, flowcharts tend to be cumbersome to modify, and they are not very useful during the preliminary stages of algorithm definition when rapid changes are occurring. The most common graphical symbols used in flowcharts are shown in Figure 3–3, and the flowchart for the algorithm in Example 2–5 is shown in Figure 3–4.

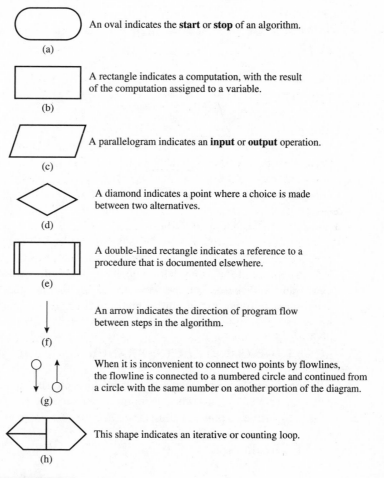

(a) An oval indicates the **start** or **stop** of an algorithm.

(b) A rectangle indicates a computation, with the result of the computation assigned to a variable.

(c) A parallelogram indicates an **input** or **output** operation.

(d) A diamond indicates a point where a choice is made between two alternatives.

(e) A double-lined rectangle indicates a reference to a procedure that is documented elsewhere.

(f) An arrow indicates the direction of program flow between steps in the algorithm.

(g) When it is inconvenient to connect two points by flowlines, the flowline is connected to a numbered circle and continued from a circle with the same number on another portion of the diagram.

(h) This shape indicates an iterative or counting loop.

FIGURE 3–3
Common symbols used in flowcharts.

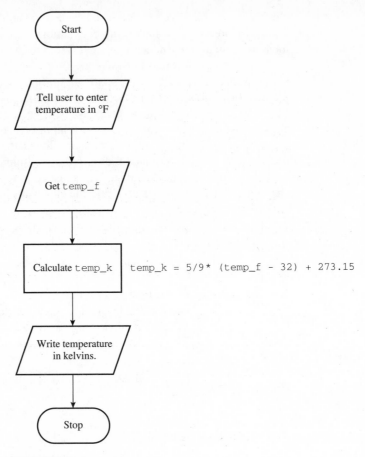

FIGURE 3–4
Flowchart for the algorithm in Example 2–5.

Throughout the examples in this book, we will illustrate the use of both pseudo-code and flowcharts. You are welcome to use the tool that gives you the best results in your own programming projects.

3.3
CONTROL CONSTRUCTS: BRANCHES

Branches are Fortran statements that permit us to select and execute specific sections of code (called *blocks*) while skipping other sections of code. They are variations of the IF statement, plus the SELECT CASE.

3.3.1 The Block IF Construct

The commonest form of the IF statement is the block IF construct. This construct specifies that a block of code will be executed if and only if a certain logical expression is true. The block IF construct has the following form:

```
IF (logical_expr) THEN
   Statement 1
   Statement 2          } Block
   ...
END IF
```

If the logical expression is true, the program executes the statements in the block between the IF and END IF statements. If the logical expression is false, then the program skips all of the statements in the block between the IF and END IF statements and executes the next statement after the END IF. The flowchart for a block IF construct is shown in Figure 3–5.

The IF (...) THEN is a single Fortran statement that must be written together on the same line, and the statements to be executed must occupy separate lines below the IF (...) THEN statement. An END IF statement must follow on a separate line. There should not be a statement number on the line containing the END IF statement. For readability, the block of code between the IF and END IF statements is usually indented by two or three spaces, but this convention is not actually required.

Good Programming Practice
Always indent the body of a block IF construct by two or more spaces to improve the readability of the code.

As an example of a block IF construct, consider the solution of a quadratic equation of the form

$$ax^2 + bx + c = 0 \qquad (3\text{--}1)$$

The solution to this equation is

$$x = \frac{-b \pm \sqrt{b^2 - 4ac}}{2a} \qquad (3\text{--}2)$$

The term $b^2 - 4ac$ is known as the *discriminant* of the equation. If $b^2 - 4ac > 0$, then there are two distinct real roots to the quadratic equation. If $b^2 - 4ac = 0$, then there is a single repeated root to the equation, and if $b^2 - 4ac < 0$, then there are two complex roots to the quadratic equation.

FIGURE 3–5
Flowchart for a simple block IF construct.

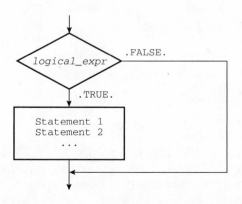

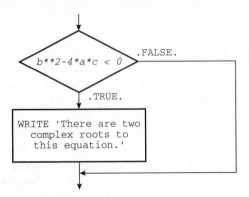

FIGURE 3–6
Flowchart showing structure to determine if a quadratic equation has two complex roots.

   Suppose that we wanted to examine the discriminant of the quadratic equation and tell a user if the equation has complex roots. In pseudocode the block `IF` construct to do this task would take the following form:

```
IF (b**2 - 4.*a*c) < 0. THEN
    Write message that equation has two complex roots.
END of IF
```

In Fortran the block `IF` construct is

```
IF ( (b**2 - 4.*a*c) < 0.) THEN
    WRITE (*,*) 'There are two complex roots to this equation.'
END IF
```

The flowchart for this construct is shown in Figure 3–6.

3.3.2 The `ELSE` and `ELSE IF` Clauses

In the simple block `IF` construct, a block of code is executed if the controlling logical expression is true. If the controlling expression is false, all the statements in the construct are skipped.

   Sometimes we may want to execute one set of statements if some condition is true and different sets of statements if other conditions are true. If fact, there might be many different options to consider. An `ELSE` clause and one or more `ELSE IF` clauses may be added to the block `IF` construct for this purpose. The block `IF` construct with an `ELSE` clause and an `ELSE IF` clause has this form:

```
IF (logical_expr_1) THEN
    Statement 1    ⎫
    Statement 2    ⎬  Block 1
    ...            ⎭
ELSE IF (logical_expr_2) THEN
    Statement 1    ⎫
    Statement 2    ⎬  Block 2
    ...            ⎭
ELSE
    Statement 1    ⎫
    Statement 2    ⎬  Block 3
    ...            ⎭
END IF
```

If *logical_expr_1* is true, then the program executes the statements in block 1 and skips to the first executable statement following the END IF. Otherwise, the program checks for the status of *logical_expr_2*. If *logical_expr_2* is true, then the program executes the statements in block 2 and skips to the first executable statement following the END IF. If both logical expressions are false, then the program executes the statements in block 3.

The ELSE and ELSE IF statements must occupy lines by themselves. There should not be a statement number on a line containing an ELSE or an ELSE IF statement.

A block IF construct can have any number of ELSE IF clauses. The logical expression in each clause will be tested only if the logical expressions in every clause above it are false. Once one of the expressions proves to be true and the corresponding code block is executed, the program skips to the first executable statement following the END IF.

The flowchart for a block IF construct with an ELSE IF and an ELSE clause is shown in Figure 3–7.

To illustrate the use of the ELSE and ELSE IF clauses, let's reconsider the quadratic equation. Suppose that we wanted to examine the discriminant of a quadratic equation and to tell a user whether the equation has two complex roots, two identical real roots, or two distinct real roots. In pseudocode this construct would take the following form:

```
IF (b**2 - 4.*a*c) < 0. THEN
    Write message that equation has two complex roots.
ELSE IF (b**2 - 4.*a*c) == 0. THEN
    Write message that equation has two identical real roots.
ELSE
    Write message that equation has two distinct real roots.
END IF
```

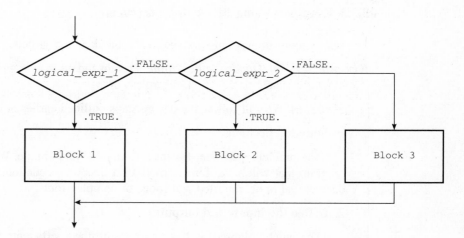

FIGURE 3–7
Flowchart for a block IF construct with an ELSE IF (...) THEN clause and an ELSE clause.

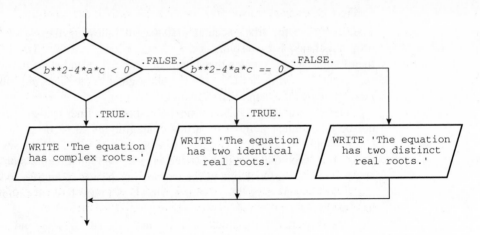

FIGURE 3–8
Flowchart showing structure to determine whether a quadratic equation has two complex roots, two identical real roots, or two distinct real roots.

The Fortran statements to do this are

```
IF ( (b**2 - 4.*a*c) < 0. ) THEN
   WRITE (*,*) 'This equation has two complex roots.'
ELSE IF ( (b**2 - 4.*a*c) == 0. ) THEN
   WRITE (*,*) 'This equation has two identical real roots.'
ELSE
   WRITE (*,*) 'This equation has two distinct real roots.'
END IF
```

The flowchart for this construct is shown in Figure 3–8.

3.3.3 Examples Using Block IF Constructs

The following examples illustrate the use of block IF constructs.

EXAMPLE 3–1 The Quadratic Equation: Design and write a program to solve for the roots of a quadratic equation, regardless of type.

SOLUTION We will follow the design steps outlined earlier in the chapter.

1. **State the problem.**

   The problem statement for this example is very simple. We want to write a program that will solve for the roots of a quadratic equation, whether they are distinct real roots, repeated real roots, or complex roots.

2. **Define the inputs and outputs.**

   The inputs required by this program are the coefficients a, b, and c of the quadratic equation

$$ax^2 + bx + c = 0 \tag{3–1}$$

The output from the program will be the roots of the quadratic equation, whether they are distinct real roots, repeated real roots, or complex roots.

3. **Design the algorithm.**

   This task can be broken down into three major sections, whose functions are input, processing, and output.

```
Read the input data
Calculate the roots
Write out the roots
```

We will now break each of the above major sections into smaller, more detailed pieces. There are three possible ways to calculate the roots, depending on the value of the discriminant, so it is logical to implement this algorithm with a three-branched IF statement. The resulting pseudocode is

```
Prompt the user for the coefficients a, b, and c.
Read a, b, and c
Echo the input coefficients
discriminant ← b**2 - 4. * a * c
IF discriminant > 0 THEN
    x1 ← ( -b + sqrt(discriminant) ) / ( 2. * a )
    x2 ← ( -b - sqrt(discriminant) ) / ( 2. * a )
    Write message that equation has two distinct real roots.
    Write out the two roots.
ELSE IF discriminant == 0 THEN
    x1 ← -b / ( 2. * a )
    Write message that equation has two identical real roots.
    Write out the repeated root.
ELSE
    real_part ← -b / ( 2. * a )
    imag_part ← sqrt ( abs ( discriminant ) ) / ( 2. * a )
    Write message that equation has two complex roots.
    Write out the two roots.
END IF
```

The flowchart for this program is shown in Figure 3–9.

4. **Turn the algorithm into Fortran statements.**

   The final Fortran code is shown in Figure 3–10.

FIGURE 3–10
Program to solve for the roots of a quadratic equation.

```
PROGRAM roots

! Purpose:
!   This program solves for the roots of a quadratic equation of the
!   form a*x**2 + b*x + c = 0.  It calculates the answers regardless
!   of the type of roots that the equation possesses.
!
! Record of revisions:
!    Date        Programmer           Description of change
!    ====        ==========           =====================
!    9/06/95     S. J. Chapman        Original code
!
```

(continued)

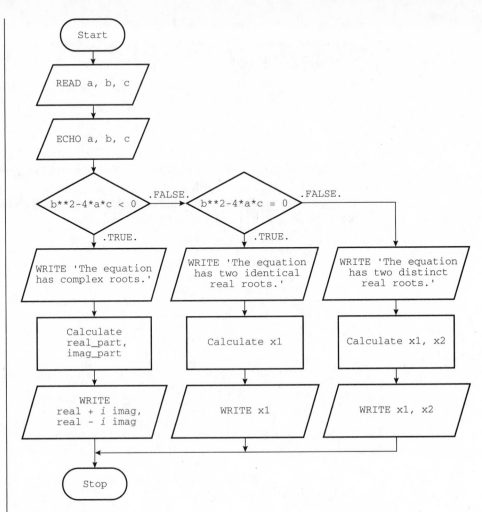

FIGURE 3–9
Flowchart of program `roots`.

(Figure 3–10 continued)

```
IMPLICIT NONE

! Declare the variables used in this program
REAL :: a                ! Coefficient of x**2 term of equation
REAL :: b                ! Coefficient of x term of equation
REAL :: c                ! Constant term of equation
REAL :: discriminant     ! Discriminant of the equation
REAL :: imag_part        ! Imaginary part of equation (for complex roots)
REAL :: real_part        ! Real part of equation (for complex roots)
REAL :: x1               ! First solution of equation (for real roots)
REAL :: x2               ! Second solution of equation (for real roots)

! Prompt the user for the coefficients of the equation
WRITE (*,*) 'This program solves for the roots of a quadratic '
WRITE (*,*) 'equation of the form A * X**2 + B * X + C = 0. '
```

(continued)

(concluded)

```
WRITE (*,*) 'Enter the coefficients A, B, and C: '
READ  (*,*) a, b, c

! Echo back coefficients
WRITE (*,*) 'The coefficients A, B, and C are: ', a, b, c

! Calculate discriminant
discriminant = b**2 - 4. * a * c

! Solve for the roots, depending upon the value of the discriminant
IF ( discriminant > 0. ) THEN ! there are two real roots, so ...

   x1 = ( -b + sqrt(discriminant) ) / ( 2. * a )
   x2 = ( -b - sqrt(discriminant) ) / ( 2. * a )
   WRITE (*,*) 'This equation has two real roots:'
   WRITE (*,*) 'X1 = ', x1
   WRITE (*,*) 'X2 = ', x2

ELSE IF ( discriminant == 0. ) THEN ! there is one repeated root, so ...

   x1 = ( -b ) / ( 2. * a )
   WRITE (*,*) 'This equation has two identical real roots:'
   WRITE (*,*) 'X1 = X2 = ', x1

ELSE ! there are complex roots, so ...

   real_part = ( -b ) / ( 2. * a )
   imag_part = sqrt ( abs ( discriminant ) ) / ( 2. * a )
   WRITE (*,*) 'This equation has complex roots:'
   WRITE (*,*) 'X1 = ', real_part, ' +i ', imag_part
   WRITE (*,*) 'X2 = ', real_part, ' -i ', imag_part

END IF

END PROGRAM
```

5. Test the program.

Next we must test the program using real input data. Since there are three possible paths through the program, we must test all three paths before we can be certain that the program is working properly. From Equation (3–2) we can verify the solutions to the following equations:

$$x^2 + 5x + 6 = 0 \qquad x = -2, \text{ and } x = -3$$

$$x^2 + 4x + 4 = 0 \qquad x = -2$$

$$x^2 + 2x + 5 = 0 \qquad x = -1 \pm i2$$

If this program is compiled and then run three times with the above coefficients, the results are as shown. (User inputs appear in bold face.)

```
C>roots
This program solves for the roots of a quadratic
equation of the form A * X**2 + B * X + C = 0.
Enter the coefficients A, B, and C:
1., 5., 6.
The coefficients A, B, and C are:        1.000000    5.000000    6.000000
```

```
This equation has two real roots:
X1 =        -2.000000
X2 =        -3.000000

C>roots
This program solves for the roots of a quadratic
equation of the form A * X**2 + B * X + C = 0.
Enter the coefficients A, B, and C:
1., 4., 4.
The coefficients A, B, and C are:        1.000000    4.000000    4.000000
This equation has two identical real roots:
X1 = X2 =        -2.000000

C>roots
This program solves for the roots of a quadratic
equation of the form A * X**2 + B * X + C = 0.
Enter the coefficients A, B, and C:
1., 2., 5.
The coefficients A, B, and C are:        1.000000    2.000000    5.000000
This equation has complex roots:
X1 =        -1.000000 +i      2.000000
X2 =        -1.000000 -i      2.000000
```

The program gives the correct answers for our test data in all three possible cases.

EXAMPLE 3–2 *Evaluating a Function of Two Variables:* Write a Fortran program to evaluate a function $f(x,y)$ for any two user-specified values x and y. The function $f(x,y)$ is defined as follows.

$$f(x,y) = \begin{cases} x + y & x \geq 0 \text{ and } y \geq 0 \\ x + y^2 & x \geq 0 \text{ and } y < 0 \\ x^2 + y & x < 0 \text{ and } y \geq 0 \\ x^2 + y^2 & x < 0 \text{ and } y < 0 \end{cases}$$

SOLUTION The function $f(x,y)$ is evaluated differently depending on the signs of the two independent variables x and y. To determine the proper equation to apply, it will be necessary to check for the signs of the x and y user-supplied values.

1. **State the problem.**

    This problem statement is very simple. Evaluate the function $f(x,y)$ for any user-supplied values of x and y.

2. **Define the inputs and outputs.**

    The inputs required by this program are the values of the independent variables x and y. The output from the program will be the value of the function $f(x,y)$.

3. **Design the algorithm.**

    This task can be broken down into three major sections, whose functions are input, processing, and output.

```
Read the input values x and y
Calculate f(x,y)
Write out f(x,y)
```

We will now break each of the above major sections into smaller, more detailed pieces. There are four possible ways to calculate the function $f(x,y)$, depending on the values of *x* and *y*, so it is logical to implement this algorithm with a four-branched IF statement. The resulting pseudocode is

```
Prompt the user for the values x and y.
Read x and y
Echo the input coefficients
If x ≥ 0 and y ≥ 0 THEN
    fun ← x + y
ELSE IF x ≥ 0 and y < 0 THEN
    fun ← x + y**2
ELSE IF x < 0 and y ≥ 0 THEN
    fun ← x**2 + y
ELSE
    fun ← x**2 + y**2
END IF
Write out f(x,y)
```

The flowchart for this program is shown in Figure 3–11.

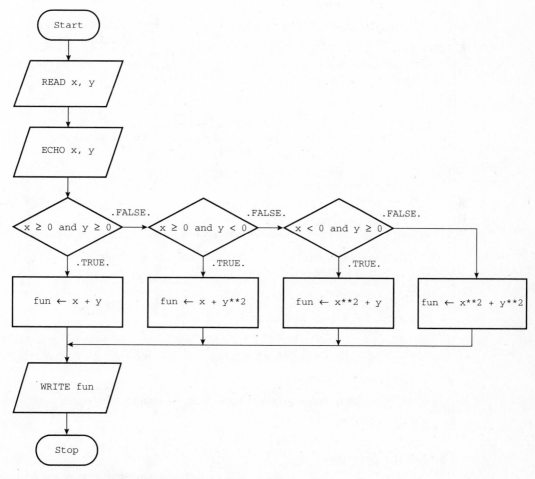

FIGURE 3–11
Flowchart of program funxy.

4. **Turn the algorithm into Fortran statements.**

The final Fortran code is shown in Figure 3–12.

FIGURE 3–12
Program funxy from Example 3–2.

```
PROGRAM funxy
!
!  Purpose:
!    This program solves the function f(x,y) for a user-specified x and y,
!    where f(x,y) is defined as:
!
!
!                        _
!                       |
!                       |    X + Y              X >= 0 and Y >= 0
!                       |    X + Y**2           X >= 0 and Y < 0
!           F(X,Y) =  |    X**2 + Y           X < 0  and Y >= 0
!                       |    X**2 + Y**2        X < 0  and Y < 0
!                       |_
!
!
!  Record of revisions:
!     Date        Programmer          Description of change
!     ====        ==========          =====================
!    09/08/95    S. J. Chapman        Original code
!
IMPLICIT NONE

! Declare the variables used in this program.
REAL :: x                    ! First independent variable
REAL :: y                    ! Second independent variable
REAL :: fun                  ! Resulting function

! Prompt the user for the values x and y
WRITE (*,*) 'Enter the coefficients x and y: '
READ  (*,*) x, y

! Write the coefficients of x and y.
WRITE (*,*) 'The coefficients x and y are: ', x, y

! Calculate the function f(x,y) based upon the signs of x and y.
IF ( ( x >= 0. ) .AND. ( y >= 0. ) ) THEN
   fun = x + y
ELSE IF ( ( x >= 0. ) .AND. ( y < 0. ) ) THEN
   fun = x + y**2
ELSE IF ( ( x < 0. ) .AND. ( y >= 0. ) ) THEN
   fun = x**2 + y
ELSE
   fun = x**2 + y**2
END IF

! Write the value of the function.
WRITE (*,*) 'The value of the function is: ', fun

END PROGRAM
```

5. **Test the program.**

Next we must test the program using real input data. Since there are four possible paths through the program, we must test all four paths before we can be certain that the program is working properly. To test all four possible paths, we will execute the program with the four sets of input values $(x,y) = (2,3)$, $(-2,3)$, $(2,-3)$, and $(-2,-3)$. Calculating by hand, we see that

$$f(2,3) = 2 + 3 = 5$$

$$f(2,-3) = 2 + (-3)^2 = 11$$

$$f(-2,3) = (-2)^2 + 3 = 7$$

$$f(-2,-3) = (-2)^2 + (-3)^2 = 13$$

If this program is compiled and then run four times with the above values, the results are

```
C>funxy
Enter the coefficients X and Y:
2. 3.
The coefficients X and Y are:          2.000000        3.000000
The value of the function is:          5.000000

C>funxy
Enter the coefficients X and Y:
2. -3.
The coefficients X and Y are:          2.000000       -3.000000
The value of the function is:         11.000000

C>funxy
Enter the coefficients X and Y:
-2. 3.
The coefficients X and Y are:         -2.000000        3.000000
The value of the function is:          7.000000

C>funxy
Enter the coefficients X and Y:
-2. -3.
The coefficients X and Y are:         -2.000000       -3.000000
The value of the function is:         13.000000
```

The program gives the correct answers for our test values in all four possible cases.

3.3.4 Name Block IF Constructs

It is possible to assign a name to a block IF construct. The general form of the construct with a name attached is

```
[name:] IF (logical_expr_1) THEN
    Statement 1
    Statement 2              } Block 1
    ...
ELSE IF (logical_expr_2) THEN [name]
    Statement 1
    Statement 2              } Block 2
    ...
ELSE [name]
    Statement 1
    Statement 2              } Block 3
    ...
END IF [name]
```

where *name* may be up to 31 alphanumeric characters long, beginning with a letter. The name given to the IF construct must be unique within each program unit and must not be the same as any constant or variable name within the program unit. If a name is assigned to an IF, then the same name must appear on the associated END IF. Names are optional on the ELSE and ELSE IF statements of the construct, but if they are used, they must be the same as the name on the IF.

Why would we want to name an IF construct? For simple examples like the ones we have seen so far, there is no particular reason to do so. The principal reason for using names is to help us (and the compiler) keep IF constructs straight in our own minds when they get very complicated. For example, suppose that we have a complex IF construct that is hundreds of lines long, spanning many pages of listings. If we name all of the parts of such a construct, then we can tell at a glance which construct a particular ELSE or ELSE IF statement belongs to. Names on constructs make a programmer's intentions explicitly clear and can help the compiler flag the specific location of an error when one occurs.

Good Programming Practice

Assign a name to any large and complicated IF constructs in your program to help you keep the parts of the construct associated together in your own mind.

3.3.5 Notes Concerning the Use of Logical IF Constructs

The block IF construct is very flexible. It must have one IF (...) THEN statement and one END IF statement. In between, it can have any number of ELSE IF clauses and may also have one ELSE clause. With this combination of features, it is possible to implement any desired branching construct.

In addition, block IF constructs may be **nested.** Two block IF constructs are said to be "nested" if one of them lies entirely within a single code block of the other one. The following two IF constructs are properly nested.

```
outer: IF (x > 0.) THEN
    ...
  inner: IF (y < 0.) THEN
      ...
    END IF inner
    ...
  END IF outer
```

It is a good idea to name IF constructs when they are being nested, since the name explicitly indicates which IF a particular END IF is associated with. If the constructs are not named, the Fortran compiler always associates a given END IF with the most recent IF statement. This method works well for a properly written program but can cause the compiler to produce confusing error messages in cases where the programmer makes a coding error. For example, suppose we have a large program containing a construct such as

```
PROGRAM mixup
...
IF (test1) THEN
   ...
   IF (test2) THEN
      ...
      IF (test3) THEN
         ...
      END IF
      ...
   END IF
   ...
END IF
...
END PROGRAM
```

This program contains three nested IF constructs that may span hundreds of lines of code. Now suppose that the first END IF statement is accidentally deleted during an editing session. When that happens, the compiler will automatically associate the second END IF with the innermost IF (test3) construct and the third END IF with the middle IF (test2). When the compiler reaches the END PROGRAM statement, it will notice that the first IF (test1) construct was never ended and will generate an error message saying that an END IF is missing. Unfortunately, the compiler can't tell *where* the problem occurred, so we will have to go back and manually search the entire program to locate the problem.

In contrast, consider what happens if we assign names to each IF construct. The resulting program would be

```
PROGRAM mixup_1
...
outer: IF (test1) THEN
   ...
   ...
   middle: IF (test2) THEN
      ...
      ...
      inner: IF (test3) THEN
         ...
         ...
      END IF inner
      ...
   END IF middle
   ...
END IF outer
...
END PROGRAM
```

Suppose that the first END IF statement is again accidentally deleted during an editing session. When that happens, the compiler will notice that there is no END IF associated with the inner IF, and it will generate an error message as soon as it encounters the END IF middle statement. Furthermore, the error message will explicitly state that the problem is associated with the inner IF construct, so we know just where to go to fix it.

It is sometimes possible to implement an algorithm using either ELSE IF clauses or nested IF statements. In that case a programmer may choose whichever style he or she prefers.

EXAMPLE 3–3 *Assigning Letter Grades:* Suppose that we are writing a program that reads in a numerical grade and assigns a letter grade to it according to the following table:

$$
\begin{array}{lll}
95 & < \text{GRADE} & A \\
86 & < \text{GRADE} \leq 95 & B \\
76 & < \text{GRADE} \leq 86 & C \\
66 & < \text{GRADE} \leq 76 & D \\
0 & < \text{GRADE} \leq 66 & F
\end{array}
$$

Write an IF construct that will assign these grades using (*a*) multiple ELSE IF clauses and (*b*) nested IF constructs.

SOLUTION

a. One possible structure using ELSE IF clauses is

```
IF ( grade > 95.0 ) THEN
    WRITE (*,*) 'The grade is A.'
ELSE IF ( grade > 86.0 ) THEN
    WRITE (*,*) 'The grade is B.'
ELSE IF ( grade > 76.0 ) THEN
    WRITE (*,*) 'The grade is C.'
ELSE IF ( grade > 66.0 ) THEN
    WRITE (*,*) 'The grade is D.'
ELSE
    WRITE (*,*) 'The grade is F.'
END IF
```

b. One possible structure using nested IF constructs is

```
if1: IF ( grade > 95.0 ) THEN
   WRITE (*,*) 'The grade is A.'
ELSE
   if2: IF ( grade > 86.0) THEN
      WRITE (*,*) 'The grade is B.'
   ELSE
      if3: IF ( grade > 76.0 ) THEN
         WRITE (*,*) 'The grade is C.'
      ELSE
         if4: IF ( grade > 66.0) THEN
            WRITE (*,*) 'The grade is D.'
         ELSE
            WRITE (*,*) 'The grade is F.'
         END IF if4
      END IF if3
   END IF if2
END IF if1
```

Example 3–3 demonstrates that if a program contains many mutually exclusive options, a single IF construct with ELSE IF clauses will be simpler than a nested IF construct.

Good Programming Practice
For branches that have many mutually exclusive options, use a single IF construct with ELSE IF clauses rather than nested IF constructs.

3.3.6 The Logical IF Statement

There is an alternative form of the logical IF construct described in Section 3.3.1. It is just a single statement of the form

IF (*logical_expr*) Statement

where Statement is an executable Fortran statement. If the logical expression is true, the program executes the statement on the same line with it. Otherwise, the program skips to the next executable statement in the program. This form of the logical IF is equivalent to a block IF construct with only one statement in the IF block.

3.3.7 The CASE Construct

The CASE construct is another form of branching construct. It permits a programmer to select a particular code block to execute based on the value of a single integer, character, or logical expression. The general form of a CASE construct is

```
[name:] SELECT CASE (case_expr)
CASE (case_selector_1) [name]
   Statement 1
   Statement 2          } Block 1
   ...
CASE (case_selector_2) [name]
   Statement 1
   Statement 2          } Block 2
   ...
 ...
CASE DEFAULT [name]
   Statement 1
   Statement 2          } Block n
   ...
END SELECT [name]
```

If the value of *case_expr* is in the range of values included in *case_selector_1* then the first code block will be executed. Similarly, if the value of *case_expr* is in the range of values included in *case_selector_2,* then the second code block will be executed. The same idea applies for any other cases in the construct. The default code block is optional. If it is present, the default code block will be executed whenever the value of *case_expr* is outside the range of all of the case selectors. If it is not present and the value of *case_expr* is outside the range of all of the case selectors, then none of the code blocks will be executed. The pseudocode for the case construct looks just like its Fortran implementation; a flowchart for this construct is shown in Figure 3–13.

A name may be assigned to a CASE construct, if desired. The name must be unique within each program unit. If a name is assigned to a SELECT CASE statement, then the same name must appear on the associated END SELECT. Names are optional on the CASE statements of the construct, but if they are used, they must be the same as the name on the SELECT CASE statement.

The *case_expr* may be any integer, character, or logical expression. Each case selector must be an integer, character, or logical value or range of values. All case selectors must be *mutually exclusive;* no single value can appear in more than one case selector.

3

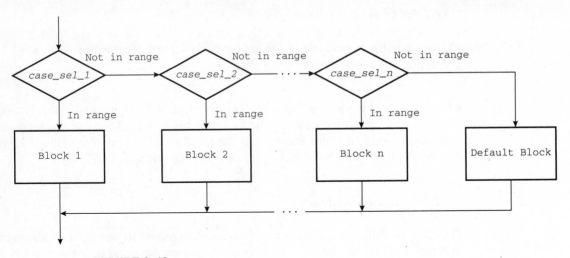

FIGURE 3–13
Flowchart for a CASE construct.

Let's look at a simple example of a CASE construct. This example prints out a message based on the value of an integer variable.

```
INTEGER :: temp_c              ! Temperature in degrees C
...
temp: SELECT CASE (temp_c)
CASE (:-1)
    WRITE (*,*) "It's below freezing today!"
CASE (0)
    WRITE (*,*) "It's exactly at the freezing point."
CASE (1:20)
    WRITE (*,*) "It's cool today."
CASE (21:33)
    WRITE (*,*) "It's warm today."
CASE (34:)
    WRITE (*,*) "It's hot today."
END SELECT temp
```

The value of temp_c controls which case is selected. If the temperature is less than 0, then the first case will be selected and the message will be It's below freezing today. If the temperature is exactly 0, then the second case will be selected, and so forth. Note that the cases do not overlap—a given temperature can appear in only one of the cases.

The *case_selector* can take one of four forms:

case_value	Execute block if *case_value* == *case_expr*
low_value	Execute block if *low_value* <= *case_expr*
high_value	Execute block if *case_expr* <= *high_value*
low_value: high_value	Execute block if *low_value* <= *case_expr* <= *high_value*

or it can be a list of any combination of these forms separated by commas.

The following statements determine whether an integer between 1 and 10 is even or odd and then print out an appropriate message. It illustrates the use of a list of values as case selectors and also the use of the CASE DEFAULT block.

```
INTEGER :: value
...
SELECT CASE (value)
CASE (1,3,5,7,9)
   WRITE (*,*) 'The value is odd.'
CASE (2,4,6,8,10)
   WRITE (*,*) 'The value is even.'
CASE (11:)
   WRITE (*,*) 'The value is too high.'
CASE DEFAULT
   WRITE (*,*) 'The value is negative or zero.'
END SELECT
```

Quiz 3–1

This quiz provides a quick check to see if you understand the concepts introduced in section 3.3. If you have trouble with the quiz, reread the section, ask your instructor, or discuss the material with a fellow student. The answers to this quiz are found in the back of the book.

Write Fortran statements that perform the following functions:

1. If x is greater than or equal to zero, then assign the square root of x to variable sqrt_x and print out the result. Otherwise, print out an error message about the argument of the square root function and set sqrt_x to zero.

2. A variable fun is calculated as numerator / denominator. If the absolute value of denominator is less than 1.0E-10, write Divide by 0 error. Otherwise, calculate and print out fun.

3. The cost per mile for a rented vehicle is 50 cents for the first 100 miles, 30 cents for the next 200 miles, and 20 cents for all miles in excess of 300 miles. Write Fortran statements that determine the total cost and the average cost per mile for a given number of miles (stored in variable distance).

Examine the following Fortran statements. Are they correct or incorrect? If they are correct, what is the output? If they are incorrect, what is wrong with them?

```
4. IF ( volts > 125. ) THEN
      WRITE (*,*) 'WARNING: High voltage on line.'
   IF ( volts < 105. ) THEN
      WRITE (*,*) 'WARNING: Low voltage on line.'
   ELSE
      WRITE (*,*) 'Line voltage is within tolerances.'
   END IF
```

(continued)

3

(concluded)

```
5. PROGRAM test
   LOGICAL :: warn
   REAL :: distance
   REAL, PARAMETER :: limit = 100.
   warn = .TRUE.
   distance = 55. + 10.
   IF ( distance > limit .OR. warn ) THEN
      WRITE (*,*) 'Warning: Distance exceeds limit.'
   ELSE
      WRITE (*,*) 'Distance = ', distance
   END IF

6. REAL, PARAMETER :: pi = 3.141593
   REAL :: a = 10.
   SELECT CASE ( a * sqrt(pi) )
   CASE (0:)
      WRITE (*,*) 'a > 0'
   CASE (:0)
      WRITE (*,*) 'a < 0'
   CASE DEFAULT
      WRITE (*,*) 'a = 0'
   END SELECT

7. CHARACTER(len=6) :: color = 'yellow'
   SELECT CASE ( color )
   CASE ('red')
      WRITE (*,*) 'Stop now!'
   CASE ('yellow')
      WRITE (*,*) 'Prepare to stop.'
   CASE ('green')
      WRITE (*,*) 'Proceed through intersection.'
   CASE DEFAULT
      WRITE (*,*) 'Illegal color encountered.'
   END SELECT

8. IF ( temperature > 37. ) THEN
      WRITE (*,*) 'Human body temperature exceeded.'
   ELSE IF ( temperature > 100. )
      WRITE (*,*) 'Boiling point of water exceeded.'
   END IF
```

3.4
CONTROL CONSTRUCTS: LOOPS

Loops are Fortran constructs that permit us to execute a sequence of statements more than once. The two basic forms of loop constructs are **while loops** and **iterative loops** (or **counting loops**). The major difference between these two types of loops is in how the repetition is controlled. The code in a while loop is repeated an indefinite number of times until some user-specified condition is satisfied. By contrast, the code in an iterative loop is repeated a specified number of times, and the number of repetitions is known before the loop starts.

3.4.1 The While Loop

A *while loop* is a block of statements that are repeated indefinitely as long as some condition is satisfied. The general form of a while loop in Fortran 90/95 is

```
DO
   ...
   IF (logical_expr) EXIT        ⎫
   ...                           ⎬ Code block
END DO                           ⎭
```

The block of statements between the DO and END DO are repeated indefinitely until the `logical_expr` becomes true and the EXIT statement is executed. After the EXIT statement is executed, control transfers to the first statement after the END DO.

A while loop may contain one or more IF statements to terminate its execution. An IF statement may be located anywhere within the body of the loop, and it is executed once each time that the loop is repeated. If the `logical_expr` in the IF is false when the statement is executed, the loop continues to execute. If the `logical_expr` in the IF is true when the statement is executed, control transfers immediately to the first statement after the END DO. If the logical expression is true the first time we reach the while loop, the statements in the loop below the IF will never be executed at all!

The pseudocode corresponding to a while loop is

```
WHILE
   ...
   IF logical_expr EXIT
   ...
End of WHILE
```

and the flowchart for this construct is shown in Figure 3–14.

Example 3–4 shows a statistical analysis program that is implemented using a while loop.

EXAMPLE 3–4 Statistical Analysis: Scientists and engineers often work with large sets of numbers, each of which is a measurement of some particular property that we are interested in. A simple example would be the grades on the first test in this course. Each grade would be a measurement of how much a particular student has learned in the course to date.

Much of the time, we are not interested in looking closely at every single measurement that we make. Instead, we want to summarize the results of a set of measurements with a few numbers that tell us a lot about the overall data set. Two such numbers are the *average* (or *arithmetic mean*) and the *standard deviation* of the set of measurements. The average or arithmetic mean of a set of numbers is defined as

$$\bar{x} = \frac{1}{N} \sum_{i=1}^{N} x_i \qquad (3\text{--}3)$$

FIGURE 3–14
Flowchart for a while loop.

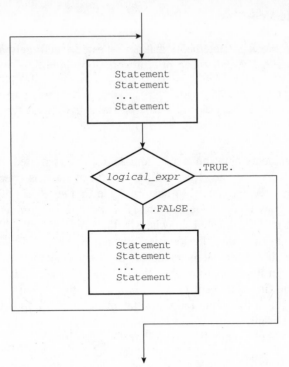

where x_i is sample i out of N samples. The standard deviation of a set of numbers is defined as

$$s = \sqrt{\frac{N \sum\limits_{i=1}^{N} x_i^2 - \left(\sum\limits_{i=1}^{N} x_i \right)^2}{N(N-1)}} \qquad (3\text{–}4)$$

Standard deviation is a measure of the amount of scatter on the measurements; the greater the standard deviation, the more scattered the points in the data set are.

Implement an algorithm that reads in a set of measurements and calculates the mean and the standard deviation of the input data set.

SOLUTION This program must be able to read in an arbitrary number of measurements and then calculate the mean and standard deviation of those measurements. We will use a while loop to accumulate the input measurements before performing the calculations.

When all the measurements have been read, we must have some way of telling the program that there is no more data to enter. For now, we will assume that all the input measurements are either positive or zero, and we will use a negative input value as a *flag* to indicate that there is no more data to read. If a negative value is entered, then the program will stop reading input values and will calculate the mean and standard deviation of the data set.

1. **State the problem.**

Since we assume that the input numbers must be positive or zero, a proper statement of this program would be: Calculate the average and the standard deviation of a set of measurements, assuming that all of the measurements are either positive or zero and assuming that we do not know in advance how many measurements are included in the data set. A negative input value will mark the end of the set of measurements.

2. **Define the inputs and outputs.**

The inputs required by this program are an unknown number of positive or zero real (floating-point) numbers. The outputs from this program are a printout of the mean and the standard deviation of the input data set. In addition, we will print out the number of data points input to the program to check that the input data was read correctly.

3. **Design the algorithm.**

This program can be broken down into three major steps:

```
Accumulate the input data.
Calculate the mean and standard deviation.
Write out the mean, standard deviation, and number of points.
```

The first major step of the program is to accumulate the input data. To do this, we will have to prompt the user to enter the desired numbers. When the numbers are entered, we will have to keep track of the number of values entered, plus the sum and the sum of the squares of those values. The pseudocode for these steps is

```
Initialize n, sum_x, and sum_x2 to 0
WHILE
    Prompt user for next number
    Read in next x
    IF x < 0. EXIT
    n ← n + 1
    sum_x ← sum_x + x
    sum_x2 ← sum_x2 + x**2
End of WHILE
```

Note that we have to read in the first value before the IF () EXIT test so that the while loop can have a value to test the first time it executes.

Next, we must calculate the mean and standard deviation. The pseudocode for this step is the Fortran versions of Equations (3–3) and (3–4).

```
x_bar ← sum_x / REAL(n)
std_dev ← SQRT((REAL(n)*sum_x2 - sum_x**2) / (REAL(n)*REAL(n-1)))
```

Finally, we must write out the results.

```
Write out the mean value x_bar.
Write out the standard deviation std_dev.
Write out the number of input data points n.
```

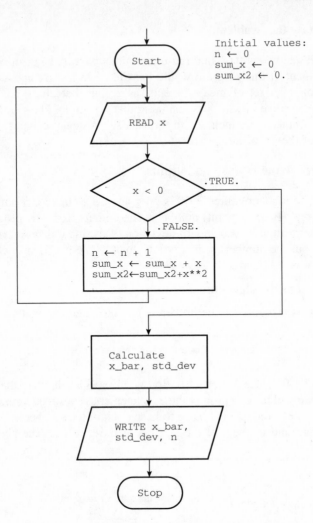

FIGURE 3–15
Flowchart for the statistical analysis program of Example 3–4.

The flowchart for this program is shown in Figure 3–15.

4. **Turn the algorithm into Fortran statements.**

The final Fortran program is shown in Figure 3–16.

FIGURE 3–16
Program to calculate the mean and standard deviation of a set of nonnegative real numbers.

```
PROGRAM stats_1
!
!  Purpose:
!    To calculate mean and the standard deviation of an input
!    data set containing an arbitrary number of input values.
!
!  Record of revisions:
!     Date         Programmer              Description of change
```

(continued)

(concluded)

```
!       ====         ==========            ======================
!     09/10/95    S. J. Chapman         Original code
!
IMPLICIT NONE

! Declare and initialize the variables used in this program.
INTEGER :: n =0        ! The number of input samples.
REAL :: std_dev = 0.   ! The standard deviation of the input samples.
REAL :: sum_x = 0.     ! The sum of the input values.
REAL :: sum_x2 = 0.    ! The sum of the squares of the input values.
REAL :: x = 0.         ! An input data value.
REAL :: x_bar          ! The average of the input samples.

! While Loop to read input values.
DO
   ! Read in next value
   WRITE (*,*) 'Enter number: '
   READ  (*,*) x
   WRITE (*,*) 'The number is ', x

   ! Test for loop exit
   IF ( x < 0 ) EXIT

   ! Otherwise, accumulate sums.
   n      = n + 1
   sum_x  = sum_x + x
   sum_x2 = sum_x2 + x**2
END DO

! Calculate the mean and standard deviation
x_bar = sum_x / real(n)
std_dev = sqrt( (real(n) * sum_x2 - sum_x**2) / (real(n) * real(n-1)) )

! Tell user.
WRITE (*,*) 'The mean of this data set is: ', x_bar
WRITE (*,*) 'The standard deviation is:    ', std_dev
WRITE (*,*) 'The number of data points is: ', n

END PROGRAM
```

5. Test the program.

To test this program, we will calculate the answers by hand for a simple data set and then compare the answers to the results of the program. If we used three input values: 3, 4, and 5, then the mean and standard deviation would be

$$\bar{x} = \frac{1}{N} \sum_{i=1}^{N} x_i = \frac{1}{3} \, 12 = 4$$

$$s = \sqrt{\frac{N \sum_{i=1}^{N} x_i^2 - \left(\sum_{i=1}^{N} x_i \right)^2}{N(N-1)}} = 1$$

When the above values are fed into the program, the results are

```
C>stats_1
Enter number:
3.
The number is        3.000000
Enter number:
```

```
4.
The number is              4.000000
Enter number:
5.
The number is              5.000000
Enter number:
-1.
The number is             -1.000000
The mean of this data set is:          4.000000
The standard deviation is:             1.000000
The number of data points is:                 3
```

The program gives the correct answers for our test data set.

In the preceding example, we failed to follow the design process completely. This failure has left the program with a fatal flaw! Did you spot it?

We have failed because *we did not completely test the program for all possible types of inputs.* Look at the example once again. If we enter either no numbers or only one number, then we will be dividing by zero in the above equations! The division-by-zero error will cause the program to abort. We need to modify the program to detect this problem, inform the user of it, and stop gracefully.

A modified version of the program called stats_2 is shown in Figure 3–17. Here we check to see if there are enough input values before performing the calculations. If not, the program will print out an intelligent error message and quit. Test the modified program for yourself.

FIGURE 3–17
A modified statistical analysis program that avoids the divide-by-zero problems inherent in program stats_1.

```
PROGRAM stats_2
!
!  Purpose:
!    To calculate mean and the standard deviation of an input
!    data set containing an arbitrary number of input values.
!
!  Record of revisions:
!      Date        Programmer           Description of change
!      ====        ==========           =====================
!    09/10/95   S. J. Chapman        Original code
! 1. 09/11/95   S. J. Chapman        Correct divide-by-0 error if
!                                    0 or 1 input values given.
!
IMPLICIT NONE

! Declare the variables used in this program.
INTEGER :: n =0        ! The number of input samples.
REAL :: std_dev = 0.   ! The standard deviation of the input samples.
REAL :: sum_x - 0.     ! The sum of the input values.
REAL :: sum_x2 = 0.    ! The sum of the squares of the input values.
REAL :: x = 0.         ! An input data value.
REAL :: x_bar          ! The average of the input samples.

!  While Loop to read input values.
DO

   ! Read in next value
   WRITE (*,*) 'Enter number: '
```

(continued)

(concluded)

```
    READ  (*,*) x
    WRITE (*,*) 'The number is ', x

    ! Test for loop exit
    IF ( x < 0 ) EXIT

    ! Otherwise, accumulate sums.
    n       = n + 1
    sum_x   = sum_x + x
    sum_x2  = sum_x2 + x**2
END DO

! Check to see if we have enough input data.
IF ( n < 2 ) THEN ! Insufficient information

    WRITE (*,*) 'At least 2 values must be entered!'

ELSE ! There is enough information, so
      ! calculate the mean and standard deviation

    x_bar = sum_x / real(n)
    std_dev = sqrt( (real(n) * sum_x2 - sum_x**2) / (real(n)*real(n-1)))

    ! Tell user.
    WRITE (*,*) 'The mean of this data set is:', x_bar
    WRITE (*,*) 'The standard deviation is:   ', std_dev
    WRITE (*,*) 'The number of data points is:', n

END IF
END PROGRAM
```

3.4.2 The DO WHILE Loop

Fortran 90/95 has an alternate form of the while loop, called the DO WHILE loop. The DO WHILE construct has the following form:

```
        DO WHILE (logical_expr)
            . . .                      ⎫  Statement 1
            . . .                      ⎪  Statement 2
            . . .                      ⎬  ...
            . . .                      ⎭  Statement n
        END DO
```

If the logical expression is true, statements 1 through n will be executed and then control will return to the DO WHILE statement. If the logical expression is still true, the statements will be executed again. This process will be repeated until the logical expression becomes false. When control returns to the DO WHILE statement and the logical expression is false, the program will execute the first statement after the END DO.

This construct is a special case of the more general while loop, in which the exit test must always occur at the top of the loop. There is no reason to ever use this construct, since the general while loop does the same job with more flexibility.

Good Programming Practice
Do not use DO WHILE loops in new programs. Use the more general while loop instead.

3.4.3 The Iterative or Counting Loop

In the Fortran language, a loop that executes a block of statements a specified number of times is called an **iterative DO loop** or a **counting loop.** The counting loop construct has the form

```
DO index = istart, iend, incr
   Statement 1
   ...            } Body
   Statement n
END DO
```

where index is an integer variable used as the loop counter (also known as the **loop index**). The integer quantities istart, iend, and incr are the *parameters* of the counting loop; they control the values of the variable index during execution. The parameter incr is optional; if it is missing, it is assumed to be 1.

    The statements between the DO statement and the END DO statement are known as the *body* of the loop. They are executed repeatedly during each pass of the DO loop.

    The counting loop construct functions as follows:

1. Each of the three DO loop parameters istart, iend, and incr may be a constant, a variable, or an expression. If they are variables or expressions, then their values are calculated before the start of the loop and the resulting values are used to control the loop.
2. At the beginning of the execution of the DO loop, the program assigns the value istart to control variable index. If index*incr $\leq$ iend*incr, the program executes the statements within the body of the loop.
3. After the statements in the body of the loop have been executed, the control variable is recalculated as

$$index = index + incr$$

    If index*incr is still less than or equal to iend*incr, the program executes the statements within the body again.
4. Step 2 is repeated as long as index*incr $\leq$ iend*incr. When this condition is no longer true, execution skips to the first statement following the end of the DO loop.

The number of iterations to be performed by the DO loop may be calculated using the Equation (3–5).

$$iter = \frac{iend - istart + incr}{incr} \tag{3-5}$$

    Let's look at a number of specific examples to make the operation of the counting loop clearer. First, consider the following example:

```
DO i = 1, 10
   Statement 1
   ...
   Statement n
END DO
```

In this case, statements 1 through n will be executed 10 times. The index variable i will be 1 on the first time, 2 on the second time, and so on. The index variable will be 10 on the last pass through the statements. When control is returned to the DO statement after the 10th pass, the index variable i will be increased to 11. Since $11 \times 1 > 10 \times 1$, control will transfer to the first statement after the END DO statement.

Second, consider the following example:

```
DO i = 1, 10, 2
    Statement 1
    ...
    Statement n
END DO
```

In this case, statements 1 through n will be executed five times. The index variable i will be 1 on the first time, 3 on the second time, and so on. The index variable will be 9 on the fifth and last pass through the statements. When control is returned to the DO statement after the fifth pass, the index variable i will be increased to 11. Since $11 \times 2 > 10 \times 2$, control will transfer to the first statement after the END DO statement.

Third, consider the following example:

```
DO i = 1, 10, -1
    Statement 1
    ...
    Statement n
END DO
```

Here, statements 1 through n will *never be executed*, since `index*incr > iend*incr` on the very first time that the DO statement is reached. Instead, control will transfer to the first statement after the END DO statement.

Finally, consider the example:

```
DO i = 3, -3, -2
    Statement 1
    ...
    Statement n
END DO
```

In this case, statements 1 through n will be executed four times. The index variable i will be 3 on the first time, 1 on the second time, -1 on the third time, and -3 on the fourth time. When control is returned to the DO statement after the fourth pass, the index variable i will be decreased to -5. Since $-5 \times -2 > -3 \times -2$, control will transfer to the first statement after the END DO statement.

The pseudocode corresponding to a counting loop is

```
DO for index = istart to iend by incr
    Statement 1
    ...
    Statement n
End of DO
```

and the flowchart for this construct is shown in Figure 3–18.

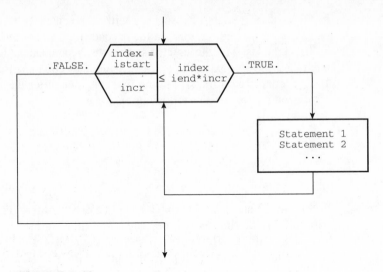

FIGURE 3–18
Flowchart for a DO loop construct.

Example 3–5 The Factorial Function: To illustrate the operation of a counting loop, we will use a DO loop to calculate the factorial function. The factorial function is defined as

N! = 1   N = 0
N! = N * (N-1) * (N-2) * ... * 3 * 2 * 1   N > 0

SOLUTION The Fortran code to calculate N factorial for positive value of N would be

```
n_factorial = 1
DO i = 1, n
   n_factorial = n_factorial * i
END DO
```

Suppose that we wish to calculate the value of 5!. If n is 5, the DO loop parameters will be istart = 1, iend = 5, and incr = 1. This loop will be executed 5 times, with the variable i taking on values of 1, 2, 3, 4, and 5 in the successive loops. The resulting value of n_factorial will be $1 \times 2 \times 3 \times 4 \times 5 = 120$.

Example 3–6 Calculating the Day of Year: The *day of year* is the number of days (including the current day) that have elapsed since the beginning of a given year. It is a number in the range 1 to 365 for ordinary years and 1 to 366 for leap years. Write a Fortran program that accepts a day, month, and year, and calculates the day of year corresponding to that date.

SOLUTION To determine the day of year, this program will need to sum up the number of days in each month preceding the current month plus the number of elapsed days in the current month. A DO loop will be used to perform this sum. Since the number of days in each month varies, it is necessary to determine the correct number of days to add for each month. A CASE construct will be used to determine the proper number of days to add for each month.

During a leap year an extra day must be added to the day of year for any month after February. This extra day accounts for the presence of February 29 in the leap year. Therefore, to perform the day of year calculation correctly, we must determine which years are leap years. In the Gregorian calendar, leap years are determined by the following rules:

1. Years evenly divisible by 400 are leap years.
2. Years evenly divisible by 100 but *not* by 400 are not leap years.
3. All years divisible by 4 but *not* by 100 are leap years.
4. All other years are not leap years.

We will use the MOD (for modulo) function to determine whether or not a year is evenly divisible by a given number. If the result of the MOD function is zero, then the year was evenly divisible.

A program to calculate the day of year is shown in Figure 3–19. Note that the program sums up the number of days in each month before the current month and that it uses a CASE construct to determine the number of days in each month.

FIGURE 3–19
A program to calculate the equivalent day of year from a given day, month, and year.

```
PROGRAM doy
! Purpose:
!   This program calculates the day of year corresponding to a
!   specified date.  It illustrates the use of the CASE construct.
!
!   Record of revisions:
!       Date         Programmer          Description of change
!       ====         ==========          =====================
!       9/09/95    S. J. Chapman         Original code
!
IMPLICIT NONE

! Declare the variables used in this program
INTEGER :: day          ! Day (dd)
INTEGER :: day_of_year  ! Day of year
INTEGER :: i            ! Index variable
INTEGER :: leap_day     ! Extra day for leap year
INTEGER :: month        ! Month (mm)
INTEGER :: year         ! Year (yyyy)

! Get day, month, and year to convert
WRITE (*,*) 'This program calculates the day of year given the '
WRITE (*,*) 'current date.  Enter current month (1-12), day(1-31),'
WRITE (*,*) 'and year in that order:  '
READ (*,*) month, day, year

! Check for leap year, and add extra day if necessary
IF ( MOD(year,400) == 0 ) THEN
   leap_day = 1              ! Years divisible by 400 are leap years
ELSE IF ( MOD(year,100) == 0 ) THEN
   leap_day = 0              ! Other centuries are not leap years
ELSE IF ( MOD(year,4) == 0 ) THEN
   leap_day = 1              ! Otherwise every 4th year is a leap year
```

(continued)

```
(concluded)
ELSE
   leap_day = 0              ! Other years are not leap years
END IF

! Calculate day of year
day_of_year = day
DO i = 1, month-1

   ! Add days in months from January to last month
   SELECT CASE (i)
   CASE (1,3,5,7,8,10,12)
      day_of_year = day_of_year + 31
   CASE (4,5,9,11)
      day_of_year = day_of_year + 30
   CASE (2)
      day_of_year = day_of_year + 28 + leap_day
   END SELECT

END DO

! Tell user
WRITE (*,*) 'Day        = ', day
WRITE (*,*) 'Month      = ', month
WRITE (*,*) 'Year       = ', year
WRITE (*,*) 'day of year = ', day_of_year

END PROGRAM
```

We will use the following known results to test the program:

1. Year 1999 is not a leap year. January 1 must be day of year 1, and December 31 must be day of year 365.
2. Year 2000 is a leap year. January 1 must be day of year 1, and December 31 must be day of year 366.
3. Year 2001 is not a leap year. March 1 must be day of year 60, since January has 31 days, February has 28 days, and this is the first day of March.

If this program is compiled and then run five times with the above dates, the results are

```
C>doy

This program calculates the day of year given the
current date.  Enter current month (1-12), day(1-31),
and year in that order:  1 1 1999

Day        =           1
Month      =           1
Year       =        1999
day of year =          1

C>doy

This program calculates the day of year given the
current date.  Enter current month (1-12), day(1-31),
and year in that order:  12 31 1999

Day        =          31
Month      =          12
```

```
Year          =          1999
day of year =           365

C>doy

This program calculates the day of year given the
current date.  Enter current month (1-12), day(1-31),
and year in that order:  1 1 2000

Day           =          1
Month         =          1
Year          =          2000
day of year =            1

C>doy

This program calculates the day of year given the
current date.  Enter current month (1-12), day(1-31),
and year in that order:  12 31 2000

Day           =          31
Month         =          12
Year          =          2000
day of year =            366

C>doy

This program calculates the day of year given the
current date.  Enter current month (1-12), day(1-31),
and year in that order:  3 1 2001

Day           =          1
Month         =          3
Year          =          2001
day of year =            60
```

The program gives the correct answers for our test dates in all five test cases.

Example 3–7 Statistical Analysis: Implement an algorithm that reads in a set of measurements and calculates the mean and the standard deviation of the input data set, when any value in the data set can be positive, negative, or zero.

Solution This program must be able to read in an arbitrary number of measurements and then calculate the mean and standard deviation of those measurements. Each measurement can be positive, negative, or zero.

Since we cannot use a data value as a flag this time, we will ask the user for the number of input values and then use a DO loop to read in those values. A flowchart for this program is shown in Figure 3–20. Note that the while loop has been replaced by a counting loop. The modified program that permits the use of any input value is shown in Figure 3–21. Verify its operation for yourself by finding the mean and standard deviation of the following 5 input values: 3., −1., 0., 1., and −2.

FIGURE 3–21
Modified statistical analysis program that works with both positive and input values.

```
PROGRAM stats_3
!
! Purpose:
!   To calculate mean and the standard deviation of an input
!   data set, where each input value can be positive, negative,
```

(continued)

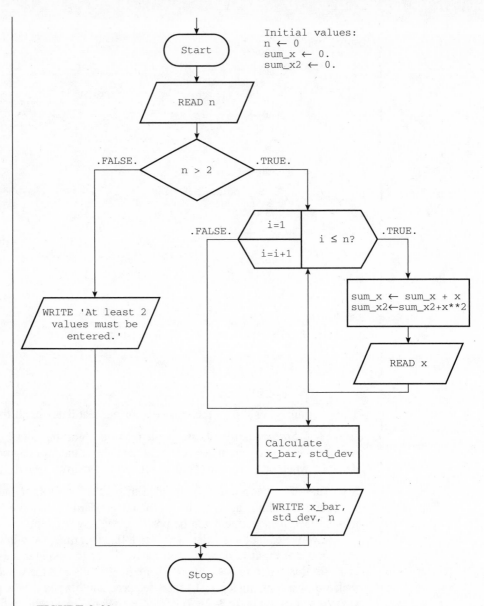

Initial values:
n ← 0
sum_x ← 0.
sum_x2 ← 0.

FIGURE 3–20
Flowchart for modified statistical analysis program using a DO loop.

(Figure 3–21 continued)
```
!    or zero.
!
!  Record of revisions:
!     Date         Programmer          Description of change
!     ====         ==========          =====================
!   09/11/95    S. J. Chapman          Original code
```

(continued)

```
(concluded)
!
IMPLICIT NONE

! Declare the variables used in this program.
INTEGER :: i              ! Loop index.
INTEGER :: n = 0          ! The number of input samples.
REAL :: std_dev           ! The standard deviation of the input samples.
REAL :: sum_x = 0.        ! The sum of the input values.
REAL :: sum_x2 = 0.       ! The sum of the squares of the input values.
REAL :: x = 0.            ! An input data value.
REAL :: x_bar             ! The average of the input samples.

! Get the number of points to input.
WRITE (*,*) 'Enter number of points: '
READ (*,*) n

! Check to see if we have enough input data.
IF ( n < 2 ) THEN ! Insufficient data

   WRITE (*,*) 'At least 2 values must be entered.'

ELSE ! we will have enough data, so let's get it.

   ! Loop to read input values.
   DO i = 1, n

      ! Read values
      WRITE (*,*) 'Enter number: '
      READ (*,*) x
      WRITE (*,*) 'The number is ', x

      ! Accumulate sums.
      sum_x = sum_x + x
      sum_x2 = sum_x2 + x**2

   END DO

   ! Now calculate statistics.
   x_bar = sum_x / real(n)
   std_dev = sqrt((real(n)*sum_x2 - sum_x**2) / (real(n)*real(n-1)))

   ! Tell user.
   WRITE (*,*) 'The mean of this data set is:', x_bar
   WRITE (*,*) 'The standard deviation is:   ', std_dev
   WRITE (*,*) 'The number of data points is:', n

END IF

END PROGRAM
```

Details of operation

Now that we have seen examples of a counting DO loop in operation, we will examine some of the important details required to use DO loops properly.

1. It is not necessary to indent the body of the DO loop as we have shown above. The Fortran compiler will recognize the loop even if every statement in it starts in column 1. However, the code is much more readable if the body of the DO loop is indented, so you should always indent the bodies of your DO loops.

Good Programming Practice
Always indent the body of a DO loop by two or more spaces to improve the readability of the code.

2. The index variable of a DO loop must not be modified anywhere within the DO loop. Since the index variable is used to control the repetitions in the DO loop, changing it could produce unexpected results. In the worst case, modifying the index variable could produce an *infinite loop* that never completes. Consider the following example:

```
PROGRAM bad_1
INTEGER :: i
DO i = 1, 4
   i = 2
END DO
END PROGRAM
```

If i is reset to 2 every time through the loop, the loop will never end because the index variable can never be greater than 4! This loop will run forever unless the program containing it is killed. Almost all Fortran compilers will recognize this problem and will generate a compile-time error if a program attempts to modify an index variable within a loop.

Programming Pitfalls
Never modify the value of a DO loop index variable while inside the loop.

3. If the number of iterations calculated from Equation (3–5) is less than or equal to zero, the statements within the DO loop are never executed at all. For example, the statements in the following DO loop will never be executed

```
DO i = 3, 2
   ...
END DO
```

since

$$\text{iter} = \frac{\text{iend} - \text{istart} + \text{incr}}{\text{incr}} = \frac{2 - 3 + 1}{1} = 0$$

4. It is possible to design counting DO loops that count down as well as up. The following DO loop executes three times with i being 3, 2, and 1 in the successive loops.

```
DO i = 3, 1, -1
   ...
END DO
```

5. The index variable and control parameters of a DO loop should always be of type integer.

> The use of real variables as DO loop indices and DO loop control parameters used to be a legal but undesirable feature of Fortran. It was declared obsolescent in Fortran 90 and has been completely deleted from Fortran 95.

6. It is possible to branch out of a DO loop at any time while the loop is executing. If program execution does branch out of a DO loop before it would otherwise finish, the loop index variable retains the value that it had when the branch occurs. Consider the following example:

```
INTEGER :: i
DO i = 1, 5
   ...
   IF (i >= 3) EXIT
   ...
END DO
WRITE (*,*) i
```

Execution will branch out of the DO loop and go to the WRITE statement on the third pass through the loop. When execution gets to the WRITE statement, variable i will contain a value of 3.

7. If a DO loop completes normally, *the value of the index variable is undefined when the loop is completed*. In the following example, the value written out by the WRITE statement is not defined in the Fortran standard.

```
INTEGER :: i
DO i = 1, 5
   ...
END DO
WRITE (*,*) i
```

On many computers, after the loop has completed, the index variable i will contain the first value of the index variable to fail the index*incr ≤ iend*incr test. In the preceding code, the variable would usually contain a 6 after the loop is finished. However, don't count on it! Since the value is officially undefined in the Fortran standard, some compilers may produce a different result. If your code depends on the value of the index variable after the loop is completed, you may get different results as the program is moved between computers.

Good Programming Practice
Never depend on an index variable to retain a specific value after a DO loop completes normally.

---

8. It is illegal for program execution to branch out into the body of a loop. The following code will generate a compile-time error on a Fortran compiler.

```
INTEGER :: i
DO i = 1, 5
   ...
200
   ...
   END DO
...
GO TO 200
```

3.4.4 The CYCLE and EXIT Statements

Two additional statements that can be used to control the operation of while loops and counting DO loops are CYCLE and EXIT.

If the CYCLE statement is executed in the body of a loop, the execution of the body will stop and control will be returned to the top of the loop. The loop index will be incremented, and execution will resume again if the index has not reached its limit. An example of the CYCLE statement in a DO loop follows, and the flowchart for this loop appears in Figure 3–22a.

```
PROGRAM test_cycle
INTEGER :: i
DO i = 1, 5
   IF ( i == 3 ) CYCLE
   WRITE (*,*) i
END DO
WRITE (*,*) 'End of loop!'
END PROGRAM
```

When this program is executed, the output is

```
C>test_cycle
        1
        2
        4
        5
End of loop!
```

Note that the CYCLE statement was executed on the iteration when i was 3 and control returned to the top of the loop without executing the WRITE statement.

If the EXIT statement is executed in the body of a loop, the execution of the body will stop and control will be transferred to the first executable statement after the loop. An example of the EXIT statement in a DO loop follows, and the flowchart for this loop appears in Figure 3–22b.

```
PROGRAM test_exit
INTEGER :: i
DO i = 1, 5
   IF ( i == 3 ) EXIT
   WRITE (*,*) i
END DO
WRITE (*,*) 'End of loop!'
END PROGRAM
```

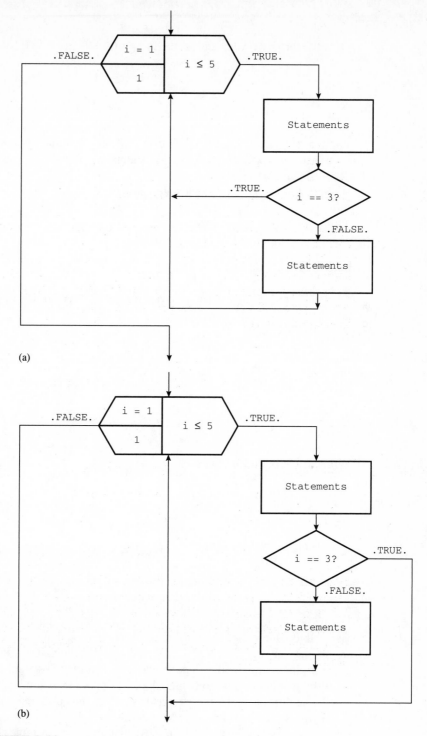

FIGURE 3–22
(a) Flowchart of a DO loop containing a CYCLE statement. (b) Flowchart of a DO loop containing an EXIT statement.

When this program is executed, the output is

```
C>test_exit
          1
          2
End of loop!
```

Note that the EXIT statement was executed on the iteration when i was 3, and control transferred to the first executable statement after the loop without executing the WRITE statement.

Both the CYCLE and EXIT statements work with both while loops and counting DO loops.

3.4.5 Named Loops

It is possible to assign a name to a loop. The general form of a while loop with a name attached is

```
[name:] DO
    Statement
    Statement
    ...
    IF ( logical_expr ) CYCLE [name]
    ...
    IF (logical_expr ) EXIT [name]
    ...
END DO [name]
```

and the general form of a counting loop with a name attached is

```
[name:] DO index = istart, iend, incr
    Statement
    Statement
    ...
    IF ( logical_expr ) CYCLE [name]
    ...
END DO [name]
```

where *name* may be up to 31 alphanumeric characters long, beginning with a letter. The name given to the loop must be unique within each program unit. If a name is assigned to a loop, then the same name must appear on the associated END DO. Names are optional on any CYCLE and EXIT statements associated with the loop, but if they are used, they must be the same as the name on the DO statement.

Why would we want to name a loop? For simple examples like the ones we have seen so far, there is no particular reason to do so. The principal reason for using names is to help us (and the compiler) keep loops straight in our own minds when they get very complicated. For example, suppose that we have a complex loop that is hundreds of lines long, spanning many pages of listings. The body of that loop may contain many smaller loops. If we name all of the parts of the loop, then we can tell at a glance which construct a particular END DO, CYCLE, or EXIT statement belongs to.

Names on constructs make our intentions explicitly clear and can help the compiler flag the specific locations of an error when one occurs.

Good Programming Practice
Assign a name to any large and complicated loops in your program to clarify which statements are associated with the loop.

3.4.6 Nesting Loops and Block `IF` Constructs

Nesting loops

If one loop is completely inside another loop, the two loops are called **nested loops.** The following example shows two nested DO loops used to calculate and write out the product of two integers.

```
PROGRAM nested_loops
INTEGER :: i, j, product
DO i = 1, 3
   DO j = 1, 3
      product = i * j
      WRITE (*,*) i, ' * ', j, ' = ', product
   END DO
END DO
END PROGRAM
```

In this example the outer DO loop will assign a value of 1 to index variable i, and then the inner DO loop will be executed. The inner DO loop will be executed three times with index variable J having values 1, 2, and 3. When the entire inner DO loop has been completed, the outer DO loop will assign a value of 2 to index variable i, and the inner DO loop will be executed again. This process repeats until the outer DO loop has executed three times, and the resulting output is

```
1 *    1 =    1
1 *    2 =    2
1 *    3 =    3
2 *    1 =    2
2 *    2 =    4
2 *    3 =    6
3 *    1 =    3
3 *    2 =    6
3 *    3 =    9
```

Note that the inner DO loop executes completely before the index variable of the outer DO loop is incremented.

When a Fortran compiler encounters an END DO statement, it associates that statement with the innermost currently open loop. Therefore, the first END DO statement above closes the DO j = 1, 3 loop, and the second END DO statement above closes the DO i = 1, 3 loop. This fact can produce hard-to-find errors if an END DO statement is accidentally deleted somewhere within a nested loop construct. If each nested loop is named, then the error will be much easier to find.

3

To illustrate this problem, let's "accidentally" delete the inner END DO statement in the previous example and compile the program with the Digital Visual Fortran 5.0 compiler.

```
PROGRAM bad_nested_loops_1
INTEGER :: i, j, product
DO i = 1, 3
    DO j = 1, 3
        product = i * j
        WRITE (*,*) i, ' * ', j, ' = ', product
END DO
END PROGRAM
```

The output of the compiler is

```
C>f132 bad_nested_loops_1.f90
DIGITAL Visual Fortran Optimizing Compiler Version: V5.0
Copyright (c) 1997 Digital Equipment Corp. All rights reserved.

bad_nes1.f90
bad_nes1.f90(3): Error: An unterminated block exists.
DO i = 1, 3
  ^
```

The compiler reports a problem with the loop construct, but it could not detect the problem until the END PROGRAM statement is reached, and it cannot tell where the problem occurred. If the program is very large, we would be faced with a difficult task when we tried to locate the problem.

Now let's name each loop and "accidentally" delete the inner END DO statement.

```
PROGRAM bad_nested_loops_2
INTEGER :: i, j, product
outer: DO i = 1, 3
    inner: DO j = 1, 3
        product = i * j
        WRITE (*,*) i, ' * ', j, ' = ', product
END DO outer
END PROGRAM
```

When we compile the modified program with the Digital Visual Fortran compiler, the output is

```
C>f132 bad_nested_loops_2.f90
DIGITAL Visual Fortran Optimizing Compiler Version: V5.0
Copyright (c) 1997 Digital Equipment Corp. All rights reserved.

bad_nes2.f90
bad_nes2.f90(7) : Error: The block construct names must match, and they do not.
   [OUTER]
END DO outer
-------^
bad_nes2.f90(3) : Error: An unterminated block exists.
outer: DO i = 1, 3
  ^
```

The compiler reports a problem with the loop construct, and it reports which loops were involved in the problem. This information can be a major aid in debugging the program.

Good Programming Practice
Assign names to all nested loops so that they will be easier to understand and debug.

If DO loops are nested, they must have independent index variables. Remember that you cannot change an index variable within the body of a DO loop. Therefore, you cannot use the same index variable for two nested DO loops, since the inner loop would be attempting to change the index variable of the outer loop within the body of the outer loop.

Also, if two loops are to be nested, one of them must lie completely within the other one. The following DO loops are incorrectly nested, and a compile-time error will be generated for this code.

```
outer: DO i = 1, 3
   ...
   inner: DO j = 1, 3
      ...
END DO outer
   ...
   END DO inner
```

The CYCLE and EXIT statements in nested loops

If a CYCLE or EXIT statement appears inside an unnamed set of nested loops, then the CYCLE or EXIT statement refers to the *innermost* loop in which it appears. For example, consider the following program:

```
PROGRAM test_cycle_1
INTEGER :: i, j, product
DO i = 1, 3
   DO j = 1, 3
      IF ( j == 2) CYCLE
      product = i * j
      WRITE (*,*) i, ' * ', j, ' = ', product
   END DO
END DO
END PROGRAM
```

If the inner loop counter j is equal to 2, then the CYCLE statement will be executed, which will cause the remainder of the code block of the innermost DO loop to be skipped. Execution of the innermost loop will start over with j increased by 1. The resulting output values are

```
1  *    1  =    1
1  *    3  =    3
2  *    1  =    2
2  *    3  =    6
3  *    1  =    3
3  *    3  =    9
```

Each time the inner loop variable had the value 2, execution of the inner loop was skipped.

It is also possible to make the CYCLE or EXIT statement refer to the *outer* loop of a nested construct of named loops by specifying a loop name in the statement. In the following example, when the inner loop counter j is equal to 2, the CYCLE outer statement will be executed. Executing the CYCLE statement will cause the remainder of the code block of the outer DO loop to be skipped, and execution of the outer loop will start over with i increased by 1.

```
PROGRAM test_cycle_2
INTEGER :: i, j, product
outer: DO i = 1, 3
    inner: DO j = 1, 3
        IF ( j == 2) CYCLE outer
        product = i * j
        WRITE (*,*) i, ' * ', j, ' = ', product
    END DO inner
END DO outer
END PROGRAM
```

The resulting output values are

```
1  *    1  =    1
2  *    1  =    2
3  *    1  =    3
```

You should always use loop names with CYCLE or EXIT statements in nested loops to make sure that the statements affect the proper loop.

Good Programming Practice
Use loop names with CYCLE or EXIT statements in nested loops to make sure that the statements affect the proper loop.

Nesting loops within IF constructs and vice versa

It is possible to nest loops within block IF constructs or block IF constructs within loops. If a loop is nested within a block IF construct, the loop must lie entirely within a single code block of the IF construct. For example, the following statements are illegal because the loop stretches between the IF and the ELSE code blocks of the IF construct.

```
outer: IF ( a < b ) THEN
    ...
    inner: DO i = 1, 3
```

```
          . . .
     ELSE
          . . .
          END DO inner
          . . .
     END IF outer
```

In contrast, the following statements are legal, since the loop lies entirely within a single code block of the IF construct.

```
     outer: IF ( a < b ) THEN
          . . .
          inner: DO i = 1, 3
               . . .
          END DO inner
          . . .
     ELSE
          . . .
     END IF outer
```

EXAMPLE 3–8 *Physics—The Flight of a Ball:* If we assume negligible air friction and ignore the curvature of the earth, a ball that is thrown into the air from any point on the earth's surface will follow a parabolic flight path (see Figure 3–23a). The height of the ball at any time t after it is thrown is given by Equation (3–6):

$$y(t) = y_o + v_{yo} t + \frac{1}{2}g\, t^2 \tag{3–6}$$

where y_o is the initial height of the object above the ground, v_{yo} is the initial vertical velocity of the object, and g is the acceleration due to the earth's gravity. The horizontal distance (range) traveled by the ball as a function of time after it is thrown is given by Equation (3–7)

$$x(t) = x_o + v_{xo} t \tag{3–7}$$

where x_o is the initial horizontal position of the ball on the ground and v_{xo} is the initial horizontal velocity of the ball.

If the ball is thrown with some initial velocity v_o at an angle of θ degrees with respect to the earth's surface, then the initial horizontal and vertical components of velocity will be (see Figure 3–23b)

$$v_{xo} = v_o \cos \theta \tag{3–8}$$

$$v_{yo} = v_o \sin \theta \tag{3–9}$$

Assume that the ball is initially thrown from position $(x_o, y_o) = (0,0)$ with an initial velocity v of 20 meters per second at an initial angle of θ degrees. Design, write, and test a program that will determine the horizontal distance traveled by the ball from the time it was thrown until it touches the ground again. The program should calculate this distance for all angles θ from 0 to 90° in 1° steps. Determine the angle θ that maximizes the range of the ball.

SOLUTION To solve this problem we must determine an equation for the range of

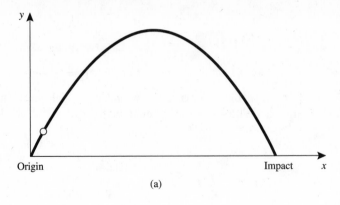

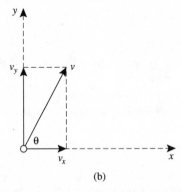

FIGURE 3–23
(a) When a ball is thrown upwards, it follows a parabolic trajectory. *(b)* The horizontal and vertical components of a velocity vector *v* at an angle θ with respect to the horizontal.

the thrown ball. We can do so by first finding the time that the ball remains in the air and then finding the horizontal distance that the ball can travel during that time.

We can calculate the time that the ball will remain in the air after it is thrown from Equation (3–6). The ball will touch the ground at the time t for which $y(t) = 0$. Remembering that the ball will start from ground level ($y(0) = 0$) and solving for t, we get

$$y(t) = y_o + v_{yo}\, t + \frac{1}{2} g\, t^2$$

$$0 = 0 + v_{yo}\, t + \frac{1}{2} g\, t^2$$

$$0 = \left(v_{yo} + \frac{1}{2} g\, t \right) t$$

Therefore, the ball will be at ground level at time $t_1 = 0$ (when we threw it), and at time:

$$t_2 = -\frac{2v_{yo}}{g}$$

We can calculate the horizontal distance that the ball will travel in time t_2 from Equation (3–7):

$$range = x(t_2) = x_o + v_{xo}\, t_2$$

$$range = 0 + v_{xo}\left(-\frac{2v_{yo}}{g}\right)$$

$$range = -\frac{2v_{xo}v_{yo}}{g}$$

We can substitute Equations (3–8) and (3–9) for v_{xo} and v_{yo} to get an equation expressed in terms of the initial velocity v and initial angle θ:

$$range = -\frac{2(v_o \cos \theta)(v_o \sin \theta)}{g}$$

$$range = -\frac{2v_o^2}{g} \cos \theta \sin \theta \qquad\qquad (3\text{–}10)$$

From the problem statement, we know that the initial velocity v_o is 20 meters per second and that the ball will be thrown at all angles from $0°$ to $90°$ in $1°$ steps. Finally, any elementary physics textbook will tell us that the acceleration due to the earth's gravity is -9.81 meters per second squared.

Now let's apply our design technique to this problem.

1. **State the problem.**

A proper statement of this problem is: Calculate the range that a ball will travel when it is thrown with an initial velocity v_o at an initial angle θ. Calculate this range for a v_o of 20 meters per second and all angles between $0°$ and $90°$, in $1°$ increments. Determine the angle θ that will result in the maximum range for the ball. Assume that there is no air friction.

2. **Define the inputs and outputs.**

As the problem is defined above, no inputs are required. We know from the problem statement what v_o and θ will be, so we do not need to read them in. The outputs from this program will be a table showing the range of the ball for each angle θ and the angle θ for which the range is maximum.

3. **Design the algorithm.**

This program can be broken down into the following major steps:

```
DO for theta = 0 to 90 degrees
    Calculate the range of the ball for each angle theta
    Determine if this theta yields the maximum range so far
```

```
      Write out the range as a function of theta
      END of DO
      WRITE out the theta yielding maximum range
```

An iterative DO loop is appropriate for this algorithm, since we are calculating the range of the ball for a specified number of angles. We will calculate the range for each value of θ and compare each range with the maximum range found so far to determine which angle yields the maximum range. Note that the trigonometric functions work in radians, so the angles in degrees must be converted to radians before the range is calculated. The detailed pseudocode for this algorithm follows.

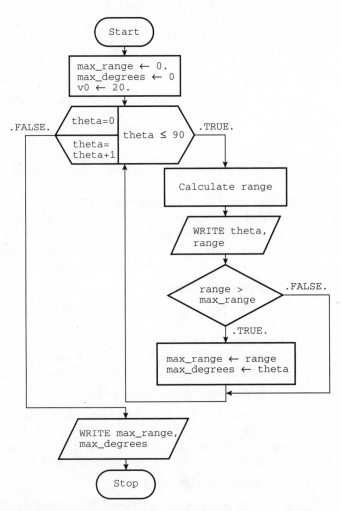

FIGURE 3–24
Flowchart for a program to determine the angle θ at which a ball thrown with an initial velocity v_o of 20 m/s will travel the farthest.

```
        Initialize max_range and max_degrees to 0
        Initialize v0 to 20 meters/second
        DO for theta = 0 to 90 degrees
           radian ← theta * degrees_2_rad          (Convert degrees to radians)
           angle ← (-2. * v0**2 / gravity ) * sin(radian) * cos(radian)
           Write out theta and range
           IF range > max_range then
               max_range ← range
               max_degrees ← theta
           END of IF
        END of DO
        Write out max_degrees, max_range
```

The flowchart for this program is shown in Figure 3–24.

4. **Turn the algorithm into Fortran statements.**

The final Fortran program is shown in Figure 3–25.

FIGURE 3–25
Program `ball` to determine the angle that maximizes the range of a thrown ball.

```
PROGRAM ball
!
!  Purpose:
!    To calculate distance traveled by a ball thrown at a specified
!    angle THETA and at a specified velocity V0 from a point on the
!    surface of the earth, ignoring the effects of air friction and
!    the earth's curvature.
!
!  Record of revisions:
!      Date          Programmer          Description of change
!      ====          ==========          =====================
!    12/09/95     S. J. Chapman          Original code
!
IMPLICIT NONE

! Declare parameters
REAL, PARAMETER :: degrees_2_rad = 0.01745329 ! Deg ==> rad conv.

! Declare variables
REAL :: gravity = -9.81 ! Accel. due to gravity (m/s**2)
INTEGER :: max_degrees  ! angle at which the max rng occurs (degrees)
REAL :: max_range       ! Maximum range for the ball at vel v0 (meters)
REAL :: range           ! Range of the ball at a particular angle (meters)
REAL :: radian          ! Angle at which the ball was thrown (in radians)
INTEGER :: theta        ! Angle at which the ball was thrown (in degrees)
REAL :: v0              ! Velocity of the ball (in m/s)

! Initialize variables.
max_range = 0.
max_degrees = 0
v0 = 20.

! Loop over all specified angles.

loop: DO theta = 0, 90
```

(continued)

(concluded)

```
    ! Get angle in radians
    radian = real(theta) * degrees_2_rad

    ! Calculate range in meters.
    range = (-2. * v0**2 / gravity) * sin(radian) * cos(radian)

    ! Write out the range for this angle.
      WRITE (*,*) 'THETA = ', theta, ' degrees; Range = ', range, &
                  ' meters'

    ! Compare the range to the previous maximum range. If this
    ! range is larger, save it and the angle at which it occurred.
    IF ( range > max_range ) THEN
        max_range = range
        max_degrees = theta
    END IF

END DO loop

! Skip a line, and then write out the maximum range and the angle
! at which it occurred.
WRITE (*,*) ' '
WRITE (*,*) 'Max range = ', max_range, ' at ', max_degrees, ' degrees'

END PROGRAM
```

The degrees-to-radians conversion factor is always a constant, so in the program it is given a name using the PARAMETER attribute, and all references to the constant within the program use that name. The acceleration due to gravity at sea level can be found in any physics text. It is about 9.81 m/sec^2, directed downward (so $g = -9.81$).

5. Test the program.

To test this program, we will calculate the answers by hand for a few of the angles and compare the results with the output of the program.

$$\theta = 0°: \qquad range = -\frac{2(20^2)}{-9.81} \cos 0 \sin 0 = 0 \text{ meters}$$

$$\theta = 5°: \qquad range = -\frac{2(20^2)}{-9.81} \cos \left(\frac{5\pi}{180}\right) \sin \left(\frac{5\pi}{180}\right) = 7.080 \text{ meters}$$

$$\theta = 40°: \qquad range = -\frac{2(20^2)}{-9.81} \cos \left(\frac{40\pi}{180}\right) \sin \left(\frac{40\pi}{180}\right) = 40.16 \text{ meters}$$

$$\theta = 45°: \qquad range = -\frac{2(20^2)}{-9.81} \cos \left(\frac{45\pi}{180}\right) \sin \left(\frac{45\pi}{180}\right) = 40.77 \text{ meters}$$

When program `ball` is executed, a 90-line table of angles and ranges is produced. To save space, only a portion of the table is reproduced below.

```
C>ball

Theta =                0 degrees; Range =    0.000000E+00 meters
Theta =                1 degrees; Range =        1.423017 meters
Theta =                2 degrees; Range =        2.844300 meters
Theta =                3 degrees; Range =        4.262118 meters
Theta =                4 degrees; Range =        5.674743 meters
Theta =                5 degrees; Range =        7.080455 meters
   . . .
Theta =               40 degrees; Range =       40.155260 meters
Theta =               41 degrees; Range =       40.377900 meters
Theta =               42 degrees; Range =       40.551350 meters
Theta =               43 degrees; Range =       40.675390 meters
Theta =               44 degrees; Range =       40.749880 meters
Theta =               45 degrees; Range =       40.774720 meters
Theta =               46 degrees; Range =       40.749880 meters
Theta =               47 degrees; Range =       40.675390 meters
Theta =               48 degrees; Range =       40.551350 meters
Theta =               49 degrees; Range =       40.377900 meters
Theta =               50 degrees; Range =       40.155260 meters
   . . .
Theta =               85 degrees; Range =        7.080470 meters
Theta =               86 degrees; Range =        5.674757 meters
Theta =               87 degrees; Range =        4.262130 meters
Theta =               88 degrees; Range =        2.844310 meters
Theta =               89 degrees; Range =        1.423035 meters
Theta =               90 degrees; Range =    1.587826E-05 meters

Max range =            40.774720 at            45 degrees
```

The program output matches our hand calculation for the angles calculated above to the four-digit accuracy of the hand calculation. Note that the maximum range occurred at an angle of 45°.

Quiz 3–2

This quiz provides a quick check to see if you understand the concepts introduced in section 3.4. If you have trouble with the quiz, reread the section, ask your instructor, or discuss the material with a fellow student. The answers to this quiz are found in the back of the book.

Examine the following DO loops and determine how many times each loop will be executed. Assume that all of the index variables shown are of type integer.

1. `DO index = 7, 10`

2. `DO j = 7, 10, -1`

3. `DO index = 1, 10, 10`   *(continued)*

4. DO loop_counter = -2, 10, 2

5. DO time = -2, -10, -1

6. DO i = -10, -7, -3

Examine the following loops and determine the value in `ires` at the end of each of the loops. Assume that `ires`, `incr`, and all index variables are integers.

7.
```
ires = 0
DO index = 1, 10
   ires = ires + 1
END DO
```

8.
```
ires = 0
DO index = 1, 10
   ires = ires + index
END DO
```

9.
```
ires = 0
DO index = 1, 10
  IF ( ires == 10 ) CYCLE
   ires = ires + index
END DO
```

10.
```
ires = 0
DO index1 = 1, 10
   DO index2 = 1, 10
      ires = ires + 1
   END DO
END DO
```

11.
```
ires = 0
DO index1 = 1, 10
   DO index2 = index1, 10
      IF ( index2 > 6 ) EXIT
      ires = ires + 1
   END DO
END DO
```

Examine the following Fortran statements and tell whether or not they are valid. If they are invalid, indicate the reason why they are invalid.

12.
```
loop1: DO i = 1, 10
   loop2: DO j = 1, 10
      loop3: DO i = i, j
         ...
      END DO loop3
   END DO loop2
END DO loop1
```

13.
```
loop1: DO i = 1, 10
   loop2: DO j = i, 10
      loop3: DO k = i, j
         ...
      END DO loop3
   END DO loop2
END DO loop1
```

(continued)

(concluded)

```
14. loopx: DO i = 1, 10
      ...
        loopy: DO j = 1, 10
          ...
        END DO loopx
    END DO loopy
```

■ 3.5

MORE ON DEBUGGING Fortran PROGRAMS

Making a mistake is much easier when writing a program containing branches and loops than when writing simple sequential programs. Even after going through the full design process, a program of any size is almost guaranteed not to be completely correct the first time it is used. Suppose that we have built the program and tested it, only to find that the output values are in error. How do we go about finding the bugs and fixing them?

The best approach to locating the error is to use a symbolic debugger if one is supplied with your compiler. You must ask your instructor, or else check with your system's manuals to determine how to use the symbolic debugger supplied with your particular compiler and computer.

An alternative approach to locating the error is to insert WRITE statements into the code to print out important variables at key points in the program. When the program is run, the WRITE statements will print out the values of the key variables. You can compare these values to the ones you expect, and the places where the actual and expected values differ will serve as a clue to help you locate the problem. For example, to verify the operation of a counting loop, you could add the following WRITE statements to the program:

```
WRITE (*,*) 'At loop1: ist, ien, inc = ', ist, ien, inc
loop1: DO i = ist, ien, inc
    WRITE (*,*) 'In loop1: i = ', i
  ...
END DO loop1
WRITE (*,*) 'loop1 completed'
```

When the program is executed, its output listing will contain detailed information about the variables controlling the DO loop and just how many times the loop was executed. You could use similar WRITE statements to debug the operation of a block IF construct.

```
WRITE (*,*) 'At if1: var1 = ', var1
if1: IF ( sqrt(var1) > 1. ) THEN
   WRITE (*,*) 'At if1: sqrt(var1) > 1.'
   ...
ELSE IF ( sqrt(var1) < 1. ) THEN
   WRITE (*,*) 'At if1: sqrt(var1) < 1.'
   ...
ELSE
   WRITE (*,*) 'At if1: sqrt(var1) == 1.'
   ...
END IF if1
```

Once you have located the portion of the code in which the error occurs, you can examine the specific statements in that area to locate the problem. A list of some common errors follows. Be sure to check for them in your code.

1. *If the problem is in an* IF *construct, check to see if you used the proper relational operator in your logical expressions.* Did you use > when you really intended >=, etc.? Logical errors of this sort can be very hard to spot, since the compiler will not give an error message for them. Be especially careful of logical expressions that are very complex, since they will be hard to understand and very easy to mess up. You should use extra parentheses to make them easier to understand. If the logical expressions are really large, consider breaking them down into simpler expressions that are easier to follow.

2. *Another common problem with* IF *statements occurs when real variables are tested for equality.* Because of small round-off errors during floating-point arithmetic operations, two numbers that theoretically should be equal will differ by a tiny amount and the test for equality will fail. When working with real variables, a good approach is to replace a test for equality with a test for *near equality*. For example, instead of testing to see if x is equal to $10.$, you should test to see if $|x - 10.| < 0.0001$. Any value of x between 9.9999 and 10.0001 will satisfy the latter test, so round-off errors will not cause problems. In Fortran statements

    ```
    IF ( x == 10. ) THEN
    ```

    would be replaced by

    ```
    IF ( ABS(x - 10.) <= 0.0001 ) THEN
    ```

3. *Most errors in counting* DO *loops involve mistakes with the loop parameters.* If you add WRITE statements to the DO loop as previously shown, the problem should be fairly clear. Did the DO loop start with the correct value? Did it end with the correct value? Did it increment at the proper step? If not, check the parameters of the DO loop closely. You will probably spot an error in the control parameters.

4. Errors in while loops are usually related to errors in the logical expression used to control their function. You can detect these errors by examining the IF (*logical_expr*) EXIT statement of the while loop with WRITE statements.

■ 3.6
SUMMARY

Chapter 3 describes the basic types of Fortran branches and loops. The principal type of branch is the block IF-ELSE IF-ELSE-END IF construct. This construct is very flexible. It can have as many ELSE IF clauses as needed to construct any desired test. Furthermore, block IF constructs can be nested to produce more complex tests. A second type of branch is the CASE construct. It may be used to select among mutually exclusive alternatives specified by an integer, character, or logical control expression.

Fortran also supports two basic types of loops: the while loop and the iterative or counting DO loop. The while loop is used to repeat a section of code when we do not know in advance how many times the loop must be repeated. The counting DO loop is used to repeat a section of code when we know in advance how many times the loop should be repeated.

It is possible to exit from a loop at any time using the EXIT statement. It is also possible to jump back to the top of a loop using the CYCLE statement. If loops are nested, an EXIT or CYCLE statement refers by default to the innermost loop.

3.6.1 Summary of Good Programming Practice

You should adhere to the following guidelines when programming with branch or loop constructs. When you follow the guidelines consistently, your code will contain fewer bugs, will be easier to debug, and will be more understandable to anyone who may need to work with it in the future.

1. Always indent code blocks in block IF, DO, and CASE constructs to make them more readable.
2. Be cautious about testing for equality with real variables in an IF construct, since round-off errors may cause two variables that should be equal to fail a test for equality. Instead, test to see if the variables are nearly equal within the round-off error to be expected on your computer.
3. Use a while loop to repeat sections of code when you don't know in advance how often the loop will be executed.
4. Use a counting DO loop to repeat sections of code when you know in advance how often the loop will be executed.
5. Never attempt to modify the values of a DO loop index while inside the loop.
6. Assign names to large and complicated loops or IF constructs, especially if they are nested.
7. Use loop names with CYCLE and EXIT statements in nested loops to make certain that the action of the CYCLE or EXIT statement affects the proper loop.

3.6.2 Summary of Fortran Statements and Constructs

The following summary describes the Fortran 90/95 statements and constructs introduced in this chapter.

Block IF Construct

```
[name:] IF ( logical_expr_1 ) THEN
    Block 1
ELSE IF ( logical_expr_2 ) THEN [name]
    Block 2
ELSE [name]
    Block 3
END IF [name]
```

Description:

The block IF construct permits the execution of a code block based on the results of one or more logical expressions. If $logical\_expr\_1$ is true, the first code block will be executed. If $logical\_expr\_1$ is false and $logical\_expr\_2$ is true, the second code block will be executed. If both logical expressions are false, the third code block will be executed. After any block is executed, control jumps to the first statement after the construct.

A block IF construct must have one and only one IF ( ) THEN statement. The construct may also have zero or more ELSE IF clauses and at most one ELSE clause. The name is optional, but if it is used on the IF statement, then it must be used on the END IF statement. The name is optional on the ELSE IF and ELSE statements even if it is used on the IF and END IF statements.

CASE Construct

```
[name:] SELECT CASE (case_expr)
CASE (case_selector_1) [name]
    Block 1
CASE (case_selector_2) [name]
    Block 2
CASE DEFAULT [name]
    Block n
END SELECT [name]
```

Description:

The CASE construct executes a specific block of statements based on the value of the $case\_expr$, which can be an integer, character, or logical value. Each case selector specifies one or more possible values for the case expression. If the $case\_expr$ is a value included in a given case selector, then the corresponding block of statements is executed and control will jump to the first executable statement after the end of the construct. If no case selector is executed, then the CASE DEFAULT block will be executed if present and control will jump to the first executable statement after the end of the construct. If CASE DEFAULT is not present, the construct does nothing.

A CASE construct must have one SELECT CASE statement and one END SELECT statement as well as one or more CASE statements. One CASE DEFAULT statement may be included. Note that all case selectors must be *mutually exclusive*. The name is optional, but if it is used on the SELECT CASE statement, then it must also be used on the END SELECT statement. The name is optional on the CASE statements even if it is used on the SELECT CASE and END SELECT statements.

CYCLE Statement

```
CYCLE [name]
```

Example:

```
CYCLE inner
```

Description:

The CYCLE statement may appear within any DO loop. When the statement is executed, all the statements below it within the loop are skipped and control returns to the top of the loop. In while loops, execution resumes from the top of the loop. In counting loops, the loop index is incremented, and if the index is still less than its limit, execution resumes from the top of the loop.

An unnamed CYCLE statement always causes the innermost loop containing the statement to cycle. A named CYCLE statement causes the named loop to cycle, even if it is not the innermost loop.

DO Loop (Iterative or Counting Loop) Construct

```
[name:] DO index = istart, iend, incr
   ...
END DO [name]
```

Example:

```
loop: DO index = 1, last_value, 3
   ...
END DO loop
```

Description:

The iterative DO loop is used to repeat a block of code a known number of times. During the first iteration of the DO loop, the variable $index$ is set to the value $istart$. $index$ is incremented by $incr$ in each successive loop until $index*incr > iend*incr$, at which time the loop terminates. The loop name is optional, but if it is used on the DO statement, then it must be used on the END DO statement. The loop variable $index$ is incremented and tested *before* each loop, so the DO loop code will never be executed at all if $istart*incr > iend*incr$.

DO WHILE Construct

```
[name:] DO WHILE ( logical_expr )
   ...
END DO [name]
```

Example:

```
loop: DO WHILE ( x >= 0. )
   ...
   ...
   ...
END DO loop
```

Description:

The DO WHILE construct is used to repeat a block of code for as long as a specified $logical\_expr$ is true. At the beginning of each pass through the loop, the $logical\_expr$ is evaluated. If it is true, the code in the loop is executed. If it is false, execution skips to the statement following the end of the loop.

This construct is a special case of the more general while construct and should not be used in new code. The more general while loop is preferred.

EXIT Statement

```
EXIT [name]
```

Example:

```
EXIT loop1
```

Description:

The EXIT statement may appear within any DO loop. When an EXIT statement is encountered, the program stops executing the loop and jumps to the first executable statement after the END DO.

An unnamed EXIT statement always causes the *innermost* loop containing the statement to exit. A named EXIT statement causes the named loop to exit, even if it is not the innermost loop.

Logical IF Statement

```
IF ( logical_expr ) statement
```

Description:

The logical IF statement is a special case of the block IF construct. If $logical\_expr$ is true, then the statement on the line with the IF is executed.

Execution continues at the line after the IF statement.

This statement may be used instead of the block IF construct if only one statement needs to be executed as a result of the logical condition.

While Loop Construct

```
[name:] DO
    ...
    IF ( logical_expr ) EXIT [name]
    ...
END DO [name]
```

Example:

```
loop1: DO
    ...
    IF ( istatus /= 0 ) EXIT loop1
    ...
END DO loop1
```

Description:

The while loop is used to repeat a block of code until a specified `logical_expr` becomes true. It differs from a counting DO loop in that we do not know in advance how many times the loop will be repeated. When the IF statement of the loop is executed with the `logical_expr` true, execution skips to the statement following the end of the loop.

The name of the loop is optional, but if a name is included on the DO statement, then the same name must appear on the END DO statement. The name on the EXIT statement is optional; it may be left out even if the DO and END DO are named.

3

■ 3.7

EXERCISES

3–1 The tangent function is defined as $\tan \theta = \sin \theta / \cos \theta$. This expression can be evaluated to solve for the tangent as long as the magnitude of $\cos \theta$ is not too near to 0. (If $\cos \theta$ is 0, evaluating the equation for $\tan \theta$ will produce a divide-by-zero error.) Assume that θ is given in degrees and write Fortran statements to evaluate $\tan \theta$ as long as the magnitude of $\cos \theta$ is greater than or equal to 10^{-20}. If the magnitude of $\cos \theta$ is less than 10^{-20}, write out an error message instead.

3–2 Write the Fortran statements required to calculate $y(t)$ from the equation

$$y(t) = \begin{cases} -3t^2 + 5 & t \geq 0 \\ 3t^2 + 5 & t < 0 \end{cases}$$

for values of t between -9 and 9 in steps of 3.

3–3 Write the Fortran statements required to calculate and print out the squares of all even integers between 0 and 50.

3–4 Write a Fortran program to evaluate the equation $y(x) = x^2 - 3x + 2$ for all values of x between -1 and 3 in steps of 0.1.

3–5 Write a Fortran program to calculate the factorial function, as defined in Example 3–5. Be sure to handle the special cases of 0! and of illegal input values.

3–6 The following Fortran statements are intended to alert a user to dangerously high oral thermometer readings (values are in degrees Fahrenheit). Are they correct or incorrect? If they are incorrect, explain why and correct them.

```
IF ( temp < 97.5 ) THEN
   WRITE (*,*) 'Temperature below normal'
ELSE IF ( temp > 97.5 ) THEN
   WRITE (*,*) 'Temperature normal'
ELSE IF ( temp > 99.5 ) THEN
   WRITE (*,*) 'Temperature slightly high'
ELSE IF ( temp > 103.0 ) THEN
   WRITE (*,*) 'Temperature dangerously high'
END IF
```

3–7 The cost of sending a package by an express delivery service is $10.00 for the first 2 pounds, and $3.75 for each pound or fraction thereof over 2 pounds. If the package weighs more than 70 pounds, a $10.00 excess weight surcharge is added to the cost. No package over 100 pounds will be accepted. Write a program that accepts the weight of a package in pounds and computes the cost of mailing the package. Be sure to handle the case of overweight packages.

3–8 What is the difference in behavior between a CYCLE statement and an EXIT statement?

3–9 Modify program stats_2 to use the DO WHILE construct instead of the while construct currently in the program.

3–10 The inverse sine function ASIN(x) is defined only for the range $-1.0 \le x \le 1.0$. If x is outside this range, an error will occur when the function is evaluated. The following Fortran statements calculate the inverse sine of a number if it is in the proper range or print an error message if it is not. Assume that x and inverse_sine are real. Is this code correct or incorrect? If it is incorrect, explain why and correct it.

```
test: IF ( ABS(x) <= 1. ) THEN
   inverse_sine = ASIN(x)
ELSE test
   WRITE (*,*) x, ' is out of range!'
END IF test
```

3–11 In Example 3–2 we wrote a program to evaluate the function $f(x,y)$ for any two user-specified values x and y, where the function $f(x,y)$ was defined as follows:

$$f(x,y) = \begin{cases} x + y & x \ge 0 \text{ and } y \ge 0 \\ x + y^2 & x \ge 0 \text{ and } y < 0 \\ x^2 + y & x < 0 \text{ and } y \ge 0 \\ x^2 + y^2 & x < 0 \text{ and } y < 0 \end{cases}$$

The problem was solved by using a single logical IF construct with four code blocks to calculate $f(x,y)$ for all possible combinations of x and y. Rewrite program funxy to use nested IF constructs, where the outer construct evaluates the value of x and the inner constructs evaluate the value of y. Be sure to assign names to each of your constructs.

3–12 Suppose that a student has the option of enrolling for a single elective during a term. The student must select a course from a limited list of options: English, History, Astronomy, or Literature. Construct a fragment of Fortran code that will prompt the student for his or her choice, read in the choice, and use the answer as the case expression for a CASE construct. Be sure to include a default case to handle invalid inputs.

3–13 Examine the following DO statements and determine how many times each loop will be executed. Assume that all loop index variables are integers.

a. DO irange = -32768, 32767
b. DO j = 100, 1, -10
c. DO kount = 2, 3, 4
d. DO index = -4, -7
e. DO i = -10, 10, 10
f. DO

3–14 Examine the following iterative DO loops. Determine the value of ires at the end of each of the loops, and also the number of times each loop executes. Assume that all variables are integers.

a.
```
ires = 0
DO index = -10, 10
    ires = ires + 1
END DO
```

b.
```
ires = 0
loop1: DO index1 = 1, 20, 5
    IF ( index1 <= 10 ) CYCLE
    loop2: DO index2 = index1, 20, 5
        ires = ires + index2
    END DO loop2
END DO loop1
```

c.
```
ires = 0
loop1: DO index1 = 10, 4, -2
    loop2: DO index2 = 2, index1, 2
        IF ( index2 > 6 ) EXIT loop2
        ires = ires + index2
    END DO loop2
END DO loop1
```

d.
```
ires = 0
loop1: DO index1 = 10, 4, -2
    loop2: DO index2 = 2, index1, 2
        IF ( index2 > 6 ) EXIT loop1
        ires = ires + index2
    END DO loop2
END DO loop1
```

3–15 Examine the following while loops. Determine the value of ires at the end of each loop and the number of times each loop executes. Assume that all variables are integers.

a.
```
ires = 0
loop1: DO
    ires = ires + 1
    IF ( (ires / 10 ) * 10 == ires ) EXIT
END DO loop1
```

b.
```
ires = 2
loop2: DO
    ires = ires**2
    IF ( ires > 200 ) EXIT
END DO loop2
```

```
c. ires = 2
   DO WHILE ( ires > 200 )
       ires = ires**2
   END DO
```

3–16 Modify program `ball` from Example 3–8 to read in the acceleration due to gravity at a particular location and to calculate the maximum range of the ball for that acceleration. After modifying the program, run it with accelerations of -9.8 m/sec^2, -9.7 m/sec^2, and -9.6 m/sec^2. What effect does the reduction in gravitational attraction have on the range of the ball? What effect does the reduction in gravitational attraction have on the best angle θ at which to throw the ball?

3–17 Modify program `ball` from Example 3–8 to read in the initial velocity with which the ball is thrown. After modifying the program, run it with initial velocities of 10 m/sec, 20 m/sec, and 30 m/sec. What effect does changing the initial velocity v_o have on the range of the ball? What effect does it have on the best angle θ at which to throw the ball?

3–18 Program `doy` in Example 3–6 calculates the day of year associated with any given month, day, and year. As written, this program does not check to see if the data entered by the user is valid. It will accept nonsense values for months and days and then do calculations with them to produce meaningless results. Modify the program so that it checks the input values for validity before using them. If the inputs are invalid, the program should tell the user what is wrong and quit. The year should be a number greater than zero, the month should be a number between 1 and 12, and the day should be a number between 1 and a maximum that depends on the month. Use a CASE construct to implement the bounds checking performed on the day.

3–19 Write a Fortran program to evaluate the function

$$y(x) = \ln \frac{1}{1 - x}$$

for any user-specified value of x, where ln is the natural logarithm (logarithm to the base e). Write the program with a while loop so that the program repeats the calculation for each legal value of x entered into the program. When an illegal value of x is entered, terminate the program.

3–20 Write a Fortran program to convert all lowercase characters in a user-supplied character string to uppercase, without changing the uppercase and nonalphabetic characters in the string. Assume that your computer uses the ASCII collating sequence.

3–21 Current Through a Diode   The current flowing through the semiconductor diode shown in Figure 3–26 is given by the equation

$$i_D = I_o(e^{qv_D/kt} - 1) \tag{3–11}$$

where

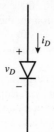

FIGURE 3–26
A semiconductor diode.

3

i_D = the voltage across the diode, in volts.
v_D = the current flow through the diode, in amps.
I_o = the leakage current of the diode, in amps.
q = the charge on an electron, 1.602×10^{-19} coulombs.
k = Boltzmann's constant, 1.38×10^{-23} joule/K.
T = temperature, in kelvins (K).

The leakage current I_o of the diode is 2.0 μA. Write a computer program to calculate the current flowing through this diode for all voltages from -1.0 V to $+0.8$ V in 0.1 V steps. Repeat this process for the following temperatures: 75°F, 100°F, and 125°F. Use the program of Example 2–4 to convert the temperatures from °F to kelvins.

3–22 Tension on a Cable   A 200-pound object is to be hung from the end of a rigid 8-foot horizontal pole of negligible weight, as shown in Figure 3–27. The pole is attached to a wall by a pivot and is supported by an 8-foot cable that is attached to the wall at a higher point. The tension on this cable is given by the equation

$$T = \frac{W \cdot lc \cdot lp}{d\sqrt{lp^2 - d^2}} \tag{3–12}$$

where T is the tension on the cable, W is the weight of the object, lc is the length of the cable, lp is the length of the pole, and d is the distance along the pole at which the

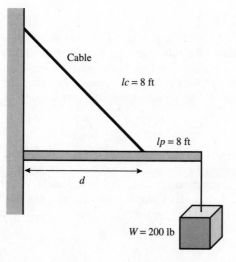

FIGURE 3–27
A 200-pound weight suspended from a rigid bar supported by a cable.

cable is attached. Write a program to determine the distance d at which to attach the cable to the pole in order to minimize the tension on the cable. The program should calculate the tension on the cable at 0.1-foot intervals from $d = 1$ foot to $d = 7$ feet and should locate the position d that produces the minimum tension.

3–23 **Bacterial Growth**   Suppose that a biologist performs an experiment in which he or she measures the rate at which a specific type of bacterium reproduces asexually in different culture media. The experiment shows that in medium A the bacteria reproduce once every 60 minutes, and in medium B the bacteria reproduce once every 90 minutes. Assume that a single bacterium is placed on each culture medium at the beginning of the experiment. Write a Fortran program that calculates and writes out the number of bacteria present in each culture at intervals of 3 hours from the beginning of the experiment until 24 hours have elapsed. How do the numbers of bacteria compare on the two media after 24 hours?

3–24 **Decibels**   Engineers often measure the ratio of two power measurements in *decibels,* or dB. The equation for the ratio of two power measurements in decibels is

$$dB = 10 \log_{10} \frac{P_2}{P_1} \qquad (3\text{–}13)$$

where P_2 is the power level being measured and P_1 is some reference power level. Assume that the reference power level P_1 is 1 watt and write a program that calculates the decibel level corresponding to power levels between 1 and 20 watts in 0.5 W steps.

3–25 **Infinite Series**   Trigonometric functions are usually calculated on computers by using a *truncated infinite series*. An *infinite series* is an infinite set of terms that together add up to the value of a particular function or expression. For example, one infinite series used to evaluate the sine of a number is

$$\sin x = x - \frac{x^3}{3!} + \frac{x^5}{5!} - \frac{x^7}{7!} + \frac{x^9}{9!} + \cdots \qquad (3\text{–}14a)$$

or

$$\sin x = \sum_{n=1}^{\infty} (-1)^{n-1} \frac{x^{2n-1}}{(2n-1)!} \qquad (3\text{–}14b)$$

where x is in units of radians.

Since a computer does not have enough time to add an infinite number of terms for every sine that is calculated, the infinite series is *truncated* after a finite number of terms. The number of terms that should be kept in the series is just enough to calculate the function to the precision of the floating point numbers on the computer on which the function is being evaluated. The truncated infinite series for $\sin x$ is

$$\sin x = \sum_{n=1}^{N} (-1)^{n-1} \frac{x^{2n-1}}{(2n-1)!} \qquad (3\text{–}15)$$

where N is the number of terms to retain in the series.

Write a Fortran program that reads in a value for x in degrees and then calculates the sine of x using the sine intrinsic function. Next calculate the sine of x using Equation (3–15), with N = 1, 2, 3, . . . , 10. Compare the true value of $\sin x$ with the values calculated using the truncated infinite series. How many terms are required to calculate $\sin x$ to the full accuracy of your computer?

3–26 Geometric Mean   The *geometric mean* of a set of numbers x_1 through x_n is defined as the *n*th root of the product of the numbers:

$$\text{geometric mean} = \sqrt[n]{x_1 x_2 x_3 \ldots x_n} \qquad (3\text{–}16)$$

Write a Fortran program that will accept an arbitrary number of positive input values and calculate both the arithmetic mean (i.e., the average) and the geometric mean of the numbers. Use a while loop to get the input values and terminate the inputs if a user enters a negative number. Test your program by calculating the average and geometric mean of the four numbers 10, 5, 2, and 5.

3–27 RMS Average   The *root-mean-square* (rms) *average* is another way of calculating a mean for a set of numbers. The rms average of a series of numbers is the square root of the arithmetic mean of the squares of the numbers:

$$\text{rms average} = \sqrt{\frac{1}{N}\sum_{i=1}^{N} x_i^{2}} \qquad (3\text{–}17)$$

Write a Fortran program that will accept an arbitrary number of positive input values and calculate the rms average of the numbers. Prompt the user for the number of values to be entered and use a DO loop to read in the numbers. Test your program by calculating the rms average of the four numbers 10, 5, 2, and 5.

3–28 Harmonic Mean   The *harmonic mean* is yet another way of calculating a mean for a set of numbers. The harmonic mean of a set of numbers is given by the equation:

$$\text{harmonic mean} = \frac{N}{\dfrac{1}{x_1} + \dfrac{1}{x_2} + \cdots + \dfrac{1}{x_N}} \qquad (3\text{–}18)$$

Write a Fortran program that will read in an arbitrary number of positive input values and calculate the harmonic mean of the numbers. Use any method that you desire to read in the input values. Test your program by calculating the harmonic mean of the four numbers 10, 5, 2, and 5.

3–29 Write a single Fortran program that calculates the arithmetic mean (average), rms average, geometric mean, and harmonic mean for a set of numbers. Use any method that you desire to read in the input values. Compare these values for each of the following sets of numbers:

a.   4, 4, 4, 4, 4, 4, 4
b.   4, 3, 4, 5, 4, 3, 5
c.   4, 1, 4, 7, 4, 1, 7
d.   1, 2, 3, 4, 5, 6, 7

3–30 Mean Time Between Failure Calculations   The reliability of a piece of electronic equipment is usually measured in terms of mean time between failures (MTBF), where MTBF is the average time that the piece of equipment can operate before a failure occurs in it. For large systems containing many pieces of electronic equipment, it is customary to determine the MTBF of each component and to calculate the overall MTBF of the system from the failure rates of the individual components. If the system is structured like the one shown in Figure 3–28, every component must work in order for the whole system to work. The overall system MTBF can be calculated as

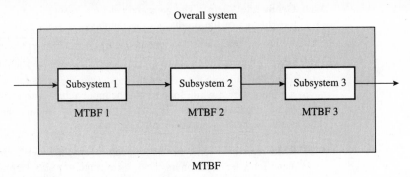

Overall system

FIGURE 3–28
An electronic system containing three subsystems with known MTBFs.

$$MTBF_{sys} = \cfrac{1}{\cfrac{1}{MTBF_1} + \cfrac{1}{MTBF_2} + \cdots + \cfrac{1}{MTBF_n}} \qquad (3\text{--}19)$$

Write a program that reads in the number of series components in a system and the MTBF for each component and then calculates the overall MTBF for the system. To test your program, determine the MTBF for a radar system consisting of an antenna subsystem with an MTBF of 2000 hours, a transmitter with an MTBF of 800 hours, a receiver with an MTBF of 3000 hours, and a computer with an MTBF of 5000 hours.

3–31 Refraction When a ray of light passes from a region with an index of refraction n_1 into a region with a different index of refraction n_2, the light ray is bent (see Figure 3–29). The angle at which the light is bent is given by *Snell's law*

$$n_1 \sin \theta_1 = n_2 \sin \theta_2 \qquad (3\text{--}20)$$

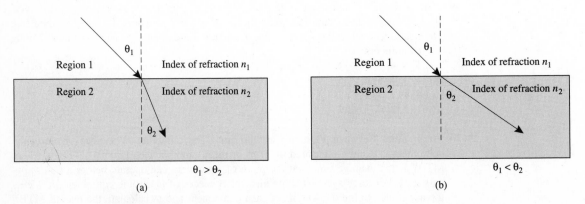

FIGURE 3–29
A ray of light bends as it passes from one medium into another one. *(a)* If the ray of light passes from a region with a low index of refraction into a region with a higher index of refraction, the ray of light bends more towards the vertical. *(b)* If the ray of light passes from a region with a high index of refraction into a region with a lower index of refraction, the ray of light bends away from the vertical.

where θ_1 is the angle of incidence of the light in the first region and θ_2 is the angle of incidence of the light in the second region. Using Snell's Law, it is possible to predict the angle of incidence of a light ray in region 2 if the angle of incidence θ_1 in region 1 and the indices of refraction n_1 and n_2 are known. The equation to perform this calculation is

$$\theta_2 = \sin^{-1}\left(\frac{n_1}{n_2} \sin \theta_1\right) \tag{3-21}$$

Write a Fortran program to calculate the angle of incidence (in degrees) of a light ray in region 2 given the angle of incidence θ_1 in region 1 and the indices of refraction n_1 and n_2. (*Note:* If $n_1 > n_2$, then for some angles θ_1, Equation (3-21) will have no real solution because the absolute value of the quantity $\left(\dfrac{n_1}{n_2} \sin \theta_1\right)$ will be greater than 1.0.

Consequently, all light is reflected back into region 1, and no light passes into region 2 at all. Your program must be able to recognize and properly handle this condition.) Test your program by running it for the following two cases: (a) $n_1 = 1.0$, $n_2 = 1.7$, and $\theta_1 = 45°$; (b) $n_1 = 1.7$, $n_2 = 1.0$, and $\theta_1 = 45°$.

4

Basic I/O Concepts

In the previous chapters, we read values into and wrote them out of our programs using list-directed READ and WRITE statements. List-directed i/o statements are said to be in **free format.** Free format is specified by the second asterisk in the READ (*,*) and WRITE (*,*) statements. As we saw, the results of writing out data in free format are not always pretty because the output often contains many extra spaces. In this chapter we will learn how to write out data using **formats** that specify the exact way in which the numbers should be printed out.

Format may be used either when writing or when reading data. Since they are most useful during output, we will examine formatted WRITE statements first and postpone formatted READ statements until later in the chapter.

The second major topic introduced in this chapter is disk file processing. We will learn the basics of how to read from and write to disk files. Advanced disk file processing is discussed in Chapter 10.

■ 4.1

FORMATS AND FORMATTED WRITE STATEMENTS

A format may be used to specify the exact manner in which variables are to be printed out by a program. In general, a format can specify both the horizontal and the vertical position of the variables on the paper and also the number of significant digits to be printed out. A typical formatted WRITE statement for an integer i and a real variable result follows.

```
WRITE (*,100) i, result
100 FORMAT (' The result for iteration ', I3,' is ', F7.3)
```

The FORMAT statement contains the formatting information used by the WRITE statement. The number 100 that appears within the parentheses in the WRITE statement is the statement label of the FORMAT statement describing how the values contained in i and result are to be printed out. I3 and F7.3 are the **format descriptors** associated with variables i and result, respectively. In this case the FORMAT statement specifies that the program should first write out the phrase 'The result for iteration ', followed by the value of variable i. The format descriptor I3 specifies that a space three characters wide should be used to print out the value of variable i. The value of i will be followed by the phrase ' is ' and then the value of the variable result. The format descriptor F7.3 specifies that a space seven characters wide should be used to print out the value of variable result and that it should be printed with three digits to the right of the decimal point. The resulting output line is shown below, compared to the same line printed with free format.

```
The result for iteration  21 is   3.142                    (formatted)
 The result for iteration            21 is        3.141593  (free format)
```

4

Note that we are able to eliminate both extra blank spaces and undesired decimal places by using format statements. Note also that the value in variable result was rounded before it was printed out in F7.3 format. (Only the value printed out has been rounded; the contents of variable result are unchanged.) Formatted I/O will permit us to create neat output listings from our programs.

In addition to FORMAT statements, formats may be specified in character constants or variables. If a character constant or variable is used to contain the format, then the constant or the name of the variable appears within the parentheses in the WRITE statement. For example, the following three WRITE statements are equivalent:

```
WRITE (*,100) i, x                  ! Format in FORMAT statement
100 FORMAT (1X,I6,F10.2)

CHARACTER(len=20) :: string         ! Format in character variable
string = '(1X,I6,F10.2)'
WRITE (*,string) i, x

WRITE (*,'(1X,I6,F10.2)') i, x      ! Format in character constant
```

In the above example, each format descriptor was separated from its neighbors by commas. With a few exceptions, multiple format descriptors in a single format must be separated by commas.

4.2
OUTPUT DEVICES

To understand the structure of a FORMAT statement, we must know something about the **output devices** on which our data will be displayed. When we run a Fortran program, the output of the program is displayed on an output device. Many types of output devices are used with computers. Some output devices produce permanent paper copies of the data, while others just display it temporarily for us to see. Common output devices include line printers, laser printers, and terminals.

A common way to get a paper copy of the output of a program is on a **line printer.** A line printer is a type of printer that got its name because it prints out data a line at a time. Since it was the first common computer output device, Fortran output specifications were designed with the line printer in mind. Other more modern output devices are generally built to be compatible with the line printer so that the same output statement can be used for any of the devices.

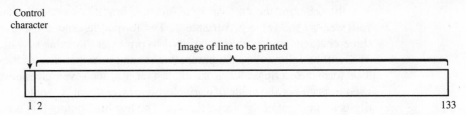

Control
character

Image of line to be printed

1 2   133

FIGURE 4–1
The output buffer is usually 133 characters long. The first character is the control character, and the next 132 characters are an image of what is to be printed on the line.

A line printer prints on computer paper that is divided into pages on a continuous roll. There are perforations between the pages so that it is easy to separate them. The most common size of computer paper in the United States is 11 inches high by $14\frac{7}{8}$ inches wide. Each page is divided into a number of lines, and each line is divided into 132 columns, with one character per column. Since most line printers print either 6 lines per inch or 8 lines per vertical inch, the printers can print either 60 or 72 lines per page. (This output assumes a 0.5-inch margin at the top and the bottom of each page; if the margin is larger, fewer lines can be printed.) The format specifies where to print a line on a page (vertical position) and also where within the line to print each variable (horizontal position).

The computer builds a complete image of each line in memory before sending it to an output device. The computer memory containing the image of the line is called the **output buffer** (see Figure 4–1). The output buffer for a line printer is usually 133 characters wide. The first character in the buffer, known as the **control character,** specifies the vertical spacing for the line. The remaining 132 characters in the buffer contain the data to be printed on that line.

The line printer does not print the control character on the page. Instead, the control character provides vertical positioning control information to the printer. Table 4–1 shows the vertical spacing resulting from various control characters. A '1' character causes the printer to skip the remainder of the current page and print the current line at the top of the next page. A blank character causes the printer to print the current line right below the previous one, while a '0' character causes the printer to skip a line before the current line is printed. A '+' character specifies no spacing; in this case the new line will overwrite the previous line. If any other character is used as the control character, the result should be the same as for a blank.

TABLE 4–1
Fortran control characters

Control character	Action
1	Skip to new page.
blank	Single spacing.
0	Double spacing.
+	No spacing (print over previous line).

For list-directed output [WRITE (*,*)], a blank control character is automatically inserted at the beginning of each output buffer. Therefore, list-directed output is always printed in single-spaced lines.

The following FORMAT statements illustrate the use of the control character. They will print a heading at the top of a new page, skip one line, and then print column headings for Table 4–1 below it.

```
WRITE (*,100)
100 FORMAT ('1','This heading is at the top of a new page.')
WRITE (*,110)
110 FORMAT ('0',' Control Character     Action ')
WRITE (*,120)
120 FORMAT (' ',' =================     ====== ')
```

The results of executing these Fortran statements are shown in Figure 4–2.

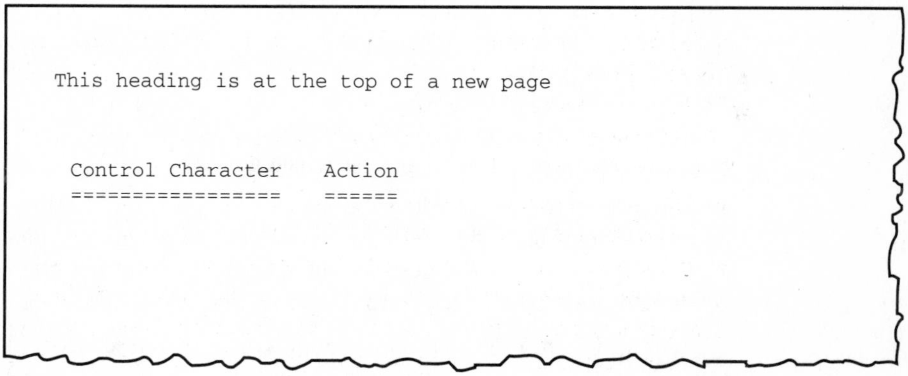

```
    This heading is at the top of a new page


    Control Character    Action
    =================    ======
```

FIGURE 4–2

You must be careful to avoid unpleasant surprises when writing output format statements. For example, the following statements will behave in an unpredictable fashion.

```
WRITE (*,100) n
100 FORMAT (I3)
```

The format descriptor I3 specifies that we want to print the value of variable n in the first three characters of the output buffer. If the value of n is 25, the three positions are filled with b25 (where b denotes a blank). Because the first character is interpreted as a control character, the printer will space down one line and print out 25 in the first two columns of the new line. On the other hand, if n is 125, then the first three characters of the output buffer are filled with 125. Because the first character is interpreted as a control character, the printer will *skip to a new page* and print out 25 in the first two columns of the new line. This result is certainly not what we intended! You should be very careful not to write any format descriptors that include column 1, since they can produce erratic printing behavior and fail to display the correct results.

Programming Pitfalls
Never write a format descriptor that includes column 1 of the output line. Erratic paging behavior and incorrectly displayed values may result if you do so.

To help avoid this error, you should write out each control character separately in the FORMAT statement. For example, the following FORMAT statements are equivalent:

```
100 FORMAT ('1','Count = ', I3)
100 FORMAT ('1Count = ', I3)
```

Each of these statements produces the same output buffer, containing a 1 in the control character position. However, the control character is more obvious in the first statement than it is in the second one.

■ 4.3
FORMAT DESCRIPTORS

Format descriptors fall into four basic categories:

1. Format descriptors that describe the *vertical position* of a line of text.
2. Format descriptors that describe the *horizontal position* of data in a line.
3. Format descriptors that describe the output format of a particular value.
4. Format descriptors that control the repetition of portions of a format.

We will deal with some common examples of format descriptors in this chapter. Other less common format descriptors are discussed in Chapter 10. Table 4–2 contains a list of symbols used with format descriptors, together with their meanings.

4.3.1 Integer Output—The I Descriptor

The descriptor used to describe the display format of integer data is the I descriptor. It has the general form

■ **TABLE 4–2**
Symbols used with format descriptors

Symbol	Meaning
c	Column number.
d	Number of digits to right of decimal place for real input or output.
m	Minimum number of digits to be displayed.
n	Number of spaces to skip.
r	**Repeat count**—the number of times to use a descriptor or group of descriptors.
w	**Field width**—the number of characters to use for the input or output.

$$rIw \quad \text{or} \quad rIw.m$$

where *r*, *w*, and *m* have the meanings given in Table 4–2. Integer values are *right justified* in their fields; that is, integers are printed out so that the last digit of the integer occupies the right-most column of the field. If an integer is too large to fit into the field in which it is to be printed, then the field is filled with asterisks. For example, the following statements

```
INTEGER :: index  = -12, junk =    4, number = -12345
WRITE (*,200) index, index+12, junk, number
WRITE (*,210) index, index+12, junk, number
WRITE (*,220) index, index+12, junk, number
200 FORMAT (' ', 2I5,    I6, I10 )
210 FORMAT (' ', 2I5.0, I6, I10.8 )
220 FORMAT (' ', 2I5.3, I6, I5 )
```

will produce the output

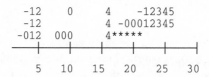

4.3.2 Real Output—The F Descriptor

One format descriptor used to describe the display format of real data is the F descriptor. It has the form

$$rFw.d$$

where *r*, *w*, and *d* have the meanings given in Table 4–2. Real values are printed *right justified* within their fields. If necessary, the number will be rounded off before it is displayed. For example, suppose that the variable pi contains the value 3.141593. If this variable is displayed using the F7.3 format descriptor, the displayed value will be ⌀⌀3.142. On the other hand, if the displayed number includes more significant digits than the internal representation of the number, extra zeros will be appended to the right of the decimal point. If the variable pi is displayed with an F10.8 format descriptor, the resulting value will be 3.14159300. If a real number is too large to fit into the field in which it is to be printed, then the field is filled with asterisks.

For example, the following statements

```
REAL :: a = -12.3, b = .123, c = 123.456
WRITE (*,200) a, b, c
WRITE (*,210) a, b, c
200 FORMAT (' ', 2F6.3, F8.3 )
210 FORMAT (' ', 3F10.2 )
```

will produce the output

4.3.3 Real Output—The E Descriptor

Real data can be printed in **exponential notation** using the E descriptor. Scientific notation is a popular way for scientists and engineers to display very large or very small numbers. It consists of expressing a number as a normalized value between 1 and 10 multiplied by 10 raised to a power.

To understand the convenience of scientific notation, let's consider the following two examples from chemistry and physics. *Avogadro's number* is the number of atoms in a mole of a substance. It can be written out as 602,000,000,000,000,000,000,000, or it can be expressed in scientific notation as 6.02×10^{23}. On the other hand, the charge on an electron is 0.0000000000000000001602 coulomb. This number can be expressed in scientific notation as 1.602×10^{-19}. Scientific notation is clearly a much more convenient way to write these numbers!

The E format descriptor has the form

   *r*E*w.d*

where *r*, *w*, and *d* have the meanings given in Table 4–2. Unlike normal scientific notation, the real values displayed in exponential notation with the E descriptor are normalized to a range between 0.1 and 1.0. That is, they are displayed as a number between 0.1 and 1.0 multiplied by a power of 10. For example, the standard scientific notation for the number 4096.0 would be 4.096×10^3, while the computer output with the E descriptor would be 0.4096×10^4. Since it is not easy to represent exponents on a line printer, the computer output would appear on the printer as `0.4096E+04`.

If a real number cannot fit into the field in which it is to be printed, then the field is filled with asterisks. You should be especially careful with field sizes when working with the E format descriptor, since many items must be considered when sizing the output field. For example, suppose that we want to print out a variable in the E format with four significant digits of accuracy. Then a field width of 11 characters is required: 1 for the sign of the mantissa, 2 for the zero and decimal point, 4 for the actual mantissa, 1 for the E, 1 for the sign of the exponent, and 2 for the exponent itself.

   `±0.ddddE±ee`

In general, the width of an E format descriptor field must satisfy the expression

$$w \geq d + 7 \tag{4–1}$$

or the field may be filled with asterisks.[1]

For example, the following statements

```
REAL :: a = 1.2346E6, b = 0.001, c = -77.7E10 , d = -77.7E10
WRITE (*,200) a, b, c, d
200 FORMAT (' ', 2E14.4, E13.6, E11.6 )
```

---

[1]If the number to be displayed in the field is positive, then the field width *w* need be only six characters larger than *d*. If the number is negative, an extra character is needed for the minus sign. Hence, in general *w* must be $\geq d + 7$. Also, note that some compilers suppress the leading zero so that one less column is required.

will produce the output[2]

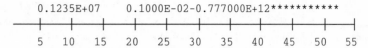

```
     0.1235E+07    0.1000E-02-0.777000E+12**********
  ─┼──┼──┼──┼──┼──┼──┼──┼──┼──┼──┼─
   5  10  15  20  25  30  35  40  45  50  55
```

Notice that the fourth field is all asterisks, since the format descriptor does not satisfy Equation (4–1).

4.3.4 True Scientific Notation—The ES Descriptor

As mentioned above, the output of the E format descriptor doesn't exactly match conventional scientific notation. Conventional scientific notation expresses a number as a value between 1.0 and 10.0 times a power of 10, while the E format expresses the number as a value between 0.1 and 1.0 times a power of 10.

We can make the computer output match conventional scientific notation by using a slightly modified version of the E descriptor called the ES descriptor. The ES descriptor is exactly the same as the E descriptor except that the number to be output will be displayed with a mantissa in the range between 1 and 10. The ES format descriptor has the form

rESw.d

where r, w, and d have the meanings given in Table 4–2. The formula for the minimum width of an ES format descriptor is the same as the formula for the width of an E format descriptor, but the ES descriptor can display one more significant digit in a given width because the leading zero is replaced by a significant digit. The ES field must satisfy the expression

$$w \geq d + 7 \tag{4–1}$$

or the field may be filled with asterisks.[3]

For example, the following statements

```
REAL :: a = 1.2346E6, b = 0.001, c = -77.7E10
WRITE (*,200) a, b, c
200 FORMAT (' ', 2ES14.4, ES12.6 )
```

---

[2]The presence of the leading zero in an E format descriptor is optional, and whether or not it appears differs among compiler vendors. For example, the Lahey Fortran compiler displays leading zeros, while the Microsoft Fortran compiler does not. The following two lines show the output produced by the Lahey and Microsoft compilers for this example.

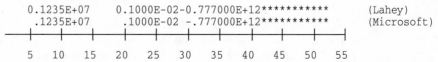

```
   0.1235E+07    0.1000E-02-0.777000E+12**********   (Lahey)
    .1235E+07     .1000E-02 -.777000E+12**********   (Microsoft)
  ─┼──┼──┼──┼──┼──┼──┼──┼──┼──┼──┼─
   5  10  15  20  25  30  35  40  45  50  55
```

[3]If the number to be displayed in the field is positive, then the field width w need be only six characters larger than d. If the number is negative, an extra character is needed for the minus sign. Hence, in general $w \geq d + 7$.

will produce the output

```
         1.2346E+06    1.0000E-03************
       ──┼────┼────┼────┼────┼────┼────┼────┼──
         5   10   15   20   25   30   35   40
```

The third field is all asterisks, since the format descriptor does not satisfy Equation (4–1).

 Good Programming Practice
When displaying very large or very small numbers, use the ES format descriptor to cause them to be displayed in conventional scientific notation. This display will help a reader to quickly understand the output numbers.

4.3.5 Logical Output—The L Descriptor

The descriptor used to display logical data has the form

rLw

where r and w have the meanings given in Table 4–2. The value of a logical variable can be only .TRUE. or .FALSE.. The output of a logical variable is either a T or an F, right justified in the output field.

For example, the following statements

```
LOGICAL :: output = .TRUE., debug = .FALSE.
WRITE (*,200) output, debug
200 FORMAT (' ', 2L5 )
```

will produce the output

```
              T    F
          ────┼────┼────┼──
             5   10   15
```

4.3.6 Character Output—The A Descriptor

Character data is displayed using the A format descriptor.

rA or rAw

where r and w have the meanings given in Table 4–2. The rA descriptor displays character data in a field whose width is the same as the number of characters being displayed, while the rAw descriptor displays character data in a field of fixed width w. If the width w of the field is longer than the length of the character variable, the variable is printed out *right justified* in the field. If the width of the field is shorter than the length of the character variable, only the first w characters of the variable will be printed out in the field.

For example, the following statements

```
CHARACTER(len=17) :: string = 'This is a string.'
WRITE (*,10) string
WRITE (*,11) string
WRITE (*,12) string
10 FORMAT (' ', A)
11 FORMAT (' ', A20)
12 FORMAT (' ', A6)
```

will produce the output

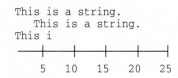

4.3.7 Horizontal Positioning—The X and T Descriptor

Two format descriptors are available to control the spacing of data in the output buffer and, therefore, on the final output line. They are the X descriptor, which inserts spaces into the buffer, and the T descriptor, which "tabs" over to a specific column in the buffer. The X descriptor has the form

nX

where n is the number of blanks to insert. It is used to add one or more blanks between two values on the output line. The T descriptor has the form

Tc

where c is the column number to go to. It is used to jump directly to a specific column in the output buffer. The T descriptor works much like a tab character on a typewriter except that it is possible to jump to any position in the output line, even if we are already past that position in the FORMAT statement.

For example, the following statements

```
CHARACTER(len=10) :: first_name = 'James     '
CHARACTER :: initial = 'R'
Character(len=16) :: last_name = 'Johnson    '
CHARACTER(len=9) :: class = 'COSC 2301'
INTEGER :: grade = 92
WRITE (*,100) first_name, initial, last_name, grade, class
100 FORMAT (1X, A10, 1X, A1, 1X, A10, 4X, I3, T51, A9)
```

will produce the output

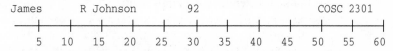

The first 1X descriptor produces a blank control character, so this output line is printed on the next line of the printer. The first name begins in column 1, the middle initial begins in column 12, the last name begins in column 14, the grade begins in column 28, and the course name begins in column 50. (The course name begins in column 51 of the buffer, but it is printed in column 50, since the first character in the output buffer is the control character.) This same output structure could have been created with the following statements:

```
WRITE (*,110) first_name, initial, last_name, class, grade
110 FORMAT (1X, A10, T13, A1, T15, A10, T51, A9, T29, I3)
```

In this example we are actually jumping backward in the output line when we print out the grade.

Since you may freely move anywhere in the output buffer with the T descriptor, it is possible to accidentally overwrite portions of your output data before the line is printed. For example, if we change the tab descriptor for class from T51 to T17

```
WRITE (*,120) first_name, initial, last_name, class, grade
120 FORMAT (1X, A10, T13, A1, T15, A10, T17, A9, T29, I3)
```

the program will produce the following output:

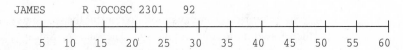

```
JAMES      R JOCOSC 2301    92
```

        5   10   15   20   25   30   35   40   45   50   55   60

 Programming Pitfalls
When using the T descriptor, be careful that your fields do not overlap.

4.3.8 Repeating Groups of Format Descriptors

We have seen that many individual format descriptors can be repeated by preceding them with a repeat count. For example, the format descriptor 2I10 is the same as the pair of descriptors I10,I10.

We can also repeat *groups* of format descriptors by enclosing the group within parentheses and placing a repetition count in front of the parentheses. For example, the following two FORMAT statements are equivalent:

```
320 FORMAT ( 1X, I6, I6, F10.2, F10.2, I6, F10.2, F10.2 )
320 FORMAT ( 1X, I6, 2(I6, 2F10.2) )
```

Groups of format descriptors may be nested if desired. For example, the following two FORMAT statements are equivalent:

```
330 FORMAT ( 1X, I6, F10.2, A, F10.2, A, I6, F10.2, A, F10.2, A )
330 FORMAT ( 1X, 2(I6, 2(F10.2, A)) )
```

However, don't go overboard with nesting. The more complicated you make your FORMAT statements, the harder it will be for you or someone else to understand and debug them.

4.3.9 Changing Output Lines—The Slash (/) Descriptor

The *slash (/) descriptor* sends the current output buffer to the printer and starts a new output buffer. With slash descriptors, a single `WRITE` statement can display output values on more than one line. Several slashes can be used together to skip several lines. The slash is one of the special descriptors that does not have to be separated from other descriptors by commas. However, you may use commas if you wish.

For example, suppose that we need to print out the results of an experiment in which we have measured the amplitude and phase of a signal at a certain time and depth. Assume that the integer variable `index` is 10 and the real variables `time`, `depth`, `amplitude`, and `phase` are 300., 330., 850.65, and 30., respectively. Then the statements

```
      WRITE (*,100) index, time, depth, amplitude, phase
100 FORMAT ('1',T20,'Results for Test Number ',I3,///, &
         1X,'Time      = ',F7.0/, &
         1X,'Depth     = ',F7.1,' meters',/, &
         1X,'Amplitude = ',F8.2/ &,
         1X,'Phase     = ',F7.1)
```

generate seven separate output buffers. The first buffer contains a `'1'` as the control character, so it skips to a new page and puts a title on the page. The next two output buffers are empty, so two blank lines are printed. The final four output buffers have a blank control character, so the four values for `time`, `depth`, `amplitude`, and `phase` are printed on successive lines. The output appears in Figure 4–3.

```
                  Results for Test Number 10



      Time      =   300.
      Depth     =   330.0 meters
      Amplitude =   850.65
      Phase     =    30.2
```

FIGURE 4–3

Notice the `1X` descriptors after each slash. These descriptors place a blank in the control character of each output buffer to ensure that the output advances by one line between buffers.

4.3.10 How Formats Are Used During `WRITE`s

Most Fortran compilers verify the syntax of `FORMAT` statements and character constants containing formats at compilation time, but do not otherwise process them.

Character variables containing formats are not even checked at compilation time for valid syntax, since the format may be modified dynamically during program execution. In all cases, formats are saved unchanged as character strings within the compiled program. When the program is executed, the characters in a format are used as a template to guide the operation of the formatted WRITE.

At execution time, the list of output variables associated with the WRITE statement is processed together with the format of the statement. The program begins at the left end of the variable list and the left end of the format; it scans from left to right, associating the first variable in the output list with the first format descriptor in the format and so on. The variables in the output list must be of the same type and in the same order as the format descriptors in the format, or a run-time error will occur. For example, the program in Figure 4–4 will compile and link correctly, since all the statements in it are legal Fortran statements, and the program doesn't check for correspondence between the format descriptors and the data types until it runs. However, it will abort at run time, when the check shows a real format descriptor corresponding to an integer variable.

Programming Pitfalls
Make sure that you have a one-to-one correspondence between the types of the data in a WRITE statement and the types of the format descriptors in the associated FORMAT statement, or your program will fail at execution time.

As the program moves from left to right through the variable list of a WRITE statement, it also scans from left to right through the associated format. However, the order in which the contents of a format are used may be modified by the inclusion of repetition counters and parentheses. Formats are scanned according to the following rules:

1. *Formats are scanned in order from left to right.* The first variable format descriptor in the format is associated with the first value in the output list of the WRITE statement and so forth. The type of each format descriptor must match the type of the data being output. In the following example, descriptor I5 is associated with variable i, I10 with variable j, I15 with variable k, and F10.2 with variable a.

```
WRITE (*,10) i, j, k, a
10 FORMAT (1X, I5, I10, I15, F10.2)
```

2. *If a format descriptor has a repetition count associated with it, the descriptor will be used the number of times specified in the repetition count before the next descriptor will be used.* In the following example, descriptor I5 is associated with variable i and again with variable j. After it has been used twice, I10 is associated with variable k, and F10.2 is associated with variable a.

```
WRITE (*,20) i, j, k, a
20 FORMAT (1X, 2I5, I10, F10.2)
```

FIGURE 4-4
A Fortran program showing a run-time error resulting from a data / format descriptor mismatch.
Note that the Fortran compiler did not check for format correspondence, so it missed the error.

```
C>f132 /FsCON bad_format.f90
Microsoft (R) Fortran PowerStation  Version 3.00.0407
Copyright (C) Microsoft Corp 1984-1995. All rights reserved.

bad_format.f90
                                                          PAGE   1
                                                          09-17-95
                                                          06:41:24


    Line#  Source Line    Microsoft Fortran PowerStation Compiler. Version 3.0

    1  PROGRAM bad_format
    2  IMPLICIT NONE
    3  INTEGER :: i = 10, j = 20
    4  WRITE (*,100) i, j
    5  100 FORMAT ( I10, F10.0 )
    6  END PROGRAM

No errors detected
Microsoft (R) 32-Bit Incremental Linker Version 2.60.5135
Copyright (C) Microsoft Corp 1992-1995. All rights reserved.

C>bad_format

run-time error F6207: WRITE(CON)
- I edit descriptor expected for INTEGER
```

3. *If a group of format descriptors included within parentheses has a repetition count associated with it, the entire group will be used the number of times specified in the repetition count before the next descriptor will be used.* Each descriptor within the group will be used in order from left to right during each repetition. In the following example, descriptor F10.2 is associated with variable a. Next the group in parentheses is used twice, so I5 is associated with i, E14.6 is associated with b, I5 is associated with j, and E14.6 is associated with c. Finally, F10.2 is associated with d.

```
WRITE (*,30) a, i, b, j, c, d
30 FORMAT (1X, F10.2, 2(I5, E14.6), F10.2)
```

4. If the WRITE statement runs out of variables before the end of the format, *the use of the format stops at the first format descriptor without a corresponding variable or at the end of the format, whichever comes first.* For example, the statements

```
INTEGER :: m = 1
WRITE (*,40) m
40 FORMAT (1X, 'M = ', I3, 'N = ', I4, 'O = ', F7.2)
```

will produce the output

since the use of the format stops at I4, which is the first unmatched format descriptor. The statements

```
REAL :: voltage = 13800.
WRITE (*,50) voltage / 1000.
50 FORMAT (1X, 'Voltage = ', F8.1, ' kV')
```

will produce the output

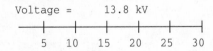

since there are no unmatched descriptors, and the use of the format stops at the end of the statement.

5. If the scan reaches the end of the format before the WRITE statement runs out of values, the program sends the current output buffer to the printer and starts over *at the right-most open parenthesis in the format that is not preceded by a repetition count.* For example, the statements

```
INTEGER :: j = 1, k = 1, l = 3, m = 4, n = 5
WRITE (*,60) j, k, l, m, n
60 FORMAT (1X,'value = ', I3)
```

will produce the output

```
value =   1
value =   2
value =   3
value =   4
value =   5
```
```
   +    +    +    +    +    +
   5   10   15   20   25   30
```

When the program reaches the end of the FORMAT statement after it prints j with the I3 descriptor, it sends that output buffer to the printer and goes back to the right-most open parenthesis not preceded by a repetition count. In this case the right-most open parenthesis without a repetition count is the opening parenthesis of the statement, so the entire statement is used again to print k, l, m, and n. By contrast, the statements

```
INTEGER :: j = 1, k = 1, l = 3, m = 4, n = 5
WRITE (*,60) j, k, l, m, n
60 FORMAT (1X,'Value = ',/, (1X,'New Line',2(3X,I5)))
```

will produce the output

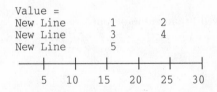

In this case the entire FORMAT statement is used to print values j and k. Since the right-most open parenthesis not preceded by a repetition count is the one just before 1X, 'New Line', that part of the statement is used again to print l, m, and n. Note that the open parenthesis associated with (3X, I5) was ignored because it was associated with a repetition count.

EXAMPLE 4–1 *Generating a Table of Information:* A good way to illustrate the use of formatted WRITE statements is to generate and print out a table of data. The program in Figure 4–5 generates the square roots, squares, and cubes of all integers between 1 and 10 and then presents the data in a table with appropriate headings.

FIGURE 4–5

A Fortran program to generate a table of square roots, squares, and cubes.

```
PROGRAM table
!
!   Purpose:
!     To illustrate the use of formatted WRITE statements.  This
!     program generates a table containing the square roots, squares,
!     and cubes of all integers between 1 and 10.  The table includes
!     a title and column headings.
!
!   Record of revisions:
!       Date          Programmer          Description of change
!       ====          ==========          =====================
!     09/15/95    S. J. Chapman        Original code
IMPLICIT NONE

INTEGER :: cube          ! The cube of i
INTEGER :: i             ! Index variable
INTEGER :: square        ! The square of i
REAL    :: square_root   ! The square root of i

! Print the title of the table on a new page.
WRITE (*,100)
100 FORMAT ('1', T3, 'Table of Square Roots, Squares, and Cubes')

! Print the column headings.
WRITE (*,110)
110 FORMAT ('0',T4,'Number',T13,'Square Root',T29,'Square',T39,'Cube')
WRITE (*,120)
120 FORMAT (1X,T4,'======',T13,'===========',T29,'======',T39,'===='/)

! Generate the required values, and print them out.
DO i = 1, 10
   square_root = SQRT ( REAL(i) )
   square = i**2
   cube = i**3
   WRITE (*,130) i, square_root, square, cube
   130 FORMAT (T4, I4, T13, F10.6, T27, I6, T37, I6)
END DO

END PROGRAM
```

This program uses the tab format descriptor to set up neat columns of data for the table. When this program is compiled and executed on a PC, the result is

```
C>table

      Table of Square Roots, Squares, and Cubes

      Number    Square Root     Square    Cube
      ======    ===========     ======    ====
         1       1.000000          1         1
         2       1.414214          4         8
         3       1.732051          9        27
         4       2.000000         16        64
         5       2.236068         25       125
         6       2.449490         36       216
         7       2.645751         49       343
         8       2.828427         64       512
         9       3.000000         81       729
        10       3.162278        100      1000
```

EXAMPLE 4–2 Charge on a Capacitor: A *capacitor* is an electrical device that stores electric charge. It essentially consists of two flat plates with an insulating material (the *dielectric*) between them (see Figure 4–6). The capacitance of a capacitor is defined as

$$C = \frac{Q}{V} \qquad (4\text{–}2)$$

where Q is the amount of charge stored in a capacitor in units of coulombs and V is the voltage between the two plates of the capacitor in volts. The units of capacitance are farads (F), with 1 farad = 1 coulomb per volt. When a charge is present on the plates of the capacitor, there is an electric field between the two plates. The energy stored in this electric field is given by the equation

$$E = \frac{1}{2} CV^2 \qquad (4\text{–}3)$$

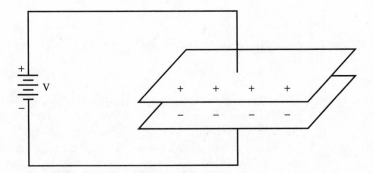

FIGURE 4–6
A capacitor consists of two metal plates separated by an insulating material.

where E is the energy in joules. Write a program that will perform one of the following calculations:

1. For a known capacitance and voltage, calculate the charge on the plates, the number of electrons on the plates, and the energy stored in the electric field.
2. For a known charge and voltage, calculate the capacitance of the capacitor, the number of electrons on the plates, and the energy stored in the electric field.

SOLUTION This program must be able to ask the user which calculation he or she wishes to perform, read in the appropriate values for that calculation, and write out the results in a reasonable format. Note that this problem will require us to work with very small and very large numbers, so we will have to pay special attention to the FORMAT statements in the program. For example, capacitors are typically rated in microfarads (μF or 10^{-6} F) or picofarads (pF or 10^{-12} F), and there are 6.241461×10^{18} electrons per coulomb of charge.

1. **State the problem.**

The problem may be succinctly stated as follows:

a. For a known capacitance and voltage, calculate the charge on a capacitor, the number of electrons stored, and the energy stored in its electric field.
b. For a known charge and voltage, calculate the capacitance of the capacitor, the number of electrons stored, and the energy stored in its electric field.

2. **Define the inputs and outputs.**

There are two possible sets of input values to this program:

a. Capacitance in farads and voltage in volts.
b. Charge in coulombs and voltage in volts.

The outputs from the program in either mode will be the capacitance of the capacitor, the voltage across the capacitor, the charge on the plates of the capacitor, and the number of electrons on the plates of the capacitor. The output must be printed out in a reasonable and understandable format.

3. **Describe the algorithm.**

This program can be broken down into four major steps:

```
Decide which calculation is required
Get the input data for that calculation
Calculate the unknown quantities
Write out the capacitance, voltage, charge, and number of electrons
```

The first major step of the program is to decide which calculation is required. There are two types of calculations: type 1 requires capacitance and voltage, while type 2 requires charge and voltage. We must prompt the user for the type of input data, read his or her answer, and then read in the appropriate data. The pseudocode for these steps follows.

```
Prompt user for the type of calculation "type"
WHILE
    Read type
    IF type == 1 or type == 2 EXIT
    Tell user of invalid value
End of WHILE

If type == 1 THEN
    Prompt the user for the capacitance c in farads
    Read capacitance c
    Prompt the user for the voltage v in volts
    Read voltage v
ELSE IF type == 2 THEN
    Prompt the user for the charge "charge" in coulombs
    Read "charge"
    Prompt the user for the voltage v in volts
    Read voltage v
END IF
```

Next we must calculate unknown values. For type 1 calculations, the unknown values are charge, the number of electrons, and the energy in the electric field, while for type 2 calculations, the unknown values are capacitance, the number of electrons, and the energy in the electric field. The pseudocode for this step follows.

```
IF type == 1 THEN
    charge ← c * v
ELSE
    c ← charge / v
END IF
electrons ← charge * electrons_per_coulomb
energy ← 0.5 * c * v**2
```

where `electrons_per_coulomb` is the number of electrons per coulomb of charge (6.241461×10^{18}). Finally we must write out the results in a useful format.

```
WRITE v, c, charge, electrons, energy
```

The flowchart for this program is shown in Figure 4–7.

4. **Turn the algorithm into Fortran statements.**

The final Fortran program is shown in Figure 4–8.

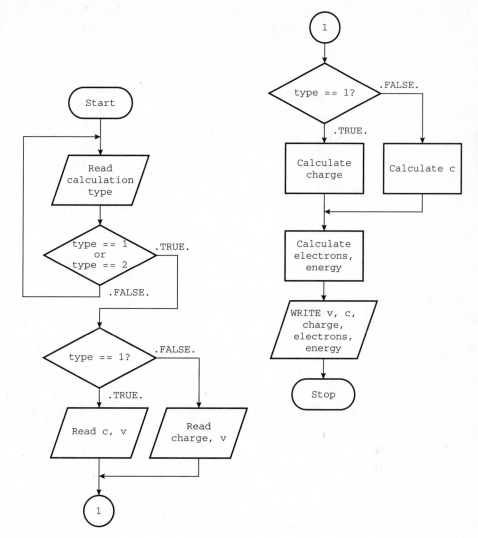

FIGURE 4–7
Flowchart for the program to calculate information about a capacitor.

FIGURE 4–8
Program to perform capacitor calculations.

```
PROGRAM capacitor
!
! Purpose:
!   To calculate the behavior of a capacitor as follows:
!   1.  If capacitance and voltage are known, calculate
!       charge, number of electrons, and energy stored.
!   2.  If charge and voltage are known, calculate capac-
!       itance, number of electrons, and energy stored.
!
```

(continued)

```
!   Record of revisions:
!       Date       Programmer            Description of change
!       ====       ==========            =====================
!     09/15/95    S. J. Chapman          Original code
!
IMPLICIT NONE

! List of parameters:
REAL, PARAMETER :: electrons_per_coulomb = 6.24146E18

! List of variables:
REAL :: c            ! Capacitance of the capacitor (farads).
REAL :: charge       ! Charge on the capacitor (coulombs).
REAL :: electrons    ! Number of electrons on the plates of the
capacitor.
REAL :: energy       ! Energy stored in the electric field (joules).
INTEGER :: type      ! Type of input data available for the calculation:
                     !   1:  C and V
                     !   2:  CHARGE and V
REAL :: v            ! Voltage on the capacitor (volts).

! Prompt user for the type of input data available.
WRITE (*, 100)
100 FORMAT (' This program calculates information about a ' &
            'capacitor.',/, ' Please specify the type of &
information',&
            ' available from the following list:',/,&
            '    1 -- capacitance and voltage ',/,&
            '    2 -- charge and voltage ',//,&
            ' Select option 1 or 2: ')

! Get response and validate it.
DO
   READ (*,*) type
   IF ( (type == 1) .OR. (type == 2) ) EXIT
   WRITE (*,110) type
   110 FORMAT (' Invalid response: ', I6, '.  Please enter 1 or 2:')
END DO

! Get additional data based upon the type of calculation.
input: IF ( type == 1 ) THEN

   WRITE (*,120)                     ! Get capacitance.
   120 FORMAT (' Enter capacitance in farads: ' )
   READ (*,*) c
   WRITE (*,130)                     ! Get voltage.
   130 FORMAT (' Enter voltage in volts: ' )
   READ (*,*) v

ELSE

   WRITE (*,140)                     ! Get charge.
   140 FORMAT (' Enter charge in coulombs: ' )
   READ (*,*) charge
   WRITE (*,130)                     ! Get voltage.
   READ (*,*) v

END IF input
```

(continued)

(concluded)

```
! Calculate the unknown quantities.
calculate: IF ( type == 1 ) THEN
    charge = c * v                              ! Charge
ELSE
    c = charge / v                              ! Capacitance
END IF calculate
electrons = charge * electrons_per_coulomb     ! Electrons
energy = 0.5 * c * v**2                         ! Energy

! Write out answers.
WRITE (*,150) v, c, charge, electrons, energy
150 FORMAT (' For this capacitor: ',/, &
            '    Voltage             = ', F10.2, ' V',/, &
            '    Capacitance         = ', ES10.3, ' F',/, &
            '    Total charge        = ', ES10.3, 'C',/, &
            '    Number of electrons = ', ES10.3,/, &
            '    Total energy        = ', F10.4, ' joules ' )

END PROGRAM
```

5. Test the program.

To test this program, we will calculate the answers by hand for a simple data set and then compare the answers to the results of the program. If we use a voltage of 100 V and a capacitance of 100 μF, the resulting charge on the plates of the capacitor is 0.01 C, there are 6.241×10^{16} electrons on the capacitor, and the energy stored is 0.5 joule.

Running these values through the program using both options 1 and 2 yields the following results:

```
C>capacitor

This program calculates information about a capacitor.
Please specify the type of information available from the following list:
  1 -- capacitance and voltage
  2 -- charge and voltage

Select option 1 or 2:
1
Enter capacitance in farads:
100.e-6
Enter voltage in volts:
100.
For this capacitor:
  Voltage             =    100.00 V
  Capacitance         = 1.000E-04 F
  Total charge        = 1.000E-02 C
  Number of electrons = 6.241E+16
  Total energy        =    .5000 joules

C>capacitor

This program calculates information about a capacitor.
Please specify the type of information available from the following list:
  1 -- capacitance and voltage
  2 -- charge and voltage
```

```
Select option 1 or 2:
2
Enter charge in coulombs:
0.01
Enter voltage in volts:
100.
For this capacitor:
  Voltage             =      100.00 V
  Capacitance         =   1.000E-04 F
  Total charge        =   1.000E-02 C
  Number of electrons =   6.241E+16
  Total energy        =       .5000 joules
```

The program gives the correct answers for our test data set.

Quiz 4–1

This quiz provides a quick check to see if you understand the concepts introduced in sections 4.1 through 4.3. If you have trouble with the quiz, reread the sections, ask your instructor, or discuss the material with a fellow student. The answers to this quiz are found in the back of the book. Unless otherwise stated, assume that variables beginning with the letters I-N are integers and that all other variables are reals.

Write Fortran statements that perform these operations:

1. Skip to a new page and print the title 'This is a test!' starting in column 25.
2. Skip a line and then display the values of i, j, and data_1 in fields 10 characters wide. Allow two decimal points for the real variable.
3. Beginning in column 12, write out the string 'The result is' followed by the value of result expressed to five significant digits in correct scientific notation.

Assume that real variables a, b, and c are initialized with -0.0001, 6.02×10^{23}, and 3.141593, respectively, and that integer variables i, j, and k are initialized with 32767, 24, and -1010101, respectively. What will be printed out by each of the following sets of statements?

4. WRITE (*,10) a, b, c
   10 FORMAT (1X,3F10.4)

5. WRITE (*,20) a, b, c
   20 FORMAT (1X,F10.3, 2X, E10.3, 2X, F10.5)

6. WRITE (*,40) a, b, c
   40 FORMAT (1X,ES10.4, ES11.4, F10.4)

7. WRITE (*, '(1X,I5)') i, j, k

(continued)

(concluded)

8. ```
   CHARACTER(len=30) :: fmt
   fmt = "(1X,I8, 2X, I8.8, 2X, I8)"
   WRITE (*,fmt) i, j, k
   ```

Assume that string_1 is a 10-character variable initialized with the string 'ABCDEFGHIJ' and that string_2 is a 5-character variable initialized with the string '12345'. What will be printed out by each of the following sets of statements?

9. ```
   WRITE (*,"(1X,2A10)") string_1, string_2
   ```

10. ```
    WRITE (*,80) string_1, string_2
    80 FORMAT (T21,A10,T24,A5)
    ```

11. ```
    WRITE (*,100) string_1, string_2
    100 FORMAT (1X,A5,2X,A5)
    ```

Examine the following Fortran statements. Are they correct or incorrect? If they are incorrect, why are they incorrect? Assume default typing for variable names where they are not otherwise defined.

12. ```
    WRITE (*,100) istart, istop, step
    100 FORMAT (2I6,F10.4)
    ```

13. ```
    LOGICAL :: test
    CHARACTER(len=6) :: name
    INTEGER :: ierror
    WRITE (*,200) name, test, ierror
    200 FORMAT (1X,'Test name: ',A,/,' Completion status : ',&
        I6, ' Test results: ', L6 )
    ```

What output will be generated by the following program? Describe the output from this program, including both the horizontal and vertical position of each output item.

14. ```
    INTEGER :: index1 = 1, index2 = 2
    REAL :: x1 = 1.2, y1 = 2.4, x2 5 2.4, y2 = 4.8
    WRITE (*,120) index1, x1, y1, index2, x2, y2
    120 FORMAT ('1',T11,'Output Data',/, &
                ' ',T11,'===========',//,&
                (' ','POINT(',I2,') = ',2F14.6))
    ```

4.4

FORMATTED READ STATEMENTS

An *input device* is a piece of equipment that can enter data into a computer. The most common input device on a modern computer is a keyboard. As data is entered into the input device, it is stored in an **input buffer** in the computer's memory. Once an
    ```

entire line has been typed into the input buffer, the user hits the ENTER key on his or her keyboard, and the input buffer is made available for processing by the computer.

A READ statement reads one or more data values from the input buffer associated with an input device. The particular input device to read from is specified by the i/o unit number in the READ statement, as we will explain later in the chapter. A **formatted READ statement** allows you to specify the exact manner in which the contents of an input buffer are to be interpreted.

In general, a format specifies which columns of the input buffer are to be associated with a particular variable and how those columns are to be interpreted. Here is a typical formatted READ statement:

```
READ (*,100) increment
100 FORMAT (6X,I6)
```

This statement specifies that the first six columns of the input buffer are to be skipped and that the contents of columns 7 through 12 are to be interpreted as an integer, with the resulting value stored in variable increment. As with WRITEs, formats may be stored in FORMAT statements, character constants, or character variables.

Formats associated with READs use many of the same format descriptors as formats associated with WRITEs. However, the interpretation of those descriptors is somewhat different. The meanings of the format descriptors commonly found with READs are described in the following sections.

4.4.1 Integer Input—The I Descriptor

The descriptor used to read integer data is the I descriptor. It has the general form

rIw

where r and w have the meanings given in Table 4–2. An integer value may be placed anywhere within its field, and it will be read and interpreted correctly.

4.4.2 Real Input—The F Descriptor

The format descriptor used to describe the input format of real data is the F descriptor. It has the form

$rFw.d$

where r, w, and d have the meanings given in Table 4–2. The interpretation of real data in a formatted READ statement is rather complicated. The input value in an F input field may be a real number with a decimal point, a real number in exponential notation, or a number without a decimal point. If a real number with a decimal point or a real number in exponential notation is present in the field, then the number is always interpreted correctly. For example, consider the following statement:

```
READ (*,'(3F10.4)') a, b, c
```

Assume that the input data for this statement is

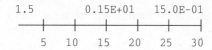

After the statement is executed, all three variables will contain the number 1.5.

If a number without a decimal point appears in the field, then a decimal point is assumed to be in the position specified by the *d* term of the format descriptor. For example, if the format descriptor is `F10.4`, then the four right-most digits of the number are assumed to be the fractional part of the input value and the remaining digits are assumed to be the integer part of the input value. Consider the following Fortran statements:

```
READ (*,110) a, b, c
110 FORMAT (3F10.4)
```

Assume that the input data for these statements is

```
            15     150      15000
  ┼     ┼     ┼     ┼     ┼     ┼
  5    10    15    20    25    30
```

After these statements are executed, a will contain 0.0015, b will contain 0.0150, and c will contain 1.5000. The use of values without decimal points in a real input field is very confusing. It is a relic from an earlier version of Fortran that you should never use in your programs.

Good Programming Practice
Always include a decimal point in any real values used with a formatted `READ` statement.

The `E` and `ES` format descriptors are completely identical to the `F` descriptor for inputting data. They may be used in the place of the `F` descriptor, if desired.

4.4.3 Logical Input—The `L` Descriptor

The descriptor used to read logical data has the form

rLw

where *r* and *w* have the meanings given in Table 4–2. The value of a logical variable can be only `.TRUE.` or `.FALSE.`. The input value must be either a `T` or an `F`, appearing as the first nonblank character in the input field. If any other character is the first nonblank character in the field, a run-time error will occur. The logical input format descriptor is rarely used.

4.4.4 Character Input—The A Descriptor

Character data is read using the A format descriptor

rA   or rAw

where r and w have the meanings given in Table 4–2. The rA descriptor reads character data in a field whose width is the same as the length of the character variable being read, while the rAw descriptor reads character data in a field of fixed width w. If the width w of the field is larger than the length of the character variable, the data from the right-most portion of the field is loaded into the character variable. If the width of the field is smaller than the length of the character variable, the characters in the field will be stored in the left-most characters of the variable and the remainder of the variable will be padded with blanks.

For example, consider the following statements:

```
CHARACTER(len=10) :: string_1, string_2
CHARACTER(len=5)  :: string_3
CHARACTER(len=15) :: string_4, string_5
READ (*,'(A)')    string_1
READ (*,'(A10)')  string_2
READ (*,'(A10)')  string_3
READ (*,'(A10)')  string_4
READ (*,'(A)')    string_5
```

Assume that the input data for these statements is

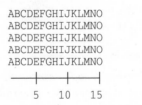

After the statements are executed, variable `string_1` will contain `'ABCDEFGHIJ'`, since `string_1` is 10 characters long and the A descriptor will read as many characters as the length of the variable. Variable `string_2` will contain `'ABCDEFGHIJ'`, since `string_2` is 10 character long and the A10 descriptor will read 10 characters. Variable `string_3` is only 5 characters long, and the A10 descriptor is 10 characters long, so `string_3` will contain the 5 right-most of the 10 characters in the field `'FGHIJ'`. Variable `string_4` will contain `'ABCDEFGHIJ bbbbb'`, since `string_4` is 15 characters long and the A10 descriptor will read only 10 characters. Finally `string_5` will contain `'ABCDEFGHIJKLMNO'`, since `string_5` is 15 characters long and the A descriptor will read as many characters as the length of the variable.

4.4.5 Horizontal Positioning—The X and T Descriptors

The X and T format descriptors may be used when reading formatted input data. The chief use of the X descriptor is to skip over fields in the input data that we do not wish to read. The T descriptor may be used for the same purpose, but it may also be used to read the same data twice in two different formats. For example, the following code reads the values in characters 1 through 6 of the input buffer twice—once as an integer and once as a character string.

```
CHARACTER(len=6) :: string
INTEGER :: input
READ (*,'(I6,T1,A6)') input, string
```

4.4.6 Vertical Positioning—The Slash (/) Descriptor

The slash (/) format descriptor causes a formatted READ statement to discard the current input buffer, get another one from the input device, and start processing from the beginning of the new input buffer. For example, the following formatted READ statement reads the values of variables a and b from the first input line, skips down two lines, and reads the values of variables c and d from the third input line.

```
REAL :: a, b, c, d
READ (*,300) a, b, c, d
300 FORMAT (2F10.2,//,2F10.2)
```

If the input data for these statements is

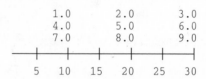

then the contents of variables a, b, c, and d will be 1.0, 2.0, 7.0, and 8.0, respectively.

4.4.7 How Formats Are Used During READs

Most Fortran compilers verify the syntax of FORMAT statements and character constants containing formats at compilation time, but do not otherwise process them. Character variables containing formats are not even checked at compilation time for valid syntax, since the format may be modified dynamically during program execution. In all cases, formats are saved unchanged as character strings within the compiled program. When the program is executed, the characters in a format are used as a template to guide the operation of the formatted READ.

At execution time the list of input variables associated with the READ statement is processed together with the format of the statement. The rules for scanning a format are essentially the same for READs and for WRITEs. The order of scanning, repetition counts, and the use of parentheses are identical.

When the number of variables to be read and the number of descriptors in the format differ, formatted READs behave as follows:

1. If the READ statement runs out of variables before the end of the format, the use of the format stops after the last variable has been read. The next READ statement will start with a new input buffer, and all of the other data in the original input buffer will be lost. For example, consider the following statements

```
READ (*,30) i, j
READ (*,30) k, l, m
30 FORMAT (5I5)
```

and the following input data

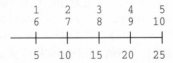

After the first statement is executed, the values of i and j will be 1 and 2, respectively. The first READ ends at that point, so that input buffer is thrown away without ever using the remainder of the buffer. The next READ uses the second input buffer, so the values of k, l, and m will be 6, 7, and 8.

2. If the scan reaches the end of the format before the READ statement runs out of variables, the program discards the current input buffer. It gets a new input buffer and resumes in the format at the right-most open parenthesis that is not preceded by a repetition count, for example, the statements

```
READ (*,40) i, j, k, l, m
40 FORMAT (I5,(T6,2I5))
```

and the input data

```
  1     2     3     4     5
  6     7     8     9    10
  +-----+-----+-----+-----+
  5    10    15    20    25
```

When the READ statement is executed, variables i, j, and k will be read from the first input buffer. They will contain 1, 2, and 3, respectively. The FORMAT statement ends at that point, so the first input buffer is discarded, and the next one is used. The FORMAT statement starts over at the right-most open parenthesis not preceded by a repetition count, so variables l and m will contain 7 and 8, respectively.

Quiz 4–2

This quiz provides a quick check to see if you understand the concepts introduced in section 4.4. If you have trouble with the quiz, reread the section, ask your instructor, or discuss the material with a fellow student. The answers to this quiz are found in the back of the book. Unless otherwise stated, assume that variables beginning with the letters I-N are integers and that all other variables are reals.

Write Fortran statements that perform the following functions:

1. Read the values of a real variable amplitude from columns 10–20, an integer variable count from columns 30–35, and a character variable identity from columns 60–72 of the current input buffer.

(continued)

(concluded)

2. Read a 25-character variable called `title` from columns 10–34 of the first input line; then read five integer variables `i1` through `i5` from columns 5–12 on each of the next five lines.

3. Read columns 11–20 from the current input line into a character variable `string`, skip two lines, and read columns 11–20 into an integer variable `number`. Use a single formatted READ statement.

What will be stored in each of the following variables?

4. `READ (*,'(3F10.4)') a, b, c`

With the input data:

5. `READ (*,20) a, b, c`
`20 FORMAT (E10.2,F10.2,/,20X,F10.2)`

With the input data:

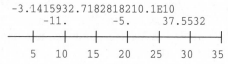

6. `READ (*,'(3I5)') i, j, k`

With the input data:

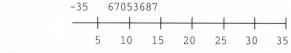

7. `CHARACTER(len=5)  :: string_1`
`CHARACTER(len=10) :: string_2, string_4`
`CHARACTER(len=15) :: string_3`
`READ (*,'(4A10)') string_1, string_2, string_3, string_4`

With the input data:

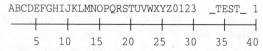

Examine the following Fortran statements. Are they correct or incorrect? If they are incorrect, why are they incorrect? If they are correct, what do they do?

8. `READ (*,100) nvals, time1, time2`
`100 FORMAT (10X,I10,F10.2,F10.4)`

9. `READ (*,220) junk, scratch`
`220 FORMAT ( T60,I15,/,E15.3)`

10. `READ (*,220) icount, range, azimuth, elevation`
`220 FORMAT ( I6, 4X, F20.2)`

■ 4.5

AN INTRODUCTION TO FILES AND FILE PROCESSING

The programs that we have written up to now have involved relatively small amounts of input and output data. We have typed in the input data from the keyboard each time that a program has been run, and the output data has gone directly to a terminal or printer. This method is acceptable for small data sets, but it rapidly becomes prohibitive when working with large volumes of data. Imagine having to type in 100,000 input values each time a program is run! Such a process would be both time-consuming and prone to typing errors. We need a convenient way to read in and write out large data sets and to be able to use them repeatedly without retyping.

Fortunately, computers have a standard structure for holding data that we will be able to use in our programs. This structure is called a **file.** A file consists of many lines of related data that can be accessed as a unit. Each line of information in a file is called a **record.** Fortran can read information from a file or write information to a file one record at a time.

The files on a computer can be stored on various types of devices, which are collectively known as *secondary memory.* (The computer's RAM is its primary memory.) Secondary memory is slower than the computer's main memory, but it still allows relatively quick access to the data. Common secondary storage devices include hard disk drives, floppy disk drives, and magnetic tapes.

In the early days of computers, magnetic tapes were the most common type of secondary storage device. Computer magnetic tapes store data in a manner similar to the audio cassette tapes that we use to play music. Like audio tapes, computer magnetic tapes must be read (or "played") in order from beginning to end. When we read data in consecutive order one record after another in this manner, we are using **sequential access.** Other devices such as hard disks have the ability to jump from one record to another anywhere within a file. When we jump freely from one record to another following no specific order, we are using **direct access.** For historical reasons, sequential access is the default access technique in Fortran even if we are working with devices capable of direct access.

To use files within a Fortran program, we will need some way to select the desired file and to read from or write to it. Fortunately, Fortran has a wonderfully flexible method to read from and write to files, whether they are on disk, magnetic tape, or some other device attached to the computer. This mechanism is known as the **input/ output unit** (i/o unit, sometimes called a "logical unit," or simply a "unit.") The i/o unit corresponds to the first asterisk in the READ (*,*) and WRITE (*,*) statements. If that asterisk is replaced by an i/o unit number, then the corresponding read or write will be to the device assigned to that unit instead of to the standard input or output device. The statements to read or write any file or device attached to the computer are exactly the same except for the i/o unit number in the first position, so we already know most of what we need to know to use file i/o. An i/o unit number must be of type INTEGER.

Several Fortran statements may be used to control disk file input and output. The statements discussed in this chapter are summarized in Table 4–3.

TABLE 4–3
Fortran input/output statements

I/O statement	Function
OPEN	Associate a specific disk file with a specific i/o unit number.
CLOSE	End the association of a specific disk file with a specific i/o unit number.
READ	Read data from a specified i/o unit number.
WRITE	Write data to a specified i/o unit number.
REWIND	Move to the beginning of a file.
BACKSPACE	Move back one record in a file.

4

I/o unit numbers are assigned to disk files or devices using the OPEN statement and detached from them using the CLOSE statement. Once a file is attached to an i/o unit using the OPEN statement, we can read and write in exactly the same manner that we already know. When we are through with the file, the CLOSE statement closes the file and releases the i/o unit to be assigned to some other file. The REWIND and BACKSPACE statements change the current reading or writing position in a file while it is open.

Certain unit numbers are predefined to be connected to certain input or output devices so that we don't need an OPEN statement to use these devices. These pre-defined units vary from processor to processor.[4] Typically, i/o unit 5 is predefined to be the *standard input device* for your program (the keyboard if you are running at a terminal or the input batch file if you are running in batch mode). Similarly, i/o unit 6 is usually predefined to be the *standard output device* for your program (the screen if you are running at a terminal or the line printer if you are running in batch mode). These assignments date back to the early days of Fortran on IBM computers, and most other vendors use them in their Fortran compilers. However, you cannot count on these associations always being true for every processor. If you need to read from and write to the standard devices, always use the asterisk instead of the standard unit number for that device. The asterisk is guaranteed to work correctly on any computer system.

Good Programming Practice
Always use asterisks instead of i/o unit numbers when referring to the standard input or standard output devices. The standard i/o unit numbers vary from processor to processor, but the asterisk works correctly on all processors.

---

[4]A *processor* is defined as the combination of a specific computer with a specific compiler.

If we want to access any files or devices other than the predefined standard devices, we must first use an OPEN statement to associate the file or device with a specific i/o unit number. Once the association has been established, we can use ordinary Fortran READs and WRITEs with that unit to work with the data in the file.[5]

4.5.1 The OPEN Statement

The OPEN statement associates a file with a given i/o unit number. Its form is

$$\text{OPEN} \; (open\_list)$$

where *open_list* contains a series of clauses specifying the i/o unit number, the file name, and information about how to access the file. The clauses in the list are separated by commas. The full list of possible clauses in the OPEN statement is given in Chapter 10. For now, we will introduce only the five most important items from the list.

1. A UNIT= clause indicating the i/o unit number to associate with this file. This clause has the form

$$\text{UNIT=} \; int\_expr$$

   where *int_expr* can be a nonnegative integer value.
2. A FILE= clause specifying the name of the file to be opened. This clause has the form

$$\text{FILE=} \; char\_expr$$

   where *char_expr* is a character value containing the name of the file to be opened.
3. A STATUS= clause specifying the status of the file to be opened. This clause has the form

$$\text{STATUS=} \; char\_expr$$

   where *char_expr* is one of the following: 'OLD', 'NEW', 'REPLACE', 'SCRATCH', or 'UNKNOWN'.
4. An ACTION= clause specifying whether a file is to be opened for reading only, for writing only, or for both reading and writing. This clause has the form

$$\text{ACTION=} \; char\_expr$$

   where *char_expr* is one of the following: 'READ', 'WRITE', or 'READWRITE'. If no action is specified, the file is opened for both reading and writing.
5. An IOSTAT= clause specifying the name of an integer variable in which the status of the open operation can be returned. This clause has the form

$$\text{IOSTAT=} \; int\_var$$

---

[5]Some Fortran compilers attach default files to logical units that have not been opened. For example, in VAX Fortran, a write to an unopened LU 26 will automatically go into a file called FOR026.DAT. You should never use this feature, since it is nonstandard and varies from processor to processor. Your programs will be much more portable if you always use an OPEN statement before writing to a file.

where *int_var* is an integer variable. If the OPEN statement is successful, a zero will be returned in the integer variable. If it is not successful, a positive number corresponding to a system error message will be returned in the variable. The system error messages vary from processor to processor, but a zero always means success.

The above clauses may appear in any order in the OPEN statement. Some examples of correct OPEN statements follow.

Case 1: Opening a file for input

The following statement opens a file named EXAMPLE.DAT and attaches it to i/o unit 8.

```
INTEGER :: ierror
OPEN (UNIT=8, FILE='EXAMPLE.DAT', STATUS='OLD', ACTION='READ', &
      IOSTAT=ierror)
```

The STATUS= 'OLD' clause specifies that the file already exists; if it does not exist, then the OPEN statement will return an error code in variable ierror. This is the proper form of the OPEN statement for an *input file*. If we are opening a file to read input data from, then the file had better be present with data in it! If it is not there, something is obviously wrong. By checking the returned value in ierror, we can tell that there is a problem and take appropriate action.

The ACTION='READ' clause specifies that the file should be read only. If an attempt is made to write to the file, an error will occur. This behavior is appropriate for an input file.

Case 2: Opening a file for output

The following statements open a file named OUTDAT and attach it to i/o unit 25.

```
INTEGER :: unit, ierror
CHARACTER(len=6) :: filename
unit = 25
filename = 'OUTDAT'
OPEN (UNIT=unit, FILE=filename, STATUS='NEW', ACTION='WRITE', &
      IOSTAT=ierror)
```

or

```
OPEN (UNIT=unit, FILE=filename, STATUS='REPLACE', ACTION='WRITE', &
      IOSTAT=ierror)
```

The STATUS='NEW' clause specifies that the file is a new file; if it already exists, then the OPEN statement will return an error code in variable ierror. This is the proper form of the OPEN statement for an *output file* if we want to make sure that we don't overwrite the data in a file that already exists.

The STATUS='REPLACE' clause specifies that a new file should be opened for output whether a file by the same name exists or not. If the file already exists, the program will delete it, create a new file, and open it for output. The old contents of the file will be lost. If it does not exist, the program will create a new file by that name and open it. This is the proper form of the OPEN statement for an output file if we want to open the file whether or not a previous file exists with the same name.

The ACTION='WRITE' clause specifies that the file should be write only. If an attempt is made to read from the file, an error will occur. This behavior is appropriate for an output file.

Case 3: Opening a scratch file

The following statement opens a scratch file and attaches it to i/o unit 12.

```
OPEN (UNIT=12, STATUS='SCRATCH', IOSTAT=ierror)
```

A *scratch file* is a temporary file that is created by the program and will be deleted automatically when the file is closed or when the program terminates. You can use this type of file for saving intermediate results while a program is running, but you cannot use it to save anything that you want to keep after the program finishes. Notice that no file name is specified in the OPEN statement. In fact, it is an error to specify a file name with a scratch file. Since no ACTION= clause is included, the file has been opened for both reading and writing.

Good Programming Practice

Always be careful to specify the proper status in OPEN statements, depending on whether you are reading from or writing to a file. This practice will help prevent errors such as accidentally overwriting data files that you want to keep.

4.5.2 The CLOSE Statement

The CLOSE statement closes a file and releases the i/o unit number associated with it. Its form is

```
CLOSE (close_list)
```

where `close_list` must contain a clause specifying the i/o number and may specify other options that are discussed with the advanced i/o material in Chapter 10. If a program does not have a CLOSE statement for a given file, that file will be closed automatically when the program terminates.

After a nonscratch file is closed, it may be reopened at any time using a new OPEN statement. When it is reopened, it may be associated with the same i/o unit or with a different i/o unit. After the file is closed, you can reassign the i/o unit that was associated with the file to any other file in a new OPEN statement.

4.5.3 READs and WRITEs to Disk Files

Once a file has been connected to an i/o unit via the OPEN statement, it is possible to read from or write to the file using the same READ and WRITE statements that we have been using. For example, the statements

```
OPEN (UNIT=8, FILE='INPUT.DAT',STATUS='OLD',IOSTAT=ierror)
READ (8,*) x, y, z
```

will read the values of variables x, y, and z using list-directed i/o from the file INPUT.DAT, and the statements

```
OPEN (UNIT=9,FILE='OUTPUT.DAT',STATUS='REPLACE',IOSTAT=ierror)
WRITE (9,100) x, y, z
100 FORMAT (' X = ', F10.2, ' Y = ', F10.2, ' Z = ', F10.2 )
```

will write the values of variables x, y, and z to the file OUTPUT.DAT in the specified format.

4.5.4 The IOSTAT= Clause in the READ Statement

The IOSTAT= clause is an important additional feature that you may add to the READ statement when you are working with disk files. The form of this clause is

$$IOSTAT=\ int\_var$$

where *int_var* is an integer variable. If the READ statement is successful, a zero will be returned in the integer variable. If it is not successful because of a file or format error, a positive number corresponding to a system error message will be returned in the variable. If it is not successful because the end of the input data file has been reached, a negative number will be returned in the variable.[6]

If no IOSTAT= clause is present in a READ statement, any attempt to read a line beyond the end of a file will abort the program. This behavior is unacceptable in a well-designed program. We often want to read all the data from a file until the end is reached and then perform some sort of processing on that data. The IOSTAT= clause is useful in this situation. If an IOSTAT= clause is present, the program will not abort on an attempt to read a line beyond the end of a file. Instead, the READ will complete with the IOSTAT variable set to a negative number. We can then test the value of the variable and process the data accordingly.

Good Programming Practice
Always include the IOSTAT= clause when reading from a disk file. This clause provides a graceful way to detect end-of-data conditions on the input files.

EXAMPLE 4–3 Reading Data from a File: It is very common to read a large data set into a program from a file and then to process the data in some fashion. Often, the program will have no way of knowing in advance just how much data is present in the file. In that case the program needs to read the data in a while loop until it reaches the end of the data set and then must detect the end of the data. Once it has read in all of the data, the program can process the data set as required.

---

[6]An alternative method of detecting file read errors and end-of-file conditions uses ERR= and END= clauses. These clauses of the READ statement are described in Chapter 10. The IOSTAT= clause lends itself better to structured programming than the other clauses do, so the alternatives are being postponed to the later chapter.

Let's illustrate this process by writing a program that can read in an unknown number of real values from a disk file and detect the end of the data in the disk file.

SOLUTION This program must open the input disk file and then read the values from it, using the IOSTAT= clause to detect problems. If the IOSTAT variable contains a negative number after a READ, then the end of the file has been reached. If the IOSTAT variable contains a zero after a READ, then everything was OK. If the IOSTAT variable contains a positive number after a READ, then a READ error occurred. In this example the program should stop if a READ error occurs.

1. **State the problem.**

The problem may be succinctly stated as follows: Write a program that can read an unknown number of real values from a user-specified input data file and detect the end of the data file when it occurs.

2. **Define the inputs and outputs.**

The inputs to this program consist of
a. The name of the file to be opened.
b. The data contained in that file.

The outputs from the program will be the input values in the data file. At the end of the file, an informative message will be written out telling how many valid input values were found.

3. **Describe the algorithm.**

The pseudocode for this program is

```
Initialize nvals to 0
Prompt user for file name
Get the name of the input file
OPEN the input file
Check for errors on OPEN

If no OPEN error THEN
    ! Read input data
    WHILE
        READ value
        IF status /= 0 EXIT
        nvals ← nvals + 1
        WRITE valid data to screen
    END of WHILE

    ! Check to see if the WHILE terminated due to end of file
    ! or READ error
    IF status > 0
        WRITE 'READ error occurred on line', nvals
    ELSE
        WRITE number of valid input values nvals
    END of IF ( status > 0 )
END of IF ( no OPEN error )
END PROGRAM
```

A flowchart for the program is shown in Figure 4–9.

4. **Turn the algorithm into Fortran statements.**

The final Fortran program is shown in Figure 4–10.

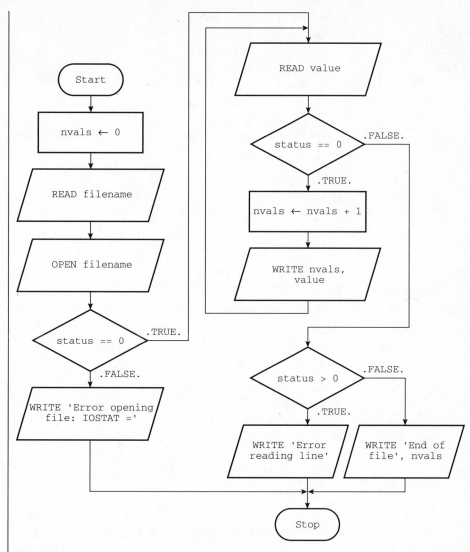

FIGURE 4–9
Flowchart for a program to read an unknown number of values from an input data file.

FIGURE 4–10
Program to read an unknown number of values from a user-specified input disk file.

```
PROGRAM read
!
!  Purpose:
!    To illustrate how to read an unknown number of values from
!    an input data file, detecting both any formatting errors and
!    the end of file.
!
```

(continued)

(concluded)

```
!  Record of revisions:
!      Date         Programmer          Description of change
!      ====         ==========          =====================
!    09/18/95     S. J. Chapman         Original code
!
IMPLICIT NONE

! Declare variables
CHARACTER(len=20) :: filename       ! Name of file to open
INTEGER :: nvals = 0                ! Number of values read in
INTEGER :: status                  ! I/O status
REAL :: value                      ! The real value read in

! Get the file name and echo it back to the user.
WRITE (*,*) 'Please enter input file name: '
READ (*,*) filename
WRITE (*,1000) filename
1000 FORMAT (' ','The input file name is: ', A)

! Open the file and check for errors on open.
OPEN (UNIT=3, FILE=filename, STATUS='OLD', ACTION='READ', &
      IOSTAT=status )
openif: IF ( status == 0 ) THEN

   ! OPEN was ok.  Read values.
   readloop: DO
      READ (3,*,IOSTAT=status) value      ! Get next value
      IF ( status /= 0 ) EXIT             ! EXIT if not valid
      nvals = nvals + 1                   ! Valid: increase count
      WRITE (*,1010) nvals, value         ! Echo to screen
      1010 FORMAT (' ','Line ', I6, ': Value = ',F10.4)
   END DO readloop

   ! The WHILE loop has terminated.  Was it because of a READ
   ! error or because of the end of the input file?
   readif: IF ( status > 0 ) THEN ! a READ error occurred.  Tell user.

      WRITE (*,1020) nvals + 1
      1020 FORMAT ('0','An error occurred reading line ', I6)

   ELSE ! the end of the data was reached.  Tell user.

      WRITE (*,1030) nvals
      1030 FORMAT ('0','End of file reached.  There were ', I6, &
                   ' values in the file.')

   END IF readif

ELSE openif
   WRITE (*,1040) status
   1040 FORMAT (' ','Error opening file: IOSTAT = ', I6 )
END IF openif

! Close file
CLOSE ( UNIT=8 )

END PROGRAM
```

Note that the input file is opened with STATUS='OLD', since we are reading from the file and the input data must already exist before the program is executed.

5. **Test the program.**

To test this program, we will create two input files: one with valid data and one with an input data error. We will run the program with both input files and verify that it works correctly both for valid data and for data containing input errors. Also, we will run the program with an invalid file name to show that it can properly handle missing input files.

The valid input file is called READ1.DAT. It contains the following lines.

```
-17.0
30.001
1.0
12000.
-0.012
```

The invalid input file is called READ2.DAT. It contains the following lines:

```
-17.0
30.001
ABCDEF
12000.
-0.012
```

Running these files through the program yields the following results:

```
C>read
Please enter input file name:
'read1.dat'
The input file name is: read1.dat
Line      1: Value =    -17.0000
Line      2: Value =     30.0010
Line      3: Value =      1.0000
Line      4: Value = 12000.0000
Line      5: Value =     -.0120

End of file reached.   There were      5 values in the file.

C>read
Please enter input file name:
'read2.dat'
The input file name is: read2.dat
Line      1: Value =    -17.0000
Line      2: Value =     30.0010

An error occurred reading line        3
```

Finally, let's test the program with an invalid input file name.

```
C>read
Please enter input file name:
'JUNK.DAT'
The input file name is: JUNK.DAT
Error opening file: IOSTAT =   6416
```

The number of the IOSTAT error reported by this program will vary from processor to processor, but it will always be positive. You must consult a listing of the run-time error codes for your particular compiler to find the exact meaning of the error code that your computer reports. For the Fortran compiler used here, run-time error 6416 means "File not found."

This program correctly read all of the values in the input file and detected the end of the data set when it occurred.

4.5.5 File Positioning

As we stated previously, ordinary Fortran files are sequential—they are read in order from the first record in the file to the last record in the file. However, we sometimes need to read a piece of data more than once or to process a whole file more than once during a program. How can we skip around within a sequential file?

Fortran provides two statements to help us move around within a sequential file. They are the BACKSPACE statement, which moves back one record each time it is called, and the REWIND statement, which restarts the file at its beginning. The forms of these statements are

```
BACKSPACE (UNIT=lu)
```

and

```
REWIND (UNIT=lu)
```

where lu is the i/o unit number associated with the file that we want to use.[7]

Both statements can also include IOSTAT= clauses to detect errors during the backspace or rewind operation without causing the program to abort.

EXAMPLE 4–4 Using File Positioning Commands: We will now illustrate the use of scratch files and file-positioning commands in a simple problem. Write a program that accepts a series of nonnegative real values and stores them in a scratch file. After the data is input, the program should ask the user what data record he or she wants to see and then recover and display that value from the disk file.

SOLUTION Since the program is expected to read only positive or zero values, we can use a negative value as a flag to terminate the input to the program. The Fortran program in Figure 4–11 opens a scratch file and then reads input values from the user. If a value is nonnegative, it is written to the scratch file. When a negative value is encountered, the program asks the user for the record to display. It checks to see if a valid record number was entered. If the record number is valid, the program rewinds the file and reads forward to that record number. Finally, it displays the contents of that record to the user.

---

[7]Alternative forms of these statements are described in Chapter 10.

FIGURE 4-11
Sample program illustrating the use of file-positioning commands.

```
PROGRAM scratch
!
!  Purpose:
!    To illustrate the use of a scratch file and positioning
!    commands as follows:
!    1.  Read in an arbitrary number of positive or zero
!        values, saving them in a scratch file.  Stop
!        reading when a negative value is encountered.
!    2.  Ask the user for a record number to display.
!    3.  Rewind the file, get that value, and display it.
!
!  Record of revisions:
!     Date        Programmer          Description of change
!     ====        ==========          =====================
!    09/18/95    S. J. Chapman         Original code
!
IMPLICIT NONE

! List of parameters:
INTEGER, PARAMETER :: lu = 8  ! i/o unit for scratch file

! List of variables:
REAL :: data               ! Data value stored in a disk file
INTEGER :: icount = 0      ! The number of input data records
INTEGER :: irec            ! Record number to recover and display
INTEGER :: j               ! Loop index

! Open the scratch file
OPEN (UNIT=lu, STATUS='SCRATCH')

! Prompt user and get input data.
WRITE (*, 100)
100 FORMAT (1X,'Enter positive or zero input values. ',/, &
            1X,'A negative value terminates input.' )

! Get the input values, and write them to the scratch file
DO
   WRITE (*, 110) icount + 1      ! Prompt for next value
   110 FORMAT (1X,'Enter sample ',I4,':' )
   READ(*,*) data                 ! Read value
   IF ( data < 0. ) EXIT          ! Exit on negative numbers
   icount = icount + 1            ! Valid value: bump count
   WRITE (lu,120) data            ! Write data to scratch file
   120 FORMAT ( 1X, ES16.6 )
END DO
! Now we have all of the records.  Ask which record to see.
! icount records are in the file.
WRITE (*,130) icount
130 FORMAT (1X,'Which record do you want to see (1 to ',I4, ')? ')
READ (*,*) irec

! Do we have a legal record number?  If so, get the record.
! If not, tell the user and stop.
IF ( (irec >= 1) .AND. (irec <= icount) ) THEN

   ! This is a legal record.  Rewind the scratch file.
   REWIND (UNIT=lu)
```

(continued)

(concluded)

```
    ! Read forward to the desired record.
    DO j = 1, irec
        READ (lu,*) data
    END DO

    ! Tell user.
    WRITE (*,140) irec, data
    140 FORMAT (1X,'The value of record ', I4, ' is ' , ES14.5 )

ELSE

    ! We have an illegal record number.  Tell user.
    WRITE (*,150) irec
    150 FORMAT (1X,'Illegal record number entered: ', I8)

END IF

END PROGRAM
```

Let us test the program with valid data.

```
C>scratch

Enter positive or zero input values.
A negative input value terminates input.
Enter sample    1:
234.
Enter sample    2:
12.34
Enter sample    3:
0.
Enter sample    4:
16.
Enter sample    5:
11.235
Enter sample    6:
2.
Enter sample    7:
-1
Which record do you want to see (1 to    6)?
5
The value of record    5 is    1.12350E+01
```

Next we should test the program with an invalid record number to see that the
error condition is handled properly.

```
C>scratch

Enter positive or zero input values.
A negative input value terminates input.
Enter sample    1:
234.
Enter sample    2:
12.34
Enter sample    3:
0.
```

```
Enter sample    4:
16.
Enter sample    5:
11.235
Enter sample    6:
2.
Enter sample    7:
-1
Which record do you want to see (1 to    6):
7
Illegal record number entered:          7
```

The program appears to be functioning correctly.

EXAMPLE 4–5 Fitting a Line to a Set of Noisy Measurements: The velocity of a falling object in the presence of a constant gravitational field is given by the equation

$$v(t) = at + v_0 \qquad (4\text{--}4)$$

where $v(t)$ is the velocity at any time t, a is the acceleration due to gravity, and v_0 is the velocity at time 0. This equation is derived from elementary physics— it is known to every freshman physics student. If we plot velocity versus time for the falling object, our (v,t) measurement points should fall along a straight line. However, the same freshman physics student also knows that if we go out into the laboratory and attempt to *measure* the velocity versus time of an object, our measurements will *not* fall along a straight line. They may come close, but they will never line up perfectly. Why not? Because we can never make perfect measurements. The measurements always contain some *noise* which distorts them.

There are many cases in science and engineering where there are noisy sets of data such as this, and we wish to estimate the straight line that "best fits" the data. This problem is called the *linear regression* problem. Given a noisy set of measurements (x,y) that appear to fall along a straight line, how can we find the equation of the line

$$y = mx + b \qquad (4\text{--}5)$$

that "best fits" the measurements? If we can determine the regression of coefficients m and b, then we can use this equation to predict the value of y at any given x by evaluating Equation (4–5) for that value of x.

A standard method for finding the regression coefficients m and b is the *method of least squares*. This method is named *least squares* because it produces the line $y = mx + b$ for which the sum of the squares of the differences between the observed y values and the predicted y values is as small as possible. The slope of the least-squares line is given by

$$m = \frac{(\Sigma xy) - (\Sigma x)\bar{y}}{(\Sigma x^2) - (\Sigma x)\bar{x}} \qquad (4\text{--}6)$$

and the intercept of the least squares line is given by

$$b = \bar{y} - m\bar{x} \qquad (4\text{--}7)$$

where

Σx is the sum of the x values.

Σx^2 is the sum of the squares of the x values.

Σxy is the sum of the products of the corresponding x and y values.

$\bar{x}$ is the mean (average) of the x values.

$\bar{y}$ is the mean (average) of the y values.

Write a program that calculates the least-squares slope m and y-axis intercept b for a given set of noisy measured data points (x,y) that are to be found in an input data file.

SOLUTION

1. State the problem.

Calculate the slope m and intercept b of a least-squares line that best fits an input data set consisting of an arbitrary number of (x,y) pairs. The input (x,y) data resides in a user-specified input file.

2. Define the inputs and outputs.

The inputs required by this program are pairs of points (x,y), where x and y are real quantities. Each pair of points will be located on a separate line in the input disk file. The number of points in the disk file is not known in advance.

The outputs from this program are the slope and intercept of the least-squares fitted line plus the number of points going into the fit.

3. Describe the algorithm.

This program can be broken down into four major steps:

```
Get the name of the input file and open it
Accumulate the input statistics
Calculate the slope and intercept
Write out the slope and intercept
```

The first major step of the program is to get the name of the input file and to open the file. We will have to prompt the user to enter the name of the input file. After the file is opened, we must check to see that the open was successful. Next we must read the file and keep track of the number of values entered, plus the sums Σx, Σy, Σx^2, and Σxy. The pseudocode for these steps follows.

```
Initialize n, sum_x, sum_x2, sum_y, and sum_xy to 0
Prompt user for input file name
Open file "filename"
Check for error on OPEN

WHILE
    READ x, y from file "filename"
    IF ( end of file ) EXIT
    n ← n + 1
    sum_x ← sum_x + x
    sum_y ← sum_y + y
    sum_x2 ← sum_x2 + x**2
    sum_xy ← sum_xy + x*y
End of WHILE
```

Next we must calculate the slope and intercept of the least-squares line. The pseudocode for this step is the Fortran versions of Equations (4–5) and (4–6).

```
x_bar ← sum_x / real(n)
y_bar ← sum_y / real(n)
slope ← (sum_xy - sum_x * y_bar) / ( sum_x2 - sum_x * x_bar)
y_int ← y_bar - slope * x_bar
```

Finally, we must write out the results.

```
Write out slope "slope" and intercept "y_int".
```

4. **Turn the algorithm into Fortran statements.**

The final Fortran program is shown in Figure 4–12.

FIGURE 4–12
The least-squares fit program of Example 4–5.

```
PROGRAM least_squares_fit
!
!  Purpose:
!    To perform a least-squares fit of an input data set
!    to a straight line and then print out the resulting slope
!    and intercept values.  The input data for this fit
!    comes from a user-specified input data file.
!
!  Record of revisions:
!      Date        Programmer         Description of change
!      ====        ==========         =====================
!    09/28/95    S. J. Chapman        Original code
!
IMPLICIT NONE

! List of parameters:
INTEGER, PARAMETER :: lu = 18 ! I/o unit for disk I/O

! List of variables.  Note that cumulative variables are all
! initialized to zero.
CHARACTER(len=24) :: filename ! Input file name (<= 24 chars)
INTEGER :: ierror             ! Status flag from I/O statements
INTEGER :: n = 0              ! Number of input data pairs (x,y)
REAL :: slope                 ! Slope of the line
REAL :: sum_x = 0.            ! Sum of all input X values
REAL :: sum_x2 = 0.           ! Sum of all input X values squared
REAL :: sum_xy = 0.           ! Sum of all input X*Y values
REAL :: sum_y = 0.            ! Sum of all input Y values
REAL :: x                     ! An input X value
REAL :: x_bar                 ! Average X value
REAL :: y                     ! An input Y value
REAL :: y_bar                 ! Average Y value
REAL :: y_int                 ! Y-axis intercept of the line

! Prompt user and get the name of the input file.
WRITE (*,1000)
1000 FORMAT (1X,'This program performs a least-squares fit of an ',/, &
             1X,'input data set to a straight line. Enter the name',/ &
             1X,'of the file containing the input (x,y) pairs: ' )
READ (*,'(A)') filename
```

(continued)

(concluded)

```
! Open the input file
OPEN (UNIT=lu, FILE=filename, STATUS='OLD', ACTION='READ', &
      IOSTAT=ierror )

! Check to see if the OPEN failed.
errorcheck: IF ( ierror > 0 ) THEN

   WRITE (*,1020) filename
   1020 FORMAT (1X,'ERROR: File ',A,' does not exist!')

ELSE

   ! File opened successfully. Read the (x,y) pairs from
   ! the input file.
   DO
      READ (lu,*,IOSTAT=ierror) x, y    ! Get pair
      IF ( ierror /= 0 ) EXIT
      n      = n + 1                    !
      sum_x  = sum_x + x                ! Calculate
      sum_y  = sum_y + y                !    statistics
      sum_x2 = sum_x2 + x**2            !
      sum_xy = sum_xy + x * y           !
   END DO

   ! Now calculate the slope and intercept.
   x_bar = sum_x / real(n)
   y_bar = sum_y / real(n)
   slope = (sum_xy - sum_x * y_bar) / ( sum_x2 - sum_x * x_bar)
   y_int = y_bar - slope * x_bar

   ! Tell user.
   WRITE (*, 1030 ) slope, y_int, n
   1030 FORMAT ('0','Regression coefficients for the least-squares line:',&
            /,1X,'  slope (m)     = ', F12.3 &
            /,1X,'  Intercept (b) = ', F12.3,&
            /,1X,'  No of points  = ', I12 )

   ! Close input file, and quit.
   CLOSE (UNIT=lu)

END IF errorcheck

END PROGRAM
```

5. Test the program.

To test this program, we will try a simple data set. For example, if every point in the input data set actually falls along a line, then the resulting slope and intercept should be exactly the slope and intercept of that line. Thus the data set

```
1.1,  1.1
2.2,  2.2
3.3,  3.3
4.4,  4.4
5.5,  5.5
6.6,  6.6
7.7,  7.7
```

should produce a slope of 1.0 and an intercept of 0.0. If we place these values in a file called INPUT and run the program, the results are

```
C>least_squares_fit

This program performs a least-squares fit of an
input data set to a straight line.  Enter the name
of the file containing the input (x,y) pairs:
INPUT
Regression coefficients for the least-squares line:
    slope (m)     =        1.000
    Intercept (b) =         .000
    No of points  =            7
```

Now let's add some noise to the measurements. The data set becomes

```
1.1, 1.01
2.2, 2.30
3.3, 3.05
4.4, 4.28
5.5, 5.75
6.6, 6.48
7.7, 7.84
```

If these values are placed in a file called INPUT1 and the program is run on that file, the results are

```
C>least_squares_fit

This program performs a least-squares fit of an
input data set to a straight line.  Enter the name
of the file containing the input (x,y) pairs:
INPUT1
Regression on coefficients for the least-squares line:
    slope (m)     =        1.024
    Intercept (b) =        -.120
    No of points  =            7
```

If we calculate the answer by hand, it is easy to show that the program gives the correct answers for our two test data sets. The noisy input data set and the resulting least-squares fitted line are shown in Figure 4–13.

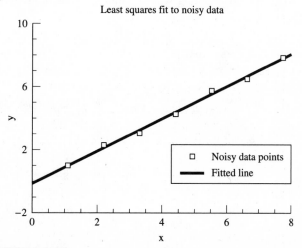

FIGURE 4–13
A noisy input data set and the resulting least-squares fitted line.

The program in Example 4–5 has a problem—it cannot distinguish between the end of an input file and a read error (such as character data instead of real data) in the input file. How would you modify the program to distinguish between these two possible cases?

Quiz 4–3

This quiz provides a quick check to see if you understand the concepts introduced in section 4.5. If you have trouble with the quiz, reread the section, ask your instructor, or discuss the material with a fellow student. The answers to this quiz are found in the back of the book.

Write Fortran statements that perform the functions described below. Unless otherwise stated, assume that variables beginning with the letters I-N are integers and that all other variables are reals.

1. Open an existing file named IN052691 on i/o unit 25 for read-only input and check the status to see if the OPEN was successful.
2. Open a new output file, making sure that you do not overwrite any existing file by the same name. The name of the output file is stored in character variable out_name.
3. Close the file attached to unit 24.
4. Read variables first and last from i/o unit 8 in free format, checking for end of data during the READ.
5. Backspace eight lines in the file attached to i/o unit 13.

Examine the following Fortran statements. Are they correct or incorrect? If they are incorrect, why are they incorrect? Unless otherwise stated, assume that variables beginning with the letters I-N are integers and that all other variables are reals.

6. OPEN (UNIT=35, FILE='DATA1', STATUS='REPLACE',IOSTAT=ierror)
   READ (35,*) n, data1, data2

7. OPEN (UNIT=11, FILE='DATA1', STATUS='SCRATCH',IOSTAT 5 ierror)

8. OPEN (UNIT=15,STATUS='SCRATCH',ACTION='READ',IOSTAT=ierror)

9. OPEN (UNIT=x, FILE='JUNK', STATUS='NEW',IOSTAT=ierror)

10. OPEN (UNIT=9, FILE='TEMP.DAT', STATUS='OLD',ACTION='READ', &
        IOSTAT=ierror)
    READ (9,*) x, y

■ 4.6
SUMMARY

This chapter presents a basic introduction to formatted WRITE and READ statements and to the use of disk files for input and output of data.

In a formatted WRITE statement, the second asterisk of the unformatted WRITE statement (WRITE (*,*)) is replaced by a FORMAT statement number or by a character constant or variable containing the format. The format describes how the output data is to be displayed. It consists of format descriptors that describe the vertical and horizontal position of the data on a page, as well as the display format for integer, real, logical, and character data types.

The format descriptors discussed in this chapter are summarized in Table 4–4.

Formatted READ statements use a format to describe how the input data is to be interpreted. All of the above format descriptors are also legal in formatted READ statements.

A disk file is opened using the OPEN statement, read and written using READ and WRITE statements, and closed using the CLOSE statement. The OPEN statement associates a file with an i/o unit number, and the READ statements and WRITE statements in the program use that i/o unit number to access the file. When the file is closed, the association is broken.

It is possible to move around within a sequential disk file using the BACKSPACE and REWIND statements. The BACKSPACE statement moves the current position in the file backward by one record whenever it is executed, and the REWIND statement moves the current position back to the first record in the file.

■ **TABLE 4–4**
Fortran 90/95 format descriptors discussed in Chapter 4

FORMAT descriptors		Usage
A	Aw	Character data.
E$w.d$		Real data in exponential notation.
ES$w.d$		Real data in scientific notation.
F$w.d$		Real data in decimal notation.
Iw	I$w.m$	Integer data.
Lw		Logical data.
Tc		Tab: move to column c of current line.
nX		Horizontal spacing: skip n spaces.
/		Vertical spacing: move down one line.
where:	c	column number
	d	number of digits to right of decimal place
	m	minimum number of digits to be displayed
	n	number of spaces to skip
	w	field width in characters

4.6.1 Summary of Good Programming Practice

You should adhere to the following guidelines when programming with formatted output statements or with disk i/o. If you follow these guidelines consistently, your code will contain fewer bugs, will be easier to debug, and will be more understandable to others who may need to work with it in the future.

1. The first column of any output line is reserved for a control character. Never put anything in the first column except for the control character. Be especially careful not to write a format descriptor that includes column 1, since the value of the data being written out could cause the program to behave erratically.
2. Always be careful to match the type of data in a WRITE statement to the type of descriptors in the corresponding format. Integers should be associated with I format descriptors; reals with E, ES, or F format descriptors; logicals with L descriptors; and characters with A descriptors. A mismatch between data types and format descriptors will result in an error at execution time.
3. Use the ES format descriptor instead of the E descriptor when displaying data in exponential format to make the output data appear to be in conventional scientific notation.
4. Use an asterisk instead of an i/o unit number when reading from the standard input device or writing to the standard output device. This technique makes your code more portable, since the asterisk is the same on all systems, while the actual unit numbers assigned to standard input and standard output devices may vary from system to system.
5. Always open input files with STATUS='OLD'. By definition, an input file must already exist if we are to read data from it. If the file does not exist, this is an error, and the STATUS='OLD' will catch that error. In addition, you should open input files with ACTION='READ' to prevent accidental overwriting of the input data.
6. Open output files with STATUS='NEW' or STATUS='REPLACE', depending on whether or not you want to preserve the existing contents of the output file. If the file is opened with STATUS='NEW', it should be impossible to overwrite an existing file, so the program cannot accidentally destroy data. If you don't care about the existing data in the output file, open the file with STATUS='REPLACE'; the file will be overwritten if it exists. Open scratch files with STATUS='SCRATCH' so that they will be automatically deleted upon closing.
7. Always include the IOSTAT= clause when reading from disk files to detect an end-of-file or error condition.

4.6.2 Summary of Fortran Statements and Structures

The following summary describes the Fortran statements and structures introduced in this chapter.

BACKSPACE Statement

```
BACKSPACE (UNIT=lu)
```

Example:

```
BACKSPACE (UNIT=8)
```

Description:
The BACKSPACE statement moves the current position of a file pointer back by one record.

CLOSE Statement

```
CLOSE (close_list)
```

Example:

```
CLOSE (UNIT=8)
```

Description:
The CLOSE statement closes the file associated with an i/o unit number.

FORMAT Statement

```
label FORMAT (format descriptor, ... )
```

Example:

```
100    FORMAT (' This is a test: ', I6 )
```

Description:
The FORMAT statement describes the position and format of the data being read or written.

Formatted READ Statement

READ (*unit,format*) *input_list*

Examples:

READ (1,100) time, speed
100 FORMAT (F10.4, F18.4)
READ (1, '(I6)') index

Description:

The formatted READ statement reads data from an input buffer according to the format descriptors specified in the format. The format is a character string that may be specified in a FORMAT statement, a character constant, or a character variable.

Formatted WRITE Statement

WRITE (*unit,format*) *output_list*

Examples:

WRITE (*,100) i, j, slope
100 FORMAT (1X, 2I10, F10.2)
WRITE (*,'(1X, 2I10, F10.2)') i, j, slope

Description:

The formatted WRITE statement outputs the data in the output list according to the format descriptors specified in the format. The format is a character string that may be specified in a FORMAT statement, a character constant, or a character variable.

OPEN Statement

OPEN (*open_list*)

Example:

OPEN (UNIT=8, FILE='IN', STATUS='OLD', ACTION='READ', &
      IOSTAT=ierror)

Description:

The OPEN statement associates a file with an i/o unit number so that it can be accessed by READ or WRITE statements.

REWIND Statement

$$\text{REWIND (UNIT=}lu\text{)}$$

Example:

$$\text{REWIND (UNIT=8)}$$

Description:
  The REWIND statement moves the current position of a file pointer back to the beginning of the file.

4

■ 4.7

EXERCISES

4–1 What is the purpose of a format? In what three ways can formats be specified?

4–2 What is the effect of each of the following characters when it appears in the control character of the Fortran output buffer?
   a. '1'
   b. ' '
   c. '0'
   d. '+'
   e. '2'

4–3 What is printed out by the following Fortran statements?
   a.
```
INTEGER :: i
i = -123
WRITE (*,100) i
100 FORMAT ('1','i = ', I6.5)
```

   b.
```
REAL :: a, b, sum, difference
a = 1.0020E6
b = 1.0001E6
sum = a + b
difference = a - b
WRITE (*,101) a, b, sum, difference
101 FORMAT (1X,'A = ',ES14.6,' B = ',E14.6, &
' Sum = ',E14.6,' Difference = ',F14.6)
```

   c.
```
INTEGER :: i1, i2
i1 = 10
i2 = 4**2
WRITE (*,300) i1 > i2
300 FORMAT (' ','Result = ', L6)
```

4–4 What is printed out by the following Fortran statements?

```
REAL :: a = 1.602E-19, b = 57.2957795, c = -1.
WRITE (*,100) a, b, c
100 FORMAT (' ',ES14.7,2(1X,E13.7))
```

4–5 For the Fortran statements and input data given below, state what the values of each variable will be when the READ statement has been completed.

Statements:

```
CHARACTER(5) :: a
CHARACTER(10) :: b
CHARACTER(15) :: c
READ (*,'(3A10)') a, b, c
```

Input Data:

```
This is a test of reading characters.
——+——+——+——+——+——+——+——+——+——
   5   10   15   20   25   30   35   40   45
```

4–6 For the Fortran statements and input data given below, state what the values of each variable will be when the READ statements have completed.
   a. Statements

```
INTEGER :: item1, item2, item3, item4, item5
INTEGER :: item6, item7, item8, item9, item10
READ (*,*) item1, item2, item3, item4, item5, item6
READ (*,*) item7, item8, item9, item10
```

Input Data:

```
    -300        -250        -210        -160        -135
    -105         -70         -55         -28         -11
      17          55         102         165         225
——+——+——+——+——+——+——+——+——+——+——
   5   10   15   20   25   30   35   40   45   50
```

   b. Statements:

```
INTEGER :: item1, item2, item3, item4, item5
INTEGER :: item6, item7, item8, item9, item10
READ (*,8) item1, item2, item3, item4, item5, item6
READ (*,8) item7, item8, item9, item10
8 FORMAT (4I10)
```

Input Data:
Same as for part *a* above.

4–7 **Table of Logarithms**   Write a Fortran program to generate a table of the base 10 logarithms between 1 and 10 in steps of 0.1. The table should start on a new page, and it should include a title describing the table and the row and column headings. This table should be organized as follows:

	X.0	X.1	X.2	X.3	X.4	X.5	X.6	X.7...
1.0	0.000	0.041	0.079	0.114	...			
2.0	0.301	0.322	0.342	0.362	...			
3.0	...							
4.0	...							
5.0	...							
6.0	...							
7.0	...							
8.0	...							
9.0	...							
10.0	...							

4–8 Example 4–3 illustrates the technique of reading an arbitrary amount of real data from an input data file. Modify that program to read in the data from an input data file and to calculate the mean and standard deviation of the samples in the file.

4–9 A real number `length` is to be displayed in F$w.d$ format with four digits to the right of the decimal point ($d = 4$). If the number is known to lie within the range `-10000. <= length <= 10000.`, what is the minimum field width w that will always be able to display the value of `length`?

4–10 In what columns will the following characters be printed? Why?

```
WRITE (*,'(T30,A)') 'Rubbish!'
```

4–11 Write Fortran statements to perform the functions described below. Assume that variables beginning with I–N are integers and that all other variables are reals.
   a. Skip to a new page and print the title `'INPUT DATA'` starting in column 40.
   b. Skip a line; then display the data point number `ipoint` in columns 6–10 and the data point value `data_1` in columns 15–26. Display the data value in scientific notation with seven significant digits.

4–12 What is the minimum field width necessary to display any real data value in E or ES format with 6 significant bits of accuracy?

4–13 Write a Fortran program that reads in a time in seconds since the start of the day (this value will be somewhere between 0. and 86400.) and writes out the time in the form HH:MM:SS using the 24-hour clock convention. Use the I$w.m$ format descriptor to ensure that leading zeros are preserved in the MM and SS fields. Also, be sure to check the input number of seconds for validity and write an appropriate error message if an invalid number is entered.

4–14 Gravitational Acceleration The acceleration due to the Earth's gravity at any height h above the surface of the Earth is given by the equation

$$g = -G \frac{M}{(R + h)^2} \qquad (4\text{--}8)$$

where G is the gravitational constant (6.672×10^{-11} N m^2/kg^2), M is the mass of the earth (5.98×10^{24} kg), R is the mean radius of the Earth (6371 km), and h is the height above the Earth's surface. If M is measured in kg and R and h are measured in meters, then the resulting acceleration will be in units of meters per second squared. Write a program to calculate the acceleration due to the Earth's gravity in 500-km increments at heights from 0 km to 40,000 km above the surface of the Earth. Print out the results in a table of height versus acceleration with appropriate labels, including the units of the output values.

4–15 What is the proper STATUS to use when opening a file for reading input data? What is the proper STATUS to use when opening a file for writing output data? What is the proper STATUS to use when opening a temporary storage file?

4–16 What is the proper ACTION to use when opening a file for reading input data? What is the proper ACTION to use when opening a file for writing output data? What is the proper ACTION to use when opening a temporary storage file?

4–17 Is a CLOSE statement always required in a Fortran program that uses disk files? Why or why not?

4–18 Write Fortran statements to perform the following functions. Assume that file INPUT.DAT contains a series of real values organized with one value per record.
    a. Open an existing file named INPUT.DAT on i/o unit 98 for input and a new file named NEWOUT.DAT on i/o unit 99 for output.
    b. Read data values from file INPUT.DAT until the end of file is reached. Write all positive data values to the output file.
    c. Close the input and output data files.

4–19 Write a program that reads an arbitrary number of real values from a user-specified input data file, rounds the values to the nearest integer, and writes the integers out to a user-specified output file. Open the input and output files with the appropriate status and be sure to handle end-of-file and error conditions properly.

4–20 Write a program that opens a scratch file and writes the integers 1 through 10 in the first 10 records. Move back six squares in the file and read the value stored in that record. Save that value in variable x. Move back three records in the file and read the value stored in that record. Save that value in variable y. Multiple the two values x and y together. What is their product?

4–21 Examine the following Fortran statements. Are they correct or incorrect? If they are incorrect, why are they incorrect? (Unless otherwise indicated, assume that variables beginning with I-N are integers and that all other variables are reals.)

    a.
```
OPEN (UNIT=1, FILE='INFO.DAT', STATUS='NEW', IOSTAT=ierror)
READ (1,*) i, j, k
```

    b.
```
OPEN (UNIT=17, FILE='TEMP.DAT', STATUS='SCRATCH', IOSTAT=ierror)
```

    c.
```
OPEN (UNIT=99, FILE='INFO.DAT', STATUS='NEW', &
```

```
          ACTION='READWRITE', IOSTAT=ierror)
     WRITE (1,*) i, j, k
```

d.
```
INTEGER :: unit = 8
OPEN (UNIT=unit, FILE='INFO.DAT', STATUS='OLD', IOSTAT=ierror)
READ (8,*) unit
CLOSE (UNIT=unit)
```

e.
```
OPEN (UNIT=9, FILE='OUTPUT.DAT', STATUS='NEW', ACTION='WRITE', &
      IOSTAT=ierror)
WRITE (9,*) mydat1, mydat2
WRITE (9,*) mydat3, mydat4
CLOSE (UNIT=9)
```

4–22 Table of Sines and Cosines   Write a program to generate a table containing the sine and cosine of θ for θ between 0° and 90° in 1° increments. The program should properly label each of the columns in the table.

4–23 Interest Calculations   Suppose that you have a sum of money P in an interest-bearing account at a local bank (P stands for *present value*). If the bank pays you interest on the money at a rate of i percent per year and compounds the interest monthly, the amount of money that you will have in the bank after n months is given by the equation

$$F = P\left(1 + \frac{i}{1200}\right)^n \tag{4–9}$$

where F is the future value of the account and $\frac{i}{12}$ is the monthly percentage interest rate. (The extra factor of 100 in the denominator converts the interest rate from percentages to fractional amounts.) Write a Fortran program that will read an initial amount of money P and an annual interest rate i and will then calculate and write out a table showing the future value of the account every month for the next five years. The table should be written to an output file called `interest`. Be sure to properly label the columns of your table.

4–24 Write a program to read a set of integers from an input data file and locate the largest and smallest values within the data file. Print out the largest and smallest values, together with the lines on which they were found. Assume that you do not know the number of values in the file before the file is read.

4–25 Means   In Exercise 3–31, we wrote a Fortran program that calculated the arithmetic mean (average), rms average, geometric mean, and harmonic mean for a set of numbers. Modify the program to read an arbitrary number of values from an input data file and calculate the means of those numbers. To test the program, place the following values into an input data file and run the program on that file: 1.0, 2.0, 5.0, 4.0, 3.0, 2.1, 4.7, and 3.0.

4–26 Converting Radians to Degrees/Minutes/Seconds   Angles are often measured in degrees (°), minutes ('), and seconds ("), with 360 degrees in a circle, 60 minutes in a degree, and 60 seconds in a minute. Write a program that reads angles in radians from an input disk file and converts them into degrees, minutes, and seconds. Test your program by placing the following four angles expressed in radians into an input file and reading that file into the program: 0.0, 1.0, 3.141592, and 6.0.

4-27 The program `least_squares_fit` from Example 4–5 has a logical error. The error can cause the program to abort with a divide-by-zero error. It slipped through the example because we did not test the program exhaustively for all possible inputs. Find the error and rewrite the program to eliminate it.

4-28 **Dynamically Modifying Format Descriptors** Write a program to read a set of four real values in free format from each line of an input data file and print them out on the standard output device. Each value should be printed in `F14.6` format if it is exactly zero or if it lies in the range $0.01 \le |\text{value}| < 1000.0$ and in `ES14.6` format otherwise. (*Hint:* Define the output format in a character variable and modify it to match each line of data as it is printed.) Test your program on the following data set:

```
  0.00012      -250.     6.02E23      -0.012
      0.0     12345.6     1.6E-19      -1000.
```

```
  +----+----+----+----+----+----+----+----+----+----+
       5   10   15   20   25   30   35   40   45   50
```

4-29 **Correlation Coefficient** The method of least squares is used to fit a straight line to a noisy input data set consisting of pairs of values (x,y). As we saw in Example 4–5, the best fit to equation

$$y = mx + b \qquad (4\text{--}5)$$

is given by

$$m = \frac{(\Sigma xy) - (\Sigma x)\bar{y}}{(\Sigma x^2) - (\Sigma x)\bar{x}} \qquad (4\text{--}6)$$

and

$$b = \bar{y} - m\,\bar{x} \qquad (4\text{--}7)$$

where

Σx is the sum of the x values.
Σx^2 is the sum of the squares of the x values.
Σxy is the sum of the products of the corresponding x and y values.
$\bar{x}$ is the mean (average) of the x values.
$\bar{y}$ is the mean (average) of the y values.

Figure 4–14 shows two data sets and the least-squares fits associated with each one. As you can see, the low-noise data fits the least-squares line much better than the noisy data does. It would be useful to have some quantitative way to describe how well the data fits the least-squares line given by Equations (4–5), (4–6), and (4–7).

The standard statistical measure of the "goodness of fit" of a data set to a least-squares line is called a *correlation coefficient.* The correlation coefficient is equal to 1.0 when there is a perfect positive linear relationship between data x and y, and it is equal to -1.0 when there is a perfect negative linear relationship between data x and y. The correlation coefficient is 0.0 when there is no linear relationship between x and y. The correlation coefficient is given by the equation

$$r = \frac{n(\Sigma xy) - (\Sigma x)(\Sigma y)}{\sqrt{[(n\Sigma x^2) - (\Sigma x)^2][(n\Sigma y^2) - (\Sigma y)^2]}} \qquad (4\text{--}10)$$

where r is the correlation coefficient and n is the number of data points included in the fit.

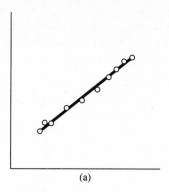
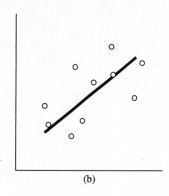

FIGURE 4–14
Two least-squares fits: *(a)* with good, low-noise data; *(b)* with very noisy data.

Write a program to read an arbitrary number of (x,y) data pairs from an input data file and to calculate and print out both the least-squares fit to the data and the correlation coefficient for the fit. If the correlation coefficient is small, ($|r| < 0.2$), write out a warning message to the user.

5

Arrays

An **array** is a group of variables or constants, all of the same type, that are referred to by a single name. The values in the group occupy consecutive locations in the computer's memory (see Figure 5–1). An individual value within the array is called an **array element;** it is identified by the name of the array together with a **subscript** pointing to the particular location within the array. For example, the first variable shown in Figure 5–1 is referred to as a(1), and the fifth variable shown in the figure is referred to as a(5). The subscript of an array is of type INTEGER. Either constants or variables may be used for array subscripts.

Arrays can be extremely powerful tools. They permit us to apply the same algorithm over and over again to many different data items with a simple DO loop. For example, suppose that we need to take the square root of 100 different real numbers. If the numbers are stored as elements of an array a consisting of 100 real values, then the code

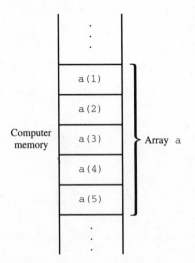

FIGURE 5–1
The elements of an array occupy successive locations in a computer's memory.

```
DO i = 1, 100
   a(i) = SQRT(a(i))
END DO
```

will take the square root of each number and store it back into its original memory location. If we wanted to take the square root of 100 real numbers without using arrays, we would have to write out

```
a1   = SQRT(a1)
a2   = SQRT(a2)
     ...
a100 = SQRT(a100)
```

as 100 separate statements! Arrays are obviously a much cleaner and shorter way to handle repeated similar operations.

Arrays are very powerful tools for manipulating data in Fortran. We can manipulate and perform calculations with individual elements of arrays one by one, with whole arrays at once, or with various subsets of arrays. You will first learn how to declare arrays in Fortran programs, and then you will learn how to use individual array elements, whole arrays, and array subsets in Fortran statements.

■ 5.1

DECLARING ARRAYS

Before an array can be used, its type and the number of elements it contains must be declared to the compiler in a type declaration statement that tells the compiler what sort of data is to be stored in the array and how much memory is required to hold it. For example, a real array voltage containing 16 elements could be declared as follows:[1]

```
REAL, DIMENSION(16) :: voltage
```

The **DIMENSION attribute** in the type declaration statement declares the size of the array being defined. The elements in array voltage would be addressed as voltage(1), voltage(2), etc., up to voltage(16). Similarly, an array of fifty 20-character variables could be declared as follows:

```
CHARACTER(len=20), DIMENSION(50) :: last_name
```

Each element in array last_name would be a 20-character variable, and the elements would be addressed as last_name(1), last_name(2), etc.

Arrays may be declared with more than one subscript so that they may be organized into two or more dimensions. These arrays are convenient for representing data

---

[1] An alternative way to declare an array is to attach the dimension information directly to the array name:

```
REAL :: voltage(16)
```

This declaration style is provided for backward compatibility with earlier versions of Fortran. It is fully equivalent to the array declaration shown above.

that is normally organized into multiple dimensions, such as map information. The number of subscripts declared for a given array is called the **rank** of the array. Both array `voltage` and array `last_name` are rank-1 arrays, since they have only one subscript. We shall see more complex arrays later in the chapter.

The number of elements in a given dimension of an array is called the **extent** of the array in that dimension. The extent of the first (and only) subscript of array `voltage` is 16, and the extent of the first (and only) subscript of array `last_name` is 50. The **shape** of an array is defined as the combination of its rank and the extent of the array in each dimension. Two arrays have the same shape if they have the same rank and the same extent in each dimension. Finally the **size** of an array is the total number of elements declared in that array. For simple rank-1 arrays, the size of the array is the same as the extent of its single subscript. Therefore, the size of array `voltage` is 16, and the size of array `last_name` is 50.

Array constants may also be defined. An array constant is an array consisting entirely of constants. It is defined by placing the constant values between special delimiters, called **array constructors.** The starting delimiter of an array constructor is (/, and the ending delimiter of an array constructor is /). For example, the following expression defines an array constant containing five integer elements:

```
(/ 1, 2, 3, 4, 5 /)
```

5.2
USING ARRAY ELEMENTS IN Fortran STATEMENTS

This section contains some of the practical details involved in using arrays in Fortran programs.

5.2.1 Array Elements Are Just Ordinary Variables

Each element of an array is a variable just like any other variable, and an array element may be used in any place where an ordinary variable of the same type may be used. Array elements may be included in arithmetic and logical expressions, and the results of an expression may be assigned to an array element. For example, assume that arrays `index` and `temp` are declared as

```
INTEGER, DIMENSION(10) :: index
REAL, DIMENSION(3) :: temp
```

Then the following Fortran statements are perfectly valid:

```
index(1) = 1
temp(3) = REAL(index(1)) / 4.
WRITE (*,*) ' index(1) = ', index(1)
```

Under certain circumstances, entire arrays or subsets of arrays can be used in expressions and assignment statements. These circumstances are explained in section 5.3.

5.2.2 Initialization of Array Elements

Just as with ordinary variables, the values in an array must be initialized before use. If an array is not initialized, the contents of the array elements are undefined. In the following Fortran statements, array j is an example of an **uninitialized array.**

```
INTEGER, DIMENSION(10) :: j
WRITE (*,*) ' j(1) = ', j(1)
```

The array j has been declared by the type declaration statement, but no values have been placed into it yet. Since the contents of an uninitialized array are unknown and can vary from computer to computer, the elements of the array should never be used until they are initialized to known values.

5

Good Programming Practice

Always initialize the elements in an array before they are used.

The elements in an array may be initialized by one of three techniques:

1. Using assignment statements.
2. Using type declaration statements at compilation time.
3. Using READ statements.

Initializing arrays with assignment statements

Initial values may be assigned to the array using assignment statements, either element by element in a DO loop or all at once with an array constructor. For example, the following DO loop will initialize all the elements of array array1 to 0.0 one element at a time:

```
REAL, DIMENSION(10) :: array1
DO i = 1, 10
   array1(i) = 0.0
END DO
```

The following assignment statement accomplishes the same function all at once using an array constructor:

```
REAL, DIMENSION(10) :: array1
array1 = (/0.,0.,0.,0.,0.,0.,0.,0.,0.,0./)
```

The simple program shown in Figure 5–2 calculates the squares of the numbers in array number and then prints out the numbers and their squares. Note that the values in array number are initialized element by element with a DO loop.

Initializing arrays in type declaration statements

Initial values may be loaded into an array at compilation time by declaring their values in a type declaration statement. To initialize an array in a type declaration statement, we use an array constructor to declare its initial values in that statement. For

FIGURE 5–2

A program to calculate the squares of the integers from 1 to 10, using assignment statements to initialize the values in array `number`.

```
PROGRAM squares

IMPLICIT NONE

INTEGER :: i
INTEGER, DIMENSION(10) :: number, square

! Initialize number and calculate square.
DO i = 1, 10
   number(i) = i                    ! Initialize number
   square(i) = number(i)**2         ! Calculate square
END DO

!Write out each number and its square.
DO i = 1, 10
   WRITE (*,100) number(i), square(i)
   100 FORMAT (1X,'Number = ',I6,'  Square = ',I6)
END DO

END PROGRAM
```

example, the following statement declares a five-element integer array `array2` and initializes the elements of `array2` to 1, 2, 3, 4, and 5.

```
INTEGER, DIMENSION(5) : array2 = (/ 1, 2, 3, 4, 5 /)
```

The five-element array constant `(/ 1, 2, 3, 4, 5 /)` was used to initialize the five-element array `array2`. In general, the number of elements in the constant must match the number of elements in the array being initialized. Either too few or too many elements will result in a compiler error.

This method works well to initialize small arrays, but what do we do if the array has 100 (or even 1000) elements? Writing out the initial values for a 100-element array would be very tedious and repetitive. To initialize larger arrays, we can use an **implied DO loop.** An implied DO loop has the general form

$$(arg1,\ arg2,\ \dots,\ index = istart,\ iend,\ incr)$$

where *arg1*, *arg2*, etc. are values evaluated each time the loop is executed, and *index*, *istart*, *iend*, and *incr* function exactly as they do for ordinary counting DO loops. For example, the `array2` declaration above could be written using an implied DO loop as

```
INTEGER, DIMENSION(5) :: array2 = (/ (i, i=1,5) /)
```

and a 1000-element array could be initialized to have the values 1, 2, . . . , 1000 using an implied DO loop as follows:

```
INTEGER, DIMENSION(1000) :: array3 = (/ (i, i=1,1000) /)
```

Implied DO loops can be nested or mixed with constants to produce complex patterns. For example, the following statements initialize the elements of `array4` to zero if they are not divisible by five and to the element number if they are divisible by five.

```
INTEGER, DIMENSION(25) :: array4 = (/ ((0,i=1,4),5*j, j=1,5) /)
```

Finally, all the elements of an array can be initialized to a single constant value by simply including the constant in the type declaration statement. In the following example, all of the elements of array5 are initialized to 1.0:

```
REAL, DIMENSION(100) :: array5 = 1.0
```

The program in Figure 5–3 illustrates the use of type declaration statements to initialize the values in an array. It calculates the square roots of the numbers in array value and then prints out the numbers and their square roots.

FIGURE 5–3
A program to calculate the square roots of the integers from 1 to 10, using a type specification statement to initialize the values in array value.

```
PROGRAM square_roots

IMPLICIT NONE

INTEGER :: i
REAL, DIMENSION(10) :: value = (/ (i, i=1,10) /)
REAL, DIMENSION(10) :: square_root

! Calculate the square roots of the numbers.
DO i = 1, 10
   square_root(i) = SQRT(value(i))
END DO

! Write out each number and its square root.
DO i = 1, 10
   WRITE (*,100) value(i), square_root(i)
   100 FORMAT (1X,'Value = ',F5.1,'  Square Root = ',F10.4)
END DO

END PROGRAM
```

Initializing arrays with READ statements

Arrays may also be initialized with READ statements. The use of arrays in I/O statements is described in detail in section 5.4.

5.2.3 Changing the Subscript Range of an Array

The elements of an n-element array are normally addressed using the subscripts 1, 2, ..., n. Thus the elements of array arr declared with the statement

```
REAL, DIMENSION(5) :: arr
```

would be addressed as arr(1), arr(2), arr(3), arr(4), and arr(5). In some problems, however, it is more convenient to address the array elements with other subscripts. For example, the possible grades on an exam might range from 0 to 100. If we wished to accumulate statistics on the number of people scoring any given grade, it would be convenient to have a 101-element array whose subscripts ranged from 0 to 100 instead of 1 to 101. If the subscripts ranged from 0 to 100, each student's exam grade could be used directly as an index into the array.

For such problems, Fortran provides a way to specify the range of numbers that will be used to address the elements of an array. To specify the subscript range, we include the starting and ending subscript numbers in the declaration statement and separate the two numbers with a colon.

```
REAL, DIMENSION(lower_bound:upper_bound) :: array
```

For example, the following arrays all consist of five elements:

```
REAL, DIMENSION(5) :: a1
REAL, DIMENSION(-2:2) :: b1
REAL, DIMENSION(5:9) :: c1
```

Array a1 is addressed with subscripts 1 through 5, array b1 is addressed with subscripts -2 through 2, and array c1 is addressed with subscripts 5 through 9. All three arrays have the same shape, since they have the same number of dimensions and the same extent in each dimension.

In general, the number of elements in a given dimension of an array can be found from the equation

$$\text{extent} = \text{upper\_bound} - \text{lower\_bound} + 1 \qquad (5\text{--}1)$$

The simple program squares_2 shown in Figure 5–4 calculates the squares of the numbers in array number and then prints out the numbers and their squares. The arrays in this example contain 11 elements, addressed by the subscripts $-5, -4, \ldots,$ $0, \ldots, 4, 5$.

FIGURE 5–4
A program to calculate the squares of the integers from -5 to 5, using array elements addressed by subscripts -5 through 5.

```
PROGRAM squares_2

IMPLICIT NONE

INTEGER :: i
INTEGER, DIMENSION(-5:5) :: number, square

! Initialize number and calculate square.
DO i = -5, 5
   number(i) = i                   ! Initialize number
   square(i) = number(i)**2        ! Calculate square
END DO

! Write out each number and its square.
DO i = -5, 5
   WRITE (*,100) number(i), square(i)
   100 FORMAT (1X,'Number = ',I6,' Square = ',I6)
END DO

END PROGRAM
```

When program `squares_2` is executed, the results are

```
C>squares_2
Number =      -5  Square =      25
Number =      -4  Square =      16
Number =      -3  Square =       9
Number =      -2  Square =       4
Number =      -1  Square =       1
Number =       0  Square =       0
Number =       1  Square =       1
Number =       2  Square =       4
Number =       3  Square =       9
Number =       4  Square =      16
Number =       5  Square =      25
```

5.2.4 Out-of-Bounds Array Subscripts

Each element of an array is addressed using an integer subscript. The range of integers that can be used to address array elements depends on the declared extent of the array. For a real array declared as

```
REAL, DIMENSION(5) :: a
```

the integer subscripts 1 through 5 address elements in the array. *Any other integers* (less than 1 or greater than 5) *could not be used as subscripts since they do not correspond to allocated memory locations.* Such integer subscripts are said to be **out of bounds** for the array. But what would happen if we make a mistake and try to access the out-of-bounds element a(6) in a program?

The answer to this question is very complicated, since it varies from processor to processor. On some processors a running Fortran program will check every subscript used to reference an array to see if it is in bounds. If an out-of-bounds subscript is detected, the program will issue an informative error message and stop. Unfortunately, such **bounds checking** requires a lot of computer time, and the program will run very slowly. To make programs run faster, most Fortran compilers make bounds checking optional. If it is turned on, programs run slower, but they are protected from out-of-bounds references. If it is turned off, programs will run much faster, but out-of-bounds references will not be checked. If your Fortran compiler has a bounds-checking option, you should always turn it on during debugging to help detect programming errors. Once the program has been debugged, bounds checking can be turned off if necessary to increase the execution speed of the final program.

Good Programming Practice

Always turn on your Fortran compiler's bounds-checking option during program development and debugging to help you catch programming errors producing out-of-bounds references. You can turn off the bounds-checking option if necessary for greater speed in the final program.

What happens in a program if an out-of-bounds reference occurs and the bounds-checking option is not turned on? Sometimes, the program will abort. Much of the time, though, the computer will simply go to the location in memory at which the referenced array element would have been if it had been allocated and use that memory location. For example, the array a declared above has five elements in it. If a(6) were used in a program, the computer would access the first word beyond the end of array a. Since that memory location will be allocated for a totally different purpose, the program can fail in subtle and bizarre ways that can be almost impossible to track down. Be careful with your array subscripts and always use the bounds checker when you are debugging!

The program shown in Figure 5–5 illustrates the behavior of a Fortran program containing incorrect array references with and without bounds checking turned on. This simple program declares a five-element real array a and a five-element real array b. Array a is initialized with the values 1., 2., 3., 4., and 5., and array b is initialized with the values 10., 20., 30., 40., and 50. Many Fortran compilers will allocate the memory for array b immediately after the memory for array a, as shown in Figure 5–6.

The program in Figure 5–5 uses a DO loop to write out the values in the elements 1 through 6 of array a, despite the fact that array a only has five elements. Therefore, it will attempt to access the out-of-bounds array element a(6).

FIGURE 5–5
A simple program to illustrate the effect of out-of-bounds array references with and without bounds checking turned on.

```
PROGRAM bounds
!
!   Purpose:
!     To illustrate the effect of accessing an out-of-bounds
!     array element.
!
!   Record of revisions:
!       Date          Programmer           Description of change
!       ====          ==========           =====================
!     09/20/95      S. J. Chapman          Original code
!
IMPLICIT NONE

! Declare and initialize the variables used in this program.

INTEGER :: i                    ! Loop index
REAL, DIMENSION(5) :: a = (/ 1., 2., 3., 4., 5./)
REAL, DIMENSION(5) :: b = (/10.,20.,30.,40.,50./)

! Write out the values of array a
DO i = 1, 6
   WRITE (*,100) i, a(i)
   100 FORMAT ( 1X,'a(', I1, ') = ', F6.2 )
END DO

END PROGRAM
```

If this program is compiled with the Lahey Fortran 90 compiler on a PC-compatible computer with bounds checking turned *on,* the result is

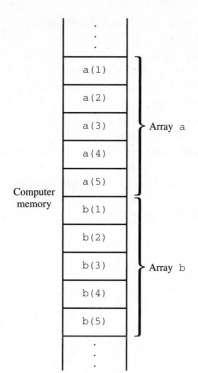

FIGURE 5–6
A computer memory showing a five-element array a immediately followed by a five-element array b. If bounds checking is turned off, some processors may not recognize the end of array a and may treat the memory location after the end of a as a(6).

```
C>bounds

a(1) =    1.00
a(2) =    2.00
a(3) =    3.00
a(4) =    4.00
a(5) =    5.00
a(6
Array subscript exceeds allocated area (see "Arrays" in the Lahey Fortran 90
  Language Reference).
  Error occurred in bounds.f90 at line 26.
```

The program checked each array reference and aborted when an out-of-bounds expression was encountered. Note that the error message tells us not only what is wrong but also the line number at which it occurred. If bounds checking is turned *off*, the result is

```
C>bounds

a(1) =    1.00
a(2) =    2.00
a(3) =    3.00
a(4) =    4.00
a(5) =    5.00
a(6) =   10.00
```

When the program tried to write out a(6), it wrote out the contents of the first memory location after the end of the array. This location just happened to be the first element of array b.

5.2.5 The Use of Named Constants with Array Declarations

In many Fortran programs, arrays are used to store large amounts of information. The amount of information that a program can process depends on the size of the arrays it contains. If the arrays are relatively small, the program will be small and will not require much memory to run, but the program will only be able to handle a small amount of data. On the other hand, if the arrays are large, the program will be able to handle a lot of information but will require a lot of memory to run. The array sizes in such a program are frequently changed to make the program run better for different problems or on different processors.

You should always declare the array sizes using named constants. Named constants make it easy to resize the arrays in a Fortran program. You can change the sizes of all arrays in the following code by simply changing the single named constant `isize`.

```
INTEGER, PARAMETER :: isize = 1000
REAL :: array1(isize)
REAL :: array2(isize)
REAL :: array3(2*isize)
```

This naming convention may seem like a small point, but it is *very* important to the proper maintenance of large Fortran programs. If all related array sizes in a program are declared using named constants and if those same named constants are used in any size tests in the program, then modifying the program later will be relatively simple. Imagine what it would be like if you had to locate and change every reference to array sizes within a 50,000-line program! The process could take weeks to complete and debug. By contrast, the size of a well-designed program could be modified in five minutes by changing only one statement in the code.

Good Programming Practice

Always use named constants to declare the sizes of arrays in a Fortran program to make them easy to change.

EXAMPLE 5–1 Finding the Largest and Smallest Values in a Data Set: To illustrate the use of arrays, we will write a simple program that reads in data values and then finds the largest and smallest numbers in the data set. The program will then write out the values, with the word LARGEST printed next to the largest value and the word SMALLEST printed by the smallest value in the data set.

SOLUTION This program must ask the user for the number of values to read and then read the input values into an array. Once the values are all read, the program must go through the data to find the largest and smallest values in the data set. Finally, it must print out the values, with the appropriate annotations beside the largest and smallest values in the data set.

1. **State the problem.**

We have not yet specified the type of data to be processed. If we are processing integer data, then the problem may be stated as follows: Develop a program to read a user-specified number of integer values from the standard input device, locate the largest and smallest values in the data set, and write out all of the values with the words 'LARGEST' and 'SMALLEST' printed next to the largest and smallest values in the data set.

2. **Define the inputs and outputs.**

This program has two types of inputs:

a. An integer containing the number of integer values to read. This value will come from the standard input device.
b. The integer values in the data set. These values will also come from the standard input device.

The outputs from this program are the values in the data set, with the word 'LARGEST' printed by the largest value and the word 'SMALLEST' printed next to the smallest value.

3. **Describe the algorithm.**

The program can be broken down into four major steps:

```
Get the number of values to read
Read the input values into an array
Find the largest and smallest values in the array
Write out the data with the words 'LARGEST' and 'SMALLEST' at the
    appropriate places
```

The first two major steps of the program are to get the number of values to read in and to read the values into an input array. We must prompt the user for the number of values to read. If that number is less than or equal to the size of the input array, then we should read in the data values. Otherwise, we should warn the user and quit. The detailed pseudocode for these steps follows.

```
Prompt user for the number of input values nvals
Read in nvals
IF nvals <= max_size then
    DO for j = 1 to nvals
        Read in input values
    End of DO
    ...
    ...(Further processing here)
    ...
ELSE
    Tell user that there are too many values for array size
End of IF
END PROGRAM
```

Next we must locate the largest and smallest values in the data set. We will use variables ilarge and ismall as pointers to the array elements having the largest and smallest values. The pseudocode to find the largest and smallest values follows.

```
                              ! Find largest value
                              temp ← input(1)
                              ilarge ← 1
                              DO for j = 2 to nvals
                                  IF input(j) > temp then
                                      temp ← input(j)
                                      ilarge ← j
                                  End of IF
                              End of DO

                              ! Find smallest value
                              temp ← input(1)
                              ismall ← 1
                              DO for j = 2 to nvals
                                  IF input(j) < temp then
                                      temp ← input(j)
                                      ismall ← j
                                  End of IF
                              End of DO
```

The final step is writing out the values with the largest and smallest numbers labeled.

```
                    DO for j = 1 to nvals
                        IF ismall == j then
                            Write input(j) and 'SMALLEST'
                        ELSE IF ilarge == j then
                            Write input(j) and 'LARGEST'
                        ELSE
                            Write input(j)
                    End of DO
```

4. **Turn the algorithm into Fortran statements.**

   The resulting Fortran program is shown in Figure 5–7.

FIGURE 5–7
A program to read in a data set from the standard input device, find the largest and smallest values, and print the values with the largest and smallest values labeled.

```
PROGRAM extremes
!
!  Purpose:
!    To find the largest and smallest values in a data set
!    and to print out the data set with the largest and smallest
!    values labeled.
!
!  Record of revisions:
!      Date          Programmer           Description of change
!      ====          ==========           =====================
!    09/21/95     S. J. Chapman           Original code
!
IMPLICIT NONE

! List of parameters:
INTEGER, PARAMETER :: max_size = 10      ! Max size of data set

! List of variables:
INTEGER, DIMENSION(max_size) :: input    ! Input values
INTEGER :: ilarge                        ! Pointer to largest value
```

(continued)

(concluded)

```
INTEGER :: ismall                           ! Pointer to smallest value
INTEGER :: j                                ! DO loop index
INTEGER :: nvals                            ! Number of vals in data set
INTEGER :: temp                             ! Temporary variable

! Get number of values in data set
WRITE (*,*) 'Enter number of values in data set:'
READ (*,*) nvals

! Is the number <= max_size?
size: IF ( nvals <= max_size) THEN

   ! Get input values.
   in: DO j = 1, nvals
      WRITE (*,100) 'Enter value ', j
      100 FORMAT (' ',A,I3,': ')
      READ (*,*) input(j)
   END DO in

   ! Find the largest value.
   temp = input(1)
   ilarge = 1
   large: DO j = 2, nvals
      IF ( input(j) > temp ) THEN
         temp = input(j)
         ilarge = j
      END IF
   END DO large

   ! Find the smallest value.
   temp = input(1)
   ismall = 1
   small: DO j = 2, nvals
      IF ( input(j) < temp ) THEN
         temp = input(j)
         ismall = j
      END IF
   END DO small

   ! Write out list.
   WRITE (*,110)
   110 FORMAT ('0','The values are:')
   out: DO j = 1, nvals
      IF ( j == ilarge ) THEN
         WRITE (*,'(1X,I6,2X,A)') input(j), 'LARGEST'
      ELSE IF ( J == ismall ) THEN
         WRITE (*,'(1X,I6,2X,A)') input(j), 'SMALLEST'
      ELSE
         WRITE (*,'(1X,I6)') input(j)
      END IF
   END DO out

ELSE size

   ! nvals > max_size.  Tell user and quit.
   WRITE (*,120) nvals, max_size
   120 FORMAT (1X,'Too many input values: ', I6, ' > ', I6)

END IF size

END PROGRAM
```

5

5. **Test the program.**

To test this program, we will use two data sets, one with 6 values and one with 12 values. Running this program with six values yields the following result:

```
C>extremes
Enter number of values in data set:
6
Enter value    1:
-6
Enter value    2:
5
Enter value    3:
-11
Enter value    4:
16
Enter value    5:
9
Enter value    6:
0

The values are:
  -6
   5
 -11 SMALLEST
  16 LARGEST
   9
   0
```

The program correctly labeled the largest and smallest values in the data set. Running this program with 12 values yields the following result:

```
C>extremes
Enter number of values in data set:
12
Too many input values:     12 >     10
```

The program recognized that there were too many input values, and it quit. Thus the program gives the correct answers for both of our test data sets.

The program in Figure 5–7 used the named constant max_size to declare the size of the array and also in all comparisons related to the array. As a result, we could change this program to process up to 1000 values by simply changing the value of max_size from 10 to 1000.

■ 5.3

USING WHOLE ARRAYS AND ARRAY SUBSETS IN Fortran STATEMENTS

Both whole arrays and array subsets may be used in Fortran statements. When they are, the operations are performed on all of the specified array elements simultaneously. This section teaches you how to use whole arrays and array subsets in Fortran statements.

5.3.1 Whole Array Operations

Under certain circumstances, **whole arrays** may be used in arithmetic calculations as though they were ordinary variables. If two arrays are the same *shape,* then they can be used in ordinary arithmetic operations and the operation will be applied on an element-by-element basis. Consider the program in Figure 5–8 in which arrays a, b, c, and d all have four elements. Each element in array c is calculated as the sum of the corresponding elements in arrays a and b, using a DO loop. Array d is calculated as the sum of arrays a and b in a single assignment statement (see Figure 5–9).

FIGURE 5–8
A program illustrating both element-by-element addition and whole array addition.

```
PROGRAM add_arrays

IMPLICIT NONE
INTEGER :: i
REAL, DIMENSION(4) :: a = (/ 1., 2., 3., 4./)
REAL, DIMENSION(4) :: b = (/ 5., 6., 7., 8./)
REAL, DIMENSION(4) :: c, d

! Element-by-element addition
DO i = 1, 4
   c(i) = a(i) + b(i)
END DO

! Whole array addition
d = a + b

! Write out results
WRITE (*,100) 'c', c
WRITE (*,100) 'd', d
100 FORMAT (' ',A,' = ',5(F6.1,1X))

END PROGRAM
```

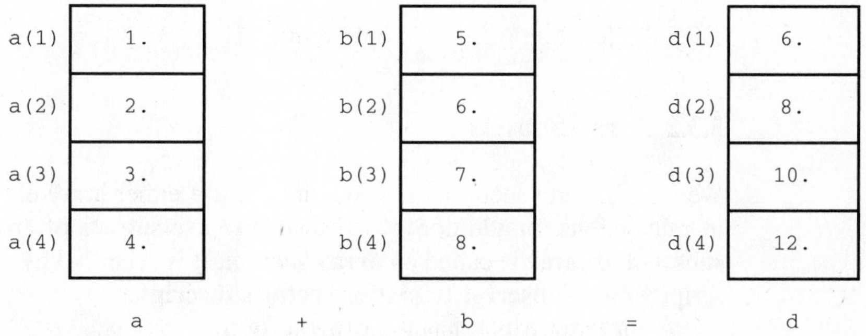

a(1)	1.	b(1)	5.	d(1)	6.
a(2)	2.	b(2)	6.	d(2)	8.
a(3)	3.	b(3)	7.	d(3)	10.
a(4)	4.	b(4)	8.	d(4)	12.
	a	+	b	=	d

FIGURE 5–9
When an operation is applied to two arrays of the same shape, the operation is performed on the arrays on an element-by-element basis.

When this program is executed, the results are exactly the same for both calculations:

```
C>add_arrays
c =      6.0     8.0    10.0    12.0
d =      6.0     8.0    10.0    12.0
```

Two arrays can be used as operands in an intrinsic operation (addition, etc.) if and only if they have the *same shape*. That is, they must have the *same number of dimensions* (the same *rank*) and *the same number of elements in each dimension* (the same *extent*). Two arrays of the same shape are said to be **conformable.** Note that although the two arrays must be the same shape, they do not have to have the same subscript range in each dimension. The following arrays can be added freely, even though the subscript ranges used to address their elements are different:

```
REAL, DIMENSION(1:4) :: a = (/ 1., 2., 3., 4./)
REAL, DIMENSION(5:8) :: b = (/ 5., 6., 7., 8./)
REAL, DIMENSION(101:104) :: c
c = a + b
```

If two arrays are not conformable, then any attempt to perform arithmetic operations with them will produce a compile-time error.

Scalar values are also conformable with arrays. In that case, the scalar value is applied equally to every element of the array. For example, after the following piece of code is executed, array c will contain the values [10., 20., 30., 40.].

```
REAL, DIMENSION(4) :: a = (/ 1., 2., 3., 4./), c
REAL :: b = 10
c = a * b
```

Many Fortran 90/95 intrinsic functions that are used with scalar values will also accept arrays as input arguments and return arrays as results. The returned arrays will contain the result of applying the function to the input array on an element-by-element basis. These functions are called **elemental intrinsic functions,** since they operate on arrays on a element-by-element basis. Most common functions are elemental, including ABS, SIN, COS, EXP, and LOG. A complete list of elemental functions is contained in Appendix B. For example, consider an array a defined as

```
REAL, DIMENSION(4) :: a = (/ -1., 2., -3., 4./)
```

Then the function ABS(a) would return [1., 2., 3., 4.].

5.3.2 Array Subsets

We have already seen that it is possible to use either array elements or entire arrays in calculations. In addition, it is possible to use subsets of arrays in calculations. A subset of an array is called an **array section.** It is specified by replacing an array subscript with a **subscript triplet** or **vector subscript.**

A subscript triplet has the general form

$$subscript\_1 : subscript\_2 : stride$$

where *subscript_1* is the first subscript to be included in the array subset, *subscript_2* is the last subscript to be included in the array subset, and *stride* is the subscript increment through the data set. It works much like an implied DO loop. A subscript triplet specifies the ordered set of all array subscripts starting with *subscript_1* and ending with *subscript_2*, advancing at a rate of `stride` between values. For example, let's define an array `array` as

```
INTEGER, DIMENSION(10) :: array = (/1,2,3,4,5,6,7,8,9,10/)
```

Then the array subset `array(1:10:2)` would be an array containing only elements `array(1)`, `array(3)`, `array(5)`, `array(7)`, and `array(9)`.

Any or all of the components of a subscript triplet may be defaulted. If *subscript_1* is missing from the triplet, it defaults to the subscript of the first element in the array. If *subscript_2* is missing from the triplet, it defaults to the subscript of the last element in the array. If `stride` is missing from the triplet, it defaults to one. All of the following possibilities are examples of legal triplets:

```
subscript_1 : subscript_2 : stride
subscript_1 : subscript_2
subscript_1 :
subscript_1 :: stride
: subscript_2
: subscript_2 : stride
:: stride
:
```

EXAMPLE 5–2 Specifying Array Sections with Subscript Triplets: Assume the following type declarations statements:

```
INTEGER :: i = 3, j = 7
REAL, DIMENSION(10) :: a = (/1.,-2.,3.,-4.,5.,-6.,7.,-8.,9.,-10./)
```

Determine the number of elements in and the contents of the array sections specified by each of the following subscript triplets:

a. `a(:)`
b. `a(i:j)`
c. `a(i:j:i)`
d. `a(i:j:j)`
e. `a(i:)`
f. `a(:j)`
g. `a(::i)`

SOLUTION

a. `a(:)` is identical to the original array: [1.,−2.,3.,−4.,5.,−6.,7.,−8.,9.,−10.]
b. `a(i:j)` is the array subset starting at element 3 and ending at element 7, with a default stride of 1: [3.,−4.,5.,−6.,7.]
c. `a(i:j:i)` is the array subset starting at element 3 and ending at element 7, with a stride of 3: [3.,−6.]
d. `a(i:j:j)` is the array subset starting at element 3 and ending at element 7, with a stride of 7: [3.]
e. `a(i:)` is the array subset starting at element 3 and by default ending at element 10 (the end of the array), with a default stride of 1: [3.,−4.,5.,−6.,7., −8.,9.,−10.]

    f. `a(:j)` is the array subset starting by default at element 1 and ending at element 7, with a default stride of 1: [1.,−2.,3.,−4.,5.,−6.,7.]

    g. `a(::i)` is the array subset starting by default at element 1 and ending by default at element 10, with a stride of 3: [1.,−4.,7.,−10.]

Subscript triplets select ordered subsets of array elements for use in calculations. In contrast, vector subscripts allow arbitrary combinations of array elements to be selected for use in an operation. A *vector subscript* is a one dimensional integer array specifying the array elements to be used in a calculation. The array elements may be specified in any order, and array elements may be specified more than once. The resulting array will contain one element for each subscript specified in the vector. For example, consider the following type declaration statements:

```
INTEGER, DIMENSION(5) :: vec = (/1, 6, 4, 1, 9 /)
REAL, DIMENSION(10) :: a = (/1.,-2.,3.,-4.,5.,-6.,7.,-8.,9.,-10./)
```

With these definitions, `a(vec)` would be the array [1., −6., −4., 1., 9.].

If a vector subscript includes any array element more than once, then the resulting array section is called a **many-one array section.** Such an array section cannot be used on the left side of an assignment statement, because it would specify that two or more different values should be assigned to the same array element at the same time! For example, consider the following Fortran statements:

```
INTEGER, DIMENSION(5) :: vec = (/1, 2, 1 /)
REAL, DIMENSION(10) :: a = (/10.,20.,30./)
REAL, DIMENSION(2) :: b
b(vec) = a
```

The assignment statement attempts to assign both the value 10. and the value 30. to array element `b(1)`, which is impossible.

■ 5.4
INPUT AND OUTPUT

It is possible to perform I/O operations on either individual array elements or entire arrays. Both types of I/O operations are described in this section.

5.4.1 Input and Output of Array Elements

You already know that an *array element* is a variable just like any other variable and that an array element may be used in any place where an ordinary variable of the same type may be used. Therefore, `READ` and `WRITE` statements containing array elements are just like `READ` and `WRITE` statements for any other variables. To write out specific elements from an array, just name them in the argument list of the `WRITE` statement. For example, the following code writes out the first five elements of the real array `a`.

```
WRITE (*,100) a(1), a(2), a(3), a(4), a(5)
100 FORMAT (1X,'a = ', 5F10.2)
```

5.4.2 The Implied DO Loop

The implied DO loop is also permitted in I/O statements. It allows an argument list to be written many times as a function of an index variable. Every argument in the argument list is written once for each value of the index variable in the implied DO loop. With an implied DO loop, the previous statement becomes

```
       WRITE (*,100) ( a(i), i = 1, 5 )
   100 FORMAT (1X,'a = ', 5F10.2)
```

The argument list in this case contains only one item: $a(i)$. This list is repeated once for each value of the index variable i. Since i takes on the values from 1 to 5, the array elements $a(1), a(2), a(3), a(4)$, and $a(5)$ will be written.

The general form of a WRITE or READ statement with an implied DO loop is

```
   WRITE (unit,format) (arg1, arg2, ..., index = istart, iend, incr)
   READ  (unit,format) (arg1, arg2, ..., index = istart, iend, incr)
```

where *arg1*, *arg2*, etc., are the values to be written or read. The variable *index* is the DO loop index, and *istart*, *iend*, and *incr* are, respectively, the starting value, ending value, and increment of the loop index variable. The index and all of the loop control parameters should be of type INTEGER.

For a WRITE statement containing an implied DO loop, each argument in the argument list is written once each time the loop is executed. Therefore, a statement like

```
       WRITE (*,1000) (i, 2*i, 3*i, i = 1, 3)
   1000 FORMAT (1X,9I6)
```

will write out nine values on a single line:

```
     1    2    3    2    4    6    3    6    9
```

Now let's look at a slightly more complicated example using arrays with an implied DO loop. Figure 5–10 shows a program that calculates the square root and cube root of a set of numbers and then prints out a table of square and cube roots. The program computes square roots and cube roots for all numbers between 1 and max_size, where max_size is a parameter. What will the output of this program look like?

FIGURE 5–10

A program that computes the square and cube roots of a set of numbers and then writes them out using an implied DO loop.

```
PROGRAM square_and_cube_roots
!
!  Purpose:
!    To calculate a table of numbers, square roots, and cube roots
!    using an implied DO loop to output the table.
!
!  Record of revisions:
!     Date         Programmer            Description of change
!     ====         ==========            =====================
!    08/22/95      S. J. Chapman         Original code
!
IMPLICIT NONE
```

(continued)

(concluded)

```
! List of parameters:
INTEGER, PARAMETER :: max_size = 10

! List of variables:
INTEGER :: j                             ! Loop index
REAL, DIMENSION(max_size) :: value        ! Array of numbers
REAL, DIMENSION(max_size) :: square_root ! Array of square roots
REAL, DIMENSION(max_size) :: cube_root   ! Array of cube roots

! Calculate the square roots & cube roots of the numbers.
DO j = 1, max_size
   value(j) = real(j)
   square_root(j) = sqrt(value(j))
   cube_root(j) = value(j)**(1./3.)
END DO

! Write out each number, its square root, and its cube root.
WRITE (*,100)
100 FORMAT ('0',20X,'Table of Square and Cube Roots',/,&
            4X,' Number      Square Root  Cube Root', &
            3X,' Number      Square Root  Cube Root',/,&
            4X,' ======      ===========  =========',&
            3X,' ======      ===========  =========')
WRITE (*,110) (value(j), square_root(j), cube_root(j), j = 1, max_size)
100 FORMAT (2(4X,F6.0,9X,F6.4,6X,F6.4))

END PROGRAM
```

The implied DO loop in this example will be executed 10 times, with j taking on every value between 1 and 10 (the loop increment is defaulted to 1 here). During each iteration of the loop, the entire argument list will be written out. Therefore, this WRITE statement will write out 30 values, six per line. The resulting output is

```
                Table of Square and Cube Roots
 Number     Square Root   Cube Root    Number     Square Root   Cube Root
 ======     ===========   =========    ======     ===========   =========
   1.         1.0000        1.0000       2.          1.4142        1.2599
   3.         1.7321        1.4422       4.          2.0000        1.5874
   5.         2.2361        1.7100       6.          2.4495        1.8171
   7.         2.6458        1.9129       8.          2.8284        2.0000
   9.         3.0000        2.0801      10.          3.1623        2.1544
```

Nested implied DO loops

Like ordinary DO loops, implied DO loops may be *nested*. If they are nested, the inner loop will execute completely for each step in the outer loop. As a simple example, consider the following statements:

```
WRITE (*,100) ((i, j, j = 1, 3), i = 1, 2)
100 FORMAT (1X,I5,1X,I5)
```

Two implied DO loops appear in this WRITE statement. The index variable of the inner loop is j, and the index variable of the outer loop is i. When the WRITE statement is executed, variable j will take on values 1, 2, and 3 while i is 1, and then 1, 2, and 3 while i is 2. The output from this statement will be

```
               1     1
               1     2
               1     3
               2     1
               2     2
               2     3
```

Nested implied DO loops are important when working with arrays having two or more dimensions, as you will see later in the chapter.

The difference between I/O with standard DO loops and I/O with implied DO loops

Array input and output can be performed either with a standard DO loop containing I/O statements or with an implied DO loop. However, there are subtle differences between the two types of loops. To better understand those differences, let's compare the same output statement written with both types of loops. We will assume that integer array arr is initialized as follows

```
INTEGER, DIMENSION(5) :: arr = (/ 1, 2, 3, 4, 5 /)
```

and compare output using a regular DO loop with output using an implied DO loop. An output statement using an ordinary DO loop is shown next:

```
DO i = 1, 5
    WRITE (*,1000) arr(i), 2.*arr(i). 3*arr(i)
    1000 FORMAT (1X,6I6)
END DO
```

In this loop the WRITE statement is executed five times. In fact, this loop is equivalent to the following statements:

```
WRITE (*,1000) arr(1), 2.*arr(1). 3*arr(1)
WRITE (*,1000) arr(2), 2.*arr(2). 3*arr(2)
WRITE (*,1000) arr(3), 2.*arr(3). 3*arr(3)
WRITE (*,1000) arr(4), 2.*arr(4). 3*arr(4)
WRITE (*,1000) arr(5), 2.*arr(5). 3*arr(5)
1000 FORMAT (1X,6I6)
```

An output statement using an implied DO loop is shown next:

```
WRITE (*;1000) (arr(i), 2.*arr(i). 3*arr(i), i = 1, 5)
1000 FORMAT (1X,6I6)
```

Here, there is only one WRITE statement, but the WRITE statement has 15 arguments. In fact, the WRITE statement with the implied DO loop is equivalent to

```
WRITE (*,1000) arr(1), 2.*arr(1). 3*arr(1), &
               arr(2), 2.*arr(2). 3*arr(2), &
               arr(3), 2.*arr(3). 3*arr(3), &
               arr(4), 2.*arr(4). 3*arr(4), &
               arr(5), 2.*arr(5). 3*arr(5)
1000 FORMAT (1X,6I6)
```

The principal difference between having many WRITE statements with few arguments and one WRITE statement with many arguments is in the behavior of the associated FORMAT statement. Remember that each WRITE statement starts at the beginning of the FORMAT statement. Therefore, each of the five WRITE statements in the standard DO loop will start over at the beginning of the FORMAT statement, and only the first three of the six I6 descriptors will be used. The output of the standard DO loop will be

```
1     2     3
2     4     6
3     6     9
4     8    12
5    10    15
```

On the other hand, the implied DO loop produces a single WRITE statement with 15 arguments, so the associated FORMAT statement will be used completely $2\frac{1}{2}$ times. The output of the implied DO loop will be

```
1     2     3     2     4     6
3     6     9     4     8    12
5    10    15
```

The same concept applies to a comparison of READ statements using standard DO loops with READ statements using implied DO loops. (See Exercise 5–9 at the end of the chapter.)

5.4.3 Input and Output of Whole Arrays and Array Sections

Entire arrays or array sections may also be read or written with READ and WRITE statements. If an array name is mentioned without subscripts in a Fortran I/O statement, then the compiler assumes that every element in the array is to be read in or written out. If an array section is mentioned in a Fortran I/O statement, then the compiler assumes that the entire section is to be read in or written out. Figure 5–11 shows

FIGURE 5–11
An example program illustrating array I/O.

```
PROGRAM array_io
!
!  Purpose:
!    To illustrate array I/O.
!
!  Record of revisions:
!    Date        Programmer         Description of change
!    ====        ==========         =====================
!    10/10/95    S. J. Chapman      Original code
!
IMPLICIT NONE

! List of variables
REAL, DIMENSION(5) :: a = (/1.,2.,3.,20.,10./) ! 5-element test array
INTEGER, DIMENSION(4) :: vec = (/4,3,4,5/)      ! vector subscript

! Output entire array.
WRITE (*,100) a
100 FORMAT ( 2X, 5F8.3 )

! Output array section selected by a triplet.
WRITE (*,100) a(2::2)

! Output array section selected by a vector subscript.
WRITE (*,100) a(vec)

END PROGRAM
```

a simple example of using an array and two array sections in I/O statements. The output from this program is

```
1.000    2.000    3.000   20.000   10.000
2.000   20.000
20.000    3.000   20.000   10.000
```

Quiz 5–1

This quiz provides a quick check to see if you understand the concepts introduced in sections 5.1 through 5.4. If you have trouble with the quiz, reread the sections, ask your instructor, or discuss the material with a fellow student. The answers to this quiz are found in the back of the book.

For questions 1 to 3, determine the length of the array specified by each of the following declaration statements and the valid subscript range for each array.

1. `INTEGER :: itemp(15)`

2. `LOGICAL :: test(0:255)`

3. ```
   INTEGER, PARAMETER :: i1 = -20
   INTEGER, PARAMETER :: i2 = -1
   REAL, DIMENSION(i1:i1*i2) :: a
   ```

Determine which of the following Fortran statements are valid. For each valid statement, specify what will happen in the program. Assume default typing for any variable not explicitly typed.

4. ```
   REAL :: phase(0:11) = (/0., 1., 2., 3., 3., 3., &
                           3., 3., 3., 2., 1., 0. /)
   ```

5. `REAL, DIMENSION(10) :: phase = 0.`

6. ```
   INTEGER :: data1(256)
   data1 = 0
   data1(10:256:10) = 1000
   WRITE (*,100) data1
   100 FORMAT (1X,10I8)
   ```

7. ```
   REAL, DIMENSION(21:31) :: array1 = 10.
   REAL, DIMENSION(10) :: array2 = 3.
   WRITE (*,100) array1 + array2
   100 FORMAT (1X,10I8)
   ```

8. ```
   INTEGER :: i, j
   INTEGER, DIMENSION(10) :: sub1
   INTEGER, DIMENSION(0:9) :: sub2
   INTEGER, DIMENSION(100) :: in = &
        (/((0,i=1,9),j*10,j=1,10)/)
   sub1 = in(10:100:10)
   sub2 = sub1 / 10
   WRITE (*,100) sub1 * sub2
   100 FORMAT (1X,10I8)
   ```

(continued)
   ```

(concluded)

```
 9. REAL, DIMENSION(-3:0) :: error
    error(-3) = 0.00012
    error(-2) = 0.0152
    error(-1) = 0.0
    WRITE (*,500) error
    500 FORMAT (T6,error = ,/,(3X,I6))

10. INTEGER, PARAMETER :: max = 10
    INTEGER :: i
    INTEGER, DIMENSION(max) :: ivec1 = (/(i,i=1,10)/)
    INTEGER, DIMENSION(max) :: ivec2 = (/(i,i=10,1,-1)/)
    REAL, DIMENSION(max) :: data1
    data1 = real(ivec1)**2
    WRITE (*,500) data1(ivec2)
    500 FORMAT (1X,'Output = ',/,5(3X,F7.1))

11. INTEGER, PARAMETER :: npoint = 10
    REAL, DIMENSION(npoint) :: mydata
    DO i = 1, npoint
       READ (*,*) mydata
    END DO
```

5.5
EXAMPLE PROBLEMS

Now we will examine two problems that illustrate the use of arrays.

EXAMPLE 5–3 Sorting Data: Many scientific and engineering applications need to sort a random input data set so that the numbers in the data set are either all in *ascending order* (lowest to highest) or all in *descending order* (highest to lowest). For example, suppose that you were a zoologist studying a large population of animals and that you wanted to identify the largest 5 percent of the animals in the population. The most straightforward way to approach this problem would be to sort the sizes of all of the animals in the population into ascending order and take the top 5 percent of the values.

Sorting data into ascending or descending order seems to be an easy job. After all, we do it all the time. It is a simple matter for us to sort the data (10, 3, 6, 4, 9) into the order (3, 4, 6, 9, 10). How do we do it? We first scan the input data list (10, 3, 6, 4, 9) to find the smallest value in the list (3), then scan the remaining input data (10, 6, 4, 9) to find the next smallest value (4), and so on until the complete list is sorted.

In fact, sorting can be a very difficult job. As the number of values to be sorted increases, the time required to perform the simple sort described here increases rapidly, since we must scan the input data set once for each value sorted. For very large data sets, this technique just takes too long to be practical. Even worse, how would we sort the data if there were too many numbers to fit into the main memory of the computer? The development of efficient sorting techniques for large data sets is an active area of research and is the subject of whole courses and books.

In this example we confine ourselves to the simplest possible algorithm to illustrate the concept of sorting. This simplest algorithm is called the *selection sort.* It is a computer implementation of the mental math just described. The basic algorithm for the selection sort is

1. Scan the list of numbers to be sorted to locate the smallest value in the list. Place that value at the front of the list by swapping it with the value currently at the front of the list. If the value at the front of the list is already the smallest value, then do nothing.
2. Scan the list of numbers from position 2 to the end to locate the next smallest value in the list. Place that value in position 2 of the list by swapping it with the value currently at that position. If the value in position 2 is already the next smallest value, then do nothing.
3. Scan the list of numbers from position 3 to the end to locate the third smallest value in the list. Place that value in position 3 of the list by swapping it with the value currently at that position. If the value in position 3 is already the third smallest value, then do nothing.
4. Repeat this process until you reach the next-to-last position in the list. After the next-to-last position in the list has been processed, the sort is complete.

Note that if we are sorting N values, this sorting algorithm requires $N - 1$ scans through the data to accomplish the sort.

This process is illustrated in Figure 5–12. Since the data set to be sorted has five values, we will make four scans through the data. During the first pass through the entire data set, the minimum value is 3, so the 3 is swapped with the 10, which was in position 1. Pass 2 searches for the minimum value in positions 2 through 5. That minimum is 4, so the 4 is swapped with the 10 in position 2. Pass 3

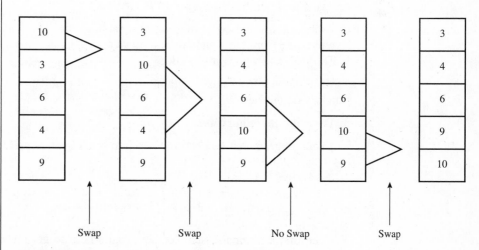

FIGURE 5–12
An example problem demonstrating the selection sort algorithm.

searches for the minimum value in positions 3 through 5. That minimum is 6, which is already in position 3, so no swapping is required. Finally, pass 4 searches for the minimum value in positions 4 through 5. That minimum is 9, so the 9 is swapped with the 10 in position 4, and the sort is completed.

> **Programming Pitfalls**
> The selection sort algorithm is the easiest sorting algorithm to under-
> stand, but it is computationally inefficient. *It should never be applied
> to sort really large data sets* (say, sets with more than 1000 elements).
> Over the years, computer scientists have developed much more efficient
> sorting algorithms. We will encounter one such algorithm (the *heapsort
> algorithm*) in Chapter 13.

We will now develop a program to read in a data set from a file, sort it into ascending order, and display the sorted data set.

SOLUTION This program must be able to ask the user for the name of the file to be sorted, open that file, read the input data, sort the data, and write out the sorted data. The design process for this problem follows.

1. State the problem.

We have not yet specified the type of data to be sorted. If the data is real, then the problem may be stated as follows: Develop a program to read an arbi-trary number of real input data values from a user-supplied file, sort the data into ascending order, and write the sorted data to the standard output device.

2. Define the inputs and outputs.

This program has two types of inputs:

a. A character string containing the file name of the input data file. This string will come from the standard input device.
b. The real data values in the file.

The outputs from this program are the sorted real data values written to the standard output device.

3. Describe the algorithm.

This program can be broken down into five major steps:

```
Get the input file name
Open the input file
Read the input data into an array
Sort the data in ascending order
Write the sorted data
```

The first three major steps of the program are to get the name of the input file, to open the file, and to read in the data. We must prompt the user for the in-put file name, read in the name, and open the file. If the file open is successful, we must read in the data, keeping track of the number of values that have been

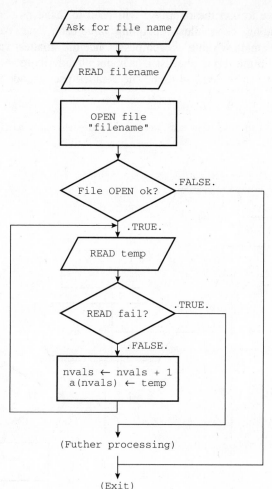

FIGURE 5–13
Flowchart for reading values to sort from an input file.

read. Since we don't know how many data values to expect, a while loop is appropriate for the READ. A flowchart for these steps is shown in Figure 5–13, and the detailed pseudocode follows.

```
Prompt user for the input file name "filename"
Read the file name "filename"
OPEN file "filename"
IF OPEN is successful THEN
    WHILE
        Read value into temp
        IF read not successful EXIT
        nvals ← nvals + 1
        a(nvals) ← temp
    End of WHILE
    ...
    ...                     (Insert sorting step here)
    ...                     (Insert writing step here)
End of IF
```

Next we have to sort the data. We will need to make `nvals-1` passes through the data, finding the smallest remaining value each time. We will use a pointer to locate the smallest value in each pass. Once the smallest value is found, it will be swapped to the top of the list if it is not already there. A flowchart for these steps is shown in Figure 5–14, and the detailed pseudocode follows.

```
DO for i = 1 to nvals-1

    ! Find the minimum value in a(i) through a(nvals)
    iptr ← i
```

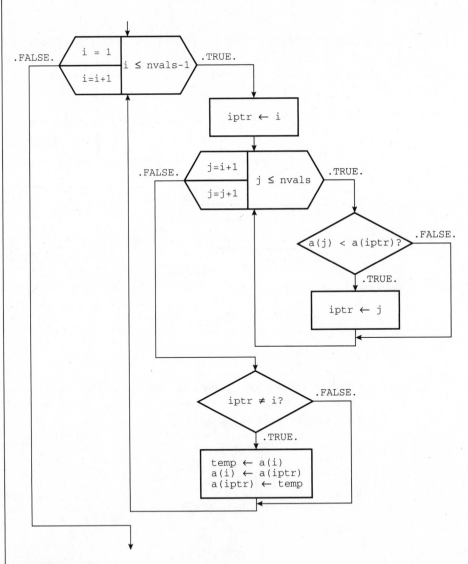

FIGURE 5–14
Flowchart for sorting values with a selection sort.

```
            DO for j = i+1 to nvals
                IF a(j) < a(iptr) THEN
                    iptr ← j
                END of IF
            END of DO

            ! iptr now points to the min value, so swap a(iptr) with
            ! a(i) if iptr /= i.
            IF i /= iptr THEN
                temp ← a(i)
                a(i) ← a(iptr)
                a(iptr) ← temp
            END of IF
        END of DO
```

The final step is writing out the sorted values. No refinement of the pseudocode is required for that step. The final pseudocode is the combination of the reading, sorting, and writing steps.

4. **Turn the algorithm into Fortran statements.**

The resulting Fortran program is shown in Figure 5–15.

FIGURE 5–15

A program to read values from an input data file and to sort them into ascending order.

```
PROGRAM sort1
!
!  Purpose:
!    To read in a real input data set, sort it into ascending order
!    using the selection sort algorithm, and write the sorted
!    data to the standard output device.
!
!  Record of revisions:
!      Date         Programmer          Description of change
!      ====         ==========          =====================
!    09/20/95     S. J. Chapman         Original code
!
IMPLICIT NONE

! List of parameters:
INTEGER, PARAMETER :: max_size = 10

! List of variables:
REAL, DIMENSION(max_size) :: a   ! Data array to sort
CHARACTER(len=20) :: filename     ! Input data file name
INTEGER :: i                      ! Loop index
INTEGER :: iptr                   ! Pointer to smallest value
INTEGER :: j                      ! Loop index
INTEGER :: nvals = 0              ! Number of data values to sort
INTEGER :: status                 ! I/O status: 0 for success
REAL :: temp                      ! Temporary variable for swapping

! Get the name of the file containing the input data.
WRITE (*,1000)
1000 FORMAT (1X,'Enter the file name with the data to be sorted: ')
READ (*,'(A20)') filename
```

(continued)

(concluded)

```fortran
! Open input data file.  Status is OLD because the input data must
! already exist.
OPEN ( UNIT=9, FILE=filename, STATUS='OLD', ACTION='READ', &
       IOSTAT=status )

! Was the OPEN successful?
fileopen: IF ( status == 0) THEN          ! Open successful

   ! The file was opened successfully, so read the data to sort
   ! from it, sort the data, and write out the results.
   ! First read in data.
   DO
      READ (9, *, IOSTAT=status) temp      ! Get value
      IF ( status /= 0 ) EXIT              ! Exit on end of data
      nvals = nvals + 1                    ! Bump count
      a(nvals) = temp                      ! Save value in array
   END DO

   ! Now, sort the data.
   outer: DO i = 1, nvals-1

      ! Find the minimum value in a(i) through a(nvals)
      iptr = i
      inner: DO j = i+1, nvals
         minval: IF ( a(j) < a(iptr) ) THEN
            iptr = j
         END IF minval
      END DO inner

      ! iptr now points to the minimum value, so swap a(iptr) with
      ! a(i) if i /= iptr.
      swap: IF ( i /= iptr ) THEN
         temp    = a(i)
         a(i)    = a(iptr)
         A(iptr) = temp
      END IF swap

   END DO outer

   ! Now write out the sorted data.
   WRITE (*,'(1X,A)') 'The sorted output data values are: '
   WRITE (*,'(4X,F10.4)') ( a(i), i = 1, nvals )

ELSE fileopen

   ! Else file open failed.  Tell user.
   WRITE (*,1050) status
   1050 FORMAT (1X,'File open failed--status = ', I6)

END IF fileopen

END PROGRAM
```

5. **Test the program.**

To test this program, we will create an input data file and run the program with it. The data set will contain a mixture of positive and negative numbers as well as at least one duplicated value to see if the program works properly under those conditions. The following data set will be placed in file `INPUT2`:

```
13.3
12.
-3.0
 0.
 4.0
 6.6
 4.
-6.
```

Running these file values through the program yields the following result:

```
C>sort1
Enter the file name containing the data to be sorted:
input2
The sorted output data values are:
     -6.0000
     -3.0000
       .0000
      4.0000
      4.0000
      6.6000
     12.0000
     13.3000
```

The program gives the correct answers for our test data set. Note that it works for both positive and negative numbers as well as for repeated numbers.

To be certain that our program works properly, we must test it for every possible type of input data. This program worked properly for the test input data set, but will it work for *all* input data sets? Study the code now and see if you can spot any flaws before continuing to the next paragraph.

The program has a major flaw that must be corrected. If there are more than 10 values in the input data file, this program will attempt to store input data in memory locations a(11), a(12), etc., which have not been allocated in the program (this is an out-of-bounds or **array overflow** condition). If bounds checking is turned on, the program will abort when we try to write to a(11). If bounds checking is not turned on, the results are unpredictable and vary from computer to computer. This program must be rewritten to prevent it from attempting to write into locations beyond the end of the allocated array. This can be done by checking to see if the number of values exceeds max_size before storing each number into array a. The corrected flowchart for reading in the data is shown in Figure 5–16, and the corrected program is shown in Figure 5–17.

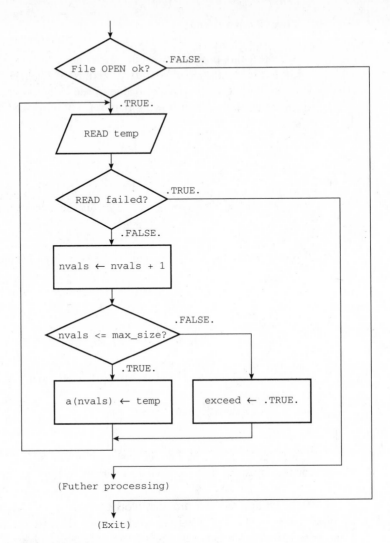

FIGURE 5–16
Corrected flowchart for reading the values to sort from an input file
without causing an array overflow.

FIGURE 5–17
A corrected version of the sort program that detects array overflows.

```
PROGRAM sort2
!
!  Purpose:
!    To read in a real input data set, sort it into ascending order
!    using the selection sort algorithm, and write the sorted
!    data to the standard output device.
!
```

(continued)

```
!  Record of revisions:
!      Date         Programmer          Description of change
!      ====         ==========          =====================
!    09/20/95     S. J. Chapman         Original code
! 1  09/23/95     S. J. Chapman         Modified to protect against array
!                                       overflow.
!
IMPLICIT NONE

! List of parameters:
INTEGER, PARAMETER :: max_size = 10

! List of variables:
REAL, DIMENSION(max_size) :: a     ! Data array to sort
LOGICAL :: exceed = .FALSE.        ! Logical indicating that array
                                   ! limits are exceeded
CHARACTER(len=20) :: filename      ! Input data file name
INTEGER :: i                       ! Loop index
INTEGER :: iptr                    ! Pointer to smallest value
INTEGER :: j                       ! Loop index
INTEGER :: nvals = 0               ! Number of data values to sort
INTEGER :: status                  ! I/O status: 0 for success
REAL :: temp                       ! Temporary variable for swapping

! Get the name of the file containing the input data.
WRITE (*,1000)
1000 FORMAT (1X,'Enter the file name with the data to be sorted: ')
READ (*,'(A20)') filename

! Open input data file.  Status is OLD because the input data must
! already exist.
OPEN ( UNIT=9, FILE=filename, STATUS='OLD', ACTION='READ', &
       IOSTAT=status )

! Was the OPEN successful?
fileopen: IF ( status == 0 ) THEN           ! Open successful

   ! The file was opened successfully, so read the data to sort
   ! from it, sort the data, and write out the results.
   ! First read in data.
   DO
      READ (9, *, IOSTAT=status) temp        ! Get value
      IF ( status /= 0 ) EXIT                ! Exit on end of data
      nvals = nvals + 1                      ! Bump count
      size: IF ( nvals <= max_size) THEN     ! Too many values?
         a(nvals) = temp                     ! No: Save value in array
      ELSE
         exceed = .TRUE.                     ! Yes: Array overflow
      END IF size
   END DO

   ! Was the array size exceeded?  If so, tell user and quit.
   toobig: IF ( exceed ) THEN
      WRITE (*,1010) nvals, max_size
      1010 FORMAT (' Maximum array size exceeded: ', I6, ' > ', I6 )
   ELSE toobig

      ! Limit not exceeded: sort the data.
      outer: DO i = 1, nvals-1
```

(continued)

(concluded)

```
        ! Find the minimum value in a(i) through a(nvals)
        iptr = i
        inner: DO j = i+1, nvals
           minval: IF ( a(j) < a(iptr) ) THEN
              iptr = j
           END IF minval
        END DO inner

        ! iptr now points to the minimum value, so swap a(iptr) with
        !   a(i) if i /= iptr.
        swap: IF ( i /= iptr ) THEN
              temp = a(i)
              a(i) = a(iptr)
           a(iptr) = temp
        END IF swap

     END DO outer

     ! Now write out the sorted data.
     WRITE (*,'(A)') ' The sorted output data values are: '
     WRITE (*,'(4X,F10.4)') ( a(i), i = 1, nvals )

  END IF toobig

ELSE fileopen

   ! Else file open failed.  Tell user.
   WRITE (*,1050) status
   1050 FORMAT (1X,'File open failed--status = ', I6)

END IF fileopen

END PROGRAM
```

In the test for array overflow conditions, we have used a logical variable exceed. If the next value to be read into the array would result on an array overflow, then exceed is set to true and the value is not stored. When all values have been read from the input file, the program checks to see if the array size would have been exceeded. If so, it writes out an error message and quits. If not, it calculates the mean, median, and standard deviation of the numbers.

This program also illustrates the proper use of named constants to allow the size of a program to be changed easily. The size of array a is set by parameter max_size, and the test for array overflow within the code also uses parameter max_size. The maximum sorting capacity of this program could be changed from 10 to 1000 by simply modifying the definition of the named constant max_size at the top of the program.

EXAMPLE 5–4 *The Median:* In Chapter 3 we examined two common statistical measures of data: averages (or means) and standard deviations. Another common statistical measure of data is the median. The *median* of a data set is the value such that half of the numbers in the data set are larger than the value and half of the numbers in the data set are smaller than the value. If the data set has an even number of values, then there cannot be a value exactly in the middle. In that case the median is usually defined as the average of the two elements in the middle. The median value of a data set is often close to the average value of the data set, but not always. For example, consider the following data set:

```
  1
  2
  3
  4
100
```

The average or mean of this data set is 22, while the median of this data set is 3!

An easy way to compute the median of a data set is to sort it into ascending order and then to select the value in the middle of the data set as the median. If the data set has an even number of values, then average the two middle values to get the median.

Write a program to calculate the mean, median, and standard deviation of an input data set, which is read from a user-specified file.

SOLUTION This program must be able to read in an arbitrary number of measurements from a file and then calculate the mean and standard deviation of those measurements.

1. **State the problem.**

Calculate the average, median, and standard deviation of a set of measurements that are read from a user-specified input file and then write those values out on the standard output device.

2. **Define the inputs and outputs.**

This program has two types of inputs:

a. A character string containing the file name of the input data file. This string will come from the standard input device.
b. The real data values in the file.

The outputs from this program are the average, median, and standard deviation of the input data set. They are written to the standard output device.

3. **Describe the algorithm.**

This program can be broken down into six major steps:

```
Get the input file name
Open the input file
Read the input data into an array
Sort the data in ascending order
Calculate the average, median, and standard deviation
Write average, median, and standard deviation
```

The detailed pseudocode for the first four steps is similar to that of the previous example:

```
Initialize variables.
Prompt user for the input file name "filename"
Read the file name "filename"
OPEN file "filename"
IF OPEN is successful THEN
    WHILE
        Read value into temp
        IF read not successful EXIT
        nvals ← nvals + 1
        IF nvals <= max_size then
            a(nvals) ← temp
        ELSE
            exceed ← .TRUE.
        End of IF
    End of WHILE

    ! Notify user if array size exceeded.
    IF array size exceeded then
        Write out message to user
    ELSE
        ! Sort the data
        DO for i = 1 to nvals-1

            ! Find the minimum value in a(i) through a(nvals)
            iptr ← i
            DO for j = i+1 to nvals
                IF a(j) < a(iptr)  THEN
                    iptr ← j
                END of IF
            END of DO (for j = i+1 to nvals)

            ! iptr now points to the min value, so swap a(iptr)
            ! with a(i) if iptr /= i.
            IF i /= iptr THEN
                temp ← a(i)
                a(i) ← a(iptr)
                a(iptr) ← temp
            END of IF
        END of DO (for i = 1 to nvals-1)

        (Add code here)

    End of IF (array size exceeded...)

End of IF (open successful...)
```

The fifth step is to calculate the required average, median, and standard deviation. However, we must first accumulate some statistics on the data (Σx and Σx^2) and then apply the definitions of average, median, and standard deviation given previously. The pseudocode for this step follows.

```
DO for i = 1 to nvals
    sum_x ← sum_x + a(i)
    sum_x2 ← sum_x2 + a(i)**2
End of DO
IF nvals >= 2 THEN
    x_bar ← sum_x / real(nvals)
    std_dev ← sqrt((real(nvals)*sum_x2-
            sum_x**2)/(real(nvals)*real(nvals-1)))
```

```
            IF nvals is an even number THEN
                median ← (a(nvals/2) + a(nvals/2+1)) / 2.
            ELSE
                median ← a(nvals/2+1)
            END of IF
        END of IF
```

We will decide if nvals is an even number by using the modulo function mod(nvals,2). If nvals is even, this function will return a 0; if nvals is odd, it will return a 1. Finally, we must write out the results.

```
    Write out average, median, standard deviation, and no. of points
```

4. **Turn the algorithm into Fortran statements.**

The resulting Fortran program is shown in Figure 5–18.

FIGURE 5–18

A program to read in values from an input data file and to calculate their mean, median, and standard deviation.

```
PROGRAM stat_4
!
!  Purpose:
!    To calculate mean, median, and standard deviation of an input
!    data set read from a file.
!
!  Record of revisions:
!      Date          Programmer          Description of change
!      ====          ==========          =====================
!    09/26/95      S. J. Chapman         Original code
!
IMPLICIT NONE

! List of parameters:
INTEGER, PARAMETER :: max_size = 100

! List of variables:
REAL, DIMENSION(max_size) :: a      ! Data array to sort
LOGICAL :: exceed = .FALSE.         ! Logical indicating that array
                                    ! limits are exceeded
CHARACTER(len=20) :: filename       ! Input data file name
INTEGER :: i                        ! Loop index
INTEGER :: iptr                     ! Pointer to smallest value
INTEGER :: j                        ! Loop index
REAL :: median                      ! The median of the input samples
INTEGER :: nvals = 0                ! Number of data values to sort
INTEGER :: status                   ! I/O status: 0 for success
REAL :: std_dev                     ! Standard deviation of input samples
REAL :: sum_x = 0.                  ! Sum of input values
REAL :: sum_x2 = 0.                 ! Sum of input values squared
REAL :: temp                        ! Temporary variable for swapping
REAL :: x_bar                       ! Average of input values

! Get the name of the file containing the input data.
WRITE (*,1000)
1000 FORMAT (1X,'Enter the file name with the data to be sorted: ')
READ (*,'(A20)') filename
```

(continued)

```fortran
! Open input data file.  Status is OLD because the input data must
! already exist.
OPEN ( UNIT=9, FILE=filename, STATUS='OLD', ACTION='READ', &
       IOSTAT=status )

! Was the OPEN successful?
fileopen: IF ( status == 0 ) THEN            ! Open successful

   ! The file was opened successfully, so read the data to sort
   ! from it, sort the data, and write out the results.
   ! First read in data.
   DO
      READ (9, *, IOSTAT=status) temp       ! Get value
      IF ( status /= 0 ) EXIT               ! Exit on end of data
      nvals = nvals + 1                     ! Bump count
      size: IF ( nvals <= max_size ) THEN   ! Too many values?
         a(nvals) = temp                    ! No: Save value in array
      ELSE
         exceed = .TRUE.                    ! Yes: Array overflow
      END IF size
   END DO

! Was the array size exceeded?  If so, tell user and quit.
toobig: IF ( exceed ) THEN
   WRITE (*,1010) nvals, max_size
   1010 FORMAT (' Maximum array size exceeded: ', I6, '>', I6 )
ELSE

   ! Limit not exceeded: sort the data.
   outer: DO i = 1, nvals-1

      ! Find the minimum value in a(i) through a(nvals)
      iptr = i
      inner: DO j = i+1, nvals
         minval: IF ( a(j) < a(iptr) ) THEN
            iptr = j
         END IF minval
      END DO inner

         ! iptr now points to the minimum value, so swap A(iptr)
         ! with a(i) if i /= iptr.
         swap: IF ( i /= iptr ) THEN
            temp     = a(i)
            a(i)     = a(iptr)
            a(iptr) = temp
         END IF swap

   END DO outer

   ! The data is now sorted.  Accumulate sums to calculate
   ! statistics.
   sums: DO i = 1, nvals
      sum_x  = sum_x + a(i)
      sum_x2 = sum_x2 + a(i)**2
   END DO sums

   ! Check to see if we have enough input data.
   enough: IF ( nvals < 2) THEN

      ! Insufficient data.
      WRITE (*,*) ' At least 2 values must be entered.'
```

(continued)

(concluded)

```
      ELSE

         ! Calculate the mean, median, and standard deviation
         x_bar   = sum_x / real(nvals)
         std_dev = sqrt( (real(nvals) * sum_x2 - sum_x**2) &
                   / (real(nvals) * real(nvals-1)) )
         even: IF ( mod(nvals,2) == 0 ) THEN
            median = ( a(nvals/2) + a(nvals/2+1) ) / 2.
         ELSE
            median = a(nvals/2+1)
         END IF even

         ! Tell user.
         WRITE (*,*) 'The mean of this data set is:  ', x_bar
         WRITE (*,*) 'The median of this data set is:', median
         WRITE (*,*) 'The standard deviation is:     ', std_dev
         WRITE (*,*) 'The number of data points is:  ', nvals

      END IF enough

   END IF toobig

ELSE fileopen

   ! Else file open failed.  Tell user.
   WRITE (*,1050) status
   1050 FORMAT (1X,'File open failed--status = ', I6)

END IF fileopen

END PROGRAM
```

5. Test the program.

To test this program, we will calculate the answers by hand for a simple data set and then compare the answers to the results of the program. If we use five input values—5, 3, 4, 1, and 9—then the mean and standard deviation would be

$$\bar{x} = \frac{1}{N} \sum_{i=1}^{N} x_i = \frac{1}{5} 22 = 4.4$$

$$s = \sqrt{\frac{N \sum_{i=1}^{N} x_i^2 - \left(\sum_{i=1}^{N} x_i \right)^2}{N(N-1)}} = 2.966$$

$$\text{median} = 4$$

If these values are placed in the file INPUT4 and the program is run with that file as an input, the results are

```
C>stat_4
Enter the file name containing the input data:
input4
  The mean of this data set is:            4.400000
  The median of this data set is:          4.000000
  The standard deviation is:               2.966479
  The number of data points is:                   5
```

The program gives the correct answers for our test data set.

Note the use of names on loops and branches in the above program. These names help us to keep the loops and branches straight. This technique becomes more and more important as programs get larger. Even in this simple program, loops and branches are nested four deep at some points!

■ 5.6
TWO-DIMENSIONAL OR RANK-2 ARRAYS

The arrays that we have worked with so far in this chapter are one-dimensional arrays or rank-1 arrays (also known as vectors). These arrays can be visualized as a series of values laid out in a column with a single subscript used to select the individual array elements (Figure 5–19a). Such arrays are useful to describe data that is a function of one independent variable, such as a series of temperature measurements made at fixed intervals of time.

Some types of data are functions of more than one independent variable. For example, we might wish to measure the temperature at five different locations at four different times. In this case, our 20 measurements could logically be grouped into five different columns of four measurements each with a separate column for each location (Figure 5–19b). Fortran has a mechanism especially designed to hold this sort of data—a two-dimensional or rank-2 array (also called a matrix).

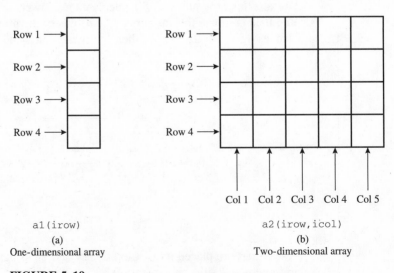

al(irow)

(a)

One-dimensional array

a2(irow,icol)

(b)

Two-dimensional array

FIGURE 5–19
Representations of one- and two-dimensional arrays.

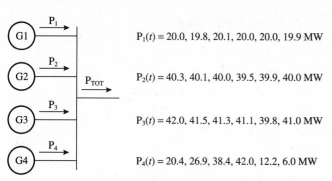

$P_1(t) = 20.0, 19.8, 20.1, 20.0, 20.0, 19.9$ MW

$P_2(t) = 40.3, 40.1, 40.0, 39.5, 39.9, 40.0$ MW

$P_3(t) = 42.0, 41.5, 41.3, 41.1, 39.8, 41.0$ MW

$P_4(t) = 20.4, 26.9, 38.4, 42.0, 12.2, 6.0$ MW

(a) Power measurements from four generators at six different times.

	G1	G2	G3	G4
Time 1	20.0	40.3	42.0	20.4
Time 2	19.8	40.1	41.5	26.9
Time 3	20.1	40.0	41.3	38.4
Time 4	20.0	39.5	41.1	42.0
Time 5	20.0	39.9	39.8	12.2
Time 6	19.9	40.0	41.0	6.0

(b) Two-dimensional matrix of power measurements.

FIGURE 5–20
(*a*) A power generating station consisting of four generators. The power output of each generator is measured at six different times. (*b*) Two-dimensional matrix of power measurements.

Rank-2 arrays are arrays whose elements are addressed with two subscripts, and any particular element in the array is selected by simultaneously choosing values for both of them. For example, Figure 5–20*a* shows a set of four generators whose power output has been measured at six different times. Figure 5–20*b* shows an array consisting of the six power measurements for each of the four generators. In this example each row specifies a measurement time, and each column specifies a generator number. The array element containing the power supplied by generator 3 at time 4 would be power(4,3); its value is 41.1 MW.

5.6.1 Declaring Rank-2 Arrays

The type and size of a rank-2 array must be declared to the compiler using a type declaration statement. Some example array declarations follow:

1. REAL, DIMENSION(3,6) :: sum

   This type statement declares a real array consisting of three rows and six columns for a total of 18 elements. The legal values of the first subscript are 1 to 3, and the legal values of the second subscript are 1 to 6. Any other subscript values are out of bounds.

2. INTEGER, DIMENSION(0:100,0:20) :: hist

   This type statement declares an integer array consisting of 101 rows and 21 columns for a total of 2121 elements. The legal values of the first subscript are 0 to 100, and the legal values of the second subscript are 0 to 20. Any other subscript values are out of bounds.

3. `CHARACTER(len=6), DIMENSION(-3:3,10) :: counts`

This type statement declares an array consisting of seven rows and 10 columns, for a total of 70 elements. Its type is `CHARACTER` with each array element capable of holding six characters. The legal values of the first subscript are -3 to 3, and the legal values of the second subscript are 1 to 10. Any other subscript values are out of bounds.

5.6.2 Rank-2 Array Storage

You have already learned that a rank-1 array of length N occupies N successive locations in the computer's memory. Similarly, a rank-2 array of size M by N occupies $M \times N$ successive locations in the computer's memory. How are the elements of the array arranged in the computer's memory? Fortran always allocates array elements in **column major order.** That is, Fortran allocates the first column in memory, then the second, then the third, etc., until all columns have been allocated. Figure 5–21 illustrates this memory allocation scheme for a 3×2 array a. As we can see from the picture, the array element a(2,2) is really the fifth location reserved in memory. The order of memory allocation will become important when we discuss data initialization and I/O statements later in this section.[2]

5.6.3 Initializing Rank-2 Arrays

Rank-2 arrays may be initialized with assignment statements, in type declaration statements, or in Fortran `READ` statements.

Initializing rank-2 arrays with assignment statements

Initial values may be assigned to an array on an element-by-element basis using assignment statements in a nested `DO` loop or all at once with an array constructor. For example, suppose we have a 4×3 integer array istat that we wish to initialize with the values shown in Figure 5–22a.

This array could be initialized at run time on an element-by-element basis with `DO` loops:

```
INTEGER, DIMENSION(4,3) :: istat
DO i = 1, 4
   DO j = 1, 3
      istat(i,j) = j
   END DO
END DO
```

---

[2]The Fortran 90/95 standard does not actually *require* that the elements of an array occupy successive locations in memory. It only requires that they *appear* to be successive when addressed with appropriate subscripts or when used in operations such as I/O statements. To keep this distinction clear, we will refer to the *notional order* of the elements in memory, with the understanding that the actual order implemented by the processor could be anything. (As a practical matter, though, every Fortran compiler that the author has ever seen allocates the elements of an array in successive memory locations.) The allocation of array elements in memory was deliberately not constrained by the standard to make it easier to implement Fortran on massively parallel computers, where different memory models might be appropriate.

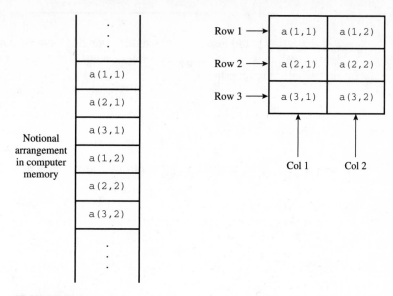

FIGURE 5–21
Notional memory allocation for a 3 x 2 rank-2 array a.

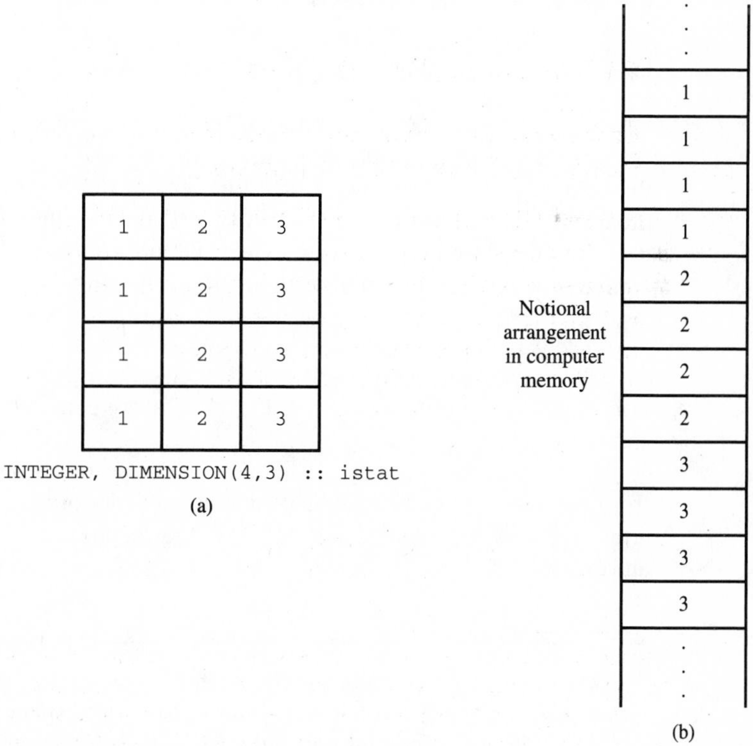

```
INTEGER, DIMENSION(4,3) :: istat
```

(a)

Notional
arrangement
in computer
memory

(b)

FIGURE 5–22
(*a*) Initial values for integer array istat. (*b*) Notional layout of values in memory for array istat.

The array could also be initialized in a single statement with an array constructor. However, this is not as simple as it might seem. The notional data pattern in memory that would initialize the array is shown in Figure 5–22b. It consists of four 1s, followed by four 2s, followed by four 3s. The array constructor that would produce this pattern in memory is

```
(/ 1,1,1,1,2,2,2,2,3,3,3,3 /)
```

so it would seem that the array could be initialized with the assignment statement

```
istat = (/ 1,1,1,1,2,2,2,2,3,3,3,3 /)
```

Unfortunately, *this assignment statement will not work.* The array constructor produces a 1 × 12 array, while array istat is a 4 × 3 array. Although they both have the same number of elements, the two arrays are not *conformable* because they have different shapes and so cannot be used in the same operation. This assignment statement will produce a compile-time error on a Fortran 90/95 compiler.

Array constructors always produce rank-1 arrays. So how can we overcome this limitation to use array constructors to initialize rank-2 vectors? Fortran 90/95 provides a special intrinsic function, called RESHAPE, that changes the shape of an array without changing the number of elements in it. The form of the RESHAPE function is

```
output = RESHAPE ( array1, array2 )
```

where array1 contains the data to reshape and array2 is a rank-1 array describing the new shape. The number of elements in array2 is the number of dimensions in the output array, and the value of each element in array2 is the extent of each dimension. The number of elements in array1 must be the same as the number of elements in the shape specified in array2, or the RESHAPE function will fail. The assignment statement to initialize array istat becomes

```
istat = RESHAPE ( (/ 1,1,1,1,2,2,2,2,3,3,3,3 /), (/4,3/) )
```

The RESHAPE function converts the 1 × 12 array constructor into a 4 × 3 array that can be assigned to istat.

Note that when RESHAPE changes the shape of an array, it maps the elements from the old shape to the new shape in column major order. Thus the first element in the array constructor becomes istat(1,1), the second element becomes istat(2,1), and so on.

Good Programming Practice

Use the RESHAPE function to change the shape of an array. This technique is especially useful when used with an array constructor to create array constants of any desired shape.

Initializing rank-2 arrays with type declaration statements

Initial values may also be loaded into the array at compilation time using type declaration statements. When a type declaration statement is used to initialize a rank-2 array, the data values are loaded into the array in the order in which memory is notionally allocated by the Fortran compiler. Since arrays are allocated in column order, the values listed in the type declaration statement must be in column order. That is, all the elements in column 1 must be listed in the statement first, followed by all of the elements in column 2, and so on. Array istat contains four rows and three columns; therefore, to initialize the array with a type declaration statement, the four values of column 1 must be listed first, then the four values for column 2, and finally the four values for column 3.

The values used to initialize the array must have the same shape as the array, so the RESHAPE function must be used as well. Therefore, array istat could be initialized at compilation time with the following statement:

```
INTEGER, DIMENSION(4,3) :: istat(4,3) = &
       RESHAPE ( (/ 1,1,1,1,2,2,2,2,3,3,3,3 /), (/4,3/) )
```

Initializing rank-2 arrays with READ statements

Arrays may be initialized with Fortran READ statements. If an array name appears without subscripts in the argument list of a READ statement, the program will attempt to read values for all of the elements in the array; the values will be assigned to the array elements in the order in which they are notionally stored in the computer's memory. Therefore, if file INITIAL.DAT contains the values

```
1 1 1 1 2 2 2 2 3 3 3 3
```

then the following code will initialize array istat to have the values shown in Figure 5–22.

```
INTEGER, DIMENSION(4,3) :: istat
OPEN (7, FILE='initial.dat', STATUS='OLD', ACTION='READ')
READ (7,*) istat
```

Implied DO loops may be used in READ statements to change the order in which array elements are initialized or to initialize only a portion of an array. For example, if file INITIAL1.DAT contains the values

```
1 2 3 1 2 3 1 2 3 1 2 3
```

then the following code will initialize array istat to have the values shown in Figure 5–22.

```
INTEGER :: i, j
INTEGER, DIMENSION(4,3) :: istat
OPEN (7, FILE='initial1.dat', STATUS='OLD', ACTION='READ')
READ (7,*) ((istat(i,j), j=1,3), i=1,4)
```

The values would have been read from file INITIAL1.DAT in a different order than in the previous example, but the implied DO loops would ensure that the proper input values went into the proper array elements.

5.6.4 Example Problem

EXAMPLE 5–5 Electric Power Generation: Figure 5–20*b* shows a series of electrical output power measurements at six different times for four different generators at the Acme Electric Power generating station. Write a program to read these values from a disk file, calculate the average power supplied by each generator over the measurement period, and calculate the total power supplied by all of the generators at each time in the measurement period.

SOLUTION

1. **State the problem.**

    Calculate the average power supplied by each generator in the station over the measurement period and calculate the total instantaneous power supplied by the generating station at each time within the measurement period. Write those values out on the standard output device.

2. **Define the inputs and outputs.**

    This program has two types of inputs:

a. A character string containing the file name of the input data file. This string will come from the standard input device.
b. The 24 real data values in the file, representing the power supplied by each of the four generators at each of six times. The data in the input file must be organized so that the six values associated with generator G1 appear first, followed by the six values associated with generator G2, and so on.

    The outputs from this program are the average power supplied by each generator in the station over the measurement period and the total instantaneous power supplied by the generating station at each time within the measurement period.

3. **Describe the algorithm.**

    This program can be broken down into six major steps:

```
Get the input file name
Open the input file
Read the input data into an array
Calculate the total instantaneous output power at each time
Calculate the average output power of each generator
Write the output values
```

    The detailed pseudocode for this problem follows.

```
Prompt user for the input file name "filename"
Read file name "filename"
OPEN file "filename"
IF OPEN is successful THEN
   Read array power
```

```
                    ! Calculate the instantaneous output power of the station
                    DO for itime = 1 to 6
                       DO for igen = 1 to 4
                          power_sum(itime) ← power(itime,igen) + power_sum(itime)
                       END of DO
                    END of DO

                    ! Calculate the average output power of each generator
                    DO for igen = 1 to 4
                       DO for itime = 1 to 6
                          power_ave(igen) ← power(itime,igen) + power_ave(igen)
                       END of DO
                       power_ave(igen) ← power_ave(igen) / 6
                    END of DO

                    ! Write out the total instantaneous power at each time
                    Write out power_sum for itime = 1 to 6

                    ! Write out the average output power of each generator
                    Write out power_ave for igen = 1 to 4

                 End of IF
```

4. **Turn the algorithm into Fortran statements.**

The resulting Fortran program is shown in Figure 5–23.

FIGURE 5–23

Program to calculate the instantaneous power produced by a generating station and the average power produced by each generator within the station.

```
PROGRAM generate
!
!  Purpose:
!    To calculate total instantaneous power supplied by a generating
!    station at each instant of time and to calculate the average
!    power supplied by each generator over the period of measurement.
!
!  Record of revisions:
!     Date          Programmer          Description of change
!     ====          ==========          =====================
!    09/27/95    S. J Chapman           Original code
!
IMPLICIT NONE

! List of parameters:
INTEGER, PARAMETER :: max_gen = 4      ! Max number of generators
INTEGER, PARAMETER :: max_time = 6     ! Max number of times

! List of variables:
CHARACTER(len=20) :: filename          ! Input data file name
INTEGER :: igen                        ! Loop index: generators
INTEGER :: itime                       ! Loop index: time
REAL, DIMENSION(max_time,max_gen) :: power
                                       ! Pwr of each gen at each time
REAL, DIMENSION(max_gen) :: power_ave  ! Ave power of each gen over all times
REAL, DIMENSION(max_time) :: power_sum ! Total power of station at each time
INTEGER :: status                      ! I/O status: 0 = success
```

(continued)

(concluded)

```
! Initialize sums to zero.
power_ave = 0.
power_sum = 0.

! Get the name of the file containing the input data.
WRITE (*,1000)
1000 FORMAT (' Enter the file name containing the input data: ')
READ (*,'(A20)') filename

! Open input data file.  Status is OLD because the input data must
! already exist.
OPEN ( UNIT=9, FILE=filename, STATUS='OLD', ACTION='READ', &
       IOSTAT=status )

! Was the OPEN successful?
fileopen: IF ( status == 0 ) THEN

   ! The file was opened successfully, so read the data to process.
   READ (9, *, IOSTAT=status) power

   ! Calculate the instantaneous output power of the station at
   ! each time.
   sum1: DO itime = 1, max_time
      sum2: DO igen = 1, max_gen
         power_sum(itime) = power(itime,igen) + power_sum(itime)
      END DO sum2
   END DO sum1

   ! Calculate the average output power of each generator over the
   ! time being measured.
   ave1: DO igen = 1, max_gen
      ave2: DO itime = 1, max_time
         power_ave(igen) = power(itime,igen) + power_ave(igen)
      END DO ave2
      power_ave(igen) = power_ave(igen) / REAL(max_time)
   END DO ave1

   ! Tell user.
   out1: DO itime = 1, max_time
      WRITE (*,1010) itime, power_sum(itime)
      1010 FORMAT (' The instantaneous power at time ', I1, ' is ', &
                     F7.2, ' MW.')
   END DO out1

   out2: DO igen = 1, max_gen
      WRITE (*,1020) igen, power_ave(igen)
      1020 FORMAT (' The average power of generator ', I1, ' is ', &
                     F7.2, ' MW.')
   END DO out2

ELSE fileopen

   ! Else file open failed.  Tell user.
   WRITE (*,1030) status
   1030 FORMAT (1X,'File open failed--status = ', I6)

END IF fileopen

END PROGRAM
```

5. **Test the program.**

To test this program, we will place the data from Figure 5–20b into a file called GENDAT. The contents of file GENDAT follow.

```
20.0   19.8   20.1   20.0   20.0   19.9
40.3   40.1   40.0   39.5   39.9   40.0
42.0   41.5   41.3   41.1   39.8   41.0
20.4   26.9   38.4   42.0   12.2    6.0
```

Note that each row of the file corresponds to a specific generator, and each column corresponds to a specific time. Next we will calculate the answers by hand for one generator and one time and then compare the results with those from the program. At time 3, the total instantaneous power being supplied by all of the generators is

$$P_{TOT} = 20.1 \text{ MW} + 40.0 \text{ MW} + 41.3 \text{ MW} + 38.4 \text{ MW} = 139.8 \text{ MW}$$

The average power for generator 1 is

$$P_{G1,AVE} = \frac{(20.0 + 19.8 + 20.1 + 20.0 + 20.0 + 19.9)}{6} = 19.97 \text{ MW}$$

The output from the program is

```
C>generate
Enter the file name containing the input data:
gendat
The instantaneous power at time 1 is  122.70 MW.
The instantaneous power at time 2 is  128.30 MW.
The instantaneous power at time 3 is  139.80 MW.
The instantaneous power at time 4 is  142.60 MW.
The instantaneous power at time 5 is  111.90 MW.
The instantaneous power at time 6 is  106.90 MW.
The average power of generator  1 is   19.97 MW.
The average power of generator  2 is   39.97 MW.
The average power of generator  3 is   41.12 MW.
The average power of generator  4 is   24.32 MW.
```

so the numbers match, and the program appears to be working correctly.

Note that in this problem the raw data array power was organized as a 6×4 matrix (six times by four generators), but the input data file was organized as a 4×6 matrix (four generators by six times)! This reversal is caused by the fact that Fortran stores array data in columns but reads in data along lines. In order for the columns to be filled correctly in memory, the data had be transposed in the input file! Needless to say, this requirement can be very confusing for people having to work with the program and its input data.

This program would be much better if we could organize the data in the input file to match the organization of the data within the computer—which we can do with implied DO loops. If we were to replace the statement

```
READ (9,*,IOSTAT=status) power
```

with the statement

```
READ (9,*,IOSTAT=status) ((power(itime,igen), igen=1,max_gen), itime=1, max_time)
```

then the data along a row in the input file would go into the corresponding row of the matrix in the computer's memory. With the new READ statement, the input data file could be structured as follows:

```
20.0    40.3    42.0    20.4
19.8    40.1    41.5    26.9
20.1    40.0    41.3    38.4
20.0    39.5    41.1    42.0
20.0    39.9    39.8    12.2
19.9    40.0    41.0     6.0
```

After the READ statement, the contents of array power would be

$$
\text{power} = \begin{bmatrix}
20.0 & 40.3 & 42.0 & 20.4 \\
19.8 & 40.1 & 41.5 & 26.9 \\
20.1 & 40.0 & 41.3 & 38.4 \\
20.0 & 39.5 & 41.1 & 42.0 \\
20.0 & 39.9 & 39.8 & 12.2 \\
19.9 & 40.0 & 41.0 & 6.0
\end{bmatrix}
$$

Good Programming Practice

Use DO loops, implied DO loops, or both when reading or writing rank-2 arrays in order to keep the structure of the matrix in the file the same as the structure of the matrix within the program. This correspondence makes the programs easier to understand.

5.6.5 Whole Array Operations and Array Subsets

Two arrays may be used together in arithmetic operations and assignment statements as long as they are conformable (that is, as long as they either have the same shape or one of them is a scalar). If they are conformable, then the corresponding operation will be performed on an element-by-element basis.

Array subsets may be selected from rank-2 arrays using subscript triplets or vector subscripts. A separate subscript triplet or vector subscript is used for each dimension in the array. For example, consider the following 5×5 array:

$$
a = \begin{bmatrix}
1 & 2 & 3 & 4 & 5 \\
6 & 7 & 8 & 9 & 10 \\
11 & 12 & 13 & 14 & 15 \\
16 & 17 & 18 & 19 & 20 \\
21 & 22 & 23 & 24 & 25
\end{bmatrix}
$$

The array subset corresponding to the first column of this array is selected as a(:,1):

$$
a(:,1) = \begin{bmatrix}
1 \\
6 \\
11 \\
16 \\
21
\end{bmatrix}
$$

The array subset corresponding to the first row is selected as $a(1,:)$:

$$a(1,:) = \begin{bmatrix} 1 & 2 & 3 & 4 & 5 \end{bmatrix}$$

Array subscripts may be used independently in each dimension. For example, the array subset $a(1:3,1:5:2)$ selects rows 1 through 3 and columns 1, 3, and 5 from array a. This array subset is

$$a(1:3,1:5:2) = \begin{bmatrix} 1 & 3 & 5 \\ 6 & 8 & 10 \\ 11 & 13 & 15 \end{bmatrix}$$

Similar combinations of subscripts can be used to select any rows or columns out of a rank-2 array.

■ 5.7

MULTIDIMENSIONAL OR RANK-N ARRAYS

Fortran supports more complex arrays with up to seven different subscripts. These larger arrays are declared, initialized, and used in the same manner as the rank-2 arrays described in the previous section.

Multidimensional or rank-n arrays are notionally allocated in memory in a manner that is an extension of the column order used for rank-2. Memory allocation for a $2 \times 2 \times 2$ rank-3 array is illustrated in Figure 5–24. Note that the first subscript

Notional
arrangement
in computer
memory

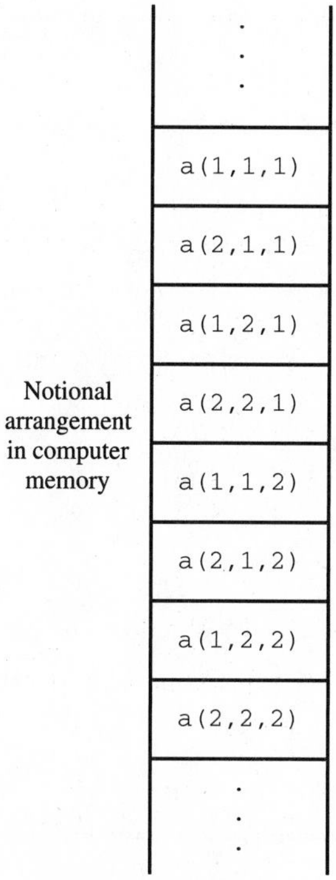

FIGURE 5–24
Notional memory allocation for a $2 \times 2 \times 2$ array a. Array elements are allocated so that the first subscript changes most rapidly, the second subscript the next most rapidly, and the third subscript the least rapidly.

runs through its complete range before the second subscript is incremented, and the second subscript runs through its complete range before the third subscript is incremented. This process repeats for whatever number of subscripts are declared for the array, with the first subscript always changing most rapidly and the last subscript always changing most slowly. We must keep this allocation structure in mind if we wish to initialize or perform I/O operations with multidimensional arrays.

Quiz 5–2

This quiz provides a quick check to see if you understand the concepts introduced in sections 5.6 and 5.7. If you have trouble with the quiz, reread the sections, ask your instructor, or discuss the material with a fellow student. The answers to this quiz are found in the back of the book.

For questions 1 to 3, determine the number of elements in the array specified by the declaration statements and the valid subscript range(s) for each array.

1. `REAL, DIMENSION(-64:64,0:4) :: data_input`

2. ```
   INTEGER, PARAMETER :: min_u = 1, max_u = 70
   INTEGER, PARAMETER :: maxfil = 3
   CHARACTER(len=24), DIMENSION(maxfil,min_u:max_u) :: filenm
   ```

3. `INTEGER, DIMENSION(-3:3,-3:3,6) :: in`

Determine which of the following Fortran statements are valid. For each valid statement, specify what will happen in the program. Assume default typing for any variables that are not explicitly typed.

4. ```
   REAL, DIMENSION(0:11,2) :: dist
   dist = (/ 0.00,  0.25,  1.00,  2.25,  4.00,  6.25, &
             9.00, 12.25, 16.00, 20.25, 25.00, 30.25, &
            -0.00, -0.25, -1.00, -2.25, -4.00, -6.25, &
            -9.00,-12.25,-16.00,-20.25,-25.00,-30.25/)
   ```

5. ```
   REAL, DIMENSION(0;11,2) :: dist
   dist = RESHAPE((/0.00, 0.25, 1.00, 2.25, 4.00, 6.25, &
                    9.00,12.25,16.00,20.25,25.00,30.25, &
                    0.00, 0.25, 1.00, 2.25, 4.00, 6.25, &
                    9.00,12.25,16.00,20.25,25.00,30.25/)&
                    , (/12,2/))
   ```

6. ```
   REAL, DIMENSION(-2:2,-1:0) :: data1 = &
         RESHAPE ( (/ 1.0, 2.0, 3.0, 4.0, 5.0, &
                      6.0, 7.0, 8.0, 9.0, 0.0 /), &
                   (/ 5, 2 /) )
   REAL, DIMENSION(0:4,2) :: data2 = &
         RESHAPE ( (/ 0.0, 9.0, 8.0, 7.0, 6.0, &
                      5.0, 4.0, 3.0, 2.0, 1.0 /), &
                   (/ 5, 2 /) )
   REAL, DIMENSION(5,2) :: data_out
   data_out = data1 + data2
   WRITE (*,*) data_out(:,1)
   WRITE (*,*) data_out(3,:)
   ```

(continued)

(concluded)

7.
```fortran
INTEGER, DIMENSION(4) :: list1 = (/1,4,2,2/)
INTEGER, DIMENSION(3) :: list2 = (/1,2,3/)
INTEGER, DIMENSION(5,5) :: array
DO i = 1,5
   DO j = 1,5
      array(i,j) = i + 10 * j
   END DO
END DO
WRITE (*,*) array(list1, list2)
```

8.
```fortran
INTEGER, DIMENSION(4) :: list = (/2,3,2,1/)
INTEGER, DIMENSION(10) :: vector = (/ (10*k, k = -4,5) /)
vector(list) = (/ 1, 2, 3, 4 /)
WRITE (*,*) vector
```

Suppose that a file INPUT is opened on i/o unit 2 and contains the following data:

11.2	16.5	31.3	3.1414	16.0	12.0
1.1	9.0	17.1	11.	15.0	-1.3
10.0	11.0	12.0	13.0	14.0	5.0
15.1	16.7	18.9	21.1	24.0	-22.2

What data would be read from file INPUT by each of the following statements? What would the value of mydata(2,4) be in each case?

9.
```fortran
REAL, DIMENSION(3,5) :: mydata
READ (2,*) mydata
```

10.
```fortran
REAL, DIMENSION(0:2,2:6) :: mydata
READ (2,*) mydata
```

11.
```fortran
REAL, DIMENSION(3,5) :: mydata
READ (2,*) ((mydata(i,j), j=1,5), i=1,3)
```

12.
```fortran
REAL, DIMENSION(3,5) :: mydata
DO i = 1, 3
   READ (2,*) (mydata(i,j), j=1,5)
END DO
```

Answer the following questions:

13. What is the value of dist(6,2) in question 5 of this quiz?

14. What is the rank of mydata in question 10 of this quiz?

15. What is the shape of mydata in question 10 of this quiz?

16. What is the extent of the first dimension of data_input in question 1 of this quiz?

17. What is the maximum number of dimensions that an array can have in Fortran 90/95?

■ 5.8
USING Fortran INTRINSIC FUNCTIONS WITH ARRAYS

Fortran 90/95 has three classes of intrinsic functions: **elemental functions, inquiry functions,** and **transformational functions.** Some functions from each class are designed for use with array arguments. We will now examine a few of them. A complete description of all Fortran intrinsic functions and subroutines is found in Appendix B.

5.8.1 Elemental Intrinsic Functions

Elemental intrinsic functions are functions that are specified for scalar arguments, but which may also be applied to array arguments. If the argument of an elemental function is a scalar, then the result of the function will be a scalar. If the argument of the function is an array, then the result of the function will be an array of the same shape as the input array. Note that if the function has more than one input argument, all of the arguments must have the same shape. If an elemental function is applied to an array, the result will be the same as if the functions were applied to each element of the array on an element-by-element basis. Thus the following two sets of statements are equivalent:

```
REAL, DIMENSION(4) :: x = (/ 0., 3.141592, 1., 2. /)
REAL, DIMENSION(4) :: y
INTEGER :: i

y = SIN(x)                          ! Whole array at once

DO i = 1,4
   y(i) = SIN(x(i))                 ! Element by element
END DO
```

Most Fortran intrinsic functions that accept scalar arguments are elemental and can be used with arrays. This category includes such common functions as ABS, SIN, COS, TAN, EXP, LOG, LOG10, MOD, and SQRT.

5.8.2 Inquiry Intrinsic Functions

Inquiry intrinsic functions are functions whose value depends on the properties of an object being investigated. For example, the function UBOUND(arr) is an inquiry function that returns the largest subscript(s) of array arr. A list of some of the common array inquiry functions appears in Table 5–1. Any function arguments shown in italics are optional; they may or may not be present when the function is invoked.

These functions are useful for determining the properties of an array, such as its size, shape, extent, and the legal subscript range in each extent. They will be especially important once we begin passing arrays to procedures in Chapter 6.

EXAMPLE 5–6 ***Determining the Properties of an Array:*** To illustrate the use of the array inquiry functions, we will declare a rank-2 array a and use the functions to determine its properties.

▮ **TABLE 5–1**
Some common array inquiry functions

Function name and calling sequence	Purpose
ALLOCATED(ARRAY)	Determines allocation status of an allocatable array (see section 5.11).
LBOUND(ARRAY, *DIM*)	Returns all of the lower bounds of ARRAY if *DIM* is absent or a specified lower bound of ARRAY if *DIM* is present. The result is a rank-1 array if *DIM* is absent or a scalar if *DIM* is present.
SHAPE(SOURCE)	Returns the shape of array SOURCE.
SIZE(ARRAY, *DIM*)	Returns either the extent of ARRAY along a particular dimension if *DIM* is present; otherwise, it returns the total number of elements in the array.
UBOUND(ARRAY, *DIM*)	Returns all of the upper bounds of ARRAY if *DIM* is absent or a specified upper bound of ARRAY if *DIM* is present. The result is a rank-1 array if *DIM* is absent or a scalar if *DIM* is present.

5

SOLUTION The program in Figure 5–25 invokes the functions SHAPE, SIZE, LBOUND, and UBOUND to determine the properties of the array.

FIGURE 5–25
Program to determine the properties of an array.

```
PROGRAM check_array
!
!   Purpose:
!     To illustrate the use of array inquiry functions.
!
!   Record of revisions:
!      Date          Programmer           Description of change
!      ====          ==========           =====================
!    04/02/96      S. J. Chapman          Original code
!
IMPLICIT NONE

! List of variables:
REAL,DIMENSION(-5:5,0:3) :: a = 0. ! Array to examine

! Get the shape, size, and bounds of the array.
WRITE (*,100) SHAPE(a)
100 FORMAT (1X,'The shape of the array is:           ',7I6)

WRITE (*,110) SIZE(a)
110 FORMAT (1X,'The size of the array is:            ',I6)

WRITE (*,120) LBOUND(a)
120 FORMAT (1X,'The lower bounds of the array are:  ',7I6)

WRITE (*,130) UBOUND(a)
130 FORMAT (1X,'The upper bounds of the array are:  ',7I6)

END PROGRAM
```

When the program is executed, the results are

```
C>check_array
The shape of the array is:              11    4
The size of the array is:               44
The lower bounds of the array are:      -5    0
The upper bounds of the array are:       5    3
```

These are obviously the correct answers for array a.

5.8.3 Transformational Intrinsic Functions

Transformational intrinsic functions are functions that have one or more array-valued arguments or an array-valued result. Unlike elemental functions, which operate on an element-by-element basis, transformational functions operate on arrays as a whole. The output of a transformational function will often not have the same shape as the input arguments. For example, the function DOT_PRODUCT has two vector input arguments of the same size and produces a scalar output.

Fortran has *many* transformational intrinsic functions. Some of the more common ones are summarized in Table 5–2. Some of the functions in Table 5–2 have additional optional arguments that are not mentioned. The complete details of each function, including any additional arguments, are found in Appendix B. Any function arguments shown in italics are optional, they may or may not be present when the function is invoked.

We have already used the RESHAPE function to initialize arrays. A number of other transformational functions will appear in the exercises at the end of this chapter.

5.9

MASKED ARRAY ASSIGNMENT: THE WHERE CONSTRUCT

We have already seen that Fortran permits us to use either array elements or entire arrays in array assignment statements. For example, we could take the logarithm of the elements in a rank-2 array value in either of the following ways:

```
DO i = 1, ndim1                                  logval = LOG ( value )
   DO j = 1, ndim2
      logval(i,j) = LOG(value(i,j))
   END DO
END DO
```

Both of the above examples take the logarithm of all of the elements in array value and store the result in array logval.

Suppose that we would like to take the logarithm of *some* of the elements of array value, but not all of them. For example, suppose that we only want to take the logarithm of positive elements, since the logarithms of zero and negative numbers are not defined and produce run-time errors. One way to do so would be on an element-by-element basis using a combination of DO loops and an IF construct. For example:

TABLE 5–2
Some common transformational functions

Function name and calling sequence	Purpose
ALL(MASK)	Logical function that returns TRUE if *all* the values in array MASK are true.
ANY(MASK)	Logical function that returns TRUE if *any* of the values in array MASK are true.
COUNT(MASK)	Returns the number of TRUE elements in array MASK.
DOT_PRODUCT(VECTOR_A, VECTOR_B)	Calculates the dot product of two equal-sized vectors.
MATMUL(MATRIX_A, MATRIX_B)	Performs matrix multiplication on to conformable matrices.
MAXLOC(ARRAY, *MASK*)	Returns the *location* of the maximum value in ARRAY among those elements for which *MASK* was true. The result is a rank-1 array with one element for each subscript in ARRAY. (*MASK* is optional.)
MAXVAL(ARRAY, *MASK*)[1]	Returns the maximum value in ARRAY among those elements for which *MASK* was true. (*MASK* is optional.)
MINLOC(ARRAY, *MASK*)	Returns the *location* of the minimum value in ARRAY among those elements for which *MASK* was true. The result is a rank-1 array with one element for each subscript in ARRAY. (*MASK* is optional.)
MINVAL(ARRAY, *MASK*)[1]	Returns the minimum value in ARRAY among those elements for which *MASK* was true. (*MASK* is optional.)
PRODUCT(ARRAY, *MASK*)[1]	Calculates the product of the elements in ARRAY for which the *MASK* is true. *MASK* is optional; if not present, it calculates the product of all of the elements in the array.
RESHAPE(SOURCE, SHAPE)	Constructs an array of the specified shape from the elements of array SOURCE. SHAPE is a rank-1 array containing the extents of each dimension in the array to be built.
SUM(ARRAY, *MASK*)[1]	Calculates the sum of the elements in ARRAY for which the *MASK* is true. *MASK* is optional; if not present, it calculates the sum of all of the elements in the array.
TRANSPOSE(MATRIX)	Returns the transpose of a rank-2 array.

[1]If a MASK is specified in these functions, it must be specified in the form MASK=*mask_expr*, where *mask_expr* is the logical array specifying the mask. The reason for this form is explained in Chapter 9 and Appendix B.

```
DO i = 1, ndim1
    DO j = 1, ndim2
        IF ( value(i,j) > 0. ) THEN
            logval(i,j) = LOG(value(i,j))
        ELSE
            logval(i,j) = -99999.
        END IF
    END DO
END DO
```

We can also perform this calculation all at once using a special form of array assignment statement known as **masked array assignment.** A masked array assignment statement is an assignment statement whose operation is controlled by a logical array of the *same shape* as the array in the assignment. The assignment operation is only performed for the elements of the array that correspond to true values in the mask. In Fortran 90/95, masked array assignments are implemented using the WHERE construct or statement.

5.9.1 The Fortran 90 WHERE Construct

The general form of a Fortran WHERE construct is

```
[name:] WHERE (mask_expr)
    Array Assignment Statement(s)      ! Block 1
ELSEWHERE [name]
    Array Assignment Statement(s)      ! Block 2
END WHERE [name]
```

where `mask_expr` is a logical array of the same shape as the array(s) being manipulated in the array assignment statements in the construct. This construct applies the operation or set of operations in block 1 to all the elements of the array for which `mask_expr` is true and applies the operation or set of operations in block 2 to all the elements of the array for which `mask_expr` is false.

A name may be assigned to a WHERE construct if desired. If the WHERE statement at the beginning of a construct is named, then the associated END WHERE statement must have the same name. The name is optional on an ELSEWHERE statement even if it is used on the corresponding WHERE and END WHERE statements.

The preceding example could be implemented with a WHERE construct as follows:

```
WHERE ( value > 0. )
    logval = LOG(value)
ELSEWHERE
    logval = -99999.
END WHERE
```

The expression `value > 0.` produces a logical array whose elements are true where the corresponding elements of `value` are greater than zero and false where the corresponding elements of `value` are less than or equal to zero. This logical array then serves as a mask to control the operation of the array assignment statement.

The WHERE construct is generally more elegant than element-by-element operations, especially for multidimensional arrays.

Good Programming Practice
Use WHERE constructs to modify and assign array elements when you want to modify and assign only those elements that pass some test.

5.9.2 The Fortran 95 WHERE Construct

Fortran 95 extends the WHERE construct with the ability to have zero or more masked ELSEWHERE clauses. The general form of a Fortran 95 WHERE construct is

```
[name:] WHERE (mask_expr1)
    Array Assignment Statement(s)      ! Block 1
ELSEWHERE (mask_expr2) [name]
    Array Assignment Statement(s)      ! Block 2
ELSEWHERE [name]
    Array Assignment Statement(s)      ! Block 3
END WHERE [name]
```

where each *mask_expr* is a logical array of the same shape as the array(s) being manipulated in the array assignment statements. This construct applies the operation or set of operations in block 1 to all the elements of the array for which *mask_expr1* is true. It applies the operation or set of operations in block 2 to all the elements of the array for which *mask_expr1* is false and *mask_expr2* is true. Finally, it applies the operation or set of operations in block 3 to all the elements of the array for which both *mask_expr1* and *mask_expr2* are false. A Fortran 95 WHERE construct can have as many masked ELSEWHERE clauses as desired.

Note that *no more than one block of statements will be executed for any given element in the array.*

5.9.3 The WHERE Statement

Fortran 90/95 also includes a single-line WHERE statement:

```
WHERE (mask_expr) Array Assignment Statement
```

The assignment statement is applied to those elements of the array for which the mask expression is true.

EXAMPLE 5–7 Limiting the Maximum and Minimum Values in an Array: Suppose that we are writing a program to analyze an input data set whose values should be in the range $[-1000,1000]$. If numbers greater than 1000 or less than -1000 would cause problems with our processing algorithm, we might want to put in a test limiting all data values to the acceptable range. Write such a test for a 10,000-element rank-1 real array input using both DO and IF constructs and a WHERE construct.

SOLUTION The test using DO and IF construct is

```
DO i = 1, 10000
   IF ( input(i) > 1000. ) THEN
      input(i) = 1000.
   ELSE IF ( input(i) < -1000. ) THEN
      input(i) = -1000.
   END IF
END DO
```

The test using a WHERE construct is

```
WHERE ( ABS(input) > 1000. )
    input = SIGN(1000.,input)
END WHERE
```

The WHERE construct is simpler than the DO and IF constructs for this example.

5.10

THE FORALL CONSTRUCT

Fortran 95 includes a new construct that is designed to permit a set of operations to be applied on an element-by-element basis to a subset of the elements in an array. The elements to be operated on may be chosen by *both* a subscript index *and* a logical condition. The operations will only be applied to those elements of the array that satisfy both the index constraints and the logical condition. This new construct is called the FORALL construct.

5.10.1 The Form of the FORALL Construct

The general form of the FORALL construct is

```
[name:] FORALL (in1=triplet1[, in2=triplet2, ..., logical_expr])
    Statement 1
    Statement 2
    ...
    Statement n
END FORALL [name]
```

Each index in the FORALL statement is specified by a subscript triplet of the form

```
subscript_1 : subscript_2 : stride
```

where $subscript\_1$ is the starting value of the index, $subscript\_2$ is the ending value, and $stride$ is the index step. Statements 1 through n in the body of the construct are assignment statements that manipulate the elements of arrays having the selected indices and satisfying the logical expression on an element-by-element basis.

A name may be assigned to a FORALL construct if desired. If the FORALL statement at the beginning of a construct is named then the associated END FORALL statement must have the same name.

A simple example of a FORALL follows. These statements create a 10×10 identity matrix, which has ones along the diagonal and zeros everywhere else.

```
REAL, DIMENSION(10,10) :: i_matrix = 0.
...
FORALL ( i=1:10 )
    i_matrix(i,i) = 1.0
END FORALL
```

As a more complex example, let's suppose that we want to take the reciprocal of all of the elements in an n × m array work. We might try to use the simple assignment statement

```
work = 1. / work
```

but this statement would cause a run-time error and abort the program if any of the elements of work happen to be zero. A FORALL construct that avoids this problem is

```
FORALL ( i=1:n, j=1:m, work(i,j) /= 0. )
   work(i,j) = 1. / work(i,j)
END FORALL
```

5.10.2 The Significance of the FORALL Construct

In general, any expression that can be written in a FORALL construct can also be written as a set of nested DO loops combined with a block IF construct. For example, the previous FORALL example could be written as

```
DO i = 1, n
   DO j = 1, m
      IF ( work(i,j) /= 0.
         work(i,j) = 1. / work(i,j)
      END IF
   END DO
END DO
```

What is the difference between these two sets of statements, and why was the FORALL construct added to the Fortran 95 language?

The answer is that *the statements in the* DO *loop structure must be executed in a strict order, while the statements in the* FORALL *construct may be executed in any order.* In the DO loops, the elements of array work are processed in the following strict order:

```
work(1,1)
work(1,2)
. . .
work(1,m)
work(2,1)
work(2,2)
. . .
work(2,m)
. . .
work(n,m)
```

In contrast, the FORALL construct processes the same set of elements *in any order selected by the processor.* This freedom means that massively parallel computers can optimize the program for maximum speed by parceling out each element to a separate processor, and the processors can finish their work in any order without impacting the final answer.

If the body of a FORALL construct contains more than one statement, then the processor completely finishes all of the selected elements of the first statement before starting any of the elements of the second statement. In the following example, the values for a(i,j) that are calculated in the first statement are used to calculate b(i,j) in the second statement. All of the a values are calculated before the first b value is calculated

```
FORALL (i=2:n-1, j=2:n-1)
   a(i,j) = SQRT(a(i,j))
   b(i,j) = 1.0 / a(i,j)
END FORALL
```

Because each element must be capable of being processed independently, the body of a FORALL construct cannot contain transformational functions whose results depend on the values in the entire array. However, the body can contain nested FORALL and WHERE constructs.

5.10.3 The FORALL Statement

Fortran 95 also includes a single-line FORALL statement:

```
FORALL (ind1=triplet1[, ..., logical_expr]) Assignment Statement
```

The assignment statement is executed for those indices and logical expressions that satisfy the FORALL control parameters. This simpler form is the same as a FORALL construct with only one statement.

Fortran on Massively Parallel Supercomputers

Much of the recent evolution of Fortran has been driven by the development of massively parallel supercomputers. Such computers consist of from tens to thousands of identical CPUs that divide up a task and solve different parts of it in parallel.

Typical of these new computers is the Cray T3E. The T3E contains from 16 to 2048 separate processors, each of which is a very-high-speed DEC Alpha microprocessor capable of 600,000,000 floating-point operations per second (600 MFLOPS). The basic 16-processor version of the T3E is theoretically capable of 9600 MFLOPs, and the largest version with 2048 processors is theoretically capable of 1,200,000 MFLOPS!

The Cray T3E supercomputer *(Courtesy of CRAY Research, Inc.)*   *(continued)*

(concluded)

While these new supercomputers are theoretically capable of incredible speeds, they can only achieve high speeds on a real application if that application can be broken apart into many pieces, each of which can be executed in parallel on a different processor. Compilers for such machines must be smart enough to identify segments of code that can be separated and send them to different processors for execution.

Fortran compilers for such machines examine all DO loops to see if the iterations of the loops can be separated and sent to different processors in parallel. Sometimes the compiler can determine that the iterations of a DO loop are independent, but often it cannot. Fortran compilers for such computers provide special directives to allow the programmer to tell the compiler which loops may be broken apart and processed in parallel.

It is a good idea to replace DO loops with WHERE and FORALL constructs wherever possible on massively parallel computers because both constructs are designed to be easily separable. The WHERE is a masked assignment statement in which the action to be applied to any element only depends on the mask for that element. Therefore, each element of the array and the corresponding element of the mask can be sent to a separate processor, and the array can be reassembled after all the calculations have been performed in parallel.

Similarly, the indices and mask in the FORALL construct determine which array elements to apply the assignment statements in the construct to, but not the time order in which the calculations must be done. Therefore each calculation can be sent to a separate parallel processor, and the results can be reassembled after the calculations are complete.

User-defined pure and elemental functions are introduced in Chapter 6. These functions also help Fortran to run more efficiently on massively parallel computers because they can be executed in parallel without the multiple copies of the function interfering with each other.

5.11

ALLOCATABLE ARRAYS

In all the examples that we have seen so far, the size of each array was declared in a type declaration statement at the beginning of the program. This type of array declaration is called **static memory allocation,** since the size of each array is set at compilation time and never changes. The size of each array must be made large enough to hold the largest problem that a particular program will ever have to solve, which can be a very serious limitation. If we declare the array sizes to be large enough to handle the largest problem that we will ever need to solve, then the program will waste memory 99 percent of the time that it is run. In addition, the program might not run at all on small computers that don't have enough memory to hold it. However, if the arrays are made small, then the program cannot solve large problems.

What can a programmer do about this problem? If the program is well designed, then the array limitations could be modified by just changing one or two array size parameters in the source code and recompiling it. This process will work for in-house programs for which the source code is available, but it is not very elegant. It won't work at all for programs whose source code is unavailable, such as programs that you buy from someone else.

A much better solution is to design a program that uses **dynamic memory allocation.** It dynamically sets the sizes of the arrays each time it is executed to be just large enough to solve the current problem. This approach does not waste computer memory and will allow the same program to run on both small and large computers.

A Fortran array using dynamic memory is declared using the ALLOCATABLE attribute in the type declaration statement and is actually allocated with an ALLOCATE statement. When the program is through using the memory, it should free it up for other uses with a DEALLOCATE statement. The structure of a typical array declaration with the ALLOCATABLE attribute[3] is

```
REAL, ALLOCATABLE, DIMENSION(:,:) :: arr1
```

Note that colons are used as placeholders in the declaration, since we do not know how big the array will actually be. The *rank* of the array is declared in the type declaration statement, but not the *size* of the array.

An array declared with colons for dimensions is known as a **deferred-shape array** because the actual shape of the array is deferred until the memory for the array is allocated. (In contrast, an array whose size is explicitly declared in a type declaration statement is known as an **explicit-shape array.**)

When the program executes, the actual size of the array will be specified with an ALLOCATE statement. The form of an ALLOCATE statement is

```
ALLOCATE (list of arrays to allocate, STAT=status)
```

A typical example is

```
ALLOCATE (arr1(100,0:10), STAT=status)
```

This statement allocates a 100×11 array arr1 at execution time. The STAT= clause is optional. If it is present, it returns an integer status. The status will be 0 for successful allocation and a compiler-dependent positive number if the allocation process fails. The most common source of failure is not having enough free memory to allocate the array. If the allocation fails and the STAT= clause is not present, then the program will abort. You should always use the STAT= clause so that the program can terminate gracefully if not enough memory is available to allocate the array.

> ***Good Programming Practice***
> Always include the STAT= clause in any ALLOCATE statement, and always check the returned status, so that a program can be shut down gracefully if there is insufficient memory to allocate the necessary arrays.

---

[3]An array may also be declared to be allocatable in a separate ALLOCATABLE statement of the form

```
ALLOCATABLE :: arr1
```

It is preferable *not* to use this statement, since it is always possible to specify the ALLOCATABLE attribute in a type declaration statement and the array will appear in a type declaration statement anyway. The only time when a separate ALLOCATABLE statement is necessary is when default typing is used and there is no type declaration statement. Since we should *never* use default typing in any program, there is never a need for this statement.

An allocatable array *may not be used in any way* in a program until memory is allocated for it. Any attempt to use an allocatable array that is not currently allocated will produce a run-time error and cause the program to abort. Fortran 90/95 includes the logical intrinsic function ALLOCATED() to allow a program to test the allocation status of an array before attempting to use it. For example, the following code tests the status of allocatable array input_data before attempting to reference it:

```
REAL, ALLOCATABLE, DIMENSION(:) :: input_data
...
IF ( ALLOCATED(input_data) ) THEN
   READ (8,*) input_data
ELSE
   WRITE (*,*) 'Warning-Array not allocated!'
END IF
```

This function can be very helpful in large programs involving many procedures in which memory is allocated in one procedure and used in a different one.

At the end of the program or procedure in which an allocatable array is used, you should *deallocate* the memory to make it available for reuse with a DEALLOCATE statement. The structure of a DEALLOCATE statement is

```
DEALLOCATE (list of arrays to deallocate, STAT=status)
```

A typical example is

```
DEALLOCATE (arr1, STAT=status)
```

where the status clause has the same meaning as it has in the ALLOCATE statement. After a DEALLOCATE statement is executed, the data in the deallocated arrays is no longer available for use.

You should always deallocate any allocatable arrays once you are finished with them. This practice is especially important for arrays allocated in subroutines and functions, as you will see in the next chapter.

Good Programming Practice
Always deallocate dynamic arrays with a DEALLOCATE statement as soon as you are through using them.

EXAMPLE 5–8 *Using Allocatable Arrays:* To illustrate the use of allocatable arrays, we will rewrite the statistical analysis program of Example 5–4 to dynamically allocate only the amount of memory needed to solve the problem. To determine how much memory to allocate, the program will read the input data file and count the number of values. It will then allocate the array, rewind the file, read in the values, and calculate the statistics.

SOLUTION The modified program with allocatable arrays is shown in Figure 5–26.

FIGURE 5-26
A modified form of the statistics program that uses allocatable arrays.

```
PROGRAM stat_5
!
!   Purpose:
!     To calculate mean, median, and standard deviation of an input
!     data set read from a file.  This program uses allocatable arrays
!     to use only the memory required to solve each problem.
!
!   Record of revisions:
!        Date          Programmer          Description of change
!        ====          ==========          =====================
!     09/26/95      S. J. Chapman          Original code
! 1.  09/30/95      S. J. Chapman          Modified for dynamic memory
!
IMPLICIT NONE

! List of variables:
REAL,ALLOCATABLE,DIMENSION(:) :: a ! Data array to sort
CHARACTER(len=20) :: filename     ! Input data file name
INTEGER :: i                      ! Loop index
INTEGER :: iptr                   ! Pointer to smallest value
INTEGER :: j                      ! Loop index
REAL :: median                    ! The median of the input samples
INTEGER :: nvals = 0              ! The number of values to process
INTEGER :: status                 ! Status: 0 for success
REAL :: std_dev                   ! Standard deviation of input samples
REAL :: sum_x = 0.                ! Sum of input values
REAL :: sum_x2 = 0.               ! Sum of input values squared
REAL :: temp                      ! Temporary variable for swapping
REAL :: x_bar                     ! Average of input values

! Get the name of the file containing the input data.
WRITE (*,1000)
1000 FORMAT (1X, 'Enter the file name with the data to be sorted:')
READ (*,'(A20)') filename

! Open input data file. Status is OLD because the input data must
! already exist.
OPEN ( UNIT=9, FILE=filename, STATUS='OLD', ACTION='READ', &
       IOSTAT=status )

! Was the OPEN successful?
fileopen: IF ( status == 0 ) THEN          ! Open successful

   ! The file was opened successfully, so read the data to find
   ! out how many values are in the file and allocate the
   ! required space.
   DO
      READ (9, *, IOSTAT=status) temp      ! Get value
      IF ( status /= 0 ) EXIT              ! Exit on end of data
      nvals = nvals + 1                    ! Bump count
   END DO

   ! Allocate memory
   WRITE (*,*) ' Allocating a: size = ', nvals
   ALLOCATE ( a(nvals), STAT=status)        ! Allocate memory
```

(continued)

```
      ! Was allocation successful? If so, rewind file, read in
      ! data, and process it.
      allocate_ok: IF ( status == 0 ) THEN

         REWIND ( UNIT=9 )                        ! Rewind file

         ! Now read in the data. We know that there are enough
         ! values to fill the array.
         READ (9, *) a                            ! Get values

         ! Sort the data.
         outer: DO i = 1, nvals-1

            ! Find the minimum value in a(i) through a(nvals)
            iptr = i
            inner: DO j = i+1, nvals
               minval: IF ( a(j) < a(iptr) ) THEN
                  iptr = j
               END IF minval
            END DO inner

            ! iptr now points to the minimum value, so swap a(iptr)
            ! with a(i) if i /= iptr.
            swap: IF ( i /= iptr ) THEN
               temp     = a(i)
               a(i)     = a(iptr)
               a(iptr) = temp
            END IF swap

         END DO outer

         ! The data is now sorted. Accumulate sums to calculate
         ! statistics.
         sums: DO i = 1, nvals
            sum_x  = sum_x + a(i)
            sum_x2 = sum_x2 + a(i)**2
         END DO sums

         ! Check to see if we have enough input data.
         enough: IF ( nvals < 2) THEN

            ! Insufficient data.
            WRITE (*,*) ' At least 2 values must be entered.'

         ELSE

            ! Calculate the mean, median, and standard deviation
            x_bar   = sum_x / real(nvals)
            std_dev = sqrt( (real(nvals) * sum_x2 - sum_x**2) &
                     / (real(nvals) * real(nvals-1)) )
            even: IF ( mod(nvals,2) == 0 ) THEN
               median = ( a(nvals/2) + a(nvals/2+1) ) / 2.
            ELSE
               median = a(nvals/2+1)
            END IF even

            ! Tell user.
            WRITE (*,*) 'The mean of this data set is:   ', x_bar
            WRITE (*,*) 'The median of this data set is: ', median
            WRITE (*,*) 'The standard deviation is:      ', std_dev
            WRITE (*,*) 'The number of data points is:   ', nvals

         END IF enough
```

(continued)

(concluded)

```
        ! Deallocate the array now that we are done.
        DEALLOCATE ( a, STAT=status )

   END IF allocate_ok

ELSE fileopen

   ! Else file open failed. Tell user.
   WRITE (*,1050) status
   1050 FORMAT (1X,'File open failed--status = ', I6)

END IF fileopen

END PROGRAM
```

To test this program, we will run it with the same data set as Example 5–4.

```
C>stat_5
Enter the file name containing the input data:
input4
Allocating a: size =              5
The mean of this data set is:        4.400000
The median of this data set is:      4.000000
The standard deviation is:           2.966479
The number of data points is:        5
```

The program gives the correct answers for our test data set.

Quiz 5–3

This quiz provides a quick check to see if you understand the concepts introduced in sections 5.8 through 5.11. If you have trouble with the quiz, reread the sections, ask your instructor, or discuss the material with a fellow student. The answers to this quiz are found in the back of the book.

For questions 1 to 5, determine what will be printed out by the WRITE statements.

```
1. REAL, DIMENSION(-3:3,0:50) :: values
   WRITE (*,*) LBOUND(values,1)
   WRITE (*,*) UBOUND(values,2)
   WRITE (*,*) SIZE(values,1)
   WRITE (*,*) SIZE(values)
   WRITE (*,*) SHAPE(values)

2. REAL, ALLOCATABLE, DIMENSION(:,:,:) :: values
   ...
   ALLOCATE( values(3,4,5), STAT=istat )
   WRITE (*,*) UBOUND(values,2)
   WRITE (*,*) SIZE(values)
   WRITE (*,*) SHAPE(values)
```

(continued)

(concluded)

3.
```fortran
REAL, DIMENSION(5,5) :: input1
DO i = 1, 5
   DO j = 1, 5
      input1(i,j) = i+j-1
   END DO
END DO
WRITE (*,*) MAXVAL(input1)
WRITE (*,*) MAXLOC(input1)
```

4.
```fortran
REAL, DIMENSION(2,2) :: arr1
arr1 = RESHAPE( (/3.,0.,-3.,5./), (/2,2/) )
WRITE (*,*) SUM( arr1 )
WRITE (*,*) PRODUCT( arr1 )
WRITE (*,*) PRODUCT( arr1, MASK=arr1 /= 0. )
WRITE (*,*) ANY(arr1 > 0.)
WRITE (*,*) ALL(arr1 > 0.)
```

5.
```fortran
INTEGER, DIMENSION(2,3) :: arr2
arr2 = RESHAPE( (/3,0,-3,5,-8,2/), (/2,3/) )
WHERE ( arr2 > 0 )
   arr2 = 2 * arr2
END WHERE
WRITE (*,*) SUM( arr2, MASK=arr2 > 0. )
```

6. Rewrite question 3 using a `FORALL` construct to initialize `input1`.

Determine which of the following sets of Fortran statements are valid. For each set of valid statements, specify what will happen in the program. For each set of invalid statements, specify what is wrong. Assume default typing for any variables that are not explicitly typed.

7.
```fortran
REAL, DIMENSION(6) :: dist1
REAL, DIMENSION(5) :: time
dist1 = (/ 0.00, 0.25, 1.00, 2.25, 4.00, 6.25 /)
time = (/ 0.0, 1.0, 2.0, 3.0, 4.0 /)
WHERE ( time > 0. )
   dist1 = SQRT(dist1)
END WHERE
```

8.
```fortran
REAL, DIMENSION(:), ALLOCATABLE :: time
time = (/ 0.00,  0.25,  1.00,  2.25, 4.00, 6.25, &
          9.00, 12.25, 16.00, 20.25 /)
WRITE (*,*) time
```

9.
```fortran
INTEGER, DIMENSION(5,5) :: data1 = 0.
FORALL (i=1:5:2, j=1:5, i-j>=0 )
   data1(i,j) = i - j + 1
END FORALL
WRITE (*,100) ((data1(i,j), j=1,5), i=1,5)
100 FORMAT (1X,5I6)
```

10.
```fortran
REAL, DIMENSION(:,:), ALLOCATABLE :: test
WRITE (*,*) ALLOCATED(test)
```

▨ 5.12

WHEN SHOULD YOU USE AN ARRAY?

You have now learned *how* to use arrays in your Fortran programs, but you have not yet learned *when* to use them. At this point in a typical Fortran course, many students are tempted to use arrays to solve problems whether they are needed or not, just because they know how to do so. How can you decide whether or not it makes sense to use an array in a particular problem?

In general, if much or all of the input data must be in memory at the same time to solve a problem efficiently, then the use of arrays to hold that data is appropriate for that problem. Otherwise, arrays are not needed. For example, let's contrast the statistics programs in Examples 3–5 and 5–4. Example 3–5 calculated the mean and standard deviation of a data set, while Example 5–4 calculated the mean, median, and standard deviation of a data set.

Recall that the equations for the mean and standard deviation of a data set are

$$\bar{x} = \frac{1}{N} \sum_{i=1}^{N} x_i \tag{3-3}$$

and

$$s = \sqrt{\frac{N \sum\limits_{i=1}^{N} x_i^2 - \left(\sum\limits_{i=1}^{N} x_i \right)^2}{N(N-1)}} \tag{3-4}$$

The sums in Equations (3–3) and (3–4) that are required to find the mean and standard deviation can easily be formed as data values are read in one by one. There is no need to wait until all of the data are read before starting to build the sums. Therefore, a program to calculate the mean and standard deviation of a data set does not need to use arrays. You could use an array to hold all of the input values before calculating the mean and standard deviation, but since the array is not necessary, you should not do so. Example 3–5 works fine and is built entirely without arrays.

On the other hand, finding the median of a data set requires that the data be sorted into ascending order. Since sorting requires all data to be in memory, a program that calculates the median must use an array to hold all of the input data before the calculations start. Therefore, Example 5–4 uses an array to hold its input data.

Two major problems are associated with using unnecessary arrays:

1. *Unnecessary arrays waste memory.* Unnecessary arrays can eat up a lot of memory, making a program larger than it needs to be. A large program requires more memory to run it, which makes the computer that it runs on more expensive. In some cases the extra size may prevent a program from running on a particular computer.
2. *Unnecessary arrays restrict program capabilities.* To understand this point, let's consider an example program that calculates the mean and standard deviation of a data set. If the program is designed with a 1000-element static input array, then it will only work for data sets with up to 1000 elements. If we encounter a data

set with more than 1000 elements, the program would have to be recompiled and relinked with a larger array size. On the other hand, a program that calculates the mean and standard deviation of a data set as the values are input has no upper limit on data set size.

 Good Programming Practice

Do not use arrays to solve a problem unless they are actually needed.

■ **5.13**
SUMMARY

5

Chapter 5 introduces arrays and their use in Fortran programs. An array is a group of variables, all of the same type, which are referred to by a single name. An individual variable within the array is called an array element. Individual array elements are addressed by means of one or more (up to seven) subscripts.

An array is declared using a type declaration statement by naming the array and specifying the maximum (and, optionally, the minimum) subscript values with the DIMENSION attribute. The compiler uses the declared subscript ranges to reserve space in the computer's memory to hold the array. The array elements are allocated in the computer's memory in an order such that the first subscript of the array changes most rapidly and the last subscript of the array changes most slowly.

As with any variable, an array must be initialized before use. An array may be initialized at compile time using array constructors in the type declaration statements or at run time using array constructors, DO loops, or Fortran READs.

Individual array elements may be used freely in a Fortran program just like any other variable. They may appear in assignment statements on either side of the equal sign. Entire arrays and array sections may also be used in calculations and assignment statements as long as the arrays are conformable with each other. Arrays are conformable if they have the same number of dimensions (rank) and the same extent in each dimension. A scalar is also conformable with any array. An operation between two conformable arrays is performed on an element-by-element basis. Scalar values are also conformable with arrays.

Fortran 90/95 contains three basic types of intrinsic functions: elemental functions, inquiry functions, and transformational functions. Elemental functions are defined for a scalar input and produce a scalar output. When applied to an array, an elemental function produces an output that is the result of applying the operation separately to each element of the input array. Inquiry functions return information about an array, such as its size or bounds. Transformational functions operate on entire arrays and produce an output that is based on all the elements of the array.

The WHERE construct permits an array assignment statement to be performed on only those elements of an array that meet specified criteria. It is useful for preventing errors caused by out-of-range data values in the array.

The FORALL construct is a method of applying an operation to many elements of an array without specifying the order in which the operation must be applied to the individual elements. It is only found in Fortran 95.

Arrays may either be static or allocatable. The size of static arrays are declared at compilation time, and they may be modified only by recompiling the program. The size of dynamic arrays may be declared at execution time, allowing a program to adjust its memory requirements to fit the size of the problem to be solved. Allocatable arrays are declared using the ALLOCATABLE attribute, are allocated during program execution using the ALLOCATE statement, and are deallocated using the DEALLOCATE statement.

Arrays are especially useful for working with data values that change as a function of one or more variables (time, location, etc.). Once the data values are stored in an array, they can be easily manipulated to derive statistics or other information.

5.13.1 Summary of Good Programming Practice

You should adhere to the following guidelines when working with arrays.

1. Decide whether an array is really needed to solve a problem *before* writing the program. If arrays are not needed, don't use them!
2. Declare all array sizes using named constants. If the sizes are declared using named constants and if those same named constants are used in any size tests within the program, then it will be very easy to modify the maximum capacity of the program at a later time.
3. Initialize all arrays before use. The results of using an uninitialized array are unpredictable and vary from processor to processor.
4. Use the bounds-checking option of your compiler. The most common problem when programming with arrays is attempting to read from or write to locations outside the bounds of the array. To detect this problem, always turn on the bounds-checking option of your compiler during program testing and debugging. Because bounds checking slows down the execution of a program, you may turn off the bounds-checking option once debugging is completed.
5. Use the RESHAPE function to change the shape of an array. This function is especially useful when used with an array constructor to create array constants of any desired shape.
6. Use implicit DO loops to read in or write out rank-2 arrays so that each row of the array appears as a row of the input or output file. This correspondence makes it easier for a programmer to relate the data in the file to the data present within the program.
7. Use WHERE constructs to modify and assign array elements when you want to modify and assign only those elements that pass some test.
8. Use allocatable arrays to produce programs that automatically adjust their memory requirements to the size of the problem being solved. Declare allocatable arrays with the ALLOCATABLE attribute, allocate memory to them with the ALLOCATE statement, and deallocate memory with the DEALLOCATE statement.

9. Always include the STAT= clause in any ALLOCATE statement, and always check the returned status, so that a program can be shut down gracefully if there is insufficient memory to allocate the necessary arrays.

5.13.2 Summary of Fortran Statements and Constructs

Type Declaration Statements with Arrays

```
type, DIMENSION( [i1:]i2, [j1:]j2,...) :: array1, ...
```

Examples:

```
REAL, DIMENSION(100) :: array
INTEGER, DIMENSION(-5:5,2) :: i
```

Description:
   These type declaration statements declare the type, shape, and size of an array.

ALLOCATABLE Attribute

```
type, ALLOCATABLE, DIMENSION(:,[:, ...]) :: array1, ...
```

Examples:

```
REAL, ALLOCATABLE, DIMENSION(:) :: array1
INTEGER, ALLOCATABLE, DIMENSION(:,:,:) :: indices
```

Description:
   The ALLOCATABLE attribute declares that the size of an array is dynamic. The size will be specified in an ALLOCATE statement at run time. The type declaration statement must specify the rank of the array, but not the extent in each dimension. Each dimension is specified using a colon as a placeholder.

ALLOCATABLE Statement

```
ALLOCATABLE :: array1, ...
```

Example:

```
ALLOCATABLE :: array1
```

Description:
   The ALLOCATABLE statement declares that the size of an array is dynamic. It duplicates the function of the ALLOCATABLE attribute associated with a type declaration statement. **Do not use this statement.** Use the ALLOCATABLE attribute instead.

5

ALLOCATE Statement

```
ALLOCATE (array1( [i1:]i2, [j1:]j2, ... ), ..., STAT=status)
```

Examples:

```
ALLOCATE (array1(10000), STAT=istat)
ALLOCATE (indices(-10:10,-10:10,5), STAT=allocate_status)
```

Description:

The ALLOCATE statement dynamically allocates memory to an array that was previously declared allocatable. The extent of each dimension is specified in the ALLOCATE statement. The returned status will be zero for successful completion and will be a machine-dependent positive number in the case of an error.

DEALLOCATE Statement

```
DEALLOCATE (array1, ... , STAT=status)
```

Example:

```
DEALLOCATE (array1, indices, STAT=status)
```

Description:

The DEALLOCATE statement dynamically deallocates the memory that an ALLOCATE statement assigned to one or more allocatable arrays. After the statement executes, the memory associated with those arrays is no longer accessible. The returned status will be zero for successful completion and will be a machine-dependent positive number in the case of an error.

FORALL Construct

```
[name: ] FORALL (index1=triplet1[, ..., logical_expr])
   Assignment Statement(s)
END FORALL [name]
```

Example:

```
FORALL (i=1:3, j=1:3, i > j)
   arr1(i,j) = ABS(i-j) + 3
END FORALL
```

Description:

The FORALL construct permits assignment statements to be executed for indices that meet the triplet specifications and the optional logical expression, but this construct does not specify the order in which the statements are executed. There may be as many indices as desired, and each index will be specified by a subscript triplet. The logical expression is applied as a mask to the indices, and the combinations of specified indices for which the logical expression is true will be executed. This construct is only available in Fortran 95.

FORALL Statement

```
FORALL (index1=triplet1[, ..., logical_expr]) Assignment Statement
```

Description:

The FORALL statement, a simplified version of the FORALL construct, contains only one assignment statement. This statement is only available in Fortran 95.

Implied DO Loop Structure

```
READ (unit,format) (arg1, arg2, ... , index = istart, iend, incr)
WRITE (unit,format) (arg1, arg2, ... , index = istart, iend, incr)
(/ (arg1, arg2, ... , index = istart, iend, incr) /)
```

Examples:

```
WRITE (*,*) ( array(i), i = 1, 10 )
INTEGER, DIMENSION(100) :: values
values = (/ (i, i=1,100) /)
```

Description:

The implied DO loop is used to repeat the values in an argument list a known number of times. The values in the argument list may be functions of the DO loop index variable. During the first iteration of the DO loop, the variable index is set to the value istart. index is incremented by incr in each successive loop until its value exceeds iend, at which time the loop terminates.

WHERE Construct

```
[name:] WHERE ( mask_expr1 )
   Block 1
ELSEWHERE ( mask_expr2 ) [name]
   Block 2
ELSEWHERE [name]
   Block 3
END WHERE [name]
```

Description:

The WHERE construct permits operations to be applied to the elements of an array that match a given criterion. A different set of operations may be applied to the elements that do not match. Each mask_expr must be a logical array of the same shape as the arrays being manipulated within the code blocks. If a given element of the mask_expr1 is true, then the array assignment statements in block 1 will be applied to the corresponding element in the arrays being operated on. If an element of the mask_expr1 is false and the corresponding element of the mask_expr2 is true, then the array assignment statements in block 2 will be applied to the corresponding element in the arrays being operated on. If both mask expressions are false, then the array assignment statements in block 3 will be applied to the corresponding element in the arrays being operated on.

The ELSEWHERE clauses are optional in this construct. The construct can have as many masked ELSE-WHERE clauses as desired and up to one plain ELSEWHERE clause.

The masked ELSEWHERE clauses are only available in Fortran 95.

WHERE Statement

    WHERE (*mask expression*) *array_assignment_statement*

Description:
  The WHERE statement, a simplified version of the WHERE construct, has only one array assignment statement and no ELSEWHERE clause.

▧ 5.14

EXERCISES

5–1 How may arrays be declared?

5–2 What is the difference between an array and an array element?

5–3 Execute the following Fortran program on your computer with bounds checking turned on and then with bounds checking turned off. What happens in each case?

```
PROGRAM bounds
IMPLICIT NONE
REAL, DIMENSION(5) :: test = (/ 1., 2., 3., 4., 5. /)
REAL, DIMENSION(5) :: test1
INTEGER :: i
DO i = 1, 6
   test(i) = SQRT(test(i))
   WRITE (*,100) 'SQRT(',test(i), ') = ', test1(i)
   100 FORMAT (1X,A,F6.3,A,F14.4)
END DO
END PROGRAM
```

5–4 Determine the shape and size of the arrays specified by the following declaration statements; also determine the valid subscript range for each dimension of each array.

  a. CHARACTER(len=80), DIMENSION(60) :: line

  b. INTEGER, PARAMETER :: istart = 32
      INTEGER, PARAMETER :: istop = 256
      INTEGER, DIMENSION(istart:istop) :: char

  c. INTEGER, PARAMETER :: num_class = 3
      INTEGER, PARAMETER :: num_student = 35
      LOGICAL, DIMENSION(num_student,num_class) :: passfail

  d. REAL, DIMENSION(-5:5,-5:5,-5:5,-5:5,-5:5) :: range

5–5 Determine which of the following Fortran program fragments are valid. For each valid statement, specify what will happen in the program. (Assume default typing for any variables that are not explicitly typed within the program fragments.)

  a. INTEGER, DIMENSION(100) :: icount, jcount
      ...
      icount = (/ (i, i=1, 100) /)
      jcount = icount + 1

b.
```
REAL, DIMENSION(6,4) :: b
...
DO i = 1, 6
   DO j = 1, 4
      temp    = b(i,j)
      b(i,j)  = b(j,i)
      b(j,i)  = temp
   END DO
END DO
```

c.
```
REAL, DIMENSION(10) :: value
value(1:10:2) = (/ 5., 4., 3., 2., 1. /)
value(2:11:2) = (/ 10., 9., 8., 7., 6. /)
WRITE (*,100) value
100 FORMAT ('1','Value = ',/,(F10.2))
```

d.
```
INTEGER, DIMENSION(9) :: info
info = (/1,-3,0,-5,-9,3,0,1,7/)
WHERE ( info > 0 )
   info = -info
ELSEWHERE
   info = -3 * info
END WHERE
WRITE (*,*) info
```

e.
```
INTEGER, DIMENSION(8) :: info
info = (/1,-3,0,-5,-9,3,0,7/)
WRITE (*,*) info <= 0
```

f.
```
REAL, DIMENSION(4,4) :: z = 0.
...
FORALL ( i=1:4, j=1:4 )
   z(i,j) = ABS(i-j)
END FORALL
```

5–6 Define these array terms: *(a)* size, *(b)* shape, *(c)* extent, *(d)* rank, *(e)* conformable.

5–7 Given a 5×5 array `my_array` containing the following values, determine the shape and contents of each of the following array sections.

$$my\_array = \begin{bmatrix} 1 & 2 & 3 & 4 & 5 \\ 6 & 7 & 8 & 9 & 10 \\ 11 & 12 & 13 & 14 & 15 \\ 16 & 17 & 18 & 19 & 20 \\ 21 & 22 & 23 & 24 & 25 \end{bmatrix}$$

a. `my_array(3,:)`

b. `my_array(:,2)`

c. `my_array(1:5:2,:)`

d. `my_array(:,2:5:2)`

e. `my_array(1:5:2,1:5:2)`

f.
```
INTEGER, DIMENSION(3) :: list = (/ 1, 2, 4 /)
my_array(:,list)
```

5–8 What will be the output from each of the WRITE statements in the following program? Why is the output of the two statements different?

```
PROGRAM test_output
IMPLICIT NONE
INTEGER, DIMENSION(0:1,0:3) :: my_data
INTEGER :: i, j
my_data(0,:) = (/ 1, 2, 3, 4 /)
my_data(1,:) = (/ 5, 6, 7, 8 /)
!
DO i = 0,1
   WRITE (*,100) (my_data(i,j), j=0,3)
   100 FORMAT (6(1X,I4))
END DO
WRITE (*,100) ((my_data(i,j), j=0,3), i=0,1)
END PROGRAM
```

5–9 An input data file INPUT1 contains the following values:

27	17	10	8	6
11	13	-11	12	-21
-1	0	0	6	14
-16	11	21	26	-16
04	99	-99	17	2

Assume that file INPUT1 has been opened on i/o unit 8 and that array values is a 4 × 4 integer array in which the elements have been initialized to zero. What will be the contents of array values after each of the following READ statements has been executed?

a. DO i = 1, 4
       READ (8,*) (values(i,j), j = 1, 4)
    END DO

b. READ (8,*) ((values(i,j), j = 1, 4), i=1,4)

c. DO i = 1, 4
       READ (8,*) values(i,:)
    END DO

d. READ (8,*) values

5–10 What will be printed out by the following program?

```
PROGRAM test
IMPLICIT NONE
INTEGER, PARAMETER :: n = 5, m = 10
INTEGER, DIMENSION(n:m,m-n:m+n) :: info

WRITE (*,100) SHAPE(info)
100 FORMAT (1X,'The shape of the array is:          ',2I6)
WRITE (*,110) SIZE(info)
110 FORMAT (1X,'The size of the array is:           ',I6)
WRITE (*,120) LBOUND(info)
120 FORMAT (1X,'The lower bounds of the array are: ',2I6)
WRITE (*,130) UBOUND(info)
130 FORMAT (1X,'The upper bounds of the array are: ',2I6)

END PROGRAM
```

5–11 Polar to Rectangular Conversion   A *scalar quantity* is a quantity that can be represented by a single number. For example, the temperature at a given location is a scalar.
In contrast, a *vector* is a quantity that has both a magnitude and a direction associated
with it. For example, the velocity of an automobile is a vector, since it has both a magnitude and a direction.

Vectors can be defined either by a magnitude and a direction or by the components
of the vector projected along the axes of a rectangular coordinate system. The two representations are equivalent. For two-dimensional vectors, we can convert back and forth
between the representations using the equations

$$\mathbf{V} = V\angle\theta = V_x\mathbf{i} + V_y\mathbf{j}$$

$$V_x = V\cos\theta$$

$$V_y = V\sin\theta$$

$$V = \sqrt{V_x^2 + V_y^2}$$

$$\theta = \tan^{-1}\frac{V_y}{V_x}$$

where $\mathbf{i}$ and $\mathbf{j}$ are the unit vectors in the x and y directions, respectively. The representation of the vector in terms of magnitude and angle is known as *polar coordinates,* and
the representation of the vector in terms of components along the axes is known as *rectangular coordinates.* Figure 5–27 shows the relationship between the two representations.
Write a program that reads the polar coordinates (magnitude and angle) of a two-
dimensional vector into a rank-1 array polar (polar(1) will contain the magnitude
V, and polar(2) will contain the angle θ in degrees), converts the vector from polar
to rectangular form, and stores the result in a rank-1 array rect. The first element of
rect should contain the x-component of the vector, and the second element should contain the y-component of the vector. After the conversion, display the contents of array
rect. Test your program by converting the following polar vectors to rectangular form:
a. $5\angle-36.87°$
b. $10\angle45°$
c. $25\angle233.13°$

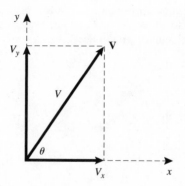

FIGURE 5–27
Representations of a vector.

5–12 Rectangular to Polar Conversion   Write a program that reads the rectangular components of a two-dimensional vector into a rank-1 array `rect` (`rect(1)` will contain the component V_x and `rect(2)` will contain the component V_y), converts the vector from rectangular to polar form, and stores the result in a rank-1 array `polar`. The first element of `polar` should contain the magnitude of the vector, and the second element should contain the angle of the vector in degrees. After the conversion, display the contents of array `polar`. (*Hint:* Look up function ATAN2 in Appendix B.) Test your program by converting the following rectangular vectors to polar form:

a. 3 **i** − 4 **j**
b. 5 **i** + 5 **j**
c. −5 **i** + 12 **j**

5–13   Assume that `values` is a 101-element array, containing a list of measurements from a scientific experiment, which has been declared by the statement

```
REAL, DIMENSION(-50:50) :: values
```

Write the Fortran statements that would count the number of positive values, negative values, and zero values in the array and then write out a message summarizing how many values of each type were found.

5–14   Rewrite the Fortran statements of Exercise 5–13, taking advantage of the transformational intrinsic function COUNT.

5–15   Write Fortran statements that would print out every fifth value in the array `values` described in Exercise 5–13. Write two versions of the statements, one using a DO loop to perform the output and one using array sections to perform the output. The output should take the following form:

```
values(-50) = xxx.xxxx
values(-45) = xxx.xxxx
...
values( 50) = xxx.xxxx
```

5–16   Write a program that can read in a rank-2 array from an input disk file and calculate the sums of all the data in each row and of each column in the array. Two numbers on the first line in the input file will specify the size of the array to read in, and the elements in each row of the array appear on a single line of the input file. Size the program to handle arrays of up to 100 rows and 100 columns. An example of an input data file containing a 2 row × 4 column array follows.

```
   2         4
-24.0    -1121.      812.1     11.1
 35.6     8.1E3    135.23    -17.3
```

Write out the results in the form:

```
Sum of row   1 =
Sum of row   2 =
    ...
Sum of col   1 =
    ...
```

5–17 Test the program that you wrote in Exercise 5–16 by running it on the following array:

$$\text{array} = \begin{bmatrix} 33. & -12. & 16. & 0.5 & -1.9 \\ -6. & -14. & 3.5 & 11. & 2.1 \\ 4.4 & 1.1 & -7.1 & 9.3 & -16.1 \\ 0.3 & 6.2 & -9.9 & -12. & 6.8 \end{bmatrix}$$

5–18 Modify the program you wrote in Exercise 5–16 to use allocatable arrays that are adjusted to match the number of rows and columns in the problem each time the program is run.

5–19 Dot Product   A three-dimensional vector can be represented in rectangular coordinates as

$$\mathbf{V} = V_x \, \mathbf{i} + V_y \, \mathbf{j} + V_z \, \mathbf{k}$$

where V_x is the component of vector $\mathbf{V}$ in the x direction, V_y is the component of vector $\mathbf{V}$ in the y direction, and V_z is the component of vector $\mathbf{V}$ in the z direction. Such a vector can be stored in a rank-1 array containing three elements, since there are three dimensions in the coordinate system. The same idea applies to an n-dimensional vector. An n-dimensional vector can be stored in a rank-1 array containing n elements. This is the reason why rank-1 arrays are sometimes called vectors.

One common mathematical operation between two vectors is the *dot product*. The dot product of two vectors $\mathbf{V}_1 = V_{x1} \, \mathbf{i} + V_{y1} \, \mathbf{j} + V_{z1} \, \mathbf{k}$ and $\mathbf{V}_2 = V_{x2} \, \mathbf{i} + V_{y2} \, \mathbf{j} + V_{z2} \, \mathbf{k}$ is a scalar quantity defined by the equation

$$\mathbf{V}_1 \cdot \mathbf{V}_2 = V_{x1}V_{x2} + V_{y1}V_{y2} + V_{z1}V_{z2}$$

Write a Fortran program that will read two vectors $\mathbf{V}_1$ and $\mathbf{V}_2$ into 2 one-dimensional arrays in computer memory and then calculate their dot product according to the equation given above. Test your program by calculating the dot product of vectors $\mathbf{V}_1 = 5 \, \mathbf{i} - 3 \, \mathbf{j} + 2 \, \mathbf{k}$ and $\mathbf{V}_2 = 2 \, \mathbf{i} + 3 \, \mathbf{j} + 4 \, \mathbf{k}$.

5–20 Power Supplied to an Object   If an object is being pushed by a force $\mathbf{F}$ at a velocity $\mathbf{v}$, then the power supplied to the object by the force is given by the equation

$$P = \mathbf{F} \cdot \mathbf{v}$$

where the force $\mathbf{F}$ is measured in newtons, the velocity $\mathbf{v}$ is measured in meters per second, and the power P is measured in watts (see Fig. 5–28). Use the Fortran program written in Exercise 5–19 to calculate the power supplied by a force of $\mathbf{F} = 4 \, \mathbf{i} + 3 \, \mathbf{j} - 2 \, \mathbf{k}$ newtons to an object moving with a velocity of $\mathbf{v} = 4 \, \mathbf{i} - 2 \, \mathbf{j} + 1 \, \mathbf{k}$ meters per second.

5–21 Write a set of Fortran statements that would search a rank-3 array `arr` and limit the maximum value of any array element to be less than or equal to 1000. If any element exceeds 1000, its value should be set to 1000. Assume that array `arr` has dimensions $1000 \times 10 \times 30$. Write two sets of statements, one checking the array elements one at a time using DO loops and one using the WHERE construct. Which approach is easier?

FIGURE 5–28
A force $\mathbf{F}$ applied to an object moving with velocity $\mathbf{v}$.

5–22 Cross Product Another common mathematical operation between two vectors is the *cross product.* The cross product of two vectors $V_1 = V_{x1}\ i + V_{y1}\ j + V_{z1}\ k$ and $V_2 = V_{x2}\ i + V_{y2}\ j + V_{z2}\ k$ is a vector quantity defined by the equation

$$V_1 \times V_2 = (V_{y1}V_{z2} - V_{y2}V_{z1})\ i + (V_{z1}V_{x2} - V_{z2}V_{x1})\ j + (V_{x1}V_{y2} - V_{x2}V_{y1})\ k$$

Write a Fortran program that will read two vectors V_1 and V_2 into arrays in computer memory and then calculate their cross product according to the preceding equation. Test your program by calculating the cross product of vectors $V_1 = 5\ i - 3\ j + 2\ k$ and $V_2 = 2\ i + 3\ j + 4\ k$.

5–23 Velocity of an Orbiting Object The vector angular velocity ω of an object moving with a velocity v at a distance r from the origin of the coordinate system is given by the equation

$$v = r \times \omega$$

where r is the distance in meters, ω is the angular velocity in radians per second, and v is the velocity in meters per second (see Figure 5–29). If the distance from the center of the earth to an orbiting satellite is $r = 300000\ i + 400000\ j + 50000\ k$ meters and the angular velocity of the satellite is $\omega = -6 \times 10^{-3}\ i + 2 \times 10^{-3}\ j - 9 \times 10^{-4}\ k$ radians per second, what is the velocity of the satellite in meters per second? Use the program written in Exercise 5–22 to calculate the answer.

5–24 Program `stat_4` in Example 5–4 will behave incorrectly if a user enters an invalid value in the input data set. For example, if the user enters the characters `1.o` instead of `1.0` on a line, then the `READ` statement will return a nonzero status for that line. This nonzero status will be misinterpreted as the end of the data set, and only a portion of the input data will be processed. Modify the program to protect against invalid values in the input data file. If a bad value is encountered in the input data file, the program should display the line number containing the bad value and skip it. The program should process all of the good values in the file, even those after a bad value.

5–25 The location of any point P in a three-dimensional space can be represented by a set of three values (x, y, z), where x is the distance along the x-axis to the point, y is the distance along the y-axis to the point, and z is the distance along the z-axis to the point. If two points P_1 and P_2 are represented by the values (x_1, y_1, z_1) and (x_2, y_2, z_2), then the distance between the points P_1 and P_2 can be calculated from the equation

$$distance = \sqrt{(x_1 - x_2)^2 + (y_1 - y_2)^2 + (z_1 - z_2)^2}$$

FIGURE 5–29

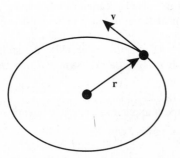

Write a Fortran program to read in two points (x_1, y_1, z_1) and (x_2, y_2, z_2) and to calculate the distance between them. Test your program by calculating the distance between the points $(-1, 4, 6)$ and $(1, 5, -2)$.

5–26 Average Annual Temperature As a part of a meteorological experiment, average annual temperature measurements were collected at 36 locations specified by latitude and longitude as shown in the following chart:

	90.0°W long	90.5°W long	91.0°W long	91.5°W long	92.0°W long	92.5°W long
30.0°N lat	68.2	72.1	72.5	74.1	74.4	74.2
30.5°N lat	69.4	71.1	71.9	73.1	73.6	73.7
31.0°N lat	68.9	70.5	70.9	71.5	72.8	73.0
31.5°N lat	68.6	69.9	70.4	70.8	71.5	72.2
32.0°N lat	68.1	69.3	69.8	70.2	70.9	71.2
32.5°N lat	68.3	68.8	69.6	70.0	70.5	70.9

Write a Fortran program that calculates the average annual temperature along each latitude and along each longitude included in the experiment. Finally, calculate the average annual temperature for all the locations in the experiment. Take advantage of intrinsic functions where appropriate to make your program simpler.

5–27 Matrix Multiplication Matrix multiplication is only defined for two matrices in which *the number of columns in the first matrix is equal to the number of rows in the second matrix*. If matrix A is an $N \times L$ matrix, and matrix B is an $L \times M$ matrix, then the product $C = A \times B$ is an $N \times M$ matrix whose elements are given by the equation

$$c_{ik} = \sum_{j=1}^{L} a_{ij} b_{jk}$$

For example, if matrices A and B are 2×2 matrices

$$A = \begin{bmatrix} 3.0 & -1.0 \\ 1.0 & 2.0 \end{bmatrix} \quad \text{and} \quad B = \begin{bmatrix} 1.0 & 4.0 \\ 2.0 & -3.0 \end{bmatrix}$$

then the elements of matrix C will be

$$c_{11} = a_{11}b_{11} + a_{12}b_{21} = (3.0)(1.0) + (-1.0)(2.0) = 1.0$$
$$c_{12} = a_{11}b_{12} + a_{12}b_{22} = (3.0)(4.0) + (-1.0)(-3.0) = 15.0$$
$$c_{21} = a_{21}b_{11} + a_{22}b_{21} = (1.0)(1.0) + (2.0)(2.0) = 5.0$$
$$c_{22} = a_{21}b_{12} + a_{22}b_{22} = (1.0)(4.0) + (2.0)(-3.0) = -2.0$$

Write a program that can read two matrices of arbitrary size from two input disk files and multiply them if they are of compatible sizes. If they are of incompatible sizes, an appropriate error message should be printed. Two integers on the first line in each file will specify the number of rows and columns in each matrix, and the elements in each row of the matrix will appear on a single line of the input file. Use allocatable arrays to hold both the input matrices and the resulting output matrix. Verify your program by creating two input data files containing matrices of the compatible sizes, calculating the resulting values, and checking the answers by hand. Also, verify the proper behavior of the program if it is given two matrices of incompatible sizes.

5–28 Use the program produced in Exercise 5–27 to calculate $C = A \times B$ where

$$A = \begin{bmatrix} 1. & -5. & 4. & 2. \\ -6. & -4. & 2. & 2. \end{bmatrix} \quad \text{and} \quad B = \begin{bmatrix} 1. & -2. & -1. \\ 2. & 3. & 4. \\ 0. & -1. & 2. \\ 0. & -3. & 1. \end{bmatrix}$$

How many rows and how many columns are present in the resulting matrix C?

5–29 Fortran 90/95 includes an intrinsic function MATMUL to perform matrix multiplication. Rewrite the program of Exercise 5–27 to use function MATMUL to multiply the matrices together.

5–30 Relative Maxima A point in a rank-2 array is said to be a *relative maximum* if it is higher than any of the eight points surrounding it. For example, the element at position (2,2) in the following array is a relative maximum, since it is larger than any of the surrounding points.

$$\begin{bmatrix} 11 & 7 & -2 \\ -7 & 14 & 3 \\ 2 & -3 & 5 \end{bmatrix}$$

Write a program to read a matrix A from an input disk file and to scan for all relative maxima within the matrix. The first line in the disk file should contain the number of rows and the number of columns in the matrix, and then the next lines should contain the values in the matrix, with all of the values in a given row on a single line of the input disk file. (Be sure to use the proper form of implied DO statements to read in the data correctly.) Use allocatable arrays. The program should only consider interior points within the matrix, since any point along an edge of the matrix cannot be completely surrounded by points lower than itself. Test your program by finding all the relative maxima in the following matrix, which can be found in file FINDPEAK.

$$A = \begin{bmatrix} 2. & -1. & -2. & 1. & 3. & -5. & 2. & 1. \\ -2. & 0. & -2.5 & 5. & -2. & 2. & 1. & 0. \\ -3. & -3. & -3. & 3. & 0. & 0. & -1. & -2. \\ -4.5 & -4. & -7. & 6. & 1. & -3. & 0. & 5. \\ -3.5 & -3. & -5. & 0. & 4. & 17. & 11. & 5. \\ -9. & -6. & -5. & -3. & 1. & 2. & 0. & 0.5 \\ -7. & -4. & -5. & -3. & 2. & 4. & 3. & -1. \\ -6. & -5. & -5. & -2. & 0. & 1. & 2. & 5. \end{bmatrix}$$

5–31 Temperature Distribution on a Metallic Plate Under steady-state conditions, the temperature at any point on the surface of a metallic plate will be the average of the temperatures of all points surrounding it. This fact can be used in an iterative procedure to calculate the temperature distribution at all points on the plate.

Figure 5–30 shows a square plate divided in 100 squares or nodes by a grid. The temperatures of the nodes form a two-dimensional array T. The temperature in all nodes at the edges of the plate is constrained to be 20°C by a cooling system, and the temperature of the node (3,8) is fixed at 100°C by exposure to boiling water.

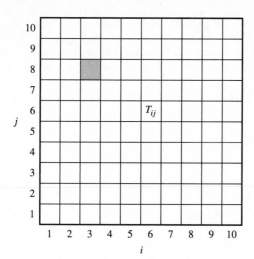

FIGURE 5–30
A metallic plate divided into 100 small segments.

A new estimate of the temperature $T_{i,j}$ in any given node can be calculated from the average of the temperatures in all segments surrounding it:

$$T_{ij,new} = \frac{1}{4}(T_{i+1,j} + T_{i-1,j} + T_{i,j+1} + T_{i,j-1}) \qquad (5\text{–}2)$$

To determine the temperature distribution on the surface of a plate, an initial assumption must be made about the temperatures in each node. Then Equation (5–2) is applied to each node whose temperature is not fixed to calculate a new estimate of the temperature in that node. These updated temperature estimates are used to calculate newer estimates, and the process is repeated until the new temperature estimates in each node differ from the old ones by only a small amount. At that point, a steady-state solution has been found.

Write a program to calculate the steady-state temperature distribution throughout the plate, making an initial assumption that all interior segments are at a temperature of 50°C. Remember that all outside segments are fixed at a temperature of 20°C and segment (3,8) is fixed at a temperature of 100°C. The program should apply Equation (5–2) iteratively until the maximum temperature change between iterations in any node is less than 0.01°. What will the steady-state temperature of segment (5,5) be?

6

Procedures and Structured Programming

Chapter 3 explained the importance of good program design. The basic technique that we employed is top-down design. In *top-down design* the programmer starts with a statement of the problem to be solved and the required inputs and outputs. He or she describes the algorithm to be implemented by the program in broad outline and then applies *decomposition* to break down the algorithm into logical subdivisions called subtasks. Then the programmer breaks down each subtask until he or she winds up with many small pieces, each of which does a simple, clearly understandable job. Finally, the programmer turns individual pieces into Fortran code.

Although we have followed this design process in our examples, the results have been somewhat restricted because we have had to combine the final Fortran code generated for each subtask into a single large program. We have not had a way to code, verify, and test each subtask independently before combining them into the final program.

Fortunately, Fortran has a special mechanism designed to make subtasks easy to develop and debug independently before building the final program. Programmers can code each subtask as a separate **program unit**[1] called an **external procedure** and then compile, test, and debug each external procedure independently of all of the other subtasks (procedures) in the program.[2]

Fortran has two kinds of external procedures: **subroutines** and **function subprograms** (or just **functions**). *Subroutines* are invoked by naming them in a separate CALL statement; they can return multiple results through calling arguments. *Function subprograms* are invoked by naming them in an expression; their result is a *single*

---

[1]A *program unit* is a separately compiled portion of a Fortran program. Main programs, subroutines, and function subprograms are all program units.

[2]Fortran also supports **internal procedures,** which are procedures entirely contained within another program unit. Internal procedures are described in Chapter 9. All references in this chapter to procedures, subroutines, and functions refer to external procedures, external subroutines, and external functions.

value that is used in the evaluation of the expression. Both type of procedures are described in this chapter.

Well-designed procedures enormously reduce the effort required on a large programming project. Their benefits include

1. **Independent testing of subtasks.** Each subtask can be coded and compiled as an independent unit. The subtask can be tested separately to ensure that it performs properly by itself before combining it into the larger program. This step is known as **unit testing.** It eliminates a major source of problems before the final program is even built.

2. **Reusable code.** In many cases different parts of a program can use the same basic subtask. For example, you may need to sort a list of values into ascending order many times within a program, or even in other programs. You could design, code, test, and debug a *single* procedure to do the sorting and then reuse that procedure whenever sorting is required. This *reusable code* has two major advantages: it reduces the total programming effort required, and it simplifies debugging, since the sorting function only needs to be debugged once.

3. **Isolation from unintended side effects.** Subprograms communicate with the main programs that invoke them through a list of variables called an **argument list.** *The only variables in the main program that can be changed by the procedure are those in the argument list.* This restriction is very important, since accidental programming mistakes can only affect the variables in the procedure in which the mistake occurred.

Once a large program is written and released, it has to be maintained. Program *maintenance* involves fixing bugs and modifying the program to handle new and unforeseen circumstances. The programmer who modifies a program during maintenance is often not the person who originally wrote it. The programmer modifying a poorly written program may make a change in one region of the code that causes unintended side effects in an unrelated part of the program. This situation happens because variable names are reused in different portions of the program. When the maintenance programmer changes the values left behind in some of the variables, those values are accidentally picked up and used in other portions of the code.

The use of well-designed procedures minimizes this problem by **data hiding.** All the variables in the procedure except for those in the argument list are hidden from the main program, and therefore mistakes or changes in those variables cannot accidentally cause unintended side effects in the main program or in other procedures.

 Good Programming Practice

Break large program tasks into procedures whenever practical to achieve the important benefits of independent component testing, reusability, and isolation from undesired side effects.

We will now examine the two different types of Fortran 90/95 procedures subroutines and functions.

■ **6.1**

SUBROUTINES

A subroutine is a Fortran procedure that is invoked by naming it in a CALL statement and that receives its input values and returns its results through an argument list. The general form of a subroutine is

```
SUBROUTINE subroutine_name ( argument_list )
    ...
        (Declaration section)
    ...
        (Execution section)
    ...
RETURN
END SUBROUTINE [name]
```

The SUBROUTINE statement marks the beginning of a subroutine. It specifies the name of the subroutine and the argument list associated with it. The subroutine name must follow standard Fortran conventions: it may be up to 31 characters long and contain both alphabetic characters and digits, but the first character must be alphabetic. The argument list contains a list of the variables, arrays, or both that are being passed from the calling program to the subroutine. These variables are called **dummy arguments,** since the subroutine does not actually allocate any memory for them. They are just placeholders for actual arguments which will be passed from the calling program unit when the subroutine is invoked.

Note that like any Fortran program, a subroutine must have a declaration section and an execution section. When a program calls the subroutine, the execution of the calling program is suspended and the execution section of the subroutine is run. When a RETURN or END SUBROUTINE statement is reached in the subroutine, the calling program starts running again at the line following the subroutine call.

Each subroutine is an independent program unit, beginning with a SUBROUTINE statement and terminated by an END SUBROUTINE statement. It is compiled separately from the main program and from any other procedures. Because each program unit in a program is compiled separately, statement labels and local variable names may be reused in different routines without causing an error.

Any executable program unit may call a subroutine, including another subroutine. (However, a subroutine may not call itself unless it is declared to be **recursive;** recursion is explained in Chapter 9.) To call a subroutine, the calling program places a CALL statement in its code. The form of a CALL statement is

```
CALL subroutine_name ( argument_list )
```

where the order and type of the **actual arguments** in the argument list must match the order and type of the dummy arguments declared in the subroutine.

The simple subroutine shown in Figure 6–1 calculates the hypotenuse of a right triangle from the lengths of the other two sides.

FIGURE 6–1

A simple subroutine to calculate the hypotenuse of a right triangle.

```
SUBROUTINE calc_hypotenuse ( side_1, side_2, hypotenuse )
!
! Purpose:
! To calculate the hypotenuse of a right triangle from the two
! other sides.
!
! Record of revisions:
!    Date        Programmer        Description of change
!    ====        ==========        =====================
!    08/27/95    S. J.Chapman      Original code
!
IMPLICIT NONE

! Declare calling parameters:
REAL, INTENT(IN) :: side_1        ! Length of side 1
REAL, INTENT(IN) :: side_2        ! Length of side 2
REAL, INTENT(OUT) :: hypotenuse   ! Length of hypotenuse

! Declare local variables:
REAL :: temp                      ! Temporary variable

! Calculate hypotenuse
temp = side_1**2 + side_2**2
hypotenuse = SQRT ( temp )

RETURN
END SUBROUTINE
```

The preceding subroutine has three arguments in its dummy argument list. Arguments side_1 and side_2 are placeholders for real values containing the lengths of sides 1 and 2 of the triangle. These dummy arguments are used to pass data to the subroutine but are not changed inside the subroutine, so they are declared to be input values with the INTENT(IN) attribute. Dummy argument hypotenuse is a placeholder for a real variable that will receive the length of the hypotenuse of the triangle. The value of hypotenuse is set in the subroutine, so it is declared to be an output variable with the INTENT(OUT) attribute.

The variable temp is actually defined within the subroutine. It is used in the subroutine, but it is not accessible to any calling program. Variables used within a subroutine that are not accessible by calling programs are called **local variables.**

Finally, the RETURN statement in the subroutine is optional. Execution automatically returns to the calling program when the END SUBROUTINE statement is reached. A RETURN statement is only necessary when we wish to return to the calling program before reaching the end of the subroutine. As a result, the RETURN statement is rarely used.

Programmers write a **test driver program** to test a subroutine. The test driver program is a small program that calls the subroutine with a sample data set for the specific purpose of testing it. A test driver program for subroutine calc_hypotenuse is shown in Figure 6–2.

FIGURE 6-2
A test driver program for subroutine `calc_hypotenuse`.

```
PROGRAM test_hypotenuse
!
!   Purpose:
!     Program to test the operation of subroutine calc_hypotenuse.
!
!   Record of revisions:
!       Date        Programmer          Description of change
!       ====        ==========          =====================
!     08/27/95    S. J.Chapman          Original code
!
IMPLICIT NONE

! Declare variables:
REAL :: s1                ! Length of side 1
REAL :: s2                ! Length of side 2
REAL :: hypot             ! Hypotenuse

! Get the lengths of the two sides.
WRITE (*,*) 'Program to test subroutine calc_hypotenuse: '
WRITE (*,*) 'Enter the length of side 1: '
READ (*,*) s1
WRITE (*,*) 'Enter the length of side 2: '
READ (*,*) s2
```

```
! Call calc_hypotenuse.
CALL calc_hypotenuse ( s1, s2, hypot )
```

```
! Write out hypotenuse.
WRITE (*,1000) hypot
1000 FORMAT (1X,'The length of the hypotenuse is: ', F10.4 )

END PROGRAM
```

The preceding program calls subroutine `calc_hypotenuse` with an actual argument list of variables s1, s2, and `hypot`. Therefore, wherever the dummy argument `side_1` appears in the subroutine, variable s1 is really used instead. Similarly, the hypotenuse is really written into variable `hypot`.

6.1.1 Example Problem—Sorting

Let us now reexamine the sorting problem of Example 5–3, using subroutines where appropriate.

EXAMPLE 6-1 Sorting Data: Develop a program to read in a data set from a file, sort it into ascending order, and display the sorted data set. Use subroutines where appropriate.

SOLUTION The program in Example 5–3 read an arbitrary number of real input data values from a user-supplied file, sorted the data into ascending order, and wrote the sorted data to the standard output device. The sorting process is a good candidate for a subroutine, since only the array a and its length nvals must be exchanged between the sorting process and the rest of the program. The rewritten program using a sorting subroutine is shown in Figure 6–3.

FIGURE 6–3

Program to sort real data values into ascending order using a `sort` subroutine.

```fortran
PROGRAM sort3
!
! Purpose:
! To read in a real input data set, sort it into ascending order
! using the selection sort algorithm, and to write the sorted
! data to the standard output device. This program calls subroutine
! "sort" to do the actual sorting.
!
! Record of revisions:
!     Date         Programmer          Description of change
!     ====         ==========          =====================
!   09/28/95    S. J. Chapman       Original code
!
IMPLICIT NONE

! List of parameters:
INTEGER, PARAMETER :: max_size = 10

! List of variables:
REAL, DIMENSION(max_size) :: a    ! Data array to sort
LOGICAL :: exceed = .FALSE.       ! Logical indicating that array
                                  ! limits are exceeded
CHARACTER(len=20) :: filename     ! Input data file name
INTEGER :: i                      ! Loop index
INTEGER :: nvals = 0              ! Number of data values to sort
INTEGER :: status                 ! I/O status: 0 for success
REAL :: temp                      ! Temporary variable for reading

! Get the name of the file containing the input data.
WRITE (*,*) 'Enter the file name with the data to be sorted: '
READ (*,'(A20)') filename

! Open input data file. Status is OLD because the input data must
! already exist.
OPEN ( UNIT=9, FILE=filename, STATUS='OLD', ACTION='READ', &
IOSTAT = status )

! Was the OPEN successful?
fileopen: IF ( status == 0 ) THEN   ! Open successful

   ! The file was opened successfully, so read the data to sort
   ! from it, sort the data, and write out the results.
   ! First read in data.
   DO
      READ (9, *, IOSTAT=status) temp    ! Get value
      IF ( status /= 0 ) EXIT            ! Exit on end of data
      nvals = nvals + 1                  ! Bump count
      size: IF ( nvals <= max_size ) THEN ! Too many values?
         a(nvals) = temp                 ! No: Save value in array
      ELSE
         exceed = .TRUE.                 ! Yes: Array overflow
      END IF size
   END DO
   ! Was the array size exceeded? If so, tell user and quit.
   toobig: IF ( exceed ) THEN
      WRITE (*,1010) nvals, max_size
      1010 FORMAT (' Maximum array size exceeded: ', I6, ' > ', I6 )
```

(continued)

(continued)

```fortran
    ELSE

        ! Limit not exceeded: sort the data.
        CALL sort (a, nvals)

        ! Now write out the sorted data.
        WRITE (*,1020) ' The sorted output data values are: '
        1020 FORMAT (A)
        WRITE (*,1030) ( a(i), i = 1, nvals )
        1030 FORMAT (4X,F10.4)

    END IF toobig

ELSE fileopen

    ! Else file open failed.  Tell user.
    WRITE (*,1040) status
    1040 FORMAT (1X,'File open failed--status = ', I6)

END IF fileopen

END PROGRAM

SUBROUTINE sort (arr, n)
!
! Purpose:
!   To sort real array "arr" into ascending order using a selection
!   sort.
!
IMPLICIT NONE

! Declare calling parameters:
INTEGER, INTENT(IN) :: n                    ! Number of values
REAL, DIMENSION(n), INTENT(INOUT) :: arr  ! Array to be sorted

! Declare local variables:
INTEGER :: i                    ! Loop index
INTEGER :: iptr                 ! Pointer to smallest value
INTEGER :: j                    ! Loop index
REAL :: temp                    ! Temp variable for swaps

! Sort the array
outer: DO i = 1, n-1

    ! Find the minimum value in arr(i) through arr(n)
    iptr = i
    inner: DO j = i+1, n
        minval: IF ( arr(j) < arr(iptr) ) THEN
            iptr = j
        END IF minval
    END DO inner

    ! iptr now points to the minimum value, so swap arr(iptr)
    ! with arr(i) if i /= iptr.
    swap: IF ( i /= iptr ) THEN
        temp      = arr(i)
        arr(i)    = arr(iptr)
        arr(iptr) = temp
    END IF swap
```

(continued)

(concluded)

```
END DO outer

END SUBROUTINE sort
```

We can test this new program just as we tested the original program; the results are identical. If the following data set is placed in file INPUT2

```
                              13.3
                              12.
                             -3.0
                              0.
                              4.0
                              6.6
                              4.
                             -6.
```

then the results of the test run will be

```
C>sort3
Enter the file name containing the data to be sorted:
input2
The sorted output data values are:
      -6.0000
      -3.0000
        .0000
       4.0000
       4.0000
       6.6000
      12.0000
      13.3000
```

The program gives the correct answers for our test data set, as it did before.

Subroutine sort performs the same function as the sorting code in the original example, but now sort is an independent subroutine that we can reuse unchanged whenever we need to sort any array of real numbers.
Note that the array was declared in the sort subroutine as

```
REAL, DIMENSION(n), INTENT(INOUT) :: arr  ! Array to be sorted
```

The statement tells the Fortran compiler that dummy argument arr is an array whose length is n, where n is also a calling argument. The dummy argument arr is only a placeholder for whatever array is passed as an argument when the subroutine is called. The actual size of the array will be the size of the array that is passed from the calling program.

Also, note that dummy argument arr was used both to pass the data to subroutine sort and to return the sorted data to the calling program. Since it is used for both input and output, it is declared with the INTENT(INOUT) attribute.

6.1.2 The INTENT Attribute

Dummy subroutine arguments can have an INTENT attribute associated with them. The INTENT attribute is associated with the type declaration statement that declares each dummy argument. The attribute can take one of three forms:

INTENT(IN)	Dummy argument is used only to pass input data to the subroutine.
INTENT(OUT)	Dummy argument is used only to return results to the calling program.
INTENT(INOUT)	Dummy argument is used both to pass input data to the subroutine and to return results to the calling program.

The purpose of the INTENT attribute is to tell the compiler how the programmer wants to use each dummy argument. Some dummy arguments may only provide input data to the subroutine, and some may only return results from the subroutine. Finally, some may both provide data and return results. You should *always* declare the appropriate INTENT attribute for each argument.[3]

Once the compiler knows what we intend to do with each dummy argument, it can use that information to help catch programming errors at compile time. For example, suppose that a subroutine accidentally modifies an input argument. Changing that input argument will cause the value of the corresponding variable in the calling program to be changed, and the changed value will be used in all subsequent processing. This type of programming error can be very hard to locate, since it is caused by the interaction between procedures.

In the following example subroutine sub1 calculates an output value but also accidentally modifies its input value.

```
SUBROUTINE sub1(input,output)

REAL, INTENT(IN) :: input
REAL, INTENT(OUT) :: output

output = 2. * input
input = -1.                ! This line is an error!
END SUBROUTINE
```

If we declare out intent for each dummy argument, the compiler can spot this error for us at compilation time. When this subroutine is compiled with the Lahey Fortran 90 compiler, the results are

```
1 SUBROUTINE sub1(input,output)
2
3 REAL, INTENT(IN) :: input
4 REAL, INTENT(OUT) :: output
5
6 output = 2. * input
7 input = -1.
```

---

[3]The intent of a dummy argument may also be declared in a separate INTENT statement of the form

```
INTENT(IN) :: arg1, arg2, . . .
```

```
FATAL -- Dummy argument (INPUT) with INTENT(IN) attribute must not be
redefined or become undefined within procedure (see "Procedure Arguments"
in
 the Lahey Fortran 90 Language Reference).

   8 END SUBROUTINE
Bytes of stack required for this program unit: 0.
```

The INTENT attribute is only valid for dummy procedure arguments. It is an error to declare the intent of local variables in a subroutine or of variables in a main program.

As you will see later, declaring the intent of each dummy argument also helps programmers spot errors that occur in the calling sequence *between* procedures. You should always declare the intent of every dummy argument in every procedure.

Good Programming Practice

Always declare the intent of every dummy argument in every procedure.

6.1.3 Variable Passing in Fortran: The Pass-by-Reference Scheme

Fortran programs communicate with their subroutines using a **pass-by-reference** scheme. When a subroutine call occurs, the main program passes a pointer to the location in memory of each argument in the actual argument list. The subroutine looks at the memory locations pointed to by the calling program to get the values of the dummy arguments it needs. This process is illustrated in Figure 6–4.

The figure shows a main program test calling a subroutine sub1. Three actual arguments are being passed to the subroutine, a real variable a, a four-element real array b, and an integer variable next. These variables are assumed to occupy memory addresses 001, 002–005, and 006, respectively, in a specific computer. Three dummy arguments are declared in sub1: a real variable x, a real array y, and an integer variable i. When the main program calls sub1, *what is passed to the subroutine are the pointers to the memory locations containing the calling arguments:* 001, 002, and 006. Whenever variable x is referred to in the subroutine, the contents of memory location 001 are accessed, and so on. This parameter passing scheme is called pass-by-reference, since only pointers to the values are passed to the subroutine, not the actual values themselves.

Some possible pitfalls associated with the pass-by-reference scheme. The programmer must ensure that the values in the calling argument list match the subroutine's calling parameters in number, type, and order. If a mismatch occurs, the Fortran program will not be able to recognize that fact and will misuse the parameters without informing you of the problem. This is the most common error that programmers make when using Fortran subroutines. The program shown in Figure 6–5 illustrates the effects of this error.

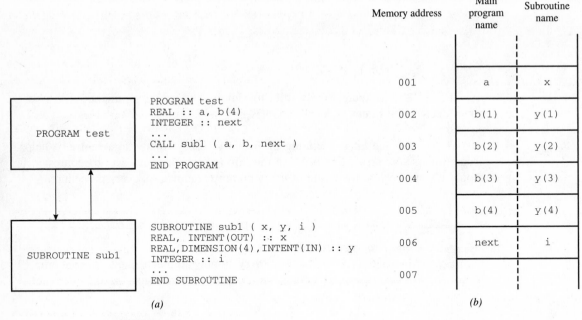

(a)   *(b)*

FIGURE 6–4
The pass-by-reference memory scheme. Note that only pointers to the memory addresses of the actual arguments are passed to the subroutine.

FIGURE 6–5
Example illustrating the effects of a type mismatch when calling a subroutine.

```
PROGRAM bad_call
!
!  Purpose:
!     To illustrate misinterpreted calling arguments.
!
IMPLICIT NONE
REAL :: x = 1.                 ! Declare real variable x.
CALL bad_argument ( x )        ! Call subroutine.
END PROGRAM

SUBROUTINE bad_argument ( i )
IMPLICIT NONE
INTEGER :: i                   ! Declare argument as integer.
WRITE (*,*), 'I = ', i         ! Write out i.
END SUBROUTINE
```

The argument in the call to subroutine `bad_argument` is real, but the corresponding dummy argument is type integer. Fortran will pass the address of the real variable x to the subroutine, which will then treat it as an integer. The results are quite bad. When the program is compiled with the Digital Visual Fortran compiler, we get this result:

```
C>bad_call
I =  1065353216
```

Another serious problem can occur if a variable is placed in the calling argument list in a position at which an array is expected. The subroutine cannot tell the difference between a variable and an array, so it will treat the variable and the variables following it in memory as though they were all part of one big array! This behavior can produce a world of problems. A subroutine containing a variable named x in its calling sequence could wind up modifying another variable y that wasn't even passed to the subroutine, just because y happens to be allocated after x in the computer's memory. Problems like that can be *extremely* difficult to find and debug.

Section 6.5 explains how to get a Fortran 90/95 compiler to automatically check the number, type, intent, and order of each argument in each subroutine call so that the compiler can catch these errors at compilation time.

> ### Programming Pitfalls
> Make sure that the values in the argument list of a subroutine call match the subroutine's declared parameters in number, type, and order. Very bad results may occur if you do not ensure that the arguments match properly.

6.1.4 Passing Arrays to Subroutines

A calling argument is passed to a subroutine by passing a pointer to the memory location of the argument. If the argument happens to be an array, then the pointer points to the first value in the array. However, the subroutine needs to know both the location and the size of the array to ensure that it stays within the boundaries of the array and to perform array operations. How can we supply this information to the subroutine?

There are three possible approaches to specifying the length of a dummy array in a subroutine. One approach is to pass the bounds of each dimension of the array to the subroutine as arguments in the subroutine call and to declare the corresponding dummy array to be that length. The dummy array is thus an **explicit-shape dummy array,** since each of its bounds is explicitly specified. This technique enables the subroutine to know the shape of each dummy array when it is executed. Since the shape of the array is known, the bounds checkers on most Fortran compilers will be able to detect and report out-of-bounds memory references. For example, the following code declares two arrays data1 and data2 to be of extent n and then processes nvals values in the arrays. If an out-of-bounds reference occurs in this subroutine, the compiler can detect and report the error.

```
SUBROUTINE process ( data1, data2, n, nvals )
INTEGER, INTENT(IN) :: n, nvals
REAL, INTENT(IN),  DIMENSION(n) :: data1  ! Explicit shape
REAL, INTENT(OUT), DIMENSION(n) :: data2  ! Explicit shape
```

```
      DO i = 1, nvals
         data2(i) = 3. * data1(i)
      END DO
      END SUBROUTINE process
```

When we use explicit-shape dummy arrays, the compiler knows the size and shape of each dummy array. Since the size and shape of each array is known, it is possible to use array operations and array sections with the dummy arrays. The following subroutine uses array sections; it will work because the dummy arrays are explicit-shape arrays.

```
      SUBROUTINE process2 ( data1, data2, n, nvals )
      INTEGER, INTENT(IN) :: nvals
      REAL, INTENT(IN),  DIMENSION(n) :: data1  ! Explicit shape
      REAL, INTENT(OUT), DIMENSION(n) :: data2  ! Explicit shape

      data2(1:nvals) = 3. * data1(1:nvals)
      END SUBROUTINE process2
```

A second approach is to declare all dummy arrays in a subroutine as **assumed-shape dummy arrays** and to create an explicit interface to the subroutine. This approach is explained in section 6.5.

The third (and oldest) approach is to declare the length of each dummy array with an asterisk as an **assumed-size dummy array.** In this case the compiler knows nothing about the length of the actual array passed to the subroutine. Bounds checking, whole array operations, and array sections will not work for assumed-size dummy arrays, because the compiler does not know the actual size and shape of the array. For example, the following code first declares two assumed-size dummy arrays data1 and data2 and then processes nvals values in the arrays.

```
      SUBROUTINE process3 ( data1, data2, nvals )
      REAL, INTENT(IN),  DIMENSION(*) :: data1  ! Assumed size
      REAL, INTENT(OUT), DIMENSION(*) :: data2  ! Assumed size
      INTEGER, INTENT(IN) :: nvals

      DO i = 1, nvals
         data2(i) = 3. * data(i)
      END DO
      END SUBROUTINE process3
```

Arrays data1 and data2 had better be at least nvals values long. If they are not, the Fortran code will either abort with an error at run time or else overwrite other locations in memory. Subroutines written like this are hard to debug, since the bounds checking option of most compilers will not work for unknown-length arrays. The subroutines also cannot use whole array operations or array sections.

Assumed-size dummy arrays are a holdover from earlier versions of Fortran. You should never use them in any new programs.

EXAMPLE 6–2 Bounds Checking in Subroutines: Write a simple Fortran program containing a subroutine that oversteps the limits of an array in its argument list. Compile and execute the program both with bounds checking turned off and with bounds checking turned on.

Solution The program in Figure 6–6 allocates a five-element array a. It initial-

Good Programming Practice

Use explicit-shape or assumed-shape dummy arrays in all new procedures. These arrays permit whole array operations to be used within the
procedure. They also allow for easier debugging, since the compiler can
detect out-of-bounds references. Never use *assumed-size dummy arrays.*
They are undesirable and are likely to be eliminated from a future version of the Fortran language.

6

izes all the elements of a to zero and then calls subroutine sub1. Subroutine sub1
modifies six elements of array a, despite the fact that a has only five elements.

FIGURE 6–6

A program illustrating the effect of exceeding the boundaries of an array in a subroutine.

```
PROGRAM array2
!
!   Purpose:
!     To illustrate the effect of accessing an out-of-bounds
!     array element.
!
! Record of revisions:
!     Date          Programmer            Description of change
!     ====          ==========            =====================
!   10/03/95      S. J. Chapman           Original code
!
IMPLICIT NONE

! Declare and initialize the variables used in this program.
INTEGER :: i                              ! Loop index
REAL, DIMENSION(5) :: a = 0.              ! Array

! Call subroutine sub1.
CALL sub1( a, 5, 6 )

! Write out the values of array a
DO i = 1, 6
   WRITE (*,100) i, a(i)
   100 FORMAT ( 1X,'A(', I1, ') = ', F6.2 )
END DO

END PROGRAM

SUBROUTINE sub1 ( a, ndim, n )
IMPLICIT NONE
INTEGER, INTENT(IN) :: ndim               ! size of array
REAL, INTENT(OUT), DIMENSION(ndim) :: a   ! Dummy argument
INTEGER, INTENT(IN) :: n                  ! # elements to process
INTEGER :: i                              ! Loop index

DO i = 1, n
   a(i) = i
END DO

END SUBROUTINE sub1
```

When this program is compiled with the Digital Visual Fortran 90 compiler with bounds checking turned *off*, the result is

```
C>array2

run-time error F6981: WRITE(CON)
- initial left parenthesis expected in format
```

In this case the subroutine has written beyond the end of array a and has actually written over a part of the main program stored in memory. This behavior can produce a very subtle and hard to find bug! The subroutine actually destroyed a part of the FORMAT statement by writing beyond the end of array a.

If the program is recompiled with the Digital Visual Fortran 90 compiler with bounds checking turned *on,* the result is

```
C>array2

array2.f90(38) : run-time error F6096: $DEBUG
- array or substring subscript expression out of range

Execution traceback:
              from SUB1 in fig6-6.f90(38)
              from main program in fig6-6.f90(19)
```

Here the program detected the out-of-bounds reference and shut down after telling the user where the problem occurred.

6.1.5 Passing Character Variables to Subroutines

When a character variable is used as a dummy subroutine argument, the length of the character variable is declared with an asterisk. Since no memory is actually allocated for dummy arguments, the compiler does not need to know the length of the character argument when the subroutine is compiled. A typical dummy character argument follows.

```
SUBROUTINE sample ( string )
CHARACTER(len=*), INTENT(IN) :: string
...
```

When the subroutine is called, the length of the dummy character argument will be the length of the actual agreement passed from the calling program. If we need to know the length of the character string passed to the subroutine during execution, we can use the intrinsic function LEN() to determine it. For example, the following simple subroutine displays the length of any character argument passed to it.

```
SUBROUTINE sample ( string )
CHARACTER(len=*), INTENT(IN) :: string
WRITE (*,'(1X,A,I3)') 'Length of variable = ', LEN(string)
END SUBROUTINE
```

6.1.6 Error Handling in Subroutines

What happens if a program calls a subroutine with insufficient or invalid data for proper processing? For example, suppose that we are writing a subroutine that subtracts two input variables and takes the square root of the result. What should we do if the difference of the two variables is a negative number?

```
SUBROUTINE process (a, b, result)
IMPLICIT NONE
REAL, INTENT(IN) :: a, b
REAL, INTENT(OUT) :: result
REAL :: temp
temp = a - b
result = SQRT ( temp )
END SUBROUTINE
```

For example, suppose that a is 1 and b is 2. If we just process the values in the subroutine, a run-time error will occur when we attempt to take the square root of a negative number. The program will abort. This is clearly not an acceptable result.

An alternative version of the subroutine follows. In this version, we test for a negative number. If a negative number is present, we print out an informative error message and stop.

```
SUBROUTINE process (a, b, result)
IMPLICIT NONE
REAL, INTENT(IN) :: a, b
REAL, INTENT(OUT) :: result
REAL :: temp
temp = a - b
IF ( temp >= 0. ) THEN
   result = SQRT ( temp )
ELSE
   WRITE (*,*) 'Square root of negative value in subroutine PROCESS!'
   STOP
END IF
END SUBROUTINE
```

Although better than the previous example, this design is also bad. If `temp` is ever negative, the program will stop without returning from subroutine `process`, and the user will lose all the data and processing that has occurred up to that point in the program.

A much better way to design the subroutine is to detect the possible error condition and to report it to the calling program by setting a value into an **error flag.** The calling program can then take appropriate actions about the error. For example, the program can be designed to recover from the error if possible. If not, it can at least write out an informative error message, save the partial results calculated so far, and then shut down gracefully.

In the following example, a zero returned in the error flag means successful completion, and a one means that the square-root-of-a-negative-number error occurred.

```
SUBROUTINE process (a, b, result, error)
IMPLICIT NONE
REAL, INTENT(IN) :: a, b
REAL, INTENT(OUT) :: result
```

```
INTEGER, INTENT(OUT) :: error
REAL :: temp
temp = a - b
IF ( temp >= 0. ) THEN
   result = SQRT ( temp )
   error = 0
ELSE
   result = 0
   error = 1
END IF
END SUBROUTINE
```

Programming Pitfalls
Never include `STOP` statements in any of your subroutines. If you do, you might create a working program, and release it to users, only to find that it mysteriously halts from time to time on certain unusual data sets.

Good Programming Practice
If error conditions can occur within a subroutine, you should test for them and set an error flag to be returned to the calling program. The calling program should test for the error conditions after a subroutine call and take appropriate actions.

Quiz 6–1

This quiz provides a quick check to see if you understand the concepts introduced in section 6.1. If you have trouble with the quiz, reread the section, ask your instructor, or discuss the material with a fellow student. The answers to this quiz are found in the back of the book.

For questions 1 through 3, determine whether the subroutine calls are correct. If they are in error, specify what is wrong with them.

```
1. PROGRAM test1
   REAL, DIMENSION(120) :: a
   REAL :: average, sd
   INTEGER :: n
   ...
   Call ave_sd ( a, 120, n, average, sd )
   ...
   END PROGRAM
   SUBROUTINE ave_sd( array, nvals, n, average, sd )
```
(continued)

```
(concluded)
      REAL, INTENT(IN) :: nvals, n
      REAL, INTENT(IN), DIMENSION(nvals) :: array
      REAL, INTENT(OUT) :: average, sd
      ...
      END SUBROUTINE

2.  PROGRAM test2
    CHARACTER(len=12) :: str1, str2
    str1 = 'ABCDEFGHIJ'
    CALL swap_str (str1, str2)
    WRITE (*,*) str1, str2
    END PROGRAM
    SUBROUTINE swap_str (string1, string2)
    CHARACTER(len=*),INTENT(IN) :: string1
    CHARACTER(len=*),INTENT(OUT) :: string2
    INTEGER :: i, length
    length = LEN(string1)
    DO i = 1, length
        string2(length-i+1:length-i+1) = string1(i:i)
    END DO
    END SUBROUTINE

3.  PROGRAM test3
    INTEGER, DIMENSION(25) :: idata
    REAL :: sum
    ...

    CALL sub3 ( idata, sum )
    ...
    END PROGRAM
    SUBROUTINE sub3( iarray, sum )
    INTEGER, INTENT(IN), DIMENSION(*) :: iarray
    REAL, INTENT(OUT) :: sum
    INTEGER :: i
    sum = 0.
    DO i = 1, 30
       sum = sum + iarray(i)
    END DO
    END SUBROUTINE
```

6 (margin tab)

6.1.7 Examples

Example 6–3 Statistics Subroutines: Develop a set of reusable subroutines capable of determining the statistical properties of a data set of real numbers in an array. The set of subroutines should include the following subroutines:

1. A subroutine to determine the maximum value in a data set and the sample number containing that value.
2. A subroutine to determine the minimum value in a data set and the sample number containing that value.
3. A subroutine to determine the average (mean) and standard deviation of the data set.

4. A subroutine to determine the median of the data set.

SOLUTION We will be generating four subroutines, each of which works on a common input data set consisting of an array of real numbers.

1. **State the problem.**

   The problem is clearly stated above. We will write four different subroutines: rmax to find the maximum value and the location of that value in a real array, rmin to find the minimum value and the location of that value in a real array, ave_sd to find the average and standard deviation of a real array, and median to find the median of a real array.

2. **Define the inputs and outputs.**

   The input to each subroutine will be an array of values plus the number of values in the array. The outputs will be as follows:

   1. The output of subroutine rmax will be a real variable containing the maximum value in the input array and an integer variable containing the offset in the array at which the maximum value occurred.
   2. The output of subroutine rmin will be a real variable containing the minimum value in the input array and an integer variable containing the offset in the array at which the minimum value occurred.
   3. The output of subroutine ave_sd will be two real variables containing the average and standard deviation of the input array.
   4. The output of subroutine median will be a real variable containing the median value of the input array.

3. **Describe the algorithm.**

   The pseudocode for the rmax routine is

   ```
   ! Initialize "real_max" to the first value in the array
   ! and "imax" to 1.
   real_max ← a(1)
   imax ← 1

   ! Find the maximum value in a(1) through a(n)
   DO for i = 2 to n
      IF a(i) > real_max THEN
         real_max ← a(i)
         imax ← i
      END of IF
   END of DO
   ```

   The pseudocode for the rmin routine is

   ```
   ! Initialize "real_min" to the first value in the array
   ! and "imin" to 1.
   real_min ← a(1)
   imin ← 1

   ! Find the maximum value in a(1) through a(n)
   ```

```
                        DO for i = 2 to n
                           IF a(i) < real_min THEN
                              real_min ← a(i)
                              imin ← i
                           END of IF
                        END of DO
```

The pseudocode for the `ave_sd` routine is essentially the same as that in Example 5–4. It will not be repeated here. For the `median` calculation, we will be able to take advantage of the `sort` subroutine that we have already written. (Here is an example of reusable code saving us time and effort.) The pseudocode for the `median` subroutine is

```
                   CALL sort ( a, n )
                   IF n is an even number THEN
                      med ← (a(n/2) + a(n/2+1)) / 2.
                   ELSE
                      med ← a(n/2+1)
                   END of IF
```

4. **Turn the algorithm into Fortran statements.**

The resulting Fortran subroutines are shown in Figure 6–7.

FIGURE 6–7
The subroutines `rmin`, `rmax`, `ave_sd`, and `median`.

```
SUBROUTINE rmax ( a, n, real_max, imax )
!
!  Purpose:
!    To find the maximum value in an array and the location
!    of that value in the array.
!
IMPLICIT NONE

! List of calling arguments:
INTEGER, INTENT(IN) :: n                    ! No. of vals in array a.
REAL, INTENT(IN), DIMENSION(n) ::  a  ! Input data.
REAL, INTENT(OUT) :: real_max               ! Maximum value in a.
INTEGER, INTENT(OUT) :: imax                ! Location of max value.

!  List of local variables:
INTEGER :: i                                ! Index variable

! Initialize the maximum value to first value in array.
real_max  = a(1)
imax = 1

! Find the maximum value.
DO i = 2, n
   IF ( a(i) > real_max ) THEN
      real_max = a(i)
      imax = i
   END IF
END DO

END SUBROUTINE rmax
```

(continued)

(continued)

```
SUBROUTINE rmin( a, n, real_min, imin )
!
!  Purpose:
!    To find the minimum value in an array and the location
!    of that value in the array.
!
IMPLICIT NONE

! List of calling arguments:
INTEGER, INTENT(IN) :: n                   ! No. of vals in array a.
REAL, INTENT(IN), DIMENSION(N) :: a   ! Input data.
REAL, INTENT(OUT) :: real_min              ! Minimum value in a.
INTEGER, INTENT(OUT) :: imin               ! Location of min value.

! List of local variables:
INTEGER :: i                               ! Index variable

! Initialize the minimum value to first value in array.
real_min  = a(1)
imin = 1

! Find the minimum value.
DO i = 2, N
   IF ( a(i) < real_min ) THEN
      real_min  = a(i)
      imin = i
   END IF
END DO

END SUBROUTINE rmin
SUBROUTINE ave_sd ( a, n, ave, std_dev, error )
!
! Purpose:
!   To calculate the average and standard deviation of an array.
!
IMPLICIT NONE

! List of calling arguments:
INTEGER, INTENT(IN) :: n                   ! No. of vals in array a.
REAL, INTENT(IN), DIMENSION(n) :: a   ! Input data.
REAL, INTENT(OUT) :: ave                   ! Average of a.
REAL, INTENT(OUT) :: std_dev               ! Standard deviation.
INTEGER, INTENT(OUT) :: error              ! Flag:  0 -- no error
                                           !        1 -- sd invalid
                                           !        2 -- ave * sd invalid

! List of local variables:
INTEGER :: i                               ! Loop index
REAL :: sum_x                              ! Sum of input values
REAL :: sum_x2                             ! Sum of input values squared

! Initialize the sums to zero.
sum_x  = 0.
sum_x2 = 0.

! Accumulate sums.
DO i = 1, n
   sum_x  = sum_x + a(i)
   sum_x2 = sum_x2 + a(i)**2
```

(continued)

(concluded)

```
END DO

! Check to see if we have enough input data.
IF ( n >= 2 ) THEN ! we have enough data

   ! Calculate the mean and standard deviation
   ave     = sum_x / REAL(n)
   std_dev = SQRT( REAL(n) * sum_x2 - sum_x**2) &
            / (REAL(n) * REAL(n - 1)) )
   error = 0

ELSE IF ( n == 1 ) THEN ! no valid std_dev

   ave = sum_x
   std_dev = 0.              ! std_dev invalid
   error = 1

ELSE

   ave = 0.                  ! ave invalid
   std_dev = 0.              ! std_dev invalid
   error = 2

END IF
END SUBROUTINE ave_sd
SUBROUTINE median ( a, n, med )
!
! Purpose:
!    To calculate the median value of an array.
!
IMPLICIT NONE

! List of calling arguments:
INTEGER, INTENT(IN) :: n               ! No. of vals in array a.
REAL, INTENT(IN), DIMENSION(N) :: a    ! Input data.
REAL, INTENT(OUT) :: med               ! Median value of a.

! Sort the data into ascending order.
CALL sort ( a, n )

! Get median.
IF ( MOD(n,2) == 0 ) THEN
   med = ( a(n/2) + a(n/2+1) ) / 2.
ELSE
   med = a(n/2+1)
END IF
END SUBROUTINE median
```

5. **Test the resulting Fortran programs.**

To test these subroutines, it is necessary to write a driver program to read the input data, call the subroutines, and write out the results. This test is left as Exercise 6–14 at the end of the chapter.

EXAMPLE 6–4 Gauss-Jordan Elimination: Many important problems in science and engineering require the solution of a system of N simultaneous linear equations in N unknowns. Some of these problems require the solution of small systems of equations, say 3 × 3 or 4 × 4. Such problems are relatively easy to solve. Other problems might require the solution of really large sets of simultaneous equations, like 1000 equations in 1000 unknowns. These problems are *much* harder to solve, and the solution requires a variety of special iterative techniques. A whole branch of the science of numerical methods is devoted to different ways to solve systems of simultaneous linear equations.

We will now develop a subroutine to solve a system of simultaneous linear equations using the straightforward approach known as Gauss-Jordan elimination. The subroutine that we develop should work fine for systems of up to about 20 equations in 20 unknowns.

Gauss-Jordan elimination depends on the fact that you can multiply one equation in a system of equations by a constant and add it to another equation, and the new system of equations will still be equivalent to the original one. In fact, this method works in exactly the same way that we solve systems of simultaneous equations by hand.

To understand the technique, consider the 3 × 3 system of equations shown below.

$$
\begin{array}{llll}
1.0 \ x1 \ + \ 1.0 \ x2 \ + \ 1.0 \ x3 \ = \ 1.0 \\
2.0 \ x1 \ + \ 1.0 \ x2 \ + \ 1.0 \ x3 \ = \ 2.0 \\
1.0 \ x1 \ + \ 3.0 \ x2 \ + \ 2.0 \ x3 \ = \ 4.0
\end{array}
\tag{6-1}
$$

We would like to manipulate this set of equations by multiplying one of the equations by a constant and adding it to another equation until we eventually wind up with a set of equations of the form

$$
\begin{array}{llll}
1.0 \ x1 \ + \ 0.0 \ x2 \ + \ 0.0 \ x3 \ = \ b1 \\
0.0 \ x1 \ + \ 1.0 \ x2 \ + \ 0.0 \ x3 \ = \ b2 \\
0.0 \ x1 \ + \ 0.0 \ x2 \ + \ 1.0 \ x3 \ = \ b3
\end{array}
\tag{6-2}
$$

When we get to this form, the solution to the system will be obvious: x1 = b1, x2 = b2, and x3 = b3.

To get from Equations (6–1) to Equations (6–2), we must go through three steps:

1. Eliminate all coefficients of x1 except in the first equation.
2. Eliminate all coefficients of x2 except in the second equation.
3. Eliminate all coefficients of x3 except in the third equation.

First we will eliminate all coefficients of x1 except that in the first equation. If we multiply the first equation by −2 and add it to the second equation, and multiply the first equation by −1 and add it to the third equation, the results are

$$
\begin{array}{llll}
1.0 \ x1 \ + \ 1.0 \ x2 \ + \ 1.0 \ x3 \ = \ 1.0 \\
0.0 \ x1 \ - \ 1.0 \ x2 \ - \ 1.0 \ x3 \ = \ 0.0 \\
0.0 \ x1 \ + \ 2.0 \ x2 \ + \ 1.0 \ x3 \ = \ 3.0
\end{array}
\tag{6-3}
$$

Next we will eliminate all coefficients of $x2$ except in the second equation. If we add the second equation as it is to the first equation, and multiply the second equation by 2 and add it to the third equation, the results are

$$
\begin{aligned}
1.0 \ \ x1 \ + \ 0.0 \ \ x2 \ + \ 0.0 \ \ x3 \ &= \ 1.0 \\
0.0 \ \ x1 \ - \ 1.0 \ \ x2 \ - \ 1.0 \ \ x3 \ &= \ 0.0 \\
0.0 \ \ x1 \ + \ 0.0 \ \ x2 \ - \ 1.0 \ \ x3 \ &= \ 3.0
\end{aligned}
\qquad (6\text{–}4)
$$

Finally we will eliminate all coefficients of $x3$ except in the third equation. In this case, there is no coefficient of $x3$ in the first equation, so we don't have to do anything there. If we multiply the third equation by -1 and add it to the second equation, the results are

$$
\begin{aligned}
1.0 \ \ x1 \ + \ 0.0 \ \ x2 \ + \ 0.0 \ \ x3 \ &= \ \ \ 1.0 \\
0.0 \ \ x1 \ - \ 1.0 \ \ x2 \ + \ 0.0 \ \ x3 \ &= \ -3.0 \\
0.0 \ \ x1 \ + \ 0.0 \ \ x2 \ - \ 1.0 \ \ x3 \ &= \ \ \ 3.0
\end{aligned}
\qquad (6\text{–}5)
$$

The last step is almost trivial. If we divide equation 1 by the coefficient of $x1$, equation 2 by the coefficient of $x2$, and equation 3 by the coefficient of $x3$, then the solution to the equations will appear on the right hand side of the equations.

$$
\begin{aligned}
1.0 \ \ x1 \ + \ 0.0 \ \ x2 \ + \ 0.0 \ \ x3 \ &= \ \ \ 1.0 \\
0.0 \ \ x1 \ + \ 1.0 \ \ x2 \ + \ 0.0 \ \ x3 \ &= \ \ \ 3.0 \\
0.0 \ \ x1 \ + \ 0.0 \ \ x2 \ + \ 1.0 \ \ x3 \ &= \ -3.0
\end{aligned}
\qquad (6\text{–}6)
$$

The final answer is $x1 = 1$, $x2 = 3$, and $x3 = -3$!

Sometimes this technique does not produce a solution. This happens when the set of equations being solved are not all *independent*. For example, consider the following 2×2 system of simultaneous equations:

$$
\begin{aligned}
2.0 \ \ x1 \ + \ 3.0 \ \ x2 \ &= \ 4.0 \\
4.0 \ \ x1 \ + \ 6.0 \ \ x2 \ &= \ 8.0
\end{aligned}
\qquad (6\text{–}7)
$$

If equation 1 is multiplied by -2 and added to equation 1, we get:

$$
\begin{aligned}
2.0 \ \ x1 \ + \ 3.0 \ \ x2 \ &= \ 4.0 \\
0.0 \ \ x1 \ + \ 0.0 \ \ x2 \ &= \ 0.0
\end{aligned}
\qquad (6\text{–}8)
$$

We have no way to solve this system for a unique solution, since infinitely many values of $x1$ and $x2$ satisfy Equations (6–8). These conditions can be recognized by the fact that the coefficient of $x2$ in the second equation is 0. The solution to this system of equations is said to be nonunique. Our computer program will have to test for problems like this, and report them with an error code.

We will now write a subroutine to solve a system of N simultaneous equations in N unknowns. The computer program will work in exactly the manner shown above, except that at each step in the process, we will reorder the equations. In the first step, we will reorder the N equations so that the first equation is the one with the largest coefficient (absolute value) of the first variable. In the second step, we will reorder equations 2 through N so that the second equation is the one with the largest coefficient (absolute value) of the second variable. We repeat this process for each step in the solution. Reordering the equations is important, because it reduces round-off errors in large systems of equations and also avoids divide-by-zero errors. (This reordering of equations is called the *maximum pivot* technique in the literature of numerical methods.)

SOLUTION The solution to this example is:

1. State the problem.

Write a subroutine to solve a system of N simultaneous equations in N unknowns using Gauss-Jordan elimination and the maximum pivot technique to avoid round-off errors. The subroutine must be able to detect singular sets of equations and set an error flag if they occur.

2. Define the inputs and outputs.

The input to the subroutine consists of an N × N matrix a with the coefficients of the variables in the simultaneous equations and a vector b with the contents of the right-hand sides of the equations. The outputs from the subroutine are the solutions to the set of equations (in vector b), and an error flag. Note that the matrix of coefficients a will be destroyed during the solution process.

3. Describe the algorithm.

The pseudocode for this subroutine is

```
DO for irow = 1 to n

    ! Find peak pivot for column irow in rows i to n
    ipeak ← irow
    DO for jrow = irow+1 to n
        IF |a(jrow,irow)| > |a(ipeak,irow)| then
            ipeak ← jrow
        END of IF
    END of DO

    ! Check for singular equations
    IF |a(ipeak,irow)| < epsilon THEN
        Equations are singular; set error code & exit
    END of IF

    ! Otherwise, if ipeak /= irow, swap equations irow & ipeak
    IF ipeak <> irow
        DO for kcol = 1 to n
            temp ← a(ipeak,kcol)
            a(ipeak,kcol) ← a(irow,kcol)
            a(irow,kcol) ← temp
        END of DO
        temp ← b(ipeak)
        b(ipeak) ← b(irow)
        b(irow) ← temp
    END of IF
```

```
            ! Multiply equation irow by -a(jrow,irow)/a(irow,irow),
            ! and add it to Eqn jrow
            DO for jrow = 1 to n except for irow
                factor ← -a(jrow,irow)/a(irow,irow)
                DO for kcol = 1 to n
                    a(jrow,kcol) ← a(irow,kcol) * factor + a(jrow,kcol)
                END of DO
                b(jrow) ← b(irow) * factor + b(jrow)
            END of DO
        END of DO

    ! End of main loop over all equations.  All off-diagonal
    ! terms are now zero.  To get the final answer, we must
    ! divide each equation by the coefficient of its on-diagonal
    ! term.
    DO for irow = 1 to n
        b(irow) ← b(irow) / a(irow,irow)
        a(irow,irow) ← 1.
    END of DO
```

4. **Turn the algorithm into Fortran statements.**

The resulting Fortran subroutine is shown in Figure 6–8. Note that the sizes of arrays a and b are passed explicitly to the subroutine as a(ndim,ndim) and b(ndim). This technique allows us to use the compiler's bounds checker while we are debugging the subroutine. Note also that the subroutine's large outer loops and IF structures are all named to help us to understand and keep track of them.

FIGURE 6–8
Subroutine simul.

```
SUBROUTINE simul ( a, b, ndim, n, error )
!
!   Purpose:
!     Subroutine to solve a set f n linear equations in n
!     unknowns using Gaussian elimination and the maximum
!     pivot technique.
!
! Record of revisions:
!     Date         Programmer        Description of change
!     ====         ==========        =====================
!   10/16/95     S. J. Chapman      Original code
!
IMPLICIT NONE

! Declare calling arguments:
INTEGER, INTENT(IN) :: ndim            ! Dimension of arrays a and b
REAL, INTENT(INOUT), DIMENSION(ndim,ndim) :: a
                                       ! Array of coefficients (n x n).
                                       ! This array is of size ndim x
                                       ! ndim, but only n x n of the
                                       ! coefficients are being used.
                                       ! The declared dimension ndim
                                       ! must be passed to the sub, or
                                       ! it won't be able to interpret
                                       ! subscripts correctly.  (This
```

(continued)

(continued)

```
                                              ! array is destroyed during
                                              ! processing.)
REAL, INTENT(INOUT), DIMENSION(ndim) :: b
                                              ! Input: Right-hand side of eqns.
                                              ! Output: Solution vector.
INTEGER, INTENT(IN) :: n                      ! Number of equations to solve.
INTEGER, INTENT(OUT) :: error                 ! Error flag:
                                              !   0 -- No error
                                              !   1 -- Singular equations

! Declare local parameters
REAL, PARAMETER :: epsilon = 1.0E-6  ! A "small" number for comparison
                                     ! when determining singular eqns

! Declare local variables:
REAL :: factor                       ! Factor to multiply eqn irow by
                                     ! before adding to eqn jrow
INTEGER :: irow                      ! Number of the equation currently
                                     ! currently being processed
INTEGER :: ipeak                     ! Pointer to equation containing
                                     ! maximum pivot value
INTEGER :: jrow                      ! Number of the equation compared
                                     ! to the current equation
INTEGER :: kcol                      ! Index over all columns of eqn
REAL :: temp                         ! Scratch value
! Process n times to get all equations...
mainloop: DO irow = 1, n

   ! Find peak pivot for column irow in rows irow to n
   ipeak = irow
   max_pivot: DO jrow = irow+1, n
      IF (ABS(a(jrow,irow)) > ABS(a(ipeak,irow))) THEN
         ipeak = jrow
      END IF
   END DO max_pivot

   ! Check for singular equations.
   singular: IF ( ABS(a(ipeak,irow)) < epsilon ) THEN
      error = 1
      RETURN
   END IF singular

   ! Otherwise, if ipeak /= irow, swap equations irow & ipeak
   swap_eqn: IF ( ipeak /= irow ) THEN
      DO kcol = 1, n
         temp        = a(ipeak,kcol)
         a(ipeak,kcol) = a(irow,kcol)
         a(irow,kcol) = temp
      END DO
      temp     = b(ipeak)
      b(ipeak) = b(irow)
      b(irow)  = temp
   END IF swap_eqn

   ! Multiply equation irow by -a(jrow,irow)/a(irow,irow),
   ! and add it to Eqn jrow (for all eqns except irow itself).
   eliminate: DO jrow = 1, n
      IF ( jrow /= irow ) THEN
         factor = -a(jrow,irow)/a(irow,irow)
```

(continued)

(concluded)

```
            DO kcol = 1, n
               a(jrow,kcol) = a(irow,kcol)*factor + a(jrow,kcol)
            END DO
            b(jrow) = b(irow)*factor + b(jrow)
         END IF
      END DO eliminate
END DO mainloop

! End of main loop over all equations.  All off-diagonal
! terms are now zero.  To get the final answer, we must
! divide each equation by the coefficient of its on-diagonal
! term.
divide: DO irow = 1, n
   b(irow)     = b(irow) / a(irow,irow)
   a(irow,irow) = 1.
END DO divide

! Set error flag to 0 and return.
error = 0
END SUBROUTINE simul
```

5. Test the resulting Fortran programs.

To test this subroutine, it is necessary to write a driver program. The driver program will open an input data file to read the equations to be solved. The first line of the file will contain the number of equations n in the system, and each of the next n lines will contain the coefficients of one of the equations. To show that the simultaneous equation subroutine is working correctly, we will display the contents of arrays a and b both before and after the call to simul.

The test driver program for subroutine simul is shown in Figure 6–9.

FIGURE 6–9

Test driver routine for subroutine simul.

```
PROGRAM test_simul
!
! Purpose:
!   To test subroutine simul, which solves a set of N linear
!   equations in N unknowns.
!
!   Record of revisions:
!      Date        Programmer        Description of change
!      ====        ==========        =====================
!   10/15/95    S. J. Chapman       Original code
!
IMPLICIT NONE

! Declare parameters:
INTEGER, PARAMETER :: max_size = 10    ! Max number of eqns

! Declare variables:
INTEGER :: i, j, n, istat, error
REAL, DIMENSION(max_size,max_size) :: a
REAL, DIMENSION(max_size) :: b
```

(continued)

(continued)

```
CHARACTER(len=20) file_name

! Get the name of the disk file containing the equations.
WRITE (*,1000)
1000 FORMAT (' Enter the file name containing the eqns: ')
READ (*,'(A20)') file_name

! Open input data file.  Status is OLD because the input data must
! already exist.

OPEN ( UNIT=1, FILE=file_name, STATUS='OLD', ACTION='READ', &
IOSTAT=istat )

! Was the OPEN successful?
fileopen: IF ( istat == 0 ) THEN
    ! The file was opened successfully, so read the number of
    ! equations in the system.
    READ (1,*) n

    ! If the number of equations is < = max_size, read them in
    ! and process them.
    size_ok: IF ( n <= max_size ) THEN
        DO i = 1, n
            READ (1,*) (a(i,j), j=1,n), b(i)
        END DO

        ! Display coefficients.
        WRITE (*,1020)
        1020 FORMAT (/,1X,'Coefficients before call:')
        DO i = 1, n
            WRITE (*,1030) (a(i,j), j=1,n), b(i)
            1030 FORMAT (1X,7F11.4)
        END DO

        ! Solve equations.
        CALL simul (a, b, max_size, n, error )
        ! Check for error.
        error_check: IF ( error /= 0 ) THEN

            WRITE (*,1040)
            1040 FORMAT (/1X,'Zero pivot encountered!', &
                        //1X,'There is no unique solution to this system.')

        ELSE error_check

            ! No errors. Display coefficients.
            WRITE (*,1050)
            1050 FORMAT (/,1X,'Coefficients after call:')
            DO i = 1, n
                WRITE (*,1030) (a(i,j), j= 1,n), b(i)
            END DO

            ! Write final answer.
            WRITE (*,1060)
            1060 FORMAT (/,1X,'The solutions are:')
            DO i = 1, n
                WRITE (*,1070) i, b(i)
                1070 FORMAT (3X,'X(', I2,') = ',F16.6)
            END DO
```

(continued)

(concluded)

```
     END IF error_check
   END IF size_ok
ELSE fileopen

   ! Else file open failed.   Tell user.
   WRITE (*,1080) istat
   1080 FORMAT (1X,'File open failed--status = ', I6)

END IF fileopen
END PROGRAM
```

To test the subroutine, we need to call it with two different data sets. One of them should have a unique solution, and the other one should be singular. We will test the system with two sets of equations. The original equations that we solved by hand will be placed in file INPUTS1

$$1.0 \ X1 \ + \ 1.0 \ X2 \ + \ 1.0 \ X3 \ = \ 1.0$$
$$2.0 \ X1 \ + \ 1.0 \ X2 \ + \ 1.0 \ X3 \ = \ 2.0 \qquad\qquad (6\text{--}1)$$
$$1.0 \ X1 \ + \ 3.0 \ X2 \ + \ 2.0 \ X3 \ = \ 4.0$$

and the following set of equations will be placed in file INPUTS2:

$$1.0 \ X1 \ + \ 1.0 \ X2 \ + \ 1.0 \ X3 \ = \ 1.0$$
$$2.0 \ X1 \ + \ 6.0 \ X2 \ + \ 4.0 \ X3 \ = \ 8.0$$
$$1.0 \ X1 \ + \ 3.0 \ X2 \ + \ 2.0 \ X3 \ = \ 4.0$$

The second equation of this set is a multiple of the third equation, so the second set of equations is singular. When we run program test_simul with these data sets, the results are

```
C>test_simul
Enter the file name containing the eqns:
inputs1

Coefficients before call:
     1.0000      1.0000      1.0000      1.0000
     2.0000      1.0000      1.0000      2.0000
     1.0000      3.0000      2.0000      4.0000

Coefficients after call:
     1.0000       .0000       .0000      1.0000
      .0000      1.0000       .0000      3.0000
      .0000       .0000      1.0000     -3.0000

The solutions are:
  X( 1) =         1.000000
  X( 2) =         3.000000
  X( 3) =        -3.000000

C>test_simul
Enter the file name containing the eqns:
inputs2
```

```
Coefficients before call:
      1.0000     1.0000     1.0000     1.0000
      2.0000     6.0000     4.0000     8.0000
      1.0000     3.0000     2.0000     4.0000

Zero pivot encountered!

There is no unique solution to this system.
```

The subroutine appears to be working correctly for both unique and singular sets of simultaneous equations.

6.2

THE SAVE ATTRIBUTE AND STATEMENT

According to the Fortran 90 and 95 standards, *the values of all the local variables and arrays in a procedure become undefined whenever we exit the procedure.* The next time that the procedure is invoked, the values of the local variables and arrays may or may not be the same as they were the last time we left it, depending on the behavior of the particular compiler being used. If we write a procedure that depends on having its local variables undisturbed between calls, the procedure will work fine on some computers and fail miserably on others!

Fortran provides a way to guarantee that local variables and arrays are saved unchanged between calls to a procedure: the SAVE attribute. The SAVE attribute appears in a type declaration statement like any other attribute. *Any local variables declared with the SAVE attribute will be saved unchanged between calls to the procedure.* For example, a local variable sums could be declared with the SAVE attribute as

```
REAL, SAVE :: sums
```

In addition, *any local variable that is initialized in a type declaration statement is automatically saved.* The SAVE attribute may be specified explicitly, if desired, but the value of the variable will be saved whether or not the attribute is explicitly included. Thus the following two variables are both saved between invocations of the procedure containing them.

```
REAL, SAVE :: sum_x = 0.
REAL :: sum_x2 = 0.
```

Fortran also includes a SAVE statement. It is a nonexecutable statement that goes into the declaration portion of the procedure along with the type declaration statements. Any local variables listed in the SAVE statement will be saved unchanged between calls to the procedure. If no variables are listed in the SAVE statement, then *all* local variables will be saved unchanged. The format of the SAVE statement is

```
SAVE :: var1, var2, ...
```

or simply

```
SAVE
```

The SAVE attribute may not appear associated with dummy arguments or with data items declared with the PARAMETER attribute. Similarly, neither of these items may appear in a SAVE statement.

> **Good Programming Practice**
> If a procedure requires that the value of a local variable not change between successive invocations, include the SAVE attribute in the variable's type declaration statement, include the variable in a SAVE statement, or initialize the variable in its type declaration statement. If you do not do so, the subroutine will work correctly on some processors but will fail on others.

EXAMPLE 6–5 Running Averages: It is sometimes desirable to keep running statistics on a data set as the values are being entered. The subroutine running_average shown in Figure 6–10 accumulates running averages and standard deviations for use in problems where we would like to keep statistics on data as it is coming in to the program. As each new data value is added, the running averages and standard deviations of all data up to that point are updated. The running sums used to derive the statistics are reset when the subroutine is called with the logical argument reset set to TRUE. Note that the sums n, sum_x, and sum_x2 are being accumulated in local variables in this subroutine. To ensure that they remain unchanged between subroutine calls, *those local variables must appear in a SAVE statement or with a SAVE attribute.*

FIGURE 6–10
A subroutine to calculate the running mean and standard deviation of an input data set.

```
SUBROUTINE running_average ( x, ave, std_dev, nvals, reset )
!
!  Purpose:
!    To calculate the running average, standard deviation,
!    and number of data points as data values x are received.
!    If "reset" is .TRUE., clear running sums and exit.
!
!  Record of revisions:
!     Date        Programmer          Description of change
!     ====        ==========          =====================
!    10/19/95    S. J. Chapman        Original code
!
IMPLICIT NONE

! List of calling arguments:
REAL, INTENT(IN) :: x               ! Input data value.
REAL, INTENT(OUT) :: ave            ! Running average.
REAL, INTENT(OUT) :: std_dev        ! Running standard deviation.
INTEGER, INTENT(OUT) :: nvals       ! Current number of points.
```

(continued)

(concluded)

```fortran
LOGICAL, INTENT(IN) :: reset       ! Reset flag: clear sums if true

! List of local variables:
INTEGER, SAVE :: n                 ! Number of input values.
REAL, SAVE :: sum_x                ! Sum of input values.
REAL, SAVE :: sum_x2               ! Sum of input values squared.
! If the reset flag is set, clear the running sums at this time.
calc_sums: IF ( reset ) THEN
   n = 0     ; sum_x = 0.    ; sum_x2 = 0.
   ave = 0. ; std_dev = 0.  ; nvals = 0
ELSE

   ! Accumulate sums.
   n      = n + 1
   sum_x  = sum_x + x
   sum_x2 = sum_x2 + x**2

   ! Calculate average.
   ave = sum_x / REAL(n)

   ! Calculate standard deviation.
   IF ( n >= 2 ) THEN
      std_dev = SQRT( (REAL(n) * sum_x2 - sum_x**2) &
               / (REAL(n) * REAL(n-1)) )
   ELSE
      std_dev = 0.
   END IF

   ! Number of data points.
   nvals = n

END IF calc_sums

END SUBROUTINE running_average
```

A test driver for this subroutine is shown in Figure 6–11.

FIGURE 6–11
A test driver program to test subroutine running_average.

```fortran
PROGRAM test_running_average
!
!  Purpose:
!     To test running average subroutine.
!
IMPLICIT NONE

! Declare variables:
INTEGER :: istat                 ! I/O status
REAL :: ave                      ! Average
REAL :: std_dev                  ! Standard deviation
INTEGER :: nvals                 ! Number of values
REAL :: x                        ! Input data value
CHARACTER(len=20) file_name      ! Input data file name
```

(continued)

(concluded)

```
! Clear the running sums.
CALL running_average ( 0., ave, std_dev, nvals, .TRUE. )

! Get the name of the file containing the input data.
WRITE (*,*) ' Enter the file name containing the data: '
READ (*,'(A20)') file_name
! Open input data file. Status is OLD because the input data must
! already exist.
OPEN ( UNIT=21, FILE=file_name, STATUS = 'OLD', ACTION = 'READ', &
       IOSTAT=istat )

! Was the OPEN successful?
openok: IF ( istat == 0 ) THEN

   ! The file was opened successfully, so read the data to calculate
   !   running averages for.
   calc: DO
      READ (21,*,IOSTAT=istat) x       ! Get next value
      IF ( istat /= 0 ) EXIT           ! EXIT if not valid.

      ! Get running average & standard deviation
      CALL running_average ( x, ave, std_dev, nvals, .FALSE. )

      ! Now write out the running statistics.
      WRITE (*,1020) 'Value = ', x, ' Ave = ', ave, &
                     ' Std_dev = ', std_dev, &
                     ' Nvals = ', nvals
      1020 FORMAT (1X,3(A,F10.4),A,I6)
   END DO calc

ELSE openok

   ! Else file open failed.  Tell user.
   WRITE (*,1030) istat
   1030 FORMAT (1X,'File open failed--status = ', I6)

END IF openok

END PROGRAM
```

To test this subroutine, we will calculate running statistics by hand for a set of five numbers and compare the hand calculations to the results from the computer program. Recall that the average and standard deviation are defined as

$$\bar{x} = \frac{1}{N} \sum_{i=1}^{N} x_i \tag{3-3}$$

and

$$s = \sqrt{\frac{N \sum\limits_{i=1}^{N} x_i^2 - \left(\sum\limits_{i=1}^{N} x_i \right)^2}{N(N-1)}} \tag{3-4}$$

where x_i is sample i out of N samples. If the five values are

$$3., \quad 2., \quad 3., \quad 4., \quad 2.8$$

then the running statistics calculated by hand would be

Value	n	$\sum x$	$\sum x^2$	Average	Std_dev
3.0	1	3.0	9.0	3.00	0.000
2.0	2	5.0	13.0	2.50	0.707
3.0	3	8.0	22.0	2.67	0.577
4.0	4	12.0	38.0	3.00	0.816
2.8	5	14.8	45.84	2.96	0.713

The output of the test program for the same data set is

```
C>test_running_average
Enter the file name containing the data:
input6
Value =      3.0000  Ave =      3.0000  Std_dev =      0.0000 Nvals =        1
Value =      2.0000  Ave =      2.5000  Std_dev =      0.7071 Nvals =        2
Value =      3.0000  Ave =      2.6667  Std_dev =      0.5774 Nvals =        3
Value =      4.0000  Ave =      3.0000  Std_dev =      0.8165 Nvals =        4
Value =      2.0000  Ave =      2.9600  Std_dev =      0.7127 Nvals =        5
```

so the results of the program agree with the hand calculations.

6.3

AUTOMATIC ARRAYS

In Chapter 5 you learned how to declare and allocate memory for **allocatable arrays.** Allocatable arrays could be adjusted to exactly the size required by the particular problem being solved. We can also use allocatable arrays to create temporary working arrays when they are needed in subroutines. To do so, the temporary arrays would have to be allocated with an ALLOCATE statement each time the subroutine is called and then deallocated with a DEALLOCATE statement before the subroutine execution ends.

However, we have a simpler way to create temporary working arrays in procedures. Fortran 90/95 provides way to automatically create temporary arrays while a procedure is executing and to automatically destroy them when execution returns from the procedure. These arrays are called **automatic arrays.** An *automatic array* is a local explicit-shape array with nonconstant bounds. (The bounds are specified either by dummy arguments or through data from modules, as explained in the next section.)

Array temps in the following code is an automatic array. Whenever subroutine sub1 is executed, dummy arguments n and m are passed to the subroutine. Note that arrays x and y are explicit-shape dummy arrays of size n × m that have been *passed to* the subroutine, while array temp is an automatic array that is *created* within the subroutine. When the subroutine starts to execute, an array temp of size n × m is automatically created, and when the subroutine ends, the array is automatically destroyed.

```
SUBROUTINE sub1 ( x, y, n, m )
IMPLICIT NONE
INTEGER, INTENT(IN) :: n, m
REAL, INTENT(IN), DIMENSION(n,m) :: x  ! Dummy array
```

```
REAL, INTENT(OUT), DIMENSION(n,m) :: y ! Dummy array
REAL, DIMENSION(n,m) :: temp            ! Automatic array
temp = 0.
...
END SUBROUTINE
```

Automatic arrays may not be initialized in their type declaration statements, but they may be initialized by assignment statements at the beginning of the procedure in which they are created. They may be passed as calling arguments to other procedures invoked by the procedure in which they are created. However, they cease to exist when the procedure in which they are created executes a RETURN or END statement. It is illegal to specify the SAVE attribute for an automatic array.

6.3.1 Comparing Automatic Arrays and Allocatable Arrays

Both automatic arrays and allocatable arrays may be used to create temporary working arrays in a program. What is the difference between them, and when should we choose one type of array or another for a particular application? The major differences between the two types of arrays follow.

1. Automatic arrays are allocated automatically whenever a procedure containing them is entered, while allocatable arrays must be allocated and deallocated manually. This feature favors the use of automatic arrays when the temporary memory is only needed within a single procedure and any procedures that it may invoke.
2. Allocatable arrays are more general and flexible, since they may be created and destroyed in separate procedures. For example, in a large program we might create a special subroutine to allocate all arrays to be just the proper size to solve the current problem, and we might create a different subroutine to deallocate them after they have been used. Also, allocatable arrays may be used in a main program, while automatic arrays may not.
3. Fortran 90 allocatable arrays have a disadvantage in that it is possible to create "memory leaks" with them. For example, suppose that we allocate a local allocatable array in subroutine and then return from the subroutine without deallocating the array. The memory allocated to the array remains allocated and is unavailable for any other use until the program terminates. An example of this problem is

```
SUBROUTINE mysub(...)
...
REAL, DIMENSION(:,:), ALLOCATABLE :: temp1  ! Local
ALLOCATE (temp1(1000,1000), STATUS=istat)
...
...
END SUBROUTINE
```

The memory allocated to array temp1 will remain unavailable for reuse until the program terminates.

Automatic arrays should normally be used to create temporary working arrays within a single procedure; allocatable arrays should be used to create arrays in main programs or arrays that will be created and destroyed in different procedures. Allocatable arrays should always be explicitly deallocated after they are no longer needed to avoid memory leaks.

Good Programming Practice
Use automatic arrays to create local temporary working arrays in procedures. Use allocatable arrays to create arrays in main programs or arrays that will be created and destroyed in different procedures. Allocatable arrays should always be explicitly deallocated after they are no longer needed to avoid memory leaks.

Allocatable arrays have an additional feature in Fortran 95. If a local allocatable array is allocated in a Fortran 95 procedure, then by default it will be automatically deallocated when that procedure ends. This feature is designed to eliminate the memory leak problem mentioned above.

If the contents of a local allocatable array must be preserved between invocations of a procedure, the array can be declared with the SAVE attribute and it will not be deallocated automatically. Instead, the contents of the array will be preserved unchanged.

6.3.2 Example Program

EXAMPLE 6–6 Using Automatic Arrays in a Procedure: As an example of using automatic arrays in a procedure, we will write a new version of subroutine simul that does not destroy its input data while calculating the solution.

To avoid destroying the data, we will add a new dummy argument to return the solution to the system of equations. This argument will be called soln; it will have INTENT(OUT), since it will only be used for output. Dummy arguments a and b will now have INTENT(IN), since they will not be modified at all in the subroutine. In addition, we will take advantages of array sections to simplify the nested DO loops found in the original subroutine simul.

The resulting subroutine is shown in Figure 6–12. Note that arrays a1 and temp1 are automatic arrays, since they are local to the subroutine but their bounds are passed to the subroutine as dummy arguments. Arrays a, b, and soln are explicit-shape dummy arrays because they appear in the argument list of the subroutine.

FIGURE 6–12
A rewritten version of subroutine simul using allocatable arrays. This version does not destroy its input arrays. The declarations of automatic arrays a1 and temp1 and the use of array sections are shown in bold face.

```
SUBROUTINE simul2 ( a, b, soln, ndim, n, error )
!
```

(continued)

(continued)

```
!  Purpose:
!    Subroutine to solve a set of N linear equations in N
!    unknowns using Gaussian elimination and the maximum
!    pivot technique. This version of simul has been
!    modified to use an array sections and allocatable arrays
!    It DOES NOT DESTROY the original input values.
!
!  Record of revisions:
!      Date        Programmer          Description of change
!      ====        ==========          =====================
!    10/16/95    S. J. Chapman         Original code
! 1. 03/02/96    S. J. Chapman         Add allocatable arrays
!
IMPLICIT NONE

! Declare calling arguments:
INTEGER, INTENT(IN) :: ndim              ! Dimension of arrays a and b
REAL, INTENT(IN), DIMENSION(ndim,ndim)   ! :: a
                                         ! Array of coefficients (N x N).
                                         ! This array is of size ndim x
                                         ! ndim, but only N x N of the
                                         ! coefficients are being used.
REAL, INTENT(IN), DIMENSION(ndim) :: b
                                         ! Input: Right-hand side of eqns.
REAL, INTENT(OUT), DIMENSION(ndim) :: soln
                                         ! Output: Solution vector.
INTEGER, INTENT(IN) :: n                 ! Number of equations to solve.
INTEGER, INTENT(OUT) :: error            ! Error flag:
                                         !    0 -- No error
                                         !    1 -- Singular equations

! Declare local parameters
REAL, PARAMETER :: epsilon = 1.0E-6      ! A "small" number for comparison
                                         ! when determining singular eqns.

! Declare local variables:
REAL, DIMENSION(n,n) :: a1               ! Copy of "a" which will be
                                         ! destroyed during the solution
REAL :: factor                           ! Factor to multiply eqn irow by
                                         ! before adding to eqn jrow
INTEGER :: irow                          ! Number of the equation currently
                                         ! currently being processed
INTEGER :: ipeak                         ! Pointer to equation containing
                                         ! maximum pivot value
INTEGER :: jrow                          ! Number of the equation compared
                                         ! to the current equation
REAL :: temp                             ! Scratch value
REAL, DIMENSION(n) :: temp1              ! Scratch array

! Make copies of arrays "a" and "b" for local use
a1 = a(1:n,1:n)
soln = b(1:n)

! Process N times to get all equations...
mainloop: DO irow = 1, n

   ! Find peak pivot for column irow in rows irow to N
   ipeak = irow
   max_pivot: DO jrow = irow+1, n
```

(concluded)

```
            IF (ABS(a(jrow,irow))  > ABS(a1(ipeak,irow))) THEN
                ipeak = jrow        END IF
        END DO max_pivot

        ! Check for singular equations.
        singular: IF ( ABS(a(ipeak,irow)) < epsilon ) THEN
            error = 1
            RETURN
        END IF singular

        ! Otherwise, if ipeak /= irow, swap equations irow & ipeak
        swap_eqn: IF ( ipeak /= irow ) THEN
            temp1 = a1(ipeak,1:n)
            a1(ipeak,1:n) = a1(irow,1:n)    ! Swap rows in a
            a1(irow,1:n) = temp1
            temp = soln(ipeak,kcol)
            soln(ipeak) = soln(irow)        ! Swap rows in b
            soln(irow) = temp
        END IF swap_eqn

        ! Multiply equation irow by −a1(jrow,irow)/a1(irow,irow),
        ! and add it to Eqn jrow (for all eqns except irow itself).
        eliminate: DO jrow = 1, n
            IF ( jrow /= irow ) THEN
                factor = −a1(jrow,irow)/a(irow,irow)
                a1(jrow,:) = a1(irow,1:n)*factor + a1(jrow,1:n)
                soln(jrow) = soln(irow)*factor + soln(jrow)
            END IF
        END DO eliminate
    END DO mainloop

    ! End of main loop over all equations.  All off-diagonal terms
    ! are now zero.  To get the final answer, we must divide
    ! each equation by the coefficient of its on-diagonal term.
    divide: DO irow = 1, n
        soln(irow) = soln(irow) / a1(irow,irow)
        a1(irow,irow) = 1.
    END DO divide

    ! Set error flag to 0 and return.
    error = 0

END SUBROUTINE simul2
```

Testing this subroutine is left as an exercise to the student (see exercise 6–35).

6.4

SHARING DATA USING MODULES

We have seen that programs exchange data with the subroutines they call through an argument list. Each item in the argument list of the program's CALL statement must be matched by a dummy argument in the argument list of the subroutine being invoked. A pointer to the location of each argument is passed from the calling program to the subroutine for use in accessing the arguments.

In addition to the argument list, Fortran programs, subroutines, and functions can also exchange data through modules. A **module** is a separately compiled program unit that contains the definitions and initial values of the data that we wish to share between program units.[4] If the module's name is included in a USE statement within a program unit, then the data values declared in the module may be used within that program unit. Each program unit that uses a module will have access the same data values, so modules provide a way to share data between program units.

A module begins with a MODULE statement, which assigns a name to the module. The name may be up to 31 characters long and must follow the standard Fortran naming conventions The module ends with an END and MODULE statement, which may optionally include the module's name. The declarations of the data to be shared are placed between these two statements. A sample module is shown in Figure 6–13.

6

FIGURE 6–13
A simple module used to share data among program units.

```
MODULE test
!
!  Purpose:
!  To declare data to share between two routines.

IMPLICIT NONE
SAVE

INTEGER, PARAMETER :: num_vals = 5      ! Max number of values in array
REAL, DIMENSION(num_vals) :: values     ! Data values

END MODULE test
```

The SAVE statement guarantees that all data values declared in the module will be preserved between references in different procedures. It should always be included in any module that declares sharable data.

To use the values in this module, a program unit must declare the module name in a USE statement. The form of a USE statement is

USE *module_name*

USE statements must appear before any other statements in a program unit (except for the PROGRAM or SUBROUTINE statement and except for comments, which may appear anywhere). The process of accessing information in a module with a USE statement is known as **USE association.**

An example that uses module test to share data between a main program and a subroutine is shown in Figure 6–14.

FIGURE 6–14
An example program using a module to share data between a main program and a subroutine.

```
PROGRAM test_module
!
!  Purpose:
```

(continued)

---
[4]Modules also have other functions, as explained in section 6.5 and in Chapter 9.

(concluded)

```
!  To illustrate sharing data via a module.
!
USE test                        ! Make data in module "test" visible
IMPLICIT NONE
REAL, PARAMETER :: pi = 3.141592  ! pi

values = pi * (/ 1., 2., 3., 4., 5. /)

CALL sub1                       ! Call subroutine

END PROGRAM
SUBROUTINE sub1
!
!  Purpose:
!    To illustrate sharing data via a module.
!
USE test                        ! Make data in module "test" visible
IMPLICIT NONE

WRITE (*,*) values

END SUBROUTINE sub1
```

The contents of module `test` are being shared between the main program and subroutine `sub1`. Any other subroutines or functions within the program could also have access to the data by including the appropriate USE statements.

Modules are especially useful for sharing large volumes of data among many program units. Modules are also useful for sharing data among a group of related procedures while keeping it invisible from the invoking program unit.

Good Programming Practice

You may use modules to pass large amounts of data between procedures within a program. If you do so, always include the SAVE statement within the module to ensure that the contents of the module remain unchanged between uses. To access the data in a particular program unit, include a USE statement as the *first noncomment statement* after the PROGRAM, SUBROUTINE, or FUNCTION statement within the program unit.

EXAMPLE 6–7 Random Number Generator: It is always impossible to make perfect measurements in the real world because some *measurement noise* will always be associated with each measurement. This fact is an important consideration in the design of systems to control the operation of such real-world devices as airplanes and refineries. A good engineering design must take these measurement errors into account so that the noise in the measurements will not lead to unstable behavior (no plane crashes or refinery explosions!)

Most engineering designs are tested by running *simulations* of the operation of the system before it is ever built. These simulations involve creating mathematical models of the behavior of the system and feeding the models a realistic string of input data. If the models respond correctly to the simulated input data, then we can have reasonable confidence that the real-world system will respond correctly to the real-world input data.

The simulated input data supplied to the models must be corrupted by a simulated measurement noise, which is just a string of random numbers added to the ideal input data. The simulated noise is usually produced by a *random number generator*.

A random number generator is a procedure that will return a different and apparently random number each time it is called. Since the numbers are in fact generated by a deterministic algorithm, they only appear to be random.[5] However, if the algorithm used to generate them is complex enough, the numbers will be random enough to use in the simulation.

One simple random number generator algorithm is shown below.[6] It relies on the unpredictability of the modulo function when applied to large numbers. Consider the following equation:

$$n_{i+1} = \text{MOD}\,(8121n_i + 28411, 134456) \tag{6-9}$$

Assume that n_i is a nonnegative integer. Then because of the modulo function, n_{i+1} will be a number between 0 and 134455 inclusive. Next n_{i+1} can be fed into the equation to produce a number n_{i+2} that is also between 0 and 134455. This process can be repeated forever to produce a series of numbers in the range [0, 134455]. If we didn't know the numbers 8121, 28411, and 134456 in advance, we could not guess the order in which the values of n would be produced. Furthermore, it turns out that there is an equal (or uniform) probability that any given number will appear in the sequence. Because of these properties, Equation (6–9) can serve as the basis for a simple random number generator with a uniform distribution.

We will now use Equation (6–9) to design a random number generator whose output is a real number in the range [0.0, 1.0).[7]

SOLUTION We will write a subroutine that generates one random number in the range $0 \le ran < 1.0$ each time that it is called. The random number will be based on the equation

$$ran_i = \frac{n_i}{134456} \tag{6-10}$$

where n_i is a number in the range 0 to 134455 produced by Equation (6–9).

---

[5] For this reason some people refer to these procedures as *pseudorandom number generators*.
[6] This algorithm is adapted from the discussion found in Chapter 7 of *Numerical Recipes: The Art of Scientific Programming* by Press, Flannery, Teukolsky, and Vetterling, Cambridge University Press, 1986.
[7] The notation [0.0, 1.0) implies that the range of the random numbers is between 0.0, and 1.0, including the number 0.0 but excluding the number 1.0.

The particular sequence produced by Equations (6–9) and (6–10) will depend on the initial value of n_0 (called the *seed*) of the sequence. We must provide a way for the user to specify n_0 so that the sequence may be varied from run to run.

1. **State the problem.**

Write a subroutine random0 that will generate and return a single number ran with a uniform probability distribution in the range $0 \le \text{ran} < 1.0$, based on the sequence specified by Equations (6–9) and (6–10). The initial value of the seed n_0 will be specified by a call to subroutine seed.

2. **Define the inputs and outputs.**

The two subroutines in this problem are seed and random0. The input to subroutine seed is an integer to serve as the starting point of the sequence. There is no output from this subroutine. There is no input to subroutine random0, and the output from the subroutine is a single real value in the range [0.0, 1.0).

3. **Describe the algorithm.**

The pseudocode for subroutine random0 is very simple:

```
SUBROUTINE random0 ( ran )
n ← MOD (8121 * n + 28411, 134456 )
ran ← REAL(n) / 134456.
END SUBROUTINE
```

where the value of n is saved between calls to the subroutine. The pseudocode for subroutine seed is also trivial:

```
SUBROUTINE seed ( iseed )
n ← ABS ( iseed )
END SUBROUTINE
```

The absolute value function is used so that the user can enter any integer as the starting point. The user will not have to know in advance that only positive integers are legal seeds.

The variable n will be placed in a module so that it may be accessed by both subroutines. In addition, we will initialize n to a reasonable value so that we get good results even if subroutine seed is not called to set the seed before the first call to random0.

4. **Turn the algorithm into Fortran statements.**

The resulting Fortran subroutines are shown in Figure 6–15.

FIGURE 6–15
Subroutines to generate a random number sequence and to set the seed of the sequence.

```
MODULE ran001
!
! Purpose:
!   To declare data shared between subs random0 and seed.
!
```

(continued)

(concluded)

```
!  Record of revisions:
!      Date        Programmer          Description of change
!      ====        ==========          =====================
!    10/17/95     S. J. Chapman        Original code
!
IMPLICIT NONE
INTEGER, SAVE :: n = 9876
END MODULE ran001

SUBROUTINE random0 ( ran )
!
!  Purpose:
!     Subroutine to generate a pseudorandom number with a uniform
!     distribution in the range 0. < = ran < 1.0.
!
!  Record of revisions:
!      Date        Programmer          Description of change
!      ====        ==========          =====================
!    10/17/95     S. J. Chapman        Original code
!

USE ran001                          ! Shared seed
IMPLICIT NONE

! List of calling arguments:
REAL, INTENT(OUT) :: ran            ! Random number

n = MOD (8121 * n + 28411, 134456 )  ! Next number
ran = REAL(n) / 134456.              ! ran

END SUBROUTINE random0

SUBROUTINE seed ( iseed )
!
!  Purpose:
!  To set the seed for random number generator random0.
!
!  Record of revisions:
!      Date        Programmer          Description of change
!      ====        ==========          =====================
!    10/17/95     S. J. Chapman        Original code
!
USE ran001                          ! Shared seed
IMPLICIT NONE

! List of calling arguments:
INTEGER, INTENT(IN) :: iseed        ! Value to initialize sequence

n = ABS ( iseed )                   ! Set seed.

END SUBROUTINE seed
```

5. Test the resulting Fortran programs.

If the numbers generated by these routines are truly uniformly distributed random numbers in the range $0 \le ran < 1.0$, then the average of many numbers should be close to 0.5. To test the results, we will write a test program that prints out the first 10 values produced by random0 to see if they are indeed in the range

$0 \leq ran < 1.0$. Then the program will average five consecutive 1000-sample intervals to see how close the averages come to 0.5. The test code to call subroutines seed and random0 is shown in Figure 6–16.

FIGURE 6–16

Test driver program for subroutines seed and random0.

```
PROGRAM test_random0
!
!  Purpose:
!    Subroutine test the random number generator random0.
!
!  Record of revisions:
!     Date       Programmer        Description of change
!     ====       ==========        =====================
!    10/17/95   S. J. Chapman      Original code
!
IMPLICIT NONE

! List of local variables
REAL :: ave             ! Average of random numbers
INTEGER :: i            ! DO loop index
INTEGER :: iseed        ! Seed for random number sequence
INTEGER :: iseq         ! DO loop index
REAL :: ran             ! A random number
REAL :: sum             ! Sum of random numbers

! Get seed.
WRITE (*,*) 'Enter seed: '
READ (*,*) iseed

! Set seed.
CALL SEED ( iseed )

! Print out 10 random numbers.
WRITE (*,*) '10 random numbers:'
DO i = 1, 10
   CALL random0 ( ran )
   WRITE (*,'(3X,F16.6)') ran
END DO

! Average 5 consecutive 1000-value sequences.
WRITE (*,*) 'Averages of 5 consecutive 1000-sample sequences:'
DO iseq = 1, 5
   sum = 0.
   DO i = 1, 1000
      CALL random0 ( ran )
      sum = sum + ran
   END DO
   ave = sum / 1000.
   WRITE (*,'(3X,F16.6)') ave
END DO

END PROGRAM
```

The results of compiling and running the test program follow.

```
C>test_random0
Enter seed:
12
```

```
10 random numbers:
            .936091
            .203204
            .431167
            .719105
            .064103
            .789775
            .974839
            .881686
            .384951
            .400086
Averages of 5 consecutive 1000-sample sequences:
            .504282
            .512665
            .496927
            .491514
            .498117
```

6

The numbers do appear to be between 0.0 and 1.0, and the averages of long sets of these numbers are nearly 0.5, so these subroutines appear to be functioning correctly. You should try them again using different seeds to see if they behave consistently.

Fortran 90/95 includes an intrinsic subroutine RANDOM_NUMBER to generate sequences of random numbers. That subroutine will typically produce more nearly random results than the simple subroutine developed in this example. The full details of how to use subroutine RANDOM_NUMBER appear in Appendix B.

■ 6.5
MODULE PROCEDURES

In addition to data, modules may also contain complete subroutines and functions, which are known as **module procedures.** These procedures are compiled as a part of the module and are made available to a program unit by including a USE statement containing the module name in the program unit. Procedures that are included within a module must follow any data objects declared in the module and must be preceded by a CONTAINS statement. The CONTAINS statement tells the compiler that the following statements are included procedures.

The following example of a module procedure, subroutine sub1, is contained within module my_subs.

```
MODULE my_subs
IMPLICIT NONE

(Declare shared data here)

CONTAINS
   SUBROUTINE sub1 ( a, b, c, x, error )
   IMPLICIT NONE
   REAL, DIMENSION(3), INTENT(IN) :: a
   REAL, INTENT(IN) :: b, c
   REAL, INTENT(OUT) :: x
   LOGICAL, INTENT(OUT) :: error
```

```
           . . .
        END SUBROUTINE sub1
     END MODULE my_subs
```

Subroutine `sub1` is made available for use in a calling program unit if the statement "USE my_subs" is included as the first noncomment statement within the program unit. The subroutine can be called with a standard CALL statement, for example:

```
     PROGRAM main_prog
     USE my_subs
     IMPLICIT NONE
     ...
     CALL sub1 ( a, b, c, x, error )
     ...
     END PROGRAM
```

6.5.1 Using Modules to Create Explicit Interfaces

Why would we bother to include a procedure in a module? We already know that it is possible to separately compile a subroutine and to call it from another program unit, so why go through the extra steps of including the subroutine in a module, compiling the module, declaring the module in a USE statement, and then calling the subroutine?

The answer is that when a procedure is compiled within a module and the module is used by a calling program, all the details of the procedure's interface are made available to the compiler. When the calling program is compiled, the compiler can automatically check the number of arguments in the procedure call, the type of each argument, whether or not each argument is an array, and the INTENT of each argument. In short, the compiler can catch most of the common errors that a programmer might make when using procedures!

A procedure compiled within a module and accessed by USE association is said to have an **explicit interface.** The Fortran compiler explicitly knows all the details about every argument in the procedure whenever the procedure is used, and the compiler checks the interface to ensure that it is being used properly.

In contrast, procedures not in a module are said to have an **implicit interface.** A Fortran compiler has no information about these procedures when it is compiling a program unit that invokes them, so it just *assumes* that the programmer got the number, type, intent, etc. of the arguments right. If the programmer actually got the calling sequence wrong, then the program will fail in strange and hard-to-find ways.

To illustrate this point, let's reexamine the program in Figure 6–5. That program has an implicit interface between program `bad_call` and subroutine `bad_argument`. A real value was passed to the subroutine when an integer argument was expected, and the number was misinterpreted by the subroutine. As we saw from that example, the Fortran compiler did not catch the error in the calling arguments.

Figure 6–17 shows the program rewritten to include the subroutine within a module.

FIGURE 6–17
Example illustrating the effects of a type mismatch when calling a subroutine included within a module.

```
MODULE my_subs
CONTAINS
   SUBROUTINE bad_argument ( i )
   IMPLICIT NONE
   INTEGER, INTENT(IN) :: i      ! Declare argument as integer.
   WRITE (*,*) ' I = ', i        ! Write out i.
   END SUBROUTINE
END MODULE

PROGRAM bad_call
!
!  Purpose:
!    To illustrate misinterpreted calling arguments.
!
USE my_subs
IMPLICIT NONE
REAL :: x = 1.                  ! Declare real variable x.
CALL bad_argument ( x )         ! Call subroutine.
END PROGRAM
```

When this program is compiled, the Fortran compiler will catch the argument mismatch for us.

```
C>f90 fig6-17.f90
DIGITAL Visual Fortran Optimizing Compiler Version: V5.0
Copyright (c) 1997 Digital Equipment Corp. All rights reserved.

fig 6-17.f90
fig6-17.f90(18) : Error: The type of the actual argument differs from the type
of the dummy argument. [X]
CALL bad_argument ( x )        ! Call subroutine.
--------------------^
```

There is _____ 'her way to allow a Fortran compiler to explicitly check proce-
_____ NTERFACE block. We will learn more about it in Chapter 9.

e Arrays

n explicit interface, the full details the type, order, intent, and
ummy arguments are known to the calling program unit, and
ing program's actual arguments are known to the procedure.
ure can know the shape and size of actual arrays passed to
ation to manipulate the arrays. Since this information is al-
explicit interface, we do not have to declare each dummy
:it-shape dummy array with the bounds of the array passed

ents can be declared as **assumed-shape dummy arrays.**
ys are special forms of dummy array arguments that _as-
calling array arguments_ when the procedure is invoked.
clared with a specific type and rank, but with colons in

each dimension instead of bounds. For example, array `arr1` in the following type declaration statement is an assumed-shape array.

```
REAL, DIMENSION(:,:) :: arr1
```

Whole array operations, array sections, and array intrinsic functions can all be used with assumed-shape dummy arrays. If needed, the actual size and extent of an assumed-shape array can be determined by using the array inquiry functions in Table 5–1. However, the upper and lower bounds of each dimension cannot be determined, since only the *shape* of the actual array but not the *bounds* are passed to the procedure. If the actual bounds are needed for some reason in a particular procedure, then we must use an explicit-shape dummy array.

Assumed-shape dummy arrays are generally better than explicit-shape dummy arrays in that we don't have to pass every bound from the calling program unit to a procedure. However, assumed-shape arrays work only if a procedure has an explicit interface.

EXAMPLE 6–8 Using Assumed-Shape Dummy Arrays: A simple procedure using an assumed-shape dummy array is shown in Figure 6–18. This procedure declares an assumed-shape dummy array `array`, and then determines its size, shape and bounds using array intrinsic functions. Note that the subroutine is contained in a module, so it has an explicit interface.

FIGURE 6–18
Subroutine to illustrate the use of assumed-shape arrays.

```
MODULE test_module
!  Purpose:
!    To illustrate the use of assumed-shape arrays.
!
CONTAINS
   SUBROUTINE test_array(array)
   IMPLICIT NONE
   REAL, DIMENSION(:,:) :: array      ! Assumed-shape array
   INTEGER :: i1, i2                  ! Bounds of first dimension
   INTEGER :: j1, j2                  ! Bounds of second dimension

   ! Get details about array.
   i1 = LBOUND(array,1)
   i2 = UBOUND(array,1)
   j1 = LBOUND(array,2)
   j2 = UBOUND(array,2)
   WRITE (*,100) i1, i2, j1, j2
   100 FORMAT (1X,'The bounds are:  (',I2,':',I2,',',I2,':',I2,')')
   WRITE (*,110) SHAPE(array)
   110 FORMAT (1X,'The shape is:    ',2I4)
   WRITE (*,120) SIZE(array)
   120 FORMAT (1X,'The size is:     ',I4)
   END SUBROUTINE test_array
END MODULE test_module

PROGRAM assumed_shape
!
!  Purpose:
```

(continued)

(concluded)

```
!     To illustrate the use of assumed-shape arrays.
!
USE test_module
IMPLICIT NONE

! Declare local variables
REAL, DIMENSION(-5:5,-5:5) :: a = 0.  ! Array a
REAL, DIMENSION(10,2) :: b = 1.       ! Array b

! Call test_array with array a.
WRITE (*,*) 'Calling test_array with array a:'
CALL test_array(a)

! Call test_array with array b.
WRITE (*,*) 'Calling test_array with array b:'
CALL test_array(b)

END PROGRAM
```

When program assumed_shape is executed, the results are

```
C>assumed_shape
Calling test_array with array a:
The bounds are: ( 1:11, 1:11)
The shape is:       11  11
The size is:       121
Calling test_array with array b:
The bounds are: ( 1:10, 1: 2)
The shape is:       10   2
The size is:        20
```

Note that the subroutine has complete information about the rank, shape, and size of each array passed to it, but not about the bounds used for the array in the calling program.

A Profusion (and Confusion!) of Fortran Array Types

The large variety of Fortran arrays can be confusing. Let's step back and review the different array types to see just where each type is used and how they relate to each other.

1. Explicit-Shape Arrays with Construct Bounds

Explicit-shape arrays with constant bounds are nondummy arrays whose shape is explicitly specified in their type declaration statements. They may be declared either in main programs or in procedures, but they *do not appear* in the dummy argument list of a procedure. Explicit-shape arrays with constant bounds allocate fixed, permanent arrays for use in a program. They may be initialized in their type declaration statements.

If an explicit-shape array with constant bounds is allocated in a procedure, the data stored in it is guaranteed to be intact from invocation to invocation only if the array is declared with the SAVE attribute or if the array is initialized in the type declaration statement.

Two examples of explicit-shape arrays with constant bounds are

```
INTEGER, PARAMETER :: ndim = 100
REAL, DIMENSION(ndim,ndim) :: input_data = 1.
REAL, DIMENSION(-3:3) :: scratch = 0.
```

(continued)

(continued)

2. Dummy Arrays

Dummy arrays are arrays that appear in the dummy argument list of procedures. They are placeholders for the actual arrays passed to the procedure when it is invoked. No actual memory is allocated for dummy arrays. The three types of dummy arrays are *explicit-shape dummy arrays, assumed-shape dummy arrays,* and *assumed-size dummy arrays.*

a. *Explicit-shape dummy arrays* are arrays that appear in the dummy argument list of a procedure and whose dimensions are explicitly declared by arguments in the procedure's argument list. All the advanced features of Fortran arrays can be used with explicit-shape dummy arrays, including whole array operations, array sections, and array intrinsic functions. An example of an explicit-shape dummy array is

```
SUBROUTINE test ( array, n, m1, m2 )
INTEGER, INTENT(IN) :: n, m1, m2
REAL, DIMENSION(n,m1:m2) :: array
```

b. *Assumed-shape dummy arrays* are arrays that appear in the dummy argument list of a procedure and whose dimensions are declared by colons. The type declaration statement specifies the type and rank of the array, but not the extent of each dimension. *An assumed-shape dummy array is only usable in a procedure with an explicit interface.* These arrays assume the shape of whatever actual array is passed to the procedure when it is invoked. All the advanced features of Fortran arrays can be used with assumed-shape dummy arrays, including whole array operations, array sections, and array intrinsic functions. An example of an assumed-shape dummy array is

```
SUBROUTINE test ( array )
REAL, DIMENSION(:,:) :: array
```

c. *Assumed-size dummy arrays* are arrays that appear in the dummy argument list of a procedure and whose last dimension is declared with an asterisk. The size of all dimensions except for the last must be explicitly specified so that the procedure can determine how to locate specific array elements in memory. An assumed-size dummy array cannot be used with whole array operations or with many of the array intrinsic functions, because the shape of the actual array is unknown. Assumed-size dummy arrays are a holdover from earlier versions of Fortran; *they should never be used in any new programs.* An example of an assumed-size dummy array is

```
SUBROUTINE test ( array )
REAL, DIMENSION(10,*) :: array
```

3. Automatic Arrays

Automatic arrays are explicit-shape arrays with nonconstant bounds that appear in procedures. They do *not* appear in the procedure's argument list. The bounds are passed to the procedure either via the argument list or by shared data in a module.

When the procedure is invoked, an array of the shape and size specified by the nonconstant bounds is *automatically* created. When the procedure ends, the array is automatically destroyed. If the procedure is invoked again, a new array will be created that could be either the same shape as or a different shape from the previous one. Data is not preserved in automatic arrays between invocations of the procedure, and it is illegal to specify either a SAVE attribute or a default initialization for an automatic array. An example of an automatic array is

```
SUBROUTINE test ( n, m )
INTEGER, INTENT(IN) :: n, m
REAL, DIMENSION(n,m) :: array
```

4. Deferred-Shape Arrays

Deferred-shape arrays are allocatable arrays or pointer arrays. (Pointer arrays are covered in Chapter 11.) A deferred-shape array is declared in a type declaration statement with an ALLOCATABLE (or POINTER) attribute and with the dimensions declared by colons. It may appear in either main programs or procedures. The array may not be used in any fashion (except as an argument to the ALLOCATED function) until memory is actually allocated for it. Memory is allocated using an ALLOCATE statement and deallocated using a DEALLOCATE statement. A deferred-shape array may not be initialized in its type declaration statement.

(concluded)

If an allocatable array is declared and allocated in a procedure, and if it is desired to keep the array between invocations of the procedure, the array must be declared with the SAVE attribute. If the array is not needed, it should be explicitly deallocated to avoid possible problems with "memory leaks." An example of a deferred-shape array is

```
INTEGER, ALLOCATABLE :: array(:,:)
ALLOCATE ( array(1000,1000), STATUS=istat)
...
DEALLOCATE ( array, STATUS = istat)
```

6

Good Programming Practice
Use either assumed-shape arrays or explicit-shape arrays as dummy array arguments in procedures. If assumed-shape arrays are used, an explicit interface is required. Whole array operations, array sections, and array intrinsic functions may be used with the dummy array arguments in either case. *Never use assumed-size arrays in any new program.*

QUIZ 6–2

This quiz provides a quick check to see if you understand the concepts introduced in sections 6.2 through 6.5. If you have trouble with the quiz, reread the sections, ask your instructor, or discuss the material with a fellow student. The answers to this quiz are found in the back of the book.

1. When should you use a SAVE statement or attribute in a program or procedure? Why should it be used?

2. What is the difference between an automatic array and an allocatable array? When should each of them be used?

3. Why should you gather up the procedures in a program and place them into a module?

4. What are the advantages and disadvantages of assumed-shape dummy arrays?

For questions 5 through 8, determine whether any errors occur in the programs. If possible, tell what the output from each program will be.

5.
```
PROGRAM test1
IMPLICIT NONE
INTEGER, DIMENSION(10) :: i
INTEGER :: j
DO j = 1, 10
   CALL sub1 ( i(j) )
```

(continued)

(concluded)

```
      WRITE (*,*) ' I = ', i(j)
   END DO
   END PROGRAM test1
   SUBROUTINE sub1 ( ival )
   IMPLICIT NONE
   INTEGER, INTENT(INOUT) :: ival
   INTEGER :: isum
   isum = isum + 1
   ival = isum
   END SUBROUTINE sub1
```

6.
```
   MODULE mydata
   IMPLICIT NONE
   REAL, SAVE, DIMENSION(8) :: a
   REAL, SAVE :: b
   END MODULE mydata

   PROGRAM test2
   USE mydata
   IMPLICIT NONE
   a = (/ 1.,2.,3.,4.,5.,6.,7.,8. /)
   b = 37.
   CALL sub2
   END PROGRAM test2

   SUBROUTINE sub2
   USE mydata
   IMPLICIT NONE
   WRITE (*,*) 'a(5) = ', a(5)
   END SUBROUTINE sub2
```

7.
```
   MODULE mysubs
   CONTAINS
      SUBROUTINE sub3(x,y)
      REAL, INTENT(IN) :: x
      REAL, INTENT(OUT) :: y
      y = 3. * x - 1.
      END SUBROUTINE sub3
   END MODULE

   PROGRAM test3
   USE mysubs
   IMPLICIT NONE
   REAL :: a = 5.
   CALL sub3 (a, -3.)
   END PROGRAM
```

8.
```
   PROGRAM test4
   IMPLICIT NONE
   REAL, DIMENSION(2,2) :: a = 1., b = 2.
   CALL sub4(a, b)
   WRITE (*,*) a
   END PROGRAM
   SUBROUTINE sub4(a,b)
   REAL, DIMENSION(:,:), INTENT(INOUT) :: a
   REAL, DIMENSION (:,:) INTENT(IN) :: b
   a = a + b
   END SUBROUTINE sub4
```

■ 6.6

Fortran FUNCTIONS

A Fortran function is a procedure whose result is a single number, logical value, character string, or array. The result of a function is a single value or single array that can be combined with variables and constants to form Fortran expressions. These expressions may appear on the right side of an assignment statement in the calling program. Fortran has two different types of functions: **intrinsic functions** and **user-defined functions** (or function subprograms).

Intrinsic functions are built into the Fortran language, such as `SIN(X)` and `LOG(X)`. Some of these functions were described in Chapters 2 and 5; all of them are detailed in Appendix B. User-defined functions or function subprograms are functions defined by individual programmers to meet a specific need not addressed by the standard intrinsic functions. They are used just like intrinsic functions in expressions. The general form of a user-defined Fortran function is

```
FUNCTION name ( argument_list )
...
(Declaration section must declare type of name)
...
(Execution section)
...
name = expr
RETURN
END FUNCTION [name]
```

The function must begin with a `FUNCTION` statement and end with an `END FUNCTION` statement. The name of the function may contain up to 31 alphabetic, numeric, and underscore characters, but the first letter must be alphabetic. The name must be specified in the `FUNCTION` statement and is optional on the `END FUNCTION` statement.

A function is invoked by naming it in an expression. When a function is invoked, execution begins at the top of the function and ends when either a `RETURN` statement or the `END FUNCTION` statement is reached. Because execution always ends at the `END FUNCTION` statement, the `RETURN` statement is not actually required in most functions and is rarely used. When the function returns, the returned value is used to continue evaluating the Fortran expression in which the function was named.

The name of the function must appear on the left side of a least one assignment statement in the function. The value assigned to *name* when the function returns to the invoking program unit will be the value of the function.

The argument list of the function may be blank if the function can perform all its calculations with no input arguments. The parentheses around the argument list are required even if the list is blank.

Since a function returns a value, it is necessary to assign a type to the function. If `IMPLICIT NONE` is used, the type of the function must be declared both in the function procedure and in the calling programs. If `IMPLICIT NONE` is not used, the default type of the function will follow the standard rules of Fortran unless they are overridden by a type declaration statement. The type declaration of a user-defined Fortran function can take one of two equivalent forms:

```
INTEGER FUNCTION my_function ( i, j )
```

or

```
FUNCTION my_function ( i, j )
INTEGER :: my_function
```

An example of a user-defined function is shown in Figure 6–19. Function `quadf` evaluates a quadratic expression with user-specified coefficients at a user-specified value `x`.

FIGURE 6–19

A function to evaluate a quadratic polynomial of the form $quad(x) = a\, x^2 + b\, x + c$.

```
REAL FUNCTION quadf ( x, a, b, c )
!
!  Purpose:
!  To evaluate a quadratic polynomial of the form
!     quadf = a * x**2 + b * x + c
!
!  Record of revisions:
!     Date        Programmer          Description of change
!     ====        ==========          =====================
!   10/22/95    S. J. Chapman        Original code
!
IMPLICIT NONE

! Declare calling arguments.
REAL, INTENT(IN) :: x        ! Value to evaluate expression for
REAL, INTENT(IN) :: a        ! Coefficient of X**2 term
REAL, INTENT(IN) :: b        ! Coefficient of X term
REAL, INTENT(IN) :: c        ! Coefficient of constant term

! Evaluate expression.
quadf = a * x**2 + b * x + c

END FUNCTION
```

This function produces a result of type real. Note that the INTENT attribute is not used with the declaration of the function name `quadf`, since it must always be used for output only. A simple test program using the function is shown in Figure 6–20.

FIGURE 6–20

A test driver program for function `quadf`.

```
PROGRAM test_quadf
!
!  Purpose:
!  Program to test function quadf.
!
IMPLICIT NONE

REAL :: quadf                 ! Declare function
REAL :: a, b, c, x            ! Declare local variables

! Get input data.
WRITE (*,*) 'Enter quadratic coefficients a, b, and c: '
```

(continued)

(concluded)

```
READ (*,*) a, b, c
WRITE (*,*) 'Enter location at which to evaluate equation: '
READ (*,*) x

! Write out result.
WRITE (*,100) ' quadf(', x, ') = ', quadf(x,a,b,c)
100 FORMAT (A,F10.4,A,F12.4)

END PROGRAM
```

Notice that function `quadf` is declared as type real both in the function itself and in the test program. In this example function `quadf` was used in the argument list of a `WRITE` statement. It could also have been used in assignment statements or wherever a Fortran expression is permissible.

Good Programming Practice

Be sure to declare the type of any user-defined functions both in the function itself and in any routines that call the function.

6.6.1 Unintended Side Effects in Functions

Input values are passed to a function through its argument list. Functions use the same argument-passing scheme as subroutines. A function receives pointers to the locations of its arguments, and it can deliberately or accidentally modify the contents of those memory locations. Therefore, *a function subprogram can modify its own input arguments.* If any of the function's dummy arguments appear on the right side of an assignment statement within the function, then the values of the input variables corresponding to those arguments will be changed. A function that modifies the values in its argument list is said to have **side effects.**

By definition, a function should produce a *single output value* using one or more input values, and it should have no side effects. The function should *never* modify its own input arguments. If a programmer needs to produce more than one output value from a procedure, then the procedure should be written as a subroutine and not as a function. To ensure that a function's arguments are not accidentally modified, they should always be declared with the `INTENT(IN)` attribute.

Good Programming Practice

A well-designed Fortran function should produce a single output value from one or more input values. It should never modify its own input arguments. To ensure that a function does not accidentally modify its input arguments, always declare the arguments with the `INTENT(IN)` attribute.

Quiz 6-3

This quiz provides a quick check to see if you understand the concepts introduced in section 6.6 If you have trouble with the quiz, reread the section, ask your instructor, or discuss the material with a fellow student. The answers to this quiz are found in the back of the book.

Write a user-defined function to perform the following calculations:

1. $f(x) = \dfrac{x - 1}{x + 1}$

2. The hyperbolic tangent function $\tanh(x) = \dfrac{e^x - e^{-x}}{e^x + e^{-x}}$

3. The factorial function $n! = (n)(n - 1)(n - 2) \ldots (2)(1)$

4. Write a logical function that has two input arguments x and y. The function should return a true value if $x^2 + y^2 > 1.0$, and a false value otherwise.

For questions 5 to 7, determine whether there are any errors in these functions. If so, show how to correct them.

5.
```
REAL FUNCTION average ( x, n )
IMPLICIT NONE
INTEGER, INTENT(IN) :: n
REAL, DIMENSION(n), INTENT(IN) :: x
INTEGER :: j
REAL :: sum
DO j = 1, n
   sum = sum + x(j)
END DO
average = sum / n
END FUNCTION average
```

6.
```
FUNCTION fun_2 ( a, b, c )
IMPLICIT NONE
REAL, INTENT(IN) :: a, b, c
a = 3. * a
fun_2 = a**2 - b + c
END FUNCTION
```

7.
```
LOGICAL FUNCTION badval ( x, y )
IMPLICIT NONE
REAL, INTENT(IN) :: x, y
badval = x > y
END FUNCTION
```

EXAMPLE 6-9 The sinc Function: The sinc function is defined by the equation

$$\text{sinc}(x) = \frac{\sin(x)}{x} \tag{6-11}$$

This function occurs in many different types of engineering analysis problems.

For example, the sinc function describes the frequency spectrum of a rectangular time pulse. A plot of the function sinc(x) versus x is shown in Figure 6–21. Write a user-defined Fortran function to calculate the sinc function.

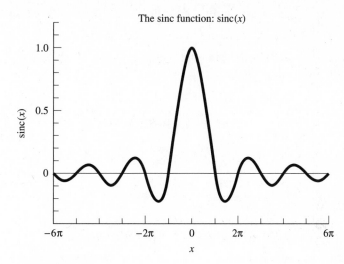

The sinc function: sinc(x)

FIGURE 6–21
Plot of sinc(x) versus x.

SOLUTION The sinc function looks easy to implement, but a calculation problem occurs when $x = 0$. The value of sinc(0) = 1, since

$$\text{sinc}(0) = \lim_{x \to 0}\left(\frac{\sin(x)}{x}\right) = 1$$

Unfortunately, a computer program would blow up on the division by 0. We must include a logical IF construct in the function to handle the special case where x is nearly 0.

1. **State the problem.**

   Write a Fortran function that calculates sinc(x).

2. **Define the inputs and outputs.**

   The input to the function is the real argument x. The function is of type real, and its output is the value of sinc(x).

3. **Describe the algorithm.**

   The pseudocode for this function is

```
IF |x| > epsilon THEN
    sinc ← SIN(x) / x
ELSE
    sinc ← 1.
END IF
```

where `epsilon` is chosen to ensure that the division does not cause divide-by-zero errors. For most computers, a good choice for `epsilon` is 1.0E-30.

4. **Turn the algorithm into Fortran statements.**

The resulting Fortran subroutines are shown in Figure 6–22.

FIGURE 6–22

The Fortran function `sinc(x)`.

```
FUNCTION sinc ( x )
!
!  Purpose:
!    To calculate the sinc function
!        sinc(x) = sin(x) / x
!
!  Record of revisions:
!     Date        Programmer          Description of change
!     ====        ==========          =====================
!    10/22/95    S. J. Chapman        Original code
!
IMPLICIT NONE

! List of calling arguments:
REAL, INTENT(IN) :: x         ! Value for which to evaluate sinc
REAL :: sinc                  ! Output value sinc(x)

! List of local parameters:
REAL, PARAMETER :: epsilon = 1.0E-30  ! the smallest value for which
                                      ! to calculate SIN(x)/x
! Check to see of ABS(x) > epsilon.
IF ( ABS(x) > epsilon ) THEN
   sinc = SIN(x) / x
ELSE
   sinc = 1.
END IF

END FUNCTION sinc
```

5. **Test the resulting Fortran program.**

To test this function, we need to write a driver program to read an input value, call the function, and write out the results. We will calculate several values of sinc(x) on a hand calculator and compare them with the results of the test program. Note that we must verify the function of the program for input values both greater than and less than `epsilon`.

A test driver program is shown in Figure 6–23.

FIGURE 6–23

A test driver program for the function `sinc(x)`.

```
PROGRAM test_sinc
!
!  Purpose:
!    To test the sinc function sinc(x)
!
```

(continued)

(concluded)

```
IMPLICIT NONE
! Declare function types:
REAL :: sinc                ! sinc function

! Declare local variables:
REAL :: x                   ! Input value to evaluate

! Get value to evaluate
WRITE (*,*) 'Enter x : '
READ (*,*) x

! Write answer.
WRITE (*,'(1X,A,F8.5)') 'sinc(x) = ', sinc(x)

END PROGRAM
```

Hand calculations yield the following values for sinc(x):

x	sinc(x)
0	1.00000
10^{-29}	1.00000
$\dfrac{\pi}{2}$	0.63662
π	0.00000

The results from the test program for these input values follow.

```
C>test_sinc
Enter x:
0
sinc(x) =  1.0000

C>test_sinc
Enter x:
1.E-29
sinc(x) =  1.0000

C>test_sinc
Enter x:
1.570796
sinc(x) = 0.63662

C>test_sinc
Enter x:
3.141593
sinc(x) =  0.0000
```

The function appears to be working correctly.

■ 6.7
PURE AND ELEMENTAL PROCEDURES

As we mentioned in previous chapters, the Fortran language has been evolving in ways to make it easier to execute on massively parallel processors. As a part of this evolution, Fortran 95 has introduced two new classifications of procedures: **pure procedures** and **elemental procedures.**

6.7.1 Pure Procedures

Pure functions are functions that do not have side effects. That is, they do not modify their input arguments, and they do not modify any other data (such as data in modules) that is visible outside the function. In addition, local variables may not have the SAVE attribute and may not be initialized in type declaration statements (since such initialization implies the SAVE attribute). Any procedures invoked by a pure function must also be pure.

Because pure functions do not have side effects, it is safe to invoke them in a FORALL construct, where they might be executed in any order. The ability to use FORALL constructs is very helpful on massively parallel processors because each processor can take one combination of control indices from the FORALL construct and execute it in parallel with the others.

Every argument in a pure function must be declared with INTENT(IN), and any subroutine or functions invoked by the function must itself be pure. In addition, the function must not do any external file I/O operations and must not contain a STOP statement. These constraints are easy to abide by—all the functions that we have created so far are pure.

In Fortran 95 a pure function is declared by adding a PURE prefix to the function statement. For example, the following function is pure:

```
PURE FUNCTION length (x, y)
IMPLICIT NONE
REAL, INTENT(IN) :: x, y
REAL :: length
length = SQRT(x**2 + y**2)
END FUNCTION length
```

Pure subroutines are subroutines that do not have side effects. Their constraints are exactly the same as those on pure functions except that they are permitted to modify arguments declared with INTENT(OUT) or INTENT(INOUT). Pure subroutines are declared by adding the PURE prefix to the SUBROUTINE statement.

6.7.2 Elemental Procedures

Elemental functions are functions that are specified for scalar arguments, but which may also be applied to array arguments. If the argument(s) of an elemental function are scalars, then the result of the function will be a scalar. If the argument(s) of the function are arrays, then the result of the function will be an array of the same shape as the input argument(s). Elemental intrinsic functions are available both in Fortran 90 and Fortran 95, but user-defined elemental functions are new to Fortran 95.

User-defined elemental functions must be PURE functions and must satisfy the following additional constraints:

1. All dummy arguments must be scalars and must not have the POINTER attribute. (You will learn about pointers in Chapter 11.)
2. The function result must be a scalar and must not have the POINTER attribute.
3. Dummy arguments must not be used in type declaration statements except as arguments of certain intrinsic functions. This constraint prohibits the use of automatic arrays in elemental functions.

In Fortran 95 a user-defined elemental function is declared by adding an ELEMENTAL prefix to the function statement. For example, the function sinc(x) from Figure 6–22 is elemental, so in Fortran 95 it would be declared as

```
ELEMENTAL FUNCTION sinc( x )
```

Elemental subroutines are subroutines that are specified for scalar arguments, but which may also be applied to array arguments. They must meet the same constraints as elemental functions. In Fortran 95 an elemental subroutine is declared by adding an ELEMENTAL prefix to the subroutine statement. For example:

```
ELEMENTAL SUBROUTINE convert(x, y, z)
```

6.8

PASSING PROCEDURES AS ARGUMENTS TO OTHER PROCEDURES

When a procedure is invoked, the actual argument list is passed to the procedure as a series of pointers to specific memory locations. How the memory at each location is interpreted depends on the type and size of the dummy arguments declared in the procedure.

This pass-by-reference approach can be extended to permit us to pass a pointer to a *procedure* instead of a pointer to a memory location. Both functions and subroutines can be passed as calling arguments. For simplicity, we will first discuss passing user-defined functions to procedures and then discuss passing subroutines to procedures.

6.8.1 Passing User-Defined Functions as Arguments

If a user-defined function is named as an actual argument in a procedure call, then a *pointer to that function* is passed to the procedure. If the corresponding formal argument in the procedure is used as a function, then when the procedure is executed, the function in the calling argument list will be used in place of the dummy function name in the procedure. Consider the following example:

```
PROGRAM :: test
REAL, EXTERNAL :: fun_1, fun_2
REAL :: x, y, output
...
CALL evaluate ( fun_1, x, y, output )
CALL evaluate ( fun_2, x, y, output )
...
END PROGRAM
SUBROUTINE evaluate ( fun, a, b, result )
REAL, EXTERNAL :: fun
REAL, INTENT(IN) :: a, b
REAL, INTENT(OUT) :: result
result = b * fun(a)
END SUBROUTINE evaluate
```

Assume that `fun_1` and `fun_2` are two user-supplied functions. Then a pointer to function `fun_1` is passed to subroutine `evaluate` on the first occasion that it is called, and function `fun_1` is used in place of the dummy formal argument `fun` in the subroutine. A pointer to function `fun_2` is passed to subroutine `evaluate` the second time that it is called, and function `fun_2` is used in place of the dummy formal argument `fun` in the subroutine.

User-supplied functions may only be passed as calling arguments if they are declared to be external in the calling and the called procedures. When a name in an argument list is declared to be external, this tells the compiler that a separately compiled function is being passed in the argument list instead of a variable. A function may be declared to be external either with an `EXTERNAL` attribute or in an `EXTERNAL` statement. The `EXTERNAL` attribute is included in a type declaration statement, just like any other attribute. An example is

```
REAL, EXTERNAL :: fun_1, fun_2
```

The `EXTERNAL` statement is a specification statement of the form

```
EXTERNAL fun_1, fun_2
```

Both of the above forms state that `fun_1`, `fun_2`, etc. are names of procedures that are defined outside of the current routine. If used, the `EXTERNAL` statement must appear in the declaration section before the first executable statement.

EXAMPLE 6–10 Passing Functions to Procedures in an Argument List: The function `ave_value` in Figure 6–24 determines the average amplitude of a function between user-specified limits `first_value` and `last_value` by sampling the function at n evenly spaced points and then calculating the average amplitude between those points. The function to be evaluated is passed to function `ave_value` as the dummy argument `func`.

FIGURE 6–24
Function `ave_value` calculates the average amplitude of a function between two points `first_value` and `last_value`. The function is passed to function `ave_value` as a calling argument.

```
REAL FUNCTION ave_value ( func, first_value, last_value, n )
!
```

(continued)

(concluded)

```
!  Purpose:
!     To calculate the average value of function "func" over the
!     range [first_value, last_value] by taking n evenly spaced
!     samples over the range and then averaging the results Function
!     "func" is passed to this routine via a dummy argument.
!
!  Record of Revisions:
!     Date          Programmer              Description of change
!     ====          ==========              =====================
!     10/25/95    S. J. Chapman             Original code
!
IMPLICIT NONE

! Declare calling arguments:
REAL, EXTERNAL :: func             ! Function to be evaluated
REAL, INTENT(IN) :: first_value    ! First value in range
REAL, INTENT(IN) :: last_value     ! Last value in range
INTEGER, INTENT(IN) :: n           ! Number of samples to average

! List of local variables:
REAL :: delta              ! Step size between samples
INTEGER :: i               ! Index variable
REAL :: sum                ! Sum of values to average

! Get step size.
delta = ( last_value - first_value ) / REAL(n-1)

! Accumulate sum.
sum = 0.
DO i = 1, n
   sum = sum + func ( REAL(i-1) * delta )
END DO

! Get average.
ave_value = sum / REAL(n)

END FUNCTION
```

A test driver program to test function `ave_value` is shown in Figure 6–25. In that program, function `ave_value` is called with the user-defined function `my_function` as a calling argument. Note that `my_function` is declared as EXTERNAL in the test driver program `test_ave_value`. The function `my_function` is averaged over 101 samples in the interval [0,1], and the results are printed out.

FIGURE 6–25
Test driver program for function `ave_value`, illustrating how to pass a user-defined function as a calling argument.

```
PROGRAM test_ave_value
!
!  Purpose:
!     To test function ave_value by calling it with a user-defined
!     function my_func.
!
!  Record of revisions:
```

(continued)

(concluded)

```
!      Date        Programmer          Description of change
!      ====        ==========          =====================
!    10/25/95    S. J. Chapman         Original code
!
IMPLICIT NONE

! Declare functions:
REAL :: ave_value                    ! Average value of function
REAL, EXTERNAL :: my_function        ! Function to evaluate

! Declare local variables:
REAL :: ave                          ! Average of my_function

! Call function with func=my_function.
ave = ave_value ( my_function, 0., 1., 101 )
WRITE (*,1000) 'my_function', ave
1000 FORMAT (1X,'The average value of ',A,' between 0. and 1. is ', &
             F16.6,'.')

END PROGRAM

REAL FUNCTION my_function( x )
IMPLICIT NONE
REAL, INTENT(IN) :: x
my_function = 3. * x
END FUNCTION
```

When program `test_ave_value` is executed, the results are

```
C>test_ave_value
The average value of my_function between 0. and 1. is         1.500000.
```

Since for this case `my_function` is a straight line between (0,0) and (1,3), it is obvious that the average value was correctly calculated as 1.5.

6.8.2 Passing Subroutines as Arguments

Subroutines may also be passed to procedures as calling arguments. If a subroutine is to be passed as a calling argument, it must be declared in an EXTERNAL statement. The corresponding dummy argument should appear in a CALL statement in the procedure.

■ 6.9
SUMMARY

Chapter 6 introduces Fortran procedures. Procedures are independently compiled program units with their own declaration sections, execution sections, and termination sections. They are extremely important to the design, coding, and maintenance of large programs. Procedures permit the independent testing of subtasks as a project is being built, allow time savings through reusable code, and improve reliability through variable hiding.

There are two types of procedures: subroutines and functions. Subroutines are procedures whose results include one or more values. A subroutine is defined using a SUBROUTINE statement and is executed using a CALL statement. Input data is passed to a subroutine and results are returned from the subroutine through argument lists on the SUBROUTINE statement and CALL statement. When a subroutine is called, pointers are passed to the subroutine pointing to the locations of each argument in the argument list. The subroutine reads from and writes to those locations.

We can control the use of each argument in a subroutine's argument list by specifying an INTENT attribute in the argument's type declaration statement. Each argument can be specified as input only (IN), output only (OUT), or both input and output (INOUT). The Fortran compiler checks to see that each argument is used properly and so can catch many programming errors at compile time.

Data can also be passed to subroutines through modules. A module is a separately compiled program unit that can contain data declarations, procedures, or both. The data and procedures declared in the module are available to any procedure that includes the module with a USE statement. Two procedures can share data by placing the data and a module and having both procedures USE the module.

If procedures are placed in a module and that module is used in a program, then the procedures have an explicit interface. The compiler will automatically check to ensure that number, type, and use of all arguments in each procedure call match the argument list specified for the procedure. This feature can match many common errors.

Fortran functions are procedures whose results are a single number, logical value, character string, or array. The two types of Fortran functions are intrinsic (built in) functions, and user-defined functions. Some intrinsic functions were discussed in Chapters 2 and 5, and all intrinsic functions are included in Appendix B. User-defined functions are declared using the FUNCTION statement and are executed by naming the function as a part of a Fortran expression. Data may be passed to a user-defined function through calling arguments or via modules. A properly designed Fortran function should not change its input arguments. It should *only* change the single output value.

It is possible to pass a function or subroutine to a procedure via a calling argument, provided that the function or subroutine is declared EXTERNAL in the calling program.

6.9.1 Summary of Good Programming Practice

The following guidelines should be adhered to when working with subroutines and functions.

1. Break large program tasks into smaller, more understandable procedures whenever possible.
2. Always specify the INTENT of every dummy argument in every procedure to help catch programming errors.
3. Make sure that the actual argument list in each procedure invocation matches the dummy argument list in *number, type, intent,* and *order.* Placing procedures in a module and then accessing the procedures by USE association creates an explicit interface, which will allow the compiler to automatically check that the argument lists are correct.

4. Test for possible error conditions within a subroutine and set an error flag to be returned to the calling program unit. The calling program unit should test for error conditions after the subroutine call and also take appropriate actions if an error occurs.

5. Always use either explicit-shape dummy arrays or assumed-shape dummy arrays for dummy array arguments. Never use assumed-size dummy arrays in any new program.

6. If a procedure requires that the value of a local variable not change between successive invocations of the procedure, specify the SAVE attribute in the variable's type declaration statement, include the variable in a SAVE statement, or initialize the variable in its type declaration statement.

7. Use automatic arrays to create local temporary working arrays in procedures. Use allocatable arrays to create arrays in main programs or arrays that will be created and destroyed in different procedures. Allocatable arrays should always be explicitly deallocated after they are no longer needed to avoid "memory leaks."

8. Modules may be used to pass large amounts of data between procedures within a program. The data values may are declared only once in the module, and all procedures needing access to that data must use that module. Be sure to include a SAVE statement in the module to guarantee that the data is preserved between accesses by different procedures.

9. Collect the procedures that you use in a program and place them in a module. When the procedures are in a module, the Fortran compiler will automatically verify the calling argument list each time that they are used.

10. Be sure to declare the type of any function both in the function itself and in any program units that invoke the function.

11. A well-designed Fortran function should produce a single output value from one or more input values. It should never modify its own input arguments. To ensure that a function does not accidentally modify its input arguments, always declare the arguments with the INTENT(IN) attribute.

6.9.2 Summary of Fortran Statements and Structures

CALL Statement

> CALL *subname(arg1, arg2, ...)*

Example:

> CALL sort (number, data1)

Description:
   This statement transfers execution from the current program unit to the subroutine, passing pointers to the calling arguments. The subroutine executes until either a RETURN or an END SUBROUTINE statement is encountered, and then execution will continue in the calling program unit at the next executable statement following the CALL statement.

CONTAINS Statement

```
                    CONTAINS
```

Example:

```
        MODULE test
           . . .
              CONTAINS
              SUBROUTINE sub1(x, y)
              ...
           END SUBROUTINE sub1
           END MODULE
```

Description:

The CONTAINS statement specifies that the following statements are separate procedure(s) within a module. The CONTAINS statement and the module procedures following it must appear after any type and data definitions within the module.

6

ELEMENTAL Prefix

```
          ELEMENTAL FUNCTION name ( arg1, ...)
          ELEMENTAL SUBROUTINE name( arg1, ...)
```

Example:

```
          ELEMENTAL FUNCTION my_fun (a, b, c)
```

Description:

This prefix declares that a Fortran 95 procedure is ELEMENTAL, which means that it is defined with scalar inputs and outputs but can be used with array inputs and outputs. When it is used with arrays, the operation defined by the elemental procedure is applied on an element-by-element basis to every element in the input array.

END Statements

```
          END FUNCTION [name]
          END MODULE [name]
          END SUBROUTINE [name]
```

Example:

```
          END FUNCTION my_function
          END MODULE my_mod
              END SUBROUTINE my_sub
```

Description:

These statements end user-defined Fortran functions, modules, and subroutines, respectively. The name of the function, module, or subroutine may optionally be included but is not required.

EXTERNAL Attribute

```
type, EXTERNAL :: name1, name2, ...
```

Example:

```
REAL, EXTERNAL :: my_function
```

Description:

This attribute declares that a particular name is an externally defined function. It is equivalent to naming the function in an EXTERNAL statement.

EXTERNAL Statement

```
EXTERNAL name1, name2, ...
```

Example:

```
EXTERNAL my_function
```

Description:

This statement declares that a particular name is an externally defined procedure. Either it or the EXTERNAL attribute must be used in the calling program unit and in the called procedure if the procedure specified in the EXTERNAL statement is to be passed as an actual argument.

FUNCTION Statement

```
[type] FUNCTION name( arg1, arg2, ... )
```

Example:

```
INTEGER FUNCTION max_value ( num, iarray )
FUNCTION gamma (x)
```

Description:

This statement declares a user-defined Fortran function. The type of the function may be declared in the FUNCTION statement, or it may be declared in a separate type declaration statement. The function is executed by naming it in an expression in the calling program. The dummy arguments are placeholders for the calling arguments passed when the function is executed. If a function has no arguments, then it must be declared with an empty pair of parentheses [name()].

INTENT Attribute

```
type, INTENT(intent_type) :: name1, name2, ...
```

Example:

```
REAL, INTENT(IN) :: value
INTEGER, INTENT(OUT) :: count
```

(continued)

(concluded)

Description:

This attribute declares the intended use of a particular dummy procedure argument. Possible values of `intent_type` are `IN`, `OUT`, and `INOUT`. The `INTENT` attribute allows the Fortran compiler to know the intended use of the argument and to check that it is used in the way intended. This attribute may only appear on dummy arguments in procedures.

INTENT Statements

```
INTENT(intent_type) :: name1, name2,
...
```

Example:

```
INTENT(IN) :: a, b
INTENT(OUT) :: result
```

Description:

This statement declares the intended use of a particular dummy procedure argument. Possible values of `intent_type` are `IN`, `OUT`, and `INOUT`. The `INTENT` statement allows the Fortran compiler to know the intended use of the argument and to check that it is used in the way intended. Only dummy arguments may appear in `INTENT` statements. *Do not use this statement; use the* `INTENT` *attribute instead.*

MODULE Statement

```
MODULE name
```

Example:

```
MODULE my_data_and_subs
```

Description:

This statement declares a module. The module may contain data, procedures, or both. The data and procedures are made available for use in a program unit by declaring the module name in a `USE` statement (`USE` association).

PURE Prefix

```
PURE FUNCTION name( arg1, ...)
PURE SUBROUTINE name( arg1, ...)
```

Example:

```
PURE FUNCTION my_fun (a, b, c)
```

Description:

This prefix declares that a Fortran 95 procedure is `PURE`, which means that it has no side effects.

RETURN Statement

```
                        RETURN
```

Example:

```
                        RETURN
```

Description:

    When this statement is executed in a procedure, control returns to the program unit that invoked the procedure. This statement is optional at the end of a subroutine or function, since execution will automatically return to the calling routine whenever an END SUBROUTINE or END FUNCTION statement is reached.

SAVE Attribute

```
             type, SAVE :: name1, name2, ...
```

Example:

```
             REAL, SAVE :: sum
```

Description:

    This attribute declares that the value of a local variable in a procedure must remain unchanged between successive invocations of the procedure. It is equivalent to the naming the variable in a SAVE statement.

SAVE Statement

```
                  SAVE [var1, var2, ...]
```

Example:

```
             SAVE count, index
             SAVE
```

Description:

    This statement declares that the value of a local variable in a procedure must remain unchanged between successive invocations of the procedure. If a list of variables is included, only those variables will be saved. If no list is included, every local variable in the procedure or module will be saved.

SUBROUTINE Statement

```
             SUBROUTINE name( arg1, arg2, ... )
```

Example:

```
             SUBROUTINE sort ( num, data1 )
```

Description:

    This statement declares a Fortran subroutine. The subroutine is executed with a CALL statement. The dummy arguments are placeholders for the calling arguments passed when the subroutine is executed.

USE Statement

$$USE \ module1, \ module2, \ ...$$

Example:

$$USE \ my\_data$$

Description:
This statement makes the contents of one or more modules available for use in a program unit. USE statements must be the first noncomment statements within the program unit after the PROGRAM, SUBROUTINE, or FUNCTION statement.

6

6.10

EXERCISES

6-1 What is the difference between a subroutine and a function?

6-2 When a subroutine is called, how is data passed from the calling program to the subroutine, and how are the results of the subroutine returned to the calling program?

6-3 What are the advantages and disadvantages of the pass-by-reference scheme used in Fortran?

6-4 What are the advantages and disadvantages of using explicit-shape dummy arrays in procedures? What are the advantages and disadvantages of using assumed-shape dummy arrays? Why should assumed-size dummy arrays never be used?

6-5 Suppose that a 15-element array a is passed to a subroutine as a calling argument. What will happen if the subroutine attempts to write to element a(16)?

6-6 Suppose that a real value is passed to a subroutine in an argument that is declared to be an integer in the subroutine. Is there any way for the subroutine to tell that the argument type is mismatched? What happens on your computer when the following code is executed?

```
PROGRAM main
IMPLICIT NONE
REAL :: x
x = -5.
CALL sub1 ( x )
END PROGRAM
SUBROUTINE sub1 ( i )
IMPLICIT NONE
INTEGER, INTENT(IN) :: i
WRITE (*,*) ' I = ', i
END SUBROUTINE
```

6-7 How could the program in exercise 6-6 be modified to ensure that the Fortran compiler catches the argument mismatch between the actual argument in the main program and the dummy argument in subroutine sub1?

6–8 What is the purpose of the INTENT attribute? Where can it be used? Why should it be used?

6–9 Determine whether the following subroutine calls are correct. If they are in error, specify what is wrong with them.

a.
```
PROGRAM sum_sqrt
IMPLICIT NONE
INTEGER, PARAMETER :: length = 20
INTEGER :: result
REAL :: test(length) = &
     (/  1., 2., 3., 4., 5., 6., 7., 8., 9., 10., &
        11., 12., 13., 14., 15., 16., 17., 18., 19., 20. /)
...
CALL test_sub ( length, test, result )
...
END PROGRAM sum_sqrt
SUBROUTINE test_sub ( length, array, res )
IMPLICIT NONE
INTEGER, INTENT(IN) :: length
REAL, INTENT(OUT) :: res
INTEGER, INTENT(IN) :: array(length)
INTEGER, INTENT(INOUT) :: i
DO i = 1, length
   res = res + SQRT(array(i))
END DO
END SUBROUTINE test_sub
```

b.
```
PROGRAM test
IMPLICIT NONE
CHARACTER(len=8) :: str = '1AbHz05Z'
CHARACTER :: largest
CALL max_char (str, largest)
WRITE (*,100) str, largest
100 FORMAT (' The largest character in ', A, ' is ', A)
END PROGRAM
SUBROUTINE max_char(string, big)
IMPLICIT NONE
CHARACTER(len=10), INTENT(IN) :: string
CHARACTER, INTENT(OUT) :: big
INTEGER :: i
big = string(1:1)
DO i = 2, 10
   IF ( string(i:i) > big ) THEN
      big = string(i:i)
   END IF
END DO
END SUBROUTINE
```

6–10 What is the purpose of the SAVE statement and attribute? When should they be used?

6–11 Is the following program correct or incorrect? If it is incorrect, what is wrong with it? If it is correct, what values will be printed out?

```
MODULE my_constants
IMPLICIT NONE
REAL, PARAMETER :: pi = 3.141593   ! Pi
REAL, PARAMETER :: g = 9.81        ! Accel. due to gravity
END MODULE my_constants
PROGRAM main
IMPLICIT NONE
```

```
      USE my_constants
      WRITE (*,*) 'SIN(2*pi) = ' SIN(2.*pi)
      g = 17.
      END PROGRAM
```

6–12 Modify the selection sort routine developed in this chapter so that it sorts real values in descending order.

6–13 Write a subroutine `ucase` that accepts a character string, and converts any lowercase letter in the string to uppercase without affecting any nonalphabetic characters in the string. Make sure that the subroutine would work on computers with either ASCII or EBCDIC character sets. (*Hint:* Look up functions `ACHAR` and `IACHAR`.)

6–14 Write a driver program to test the statistical subroutines developed in Example 6–3. Be sure to test the routines with a variety of input data sets. Did you discover any problems with the subroutines?

6–15 Write a subroutine that uses subroutine `random0` to generate a random number in the range $[-1.0, 1.0)$.

6–16 **Dice Simulation** It is often useful to be able to simulate the throw of a fair die. Write a Fortran function `dice()` that simulates the throw of a fair die by returning some random integer between 1 and 6 every time that it is called. (*Hint:* Call `random0` to generate a random number. Divide the possible values out of `random0` into six equal intervals and return the number of the interval that a given random number falls into.)

6–17 **Road Traffic Density** Subroutine `random0` produces a number with a *uniform probability distribution* in the range [0.0, 1.0). This subroutine is suitable for simulating random events if each outcome has an equal probability of occurring. However, in many events, the probability of occurrence is *not* equal for every event, and a uniform probability distribution is not suitable for simulating such events.

For example, when traffic engineers studied the number of cars passing a given location in a time interval of length t, they discovered that the probability of k cars passing during the interval is given by the equation

$$P(k, t) = e^{-\lambda t} \frac{(\lambda t)^k}{k!} \text{ for } t \geq 0, \lambda > 0, \text{ and } k = 0, 1, 2, \ldots \qquad (6\text{--}12)$$

This probability distribution is known as the *Poisson distribution,* it occurs in many applications in science and engineering. For example, the number of calls k to a telephone switchboard in time interval t, the number of bacteria k in a specified volume t of liquid, and the number of failures k of a complicated system in time interval t all have Poisson distributions.

Write a function to evaluate the Poisson distribution for any k, t, and λ. Test your function by calculating the probability of 0, 1, 2, $\ldots$, 5 cars passing a particular point on a highway in 1 minute, given that λ is 1.6 per minute for that highway.

6–18 What are two purposes of a module? What are the special advantages of placing procedures within modules?

6–19 Write three Fortran functions to calculate the hyperbolic sine, cosine, and tangent functions:

$$\sinh(x) = \frac{e^x - e^{-x}}{2} \qquad \cosh(x) = \frac{e^x + e^{-x}}{2} \qquad \tanh(x) = \frac{e^x - e^{-x}}{e^x + e^{-x}}$$

Use your functions to calculate the hyperbolic sines, cosines, and tangents of the following values: -2, -1.5, -1.0, -0.5, -0.25, 0.0, 0.25, 0.5, 1.0, 1.5, and 2.0. Sketch the shapes of the hyperbolic sine, cosine, and tangent functions.

6–20 Cross Product Write a function to calculate the cross product of two vectors $\mathbf{V}_1$ and $\mathbf{V}_2$:

$$\mathbf{V}_1 \times \mathbf{V}_2 = (V_{y1}V_{z2} - V_{y2}V_{z1})\,\mathbf{i} + (V_{z1}V_{x2} - V_{z2}V_{x1})\,\mathbf{j} + (V_{x1}V_{y2} - V_{x2}V_{y1})\,\mathbf{k}$$

where $\mathbf{V}_1 = V_{x1}\mathbf{i} + V_{y1}\mathbf{j} + V_{z1}\mathbf{k}$ and $\mathbf{V}_2 = V_{x2}\mathbf{i} + V_{y2}\mathbf{j} + V_{z2}\mathbf{k}$. Note that this function will return a real array as its result. Use the function to calculate the cross product of the two vectors $\mathbf{V}_1 = [-2, 4, 0.5]$ and $\mathbf{V}_2 = [0.5, 3, 2]$.

6–21 Matrix Multiplication Write a subroutine to calculate the product of two matrices if they are of compatible sizes and if the output array is large enough to hold the result. If the matrices are not of compatible sizes or if the output array is too small, set an error flag and return to the calling program. The dimensions of all three arrays a, b, and c should be passed to the subroutines from the calling program so that explicit-shape dummy arrays can be used and size checking can be done. (*Note:* The definition of matrix multiplication appears in exercise 5–27.) Check your subroutine by multiplying the following two pairs of arrays both with the subroutine and with the intrinsic subroutine MATMUL.

a.
$$a = \begin{bmatrix} 2 & -1 & 2 \\ -1 & -3 & 4 \\ 2 & 4 & 2 \end{bmatrix} \qquad b = \begin{bmatrix} 1 & 2 & 3 \\ 2 & 1 & 2 \\ 3 & 2 & 1 \end{bmatrix}$$

b.
$$a = \begin{bmatrix} 1 & -1 & -2 \\ 2 & 2 & 0 \\ 3 & 3 & 3 \\ 5 & 4 & 4 \end{bmatrix} \qquad b = \begin{bmatrix} -2 \\ 5 \\ 2 \end{bmatrix}$$

6–22 Write a new version of the matrix multiplication subroutine from exercise 6–21 that uses an explicit interface and assumed-shape arrays. Before multiplying the matrices, this version should check to ensure that the input arrays are compatible and that the output array is large enough to hold the product of the two matrices. It can check for compatibility using the inquiry intrinsic functions found in Table 5–1. If these conditions are not satisfied, the subroutine should set an error flag and return.

6–23 Sort with Carry It is often useful to sort an array arr1 into ascending order, while simultaneously carrying along a second array arr2. In such a sort, each time an element of array arr1 is exchanged with another element of arr1, the corresponding elements of array arr2 are also swapped. When the sort is over, the elements of array arr1 are in ascending order, while the elements of array arr2 that were associated with particular elements of array arr1 are still associated with them. For example, suppose we have the following two arrays:

```
Element    arr1    arr2
  1.        6.      1.
  2.        1.      0.
  3.        2.     10.
```

After sorting array arr1 while carrying along array arr2, the contents of the two arrays will be

Element	arr1	arr2
1.	1.	0.
2.	2.	10.
3.	6.	2.

Write a subroutine to sort one real array into ascending order while carrying along a second one. Test the subroutine with the following two 9-element arrays:

```
REAL, DIMENSION(9) :: &
  a = (/  1., 11., -6., 17.,-23.,  0.,  5.,  1., -1. /)
REAL, DIMENSION(9) :: &
  b = (/ 31.,101., 36.,-17.,  0., 10., -8., -1., -1. /)
```

6–24 Minima and Maxima of a Function Write a subroutine that attempts to locate the maximum and minimum values of an arbitrary function $f(x)$ over a certain range. The function being evaluated should be passed to the subroutine as a calling argument. The subroutine should have the following input arguments:

first_value   -- The first value of x to search.

last_value   -- The last value of x to search.

num_steps   -- The number of steps to include in the search.

func   -- The name of the function to search.

The subroutine should have the following output arguments:

xmin   -- The value of x at which the minimum was found.

min_value   -- The minimum value of $f(x)$ found.

xmax   -- The value of x at which the maximum was found.

max_value   -- The maximum value $f(x)$ found.

6–25 Write a test driver program for the subroutine generated in the previous problem. The test driver program should pass to the subroutine the user-defined function $f(x) = x^3 - 5x^2 + 5x + 2$ and search for the minimum and maximum in 200 steps over the range $-1 \le x \le 3$. It should print out the resulting minimum and maximum values.

6–26 Derivative of a Function The *derivative* of a continuous function $f(x)$ is defined by the equation

$$\frac{d}{dx} f(x) = \lim_{\Delta x \to 0} \frac{f(x + \Delta x) - f(x)}{\Delta x} \tag{6–13}$$

In a sampled function, this definition becomes

$$f'(x_i) = \frac{f(x_{i+1}) - f(x_i)}{\Delta x} \tag{6–14}$$

where $\Delta x = x_{i+1} - x_i$. Assume that a vector vect contains nsamp samples of a function taken at a spacing of dx per sample. Write a subroutine that will calculate the derivative of this vector from Equation (6–14). The subroutine should check to make sure that dx is greater than zero to prevent divide-by-zero errors in the subroutine.

To check your subroutine, you should generate a data set whose derivative is known and compare the result of the subroutine with the known correct answer. A good choice for a test function is sin x. From elementary calculus we know that $\frac{d}{dx}(\sin x) = \cos x$. Generate an input vector containing 100 values of the function sin x, starting at $x = 0$ and using a step size Δx of 0.05. Take the derivative of the vector with your subroutine and then compare the resulting answers to the known correct answer. How close did your subroutine come to calculating the correct value for the derivative?

6–27 Derivative in the Presence of Noise We will now explore the effects of input noise on the quality of a numerical derivative. First generate an input vector containing 100 val-

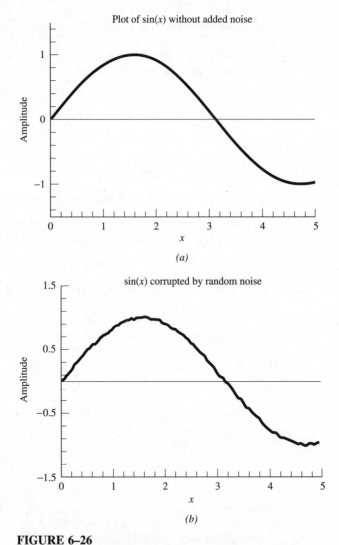

FIGURE 6–26
(a) A plot of sin x as a function of x with no noise added to the data. (b) A plot of sin x as a function of x with a 2 percent peak amplitude uniform random noise added to the data.

ues of the function sin x, starting at $x = 0$ and using a step size Δx of 0.05, just as you did in the previous problem. Next use subroutine random0 to generate a small amount of random noise with a maximum amplitude of ± 0.02 and add that random noise to the samples in your input vector. Note that the peak amplitude of the noise is only 2 percent of the peak amplitude of your signal, since the maximum value is sin x is 1. Now take the derivative of the function using the derivative subroutine that you developed in the last problem. How close to the theoretical value of the derivative did you come?

6–28 Linear Least-Squares Fit Develop a subroutine that will calculate slope m and intercept b of the least-squares line that best fits an input data set. The input data points (x, y) will be passed to the subroutine in two input arrays, X and Y. The equations describing the slope and intercept of the least-squares line are

$$y = mx + b \tag{4-5}$$

$$m = \frac{(\sum xy) - (\sum x)\bar{y}}{(\sum x^2) - (\sum x)\bar{x}} \tag{4-6}$$

and

$$b = \bar{y} - m\bar{x} \tag{4-7}$$

where

$\sum x$ is the sum of the x values.

$\sum x^2$ is the sum of the squares of the x values.

$\sum xy$ is the sum of the products of the corresponding x and y values.

$\bar{x}$ is the mean (average) of the x values.

$\bar{y}$ is the mean (average) of the y values.

Test your routine using a test driver program and the following 20-point input data set:

Sample data to test least-squares-fit routine

No.	x	y	No.	x	y
1	−4.91	−8.18	11	−0.94	0.21
2	−3.84	−7.49	12	0.59	1.73
3	−2.41	−7.11	13	0.69	3.96
4	−2.62	−6.15	14	3.04	4.26
5	−3.78	−5.62	15	1.01	5.75
6	−0.52	−3.30	16	3.60	6.67
7	−1.83	−2.05	17	4.53	7.70
8	−2.01	−2.83	18	5.13	7.31
9	0.28	−1.16	19	4.43	9.05
10	1.08	0.52	20	4.12	10.95

6–29 Correlation Coefficient of Least-Squares Fit Develop a subroutine that will calculate both the slope m and intercept b of the least-squares line that best fits an input data set and also the correlation coefficient of the fit. The input data points (x,y) will be passed to the subroutine in two input arrays, x and y. The equations describing the slope and intercept of the least-squares line are given in the previous problem, and the equation for the correlation coefficient is

$$r = \frac{n(\Sigma xy) - (\Sigma x)(\Sigma y)}{\sqrt{[(n\Sigma x^2) - (\Sigma x)^2][(n\Sigma y^2) - (\Sigma y)^2]}} \qquad (4\text{--}10)$$

where

$\sum x$ is the sum of the x values.

$\sum y$ is the sum of the y values.

$\sum x^2$ is the sum of the squares of the x values.

$\sum y^2$ is the sum of the squares of the y values.

$\sum xy$ is the sum of the products of the corresponding x and y values.

n is the number of points included in the fit.

Test your routine using a test driver program and the 20−point input data set given in the previous problem.

6–30 The Birthday Problem In a group of n people, what is the probability that two or more of them have the same birthday? It is possible to determine the answer to this question by simulation. Write a function that calculates the probability that two or more of n people will have the same birthday, where n is a calling argument. (Hint: The function should create an array of size n and generate n birthdays in the range 1 to 365 randomly. It should then check to see if any of the n birthdays are identical. The functions should perform this experiment at least 5000 times and calculate the fraction of those times in which two or more people had the same birthday.) Write a main program that calculates and prints out the probability that 2 or more of n people will have the same birthday for $n = 2, 3, \ldots, 40$.

6–31 Elapsed Time Measurement When testing the operation of procedures, it is very useful to have an set of *elapsed time subroutines*. By starting a timer before a procedure executes and then checking the time after the execution is completed, we can see how fast or slow the procedure is. Programmers can use this technique to identify the time-consuming portions of their programs, and rewrite them if necessary to make them faster.

Write a pair of subroutines named set_timer and elapsed_time to calculate the elapsed time in seconds between the last time that subroutine set_timer was called and the time that subroutine elapsed_time is being called. When subroutine set_timer is called, it should get the current time and store it into a variable in a module. When subroutine elapsed_time is called, it should get the current time and then calculate the difference between the current time and the stored time in the module. The elapsed time in seconds between the two calls should be returned to the calling program unit in an argument of subroutine elapsed_time. (*Note*: The intrinsic subroutine to read the current time is called DATE_AND_TIME; see Appendix B.)

6–32 Use subroutine random0 to generate a set of three arrays of random numbers. The three arrays should be 100, 1000, and 10,000 elements long. Then use your elapsed time subroutines to determine the time that it takes subroutine sort to sort each array. How does the elapsed time to sort increase as a function of the number of elements being sorted?

(*Hint*: On a fast computer, you will need to sort each array many times and calculate the average sorting time in order to overcome the quantization error of the system clock.)

6–33 Evaluating Infinite Series The value of the exponential function e^x can be calculated by evaluating the following infinite series:

$$e^x = \sum_{n=0}^{\infty} \frac{x^n}{n!}$$

Write a Fortran function that calculates e^x using the first 12 terms of the infinite series. Compare the result of your function with the result of the intrinsic function EXP(x) for $x = -10, -5., -1., 0., 1., 5., 10.,$ and 15.

6–34 Use subroutine random0 to generate an array containing 10,000 random numbers between 0.0 and 1.0. Then use the statistics subroutines developed in this chapter to calculate the average and standard deviation of values in the array. The theoretical average of a uniform random distribution in the range [0,1) is 0.5, and the theoretical standard deviation of the uniform random distribution is $\frac{1}{\sqrt{12}}$. How close does the random array generated by random0 come to behaving like the theoretical distribution?

6–35 Write a test driver program to test subroutine simul2 in Figure 6–12. Use the two data sets in Example 6–4 to test the subroutine.

6–36 Gaussian (Normal) Distribution Subroutine random0 returns a uniformly distributed random variable in the range [0,1], which means that there is an equal probability of any given number in the range occurring on a given call to the subroutine. Another type of random distribution is the Gaussian distribution, in which the random value takes on the classic bell-shaped curve shown in Figure 6–27. A Gaussian distribution with an average of 0.0 and a standard deviation of 1.0 is called a standardized normal distribution, and the probability of any given value occurring in the *standardized normal distribution*

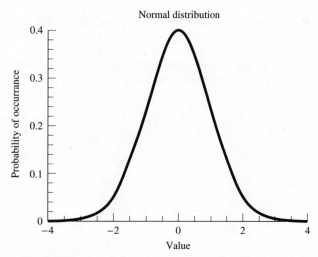

FIGURE 6–27
A normal probability distribution.

is given by the equation

$$p(x) = \frac{1}{\sqrt{2\pi}} e^{-x^2/2} \tag{6-15}$$

It is possible to generate a random variable with a standardized normal distribution starting from a random variable with a uniform distribution in the range $[-1,1)$ as follows:

a. Select two uniform random variables x_1 and x_2 from the range $[-1,1)$ such that $x_1^2 + x_2^2 < 1$. To do so, generate two uniform random variables in the range $[-1,1)$ and see if the sum of their squares happens to be less than 1. If so, use them. If not, try again.

b. Then each of the values y_1 and y_2 in the equations below will be a normally distributed random variable.

$$y_1 = \sqrt{\frac{-2 \ln r}{r}} \, x_1 \tag{6-16}$$

$$y_2 = \sqrt{\frac{-2 \ln r}{r}} \, x_2 \tag{6-17}$$

where

$$r = \sqrt{x_1^2 + x_2^2} \tag{6-18}$$

and ln is the natural logarithm.

Write a subroutine that returns a normally distributed random value each time that it is called. Test your subroutine by getting 1000 random values and calculating the standard deviation. How close to 1.0 was the result?

6–37 Gravitational Force The gravitational force F between two bodies of masses m_1 and m_2 is given by the equation

$$F = \frac{Gm_1m_2}{r^2} \tag{6-19}$$

where G is the gravitation constant (6.672×10^{-11} N m^2/kg^2), m_1 and m_2 are the masses of the bodies in kilograms, and r is the distance between the two bodies. Write a function to calculate the gravitational force between two bodies given their masses and the distance between them. Test your function by determining the force on an 800 kg satellite in orbit 38,000 km above Earth. (The mass of Earth is 5.98×10^{24} kg.)

More about Character Variables

A *character variable* is a variable that contains character information. In this context, a "character" is any symbol found in a **character set.** Two basic character sets are in common use in the United States. ASCII (American Standard Code for Information Interchange), and EBCDIC (Extended Binary Coded Decimal Interchange Code). The EBCDIC character set is used in IBM mainframes and those computers compatible with them, while the ASCII character set is used on essentially all the other computers in the world. Both character sets include the digits 0-9, the uppercase letters A-Z, the lowercase letters a-z, and other specialized symbols such as +, -, *, /, and !. Most symbols appear in both character sets, but they are represented by different patterns of bits in each set. The complete ASCII and EBCDIC character sets are given in Appendix A.

In many countries outside the United States, an international version of the ASCII character set is used. This set is known as the ISO 646 standard. It is the same as ASCII except that 10 specific characters may be replaced with the extra symbols needed in a particular country, such as £, å, ñ, and ø. This character set can create problems when a program is moved from one country to another, because some symbols will change and printed information might become corrupted.

An extended ASCII character set has become popular with the rise of the PC. The first 128 symbols of this character set are identical to ASCII. The next 128 symbols include the special letters and diacritical marks needed to write most European languages. Programs that use the extended ASCII character set can be moved from country to country more easily.

Fortran generally does not care about the difference between character sets. It stores each symbol in 1 byte of computer memory, whether that symbol is from an ASCII or an EBCDIC character set. All reads, writes, and assignments are the same regardless of character set. However, some character comparisons and manipulations are character-set dependent. If not handled properly, these dependencies could cause trouble when we try to move programs from one processor to another. I will point out these dependencies and how to avoid them as they arise.

Many countries use character sets not based on the Roman alphabet. For example, Russian and many Eastern European languages are written in the Cyrillic character set (ФИСВУАПРШ, etc.). Hebrew and Arabic also have their own character sets. Finally, many Oriental languages are written with ideograms, with each language using several thousand characters. Fortran 90/95 includes special provisions for supporting alternative character sets for these languages (see Chapter 8).

7.1

CHARACTER COMPARISON OPERATIONS

Character strings may be compared to each other using either relational operators or special character comparison functions called *lexical functions*. Lexical functions have an advantage over the relational operators when program portability is considered.

7.1.1 The Relational Operators with Character Data

Character strings can be compared in logical expressions using the **relational** operators ==, /-, <, <=, >, and >=. The result of the comparison is a logical value that is either true or false. For instance, the expression '123' == '123' is true, while the expression '123' == '1234' is false.

How are two characters compared to determine if one is greater than the other? The comparison is based on the **collating sequence** of the characters. The *collating sequence* of the characters is the order in which they occur within a specific character set. For example, the character 'A' is character number 65 in the ASCII character set, while the character 'B' is character number 66 in the set (see Appendix A). Therefore, the logical expression 'A' < 'B' is true in the ASCII character set. On the other hand, the character 'a' is character 97 in the ASCII set, so 'a' is greater than 'A'.

Comparisons based on collating sequence are inherently dangerous, since different character sets have different collating sequences. For example, in the EBCDIC character set, 'a' is less than 'A', just the opposite of the ASCII character set. Code that depends on collating sequence is likely to fail when moved between processors!

We can make some comparisons safely regardless of character set. The letters 'A' to 'Z' are always in alphabetical order, the numbers '0' to '9' are always in numerical sequence, and the letters and numbers are not intermingled in the collating sequence. Beyond that, however, all bets are off. The relationships among the special symbols and the relationship between the uppercase and lowercase letters may differ for different character sets. We must be very careful when comparing strings with relational operators!

How are two strings compared to determine if one is greater than the other? The comparison begins with the first character in each string. If they are the same, then the second two characters are compared. This process continues until the first difference is found between the strings. For example, 'AAAAAB' > 'AAAAAA'.

What happens if the strings are different lengths? The comparison begins with the first letter in each string and progresses through each letter until a difference is found. If the two strings are the same all the way to the end of one of them, then the other string is considered the larger of the two. Therefore, `'AB' > 'AAAA'` and `'AAAAA' > 'AAAA'`.

EXAMPLE 7–1 *Alphabetizing Words:* A common task is to alphabetize lists of character strings (names, places, etc.). Write a subroutine that will accept a character array and alphabetize the data in the array.

SOLUTION Since relational operators work for character strings the same way that they work for real values, we can easily modify the sorting subroutine that we developed in Chapter 6 to alphabetize an array of character variables. All we have to do is to substitute character array declarations for the real declarations in the sorting routines. The rewritten program is shown in Figure 7–1.

FIGURE 7–1
A program to alphabetize character strings using a version of the selection sort algorithm adapted for character strings.

```
PROGRAM sort4
!
!  Purpose:
!    To read in a character input data set, sort it into ascending
!    order using the selection sort algorithm, and write the
!    sorted data to the standard output device. This program calls
!    subroutine "sortc" to do the actual sorting.
!
!  Record of revisions:
!      Date        Programmer          Description of change
!      ====        ==========          =====================
!    11/15/95    S. J. Chapman         Original code
!
IMPLICIT NONE

! List of parameters:
INTEGER, PARAMETER :: max_size = 10      ! Max number to sort

! List of variables:
CHARACTER(len=20), DIMENSION(max_size) :: a
                                  ! Data array to sort
LOGICAL :: exceed = .FALSE.       ! Logical indicating that array
                                  !   limits are exceeded
CHARACTER(len=20) :: filename     ! Input data file name
INTEGER :: i                      ! Loop index
INTEGER :: nvals=0                ! Number of data values to sort
INTEGER :: status                 ! I/O status: 0 for success
CHARACTER(len=20) :: temp         ! Temporary variable for reading

! Get the name of the file containing the input data.
WRITE (*,*) 'Enter the file name with the data to be sorted: '
READ (*,'(A20)') filename

! Open input data file. Status is OLD because the input data must
! already exist.
OPEN ( UNIT=9, FILE=filename, STATUS='OLD', ACTION='READ', &
       IOSTAT=status )
```

(continued)

(continued)

```
! Was the OPEN successful?
fileopen: IF ( status == 0 ) THEN          ! Open successful

   ! The file was opened successfully, so read the data to sort
   ! from it, sort the data, and write out the results.
   ! First read in data.
   DO
      READ (9, *, IOSTAT=status) temp       ! Get value
      IF ( status /= 0 ) EXIT               ! Exit on end of data
      nvals = nvals + 1                     ! Bump count
      size: IF ( nvals <= max_size ) THEN   ! Too many values?
         a(nvals) = temp                    ! No: Save value in array
      ELSE
         exceed = .TRUE.                    ! Yes: Array overflow
      END IF size
   END DO

   ! Was the array size exceeded?  If so, tell user and quit.
   toobig: IF ( exceed ) THEN
      WRITE (*,1010) nvals, max_size
      1010 FORMAT (' Maximum array size exceeded: ', I6, ' > ', I6 )
   ELSE

      ! Limit not exceeded: sort the data.
      CALL sortc (a, nvals)

      ! Now write out the sorted data.
      WRITE (*,*) 'The sorted output data values are: '
      WRITE (*,'(4X,A)') ( a(i), i = 1, nvals )

   END IF toobig
ELSE fileopen

   ! Else file open failed.  Tell user.
   WRITE (*,1020) status
   1020 FORMAT (1X,'File open failed--status = ', I6)

END IF fileopen

END PROGRAM

SUBROUTINE sortc (array, n )
!
!  Purpose:
!    To sort a character array into ascending order using a
!    selection sort.
!
!  Record of revisions:
!      Date        Programmer          Description of change
!      ====        ==========          =====================
!    11/15/95    S. J. Chapman         Original code
!
IMPLICIT NONE

! Declare calling parameters:
INTEGER, INTENT(IN) :: n                     ! Number of values
CHARACTER(len=20), DIMENSION(n), INTENT(INOUT) :: array
                                             ! Array to be sorted
! Declare local variables:
```

(concluded)

```
INTEGER :: i              ! Loop index
INTEGER :: iptr           ! Pointer to smallest value
INTEGER :: j              ! Loop index
CHARACTER(len=20) :: temp ! Temp variable for swaps

! Sort the array
outer: DO i = 1, n-1

   ! Find the minimum value in array(i) through array(n)
   iptr = i
   inner: DO j = i+1, n
      minval: IF ( array(j) < array(iptr) ) THEN
         iptr = j
      END IF minval
   END DO inner

   ! iptr now prints to the minimum value, so swap array(iptr)
   ! with array(i) if i /= iptr.
   swap: IF ( i /= iptr ) THEN
      temp       = array(i)
      array(i)   = array(iptr)
      array(iptr) = temp
   END IF swap

END DO outer

END SUBROUTINE sortc
```

To test this program, we will place the following character values in file INPUTC:

```
Fortran
fortran
ABCD
ABC
XYZZY
9.0
A9IDL
```

If we compile and execute the program on a computer with an ASCII collating sequence, the results of the test run will be

```
C>sort4
Enter the file name containing the data to be sorted:
inputc
The sorted output data values are:
  9.0
  A9IDL
  ABC
  ABCD
  Fortran
  XYZZY
  fortran
```

Note that the number 9 was placed before any of the letters and that the lowercase letters were placed after the uppercase letters. These locations are in accordance with the ASCII table in Appendix A.

If this program were executed on a computer with the EBCDIC character set and collating sequence, the answer would have been different than the one shown here. In exercise 7–3, you will be asked to work out the expected output of this program if it were executed on an EBCDIC computer.

7.1.2 The Lexical Functions LLT, LLE, LGT, and LGE

The result of the sort subroutine in the previous example depended on the character set used by the processor on which it was executed. This dependence is bad, since it makes our Fortran program less portable between processors. We need some way to ensure that programs produce the *same answer* regardless of the computer on which they are compiled and executed.

Fortunately, the Fortran language includes a set of four logical intrinsic functions for just this purpose: LLT (lexically less than), LLE (lexically less than or equal to), LGT (lexically greater than), and LGE (lexically greater than or equal to). These functions are the exact equivalent of the relational operators $<$, $<=$, $>$, and $>=$, except that the lexical functions always compare characters according to the ASCII collating sequence, regardless of the computer they are running on. If these **lexical functions** are used instead of the relational operators to compare character strings, the results will be the same on every computer!

In the following example, character variables string1 and string2 are being compared using the relational operator < and the logical function LLT. The value of result1 will vary from processor to processor, but the value of result2 will always be true on any processor.

```
LOGICAL :: result1, result2
CHARACTER(len=6) :: string1, string2
string1 = 'A1'
string2 = 'a1'
result1 = string1 < string2
result2 = LLT( string1, string2 )
```

> ***Good Programming Practice***
> If there is any chance that your program will have to run on computers with both ASCII and EBCDIC character sets, use the logical functions LLT, LLE, LGT, and LGE to test for inequality between two character strings. Do not use the relational operators <, <=, >, and >= with character strings, since their results may vary from computer to computer.

7.2
INTRINSIC CHARACTER FUNCTIONS

The Fortran language contains several additional intrinsic functions that are important for manipulating character data. Seven of these functions are CHAR, ICHAR,

`ACHAR`, `IACHAR`, `LEN`, `LEN_TRIM`, and `INDEX`. Some common character intrinsic functions are summarized in Table 7–1.

The `CHAR` function converts an input integer value into a corresponding output character. For example:

```
CHARACTER :: out
INTEGER :: input = 65
out = CHAR(input)
```

The input to the `CHAR` function is a single integer argument, and the output from the function is the character whose collating sequence number matches the input argument for the particular processor. For example, if a processor uses the ASCII collating sequence, then `CHAR(65)` is the character `'A'`.

The `ICHAR` function converts an input character into a corresponding output integer. For example:

```
CHARACTER :: input = 'A'
INTEGER :: out
out = ICHAR(input)
```

The input to the `ICHAR` function is a single character, and the output from the function is the integer whose collating sequence number matches the input character for the particular processor. For example, if a processor uses the ASCII collating sequence, then `ICHAR('A')` is the integer 65.

The functions `ACHAR` and `IACHAR` are exactly the same as the functions `CHAR` and `ICHAR` except that the former work with the ASCII collating sequence regardless of the character set used by a particular processor. Therefore, the results of the functions `ACHAR` and `IACHAR` will be the same on any computer. You should use `ACHAR` and `IACHAR` to improve the portability of the programs that you write.

Good Programming Practice

Use functions `ACHAR` and `IACHAR` instead of `CHAR` and `ICHAR`, since the results of the first set of functions are independent of the processor on which they are executed, while the results of the second set of functions vary depending on the collating sequence of the particular processor on which they are executed.

Function `LEN` returns the declared length of a character string. The input to `LEN` is a character string `str1`, and the output from the function is an integer containing the number of characters in `str1`. An example of the `LEN` function follows.

```
CHARACTER(len=20) :: str1
INTEGER :: out
str1 = 'ABC XYZ'
out = LEN(str1)
```

The output from `LEN` is 20. Note that the output of `LEN` is the declared size of the string, *not* the number of nonblank characters in the string.

Function `LEN_TRIM` returns the length of a character string without trailing blanks. The input to `LEN_TRIM` is a character string `str1`, and the output from the function is an integer containing the number of characters in `str1`, excluding trailing blanks. If `str1` is entirely blank, then function `LEN_TRIM` returns a zero. An example of the `LEN_TRIM` function follows.

```
CHARACTER(len=20) :: str1
INTEGER :: out
str1 = 'ABC XYZ'
out = LEN_TRIM(str1)
```

The output from `LEN_TRIM` is 7.

The `INDEX` function searches for a pattern in a character string. The inputs to the function are two strings: `str1` containing the string to search and `str2` containing the pattern that we are looking for. The output from the function is an integer containing the position in the character string `str1` at which the pattern was found. If no match is found, `INDEX` returns a zero. An example of the `INDEX` function follows.

```
CHARACTER(len=20) :: str1 = 'THIS IS A TEST!'
CHARACTER(len=20) :: str2 = 'TEST'
INTEGER :: out
out = INDEX(str1,str2)
```

The output of this function is the integer 11, since `TEST` begins at character 11 in the input character string.

If `str2` were `'IS'`, then what would be the value of `INDEX(str1,str2)`? The answer is 3, since `'IS'` occurs within the word `'THIS'`. The `INDEX` function will never see the word `'IS'` because it stops searching at the first occurrence of the search pattern in the string.

The `INDEX` function can also have an optional third argument *back*. If present, the argument *back* must be a logical value. If *back* is present and true, then the search starts from the end of string `str1` instead of from the beginning. An example of the `INDEX` function with the optional third argument follows.

```
CHARACTER(len=20) :: str1 = 'THIS IS A TEST!'
CHARACTER(len=20) :: str2 = 'IS'
INTEGER :: out
OUT = INDEX(str1,str2,.TRUE.)
```

The output of this function is the integer 6, since the last occurrence of `IS` begins at character 6 in the input character string.

7.3

PASSING CHARACTER VARIABLES TO SUBROUTINES AND FUNCTIONS

In Example 7–1 we created a subroutine to alphabetize an array of character variables. The character array in that subroutine was declared as

```
INTEGER, INTENT(IN) :: n
CHARACTER(len=20), DIMENSION(n), INTENT(INOUT) :: array
```

▨ TABLE 7–1
Some common character intrinsic functions

Function name and argument(s)	Argument types	Result type	Comments
ACHAR(ival)	INT	CHAR	Returns the character corresponding to ival in the ASCII collating sequence.
CHAR(ival)	INT	CHAR	Returns the character corresponding to ival in the processor's collating sequence.
IACHAR(char)	CHAR	INT	Returns the integer corresponding to char in the ASCII collating sequence.
ICHAR(char)	CHAR	INT	Returns the integer corresponding to char in the processor's collating sequence.
INDEX(str1,str2,back)	CHAR, LOG	INT	Returns the character number of the first location in str1 to contain the pattern in str2 (0 = no match). Argument back is optional; if present and true, then the search starts from the end of str1 instead of from the beginning.
LEN(str1)	CHAR	INT	Returns length of str1.
LEN_TRIM(str1)	CHAR	INT	Returns length of str1, excluding any trailing blanks.
LLT(str1,str2)	CHAR	LOG	TRUE if str1 < str2 according to the ASCII collating sequence.
LLE(str1,str2)	CHAR	LOG	TRUE if str1 <= str2 according to the ASCII collating sequence.
LGT(str1,str2)	CHAR	LOG	TRUE if str1 > str2 according to the ASCII collating sequence.
LGE(str1,str2)	CHAR	LOG	TRUE if str1 >= str2 according to the ASCII collating sequence.

This subroutine will sort a character array with any number of elements, but it will *only* sort the array when each element in the array is 20 characters long. If we wanted to sort data in an array whose elements were a different length, we would need a whole new subroutine to do it! This behavior is unreasonable. We should be able to write a single subroutine to process character data in a given fashion regardless of the number of characters in each element.

Fortran contains a feature to support this requirement. The language allows a special form of the character type declaration for dummy character arguments in procedures. This special declaration takes the form

```
CHARACTER(len=*) :: char_var
```

where *char_var* is the name of a dummy character argument. This declaration says that dummy argument *char_var* is a character variable, but the length of the character variable is not explicitly known at compilation time. If the procedure using *char_var* needs to know its length, it can call function LEN to get that information. The dummy arguments in subroutine sortc could have been declared as

```
INTEGER, INTENT(IN) :: n
CHARACTER(len=*), DIMENSION(n), INTENT(INOUT) :: array
```

If they were declared in this manner, the subroutine would work equally well for arrays of character variables containing elements of any length.

Good Programming Practice

Use the CHARACTER(len=*) type statement to declare dummy character arguments in procedures. This feature allows the procedure to work with strings of arbitrary lengths. If the procedure needs to know the actual length of a particular variable, it may call the LEN function with that variable as a calling argument.

Remember that dummy arguments are just placeholders for the variables that will be passed to the procedure when it is invoked. No actual memory is allocated for the dummy arguments. Since no memory is being allocated, the Fortran compiler does not need to know the length of the character variables that will be passed to the procedure in advance. Therefore, we can use the CHARACTER(len=*) type declaration statement for dummy character arguments in a procedure.

On the other hand, any character variables that are local to the procedure must be declared with explicit lengths. Memory will be allocated in the procedure for these local variables, and we must explicitly specify the length of each local variable for the compiler to know how much memory to allocate for it. This fact creates a problem for local variables that must be the same length as a dummy argument passed to the procedure. For example, in subroutine sortc, the variable temp that was used for swapping must be the same length as an element of the dummy argument array.

How can we adjust the size of a temporary variable to fit the size of a dummy array whenever the subroutine is called? If we declare the length of the variable to be the length of a dummy subroutine argument, then when the subroutine is executed, an **automatic character variable** of that size will be allocated. (This is very similar to the behavior of automatic arrays described in the last chapter.) When the subroutine execution ends, that automatic variable will be destroyed. Like automatic arrays, this automatic character variable may not be initialized in its type declaration statement.

For example, the following statements create an automatic character variable `temp` of the same length as the dummy argument `string`.

```
SUBROUTINE sample ( string )
CHARACTER(len=*) :: string
CHARACTER(len=len(string)) :: temp
```

A version of the character sort subroutine that will work for character arrays of any length, with any number of elements, and on any processor is shown in Figure 7–2.

FIGURE 7–2
A modified version of subroutine `sortc` that will work for arrays of any size and array elements of any length.

```
SUBROUTINE sortc (array, n )
!
! Purpose:
!   To sort character array "array" into ascending order using
!   a selection sort. This version of the subroutine sorts
!   according to the ASCII collating sequence. It works for
!   character arrays with any number of elements, with array
!   elements of any length, and on processors regardless of
!   character set.
!
! Record of revisions:
!      Date        Programmer          Description of change
!      ====        ==========          =====================
!    11/15/95    S. J. Chapman         Original code
! 1. 11/20/95    S. J. Chapman         Modified to work with lexical
!                                      fns and arbitrary element
!                                      lengths
!
IMPLICIT NONE

! Declare calling parameters:
INTEGER, INTENT(IN) :: n                 ! Number of values
CHARACTER(len=*), DIMENSION(n), INTENT(INOUT) :: array
                                         ! Array to be sorted
! Declare local variables:
INTEGER :: i                  ! Loop index
INTEGER :: iptr               ! Pointer to smallest value
INTEGER :: j                  ! Loop index
CHARACTER(len=len(array)) :: temp  ! Temp variable for swaps

! Sort the array
outer: DO i = 1, n-1

   ! Find the minimum value in array(i) through array(n)
   iptr = i
   inner: DO j = i+1, n
     minval: IF ( LLT(array(j),array(iptr)) ) THEN
        iptr = j
```

(continued)

(concluded)

```
      END IF minval
   END DO inner

   ! iptr now prints to the minimum value, so swap array(iptr)
   ! with array(i) if i /=  iptr.
   swap: IF ( i / = iptr ) THEN
      temp        = array(i)
      array(i)    = array(iptr)
      array(iptr) = temp
   END IF swap

END DO outer

END SUBROUTINE sortc
```

7

EXAMPLE 7–2 Shifting Strings to Uppercase: We saw in Example 7–1 that lower-case character strings were not alphabetized properly with uppercase strings, since the collating sequence positions of the lowercase letters were different from the collating sequence numbers of the corresponding uppercase letters. The difference between upper- and lowercase letters also causes a problem when we are attempting to match a pattern within a character variable, since 'STRING' is not the same as 'string' or 'String'. It is often desirable to shift all character variables to uppercase to make matching and sorting easier. Write a subroutine to convert all lowercase letters in a character string to uppercase without changing any other characters in the string.

SOLUTION The problem is complicated by the fact that we don't know which collating sequence is used by the computer that the subroutine will be running on. Appendix A shows the two common collating sequences, ASCII and EBCDIC; note the fixed offset between an uppercase letter and the corresponding lowercase letter in each collating sequence. However, that offset is different for the two sequences. Furthermore, the EBCDIC sequence inserts some nonalphabetic characters into the middle of the alphabet. These characters should not be affected by the uppercase shift. The ASCII character set is much simpler, since all letters are in order and no nonalphabetic characters are mixed into the middle of the alphabet.

Fortunately, if we use the lexical functions for comparisons and the ACHAR and IACHAR functions for conversions, then we can act as though the processor were ASCII and be assured of correct results regardless of the collating sequence of the actual machine.

1. State the problem.

Write a subroutine to convert all lowercase letters in a character string to uppercase without affecting numeric and special characters. Design the subroutine to work properly on any processor by using functions that are independent of collating sequence.

2. Define the inputs and outputs.

The input to the subroutine is the character argument `string`. The output from the subroutine is also in `string`, which can be any length.

3. Define the algorithm.

Looking at the ASCII table in Appendix A, we note that the uppercase letters begin at sequence number 65, and the lowercase letters begin at sequence number 97. Exactly 32 numbers separate each uppercase letter and its lowercase equivalent. Furthermore, no other symbols are mixed into the middle of the alphabet.

These facts give us our basic algorithm for shifting strings to uppercase. We will determine if a character is lowercase by deciding if it is between `'a'` and `'z'` in the ASCII character set. If it is, then we will subtract 32 from its sequence number to convert it to uppercase using the ACHAR and IACHAR functions. The initial pseudocode for this algorithm is

```
Determine if character is lower case.  If so,
   Convert to integer form
   Subtract 32 from the integer
   Convert back to character form
End of IF
```

The final pseudocode for this subroutine is

```
! Get length of string
length ← LEN(string)

DO for i = 1 to length
   IF LGE(string(i:i),'a') .AND. LLE(string(i:i),'z') THEN
      string(i:i) ← ACHAR ( IACHAR (string(i:i) - 32 ) )
   END of IF
END of DO
```

where `length` is the length of the input character string.

4. Turn the algorithm into Fortran statements.

The resulting Fortran subroutines are shown in Figure 7–3.

FIGURE 7–3
Subroutine `ucase`.

```
SUBROUTINE ucase ( string )
!
!  Purpose:
!    To shift a character string to uppercase on any processor,
!    regardless of collating sequence.
!
!  Record of revisions:
!     Date        Programmer          Description of change
!     ====        ==========          =====================
!    11/25/95   S. J. Chapman        Original code
```

(continued)

(concluded)

```
!
IMPLICIT NONE

! Declare calling parameters:
CHARACTER(len=*), INTENT(INOUT) :: string

! Declare local variables:
INTEGER :: i                       ! Loop index
INTEGER :: length                  ! Length of input string

! Get length of string
length = LEN ( string )

! Now shift lowercase letters to uppercase.
DO i = 1, length
   IF ( LGE(string(i:i),'a') .AND. LLE(string(i:i),'z') ) THEN
      string(i:i) = ACHAR ( IACHAR ( string(i:i) ) - 32 )
   END IF
END DO

END SUBROUTINE ucase
```

5. **Test the resulting Fortran program.**

To test this subroutine, we will write a driver program to read a character string, call the subroutine, and write out the results. A test driver program is shown in Figure 7–4.

FIGURE 7–4

Test driver program for subroutine ucase.

```
PROGRAM test_ucase
!
!  Purpose:
!    To test subroutine ucase.
!
IMPLICIT NONE
CHARACTER(len=20) string
WRITE (*,*) 'Enter test string (up to 20 characters): '
READ (*,'(A20)') string
CALL ucase(string)
WRITE (*,*) 'The shifted string is: ', string
END PROGRAM
```

The results from the test program for two input strings follow.

```
C>test_ucase
   Enter test string (up to 20 characters):
This is a test!...
   The shifted string is: THIS IS A TEST!...
C>test_ucase
   Enter test string (up to 20 characters):
abcf1234^&*$po()-
   The shifted string is: ABCF1234^&*$PO()-
```

The subroutine is shifting all lowercase letters to uppercase while leaving everything else alone. It appears to be working correctly.

■ 7.4

VARIABLE-LENGTH CHARACTER FUNCTIONS

You already know that subroutines can work with strings of variable lengths by declaring them with the CHARACTER(len=*) declaration. Fortran also provides a way to write a character function that can return a string of arbitrary length. We can create an **automatic-length character function,** where the length returned by the function is specified by a calling argument. Figure 7–5 shows a simple example. Function abc returns the first n characters of the alphabet, where n is specified in the call to the function.

Automatic-length character functions must be declared with an explicit interface, so that the compiler knows the details of the returned character string.

FIGURE 7–5
A sample function that returns a variable-length character string.

```
MODULE character_subs

CONTAINS
   FUNCTION abc( n )
   !
   !  Purpose:
   !    To return a string containing the first N characters
   !    of the alphabet.
   !
   !  Record of revisions:
   !      Date         Programmer          Description of change
   !      ====         ==========          =====================
   !.   11/25/95    S. J. Chapman        Original code
   !
   IMPLICIT NONE

   ! Declare calling parameters:
   INTEGER, INTENT(IN) :: n                ! Length of string to return
   CHARACTER(len=n) abc                    ! Returned string

   ! Declare local variables:
   character(len=26) :: alphabet = 'abcdefghijklmnopqrstuvwxyz'

   ! Get string to return
   abc = alphabet(1:n)

   END FUNCTION abc

END MODULE
```

A test driver program for this function is shown in Figure 7–6. The module containing the function must be named in a USE statement in the calling program.

FIGURE 7–6
Program to test function abc.

```
PROGRAM test_abc
```

(continued)

(concluded)

```
!
!   Purpose:
!     To test function abc.
!
USE character_subs
IMPLICIT NONE

INTEGER :: n                              ! String length

WRITE (*,*) 'Enter string length:'    ! Get string length
READ (*,*), n

WRITE (*,*) 'The string is: ', abc(n) ! Tell user

END PROGRAM
```

When this program is executed, the results are

```
C>test_abc
Enter string length:
10
The string is: abcdefghij

C>test_abc
Enter string length:
3
The string is: abc
```

The length of the character function abc could also be declared with an asterisk instead of a passed length:

```
CHARACTER(len=*) abc ! Returned string
```

 This declaration would have created an **assumed-length character function.** The behavior of the resulting function is exactly the same as in the example above. However, assumed-length character functions have been declared obsolescent in Fortran 95 and are candidates for deletion in future versions of the language. Do not use them in any of your programs.

Quiz 7–1

This quiz provides a quick check to see if you understand the concepts introduced in sections 7.1 through 7.4. If you have trouble with the quiz, reread the sections, ask your instructor, or discuss the material with a fellow student. The answers to this quiz are found in the back of the book.

(continued)

(concluded)

For questions 1 to 3, state the result of the following expressions. If the result depends on the character set used, state the result for both the ASCII and EBCDIC character sets.

1. `'abcde' < 'ABCDE'`

2. `LLT ('abcde','ABCDE')`

3. `'1234' == '1234 '`

For questions 4 and 5, state whether each statement is legal or not. If a statement is legal, tell what it does. If it is not legal, explain why.

4.
```
FUNCTION day(iday)
IMPLICIT NONE
INTEGER, INTENT(IN) :: iday
CHARACTER(len=3) :: day
CHARACTER(len=3), DIMENSION(7) :: days = &
    (/'SUN', 'MON', 'TUE', 'WED', 'THU', 'FRI', 'SAT'/)
IF ( ( iday >= 1 ) .AND. ( iday <= 7 ) ) THEN
    day = days(iday)
END IF
END FUNCTION day
```

5.
```
FUNCTION swap_string(string)
IMPLICIT NONE
CHARACTER(len=*), INTENT(IN) :: string
CHARACTER(len=len(string)) :: swap_string
INTEGER :: length, i
length = LEN(string)
DO i = 1, length
    swap_length(length-i+1:length-i+1) = string(i:i)
END DO
END FUNCTION
```

For question 6, state the contents of each variable after the code is executed.

6.
```
CHARACTER(len=80) :: line
INTEGER :: ipos1, ipos2, ipos3, ipos4
line = 'This is a test line containing some input data!'
ipos1 = INDEX (LINE, 'in')
ipos2 = INDEX (LINE, 'Test')
ipos3 = INDEX (LINE, 't 1')
ipos4 = INDEX (LINE, 'in', .TRUE.)
```

7.5

INTERNAL FILES

We learned how to manipulate numeric data in the previous chapters of this book and how to manipulate character data earlier in this chapter. However, we have *not* learned yet how to convert numeric data into character data, and vice versa. Fortran uses a special mechanism, known as **internal files,** for such conversions.

Internal files are a special extension of the Fortran I/O system in which the READs and WRITEs occur to internal character buffers (internal files) instead of to disk files (external files). Anything that can be written to an external file can also be written to an internal file where it will be available for further manipulation. Likewise, anything that can be read from an external file can be read from an internal file.

The general form of a READ from an internal file is

```
READ (buffer,format) arg1, arg2, ...
```

where *buffer* is the input character buffer, *format* is the format for the READ, and *arg1*, *arg2*, etc. are the variables whose values are to be read from the buffer. The general form of a WRITE to an internal file is

```
WRITE (buffer,format) arg1, arg2, ...
```

where *buffer* is the output character buffer, *format* is the format for the WRITE, and *arg1*, *arg2*, etc. are the values to be written to the buffer.

A common use of internal files is to convert character data into numeric data, and vice versa. For example, if the character variable input contains the string '135.4', then the following code will convert the character data into a real value:

```
CHARACTER(len=5) :: input = '135.4'
REAL :: value
READ (input,*) value
```

Certain I/O features are not available with internal files. For example, the OPEN, CLOSE, BACKSPACE, and REWIND statements may not be used with them.

Good Programming Practice

Use internal files to convert data from character format to numeric format, and vice versa.

7.6

EXAMPLE PROBLEMS

EXAMPLE 7–3 Varying a Format to Match the Data to Be Output: So far, we have used three format descriptors to write real data values. The F*w.d* format descriptor displays the data in a format with a fixed decimal point, and the E*w.d* and ES*w.d* format descriptors display the data in exponential notation. The F format descriptor displays data in a way that is easier for a person to understand quickly, but it will fail to display the number correctly if the absolute value of the number is either too small or too large. The E and ES format descriptors will display the number correctly regardless of size, but it is harder for a person to read at a glance.

Write a Fortran function that converts a real number into characters for display in a 12-character-wide field. The function should check the size of the number to be printed out and modify the format statement to display the data in `F12.4` format for as long as possible until the absolute value of the number gets either too big or too small. When the number is out of range for the `F` format, the function should switch to `ES` format.

SOLUTION In the `F12.4` format, the function displays four digits to the right of the decimal place. One additional digit is required for the decimal point, and another one is required for the minus sign if the number is negative. After subtracting those characters, seven characters are left for positive numbers, and six characters are left for negative numbers. Therefore, we must convert the number to exponential notation for any positive number larger than 9,999,999 and for any negative number smaller than $-999,999$.

If the absolute value of the number to be displayed is smaller than 0.01, then the display should shift to `ES` format, because the `F12.4` format will not display enough significant digits. However, an exact zero value should be displayed in normal `F` format rather than in exponential format.

When it is necessary to switch to exponential format, we will use the `ES12.5` format, since the number appears in ordinary scientific notation.

1. State the problem.

Write a function to convert a real number into 12 characters for display in a 12-character-wide field. Display the number in `F12.4` format, unless the number overflows the format descriptor or gets too small to display with enough precision in an `F12.4` field. When it is not possible to display the number in `F12.4` format, switch to the `ES12.5` format. However, display an exact zero in `F12.4` format.

2. Define the inputs and outputs.

The input to the function is a real number passed through the argument list. The function returns a 12-character expression containing the number in a form suitable for displaying.

3. Describe the algorithm.

The basic requirements for this function were discussed in the problem statement. The pseudocode to implement these requirements follows.

```
IF value > 9999999. THEN
   Use ES12.5 format
ELSE IF value < -999999. THEN
   Use ES12.5 format
ELSE IF value == 0. THEN
   Use F12.4 format
ELSE IF ABS(value) < 0.01 THEN
   Use ES12.5 format
ELSE
```

```
              USE F12.4 format
          END of IF
          WRITE value to buffer using specified format
```

4. Turn the algorithm into Fortran statements.

The resulting Fortran function is shown in Figure 7–7. Function real_to_char illustrates both how to use internal files and how to use a character variable to contain format descriptors. The proper format descriptor for the real-to-character conversion is stored in variable fmt, and an internal WRITE operation is used to write the character string into buffer string.

FIGURE 7–7

Character function real_to_char.

```
FUNCTION real_to_char ( value )
!
!   Purpose:
!     To convert a real value into a 12-character string, with the
!     number in as readable a format as possible considering
!     its range. This routine prints out the number according to the
!     following rules:
!        1. value > 9999999.                        ES12.5
!        2. value < -999999.                        ES12.5
!        3. 0.    < ABS(value) < 0.01               ES12.5
!        4. value = 0.0                             F12.4
!        5. Otherwise                               F12.4
!
!   Record of revisions:
!      Date       Programmer        Description of change
!      ====       ==========        =====================
!     11/26/95    S. J. Chapman     Original code
!
IMPLICIT NONE

! Declare calling arguments:
REAL, INTENT(IN) :: value             ! value to convert to char form
CHARACTER (len=12) :: real_to_char    ! Output character string

! Declare local variables:
CHARACTER(len=9) :: fmt               ! Format descriptor
CHARACTER(len=12) :: string           ! Output string

! Clear string before use
string = ' '

! Select proper format
IF ( value > 9999999. ) THEN
   fmt = '(ES12.5)'
ELSE IF ( value < -999999. ) THEN
   fmt = '(ES12.5)'
ELSE IF ( value == 0. ) THEN
   fmt = '(F12.4)'
ELSE IF ( ABS(value) < 0.01 ) THEN
   fmt = '(ES12.5)'
ELSE
   fmt = '(F12.4)'
```

(continued)

(concluded)

```
END IF

! Convert value to character form.
WRITE (string,fmt) value
real_to_char = string

END FUNCTION real_to_char
```

5. **Test the resulting Fortran program.**

To test this function, we will write a driver program to read a real number, call the function, and write out the results. A test driver program is shown in Figure 7–8.

FIGURE 7–8
Test driver program for function real_to_char.

```
PROGRAM test_real_to_char
!
!  Purpose:
!    To test function real_to_char.
!
!  Record of revisions:
!     Date         Programmer        Description of change
!     ====         ==========        =====================
!    11/26/95    S. J. Chapman       Original code
!
! External routines:
!    real_to_char -- Convert real to character string
!    ucase        -- Shift string to uppercase
!
IMPLICIT NONE

! Declare external functions:
CHARACTER(len=12), EXTERNAL :: real_to_char

! Declare local variables:
CHARACTER :: ch                 ! Character to hold Y/N response.
CHARACTER(len=12) :: result     ! Character output
REAL :: value                   ! Value to be converted

while: DO

   !Prompt for input value.
   WRITE (*,'(1X,A)') 'Enter value to convert:'
   READ (*,*) value

   ! Write converted value and see if we want another.
   result = real_to_char(value)
   WRITE (*,'(1X,A,A,A)') 'The result is ', result, &
                          ': Convert another one? (Y/N) [N]'
   ! Get answer.
   READ (*,'(A)') ch

   ! Convert answer to uppercase to make match.
   CALL ucase ( ch )
   ! Do another?
```

(continued)

(concluded)

```
    IF ( ch /=  'Y' ) EXIT

END DO while

END PROGRAM
```

To verify that this function is working correctly for all cases, we must supply test values that fall within each of the ranges that it is designed to work for. Therefore, we will test it with the following numbers:

```
0.
0.001234567
1234.567
12345678.
-123456.7
-1234567.
```

The results from the test program for the six input values follow.

```
C>test_real_to_char
Enter value to convert:
0.
The result is       .0000: Convert another one? (Y/N) [N]
y
Enter value to convert:
0.001234567
The result is  1.234567E-03: Convert another one? (Y/N) [N]
Y
Enter value to convert:
1234.567
The result is     1234.5670: Convert another one? (Y/N) [N]
Y
Enter value to convert:
12345678.
The result is 1.234567E+07: Convert another one? (Y/N) [N]
y
Enter value to convert:
-123456.7
The result is -123456.7000: Convert another one? (Y/N) [N]
y
Enter value to convert:
-1234567.
The result is -1.234567E+06: Convert another one? (Y/N) [N]
n
```

The function appears to be working correctly for all possible input values.

The test program test_real_to_char also contains a few interesting features. Since we would normally use the program to test more than one value, it is structured as a while loop. The program prompts the user to determine whether or not to repeat the loop. The first character of the user's response is stored in variable ch and is compared to the character 'Y'. If the user responded with a 'Y', the loop is repeated; otherwise, it is terminated. Note that subroutine ucase is called to shift the contents of ch to uppercase, so that both 'y' and 'Y' will be interpreted as yes answers. This form of repetition control is very useful in interactive Fortran programs.

EXAMPLE 7–4 *Plotting Data:* Engineers often want to get a quick plot of a data set so that they can visualize it. A plot will show patterns in the data that are not obvious when a person is just scanning a column of numbers.

The best plots available are the high-resolution plots generated by plotters, laser printers, and similar devices, using special programs to generate the control codes used by the devices. These devices and programs may not always be available. Even if they are available, there is no *standard* way of plotting from a Fortran program onto various plotting devices. Programs will have to be adapted to each device individually; they are, therefore, inherently nonportable.

Anyone with access to a computer can always plot a data set by creating a *line-printer plot* with a simple Fortran subroutine. Although the plot will be relatively coarse, it will be device independent and totally portable. Line-printer plots can be very convenient for quick-and-dirty looks at a data set.

A line-printer plot is a plot composed of characters placed in specific columns corresponding to the values in the data set. It is low resolution because the number of columns on a line printer are limited. However, it does have the advantage of being free, and it can be moved anywhere.

We will write a subroutine to make a line-printer plot of a data set whose samples were taken at regular intervals. (Exercise 7–17 asks you to write a more general plotting subroutine that supports samples taken at arbitrary intervals.) The upper and lower limits of the plot should be under user control, and the subroutine should be able to calculate default limits based on the values in the data set.

SOLUTION The plot subroutine will need to plot the data in a fixed number of columns small enough to fit the line printer that the plot will be printed on. Since we do not know how wide a particular printer will be, this plot will be designed to fit an 80-column printer, which is the smallest size normally encountered. If we allocate 15 characters for printing out the values of the data points, then the plotting area can be 65 characters wide.

The plotting routine will first need to determine the minimum and maximum values to plot. These values can either be passed from the calling program, or they can be calculated from the largest and smallest numbers in the data set. Once we know what the largest and smallest values to plot are, we can divide the difference between those numbers into 65 evenly spaced bins. For each data point, if the point falls within a specific bin, then an asterisk will be printed in that bin.

1. **State the problem.**

Write a subroutine that will generate an 80-character-wide line-printer plot on a user-specified i/o unit number for an input data set containing values sampled at regular intervals. The maximum and minimum values to plot may either be specified by the calling routine or be calculated by default in the plot subroutine. The subroutine should also write out the actual values being plotted.

2. **Define the inputs and outputs.**

The inputs to this subroutine are

a. A real array y containing the data to plot.

b. The number of points `npts` in the array.

c. The minimum value `minval` and the maximum value `maxval` to plot.

d. A default flag `default` to tell the subroutine to calculate its own plotting limits.

e. The i/o unit number `unit` to send the plot to.

The outputs from the program are the individual lines of the plot sent to the specified i/o unit.

3. **Describe the algorithm.**

The basic pseudocode for this program follows.

```
IF default THEN
    Calculate the limits of the plot
End of IF
Write out an upper border for the plot
DO for i = 1 to npts
    Set left & right borders of plot
    Set zero position for plot
    Place asterisk in column corresponding to y(i)
    Write out y(i) and plot line
End of DO
Write out a lower border for the plot
Write out number of points plotted
```

4. **Turn the algorithm into Fortran statements.**

The resulting Fortran subroutine is shown in Figure 7–9. Note that we are using intrinsic functions `MAXVAL` and `MINVAL` to determine the smallest and largest values in the input array and using function `real_to_char` to print out the values of the data points in an easy-to-read manner that works for all possible input values. We are taking advantage of our previous work and not reinventing the wheel!

FIGURE 7–9

Subroutine `plot`.

```
SUBROUTINE plot ( y, npts, minplt, maxplt, default, unit )
!
! Purpose:
!   Subroutine to plot the points in array y.  The data in the
!   array is assumed to be at a uniform spacing.
!
! Record of revisions:
!     Date        Programmer          Description of change
!     ====        ==========          =====================
!   11/27/95    S. J. Chapman         Original code
!
IMPLICIT NONE

! Declare calling arguments:
INTEGER, INTENT(IN) :: npts            ! Number of points to plot
REAL,DIMENSION(npts),INTENT(IN) :: y   ! Input data
REAL, INTENT(IN) :: minplt             ! Minimum value of plot
REAL, INTENT(IN) :: maxplt             ! Maximum value of plot
```

(continued)

(continued)

```
LOGICAL, INTENT(IN) :: default      ! Flag to set default limits
INTEGER, INTENT(IN) :: unit         ! Output i/o unit to plot on

! External functions:
CHARACTER(len=12) :: real_to_char   ! Convert real to char str

! Declare parameters:
INTEGER, PARAMETER :: nbins = 65    ! Number of bins to plot in

! Declare local variables:
CHARACTER(len=14) :: annotation     ! Line annotation (y value)
CHARACTER(len=12) :: ch_maxamp      ! Char form of max value to plot
CHARACTER(len=12) :: ch_minamp      ! Char form of min value to plot
INTEGER :: i                        ! Loop index
INTEGER :: ibin                     ! Bin # for current y value
INTEGER :: ibin0                    ! Bin # for zero crossing
REAL :: fraction                    ! Fraction of plot width
REAL :: maxamp                      ! Max value to plot (local)
REAL :: minamp                      ! Min value to plot (local)
CHARACTER(len=65) :: plot_buffer    ! Plotting buffer
CHARACTER(len=65) :: scale          ! Scale on border of plot

! If the scales are defaulted, set min and max of Y axis.
set_range: IF ( default ) THEN
    ! Get the largest and smallest values in the array.
   maxamp = MAXVAL(y)
   minamp = MINVAL(y)
ELSE
    ! Set specified value for range of Y axis.
   maxamp = maxplt
   minamp = minplt
END IF set_range

! We will divide minamp to maxamp into 65 bins for plotting
! purposes.  Locate the zero bin if it is between minamp
! and maxamp.
IF ( (maxamp > 0.) .AND. (minamp < 0) ) THEN
   fraction = ( 0. - minamp) / (maxamp - minamp )
   ibin0 = NINT ( (nbins-1) * faction ) + 1
ELSE
   ibin0 = 0
END IF

! Set border scale, including zero mark.
annotation = ' '
scale = '+ ----------------------------&
        &----------------------------+'
IF ( ibin0 > 0 ) THEN
   scale(ibin0:ibin0) = '+'
END IF

! Print upper border.
ch_minamp = real_to_char(minamp)
ch_maxamp = real_to_char(maxamp)
WRITE (unit,'(10X,A,46X,A)') ch_minamp, ch_maxamp
WRITE (unit,'(A,1X,A)') annotation, scale

! Plot data points.
plot_points :: DO i = 1, npts
```

(concluded)

```
    ! Clear line
    plot_buffer = ' '
    annotation = ' '

    ! Set value of y data point.
    annotation(2:13) = real_to_char( y(i) )

    ! Set min and max borders.
    plot_buffer(1:1)   = '|'
    plot_buffer(65:65) = '|'

    ! Set zero line, if within borders.
    IF ( ibin0 > 0 ) THEN
       plot_buffer(ibin0:ibin0) = '|'
    END IF

    ! Plot point on array.
    fraction = ( y(i) - minamp) / (maxamp - minamp )
    ibin = NINT ( (nbins-1) * faction ) + 1
    IF ( (ibin >= 1) .AND. (ibin <= ibins) ) THEN
       plot_buffer(ibin:ibin) = '*'
    END IF
    ! Write out line.
    WRITE (unit,'(A,1X,A)') annotation, plot_buffer

END DO plot_points

! Print lower border.
annotation = ' '
WRITE (unit,'(A,1X,A)') annotation, scale
WRITE (unit,'(10X,A,46X,A)') ch_minamp, ch_maxamp

! Print out summary info.
WRITE (unit,'(/,10X,A,I12)' ) 'Number of Points = ', npts

END SUBROUTINE plot
```

5. Test the resulting Fortran program.

To test this subroutine, we will write a driver program that generates a data set based on the function

$$y(t) = 10e^{-0.2t}\sin t \tag{7-1}$$

and call the plot subroutine with that data. The test driver program test_plot is shown in Figure 7–10.

FIGURE 7–10

Test driver program for subroutine plot.

```
PROGRAM test_plot
!
!  Purpose:
!    Program to test subroutine "plot".  This program generates
!    a data set based on the function:
!       y(t) = 10. * EXP (-t/5) * SIN(t)
!    starting at t = 0 for 12 seconds, with a step size dt = 1/3.
!
```

(continued)

(concluded)

```
IMPLICIT NONE

! Declare local variables:
LOGICAL :: default = .TRUE.      ! Default plot boundaries
INTEGER :: i, unit = 6
REAL :: minplt = 0., maxplt = 0.
INTEGER :: npts = 37
REAL, DIMENSION(0:36) :: y

! Generate function.
DO i = 0, 36
   y(i) = 10. * EXP ( -REAL(i)/15. ) * SIN ( REAL(i)/3. )
END DO

! Plot data
CALL plot ( y, npts, minplt, maxplt, default, unit )

END PROGRAM
```

A plot of the input function is shown in Figure 7–11*a,* and the output of the line-printer plot is shown in Figure 7–11*b.* The line-printer plot gives us a good idea of the overall behavior of the data set.

Quiz 7–2

This quiz provides a quick check to see if you understand the concepts introduced in sections 7.5 and 7.6. If you have trouble with the quiz, reread the sections, ask your instructor, or discuss the material with a fellow student. The answers to this quiz are found in the back of the book.

For questions 1 to 3, state whether each of the following groups of statements is correct or not. If correct, describe the results of the statements.

1. ```
   CHARACTER(len=12) :: buff
   CHARACTER(len=12) :: buff1 = 'ABCDEFGHIJKL'
   INTEGER :: i = -1234
   IF ( buff1(10:10)  ==  'K' ) THEN
      buff = "(1X,I10.8)"
   ELSE
      buff = "(1X,I10)"
   END IF
   WRITE (*,buff) i
   ```

2. ```
   CHARACTER(len=80) :: outbuf
   INTEGER :: i = 123, j, k = -11
   j = 1023 / 1024
   WRITE (outbuf,*) i, j, k
   ```

3. ```
   CHARACTER(len=30) :: line = &
        '123456789012345678901234567890'
   CHARACTER(len=30) :: fmt = &
        '(3X,I6,12X,I3,F6.2)'
   INTEGER :: ival1, ival2
   REAL :: rval3
   READ (line,fmt) ival1, ival2, rval3
   ```
   ```

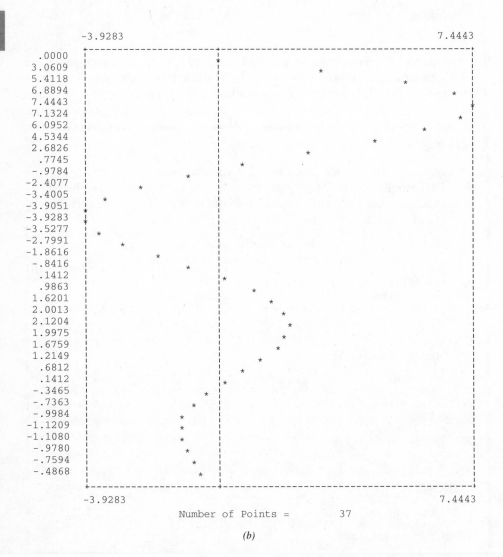

FIGURE 7–11
(*a*) Plot of function $y(t) = 10e^{-0.2t} \sin t$. (*b*) Line-printer plot of the function produced by subroutine plot.

■ 7.7
SUMMARY

A character variable is a variable that contains character information. Two character strings may be compared using the relational operators. However, the result of the comparison may differ depending on the collating sequence of the characters on a particular processor. A safer way to test character strings for inequality is to use the lexical functions, which always return the same value on any computer regardless of collating sequence.

It is possible to declare automatic character variables in procedures. The length of an automatic character variable is specified by either a dummy argument or by a value passed in a module. Each time the procedure is run, a character variable of the specified length is automatically generated; the variable is automatically destroyed when the execution of the procedure ends.

It is possible to generate character functions that can return character strings of variable length provided that an explicit interface exists between the function and any invoking program units. The easiest way to generate an explicit interface is to package the function within a module and then to use that module in the calling procedure.

Internal files provide a means to convert data from character form to numeric form, and vice versa, within a Fortran program. They involve writes to and reads from a character variable within the program.

7.7.1 Summary of Good Programming Practice

The following guidelines should be adhered to when working with character variables:

1. Use the lexical functions rather than the relational operators to compare two character strings for inequality. This action avoids potential problems when a program is moved from a processor with an ASCII character set to a processor with an EBCDIC character set.
2. Use functions ACHAR and IACHAR instead of functions CHAR and ICHAR. The results of the first set of functions are independent of the processor on which they are executed, while the results of the second set of functions vary depending on the collating sequence of the particular processor that they are executed on.
3. Use the CHARACTER(len=*) type statement to declare dummy character arguments in procedures. This feature allows the procedure to work with strings of arbitrary lengths. If the subroutine or function needs to know the actual length of a particular variable, it may call the LEN function with that variable as a calling argument.
4. Use internal files to convert data from character format to numeric format, and vice versa.

7.7.2 Summary of Fortran Statements and Structures

Internal READ Statement

```
                    READ (buffer,fmt) input_list
```

Example

```
            READ (line,'(1X, I10, F10.2)') i, slope
```

Description:

   The internal READ statement reads the data in the input list according to the formats specified in *fmt*, which can be a character string, a character variable, the label of a FORMAT statement, or *. The data is read from the internal character variable *buffer*.

Internal WRITE Statement

```
                    WRITE (buffer,fmt) output_list
```

Example

```
            WRITE (line,'(2I10,F10.2)') i, j, slope
```

Description:

   The internal WRITE statement writes the data in the output list according to the formats specified in *fmt*, which can be a character string, a character variable, the label of a FORMAT statement, or *. The data is written to the internal character variable *buffer*.

7.8

EXERCISES

7–1 Determine the contents of each variable in the following code fragment after the code has been executed:

```
CHARACTER(len=16) :: a = '1234567890123456'
CHARACTER(len=16) :: b = 'ABCDEFGHIJKLMNOP', c
IF ( a > b ) THEN
   c = a(1:6) // b(7:12) // a(13:16)
ELSE
   c = b(7:12) // a(1:6) // a(13:16)
END IF
a(7:9) = '='
```

7–2 Determine the contents of each variable in the following code fragment after the code has been executed. How does the behavior of this code fragment differ from the behavior of the code fragment in exercise 7–1?

```
CHARACTER(len=16) :: a = '1234567890123456'
CHARACTER(len=16) :: b = 'ABCDEFGHIJKLMNOP', c
IF ( LGT(a,b) ) THEN
   c = a(1:6) // b(7:12) // a(13:16)
ELSE
   c = b(7:12) // a(1:6) // a(13:16)
END IF
a(7:9) = '='
```

7–3 Determine the order in which the character strings in Example 7–1 would be sorted by the subroutine `sortc` if executed in a computer using the EBCDIC collating sequence.

7–4 Rewrite subroutine `ucase` as a character function. Note that this function must return a variable-length character string.

7–5 Write a subroutine `lcase` that properly converts a string to lowercase regardless of collating sequence.

7–6 Determine the order in which the following character strings will be sorted by the subroutine `sortc` of Example 7–1 (*a*) according to the ASCII collating sequence and (*b*) according to the EBCDIC collating sequence.

```
'This is a test!'
'?well?'
'AbCd'
'aBcD'
'1DAY'
'2nite'
'/DATA/'
'quit'
```

7–7 Determine the contents of each variable in the following code fragment after the code has been executed:

```
CHARACTER(len=132) :: buffer
REAL :: a, b
INTEGER :: i = 1700, j = 2400
a = REAL(1700 / 2400)
b = REAL(1700) / 2400
WRITE (buffer,100) i, j, a, b
100 FORMAT (T11,I10,T31,I10,T51,F10.4,T28,F10.4)
```

7–8 Write a subroutine `caps` that searches for all the words within a character variable, capitalizes the first letter of each word, and shifts the remainder of the word to lowercase. Assume that all nonalphabetic and nonnumeric characters can mark the boundaries of a word within the character variable (for example, periods and commas). Nonalphabetic characters should be left unchanged. Test your routine on the following character variables:

```
CHARACTER(len=40) :: a = 'this is a test--does it work?'
CHARACTER(len=40) :: b = 'this iS the 2nd test!'
CHARACTER(len=40) :: c = '123 WHAT NOW?!? xxxooxxx.'
```

7–9 Rewrite subroutine `caps` as a variable-length character function. Test the function using the same data as in the previous exercise.

7–10 The intrinsic function `LEN` returns the number of characters that a character variable can store, *not* the number of characters actually stored in the variable. Write a function `len_used` that returns the number of characters actually used within a variable. The function should determine the number of characters actually used by determining the positions of the first and last nonblank characters in the variable and by performing the appropriate math. Test your function with the following variables. Compare the results of function `len_used` with the results returned by `LEN` and `LEN_TRIM` for each of the values given.

```
CHARACTER(len=30) :: a(3)
a(1) = 'How many characters are used?'
a(2) = '   ...and how about this one?'
a(3) = '   !   !
```

7–11 When a relatively short character string is assigned to a longer character variable, the extra space in the variable is filled with blanks. In many circumstances, we would like to use a substring consisting of only the *nonblank* portions of the character variable. To do so, we need to know where the nonblank portions are within the variable. Write a subroutine that will accept a character string of arbitrary length and then return two integers containing the numbers of the first and last nonblank characters in the variable. Test your subroutine with several character variables of different lengths and with different contents.

7–12 Input Parameter File A common feature of large programs is an *input parameter file* in which the user can specify certain values to be used during the execution of the program. In simple programs the values in the file must be listed in a specific order, and none of them may be skipped. These values may be read with a series of consecutive `READ` statements. If a value is left out of the input file or an extra value is added to the input file, all subsequent `READ` statements are misaligned and the numbers will go into the wrong locations in the program.

In more sophisticated programs, default values are defined for the input parameters in the file. In such a system, *only the input parameters whose defaults need to be modified need to be included in the input file.* Furthermore, the values that do appear in the input file may occur in any order. Each parameter in the input file is recognized by a corresponding *keyword* indicating which value is being supplied.

For example, a numerical integration program might include default values for the starting time of the integration, the ending time of the integration, the step size to use, and whether or not to plot the output. These values could be overridden by lines in the input file. An input parameter file for this program might contain the following items:

```
start = 0.0
stop = 10.0
dt = 0.2
plot off
```

These values could be listed in any order, and some of them could be omitted if the default values are acceptable. In addition, the keywords might appear in uppercase, lowercase, or mixed case. The program will read this input file a line at a time and update the variable specified by the keyword with the value on the line.

Write a subroutine that accepts a character argument containing a line from the input parameter file and has the following output arguments:

```
REAL :: start, stop, dt
LOGICAL :: plot
```

The subroutine should check for a keyword in the line and also update the variable that matches that keyword. It should recognize the keywords `'START'`, `'STOP'`, `'DT'`, and `'PLOT'`. If the keyword `'START'` is recognized, the subroutine should check for an equal sign and then use the value to the right of the equal sign to update variable START. It should behave similarly for the other keywords with real values. If the keyword `'PLOT'` is recognized, the subroutine should check for ON or OFF and update the logical variable `'PLOT'` accordingly. (*Hint:* Shift each line to uppercase for easy recognition. Then use function INDEX to identify keywords.)

7–13 Histograms A *histogram* is a plot that shows how many times a particular measurement falls within a certain range of values. For example, suppose that there are 30 students in a class and that their scores on the last exam fell within the following ranges:

Range	No. of Students
100 - 95	3
94 - 90	6
89 - 85	9
84 - 80	7
79 - 75	4
74 - 70	2
69 - 65	1

A plot of the number of students scoring in each range of numbers is a histogram (see Figure 7–12).

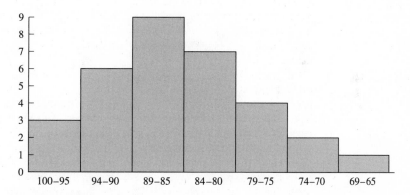

FIGURE 7–12
Histogram of student test scores.

To create this histogram, we started with a set of data consisting of 30 grades. We divided the range of possible grades on the test (0 to 100) into 20 bins and then counted how many scores fell within each bin. Then we plotted the number of grades in each bin. (Since no one scored below 65 on the exam, we didn't bother to plot all of the empty bins between 0 and 64 in Figure 7–12.)

Write a subroutine that will accept an array of real input data values, divide them into a user-specified number of bins over a user-specified range, and accumulate the number of samples that fall within each bin. The subroutine should then plot a histogram of the data values using a line-printer plot.

7-14 Use the random number subroutine `random0` that was developed in Chapter 6 to generate an array of 20,000 random numbers in the range [0,1). Use the histogram subroutine developed in the previous exercise to divide the range between 0 and 1 into 20 bins and to plot a histogram of the 20,000 random numbers. How uniform was the distribution of the numbers generated by the random number generator?

7-15 Use the normally distributed random number subroutine developed in exercise 6–36 to generate an array of 20,000 random numbers. Use the histogram subroutine developed in the exercise 7–13 to divide the range between −4 and 4 into 41 bins and to plot a histogram of the 20,000 random numbers. How well does the histogram match the probability distribution shown in Figure 6–27?

7-16 **Plotting Polynomials** A polynomial is a function of the form

$$y(x) = a_0 + a_1 x + a_2 x^2 + a_3 x^3 + \ldots$$

Write a program that can read a parameter file containing a polynomial, as well as START, STOP, and INCR keywords. Then, the program should plot the function from $x = $ START to $x = $ STOP in increments of $\Delta x = $ INCR. The polynomial will be specified by a series of COEFx cards. The COEF0 card will specify the coefficient a_0, the COEF1 card will specify the coefficient a_1, etc. The program should support reading and plotting polynomials of up to ninth order.

A typical parameter file for plotting the equation $y(x) = 7 + 3x - 2x^2$ would be:

```
COEF0 =  7.0
COEF1 =  3.0
COEF2 = -2.0
START = -2.
STOP  =  3.
INCR  =  0.2
```

7-17 **X-Y Plots** Write a subroutine that plots a series of (x,y) pairs of points over a user-specified range of x and y values. Test your subroutine by plotting the points generated by the following code fragment:

```
REAL, PARAMETER :: pi = 3.141592
REAL, DIMENSION(40) :: x, y
DO i = 1, 40
   x(i) = COS(REAL(i)*(pi/20.))
   y(i) = SIN(REAL(i)*(pi/20.))
END DO
```

7-18 **Plotting Functions of Two Variables** We sometimes need to examine data that is a function of two independent variables. For example, the function $z(x,y)$ in Equation (7–2) is a function of the two independent variables x and y.

$$z(x,y) = \sqrt{1.25x^2 + 0.75y^2} \qquad (7-2)$$

This sort of data can be represented by a two-dimensional plot with x and y as the axes. A number between 0 and 9 represents the magnitude of z at each (x,y) pair. Create a subroutine that generates a line-printer plot of a function of two variables x and y over a user-specified range. The function to plot and the range over which it is to be plotted should be passed to the subroutine as calling arguments. Test the subroutine by plotting Equation (7–2) over the range $-2 \leq x \leq 2$ and $-2 \leq y \leq 2$.

7–19 Write a program that opens a user-specified disk file containing the source code for a Fortran program. The program should copy the source code from the input file to a user-specified output file, stripping out any comments during the copying process. Assume that the Fortran source file is in free format.

7

Additional Data Types

In this chapter we will examine alternative kinds of the REAL data type and explain how to select the desired kind for a particular problem. Then we will turn our attention to two additional data types: the COMPLEX data type and the derived data type. The COMPLEX data type is used to store and manipulate complex numbers, which have both real and imaginary components. The derived data type is a mechanism for users to create special new data types to suit the needs of a particular problem.

8.1

ALTERNATIVE KINDS OF THE REAL DATA TYPE

The real data type is used to represent numbers containing decimal points. On most computers, a **default real** variable is **single precision,** which is usually 4 bytes (or 32 bits) long. It is divided into two parts, a mantissa and an exponent. In a typical implementation, 24 bits of the number are devoted to the mantissa, and 8 bits are devoted to the exponent. The 24 bits devoted to the mantissa are enough to represent six or seven significant decimal digits, so a real number can have up to about seven significant digits.[1] Similarly, the 8 bits of the exponent are enough to represent numbers as large as 10^{38} and as small as 10^{-38}.

Sometimes, a 4-byte real number cannot adequately express a value that we need to solve a problem. Scientists and engineers may need to express a number to more than seven significant digits of precision, or they may need to work with numbers larger than 10^{38} or smaller than 10^{-38}. In either case we cannot use a single precision variable to represent the number. Fortran 90/95 includes a longer version of the

---

[1] One bit is used to represent the sign of the number, and 23 bits are used to represent the magnitude of the mantissa. Since $2^{23} = 8,388,608$, it is possible to represent between six and seven significant digits with a real number.

real data type for use in these circumstances. This longer version of the real data type is also known as **double precision,** in contrast to the default single-precision real.

A double-precision real variable is usually 8 bytes (or 64 bits) long, which is twice as long as a single-precision real variable. In a typical implementation,[2] 53 bits of the number are devoted to the mantissa, and 11 bits are devoted to the exponent. The 53 bits devoted to the mantissa are enough to represent 15 to 16 significant decimal digits. Similarly, the 11 bits of the exponent are enough to represent numbers as large as 10^{308} and as small as 10^{-308}.

8.1.1 Kinds of REAL Constants and Variables

Since Fortran compilers have at least two kinds of real variables, we need some way to declare which data type we want to use in a particular problem. Fortran uses a **kind type parameter** to declare data types. Single-precision reals and double-precision reals are different kinds of the real data type, each with its own unique *kind number.* Examples of a real type declaration statement with a kind type parameter follow.

```
REAL(KIND=1) :: value_1
REAL(KIND=4) :: value_2
REAL(KIND=8), DIMENSION(20) :: array
REAL(4) :: temp
```

The kind of a real value is specified in parentheses after the REAL, either with or without the phrase KIND=. A variable declared with a kind type parameter is called a **parameterized variable.** If no kind is specified, then the default kind of real value is used. The default kind may vary among different processors, but it is usually 32-bit single precision.

What do the kind numbers mean? Unfortunately, we do not know. Each compiler vendor is free to assign any kind number to any size of variable. For example, on some compilers, a 32-bit real value might be KIND=1 and a 64-bit real value might be KIND=2. On other compilers, a 32-bit real value might be KIND=4 and a 64-bit real value might be KIND=8. Table 8–1 shows examples of kind numbers for some representative computer/compiler combinations.

Therefore, to make your programs portable between computers, you should always assign kind numbers to a named constant and then use that named constant in all type declaration statements. You will then be able to modify the program to run on different processors by changing only the value of the named constant. For example:

```
INTEGER, PARAMETER :: single = 4    ! Compiler dependent value
INTEGER, PARAMETER :: double = 8    ! Compiler dependent value
REAL(KIND=single):: value_1
REAL(KIND=double),DIMENSION(20) :: array
REAL(single) :: temp
```

---

[2]This statement refers to IEEE Standard 754 for double-precision numbers. Most new computer systems conform to this standard, but some older systems allocate their bits in a different fashion. For example, older VAX computers allocated 56 bits to the mantissa and 8 bits to the exponent of their double-precision numbers, giving them a range of 10^{-38} to 10^{38} and 16 to 17 significant digits of accuracy.

■ TABLE 8–1
KIND numbers for real values in some Fortran 90 compilers

Computer/compiler	32-bit real	64-bit real	128-bit real
Cray T90 Supercomputer/CF90	N/A	4,8*	16
DEC/DEC Fortran 90	4*	8	N/A
PC/Lahey Fortran 90	4*	8	N/A
PC/Microsoft Powerstation 4.0	4*	8	N/A
PC/NAGWare FTN90	1*	2	N/A

*Denotes the default real type for a particular processor

An even better approach for a large program would be to define the kind parameters within a module and to use that module in each procedure within the program. Then you can change the kind numbers for the entire program by editing a single file.

It is also possible to declare the kind of a real constant. The kind of a real constant is declared by appending an underscore and the kind number to the constant. The following are examples of valid real constants:

```
34.
34._4
34.E3
1234.56789_double
```

The second example is only valid if KIND= 4 is a valid kind of real on the particular processor where the program is being executed. The fourth example is only valid if double is a valid previously defined integer named constant, whose value is a valid kind number. A constant without a kind type identifier is assumed to be of the default kind, which is single precision on most processors.

In addition to the above examples, a double-precision constant in exponential notation can be declared by using a D instead of an E to declare the exponent of the constant. For example:

3.0E0   is a single-precision constant.

3.0D0   is a double-precision constant.

Good Programming Practice

Always assign kind numbers to a named constant and then use that named constant in all type declaration statements and constant declarations. This practice will allow you to port the program to other computers, which may use different kind numbers, with relative ease. For large programs, place the named constants containing the kind parameters in a single module and then use that module in every procedure within the program.

8.1.2 Determining the KIND of a Variable

Fortran 90/95 includes an intrinsic function KIND, which returns the kind number of a given constant or variable. You can use this function to determine the kind numbers in use by your compiler. For example, the program in Figure 8–1 determines the kind numbers associated with single- and double-precision variables on a particular processor.

FIGURE 8–1
Program to determine the kind numbers associated with single- and double-precision real variables on a particular computer system.

```
PROGRAM kinds
!
!   Purpose:
!     To determine the kinds of single and double precision real
!     values on a particular computer.
!
IMPLICIT NONE

! Write out the kinds of single & double precision values
WRITE (*,'(" The KIND for single precision is",I2)') KIND(0.0)
WRITE (*,'(" The KIND for double precision is",I2)') KIND(0.0D0)

END PROGRAM
```

When this program is executed on a Pentium-based PC using the Digital Visual Fortran compiler, the results are

```
C>kinds
The KIND for single precision is 4
The KIND for double precision is 8
```

When the program is executed on a Pentium-based PC using the NAGWare Fortran 90 compiler, the results are

```
C>kinds
The KIND for single precision is 1
The KIND for double precision is 2
```

As you can see, the kind numbers will vary from processor to processor. Try the program on your own computer/compiler and see what values you get.

8.1.3 Selecting Precision in a Processor-Independent Manner

A major problem encountered when porting a Fortran program from one computer to another is the fact that the terms *single precision* and *double precision* are not precisely defined. Double-precision values have approximately twice the precision of single-precision values, but the number of bits associated with each kind of real is entirely up to the computer vendor. On most computers a single-precision value is 32 bits long and a double-precision value is 64 bits long. However, on some computers such as Cray Supercomputers and the 64-bit DEC Alpha chip, single precision is 64 bits long and double precision is 128 bits long. Thus a program that runs properly in single precision on a Cray might need double precision to run properly when it is migrated to a 32-bit computer, and a program that requires double precision for proper operation on a 32-bit computer will only need single precision on a computer based on the 64-bit Alpha chip.

How can we write programs so that they can be easily ported between processors with different word sizes and still function correctly? We can use a Fortran 90/95 intrinsic function to *automatically select the proper kind of real value to use* as the program is moved between computers. This function is called SELECTED_REAL_KIND. When it is executed, it returns the kind number of the smallest type of real value that meets the specified range and precision on that particular processor. The general form of this function is

```
kind_number = SELECTED_REAL_KIND(p=precision,r=range)
```

where *precision* is the number of decimal digits of precision required and *range* is the range of the exponent required in powers of 10. The two arguments *precision* and *range* are called optional arguments; either one or both may be supplied to specify the desired characteristics of the real value. The function returns the kind number of the smallest real kind satisfying the specified requirements. It returns a -1 if the specified precision is not available from any real data type on the processor, a -2 if the specified range is not available from any real data type on the processor, and a -3 if neither is available.

All of the following statements are legal uses of this function:

```
kind_number = SELECTED_REAL_KIND(p=6,r=37)
kind_number = SELECTED_REAL_KIND(p=12)
kind_number = SELECTED_REAL_KIND(r=100)
kind_number = SELECTED_REAL_KIND(13,200)
kind_number = SELECTED_REAL_KIND(13)
kind_number = SELECTED_REAL_KIND(p=17)
```

On a Pentium-based computer using the Digital Visual Fortran compiler, the first function will return a 4 (the kind number for single precision) and the next four functions will return an 8 (the kind number for double precision). The last function will return a -1, since no real data type on an Intel Pentium-based PC has 17 decimal digits of precision. Other processors will return different results; try it on yours and see what you get.

Notice from the preceding example that the p= and r= are optional as long as *precision* and *range* are specified in that order, and the p= is optional if only the precision is specified. These characteristics of optional arguments are explained in Chapter 9.

The function SELECTED_REAL_KIND should be used with a certain amount of caution, since over-specifying your program's requirements can increase the program's size and slow down execution. For example, 32-bit computers have between six and seven decimal digits of precision in their single-precision variables. If you specify a real data type as SELECTED_REAL_KIND(6), then you will get single precision on those machines. However, if you specify a real data type as SELECTED_REAL_KIND(7), then you will get double precision and the program will be both larger and slower. Make sure that you really need that seventh decimal place before you ask for it!

Good Programming Practice

Use the function SELECTED_REAL_KIND to determine the kind numbers of the real variables needed to solve a problem. The function will return the proper kind numbers on any computer, making your programs more portable.

You can also use other intrinsic functions to determine the kind of a real value and the precision and range of the real value on a particular computer. These functions are summarized in Table 8–2. The integer function KIND() returns the kind number of a specified value. The integer function PRECISION() returns the number of decimal digits that can be stored in the real value, and the integer function RANGE() returns the exponent range that can be supported by the real value. The use of these functions is illustrated in the program in Figure 8–2.

8

FIGURE 8–2
Program to illustrate the use of function SELECTED_REAL_KIND() to select desired kinds of real variables in a processor-independent manner and the use of functions KIND(), PRECISION(), and RANGE() to get information about real values.

```
PROGRAM select_kinds
!
!  Purpose:
!    To illustrate the use of SELECTED_REAL_KIND to select
!    desired kinds of real variables in a processor-independent
!    manner.
!
!  Record of revisions:
!      Date        Programmer          Description of change
!      ====        ==========          =====================
!    12/09/95    S. J. Chapman         Original code
!
IMPLICIT NONE

! Declare parameters:
INTEGER, PARAMETER :: single = SELECTED_REAL_KIND(p=6,r=37)
INTEGER, PARAMETER :: double = SELECTED_REAL_KIND(p=13,r=200)

! Declare variables of each type:
REAL(kind=single) :: var1 = 0.
REAL(kind=double) :: var2 = 0._double

! Write characteristics of selected variables.
WRITE (*,100) 'var1', KIND(var1), PRECISION(var1), RANGE(var1)
WRITE (*,100) 'var2', KIND(var2), PRECISION(var2), RANGE(var2)
100 FORMAT(1X,A,': kind = ',I2,', Precision = ',I2,', Range = ',I3)

END PROGRAM
```

▓ **TABLE 8–2**
Common KIND-related intrinsic functions

Function	Description
SELECTED_REAL_KIND(p,r)	Return smallest kind of real value with a minimum of p decimal digits of precision and maximum range $\geq 10^r$.
SELECTED_INT_KIND(r)	Return smallest kind of integer value with a maximum range $\geq 10^r$.
KIND(X)	Return kind number of X, where X is a variable or constant of any intrinsic type.
PRECISION(X)	Return decimal precision of X, where X is a real or complex value.
RANGE(X)	Return the decimal exponent range for X, where X is an integer, real, or complex value.

When this program is executed on a Pentium-based PC using the Lahey Fortran 90 compiler, the results are

```
C>select_kinds
var1: kind = 4, Precision = 6, Range = 37
var2: kind = 8, Precision = 15, Range = 307
```

Note that the program requested 13 decimal digits of precision and a range of 200 powers of 10 for the second variable, but the variable actually assigned by the processor has 15 digits of precision and a range of 308 powers of 10. This type of real variable was the smallest size available on the processor that met or exceeded the request. Try this program on your own computer and see what values you get.

8.1.4 Mixed-Mode Arithmetic

When an arithmetic operation is performed between a double-precision real value and another real or integer value, Fortran converts the other value to double precision and performs the operation in double precision with a double-precision result. However, the automatic mode conversion *does not occur* until the double-precision number and the other number both appear in the same operation. Therefore, a portion of an expression may be evaluated in integer or single-precision real arithmetic, followed by another portion evaluated in double-precision real arithmetic.

For example, suppose that we want to add 1/3 to 1/3 and get the answer to 15 significant digits. We might try to calculate the answer with any of the following expressions:

	Expression	Result
1.	1.D0/3. + 1/3	3.333333333333333E-001
2.	1./3. + 1.D0/3.	6.666666333333333E-001
3.	1.D0/3. + 1./3.D0	6.666666666666666E-001

1. In the first expression, the single-precision constant `3.` is converted to double precision before dividing into the double-precision constant `1.D0`, producing the result `3.33333333333333E-001`. Next, the integer constant `1` is divided by the integer constant `3`, producing an integer `0`. Finally, the integer `0` is converted into double precision and added to first number, producing the final value of `3.33333333333333E-001`.

2. In the second expression, `1./3.` is evaluated in single precision producing the result `3.333333E-01`, and `1./3.D0` is evaluated in double precision, producing the result `3.33333333333333E-01`. Then the single precision result is converted to double precision and added to the double precision result to produce the final value of `6.66666633333333E-001`.

3. In the third expression, both terms are evaluated in double precision, leading to a final value of `6.66666666666666E-001`.

As we can see, adding 1/3 + 1/3 produces significantly different answers depending on the type of numbers used in each part of the expression. The third expression shown above yields the answer that we really wanted, while the first two are inaccurate to a greater or lesser degree. This result should serve as a warning: If you really need double-precision arithmetic, you should be very careful to ensure that *all* intermediate portions of a calculation are performed with double-precision arithmetic and that *all* intermediate results are stored in double-precision variables.

A special case of mixed-mode arithmetic occurs during the initialization of double-precision real variables in type declaration statements and `DATA` statements. If the constant used to initialize the variable is written in single-precision form, then the variable will only be initialized to single-precision accuracy, regardless of the number of significant digits written in the constant.[3] For example, the variable `a1` in the following program is only initialized to seven significant digits even though it is double precision:

```
PROGRAM test_initial
INTEGER, PARAMETER :: db1 = SELECTED_REAL_KIND(p=13)
REAL(KIND=db1) :: a1 = 6.666666666666666
REAL(KIND=db1) :: a2 = 6.666666666666666_db1
WRITE (*,*) a1, a2
END PROGRAM
```

When this program is executed, the result is valid to only seven significant digits:

```
C>test_initial
      6.666666507720947        6.666666666666666
```

 Programming Pitfalls
Always be careful to initialize double-precision real variables with double-precision real constants to preserve the full precision of the constant.

---

[3]FORTRAN 77 behaved differently here—it would permit all the digits of a constant to be used in an initialization statement, even if there were more digits than a single-precision value could support. This difference could cause problems when transporting a FORTRAN 77 program to Fortran 90/95.

8.1.5 Double-Precision Intrinsic Functions

All generic functions that support single-precision real values will also support double-precision real values. If the input value is single precision, then the function will be calculated with a single-precision result. If the input value is double precision, then the function will be calculated with a double-precision result.

One important intrinsic function is DBLE. This function converts any numeric input argument to double precision.

8.1.6 When to Use High-Precision Real Values

We have seen that double-precision real numbers are better than single-precision real numbers, offering more precision and greater range. If they are so good, why bother with single-precision numbers at all? Why don't we just use double-precision numbers all the time?

Programmers have several good reasons for not using double-precision numbers all the time. For one thing, every double-precision number requires twice as much memory as a single-precision number requires. This extra size makes programs using double-precision numbers much larger, and computers with more memory are required to run the programs. Another important consideration is speed. Double-precision calculations are normally *much* slower than single-precision calculations, so computer programs using double-precision calculations run more slowly than computer programs using single-precision calculations.[4] Because of these disadvantages, we should only use the double-precision numbers when they are actually needed.

Double-precision numbers are actually needed in the following situations:

1. *When the dynamic range of the calculation requires numbers whose absolute values are smaller than* 10^{-39} *or larger than* 10^{39}. In this case, the problem either must be rescaled or double-precision variables must be used.
2. *When the problem requires numbers of very different sizes to be added to or subtracted from one another.* If two numbers of very different sizes must be added or subtracted from one another, the resulting calculation will lose a great deal of precision. For example, suppose we wanted to add the number 3.25 to the number 1,000,000.0. In single precision, the result would be 1,000,003.0. In double precision, the result would be 1,000,003.25.
3. *When the problem requires two numbers of very nearly equal size to be subtracted.* When two numbers of very nearly equal size must be subtracted, small errors in the last digits of the answer become greatly exaggerated.

    For example, consider two nearly equal numbers that are the result of a series of single-precision calculations. Because of the round-off error in the calculations,

---

[4]Intel-based PC compatibles (486, Pentium, etc.) with a math coprocessor are an exception to this general rule. The math coprocessor performs hardware calculations with 80-bit accuracy regardless of the precision of the data being processed. As a result, there is little speed penalty for double-precision operations on a PC.

each of the numbers is accurate to 0.0001 percent. The first number a1 should be 1.0000000, but through round-off errors in previous calculations is actually 1.0000010, while the second number a2 should be 1.0000005, but through round-off errors in previous calculations is actually 1.0000000. The difference between these numbers should be

$$\texttt{true\_result} = \texttt{a1} - \texttt{a2} = -0.0000005$$

but the actual difference between them is

$$\texttt{actual\_result} = \texttt{a1} - \texttt{a2} = 0.0000010$$

Therefore, the error in the subtracted number is

$$\% \text{ ERROR} = \frac{\texttt{actual\_result} - \texttt{true\_result}}{\texttt{true\_result}} \times 100\%$$

$$\% \text{ ERROR} = \frac{0.0000010 - (-0.0000005)}{-0.0000005} \times 100\% = -300\%$$

The single-precision math created a 0.001 percent error in a1 and a2, and then the subtraction blew up that error so that it became a 300 percent error in the final answer! When two nearly equal numbers must be subtracted as a part of a calculation, then the entire calculation should be performed in double precision to avoid round-off error problems.

EXAMPLE 8–1 *Numerical Calculation of Derivatives:* The derivative of a function is defined mathematically as

$$\frac{d}{dx} f(x) \lim_{\Delta x \to 0} \frac{f(x + \Delta x) - f(x)}{\Delta x} \qquad (8\text{–}1)$$

The derivative of a function is a measure of the instantaneous slope of the function at the point being examined. In theory, the smaller Δx, the better the estimate of the derivative. However, the calculation can go bad if there is not enough precision to avoid roundoff errors. Note that as Δx gets small, we will be subtracting two numbers which are very nearly equal, and the effects of roundoff errors will be multiplied.

To test the effects of precision on our calculations, we will calculate the derivative of the function

$$f(x) = \frac{1}{x} \qquad (8\text{–}2)$$

for the location $x = 0.15$. This function is shown in Figure 8–3.

SOLUTION From elementary calculus, the derivative of $f(x)$ is

$$\frac{d}{dx} f(x) = \frac{d}{dx} \frac{1}{x} = -\frac{1}{x^2}$$

For $x = 0.15$

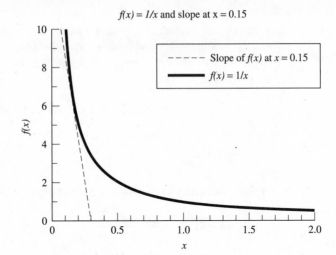

$f(x) = 1/x$ and slope at x = 0.15

FIGURE 8–3
Plot of the function $f(x) = 1/x$, showing the slope at $x = 0.15$

$$\frac{d}{dx} f(x) = -\frac{1}{x^2} = -44.44444444444...$$

We will now attempt to evaluate the derivative of Equation (8–2) for sizes of Δx from 10^{-1} to 10^{-10} using both single- and double-precision mathematics. We will print out the results for each case, together with the true analytical solution and the resulting error.

A Fortran program to evaluate the derivative of Equation (8–2) as shown in Figure 8–4.

FIGURE 8–4
Program to evaluate the derivative of the function $f(x) = 1/x$ at $x = 0.15$, using both single-precision and double-precision arithmetic.

```
PROGRAM diff
!
!   Purpose:
!     To test the effects of finite precision by differentiating
!     a function with 10 different step sizes, with both single
!     precision and double precision. The test will be based on
!     the function F(X) = 1./X.
!
!   Record of revisions:
!       Date         Programmer           Description of change
!       ====         ==========           =====================
!     12/03/95     S. J. Chapman          Original code
!
IMPLICIT NONE
```

(continued)

(concluded)

```
! Declare parameters
INTEGER, PARAMETER :: single = SELECTED_REAL_KIND(p=6,r=37)
INTEGER, PARAMETER :: double = SELECTED_REAL_KIND(p=13)

! List of local variables:
REAL(KIND=double) :: ans           ! True (analytic) answer
REAL(KIND=double) :: d_ans         ! Double-precision answer
REAL(KIND=double) :: d_error       ! Double-precision percent error
REAL(KIND=double) :: d_fx          ! Double precision F(x)
REAL(KIND=double) :: d_fxdx        ! Double precision F(x+dx)
REAL(KIND=double) :: d_dx          ! Step size
REAL(KIND=double) :: d_x =0.15D0   ! Location to evaluate dF(x)/dx
INTEGER :: i                       ! Index variable
REAL(KIND=single) :: s_ans         ! Single-precision answer
REAL(KIND=single) :: s_error       ! Single-precision percent error
REAL(KIND=single) :: s_fx          ! Single precision F(x)
REAL(KIND=single) :: s_fxdx        ! Single precision F(x+dx)
REAL(KIND=single) :: s_dx          ! Step size
REAL(KIND=single) :: s_x =0.15E0   ! Location to evaluate dF(x)/dx

  ! Print headings.
  WRITE (*,1)
  1 FORMAT (1X,'      DX      TRUE ANS      SP ANS          DP  ANS ', &
                   SP ERR   DP   ERR ')

! Calculate analytic solution at x=0.15.
ans = - ( 1.D0 / d_x**2 )

! Calculate answer from definition of differentiation
step_size: DO i = 1, 10

  ! Get delta x.
  s_dx = 1.0 / 10.0**i
  d_dx = 1.D0 / 10.D0**i

  ! Calculate single-precision answer.
  s_fxdx = 1. / (s_x + s_dx )
  s_fx   = 1./ s_x
  s_ans  = ( s_fxdx - s_fx ) / s_dx

  ! Calculate single-precision error, in percent.
  s_error = ( s_ans - REAL(ans) ) / REAL(ans) * 100.

  ! Calculate double-precision answer.
  d_fxdx = 1.D0 / ( d_x + d_dx )
  d_fx   = 1.D0 / d_x
  d_ans  = ( d_fxdx -  d_fx ) /d_dx

  ! Calculate double-precision error, in percent.
  d_error = ( d_ans - ans ) / ans * 100.

  ! Tell user.
  WRITE (*,100) d_dx, ans, s_ans, d_ans, s_error, d_error
  100 FORMAT (1X, ES10.3, F12.7, F12.7, ES22.14, F9.3, F9.3)

END DO step_size

END PROGRAM
```

When this program is compiled and executed using Microsoft Fortran 90 on a PC, the following results are obtained[5]:

```
C>diff
    DX        TRUE ANS      SP ANS        DP ANS                 SP ERR    DP ERR
1.000E-01  -44.4444444  -26.6666600  -2.66666666666667D+01    -40.000   -40.000
1.000E-02  -44.4444444  -41.6666500  -4.16666666666667D+01     -6.250    -6.250
1.000E-03  -44.4444444  -44.1498800  -4.41501103752762D+01      -.663     -.662
1.000E-04  -44.4444444  -44.4126100  -4.44148345547379D+01      -.072     -.067
1.000E-05  -44.4444444  -44.4412200  -4.44414816790584D+01      -007      -.007
1.000E-06  -44.4444444  -44.3458600  -4.44441481501912D+01      -.222     -.001
1.000E-07  -44.4444444  -42.9153400  -4.44441148151035D+01     -3.440      .000
1.000E-08  -44.4444444  -47.6837200  -4.44444414604561D+01      7.288      .000
1.000E-09  -44.4444444    .0000000   -4.44444445690806D+01   -100.000      .000
1.000E-10  -44.4444444    .0000000   -4.44444481217943D+01   -100.000      .000
```

When Δx is fairly large, both the single-precision and double-precision results give essentially the same answer. In that range the accuracy of the result is only limited by the step size. As Δx gets smaller and smaller, the single-precision answer gets better and better until $\Delta x \approx 10^{-5}$. For step sizes smaller than 10^{-5}, round-off errors start to dominate the solution. The double-precision answer gets better and better until $\Delta x \approx 10^{-9}$. For step sizes smaller than 10^{-9}, double-precision round-off errors start to get progressively worse.

In this problem the use of double precision allowed us to improve the quality of our answer from four correct significant digits to eight correct significant digits. The problem also points out the critical importance of a proper Δx size in producing a right answer. Such concerns occur in all computer programs performing scientific and engineering calculations. All such programs contain parameters that *must* be chosen correctly, or round-off errors will result in bad answers. The design of proper algorithms for use on computers is a discipline, known as *numerical analysis*.

8.1.7 Solving Large Systems of Simultaneous Linear Equations

Chapter 6 introduced the method of Gauss-Jordan elimination to solve systems of simultaneous linear equations of the following form:

$$a_{11} x_1 + a_{12} x_2 + \cdots + a_{1n} x_n = b_1$$

$$a_{21} x_1 + a_{22} x_2 + \cdots + a_{2n} x_n = b_2$$

$$\cdots$$

$$a_{n1} x_1 + a_{n2} x_2 + \cdots + a_{nn} x_n = b_n$$

(8–3)

---

[5]To reproduce these results with many compilers, it is necessary to turn off all optimizations. If the optimizer is used, the compilers store intermediate single-precision results as double-precision values in CPU registers, and the calculation is effectively performed in double precision. This practice makes single-precision arithmetic look misleadingly good.

In the Gauss-Jordan method, the first equation in the set is multiplied by a constant and added to all of the other equations in the set to eliminate x_1, and then the process is repeated with the second equation in the set multiplied by a constant and added to all of the other equations in the set to eliminate x_2, and so forth for all the equations. This type of solution is subject to cumulative round-off errors that eventually make the answers unusable. Any round-off errors in eliminating the coefficients of x_1 are propagated into even bigger errors when eliminating the coefficients of x_2, which are propagated into even bigger errors when eliminating the coefficients of x_3, and so on. For a large enough system of equations, the cumulative round-off errors will produce unacceptably bad solutions.

How big must a system of equations be before round-off error makes it impossible to solve them using Gauss-Jordan elimination? There is no easy answer to this question. Some systems of equations are more sensitive to slight round-off errors than others are. To understand this situation, let's look at the two simple sets of simultaneous equations shown in Figure 8–5. Figure 8–5a shows a plot of these two simultaneous equations:

$$3.0x - 2.0y = 3.0$$
$$5.0x + 3.0y = 5.0$$

(8–4)

The solution to this set of equations is $x = 1.0$ and $y = 0.0$. The point $(1.0, 0.0)$ is the intersection of the two lines on the plot in Figure 8–5a. Figure 8–5b shows a plot of these two simultaneous equations:

$$1.00x - 1.00y = -2.00$$
$$1.03x - 0.97y = -2.03$$

(8–5)

The solution to this set of equations is $x = -1.5$ and $y = 0.5$. The point $(-1.5, 0.5)$ is the intersection of the two lines on the plot in Figure 8–5b.

Now let's compare the sensitivity of Equations (8–4) and (8–5) to slight errors in the coefficients of the equations. (A slight error in the coefficients of the equations is similar to the effect of round-off errors on the equations.) Assume that coefficient a_{11} of Equations (8–3) is in error 1 percent so that a_{11} is really 3.03 instead of 3.00. Then the solution to the equations becomes $x = 0.995$ and $y = 0.008$, which is almost the same as the solution to the original equations. Now, let's assume that coefficient a_{11} of Equations (8–4) is in error by 1 percent, so that a_{11} is really 1.01 instead of 1.00. Then the solution to the equations becomes $x = 1.789$ and $y = 0.193$, which is a major shift compared to the previous answer. Equations (8–4) are relatively insensitive to small coefficient errors, while Equations (8–5) are *very* sensitive to small coefficient errors.

If we examine Figure 8–5b closely, we can see why Equations (8–5) are so sensitive to small changes in coefficients. The lines representing the two equations are almost parallel to each other, so a tiny change in one of the equations moves their intersection point by a very large distance. If the two lines had been exactly parallel to each other, then the system of equations would have had either no solutions or an infinite number of solutions. In the case where the lines are nearly parallel, there is a single unique solution, but its location is very sensitive to slight changes in the coef-

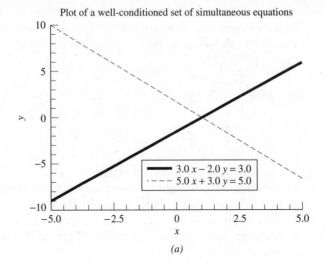

(a)

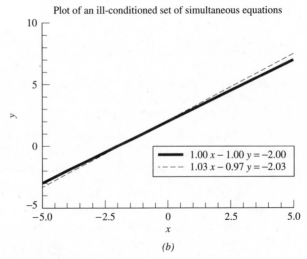

(b)

FIGURE 8–5
(a) Plot of a well-conditioned 2 × 2 set of equations.
(b) Plot of an ill-conditioned 2 × 2 set of equations.

ficients. Therefore, systems like Equations (8–5) will be very sensitive to accumulated round-off noise during Gauss-Jordan elimination.

Systems of simultaneous equations that behave well, such as Equations 8–4, are called **well-conditioned systems,** and systems of simultaneous equations that behave poorly, such as Equations 8–5, are called **ill-conditioned systems.** Well-conditioned systems of equations are relatively immune to round-off error, while ill-conditioned systems are very sensitive to round-off error.

When working with very large systems of equations or ill-conditioned systems of equations, it is helpful to work in double-precision arithmetic. Double-precision arithmetic dramatically reduces round-off errors, allowing Gauss-Jordan elimination to produce correct answers even for difficult systems of equations.

EXAMPLE 8–2 Solving Large Systems of Linear Equations: For large and/or ill-conditions systems of equations, Gauss-Jordan elimination will produce a correct answer only if double-precision arithmetic is used to reduce round-off error. Write a subroutine that uses double-precision arithmetic to solve a system of simultaneous linear equations. Test your subroutine by comparing it to the single-precision subroutine `simul` created in Chapter 6. Compare the two subroutines on both well-defined and ill-defined systems of equations.

SOLUTION The double-precision subroutine `dsimul` will be essentially the same as the single-precision subroutine `simul2` in Figure 6–12 that we developed in Chapter 6. Subroutine `simul2`, which is renamed `simul` here, is used as the starting point because that version includes both the use of array operations and automatic arrays for simplicity and flexibility. In addition, it does not destroy its input data.

1. **State the problem.**

   Write a subroutine to solve a system of N simultaneous equations in N unknowns using Gauss-Jordan elimination, double-precision arithmetic, and the maximum-pivot technique to avoid round-off errors. The subroutine must be able to detect singular sets of equations and set an error flag if they occur.

2. **Define the inputs and outputs.**

   The input to the subroutine consists of an N × N double-precision matrix a, with the coefficients of the variables in the simultaneous equations, and a double-precision vector b, with the contents of the right sides of the equations. The outputs from the subroutine are the solutions to the set of equations (in vector `soln`) and an error flag.

3. **Describe the algorithm.**

   The pseudocode for this subroutine is the same as the pseudocode for subroutine `simul2` in Chapter 6 and is not repeated here.

4. **Turn the algorithm into Fortran statements.**

   The resulting Fortran subroutine is shown in Figure 8–6.

FIGURE 8–6
Subroutine to solve a system of simultaneous equations in double precision.

```
SUBROUTINE dsimul ( a, b, soln, ndim, n, error )
!
! Purpose:
!    Subroutine to solve a set of N linear equations in N
!    unknowns, using Gauss-Jordan elimination and the maximum-
!    pivot technique. This version of simul has been
```

(continued)

(continued)

```
!     modified to use array sections and automatic arrays.
!     It uses double-precision arithmetic to avoid
!     cumulative round-off errors. It DOES NOT DESTROY the
!     original input values.
!
!   Record of revisions:
!      Date        Programmer        Description of change
!      ====        ==========        =====================
!     10/16/95    S. J. Chapman      Original code
! 1. 03/02/95    S. J. Chapman      Add automatic arrays
! 2. 05/08/96    S. J. Chapman      Double precision
!
IMPLICIT NONE

! Declare parameters
INTEGER, PARAMETER :: db1 = SELECTED_REAL_KIND(p=13)

! Declare calling arguments:
INTEGER, INTENT(IN) :: ndim                 ! Dimension of arrays a and b
REAL (KIND=db1), INTENT(IN), DIMENSION(ndim,ndim) :: a
                                            ! Array of coefficients (N x N)
                                            ! This array is of size ndim  x
                                            ! ndim, but only N x N of the
                                            ! coefficients are being used
REAL (KIND=db1), INTENT(IN), DIMENSION(ndim) :: b
                                            ! Input: Right side of eqns
REAL (KIND=db1), INTENT(OUT), DIMENSION(ndim) :: soln
                                            ! Output: Solution vector
INTEGER, INTENT(IN) :: n                    ! Number of equations to solve
INTEGER, INTENT(OUT) :: error               ! Error flag:
                                            ! 0 — No error
                                            ! 1 — Singular equations


! Declare local parameters
REAL (KIND=db1), PARAMETER :: epsilon = 1.0E-12
                                            ! A "small" number for comparison
                                            ! when determining singular eqns


! Declare local variables:
REAL (KIND=db1), DIMENSION(n,n) :: a1       ! Copy of "a" that will be
                                            ! destroyed during the solution
REAL (KIND=db1) :: factor                   ! Factor to multiply eqn irow by
                                            ! before adding to eqn jrow
INTEGER :: irow                             ! Number of the equation
                                            ! currently being processed
INTEGER :: ipeak                            ! Pointer to equation containing
                                            ! maximum-pivot value
INTEGER :: jrow                             ! Number of the equation compared
                                            ! to the current equation
REAL (KIND=db1) :: temp                     ! Scratch value
REAL (KIND=db1),DIMENSION(n) :: temp1       ! Scratch array

! Make copies of arrays "a" and "b" for local use
a1 = a(1:n,1:n)
soln = b(1:n)

! Process N times to get all equations . . .
mainloop: DO irow = 1, n

   ! Find peak pivot for column irow in rows irow to N
```

(continued)

(concluded)

```
      ipeak = irow
      max_pivot: DO jrow = irow+1, n
         IF (ABS(a1(jrow,irow)) > ABS(a1(ipeak,irow))) THEN
            ipeak = jrow
         END IF
      END DO max_pivot

      ! Check for singular equations.
      singular: IF ( ABS(a1(ipeak,irow)) < epsilon ) THEN
         error = 1
         RETURN
      END IF singular

      ! Otherwise, if ipeak /=  irow, swap equations irow & ipeak
      swap_eqn: IF ( ipeak /=  irow ) THEN
         temp1 = a1(ipeak,1:n)
         a1(ipeak,1:n) = a1(irow,1:n)        ! Swap rows in a
         a1(irow,1:n) = temp1
         temp = soln(ipeak)
         soln(ipeak) = soln(irow)            ! Swap rows in b
         soln(irow) = temp
      END IF swap_eqn

      ! Multiply equation irow by -a1(jrow,irow)/a1(irow,irow),
      ! and add it to Eqn jrow (for all eqns except irow itself).
      eliminate: DO jrow = 1, n
         IF ( jrow /=  irow ) THEN
            factor = -a1(jrow,irow)/a1(irow,irow)
            a1(jrow,1:n) = a1(irow,1:n)*factor + a1(jrow,1:n)
            soln(jrow) = soln(irow)*factor + soln(jrow)
         END IF
      END DO eliminate
   END DO mainloop

   ! End of main loop over all equations. All off-diagonal
   ! terms are now zero. To get the final answer, we must
   ! divide each equation by the coefficient of its on-diagonal
   ! term.
   divide: DO irow = 1, n
      soln(irow) = soln(irow) / a1(irow,irow)
   END DO divide

   ! Set error flag to 0 and return.
   error = 0

   END SUBROUTINE dsimul
```

5. **Test the resulting Fortran programs.**

To test this subroutine, we will write a driver program. The driver program will open an input data file to read the equations to be solved. The first line of the file will contain the number of equations N in the system, and each of the next N lines will contain the coefficients of one of the equations. The coefficients will be stored in a single-precision array and sent to subroutine simul for solution; they will also be stored in a double-precision array and sent to subroutine dsimul for solution. To verify that the solutions are correct, they will be plugged back into the original equations, and the resulting errors will be calculated. The solutions and errors for single-precision and double-precision arithmetic will be displayed in a summary table.

The test driver program for subroutine dsimul is shown in Figure 8–7. Note that it uses allocatable arrays throughout, so it will work with input data sets of any size.

FIGURE 8–7
Test driver program for subroutine dsimul.

```
PROGRAM test_dsimul
!
!  Purpose:
!    To test subroutine dsimul, which solves a set of N linear
!    equations in N unknowns.  This test driver calls subroutine
!    simul to solve the problem in single precision and for subrou-
!    tine dsimul to solve the problem in double precision. The
!    results of the two solutions together with their errors are
!    displayed in a summary table.
!
!  Record of revisions:
!      Date        Programmer          Description of change
!      ====        ==========          =====================
!    05/08/96     S. J. Chapman        Original code
!
IMPLICIT NONE

! Declare parameters
INTEGER, PARAMETER :: sgl = SELECTED_REAL_KIND(p=6)     ! Single
INTEGER, PARAMETER :: dbl = SELECTED_REAL_KIND(p=13)   ! Double

! List of local variables
REAL(KIND=sgl), ALLOCATABLE, DIMENSION(:,:) :: a
                                   ! Single-precision coefficients
REAL(KIND=sgl), ALLOCATABLE, DIMENSION(:) :: b
                                   ! Single-precision constant values
REAL(KIND=sgl), ALLOCATABLE, DIMENSION(:) :: soln
                                   ! Single-precision solution
REAL(KIND=sgl), ALLOCATABLE, DIMENSION(:) :: error
                                   ! Array of single-precision errors
REAL(KIND=sgl) :: serror_max       ! Max single-precision error
REAL(KIND=dbl), ALLOCATABLE, DIMENSION(:,:) :: da
                                   ! Double-precision coefficients
REAL(KIND=dbl), ALLOCATABLE, DIMENSION(:) :: db
                                   ! Double-precision constant values
REAL(KIND=dbl), ALLOCATABLE, DIMENSION(:) :: dsoln
                                   ! Double-precision solution
REAL(KIND=dbl), ALLOCATABLE, DIMENSION(:) :: derror
                                   ! Array of double-precision errors
REAL(KIND=dbl) :: derror_max       ! Max double-precision error
INTEGER :: error_flag              ! Error flag from subroutines
INTEGER :: i, j                    ! Loop index
INTEGER :: istat                   ! I/O status
INTEGER :: n                       ! Size of system of eqns to solve
CHARACTER(len=20) :: filename      ! Input data file name

! Get the name of the disk file containing the equations.
```

(continued)

(continued)

```
WRITE (*,*) 'Enter the file name containing the eqns: '
READ (*,'(A20)') filename

! Open input data file.  Status is OLD because the input data must
! already exist.
OPEN ( UNIT=1, FILE=filename, STATUS='OLD', ACTION='READ', &
       IOSTAT=istat )

! Was   the OPEN successful?
open_ok: IF ( istat == 0 ) THEN

   ! The file was opened successfully, so read the number of
   ! equations in the system.
   READ (1,*) n

   ! Allocate memory for that number of equations
   ALLOCATE ( a(n,n), b(n), soln(n), serror(n), &
              da(n,n), db(n), dsoln(n), derror(n), STAT=istat )

   ! If the memory is available, read in equations and
   ! process them.
   solve: IF ( istat == 0 ) THEN

      DO i = 1, n
         READ (1,*) (da(i,j), j=1,n), db(i)
      END DO

      ! Copy the coefficients in single precision for the
      ! single-precision solution.
      a = da
      b = db

      ! Display coefficients.
      WRITE (*,1010)
      1010 FORMAT (/,1X,'Coefficients:')
      DO i = 1, n
         WRITE (*,'(1X,7F11.4)') (a(i,j), j=1,n), b(i)
      END DO

      ! Solve equations.
      CALL simul  (a, b, soln, n, n, error_flag )
      CALL dsimul (da, db, dsoln, n, n, error_flag )

      ! Check for error.
      error_check: IF ( error_flag /= 0 ) THEN
         WRITE (*,1020)
         1020 FORMAT (/1X, 'Zero pivot encountered!', &
              //1X, 'There is no unique solution to this system.')

      ELSE error_check

         ! No errors. Check for round-off errors by substituting the answers in
         ! the original equations and calculating the differences.
         serror_max = 0.
         derror_max = 0._dbl
         serror = 0.
         derror = 0._dbl
         DO i = 1, n
            serror(i) = SUM ( a(i,:) * soln(:) ) - b(i)
            derror(i) = SUM ( da(i,:) * dsoln(:) ) - db(i)
```

(concluded)

```
                END DO
                serror_max = MAXVAL ( ABS ( serror ) )
                derror_max = MAXVAL ( ABS ( derror ) )

                ! Tell user about it.
                WRITE (*,1030)
                1030 FORMAT (/1X, ' i       SP x(i)        DP x(i) ', &
                      '        SP Err         DP Err ')
                WRITE (*,1040)
                1040 FORMAT ( 1X,' ===    =========     =========', &
                      '     ========     ========')
                DO i = 1, n
                   WRITE (*,1050) i, soln(i), dsoln(i), serror(i), derror(i)
                   1050 FORMAT (1X, I3, 2X, G15.6, G15.6, F15.8, F15.8)
                END DO

                ! Write maximum errors.
                WRITE (*,1060) serror_max, derror_max
                1060 FORMAT (/,1X,'Max single-precision error:',F15.8, &
                        /,1X,'Max double-precision error:',F15.8)

             END IF error_check
          END IF solve

          ! Deallocate dynamic memory
          DEALLOCATE ( a, b, soln, serror, da, db, dsoln, derror )
       ELSE open_ok
          ! Else file open failed.  Tell user.
          WRITE (*,1070) istat
          1070 FORMAT (1X, 'File open failed--status = ', I6)
       END IF open_ok

    END PROGRAM
```

To test the subroutine, we will call it with three different data sets. The first should be a well-conditioned system of equations, the second should be an ill-conditions system of equations, and the third should have no unique solution. The first system of equations that we will use to test the subroutine is the 6 × 6 system of equations shown here:

$$
\begin{aligned}
-2.0\,X_1 + 5.0\,X_2 + 1.0\,X_3 + 3.0\,X_4 + 4.0\,X_5 - 1.0\,X_6 &= 0.0 \\
2.0\,X_1 - 1.0\,X_2 - 5.0\,X_3 - 2.0\,X_4 + 6.0\,X_5 + 4.0\,X_6 &= 1.0 \\
-1.0\,X_1 + 6.0\,X_2 - 4.0\,X_3 - 5.0\,X_4 + 3.0\,X_5 - 1.0\,X_6 &= -6.0 \\
4.0\,X_1 + 3.0\,X_2 - 6.0\,X_3 - 5.0\,X_4 - 2.0\,X_5 - 2.0\,X_6 &= 10.0 \\
-3.0\,X_1 + 6.0\,X_2 + 4.0\,X_3 + 2.0\,X_4 - 6.0\,X_5 + 4.0\,X_6 &= -6.0 \\
2.0\,X_1 + 4.0\,X_2 + 4.0\,X_3 + 4.0\,X_4 + 5.0\,X_5 - 4.0\,X_6 &= -2.0
\end{aligned}
$$

(8–6)

If this system of equations is placed in a file called SYS6.WEL and program test_dsimul is run on this file, the results are

```
C>test_dsimul
Enter the file name containing the eqns:
sys6.wel

Coefficients before calls:
    -2.0000     5.0000     1.0000     3.0000     4.0000    -1.0000      .0000
     2.0000    -1.0000    -5.0000    -2.0000     6.0000     4.0000     1.0000
    -1.0000     6.0000    -4.0000    -5.0000     3.0000    -1.0000    -6.0000
```

```
        4.0000      3.0000     -6.0000     -5.0000    -2.0000    -2.0000    10.0000
       -3.0000      6.0000      4.0000      2.0000    -6.0000     4.0000    -6.0000
        2.0000      4.0000      4.0000      4.0000     5.0000    -4.0000    -2.0000
```

i	SP x(i)	DP x(i)	SP Err	DP Err
===	=========	=========	=======	========
1	.662556	.662556	00000173	.00000000
2	-.132567	-.132567	00000072	.00000000
3	-3.01373	-3.01373	.00000286	.00000000
4	2.83548	2.83548	.00000191	.00000000
5	-1.08520	1.08520	-.00000095	.00000000
6	-.836043	-.836043	-.00000119	.00000000

```
Max single-precision error:      .00000286
Max double-precision error:      .00000000
```

For this well-conditioned system, the results of single-precision and double-precision calculations were essentially identical. The second system of equations that we will use to test the subroutine is the following 6×6 system of equations. Note that the second and sixth equations are almost identical, so this system is ill-conditioned.

$$-2.0 \ X_1 + 5.0 \ X_2 \qquad + 1.0 \ X_3 + 3.0 \ X_4 + 4.0 \ X_5 - 1.0 \ X_6 = \quad 0.0$$
$$2.0 \ X_1 - 1.0 \ X_2 \qquad - 5.0 \ X_3 - 2.0 \ X_4 + 6.0 \ X_5 + 4.0 \ X_6 = \quad 1.0$$
$$-1.0 \ X_1 + 6.0 \ X_2 \qquad - 4.0 \ X_3 - 5.0 \ X_4 + 3.0 \ X_5 - 1.0 \ X_6 = -6.0 \qquad (8\text{--}7)$$
$$4.0 \ X_1 + 3.0 \ X_2 \qquad - 6.0 \ X_3 - 5.0 \ X_4 - 2.0 \ X_5 - 2.0 \ X_6 = 10.0$$
$$-3.0 \ X_1 + 6.0 \ X_2 \qquad + 4.0 \ X_3 + 2.0 \ X_4 - 6.0 \ X_5 + 4.0 \ X_6 = -6.0$$
$$2.0 \ X_1 - 1.00001 \ X_2 \ - 5.0 \ X_3 - 2.0 \ X_4 + 6.0 \ X_5 + 4.0 \ X_6 = \quad 1.0001$$

If this system of equations is placed in a file called SYS6.ILL and program test_dsimul is run on this file, the results are[6]

```
C>test_dsimul
Enter the file name containing the eqns:
sys6.ill

Coefficients before calls:
       -2.0000      5.0000      1.0000      3.0000     4.0000    -1.0000     .0000
        2.0000     -1.0000     -5.0000     -2.0000     6.0000     4.0000    1.0000
       -1.0000      6.0000     -4.0000     -5.0000     3.0000    -1.0000   -6.0000
        4.0000      3.0000     -6.0000     -5.0000    -2.0000    -2.0000   10.0000
       -3.0000      6.0000      4.0000      2.0000    -6.0000     4.0000   -6.0000
        2.0000     -1.0000     -5.0000     -2.0000     6.0000     4.0000    1.0000
```

i	SP x(i)	DP x(i)	SP Err	DP Err
===	=========	=========	=======	========
1	-44.1711	-38.5295	2.83736500	.00000000
2	-11.1934	-10.0000	-3.96770900	.00000000
3	-52.9274	-47.1544	-2.92594100	.00000000
4	29.8776	26.1372	-4.72323000	.00000000

---

[6]To reproduce these results with the Lahey Fortran 90 compiler, it is necessary to compile the program with the -o0 option, which turns off all optimizations. If the optimizer is used, the Lahey compiler stores intermediate single-precision results as double precision values in CPU registers, and the calculation is effectively performed in double precision. This practice makes single-precision arithmetic look misleadingly good.

8

```
5         -17.9852        -15.8502         4.52078600       .00000000
6         -5.69733        -5.08561         3.96770200       .00000000
```

```
Max single-precision error:      4.72323000
Max double-precision error:       .00000000
```

For this ill-conditioned system, the results of the single-precision and double-precision calculations were dramatically different. The single precision numbers $x(i)$ differ from the true answers by almost 20 percent, while the double-precision answers are almost exactly correct. Double-precision calculations are essential for a correct answer to this problem! The third system of equations that we will use to test the subroutine is the following 6×6 system of equations:

$$
\begin{aligned}
-2.0\ X_1 + 5.0\ X_2 + 1.0\ X_3 + 3.0\ X_4 + 4.0\ X_5 - 1.0\ X_6 &= 0.0 \\
2.0\ X_1 - 1.0\ X_2 - 5.0\ X_3 - 2.0\ X_4 + 6.0\ X_5 + 4.0\ X_6 &= 1.0 \\
-1.0\ X_1 + 6.0\ X_2 - 4.0\ X_3 - 5.0\ X_4 + 3.0\ X_5 - 1.0\ X_6 &= -6.0 \\
4.0\ X_1 + 3.0\ X_2 - 6.0\ X_3 - 5.0\ X_4 - 2.0\ X_5 - 2.0\ X_6 &= 10.0 \\
-3.0\ X_1 + 6.0\ X_2 + 4.0\ X_3 + 2.0\ X_4 - 6.0\ X_5 + 4.0\ X_6 &= -6.0 \\
2.0\ X_1 - 1.0\ X_2 - 5.0\ X_3 - 2.0\ X_4 + 6.0\ X_5 + 4.0\ X_6 &= 1.0
\end{aligned}
\tag{8--8}
$$

If this system of equations is placed in a file called SYS6.SNG and program test_dsimul is run on this file, the results are

```
C>test_dsimul
Enter the file name containing the eqns:
sys6.sng
```

```
Coefficients before calls:
  -2.0000     5.0000     1.0000     3.0000     4.0000    -1.0000      .0000
   2.0000    -1.0000    -5.0000    -2.0000     6.0000     4.0000     1.0000
  -1.0000     6.0000    -4.0000    -5.0000     3.0000    -1.0000    -6.0000
   4.0000     3.0000    -6.0000    -5.0000    -2.0000    -2.0000    10.0000
  -3.0000     6.0000     4.0000     2.0000    -6.0000     4.0000    -6.0000
   2.0000    -1.0000    -5.0000    -2.0000     6.0000     4.0000     1.0000
```

```
Zero pivot encountered!
```

```
There is no unique solution to this system.
```

Since the second and sixth equations of this set are identical, there is no unique solution to this system of equations. The subroutine correctly identified and flagged this situation.

Subroutine dsimul seems to be working correctly for all three cases: well-conditioned systems, ill-conditioned systems, and singular systems. Furthermore, these tests showed the clear advantage of the double-precision subroutine over the single-precision subroutine for ill-conditioned systems.

■ 8.2

ALTERNATIVE LENGTHS OF THE INTEGER DATA TYPE

The Fortran 90/95 standard also allows (but does not require) a Fortran compiler to support integers of multiple lengths. The reason for having integers of different lengths is that shorter integers could be used for variables that have a restricted range in order to reduce the size of a program, while longer integers could be used for variables that needed the extra range.

The lengths of supported integers will vary from processor to processor, and the kind type parameters associated with a given length will also vary. You will have to check with your compiler vendor to see what lengths your compiler supports. The lengths and kind type parameters of integers supported by several processors are shown in Table 8–3. (In the table, int8 is an 8-bit integer, int16 is a 16-bit integer, etc.) Both the lengths of integers supported and the kind type parameters assigned to them differ from processor to processor. This variation creates a problem when we want to write programs that are portable across different types of processors.

How can we write programs so that they can be easily ported between processors with different kind numbers and still function correctly? The best approach is to use a Fortran 90/95 intrinsic function to *automatically select the proper kind of integer to use* as the program is moved from processor to processor. This function is called `SELECTED_INT_KIND`. When it is executed, it returns the kind type parameter of the smallest kind of integer value that meets the specified range on that particular computer. The general form of this function is

$$kind\_number = SELECTED\_INT\_KIND(range)$$

where `range` is the required range of the integer in powers of 10. The function returns the kind number of the smallest integer kind satisfying the specified requirements. It returns a -1 if the specified range is not available from any integer data type on the processor.

The following examples are legal uses of this function

```
kind_number = SELECTED_INT_KIND(3)
kind_number = SELECTED_INT_KIND(9)
kind_number = SELECTED_INT_KIND(12)
```

On an Pentium-based computer using the Microsoft Fortran Powerstation 4.0 compiler, the first function will return a 2 (the kind number for 2-byte integers), since the specified range is -10^3 to $+10^3$ and a 2-byte integer can hold any number in the range $-32,768$ to $32,767$. Similarly, the second function will return a 4 (the kind number for 4-byte integers), since the specified range is -10^9 to $+10^9$ and a 4-byte integer can hold any number in the range $-2,147,483,648$ to $2,147,483,647$. The last

TABLE 8–3

KIND numbers for integer values in some Fortran 90 compilers

Computer/compiler	int8	int16	int32	int48	int64
Cray T90 Supercomputer / CF90	N/A	N/A	1, 2, 4	6*	8
DEC / DEC Fortran 90	1	2	4*	N/A	8
PC / Lahey Fortran 90	1	2	4*	N/A	N/A
PC / Microsoft Powerstation 4.0	1	2	4*	N/A	N/A
PC / NAGWare FTN90	1	2	3*	N/A	N/A

*Denotes the **default integer** type for a particular processor.

function will return a -1, since no integer data type has a range of -10^{12} to $+10^{12}$. Different results will be returned on other processors; try it on yours and see what you get.

Good Programming Practice

Use the function SELECTED_INT_KIND to determine the kind numbers of the integer variables needed to solve a problem. The function will return the proper kind numbers on any processor, making your programs more portable.

8.3

ALTERNATIVE KINDS OF THE CHARACTER DATA TYPE

Fortran 90/95 also includes a provision for supporting multiple kinds of character sets. Support for multiple character sets is optional and may not be implemented on your processor. If present, this feature allows the Fortran language to support different character sets for the many different languages found around the world, or even special "languages" such as musical notation.

The general form of a character declaration with a kind parameter is

```
CHARACTER(kind=kind_num,len=length) :: string
```

where *kind_num* is the kind number of the desired character set.

The most common use of alternate character sets is likely to be to support the 2-byte character sets required by many Oriental languages such as Chinese and Japanese. You may check your compiler's documentation to see if it supports this feature.

8.4

THE COMPLEX DATA TYPE

Complex numbers occur in many problems in science and engineering. For example, complex numbers are used in electrical engineering to represent alternating current voltages, currents, and impedances. The differential equations that describe the behavior of most electrical and mechanical systems also give rise to complex numbers. Because they are so ubiquitous, it is impossible to work as an engineer without a good understanding of the use and manipulation of complex numbers.

A complex number has the general form

$$c = a + bi \tag{8-9}$$

where c is a complex number, a and b are both real numbers, and i is $\sqrt{-1}$. The number a is called the *real part* and b is called the *imaginary part* of the complex number c. Since a complex number has two components, it can be plotted as a point on a plane (see Figure 8–8). The horizontal axis of the plane is the real axis, and the vertical axis of the plane is the imaginary axis; therefore, any complex number $a + bi$ can be represented as a single point a units along the real axis and b units along the imaginary axis. A complex number represented this way is said to be in *rectangular coordinates,* since the real and imaginary axes define the sides of a rectangle.

A complex number can also be represented as a vector of length z and angle θ pointing from the origin of the plane to the point P (see Figure 8–9). A complex number represented this way is said to be in *polar coordinates.*

$$c = a + bi = z \angle \theta$$

The relationships among the rectangular and polar coordinate terms a, b, z, and θ are

$$a = z \cos \theta \tag{8–10}$$

$$b = z \sin \theta \tag{8–11}$$

$$z = \sqrt{a^2 + b^2} \tag{8–12}$$

$$\theta = \tan^{-1} \frac{b}{a} \tag{8–13}$$

Fortran uses rectangular coordinates to represent complex numbers. Each complex number consists of a pair of real numbers (a,b) occupying successive locations in memory. The first number (a) is the real part of the complex number, and the second number (b) is the imaginary part of the complex number.

If complex numbers c_1 and c_2 are defined as $c_1 = a_1 + b_1 i$ and $c_2 = a_2 + b_2 i$, then the addition, subtraction, multiplication, and division of c_1 and c_2 are defined as follows.

$$c_1 + c_2 = (a_1 + a_2) + (b_1 + b_2)i \tag{8–14}$$

$$c_1 - c_2 = (a_1 - a_2) + (b_1 - b_2)i \tag{8–15}$$

$$c_1 \times c_2 = (a_1 a_2 - b_1 b_2) + (a_1 b_2 + b_1 a_2)i \tag{8–16}$$

$$\frac{c_1}{c_2} = \frac{a_1 a_2 + b_1 b_2}{a_2^2 + b_2^2} + \frac{b_1 a_2 - a_1 b_2}{a_2^2 + b_2^2}i \tag{8–17}$$

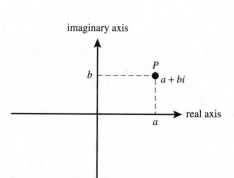

FIGURE 8–8
Representing a complex number in rectangular coordinates.

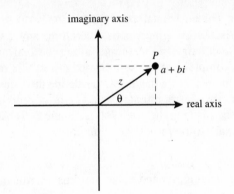

imaginary axis

real axis

FIGURE 8–9
Representing a complex number in polar coordinates.

When two complex numbers appear in a binary operation, Fortran performs the required additions, subtractions, multiplications, or divisions between the two complex numbers using the preceding formulas.

8.4.1 Complex Constants and Variables

A **complex constant** consists of two numeric constants separated by commas and enclosed in parentheses. The first constant is the real part of the complex number, and the second constant is the imaginary part of the complex number. For example, the following complex constants are equivalent to the complex numbers shown next to them:

`(1., 0.)`	$1 + 0i$
`(0.7071,0.7071)`	$0.7071 + 0.7071i$
`(0, -1)`	$-i$
`(1.01E6, 0.5E2)`	$1010000 + 50i$
`(1.12_db1, 0.1_db1)`	$1.12 + 0.1i$ (Kind is db1)

The last constant will be valid only if db1 is a named constant that has been set to a valid kind number for real data on the particular processor where the constant is used.

A complex variable is declared using a COMPLEX type declaration statement. The form of this statement is

```
COMPLEX(KIND=kind_num) :: var1, var2, etc.
```

The kind of the complex variable is optional; if it is left out, the default kind will be used. For example, the following statement declares a 256-element complex array. Remember that we are actually allocating 512 default-length values, since two real values are required for each complex number.

```
COMPLEX, DIMENSION(256) :: array
```

Any processor has at least two kinds of complex values, corresponding to the single-precision and double-precision kinds of real data. The single-precision version of the complex data type will have the same kind number as the single-precision version of the real data type, and the double-precision version of the complex data type will have the same kind number as the double-precision version of the real data type. Therefore, the intrinsic function SELECTED_REAL_KIND can also be used to specify the size of complex data in a processor-independent manner.

The **default complex** kind will always be the same as the default real kind on any given processor.

8.4.2 Initializing Complex Variables

Like other variables, complex variables may be initialized by assignment statements, in type declaration statements, or by READ statements. The following code initializes all of the elements of array array1 to (0.,0.), using an assignment statement:

```
COMPLEX, DIMENSION(256) :: array1
array1 = (0.,0.)
```

A complex number may also be initialized in a type declaration statement using a complex constant. The following code declares and initializes variable a1 to (3.141592,-3.141592), using a type declaration statement:

```
COMPLEX :: a1 = (3.141592, −3.141592)
```

When a complex number is read or written with a formatted I/O statement, the first format descriptor encountered is used for the real part of the complex number; the second format descriptor encountered is used for the imaginary part of the complex number. The following code initializes variable a1, using a formatted READ statement:

```
COMPLEX :: a1
READ (*,'(2F10.2)') a1
```

The value in the first 10 characters of the input line will be placed in the real part of variable a1, and the value in the second 10 characters of the input line will be placed in the imaginary part of variable a1. Note that no parentheses are included on the input line when we read a complex number using formatted I/O. In contrast, when we read a complex number with a *list-directed* I/O statement, the complex number must be typed exactly like a complex constant, parentheses and all. The following READ statement

```
COMPLEX :: a1
READ (*,*) a1
```

requires that the input value be typed as shown: (1.0,0.25). When a complex number is written with a free-format WRITE statement, it is output as a complex value complete with parentheses. For example, the statements

```
COMPLEX :: a1 = (1.0,0.25)
WRITE (*,*) a1
```

produce this result:

```
(1.000000,2.500000E-01)
```

8.4.3 Mixed-Mode Arithmetic

When an arithmetic operation is performed between a complex number and another number (any kind of real or integer), Fortran converts the other number into a complex number and then performs the operation, with a complex result. For example, the following code will produce an output of (300.,-300.):

```
COMPLEX :: c1 = (100.,-100.), c2
INTEGER :: i = 3
c2 = c1 * i
WRITE (*,*) c2
```

Initially, c1 is a complex variable containing the value (100.,-100.), and i is an integer containing the value 3. When the fourth line is executed, the integer i is converted into the complex number (3.,0.) and that number is multiplied by c1 to give the result (300.,-300.).

When an arithmetic operation is performed between two complex or real numbers of different kinds, both numbers are converted into the kind having the higher decimal precision before the operation. The resulting value will have the higher precision.

If a real expression is assigned to a complex variable, the value of the expression is placed in the real part of the complex variable and the imaginary part of the complex variable is set to zero. If two real values need to be assigned to the real and imaginary parts of a complex variable, then the CMPLX function (described in section 8.4.5) must be used. When a complex value is assigned to a real or integer variable, the real part of the complex number is placed in the variable and the imaginary part is discarded.

8.4.4 Using Complex Numbers with Relational Operators

It is possible to compare two complex numbers with the $==$ relational operator to see if they are equal to each other and to compare them with the $/=$ operator to see if they are not equal to each other. However, they cannot be compared with the $>$, $<$, $>=$, or $<=$ operators. The reason is that complex numbers consist of two separate parts. Suppose that we have two complex numbers $c_1 = a_1 + b_1 i$ and $c_2 = a_2 + b_2 i$, with $a_1 > a_2$ and $b_1 < b_2$. How can we possibly say which of these numbers is larger?

On the other hand, it is possible to compare the *magnitudes* of two complex numbers. The magnitude of a complex number can be calculated with the CABS intrinsic function (see section 8.4.5) or directly from Equation 8–12.

$$|c| = \sqrt{a^2 + b^2} \tag{8–12}$$

Since the magnitude of a complex number is a real value, two magnitudes can be compared with any of the relational operators.

8.4.5 COMPLEX Intrinsic Functions

Fortran includes many specific and generic functions that support complex calculations. These functions fall into three general categories:

1. **Type conversion functions.** These functions convert data to and from the complex data type. Function `CMPLX(a,b,kind)` is a generic function that converts real or integer numbers a and b into a complex number whose real part has value a and whose imaginary part has value b. The kind parameter is optional; if it is specified, then the resulting complex number will be of the specified kind. Functions `REAL()` and `INT()` convert the real part of a complex number into the corresponding real or integer data type and throw away the imaginary part of the complex number. Function `AIMAG()` converts the imaginary part of a complex number into a real number.

2. **Absolute value function.** This function calculates the absolute value of a number. Function `CABS(c)` is a specific function that calculates the absolute value of a complex number using the equation

$$CABS(c) = \sqrt{a^2 + b^2}$$

where $c = a + bi$.

3. **Mathematical functions.** These functions include exponential functions, logarithms, trigonometric functions, and square roots. The generic functions `SIN`, `COS`, `LOG10`, `SQRT`, etc. will work as well with complex data as they will with real data.

Some of the intrinsic functions that support complex numbers are listed in Table 8–4.

We must be careful when converting a complex number to a real number. If we use the `REAL()` or `DBLE()` functions to do the conversion, only the *real* portion of the complex number is translated. In many cases, what we really want is the *magnitude* of the complex number. If so, we must use `CABS()` instead of `REAL()` to do the conversion.

> ***Programming Pitfalls***
> Be careful when converting a complex number into a real number. Find out whether the real part of the number or the magnitude of the number is needed and then use the proper function to do the conversion.

We must be careful when using double-precision variables with the function `CMPLX`. The Fortran standard states that the function `CMPLX` returns a result of the default complex kind regardless of its input arguments unless another kind is explicitly specified. This standard can lead to a trap in which a programmer accidentally loses precision without being aware of it. Consider the following code in which we declare two double-precision real variables and a double-precision complex variable and then try to assign the contents of the two real variables to the complex variable. Because the kind is not specified in the `CMPLX` function, the accuracy of the information in the complex variable is reduced to single precision.

```
PROGRAM test_cmplx
INTEGER, PARAMETER :: dbl = SELECTED_REAL_KIND(p=13)
COMPLEX(KIND=dbl) :: c1 = (0.,0.)
REAL(KIND=dbl) :: a1 = 3.333333333333333_dbl
REAL(KIND=dbl) :: b1 = 6.666666666666666_dbl
```

TABLE 8–4
Some intrinsic functions that support complex numbers

Generic function	Specific function	Function value	Comments
ABS(c)	CABS(c)	$\sqrt{a^2 + b^2}$	Calculates magnitude of a complex number. (The result is a real value of the same kind as *c*.)
CMPLX(a,b,*kind*)			Combines *a* and *b* into a complex number $a + bi$. (*a*, *b* may be integer, real, or double precision.) *kind* is an optional integer. If present, it specifies the kind of the resulting complex number. If not specified, the kind will be default complex.
	CONJG(c)	c^*	Calculates the complex conjugate of *c*. If $c = a + bi$, then $c^* = a - bi$.
DBLE(c)			Converts real part of *c* into a double-precision real number.
INT(c)			Converts real part of *c* into an integer.
REAL(c,*kind*)			Converts real part of *c* into a real number. *kind* is an optional integer. If present, it specifies the kind of the resulting real number.

```
c1 = CMPLX(a1,b1)
WRITE (*,*) c1
END PROGRAM
```

When this program is executed, the result is accurate only to single precision:

```
C>test_cmplx
     (3.333333253860474,6.666666507720947)
```

To get the desired result, the CMPLX function must be rewritten with the kind of the result specified:

```
c1 = CMPLX(a1,b1,dbl)
```

Programming Pitfalls
Be careful to specify the output kind type parameter when using the CMPLX function with double-precision values. Failure to do so can produce mysterious losses of precision within a program.

EXAMPLE 8–3 ***The Quadratic Equation (Revisited):*** Write a general program to solve for the roots of a quadratic equation, regardless of type. Use complex variables so that no branches will be required based on the value of the discriminant.

SOLUTION

1. State the problem.

Write a program that will solve for the roots of a quadratic equation, whether they are distinct real roots, repeated real roots, or complex roots, without requiring tests on the value of the discriminant.

2. Define the inputs and outputs.

The inputs required by this program are the coefficients a, b, and c of the quadratic equation

$$ax^2 + bx + c = 0 \qquad\qquad (3\text{–}1)$$

The output from the program will be the roots of the quadratic equation, whether they are real, repeated, or complex.

3. Describe the algorithm.

This task can be broken down into three major sections, whose functions are input, processing, and output:

```
Read the input data
Calculate the roots
Write out the roots
```

We will now break each of the above major sections into smaller, more detailed pieces. In this algorithm, the value of the discriminant is unimportant in determining how to proceed. The resulting pseudocode follows.

```
Write 'Enter the coefficients A, B, and C: '
Read in a, b, c
discriminant ← CMPLX( b**2 - 4.*a*c, 0. )
x1 ← ( -b + SQRT(discriminant) ) / ( 2. * a )
x2 ← ( -b - SQRT(discriminant) ) / ( 2. * a )
Write 'The roots of this equation are: '
Write 'x1 = ', REAL(x1), ' +i ', AIMAG(x1)
Write 'x2 = ', REAL(x2), ' +i ', AIMAG(x2)
```

4. Turn the algorithm into Fortran statements.

The final Fortran code is shown in Figure 8–10.

FIGURE 8–10

A program to solve the quadratic equation using complex numbers.

```
PROGRAM roots_2
!
!  Purpose:
!    To find the roots of a quadratic equation
!       A * X**2 + B * X + C = 0.
!    using complex numbers to eliminate the need to branch
!    based on the value of the discriminant.
!
!  Record of revisions:
```

(continued)

(concluded)

```
!          Date        Programmer            Description of change
!          ====        ==========            =====================
!          12/23/95    S. J. Chapman         Original code
!
IMPLICIT NONE

! List of variables:
REAL :: a                    ! The coefficient of X**2
REAL :: b                    ! The coefficient of X
REAL :: c                    ! The constant coefficient
REAL :: discriminant         ! The discriminant of the quadratic eqn
COMPLEX :: x1                ! First solution to the equation
COMPLEX :: x2                ! Second solution to the equation

! Get the coefficients.
WRITE (*,1000)
1000 FORMAT (' Program to solve for the roots of a quadratic',&
        /, ' equation of the form A * X**2 + B * X + C = 0. ' )
WRITE (*,1005)
1005 FORMAT (' Enter the coefficients A, B, and C: ')
READ (*,*) a, b, c
! Calculate the discriminant
discriminant = b**2 - 4. * a * c

! Calculate the roots of the equation
x1 = ( -b + SQRT( CMPLX(discriminant,0.) ) ) ) / (2. * a)
x2 = ( -b - SQRT( CMPLX(discriminant,0.) ) ) ) / (2. * a)

! Tell user.
WRITE (*,*) 'The roots are: '
WRITE (*,100) '   x1 = '  REAL(x1), ' + i ', AIMAG(x1)
WRITE (*,100) '   x2 = ', REAL(x2), ' + i ', AIMAG(x2)
100 FORMAT (A,F10.4,A,F10.4)

END PROGRAM roots_2
```

5. Test the program.

Next, we must test the program using real input data. We will test cases in which the discriminant is greater than, less than, and equal to zero to be certain that the program is working properly under all circumstances. From Equation (3–1), we can verify the solutions to the following equations:

$$x^2 + 5x + 6 = 0 \qquad x = -2 \text{ and } x = -3$$

$$x^2 + 4x + 4 = 0 \qquad x = -2$$

$$x^2 + 2x + 5 = 0 \qquad x = -1 \pm 2i$$

When the above coefficients are fed into the program, the results are

```
C>roots_2
Program to solve for the roots of a quadratic
equation of the form A * X**2 + B * X + C.
Enter the coefficients A, B, and C:
1,5,6
```

```
The roots are:
   x1 =      -2.0000 + i          .0000
   x2 =      -3.0000 + i          .0000

C>roots_2
Program to solve for the roots of a quadratic
equation of the form A * X**2 + B * X + C.
Enter the coefficients A, B, and C:
1,4,4
The roots are:
   X1 =      -2.0000 + i          .0000
   X2 =      -2.0000 + i          .0000

C>roots_2
Program to solve for the roots of a quadratic
equation of the form A * X**2 + B * X + C.
Enter the coefficients A, B, and C:
1,2,5
The roots are:
   X1 =      -1.0000 + i         2.0000
   X2 =      -1.0000 + i        -2.0000
```

The program gives the correct answers for our test data in all three possible cases. Note how much simpler this program is compared to the quadratic root solver found in Example 3–1. The use of the complex data type has greatly simplified our program.

Quiz 8–1

This quiz provides a quick check to see if you understand the concepts introduced in sections 8.1 through 8.4. If you have trouble with the quiz, reread the sections, ask your instructor, or discuss the material with a fellow student. The answers to this quiz are found in the back of the book.

1. What kinds of real numbers and integers are supported by your compiler? What are the kind numbers associated with each one?

2. What will be written out by the following code?

```
COMPLEX :: a, b, c, d
a = ( 1., -1. )
b = ( -1., -1. )
c = ( 10., 1. )
d = ( a + b ) / c
WRITE (*,*) d
```

3. Use the definitions in Equations (8–14) through (8–17) to write a computer program that evaluates d in the preceding problem *without using complex numbers*. How much harder is it to evaluate this expression without the benefit of complex numbers?

■ 8.5

DERIVED DATA TYPES

So far, we have studied Fortran's **intrinsic data types:** integer, real, complex, logical, and character. In addition to these data types, the Fortran language permits us to create our own data types to add new features to the language or to help us solve specific classes of problems. A user-defined data type may have any number and combination of components, but each component must be either an intrinsic data type or a user-defined data type that was previously defined. User-defined data types are called **derived data types** because ultimately they must be derived from intrinsic data types.

Basically, a derived data type is a convenient way to group together all the information about a particular item. Like an array, a single derived data type can have many components. Unlike an array, the components of a derived data type may have different types. One component may be an integer while the next component is a real, the next a character string, and so forth. Furthermore, each component is known by a name instead of a number.

A derived data type is defined by a sequence of type declaration statements beginning with a TYPE statement and ending with an END TYPE statement. Between these two statements are the definitions of the components in the derived data type. The form of a derived data type is

```
TYPE [::] type_name
   component definitions
   ...
END TYPE [type_name]
```

where the double colons and the name on the END TYPE statement are optional. A derived data type can have as many component definitions as desired.

To illustrate the use of a derived data type, let's suppose that we were writing a grading program. The program would contain information about the students in a class, such as name, social security number, age, and sex. We could define a special data type called `person` to contain all the personal information about each person in the program. For example:

```
TYPE :: person
   CHARACTER(len=14) :: first_name
   CHARACTER :: middle_initial
   CHARACTER(len=14) :: last_name
   CHARACTER(len=14) :: phone
   INTEGER :: age
   CHARACTER :: sex
   CHARACTER(len=11) :: ssn
END TYPE person
```

Once the derived type `person` is defined, variables of that type may be declared as shown:

```
TYPE (person) :: john, jane
TYPE (person), DIMENSION(100) :: people
```

The latter statement declares an array of 100 variables of type `person`. Each item of a derived data type is known as a **structure.**

It is also possible to create unnamed constants of a derived data type. To do so, we use a **structure constructor.** A structure constructor consists of the name of the type followed by the components of the derived data type in parentheses. The components appear in the order in which they were declared in the definition of the derived type. For example, the variables `john` and `jane` could be initialized by constants of type `person` as follows:

```
john = person('John','R','Jones','323-6439',21,'M','123-45-6789')
jane = person('Jane','C','Bass', '332-3060',17,'F','999-99-9999')
```

A derived data type may be used as a component within another derived data type. For example, a grading program could include a derived data type called `grade_info` containing a component of the type `person` defined above to contain personal information about the students in the class. The next example defines the derived type `grade_info` and declares an array `class` to be 30 variables of this type.

```
TYPE :: grade_info
    TYPE (person) :: student
    INTEGER :: num_quizzes
    REAL, DIMENSION(10) :: quiz_grades
    INTEGER :: num_exams
    REAL, DIMENSION(10) :: exam_grades
    INTEGER :: final_exam_grade
    REAL :: average
END TYPE
TYPE (grade_info), DIMENSION(30) :: class
```

8.5.1 Working with Derived Data Types

Each component in a variable of a derived data type can be addressed independently and can be used just like any other variable of the same type. If the component is an integer, then it can be used just like any other integer, and so forth. A component is specified by a **component selector,** which consists of the name of the variable followed by a percent sign (`%`) and followed by the component name. For example, the following statement sets the component `age` of variable `john` to 35:

```
john%age = 35
```

To address a component within an array of a derived data type, *place the array subscript after the array name and before the percent sign.* For example, to set the final exam grade for student 5 in array `class` defined in section 8.5, we would write:

```
class(5)%final_exam_grade = 95
```

To address a component of a derived data type that is included within another derived data type, we simply concatenate their names separated by percent signs. Thus we could set the age of student 5 within the class with the statement:

```
class(5)%student%age = 23
```

As you can see, working with the components of a variable of a derived data type is easy. However, it is *not* easy to work with variables of derived data types as a whole.

It is legal to assign one variable of a given type to another variable of the same type, but that is almost the only operation that is defined. Other intrinsic operations such as addition, subtraction, multiplication, division, and comparison are not defined by default for these variables. You will learn how to extend these operations to work properly with derived data types in Chapter 9.

8.5.2 Input and Output of Derived Data Types

If a variable of a derived data type is included in a WRITE statement, the components of the variable are written out in the order in which they are declared in the type definition. If the WRITE statement uses formatted I/O, then the format descriptors must match the type and order of the components in the variable.

Similarly, if a variable of a derived data type is included in a READ statement, then the input data must be supplied in the order in which the components are declared in the type definition. If the READ statement uses formatted I/O, then the format descriptors must match the type and order of the components in the variable.

The program shown in Figure 8–11 illustrates the output of a variable of type person using both formatted and free-format I/O.

FIGURE 8–11
A program to illustrate output of variables of derived data types.

```
PROGRAM test_io
!
!  Purpose:
!    To illustrate I/O of variables of derived data types.
!
!  Record of revisions:
!      Date          Programmer           Description of change
!      ====          ==========           =====================
!    12/23/95      S. J. Chapman          Original code
!
IMPLICIT NONE

! Declare type person
TYPE :: person
   CHARACTER(len=14) :: first_name
   CHARACTER :: middle_initial
   CHARACTER(len=14) :: last_name
   CHARACTER(len=14) :: phone
   INTEGER :: age
   CHARACTER :: sex
   CHARACTER(len=11) :: ssn
END TYPE person

! Declare a variable of type person
TYPE (person) :: john

! Initialize variable
john = person('John','R','Jones','323-6439',21,'M','123-45-6789')
```

(continued)

(concluded)

```
! Output variable using free-format I/O
write (*,*) 'Free format: ', john

! Output variable using formatted I/O
write (*,1000) john
1000 FORMAT (' Formatted I/O:',/,4(1X,A,/),1X,I4,/,1X,A,/,1X,A)

END PROGRAM
```

When this program is executed, the results are

```
C>test_io
Free format: John      RJones      323-6439      21M123-45-6789

Formatted I/O:
John
R
Jones
323-6439
  21
M
123-45-6789
```

8.5.3 Declaring Derived Data Types in Modules

As we have seen, the definition of a derived data type can be fairly bulky. This definition must be included in every procedure that uses variables or constants of the derived type, which can present a painful maintenance problem in large programs. To avoid this problem, it is customary to define all derived data types in a program in a single module and then to use that module in all procedures needing to use the data type. This practice is illustrated in Example 8–4 below.

Good Programming Practice
For large programs using derived data types, declare the definitions of each data type in a module and then use that module in each procedure of the program that needs to access the derived data type.

EXAMPLE 8–4 Sorting Derived Data Types by Components: To illustrate the use of derived data types, we will create a small database program that permits us to read in a database of customer names and addresses and to sort and display the addresses by last name, city, or ZIP code.

SOLUTION To solve this problem, we will create a simple derived data type containing the personal information about each customer in the database and then initialize the customer database from a disk file. Once the database is initialized, we will prompt the user for the desired display order and sort the data into that order.

1. **State the problem.**

Write a program to read a database of customers from a data file and to sort and display that database in alphabetical order by last name, city, or ZIP code.

2. **Define the inputs and outputs.**

The inputs to the program are the name of the customer database file, the customer database file itself, and an input value from the user specifying the order in which the data is to be sorted. The output from the program is the customer list sorted in alphabetical order by the selected field.

3. **Describe the algorithm.**

The first step in writing this program will be to create a derived data type to hold all the information about each customer. This data type will need to be placed in a module so that each procedure in the program can use it. An appropriate data type definition is

```
TYPE :: personal_info
    CHARACTER(len=12) :: first        ! First name
    CHARACTER         :: mi           ! Middle initial
    CHARACTER(len=12) :: last         ! Last name
    CHARACTER(len=26) :: street       ! Street Address
    CHARACTER(len=12) :: city         ! City
    CHARACTER(len=2)  :: state        ! State
    INTEGER           :: zip          ! Zip code
END TYPE personal_info
```

The program can logically be broken into two sections: a main program that reads and writes the customer database and a separate procedure that sorts the data into the selected order. The top-level pseudocode for the main program is

```
Get name of customer data file
Read customer data file
Prompt for sort order
Sort data in specified order
Write out sorted customer data
```

Now we must expand and refine the pseudocode for the main program. We must describe how the data will be read in, how the sort order is selected, and how the sorting is done in more detail. A detailed version of the pseudocode for the main program follows.

```
Prompt user for the input file name "filename"
Read the file name "filename"
OPEN file "filename"
IF OPEN is successful THEN
    WHILE
        Read value into temp
        IF read not successful EXIT
        nvals ← nvals + 1
        customers(nvals) ← temp
    End of WHILE
```

```
      Prompt user for type of sort (1=last name;2=city;3=zip)
      Read choice
      SELECT CASE (choice)
      CASE (1)
         Call sort_database with last_name comparison function
      CASE (2)
         Call sort_database with city comparison function
      CASE (3)
         Call sort_database with zip code comparison function
      CASE DEFAULT
         Tell user of illegal choice
      END of SELECT CASE

      Write out sorted customer data
   END of IF
```

The sorting procedure will be a selection sort similar to any of the sorting routines that we have already encountered in Chapters 5, 6, and 7. The one tricky thing about this particular sorting process is that we do not know in advance what component of the data type we will be sorting on. Sometimes we will be sorting on the last name, while other times we will be sorting on the city or ZIP code. We must do something to make the sort procedure work properly regardless of the component of the data that we are sorting on.

The easiest way to handle this problem is to write a series of functions that compare individual components of two different variables of the data type to determine the lesser of the two. One function will compare two last names to determine which is the lesser (lower in alphabetical order), while another function will compare two city names to determine which is the lesser (lower in alphabetical order), and a third will compare two ZIP codes to determine which is the lesser (lower in numerical sequence). Once the comparison functions are written, we will be able to sort the data in any order by passing the appropriate comparison function to the sorting subroutine as a command-line argument.

The pseudocode for the last name comparison routine is

```
      LOGICAL FUNCTION lt_last (a, b)
      lt_lastname ← LLT(a%last,b%last)
```

Note that the routine uses the LLT function to ensure that the sorting order is the same on all computers regardless of collating sequence. The pseudocode for the city comparison routine is

```
      LOGICAL FUNCTION lt_city (a, b)
      lt_lastname ← LLT(a%city, b%city)
```

Finally, the pseudocode for the ZIP code comparison routine is

```
      LOGICAL FUNCTION lt_zip (a, b)
      lt_zip ← a%zip < b%zip
```

The pseudocode for the sorting routine will be the same as the pseudocode for subroutine sort in Chapter 6, except that the comparison function will be passed as a command-line argument. It is not reproduced here.

4. Turn the algorithm into Fortran statements.

The resulting Fortran subroutine is shown in Figure 8–12.

FIGURE 8–12

Program to sort a customer database according to a user-specified field.

```
MODULE types
!
!   Purpose:
!     To define the derived data type used for the customer
!     database.
!
!   Record of revisions:
!       Date        Programmer          Description of change
!       ====        ==========          =====================
!     12/27/95    S. J. Chapman         Original code
!
IMPLICIT NONE

! Declare type personal_info
TYPE :: personal_info
    CHARACTER(len=12) :: first      ! First name
    CHARACTER         :: mi         ! Middle Initial
    CHARACTER(len=12) :: last       ! Last name
    CHARACTER(len=26) :: street     ! Street Address
    CHARACTER(len=12) :: city       ! City
    CHARACTER(len=2)  :: state      ! State
    INTEGER           :: zip        ! Zip code
END TYPE personal_info

END MODULE types

PROGRAM customer_database
!
!   Purpose:
!     To read in a character input data set, sort it into ascending
!     order using the selection sort algorithm, and write the
!     sorted data to the standard output device.  This program calls
!     subroutine "sort_database" to do the actual sorting.
!
!   Record of revisions:
!       Date        Programmer          Description of change
!       ====        ==========          =====================
!     12/27/95    S. J. Chapman         Original code
!
USE types                           ! Declare the module types
IMPLICIT NONE

! List of parameters:
INTEGER, PARAMETER :: max_size = 100  ! Max addresses in database
! List of external functions:
LOGICAL, EXTERNAL :: lt_last        ! Comparison fn for last names
LOGICAL, EXTERNAL :: lt_city        ! Comparison fn for cities
LOGICAL, EXTERNAL :: lt_zip         ! Comparison fn for zip codes

! List of variables:
TYPE(personal_info), DIMENSION (max_size) :: customers
                                    ! Data array to sort
INTEGER :: choice                   ! Choice of how to sort database
LOGICAL :: exceed = .FALSE.         ! Logical indicating that array
```

(continued)

(continued)

```
                                            !      limits are exceeded
CHARACTER(len=20) :: filename    ! Input data file name
INTEGER :: i                     ! Loop index
INTEGER :: nvals = 0             ! Number of data values to sort
INTEGER :: status               ! I/O status: 0 for success
TYPE(personal_info) :: temp     ! Temporary variable for reading

! Get the name of the file containing the input data.
WRITE (*,*) 'Enter the file name with customer database: '
READ (*,'(A20)') filename

! Open input data file.  Status is OLD because the input data must
! already exist.
OPEN ( UNIT=9, FILE=filename, STATUS='OLD', IOSTAT=status )

! Was the OPEN successful?
fileopen: IF ( status == 0 ) THEN        ! Open successful

   ! The file was opened successfully, so read the customer
   ! database from it.
   DO
      READ (9, 1010, IOSTAT=status) temp    ! Get value
      1010 FORMAT (A12,1X,A1,1X,A12,1X,A26,1X,A12,1X,A2,1X,I5)
      IF ( status /= 0 ) EXIT               ! Exit on end of data
      nvals = nvals + 1                     ! Bump count
      size: IF ( nvals <= max_size ) THEN   ! Too many values?
         customers(nvals) = temp            ! No: Save value in array
      ELSE
         exceed = .TRUE.                    ! Yes: Array overflow
      END IF size
   END DO

   ! Was the array size exceeded?  If so, tell user and quit.
   toobig: IF ( exceed ) THEN
      WRITE (*,1020) nvals, max_size
      1020 FORMAT (' Maximum array size exceeded: ', I6, ' > ', I6 )
   ELSE

      ! Limit not exceeded: find out how to sort data.
      WRITE (*,1030)
      1030 FORMAT (1X,'Enter way to sort database:',/, &
                   1X,' 1 -- By last name ',/, &
                   1X,' 2 -- By city ',/, &
                   1X,' 3 -- By zip code ')
      READ (*,*) choice

      ! Sort database
      SELECT CASE ( choice )
      CASE (1)
         CALL sort_database (customers, nvals, lt_last )
      CASE (2)
         CALL sort_database (customers, nvals, lt_city)
      CASE (3)
         CALL sort_database (customers, nvals, lt_zip)
      CASE DEFAULT
         WRITE (*,*) 'Invalid choice entered!'
      END SELECT

      ! Now write out the sorted data.
```

(continued)

(continued)

```
         WRITE (*,'(A)') ' The sorted database values are: '
         WRITE (*,1040) ( customers(i), i = 1, nvals )
         1040 FORMAT (1X,A12,1X,A1,1X,A12,1X,A26,1X,A12,1X,A2,1X,I5)

      END IF toobig

   ELSE fileopen

      ! Status /= 0, so an open error occurred.
      WRITE (*,'(A,I6)') ' File open error: IOSTAT=', status

   END IF fileopen

   END PROGRAM

   SUBROUTINE sort_database (array, n, lt_fun )
   !
   !   Purpose:
   !     To sort array "array" into ascending order using a selection
   !     sort, where "array" is an array of the derived data type
   !     "personal_info".  The sort is based on the external
   !     comparison function "lt_fun", which will differ depending on
   !     which component of the derived type array is used for
   !     comparison.
   !
   !   Record of revisions:
   !      Date          Programmer          Description of change
   !      ====          ==========          =====================
   !    12/27/95    S. J. Chapman          Original code
   !
   USE types                               ! Declare the module types
   IMPLICIT NONE

   ! Declare calling parameters:
   INTEGER, INTENT(IN) :: n                         ! Number of values
   TYPE(personal_info), DIMENSION(n), INTENT(INOUT) :: array
                                           ! Array to be sorted
   LOGICAL, EXTERNAL :: lt_fun                   ! Comparison function

   ! Declare local variables:
   INTEGER :: i                    ! Loop index
   INTEGER :: iptr                 ! Pointer to smallest value
   INTEGER :: j                    ! Loop index
   TYPE(personal_info) :: temp     ! Temp variable for swaps

   ! Sort the array
   outer: DO i = 1, n-1
      ! Find the minimum value in array(i) through array(n)
      iptr = i
      inner: DO j = i+1, n
         minval: IF ( lt_fun(array(J),array(iptr)) ) THEN
            iptr = j
         END IF minval
      END DO inner

      ! iptr now points to the minimum value, so swap array(iptr)
      ! with array(i) if i /= iptr.
      swap: IF ( i /= iptr ) THEN
         temp        = array(i)
```

(continued)

(concluded)

```
        array(i)    = array(iptr)
        array(iptr) = temp
   END IF swap

END DO outer
END SUBROUTINE sort_database

LOGICAL FUNCTION lt_last (a, b)
!
!  Purpose:
!    To compare variables "a" and "b" and determine which
!    has the smaller last name (lower alphabetical order).
!
USE types                    ! Declare the module types
IMPLICIT NONE

! Declare calling arguments
TYPE (personal_info), INTENT(IN) :: a, b

! Make comparison.
lt_last = LLT ( a%last, b%last )

END FUNCTION lt_last

LOGICAL FUNCTION lt_city (a, b)
!
!  Purpose:
!    To compare variables "a" and "b" and determine which
!    has the smaller city (lower alphabetical order).
!
USE types                    ! Declare the module types
IMPLICIT NONE

! Declare calling arguments
TYPE (personal_info), INTENT(IN) :: a, b

! Make comparison.
lt_city = LLT ( a%city, b%city )

END FUNCTION lt_city

LOGICAL FUNCTION lt_zip (a, b)
!
!  Purpose:
!    To compare variables "a" and "b" and determine which
!    has the smaller zip code (lower numerical value).
!
USE types                    ! Declare the module types
IMPLICIT NONE

! Declare calling arguments
TYPE (personal_info), INTENT(IN) :: a, b

! Make comparison.
lt_zip = a%zip < b%zip

END FUNCTION lt_zip
```

5. Test the resulting Fortran programs.

To test this program, we need to create a sample customer database. A simple customer database is shown in Figure 8–13; it is stored in the disk in a file called database.

FIGURE 8–13
Sample customer database used to test the program of Example 8–4.

```
John        Q Public      123 Sesame Street    Anywhere       NY 10035
James       R Johnson     Rt. 5 Box 207C       West Monroe    LA 71291
Joseph      P Ziskend     P. O. Box 433        APO            AP 96555
Andrew      D Jackson     Jackson Square       New Orleans    LA 70003
Jane        X Doe         12 Lakeside Drive    Glenview       IL 60025
Colin       A Jeffries    11 Main Street       Chicago        IL 60003
```

To test the program, we will execute it three times using this database, once with each possible sorting option.

```
C>customer_database
Enter the file name with customer database:
database
Enter way to sort database:
  1 -- By last name
  2 -- By city
  3 -- By zip code
1
The sorted database values are:
Jane        X Doe         12 Lakeside Drive    Glenview       IL 60025
Andrew      D Jackson     Jackson Square       New Orleans    LA 70003
Colin       A Jeffries    11 Main Street       Chicago        IL 60003
James       R Johnson     Rt. 5 Box 207C       West Monro     LA 71291
John        Q Public      123 Sesame Street    Anywhere       NY 10035
Joseph      P Ziskend     P. O. Box 433        APO            AP 96555

C>customer_database
Enter the file name with customer database:
database
Enter way to sort database:
  1 -- By last name
  2 -- By city
  3 -- By zip code
2
The sorted database values are:
Joseph      P Ziskend     P. O. Box 433        APO            AP 96555
John        Q Public      123 Sesame Street    Anywhere       NY 10035
Colin       A Jeffries    11 Main Street       Chicago        IL 60003
Jane        X Doe         12 Lakeside Drive    Glenview       IL 60025
Andrew      D Jackson     Jackson Square       New Orleans    LA 70003
James       R Johnson     Rt. 5 Box 207C       West Monroe    LA 71291

C>customer_database
Enter the file name with customer database:
database
Enter way to sort database:
  1 -- By last name
  2 -- By city
  3 -- By zip code
3
The sorted database values are:
```

(continued)

(concluded)

```
John      Q Public         123 Sesame Street    Anywhere     NY 10035
Colin     A Jeffries       11 Main Street       Chicago      IL 60003
Jane      X Doe            12 Lakeside Drive    Glenview     IL 60025
Andrew    D Jackson        Jackson Square       New Orleans  LA 70003
James     R Johnson        Rt. 5 Box 207C       West Monroe  LA 71291
Joseph    P Ziskend        P. O. Box 433        APO          AP 96555
```

Note that the program is working correctly with one minor exception. When it sorted the data by city, it got APO and Anywhere out of order. Can you tell why this happened? You will be asked to rewrite this program to eliminate the problem in Exercise 8–12.

Memory Allocation for Derived Data Types

When a Fortran compiler allocates memory for a variable of a derived data type, the compiler is *not* required to allocate the elements of the derived data type in successive memory locations. Instead, it is free to place them anywhere it wants, as long as the proper element order is preserved during I/O operations. This freedom was deliberately built into the Fortran 90 and 95 standards to allow compilers on massively parallel computers to optimize memory allocations for the fastest possible performance.

However, a strict order of memory allocations is sometimes important. For example, if we want to pass a variable of a derived data type to a procedure written in another language, it is necessary for the elements of that variable to be in strict order.

If the elements of a derived data type must be allocated in consecutive memory locations for some reason, the type definition must include a special SEQUENCE statement. An example of a derived data type whose elements will always be declared in consecutive locations in memory is

```
TYPE :: vector
   SEQUENCE
   REAL :: a
   REAL :: b
   REAL :: c
END TYPE
```

8

Quiz 8–2

This quiz provides a quick check to see if you understand the concepts introduced in section 8.5. If you have trouble with the quiz, reread the sections, ask your instructor, or discuss the material with a fellow student. The answers to this quiz are found in the back of the book.

For questions 1 to 6, assume these derived data types:

```
TYPE :: position
   REAL :: x
   REAL :: y
   REAL :: z
END TYPE position
TYPE :: time
```

(continued)

(concluded)

```
                INTEGER :: second
                INTEGER :: minute
                INTEGER :: hour
                INTEGER :: day
                INTEGER :: month
                INTEGER :: year
        END TYPE time
        TYPE :: plot
            TYPE (time) :: plot_time
            TYPE (position) :: plot_position
        END TYPE
        TYPE (plot), DIMENSION(10) :: points
```

1. Write the Fortran statements to print out the date associated with the seventh plot point in format DD/MM/YYYY HH:MM:SS.

2. Write the Fortran statements to print out the position associated with the seventh plot point.

3. Write the Fortran statements required to calculate the rate of motion between the second and third plot points. You will have to calculate the difference in position and the difference in time between the two points. The rate of motion will be $\dfrac{\Delta pos}{\Delta time}$.

For questions 4 to 6, state whether the statement(s) are valid. If the statements are valid, describe what they do.

4. `WRITE (*,*) points(1)`

5. `WRITE (*,1000) points(4)`
   `1000 FORMAT (1X,3ES12.6, 6I6 )`

6. `dpos = points(2).plot_position - points(1).plot_position`

8.6

SUMMARY

This chapter introduced the concept of kinds and kind type parameters. *Kinds* are versions of the same basic data type, each differing in size, precision, range, etc.

All Fortran compilers support at least two kinds of real data, which are usually known as single precision and double precision. Double-precision data occupies twice the memory of single-precision data on most computers. Double-precision variables have both a greater range and more significant digits than single-precision variables have.

The choice of precision for a particular real value is specified by the kind type parameter in the type declaration statement. Unfortunately, the numbers associated with each kind of real value vary for different processors. The numbers can be determined by using the KIND intrinsic function on a particular processor, or the desired precision can be specified in a processor-independent manner using the SELECTED_REAL_KIND intrinsic function.

Double-precision real numbers take up more space and require more computer time to calculate than single-precision real numbers do and should not be used indiscriminately. In general, double-precision real numbers should be used when

1. A problem requires many significant digits or a large range of numbers.
2. Numbers of dramatically different sizes must be added or subtracted.
3. Two nearly equal numbers must be subtracted, and the result used in further calculations.

Fortran 90/95 permits (but does not require) a compiler to support multiple kinds of integers. Not all compilers will support multiple kinds of integers. The kind numbers associated with particular integer lengths vary from processor to processor. Fortran includes an intrinsic function SELECTED_INT_KIND to help programmers select the kind of integer required for a particular application in a processor-independent manner.

Fortran 90/95 also allows a compiler to support multiple kinds of character sets. If your compiler implements this feature, you can use it to write out character data in different languages.

Complex numbers consist of two real numbers in successive locations in memory. These two numbers are treated as though they were the real and imaginary parts of a complex number expressed in rectangular coordinates. They are processed according to the rules for complex addition, subtraction, multiplication, division, etc. There is a kind of complex number corresponding to each kind of real number available on a particular processor. The kind numbers are identical for real and complex data, so the desired precision of a complex value may be selected using the SELECTED_REAL_KIND intrinsic function.

Complex constants are written as two numbers in parentheses, separated by commas (e.g., (1.,-1.)). Complex variables are declared using a COMPLEX type declaration statement. They may be read or written using any type of real format descriptor (E, ES, F, etc.). When reading or writing complex numbers, the real and imaginary parts of the number are processed separately. The first value read will become the real part, and the next value will become the imaginary part. If list-directed input is used with complex numbers, the input value must be typed as a complex constant, complete with parentheses.

In a binary operation involving a complex number and an integer or real number, the other number is first converted to complex, and then the operation is performed using complex arithmetic. All arithmetic is performed at the highest precision of any number in the calculation.

Derived data types are data types defined by the programmer for use in solving a particular problem. They may contain any number of components, and each component may be of any intrinsic data type or any previously defined derived data type. Derived data types are defined using a TYPE ... END TYPE construct, and variables of that type are declared using a TYPE statement. Constants of a derived data type may be constructed using structure constructors. A variable or constant of a derived data type is called a structure.

The components of a variable of a derived data type may be used in a program just like any other variables of the same type. They are addressed by naming both the variable and the component separated by a percent sign (e.g., `student%age`). Variables of a derived data type may not be used with any Fortran intrinsic operations except for assignment. Addition, subtraction, multiplication, division, etc. are undefined for these variables. They may be used in I/O statements.

You will learn how to extend intrinsic operations to variables of a derived data type in Chapter 9.

8.6.1 Summary of Good Programming Practice

The following guidelines should be adhered to when working with parameterized variables, complex numbers, and derived data types:

1. Always assign kind numbers to a named constant and then use that named constant in all type declaration statements and constant declarations. For large programs with many procedures, place the kind parameters in a single module and then use that module in every procedure within the program.
2. Use the function `SELECTED_REAL_KIND` to determine the kind numbers of the real values needed to solve a problem. The function will return the proper kind numbers on any processor, making your programs more portable.
3. Use the function `SELECTED_INT_KIND` to determine the kind numbers of the integer variables needed to solve a problem.
4. Use double-precision real numbers instead of single-precision real numbers in these situations:
   a. A problem requires many significant digits or a large range of numbers.
   b. Numbers of dramatically different sizes must be added or subtracted.
   c. Two nearly equal numbers must be subtracted, and the result used in further calculations.
5. Be careful when you are converting a complex number to a real or double-precision number. If you use the `REAL()` or `DBLE()` functions, only the *real* portion of the complex number is translated. In many cases, what we really want is the *magnitude* of the complex number. If so, we must use `CABS()` instead of `REAL()` to do the conversion.
6. Be careful when you are converting a pair of double-precision real numbers into a complex number using function `CMPLX`. If you do not explicitly specify that the kind of the function result is double precision, the result will be of type default complex and precision will be lost.
7. For large programs using derived data types, declare the definitions of each data type in a module, and then use that module in each procedure of the program that needs to access the derived data type.

8.6.2 Summary of Fortran Statements and Structures

COMPLEX Statement

                    COMPLEX(KIND=*kind_no*) :: *var1(, var2, etc.)*

Example:

                    COMPLEX(KIND=single) :: volts, amps

Description:

The COMPLEX statement declares variables of the complex data type. The kind number is optional and machine dependent. If it is not present, the kind is the default complex kind for the particular machine (usually single precision).

Derived Data Type

                    TYPE *[::] type_name*
                       component 1
                       ...
                       component n
                    END TYPE *[type_name]*
                    TYPE (*type_name*) :: *var1 (, var2, ...)*

Example:

                    TYPE :: state_vector
                       LOGICAL :: valid   ! Valid data flag
                       REAL(kind=single) :: x   ! x position
                       REAL(kind=single) :: y   ! y position
                       REAL(kind=double) :: time   ! time of validity
                       CHARACTER(1en=12) :: id   ! Target ID
                    END TYPE state_vector
                    TYPE (state_vector), DIMENSION(50) :: objects

Description:

The derived data type is a structure containing a combination of intrinsic and previously defined derived data types. The type is defined by a TYPE ... END TYPE construct, and variables of that type are declared with a TYPE() statement.

8

REAL Statement with KIND Parameter

          REAL(KIND=*kind_no*) :: *var1(, var2, etc.)*

Example:

          REAL(KIND=single), DIMENSION(100) :: points

Description:

   The REAL statement is a type declaration statement that declares variables of the real data type. The kind number is optional and machine dependent. If it is not present, the kind is the default real kind for the particular machine (usually single precision).

   To specify double-precision real values, the kind must be set to the appropriate number for the particular machine. The kind number may be found by using the function KIND(0.0D0) or by using the function SELECTED_REAL_KIND.

8.7

EXERCISES

8–1 What are kinds of the REAL data type? How many kinds of real data must a compiler support according to Fortran 90/95 standard?

8–2 What kind numbers are associated with the different types of real variables available on your compiler/computer? Determine the precision and range associated with each type of real data.

8–3 What are the advantages and disadvantages of double-precision real numbers compared to single-precision real numbers? When should double-precision real numbers be used instead of single-precision real numbers?

8–4 What is an ill-conditioned system of equations? Why is it hard to find the solution to an ill-conditioned set of equations?

8–5 State whether each of the following sets of Fortran statements are legal or illegal. If they are illegal, what is wrong with them? If they are legal, what do they do?
   a. Statements:

```
INTEGER, PARAMETER :: sng = KIND(0.0)
INTEGER, PARAMETER :: dbl = KIND(0.0D0)
REAL(KIND=sng) :: a
REAL(KIND=dbl) :: b
READ (*,'(F18.2)') a, b
WRITE (*,*) a, b
```

```
Input data:

    1111111111111111111111111111111111111111111
    2222222222222222222222222222222222222222222
    ----|----|----|----|----|----|----|----|
        5   10   15   20   25   30   35   40
```

b. Statements:

```
INTEGER, PARAMETER :: single = SELECTED_REAL_KIND(p=6)
COMPLEX(kind=single), DIMENSION(5) :: a1
INTEGER :: i
DO i = 1, 5
   a1(i) = CMPLX ( i, -2*i )
END DO
IF (a1(5) > a1(3)) THEN
   WRITE (*,100) (i, a1(i), i = 1, 5)
   100 FORMAT (3X,'a1(',I2,') = (',F10.4,',',F10.4,')')
END IF
```

8–6 Derivative of a Function   Write a subroutine to calculate the derivative of a double-precision real function $f(x)$ at position $x = x_0$. The calling arguments to the subroutine should be the function $f(x)$, the location x_0 at which to evaluate the function, and the step size Δx to use in the evaluation. The output from the subroutine will be the derivative of the function at point $x = x_0$. To make your subroutine machine independent, define double precision as the kind of real value having at least 13 digits of precision. Note that the function to be evaluated should be passed to the subroutine as a calling argument! Test your subroutine by evaluating the function $f(x) = 10 \sin 20x$ at position $x = 0$.

8–7 If you have not done so previously, write a set of elapsed time subroutines for your computer, as described in Exercise 6–31. Use the elapsed time subroutines to compare the time required to solve a 10×10 system of simultaneous equations in single precision and in double precision. You will need to write two test driver programs (one single precision and one double precision) that read the coefficients of the equations, start the timer running, solve the equations, and then calculate the elapsed time. How much slower is the double-precision solution than the single-precision solution on your computer? (*Hint:* If you have a very fast computer, you might have to create an inner loop and solve the system of equations 10 or more times in order to get a meaningful elapsed time.)

Test you program on the system of equations shown below. (This set of equations is contained in file SYS10 in directory CHAP8 at the book's Web site.)

$$
\begin{aligned}
-2x_1 + 5x_2 + x_3 + 3x_4 + 4x_5 - x_6 + 2x_7 - x_8 - 5x_9 - 2x_{10} &= -5 \\
6x_1 + 4x_2 - x_3 + 6x_4 - 4x_5 - 5x_6 + 3x_7 - x_8 + 4x_9 + 3x_{10} &= -6 \\
-6x_1 - 5x_2 - 2x_3 - 2x_4 - 3x_5 + 6x_6 + 4x_7 + 2x_8 - 6x_9 + 4x_{10} &= -7 \\
2x_1 + 4x_2 + 4x_3 + 4x_4 + 5x_5 - 4x_6 + 0x_7 + 0x_8 - 4x_9 + 6x_{10} &= -0 \\
-4x_1 - x_2 + 3x_3 - 3x_4 - 4x_5 - 4x_6 - 4x_7 + 4x_8 + 3x_9 - 3x_{10} &= 5 \\
4x_1 + 3x_2 + 5x_3 + x_4 + x_5 + x_6 + 0x_7 + 3x_8 + 3x_9 + 6x_{10} &= -8 \\
x_1 + 2x_2 - 2x_3 + 0x_4 + 3x_5 - 5x_6 + 5x_7 + 0x_8 + x_9 - 4x_{10} &= 1 \\
-3x_1 - 4x_2 + 2x_3 - x_4 - 2x_5 + 5x_6 - x_7 - x_8 - 4x_9 + x_{10} &= -4 \\
5x_1 + 5x_2 - 2x_3 - 5x_4 + x_5 - 4x_6 - x_7 + 0x_8 - 2x_9 - 3x_{10} &= -7 \\
-5x_1 - 2x_2 - 5x_3 + 2x_4 + x_5 - 3x_6 + 4x_7 - x_8 - 4x_9 + 4x_{10} &= 6
\end{aligned}
$$

8–8 Write a program to determine the kinds of integers supported by your particular compiler. The program should use the function SELECTED_INT_KIND with various input ranges to determine all legal kind numbers. What are the kind numbers and ranges associated with each kind of integer?

8–9 Simultaneous Equations with Complex Coefficients   Create a subroutine csimul to solve for the unknowns in a system of simultaneous linear equations that have complex coefficients. Test your subroutine by solving this system of equations:

```
(-2+i5) x₁ + (1+i3)  x₂ + (4-i1) x₃ = (7+i5)
 (2-i1) x₁ + (-5-i2) x₂ + (6+i4) x₃ = (-10-i8)
(-1+i6) x₁ + (-4-i5) x₂ + (3-i1) x₃ = (-3-i3)
```

8–10 Amplitude and Phase of a Complex Number Write a subroutine that will accept a complex number $c = a + ib$ stored in a variable of type COMPLEX and return the amplitude amp and the phase theta (in degrees) of the complex number in two real variables. (*Hint:* Use intrinsic function ATAN2 to help calculate the phase.)

8–11 When the database was sorted by city in Example 8–4, APO was placed ahead of 'Anywhere'. Why? Rewrite the program in this example to eliminate this problem.

8–12 Create a derived data type called "polar" to hold a complex number expressed in polar (z, θ) format as shown in Figure 8–9. The derived data type will contain two components, a magnitude z and an angle θ, with the angle expressed in degrees. Write two functions that convert an ordinary complex number into a polar number and that convert a polar number into an ordinary complex number.

8–13 If two complex numbers are expressed in polar form, the two numbers may be multiplied by multiplying their magnitudes and adding their angles. That is, if $P_1 = z_1 \angle \theta_1$ and $P_2 = z_2 \angle \theta_2$, then $P_1 \cdot P_2 = z_1 z_2 \angle \theta_1 + \theta_2$. Write a function that multiplies two variables of type "polar" together using this expression and returns a result in polar form. Note that the resulting angle θ should be in the range $-180° < \theta \le 180°$.

8–14 If two complex numbers are expressed in polar form, the two numbers may be divided by dividing their magnitudes and subtracting their angles. That is, if $P_1 = z_1 \angle \theta_1$ and $P_2 = z_2 \angle \theta_2$, then $\dfrac{P_1}{P_2} = \dfrac{z_1}{z_2} \angle \theta_1 - \theta_2$. Write a function that divides two variables of type "polar" using this expression and returns a result in polar form. Note that the resulting angle θ should be in the range $-180° < \theta \le 180°$.

8–15 Euler's Equation Euler's equation defines e raised to an imaginary power in terms of sinusoidal functions as follows

$$e^{i\theta} = \cos \theta + i \sin \theta \tag{8–18}$$

Write a function to evaluate $e^{i\theta}$ for any θ using Euler's equation. Also, evaluate $e^{i\theta}$ using the intrinsic complex exponential function CEXP. Compare the answers that you get by the two methods for the cases where $\theta = 0$, $\dfrac{\pi}{2}$, and π.

8–16 A point can be located in a Cartesian plane by two coordinates (x, y), where x is the displacement of the point along the x-axis from the origin and y is the displacement of the point along the y-axis from the origin. Create a derived data type called "point" whose components are x and y. A line can be represented in a Cartesian plane by the equation

$$y = mx + b \tag{8–19}$$

where m is the slope of the line and b is the y-axis intercept of the line. Create a derived data type called "line" whose components are m and b.

8–17 The distance between two points (x_1, y_1) and (x_2, y_2) is given by the equation

$$distance = \sqrt{(x_2 - x_1)^2 + (y_2 - y_1)^2} \tag{8–20}$$

Write a function that calculates the distance between two values of type "point" as defined in exercise 8–16. The inputs should be two points, and the output should be the distance between the two points expressed as a real number.

8–18 From elementary geometry we know that two points uniquely determine a line as long as they are not coincident. Write a function that accepts two values of type "point," and returns a value of type "line" containing the slope and y-intercept of the line. If the two points are identical, the function should return zeros for both the slope and the intercept. From Figure 8–14, we can see that the slope of the line can be calculated from the equation

$$m = \frac{y_2 - y_1}{x_2 - x_1} \qquad\qquad (8\text{–}21)$$

and the intercept can be calculated from the equation

$$b = y_1 - mx_1 \qquad\qquad (8\text{–}22)$$

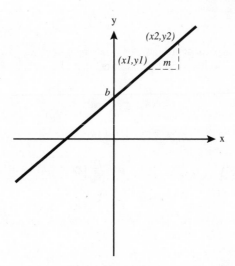

FIGURE 8–14
The slope and intercept of a line can be determined from two points $(x1, y1)$ and $(x2, y2)$ that line along the line.

8–19 Tracking Radar Targets Many surveillance radars have antennas that rotate at a fixed rate, scanning the surrounding air space. The targets detected by such radars are usually displayed on *plan position indicator* (PPI) displays, such as the one shown in Figure 8–15. As the antenna sweeps around the circle, a bright line sweeps around the PPI display. Each target detected shows up on the display as a bright spot at a particular range r and angle θ, where θ is measured in compass degrees relative to North.

Each target will be detected at a different position every time that the radar sweeps around the circle, both because the target moves and because of inherent noise in the range and angle measurement process. The radar system needs to track detected targets through successive sweeps and to estimate target position and velocity from the successive detected positions. Radar systems that accomplish such tracking automatically are known as *track-while-scan* (TWS) radars. They work by measuring the position of the target each time it is detected and passing that position to a *tracking algorithm*.

One of the simplest tracking algorithms is known as the α-β tracker. The α-β tracker works in Cartesian coordinates, so the first step in using the tracker is to convert each

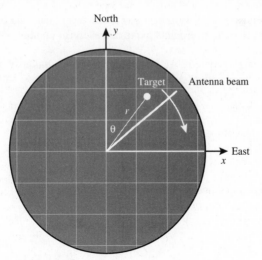

North

y

Target

Antenna beam

r

θ

East

x

FIGURE 8–15
The PPI display of a track-while-scan radar. Target detections show up as bright spots on the display. Each detection is characterized by a range, compass azimuth, and detection time (r, θ, T_n).

8

target detection from polar coordinates (r, θ) into rectangular coordinates (x, y). The tracker then computes a smoothed target position $(\bar{x}_n, \bar{y}_n)$ and velocity $(\dot{x}_n, \dot{y}_n)$ from the equations

Smoothed position:
$$\bar{x}_n = x_{pn} + \alpha (x_n - x_{pn}) \tag{8-23a}$$

$$\bar{y}_n = y_{pn} + \alpha (y_n - y_{pn}) \tag{8-23b}$$

Smoothed velocity:
$$\dot{\bar{x}}_n = \dot{\bar{x}}_{n-1} + \frac{\beta}{T_s} (x_n - x_{pn}) \tag{8-24a}$$

$$\dot{\bar{y}}_n = \dot{\bar{y}}_{n-1} + \frac{\beta}{T_s} (y_n - y_{pn}) \tag{8-24b}$$

Predicted position:
$$x_{pn} = \bar{x}_{n-1} + \dot{\bar{x}}_{n-1}T_s \tag{8-25a}$$

$$y_{pn} = \bar{y}_{n-1} + \dot{\bar{y}}_{n-1}T_s \tag{8-25b}$$

where (x_n, y_n) is the measured target position at time n, (x_{pn}, y_{pn}) is the predicted target position at time n, $(\bar{x}_n, \bar{y}_n)$ is the smoothed target velocity at time n, $(\bar{x}_{n-1}, \bar{y}_{n-1})$, $(\dot{\bar{x}}_{n-1}, \dot{\bar{y}}_{n-1})$ are the smoothed positions and velocity from time $n-1$, α is the position smoothing parameter, β is the velocity smoothing parameter, and T_s is the time between observations.

Design a Fortran program that acts as a radar tracker. The input to the program will be a series of radar target detections (r, θ, T), where r is range in meters, θ is azimuth in compass degrees, and T is the time of the detection in seconds. The program should convert the observations to rectangular coordinates on an east-north grid and then use them to update the tracker as follows:

1. Calculate the time difference T_s since the last detection.
2. Predict the position of the target at the time of the new detection using equations (8–25).

3. Update the smoothed position of the target using equations (8–23). Assume that the position smoothing parameter $\alpha = 0.7$.
4. Update the smoothed velocity of the target using equations (8–24). Assume that the velocity smoothing parameter $\beta = 0.38$.

A block diagram illustrating the operation of the tracker is shown in Figure 8–16.

The program should print out a table containing the observed position of the target, predicted position of the target, and smoothed position of the target each time that the target is measured. Finally, it should produce line-printer plots of the estimated x and y velocity components of the target.

The program should include separate derived data types to hold the detections in polar coordinates (r_n, θ_n, T_n), the detections in rectangular coordinates (x_n, y_n, T_n), and the smoothed state vectors $(\bar{x}_n, \bar{y}_n, \dot{x}_n, \dot{y}_n, T_n)$. It should include separate procedures to perform the polar-to-rectangular conversion, target predictions, and target updates. (Be careful of the polar-to-rectangular conversion—since it uses compass angles, the equations to convert to rectangular coordinates will be different than what we saw earlier!)

Test your program by supplying it with both a noise-free and a noisy input data set. Both data sets are from a plane flying in a straight line, making a turn, and flying in a straight line again. The noisy data is corrupted by a Gaussian noise with a standard deviation of 200 meters in range and 1.1° in azimuth. (The noise-free data can be found in file `track1.dat`, and the noisy data can be found in file `track2.dat` on the disk accompanying the instructor's manual, or at the Web site for this book.) How well does the tracker work at smoothing out errors? How well does the tracker handle the turn?

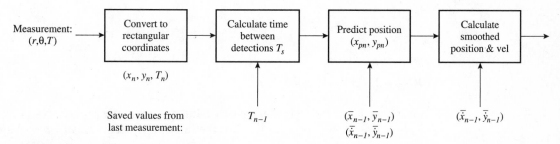

FIGURE 8–16
Block diagram of the operation of an α-β tracker. Note that the smoothed position, velocity, and time from the last update must be saved for use in the current tracker cycle.

9

Advanced Features of Procedures and Modules

This chapter introduces some of the more advanced features of Fortran 90/95 procedures and modules. These features permit us to have better control over access to the information contained in procedures and modules, allow us to write more flexible procedures that support optional arguments and varying data types, and allow us to extend the Fortran language to support new operations on both intrinsic and derived data types.

▨ 9.1

INTERNAL PROCEDURES

In Chapter 6 you learned about **external procedures** and **module procedures.** A third type of procedure in Fortran 90/95 is called the **internal procedure.** An *internal procedure* is a procedure that is entirely contained within another program unit, called the host program unit, or just the **host.** The internal procedure is compiled together with the host, and it can only be invoked from the host program unit. Like module procedures, internal procedures are introduced by a CONTAINS statement. An internal procedure must follow all of the executable statements within the host procedure and must be introduced by a CONTAINS statement.

Why would we want to use internal procedures? In some problems, low-level manipulations are performed repeatedly as a part of the solution. We can simplify these low-level manipulations by defining an internal procedure to perform them.

A simple example of an internal procedure is shown in Figure 9–1. This program accepts an input value in degrees and uses an internal procedure to calculate the secant of that value. Although the internal procedure secant is invoked only once in this simple example, it could have been invoked repeatedly in a larger problem to calculate secants of many different angles.

FIGURE 9–1
Program to calculate the secant of an angle in degrees using an internal procedure.

```
PROGRAM test
!
!  Purpose:
!    To illustrate the use of an internal procedure.
!
!  Record of revisions:
!      Date         Programmer         Description of change
!      ====         ==========         =====================
!    12/28/95      S. J. Chapman       Original code
!
IMPLICIT NONE

! Declare parameters:
INTEGER, PARAMETER :: single = KIND(0.0)     ! Single precision
REAL (KIND=single), PARAMETER :: pi = 3.141592

! Declare local variables:
REAL (kind=single) :: theta                  ! Angle in degrees

! Get desired angle
WRITE (*,*) 'Enter desired angle in degrees: '
READ (*,*) theta

! Calculate and display the result.
WRITE (*,'(A,F10.4)') ' The secant is ', secant(theta)

! Note that the WRITE above was the last executable statement.
! Now, declare internal procedure secant:
CONTAINS
   REAL FUNCTION secant(angle_in_degrees)
   !
   !  Purpose:
   !    To calculate the secant of an angle in degrees.
   !
   REAL (KIND=single) angle_in_degrees

   ! Calculate secant
   secant = 1. / cos( angle_in_degrees * pi / 180. )

   END FUNCTION secant

END PROGRAM test
```

Note that the internal function secant appears after the last executable statement in program test. It is not a part of the executable code of the host program. When program test is executed, the user is prompted for an angle; then the internal function secant is called to calculate the secant of the angle as a part of the final WRITE statement. When this program is executed, the results are

```
C>test
Enter desired angle in degrees:
45
The secant is     1.4142
```

An internal procedure functions exactly like an external procedure, with the following three exceptions:

1. The internal procedure can be invoked *only* from the host procedure. No other procedure within the program can access it.
2. The name of an internal procedure may not be passed as a command line argument to another procedure.
3. An internal procedure inherits all the data entities (parameters and variables) of its host program unit by **host association.**

The last point requires more explanation. When an internal procedure is defined within a host program unit, all the parameters and variables within the host program unit are also usable within the internal procedure. Look at Figure 9–1 again. Note the absence of an IMPLICIT NONE statement within the internal procedure, because the one in the host program applies to the internal procedure as well. Note also that both the named constants single and pi, which are defined in the host program, are used in the internal procedure.

The only time an internal procedure cannot access a data entity defined in its host is when the internal procedure defines a different data entity with the same name. In that case the data entity defined in the host is not accessible in the procedure, and the data entity in the host will be totally unaffected by any manipulations that occur within the internal procedure.

■ 9.2
SCOPE AND SCOPING UNITS

In Chapter 6 we learned that the main program and each external subroutine and function in a program are compiled independently and are then associated together by a linker. Because they were compiled independently, variable names, constant names, loop names, statement labels, and so on could be reused in the different procedures without interfering with each other. For example, the name my_data could be declared and used as a character variable in one procedure and also declared and used as an integer array in another procedure without causing a conflict. There was no conflict because the **scope** of each name or label was restricted to a single procedure.

The *scope* of an object (a variable, named constant, procedure name, statement label, etc.) is the portion of a Fortran program over which it is defined. The three levels of scope in a Fortran 90/95 program are global, local, and statement.

1. **Global** Global objects are objects that are defined throughout an entire program. The names of these objects must be unique within a program. The only global objects that we have encountered so far are the names of programs, external procedures, and modules. Each of these names must be unique within the entire program.[1]

---

[1]In some circumstances, there can be local objects with the same names as some global objects. For example, if a program contains an external subroutine called sort, then no other global object in the program can have the name sort. However, a *different subroutine* within the program could contain a local variable called sort without causing a conflict. Since the local variable is not visible outside the subroutine, it does not conflict with the global object of the same name.

2. **Local** Local objects are objects that are defined and must be unique within a single **scoping unit.** Examples of scoping units are programs, external procedures, and modules. A local object within a scoping unit must be unique within that unit, but the object name, statement label, and so on may be reused in another scoping unit without causing a conflict.

3. **Statement** The scope of certain objects may be restricted to a single statement within a program unit. The only examples that we have seen of objects whose scope is restricted to a single statement are the implied DO variable in an array constructor and the index variables in a FORALL statement. An example array constructor is

```
array = (/ (2*i, i=1,10,2) /)
```

Here the variable i is used to define the array values using an implied DO loop. This use of variable i should not interfere with the use of i in the surrounding program, because the scope of this variable is limited to this single statement.

Just what is a scoping unit? It is the portion of a Fortran program over which a local object is defined. The scoping units in a Fortran 90/95 program are

1. A main program, internal or external procedure, or module, excluding any derived type definitions or procedures contained within it.
2. A derived type definition.
3. An interface, which is introduced later in this chapter.

Local objects within each of these scoping units must be unique, but they may be reused between scoping units. The fact that a derived type definition is a scoping unit means that we can have a variable named x as a component of the derived type definition and also have a variable named x within the program containing the derived type definition, without the two variables conflicting with each other.

If one scoping unit completely surrounds another scoping unit, then it is called the **host scoping unit,** or just the *host,* of the inner scoping unit. The inner scoping unit automatically inherits the object definitions declared in the host scoping unit, unless the inner scoping unit explicitly redefines the objects. This inheritance is called **host association.** Thus an internal procedure inherits all the variables names and values defined in the host procedure unless the internal procedure explicitly redefines a variable name of its own use. If the internal procedure uses a variable name defined in the host unit without redefining it, then changes to that variable in the internal procedure will also change the variable in the host unit. In contrast, if the internal procedure redefines a variable name used in the host unit, then modifications to that local variable will not affect the value of the variable with the same name in the host unit.

Finally, objects defined in a module normally have the scope of that module, but their scope may be extended by USE association. If the module name appears in a USE statement in a program unit, then all of the objects defined in the module become objects defined in the program unit using the module and the names of those objects must be unique. If an object named x is declared within a module and that module is used in a procedure, then no other object may be named x within the procedure.

EXAMPLE 9–1 Scope and Scoping Units: When dealing with a subject as complex as scope and scoping units, it is helpful to look at an example. Figure 9–2 shows a Fortran program written specifically to explore the concept of scope. If you can answer the following questions about that program, then you will have a pretty good understanding of scope.

1. What are the scoping units within this program?
2. Which scoping units are hosts to other units?
3. Which objects in this program have global scope?
4. Which objects in this program have statement scope?
5. Which objects in this program have local scope?
6. Which objects in this program are inherited by host association?
7. Which objects in this program are made available by USE association?
8. Explain what will happen in this program as it is executed.

FIGURE 9–2
Program to illustrate the concept of scope and scoping units.

```
MODULE module_example
IMPLICIT NONE
REAL :: x = 100.
REAL :: y = 200.
END MODULE

PROGRAM scoping_test
USE module_example
IMPLICIT NONE
INTEGER :: i = 1, j = 2
WRITE (*,'(A25,2I7,2F7.1)') ' Beginning:', i, j, x, y
CALL sub1 ( i, j )
WRITE (*,'(A25,2I7,2F7.1)') ' After sub1:', i, j, x, y
CALL sub2
WRITE (*,'(A25,2I7,2F7.1)') ' After sub2:', i, j, x, y
CONTAINS
    SUBROUTINE sub2
    REAL :: x
    x = 1000.
    y = 2000.
    WRITE (*,'(A25,2F7.1)') ' In sub2:', x, y
    END SUBROUTINE sub2
END PROGRAM scoping_test

SUBROUTINE sub1 (i, j)
IMPLICIT NONE
INTEGER, INTENT(INOUT) :: i, j
INTEGER, DIMENSION(5) :: array
WRITE (*,'(A25,2I7)') ' In sub1 before sub2:', i, j
CALL sub2
WRITE (*,'(A25,2I7)') ' In sub1 after sub2:', i, j
array = (/ (1000*i, i=1,5) /)
WRITE (*,'(A25,7I7)') ' After array def in sub2: ', i, j, array
```

(continued)

(concluded)

```
CONTAINS
   SUBROUTINE sub2
   INTEGER :: i
   i = 1000
   j = 2000
   WRITE (*,'(A25,2I7)') ' In sub1 in sub2:', i, j
   END SUBROUTINE sub2
END SUBROUTINE sub1
```

SOLUTION The answers to the questions are given below.

1. *What are the scoping units within this program?*

Each module, main program, internal procedure, and external procedure is a scoping unit, so the scoping units are module `module_example`, main program `scoping_test`, external subroutine `sub1`, and the two internal subroutines `sub2`. If there had been any derived data types within the program, their definitions would also have been scoping units. Figure 9–3 illustrates the relationships among the five scoping units in this program.

2. *Which scoping units are hosts to other units?*

The main program `scoping_test` is the host scoping unit for the internal subroutine `sub2` contained within it, and the external subroutine `sub1` is the host scoping unit for the internal subroutine `sub2` contained within it. Note that the two internal subroutines are different, even though they have the same name!

3. *Which objects in this program have global scope?*

The objects within this program that have global scope are the names of the module `module_example`, the main program `scoping_test`, and the external subroutine `sub1`. These names must be unique throughout the program. For example, a single program cannot contain two external subroutines both named

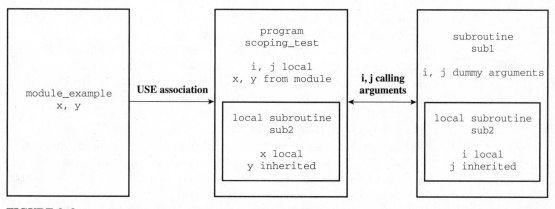

FIGURE 9–3

A block diagram illustrating the relationships among the various scoping units in program `scoping_test`.

sub1. In contrast, the names of the internal subroutines sub2 have local scope only, so it is legal to have two different local subroutines of the same name in two different scoping units.

4. *Which objects in this program have statement scope?*

The only object within this program that has statement scope is the variable i within the array definition in subroutine sub1. Because that variable has statement scope, the value of variable i in subroutine sub1 will be unchanged by the use of i to define the array.

5. *Which objects in this program have local scope?*

All other objects within this program have local scope, including the names of the internal subroutines sub2. Because each internal subroutine is local to its host scoping unit, there is no conflict involved in having two subroutines with the same name. Each of the internal subroutines is only defined within and callable from its host scoping unit.

6. *Which objects in this program are inherited by host association?*

All objects in the two internal subroutines are inherited from their host scoping units by host association with the exception of those objects explicitly redefined within the internal subroutines. Variable x is local to the first internal subroutine, while variable y is inherited from the main program, which is the host scoping unit. Similarly, variable i is local to the second internal subroutine, while variable j is inherited from the subroutine sub1, which is the host scoping unit.

7. *Which objects in this program are made available by USE association?*

Variables x and y are made available to the main program by USE association.

8. *Explain what will happen in this program as it is executed.*

When this program begins execution, variables x and y are initialized to 100. and 200., respectively, in module module_example, and variables i and j are initialized to 1 and 2, respectively, in the main program. Variables x and y are visible in the main program by USE association.

When subroutine sub1 is called, variables i and j are passed to sub1 as calling arguments. Subroutine sub1 then calls its local subroutine sub2, which sets i to 1000 and j to 2000. However, variable i is local to sub2, so changing it has no effect on variable i in sub1. Variable j is the same variable in sub1 and sub2 through host association, so when sub2 sets a new value for j, the value of j in sub1 is changed to 2000.

Next a value is assigned to the array using variable i as an array constructor. Variable i takes on values from 1 to 5 as a part of the implied DO loop, but the scope of that variable is statement only, so in the next line of the subroutine the value of variable i remains 1 as it was before the array assignment.

When execution returns from sub1 to the main program, i is still 1 and j is 2000. Next the main program calls its own local subroutine sub2.

Subroutine `sub2` sets x to 1000. and y to 2000. However, variable x is local to `sub2`, so changing it has no effect on variable x in the main program. Variable y is the same variable in the main program and in `sub2` through host association, so when `sub2` sets a new value for y, the value of y in the main program is changed to 2000.

After the call to `sub2`, the values of i, j, x, and y in the main program are 1, 2000, 100., and 2000., respectively.

We can verify our analysis of the operation of this program by executing it and examining the results:

```
C>scoping_test
            Beginning:        1       2  100.0  200.0
    In sub1 before sub2:      1       2
       In sub1 in sub2:    1000    2000
    In sub1 after sub2:      1    2000
After array def in sub2:     1    2000   1000   2000   3000   4000   5000
            After sub1:      1    2000  100.0  200.0
             In sub2: 1000.0  2000.0
            After sub2:      1    2000  100.0 2000.0
```

The output of this program matches our analysis.

It is possible to reuse a local object name for different purposes in nested scoping units. For example, the integer i was defined in subroutine `sub1` and would normally have been available to internal subroutine `sub2` by host association. However, `sub2` defined its own integer i, so in fact the integer i is different in the two scoping units. This sort of double definition is a recipe for confusion, and you should avoid using it in your code. Instead, just create a new variable name in the internal subroutine that does not conflict with any in the host.

Good Programming Practice

When working with nested scoping units, avoid redefining the meaning of objects that have the same name in both the inner and outer scoping units. This suggestion applies essentially to internal procedures. You can avoid confusion about the behavior of variables in the internal procedure by simply giving them different names from the variables in the host procedure.

9.3

RECURSIVE PROCEDURES

An ordinary Fortran 90/95 procedure may not invoke itself either directly or indirectly (that is, by either invoking itself or by invoking another procedure which then invokes the original procedure). In other words, ordinary Fortran 90/95 procedures are not recursive. However, certain classes of problems are most easily solved recursively. For example, the factorial function can be defined as

$$N! = \begin{cases} N(N-1)! & N \geq 1 \\ 1 & N = 0 \end{cases} \qquad (9-1)$$

This definition can most easily be implemented recursively, with the procedure that calculates N! calling itself to calculate $(N - 1)!$, and that procedure calling itself to calculate $(N - 2)!$, etc. until finally the procedure is called to calculate 0!.

To accommodate such problems, Fortran allows subroutines and functions to be declared recursive. If a procedure is *declared recursive,* then the Fortran compiler will implement it in such a way that it can invoke itself either directly or indirectly as often as desired.

A subroutine is declared recursive by adding the keyword RECURSIVE to the SUBROUTINE statement. Figure 9–4 shows an example subroutine that calculates the factorial function directly from Equation (9–1). It looks just like any other subroutine except that it is declared to be recursive. You will be asked to verify the proper operation of the subroutine in exercise 9–3.

FIGURE 9–4
A subroutine to recursively implement the factorial function.

```
RECURSIVE SUBROUTINE factorial ( n, result )
!
!  Purpose:
!    To calculate the factorial function
!            | n(n-1)        n >= 1
!     n ! =  |
!            | 1             n = 0
!
!  Record of revisions:
!     Date        Programmer           Description of change
!     ====        ==========           =====================
!   10/31/95   S. J. Chapman           Original code
!
IMPLICIT NONE

! List of calling arguments:
INTEGER, INTENT(IN) :: n            ! Value to calculate
INTEGER, INTENT(OUT) :: result      ! Result

! Local variable
INTEGER :: temp                     ! Temporary variable

IF ( n >= 1 ) THEN
   CALL factorial ( n-1, temp )
   result = n * temp
ELSE
   result = 1
END IF

END SUBROUTINE factorial
```

We can also define recursive Fortran functions. However, an extra complication occurs when working with recursive functions. Remember that a function is invoked by naming the function in an expression, while the value to be returned from the function is specified by assigning it to the function name. Thus, if a function were to invoke itself, the function's name would appear on the left side of an assignment statement when its return value is being set and on the right side of an assignment statement when it invoking itself recursively. This double use of the function name could certainly cause confusion.

To avoid confusion between the two uses of the function name in a recursive function, Fortran allows us to specify two different names for invoking the function recursively and for returning its result. The actual name of the function is used whenever we want the function to invoke itself, and a special dummy argument is used whenever we want to specify a value to return. The name of this special dummy argument is specified in a RESULT clause in the FUNCTION statement. For example, the following line declares a recursive function fact that uses the dummy argument answer for the value returned to the invoking program unit:

```
RECURSIVE FUNCTION fact(n) RESULT(answer)
```

If a RESULT clause is included in a function, then a function name *may not* appear in a type declaration statement in the function. The name of the dummy result variable is declared instead. For example, Figure 9–5 shows a recursive function that calculates the factorial function directly from Equation (9–1). Note that the type of the result variable answer is declared, not the type of the function name fact. You will be asked to verify the proper operation of this function in exercise 9–3.

FIGURE 9–5
A function to recursively implement the factorial function.

```
RECURSIVE FUNCTION fact(n) RESULT(answer)
!
!  Purpose:
!    To calculate the factorial function
!           |  n(n-1)!      n >= 1
!    n ! =  |
!           |  1            n = 0
!
!  Record of revisions:
!     Date          Programmer            Description of change
!     ====          ==========            =====================
!    10/31/95    S. J. Chapman            Original code
!
IMPLICIT NONE

! List of calling arguments:
INTEGER, INTENT(IN) :: n           ! Value to calculate
INTEGER :: answer                  ! Result variable

IF ( n >= 1 ) THEN
   answer = n * fact(n-1)
ELSE
   answer = 1
END IF

END FUNCTION fact
```

User-defined elemental functions, which are only present in Fortran 95, may not be recursive.

■ 9.4

KEYWORD ARGUMENTS AND OPTIONAL ARGUMENTS

In Chapter 6 we stated that when invoking a procedure, the actual argument list used to invoke the procedure must match the dummy argument list exactly in number, type, and order. If the first dummy argument is a real array, then the first actual argument must also be a real array, and so forth. If the procedure has four dummy arguments, then the procedure invocation must have four actual arguments.

This statement is usually true in Fortran 90/95. However, we can also change the order of the calling arguments in the list or specify actual arguments for only some of the procedure's dummy arguments provided that the interface to the procedure is explicit. A procedure interface can be made explicit by placing the procedure in a module and accessing that module in the invoking program by USE association. (A procedure interface can also be made explicit by using an interface block, as explained in the next section.)

If a procedure's interface is explicit, then it is possible to use **keyword arguments** in the calling program to provide increased flexibility. A keyword argument is an argument of the form

```
keyword = actual_argument
```

where keyword is the name of the dummy argument that is being associated with the actual argument. If the procedure invocation uses keyword arguments, then the calling arguments can be arranged in any order because the keywords allow the compiler to sort out which actual argument goes with which dummy argument.

Let's illustrate this idea with an example. Figure 9–6 shows a function calc that takes three real arguments first, second, and third. The function is contained inside a module to make its interface explicit. The main program invokes this function in four different ways using the same arguments. The first time that the function is invoked, it is done the conventional way, in which the actual arguments match the dummy arguments in type, number, and order:

```
WRITE (*,*) calc ( 3., 1., 2. )
```

The next two times that the function is invoked, we use keyword arguments:

```
WRITE (*,*) calc ( first=3., second=1., third=2. )
WRITE (*,*) calc ( second=1., third=2., first=3. )
```

The final time that the function is called, we use a mixture of conventional arguments and keyword arguments. The first argument is conventional, and so it is associated with the first dummy argument. The later arguments are keyword arguments, so they are associated with dummy arguments by their keywords. In general, it is legal to mix conventional calling arguments and keyword arguments, but once a keyword argument appears in the list, all of the remaining arguments must also be keyword arguments.

FIGURE 9–6
Program to illustrate the use of keyword arguments.

```
WRITE (*,*) calc ( 3., third=2., second=1. )
```

(continued)

(concluded)

```
MODULE procs
CONTAINS
   REAL FUNCTION calc ( first, second, third )
   IMPLICIT NONE
   REAL, INTENT(IN) :: first, second, third
   calc = ( first - second ) / third
   END FUNCTION calc
END MODULE procs

PROGRAM test_keywords

USE procs
IMPLICIT NONE

WRITE (*,*) calc ( 3., 1., 2. )
WRITE (*,*) calc ( first=3., second=1., third=2. )
WRITE (*,*) calc ( second=1., third=2., first=3. )
WRITE (*,*) calc ( 3., third=2., second=1.)

END PROGRAM test_keywords
```

When the program in Figure 9–6 is executed, the results are

```
C>test_keywords
          1.000000
          1.000000
          1.000000
          1.000000
```

The function calculated the same value every time regardless of the order in which the arguments were presented.

Keyword arguments allow us to change the order in which actual arguments are presented to a procedure, but by itself that feature is not very useful. It appears that all we are doing here is creating extra typing to accomplish the same goal! However, keyword arguments are useful when used with optional arguments.

An **optional argument** is a dummy procedure argument that does not always have to be present when the procedure is invoked. If it is present, then the procedure will use it. If not, then the procedure will function without it. Optional arguments are only possible in procedures with explicit interfaces. They are specified by including the OPTIONAL attribute in the declaration of a dummy argument:

```
INTEGER, INTENT(IN), OPTIONAL :: upper_limit
```

The procedure containing an optional argument must have some way to determine if the optional argument is present when the procedure is executed. This is accomplished by a logical intrinsic function PRESENT, which returns a true value if the optional argument is present and a false value if it is not present. For example, a procedure could take some action based on the presence or absence of an optional argument upper_limit as follows:

```
IF ( PRESENT(upper_limit) ) THEN
   ...
ELSE
   ...
END IF
```

Keywords are very useful for procedures with optional arguments. If the optional arguments are present and in order in the calling sequence, then no keywords are required. If only some of the optional arguments are present, but the ones that are present are in order, then no keywords are required. However, if optional arguments are out of order, or if some of the earlier optional arguments are missing while later ones are supplied, then keywords must be supplied. The compiler will use the keywords to sort out which optional arguments are present and which ones are absent.

Incidentally, we have already met an intrinsic function that uses keywords and optional arguments. Recall that the function SELECTED_REAL_KIND accepts two arguments for the desired precision p and the desired range r of the real number. The default order for the two arguments is (p, r), so if the arguments are specified in that order no keywords are necessary. If they are specified out of order or if only the range is specified, then the keywords must be used. Examples of legal uses of the function follow.

```
kind_num = SELECTED_REAL_KIND(13,100)
kind_num = SELECTED_REAL_KIND(13)
kind_num = SELECTED_REAL_KIND(r=100,p=13)
kind_num = SELECTED_REAL_KIND(r=100)
```

EXAMPLE 9–2 *Finding the Extreme Values in a Data Set:* Suppose that we want to write a subroutine that searches through a real array to locate the minimum and/or maximum values in the array and also the locations where the minimum and/or maximum values occur. This subroutine could be used in many different applications. On some occasions, we might be looking for only the maximum value in the array. At other times, we might only care about the minimum values. On still other occasions we might be interested in both values (for example, if we were setting the limits on a plotting program). Sometimes we will care where the extreme values occur within an array, and other times it will not matter.

To accommodate all of these possibilities in a single subroutine, we will write a subroutine that has four optional output arguments: the maximum value, the location of the maximum value, the minimum value, and the location of the minimum value. The values returned will depend on the arguments specified by the user in the subroutine call.

SOLUTION The subroutine is shown in Figure 9–7. It can return from one to four optional results in any possible combination. Note that the subroutine must have an explicit interface in order to support optional arguments, so it is placed inside a module.

FIGURE 9–7
A subroutine to locate the extreme values in a real array. The subroutine is embedded in a module to make its interface explicit.

```
MODULE procs

CONTAINS
```

(continued)

(continued)

```
SUBROUTINE extremes (a, n, maxval, pos_maxval, minval, pos_minval)
!
!   Purpose:
!     To find the maximum and minimum values in an array and
!     the location of those values in the array. This subroutine
!     returns its output values in optional arguments.
!
!   Record of revisions:
!       Date        Programmer          Description of change
!       ====        ==========          =====================
!     12/31/95     S. J. Chapman        Original code
!
IMPLICIT NONE

! List of calling arguments:
INTEGER, INTENT(IN) :: n                        ! # vals in array a
REAL, INTENT(IN), DIMENSION(n) :: a             ! Input data.
REAL, INTENT(OUT) , OPTIONAL :: maxval          ! Maximum value.
INTEGER, INTENT(OUT), OPTIONAL :: pos_maxval    ! Pos of maxval
REAL, INTENT(OUT), OPTIONAL :: minval           ! Minimum value.
INTEGER, INTENT(OUT), OPTIONAL :: pos_minval    ! Pos of minval

! List of local variables:
INTEGER :: i                        ! Index
REAL :: real_max                    ! Max value
INTEGER :: pos_max                  ! Pos of max value
REAL :: real_min                    ! Min value
INTEGER :: pos_min                  ! Pos of min value

! Initialize the values to first value in array.
real_max = a(1)
pos_max = 1
real_min = a(1)
pos_min = 1

! Find the extreme values in a(2) through a(n).
DO i = 2, n
   max: IF ( a(i) > real_max ) THEN
      real_max = a(i)
      pos_max = i
   END IF max
   min: IF (a (i) < real_min ) THEN
      real_min = a(i)
      pos_min = i
   END IF min
END DO

! Report the results
IF ( PRESENT(maxval) ) THEN
   maxval = real_max
END IF
IF ( PRESENT(pos_maxval) ) THEN
   pos_maxval = pos_max
END IF
IF ( PRESENT(minval) ) THEN
   minval = real_min
END IF
IF ( PRESENT(pos_minval) ) THEN
   pos_minval = pos_min
```

9

(continued)

(concluded)

```
END IF

    END SUBROUTINE extremes
END MODULE procs
```

You will be asked to verify the proper operation of this subroutine in exercise 9–4 at the end of this chapter.

Quiz 9–1

This quiz provides a quick check to see if you understand the concepts introduced in sections 9.1 through 9.4. If you have trouble with the quiz, reread the sections, ask your instructor, or discuss the material with a fellow student. The answers to this quiz are found in the back of the book.

1. What are the major differences between an internal subroutine and an external subroutine? When would you wish to use an internal subroutine?

2. What is the scope of an object in Fortran? What are the three levels of scope in Fortran?

3. What is host association? Explain how variables and constants are inherited by host association.

4. What is the value of z that is written out after the following code is executed? Explain how the value is produced.

```
PROGRAM x
REAL :: z = 10.
TYPE position
    REAL :: x
    REAL :: y
    REAL :: z
END TYPE position
TYPE (position) :: xyz
xyz = position(1., 2., 3.)
z = fun1( z )
WRITE (*,*) z
CONTAINS
    REAL FUNCTION fun1(x)
    REAL, INTENT(IN) :: x
    fun1 = (x + xyz%x) / xyz%z
    END FUNCTION fun1
END PROGRAM
```

5. What is the value of i after the following code is executed?

```
PROGRAM xyz
INTEGER :: i = 0
INTEGER, DIMENSION(6) :: count
i = i + 27
```

(continued)

(concluded)

```
        count = (/ (2*i, i=6,1,-1) /)
        i = i - 7
        WRITE (*,*) i
        END PROGRAM xyz
```

6. If the following program legal or illegal? Why or why not?

```
        PROGRAM abc
        REAL :: abc = 10.
        WRITE (*,*) abc
        END PROGRAM
```

7. What are recursive procedures? How are they declared?

8. Is the following function legal or illegal? Why or why not?

```
        RECURSIVE FUNCTION sum_1_n(n) RESULT(sum)
        IMPLICIT NONE
        INTEGER, INTENT(IN) :: n
        INTEGER :: sum_1_n
        IF ( n > 1 ) THEN
            sum = n + sum_1_n(n-1)
        ELSE
            sum = 1
        END IF
        END FUNCTION
```

9. What are keyword arguments? What requirement(s) must be met before they can be used? Why would you want to use a keyword argument?

10. What are optional arguments? What requirement(s) must be met before they can be used? Why would you want to use an optional argument?

9.5

PROCEDURE INTERFACES AND INTERFACE BLOCKS

As we have seen, a calling program unit must have an *explicit interface* to a procedure if it is to use advanced Fortran features such as keyword arguments and optional arguments. In addition, an explicit interface allows the compiler to catch many errors that occur in the calling sequences between procedures. These errors might otherwise produce subtle and hard-to-find bugs.

The easiest way to create an explicit interface is to place procedures in a module and then use that module in the calling program unit. Any procedures placed in a module will always have an explicit interface.

Unfortunately placing the procedures in a module is sometimes inconvenient or even impossible. For example, suppose that a technical organization has a large library containing hundreds of subroutines and functions written in an earlier version of Fortran that are used both in old, existing programs and in new programs. This situation is very common because various versions of Fortran have been in general use since the late

1950s. Rewriting all these subroutines and functions to place them into modules and add explicit interface characteristics such as the INTENT attribute would create a major problem. If the procedures were modified in this way, then the older programs would no longer be able to use them. Most organizations would not want to make two versions of each procedure, one with an explicit interface and one without, because duplication would create a significant configuration control problem whenever one of the library procedures is modified. Both versions of the procedure would have to be modified separately, and each one would have to be independently verified to be working properly.

The problem can be even worse, since the external library of procedures could be written in another language such as C. In that case we have no way to place the procedures in a module.

9.5.1 Creating Interface Blocks

How do we take advantage of the features of an explicit interface when placing procedures into a module is impossible or impractical? In these cases Fortran allows us to define an **interface block** in the invoking program unit. The interface block specifies all the interface characteristics of an external procedure, and the Fortran compiler uses the information in the interface block to perform its consistency checks and to apply such advanced features as keyword arguments.[2]

An interface block is created by duplicating the calling argument information of a procedure within the interface. The general form of an interface is

```
INTERFACE
    interface_body_1
    interface_body_2
    ...
END INTERFACE
```

Each *interface_body* consists of the initial SUBROUTINE or FUNCTION statement of the corresponding external procedure, the type specification statements associated with its arguments, and an END SUBROUTINE or END FUNCTION statement. These statements provide enough information for the compiler to check the consistency of the interface between the calling program and the external procedure.

When an interface is used, it is placed in the header section of the invoking program unit along with all the type declaration statements.

EXAMPLE **9–3** *Creating an Interface to an External Subroutine:* In Example 6–1 we created a subroutine sort to sort an array of real values into ascending order. Assume that it is impossible to place that subroutine into a module; therefore, we need to create an interface block to explicitly define the interface between the subroutine and a calling program unit. Use that interface to allow a program to call subroutine sort while using keyword arguments.

SOLUTION First, we must create an interface for subroutine sort. The interface

---

[2]Fortran interface blocks are essentially equivalent to prototypes in the C language.

will consist of the SUBROUTINE statement, the type declaration statements of the subroutine's dummy arguments, and the END SUBROUTINE statement. It is

```
INTERFACE
    SUBROUTINE sort (array, n)
    IMPLICIT NONE
    REAL, DIMENSION(:), INTENT(INOUT) :: array
    INTEGER, INTENT(IN) :: n
    END SUBROUTINE
END INTERFACE
```

Next, we will use this interface in the calling program's header to explicitly define the interface to subroutine sort. Figure 9–8 shows a calling program that uses the interface block to create an explicit interface to subroutine sort.

FIGURE 9–8
A simple program illustrating the use of interface blocks.

```
PROGRAM interface_example
!
!   Purpose:
!     To illustrate the use of interface blocks to create explicit
!     interfaces. This program uses an interface block to create
!     an explicit interface to subroutine "sort" and then takes
!     advantage of that interface to use keyword arguments.
!
!   Record of revisions:
!      Date         Programmer          Description of change
!      ====         ==========          =====================
!    01/02/96     S. J. Chapman         Original code
!
IMPLICIT NONE

! Declare interface to subroutine "sort"
INTERFACE
   SUBROUTINE sort(a,n)
   IMPLICIT NONE
   REAL, DIMENSION(:), INTENT(INOUT) :: a
   INTEGER, INTENT(IN) :: n
   END SUBROUTINE sort
END INTERFACE

! Declare local variables
REAL, DIMENSION(6) :: array = (/ 1., 5., 3., 2., 6., 4. /)
INTEGER :: nvals = 6

! Call "sort" to sort data into ascending order.
CALL sort ( N = nvals, A = array)
! Write out sorted array.
WRITE (*,*), array

END PROGRAM
```

When this program is compiled together with subroutine sort and executed, the results are

```
C>interface_example
      1.000000       2.000000       3.000000       4.000000
      5.000000       6.000000
```

The compiler used the interface block to correctly sort out the keyword arguments in the call to subroutine `sort`, and the program produced the correct answer.

9.5.2 Notes on the Use of Interface Blocks

How and when should interface blocks be used to best advantage in a program? When we look at the structure of an interface block, it seems that we are just creating extra work for ourselves by duplicating some of the statements from the original procedure in the interface block. When should we create an interface block, and why? The following notes provide guidance on the use of interface blocks in Fortran.

1. Whenever possible, avoid interface blocks by simply placing all of your procedures in modules and access the appropriate modules by USE association.

 Good Programming Practice
Avoid interface blocks by placing your procedures in modules whenever possible.

---

2. An interface block must not specify the interface of a procedure already in a module available by USE association. This constitutes a double definition of the explicit interface, which is illegal and will cause a compiler error.
3. A common use of interface blocks is to provide explicit interfaces to separately compiled procedures written in earlier versions of Fortran or in other languages such as C. In this case writing an interface block allows modern Fortran programs to have an explicit interface with full argument checking, while allowing older or non-Fortran programs to continue to use the procedures unchanged.
4. An easy way to make the interfaces for a large library of old subroutines or functions available to all calling program units is to place them in a module, and then to USE that module in each calling program unit. For example, the interface to subroutine `sort` could be placed in a module as follows:

```
MODULE interface_definitions
    INTERFACE
        SUBROUTINE sort (array, n)
        IMPLICIT NONE
        REAL, DIMENSION(:), INTENT(INOUT) :: array
        INTEGER, INTENT(IN) :: n
        END SUBROUTINE
        ...
        (insert other procedure interfaces here)
        ...
    END INTERFACE
END MODULE
```

Unlike module procedures, there is no CONTAINS statement when interfaces are included in a module.

Good Programming Practice

If you must create interfaces to many procedures, place all of the interfaces in a module so that they will be easily accessible to many program units by USE association.

5. Each interface is a separate scoping unit, so the same variable name may appear in an interface and in a program including that interface without causing a conflict.
6. The names used for dummy arguments in an interface block do not have to be the same as the names used for the dummy arguments in the corresponding procedures. The dummy arguments in the interface block must match the dummy arguments in the corresponding procedures in type, intent, array size, and so on, but the names themselves do not have to match. However, you should never rename the arguments in an interface. Even though such renaming is legal, it adds extra confusion and increases the possibility for error.

■ 9.6
GENERIC PROCEDURES

The Fortran 90/95 language includes both generic and specific intrinsic functions. A **generic function** is a function that can operate properly with many different types of input data, while a **specific function** is a function that requires one specific type of input data. For example, Fortran includes a generic function ABS() to take the absolute value of a number. It can function with integer data, single-precision real data, double-precision real data, or complex data. The language also includes the specific functions IABS(), which requires an integer input value; ABS(), which requires a single-precision real input value; DABS(), which requires a double-precision real input value; and CABS(), which requires a complex input value.

Now for a little secret: The generic function ABS() does not actually exist anywhere within a Fortran compiler. Instead, whenever the compiler encounters the generic function, it examines the arguments of the function and invokes the appropriate specific function for those arguments. For example, if the compiler detects the generic function ABS(−34) in a program, it will generate a call to the specific function IABS() because the calling argument of the function is an integer. When we use generic functions, we are allowing the compiler to do some of the detail work for us.

9.6.1 User-Defined Generic Procedures

Fortran 90/95 allows us to define our own generic procedures in addition to the standard ones built into the compiler. For example, we might wish to define a generic subroutine sort that is capable of sorting integer data, single-precision real data, double-precision real data, or character data depending on the arguments supplied to it. We could use that generic subroutine in our programs instead of worrying about the specific details of the calling arguments each time that we want to sort a data set.

We can implement generic procedures with a special version of the interface block called a **generic interface block.** If we add a generic name to the INTERFACE statement, then every procedure interface defined within the interface block will be assumed to be a specific version of that generic procedure. The general form of an interface block used to declare a generic procedure is

```
INTERFACE generic_name
    specific_interface_body_1
    specific_interface_body_2
    . . .
END INTERFACE
```

When the compiler encounters the generic procedure name in a program unit containing this generic interface block, it will examine the arguments associated with the call to the generic procedure to decide which specific procedure to use.

In order for the compiler to determine which specific procedure to use, each of the specific procedures in the block must be *unambiguously* distinguished from the others. For example, one specific procedure might have real input data while another one has integer input data. The compiler can then compare the generic procedure's calling sequence to the calling sequences of each specific procedure to decide which one to use. The following rules apply to the specific procedures in a generic interface block:

1. Either all the procedures in a generic interface block must be subroutines or all of the procedures in the blocking must be functions. They cannot be mixed, because the generic procedure being defined must either be a subroutine or be a function—it cannot be both.
2. Every procedure in the block must be distinguishable from all the other procedures in the block by the type, number, and position of its non-optional arguments. As long as each procedure is distinguishable from all of the other procedures in the block, the compiler will be able to decide which procedure to use by comparing the type, number, and position of the generic procedure's calling arguments with the type, number, and position of each specific procedure's dummy arguments.

Generic interface blocks may be placed in the header of a program unit that invokes the generic procedure, or they may be placed in a module that may be used in the program unit that invokes the generic procedure.

Good Programming Practice

Use generic interface blocks to define procedures that can function with different types of input data. Generic procedures will add to the flexibility of your programs, making it easier for them to handle different types of data.

As an example, suppose that a programmer has written the following four subroutines to sort data into ascending order.

Subroutine	Function
SUBROUTINE sorti (array, nvals)	Sorts integer data.
SUBROUTINE sortr (array, nvals)	Sorts single-precision real data.
SUBROUTINE sortd (array, nvals)	Sorts double-precision real data.
SUBROUTINE sortc (array, nvals)	Sorts character data.

Now he or she wishes to create a generic subroutine `sort` to sort any of these types of data into ascending order. This task can be done with the following generic interface block (parameters `single` and `double` will have to be previously defined):

```
INTERFACE sort
    SUBROUTINE sorti (array, nvals)
    IMPLICIT NONE
    INTEGER, INTENT(IN) :: nvals
    INTEGER, INTENT(INOUT), DIMENSION(nvals) :: array
    END SUBROUTINE sorti

    SUBROUTINE sortr (array, nvals)
    IMPLICIT NONE
    INTEGER, INTENT(IN) :: nvals
    REAL (KIND=single), INTENT(INOUT), DIMENSION(nvals) :: array
    END SUBROUTINE sortr

    SUBROUTINE sortd (array, nvals)
    IMPLICIT NONE
    INTEGER, INTENT(IN) :: nvals
    REAL (KIND=double), INTENT(INOUT), DIMENSION(nvals) :: array
    END SUBROUTINE sortd

    SUBROUTINE sortc (array, nvals)
    IMPLICIT NONE
    INTEGER INTENT(IN) :: nvals
    CHARACTER(len=*), INTENT(INOUT), DIMENSION(nvals) :: array
    END SUBROUTINE sortc
END INTERFACE
```

This generic interface block satisfies the requirements stated above because all the procedures are subroutines, and they can be distinguished from one another by the type of the array in their calling sequences.

9.6.2 Generic Interfaces for Procedures in Modules

In the preceding example, an explicit interface was given for each specific subroutine in the generic interface block defining the generic subroutine `sort`. This arrangement would be appropriate if each of the specific subroutines were separately compiled and did not have an explicit interface. But what happens if the individual subroutines are in a module, and so they already have explicit interfaces?

Section 9.5.2 explained that it is illegal to explicitly declare an interface for a procedure that already has an explicit interface by being in a module. Given that rule, how can we include procedures defined in modules in a generic interface block? To get around this problem, Fortran includes a special MODULE PROCEDURE statement that can be used in a generic interface block. The form of this statement is

```
MODULE PROCEDURE module_procedure_1 (, module_procedure_2, . . . )
```

where *module_procedure_1* and so on are the names of procedures whose interfaces are defined in a module that is available by USE association.

If the four sorting subroutines had been defined in a module instead of being separately compiled, then the generic interface for subroutine sort would become

```
INTERFACE sort
    MODULE PROCEDURE sorti
    MODULE PROCEDURE sortr
    MODULE PROCEDURE sortd
    MODULE PROCEDURE sortc
END INTERFACE
```

This interface block should be placed in the module in which the procedures are defined.

EXAMPLE 9–4 Creating a Generic Subroutine: Create a subroutine maxval that returns the maximum value in an array and optionally returns the location of that maximum value. This subroutine should work correctly for integer, single-precision real, double-precision real, single-precision complex, or double-precision complex data. Since relational comparisons of complex data values are meaningless, the complex versions of the subroutine should look for the maximum absolute value in the array.

SOLUTION We will be producing a generic subroutine that can work with five different types of input data, so in fact we create five different subroutines and relate them together using a generic interface block. Note that the subroutines must have an explicit interface in order to support optional arguments, so they will all be placed in a module.

1. **State the problem.**

    Write a generic subroutine to find the maximum value in an array and optionally the location of that maximum value. The subroutine should work for integer, single-precision real, double-precision real, single-precision complex, or double-precision complex data. For complex data the comparisons should be based on the magnitude of the values in the array.

2. **Define the inputs and outputs.**

    This problem has five different subroutines. The input to each subroutine will be an array of values of the appropriate type, plus the number of values in the array. The outputs will be as follows:
    a. A variable containing the maximum value in the input array.
    b. An optional integer variable containing the offset in the array at which the maximum value occurred.

The types of the input and output arguments for each of the five subroutines are specified in the following table.

Specific name	Input array type	Array length type	Output maximum value	Optional location of maximum value
maxval_i	Integer	Integer	Integer	Integer
maxval_r	Single-precision real	Integer	Single-precision real	Integer
maxval_d	Double-precision real	Integer	Double-precision real	Integer
maxval_c	Single-precision complex	Integer	Single-precision real	Integer
maxval_dc	Double-precision complex	Integer	Double-precision real	Integer

3. Describe the algorithm.

The pseudocode for the first three specific subroutines is identical.

```
! Initialize "value_max" to a(1) and "pos_max" to 1.
value_max ← a(1)
pos_max ← 1

! Find the maximum values in a(2) through a(nvals)
DO for i = 2 to nvals
   IF a(i) > value_max THEN
      value_max ← a(i)
      pos_max ← i
   END of IF
END of DO

! Report results
IF argument pos_maxval is present THEN
   pos_maxval ← pos_max
END of IF
```

The pseudocode for the two complex subroutines is slightly different because comparisons must be with the absolute values.

```
! Initialize "value_max" to ABS(a(1)) and "pos_max" to 1.
value_max ← ABS(a(1))
pos_max ← 1

! Find the maximum values in a(2) through a(nvals)
DO for i = 2 to nvals
   IF ABS(a(i)) > value_max THEN
      value_max ← ABS(a(i))
      pos_max ← i
   END of IF
END of DO

! Report results
IF argument pos_maxval is present THEN
   pos_maxval ← pos_max
END of IF
```

4. Turn the algorithm into Fortran statements.

The resulting Fortran subroutine is shown in Figure 9–9.

FIGURE 9–9

A generic subroutine maxval that finds the maximum value in an array and optionally the location of that maximum value.

```
MODULE generic_maxval
!
!  Purpose:
!    To produce a generic procedure maxval that returns the
!    maximum value in an array and optionally the location
!    of that maximum value for the following input data types:
!    integer, single-precision real, double-precision real,
!    single-precision complex, and double-precision complex.
!    Complex comparisons are done on the absolute values of the
!    values in the input array.
!
!  Record of revisions:
!     Date        Programmer        Description of change
!     ====        ==========        =====================
!   01/03/96    S. J. Chapman       Original code
!
IMPLICIT NONE

! Declare parameters:
INTEGER, PARAMETER :: sgl = SELECTED_REAL_KIND(p=6)
INTEGER, PARAMETER :: dbl = SELECTED_REAL_KIND(p=13)

! Declare generic interface.
INTERFACE maxval
   MODULE PROCEDURE maxval_i
   MODULE PROCEDURE maxval_r
   MODULE PROCEDURE maxval_d
   MODULE PROCEDURE maxval_c
   MODULE PROCEDURE maxval_dc
END INTERFACE

CONTAINS
   SUBROUTINE maxval_i ( array, nvals, value_max, pos_maxval )
   IMPLICIT NONE

   ! List of calling arguments:
   INTEGER, INTENT(IN) :: nvals                        ! # vals.
   INTEGER, INTENT(IN), DIMENSION(nvals) :: array      ! Input data.
   INTEGER, INTENT(OUT) :: value_max                   ! Max value.
   INTEGER, INTENT(OUT), OPTIONAL :: pos_maxval        ! Position

   ! List of local variables:
   INTEGER :: i                                        ! Index
   INTEGER :: pos_max                                  ! Pos of max value

   ! Initialize the values to first value in array.
   value_max = array(1)
   pos_max = 1

   ! Find the extreme values in array(2) through array(nvals).
   DO i = 2, nvals
      IF ( array(i) > value_max ) THEN
         value_max = array(i)
         pos_max = i
      END IF
```

(continued)

(continued)

```
      END DO

      ! Report the results
      IF (PRESENT(pos_maxval) ) THEN
         pos_maxval = pos_max
      END IF

      END SUBROUTINE maxval_i

      SUBROUTINE maxval_r ( array, nvals, value_max, pos_maxval )
      IMPLICIT NONE

      ! List of calling arguments:
      INTEGER, INTENT(IN) :: nvals
      REAL (KIND=sgl), INTENT(IN), DIMENSION(nvals) :: array
      REAL (KIND=sgl), INTENT(OUT) :: value_max
      INTEGER, INTENT(OUT), OPTIONAL :: pos_maxval

      ! List of local variables:
      INTEGER :: i                            ! Index
      INTEGER :: pos_max                      ! Pos of max value

      ! Initialize the values to first value in array.
      value_max = array(1)
      pos_max = 1

      ! Find the extreme values in array(2) through array(nvals).
      DO i = 2, nvals
         IF ( array(i) > value_max ) THEN
            value_max = array(i)
            pos_max = i
         END IF
      END DO

      ! Report the results
      IF ( PRESENT(pos_maxval) ) THEN
         pos_maxval = pos_max
      END IF

      END SUBROUTINE maxval_r

      SUBROUTINE maxval_d ( array, nvals, value_max, pos_maxval )
      IMPLICIT NONE

      ! List of calling arguments:
      INTEGER, INTENT(IN) :: nvals
      REAL (KIND=dbl), INTENT(IN), DIMENSION(nvals) :: array
      REAL (KIND=dbl), INTENT(OUT) :: value_max
      INTEGER, INTENT(OUT), OPTIONAL :: pos_maxval

      ! List of local variables:
      INTEGER :: i                            ! Index
      INTEGER :: pos_max                      ! Pos of max value

      ! Initialize the values to first value in array.
      value_max = array(1)
      pos_max = 1

      ! Find the extreme values in array(2) through array(nvals).
```

9

(continued)

(continued)

```fortran
   DO i = 2, nvals
      IF ( array(i) > value_max ) THEN
         value_max = array(i)
         pos_max = i
      END IF
   END DO

   ! Report the results
   IF ( PRESENT(pos_maxval) ) THEN
      pos_maxval = pos_max
   END IF

END SUBROUTINE maxval_d

SUBROUTINE maxval_c ( array, nvals value_max, pos_maxval )
IMPLICIT NONE

! List of calling arguments:
INTEGER, INTENT(IN) :: nvals
COMPLEX (KIND=sgl), INTENT(IN), DIMENSION(nvals) :: array
REAL (KIND=sgl), INTENT(OUT) :: value_max
INTEGER, INTENT(OUT), OPTIONAL :: pos_maxval

! List of local variables:
INTEGER :: i                              ! Index
INTEGER :: pos_max                        ! Pos of max value

! Initialize the values to first value in array.
value_max = ABS(array(1))
pos_max = 1

! Find the extreme values in array(2) through array(nvals).
DO i = 2, nvals
   IF ( ABS(array(i)) > value_max ) THEN
      value_max = ABS(array(i))
      pos_max = i
   END IF
END DO

! Report the results
IF ( PRESENT(pos_maxval) ) THEN
   pos_maxval = pos_max
END IF

END SUBROUTINE maxval_c

SUBROUTINE maxval_dc ( array, nvals, value_max, pos_maxval )
IMPLICIT NONE

! List of calling arguments:
INTEGER, INTENT(IN) :: nvals
COMPLEX (KIND=dbl), INTENT(IN), DIMENSION(nvals) :: array
REAL (KIND=dbl), INTENT(OUT) :: value_max
INTEGER, INTENT(OUT), OPTIONAL :: pos_maxval

! List of local variables:
INTEGER :: i                              ! Index
INTEGER :: pos_max                        ! Pos of max value
```

(continued)

(concluded)

```
! Initialize the values to first value in array.
value_max = ABS(array(1))
pos_max = 1

! Find the extreme values in array(2) through array(nvals).
DO i = 2, nvals
   IF ( ABS(array(i)) > value_max ) THEN
      value_max = ABS(array(i))
      pos_max = i
   END IF
END DO

! Report the results
IF ( PRESENT(pos_maxval) ) THEN
   pos_maxval = pos_max
END IF

END SUBROUTINE maxval_dc

END MODULE generic_maxval
```

5. Test the resulting Fortran programs.

To test this generic subroutine, we need to write a test driver program to call the subroutine with the five different types of data that it supports and then display the results. The test driver program will call the subroutine with different combinations and orders of arguments to illustrate the use of keywords and optional arguments. Figure 9–10 shows an appropriate test driver program.

FIGURE 9–10
Test driver program for generic subroutine `maxval`.

```
PROGRAM test_maxval
!
!  Purpose:
!    To test the generic subroutine maxval with five different types
!    of input data sets.
!
!  Record of revisions:
!      Date          Programmer          Description of change
!      ====          ==========          =====================
!    01/03/96     S. J. Chapman          Original code
!
USE generic_maxval
IMPLICIT NONE

! List of variables:
INTEGER, DIMENSION(6) :: array_i                    ! Integer array
REAL (KIND=sgl), DIMENSION(6) :: array_r     ! Sing. prec real arr
REAL (KIND=dbl), DIMENSION(6) :: array_d     ! Dbl. prec real arr
COMPLEX (KIND=sgl), DIMENSION(6) :: array_c  ! Sing. prec. cx arr
COMPLEX (KIND=dbl), DIMENSION(6) :: array_dc ! Sing. prec. cx arr
INTEGER :: value_max_i                              ! Max value
```

(continued)

(concluded)

```
REAL (KIND=sgl) :: value_max_r              ! Max value
REAL (KIND=dbl) :: value_max_d              ! Max value
INTEGER :: pos_maxval                         ! Pos of max value

! Initialize arrays
array_i  = (/ -13, 3, 2, 0, 25, -2 /)
array_r  = (/ -13., 3., 2., 0., 25., -2. /)
array_d  = (/ -13._dbl, 3._dbl, 2._dbl, 0._dbl, &
              25._dbl, -2._dbl /)
array_c  =  (/(1.,2.), (-4.,-6.), (4.,-7), (3.,4.), &
              (0.,1.), (6.,-8.) /)
array_dc = (/ (1._dbl,2._dbl), (-4._dbl,-6._dbl), &
              (4._dbl,-7._dbl), (3._dbl,4._dbl), &
              (0._dbl,1._dbl), (6._dbl,-8._dbl) /)

! Test integer subroutine. Include optional argument.
CALL maxval ( array_i, 6, value_max_i, pos_maxval )
WRITE (*,1000) value_max_i, pos_maxval
1000 FORMAT (' Integer args: max value = ',I3, &
             '; position = ', I3 )

! Test single prec real subroutine. Leave out optional arg.
CALL maxval ( array_r, 6, value_max_r )
WRITE (*,1010) value_max_r
1010 FORMAT (' Single precision real args: max value = ',F7.3)

! Test double prec real subroutine. Use keywords.
CALL maxval ( ARRAY=array_d, NVALS = 6, VALUE_MAX=value_max_d )
WRITE (*,1020) value_max_d
1020 FORMAT (' Double prec real args: max value = ',F7.3)

! Test single prec cmplx subroutine. Use scrambled keywords.
CALL maxval ( NVALS=6, ARRAY=arry_c, VALUE_MAX=value_max_r, &
              POS_MAXVAL=pos_maxval )
WRITE (*,1030) value_max_r, pos_maxval
1030 FORMAT (' Single precision complex args:' &
             ' max abs value = ',F7.3, &
             '; position = ', I3 )

! Test double prec complex subroutine. Leave out optional arg.
CALL maxval ( array_dc, 6, value_max_d )
WRITE (*,1040) value_max_r
1040 FORMAT (' Double precision complex args:' &
             ' max abs value = ',F7.3 )

END PROGRAM
```

When the test driver program is executed, the results are:

```
C>test_maxval
Integer arguments: max value = 25; position = 5
Single-precision real arguments: max value = 25.000
Double-precision real arguments: max value = 25.000
Single-precision complex arguments: max abs value = 10.000; position = 6
Double-precision complex arguments: max abs value = 10.000
```

As you can see, the subroutine picked out the proper maximum values and locations for each data type.

▪ 9.7

EXTENDING FORTRAN WITH USER-DEFINED OPERATORS AND ASSIGNMENTS

As explained in Chapter 8, none of the intrinsic unary and binary operators are defined for derived data types. In fact, the only operation that was defined for derived data types was the assignment of one item of a derived data type to another variable of the same type. We were able to work freely with the *components* of derived data types, but not with the derived data types themselves. This serious limitation reduces the usefulness of derived data types.

Fortunately, we have a way around this limitation. Fortran 90/95 is an *extensible* language, which means that an individual programmer can add new features to accommodate special types of problems. The first examples of this extensibility were derived data types themselves. In addition, Fortran permits the programmer to define new unary and binary operators for both intrinsic and derived data types and also to define new extensions to standard operators for derived data types. With appropriate definitions, the Fortran language can be made to add, subtract, multiply, divide, compare, and so forth two operators of a derived data type.

How can we define new operators or extend existing ones? The first step is to write a function that performs the desired task and place it into a module. For example, if we wanted to add two values of a derived data type, we would first create a function whose arguments are the two values to be added and whose result is the sum of the two values. The function will implement the instructions required to perform the addition. The next step is to associate the function with a user-defined or intrinsic operator using an interface operator block. The form of an interface operator block is

```
INTERFACE OPERATOR (operator_symbol)
   MODULE PROCEDURE function_1
   ...
END INTERFACE
```

where `operator_symbol` is any standard intrinsic operator (+ , − , *, /, > , < , etc.) or any user-defined operator. A *user-defined operator* is a sequence of up to 31 letters surrounded by periods (numbers and underscore characters are not allowed in an operator name). For example, a user-defined operator might be named .INVERSE.. Each interface body can be either a complete description of the interface to the function if the function is not in a module or a `MODULE PROCEDURE` statement if the function is in a module. In either case, the function *must* have an explicit interface.

More than one function can be associated with the same operator symbol, but the functions must be distinguishable from one another by having different types of dummy arguments. When the compiler encounters the operator symbol in a program, it invokes the function whose dummy arguments match the operands associated with the operator symbol. If no associated function has dummy arguments that match the operands, then a compilation error results.

If the function associated with an operator has two dummy arguments, then the resulting operator will be a binary operator. If the function has only one dummy argument, then the operator will be a unary operator. Once defined, the operator will be treated as a reference to the function. For binary operations the left-hand operand will become the first argument of the function, and the right-hand operand will become the second argument of the function. The function must not modify its calling arguments. To enforce this rule, it is customary to declare all function arguments with INTENT(IN).

If the operator being defined by the interface is one of Fortran's intrinsic operators (+, -, *, /, >, etc.), then we have to consider three additional constraints:

1. We cannot change the meaning of an intrinsic operator for predefined intrinsic data types. For example, we cannot change the meaning of the addition operator (+) when it is applied to two integers. However, we can *extend* the meaning of the operator by defining the actions to perform when the operator is applied to derived data types or to combinations of derived data types and intrinsic data types.
2. The number of arguments in a function must be consistent with the normal use of the operator. For example, multiplication (*) is a binary operator, so any function extending its meaning must have two arguments.
3. If a relational operator is extended, then the same extension applies regardless of which way the operator is written. For example, if we give an additional meaning to the relational operator "greater than," then the extension applies whether "greater than" is written as > or .GT.

We can extend the meaning of the assignment operator (=) in a similar fashion. To define extended meanings for the assignment operator, we use an interface assignment block:

```
INTERFACE ASSIGNMENT (=)
    MODULE PROCEDURE subroutine_1
    ...
END INTERFACE
```

For an assignment operator, the interface body must refer to a *subroutine* instead of to a function. The subroutine must have two arguments. The first argument is the output of the assignment statement and must have INTENT(OUT). The second dummy argument is the input to the assignment statement and must have INTENT(IN). The first argument corresponds to the left side of the assignment statement, and the second argument corresponds to the right side of the assignment statement.

More than one subroutine can be associated with the assignment symbol, but the subroutines must be distinguishable from one another by having different types of dummy arguments. When the compiler encounters the assignment symbol in a program, it invokes the subroutine whose dummy arguments match the types of the values on either side of the equal sign. If no associated subroutine has dummy arguments that match the values, then a compilation error results.

Good Programming Practice

Use interface operator blocks and interface assignment blocks to create new operators and to extend the meanings of existing operators to work with derived data types. Once proper operators are defined, working with derived data types can be very easy.

The best way to explain the use of user-defined operators and assignments is by an example. We will now define a new derived data type and create appropriate user-defined operations and assignments for it.

EXAMPLE 9–5 *Vectors:* The study of the dynamics of objects in motion in three dimensions is an important area of engineering. In the study of dynamics, the position and velocity of objects, forces, torques, and so forth are usually represented by three-component vectors $\mathbf{v} = x\,\hat{\mathbf{i}} + y\,\hat{\mathbf{j}} + z\,\hat{\mathbf{k}}$, where the three components (x, y, z) represent the projection of the vector $\mathbf{v}$ along the x-, y-, and z-axes, respectively, and $\hat{\mathbf{i}}, \hat{\mathbf{j}},$ and $\hat{\mathbf{k}}$ are the unit vectors along the x-, y-, and z-axes (see Figure 9–11). The solutions of many mechanical problems involve manipulating these vectors in specific ways.

The most common operations performed on these vectors follow.

1. **Addition**   Two vectors are added together by separately adding their x, y, and z components. If $\mathbf{v_1} = x_1\,\hat{\mathbf{i}} + y_1\,\hat{\mathbf{j}} + z_1\,\hat{\mathbf{k}}$ and $\mathbf{v_2} = x_2\,\hat{\mathbf{i}} + y_2\,\hat{\mathbf{j}} + z_2\,\hat{\mathbf{k}}$, then $\mathbf{v_1} + \mathbf{v_2} = (x_1 + x_2)\,\hat{\mathbf{i}} + (y_1 + y_2)\,\hat{\mathbf{j}} + (z_1 + z_2)\,\hat{\mathbf{k}}$.
2. **Subtraction**   Two vectors are subtracted by separately subtracting their x, y, and z components. If $\mathbf{v_1} = x_1\,\hat{\mathbf{i}} + y_1\,\hat{\mathbf{j}} + z_1\,\hat{\mathbf{k}}$ and $\mathbf{v_2} = x_2\,\hat{\mathbf{i}} + y_2\,\hat{\mathbf{j}} + z_2\,\hat{\mathbf{k}}$, then $\mathbf{v_1} - \mathbf{v_2} = (x_1 - x_2)\,\hat{\mathbf{i}} + (y_1 - y_2)\,\hat{\mathbf{j}} + (z_1 - z_2)\,\hat{\mathbf{k}}$.
3. **Multiplication by a scalar**   A vector is multiplied by a scalar by separately multiplying each component by the scalar. If $\mathbf{v} = x\,\hat{\mathbf{i}} + y\,\hat{\mathbf{j}} + z\,\hat{\mathbf{k}}$, then $a\mathbf{v} = ax\,\hat{\mathbf{i}} + ay\,\hat{\mathbf{j}} + az\,\hat{\mathbf{k}}$.

9

FIGURE 9–11
A three-dimensional vector.

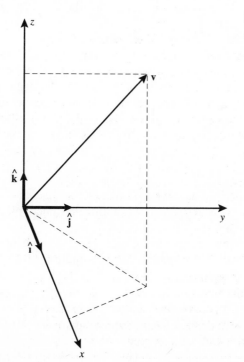

4. **Division by a scalar** A vector is divided by a scalar by separately dividing each component of the scalar. If $\mathbf{v} = x\,\hat{\mathbf{i}} + y\,\hat{\mathbf{j}} + z\,\hat{\mathbf{k}}$, then $\dfrac{\mathbf{v}}{a} = \dfrac{x}{a}\,\hat{\mathbf{i}} + \dfrac{y}{a}\,\hat{\mathbf{j}} + \dfrac{z}{a}\,\hat{\mathbf{k}}$.

5. **The dot product** The dot product of two vectors is one form of multiplication operation performed on vectors. It produces a scalar that is the sum of the products of the vector's components. If $\mathbf{v_1} = x_1\,\hat{\mathbf{i}} + y_1\,\hat{\mathbf{j}} + z_1\,\hat{\mathbf{k}}$ and $\mathbf{v_2} = x_2\,\hat{\mathbf{i}} + y_2\,\hat{\mathbf{j}} + z_2\,\hat{\mathbf{k}}$, the dot product of the vectors is $\mathbf{v_1} \cdot \mathbf{v_2} = x_1 x_2 + y_1 y_2 + z_1 z_2$.

6. **The cross product** The cross product is another multiplication operation that appears frequently between vectors. The cross product of two vectors is another vector whose direction is perpendicular to the plane formed by the two input vectors. If $\mathbf{v_1} = x_1\,\hat{\mathbf{i}} + y_1\,\hat{\mathbf{j}} + z_1\,\hat{\mathbf{k}}$ and $\mathbf{v_2} = x_2\,\hat{\mathbf{i}} + y_2\,\hat{\mathbf{j}} + z_2\,\hat{\mathbf{k}}$, then the cross product of the two vectors is defined as $\mathbf{v_1} \times \mathbf{v_2} = (y_1 z_2 - y_2 z_1)\hat{\mathbf{i}} + (z_1 x_2 - z_2 x_1)\hat{\mathbf{j}} + (x_1 y_2 - x_2 y_1)\hat{\mathbf{k}}$.

Create a derived data type called `vector`, having three components x, y, and z. Define functions to create vectors from arrays, to convert vectors to arrays, and to perform the six vector operations. Extend the intrinsic operators +, -, *, and / to have valid meanings when working with vectors and also create a new operator .DOT. for the dot product of two vectors. Finally, extend the assignment operator (=) to allow three-element arrays to be assigned to vectors and vectors to be assigned to three-element arrays.

SOLUTION To make it easy to work with vectors, we should place the definition of the data type, the manipulating functions, and the operator definitions all in a single module. That one module can then be used by any programs wanting to manipulate vectors.

Note that six operations were defined for vectors, but we must write more than six functions to implement them. For example, the multiplication of a vector by a scalar could occur in either order: vector times scalar or scalar times vector. Both orders produce the same result, but the order of command-line arguments for an implementing function is different in either case. Also, a scalar could be either an integer or a single-precision real number. To allow for all four possibilities (either order and either type of scalar), we actually have to write four functions!

1. **State the problem.**

Create a derived data type called `vector`, having three single-precision real components x, y, and z. Write the following functions and subroutines for manipulating vectors:

a. Create a vector from a three-element single-precision real array.
b. Convert a vector into a three-element single-precision real array.
c. Add two vectors.
d. Subtract two vectors.
e. Multiply a single-precision real scalar by a vector.
f. Multiply a vector by a single-precision real scalar.
g. Multiply an integer scalar by a vector.

h. Multiply a vector by an integer scalar.
i. Divide a vector by a single-precision real scalar.
j. Divide a vector by an integer scalar.
k. Calculate the dot product of two vectors.
l. Calculate the cross product of two vectors.

Associate these functions and subroutines with the appropriate operators using the interface operator constructs and interface assignment constructs.

2. Define the inputs and outputs.

Each procedure described in step 1 has its own inputs and outputs. The types of input and output arguments for each function are specified in the following table:

Specific function/ subroutine name	Input argument 1 type	Input argument 2 type	Output type
array_to_vector (subroutine)	three-element single-precision real array	N/A	vector
vector_to_array (subroutine)	Vector	N/A	three-element single-precision real array
vector_add	Vector	Vector	Vector
vector_subtract	Vector	Vector	Vector
vector_times_real	Vector	Single-precision real	Vector
real_times_vector	Single-precision real	Vector	Vector
vector_times_int	Vector	Integer	Vector
int_times_vector	Integer	Vector	Vector
vector_div_real	Vector	Single-precision real	Vector
vector_div_int	Vector	Integer	Vector
dot_product	Vector	Vector	Single-precision real
cross_product	Vector	Vector	Vector

3. Describe the algorithm.

The following definitions apply in the pseudocode for all of the routines in step 1.

vec_1	First input argument (vector).
vec_2	Second input argument (vector).
real_1	First input argument (single-precision real).
real_2	Second input argument (single-precision real).

int_1	First input argument (integer).
int_2	Second input argument (integer).
array	Input argument (single-precision real array).
vec_result	Function result (vector).
real_result	Function result (single-precision real).
array_result	Function result (single-precision real array).

Given these definitions, the pseudocode for the `array_to_vector` subroutine is

```
vec_result%x ← array(1)
vec_result%y ← array(2)
vec_result%z ← array(3)
```

The pseudocode for the `vector_to_array` subroutine is

```
array_result(1) ← vec_1%x
array_result(2) ← vec_1%y
array_result(3) ← vec_1%z
```

The pseudocode for the `vector_add` function is

```
vec_result%x ← vec_1%x + vec_2%x
vec_result%y ← vec_1%y + vec_2%y
vec_result%z ← vec_1%z + vec_2%z
```

The pseudocode for the `vector_subtract` function is

```
vec_result%x ← vec_1%x - vec_2%x
vec_result%y ← vec_1%y - vec_2%y
vec_result%z ← vec_1%z - vec_2%z
```

The pseudocode for the `vector_times_real` function is

```
vec_result%x ← vec_1%x * real_2
vec_result%y ← vec_1%y * real_2
vec_result%z ← vec_1%z * real_2
```

The pseudocode for `real_times_vector` function is

```
vec_result%x ← real_1 * vec_2%x
vec_result%y ← real_1 * vec_2%y
vec_result%z ← real_1 * vec_2%z
```

The pseudocode for the `vector_times_int` function is

```
vec_result%x ← vec_1%x * REAL(int_2)
vec_result%y ← vec_1%y * REAL(int_2)
vec_result%z ← vec_1%z * REAL(int_2)
```

The pseudocode for the `int_times_vector` function is

```
vec_result%x ← REAL(int_1) * vec_2%x
vec_result%y ← REAL(int_1) * vec_2%y
vec_result%z ← REAL(int_1) * vec_2%z
```

The pseudocode for the `vector_div_real` function is

```
                        vec_Result%x ← vec_1%x / real_2
                        vec_Result%y ← vec_1%y / real_2
                        vec_result%z ← vec_1%z / real_2
```

The pseudocode for the `vector_div_int` function is

```
                    vec_result%x ← vec_1%x / REAL(int_2)
                    vec_result%y ← vec_1%y / REAL(int_2)
                    vec_result%z ← vec_1%z / REAL(int_2)
```

The pseudocode for the `dot_product` function is

```
        real_result ← vec_1%x*vec_2%x + vec_1%y*vec_2%y + vec_1%z*vec_2%z
```

The pseudocode for the `cross_product` function is

```
                vec_result%x ← vec_1%y*vec_2%z - vec_1%z*vec_2%y
                vec_result%y ← vec_1%z*vec_2%x - vec_1%x*vec_2%z
                vec_result%z ← vec_1%x*vec_2%y - vec_1%y*vec_2%x
```

These twelve functions will be assigned to operators in interface operator and interface assignment blocks as follows:

Function	Operator
array_to_vector	=
vector_to_array	=
vector_add	+
vector_subtract	–
vector_times_real	*
real_times_vector	*
vector_times_int	*
int_times_vector	*
vector_div_real	/
vector_div_int	/
dot_product	.DOT.
cross_product	*

4. **Turn the algorithm into Fortran statements.**

The resulting Fortran module is shown in Figure 9–12.

FIGURE 9–12
A module to create a derived data type `vector` and to define mathematical operations that can be performed on values of type `vector`.

```
MODULE vectors
!
!  Purpose:
!    To define a derived data type called vector and the
!    operations that can be performed on it. The module
```

(continued)

(continued)

```
!     defines eight operations that can be performed on vectors:
!
!                        Operation                         Operator
!                        =========                         ========
!        1.  Creation from a real array                        =
!        2.  Conversion to a real array                        =
!        3.  Vector addition                                   +
!        4.  Vector subtraction                                -
!        5.  Vector-scalar multiplication (4 cases)            *
!        6.  Vector-scalar division (2 cases)                  /
!        7.  Dot product                                     .DOT.
!        8.  Cross product                                     *
!
!     It contains a total of 12 procedures to implement those
!     operations: array_to_vector, vector_to_array, vector_add,
!     vector_subtract, vector_times_real, real_times_vector,
!     vector_times_int, int_times_vector, vector_div_real,
!     vector_div_int, dot_product, and cross_product.
!
!   Record of revisions:
!       Date        Programmer          Description of change
!       ====        ==========          =====================
!     01/05/96    S. J. Chapman         Original code
!
IMPLICIT NONE

! Declare vector data types:
TYPE :: vector
   REAL :: x
   REAL :: y
   REAL :: z
END TYPE

! Declare interface operators:
INTERFACE ASSIGNMENT (=)
   MODULE PROCEDURE array_to_vector
   MODULE PROCEDURE vector_to_array
END INTERFACE

INTERFACE OPERATOR (+)
   MODULE PROCEDURE vector_add
END INTERFACE

INTERFACE OPERATOR (-)
   MODULE PROCEDURE vector_subtract
END INTERFACE

INTERFACE OPERATOR (*)
   MODULE PROCEDURE vector_times_real
   MODULE PROCEDURE real_times_vector
   MODULE PROCEDURE vector_times_int
   MODULE PROCEDURE int_times_vector
   MODULE PROCEDURE cross_product
END INTERFACE

INTERFACE OPERATOR (/)
   MODULE PROCEDURE vector_div_real
   MODULE PROCEDURE vector_div_int
END INTERFACE
```

(continued)

(continued)

```
INTERFACE OPERATOR (.DOT.)
   MODULE PROCEDURE dot_product
END INTERFACE

! Now define the implementing functions.
CONTAINS
   SUBROUTINE array_to_vector(vec_result, array)
      TYPE (vector), INTENT(OUT) :: vec_result
      REAL, DIMENSION(3), INTENT(IN) :: array
      vec_result%x = array(1)
      vec_result%y = array(2)
      vec_result%z = array(3)
   END SUBROUTINE array_to_vector

   SUBROUTINE vector_to_array(array_result, vec_1)
      REAL, DIMENSION(3), INTENT(OUT) :: array_result
      TYPE (vector), INTENT(IN) :: vec_1
      array_result(1) = vec_1%x
      array_result(2) = vec_1%y
      array_result(3) = vec_1%z
   END SUBROUTINE vector_to_array

   FUNCTION vector_add(vec_1, vec_2)
      TYPE (vector) :: vector_add
      TYPE (vector), INTENT(IN) :: vec_1, vec_2
      vector_add%x = vec_1%x + vec_2%x
      vector_add%y = vec_1%y + vec_2%y
      vector_add%z = vec_1%z + vec_2%z
   END FUNCTION vector_add

   FUNCTION vector_subtract(vec_1, vec_2)
      TYPE (vector) :: vector_subtract
      TYPE (vector), INTENT(IN) :: vec_1, vec_2
      vector_subtract%x = vec_1%x - vec_2%x
      vector_subtract%y = vec_1%y - vec_2%y
      vector_subtract%z = vec_1%z - vec_2%z
   END FUNCTION vector_subtract

   FUNCTION vector_times_real(vec_1, real_2)
      TYPE (vector) :: vector_times_real
      TYPE (vector), INTENT(IN) :: vec_1
      REAL, INTENT(IN) :: real_2
      vector_times_real%x = vec_1%x * real_2
      vector_times_real%y = vec_1%y * real_2
      vector_times_real%z = vec_1%z * real_2
   END FUNCTION vector_times_real

   FUNCTION real_times_vector(real_1, vec_2)
      TYPE (vector) :: real_times_vector
      REAL, INTENT(IN) :: real_1
      TYPE (vector), INTENT(IN) :: vec_2
      real_times_vector%x = real_1 * vec_2%x
      real_times_vector%y = real_1 * vec_2%y
      real_times_vector%z = real_1 * vec_2%z
   END FUNCTION real_times_vector

   FUNCTION vector_times_int(vec_1, int_2)
      TYPE (vector) :: vector_times_int
```

9

(continued)

(concluded)

```
      TYPE (vector), INTENT(IN) :: vec_1
      INTEGER, INTENT(IN) :: int_2
      vector_times_int%x = vec_1%x * REAL(int_2)
      vector_times_int%y = vec_1%y * REAL(int_2)
      vector_times_int%z = vec_1%z * REAL(int_2)
   END FUNCTION vector_times_int

   FUNCTION int_times_vector(int_1, vec_2)
      TYPE (vector) :: int_times_vector
      INTEGER, INTENT(IN) :: int_1
      TYPE (vector), INTENT(IN) :: vec_2
      int_times_vector%x = REAL(int_1) * vec_2%x
      int_times_vector%y = REAL(int_1) * vec_2%y
      int_times_vector%z = REAL(int_1) * vec_2%z
   END FUNCTION int_times_vector

   FUNCTION vector_div_real(vec_1, real_2)
      TYPE (vector) :: vector_div_real
      TYPE (vector), INTENT(IN) :: vec_1
      REAL, INTENT(IN) :: real_2
      vector_div_real%x = vec_1%x / real_2
      vector_div_real%y = vec_1%y / real_2
      vector_div_real%z = vec_1%z / real_2
   END FUNCTION vector_div_real

   FUNCTION vector_div_int(vec_1, int_2)
      TYPE (vector) :: vector_div_int
      TYPE (vector), INTENT(IN) :: vec_1
      INTEGER, INTENT(IN) :: int_2
      vector_div_int%x = vec_1%x / REAL(int_2)
      vector_div_int%y = vec_1%y / REAL(int_2)
      vector_div_int%z = vec_1%z / REAL(int_2)
   END FUNCTION vector_div_int

   FUNCTION dot_product(vec_1, vec_2)
      REAL :: dot_product
      TYPE (vector), INTENT(IN) :: vec_1, vec_2
      dot_product = vec_1%x*vec_2%x + vec_1%y*vec_2%y &
                  + vec_1%z*vec_2%z
   END FUNCTION dot_product

   FUNCTION cross_product(vec_1, vec_2)
      TYPE (vector) :: cross_product
      TYPE (vector), INTENT(IN) :: vec_1, vec_2
      cross_product%x = vec_1%y*vec_2%z - vec_1%z*vec_2%y
      cross_product%y = vec_1%z*vec_2%x - vec_1%x*vec_2%z
      cross_product%z = vec_1%x*vec_2%y - vec_1%y*vec_2%x
   END FUNCTION cross_product

END MODULE vectors
```

5. **Test the resulting Fortran programs.**

To test this data type and its associated operations, we need to write a test driver program that defines and manipulates vectors and then prints out the results. The program should exercise every operation defined for vectors in the module. Figure 9–13 shows an appropriate test driver program.

FIGURE 9–13
Test driver program to test the `vector` data type and associated operations.

```
PROGRAM test_vectors
!
!  Purpose:
!    To test the definitions, operations, and assignments
!    associated with the vector data type.
!
!  Record of revisions:
!     Date       Programmer          Description of change
!     ====       ==========          =====================
!    01/05/96    S. J. Chapman       Original code
!
USE vectors
IMPLICIT NONE

! List of variables:
REAL, DIMENSION(3) :: array_out          ! Output array
TYPE (vector) :: vec_1, vec_2            ! Test vectors

! Test assignments by assigning an array to vec_1 and
! assigning vec_1 to array_out.
vec_1 = (/ 1., 2., 3. /)
array_out = vec_1
WRITE (*,1000) vec_1, array_out
1000 FORMAT (' Test assignments: ',/, &
             ' vec_1 =       ', 3F8.2,/, &
             ' array_out = ', 3F8.2)

! Test addition and subtraction.
vec_1 = (/ 10., 20., 30. /)
vec_2 = (/ 1., 2., 3. /)
WRITE (*,1010) vec_1, vec_2, vec_1 + vec_2, vec_1 - vec_2
1010 FORMAT (/' Test addition and subtraction: ',/, &
             ' vec_1 =         ', 3F8.2,/, &
             ' vec_2 =         ', 3F8.2,/, &
             ' vec_1 + vec_2 = ', 3F8.2,/, &
             ' vec_1 - vec_2 = ', 3F8.2)

! Test multiplication by a scalar.
vec_1 = (/ 1., 2., 3. /)
WRITE (*,1020) vec_1, 2.*vec_1, vec_1*2., 2*vec_1, vec_1*2
1020 FORMAT (/' Test multiplication by a scalar: ',/, &
             ' vec_1 =         ', 3F8.2,/, &
             ' 2. * vec_1 =    ', 3F8.2,/, &
             ' vec_1 * 2. =    ', 3F8.2,/, &
             ' 2 * vec_1 =     ', 3F8.2,/, &
             ' vec_1 * 2 =     ', 3F8.2)

! Test division by a scalar.
vec_1 = (/ 10., 20., 30. /)
WRITE (*,1030) vec_1, vec_1/5., vec_1/5
1030 FORMAT (/' Test division by a scalar: ',/, &
             ' vec_1 =         ', 3F8.2,/, &
             ' vec_1 / 5. =    ', 3F8.2,/, &
             ' vec_1 / 5 =     ', 3F8.2)

! Test dot product.
```

9

(continued)

(concluded)

```
vec_1 = (/ 1., 2., 3. /)
vec_2 = (/ 1., 2., 3. /)
WRITE (*,1040) vec_1, vec_2, vec_1 .DOT. vec_2
1040 FORMAT (/' Test dot product: ',/, &
                  ' vec_1 =                    ', 3F8.2,/, &
                  ' vec_2 =                    ', 3F8.2,/, &
                  ' vec_1 .DOT. vec_2 = ', 3F8.2)

! Test cross product.
vec_1 = (/ 1., −1., 1. /)
vec_2 = / −1., 1., 1. /)
WRITE (*,1050) vec_1, vec_2, vec_1*vec_2
1050 FORMAT (/' Test cross products: ',/, &
                  ' vec_1 =              ', 3F8.2,/, &
                  ' vec_2 =              ', 3F8.2,/, &
                  ' vec_1 * vec_2 = ', 3F8.2)

END PROGRAM test_vectors
```

When the test driver program is executed, the results are

```
C>test_vectors
Test assignments:
vec_1 =          1.00     2.00     3.00
array_out =      1.00     2.00     3.00

Test addition and subtraction:
vec_1  =              10.00    20.00    30.00
vec_2  =               1.00     2.00     3.00
vec_1 + vec_2  =      11.00    22.00    33.00
vec_1 - vec_2  =       9.00    18.00    27.00

Test multiplication by a scalar:
vec_1  =               1.00     2.00     3.00
2. * vec_1  =          2.00     4.00     6.00
vec_1 * 2.  =          2.00     4.00     6.00
2 * vec_1   =          2.00     4.00     6.00
vec_1 * 2   =          2.00     4.00     6.00

Test division by a scalar:
vec_1 =               10.00    20.00    30.00
vec_1 / 5.  =          2.00     4.00     6.00
vec_1 / 5   =          2.00     4.00     6.00

Test dot product:
vec_1 =                        1.00     2.00     3.00
vec_2 =                        1.00     2.00     3.00
vec_1 .DOT. vec_2  =          14.00

Test cross product:
vec_1 =                        1.00    -1.00     1.00
vec_2 =                       -1.00     1.00     1.00
vec_1 * vec_2  =              -2.00    -2.00      .00
```

The results of the program are correct, and we can verify them by calculating the answers from the definitions of the operations.

What would happen in a program if we tried to perform an operation with vectors that was not defined in the module? For example, what would happen if we tried to multiply a vector by a double-precision real scalar? A compilation error would result because the compiler does not know how to perform the operation. When defining a new data type and its operations, be careful to define *every* combination of operations that you might wish to use.

9.8

RESTRICTING ACCESS TO THE CONTENTS OF A MODULE

When a module is accessed by USE association, by default all of the entities defined within that module become available for use in the program unit containing the USE statement. In the past, we have used this fact to share data between program units, to make procedures with explicit interfaces available to program units, to create new operators, and to extend the meanings of existing operators.

In Example 9–5, we created a module called vectors to extend the Fortran language. Any program unit that accesses module vectors can define its own vectors, and can manipulate them using the binary operators +, -, *, /, and .DOT.. Unfortunately, the program will also be able to invoke such functions as vector_add, vector_subtract, etc., even though it should only be using them indirectly through the use of the defined operators. These procedure names are not needed in any program unit, but they are declared, and they might conflict with a procedure name defined in the program. A similar problem could occur when many data items are defined within a module, but only a few of them are needed by a particular program unit. All of the unnecessary data items will also be available in the program unit, making it possible for a programmer to modify them by mistake.

In general, you should restrict access to any procedures or data entities in a module to only those program units that must know about them. This process is known as **data hiding.** The more access is restricted, the less chance there is of a programmer using or modifying an item by mistake. Restricting access makes programs more modular and easier to understand and maintain.

How can we restrict access to the entities in a module? Fortran 90/95 provides a way to control the access to a particular item in a module by program units outside that module: the PUBLIC and PRIVATE attributes and statements. If the PUBLIC attribute or statement is specified for an item, then the item will be available to program units outside the module. If the PRIVATE attribute or statement is specified, then the item will not be available to program units outside the module, although procedures inside the module still have access to it. The default attribute for all data and procedures in a module is PUBLIC, so by default any program unit that uses a module can have access to every data item and procedure within it.

The PUBLIC or PRIVATE status of a data item or procedure can be declared in one of two ways. We can specify the status as an attribute in a type definition statement or in an independent Fortran statement. Examples in which the attributes are declared as part of a type definition statement are

```
INTEGER, PRIVATE :: count
REAL, PUBLIC :: voltage
TYPE (vector), PRIVATE :: scratch_vector
```

This type of declaration can be used for data items and for functions, but not for subroutines. A `PUBLIC` or `PRIVATE` statement can also be used to specify the status of data items, functions, and subroutines. The form of a `PUBLIC` or `PRIVATE` statement is

```
PUBLIC [::] list of public items
PRIVATE [::] list of private items
```

If a module contains a `PRIVATE` statement without a list of private items, then by default every data item and procedure in the module is private. Any items that should be public must be explicitly listed in a separate `PUBLIC` statement. This is the preferred way to design modules, since only the items that are actually required by programs are exposed to them.

Good Programming Practice

It is good programming practice to hide any module data items or procedures that do not need to be directly accessed by external program units. The best way to hide data items and procedures is to include a `PRIVATE` statement in each module and then list the specific items that you wish to make visible in a separate `PUBLIC` statement.

As an example of the proper use of data hiding, let's reexamine module `vectors` from Example 9–5. Programs accessing this module need to define variables of type `vector` and need to perform operations involving vectors. However, the programs do not need direct access to any of the subroutines or functions in the module. The proper declarations for this circumstance are shown in Figure 9–14.

FIGURE 9–14
The first part of module `vector` modified to hide all nonessential items from external program units. Changes to the module are shown in bold type.

```
MODULE vectors
!
!  Purpose:
!    To define a derived data type called vector and the
!    operations that can be performed on it.  The module
!    defines eight operations that can be performed on vectors:
!
!             Operation                            Operator
!             =========                            ========
!      1. Creation from a real array                 =
!      2. Conversion to a real array                 =
!      3. Vector addition                             +
!      4. Vector subtraction                          -
!      5. Vector-scalar multiplication (4 cases)      *
!      6. Vector-scalar division (2 cases)            /
!      7. Dot product                               .DOT.
!      8. Cross product                               *
!
```

(continued)

(concluded)

```
!    It contains a total of 12 procedures to implement those
!    operations: array_to_vector, vector_to_array, vector_add,
!    vector_subtract, vector_times_real, real_times_vector,
!    vector_times_int, int_times_vector, vector_div_real,
!    vector_div_int, dot_product, and cross_product.  These
!    procedures are private to the module; they can only be
!    accessed from the outside via the defined operators.
!
!  Record of revisions:
!      Date          Programmer          Description of change
!      ====          ==========          =====================
!    01/05/96     S. J. Chapman          Original code
! 1. 01/06/96     S. J. Chapman          Modified to hide non-
!                                          essential items.
!
IMPLICIT NONE

! Declare all items to be private except for type vector and
! the operators defined for it.
PRIVATE
PUBLIC :: vector, assignment (=), operator (+), operator (-), &
          operator (*), operator (/), operator (.DOT.)

! Declare vector data type:
TYPE :: vector
   REAL :: x
   REAL :: y
   REAL :: z
END TYPE
```

The following notes apply to PUBLIC and PRIVATE declarations for derived data types in modules.

1. The components of a derived data type declared in a module can be made inaccessible to program units outside of the module by including a PRIVATE statement within the derived data type. Note that the derived data type as a whole is still available to outside program units, but its components cannot be accessed separately. Outside program units may freely declare variables of the derived data type, but they may not work with individual components of those variables. An example of a derived data type with private components is

```
TYPE vector
   PRIVATE
   REAL :: x
   REAL :: y
END TYPE
```

2. In contrast to the preceding situation, an entire derived data type can be declared to be private. For example:

```
TYPE, PRIVATE :: vector
   REAL :: x
   REAL :: y
END TYPE
```

In this case the data type vector is not accessible by any program units that use the module. This condition differs from the previous case in which the data type was available but its components could not be accessed separately. Such a derived data type can be used only for internal calculations within the module.

3. Finally, it is possible to declare private variables of a derived data type even though the type itself is public. For example:

```
TYPE :: vector
    REAL :: x
    REAL :: y
END TYPE
TYPE (vector), PRIVATE :: vec_1
```

In this case the derived data type vector is public and available in program units that use the module, but the variable vec_1 may be used only within the module. This type of declaration might be used for variables used in internal calculations within the module.

9.9

ADVANCED OPTIONS OF THE USE STATEMENT

When a program unit accesses a module by USE association, by default it gets access to every data item, interface, and procedure in the module. The module can restrict access to some items by declaring them to be PRIVATE. In addition to this control, a program unit using the module can further restrict the list of items being used and can also modify the names of those items.

Why would we want to further restrict the list of items from a module that is accessed by USE association in a program unit? If the program unit does not need a data item from a module, then it is good defensive programming to make that item unavailable. This action will prevent the program unit from using or modifying the item by mistake and will reduce the chance of developing hard-to-find bugs. A common problem of this sort would be to make a typographical error in a local variable name and not know it because the new name just accidentally happens to be declared in the module. Most typographical errors are caught by the compiler because the IMPLICIT NONE statement makes undeclared variables illegal. However, if the new name happens to be defined in the module, then using it will not be an error. Furthermore, since the contents of the module do not appear in the program unit listing, the programmer may not realize that a variable of that name was defined in the module! Problems like this can be hard to find.

To restrict access to certain specific items in a module, we can add an ONLY clause to the USE statement. The form of the statement is

USE *module_name*, ONLY: *only_list*

where *module_name* is the module name and *only_list* is the list of items from the module to be used, with items in the list separated by commas. As an example, we could further restrict access to operations in module vectors by using the statement

```
USE vectors, ONLY: vector, assignment(=)
```

In a procedure containing this statement, declaring a variable of type `vector` and assigning a three-element array to it would be legal, but adding two vectors together would not be legal.

It is also possible to rename a data item or procedure in the USE statement. The first reason that we might wish to rename a data item or procedure when it is used by a program unit is that the items name might be the same as the name of a local data item or an item from another module also used by the program unit. In this case renaming the item avoids a clash between the two definitions of the name.

The second reason to rename a module data item or procedure is to shorten a name declared in a module that is used very frequently in a program unit. For example, a module called `data_fit` might contain a procedure with the name `sp_real_least_squares_fit` to distinguish it from a double-precision version `dp_real_least_squares_fit`. When this module is used in a program unit, the programmer might wish to refer to the procedure by a less unwieldy name. He or she might wish to call the procedure simply `lsqfit` or something similar.

The forms of the USE statement that permit a programmer to rename a data item or procedure are

```
USE module_name, rename_list
USE module_name, ONLY: rename_list
```

where each item in the *rename_list* takes the form

```
module_name => local_name
```

In the first case, all public items in the module will be available to the program unit, but the ones in the rename list will be renamed. In the second case, only the items listed would be available, and they would be renamed. For example, the USE statement to rename the least-squares fit routine just mentioned while simultaneously restricting access to all other items in module `data_fit` would be

```
USE data_fit, ONLY: sp_real_least_squares_fit => lsqfit
```

A few complications can arise when multiple USE statements in a single program unit refer to the same module. It makes no sense to use more than one USE statement in a single routine to refer to a given module, so you should never have this problem in well-written code. However, if you do have more than one USE statement referring to the same module, the following rules apply:

1. If none of the USE statements have rename lists or ONLY clauses, then the statements are just duplicates of each other, which is legal but has no effect on the program.
2. If all the USE statements include rename lists but no ONLY clauses, then the effect is the same as if all the renamed items were listed in a single USE statement.
3. If all the USE statements include ONLY clauses, then the effect is the same as if all the lists were listed in a single USE statement.
4. If some USE statements have an ONLY clause and some do not, then the ONLY clauses have no effect on the program at all! This outcome occurs because the USE

statements without ONLY clauses allow all public items in the module to be visible in the program unit.

Quiz 9–2

This quiz provides a quick check to see if you understand the concepts introduced in sections 9.5 through 9.9. If you have trouble with the quiz, reread the sections, ask your instructor, or discuss the material with a fellow student. The answers to this quiz are found in the back of the book.

1. What is an interface block? What are the two possible locations for interface blocks in a Fortran program?

2. Why would a programmer choose to create an interface block to a procedure instead of including the procedure in a module?

3. What items must appear in the interface body of an interface block?

4. Is the following program valid? Why or why not? If it is legal, what does it do?

```
PROGRAM test
IMPLICIT NONE
TYPE :: data
   REAL :: x1
   REAL :: x2
END TYPE
CHARACTER(len=20) :: x1 = 'This is a test.'
TYPE (data) :: x2
x2%x1 = 613.
x2%x2 = 248.
WRITE (*,*) x1, x2
END PROGRAM
```

5. How is a generic procedure defined?

6. Is the following code valid? Why or why not? If it is legal, what does it do?

```
INTERFACE fit
   SUBROUTINE least_squares_fit (array, nvals, slope, intercept)
   IMPLICIT NONE
   INTEGER, INTENT(IN) :: nvals
   REAL, INTENT(IN), DIMENSION(nvals) :: array
   REAL, INTENT(OUT) :: slope
   REAL, INTENT(OUT) :: intercept
   END SUBROUTINE

   SUBROUTINE median_fit (data1, n, slope, intercept)
   IMPLICIT NONE
   INTEGER, INTENT(IN) :: n
   REAL, INTENT(IN), DIMENSION(n) :: data1
```

(continued)

(concluded)

```
      REAL, INTENT(OUT) :: slope
      REAL, INTENT(OUT) :: intercept
      END SUBROUTINE
   END INTERFACE
```

7. What is a MODULE PROCEDURE statement? What is its purpose?

8. What is the difference in structure between a user-defined operator and a user-defined assignment? How are they implemented?

9. How can access to the contents of a module be controlled? Why would we wish to limit the access to some data items or procedures in a module?

10. What is the default type of access for items in a module?

11. How can a program unit accessing a module by USE association control which items in the module it sees? Why would a programmer wish to use this technique?

12. How can a program unit accessing a module by USE association rename data items or procedures in the module? Why would a programmer wish to use this technique?

9.10
SUMMARY

This chapter introduces several advanced features of procedures and modules in Fortran 90/95. None of these features were available in earlier versions of Fortran.

An internal procedure is a procedure defined entirely within another program unit, which is called the host program unit, and is only accessible from the host program unit. Internal procedures are included in the host program unit after all the executable statements of the program unit and are preceded by a CONTAINS statement. An internal procedure has access to all the data items defined in its host program unit by host association unless the internal procedure contains a data item of the same name as a data item in the host. In that case the data item in the host is not accessible to the internal procedure.

Fortran supports three levels of scope: global, local, and statement. Global-scope objects include program, external procedure, and module names. The only statement-scope objects that we have seen so far are the variables in an implied DO loop in an array constructor and the index variables in a FORALL statement. Local-scope objects have a scope restricted to a single scoping unit. A scoping unit is a main program, a procedure, a module, a derived data type, or an interface. If one scoping unit is defined entirely inside another scoping unit, then the inner scoping unit inherits all the data items defined in the host scoping unit by host association.

Ordinarily, Fortran 90/95 subroutines and functions are not recursive—they cannot call themselves either directly or indirectly. However, they can be made recursive if they are declared to be recursive in the corresponding SUBROUTINE or FUNCTION statement. A recursive function declaration includes a RESULT clause specifying the name to be used to return the function result.

If a procedure has an explicit interface, then keyword arguments may be used to change the order in which calling arguments are specified. A keyword argument consists of the dummy argument's name followed by an equal sign and the value of the argument. Keyword arguments are very useful in supporting optional arguments.

If a procedure has an explicit interface, then optional arguments may be declared and used. An optional argument is an argument that may or may not be present in the procedure's calling sequence. An intrinsic function PRESENT() is provided to determine whether or not a particular optional argument is present when the procedure gets called. Keyword arguments are commonly used with optional arguments because optional arguments often appear out of sequence in the calling procedure.

Interface blocks are used to provide an explicit interface for procedures that are not contained in a module. They are often used to provide Fortran 90/95 interfaces to older pre-Fortran 90 code without rewriting all the code. The body of an interface block must either contain a complete description of the calling sequence to a procedure, including the type and position of every argument in the calling sequence, or a MODULE PROCEDURE statement to refer to a procedure already defined in a module.

Generic procedures are procedures that can function properly with different types of input data. A generic procedure is declared using a generic interface block, which looks like an ordinary interface block with the addition of a generic procedure name. One or more specific procedures may be declared within the body of the generic interface block. Each specific procedure must be distinguishable from all other specific procedures by the type and sequence of its non-optional dummy arguments. When a generic procedure is referenced in a program, the compiler uses the sequence of calling arguments associated with the reference to decide which specific procedure to execute.

New operators may be defined and intrinsic operators may be extended to have new meanings in Fortran 90/95. A new operator may have a name consisting of up to 31 characters surrounded by periods. New operators and extended meanings of intrinsic operators are defined using an interface operator block. The first line of the interface operator block specifies the name of the operator to be defined or extended, and its body specifies the Fortran functions that are invoked to define the extended meaning. For binary operators, each function must have two input arguments; for unary operators, each function must have a single input argument. If several functions are present in the interface body, then they must be distinguishable from one another by the type and/or order of their dummy arguments. When the Fortran compiler encounters a new or extended operator, it uses the type and order of the operands to decide which function to execute. This feature is commonly used to extend operators to support derived data types.

The assignment statement (=) may also be extended to work with derived data types by using an interface assignment block. The body of the interface assignment block must refer to one or more subroutines. Each subroutine must have exactly two dummy arguments, with the first argument having INTENT(OUT) and the second argument having INTENT(IN). The first argument corresponds to the left side of the equal sign, and the second argument corresponds to the right side of the equal sign. All subroutines in the body of an interface assignment block must be distinguishable from one another by the type and order of their dummy arguments.

It is possible to control access to the data items, operators, and procedures in a module by using the PUBLIC and PRIVATE statements or attributes. If an entity in a module is declared PUBLIC, then it will be available to any program unit that accesses the module by USE association. If an entity is declared PRIVATE, then it will not be available to any program unit that accesses the module by USE association. However, it will remain available to any procedures defined within the module.

The contents of a derived data type may be declared PRIVATE. If they are declared PRIVATE, then the components of the derived data type will not be separately accessible in any program unit that accesses the type of USE association. The data type as a whole will be available to the program unit, but its components will not be separately addressable. In addition, an entire derived data type may be declared PRIVATE. In that case neither the data type nor its components are accessible.

The USE statement has two options. The statement may be used to rename specific data items or procedures accessed from a module, which can prevent name conflicts or provide simplified names for local use. Alternatively, the ONLY clause may be used to restrict a program unit's access to only those items that appear in the list. Both options may be combined in a single USE statement.

9.10.1 Summary of Good Programming Practice

The following guidelines should be adhered to when working with the advanced features of procedures and modules:

1. When working with nested scoping units, avoid redefining the meaning of objects that have the same name in both the inner and outer scoping units. This guideline applies especially to internal procedures. You can avoid confusion about the behavior of variables in the internal procedure by simply giving them different names from the variables in the host procedure.
2. Avoid interface blocks by placing your procedures in modules whenever possible.
3. If you must create interfaces to many procedures, place all of the interfaces in a module so that they will be easily accessible to program units by USE association.
4. Use user-defined generic procedures to define procedures that can function with different types of input data.
5. Use interface operator blocks and interface assignment blocks to create new operators and to extend the meanings of existing operators to work with derived data types. Once proper operators are defined, working with derived data types can be very easy.
6. Hide any module data items or procedures that do not need to be directly accessed by external program units. The best way to do so is to include a PRIVATE statement in each module and then list the specific items that you wish to make public in a separate PUBLIC statement.

9.10.2 Summary of Fortran Statements and Structures

CONTAINS Statement

```
CONTAINS
```

Example:

```
PROGRAM main
...
CONTAINS
    SUBROUTINE sub1(x, y)
    ...
    END SUBROUTINE sub1
END PROGRAM
```

Description:

The CONTAINS statement specifies that the following statements are one or more separate procedures within the host unit. When used within a module, the CONTAINS statement marks the beginning of one or more module procedures. When used within a main program or an external procedure, the CONTAINS statement marks the beginning of one or more internal procedures. The CONTAINS statement must appear after any type, interface, and data definitions within a module and must follow the last executable statement within a main program or an external procedure.

Generic Interface Block

```
INTERFACE generic_name
    interface_body_1
    interface_body_2
    ...
END INTERFACE
```

Example:

```
INTERFACE sort
    MODULE PROCEDURE sorti
    MODULE PROCEDURE sortr
END INTERFACE
```

Description:

A generic procedure is declared using a generic interface block. A generic interface block declares the name of the generic procedure on the first line and then lists the explicit interfaces of the specific procedures associated with the generic procedure in the interface body. The explicit interface must be fully defined for any specific procedures not appearing in a module. Procedures appearing in a module are referred to with a MODULE PROCEDURE statement, since their interfaces are already known.

Interface Assignment Block

```
                        INTERFACE Assignment (=)
                            interface_body
                        END INTERFACE
```

Example:

```
                        INTERFACE ASSIGNMENT (=)
                            MODULE PROCEDURE vector_to_array
                            MODULE PROCEDURE array_to_vector
                        END INTERFACE
```

Description:

An interface assignment block extends the meaning of the assignment statement to support assignment operations between two different derived data types or between derived data types and intrinsic data types. Each procedure in the interface body must be a subroutine with two arguments. The first argument must have INTENT(OUT), and the second one must have INTENT(IN). All subroutines in the interface body must be distinguishable from each other by the order and type of their arguments.

Interface Block

```
                    INTERFACE
                        interface_body_1
                        ...
                    END INTERFACE
```

Example:

```
                    INTERFACE
                        SUBROUTINE sort(array,n)
                        INTEGER, INTENT(IN) :: n
                        REAL, INTENT(INOUT), DIMENSION(n) :: array
                        END SUBROUTINE
                    END INTERFACE
```

Description:

An interface block is used to declare an explicit interface for a separately compiled procedure. It may appear in the header of a procedure that wishes to invoke the separately compiled procedure, or it may appear in a module. The module may be used by the procedure that wishes to invoke the separately compiled procedure.

9

Interface Operator Block

```
INTERFACE OPERATOR (operator_symbol)
    interface_body
END INTERFACE
```

Example:

```
INTERFACE OPERATOR (*)
    MODULE PROCEDURE real_times_vector
    MODULE PROCEDURE vector_times_real
END INTERFACE
```

Description:

An interface operator block is used to define a new operator or to extend the meaning of an intrinsic operator to support derived data types. Each procedure in the interface must be a function whose arguments are `INTENT(IN)`. If the operator is a binary operator, then the function must have two arguments. If the operator is a unary operator, then the function must have only one argument. All functions in the interface body must be distinguishable from each other by the order and type of their arguments.

MODULE PROCEDURE Statement

```
MODULE PROCEDURE module_procedure_1 (, module_procedure_2, ... )
```

Example:

```
INTERFACE sort
    MODULE PROCEDURE sorti
    MODULE PROCEDURE sortr
END INTERFACE
```

Description:

The `MODULE PROCEDURE` statement is used in interface blocks to specify that a procedure contained in a module is to be associated with the generic procedure, operator, or assignment defined by the interface.

Recursive FUNCTION Statement

```
RECURSIVE [type] FUNCTION name( arg1, arg2, ... ) RESULT (res)
```

Example:

```
RECURSIVE FUNCTION fact( n ) RESULT (answer)
INTEGER :: answer
```

Description:

This statement declares a recursive Fortran function. A recursive function is one that can invoke itself. The type of the function may either be declared in the FUNCTION statement or in a separate type declaration statement. (The type of the result variable *res* is declared, not the type of the function name.) The value returned by the function call is the value assigned to *res* within the body of the function.

USE Statement

```
USE module_name (, rename_list, ONLY: only_list)
```

Example:

```
USE my_procs
USE my_procs, process_vector_input => input
USE my_procs, ONLY: process_vector_input => input
```

Description:

The USE statement makes the contents of the named module available to the program unit in which the statement appears. In addition to its basic function, the USE statement permits the module objects to be renamed as they are made available. The ONLY clause permits the programmer to specify that only certain objects from the module will be made available to the program unit.

▓ 9.11

EXERCISES

9–1 What are the differences between internal procedures and external procedures? When should an internal procedure be used instead of an external procedure?

9–2 In Example 8–4 the logical function lt_city failed to sort APO and Anywhere in proper order because all capital letters appear before all lowercase letters in the ASCII collating sequence. Add an internal procedure to function lt_city to avoid this problem by shifting both city names to uppercase before the comparison. Note that this procedure should not shift the names in the database to uppercase. It should only shift the names to uppercase while they are being used for the comparison.

9–3 Write test driver programs for the recursive subroutine `factorial` and the recursive function `fact` that were introduced in section 9.3. Test both procedures by calculating 5! and 10! with each one.

9–4 Write a test driver program to verify the proper operation of subroutine `extremes` in Example 9–2.

9–5 What is printed out when the following code is executed? What are the values of x, y, i, and j at each point in the program? If a value changes during the course of execution, explain why it changes.

```
PROGRAM exercise9_5
IMPLICIT NONE
REAL :: x = 12., y = -3., result
INTEGER :: i  = 6, j = 4
WRITE (*,100) ' Before call: x, y, i, j = ', x, y, i, j
100 FORMAT (A,2F6.1,2I6)
result = exec(y,i)
WRITE (*,*) ' The result is ', result
WRITE (*,100) ' After call: x, y, i, j = ', x, y, i, j
CONTAINS
    REAL FUNCTION exec(x,i)
    REAL, INTENT(IN) :: x
    INTEGER, INTENT(IN) :: i
    WRITE (*,100) ' In exec:      x, y, i, j = ', x, y, i, j
    100 FORMAT (A,2F6.1,2I6)
    exec = ( x + y ) / REAL ( i + j )
    j = i
    END FUNCTION exec
END PROGRAM
```

9–6 Is the following program correct or not? If it is correct, what is printed out when it executes? If not, what is wrong with it?

```
PROGRAM junk
IMPLICIT NONE
REAL :: a = 3, b = 4, output
INTEGER :: i = 0
call sub1(a, i, output)
WRITE (*,*) 'The output is ', output

CONTAINS
    SUBROUTINE sub1(x, j, junk)
    REAL, INTENT(IN) :: x
    INTEGER, INTENT(IN) :: j
    REAL, INTENT(OUT) :: junk
    junk = (x - j) / b
    END SUBROUTINE sub1
END PROGRAM
```

9–7 What are the three levels of scope in Fortran? Give examples of objects of each type.

9–8 What are scoping units in Fortran? Name the different types of scoping units.

9–9 What is a keyword argument? Under what circumstances can keyword arguments be used?

9-10 Assuming the following subroutine definition, are the subsequent calls legal or illegal? Assume that all calling arguments are of type real and that the subroutine interface is explicit. Explain why each illegal call is illegal.

```
SUBROUTINE my_sub (a, b, c, d, e )
REAL, INTENT(IN) :: a, d
REAL, INTENT(OUT) :: b
REAL, INTENT(IN), OPTIONAL :: c, e
IF ( PRESENT(c) ) THEN
   b = (a - c) / d
ELSE
   b = a / d
END IF
IF ( PRESENT(e) ) b = b - e
END SUBROUTINE
```

a. `CALL my_sub (1., x, y, 2., z)`
b. `CALL my_sub (10., 21., x, y, z)`
c. `CALL my_sub (x, y, 25.)`
d. `CALL my_sub (p, q, d=r)`
e. `CALL my_sub (a=p, q, d=r, e=s)`
f. `CALL my_sub (b=q, a=p, c=t, d=r, e=s)`

9-11 In Example 7–4 we created a subroutine to plot a data set on the line printer. That subroutine contained three dummy arguments to specify the limits of the plot: `minplt`, `maxplt`, and `default`. If `default` was false, then the limits specified in `minplt` and `maxplt` were used. If `default` was true, then the plot limits were calculated from the input data set. Rewrite the subroutine to make `minplt` and `maxplt` optional arguments. If they are present, use them to set the limits of the plot. Otherwise, calculate the limits from the input data set. (*Note:* It is a good idea to move the optional arguments to the end of the calling sequence.)

9-12 What is an interface block? When would interface blocks be needed in a Fortran program?

9-13 In Example 6–4 we created a subroutine `simul` to solve a system of N simultaneous equations in N unknowns. Assuming that the subroutine is independently compiled, it will not have an explicit interface. Write an interface block to define an explicit interface for this subroutine.

9-14 What is a generic procedure? How can a generic procedure be defined?

9-15 In Example 6–6 we created an improved version of the single-precision subroutine `simul` to solve a system of N simultaneous equations in N unknowns. In Example 8–2 we created a double-precision subroutine `dsimul` to solve a double-precision system of N simultaneous equations in N unknowns. In exercise 8–9 we created a complex subroutine `csimul` to solve a complex system of N simultaneous equations in N unknowns. Write a generic interface block for these three procedures.

9-16 Are the following generic interface blocks legal or illegal? Why?

a.
```
INTERFACE my_procedure
    SUBROUTINE proc_1 (a, b, c)
    REAL, INTENT(IN) ::a
    REAL INTENT(IN) ::b
    REAL, INTENT(OUT) ::c
    END SUBROUTINE proc_1
    SUBROUTINE proc_2 (x, y, out1, out2)
    REAL, INTENT(IN) ::x
    REAL, INTENT(IN) ::y
    REAL, INTENT(OUT) ::out1
    REAL, INTENT(OUT), OPTIONAL ::out2
    END SUBROUTINE proc_2
END INTERFACE
```

b.
```
INTERFACE my_procedure
    SUBROUTINE proc_1 (a, b, c)
    REAL, INTENT(IN) ::a
    REAL, INTENT(IN) ::b
    REAL, INTENT(OUT) ::c
    END SUBROUTINE proc_1
    SUBROUTINE proc_2 (x, y, z)
    INTEGER, INTENT(IN) ::x
    INTEGER, INTENT(IN) ::y
    INTEGER INTENT(OUT) ::out
    END SUBROUTINE proc_2
END INTERFACE
```

9–17 Simulating Dice Throws   Assume that a programmer is writing a game program. As a part of the program, it is necessary to simulate the throw of a pair of dice. Write a subroutine called throw to return two random values from 1 to 6 each time that it is called. The subroutine should contain an internal function called die to actually calculate the result of each toss of a die, and that function should be called twice by the subroutine to get the two results to return to the calling routine. (*Note:* You can generate a random die result by using the intrinsic subroutine RANDOM_NUMBER.)

9–18 How can a new Fortran operator be defined? What rules apply to the procedures in the body of an interface operator block?

9–19 How can an intrinsic Fortran operator be extended to have new meanings? What special rules apply to procedures in an interface operator block if an intrinsic operator is being extended?

9–20 How can the assignment operator be extended? What rules apply to the procedures in the body of an interface assignment block?

9–21 Polar Complex Numbers   A complex number may be represented in one of two ways: rectangular or polar (see Figure 9–15). The rectangular representation takes the form $c = a + bi$, where a is the real component and b is the imaginary component of the complex number. The polar representation is of the form $z \angle \theta$, where z is the magnitude of the complex number and θ is the angle of the number. The relationship between these two representations of complex numbers is

$$a = z \cos \theta \qquad\qquad (8\text{--}10)$$

$$b = z \sin \theta \qquad\qquad (8\text{--}11)$$

$$z = \sqrt{a^2 + b^2} \qquad (8\text{--}12)$$

$$\theta = \tan^{-1}\frac{b}{a} \qquad (8\text{--}13)$$

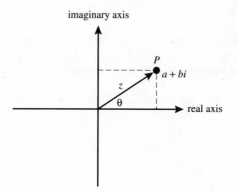

FIGURE 9–15
Representing a complex number in both rectangular and polar coordinates.

The COMPLEX data type represents a complex number in rectangular form. Define a new data type called POLAR that represents a complex number in polar form. Then write a module containing an interface assignment block and the supporting procedures to allow complex numbers to be assigned to polar numbers, and vice versa.

9–22 If two complex numbers $P_1 = z_1\angle\theta_1$ and $P_2 = z_2\angle\theta_2$ are expressed in polar form, then the product of the numbers is $P_1 \cdot P_2 = z_1 z_2\angle\theta_1 + \theta_2$. Similarly P_1 divided by P_2 is $\dfrac{P_1}{P_2} = \dfrac{z_1}{z_2}\angle\theta_1 - \theta_2$. Extend the module created in exercise 9–21 to add an interface operator block and the supporting procedures to allow two POLAR numbers to be multiplied and divided.

9–23 How can the access to data items and procedures in a module be controlled?

9–24 Are the following programs legal or illegal? Why?

a.
```
MODULE my_module
IMPLICIT NONE
PRIVATE
REAL, PARAMETER :: pi = 3.141592
REAL, PARAMETER :: two_pi = 2 * pi
END MODULE
PROGRAM test
USE my_module
IMPLICIT NONE
WRITE (*,*) 'Pi/2  = ', pi / 2.
END PROGRAM
```

b.
```
MODULE my_module
IMPLICIT NONE
PUBLIC
REAL, PARAMETER :: pi = 3.141592
REAL, PARAMETER :: two_pi = 2 * pi
END MODULE
```

```
PROGRAM test
USE my_module
IMPLICIT NONE
REAL :: two_pi
WRITE (*,*) 'Pi/2   =', pi / 2.
two_pi = 2. * pi
END PROGRAM
```

9–25 Modify the module in exercise 9–22 to allow access to only the definition of the POLAR type, the assignment operator, and the multiplication and division operators. Restrict access to the functions that implement the operator definitions.

9–26 In each of the following cases, indicate which of the items defined in the module will be available in the program that accesses it.

a.
```
MODULE module_1
IMPLICIT NONE
PRIVATE
PUBLIC pi, two_pi, name
REAL, PARAMETER :: pi = 3.141592
REAL, PARAMETER :: two_pi = 2 * pi
TYPE :: name
   CHARACTER(len=12) :: first
   CHARACTER :: mi
   CHARACTER(len=12) :: last
END TYPE
TYPE (name), PUBLIC :: name1 = name("John","Q","Doe")
TYPE (name) :: name2 = name("Jane","R","Public")
END MODULE
PROGRAM test
USE module_2, name1  =>  sample_name
...
END PROGRAM
```

b.
```
MODULE module_2
IMPLICIT NONE
REAL, PARAMETER :: pi = 3.141592
REAL, PARAMETER :: two_pi = 2 * pi
TYPE, PRIVATE :: name
   CHARACTER(len=12) :: first
   CHARACTER :: mi
   CHARACTER(len=12) :: last
END TYPE
TYPE (name), PRIVATE :: name1 = name("John","Q","Doe")
TYPE (name), PRIVATE :: name2 = name("Jane","R","Public")
END MODULE
PROGRAM test
USE module_3, ONLY: pi
...
END PROGRAM
```

10

Advanced I/O Concepts

Chapter 4 introduced the basics of Fortran input and output statements. We learned how to read data using the formatted READ statement and how to write data using the formatted WRITE statement. We also learned about the most common format descriptors, A, E, ES, F, I, L, T, X, and /. Finally, we learned how to open, close, read, write, and position sequential disk files.

This chapter deals with the more advanced features of the Fortran I/O system. It includes a description of additional format descriptors and provides more details about the operation of list-directed I/O statements. Next it provides more details about the proper use of the various Fortran I/O statements and introduces namelist I/O. Finally the chapter explains the difference between formatted and unformatted disk files and the difference between sequential access and direct access disk files. We will learn when and how to properly use each type of file.

10.1

ADDITIONAL FORMAT DESCRIPTORS

A complete list of all Fortran 90/95 format descriptors is shown in Table 10–1. Twelve of the format descriptors describe input/output data types: E, ES, EN, F, and D for single- and double-precision real values; I for integer values; B, O, and Z for either integer or real values; L for logical values; A for character values; and finally G for any type of value. Five of the format descriptors control the horizontal and vertical position of data: X, /, T, TL, and TR. The ':' character controls the way that formats associated with WRITE statements are scanned after the last variable in the WRITE statement has been output. Finally a number of undesirable and/or obsolete format descriptors are briefly mentioned. These format descriptors appear shaded in Table 10–1.

We will now discuss those format descriptors not previously described.

TABLE 10–1
Complete list of Fortran 90/95 format descriptors

FORMAT descriptors		Usage
Real data I/O descriptors		
D*w.d*		Double-precision data in exponential notation.
E*w.d*	E*w.d*E*e*	Real data in exponential notation.
EN*w.d*	EN*w.d*E*e*	Real data in engineering notation.
ES*w.d*	ES*w.d*E*e*	Real data in scientific notation.
F*w.d*		Real data in decimal notation.
Integer data I/O descriptor		
I*w*	I*w.m*	Integer data in decimal format.
Real or integer data I/O descriptors		
B*w*	B*w.m*	Data in binary format.
O*w*	O*w.m*	Data in octal format.
Z*w*	Z*w.m*	Data in hexadecimal format.
Logical data I/O descriptor		
L*w*		Logical data.
Character data I/O descriptors		
A	A*w*	Character data.
'*x . . . x*' "*x . . . x*"	*n*H*x . . . x*	Character constants (the *n*H*x . . . x* form is *obsolescent* in Fortran 90 / *deleted* in Fortran 95).
Generalized I/O descriptor		
G*w.d*	G*w.d*E*e*	Generalized edit descriptor for any type of data.
Positioning descriptors		
*n*X		Horizontal spacing: skip *n* spaces.
/		Vertical spacing: move down one line.
T*c*		Tab: move to column *c* of current line.
TL*n*		Tab: move left *n* columns in current line.
TR*n*		Tab: move right *n* columns in current line.
Scanning control descriptor		
:		Format-scanning control character.

(continued)

(concluded)

Miscellaneous descriptors (undesirable)	
kP	Scale factor for display of real data.
BN	Blank null: ignore blanks in numeric input fields.
BZ	Blank zero: interpret blanks in a numeric input field as zeros.
S	Sign control: use default system convention.
SP	Sign control: display + before positive numbers.
SS	Sign control: suppress + before positive numbers.

where

c = column number.

d = number of digits to right of decimal place.

e = number of digits in exponent.

k = scale factor (number of places to shift decimal point).

m = minimum number of digits to be displayed.

r = repetition count.

w = field width in characters.

10

10.1.1 Additional Forms of the E and ES Format Descriptors

The E, ES, and F format descriptors were described in Chapter 4. In addition to the information presented here, other (optional) forms of the E and ES descriptors allow a programmer to specify the number of digits to display in the exponent of the real number. These forms are

$$r\text{E}w.d\text{E}e \qquad \text{or} \qquad r\text{ES}w.d\text{E}e$$

where w, d, e, and r have the meanings given in Table 10–1. They function exactly as described in Chapter 4 except that the number of digits in the exponent is specified.

10.1.2 Engineering Notation—The EN Descriptor

Engineering notation is a modified version of scientific notation in which a real number is expressed as a value between 1.0 and 1000.0 times a power of 10, where the power of 10 is always a multiple of three. This form of notation is very convenient in the engineering world because 10^{-6}, 10^{-3}, 10^{3}, 10^{6}, and so on all have standard, universally recognized prefixes. For example, 10^{-6} is known by the prefix *micro*, and 10^{-3} is known by the prefix *milli*. Engineerings will commonly speak of 250 KΩ resistors and 50 nF capacitors instead of 2.5×10^{5} Ω resistors and 5×10^{-8} F capacitors.

Fortran can print out numbers in engineering notation with the EN descriptor. When writing data, the EN descriptor displays a floating-point number with a mantissa in the range between 1 and 1000 while the exponent is always a power of 10 divisible by 3. The EN format descriptor has the form

    *r*ENw.d   or   *r*ENw.dE*e*

where *w*, *d*, *e*, and *r* have the meanings given in Table 10–1.

For example, the following statements

```
a = 1.2346E7;  b = 0.0001;  c = -77.7E10
WRITE (*,'(1X,3EN15.4)') a, b, c
```

will produce the output

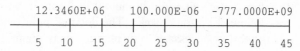

Note that all of the exponents of powers of three. When reading data, the EN descriptor behaves exactly like the E, ES, and F descriptors.

10.1.3 Double-Precision Data—The D Descriptor

 The D format descriptor is an obsolete format descriptor for use with double-precision data. The D format descriptor has the form

    *r*Dw.d

It is functionally identical to the E format descriptor except that the exponent indicator is sometimes a D instead of an E. This descriptor is only preserved for backwards compatibility with earlier versions of Fortran. *You should never use the* D *format descriptor in any new program.*

10.1.4 The Generalized (G) Format Descriptor

The F format descriptor displays real values in a fixed format. For example, the descriptor F7.3 will display a real value in the format ddd.ddd for positive numbers or -dd.ddd for negative numbers. The F descriptor produces output data in a very easy-to-read format. Unfortunately, if the number to be displayed with an F7.3 descriptor is ≥ 1000 or ≤ -100, then the output data will be replaced by a field of asterisks: *******. In contrast, the E format descriptor will display a number regardless of its range. However, numbers displayed in the E format are not as easy to interpret as numbers displayed in the F format. Although the following two numbers are identical, the one displayed in the F format is easier to understand.

```
225.671   0.225671E+03
```

Because the F format is easier to read, it would be really nice to have a format descriptor that displays numbers in the F format whenever possible but then switches to the E format when they become too big or too small. The G (generalized) format descriptor behaves in just this fashion when used with real data.

The G format descriptor has the form

$$r\text{G}w.d \qquad \text{or} \qquad r\text{G}w.d\text{E}e$$

where w, d, e, and r have the meanings given in Table 10–1. A real value displayed with a G format descriptor will be displayed either in F or in E format depending on the exponent of the number. If the real value to be displayed is represented as $\pm\, 0.dddddd \times 10^k$ and the format descriptor to be used for the display is G$w.d$, then the relationship between d and k will determine how the data is to be displayed. If $0 \leq k \leq d$, the value will be output in F format with a field width of $w - 4$ characters followed by four blanks. The decimal point will be adjusted (within the $w - 4$ characters) as necessary to display as many significant digits as possible. If the exponent is negative or is greater than d, the value will be output in E format. In either case a total of d significant digits will be displayed.

The operation of the G format descriptor with real data is illustrated in the next table. In the first example, k is -1, so the output comes out in E format. For the last example, k is 6 and d is 5, so the output again comes out in E format. For all of the examples in between, $0 \leq k \leq d$; therefore, the output comes out in F format with the decimal point adjusted to display as many significant digits as possible.

Value	Exponent	G descriptor	Output
0.012345	−1	G11.5	0.12345E-01
0.123450	0	G11.5	0.12345
1.234500	1	G11.5	1.23450
12.34500	2	G11.5	12.3450
123.4500	3	G11.5	123.450
1234.5600	4	G11.5	1234.50
12345.600	5	G11.5	12345.0
123456.00	6	G11.5	0.12345E+06

The generalized format descriptor can also be used with integer, logical, and character data. When it is used with integer data, it behaves like the I format descriptor. When it is used with logical data, it behaves like the L format descriptor. When it is used with character data, it behaves like the A format descriptor.

10.1.5 The Binary, Octal, and Hexadecimal (B, O, and Z) Descriptors

The binary (B), octal (O), and hexadecimal (Z) descriptors can be used to read or write data in binary, octal, or hexadecimal formats. They work for both integer and real data. The general forms of these descriptors are

$$rBw \quad \text{or} \quad rBw.m$$

$$rOw \quad \text{or} \quad rOw.m$$

$$rZw \quad \text{or} \quad rZw.m$$

where w, m, and r have the meanings given in Table 10–1. The format descriptors must be large enough to display all the digits in the appropriate notation, or the field will be filled with asterisks. For example, the statements

```
a = 16
b = -1
WRITE (*,'(1X,A,B16,1X,B16)')      'Binary: ', a, b
WRITE (*,'(1X,A,O11.4,1X,O11.4)')  'Octal:  ', a, b
WRITE (*,'(1X,A,Z8,1X,Z8)')        'Hex:    ', a, b
```

will produce the output

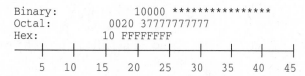

```
Binary:           10000 ****************
Octal:        0020 37777777777
Hex:          10 FFFFFFFF
```

Since numbers are stored in 2's complement format on this computer, a -1 will be 32 bits set to one. Therefore, the binary representation of b will consist of 32 ones. Since the B16 field is too small to display this number, it is filled with asterisks.

10.1.6 The Tab Descriptors

Fortran has three tab format descriptors: Tc, TLn, and TRn. You met the Tc descriptor in Chapter 4. In a formatted WRITE statement, it makes the output of the following descriptor begin at column c in the output buffer. In a formatted READ statement, it makes the field of the following descriptor begin at column c in the input buffer. For example, the following code will print the letter 'Z' in column 30 of the output line. (Remember that column 1 is used for carriage control and is not printed.)

```
WRITE (*,'(T31,A)') 'Z'
```

The Tc descriptor performs an *absolute* tab function in the sense that the output moves to column c regardless of where the previous output was. By contrast, the TLn and TRn descriptors are *relative* tab functions. TLn moves the output left by n columns, and TRn moves the output right by n columns. Where the next output will occur depends on the location of the previous output on the line. For example, the following code prints a 100 in columns 10–12 and a 200 in columns 17–19:

```
WRITE (*,'(T11,I3,TR4,I3)') 100, 200
```

10.1.7 The Colon (:) Descriptor

You have learned that if a WRITE statement runs out of variables before the end of its corresponding format, the use of the format continues until the first format descriptor without a corresponding variable or until the end of the format, whichever comes first. For example, consider the statements

```
m = 1
voltage = 13800.
WRITE (*,40) m
40 FORMAT (1X, 'M = ', I3, ' N = ', I4, ' O = ', F7.2)
WRITE (*,50) voltage / 1000.
50 FORMAT (1X, 'Voltage = ', F8.1, ' kV')
```

These statements will produce the output

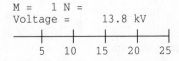

The use of the first FORMAT statement stops at I4, which is the first unmatched format descriptor. The use of the second FORMAT statement stops at the end of the statement, since no unmatched descriptors occur before that.

The colon descriptor (:) permits a user to modify the normal behavior of format descriptors during writes. The colon descriptor serves as a *conditional stopping point* for the WRITE statement. If there are more values to print out, the colon is ignored, and the execution of the formatted WRITE statement continues according to the normal rules for using formats. However, if a colon is encountered in the format and there are no more values to write out, execution of the WRITE statement stops at the colon.

To help understand the use of the colon, let's examine the simple program shown in Figure 10–1.

FIGURE 10–1
Program illustrating the use of the colon format descriptor.

```
PROGRAM test
IMPLICIT NONE
REAL, DIMENSION(8) :: x
INTEGER :: i
x = (/ 1.1, 2.2, 3.3, 4.4, 5.5, 6.6, 7.7, 8.8 /)

WRITE (*,100) (i, x(i), i = 1, 8)
100 FORMAT (/, 1X,'The output values are: '/, &
         3(5X,'X(',I2,') = ',F10.4))

WRITE (*,200) (i, x(i), i = 1, 8)
200 FORMAT (/,1X,'The output values are: '/,
         3(:,5X,'X(',I2,') = ',F10.4))

END PROGRAM
```

This program contains an eight-element array whose values we wish to print out three-abreast across the page. Note that the portion of the format descriptors inside the parentheses has a repeat count of three, so each line will contain three values printed in identical format before the program advances to the next line. If the program is compiled and executed, the result is

```
C>test
The output values are:
    X( 1) =       1.1000    X( 2) =       2.2000    X( 3) =       3.3000
    X( 4) =       4.4000    X( 5) =       5.5000    X( 6) =       6.6000
    X( 7) =       7.7000    X( 8) =       8.8000    X(

The output values are:
    X( 1) =       1.1000    X( 2) =       2.2000    X( 3) =       3.3000
    X( 4) =       4.4000    X( 5) =       5.5000    X( 6) =       6.6000
    X( 7) =       7.7000    X( 8) =       8.8000
```

The first WRITE statement and FORMAT statement run out of values to output after x(8) is written, but since it is in the middle of a format, the WRITE continues to execute until it comes to the first output descriptor without a corresponding variable. As a result, an extra 'X(' is printed out. The second WRITE statement and FORMAT are identical to the first pair except that a colon occurs at the beginning of the repeated portion of the FORMAT statement. This pair also runs out of values to output after x(8) is written. Since it is in the middle of a format, the WRITE continues to execute but immediately bumps into the colon and stops. In this case the extra 'X(' is not printed out.

The colon descriptor is most commonly used to terminate output cleanly in the middle of a line, as it was in the preceding example.

10.1.8 Scale Factors—The P Descriptor

The P descriptor adds a scale factor to any real values printed out with the E and F format descriptors. A scale factor has the form

$$n\mathrm{P}$$

where n is the number of places by which to shift the decimal point. The P scale factor may precede either E or F format descriptors. The general form of the descriptors with a scale factor are

$$n\mathrm{PrF}w.d \quad \text{and} \quad n\mathrm{PrE}w.d$$

With the F format descriptor, the P scale factor causes the displayed number to be multiplied by 10^n. With the E format descriptor, the P scale factor causes the fractional part of the displayed number to be multiplied by 10^n and causes the exponent to be decreased by n.

The P scale factor has been made redundant by the introduction of the ES and EN format descriptors in Fortran 90. *It should never be used in any new program.*

10.1.9 The Sign Descriptors

The sign format descriptors control the display of positive signs before positive numbers in an output line. There are three sign format descriptors: S, SP, and SS. The SP descriptor causes positive signs to be displayed before all positive numerical values following it in the same format statement, while the SS descriptor suppresses positive signs before all positive numerical values following it in the same format statement. The S descriptor restores the system default behavior for all positive numerical values following it. These format descriptors are almost never needed and so are little used.

10.1.10 Blank Interpretation: The BN and BZ Descriptors

The BN (blank null) and BZ (blank zero) descriptors control the way in which blanks are interpreted in input data fields. If the BN descriptor is in effect, then blanks are ignored. If the BZ descriptor is in effect, then blanks are treated as zeros. In either case, if an entire input data field is blank, then the field is interpreted as 0. *The BN and BZ descriptors are never needed in any modern program.* They are only present for backward compatibility with the I/O behavior of FORTRAN 66.

■ 10.2
DEFAULTING VALUES IN LIST-DIRECTED INPUT

List-directed input has the advantage of being very simple to use, since no FORMAT statements need be written for it. A list-directed READ statement is very useful for getting input information from a user at a terminal. The user may type the input data in any column, and the READ statement will still interpret it properly.

In addition, list-directed READ statements support *null values*. If an input data line contains two consecutive commas, then the corresponding variable in the input list will be left unchanged. This behavior permits a user to default one or more input data values to their previously defined values. Consider the following example:

```
PROGRAM test
INTEGER :: i = 1, j = 2, k = 3
WRITE (*,*) 'Enter i, j, and k: '
READ (*,*) i, j, k
WRITE (*,*) 'i, j, k = ', i, j, k
END PROGRAM
```

When this program is compiled and executed, the results are

```
C>test
Enter i, j, and k:
1000,,-2002
i, j, k =          1000           2          -2002
```

Note that the value of j was defaulted to 2, while new values were assigned to i and k. It is also possible to default all of the remaining variables on a line by concluding it with a slash.

```
C>test
Enter i, j, and k:
1000 /
i, j, k =          1000           2           3
```

Quiz 10–1

This quiz provides a quick check to see if you understand the concepts introduced in sections 10.1 and 10.2. If you have trouble with the quiz, reread the sections, ask your instructor, or discuss the material with a fellow student. The answers to this quiz are found in the back of the book.

For questions 1 to 4, determine what will be written out when the statements are executed.

1. ```
REAL :: a = 4096.07
WRITE (*,1) a, a, a, a, a
1 FORMAT (1X, F10.1, F9.2, E12.5, G12.5, G11.4)
```

2. ```
INTEGER :: i
REAL, DIMENSION(5) :: data1 = (/ -17.2,4.,4.,.3,-2.22 /)
WRITE (*,1) (i, data1(i), i=1, 5)
1 FORMAT (2(5X,'Data1(',I3,') = ',F8.4,:,',',))
```

3. ```
REAL :: x = 0.0000122, y = 123456.E2
WRITE (*,'(1X,2EN14.6,/,1X,2ES14.6)') x, y, x, y
```

4. ```
INTEGER :: i = -2002, j = 1776, k = -3
WRITE (*,*) 'Enter i, j, and k: '
READ (*,*) i, j, k
WRITE (*,1) i, j, k
1 FORMAT (' i = ',I10,' j = ',I10,' k = ',I10)
```

where the input line is

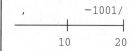

10.3

DETAILED DESCRIPTION OF Fortran I/O STATEMENTS

A summary of Fortran 90/95 I/O statements appears in Table 10–2. These statements permit us to open and close files, check the status of files, go to a specific position within a file, and to read from or write to a file. This section explains all the statements found in the table. Some of them were introduced in simplified form in Chapter 4, but even the familiar statements have many additional options.

The discussion of each I/O statement includes a table listing all the possible clauses that can be used with the statement. Clauses that should not be used in modern Fortran programs are shown with a shaded background.

10.3.1 The OPEN Statement

A disk file must be connected to an i/o unit before data can be read from or written to the file. Depending on the particular implementation of your compiler, a few files

TABLE 10–2
Fortran 90/95 I/O statements

Statement	Function
OPEN	Open a file (connect it to an i/o unit).
CLOSE	Close a file (disconnect it from an i/o unit).
INQUIRE	Check on properties of a file.
READ	Read data from a file (via an i/o unit).
PRINT	Write data to the standard output device.
WRITE	Write data to a file (via an i/o unit).
REWIND	Rewind a sequential file to the beginning.
BACKSPACE	Move back one record in a sequential file.
ENDFILE	Move to the end of a sequential file.

may be preconnected to some of the i/o units when execution begins. If preconnected files exist, it is possible to write data to them without opening them first. For example, VAX Fortran automatically preconnects a file called FILE021.DAT to i/o unit 21, and so forth. The preconnected file is automatically created the first time that a VAX Fortran program writes to it.

Unfortunately, the number and the names of preconnected files (if any) differ from processor to processor, so this feature will make your programs much less portable. You should always explicitly open any file that you use to improve the portability of your programs and to allow you to choose your own name for each file.

Good Programming Practice
Do not rely on preconnected files in your Fortran programs (except for the standard input and output devices). The number and the names of preconnected files vary from processor to processor, so using them will reduce the portability of your programs.

An i/o unit is explicitly connected to a disk file using the OPEN statement. Once we are through using a file, the file should be disconnected from the i/o unit using the CLOSE statement. After the CLOSE statement has been executed, the i/o unit will no longer be connected to the file; it may be connected to some other file using another OPEN statement.

The OPEN statement has the general form

OPEN (*open_list*)

where *open_list* consists of two or more clauses separated by commas. The possible clauses in an OPEN statement are summarized in Table 10–3. These clauses may

■ TABLE 10–3

Clauses allowed in the OPEN statement

Clause	Input or output	Purpose	Possible values
[UNIT=]*int_expr*	Input	I/O unit to attach file to. The UNIT= phrase is optional.	Processor-dependent integer.
FILE=*char_expr*	Input	Name of file to open.[1]	Character string.
STATUS=*char_expr*	Input	Specifies status for file to be opened.	'OLD', 'NEW', 'SCRATCH', 'REPLACE', 'UNKNOWN'
IOSTAT=*int_var*	Output	I/O status at end of operation.	Processor-dependent integer *int_var*. 0 = success; positive = open failure.
ACCESS=*char_expr*	Input	Specifies sequential or direct access.	'SEQUENTIAL', 'DIRECT'
FORM=*char_expr*	Input	Specifies formatted or unformatted data.	'FORMATTED', 'UNFORMATTED'
ACTION=*char_expr*	Input	Specifies whether file is read only, write only, or read/write.	'READ', 'WRITE', 'READWRITE'
RECL=*int_expr*	Input	For a formatted direct access file, the number of characters in each record. For an unformatted direct access file, the number of processor-dependent units in each record.[2]	Processor-dependent positive integer.
POSITION=*char_expr*	Input	Specifies the position of the file pointer after the file is opened.	'REWIND', 'APPEND', 'ASIS'
DELIM=*char_expr*	Input	Specifies whether list-directed character output is to be delimited by apostrophes, by quotation marks, or by nothing. (Default value is 'NONE'.)	'APOSTROPHE', 'QUOTE', 'NONE'
PAD=*variable*	Input	Specifies whether formatted input records are padded with blanks. (Default value is 'YES'.)	'YES', 'NO'
BLANK=*char_expr*	Input	Specifies whether blanks are to be treated as nulls or zeros. Nulls are the default case.[3]	'NULL', 'ZERO'

10

(continued)

(concluded)

ERR=*label*	Input	Statement label to transfer control to if open fails.[4]	Statement labels in current scoping unit.

[1]The FILE= clause is not allowed for scratch files.
[2]The RECL= clause is only defined for files connected for direct access.
[3]The BLANK= clause is only defined for files connected for formatted I/O. This clause is never needed in a modern Fortran program.
[4]The ERR= clause is never needed in a modern Fortran program. Use the IOSTAT= clause instead.

be included in the OPEN statement in any order. Some clauses are only meaningful for specific types of files and do not appear in every statement. For example, the RECL= clause is only meaningful for direct access files. Also, some combinations of clauses have contradictory meanings and will produce errors at compile time. I will point out some examples of these contradictions throughout this discussion.

The UNIT= clause

This clause specifies the **i/o unit** number to be associated with the file. The UNIT= clause must be present in any OPEN statement. The i/o unit number specified here will be used in later READ and WRITE statements to access the file. The UNIT= io_unit clause may be abbreviated to just the io_unit number if it appears as the first clause in an OPEN statement. This feature is included in Fortran 90/95 for backward compatibility with earlier versions of Fortran. Therefore, the following two statements are equivalent:

```
OPEN ( UNIT=10, ... )
OPEN ( 10, ... )
```

The FILE= clause

This clause specifies the name of the file to connect to the specified i/o unit. A file name must be supplied for all files except for scratch files.

The STATUS= clause

This clause specifies the status of the file to connect to the specified i/o unit. There are five possible file statuses: 'OLD', 'NEW', 'REPLACE', 'SCRATCH', and 'UNKNOWN'.

If the file status is 'OLD', then the file must already exist on the system when the OPEN statement is executed, or the OPEN will fail with an error. If the file status is 'NEW', then the file must *not* already exist on the system when the OPEN statement is executed, or the OPEN will fail with an error. If the file status is STATUS='REPLACE', then a new file will be opened whether it exists or not. If the file already exists, the program will delete it, create a new file, and then open it for output. The old contents of the file will be lost. If it does not exist, the program will create a new file by that name and open it.

If the file status is 'SCRATCH', then a **scratch file** will be created on the computer and attached to the i/o unit. A *scratch file* is a temporary file that is created by the computer that the program can use for temporary data storage while it is running. When a scratch file is closed or when the program ends, the file is automatically deleted from the system. Note that the FILE= clause is not used with a scratch file, since no permanent file is created. It is an error to specify a file name for a scratch file.

If the file status is 'UNKNOWN', then the behavior of the program will vary from processor to processor—the Fortran standard does not specify the behavior of this option. The most common behavior is for the program to first look for an existing file with the specified name and open it if it exists. The contents of the file are not destroyed by the act of opening it with unknown status, but the original contents can be destroyed if we later write to the file. If the file does not exist, then the computer creates a new file with that name and opens it. Unknown status should be avoided in a program because the behavior of the OPEN statement is processor dependent, which could reduce the portability of the program.

If no STATUS= clause appears in an OPEN statement, then the default status is 'UNKNOWN'.

The IOSTAT= clause

This clause specifies an integer variable that will contain the i/o status after the OPEN statement is executed. If the file is opened successfully, then the status variable will contain a zero. If the open failed, then the status variable will contain a processor-dependent positive value corresponding to the type of error that occurred.

The ACCESS= clause

This clause specifies the access method to be used with the file. The two types of access methods are 'SEQUENTIAL' and 'DIRECT'. **Sequential access** involves opening a file and reading or writing its records in order from beginning to end. Sequential access is the default access mode in Fortran, and all files that we have used so far have been sequential files. The records in a file opened with sequential access do not have to be any particular length.

If a file is opened with **direct access**, it is possible to jump directly from one record to another within the file at any time without having to read any of the records in between. All records in a file opened with direct access must be the same length.

The FORM= clause

This clause specifies the format status of the file. The two file formats are 'FOR-MATTED' and 'UNFORMATTED'. The data in **formatted files** consists of recognizable characters, numbers, and so forth. These files are called formatted because we use format descriptors (or list-directed I/O statements) to convert their data into a form usable by the computer whenever we read or write them. When we write to a formatted file, the bit patterns stored in the computer's memory are translated into a series of characters that humans can read, and those characters are written to the file. The instructions for the translation process are included in the format descriptors. All the disk files that we have used so far have been formatted files.

In contrast, **unformatted files** contain data that is an exact copy of the data stored in the computer's memory. When we write to an unformatted file, the exact bit patterns in the computer's memory are copied into the file. Unformatted files are much smaller than the corresponding formatted files, but the information in an unformatted file is coded in bit patterns that cannot be easily examined or used by people. Furthermore, the bit patterns corresponding to particular values vary among different types of computer systems, so unformatted files cannot easily be moved from one type of computer to another one.

If a file uses sequential access, the default file format is `'FORMATTED'`. If the file uses direct access, the default file format is `'UNFORMATTED'`.

The `ACTION=` clause

This clause specifies whether a file is to be opened for reading only, for writing only, or for both reading and writing. Possible values are `'READ'`, `'WRITE'`, or `'READWRITE'`. The default action is `'READWRITE'`.

The `RECL=` clause

This clause specifies the length of each record in a direct access file. For formatted files opened with direct access, this clause contains the length of each record in characters. For unformatted files this clause contains the length of each record in processor-dependent units.

The `POSITION=` clause

This clause specifies the position of the file pointer after the file is opened. The possible values are `'REWIND'`, `'APPEND'`, or `'ASIS'`. If the expression is `'REWIND'`, then the file pointer points to the first record in the file. If the expression is `'APPEND'`, then the file pointer points just after the last record in the file and just before the end-of-file marker. If the expression is `'ASIS'`, then the position of the file pointer is unspecified and processor dependent. The default position is `'ASIS'`.

The `DELIM=` clause

This clause specifies which characters are to be used to delimit character strings in list-directed output and namelist output statements. The possible values are `'QUOTE'`, `'APOSTROPHE'`, or `'NONE'`. If the expression is `'QUOTE'`, then the character strings will be delimited by quotation marks and any quotation marks in the string will be doubled. If the expression is `'APOSTROPHE'`, then the character strings will be delimited by apostrophes and any apostrophes in the string will be doubled. If the expression is `'NONE'`, then the character strings have no delimiters.

The `PAD=` clause

This clause has the possible values `'YES'` or `'NO'`. If this clause is `'YES'`, then the processor will pad out input data lines with blanks as required to match the length of the record specified in a `READ` format descriptor. If it is `'NO'`, then either the input data line must be at least as long as the record specified in the format descriptor or an error will occur. The default value is `'YES'`.

The `BLANK=` clause

This clause specifies whether blank columns in numeric fields are to be treated as blanks or as zeros. The possible values are `'ZERO'` or `'NULL'`. It is the equivalent of the BN and BZ format descriptors except that the value specified here applies to the entire file. This clause provides backward compatibility with FORTRAN 66; it should never be needed in any new Fortran program.

The ERR= clause

This clause specifies the label of a statement to jump to if the file open fails. The ERR= clause provides a way to add special code to handle file-open errors. (This clause should not be used in new programs; use the IOSTAT= clause instead.)

The importance of using the IOSTAT= clause

If a file open fails and there is no IOSTAT= clause or ERR= clause in the OPEN statement, then the Fortran program will print out an error message and abort. This behavior is very inconvenient in a large program that runs for a long period of time, since large amounts of work can be lost if the program aborts. A *much* better technique is to trap such errors and let the user tell the program how to handle the problem. The user could specify a new disk file, or he or she could let the program shut down gracefully, saving all the work done so far.

If either the IOSTAT= clause or the ERR= clause are present in the OPEN statement, then the Fortran program will not abort when an open error occurs. If an error occurs and the IOSTAT= clause is present, then a positive i/o status will be returned, specifying the type of error that occurred. The program can check for this error and provide the user with options for continuing or shutting down gracefully. For example:

```
OPEN ( UNIT=8, FILE ='test.dat', STATUS='OLD', IOSTAT=istat)

! Check for OPEN error
in_ok: IF ( istat /= 0 ) THEN
   WRITE (*,*) 'Input file OPEN failed: istat=', istat
   WRITE (*,*) 'Shutting down...'
   ...
ELSE
   normal processing
   ...
END IF in_ok
```

In general, the IOSTAT= clause should be used instead of the ERR= clause in all new programs, since the IOSTAT= clause allows more flexibility and is better suited to modern structured programming. The use of the ERR= clause encourages "spaghetti code" in which execution jumps around in a fashion that is hard to follow and hard to maintain.

> ***Good Programming Practice***
> Always use the IOSTAT= clause in OPEN statements to trap file-open errors. When an error is detected, tell the user all about the problem before shutting down gracefully or requesting an alternative file.

Examples

Some sample OPEN statements follow.

1. OPEN (UNIT=9, FILE='x.dat', STATUS='OLD', POSITION='APPEND', &
       ACTION='WRITE')

This statement opens a file named x.dat and attaches it to i/o unit 9. The status
of the file is 'OLD', so the file must already exist. The position is 'APPEND', so
the file pointer will be positioned after the last record in the file and just before
the end-of-file marker. The file is a formatted file opened for sequential access and
is write only. Since there is no IOSTAT= or ERR= clause, an open error would abort
the program containing this statement.

2. OPEN (22, STATUS='SCRATCH')

This statement creates a scratch file and attaches it to i/o unit 22. The scratch file
is automatically given some unique name by the system and is automatically deleted
when the file is closed or the program ends. It is a formatted file opened for sequential access. Since there is no IOSTAT= or ERR= clause, an open error would
abort the program containing this statement.

3. OPEN (FILE='input',UNIT=1u,STATUS='OLD',ACTION='READ',IOSTAT=istat)

This statement opens an existing file named input and attaches it to the i/o unit
corresponding to the value of variable 1u. The status of the file is 'OLD', so this
OPEN statement will fail if the file does not already exist. The file is a formatted
file opened for sequential access and is opened for reading only. A status code is
returned in variable istat. It will be 0 for a successful file open and positive for
an unsuccessful file open. Since the IOSTAT= clause is present in this statement,
an open error would not abort the program containing this statement.

10.3.2 The CLOSE Statement

Once a file is no longer needed, it should be disconnected from its i/o unit using the
CLOSE statement. After the CLOSE statement has been executed, the i/o unit will no
longer be connected to the file; it may be connected to some other file using another
OPEN statement.

A Fortran program will automatically update and close any open files whenever the
program ends. Therefore, a CLOSE statement is not actually required unless we want to
attach more than one file to the same i/o unit. However, it is good practice to close any
file with a CLOSE statement just as soon as the program is finished using it. When a file
has been opened by one program, no other program may have access to it at the same
time. By closing the file as soon as possible, the file is made available for other programs
to use. This practice is especially important for files that are shared by many people.

Good Programming Practice

Always explicitly close each disk file with a CLOSE statement as soon as possible after a program is finished using it, so that it may be available for use by others.

The CLOSE statement has the general form

$$\text{CLOSE } (close\ list)$$

where *close list* consists of one or more clauses separated by commas. The possible clauses in the CLOSE statement are summarized in Table 10–4. They may be included in the CLOSE statement in any order.

The UNIT= clause

This clause is exactly the same as the UNIT= clause in the OPEN statement. The UNIT= clause must be present in any CLOSE statement.

The STATUS= clause

This clause specifies the status of the file connected to the specified i/o unit. The two possible file statuses are 'KEEP' and 'DELETE'. If the file status is 'KEEP', then the file is kept on the file system after it is closed. If the file status is 'DELETE', then the file is deleted after it is closed. A scratch file is always deleted when it is closed; it is not legal to specify keep status for a scratch file. For any other type of file, the default status is 'KEEP'.

10

TABLE 10–4
Clauses allowed in the CLOSE statement

Clause	Input or output	Purpose	Possible values
[UNIT]=*int_expr*	Input	I/o unit to close. The UNIT= phrase is optional.	Processor-dependent integer.
STATUS=*char_expr*	Input	Specifies whether file is to be kept or deleted after closing.	'KEEP', 'DELETE'
IOSTAT=*int_var*	Output	I/O status at end of operation.	Processor-dependent integer *int_var*. 0 = success; positive = close failure.
ERR=*label*	Input	Statement label to transfer control to if open fails.[1]	Statement labels in current scoping unit.

[1] The ERR= clause is never needed in a modern Fortran program. Use the IOSTAT= clause instead.

The IOSTAT= clause

This clause specifies an integer variable that will contain the i/o status after the CLOSE statement is executed. If the file is closed successfully, then the status variable will contain a zero. If the close failed, then the status variable will contain a processor-dependent positive value corresponding to the type of error that occurred.

The ERR= clause

This clause specifies the label of a statement to jump to if the file close fails. The ERR= clause provides a way to add special codes to handle file-close errors. (This clause should not be used in new programs; use the IOSTAT= clause instead.)

Examples

Some sample CLOSE statements follow.

1. CLOSE (9)

   This statement closes the file attached to i/o unit 9. If the file is a scratch file, it will be deleted; otherwise, it will be kept. Since there is no IOSTAT= or ERR= clause, an error would abort the program containing this statement.

2. CLOSE (UNIT=22, STATUS='DELETE', IOSTAT=istat)

   This statement closes and deletes the file attached to i/o unit 22. An operation status code is returned in variable istat. It will be 0 for success and positive for failure. Since the IOSTAT= clause is present in this statement, a close error will not abort the program containing this statement.

10.3.3 The INQUIRE Statement

The INQUIRE statement allows us to check on the status or properties of a file that we want to use in a Fortran program. It is designed to provide detailed information about a file, either before or after the file has been opened.

There are three different versions of the INQUIRE statement. The first two versions of the statement are similar except for the manner in which the file is looked up. The file can be found by either specifying the FILE= clause or the UNIT= clause (but not both simultaneously!). If a file has not yet been opened, it must be identified by name. If the file is already open, it may be identified by either name or i/o unit. The INQUIRE statement has many possible output clauses. To find out a particular piece of information about a file, just include the appropriate clause in the statement. A complete list of all clauses is given in Table 10–5.

The third form of the INQUIRE statement is the inquire-by-output-list statement. This statement takes the form

        INQUIRE (IOLENGTH=*int_var*) *output_list*

◼ **TABLE 10–5**
Clauses allowed in the INQUIRE statement

Clause	Input or output	Purpose	Possible values
[UNIT=]*int_expr*	Input	I/o unit of file to check.[1]	Processor-dependent integer.
FILE=*char_expr*	Input	Name of file to check.[1]	Processor-dependent character string.
IOSTAT=*int_var*	Output	I/O status	Returns 0 for success; processor-dependent positive number for failure.
EXIST=*log_var*	Output	Does the file exist?	.TRUE., .FALSE.
OPENED=*log_var*	Output	Is the file open?	.TRUE., .FALSE.
NUMBER=*int_var*	Output	I/o unit number of file, if open. If file is not open, this value is undefined.	Processor-dependent positive number.
NAMED=*log_var*	Output	Does the file have a name? (Scratch files are unnamed.)	.TRUE., .FALSE.
NAME=*char_var*	Output	Name of file if file is named; undefined otherwise.	File name.
ACCESS=*char_var*	Output	Specifies type of access if the file is currently open.[2]	'SEQUENTIAL', 'DIRECT'
SEQUENTIAL=*char_var*	Output	Specifies if file *can be opened* for sequential access.[2]	'YES', 'NO', 'UNKNOWN'
DIRECT=*char_var*	Output	Specifies if file *can be opened* for direct access.[2]	'YES', 'NO', 'UNKNOWN'
FORM=*char_var*	Output	Specifies type of formatting for a file if the file is open.[3]	'FORMATTED', 'UNFORMATTED'
FORMATTED=*char_var*	Output	Specifies if file *can be* connected for formatted I/O.[3]	'YES', 'NO', 'UNKNOWN'
UNFORMATTED=*char_var*	Output	Specifies if file *can be* connected for unformatted I/O.[3]	'YES', 'NO', 'UNKNOWN'
RECL=*int_var*	Output	Specifies the record length of a direct access file; undefined for sequential files.	Record length is in processor-dependent units.
NEXTREC=*int_var*	Output	For a direct access file, one more than the number of the last record read from or written to the file; undefined for sequential files.	

10

(continued)

(concluded)

BLANK=*char_var*	Output	Specifies whether blanks in numeric fields are treated as nulls or zeros.[4]	'ZERO', 'NULL'
POSITION=*char_var*	Output	Specifies location of file pointer when the file is first opened. This value is undefined for unopened files, or for files opened for direct access.	'REWIND', 'APPEND', 'ASIS', 'UNDEFINED'
ACTION=*char_var*	Output	Specifies read, write, or readwrite status for opened files. This value is undefined for unopened files.[5]	'READ', 'WRITE', 'READWRITE', 'UNDEFINED'
READ=*char_var*	Output	Specifies whether file *can be* opened for read-only access.[5]	'YES', 'NO', 'UNKNOWN'
WRITE=*char_var*	Output	Specifies whether file *can be* opened for write-only access.[5]	'YES', 'NO', 'UNKNOWN'
READWRITE=*char_var*	Output	Specifies whether file *can be* opened for readwrite access.[5]	'YES', 'NO', 'UNKNOWN'
DELIM=*char_var*	Output	Specifies type of character delimiter used with list-directed and namelist I/O to this file.	'APOSTROPHE', 'QUOTE', 'NONE', 'UNKNOWN'
PAD=*char_var*	Output	Specifies whether input lines are to be padded with blanks. This value is always yes unless a file is explicitly opened with PAD='NO'.	'YES', 'NO',
IOLENGTH=*int_var*	Output	Returns the length of an unformatted record in processor dependent units. This clause is special to the third type of INQUIRE statement (see text).	
ERR=*statement label*	Input	Statement to branch to if statement fails.[6]	Statement label in current program unit.

[1]One and only one of the FILE= and UNIT= clauses may be included in any INQUIRE statement.
[2]The difference between the ACCESS= clause and the SEQUENTIAL= and DIRECT= clauses is that the ACCESS= clause tells what sort of access *is being used,* while the other two clauses tell what sort of access *can be used.*
[3]The difference between the FORM= clause and the FORMATTED= and UNFORMATTED= clauses is that the FORM= clause tells what sort of I/O *is being used,* while the other two clauses tell what sort of I/O *can be used.*
[4]The BLANK= clause is defined only for files connected for formatted I/O.
[5]The difference between the ACTION= clause and the READ=, WRITE=, and READWRITE= clauses is that the ACTION= clause specifies the action for which the file *is* open, while the other clauses specify the action for which the file *can be* opened.
[6]The ERR= clause is never needed in a modern Fortran program. Use the IOSTAT= clause instead.

where *int_var* is an integer variable and *output_list* is a list of variables, constants, and expressions like the ones that would appear in a WRITE statement. The purpose of this statement is to return the length of the unformatted record that can contain the entities in the output list. As we will see later in this chapter, unformatted direct access files have a fixed record length that is measured in processor-dependent units, and so the length changes from processor to processor. Furthermore, this record length must be specified when the file is opened. This form of the INQUIRE statement provides a processor-independent way to specify the length of records in direct access files. An example of this form of INQUIRE statement will be shown when we introduce direct access files in section 10.6.

EXAMPLE 10–1 *Preventing Output Files from Overwriting Existing Data:* In many programs, the user is asked to specify an output file into which the results of the program will be written. It is good programming practice to check to see if the output file already exists before opening it and writing into it. If it already exists, the user should be asked if he or she *really* wants to destroy the data in the file before the program overwrites it. If so, the program can open the file and write into it. If not, the program should get a new output file name and try again. Write a program that demonstrates a technique for protection against overwriting existing files.

SOLUTION The resulting Fortran program is shown in Figure 10–2.

FIGURE 10–2
Program illustrating how to prevent an output file from accidentally overwriting data.

```
PROGRAM open_file
!
! Purpose:
!   To illustrate the process of checking before overwriting an
!   output file.
!
IMPLICIT NONE

! Declare local variables:
CHARACTER(len=20) :: name          ! File name
CHARACTER :: yn                    ! Yes / No flag
LOGICAL :: lexist                  ! True if file exists
LOGICAL :: lopen = .FALSE.         ! True if file is open

! Do until file is open
openfile: DO

   ! Get output file name.
   WRITE (*,*) 'Enter output file name: '
   READ (*,'(A)') file_name

   ! Does file already exist?
   INQUIRE ( FILE=file_name, EXIST=lexist )
   exists: IF ( .NOT. lexist ) THEN
      ! It's OK, the file didn't already exist.  Open file.
```

(continued)

10

(concluded)

```
        OPEN (UNIT=9, FILE=name, STATUS='NEW', ACTION= 'WRITE')
        lopen = .TRUE.

   ELSE
        ! File exists.  Should we replace it?
        WRITE (*,*) 'Output file exists.  Overwrite it? (Y/N)'
        READ (*,'(A)') yn
        CALL ucase ( yn )   !                   Shift to upper case

        replace: IF ( yn == 'Y' ) THEN
            ! It's OK.  Open file.
            OPEN (UNIT=9, FILE=name, STATUS='REPLACE', ACTION='WRITE')
            lopen = .TRUE.
        END IF replace

   END IF exists
   IF ( lopen ) EXIT
END DO openfile

! Now write output data, and close and save file.
WRITE (9,*) 'This is the output file!'
CLOSE (9,STATUS='KEEP')

END PROGRAM
```

Test this program for yourself. Can you suggest any improvements to make this program work better? (*Hint:* What about the OPEN statements?)

Good Programming Practice

Check to see if your output file is overwriting an existing data file. If it is, make sure that the user really wants to overwrite the file before destroying the data in the file.

10.3.4 The READ Statement

The READ statement reads data from the file associated with a specified i/o unit, converts its format according to the specified FORMAT descriptors, and stores it into the variables in the I/O list. A READ statement keeps reading input lines until all the variables in *io_list* have been filled, the end of the input file is reached, or an error occurs. A READ statement has the general form

$$\text{READ } (control\_list) \; io\_list$$

where *control_list* consists of one or more clauses separated by commas. The possible clauses in a READ statement are summarized in Table 10–6. The clauses may be included in the READ statement in any order. Not all the clauses will be included in any given READ statement.

■   **TABLE 10–6**
Clauses allowed in the READ statement

Clause	Input or output	Purpose	Possible values
[UNIT=]*int_expr*	Input	I/o unit to read from.	Processor-dependent integer.
[FMT=]*statement_label* [FMT=]*char_expr* [FMT=]*	Input	Specifies the format to use when reading formatted data.	
IOSTAT=*int_var*	Output	I/O status at end of operation.	Processor-dependent integer *int_var*. 0 = success. positive = failure. −1 = end of file. −2 = end of record.
REC=*int_expr*	Input	Specifies the record number to read in a direct access file.	
NML=*namelist*	Input	Specifies namelist of I/O entities to read.	Namelists defined in the current scoping unit, or accessed through use or host association.
ADVANCE=*char_expr*	Input	Specifies whether to perform advancing or nonadvancing I/O. Valid for sequential files only.	'YES', 'NO'
SIZE=*int_var*	Output	Specifies number of characters read during nonadvancing I/O. Valid for nonadvancing I/O only.	
EOR=*label*	Input	Statement label to transfer control to if end of record is reached during nonadvancing I/O. Valid for nonadvancing I/O only.	Statement labels in current scoping unit.
END=*statement_label*	Input	Statement label to transfer control to if end of file is reached.[1]	Statement labels in current scoping unit.
ERR=*statement_label*	Input	Statement label to transfer control to if an error occurs.[1]	Statement labels in current scoping unit.

[1]The END=, ERR=, and EOR= clauses are never needed in a modern Fortran program. Use the IOSTAT= clause instead.

10

The `UNIT=` clause

This clause specifies the i/o unit number from which to read the data. An * indicates reading data from the standard input device. *The `UNIT=` clause must be present in any `READ` statement.*

The i/o unit may also be specified by naming it in the `READ` statement without the `UNIT=` keyword. This feature is included in Fortran 90/95 for backward compatibility with earlier versions of Fortran. If the i/o unit is specified in this alternative form, then it must be the first clause in the `READ` statement. The following two statements are equivalent:

```
READ ( UNIT=10, ... )
READ ( 10, ... )
```

The `FMT=` clause

This clause has the form

```
[FMT=] statement_label or [FMT=] char_expr or [FMT=] *
```

where `statement_label` is the label of a `FORMAT` statement, `char_expr` is a character string containing the format information, or * indicates list-directed I/O. A `FMT=` clause must be supplied for all formatted `READ` statements.

If the `FMT=` clause is the second clause in a `READ` statement, and if the first clause is an abbreviated unit number without the `UNIT=` keyword, then the format clause may be abbreviated by only naming the statement number, character variable, or * containing the format. This feature is included in Fortran 90/95 for backward compatibility with earlier versions of Fortran. Therefore, the following two statements are equivalent:

```
READ ( UNIT=10, FMT=100 ) data1
READ ( 10, 100 ) data1
```

The `IOSTAT=` clause

This clause specifies an integer variable that will contain the status after the `READ` statement is executed. If the read is successful, then the status variable will contain a 0. If an end of file condition is detected, then the status variable will contain a -1. If an end of record condition is encountered during nonadvancing i/o, the status variable will contain a -2. If the read fails, then the status variable will contain a positive value corresponding to the type of error that occurred.

The `REC=` clause

This clause specifies the number of the record to read in a direct access file. It is valid only for direct access files.

The `NML=` clause

This clause specifies a named list of values to read in. The details of namelist I/O are described in the section 10.4.

The `ADVANCE=` clause

This clause specifies whether or not the current input buffer should be discarded at the end of the `READ`. The possible values are `'YES'` or `'NO'`. If the value is `'YES'`, then any remaining data in the current input buffer will be discarded when the `READ` statement is completed. If the value is `'NO'`, then the remaining data in the current input buffer will be saved and used to satisfy the next `READ` statement. The default value is `'YES'`. This clause is valid only for sequential files.

The `SIZE=` clause

This clause specifies the name of an integer variable to contain the number of characters that have been read from the input buffer during a nonadvancing I/O operation. It may be specified only if the `ADVANCE='NO'` clause is specified.

The `EOR=` clause

This clause specifies the label of an executable statement to jump to if the end of the current record is detected during a nonadvancing `READ` operation. If the end of the input record is reached during a nonadvancing I/O operation, then the program will jump to the statement specified and execute it. This clause may only be specified if the `ADVANCE='NO'` clause is specified. If the `ADVANCE='YES'` clause is specified, then the read will continue on successive input lines until all the input data is read.

The `END=` clause

This clause specifies the label of an executable statement to jump to if the end of the input file is detected. The `END=` clause provides a way to handle unexpected end-of-file conditions. This clause should not be used in modern programs; use the more general and flexible `IOSTAT=` clause instead.

The `ERR=` clause

This clause specifies the label of an executable statement to jump to if a read error occurs. The most common read error is a mismatch between the type of the input data in a field and the format descriptors used to read it. For example, if the characters `'A123'` appeared by mistake in a field read with the `I4` descriptor, an error would be generated. This clause should not be used in modern programs; use the more general and flexible `IOSTAT=` clause instead.

The importance of using the `IOSTAT=` clause

If a read fails and there is no `IOSTAT=` clause or `ERR=` clause in the `READ` statement, the Fortran program will print out an error message and abort. If the end of the input file is reached and there is no `IOSTAT=` clause or `END=` clause, the Fortran program will abort. Finally, if the end of an input record is reached during nonadvancing i/o and there is no `IOSTAT=` clause or `EOR=` clause, the Fortran program will abort. If either the `IOSTAT=` clause or the `ERR=`, `END=`, and `EOR=` clauses are present in the `READ` statement, then the Fortran program will not abort when read errors, end-of-file, or end-of-record conditions occur. Instead, the programmer can do something to handle those conditions and allow the program to continue running.

The following code fragment shows how to use the IOSTAT= message to read an unknown number of input values without aborting when the end of the input file is reached. It uses a while loop to read data until the end of the input file is reached.

```
OPEN ( UNIT=8, FILE='test.dat', STATUS='OLD' )

! Read input data
nvals = 0
DO
    READ (8,100,IOSTAT=istat) temp
    ! Check for end of data
    IF ( istat < 0 ) EXIT
    nvals = nvals + 1
    array(nvals) = temp
END DO
```

The IOSTAT= clause should be used instead of the END=, ERR=, and EOR= clauses in all new programs, since the IOSTAT= clause allows more flexibility and is better suited to modern structured programming. The use of the other clauses encourages spaghetti code, in which execution jumps around in a fashion that is hard to follow and hard to maintain.

Good Programming Practice

Use the IOSTAT= clause in READ statements to prevent programs from aborting on errors, end-of-file conditions, or end-of-record conditions. When one of these conditions is detected, the program can take appropriate actions to continue processing or to shut down gracefully.

10.3.5 Alternative Form of the READ Statement

An alternative form of the READ statement only works for formatted reads or list-directed reads from the standard input device. This statement has the form

```
READ fmt, io_list
```

where *fmt* is the format specification to use when reading the list of variables in the *io_list*. The format may be the number of a FORMAT statement, the name of a character variable containing the formatting information, a character string containing the formatting information, or an asterisk. Examples of this version of the read statement follow.

```
READ 100, x, y
100 FORMAT (2F10.2)

READ '(2F10.2)', x, y
```

This version of the READ statement is much less flexible than the standard READ statement, since it can only work with the standard input device and cannot support any optional clauses. This statement is a holdover from an earlier version of FORTRAN. You will never need to use it in a modern program.

10.3.6 The WRITE Statement

The WRITE statement takes data from the variables in the I/O list, converts it according to the specified FORMAT descriptors, and writes it out to the file associated with the specified i/o unit. The WRITE statement has the general form

```
WRITE (control_list) io_list
```

where `control_list` consists of one or more clauses separated by commas. The possible clauses in a WRITE statement are the same as those in the READ statement except that there are no END= , SIZE=, or EOR= clauses in the WRITE statement.

10.3.7 The PRINT Statement

An alternative output statement called the PRINT statement works only for formatted writes or list-directed writes to the standard output device. This statement has the form

```
PRINT fmt, io_list
```

where `fmt` is the format specification to use when reading the list of variables in the `io_list`. The format may be the number of a FORMAT statement, the name of a character variable containing the formatting information, a character string containing the formatting information, or an asterisk. Examples of the PRINT statement follow.

```
PRINT 100, x, y
100 FORMAT (2F10.2)

string = '(2F10.2)'
PRINT string, x, y
```

The PRINT statement is much less flexible than the standard WRITE statement, since it can only work with the standard output device and cannot support any optional clauses. It is a holdover from earlier versions of FORTRAN. You will never need to use it in a modern program. However, many Fortran programmers are stylistically committed to using this statement through long years of habit. It does work, and programs using the PRINT statement will continue to be supported indefinitely in the future. You should recognize the statement when you see it, but in the opinion of this author, you should not use PRINT in the programs you write.

10.3.8 File-Positioning Statements

Fortran has two file-positioning statements REWIND and BACKSPACE. The REWIND statement positions the file so that the next READ statement will read the first line in the file. The BACKSPACE statement moves the file back by one line. These statements are only valid for sequential files. The statements have the general form

```
REWIND (control_list)
BACKSPACE (control_list)
```

where *control_list* consists of one or more clauses separated by commas. The possible clauses in a file-positioning statement are summarized in Table 10–7. The meanings of these clauses are the same as in the other I/O statements described in this chapter.

The i/o unit may be specified without the UNIT= keyword if it is in the first position of the control list. The following statements are examples of legal file-positioning statements:

```
REWIND (unit_in)
BACKSPACE (UNIT=12, IOSTAT=istat)
```

For compatibility with earlier versions of FORTRAN, a file-positioning statement containing only an i/o unit number can also be specified without parentheses:

```
REWIND 6
BACKSPACE unit_in
```

The IOSTAT= clause should be used instead of the ERR= clause in modern Fortran programs. The IOSTAT= clause is better suited to modern structured programming techniques.

■ **TABLE 10–7**
Clauses allowed in the REWIND, BACKSPACE, or ENDFILE statements

Clause	Input or output	Purpose	Possible values
[UNIT=]*int_expr*	Input	I/o unit to operate on. The UNIT= phrase is optional.	Processor-dependent integer.
IOSTAT=*int_var*	Output	I/O status at the end of the operation.	Processor-dependent integer *int_var*: 0 = success, positive = failure.
ERR= *statement_label*	Input	Statement label to transfer control to if an error occurs.[1]	Statement labels in current scoping unit.

[1]The ERR= clause is never needed in a modern Fortran program. Use the IOSTAT= clause instead.

10.3.9 The ENDFILE Statement

The ENDFILE statement writes an end-of-file record at the current position in a sequential file and then positions the file after the end-of-file record. After executing an ENDFILE statement on a file, no further READs or WRITEs are possible until either a BACKSPACE or a REWIND statement is executed. Until then, any further READ or WRITE statements will produce an error. This statement has the general form

$$\text{ENDFILE } (control\_list)$$

where *control_list* consists of one or more clauses separated by commas. The possible clauses in an ENDFILE statement are summarized in Table 10–7. The meanings of these clauses are the same as in the other I/O statements described above. The i/o unit may be specified without the UNIT= keyword if it is in the first position of the control list.

For compatibility with earlier version of FORTRAN, an ENDFILE statement containing only an i/o unit number can also be specified without parentheses. The following statements are examples of legal ENDFILE statements:

```
ENDFILE (UNIT=12, IOSTAT=istat)
ENDFILE 6
```

The IOSTAT= clause should be used instead of the ERR= clause in modern Fortran programs. The IOSTAT= clause is better suited to modern structured programming techniques.

■ 10.4
NAMELIST I/O

Namelist I/O is a convenient way to write out or to read in a fixed list of variable names and values. A *namelist* is just a list of variable names that are always read or written as a group. The form of a namelist is

```
NAMELIST / nl_group_name / var1 [, var2, ... ]
```

where *nl_group_name* is the name of the namelist and *var1, var2,* and so on are the variables in the list. The NAMELIST is a specification statement and must appear before the first executable statement in a program. If multiple NAMELIST statements have the same name, then the variables in all statements are concatenated and treated as though they were in a single large statement. The variables listed in a NAMELIST may be read or written as a unit using namelist-directed I/O statements.

A NAMELIST I/O statement looks like a formatted I/O statement except that the FMT= clause is replaced by a NML= clause. The form of a namelist-directed WRITE statement is

```
WRITE (UNIT=unit, NML=nl_group_name, [ ... ])
```

where unit is the i/o unit to which the data will be written and *nl_group_name* is the name of the namelist to be written. (Unlike most other clauses in I/O statements, the `nl_group_name` is not enclosed in apostrophes or quotes.) When a namelist-directed WRITE statement is executed, the names of all the variables in the namelist are printed out together with their values in a special order. The first item to be printed is an ampersand (&) followed by the namelist name. Next comes a series of output values in the form "NAME=value". These output values may either appear on a single line separated by commas or appear on separate lines, depending on the way a particular processor implements the namelist. Finally, the list is terminated by a slash (/).

For example, consider the program shown in Figure 10–3.

FIGURE 10–3
A simple program using a NAMELIST-directed WRITE statement.

```
PROGRAM write_namelist
!  Purpose:
!     To illustrate a NAMELIST-directed WRITE statement.
!
IMPLICIT NONE

! Declare variables
INTEGER :: i = 1, j = 2                        ! Integer variables
REAL :: a = -999., b = 0.                      ! Real variables
CHARACTER(len=12) :: string = 'Test string.'   ! Char variables
NAMELIST / mylist / i, j, string, a, b         ! Declare namelist

OPEN (8,FILE='output.nml',DELIM='APOSTROPHE')  ! Open output file
WRITE (UNIT=8, NML=mylist)                     ! Write namelist
CLOSE (8)                                      ! Close file

END PROGRAM
```

After this program is executed, the file `output.nml` contains the lines:

```
&MYLIST
I =            1
J =            2
STRING = 'Test string.'
A =      -999.000000
B =      0.000000E+00
/
```

The namelist output begins with an ampersand and the list name and concludes with a slash. Note that the character string is surrounded by apostrophes, because the file was opened with the clause DELIM='APOSTROPHE'.

The general form of a namelist-directed READ statement is

$$\text{READ (UNIT=}unit\text{, NML=}nl\_group\_name\text{, [...])}$$

where `unit` is the i/o unit from which the data will be read and `nl_group_name` is the name of the namelist to be read. When a namelist-directed READ statement is executed, the program searches the input file for the marker `&nl_group_name`, which indicates the beginning of the namelist. The program then reads all the values in the namelist until a slash character (/) is encountered to terminate the READ. The values in the input list may appear on any line within the input file as long as they are between the markers `&nl_group_name` and `/`. The values are assigned to the namelist variables according to the names given in the input list. The namelist READ statement does not have to set a value for every variable in the namelist. If some namelist variables are not included in the input file list, then their values will remain unchanged after the namelist READ executes.

Namelist-directed READ statements are very useful. Suppose that you are writing a program containing 100 input variables. The variables will be initialized to their usual values by default in the program. During any particular run of the program, anywhere from 1 to 10 of these values may need to be changed, but the others would remain at their default values. In this case you could include all 100 values in a namelist and include a namelist-directed READ statement in the program. When users run the program, they can just list the few values to be changed in the namelist input file; all other input variables will remain unchanged. This approach is much better than using an ordinary READ statement, since all 100 values would need to be listed in the ordinary READ's input file, even if they were not being changed during a particular run.

Consider the example in Figure 10–4, which illustrates how a namelist READ can update selected values in the namelist.

FIGURE 10–4
A simple program using a NAMELIST-directed READ statement.

```
PROGRAM read_namelist
!  Purpose:
!     To illustrate a NAMELIST-directed READ statement.
!
IMPLICIT NONE

! Declare variables
INTEGER :: i = 1, j = 2                           ! Integer variables
REAL :: a = -999., b = 0.                         ! Real variables
CHARACTER(len=12) :: string='Test string.'        ! Char variables
NAMELIST / mylist / i, j, string, a, b            ! Declare namelist

OPEN (7,FILE='input.nml',DELIM='APOSTROPHE')      ! Open input file.

! Write NAMELIST before update
WRITE (*,'(1X,A)') 'Namelist file before update: '
WRITE (UNIT=*,NML=mylist)

READ (UNIT=7,NML=mylist)                          ! Read namelist file.

! Write NAMELIST after update
WRITE (*,'(1X,A)') 'Namelist file after update: '
WRITE (UNIT=*, NML=mylist)

END PROGRAM
```

If the file input.nml contains the following data

```
                      &MYLIST
                      I =          -111
                      STRING = 'Test 1.'
                      STRING = 'Different!'
                      B =      123456.
                      /
```

then variable b will be assigned the value 123456., variable i will be assigned the value −111, and variable string will be assigned a value of 'Different!'. Note that if more than one input value exists for the same variable, the last one in the namelist is used. The values of all variables other than b, i, and string will not be changed. The result of executing this program follows.

```
C>namelist_read
Namelist file before update:
&MYLIST
I =              1
J =              2
STRING =  Test string.
A =       -999.000000
B =       0.000000E+00
/
Namelist file after update:
&MYLIST
I =            -111
J =              2
STRING =  Different!
A =       -999.000000
B =       123456.000000
/
```

If a namelist output file is opened with the character delimiter set to 'APOSTRO-PHE' or 'QUOTE', then the output file written by a namelist WRITE statement is in a form that can be directly read by a namelist READ statement. Consequently, the namelist is a great way to exchange a lot of data between separate programs or between different runs of the same program.

Good Programming Practice

Use NAMELIST I/O to save data to be exchanged between programs or between different runs of a single program. Also, you may use NAMELIST READ statements to update selected input parameters when a program begins executing.

Array names, array sections, and array elements may all appear in a NAMELIST statement. If an array name appears in a namelist, then when a namelist WRITE is executed, every element of the array is printed out in the output namelist one at a time, for example, a(1) = 3., a(2) = -1., and so on. When a namelist READ is executed, each element of the array may be set separately; only the elements whose values are to be changed need to be supplied in the input file.

Dummy arguments and variables that are created dynamically (e.g., array dummy arguments with nonconstant bounds, character variables with nonconstant lengths, automatic variables, and pointers) may not appear in a NAMELIST.

■ 10.5

UNFORMATTED FILES

All the files that we have used so far in this book have been formatted files. A formatted file contains recognizable characters, numbers, and so forth stored in a standard coding scheme such as ASCII or EBCDIC. These files are easy to distinguish because we can see the characters and numbers in the file when we display them on the screen or print them on a printer. However, to use data in a formatted file, a program must translate the characters in the file into the internal integer or real format used by the particular processor on which the program is running. The instructions for this translation are provided by format descriptors.

Formatted files have the advantage that we can readily see what sort of data they contain. However, they also have disadvantages. A processor must do a good deal of work to convert a number between the processor's internal representation and the characters contained in the file. All this work is just wasted effort if we are going to be reading the data back into another program on the same processor. Also, the internal representation of a number usually requires much less space than the corresponding ASCII or EBCDIC representation of the number found in a formatted file. For example, the internal representation of a 32-bit real value requires 4 bytes of space. The ASCII representation of the same value would be $\pm$ .dddddddE $\pm$ ee, which requires 13 bytes of space (one byte per character). Storing data in ASCII or EBCDIC format is inefficient and wasteful of disk space.

Unformatted files overcome these disadvantages by copying the information from the processor's memory directly to the disk file with no conversions at all. Since no conversions occur, no processor time is wasted formatting the data. Furthermore, the data occupies a much smaller amount of disk space. On the other hand, unformatted data cannot be examined and interpreted directly by humans. In addition, it usually cannot be moved between different types of processors, because those types of processors have different internal ways to represent integers and real values.

Formatted and unformatted files are compared in Table 10–8. In general, formatted files are best for data that people must examine or for data that may have to be moved between different types of processors. Unformatted files are best for storing information that humans will not need to examine and that will be created and used on the same type of processor. Under those circumstances unformatted files are both faster and occupy less disk space than formatted files.

Unformatted I/O statements look just like formatted I/O statements, except that the FMT= clause is left out of the control list in the READ and WRITE statements. For example, the following two statements perform formatted and unformatted writes of array arr:

```
WRITE (UNIT=10,FMT=100,IOSTAT=istat) (arr(i), i = 1, 1000)
100 FORMAT ( 1X, 5E13.6 )

WRITE (UNIT=10,IOSTAT=istat) (arr(i), i = 1, 1000)
```

A file may be either FORMATTED or UNFORMATTED, but not both. Therefore, we cannot mix formatted and unformatted I/O statements within a single file. The `IN-QUIRE` statement can be used to determine the formatting status of a file.

Good Programming Practice

Use formatted files to create data that must be readable by humans or that must be transferable between processors of different types. Use unformatted files to efficiently store large quantities of data that do not have to be directly examined and that will remain on one type of processor. Also, use unformatted files when I/O speed is critical.

10.6
DIRECT ACCESS FILES

Direct access files are files that are written and read using direct access. The records in a sequential access file must be read in order from beginning to end. By contrast, the records in a direct access file may be read in arbitrary order. Direct access files are especially useful for information that may need to be accessed in any order, such as database files.

The key to the operation of a direct access file is that every record in a direct access file must be of the same length. If each record is the same length, then it is a simple matter to calculate exactly how far the ith record is into the disk file and to read the disk sector containing that record directly without reading all of the sectors before it in the file. For example, suppose that we want to read the 120th record in a direct access file with 100-byte records. The 120th record will be located between bytes 11,901 and 12,000 of the file. The compiler can calculate the disk sector containing those bytes and read it directly.

A direct access file is opened by specifying `ACCESS='DIRECT'` in the `OPEN` statement. The length of each record in a direct access file must be specified in the `OPEN`

TABLE 10–8
Comparison of formatted and unformatted files

Formatted files	Unformatted files
Can display data on output devices.	Cannot display data on output devices.
Can easily transport data between different computers.	Cannot easily transport data between computers with different internal data representations.
Requires a relatively large amount of disk space.	Requires relatively little disk space.
Slow: requires a lot of computer time.	Fast: requires little computer time.
Truncation or rounding errors possible in formatting.	No truncation or rounding errors.

statement using the `RECL=` clause. A typical `OPEN` statement for a direct access formatted file follows.

```
OPEN ( UNIT=8, FILE='dirio.fmt', ACCESS='DIRECT', FORM='FORMATTED', &
       RECL=40 )
```

The `FORM=` clause had to be specified here, because the default form for direct access is `'UNFORMATTED'`.

For formatted files the length of each record in the `RECL=` clause is specified in units of characters. Therefore, each record in file `dirio.fmt` example is 40 characters long. For unformatted files the length specified in the `RECL=` clause may be in units of bytes, words, or some other machine-dependent quantity. You can use the `INQUIRE` statement to determine the record length required for an unformatted direct access file in a processor-independent fashion.

`READ` and `WRITE` statements for direct access files look like similar statements for sequential access files except that the `REC=` clause may be included to specify the particular record to read or write. (If the `REC=` clause is left out, then the next record in the direct access file will be read or written.) A typical `READ` statement for a direct access formatted file follows.

```
READ ( 8, '(I6)', REC=irec ) ival
```

Direct access unformatted files whose record length is a multiple of the sector size of a particular computer are the most efficient Fortran files possible on that computer. Because they are direct access, it is possible to read any record in such a file directly. Because they are unformatted, no computer time is wasted in format conversions during reads or writes. Finally, because each record is exactly one disk sector long, only one disk sector will need to be read or written for each record. (Shorter records that are not multiples of the disk sector size might stretch across two disk sectors, forcing the computer to read both sectors in order to recover the information in the record.) Because these files are so efficient, many large programs written in Fortran are designed to use them.

A simple program using a direct access formatted file is shown in Figure 10–5. This program creates a direct access formatted file named `dirio.fmt` with 40 characters per record. It fills the first 100 records with information and then directly recovers whichever record the user specifies.

FIGURE 10–5
A sample program using a direct access formatted file.

```
PROGRAM direct_access_formatted
!
!  Purpose:
!    To illustrate the use of direct access Fortran files.
!
!  Record of revisions:
!      Date        Programmer          Description of change
!      ====        ==========          =====================
!    01/14/96    S. J. Chapman         Original code
!
```

(continued)

(concluded)

```
IMPLICIT NONE

! List of local variables:
INTEGER :: i                    ! Index variable
INTEGER :: irec                 ! Number of record in file
CHARACTER(len=40) :: line       ! String containing current line.

! Open a direct access formatted file with 40 characters per record.
OPEN ( UNIT=8, FILE='dirio.fmt', ACCESS='DIRECT', &
       FORM='FORMATTED', STATUS='REPLACE', RECL=40 )

! Insert 100 records into this file.
DO i = 1, 100
   WRITE ( 8, '(A,I3,A)', REC=i ) 'This is record ', i, '.'
END DO

! Find out which record the user wants to retrieve.
WRITE (*,'(A)',ADVANCE='NO') ' Which record would you like to see? '
READ (*,'(I3)') irec

! Retrieve the desired record.
READ ( 8, '(A)', REC=irec ) line

! Display the record.
WRITE (*, '(A,/,5X,A)') ' The record is: ', line

END PROGRAM
```

When the program is compiled and executed, the results are

```
C>direct_access_formatted
Which record would you like to see? 34
The record is:
    This is record 34.
```

This program also illustrates the use of the ADVANCE='NO' clause in a WRITE statement to allow a response to be entered on the same line that the prompt is printed on. The cursor did not advance to a new line when the WRITE statement was executed.

EXAMPLE 10–2 Comparing Direct Access Formatted and Unformatted Files: To compare the operation of formatted and unformatted direct access files, create two files containing 5,000 records, each with four double-precision real values per line. One file should be formatted and the other one should be unformatted. Compare the sizes to the two files and then compare the time that it takes to recover 10,000 records in random order from each file. Use subroutine random0 from Chapter 6 to generate the values placed in the files and also the order in which the values are to be recovered. Use subroutine elapsed_time from exercise 6–31 to determine how long it takes to read each file.

SOLUTION A program to generate the files and then the access to them is shown in Figure 10–6. Note that the program uses the INQUIRE statement to determine the length for each record in the unformatted file.

FIGURE 10–6

Sample program comparing direct access unformatted files to direct access formatted files.

```
PROGRAM direct_access
!
!   Purpose:
!     To compare direct access formatted and unformatted files.
!
!   Record of revisions:
!       Date          Programmer            Description of change
!       ====          ==========            =====================
!     01/14/96      S. J. Chapman           Original code
!
IMPLICIT NONE

! List of parameters:
INTEGER, PARAMETER :: single = SELECTED_REAL_KIND(p=6)
INTEGER, PARAMETER :: double = SELECTED_REAL_KIND(p=14)
INTEGER, PARAMETER :: max_records = 5000      ! Max # of records
INTEGER, PARAMETER :: number_of_reads = 10000 ! # of reads

! List of local variables:
INTEGER :: i, j                    ! Index variable
INTEGER :: length_fmt = 80         ! Length of each record in
                                   !   formatted file
INTEGER :: length_unf              ! Length of each record in
                                   !   unformatted file
INTEGER :: irec                    ! Number of record in file
REAL (KIND=single) :: time_fmt     ! Time for formatted reads
REAL (KIND=single) :: time_unf     ! Time for unformatted reads
REAL (KIND=single) :: value        ! Value returned from random0
REAL (KIND=double), DIMENSION(4) :: values ! Values in record

! Get the length of each record in the unformatted file.
INQUIRE (IOLENGTH=length_unf) values
WRITE (*,'(A,I2)') ' The unformatted record length is ', &
                   length_unf
WRITE (*,'(A,I2)') ' The formatted record length is ', &
                   length_fmt

! Open a direct access unformatted file.
OPEN ( UNIT=8, FILE='dirio.unf', ACCESS='DIRECT', &
       FORM='UNFORMATTED', STATUS='REPLACE', RECL=length_unf )

! Open a direct access formatted file.
OPEN ( UNIT=9, FILE='dirio.fmt', ACCESS='DIRECT', &
       FORM='FORMATTED', STATUS='REPLACE', RECL=length_fmt )

! Generate records and insert into each file.
DO i = 1, max_records
   DO j = 1, 4
     CALL random0(value)                    ! Generate records
     values(j) = 30._double * value
   END DO

   ! Write to unformatted and formatted files.
```

(continued)

(concluded)

```
    WRITE (8,REC=i) values
    WRITE (9,'(4ES20.14)', REC=i) values
END DO

! Measure the time to recover random records from the
! unformatted file.
CALL set_timer
DO i = 1, number_of_reads
   CALL random0(value)
   irec=(max_records-1) * value + 1
   READ (8,REC=irec) values
END DO
CALL elapsed_time (time_unf)

! Measure the time to recover random records from the
! formatted file.
CALL set_timer
DO i = 1, number_of_reads
   CALL random0(value)
   irec = (max_records-1) * value + 1
   READ (9,'(4ES20.14)',REC=irec) values
END DO
CALL elapsed_time (time_fmt)

! Tell user.
WRITE (*,'(A,F6.2)') ' Time for reading unformatted file = ', &
                     time_unf
WRITE (*,'(A,F6.2)') ' Time for reading formatted file = ', &
                     time_fmt

END PROGRAM
```

When the program is compiled with the Microsoft Fortran Powerstation 4.0 compiler and executed on a 486/DX2-66 personal computer, the results are

```
C>direct_access
The unformatted record length is 32
The formatted record length is 80
Time for reading unformatted file =    5.11
Time for reading formatted file =     16.26
```

The length of each record in the unformatted file is 32 bytes, because the Microsoft compiler happens to measure lengths in units of bytes. On other processors the length might come out in different, processor-dependent units. If we examine the files after the program executes, we see that the formatted file is much larger than the unformatted file, even though they both store the same information.

```
C>dir dirio.*
Volume in drive C has no label
Volume Serial Number is 282E-0802
Directory of C:\BOOK\F90\Chap10

DIRIO    FMT     410,000  01-15-96  8:53p dirio.fmt
DIRIO    UNF     160,000  01-15-96  8:53p dirio.unf
        2 file(s)       570,000 bytes
        0 dir(s)     78,921,728 bytes free
```

Unformatted direct access files are both smaller and faster than formatted direct access files but are not portable between different kinds of processors.

Good Programming Practice

Use sequential access files for data that is normally read and processed sequentially. Use direct access files for data that must be read and written in any arbitrary order.

Good Programming Practice

Use direct access, unformatted files for applications where large quantities of data must be manipulated quickly. If possible, make the record length of the files a multiple of the basic disk sector size for your computer.

Quiz 10–2

This quiz provides a quick check to see if you understand the concepts introduced in sections 10.3 to 10.6. If you have trouble with the quiz, reread the sections, ask your instructor, or discuss the material with a fellow student. The answers to this quiz are found in the back of the book.

1. What is the difference between a formatted and an unformatted file? What are the advantages and disadvantages of each type of file?

2. What is the difference between a direct access file and a sequential file? What are the advantages and disadvantages of each type of file?

3. What is the purpose of the INQUIRE statement? Explain three ways it can be used.

For questions 4 to 9, determine whether the following statements are valid. If not, specify what is wrong with them. If they are valid, what do they do?

4.
```
INTEGER :: i = 29
OPEN (UNIT=i,FILE='temp.dat',STATUS='SCRATCH')
WRITE (FMT="(1X,'The unit is ',I3)",UNIT=i) i
```

5.
```
INTEGER :: i = 7
OPEN (i,STATUS='SCRATCH',ACCESS='DIRECT')
WRITE (FMT="(1X,'The unit is ',I3)",UNIT=i) i
```

6.
```
INTEGER :: i = 7, j = 0
OPEN (UNIT=i,STATUS='SCRATCH',ACCESS='DIRECT',RECL=80)
WRITE (FMT='(I10)', UNIT= i) j
CLOSE (i)
```

(continued)

(concluded)

7.
```
INTEGER :: i
REAL,DIMENSION(9) :: a = (/ (-100,i=1,5), (100,i=6,9) /)
OPEN (8,FILE='mydata',STATUS='REPLACE',IOSTAT=istat)
WRITE (8,'(1X,3EN14.7)') (a(i), i = 1, 3)
WRITE (8,*) (a(i), i = 4, 6)
WRITE (UNIT=8) (a(i), I = 7, 9)
CLOSE (8)
```

8.
```
LOGICAL :: exists
INTEGER :: lu = 11, istat
INQUIRE (FILE='mydata.dat',EXIST=exists,UNIT=lu,IOSTAT=istat)
```

9. What is in the data file `out.dat` after the following statements are executed?

```
INTEGER :: i, istat
REAL, DIMENSION(5) :: a = (/ (100.*i, i=-2,2) /)
REAL :: b = -37, c = 0
NAMELIST / local_data / a, b, c
OPEN(UNIT=3,FILE='in.dat'.,ACTION='READ',STATUS='OLD',IOSTAT=istat)
OPEN(UNIT=4,FILE='out.dat',ACTION='WRITE',IOSTAT=istat)
READ(3,NML=local_data,IOSTAT=istat)
WRITE(4,NML=local_data,IOSTAT=istat)
```

Assume that the file `in.dat` contains the following information:
```
&local_data A(2) = -17.,A(5) = 30. /
```

10

EXAMPLE 10–3 Spare Parts Inventory: Any engineering organization that maintains computers or test equipment needs to keep a supply of spare parts and consumable supplies on hand for use when equipment breaks, printers run out of paper, and so on. The organization needs to keep track of these supplies to determine how many units of each type are being used in a given period of time, how many are in stock, and when to order more of a particular item. In actual practice these functions are usually implemented with a database program. Here, we will write a simple Fortran program to keep track of stockroom supplies.

SOLUTION A program to keep track of stockroom supplies needs to maintain a database of all available supplies, their descriptions, and their quantities. A typical database record might consist of the following fields:

1. **Stock number** A unique number by which the item is known. Stock numbers start at 1 and go up to however many items are carried in the stockroom. (6 characters on disk; 1 integer in memory)
2. **Description** Description of item. (30 characters)
3. **Vendor** The company that makes or sells the item. (10 characters)
4. **Vendor number** The number by which the item is known to the vendor. (20 characters)
5. **Number in stock** (6 characters on disk; 1 integer in memory)

6. **Minimum quantity**   If less than this number of the item is in stock, it should be reordered. (6 characters on disk; 1 integer in memory)

We will create a database file on disk in which the number of each record corresponds to the stock number of the item in the record. There will be as many records as there are items in stock, and each record will be 78 bytes long to hold the 78 characters of a database record. Furthermore, it may be necessary to withdraw items from stock in any order, so we should have direct access to any record in the database. We will implement the database using a direct access formatted Fortran file with a record length of 78 bytes.

In addition, we will need a file containing information about the withdrawals from stock of various parts and supplies and about their replenishment by purchases from vendors. This *transaction file* will consist of stock numbers and quantities purchased or withdrawn. (Purchases of supplies are indicated by positive numbers, and withdrawals from stock are indicated by negative numbers.) Since the transactions in the transaction file will be read in chronological sequence, we can use a sequential file for the transaction file.

Finally, we will need a file for reorders and error messages. This output file will contain reordering messages whenever the quantity of a stock item falls below the minimum quantity. It will also contain error messages if someone tries to withdraw an item that is not currently in stock.

1. State the problem.

Write a program to maintain a database of stockroom supplies for a small company. The program will accept inputs describing the issues from the stockroom and replenishments of the stock and will constantly update the database of stockroom supplies. It will also generate reorder messages whenever the supply of an item gets too low.

2. Define the inputs and outputs.

The input to the program will be a sequential transaction file describing the issues from the stockroom and replenishments of the stocks. Each purchase or issue will be a separate line in the transaction file. Each record will consist of a stock number and quantity in free format.

The program has two outputs. One is the database itself, and the other is a message file containing reordering and error messages. The database file will consist of 78-byte records structured just as described.

3. Describe the algorithm.

When the program starts, it will open the database file, transaction file, and message file. It will then process each transaction in the transaction file, updating the database as necessary and generating required messages. Here is the high-level pseudocode for this program:

```
Open the three files
WHILE transactions file is not at end-of-file DO
  Read transaction
```

```
                    Apply to database
                    IF error or limit exceeded THEN
                       Generate error / reorder message
                    END of IF
                 END of WHILE
                 Close the three files
```

The detailed pseudocode for this program follows.

```
              ! Open files
              Open database file for DIRECT access
              Open transaction file for SEQUENTIAL access
              Open message file for SEQUENTIAL access

              ! Process transactions
              WHILE
                 Read transaction
                 IF end-of-file EXIT
                 Add / subtract quantities from database
                 IF quantity < 0 THEN
                    Generate error message
                 END of IF
                 IF quantity < minimum THEN
                    Generate reorder message
                 END of IF
              END of WHILE

              ! Close files
              Close database file
              Close transaction file
              Close message file
```

4. **Turn the algorithm into Fortran statements.**

The resulting Fortran subroutines are shown in Figure 10–7.

FIGURE 10–7
Program stock.

```
PROGRAM stock
!
!   Purpose:
!     To maintain an inventory of stockroom supplies and to generate
!     warning messages when supplies get low.
!
!   Record of revisions:
!       Date        Programmer          Description of change
!       ====        ==========          =====================
!     01/15/96    S. J. Chapman         Original code
!
IMPLICIT NONE

! Declare derived data type for a database item
TYPE :: database_record
   INTEGER :: stock_number              ! Item number
   CHARACTER(len=30) :: description      ! Description of item
   CHARACTER(len=10) :: vendor           ! Vendor of item
   CHARACTER(len=20) :: vendor_number    ! Vendor stock number
```

(continued)

(continued)

```
    INTEGER :: number_in_stock          ! Number in stock
    INTEGER :: minimum_quantity         ! Minimum quantity
END TYPE

! Declare derived data type for transaction
TYPE :: transaction_record
    INTEGER :: stock_number             ! Item number
    INTEGER :: number_in_transaction    ! Number in transaction
END TYPE

! Declare parameters:
INTEGER, PARAMETER :: lu_db = 7         ! Unit for db file
INTEGER, PARAMETER :: lu_m = 8          ! Unit for message file
INTEGER, PARAMETER :: lu_t = 9          ! Unit for trans file

! Declare local variables:
TYPE (database_record) :: item          ! Database item
TYPE (transaction_record) :: trans      ! Transaction item
CHARACTER(len=3) :: file_stat           ! File status
INTEGER :: istat                        ! I/O status
LOGICAL :: exist                        ! True if file exists

CHARACTER(len=24) :: db_file='stock.db'     ! Database file
CHARACTER(len=24) :: msg_file='stock.msg'   ! Message file
CHARACTER(len=24) :: trn_file='stock.trn'   ! Trans. file

! Begin execution: open database file, and check for error.
OPEN (lu_db, FILE=db_file, STATUS='OLD', ACCESS='DIRECT', &
      FORM='FORMATTED', RECL=78, IOSTAT=istat )
IF ( istat /= 0 ) THEN
   WRITE (*,100) db_file, istat
   100 FORMAT (' Open failed on file ',A,'. IOSTAT = ',I6)
   STOP
END IF

! Open transaction file and check for error.
OPEN (lu_t, FILE=trn_file, STATUS='OLD', ACCESS='SEQUENTIAL', &
      IOSTAT=istat )
IF ( istat /= 0 ) THEN
   WRITE (*,100) trn_file, istat
   STOP
END IF

! Open message file and position file pointer at end of file.
! Check for error.
INQUIRE (FILE=msg_file,EXIST=exist) ! Does the msg file exist?
IF ( exist ) THEN
   file_stat='OLD'                      ! Yes, append to it.
ELSE
   file_stat = 'NEW'                    ! No, create it.
END IF
OPEN (lu_m, FILE=msg_file, STATUS=file_stat, POSITION='APPEND', &
      ACCESS='SEQUENTIAL', IOSTAT=istat )
IF ( istat /= 0 ) THEN
   WRITE (*,100) msg_file, istat
   STOP
END IF

! Now begin processing loop for as long as transactions exist.
```

(continued)

(concluded)

```
process: DO
   ! Read transaction.
   READ (lu_t,*,IOSTAT=istat) trans

   ! If we are at the end of the data, exit now.
   IF ( istat /= 0 ) EXIT

   ! Get database record, and check for error.
   READ (lu_db,'(A6,A30,A10,A20,I6,I6)',REC=trans%stock_number, &
         IOSTAT=istat) item
   IF ( istat /= 0 ) THEN
      WRITE (*,'(A,I6,A,I6)') &
            ' Read failed on database file record ', &
            trans%stock_number, ' IOSTAT =', istat
      STOP
   END IF

   ! Read ok, so update record.
   item%number_in_stock = item%number_in_stock &
                     + trans%number_in_transaction

   ! Check for errors.
   IF ( item%number_in_stock < 0 ) THEN
      ! Write error message & reset quantity to zero.
      WRITE (lu_m,'(A,I6,A)') ' ERROR: Stock number ', &
            trans%stock_number, ' has quantity < 0! '
      item%number_in_stock = 0
   END IF

   ! Check for quantities < minimum.
   IF ( item%number_in_stock < item%minimum_quantity ) THEN
      ! Write reorder message to message file.
      WRITE (lu_m,110) ' Reorder stock number ', &
            trans%stock_number, ' from vendor ', &
            item%vendor, ' Description: ', &
            item%description
      110 FORMAT (A,I6,A,A,/,A,A)
   END IF

   ! Update database record
   WRITE (lu_db,'(A6,A30,A10,A20,I6,I6)',REC=trans%stock_number, &
         IOSTAT=istat) item

END DO process

! End of updates.  Close files and exit.
CLOSE ( lu_db )
CLOSE ( lu_t )
CLOSE ( lu_m )

END PROGRAM
```

5. **Test the resulting Fortran program.**

To test this subroutine, we need to create a sample database file and transaction file. The following database file has only four stock items:

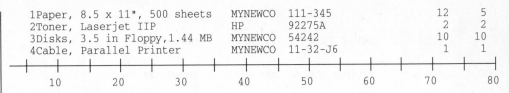

```
1Paper, 8.5 x 11", 500 sheets   MYNEWCO  111-345              12      5
2Toner, Laserjet IIP            HP       92275A                2      2
3Disks, 3.5 in Floppy,1.44 MB   MYNEWCO  54242                10     10
4Cable, Parallel Printer        MYNEWCO  11-32-J6              1       1
        10      20      30      40      50      60      70      80
```

The following transaction file contains records of the dispensing of three reams of paper and five floppy disks. In addition, two new toner cartridges arrive and are placed in stock.

```
                1      -3
                3      -5
                2       2
```

If the program is run against this transaction file, the new database is

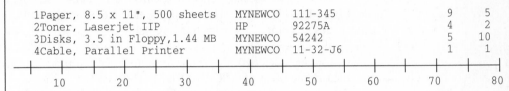

```
1Paper, 8.5 x 11", 500 sheets   MYNEWCO  111-345               9      5
2Toner, Laserjet IIP            HP       92275A                4      2
3Disks, 3.5 in Floppy,1.44 MB   MYNEWCO  54242                 5     10
4Cable, Parallel Printer        MYNEWCO  11-32-J6              1       1
        10      20      30      40      50      60      70      80
```

and the message file contains the following lines:

```
        Reorder stock number        3 from vendor MYNEWCO
            Description:  Disks, 3.5 in Floppy, 1.44 MB
```

By comparing the before and after values in the database, we can see that the program is functioning correctly.

10

Example 10–3 illustrated several advanced I/O features. The files that must exist for the program to work are opened with the 'OLD' status. The output message file may or may not previously exist; therefore, it is opened with the proper status 'OLD' or 'NEW' depending on the results of an INQUIRE statement. The example uses both direct access and sequential access files. The direct access file was used in the database, where it is necessary to be able to access any record in any order. The sequential files were used for simple input and output lists that were processed in sequential order. The message file was opened with the 'APPEND' option so that new messages could be written at the end of any existing messages.

The program also exhibits a few undesirable features. The principal one is the use of STOP statements whenever an error occurs. This statement was used here to keep the example simple for classroom purposes. However, in a real program we should either close all files and shut down gracefully when an error occurs or else offer the user a chance to fix whatever problem is detected.

A real database would have probably used direct access unformatted files, instead of formatted files. We used formatted files here to make it easy to see the before-and-after effects on the database.

▨ 10.7

SUMMARY

This chapter introduced the additional format descriptors EN, D, G, B, O, Z, P, TL, TR, S, SP, SN, BN, BZ, and :. The EN descriptor provides a way to display data in engineering notation. The G descriptor provides a way to display any form of data. The B, O, and Z descriptors display integer or real data in binary, octal, and hexadecimal format respectively. The TLn and TRn descriptors shift the position of data in the current line left and right by n characters. The colon descriptor (:) serves as a conditional stopping point for a WRITE statement. The D, P, S, SP, SN, BN, and BZ descriptors should not be used in new programs.

Then we covered advanced features of Fortran I/O statements. The INQUIRE, PRINT, and ENDFILE statements were introduced, and all options were explained for all Fortran I/O statements. This chapter introduced NAMELIST I/O and explained the advantages of namelists for exchanging data between two programs or between two runs of the same program.

Fortran includes two file forms: *formatted* and *unformatted*. Formatted files contain data in the form of ASCII or EBCDIC characters, while unformatted files contain data that is a direct copy of the bits stored in the computer's memory. Formatted I/O requires a relatively large amount of processor time, since the data must be translated every time a read or write occurs. However, formatted files can be easily moved between processors of different types. Unformatted I/O is very quick, since no translation occurs. However, unformatted files cannot be easily inspected by humans and cannot be easily moved between processors of different types.

Fortran includes two access methods: *sequential* and *direct*. Sequential access files are files intended to be read or written in sequential order. The REWIND and BACKSPACE commands provide a limited opportunity to move around within a sequential file, but the records in these files must basically be read one after another. Direct access files are files intended to be read or written in any arbitrary order. To make this possible, each record in a direct access file must be of a fixed length. If the length of each record is known, then it is possible to directly calculate where to find any specific record in the disk file and to read or write only that record. Direct access files are especially useful for large blocks of identical records that might need to be accessed in any order. A common application for direct access files is databases.

10.7.1 Summary of Good Programming Practice

The following guidelines should be adhered to when working with Fortran I/O:

1. Never use the D, P, BN, BZ, S, SP, or SS format descriptors in new programs.
2. Do not rely on preconnected files in your Fortran programs (except for the standard input and output files). The number and the names of preconnected files vary from processor to processor, so using them will reduce the portability of your programs. Instead, always explicitly open each file that you use with an OPEN statement.

3. Always use the IOSTAT= clause in OPEN statements to trap errors. When an error is detected, tell the user all about the problem before shutting down gracefully or requesting an alternative file.
4. Always explicitly close each disk file with a CLOSE statement as soon as possible after a program is finished using it so that it may be available for use by others in a multitasking environment.
5. Check to see if your output file is overwriting an existing data file. If it is, make sure that the user really wants to do so before destroying the data in the file.
6. Use the IOSTAT= clause on READ statements to prevent programs from aborting on errors, end-of-file, or end-of-record conditions. When an error or end-of-file condition is detected, the program can take appropriate actions to continue processing or to shut down gracefully.
7. Use NAMELIST I/O to save data to be exchanged between programs or between different runs of a single program. Also, you may use NAMELIST READ statements to update selected input parameters when a program begins executing.
8. Use formatted files to create data that must be readable by humans or that must be transferable between different types of computers. Use unformatted files to efficiently store large quantities of data that does not have to be directly examined and that will remain on only one type of computer. Also, use unformatted files when I/O speed is critical.
9. Use sequential access files for data that is normally read and processed sequentially. Use direct access files for data that must be read and written in any arbitrary order.
10. Use direct access, unformatted files for applications where large quantities of data must be manipulated quickly. If possible, make the record length of the files a multiple of the basic disk sector size for your computer.

10

10.7.2 Summary of Fortran Statements and Structures

BACKSPACE Statement

```
                    BACKSPACE (control_list)
or                  BACKSPACE (unit)
or                  BACKSPACE unit
```

Example:

```
                    BACKSPACE (lu,IOSTAT=istat)
                    BACKSPACE (8)
```

Description:

   The BACKSPACE statement moves the current position of a file back by one record. Possible clauses in the control list are UNIT=, IOSTAT=, and ERR=.

ENDFILE Statement

	ENDFILE (*control_list*)
or	ENDFILE (*unit*)
or	ENDFILE *unit*

Example:

```
ENDFILE (UNIT=lu, IOSTAT=istat)
ENDFILE (8)
```

Description:

The ENDFILE statement writes an end-of-file record to a file and positions the file pointer beyond the end-of-file record. Possible clauses in the control list are UNIT=, IOSTAT=, and ERR=.

INQUIRE Statement

```
INQUIRE (control_list)
```

Example:

```
LOGICAL :: lnamed
CHARACTER(len=12) :: filename, access
INQUIRE (UNIT=22, NAMED=lnamed, NAME=filename, ACCESS=access)
```

Description:

The INQUIRE statement permits a user to determine the properties of a file. The file may be specified either by its file name, or (after the file is opened) by its i/o unit number. The possible clauses in the INQUIRE statement are described in Table 10–5.

NAMELIST Statement

```
NAMELIST / nl_group_name / var1 [, var2, ...]
```

Example:

```
NAMELIST / control_data / page_size, rows, columns
WRITE (8,NML=control_data)
```

Description:

The NAMELIST statement is a specification statement that associates a group of variables in a namelist. All the variables in the namelist may be written or read as a unit using the namelist version of the WRITE and READ statements. When a namelist is read, only the values that appear in the input list will be modified by the READ. The values appear in the input list in a keyword format, and individual values may appear in any order.

PRINT Statement

```
PRINT fmt, output_list
```

Example:

```
PRINT *, intercept
PRINT '(2I6)', i, j
```

Description:

The PRINT statement outputs the data in the output list *to the standard output device* according to the formats specified in the format descriptors. The format descriptors may be in a FORMAT statement or a character string, or the format might be defaulted to list-directed I/O with an asterisk.

REWIND Statement

```
        REWIND (control_list)
or      REWIND (unit)
or      REWIND unit
```

Example:

```
        REWIND (8)
        REWIND (lu, IOSTAT=istat)
        REWIND 12
```

Description:

The REWIND statement moves the current position of a file back to the beginning of the file. Possible clauses in the control list are UNIT=, IOSTAT=, and ERR=.

■ **10.8**

EXERCISES

10–1 What is the difference between the ES and the EN format descriptor? How would the number 12345.67 be displayed by each of these descriptors?

10–2 What types of data may be displayed with the B, O, and Z descriptors? What do these descriptors do?

10–3 Write the form of the G format descriptor that will display seven significant digits of a number. What is the minimum width of this descriptor?

10–4 Write the following integers with the I8 and I8.8 format descriptors. How do the outputs compare? (a) 1024 (b) −128 (c) 30000

10–5 Write the integers from the previous exercise with the B16 (binary), O11 (octal), and Z8 (hexadecimal) format descriptors.

10–6 Use subroutine random0 developed in Chapter 6 to generate nine random numbers in the range [−100000, 100000). Display the numbers with the G11.5 format descriptor.

10–7 Suppose that you wanted to display the nine random numbers generated in the previous exercise in the following format:

```
VALUE(1) = ±xxxxxx.xx   VALUE(2) = ±xxxxxx.xx
VALUE(3) = ±xxxxxx.xx   VALUE(4) = ±xxxxxx.xx
VALUE(5) = ±xxxxxx.xx   VALUE(5) = ±xxxxxx.xx
VALUE(7) = ±xxxxxx.xx   VALUE(8) = ±xxxxxx.xx
VALUE(9) = ±xxxxxx.xx
```

```
├──┼──┼──┼──┼──┼──┼──┼──┼──┼──┤
     10    20    30    40    50
```

Write a single format descriptor that would generate this output. Use the colon descriptor appropriately in the format statement.

10–8 Suppose that the following values were to be displayed with a G10.4 format descriptor. What would each output look like?
   a. -6.38765×10^{10}
   b. -6.38765×10^{2}
   c. -6.38765×10^{-1}
   d. 2345.6
   e. .TRUE.
   f. 'String!'

10–9 Suppose that the first four values from the previous exercise were to be displayed with an EN14.6 format descriptor. What would each output look like?

10–10 Explain the operation of NAMELIST I/O. Why is it especially suitable for initializing a program or sharing data between programs?

10–11 What will be written out by the statements shown below?

```
INTEGER :: i, j
REAL, DIMENSION(3,3) :: array
NAMELIST / io / array
array = RESHAPE( (/ ((10.*i*j, j=1,3), i=0,2) /), (/3,3/) )
WRITE (*,NML=io)
```

10–12 What will be written out by the statements shown below?

```
INTEGER :: i, j
REAL, DIMENSION(3,3) :: a
NAMELIST / io / a
array = RESHAPE( (/ ((10.*i*j, j=1,3), i=0,2) /), (/3,3/) )
READ (8,NML=io)
WRITE (*,NML=io)
```

Input data on unit 8:

```
&io a(1, 1) = -100.
a(3, 1) = 6., a(1, 3) = -6. /
a(2, 2) = 1000. /
```

10–13 What is the difference between using the TR*n* format descriptor and the *n*X format descriptor to move 10 characters to the right in an output format statement?

10–14 What is printed out by the following sets of Fortran statements?

a.
```
REAL :: value = 356.248
INTEGER :: i
WRITE (*,200) 'Value = ', (value, i = 1,5)
200 FORMAT ('0',A,F10.4,G10.2,G11.5,G11.6,1PE10.3)
```

b.
```
INTEGER, DIMENSION(5) :: i
INTEGER :: j
DO j = 1, 5
   i(j) = j**2
END DO
READ (*,*) i
WRITE (*,500) i
500 FORMAT (3(10X,I5))
```

Input data:
```
-101      ,,      17        /
  20              71        ,,
```

10–15 Assume that a file is opened with the following statement:
```
OPEN ( UNIT=71, FILE='myfile')
```

What is the status of the file when it is opened this way? Will the file be opened for sequential or direct access? Where will the file pointer be? Will it be formatted or unformatted? Will the file be opened for reading, writing, or both? How long will each record be? How will list-directed character strings that are written to the file be delimited? What will happen if the file is not found? What will happen if an error occurs during the open process?

10–16 Answer the questions of the previous exercise for the following files.

a.
```
OPEN ( UNIT=21, FILE='myfile', ACCESS='DIRECT', &
       FORM='FORMATTED', RECL=80, IOSTAT=istat)
```

b.
```
OPEN ( UNIT=10, FILE='yourfile', ACCESS='DIRECT', ACTION='WRITE', &
       STATUS='REPLACE', RECL=80, IOSTAT=istat)
```

c.
```
OPEN ( 5, FILE='file_5', ACCESS='SEQUENTIAL', &
       STATUS='OLD', DELIM='QUOTE', ACTION='READWRITE', &
       POSITION='APPEND', IOSTAT=istat )
```

d.
```
OPEN ( UNIT= 1, STATUS='SCRATCH', IOSTAT=istat)
```

10–17 The IOSTAT= clause in a READ statement can return positive, negative, or zero values. What do positive values mean? negative values? zero values?

10–18 **File Copy while Trimming Trailing Blanks**   Write a Fortran program that prompts the user for an input file name and an output file name and then copies the input file to the output file, trimming trailing blanks off the end of each line before writing it out. The program should use the STATUS= and IOSTAT= clauses in the OPEN statement to confirm that the input file already exists and use the STATUS= and IOSTAT= clauses in the OPEN statement to confirm that the output file does not already exist. Be sure to use the proper ACTION= clause for each file. If the output file is already present, then prompt the user to see if it should be overwritten. If so, overwrite it, and if not, stop the program. After the copy process is completed, the program should ask the user whether or not to delete the original file. The program should set the proper status in the input file's CLOSE statement if the file is to be deleted.

10–19 Determine whether or not each of the following sets of Fortran statements is valid. If not, explain why not. If valid, describe the output from the statements.

a.
```
CHARACTER(len=10) :: acc, fmt, act, delim
INTEGER :: unit = 35
LOGICAL :: lexist, lnamed, lopen
INQUIRE (FILE='input',EXIST=lexist)
IF ( lexist ) THEN
   OPEN (unit, FILE='input', STATUS='OLD')
   INQUIRE (UNIT=unit,OPENED=lopen,EXIST=lexist, &
           NAMED=lnamed,ACCESS=acc,FORM=fmt, &
           ACTION=act, DELIM =delim)
   WRITE (*,100) lexist, lopen, lnamed, acc, fmt, &
           act, delim
   100 FORMAT (1X,'File status:  Exists = ',L1, &
           ' Opened = ', L1, ' Named = ',L1, &
           ' Access = ', A,/,' Format = ',A, &
           ' Action = ', A,/,' Delims = ',A)
END IF
```

b.
```
INTEGER :: i1 = 10
OPEN (9, FILE='file1', ACCESS='DIRECT', FORM='FORMATTED', &
      STATUS='NEW')
WRITE (9,'(I6)') i1
```

10–20 Copying a File in Reverse Order   Write a Fortran program that prompts the user for an input file name and an output file name and then copies the input file to the output file *in reverse order.* That is, the last record of the input file is the first record of the output file. The program should use the INQUIRE statement to confirm that the input file already exists and that the output file does not already exist. If the output file is already present, the prompt the user to see if it should be overwritten before proceeding. (*Hint:* Read all the lines in the input file to count them and then use BACKSPACE statements to work backwards through the file. Be careful of the IOSTAT values!)

10–21 Comparing Formatted and Unformatted Files   Write a Fortran program containing a real array with 10,000 random values in the range $[-10^6, 10^6]$. Then perform the following actions:
a. Open a formatted sequential file and write the values to the file preserving the full seven significant digits of the numbers. (Use the ES format so that numbers of any size will be properly represented.) Write 10 values per line to the file so that there are 100 lines in the file. How big is the resulting file?
b. Open an unformatted sequential file and write the values to the file. Write 10 values per line to the file so that there are 100 lines in the file. How big is the resulting file?
c. Which file was smaller, the formatted file or the unformatted file?
d. Use the subroutines set_timer and elapsed_time created in exercise 6–31 to time the formatted and unformatted writes. Which one is faster?

10–22 Comparing Sequential and Direct Access Files Write a Fortran program containing a real array with 1,000 random values in the range $[-10^5, 10^5)$. Then perform the following actions:

a. Open a formatted sequential file and write the values to the file preserving the full seven significant digits of the numbers. (Use the ES14.7 format so that numbers of any size will be properly represented.) How big is the resulting file?

b. Open a formatted direct access file with 14 characters per record and write the values to the file preserving the full seven significant digits of the numbers. (Again, use the ES14.7 format.) How big is the resulting file?

c. Open an unformatted direct access file and write the values to the file. Make the length of each record large enough to hold one number. (This parameter is computer dependent; use the INQUIRE statement to determine the length to use for the RECL= clause.) How big is the resulting file?

d. Which file was smaller, the formatted direct access file or the unformatted direct access file? How do they compare to the file sizes in the previous example?

e. Now retrieve 100 records from each of the three files in the following order: record 1, record 1000, record 2, record 999, record 3, record 998, etc. Use the subroutines set_timer and elapsed_time created in exercise 6–31 to time the reads from each file. Which one is fastest?

f. How did the sequential access file compare to the random access files when reading data in this order?

10

Pointers and Dynamic Data Structures

In earlier chapters, we have created and used variables of the five intrinsic Fortran data types and of derived data types. These variables all had two characteristics in common: they all stored some form of data, and they were almost all **static,** meaning that the number and types of variables in a program were declared before program execution and remained the same throughout program execution.[1]

Fortran 90/95 includes another type of variable that contains no data at all. Instead, it contains the *address in memory* of another variable where the data is actually stored. Because this type of variable points to another variable, it is called a **pointer.** The difference between a pointer and an ordinary variable is illustrated in Figure 11–1. Both pointers and ordinary variables have names, but pointers store the addresses of ordinary variables, whereas ordinary variables store data values.

Pointers are primarily used in situations where variables and arrays must be created and destroyed dynamically during the execution of a program and where it is not known before the program executes just how many of any given type of variable will be needed during a run. For example, suppose that a mailing list program must read in an unknown number of names and addresses, sort them into a user-specified order, and then print mailing labels in that order. The names and addresses will be stored in variables of a derived data type. If this program is implemented with static arrays, then the arrays must be as large as the largest possible mailing list ever to be processed. Most of the time the mailing lists will be much smaller, and this condition will produce a terrible waste of computer memory. If the program is implemented with allocatable arrays, then we can allocate just the required amount of memory, but we must still know in advance the total number of addresses before the first one is read. By contrast, we will now learn how to *dynamically allocate a variable for each address as it is read in* and how to use pointers to manipulate those addresses in any desired fashion. This flexibility will produce a much more efficient program.

---

[1]Allocatable arrays, automatic arrays, and automatic character variables were the limited exceptions to this rule.

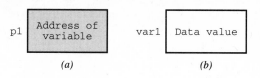

FIGURE 11–1

The difference between a pointer and an ordinary variable: (*a*) A pointer stores the *address* of an ordinary variable in its memory location. (*b*) An ordinary variable stores a data value.

We will first learn the basics of creating and using pointers and then work through several examples of how to use them to write flexible and powerful programs.

■ 11.1
POINTERS AND TARGETS

A Fortran variable is declared to be a pointer by either including the POINTER attribute in its type definition statement (the preferred choice) or by listing it in a separate POINTER statement. For example, each of the following statements declares a pointer p1 that must point to a real variable.

```
REAL, POINTER :: p1
```

or

```
REAL :: p1
POINTER :: p1
```

Note that the *type* of a pointer must be declared, even though the pointer does not contain any data of that type. Instead, it contains the *address* of a variable of the declared type. A pointer can point only to variables of its declared type. Any attempt to point to a variable of a different type will produce a compilation error.

Pointers to variables of derived data types may also be declared. For example,

```
TYPE (vector), POINTER :: vector_pointer
```

declares a pointer to a variable of derived data type vector. Pointers may also point to an array. A pointer to an array is declared with a **deferred-shape array specification,** meaning that the rank of the array is specified, but the actual extent of the array in each dimension is indicated by colons. Two pointers to arrays are

```
INTEGER, DIMENSION(:), POINTER :: ptr1
REAL, DIMENSION(:,:), POINTER :: ptr2
```

The first pointer can point to any rank-1 integer array, while the second pointer can point to any rank-2 real array.

A pointer can point to any variable or array of the pointer's type as long as the variable or array has been declared to be a **target.** A *target* is a data object whose address has been made available for use with pointers. A Fortran variable or array is declared to be a target by either including the TARGET attribute in its type definition statement (the preferred choice) or by listing it in a separate TARGET statement. For example, each of the following sets of statements declares two targets to which pointers may point.

```
REAL, TARGET :: a1 = 7
INTEGER, DIMENSION(10), TARGET :: int_array
```

or

```
REAL :: a1 = 7
INTEGER, DIMENSION(10) :: int_array
TARGET :: a1, int_array
```

They declare a real scalar value `a1` and a rank-1 integer array `int_array`. Variable `a1` may be pointed to by any real scalar point (such as the pointer `p1` declared above), and `int_array` may be pointed to by any integer rank-1 pointer (such as pointer `ptr1` above).

11.1.1 Pointer Assignment Statements

A pointer can be associated with a given target by means of a **pointer assignment statement.** A pointer assignment statement takes the form

$$pointer => target$$

where *pointer* is the name of a pointer, and *target* is the name of a variable or array of the same type as the pointer. The pointer assignment operator consists of an

11

The Significance of the TARGET Attribute

A pointer is a variable that contains the memory location of another variable, which is called the target. The target itself is just an ordinary variable of the same type as the pointer. Given that the target is just an ordinary variable, why is it necessary to attach a special TARGET attribute to the variable before a pointer can point to it? Other computer languages such as C have no such requirement.

The reason that the TARGET attribute is required has to do with the way Fortran compilers work. Fortran is normally used for large, numerically intensive mathematical problems, and most Fortran compilers are designed to produce output programs that are as fast as possible. These compilers include an *optimizer* as a part of the compilation process. The optimizer examines the code and rearranges it, unwraps loops, eliminates common subexpressions, and so forth in order to increase the final execution speed. As a part of this optimization process, some of the variables in the original program can actually disappear, having been combined out of existence or replaced by temporary values in registers. So, what would happen if the variable that we wish to point to is optimized out of existence? We would have a problem pointing to it!

It is possible for a compiler to analyze a program and determine whether or not each individual variable is ever used as a target of a pointer, but that process is tedious. The TARGET attribute was added to the language to help the compiler writers. The attribute tells a compiler that a particular variable *could* be pointed to by a pointer, and therefore it must not be optimized out of existence.

equal sign followed by a greater than sign with no space in between.[2] When this statement is executed, the memory address of the target is stored in the pointer. After the pointer assignment statement, any reference to the pointer will actually be a reference to the data stored in the target.

If a pointer is already associated with a target and another pointer assignment statement is executed using the same pointer, then the association with the first target is lost and the pointer now points to the second target. Any reference to the pointer after the second pointer assignment statement will actually be a reference to the data stored in the second target.

For example, the program in Figure 11–2 defines a real pointer p and two target variables t1 and t2. The pointer is first associated with variable t1 by a pointer assignment statement, and p is written out by a WRITE statement (Figure 11–3a). Then the pointer is associated with variable t2 by another pointer assignment statement, and p is written out by a second WRITE statement (see Figure 11–3b).

FIGURE 11–2
Program to illustrate pointer assignment statements.

```
PROGRAM test_ptr
IMPLICIT NONE
REAL, POINTER :: p
REAL, TARGET :: t1 = 10., t2 = -17.
p => t1
WRITE (*,*) 'p, t1, t2 = ', p, t1, t2
p => t2
WRITE (*,*) 'p, t1, t2 = ', p, t1, t2
END PROGRAM
```

When this program is executed, the results are

```
C>test_ptr
p, t1, t2 =     10.000000     10.000000     -17.000000
p, t1, t2 =    -17.000000     10.000000     -17.000000
```

It is important to note that p never contains either 10. or −17. Instead, it contains the addresses of the variables in which those values were stored, and the Fortran compiler treats a reference to the pointer as a reference to those addresses. Also, note that a value could be accessed either through a pointer to a variable or through the variable's name, and the two forms of access can be mixed even within a single statement.

It is also possible to assign the value of one pointer to another pointer in a pointer assignment statement:

$$pointer1 \Rightarrow pointer2$$

After such a statement, *both pointers point directly and independently to the same target*. If either pointer is changed in a later assignment, the other pointer will be unaffected and will continue to point to the original target. If *pointer2* is disassociated (does not point to a target) at the time the above pointer assignment statement

---

[2]This sign is identical in form to the rename sign in the USE statement (see Chapter 9), but it has a different meaning.

Pointers   Variables
                               t1

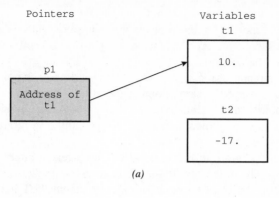

p1

Address of
t1

t2

(a)

FIGURE 11–3
The relationship between the pointer and the variables in program test_ptr. (*a*) The situation after the first executable statement: p contains the address of variable t1, and a reference to p is the same as a reference to t1. (*b*) The situation after the third executable statement: p contains the address of variable t2, and a reference to p is the same as a reference to t2.

Pointers   Variables
                               t1

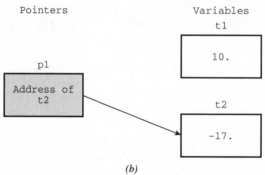

p1

Address of
t2

t2

(b)

is executed, then *pointer1* also becomes disassociated. For example, the program in Figure 11–4 defines two real pointers p1 and p2 and two target variables t1 and t2. The pointer p1 is first associated with variable t1 by a pointer assignment statement, and then pointer p2 is assigned the value of pointer p1 by another pointer assignment statement. After these statements, both pointers p1 and p2 are independently associated with variable t1. When pointer p1 is later associated with variable t2, pointer p2 remains associated with t1 (see Figure 11–5).

FIGURE 11–4
Program to illustrate pointer assignment between two pointers.

```
PROGRAM test_ptr2
IMPLICIT NONE
REAL, POINTER :: p1, p2
REAL, TARGET :: t1 = 10., t2 = -17.
p1 => t1
p2 => p1
WRITE (*,'(A,4F8.2)') ' p1, p2, t1, t2 = ', p1, p2, t1, t2
p1 => t2
WRITE (*,'(A,4F8.2)') ' p1, p2, t1, t2 = ', p1, p2, t1, t2
END PROGRAM
```

When this program is executed, the results are

```
C>test_ptr2
p1, p2, t1, t2 =      10.00  10.00  10.00  -17.00
p1, p2, t1, t2 =     -17.00  10.00  10.00  -17.00
```

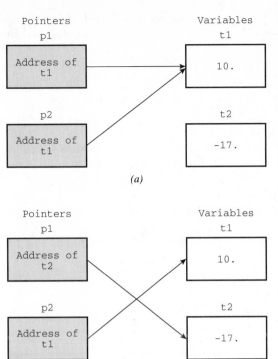

FIGURE 11–5
The relationship between the pointer and the variables in program `test_ptr2`. (*a*) The situation after the second executable statement: p1 and p2 both contain the address of variable t1, and a reference to either one is the same as a reference to t1. (*b*) The situation after the fourth executable statement: p1 contains the address of variable t2, and p2 contains the address of variable t1. Note that p2 was unaffected by the reassignment of pointer p1.

11.1.2 Pointer Association Status

The **association status** of a pointer indicates whether or not the pointer currently points to a valid target. There are three possible statuses: **undefined, associated,** and **disassociated.** When a pointer is first declared in a type declaration statement, its pointer association status is *undefined.* Once a pointer has been associated with a target by a pointer assignment statement, its association status becomes *associated.* If a pointer is later disassociated from its target and is not associated with any new target, then its association status becomes *disassociated.*

How can a pointer be disassociated from its target? It can be disassociated from one target and simultaneously associated with another target by executing a pointer assignment statement. In addition, a pointer can be disassociated from all targets by executing a NULLIFY statement. A NULLIFY statement has the form

NULLIFY (*ptr1,* [*,ptr2,* ...])

where *ptr1, ptr2,* and so on are pointers. After the statement is executed, the pointers listed in the statement are disassociated from all targets.

A pointer can only be used to reference a target when it is associated with that target. Any attempt to use a pointer when it is not associated with a target will result in an error, and the program containing the error will abort. Therefore, we must be able to tell whether or not a particular pointer is associated with a particular target, or with any target at all. The logical intrinsic function ASSOCIATED provides this information. The function comes in two forms, one containing a pointer as its only argument and one containing both a pointer and a target. The first form is

```
status = ASSOCIATED ( pointer )
```

This function returns a true value *if the pointer is associated with any target* and a false value if it is not associated with any target. The second form is

```
status = ASSOCIATED ( pointer, target )
```

This function returns a true value *if the pointer is associated with the particular target included in the function* and a false value otherwise.

A pointer's association status can be undefined only from the time that it is declared until it is first used. Thereafter, the pointer's status will always be either associated or disassociated. Because the undefined status is ambiguous, every pointer's status should be clarified as soon as it is created by either assigning it to a target or nullifying it. For example, pointers could be declared and nullified in a program as follows:

```
REAL, POINTER :: p1, p2
INTEGER, POINTER :: i1
...
(additional specification statements)
...
NULLIFY (p1, p2, i1)
```

Good Programming Practice
Always nullify or assign all pointers in a program unit as soon as they are created. This practice eliminates any possible ambiguities associated with the undefined state.

Fortran 95 provides an intrinsic function `NULL()` that can be used to nullify a pointer at the time it is declared (or at any time during the execution of a program). In Fortran 95, pointers can be declared and nullified as follows:

```
REAL, POINTER :: p1 = NULL(), p2 = NULL()
INTEGER, POINTER :: i1 = NULL()
...
(additional specification statements)
```

The details of the `NULL()` function are described in Appendix B.

The simple program shown in Figure 11–6 illustrates the use of the `NULLIFY` statement and the `ASSOCIATED` intrinsic function.

FIGURE 11–6
Program to illustrate the use of the `NULLIFY` statement and the `ASSOCIATED` function.

```
PROGRAM test_ptr3
IMPLICIT NONE
REAL, POINTER :: p1, p2, p3
REAL, TARGET :: a = 11., b = 12.5, c = 3.141592
```

(continued)

(concluded)

```
NULLIFY ( p1, p2, p3)      ! Nullify pointers
WRITE (*,*) ASSOCIATED(p1)
p1 => a                    ! p1 points to a
p2 => b                    ! p2 points to b
p3 => c                    ! p3 points to c
WRITE (*,*) ASSOCIATED(p1)
WRITE (*,*) ASSOCIATED(p1,b)
END PROGRAM
```

The pointers p1, p2, and p3 will be nullified as soon as program execution begins. Thus the result of the first ASSOCIATED(p1) function will be false. Then the pointers are associated with targets a, b, and c. When the second ASSOCIATED(p1) function is executed, the pointer will be associated, so the result of the function will be true. The third ASSOCIATED(p1,b) function checks to see if pointer p1 points to variable b. It doesn't, so the function returns false.

■ 11.2

USING POINTERS IN ASSIGNMENT STATEMENTS

Whenever a pointer appears in a Fortran expression where a value is expected, the value of the target pointed to is used instead of the pointer itself. This process is known as **dereferencing** the pointer. We have already seen an example of dereferencing in the previous section: Whenever a pointer appeared in a WRITE statement, the value of the target pointed to was printed out instead. As another example, consider two pointers p1 and p2, which are associated with variables a and b, respectively. In the ordinary assignment statement

$$p2 = p1$$

both p1 and p2 appear in places where variables are expected, so they are dereferenced, and this statement is exactly identical to the statement

$$b = a$$

By contrast, in the pointer assignment statement

$$p2 \Rightarrow p1$$

p2 appears in a place where a pointer is expected, and p1 appears in a place where a target (an ordinary variable) is expected. As a result, p1 is dereferenced, and p2 refers to the pointer itself. The result is that the target pointed to by p1 is assigned to the pointer p2.

The program shown in Figure 11–7 provides another example of using pointers in place of variables.

FIGURE 11–7
Program to illustrate the use of pointers in place of variables in assignment statements.

```
PROGRAM test_ptr4
IMPLICIT NONE
```

(continued)

(concluded)

```
REAL, POINTER :: p1, p2, p3
REAL, TARGET :: a = 11., b = 12.5, c
NULLIFY (p1, p2, p3)      ! Nullify pointers
p1 => a                   ! p1 points to a
p2 => b                   ! p2 points to b
p3 => c                   ! p3 points to c
p3 = p1 + p2              ! Same as c = a + b
WRITE (*,*) 'p3 = ', p3
p2 => p1                  ! p2 points to a
p3 = p1 + p2              ! Same as c = a + a
WRITE (*,*) 'p3 = ', p3
p3 = p1                   ! Same as c = a
p3 => p1                  ! p3 points to a
WRITE (*,*) 'p3 = ', p3
WRITE (*,*) 'a, b, c = ', a, b, c
END PROGRAM
```

In this example the first assignment statement p3 = p1 + p2 is equivalent to the statement c = a + b, since the pointers p1, p2, and p3 point to variables a, b, and c, respectively, and since ordinary variables are expected in the assignment statement. The pointer assignment statement p2 => p1 causes pointer p1 to point to a, so the second assignment statement p3 = p1 + p2 is equivalent to the statement c = a + a. Finally, the assignment statement p3 = p1 is equivalent to the statement c = a, and the pointer assignment statement p3 => p1 causes pointer p3 to point to a. The output of this program is

```
C>test_ptr4
p3 =         23.500000
p3 =         22.000000
p3 =         11.000000
a, b, c =         11.000000      12.500000      11.000000
```

The following discussion shows one way that pointers can improve the efficiency of a program. Suppose that we need to swap two 100×100-element real arrays array1 and array2 in a program. To swap these arrays, we would normally use the following code:

```
REAL, DIMENSION(100,100) :: array1, array2, temp
...
temp = array1
array1 = array2
array2 = temp
```

The code is simple enough, but note that we are moving 10,000 real values in each assignment statement! All of that moving requires a lot of time. By contrast, we could perform the same manipulation with pointers and only exchange the *addresses* of the target arrays:

```
REAL, DIMENSION(100,100), TARGET :: array1, array2
REAL, DIMENSION(:,:), POINTER :: p1, p2, temp
p1 => array1
p2 => array2
...
temp => p1
p1 => p2
p2 => temp
```

In the latter case, we only swapped the addresses, and not the entire 10,000-element arrays! This example is enormously more efficient than the previous example.

 Good Programming Practice

When sorting or swapping large arrays or derived data types, it is more efficient to exchange pointers to the data than it is to manipulate the data itself.

◼ 11.3

USING POINTERS WITH ARRAYS

A pointer can point to an array as well as a scalar. A pointer to an array must declare the type and the rank of the array that it will point to, but does *not* declare the extent in each dimension. Thus the following statements are legal:

```
REAL, DIMENSION(100,1000), TARGET :: mydata
REAL, DIMENSION(:,:), POINTER :: pointer
pointer => array
```

A pointer can point not only to an array but also to a *subset* of an array (an array section). Any array section that can be defined by a subscript triplet can be used as the target of a pointer. For example, the program in Figure 11–8 declares a 16-element integer array info and fills the array with the values 1 through 16. This array serves as the target for a series of pointers. The first pointer ptr1 points to the entire array, and the second one points to the array section defined by the subscript triplet ptr1(2::2). This array section will consist of the even subscripts 2, 4, 6, 8, 10, 12, 14, and 16 from the original array. The third pointer also uses the subscript triplet 2::2, and it points to the even elements from the list pointed to by the second pointer. This array section will consist of the subscripts 4, 8, 12, and 16 from the original array. This process of selection continues with the remaining pointers.

FIGURE 11–8

Program to illustrate the use of pointers with array sections defined by subscript triplets.

```
PROGRAM array_ptr
IMPLICIT NONE
INTEGER :: i
INTEGER, DIMENSION(16), TARGET :: info = (/ (i, i=1,16) /)
INTEGER, DIMENSION(:), POINTER :: ptr1, ptr2, ptr3, ptr4, ptr5
ptr1 => info
ptr2 => ptr1(2::2)
ptr3 => ptr2(2::2)
ptr4 => ptr3(2::2)
ptr5 => ptr4(2::2)
WRITE (*,'(A,16I3) ') ' ptr1 = ', ptr1
WRITE (*,'(A,16I3) ') ' ptr2 = ', ptr2
WRITE (*,'(A,16I3) ') ' ptr3 = ', ptr3
WRITE (*,'(A,16I3) ') ' ptr4 = ', ptr4
WRITE (*,'(A,16I3) ') ' ptr5 = ', ptr5
END PROGRAM
```

When this program is executed, the results are

```
C>array_ptr
ptr1 =    1   2   3   4   5   6   7   8   9 10 11 12 13 14 15 16
ptr2 =    2   4   6   8  10  12  14  16
ptr3 =    4   8  12  16
ptr4 =    8  16
ptr5 =   16
```

Although pointers work with array sections defined by subscript triplets, *they do not work with array sections defined by vector subscripts.* Thus the code in Figure 11–9 is illegal and will produce a compilation error.

FIGURE 11–9
Program to illustrate invalid pointer assignments to array sections defined with vector subscripts. This program will produce a compilation error.

```
PROGRAM bad
IMPLICIT NONE
INTEGER :: i
INTEGER, DIMENSION(3) :: subs = (/ 1, 8, 11 /)
INTEGER, DIMENSION(16), TARGET :: info = (/ (i, i=1,16) /)
INTEGER, DIMENSION(:), POINTER :: ptr1
ptr1 => info(subs)
WRITE (*,'(A,16I3)') ' ptr1 = ', ptr1
END PROGRAM
```

■ 11.4

DYNAMIC MEMORY ALLOCATION WITH POINTERS

One of the most powerful features of pointers is that they can be used first to dynamically create variables or arrays whenever required and then to release the space used by the dynamic variables or arrays once they are no longer needed. This procedure is similar to the procedure used to create allocatable arrays. Memory is allocated using an ALLOCATE statement, and it is deallocated using a DEALLOCATE statement. The ALLOCATE statement has the same form as the ALLOCATE statement for an allocatable array. The statement takes the form

$$\text{ALLOCATE } (pointer(size),[\ldots,] \text{ STAT}=status)$$

where *pointer* is the name of a pointer to the variable or array being created, *size* is the dimension specification if the object being created is an array, and *status* is the result of the operation. If the allocation is successful, then the status will be 0. If it fails, a processor-dependent positive integer will be returned in the status variable. The STAT= clause is optional but should always be used, since a failed allocation statement without a STAT= clause will cause a program to abort.

This statement creates an unnamed data object of the specified size and of the pointer's type, and sets the pointer to point to the object. Because the new data object is unnamed, it can be accessed only by using the pointer. After the statement is executed, the association status of the pointer will become *associated.* If the pointer was associated with another data object before the ALLOCATE statement is executed, then that association is lost.

The data object created by using the pointer ALLOCATE statement is unnamed, and so can only be accessed by the pointer. If all pointers to that memory are either nullified or reassociated with other targets, then the data object will no longer be accessible by the program. The object will still be present in memory, but it will no longer be possible to use it. Thus careless programming with pointers can result in memory being filled with unusable space. This unusable memory is commonly referred to as a "memory leak." One symptom of this problem is that a program seems to grow larger and larger as it continues to execute, until it either fills the entire computer or uses all available memory. An example of a program with a memory leak is shown in Figure 11–10. In this program 10-element arrays are allocated using both ptr1 and ptr2. The two arrays are initialized to different values, and those values are printed out. Then ptr2 is assigned to point to the same memory as ptr1 in a pointer assignment statement. After that statement, the memory that was assigned to ptr2 is no longer accessible to the program. That memory has been "lost" and will not be recovered until the program stops executing.

FIGURE 11–10
Program to illustrate memory leaks.

```
PROGRAM mem_leak
IMPLICIT NONE
INTEGER :: i, istat
INTEGER, DIMENSION(:), POINTER :: ptr1, ptr2

! Check associated status of ptrs.
WRITE (*,'(A,2L5)') ' Are ptr1, ptr2 associated? ', &
      ASSOCIATED(ptr1), ASSOCIATED(ptr2)

! Allocate and initialize memory
ALLOCATE (ptr1(1:10), STAT=istat)
ALLOCATE (ptr2(1:10), STAT=istat)
ptr1 = (/ (i, i = 1,10 ) /)
ptr2 = (/ (i, i = 11,20) /)

! Check associated status of ptrs.
WRITE (*,'(A,2L5)') ' Are ptr1, ptr2 associated? ', &
      ASSOCIATED(ptr1), ASSOCIATED(ptr2)

WRITE (*,'(A,10I3) ') ' ptr1 = ', ptr1  ! Write out data
WRITE (*,'(A,10I3) ') ' ptr2 = ', ptr2

ptr2 => ptr1                            ! Reassign ptr2

WRITE (*,'(A,10I3) ') ' ptr1 = ', ptr1  ! Write out data
WRITE (*,'(A,10I3) ') ' ptr2 = ', ptr2

NULLIFY(ptr1)                           ! Nullify pointer
DEALLOCATE(ptr2, STAT=istat)            ! Deallocate memory

END PROGRAM
```

When program mem_leak executes, the results are

```
C>mem_leak
Are ptr1, ptr2 associated?     F    F
Are ptr1, ptr2 associated?     T    T
```

```
ptr1 =    1  2  3  4  5  6  7  8  9 10
ptr2 =   11 12 13 14 15 16 17 18 19 20
ptr1 =    1  2  3  4  5  6  7  8  9 10
ptr2 =    1  2  3  4  5  6  7  8  9 10
```

Memory that has been allocated with an ALLOCATE statement should be deallocated with a DEALLOCATE statement when the program is finished using it. If the memory is not deallocated, then it will be unavailable for any other use until the program finishes executing. When memory is deallocated in a pointer DEALLOCATE statement, the pointer to that memory is nullified at the same time. Thus the following statement both deallocates the memory pointed to and nullifies the pointer ptr2:

```
DEALLOCATE(ptr2, STAT=istat)
```

The pointer DEALLOCATE statement can only deallocate memory that was created by an ALLOCATE statement. It is important to remember this fact. If the pointer in the statement happens to point to a target that was not created with an ALLOCATE statement, then the DEALLOCATE statement will fail and the program will abort unless the STAT= clause was specified. The association between such pointers and their targets can be broken by the use of the NULLIFY statement.

A potentially serious problem can occur when deallocating memory. Suppose that two pointers ptr1 and ptr2 point to the same allocated array. If pointer ptr1 is used in a DEALLOCATE statement to deallocate the array, then that pointer is nullified. However, ptr2 will *not* be nullified. *It will continue to point to the memory location where the array used to be,* even if that memory location is reused for some other purpose by the program. If that pointer is used to either read data from or write data to the memory location, it will be either reading unpredictable values or overwriting memory used for some other purpose. In either case using that pointer is a recipe for disaster! If a piece of allocated memory is deallocated, then *all* the pointers to that memory should be nullified or reassigned. One of them will be automatically nullified by the DEALLOCATE statement, and any others should be nullified in NULLIFY statement(s).

Good Programming Practice
Always nullify or reassign *all* pointers to a memory location when that memory is deallocated. One pointer will be automatically nullified by the DEALLOCATE statement, and any others should be manually nullified in NULLIFY statement(s) or reassigned in pointer assignment statements.

Figure 11–11 illustrates the effect of using a pointer after the memory to which it points has been deallocated. In this example two pointers ptr1 and ptr2 point to the same 10-element allocatable array. When that array is deallocated with ptr1, that pointer becomes disassociated. Pointer ptr2 remains associated, but now points to a piece of memory that can be freely reused by the program for other purposes. When ptr2 is accessed in the next WRITE statement, it points to an unallocated part of memory that could contain anything. Then a new two-element array is allocated using ptr1. Depending on the behavior of the compiler, this array could be allocated over the freed memory from the previous array, or it could be allocated somewhere else in memory.

FIGURE 11—11
Program to illustrate the effect of using a pointer after the memory to which it points has been deallocated.

```
PROGRAM bad_ptr
IMPLICIT NONE
INTEGER :: i, istat
INTEGER, DIMENSION(:), POINTER :: ptr1, ptr2

! Allocate and initialize memory
ALLOCATE (ptr1(1:10), STAT=istat)        ! Allocate ptr1
ptr1 = (/ (i, i = 1,10) /)               ! Initialize ptr1
ptr2 => ptr1                             ! Assign ptr2

! Check associated status of ptrs.
WRITE (*,'(A,2L5)') ' Are ptr1, ptr2 associated? ', &
      ASSOCIATED(ptr1), ASSOCIATED(ptr2)

WRITE (*,'(A,10I3)') ' ptr1 = ', ptr1    ! Write out data
WRITE (*,'(A,10I3)') ' ptr2 = ', ptr2

! Now deallocate memory associated with ptr1
DEALLOCATE(ptr1, STAT=istat)             ! Deallocate memory

! Check associated status of ptrs.
WRITE (*,'(A,2L5)') ' Are ptr1, ptr2 associated? ', &
      ASSOCIATED(ptr1), ASSOCIATED(ptr2)

! Write out memory associated with ptr2
WRITE (*,'(A,10I3)') ' ptr2 = ', ptr2

ALLOCATE (ptr1(1:2), STAT=istat)         ! Reallocate ptr1
ptr1 = (/ 21, 22 /)

WRITE (*,'(A,10I3)') ' ptr1 = ', ptr1    ! Write out data
WRITE (*,'(A,10I3)') ' ptr2 = ', ptr2

END PROGRAM
```

The results of this program will vary from compiler to compiler, since deallocated memory may be treated differently on different processors. When this program is executed on the Lahey Fortran 90 Compiler, the results are

```
C>bad_ptr
Are ptr1, ptr2 associated?     T    T
ptr1 =   1  2  3  4  5  6  7  8  9 10
ptr2 =   1  2  3  4  5  6  7  8  9 10
Are ptr1, ptr2 associated?     F    T
ptr2 =   1  2  3  4  5  6  7  8  9 10
ptr1 =  21 22
ptr2 =  21 22  3  4  5  6  7  8  9 10
```

After ptr1 was used to deallocate the memory, its pointer status changed to *disassociated,* while the status of ptr2 remained *associated.* When ptr2 was then used to examine memory, it pointed to the memory location *where the array used to be,* and saw the old values because the memory had not yet been reused. Finally, when ptr1 was used to allocate a new two-element array, some of the freed-up memory was reused.

It is possible to mix pointers and allocatable arrays in a single ALLOCATE statement or DEALLOCATE statement, if desired.

11.5
USING POINTERS AS COMPONENTS OF DERIVED DATA TYPES

Pointers may appear as components of derived data types. Pointers in derived data types may even point to the derived data type being defined. This feature is very useful, since it permits us to construct various types of dynamic data structures linked together by successive pointers during the execution of a program. The simplest such structure is a **linked list,** which is a list of values linked together in a linear fashion by pointers. For example, the following derived data type contains a real number and a pointer to another variable of the same type:

```
TYPE :: real_value
    REAL :: value
    TYPE (real_value), POINTER :: p
END TYPE
```

A linked list is a series of variables in a derived data type with the pointer from each variable pointing to the next variable in the list. The pointer in the last variable is nullified, since there is no variable after it in the list. Two pointers (say, head and tail) are also defined to point to the first and last variables in the list. Figure 11–12 illustrates this structure for variables of type real_value.

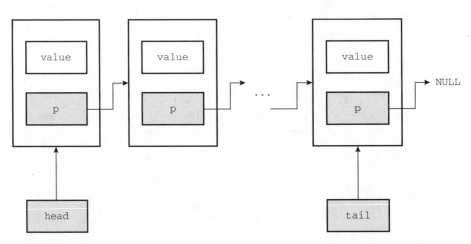

FIGURE 11–12
A typical linked list. Note that pointer in each variable points to the next variable in the list.

Linked lists are much more flexible than arrays. Recall that a static array must be declared with a fixed size when a program is compiled. As a result we must size each such array to be large enough to handle the largest problem that a program will ever be required to solve. This large memory requirement can result in a program being too large to run on some computers and also results in a waste of memory most of the time that the program is executed. Even allocatable arrays don't completely solve the problem. Allocatable arrays prevent memory waste by allowing us to allocate only the amount of memory needed for a specific problem, but we must know before we allocate the memory just how many values will be present during a particular run. In contrast, linked lists permit us to add elements one at a time, and we do not have to know in advance how many elements will ultimately be in the list.

When a program containing a linked list first starts to execute, the list has no values. In that case the `head` and `tail` pointers have nothing to point to, so they are both nullified (see Figure 11–13a). When the first value is read, a variable of the derived data type is created and the value is stored in that variable. The `head` and `tail` pointers are set to point to the variable, and the pointer in the variable is nullified (Figure 11–13b).

When the next value is read, a new variable of the derived data type is created, the value is stored in that variable, and the pointer in the variable is nullified. The pointer in the previous variable is set to point to the new variable, and the `tail` pointer is set to point to the new variable. The `head` pointer does not change (Figure 11–13c). This process is repeated as each new value is added to the list.

Once all of the values are read, the program can process them by starting at the `head` pointer and following the pointers in the list until the `tail` pointer is reached.

EXAMPLE 11–1 Creating a Linked List: In this example, we will write a simple program that reads in a list of real numbers and then writes them out. The number of values that the program can handle should be limited only by the amount of memory in the computer. This program doesn't do anything interesting by itself, but building a linked list in memory is a necessary first step in many practical problems. You will learn how to create the list in this example and then start using lists to do useful work in later examples.

11

SOLUTION We will use a linked list to hold the input values, since the size of a linked list can keep growing as long as additional memory can be allocated for new values. Each input value will be stored in a variable of the following derived data type, where the element p points to the next item in the list and the element `value` stores the input real value.

```
TYPE :: real_value
    REAL :: value
    TYPE (real_value), POINTER :: p
END TYPE
```

1. **State the problem.**

Write a program to read an arbitrary number of real values from a file and to solve them in a linked list. After all of the values have been read, the program should write them to the standard output device.

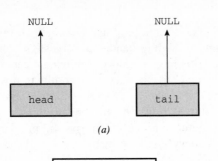

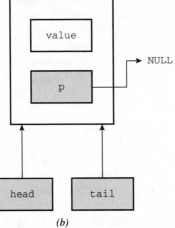

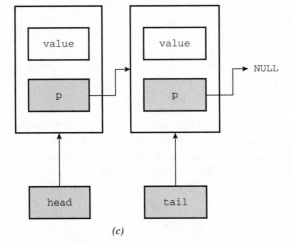

FIGURE 11–13
Building a linked list: (*a*) The initial situation with an empty list. (*b*) After adding one value to the list. (*c*) After adding a second value to the list.

2. Define the inputs and outputs.

The input to the program will be a file name and a list of real values arranged one value per line in that file. The output from the program will be the real values in the file listed to the standard output device.

3. **Describe the algorithm.**

This program can be broken down into four major steps

```
Get the input file name
Open the input file
Read the input data into a linked list
Write the data to the standard output device
```

The first three major steps of the program are to get the name of the input file, to open the file, and to read in the data. We must prompt the user for the input file name, read in the name, and open the file. If the file open is successful, we must read in the data, keeping track of the number of values read. Since we don't know how many data values to expect, a while loop is appropriate for the READ. Here is the pseudocode for these steps:

```
Prompt user for the input file name "filename"
Read the file name "filename"
OPEN file "filename"
IF OPEN is successful THEN
    WHILE
        Read value into temp
        IF read not successful EXIT
        nvals ← nvals + 1
        (ALLOCATE new list item & store value)
    END of WHILE
    ...                         (Insert writing step here)
END of IF
```

The step of adding a new item to the linked list needs to be examined more carefully. A new variable is added to the list under two possible conditions: either there is nothing in the list yet or else there are already values in the list. If the list is empty, then the head and tail pointers are nullified, so we will allocate the new variable using the head pointer and point the tail pointer to the same place. The pointer p within the new variable must be nullified because there is nothing to point to yet, and the real value will be stored in the element value of the variable.

If there are already values in the list, then the tail pointer points to the last variable in the list. In that case we will first allocate the new variable using the pointer p within the last variable in the list and then point the tail pointer to the new variable. The pointer p within the new variable must be nullified because there is nothing to point to, and the real value will be stored in the element value of the new variable. The pseudocode for these steps follows.

```
Read value into temp
IF read not successful EXIT
nvals ← nvals + 1
IF  head is not associated THEN
    ! The list is empty
    ALLOCATE head
    tail => head            ! Tail points to first value
    NULLIFY tail%p           ! Nullify p within 1st value
    tail%value ← temp        ! Store new number
ELSE
    ! The list already has values
```

11

```
        ALLOCATE tail%p
        tail => tail%p          ! Tail now points to new last value
        NULLIFY tail%p          ! Nullify p within new last value
        tail%value ← temp       ! Store new number
     END of IF
```

The final step is to write the values in the linked list. To do so, we must go back to the head of the list and follow the pointers in it to the end of the list. We will define a local pointer `ptr` to point to the value currently being printed out. The pseudocode for these steps follows.

```
        ptr => head
        WHILE ptr is associated
            WRITE ptr%value
            ptr => ptr%p
        END of WHILE
```

4. Turn the algorithm into Fortran statements.

The resulting Fortran subroutine is shown in Figure 11–14.

FIGURE 11–14
Program to read in a series of real values and store them in a linked list.

```
PROGRAM linked_list
!
!   Purpose:
!     To read in a series of real values from an input data file
!     and store them in a linked list.  After the list is read in,
!     it will be written back to the standard output device.
!
!   Record of revisions:
!      Date         Programmer          Description of change
!      ====         ==========          =====================
!    01/28/95    S. J. Chapman          Original code
!
IMPLICIT NONE

! Derived data type to store real values in
TYPE :: real_value
   REAL :: value
   TYPE (real_value), POINTER :: p
END TYPE

! List of variables:
TYPE (real_value), POINTER :: head  ! Pointer to head of list
CHARACTER(len=20) :: filename        ! Input data file name
INTEGER :: nvals = 0                  ! Number of data read
TYPE (real_value), POINTER :: ptr    ! Temporary pointer
TYPE (real_value), POINTER :: tail   ! Pointer to tail of list
INTEGER :: istat                      ! Status: 0 for success
REAL :: temp                          ! Temporary variable

! Get the name of the file containing the input data.
WRITE (*,*) 'Enter the file name with the data to be read: '
READ (*,'(A20)') filename

! Open input data file.
```

(continued)

(concluded)

```
OPEN ( UNIT=9, FILE=filename, STATUS='OLD', ACTION='READ', &
       IOSTAT=istat )

! Was the OPEN successful?
fileopen: IF ( iSTAT == 0 ) THEN            ! Open successful

   ! The file was opened successfully, so read the data from
   ! it, and store it in the linked list.
   input: DO
      READ (9, *, IOSTAT=istat) temp        ! Get value
      IF ( istat /= 0 ) EXIT                ! Exit on end of data
      nvals = nvals + 1                     ! Bump count

      IF (.NOT. ASSOCIATED(head)) THEN      ! No values in list
         ALLOCATE (head,STAT=istat)         ! Allocate new value
         tail => head                       ! Tail pts to new value
         NULLIFY (tail%p)                   ! Nullify p in new value
         tail%value = temp                  ! Store number
      ELSE                                  ! Values already in list
         ALLOCATE (tail%p,STAT=istat)       ! Allocate new value
         tail => tail%p                     ! Tail pts to new value
         NULLIFY (tail%p)                   ! Nullify p in new value
         tail%value = temp                  ! Store number
      END IF
   END DO input

   ! Now, write out the data.
   ptr => head
   output: DO
      IF ( .NOT. ASSOCIATED(ptr) ) EXIT     ! Pointer valid?
      WRITE (*,'(1X,F10.4)') ptr%value      ! Yes: Write value
      ptr => ptr%p                          ! Get next pointer
   END DO output

ELSE fileopen

   ! Else file open failed.  Tell user.
   WRITE (*,'(1X,A,I6)') 'File open failed--status = ', istat

END IF fileopen

END PROGRAM
```

5. Test the resulting Fortran program.

To test this program, we must generate a file of input data. If the following 10 real values are placed in a file called input.dat, then we can use that file to test the program: 1.0, 3.0, −4.4, 5., 2., 9.0, 10.1, −111.1, 0.0, −111.1. When the program is executed with this file, the results are

```
C>linked_list
Enter the file name with the data to be read:
input.dat
    1.0000
    3.0000
   -4.4000
    5.0000
    2.0000
```

```
        9.0000
       10.1000
     -111.1000
         .0000
     -111.1000
```

The program appears to be working properly. Note that the program does not check the status of the ALLOCATE statements. This was done deliberately to make the manipulations of the linked list as clear as possible. In any real program, these statuses should be checked to detect memory problems so that the program can shut down gracefully.

EXAMPLE 11–2 The Insertion Sort: We introduced the selection sort in Chapter 5. That algorithm sorted a list by searching for the smallest value in the list and placing it at the top. Then it searched for the smallest value in the remaining portion of the list, placed it in the second position, and so forth until all of the values were sorted.

Another possible sorting algorithm is the insertion sort. The *insertion sort* works by placing each value in its proper position in the list as it is read in. If the value is smaller than any previous value in the list, then it is placed at the top. If the value is larger than any previous value in the list, then it is placed at the bottom. If the value is in between, then the number is inserted at the appropriate place in the middle of the list.

An insertion sort of the values 7, 2, 11, −1, and 3 is shown in Figure 11–15. The first value read is a 7. Since there are no other values in the list, it is placed at the top. The next value read is a 2. Since it is smaller than the 7, it is placed above the 7 in the list. The third value read is an 11. Since it is larger than any other value in the list, it is placed at the bottom. The fourth value read is a −1. Since it is smaller than any other value in the list, it is placed at the top. The fifth value read is a 3. Since it is larger than 2 and smaller than 7, it is placed between them in the list. In the insertion sort, the list is always kept sorted as each value is read.

Linked lists are ideally suited for implementing an insertion sort, since new values can be added at the front, at the end, or anywhere in the middle of the list by simply changing pointers. Use a linked list to implement an insertion sort algorithm to sort an arbitrary number of integer values.

SOLUTION We will use a linked list to hold the input values, since it is easy to insert new values anywhere in the linked list by simply changing pointers. Each input value will be read and stored in a variable of the following derived data type, where the pointer next_value points to the next item in the list and the element value stores the input integer value.

```
TYPE :: int_value
   INTEGER :: value
   TYPE (int_value), POINTER :: next_value
END TYPE
```

Each value will be read, compared to all previous values, and inserted at the proper point in the list.

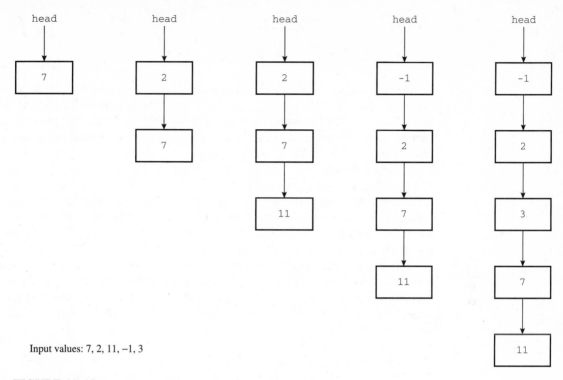

Input values: 7, 2, 11, −1, 3

FIGURE 11–15
Sorting the values 7, 2, 11, −1, and 3 with the insertion sort.

11

1. **State the problem.**

   Write a program to read an arbitrary number of integer values from a file and to sort them using an insertion sort. After all the values have been read and sorted, the program should write the sorted list out to the standard output device.

2. **Define the inputs and outputs.**

   The input to the program will be a file name and a list of integer values arranged one value per line in that file. The output from the program will be the sorted integer values listed to the standard output device.

3. **Describe the algorithm.**

   The pseudocode for this program follows.

   ```
   Prompt user for the input file name "filename"
   Read the file name "filename"
   OPEN file "filename"
   IF OPEN is successful THEN
        WHILE
            Read value into temp
            IF read not successful EXIT
            nvals ← nvals + 1
   ```

```
            ALLOCATE new data item & store value
               Insert item at proper point in list
         END of WHILE
         Write the data to the standard output device
      END of IF
```

As in Example 11–1, we can add a new variable to the list under two possible conditions: either there is nothing in the list yet or else there are already values in the list. If the list is empty, then the head and tail pointers are nullified. Therefore, we will allocate the new variable using the head pointer and point the tail pointer to the same place. The pointer next_value within the new variable must be nullified because there is nothing to point to yet, and the integer will be stored in the element value of the variable.

If there are already values in the list, then we must search to find the proper place to insert the new value into the list. There are three possibilities here. If the number is smaller than the first number in the list (pointed to by the head pointer), then we will add the value at the front of the list. If the number is greater than or equal to the last number in the list (pointed to by the tail pointer), then we will add the value at the end of the list. If the number is between those values, we will search until we locate the two values that it lies between and insert the new value there. Note that we must allow for the possibility that the new value is equal to one of the numbers already in the list. The pseudocode for these steps follows.

```
Read value into temp
IF read not successful EXIT
nvals ← nvals + 1
ALLOCATE ptr
ptr%value ← temp
IF head is not associated THEN
   ! The list is empty
   head => ptr
   tail => head
   NULLIFY tail%next_value
ELSE
   ! The list already has values.  Check for
   ! location for new value.
   IF ptr%value < head%value THEN
      ! Add at front
      ptr%next_value => head
      head => ptr
   ELSE IF ptr%value >= tail%value THEN
      ! Add at rear
      tail%next_value => ptr
      tail => ptr
      NULLIFY tail%next_value
   ELSE
      ! Find place to add value
      ptr1 => head
      ptr2 => ptr1%next_value
      DO
         IF ptr%value >= ptr1%value AND
            ptr%value < ptr2%value THEN
            ! Insert value here
            ptr%next_value => ptr2
            ptr1%next_value => ptr
            EXIT
         END of IF
```

```
                              ptr1 => ptr2
                              ptr2 => ptr2%next_value
                        END of DO
                  END of IF
            END of IF
```

The final step is to write the values in the linked list. To do so, we must go back to the head of the list and follow the pointers to the end of the list. We will use pointer `ptr` to point to the value currently being printed out. The pseudocode for these steps follows.

```
                  ptr => head
                  WHILE ptr is associated
                     WRITE ptr%value
                     ptr => ptr%next_value
                  END of WHILE
```

4. **Turn the algorithm into Fortran statements.**

The resulting Fortran subroutine is shown in Figure 11–16.

FIGURE 11–16
Program to read in a series of integer values and sort them using the insertion sort.

```
PROGRAM insertion_sort
!
!  Purpose:
!    To read a series of integer values from an input data file
!    and sort them using an insertion sort.  After the values
!    are sorted, they will be written back to the standard
!    output device.
!
!  Record of revisions:
!      Date          Programmer          Description of change
!      ====          ==========          =====================
!    01/30/95      S. J. Chapman         Original code
!
IMPLICIT NONE

! Derived data type to store real values in
TYPE :: int_value
   INTEGER :: value
   TYPE (int_value), POINTER :: next_value
END TYPE

! List of variables:
TYPE (int_value), POINTER :: head    ! Pointer to head of list
CHARACTER(len=20) :: filename         ! Input data file name
INTEGER :: istat                      ! Status: 0 for success
INTEGER :: nvals = 0                   ! Number of data read
TYPE (int_value), POINTER :: ptr     ! Ptr to new value
TYPE (int_value), POINTER :: ptr1    ! Temp ptr for search
TYPE (int_value), POINTER :: ptr2    ! Temp ptr for search
TYPE (int_value), POINTER :: tail    ! Pointer to tail of list
INTEGER :: temp                       ! Temporary variable

! Get the name of the file containing the input data.
```

(continued)

(continued)

```
WRITE (*,*) 'Enter the file name with the data to be sorted: '
READ (*,'(A20)') filename

! Open input data file.
OPEN ( UNIT=9, FILE=filename, STATUS='OLD', ACTION='READ', &
       IOSTAT=istat )

! Was the OPEN successful?
fileopen: IF ( istat == 0 ) THEN          ! Open successful

   ! The file was opened successfully, so read the data value
   ! to sort, allocate a variable for it, and locate the proper
   ! point to insert the new value into the list.
   input: DO
      READ (9, *, IOSTAT=istat) temp       ! Get value
      IF ( istat /= 0 ) EXIT input         ! Exit on end of data
      nvals = nvals + 1                     ! Bump count

      ALLOCATE (ptr,STAT=istat)            ! Allocate space
      ptr%value = temp                      ! Store number

      ! Now find out where to put it in the list.
      new: IF (.NOT. ASSOCIATED(head)) THEN ! No values in list
         head => ptr                        ! Place at front
         tail => head                       ! Tail pts to new value
         NULLIFY (ptr%next_value)           ! Nullify next ptr
      ELSE
         ! Values already in list.  Check for location.
         front: IF ( ptr%value < head%value ) THEN
            ! Add at front of list
            ptr%next_value => head
            head => ptr
         ELSE IF ( ptr%value >= tail%value ) THEN
            ! Add at end of list
            tail%next_value => ptr
            NULLIFY ( tail%next_value )
         ELSE
            ! Find place to add value
            ptr1 => head
            ptr2 => ptr1%next_value
            search: DO
               IF ( (ptr%value >= ptr1%value) .AND. &
                    (ptr%value < ptr2%value) ) THEN
                  ! Insert value here
                  ptr%next_value => ptr2
                  ptr1%next_value => ptr
                  EXIT search
               END IF
               ptr1 => ptr2
               ptr2 => ptr2%next_value
            END DO search
         END IF front
      END IF new
   END DO input

   ! Now, write out the data.
   ptr => head
   output: DO
      IF ( .NOT. ASSOCIATED(ptr) ) EXIT    ! Pointer valid?
      WRITE (*,'(1X,I10)') ptr%value        ! Yes: Write value
```

(continued)

(concluded)

```
      ptr => ptr%next_value                  ! Get next pointer
   END DO output

ELSE fileopen

   ! Else file open failed.  Tell user.
   WRITE (*,'(1X,A,I6)') 'File open failed--status = ', istat

END IF fileopen

END PROGRAM
```

5. **Test the resulting Fortran program.**

To test this program, we must generate a file of input data. If seven integer values (7, 2, 11, −1, 3, 2, and 0) are placed in a file called input1.dat, then we can use that file to test the program. When the program is executed with this file, the results are

```
            C>insertion_sort
            Enter the file name with the data to be sorted:
            input1.dat
                  -1
                   0
                   2
                   2
                   3
                   7
                  11
```

The program appears to be working properly. Note that this program also does not check the status of the ALLOCATE statements. This was done deliberately to make the manipulations as clear as possible. (At one point in the program, the DO and IF structures are nested six deep!) In any real program, these statuses should be checked to detect memory problems so that the program can shut down gracefully.

11

▓ 11.6

ARRAYS OF POINTERS

It is not possible to declare an array of pointers in Fortran. In a pointer declaration, the DIMENSION attribute refers to the dimension of the pointer's target, not to the dimension of the pointer itself. The dimension must be declared with a deferred-shape specification, and the actual size will be the size of the target with which the pointer is associated. In the following example, the subscript on the pointer refers to the corresponding position in the target array, so the value of ptr(4) is 6.

```
REAL, DIMENSION(:), POINTER :: ptr
REAL, DIMENSION(5), TARGET :: tgt = (/ -2, 5., 0., 6., 1 /)
ptr => tgt
WRITE (*,*) ptr(4)
```

Arrays of pointers are useful in many applications. Fortunately, we can create an array of pointers for those applications by using derived data types. Although it is illegal to have an array of pointers in Fortran, it is perfectly legal to have an array of any derived data type. Therefore, we can declare a derived data type containing only a pointer and then create an array of that data type! For example, the program in Figure 11–17 declares an array of a derived data type containing real pointers, each of which points to a real array.

FIGURE 11–17

Program illustrating how to create an array of pointers using a derived data type.

```
PROGRAM ptr_array
IMPLICIT NONE
TYPE :: ptr
   REAL, DIMENSION(:), POINTER :: p
END TYPE
TYPE (ptr), DIMENSION(3) :: p1
REAL, DIMENSION(4), TARGET :: a = (/ 1.,  2.,  3.,  4. /)
REAL, DIMENSION(4), TARGET :: b = (/ 5.,  6.,  7.,  8. /)
REAL, DIMENSION(4), TARGET :: c = (/ 9., 10., 11., 12. /)
p1(1).p => a
p1(2).p => b
p1(3).p => c
WRITE (*,*) p1(3).p
WRITE (*,*) p1(2).p(3)
END PROGRAM
```

With the declarations in program ptr_array, the expression p1(3).p refers to the *third* array (array c), so the first WRITE statement should print out 9., 10., 11., and 12. The expression p1(2).p(3) refers to the *third* value of the *second* array (array b), so the second WRITE statement prints out the value 7. When this program is compiled and executed with the Microsoft Fortran 90 compiler, the results are

```
C>ptr_array
       9.000000       10.000000       11.000000       12.000000
       7.000000
```

Quiz 11–1

This quiz provides a quick check to see if you understand the concepts introduced in sections 11.1 through 11.6. If you have trouble with the quiz, reread the sections, ask your instructor, or discuss the material with a fellow student. The answers to this quiz are found in the back of the book.

1. What is a pointer? What is a target? What is the difference between a pointer and an ordinary variable?

2. What is a pointer assignment statement? What is the difference between a pointer assignment statement and an ordinary assignment statement?

3. What are the possible association statuses of a pointer? How can the association status be changed?

(continued)

(concluded)

4. What is dereferencing?

5. How can memory be dynamically allocated with pointers? How can it be deallocated?

Are each of the following code segments valid or invalid? If a code segment is valid, explain what it does. If it is invalid, explain why.

6.
```
REAL, TARGET :: value = 35.2
REAL, POINTER :: ptr2
ptr2 = value
```

7.
```
REAL, TARGET :: value = 35.2
REAL, POINTER :: ptr2
ptr2 => value
```

8.
```
INTEGER, DIMENSION(10,10), TARGET :: array
REAL, DIMENSION(:,:), POINTER :: ptr3
ptr3 => array
```

9.
```
REAL, DIMENSION(10,10) :: array
REAL DIMENSION(:,:) :: ptr4
POINTER :: ptr4
TARGET :: array
ptr4 => array
```

10.
```
INTEGER, POINTER :: ptr
WRITE (*,*) ASSOCIATED(ptr)
ALLOCATE (ptr)
ptr = 137
WRITE (*,*) ASSOCIATED(ptr), ptr
NULLIFY (ptr)
```

11.
```
INTEGER, DIMENSION(:), POINTER :: ptr1, ptr2
INTEGER :: istat
ALLOCATE (ptr1(10), STAT=istat)
ptr1 = 0
ptr1(3) = 17
ptr2 => ptr1
DEALLOCATE (ptr1)
WRITE (*,*) ptr2
```

12.
```
TYPE mytype
    INTEGER, DIMENSION(:), POINTER :: array
END TYPE
TYPE (mytype), DIMENSION(10) :: p
INTEGER :: i, istat
DO i = 1, 10
   ALLOCATE (p(i).array(10), STAT=istat)
   DO j = 1, 10
     p(i).array(j) = 10*(i-1) + j
   END DO
END DO
WRITE (*,'(1X,10I4)') p(4).array
WRITE (*,'(1X,10I4)') p(7).array(1)
```

▨ 11.7

USING POINTERS IN PROCEDURES

Pointers may be used as dummy arguments in procedures and may be passed as actual arguments to procedures. In addition, a function result can be a pointer. The following restrictions apply if pointers are used in procedures:

1. If a procedure has dummy arguments with either the POINTER or TARGET attributes, then the procedure must have an explicit interface.
2. If a dummy argument is a pointer, then the actual argument passed to the procedure must be a pointer of the same type, kind, and rank.
3. A pointer dummy argument cannot have an INTENT attribute.
4. A pointer dummy argument cannot appear in an ELEMENTAL procedure in Fortran 95.

We always need to be careful when passing pointers to procedures. As programs get larger and more flexible, we will often get to a situation where pointers are allocated in one procedure, used in others, and finally deallocated and nullified in yet another. In such a complex program, it is *very* easy to make errors such as attempting to work with disassociated pointers or allocating new arrays with pointers that are already in use. It is very important that the status results be checked for all ALLOCATE and DEALLOCATE statements and that the status of pointers be checked using the ASSOCIATED function.

When a pointer is used to pass data to a procedure, we automatically know the type of the data associated with the pointer from the type of the pointer itself. If the pointer points to an array, we will know the rank of the array, but not its extent or size. If we need to know the extent or size of the array, then we can use the intrinsic functions LBOUND and UBOUND to determine the bounds of each dimension of the array.

> **EXAMPLE 11–3 Extracting the Diagonal Elements from a Matrix:** To illustrate the proper use of pointers, we will write a subroutine that accepts a pointer to a square matrix and returns a pointer to an array containing the diagonal elements of the matrix.
>
> **SOLUTION** A subroutine with appropriate error checking is shown in Figure 11–18. This example accepts a pointer to a two-dimensional square array and returns the diagonal elements of the array in a one-dimensional array that it allocates on a separate pointer. The subroutine checks the association status of the input pointer to ensure that it is currently associated, checks the array to make sure that it is square, and checks the association status of the output pointer to ensure that it is *not* currently associated. (The last test ensures that we don't accidentally reuse a pointer that is currently in use. Reusing the pointer might leave the original data inaccessible if there were no other pointer to it.) If any of the conditions fail, then an appropriate error flag is set and the subroutine returns to the calling program unit.

FIGURE 11–18

Subroutine to extract the diagonal elements from a square array. This subroutine illustrates the proper technique for working with pointers passed as calling arguments.

```
SUBROUTINE get_diagonal ( ptr_a, ptr_b, error )
!
!  Purpose:
!    To extract the diagonal elements from the rank=two
!    square array pointed to by ptr_a and store them in
!    a rank=one array allocated on ptr_b.  The following
!    error conditions are defined:
!    0 -- No error
!    1 -- ptr_a not associated on input
!    2 -- ptr_b already associated on input
!    3 -- Array on ptr_a not square
!    4 -- Unable to allocate memory for ptr_b
!
!    Record of revisions:
!       Date         Programmer         Description of change
!       ====         ==========         =====================
!       01/31/96     S. J. Chapman      Original code
!
IMPLICIT NONE

! Declare calling arguments:
INTEGER, DIMENSION(:,:), POINTER :: ptr_a ! Ptr to square array
INTEGER, DIMENSION(:), POINTER :: ptr_b   ! Ptr to output array
INTEGER, INTENT(OUT) :: error             ! Errors flag

! Declare local variables:
INTEGER :: i                         ! Loop counter
INTEGER :: istat                     ! Allocate status
INTEGER, DIMENSION(2) :: l_bound     ! Lower bounds on ptr_a
INTEGER, DIMENSION(2) :: u_bound     ! Upper bounds on ptr_a
INTEGER, DIMENSION(2) :: extent      ! Extent of array on ptr_a

! Check error conditions
error_1: IF ( .NOT. ASSOCIATED ( ptr_a ) ) THEN
   error = 1
ELSE IF ( ASSOCIATED ( ptr_b ) ) THEN
   error = 2
ELSE
   ! Check for square array
   l_bound = LBOUND ( ptr_a )
   u_bound = UBOUND ( ptr_a )
   extent = u_bound - l_bound + 1
   error_3: IF ( extent(1) /= extent(2) ) THEN
      error = 3
   ELSE
      ! Everything is ok so far, allocate ptr_b.
      ALLOCATE ( ptr_b(extent(1)), STAT=istat )
      error_4: IF ( istat /= 0 ) THEN
         error = 4
      ELSE
         ! Everything is ok, extract diagonal.
         ok: DO i = 1, extent(1)
            ptr_b(i) = ptr_a(l_bound(1)+i-1,l_bound(2)+i-1)
         END DO ok
```

(continued)

(concluded)

```
         ! Reset error flag.
         error = 0
      END IF error_4
   END IF error_3
END IF error_1

END SUBROUTINE get_diagonal
```

A test driver program for this subroutine is shown in Figure 11–19. This program tests the first three possible error conditions and also the proper operation of the subroutine when no error occurs. Because we do not have an easy way to get the memory allocation of ptr_b to fail, the driver does not have an explicit test for that condition.

FIGURE 11–19

Test driver program for subroutine get_diagonal.

```
PROGRAM test_diagonal
!
!  Purpose:
!    To test the diagonal extraction subroutine.
!
!  Record of revisions:
!     Date          Programmer          Description of change
!     ====          ==========          =====================
!    01/31/96     S. J. Chapman         Original code
!
IMPLICIT NONE

! Declare interface to subroutine diagonal:
INTERFACE
   SUBROUTINE get_diagonal ( ptr_a, ptr_b, error )
   INTEGER, DIMENSION(:,:), POINTER :: ptr_a
   INTEGER, DIMENSION(:), POINTER :: ptr_b
   INTEGER, INTENT(OUT) :: error
   END SUBROUTINE get_diagonal
END INTERFACE

! Declare local variable:
INTEGER :: i, j, k                         ! Loop counter
INTEGER :: istat                           ! Allocate status
INTEGER, DIMENSION(:,:) POINTER :: ptr_a   ! Ptr to square array
INTEGER, DIMENSION(:), POINTER :: ptr_b    ! Ptr to output array
INTEGER :: error                           ! Errors flag

! Call diagonal with nothing defined to see what happens.
CALL get_diagonal ( ptr_a, ptr_b, error )
WRITE (*,*) 'No pointers allocated: '
WRITE (*,*) ' Error = ', error

! Allocate both pointers, and call the subroutine.
ALLOCATE (ptr_a(10,10), STAT=istat )
ALLOCATE (ptr_b(10), STAT=istat )
CALL get_diagonal ( ptr_a, ptr_b, error )
```

(continued)

(concluded)

```
WRITE (*,*) 'Both pointers allocated: '
WRITE (*,*) ' Error = ', error

! Allocate ptr_a, but with unequal extents.
DEALLOCATE (ptr_a, STAT=istat)
DEALLOCATE (ptr_b, STAT=istat)
ALLOCATE (ptr_a(-5:5,10), STAT=istat )
CALL get_diagonal ( ptr_a, ptr_b, error )
WRITE (*,*) 'Array on ptr_a not square: '
WRITE (*,*) ' Error = ', error

! Allocate ptr_a only, initialize, and get results.
DEALLOCATE (ptr_a, STAT=istat)
ALLOCATE (ptr_a(-2:2,0:4), STAT=istat )
k = 0
DO j = 0, 4
   DO i = -2, 2
      k = k + 1                       ! Store the numbers 1 .. 25
      ptr_a(i,j) = k                  ! in row order in the array
   END DO
END DO
CALL get_diagonal ( ptr_a, ptr_b, error )
WRITE (*,*) 'ptr_a allocated & square; ptr_b not allocated: '
WRITE (*,*) ' Error = ', error
WRITE (*,*) ' Diag = ', ptr_b

END PROGRAM
```

When the test driver program is executed, the results are

```
C>test_diagonal
No pointers allocated:
 Error =               1
Both pointers allocated:
 Error =               2
Array on ptr_a not square:
 Error =               3
ptr_a allocated & square; ptr_b not allocated:
 Error =               0
 Diag  =               1          7         13         19         25
```

All errors were flagged properly, and the diagonal values are correct, so the subroutine appears to be working properly.

Good Programming Practice

Always test the association status of any pointers passed to a procedure as calling arguments. In a large program you can easily make mistakes that result in an attempt to use an unassociated pointer or in an attempt to reallocate an already associated pointer. (The latter case will produce a memory leak.)

It is also possible for a function to return a pointer value. If a function is to return a pointer, then the RESULT clause must be used in the function definition and the RESULT variable must be declared to be a pointer. For example, the function in Figure 11–20 accepts a pointer to a rank-1 array and returns a pointer to every fifth value in the array.

FIGURE 11–20

A pointer-valued function.

```
FUNCTION every_fifth (ptr_array) RESULT (ptr_fifth)
!
!   Purpose:
!     To produce a pointer to every fifth element in an
!     input rank one array.
!
!   Record of revisions:
!     Date        Programmer            Description of change
!     ====        ==========            =====================
!     01/31/96    S. J. Chapman         Original code
!
IMPLICIT NONE

! Declare calling arguments:
INTEGER, DIMENSION(:), POINTER :: ptr_array
INTEGER, DIMENSION(:), POINTER :: ptr_fifth

! Declare local variables:
INTEGER :: low          ! Array lower bound
INTEGER :: high         ! Array upper bound

low = LBOUND(ptr_array,1)
high = UBOUND(ptr_array,1)
ptr_fifth => ptr_array(low:high:5)

END FUNCTION every_fifth
```

A pointer-valued function must always have an explicit interface in any procedure that uses it. The explicit interface may be specified by an interface or by placing the function in a module and then using the module in the procedure. Once the function is defined, it can be used any place that a pointer expression can be used. For example, it can be used on the right side of a pointer assignment statement as follows:

```
ptr_2 => every_fifth( ptr_1 )
```

The function can also be used in a location where an integer array is expected. In that case the pointer returned by the function will automatically be dereferenced, and the values pointed to will be used. Thus the following statement is legal and will print out the values pointed to by the pointer returned from the function.

```
WRITE (*,*) every_fifth( ptr_1 )
```

Like any other function, a pointer-valued function can *not* be used on the left side of an assignment statement.

◼ 11.8

BINARY TREE STRUCTURES

We have already seen one example of a dynamic data structure: the linked list. Another very important dynamic data structure is the **binary tree.** A binary tree consists of repeated components (or **nodes**) arranged in an inverted tree structure. Each component or node is a variable of a derived data type that stores some sort of data plus *two* pointers to other variables of the same data type. A sample derived data type might be

```
TYPE :: person
    CHARACTER(len=10) :: last
    CHARACTER(len=10) :: first
    CHARACTER :: mi
    TYPE (person), POINTER :: before
    TYPE (person), POINTER :: after
END TYPE
```

This data type is illustrated in Figure 11–21. It could be extended to include further information about each person, such as address, phone number, and social security number.

An important requirement for binary trees is that the components must be sortable according to some known criterion. For our example, the components may be sortable alphabetically by last name, first name, and middle initial. If the pointers in a component are associated, then the pointer `before` must point to another component that falls before the current component in the sorting order. The pointer `after` must point to another component that falls after the current component in the sorting order.

Binary trees start from a single node (the *root node*), which is the first value read into the program. When the first value is read, a variable is created to hold it and the two pointers in the variable are nullified. When the next value is read, a new node is created to hold it. That value is compared to the value in the root node. If the new value is less than the value in the root node, then the `before` pointer of the root node is set to point to the new variable. If the new value is greater than the value in the root node, then the `after` pointer of the root node is set to point to the new variable. If a value is greater than the value in the root node but the `after` pointer is already in use, then we compare the new value to the value in the node pointed to by the `after` pointer and insert the new node in the proper position below that node. This process is repeated as new values are added, producing nodes arranged in an inverted tree structure with their values in order.

11

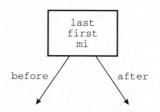

FIGURE 11–21
A typical component of a binary tree.

This process is best illustrated by an example. Let's add the following names to a binary tree structure consisting of variables of the type defined at the beginning of this section.

```
Jackson, Andrew D
Johnson, James R
Johnson, Jessie R
Johnson, Andrew C
Chapman, Stephen J
Gomez, Jose A
Chapman, Rosa P
```

The first name read in is Jackson, Andrew D. Since there is no other data yet, this name is stored in node 1, which becomes the root node of the tree, and both of the pointers in the variable are nullified (see Figure 11–22a). The next name read in is Johnson, James R. This name is stored in node 2, and both pointers in the new variable are nullified. Next the new value is compared to the root node. Since it is greater than the value in the root node, the pointer `after` of the root node is set to point to the new variable (see Figure 11–22b).

The third name read in is Johnson, Jessie R. This name is stored in node 3, and both pointers in the new variable are nullified. Next the new value is compared to the root node. It is greater than the value in the root node, but the `after` pointer of the root node already points to node 2, so we compare the new variable with the value in node 2. That value is Johnson, James R. Since the new value is greater than that value, the new variable is attached below node 2 and the `after` pointer of node 2 is set to point to it (see Figure 11–22c).

The fourth name read in is Johnson, Andrew C. This name is stored in node 4, and both pointers in the new variable are nullified. Next the new value is compared to the root node. It is greater than the value in the root node, but the `after` pointer of the root node already points to node 2, so we compare the new variable with the value in node 2. That value is Johnson, James R. Since the new value is less than that value, the new variable is attached below node 2 and the `before` pointer of node 2 is set to point to it (see Figure 11–22d).

The fifth name read in is Chapman, Stephen J. This name is stored in node 5, and both pointers in the new variable are nullified. Next the new value is compared to the root node. Since the new value is less than that value, the new variable is attached below the root node and the `before` pointer of the root node is set to point to it (see Figure 11–22e).

The sixth name read in is Gomez, Jose A. This name is stored in node 6, and both pointers in the new variable are nullified. Next the new value is compared to the root node. It is less than the value in the root node, but the `before` pointer of the root node already points to node 5, so we compare the new variable with the value in node 5. That value is Chapman, Stephen J. Since the new value is greater than that value, the new variable is attached below node 5 and the `after` pointer of node 5 is set to point to it (see Figure 11–22f).

The seventh name read in is Chapman, Rosa P. This name is stored in node 7, and both pointers in the new variable are nullified. Next the new value is compared to the root node. It is less than the value in the root node, but the `before` pointer of the root node already points to node 5, so we compare the new variable with the value in node 5. That value is Chapman, Stephen J. Since the new value is less than that value, the new variable is attached below node 5 and the `before` pointer of node 5 is set to point to it (see Figure 11–22g).

This process can be repeated indefinitely as more data values are added to the tree.

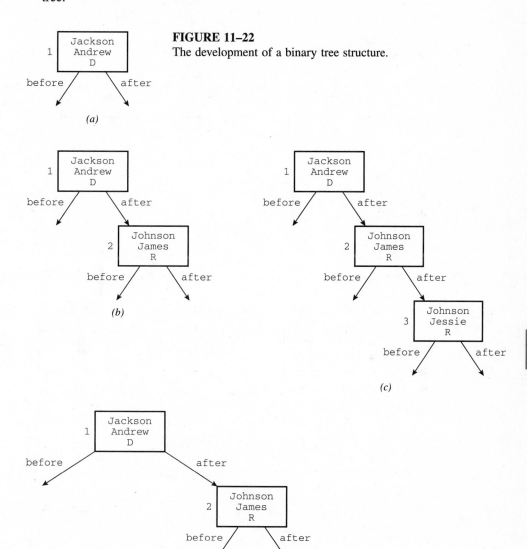

FIGURE 11–22
The development of a binary tree structure.

(a)

(b)

(c)

(d)

(continued)

(concluded)

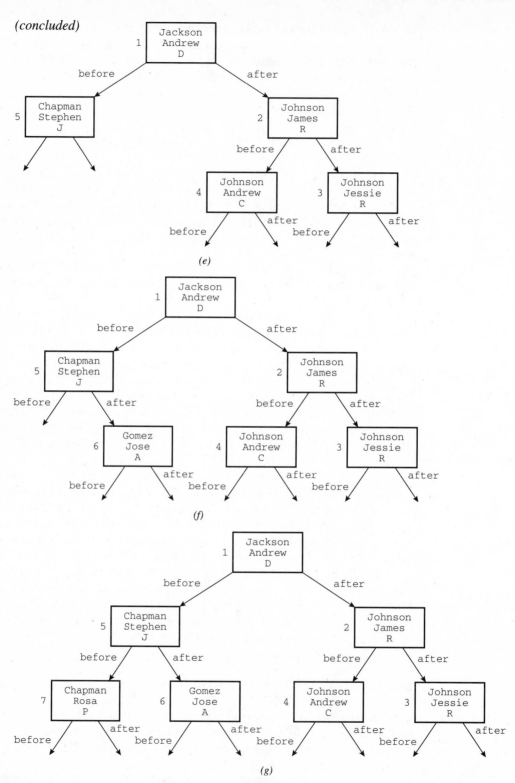

(e)

(f)

(g)

11.8.1 The Significance of Binary Tree Structures

Now let's examine the completed structure in Figure 11–22g. Notice that when the tree is finished, the values are arranged in sorted order from left to right across the structure. This fact means that the binary tree can be used as a way to sort a data set. (In this application, the binary tree is similar to the insertion sort described earlier in the chapter.)

However, there is something far more important about this data structure than the fact that it is sorted. Suppose that we wanted to search for a particular name in the original list of names. Depending on where the name appears in the list, we would have to check from one to seven names before locating the one we wanted. On average, we would have to search 3.5 names before spotting the desired one. In contrast, if the names are arranged in a binary tree structure, then starting from the root node no more than three checks would be required to locate any particular name. A binary tree is a very efficient way to search for and retrieve data values.

This advantage increases rapidly as the size of the database to be searched increases. For example, suppose that we have 32,767 values in a database. If we search through the linear list to try to find a particular value, from 1 to 32,767 values would have to be searched; the average search length would be 16,384. In contrast, 32,767 values can be stored in a binary tree structure consisting of only 15 layers, so the maximum number of values to search to find any particular value would be 15! Binary trees are a *very* efficient way to store data for easy retrieval.

In practice, binary trees may not be quite this efficient. Since the arrangement of the nodes in a binary tree depends on the order in which data was read in, more layers of nodes may appear in some parts of the tree than in others (see Figure 11–23). In that case we may have to search a few extra layers to find some of the values. However, the efficiency of a binary tree is so much greater than that of a linear list that binary trees are still better for data storage and retrieval.

The worst sort of data to store in a binary tree is sorted data. If sorted data is read, then each value is larger than the previous one, and so each new node is placed after the previous one. In the end, we wind up with a binary tree consisting of only one branch, which just reproduces the structure of the original list (see Figure 11–24). The best sort of data to store in a binary tree is random data, since random values will fill in all branches of the tree roughly equally.

Many databases are structured as binary trees. These databases often include special techniques called *hashing techniques* to partially randomize the order of the data stored in the database and so avoid the situation shown in Figure 11–24. They also often include special procedures to even out the bottom branches of the binary tree in order to make searching for data in the tree faster.

11.8.2 Building a Binary Tree Structure

Because each node of a binary tree looks and behaves just like any other node, binary trees are perfectly suited to recursive procedures. For example, suppose that we want to add a value to a binary tree. A program could read the new value, create a

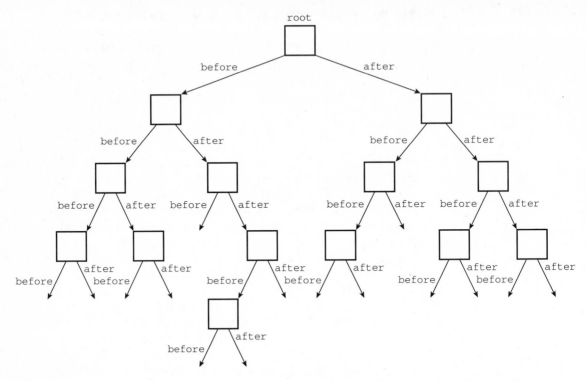

FIGURE 11–23
A binary tree structure whose lowest branches are not completely filled in.

new node for it, and call a subroutine named `insert_node` to insert the node into the tree. The subroutine will first be called with a pointer to the root node. The root node becomes the "current node" for the subroutine. If the current node doesn't exist, then the subroutine will add the new node at that location. If the current node does exist, then the subroutine will compare the value in the current node to the value in the new node. If the value in the new node is less than the value in the current node, then the subroutine will call itself recursively using the `before` pointer from the current node. If the value in the new node is greater than the value in the current node, then the subroutine will call itself recursively using the `after` pointer from the current node. Subroutine `insert_node` will continue to call itself recursively until it reaches the bottom of the tree and locates the proper place to insert the new node.

Similar recursive subroutines can be written to retrieve specific values from the binary tree or to write out all of the values in the tree in sorted order. The following example will illustrate the construction of a binary tree.

EXAMPLE 11–4 Storing and Retrieving Data in a Binary Tree: Suppose that we want to create a database containing the names and telephone numbers of a group of people. (This structure could easily accommodate more information about each person, but we will keep it simple for the purposes of this example.) Write a program to read the names and phone numbers and to store them in a binary tree.

root

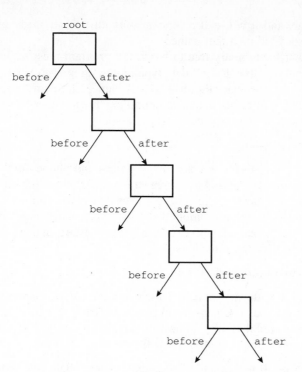

FIGURE 11–24
A binary tree resulting from
sorted input data. Note that the
tree has just become a list, and all
of the advantages of the binary
tree structure have been lost.

After reading all of the names, the program should be able to print out all of the
names and phone numbers in alphabetical order. In addition, it should be able to
recover the phone number of any individual given his or her name. Use recursive
subroutines to implement the binary tree functions.

SOLUTION The information about each person will be stored in a binary tree. We
must create a derived data type to hold the information contained in each node:
name, telephone number, and pointers to two other nodes. An appropriate derived
data type is

```
TYPE :: node
   CHARACTER(len=10) :: last
   CHARACTER(len=10) :: first
   CHARACTER :: mi
   CHARACTER(len=16) :: phone
   TYPE (node), POINTER :: before
   TYPE (node), POINTER :: after
END PROGRAM
```

The main program will read names and phone numbers from an input data file
and create nodes to hold them. When each node is created, it will call a recursive subroutine insert_node to locate the proper place in the tree to put the
new code. Once all of the names and phone numbers are read in, the main program will call recursive subroutine write_node to list out all names and phone
numbers in alphabetical order. Finally, the program will prompt the user to pro-

vide a name, and it will call recursive subroutine `find_node` to get the phone number associated with that name.

Note that for a binary tree to work, the program must have a way to compare two values of the derived data type representing each node. In this case we wish to sort and compare the data by last name, first name, and middle initial. Therefore, we will create extended definitions for the operators >, <, and == so that they can work with the derived data type.

1. State the problem.

Write a program that reads a list of names and phone numbers from an input file and stores them in a binary tree structure. After reading in all of the names, the program will print out all of the names and phone numbers in alphabetical order. Then the program prompts the user for a specific name and retrieves the phone number associated with that name. It will use recursive subroutines to implement the binary tree functions.

2. Define the inputs and outputs.

The inputs to the program are a file name and a list of names and phone numbers within the file. The names and phone numbers will be in the following order: last, first, middle initial, phone number.

The outputs from the program will be

- A list of all names and phone numbers in alphabetical order.
- The phone number associated with a user-specified name.

3. Describe the algorithm.

The basic pseudocode for the main program is

```
Get input file name
Read input data and store in binary tree
Write out data in alphabetical order
Get specific name from user
Recover and display phone number associated with that name
```

The data to be stored in the binary tree will be read from the input file using a while loop and stored using recursive subroutine `add_node`. Once all of the data has been read, the sorted data will be written out to the standard output device using subroutine `write_node`; then the user will be prompted to input the name of the record to find. Subroutine `find_node` will be used to search for the record. If the record is found, it will be displayed. Here is the detailed pseudocode for the main program:

```
Prompt user for the input file name "filename"
Read the file name "filename"
OPEN file "filename"
IF OPEN is successful THEN
    WHILE
        Create new node using pointer "temp"
        Read value into temp
        IF read not successful EXIT
        CALL add_node(root, temp) to put item in tree
```

```
            END of WHILE
            Call write_node(root) to write out sorted data
            Prompt user for name to recover; store in "temp"
            CALL find_node(root, temp, error)
            Write the data to the standard output device
         END of IF
```

It is necessary to create a module containing the definition of the derived data type and the three recursive subroutines required to manipulate the binary tree structure. To add a node to the tree, we should start by looking at the root node. If the root node does not exist, then the new node will become the root node. If the root node exists, then we should compare the name in the new node to the name in the root node to determine if the new node is alphabetically less than or greater than the root node. If it is less, then we should check the before pointer of the root node. If that pointer is null, then we will add the new node there. Otherwise, we will check the node pointed to by the before pointer and repeat the process. If the new node is alphabetically greater than or equal to the root node, then we should check the after pointer of the root node. If that pointer is null, then we will add the new node there. Otherwise, we will check the node pointed to by the after pointer and repeat the process.

For each node we examine, we perform the same steps:

1. Determine whether the new node is < or >= the current node.
2. If it is less than the current node and the before pointer is null, add the new node there.
3. If it is less than the current node and the before pointer is not null, examine the node pointed to.
4. If the new node is greater than or equal to the current node and the after pointer is null, add the new node there.
5. If it is greater than or equal to the current node and the after pointer is not null, examine the node pointed to.

Since the same pattern repeats over and over, we can implement add_node as a recursive subroutine.

```
        If ptr is not associated THEN
           ! There is no tree yet.  Add the node right here.
           ptr => new_node
        ELSE IF new_node < ptr THEN
           ! Check to see if we can attach new node here.
           IF ptr%before is associated THEN
              ! Node in use, so call add_node recursively
              CALL add_node ( ptr%before, new_node )
           ELSE
              ! Pointer not in use.  Add node here.
              ptr%before => new_node
           END of IF
        ELSE
           ! Check to see if we can attach new node to after ptr.
           IF ptr%after is associated THEN
              ! Node in use, so call add_node recursively
              CALL add_node ( ptr%after, new_node )
           ELSE
              ! Pointer not in use.  Add node here.
```

11

```
              ptr%after => new_node
           END of IF
        END of IF
```

Subroutine `write_node` is a recursive subroutine to write out the values in the tree in alphabetical order. The subroutine starts at the root node and works its way down to the left-most branch in the tree. Then it works its way along from left to right through the structure. The pseudocode follows.

```
      IF pointer "before" is associated THEN
         CALL write_node ( ptr%before )
      END of IF
      WRITE contents of current node
      IF pointer "after" is associated THEN
         CALL write_node ( ptr%after )
      END of IF
```

Subroutine `find_node` is a recursive subroutine to locate a particular node in the tree. To find a node in the tree, we start by looking at the root node. We should compare the name we are searching for to the name in the root node to determine if the name we want is alphabetically less than or greater than the root node. If it is less, then we should check the `before` pointer of the root node. If that pointer is null, then the desired node does not exist. Otherwise, we will check the node pointed to by the `before` pointer and repeat the process. If the name we are searching for is alphabetically greater than or equal to the root node, then we should check the `after` pointer of the root node. If that pointer is null, then the desired node does not exist. Otherwise, we will check the node pointed to by the `after` pointer and repeat the process. If the name we are searching for is equal to the root node, then the root node contains the data we want and we will return it. This process is repeated recursively for each node called until either the desired data is found or a null pointer is reached. Here is the pseudocode:

```
   If search_value < ptr THEN
      IF ptr%before is associated THEN
         CALL find_node ( ptr%before, search_value, error )
      ELSE ! not found
         error ← 1
      END of IF
   ELSE IF search_value == ptr THEN
      search_value = ptr
      error ← 0
   ELSE
      IF ptr%after is associated THEN
         CALL find_node ( ptr%after, search_value, error )
      ELSE ! not found
         error ← 1
      END of IF
   END of IF
```

The module must contain the definition of the derived data type and the definitions of the >, <, and == operators for that data type. We will include three INTERFACE OPERATOR blocks in the module to meet this requirement. In addition, we must write the three private functions that implement the operators. The first function is called `greater_than`, the second is called `less_than`, and the third is called `equal_to`. These functions must compare the last two names to decide whether the first is greater than, less than, or the same as the second. If the last names are the same, then the functions must compare the two first names and middle initials. Note that all names should be shifted to uppercase to avoid mixing upper- and lower-case during the comparisons. We will use a subroutine called `ushift`, which in turn calls the subroutine `ucase` that we developed in Chapter 7. The pseudocode for function `greater_than` is

```
IF last1 > last2 THEN
   greater_than = .TRUE.
ELSE IF last1 < last2 THEN
   greater_than = .FALSE.
ELSE ! Last names match
   IF first1 > first2 THEN
      greater_than = .TRUE.
   ELSE IF first1 < first 2 THEN
      greater_than = .FALSE.
   ELSE ! First names match
      IF mi1 > mi2 THEN
         greater_than = .TRUE.
      ELSE
         greater_than = .FALSE.
      END of IF
   END of IF
END of IF
```

The pseudocode for function `less_than` is

```
IF last1 < last2 THEN
   less_than = .TRUE.
ELSE IF last1 > last2 THEN
   less_than = .FALSE.
ELSE ! Last names match
   IF first1 < first2 THEN
      less_than = .TRUE.
   ELSE IF first1 > first2 THEN
      less_than = .FALSE.
   ELSE ! First names match
      IF mi1 < mi2 THEN
         less_than = .TRUE.
      ELSE
         less_than = .FALSE.
      END of IF
   END of IF
END of IF
```

The pseudocode for function `equal_to` is

```
IF last1 == last2 .AND. first1 == first2 .AND. mi1 == mi2 THEN
   equal_to = .TRUE.
ELSE
   equal_to = .FALSE.
END of IF
```

4. Turn the algorithm into Fortran statements.

The resulting Fortran program is shown in Figure 11–25. Module `btree` contains the definition of the derived data type and all the supporting subroutines and functions. This module also defines the operators >, <, and == for the derived data type. Note that only the essential procedures in the module are PUBLIC. The main program accesses the procedures in the module by USE association, so the procedures have an explicit interface.

FIGURE 11–25

A program to store a database of names and phone numbers in a binary tree structure and to retrieve a selected item from that tree.

```
MODULE btree
!
!   Purpose:
!     To define the derived data type used as a node in the
!     binary tree and to define the operations >, <, and ==
!     for this data type.  This module also contains the
!     subroutines to add a node to the tree, write out the
!     values in the tree, and find a value in the tree.
!
!   Record of revisions:
!       Date        Programmer          Description of change
!       ====        ==========          =====================
!     02/04/96    S. J. Chapman         Original code
!
IMPLICIT NONE

! Restrict access to module contents.
PRIVATE
PUBLIC :: node, OPERATOR(>), OPERATOR(<), OPERATOR(==)
PUBLIC :: add_note, write_node, find_node

! Declare type for a node of the binary tree.
TYPE :: node
   CHARACTER(len=10) :: last
   CHARACTER(len=10) :: first
   CHARACTER :: mi
   CHARACTER(len=16) :: phone
   TYPE (node), POINTER :: before
   TYPE (node), POINTER :: after
END TYPE

INTERFACE OPERATOR (>)
   MODULE PROCEDURE greater_than
END INTERFACE

INTERFACE OPERATOR (<)
   MODULE PROCEDURE less_than
END INTERFACE

INTERFACE OPERATOR (==)
   MODULE PROCEDURE equal_to
END INTERFACE

CONTAINS
   RECURSIVE SUBROUTINE add_node (ptr, new_node)
   !
   !   Purpose:
   !     To add a new node to the binary tree structure.
   !
   TYPE (node), POINTER :: ptr  ! Pointer to current pos. in tree
   TYPE (node), POINTER :: new_node ! Pointer to new node
```

(continued)

(continued)

```
IF ( .NOT. ASSOCIATED(ptr) ) THEN
   ! There is no tree yet. Add the node right here.
   ptr => new_node
ELSE IF ( new_node < ptr ) THEN
   IF ( ASSOCIATED(ptr%before) ) THEN
      CALL add_node ( ptr%before, new_node )
   ELSE
      ptr%before => new_node
   END IF
ELSE
   IF ( ASSOCIATED(ptr%after) ) THEN
      CALL add_node ( ptr%after, new_node )
   ELSE
      ptr%after => new_node
   END IF
END IF
END SUBROUTINE add_node
```

RECURSIVE SUBROUTINE write_node (ptr)
```
!
!  Purpose:
!    To write out the contents of the binary tree
!    structure in order.
!
TYPE (node), POINTER :: ptr  ! Pointer to current pos. in tree

! Write contents of previous node.
IF ( ASSOCIATED(ptr%before) ) THEN
   CALL write_node ( ptr%before )
END IF

! Write contents of current node.
WRITE (*,"(1X,A,', ',A,1X,A)") ptr%last, ptr%first, ptr%mi

! Write contents of next node.
IF ( ASSOCIATED(ptr%after) ) THEN
   CALL write_node ( ptr%after )
END IF
END SUBROUTINE write_node
```

RECURSIVE SUBROUTINE find_node (ptr, search, error)
```
!
!  Purpose:
!    To find a particular node in the binary tree structure.
!    "Search" is a pointer to the name to find and will
!    also contain the results when the subroutine finishes
!    if the node is found.
!
TYPE (node), POINTER :: ptr     ! Pointer to curr pos. in tree
TYPE (node), POINTER :: search  ! Pointer to value to find.
INTEGER :: error                ! Error: 0 = ok, 1 = not found

IF ( search < ptr ) THEN
   IF ( ASSOCIATED(ptr%before) ) THEN
      CALL find_node (ptr%before, search, error)
   ELSE
      error = 1
   END IF
ELSE IF ( search == ptr ) THEN
```

(continued)

(continued)

```
      search = ptr
      error = 0
ELSE
   IF ( ASSOCIATED(ptr%after) ) THEN
      CALL find_node (ptr%after, search, error)
   ELSE
      error = 1
   END IF
END IF
END SUBROUTINE find_node
```

LOGICAL FUNCTION greater_than (op1, op2)

```
!
!  Purpose:
!     To test to see if operand 1 is > operand 2
!     in alphabetical order.
!
TYPE (node), INTENT(IN) :: op1, op2
CHARACTER(len=10) :: last1, last2, first1, first2
CHARACTER :: mi1, mi2

CALL ushift (op1, last1, first1, mi1 )
CALL ushift (op2, last2, first2, mi2 )

IF (last1 > last2) THEN
   greater_than = .TRUE.
ELSE IF (last1 < last2 ) THEN
   greater_than = .FALSE.
ELSE ! Last names match
   IF (first1 > first2) THEN
      greater_than = .TRUE.
   ELSE IF (first1 < first2) THEN
      greater_than = .FALSE.
   ELSE ! First names match
     IF (mi1 > mi2) THEN
        greater_than = .TRUE.
     ELSE
        greater_than = .FALSE.
     END IF
   END IF
END IF
END FUNCTION greater_than
```

LOGICAL FUNCTION less_than (op1, op2)

```
!
!  Purpose:
!     To test to see if operand 1 is < operand 2
!     in alphabetical order.
!
TYPE (node), INTENT(IN) :: op1, op2
CHARACTER(len=10) :: last1, last2, first1, first2
CHARACTER :: mi1, mi2

CALL ushift (op1, last1, first1, mi1 )
CALL ushift (op2, last2, first2, mi2 )

IF (last1 < last2 ) THEN
   less_than = .TRUE.
ELSE IF (last1 > last2) THEN
   less_than = .FALSE.
```

(continued)

(continued)

```
      ELSE ! Last names match
         IF (first1 < first2) THEN
            less_than = .TRUE.
         ELSE IF (first1 > first2) THEN
            less_than = .FALSE.
         ELSE ! First names match
            IF (mi1 < mi2) THEN
               less_than = .TRUE.
            ELSE
               less_than = .FALSE.
            END IF
         END IF
      END IF
   END IF
   END FUNCTION less_than

   LOGICAL FUNCTION equal_to (op1, op2)
   !
   !  Purpose:
   !    To test to see if operand 1 is equal to operand 2
   !    alphabetically.
   !
   TYPE (node), INTENT(IN) :: op1, op2

   CHARACTER(len=10) :: last1, last2, first1, first2
   CHARACTER :: mi1, mi2

   CALL ushift (op1, last1, first1, mi1 )
   CALL ushift (op2, last2, first2, mi2 )

   IF ( (last1 == last 2). AND. (first1 == first 2) .AND. &
        (mi1 == mi2 ) ) THEN
      equal_to = .TRUE.
   ELSE
      equal_to = .FALSE.
   END IF
   END FUNCTION equal_to

   SUBROUTINE ushift ( op, last, first, mi )
   !
   !  Purpose:
   !    To create upshifted versions of all strings for
   !    comparison.
   !
   TYPE (node), INTENT(IN) :: op
   CHARACTER(len=10), INTENT(INOUT) :: last, first
   CHARACTER, INTENT(INOUT) :: mi

   last = op%last
   first = op%first
   mi = op%mi
   CALL ucase (last)
   CALL ucase (first)
   CALL ucase (mi)
   END SUBROUTINE ushift

   SUBROUTINE ucase ( string )
   !
   ! Purpose:
   !   To shift a character string to UPPER case.
   !
```

11

(continued)

(continued)

```
    ! Record of revisions:
    !    Date        Programmer           Description of change
    !    ====        ==========           =====================
    !   11/25/95    S. J. Chapman         Original code
    ! 1.11/25/95    S. J. Chapman         Modified for any collating seq
    !
    IMPLICIT NONE

    ! Declare calling parameters:
    CHARACTER(len=*), INTENT(INOUT) :: string

    ! Declare local variables:
    INTEGER :: i                  ! Loop index
    INTEGER :: length             ! Length of input string

    ! Get length of string
    length = LEN ( string )

    ! Now shift lower case letters to upper case.
    DO i = 1, length
       IF ( ( string(i:i) >= 'a' ) .AND. &
            ( string(i:i) <= 'z' ) ) THEN
          string(i:i) = ACHAR ( IACHAR ( string(i:i) ) - 32 )
       END IF
    END DO

    END SUBROUTINE ucase

END MODULE btree

PROGRAM binary_tree
!
!   Purpose:
!     To read in a series of random names and phone numbers
!     and store them in a binary tree.  After the values are
!     stored, they are written out in sorted order.  Then the
!     user is prompted for a name to retrieve, and the program
!     recovers the data associated with that name.
!
!   Record of revisions:
!      Date        Programmer           Description of change
!      ====        ==========           =====================
!    02/06/95    S. J. Chapman         Original code
!
USE btree
IMPLICIT NONE

! List of variables:
INTEGER :: error                    ! Error flag: 0=success
CHARACTER(len=20) :: filename       ! Input data file name
INTEGER :: istat                    ! Status: 0 for success
TYPE (node), POINTER :: root        ! Pointer to root node
TYPE (node), POINTER :: temp        ! Temp pointer to node

! Nullify new pointers
NULLIFY ( root, temp )

! Get the name of the file containing the input data.
WRITE (*,*) 'Enter the file name with the input data: '
READ(*,'(A20)') filename
```

(continued)

(concluded)

```
! Open input data file.  Status is OLD because the input data must
! already exist.
OPEN ( UNIT=9, FILE=filename, STATUS='OLD', ACTION='READ', &
       IOSTAT=istat )

! Was the OPEN successful?
fileopen: IF ( istat == 0 ) THEN              ! Open successful

   ! The file was opened successfully, allocate space for each
   ! node, read the data into that node, and insert it into the
   ! binary tree.
   input: DO
      ALLOCATE (temp,STAT=istat)              ! Allocate node
      NULLIFY ( temp%before, temp%after)  ! Nullify pointers

      READ (9, 100, IOSTAT=istat) temp%last, temp%first, &
         temp%mi, temp%phone                  ! Read data
      100 FORMAT (A10,1X,A10,1X,A1,1X,A16)
      IF ( istat /= 0 ) EXIT input            ! Exit on end of data
      CALL add_node(root, temp)               ! Add to binary tree
   END DO input

   ! Now, write out the sorted data.
   WRITE (*,'(/,1X,A)') 'The sorted data list is: '
   CALL write_node(root)

   ! Prompt for a name to search for in the tree.
   WRITE (*,'(/,1X,A)') 'Enter name to recover from tree:'
   WRITE (*,'(1X,A)',ADVANCE='NO') 'Last Name:        '
   READ (*,'(A)') temp%last
   WRITE (*,'(1X,A)',ADVANCE='NO') 'First Name:       '
   READ(*,'(A)') temp%first
   WRITE (*,'(1X,A)',ADVANCE='NO') 'Middle Initial: '
   READ (*,'(A)') temp%mi

   ! Locate record
   CALL find_node ( root, temp, error )
   check: IF ( error == 0 ) THEN
      WRITE (*,'(/,1X,A)') 'The record is:'
      WRITE (*,'(1X,7A)') temp%last, ', ', temp%first, ' ', &
                    temp%mi, '  ', temp%phone
   ELSE
      WRITE (*,'(/,1X,A)') 'Specified node not found!'
   END IF check

ELSE fileopen

   ! Else file open failed.  Tell user.
   WRITE (*,'(1X,A,I6)') 'File open failed--status = ', istat

END IF fileopen

END PROGRAM
```

5. Test the resulting Fortran program.

To test this program, we will create an input data file containing names and

telephone numbers, and we will execute the program with that data. The file
`tree_in.dat` will be created containing the following data:

```
Leroux      Hector     A (608) 555-1212
Johnson     James      R (800) 800-1111
Jackson     Andrew     D (713) 723-7777
Romanoff    Alexi      N (212) 338-3030
Johnson     Jessie     R (800) 800-1111
Chapman     Stephen    J (713) 721-0901
Nachshon    Bini       M (618) 813-1234
Ziskend     Joseph     J (805) 238-7999
Johnson     Andrew     C (504) 388-3000
Chi         Shuchung   F (504) 388-3123
deBerry     Jonathan   S (703) 765-4321
Chapman     Rosa       P (713) 721-0901
Gomez       Jose       A (415) 555-1212
Rosenberg   Fred       R (617) 123-4567
```

We will execute the program twice. Once we will specify a valid name to look
up, and once we will specify an invalid one, to test that the program is working
properly in both cases. When the program is executed, the results are

```
C>binary_tree
Enter the file name with the input data:
tree_in.dat

The sorted data list is:
Chapman     , Rosa       P
Chapman     , Stephen    J
Chi         , Shuchung   F
deBerry     , Jonathan   S
Gomez       , Jose       A
Jackson     , Andrew     D
Johnson     , Andrew     C
Johnson     , James      R
Johnson     , Jessie     R
Leroux      , Hector     A
Nachshon    , Bini       M
Romanoff    , Alexi      N
Rosenberg   , Fred       R
Ziskend     , Joseph     J

Enter name to recover from tree:
Last Name:      Nachshon
First Name:     Bini
Middle Initial: M

The record is:
Nachshon , Bini M (618) 813-1234

C>binary_tree
Enter the file name with the input data:
tree_in.dat

The sorted data list is:
Chapman     , Rosa       P
Chapman     , Stephen    J
Chi         , Shuchung   F
deBerry     , Jonathan   S
Gomez       , Jose       A
```

```
        Jackson     , Andrew      D
        Johnson     , Andrew      C
        Johnson     , James       R
        Johnson     , Jessie      R
        Leroux      , Hector      A
        Nachshon    , Bini        M
        Romanoff    , Alexi       N
        Rosenberg   , Fred        R
        Ziskend     , Joseph      J

        Enter name to recover from tree:
        Last Name:       Johnson
        First Name:      James
        Middle Initial:  A

        Specified node not found!
```

The program appears to be working. Please note that it properly stored data into the binary tree regardless of capitalization. (deBerry is in the proper place.)

Can you determine the tree structure that the program created. What is the maximum number of layers that the program must search through to find any particular data item in this tree?

◼ 11.9

SUMMARY

A pointer is a special type of variable that contains the *address* of another variable instead of containing a value. A pointer has a specified data type and (if it points to an array) rank, and it can point *only* to data items of that particular type and rank. Pointers are declared with the POINTER attribute in a type declaration statement or in a separate POINTER statement. The data item pointed to by a pointer is called a target. Only data items declared with the TARGET attribute in a type declaration statement or in a separate TARGET statement can be pointed to by pointers.

A pointer assignment statement places the address of a target in a pointer. The form of the statement is

```
            pointer => target
            pointer1 => pointer2
```

In the latter case, the address currently contained in *pointer2* is placed in *pointer1*, and both pointers independently point to the same target.

A pointer can have one of three possible association statuses: undefined, associated, or disassociated. When a pointer is first declared in a type declaration statement, its pointer association status is undefined. Once a pointer has been associated with a target by a pointer assignment statement, its association status becomes associated. If a pointer is later disassociated from its target and is not associated with any new target, then its association status becomes disassociated. A pointer should always be nullified or associated as soon as it is created. The function ASSOCIATED() can be used to determine the association status of a pointer.

11

Pointers can be used to dynamically create and destroy variables or arrays. Memory is allocated for data items in an ALLOCATE statement and deallocated in a DEALLOCATE statement. The pointer in the ALLOCATE statement points to the data item that is created and is the *only* way to access that data item. If that pointer is disassociated or is associated with another target before another pointer is set to point to the allocated memory, then the memory becomes inaccessible to the program. This condition is called a memory leak.

When dynamic memory is deallocated in a DEALLOCATE statement, the pointer to the memory is automatically nullified. However, if other pointers are pointing to that same memory, they must be manually nullified or reassigned. If not, the program might attempt to use them to read or write to the deallocated memory location, with potentially disastrous results.

Pointers may be used as components of derived data types, including the data type being defined. This feature permits us to create dynamic data structures, such as linked lists and binary trees, where the pointers in one dynamically allocated data item point to the next item in the chain. This flexibility is extraordinarily useful in many problems.

It is not possible to declare an array of pointers, since the DIMENSION attribute in a pointer declaration refers to the dimension of the target, not to the dimension of the pointer. When an array of pointers is needed, it can be created by defining a derived data type containing only a pointer and then creating an array of that derived data type.

Pointers may be passed to procedures as calling arguments provided that the procedure has an explicit interface in the calling program. A dummy pointer argument must not have an INTENT attribute. It is also possible for a function to return a pointer value if the RESULT clause is used and the result variable is declared to be a pointer.

11.9.1 Summary of Good Programming Practice

The following guidelines should be adhered to when working with pointers:

1. Always nullify or assign all pointers in a program unit as soon as they are created. This technique eliminates any possible ambiguities associated with the undefined allocation status.
2. When sorting or swapping large arrays or derived data types, it is more efficient to exchange pointers to the data than it is to manipulate the data itself.
3. Always nullify or reassign *all* pointers to a memory location when that memory is deallocated. One of the pointers will be automatically nullified by the DEALLOCATE statement, and any others must be manually nullified in NULLIFY statement(s) or reassigned in pointer assignment statements.
4. Always test the association status of any pointers passed to procedures as calling arguments. In a large program you can easily make mistakes that result in an attempt to use an unassociated pointer or in an attempt to reallocate an already associated pointer. (The latter case will produce a memory leak.)

11.9.2 Summary of Fortran Statements and Structures

POINTER Attribute

```
type, POINTER :: ptr1 [, ptr2, ... ]
```

Example:

```
INTEGER, POINTER :: next_value
REAL, DIMENSION(:), POINTER :: array
```

Description:

   The POINTER attribute declares the variables in the type definition statement to be pointers.

POINTER Statement

```
POINTER :: ptr1 [, ptr2, ... ]
```

Example:

```
POINTER :: p1, p2, p3
```

Description:

   The POINTER statement declares the variables in its list to be pointers. It is generally preferable to use the pointer attribute in a type declaration statement to declare a pointer instead of this statement.

11

TARGET Attribute

```
type, TARGET :: var1 [, var2, ... ]
```

Example:

```
INTEGER, TARGET :: num_values
REAL, DIMENSION(100), TARGET :: array
```

Description:

   The TARGET attribute declares the variables in the type definition statement to be legal targets for pointers.

TARGET Statement

```
TARGET :: var1 [, var2, ... ]
```

Example:

```
TARGET :: my_data
```

Description:

The TARGET statement declares the variables in its list to be legal targets for pointers. It is generally preferable to use the target attribute in a type declaration statement to declare a target instead of this statement.

■ 11.10

EXERCISES

11–1 What is the difference between a pointer variable and an ordinary variable?

11–2 How does a pointer assignment statement differ from an ordinary assignment statement? What happens in the two statements a = z and a => z?

```
INTEGER :: x = 6, z = 8
INTEGER, POINTER == a
a => x
a = z
a => z
```

11–3 Is the following program fragment correct or incorrect? If it is incorrect, explain what is wrong with it. If it is correct, what does it do?

```
REAL, POINTER :: p1
REAL :: x1 = 11.
INTEGER, POINTER ::p2
INTEGER :: x2 = 12
p1 => x1
p2 => x2
WRITE (*,'(A,4G8.2)') ' p1, p2, x1, x2 = ', p1, p2, x1, x2
p1 => p2
p2 => x1
WRITE (*,'(A,4G8.2)') ' p1, p2, x1, x2 = ', p1, p2, x1, x2
END PROGRAM
```

11–4 What are the possible association statuses of a pointer? How can you determine the association status of a given pointer?

11–5 Is the following program fragment correct or incorrect? If it is incorrect, explain what is wrong with it. If it is correct, what is printed out by the WRITE statement?

```
REAL, POINTER :: p1, p2
REAL, TARGET :: x1 = 11.1, x2 = -3.2
p1 => x1
WRITE (*,*) ASSOCIATED(p1), ASSOCIATED(p2), ASSOCIATED(p1,x2)
```

11–6 What is the purpose of the function `NULL()`, which was added to Fortran 95? What advantage does this function have over the nullify statement?

11–7 What are the proper Fortran statements to declare a pointer to an integer array and then point that pointer to every 10th element in a 1000-element target array called `my_data`?

11–8 What is printed out by the following program?

```
PROGRAM ex11_8
IMPLICIT NONE
INTEGER :: i
REAL, DIMENSION(-25:25), TARGET :: info = (/ (2.1*i, i=-25,25) /)
REAL, DIMENSION(:), POINTER :: ptr1, ptr2, ptr3
ptr1 => info(-25:25:5)
ptr2 => ptr1(1::2)
ptr3 => ptr2(3:5)
WRITE (*,'(A,11F6.1)') ' ptr1 = ', ptr1
WRITE (*,'(A,11F6.1)') ' ptr2 = ', ptr2
WRITE (*,'(A,11F6.1)') ' ptr3 = ', ptr3
WRITE (*,'(A,11F6.1)') ' ave of ptr3 = ', SUM(ptr3)/SIZE(ptr3)
END PROGRAM
```

11–9 How is dynamic memory allocated and deallocated using pointers? How does memory allocation using pointers and allocatable arrays differ?

11–10 What is a memory leak? Why is it a problem, and how can it be avoided?

11–11 Is the following program correct or incorrect? If it is incorrect, explain what is wrong with it. If it is correct, what is printed out by the WRITE statement?

```
MODULE my_sub
CONTAINS
    SUBROUTINE running_sum (sum, value)
    REAL, POINTER :: sum, value
    ALLOCATE (sum)
    sum = sum + value
    END SUBROUTINE running_sum
END MODULE
PROGRAM sum_values
USE my_sub
IMPLICIT NONE
INTEGER :: istat
REAL, POINTER :: sum, value
ALLOCATE (sum, value, STAT=istat)
WRITE (*,*) 'Enter values to add: '
DO
    READ (*,*,IOSTAT=istat) value
    IF ( istat /= 0 ) EXIT
    CALL running_sum (sum, value)
    WRITE (*,*) ' The sum is ', sum
END DO
END PROGRAM
```

11–12 Is the following program correct or incorrect? If it is incorrect, explain what is wrong with it. If it is correct, what is printed out by the WRITE statements? What happens when this program is compiled and executed on your computer?

```
PROGRAM ex11_12
IMPLICIT NONE
INTEGER :: i, istat
INTEGER, DIMENSION(:), POINTER :: ptr1, ptr2

ALLOCATE (ptr1(1:10), STAT=istat)
ptr1 = (/ (i, i = 1,10 ) /)
ptr2 => ptr1

WRITE (*,'(A,10I3)') ' ptr1 = ', ptr1
WRITE (*,'(A,10I3)') ' ptr2 = ', ptr2

DEALLOCATE(ptr1, STAT=istat)

ALLOCATE (ptr1(1:3), STAT=istat)
ptr1 = (/ -2, 0, 2, /)

WRITE (*,'(A,10I3)') ' ptr1 = ', ptr1
WRITE (*,'(A,10I3)') ' ptr2 = ', ptr2

END PROGRAM
```

11–13 Create a version of the insertion sort program that will sort a set of input character values in a case-insensitive manner (that is, uppercase and lowercase are to be treated as equivalent). Ensure that the ASCII collating sequence is used regardless of the computer on which program is executed.

11–14 Insertion Sort Using a Binary Tree versus a Linked List (*a*) Create an insertion sort subroutine to sort an array of real data using a linked list. This subroutine will be similar to the program in Example 11–2 except that the input data will be presented all at once in an array instead of being read one value at a time from the disk. (*b*) Create a set of subroutines to perform an insertion sort on an array of real data using a binary tree structure. (*c*) Compare the two ways to perform insertion sorts by generating a set of 50,000 random numbers and sorting the list with both subroutines. Time both subroutines using the elapsed time subroutines developed in exercise 6–31. Which sorting algorithm was fastest?

11–15 How can an array of pointers be generated in Fortran 90/95?

11–16 What is printed out by the following program?

```
PROGRAM ex11_16
TYPE :: ptr
   REAL, DIMENSION(:), POINTER :: p
END TYPE
TYPE (ptr), DIMENSION(4) :: p1
REAL, DIMENSION(4), TARGET :: a = (/  1.,  2.,  3.,  4. /)
REAL, DIMENSION(2), TARGET :: b = (/  5.,  6. /)
REAL, DIMENSION(3), TARGET :: c = (/  7.,  8.,  9. /)
REAL, DIMENSION(5), TARGET :: d = (/ 10., 11., 12., 13., 14. /)
p1(1)%p => a
p1(2)%p => b
p1(3)%p => c
p1(4)%p => d

WRITE (*,'(F6.1,/)') p1(1)%p(2) + p1(4)%p(4) + p1(3)%p(3)
```

```
DO i = 1,4
   WRITE (*,'(5F6.1)') p1(i)%p
END DO

END PROGRAM
```

11–17 Write a function that accepts a real input array and returns a pointer to the largest value in the array.

11–18 Write a function that accepts a pointer to a real input array and returns a pointer to the largest value in the array.

11–19 **Linear Least-Squares Fit** Write a program that reads in an unknown number of real (x,y) pairs from a file and stores them in a linked list. When all the values have been read in, the list should be passed to a subroutine that will compute the linear least-squares fit of the data to a straight line. (The equations for the linear least-squares fit were introduced in Example 4–5.)

11–20 **Doubly Linked Lists** Linked lists have the limitation that in order to find a particular element in the list, it is always necessary to search the list from the top down. There is no way to work backwards up the list to find a particular item. For example, suppose that a program had examined the 1000th item in a list and now wanted to examine the 999th item in the list. The only way to do so would be to go back to the top of the list and start over, working from item 1 down! We can get around this problem by creating a *doubly linked list*. A doubly linked list has pointers both to the next item in the list and to the previous item in the list, permitting searches to be conducted in either direction. Write a program that reads in an arbitrary number of real numbers and adds them to a doubly linked list. Then write out the numbers both in input order and in reverse input order using the pointers. Test the program by creating 20 random values between -100.0 and 100.0 and processing them with the program.

11–21 **Insertion Sort with Doubly Linked Lists** Write a version of the insertion sort program that inserts the real input values into a doubly linked list. Test the program by creating 50 random values between -1000.0 and 1000.0 and sorting them with the program. Print out the sorted values in both ascending and descending order.

11–22 Manually reconstruct the binary tree created by the program in Example 11–4 for the given test data set. How many layers are in the tree? Is the tree regular or irregular?

12

Introduction to Numerical Methods

Most Fortran programs are written to solve some sort of mathematical problem. The name Fortran itself comes from FORmula TRANslation, implying that the language is designed to translate mathematical formulas for solution on a computer. Normally, we can take any mathematical formula that works on paper (an **algorithm**), convert it into Fortran statements, and solve the problem on a computer.

However, this statement is only true within certain limits. Computers are wonderful devices, but they are not perfect. If the real-world limitations of our computers are not considered, we can create programs that take too long to run when the algorithms are implemented. Worse, we can get programs that give incorrect answers even though every mathematical equation within the program is correct! We saw a few examples of this problem when we solved for the derivative of a function and examined ill-conditioned systems of equations in Chapter 8.

The first section of this chapter explains some of the limitations of computers for solving numerical problems. It describes the major types of errors that can occur during computer calculations and problem solving. After explaining the limitations of computer mathematics, the chapter introduces a number of examples illustrating the proper use of computers to solve typical problems important in many areas of science and engineering. These examples illustrate the thought involved in designing a practical application.

The study of solution techniques for use on computers is a branch of mathematics known as *numerical analysis,* and the individual techniques used to solve problems on computers are called *numerical methods.* The study of numerical methods is a separate course in itself, with whole textbooks devoted to that topic alone. This chapter barely scratches the surface of numerical methods, but it should give you some feel for the limitations of computers and the techniques used to avoid these limitations.

Many people have spent entire careers and millions of dollars developing high-quality numerical algorithms for solving mathematical problems on computers. Some of these algorithms have been collected into libraries and are available either free of charge or for purchase (see Chapter 13). If you need to solve a difficult mathematical problem in the course of your work, use one of the high-quality procedures in these libraries to get the answer. You will waste a lot of time if you try to write your own versions of the procedures, and your resulting code will be less reliable, because it will not have been tested by so many people with so many different input data sets.

■ 12.1
THE TYPES OF ERRORS FOUND IN COMPUTER CALCULATIONS

Two major classes of errors are common in computer calculations. One of them is intrinsic to the nature of the computer itself, and the other one is due to programmer errors caused by the selection of an inappropriate model for the data being analyzed.

12.1.1 Errors Intrinsic to the Nature of a Computer

The errors intrinsic to the nature of the computer itself happen because any computer has a *finite precision*. A single-precision real number typically has 6 to 7 significant digits, and a double-precision real number typically has 14 to 15 significant digits. Many real numbers cannot be represented exactly on a computer. For example, the fraction 2/3 may be represented on a computer as 0.666667 in single precision or as 0.66666666666667 in double precision, but it can never be *exactly* correct: 0.666666666 . . . This failure to represent a number exactly is the first source of error that occurs in our calculations. Many real numbers cannot be represented exactly on a computer.

In addition, any real value on a computer has a finite **range.** A single-precision real number typically has a range of positive or negative 10^{-38} to 10^{38}, plus 0. Numbers with absolute values larger than 10^{38} will cause an *overflow* and will usually cause the computer program to abort. Numbers with absolute values smaller than 10^{-38} will cause an *underflow* and will be set to 0. A double-precision real number typically has a range of positive or negative 10^{-308} to 10^{308}, plus 0. Numbers with absolute values larger than 10^{308} will cause an overflow and will usually cause the computer program to abort. Numbers with absolute values smaller than 10^{-308} will cause an underflow and will be set to 0. Computer programs must work within these limitations.

The distinction between truncation and rounding

Whenever two numbers are added, subtracted, multiplied, or divided, inevitable **truncation** or **round-off** errors are associated with the operations. There is an important distinction between truncation and round off. When a number is truncated to n significant digits, the first n significant digits are preserved and all other digits are thrown away. In contrast, when a number is rounded off to n significant digits, the n significant digits that most closely represent the original number are preserved. For example, consider the number 2/3, which is equivalent to 0.666666666 . . . If this number is *truncated* to three significant digits, the result is 0.666. If it is *rounded* to three significant digits, the result is 0.667, since 0.667 is closer to the original number than 0.666.

12

Some computers truncate the results of their mathematical operations, while other computers round the results of their operations. In general, the computers that employ rounding will have smaller numerical errors than the computers that employ truncation. This difference between rounding and truncation may cause slight differences in numerical accuracy as a program is moved from one type of computer to another one.

To better understand the effects of limited precision, truncation, and round off on numerical calculations, let's consider a fictitious computer that has only three significant decimal digits of accuracy. This computer can perform addition, subtraction, multiplication, and division on any two numbers, but each number can only have three significant digits, and the result will have three significant digits. This computer will exhibit the same types of errors that we would find in a real computer, but they will be greatly exaggerated and much easier for us to see.

First, consider the difference between truncation and round off on calculations in this computer. For example, suppose that we wish to add together the two numbers 0.123 and 0.0456. Each of these numbers can be represented on the computer, since they have only three significant digits of precision. The correct sum of these numbers is

$$
\begin{array}{r}
0.123 \\
\underline{0.0456} \\
0.1686
\end{array}
$$

If the computer employs truncation, then the 0.0456 will be truncated to 0.045 before it is added to 0.123; the result will be

$$
\begin{array}{r}
0.123 \\
\underline{0.045} \\
0.168
\end{array}
$$

If the computer employs rounding, then the 0.0456 will be rounded to 0.046 before it is added to 0.123; the result will be

$$
\begin{array}{r}
0.123 \\
\underline{0.046} \\
0.169
\end{array}
$$

The answer using rounding is closer to the truth than the answer using truncation is.

Since truncation or round-off errors are major limitations on the accuracy of computer mathematics, most computer vendors take steps to minimize them as much as possible. A common approach is to add **guard digits** to mathematical calculations. *Guard digits* are extra digits in a mathematical calculation that are beyond the precision of the kind of real values used in the calculation. By calculating the results of each operation to more precision than the final answer, the vendor can ensure that the result of each calculation is properly rounded to minimize total error. Intel microprocessors take this idea to extremes: They perform 80-bit arithmetic on both 32-bit single-precision and 64-bit double-precision values!

Errors in adding series of numbers

Suppose that we have a long series of numbers to add. On computers with finite precision, the order in which the numbers are added affects the final answer that we get. To understand this effect, let's use our hypothetical computer with truncation to add the following series of numbers.

```
0.0488
0.0958
0.3370
0.3690
```

The true sum of these numbers is 0.8506. If the numbers are added starting with the largest number first and adding successively smaller ones while truncating results at three significant digits, the result is

```
0.369
0.337
0.706
0.095          (number truncated to three digits for addition)
0.801
0.048          (number truncated to three digits for addition)
0.849
```

If the numbers are added starting with the smallest number first and adding successively larger ones while truncating results at three significant digits, the result is

```
0.0488
0.0958
0.144          (result truncated to three digits)
0.337
0.481
0.369
0.850
```

The answer depends on the order in which the numbers are added! Note that the answer when adding the smallest numbers first is closer to the truth than the answer when adding the largest numbers first. This condition happens because fewer truncations occur when we add the numbers from smallest to largest than when we add the numbers from largest to smallest.

In general, if a series of numbers are added, they should be added in order from smallest to largest to minimize the inaccuracies caused by truncation and round-off errors.[1] This effect has practical implications for the design of many Fortran functions. Most trigonometric and transcendental functions are actually calculated as the sum of the first few terms of an infinite series. For example, the transcendental function e^x can be calculated from the infinite series

$$e^x = 1 + \frac{x}{1} + \frac{x^2}{2!} + \frac{x^3}{3!} + \frac{x^4}{4!} + \frac{x^5}{5!} + \frac{x^6}{6!} + \cdots \tag{12-1}$$

or

$$e^x = \sum_{n=0}^{\infty} \frac{x^n}{n!} \tag{12-2}$$

---

[1] A similar but smaller effect occurs on a computer that rounds off numbers instead of truncating them. It is still better to add the smaller numbers first, but the difference between adding the larger numbers first and adding the smaller numbers first will be much smaller on a machine that rounds.

2

A computer implementation of this function would include only the first few terms—just enough to attain the desired precision. Let's calculate the first few terms of this infinite series and see what they look like. If $x = 1$, then the series would reduce to

$$e^1 = 1 + \frac{1}{1} + \frac{1}{2!} + \frac{1}{3!} + \frac{1}{4!} + \frac{1}{5!} + \frac{1}{6!} + \cdots$$

$$e^1 = 1 + 1 + 0.5 + 0.166667 + 0.0416667 + 0.008333333 + 0.001388889 + \cdots$$

As you can see, these terms decrease in size rapidly as n increases. If we evaluate the first 12 terms of this series to calculate the value of e^1, we will be adding together numbers of dramatically different sizes. The error in the resulting answer will be minimized if we add the smallest one first and then work back toward the largest ones.

In terms of Fortran code, the following two calculations of e^x are *not* identical. The second one is better than the first, because it minimizes truncation errors.

```
REAL :: exp1 = 0., x = 1.
INTEGER :: i
DO i = 0, 11
   exp1 = exp1 + x**i / factorial(i)
END DO

REAL :: exp1 = 0., x = 1.
INTEGER :: i
DO i = 11, 0, -1
   exp1 = exp1 + x**i / factorial(i)
END DO
```

Good Programming Practice
When adding a large series of real numbers, add them in order from smallest to largest in order to minimize truncation errors.

Errors caused by subtraction of nearly equal numbers

A second source of errors occurs when subtracting two numbers with nearly equal values. If one number is subtracted from another nearly equal number, the resulting number will have less precision than either of the original values. That loss of precision can produce larger errors in later calculations. For example, suppose that we wish to evaluate the following expression with our three-significant-digit computer:

$$w - x + y + z$$

where $w = 0.0256$, $x = 0.0224$, $y = 0.939$, and $z = 0.879$. The correct result of this expression is 1.8212, which to three significant digits is 1.82. On the three-significant-digit computer, the result of this expression will depend on the order in which it is evaluated. In theory, this expression could be evaluated as either

$$(w - x) + (y + z)$$

or

$$(y - x) + (w + z)$$

The result of the first expression is

```
0.0256                  w
-0.0224                  x
0.0032

0.939                   y
0.879                   z
1.81                    (Result truncated to three significant digits)

1.81
0.0032                  (=0 when truncated to three significant digits)
1.81
```

The result of the second expression is

```
0.939                   y
-0.022                  x (Truncated to three digits for addition)
0.917

0.025                   w (Truncated to three digits for addition)
0.879                   z
0.904

0.917                   y - x
0.904                   w + z
1.82                    (Result truncated to three significant digits)
```

The answer depends on the order of the operations! The results were worse when two nearly equal numbers were subtracted and that result was used in further calculations.

In general, the accuracy of an answer will drop when two nearly equal numbers are subtracted. This is especially obvious when the difference between the two numbers is used in the denominator of an expression. We saw that effect dramatically in Example 8–1 while solving for the numerical derivative of a function.

Good Programming Practice
Precision is lost whenever two nearly equal numbers are subtracted, and the result is used in further calculations. If an algorithm requires you to subtract two nearly equal numbers at an intermediate point in the calculation, you may need to perform the calculation using double-precision real arithmetic.

Cumulative errors caused by multiple cascaded operations

A third source of error occurs when the errors in one operation are propagated into a later operation, producing an even larger error in that operation. That error in turn produces even larger errors in later operations in the chain. In other words, the error *propagates* and *grows* during the calculations. Because errors increase with each operation, it pays to keep the number of operations in your algorithms as small as possible.

For example, consider the two expressions $4*a*b$ and $(a+a+a+a)*b$, where $a = 0.568$ and $b = 0.502$. These expressions are theoretically equal to 1.140554, which is 1.14 when truncated to three significant digits. However, when we evaluate the expressions with our three-significant-digit truncating computer, the results are different. The first expression becomes

```
      4.00
   x  0.568
      2.27          (Result truncated to three significant digits)


      2.27
   x  0.502
      1.13          (Result truncated to three significant digits)
```

The second expression becomes

```
      0.568
   +  0.568
      1.13          (Result truncated to three significant digits)
   +  0.56          (Truncated to three significant digits for addition)
      1.69
   +  0.56          (Truncated to three significant digits for addition)
      2.25


      2.25
   x  0.502
      1.12          (Result truncated to three significant digits)
```

Here the expression containing more operations had a larger error than the expression containing fewer operations. It pays to simplify your expressions to contain as few operations as possible.

Good Programming Practice

Wherever possible, simplify your expressions to contain as few operations as possible. The fewer the cascaded operations you perform, the more accurate your final answer will be. You will get the answer faster, too!

We observed the propagation of small errors into successively larger ones while solving simultaneous equations in Chapter 8. Single-precision arithmetic generally worked well for well-conditioned systems containing a small number of equations in a small number of unknowns. However, for larger systems and for ill-conditioned systems, the answers became progressively worse. The larger systems of equations required more arithmetic operations to find solutions than the smaller ones did, so there was more chance for errors to build up during the solution process.

An example: the quadratic equation

The quadratic equation is an excellent tool for illustrating the limits of computer mathematics, since we understand the equation well and have been solving it in exercises since the beginning of the book. We know that the two solutions to a quadratic equation of the form

$$ax^2 + bx + c = 0 \tag{12–3}$$

are

$$x = \frac{-b \pm \sqrt{b^2 - 4ac}}{2a} \tag{12–4}$$

In this book we have written several programs to solve this equation, and they have all appeared to work well. However, they have worked well *only* because the coefficients of the equations have been reasonable values for the capabilities of the single-precision real numbers that were used. For example, the programs can properly calculate the two roots of the equation

$$x^2 - 5x + 4 = 0 \tag{12–5}$$

to be 1.0 and 4.0.

Let's see what happens to the quadratic equation if we use different and more challenging coefficients. Suppose that we try to solve for the roots of the equation

$$10^{30}x^2 - 5 \times 10^{30}x + 4 \times 10^{30} = 0 \tag{12–6}$$

A human can see that this equation is the same as equation (12–5) multiplied by 10^{30}, so he or she can immediately see that the roots of the equation are 1.0 and 4.0. However, when the computer tries to solve the problem with single-precision real arithmetic, both the terms b^2 and $4ac$ produce overflows, and the quadratic equation program aborts. We get no answer at all!

The above equation could be solved by simply dividing each term by 10^{30} before applying equation (12–4), but some other cases cannot be resolved so simply. For example, consider the equation

$$10^{-20}x^2 - 10^{20}x + 10^{20} = 0 \tag{12–7}$$

This equation has one root near to 1.0 and another one near to 10^{40}. If we attempt to plug these coefficients directly into Equation (12–4), the b^2 term will cause an overflow and the program will abort. If we instead divide each term of this equation by 10^{20}, the equation will become

$$10^{-40}x^2 - x + 1 = 0$$

However, single-precision real numbers cannot represent values smaller than about 10^{-38}, so the coefficient of the first term becomes 0 and the equation reduces to

$$-x + 1 = 0$$

This equation correctly finds the root $x = 1.0$, but the other one is lost completely.

Finally, consider the equation

$$x^2 - 10^5x + 1 = 0 \tag{12–8}$$

The roots of this equation are nearly 10^5 and 10^{-5}. If we attempt to plug these coefficients directly into equation (12–4), the expression becomes

$$x = \frac{10^5 \pm \sqrt{(-10^5)^2 - 4}}{2}$$

The expression under the radical becomes $10^{10} - 4$, which is just 10^{10} since most implementations of single precision real numbers only have six to seven significant digits. Therefore the equation becomes

$$x = \frac{10^5 \pm 10^5}{2}$$

and the answers become $x = 10^5$, which is correct, and $x = 0$, which is incorrect! This example shows errors caused by round off followed by the subtraction of two nearly equal numbers.

Equations (12–6), (12–7), and (12–8) illustrate three types of problems that could occur when solving mathematical equations on the computer. In the first case, all the coefficients of the equation were too large, resulting in errors representing the values in the solution to the equation. In the second case, the *range* of the coefficients was too large (10^{-20} to 10^{20}). In the third case, the *precision* of the arithmetic was too small, resulting in round-off errors under the radical. Then the subtraction of two nearly equal numbers produced an incorrect answer.

To mitigate the effects of these mathematical problems, we can try to "work harder," we can try to "work smarter," or both. We can work harder by substituting double-precision real arithmetic for single-precision real arithmetic. Since double-precision numbers have a much higher precision and a much larger range, they will be able to solve many problems that cannot be solved by single-precision numbers. Double-precision real arithmetic would have found acceptable answers for all three examples given above. The cost of using double precision is that programs will be larger and slower. Moreover, double precision numbers have their own range and precision limits. They improve the situation, but they do *not* eliminate round-off and other computer errors.

We can also work smarter by reformulating equations into mathematically equivalent forms that are not as sensitive to the limits of computer mathematics, or by solving the original equations by a different technique that is not as sensitive to the limits of computer mathematics. For example, if the quadratic equation (12–6) were *normalized* by dividing both sides of the equation by 10^{30}, then single precision arithmetic would solve the problem nicely.

Equation (12–7) is harder to solve for because simply normalizing the equation doesn't eliminate the range problems. The roots of this equation would have to be found using double-precision real arithmetic, because the range of the coefficient values (10^{40}) is simply too large to be represented by single-precision arithmetic. We must use double-precision arithmetic to solve this problem.

Equation (12–8) is an example of a large class of problems in which round-off errors followed by subtractions produce wrong answers. These errors are mostly caused by the subtraction of two nearly equal numbers that have been rounded off because of the limitations of the computer. The best way to avoid these problems is to try to modify the algorithm to avoid subtracting the two nearly equal numbers. For the quadratic equation there are two solutions: one produced by addition (which produced the correct answer) and one produced by subtraction (which produced the wrong answer). Although we can use this equation to solve for the answer produced by the addition, but we must find another way to calculate the other root.

Once we know one root of a quadratic equation, we can calculate the other from the well-known mathematical relationship

$$x_1 x_2 = \frac{c}{a} \qquad (12\text{--}9)$$

where x_1 and x_2 are the roots of the equation and c and a are two of the coefficients of the quadratic equation. Therefore, one possible way around the limitations of the computer is to use equation (12–4) only for the root found by addition and then to use equation (12–9) to solve for the other root.

It can be quite difficult to determine the best approach to solving any particular type of problem numerically on a computer. Researchers have been actively working on these problems for more than 40 years, and some high-quality algorithms have been developed. These algorithms have been collected into libraries, some of which are free and some of which must be purchased. In either case, you will write much better programs if you use the robust and well-tested procedures in these libraries to solve numerical problems instead of attempting to write your own solutions from scratch.

Good Programming Practice
Wherever possible, use predeveloped libraries of procedures to solve numerical problems such as simultaneous equations, roots of equations, fits, and so forth. The procedures in these libraries are usually better tested and more reliable than any that you could create from scratch.

12

EXAMPLE 12–1 The Quadratic Equation Revisited: It is possible to produce a more robust subroutine to solve for the roots of a quadratic equation by first normal-izing the equation and then by solving for the roots using the sum term in Equation (12–4) to get the first root, and then using Equation (12–9) to get the second root. Write such a subroutine for the case where the equation has real roots.

SOLUTION To normalize the quadratic equation, we will determine the coefficient with the largest absolute value and divide all the terms in the equation by that value. Then we will apply Equations (12–4) and (12–9) to get the two solutions. We will use the sign for the discriminant in Equation (12–4) that gives the *largest overall absolute value* in order to avoid loss of precision during subtractions. Thus if the quantity $-b$ is positive, then we will add the quantity $\sqrt{b^2 - 4ac}$ to it. If the quantity $-b$ is negative, then we will subtract the quantity $\sqrt{b^2 - 4ac}$ from it.

Note that this subroutine is only supposed to work for the case of real roots, so it must return an error if the equation has complex roots.

1. **State the problem.**

Write a subroutine to solve for the real roots of the quadratic equation

$$ax^2 + bx + c = 0$$

in a manner that is relatively insensitive to numerical errors by first normalizing the equation, then getting the first root from the equation

$$x = \frac{-b + \sqrt{b^2 - 4ac}}{2a}$$

and finally getting the second root from the equation

$$x_2 = \frac{c}{ax_1}$$

If the quadratic equation has complex roots, the subroutine should set an error flag and exit.

2. **Define the inputs and outputs.**

The inputs to this subroutine are the three coefficients of the quadratic equation a, b, and c. The outputs from this subroutine are the roots x_1 and x_2 and an integer variable error. The value of error will be 0 for successful completion and 1 if the equation has complex roots.

3. **Describe the algorithm.**

The basic pseudocode for this subroutine is

```
Normalize equations
Calculate discriminant
IF discriminant is positive THEN
    Calculate first root
    Calculate second root
    Set error to 0
ELSE
    Set error to 1
END of IF
```

The detailed pseudocode for the subroutine is

```
! Normalize equations
big ← MAX( |a|, |b|, |c|)
an ← a / big
bn ← b / big
cn ← c / big

! Calculate discriminant
discriminant ← bn**2 - 4. * an * cn

IF discriminant >= 0 THEN
    IF −bn > 0 THEN
        x1 ← ( −bn + SQRT(discriminant) ) / (2. * an)
    ELSE
        x1 ← ( −bn - SQRT(discriminant) ) / (2. * an)
    END of IF
    x2 ← cn / ( an * x1 )
```

```
      error ← 0
   ELSE
      error ← 1
   END of IF
```

4. **Turn the algorithm into Fortran statements.**

The resulting Fortran subroutine is shown in Figure 12–1.

FIGURE 12–1

Subroutine to calculate the roots of a quadratic equation in a manner that minimizes numerical problems.

```
SUBROUTINE quad ( a, b, c, x1, x2, error )
!
!   Purpose:
!       To solve for the real roots of the quadratic equation
!           a*x**2 + b*x + c = 0
!       in a robust manner by normalizing the coefficients
!       of the equation and avoiding the necessity of
!       subtracting two nearly equal numbers in the solution.
!
!   Record of revisions:
!       Date        Programmer          Description of change
!       ====        ==========          =====================
!     02/08/96    S. J. Chapman         Original code
!
IMPLICIT NONE

! Declare dummy arguments:
REAL, INTENT(IN) :: a             ! Coefficient of x**2
REAL, INTENT(IN) :: b             ! Coefficient of x
REAL, INTENT(IN) :: c             ! Constant coefficient
REAL, INTENT(OUT) :: x1           ! Root 1
REAL, INTENT (OUT) :: x2          ! Root 2
INTEGER, INTENT(OUT) :: error     ! Error flag: 0=no error
                                  !             1=complex roots

! Declare local variables
REAL :: an                 ! Normalized coefficient of x**2
REAL :: big                ! Abs value of largest coef.
REAL :: bn                 ! Normalized coefficient of x
REAL :: cn                 ! Normalized constant coefficient
REAL :: discriminant       ! Discriminant of equation
! Normalize coefficients
big = MAX ( ABS(a), ABS(b), ABS(c) )
an = a / big
bn = b / big
cn = c / big

! Calculate discriminant
discriminant = bn**2 - 4.*an*cn

! Get roots
IF ( discriminant >= 0 ) THEN
   IF ( -bn > 0 ) THEN
      x1 = ( -bn + SQRT(discriminant) ) / (2. * an)
   ELSE
      x1 = ( -bn - SQRT(discriminant) ) / (2. * an)
   END IF
```

(continued)

12

(concluded)

```
      x2 = cn / (an * x1 )
      error = 0
ELSE
      error = 1
END IF

END SUBROUTINE quad
```

5. Test the program.

We must develop a test driver program in order to test this subroutine. The program should read the input coefficients, call subroutine quad, and display the results. A suitable test driver program is shown in Figure 12–2.

FIGURE 12–2
The test driver program for subroutine quad.

```
PROGRAM test_quad
!
!   Purpose:
!     To test subroutine quad, which calculates the roots of
!     a quadratic equation in a more robust fashion.
!
!   Record of revisions:
!       Date        Programmer          Description of change
!       ====        ==========          =====================
!     02/08/96     S. J. Chapman        Original code
!
IMPLICIT NONE

! List of variables:
REAL :: a                ! Coefficient of x**2
REAL :: b                ! Coefficient of x
REAL :: c                ! Constant coefficient
REAL :: x1               ! Root 1
REAL :: x2               ! Root 2
INTEGER :: error         ! Error flag: 0 = no error
                         !             1 = complex roots
! Prompt user and get the coefficients.
WRITE (*,1000)
1000 FORMAT (1X, 'This program finds the roots of the quadratic ',/, &
             1X, 'equation a*x**2 + b*x + c = 0.  Please enter ',/, &
             1X, 'a, b, and c: ')
READ (*,*) a, b, c

! Get roots
CALL quad ( a, b, c, x1, x2, error )

! Write results.
IF ( error == 0 ) THEN
   WRITE (*,*) 'The roots are: '
   WRITE (*,'(A,ES15.7)') ' x1 = ', x1
   WRITE (*,'(A,ES15.7)') ' x2 = ', x2
ELSE
   WRITE (*,'(A,I2)') ' Error in subroutine quad = ', error
END IF

END PROGRAM
```

To properly test subroutine `quad`, we need to call it with both data sets with real roots and data sets with complex roots. The data sets with real roots should include both simple examples and hard to solve examples. We will test the subroutine with the following data sets:

1. $x^2 - 5x + 4 = 0$

    This is a simple quadratic equation with two real roots at $x = 1$ and $x = 4$. These roots should be easy to find with any quadratic equation solving program.

2. $10^{30}x^2 - 5 \times 10^{30}x + 4 \times 10^{30} = 0$

    This example is a scaled version of the previous equation. These large numbers would cause overflow errors in the straightforward quadratic equation program.

3. $10^{-20}x^2 - 5 \times 10^{-20}x + 4 \times 10^{-20} = 0$

    This example is also a scaled version of the first equation. These small numbers would cause underflows in the straightforward quadratic equation program, and that program would give the incorrect results $x_1 = x_2 = 2.5$ with no warning that anything was wrong.

4. $x^2 - 10^5 x + 1 = 0$

    This example has two roots at about $x_1 = 10^5$ and $x_2 = 10^{-5}$. The straightforward quadratic equation program has trouble with it because $b^2 >> 4ac$, and none of the significant digits of $4ac$ survive after the subtraction.

5. $x^2 - 5x + 10 = 0$

    This data set has complex roots, since the discriminant is negative.

The results when calling the subroutine with these five equations follow.

```
C>test_quad

This program finds the roots of the quadratic
equation a*x**2 + b*x + c = 0. Please enter
a, b, and c:
1.   -5.   4.

The roots are:
  x1 =    4.0000000E+00
  x2 =    1.0000000E+00

C>test_quad

This program finds the roots of the quadratic
equation a*x**2 + b*x + c = 0. Please enter
a, b, and c:
1.E30   -5.E30   4.E30

The roots are:
  x1 =    3.9999998E+00
  x2 =    1.0000001E+00

C>test_quad
```

12

```
This program finds the roots of the quadratic
equation a*x**2 + b*x + c = 0. Please enter
a, b, and c:
1.E-20  -5.E-20  4.E-20

The roots are:
  x1 =   4.0000000E+00
  x2 =   1.0000000E+00

C>test_quad

This program finds the roots of the quadratic
equation a*x**2 + b*x + c = 0. Please enter
a, b, and c:
1.0  1.0E5  1.0

The roots are:
  x1 =  -1.0000000E+05
  x2 =  -9.9999997E-06

C>test_quad

This program finds the roots of the quadratic
equation a*x**2 + b*x + c = 0. Please enter
a, b, and c:
1.0  -5.0  10.0

Error in subroutine quad = 1
```

The program seems to be working correctly for these inputs. You should try these same values in the original quadratic equation program developed in Chapter 3 to see how much better this routine functions than a straightforward implementation of Equation (12–4).

12.1.2 Errors Caused by Incorrect Models

Another common source of errors in computer programs is the use of *inappropriate models* to analyze data. For example, consider least-squares fits. You learned in earlier chapters how to calculate the line that "best fits" a data set. But what if the behavior of the input data set is not linear? In that case the least-squares fit line will be meaningless.

A falling ball provides a very good illustration of this problem. Suppose that we make noisy measurements of the position and velocity of a ball as it falls after it has been thrown downward from a 50-meter height. Since the measurements are noisy, we would like to perform a fit to the data to get a better feel for the position and velocity of the ball as a function of time. The following measurements are made as the ball falls to the ground:

TABLE 12–1

Measured position and velocity of ball versus time

Time (sec)	Position (m)	Velocity (m/s)
0.167	49.9	−5.1

(continued)

(concluded)

Time (sec)	Position (m)	Velocity (m/s)
0.333	52.2	−12.9
0.500	50.6	−15.1
0.667	47.0	−6.8
0.833	47.7	−12.3
1.000	42.3	−18.0
1.167	37.9	−5.7
1.333	38.2	−6.3
1.500	38.0	−12.7
1.667	33.8	−13.7
1.833	26.7	−26.7
2.000	24.8	−31.3
2.167	22.0	−22.9
2.333	16.5	−25.6
2.500	14.0	−25.7
2.667	5.6	−25.2
2.833	2.9	−35.0
3.000	0.8	−27.9

Note that the velocity measurements appear to be noisier than the position measurements. This result is true because the instrument used to measure velocity was not as accurate as the instrument used to measure position.

The velocity data is plotted as a function of time in Figure 12–3*a*. There is a lot of scatter in this data set, but it does appear to follow a roughly linear trend. More important, we *know* from elementary physics that the velocity of a ball thrown in the presence of a uniform gravitational field should be given by the equation

$$v(t) = a\,t + v_o \tag{12–10}$$

If we do a linear least-squares fit to this data, the result is

$$v(t) = -8.69\,t - 4.53 \tag{12–11}$$

which, considering the high noise level in the data, is in fairly good agreement with the actual conditions under which the ball was dropped. (The actual acceleration was -10 m/s^2, and the actual initial velocity was -2 m/s.)

The measured position data is plotted as a function of time in Figure 12–3*b*. There is somewhat less noise on this data set, since it was easier for us to measure position than it was to measure velocity during this particular experiment. If we do a linear least-squares fit to this data, the resulting fit is

$$y(t) = -18.87\,t + 60.47 \tag{12–12}$$

This fit is shown in Figure 12–3*b,* and it even looks reasonable. However, it is complete garbage!

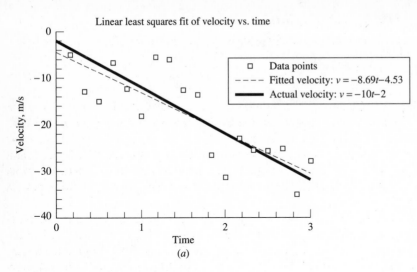

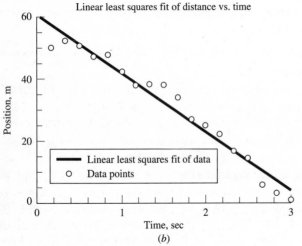

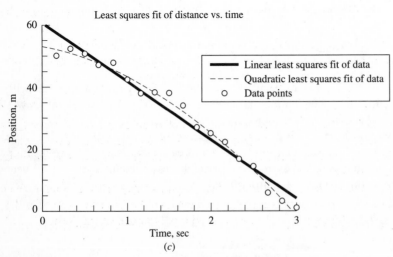

FIGURE 12–3

(*a*) Measured velocity of a ball as a function of time after it is thrown. Both the line corresponding to theoretical velocity of the ball and the least-squares fit of the velocity are shown. (*b*) Measured position of the ball as a function of time after it is thrown, together with a linear least-squares fit through the data. (*c*) Measured position of the ball as a function of time after it is thrown, together with a quadratic least-squares fit through the data.

12

We know from elementary physics that the position of a ball thrown in the presence of a uniform gravitational field is given by the equation

$$y(t) = \frac{1}{2}a\,t^2 + v_0\,t + y_0 \qquad (12\text{–}13)$$

The position of the ball as a function of time is a *quadratic* function, not a linear function. Therefore, fitting a straight line to the data is both meaningless and misleading. It is a case of garbage in, garbage out!

To properly analyze this data set, we must fit it to a parabola instead of a straight line. We will develop a technique to perform a least-squares fit to a parabola in an example later in this chapter. The position data is shown together with a best-fit parabola in Figure 12–3c.

The linear least-squares fit to the position data in Equation (12–12) is invalid. If we used it to estimate the position of the ball at time $t = 1.2$ s, we would add an additional error to our estimate because the model itself is inaccurate. Programmers must be constantly alert to recognize problems of this sort. Before attempting to write any program, they should be certain that they understand the theory behind the program well enough to detect model-based flaws.

Good Programming Practice

Think carefully about what you want to do *before* you start programming. Pay attention to the types of models appropriate to the data that you are working with. Otherwise, garbage in will yield garbage out!

EXAMPLE 12–2 Higher-Order Least-Squares Fits: As we saw in the preceding discussion, it does not make sense to perform a linear least-squares fit to a data set known in advance not to be linear. Instead, the data values should be fitted to the shape that they are theoretically expected to have. For example, the position of a falling ball as a function of time should be fitted to a parabola, since we know from elementary physics that the position of the ball will change quadratically with time.

It is possible to extend the idea of least-squares fits to find the best (in a least-squares sense) fit to a polynomial more complicated than a straight line. Any polynomial may be represented by an equation of the form

$$y(x) = c_0 + c_1 x + c_2 x^2 + c_3 x^3 + c_4 x^4 + \cdots \qquad (12\text{–}14)$$

where the order of the polynomial corresponds to the highest power of x appearing in the polynomial. To perform a least-squares fit to a polynomial of order n, we must solve for the coefficients $c_0, c_1, \ldots, c_n$ that minimize the error between the polynomial and the data points being fit.

The polynomial being fitted to the data may be of any order as long as there are at least as many distinct data points as there are coefficients to solve for. For example, the data may be fitted to a first-order polynomial of the form

$$y(x) = c_0 + c_1 x$$

as long as there are at least two distinct data points in the fit. This equation is the equation for a straight line, where c_0 is the intercept of the line and c_1 is the slope of the line. Similarly, the data may be fitted to a second-order polynomial of the form

$$y(x) = c_0 + c_1 x + c_2 x^2$$

as long as there are at least three distinct data points in the fit. This equation is a quadratic expression whose shape is parabolic.

It can be shown[2] that the coefficients of a linear least-squares fit to the polynomial $y(x) = c_0 + c_1 x$ are the solutions of the following system of equations

$$N c_0 + \left(\sum x\right) c_1 = \sum y$$

$$\left(\sum x\right) c_0 + \left(\sum x^2\right) c_1 = \sum xy$$
(12–15)

where

(x_i, y_i) is the ith sample measurement.
N is the number of sample measurements included in the fit.
$\sum x$ is the sum of the x_i values of all measurements.
$\sum x^2$ is the sum of the squares of the x_i values of all measurements.
$\sum xy$ is the sum of the products of the corresponding x_i and y_i values.

Any number of sample measurements (x_i, y_i) may be used in the fit, as long as the number of measurements is greater than or equal to 2. In exercise 12–4 at the end of this chapter, you will be asked to prove that the solution to Equations (12–15) is equivalent to Equations (4–5) and (4–6), which we have been using to perform linear least-square fits.

The formulation shown above can be extended to fits of higher-order polynomials. For example, we can show that the coefficients of a least-squares fit to the second-order polynomial $y(x) = c_0 + c_1 x + c_2 x^2$ are the solutions of the following system of equations

$$N c_0 + \left(\sum x\right) c_1 + \left(\sum x^2\right) c_2 = \sum y$$

$$\left(\sum x\right) c_0 + \left(\sum x^2\right) c_1 + \left(\sum x^3\right) c_2 = \sum xy$$
(12–16)

$$\left(\sum x^2\right) c_0 + \left(\sum x^3\right) c_1 + \left(\sum x^4\right) c_2 = \sum x^2 y$$

where the various terms have meanings similar to the ones described above. Any number of sample measurements (x_i, y_i) may be used in the fit, as long as the number of distinct measurements is greater than or equal to 3. The least-squares fit of the data to a parabola can be found by solving equations (12–16) for c_0, c_1, and c_2.

---

[2] A. Papoulis, *Probability and Statistics* (Prentice-Hall, 1990), pp. 392–393.

The same idea can be extended to fitting polynomials of any order. To fit data to a polynomial of order n, the user must solve an $n \times n$ set of simultaneous equations, and must have at least n distinct sample measurements (x_i, y_i). The general case of fitting an nth order polynomial to a data set is considered in exercise 12–5 at the end of this chapter.

For this example, we will create a subroutine to perform a least-squares fit to a second-order polynomial (a parabola), and we will use that subroutine to fit a parabola to the position data contained in Table 12–1.

SOLUTION The least-squares fit subroutine will have to calculate the coefficients of c_0, c_1, and c_2 and the constants on the right side of equations 12–16. It can then call subroutine `simul` to actually solve for the coefficients c_0, c_1, and c_2. The subroutine will have to check for two possible error conditions: not enough input data and singular equations.

1. **State the problem.**

Write a subroutine to perform a least-squares fit to a second-order polynomial (a parabola) of the form

$$y(x) = c_0 + c_1 x + c_2 x^2$$

The subroutine should accept an array of input points (x_i, y_i) to be fit. The input points will be divided into separate x and y arrays. The subroutine should test to ensure that the input array has at least three points. The subroutine should report an error if insufficient data is available or if the set of simultaneous equations is singular.

2. **Define the inputs and outputs.**

The inputs to this subroutine are

a. Two arrays of input points x and y to be fitted.
b. The number of values nvals in the x and y arrays.

The outputs from this subroutine are an array c containing the coefficients of the polynomial c(0), c(1), and c(2), and an error flag error. If the fit is successful, error should be 0. If simultaneous equations are singular, error should be 1; if there are fewer than three input points, error should be 2.

3. **Describe the algorithm.**

This program can be broken down into four major steps:

```
Check to see that there is sufficient input data
Build the coefficients of the simultaneous equations
Solve the simultaneous equations
Return the coefficients of the polynomial
```

The first step of the program is to check that there is enough data to perform the fit. If three points are not available, then we will set the error flag to 2 and get out at once. If there is enough data, then we must build the coefficients for the simultaneous equations. This step is divided into two parts: calculating the sums used as coefficients and assigning the proper sum to each coefficient. Next, we will call subroutine `simul` to solve for the coefficients of the equation. Finally, those coefficients will be returned to the calling program.

The detailed pseudocode for the subroutine follows. Note that the terms $\sum x^0$ is just `nvals` and the sum $\sum x^0 y$ is just $\sum y$. These terms are written as shown to make the summation and array section manipulation easier.

```
IF nvals < 3 Then
   error ← 2
ELSE
   ! Build sums as follows:
   Clear sums
   DO for j = 1 to nvals
      DO for i = 0 to 4
         sum_xi(i) = sum_xi(i) + x(j)**i
      END DO
      DO for i = 0 to 2
         sum_xiy(i) = sum_xiy(i) + x(j)**i + y(j)
      END DO
   END of DO
   ! Now assign sums to coefficients of equations
   a(:,1) = sum_xi(0:2)
   a(:,2) = sum_xi(1:3)
   a(:,3) = sum_xi(2:4)
   b(:) = sum_xiy(0:2)
   CALL simul ( a, b, soln, 3, 3, error )
   ! Was the solution successful?
   IF error == 0 THEN
      c ← soln
   ELSE
      c ← 0.
   END of IF
END of IF
```

4. **Turn the algorithm into Fortran statements.**

The resulting Fortran subroutine is shown in Figure 12–4. Note that the least-squares fit subroutine calls the version of subroutine `simul` that does not destroy its input coefficients. (This version was developed in Example 6–6.)

FIGURE 12–4
Subroutine `lsq_fit_2` to perform a least-squares fit to a parabola.

```
SUBROUTINE lsq_fit_2 ( x, y, nvals, c, error )
!
!  Purpose:
!    To perform a least-squares fit of an input data set
!    to the parabola
!        y(x) = c(0) + c(1) * x + c(2) * x**2,
!    and return the resulting coefficients. The input
!    data set consists of nvals (x,y) pairs contained in
!    arrays x and y. The output coefficients of the
!    quadratic fit c0, c1, and c2 are placed in array c.
!
!  Record of revisions:
!    Date        Programmer          Description of change
!    ====        ==========          =====================
!    02/10/96    S. J. Chapman       Original code
```

(continued)

(concluded)

```
!
IMPLICIT NONE

! Declare dummy arguments:
INTEGER, INTENT(IN) :: nvals              ! Number of input data pts
REAL, DIMENSION(nvals), INTENT(IN) :: x   ! Input x values
REAL, DIMENSION(nvals), INTENT(IN) :: y   ! Input y values
REAL, DIMENSION(0:2), INTENT(OUT) :: c    ! Coefficients of fit
INTEGER, INTENT(OUT) :: error             ! Error flag:
                                          !  0 = No error.
                                          !  1 = Singular eqns
                                          !  2 = Insufficient data

! Declare local variables:
REAL, DIMENSION(3,3) :: a        ! Coefficients of eqn to solve
REAL, DIMENSION(3) :: b          ! Right side of coefficient eqns
INTEGER :: i, j                  ! Index variable
REAL, DIMENSION(0:2) :: soln     ! Solution vector
REAL, DIMENSION(0:4) :: sum_xi   ! Sum of x**i values
REAL, DIMENSION(0:2) :: sum_xiy  ! Sum of x**i*y values

! First, check to make sure that we have enough input data.
check_data: IF ( nvals < 3 ) THEN

   ! Insufficient data.  Set error = 2, and get out.
   error = 2
ELSE

   sum_xi = 0.                   ! Clear sums
   sum_xiy = 0.

   ! Build the sums required to solve the equations.
   sums: DO j = 1, nvals
      DO i = 0, 4
         sum_xi(i) = sum_xi(i) + x(j)**i
      END DO
      DO i = 0, 2
         sum_xiy(i) = sum_xiy(i) + x(j)**i * y(j)
      END DO
   END DO sums

   ! Set up the coefficients of the equations.
   a(:,1) = sum_xi(0:2)
   a(:,2) = sum_xi(1:3)
   a(:,3) = sum_xi(2:4)
   b(:) = sum_xiy(0:2)

   ! Solve for the least squares fit coefficients. They will
   ! be returned in array b if error = 0.
   CALL simul ( a, b, soln, 3, 3, error )

   ! If error == 0, return the coefficients to the user.
   return: IF ( error == 0 ) THEN
      c = soln
   ELSE
      c = 0.
   END IF return
END IF check_data

END SUBROUTINE lsq_fit_2
```

12

5. Test the program.

We must develop a test driver program in order to test this subroutine. The program should read the input points from a data file, call subroutine `lsq_fit_2`, and report the results of the fit. A suitable test driver program is shown in Figure 12–5.

FIGURE 12–5

The test driver program for subroutine `lsq_fit_2`.

```
PROGRAM test_lsq_fit_2
!
!  Purpose:
!    To test subroutine lsq_fit_2, which performs a least-
!    squares fit to a parabola. The input data for this fit
!    comes from a user-specified input data file.
!
!  Record of revisions:
!     Date          Programmer          Description of change
!     ====          ==========          =====================
!   02/13/96    S. J. Chapman           Original code
!
IMPLICIT NONE

! List of parameters:
INTEGER, PARAMETER :: lu = 12            ! Unit for file i/o
INTEGER, PARAMETER :: max_vals = 1000    ! Maximum data pts

! List of variables:
REAL, DIMENSION(0:2) :: c        ! Coefficients of fit
INTEGER :: error                 ! Error flag
LOGICAL :: exceed = .FALSE.      ! Logical indicating that array
                                 ! limits are exceeded.
CHARACTER(1en=20) :: filename    ! Input data file name
INTEGER :: istat                 ! Status: 0 for success
INTEGER :: nvals = 0             ! Number of values read
REAL :: t1, t2                   ! Temporary vars for read
REAL, DIMENSION(max_vals) :: x   ! x values of (x,y) pairs
REAL, DIMENSION(max_vals) :: y   ! y values of (x,y) pairs

! Prompt user and get the name of the input file.
WRITE (*,1000)
1000 FORMAT (1X,'This program performs a least-squares fit of an ',/, &
             1X,'input data set to a parabola. Enter the name ',/, &
             1X,'of the file containing the input (x,y) pairs: ')
READ (*,'(A)') filename

! Open the input file
OPEN (UNIT=lu, FILE=filename, STATUS='OLD', ACTION='READ', &
      IOSTAT=istat )

! Was the OPEN successful?
fileopen: IF ( istat == 0 ) THEN          ! Open successful

   ! The file was opened successfully, so read the data,
   input: DO
      READ (lu,*,IOSTAT=istat) t1, t2    ! Get values
```

(continued)

(concluded)

```
          IF ( istat /= 0 ) EXIT          ! Exit on end of data
          nvals = nvals + 1               ! Bump count
          size: IF ( nvals <= max_vals ) THEN ! Too many values?
             x(nvals) = t1                ! No: Save values
             y(nvals) = t2                ! No: Save values
          ELSE
             exceed = .TRUE.                    ! Yes: Array overflow
          END IF size
       END DO input

       ! Was the array size exceeded? If so, tell user and quit.
       toobig: IF ( exceed ) THEN
          WRITE (*,1010) nvals, max_vals
          1010 FORMAT (' Max array size exceeded: ', I6, ' > ', I6 )
       ELSE

          ! Limit not exceeded: fit data to parabola.
          CALL lsq_fit_2 ( x, y, nvals, c, error )

          ! Tell user about results of fit.
          fit_error: IF ( error == 0 ) THEN
             WRITE (*, 1020 ) c, nvals
             1020 FORMAT ('0', 'Regression coefficients for the ', &
                          'least-squares fit parabola: ', &
                          /,1X,' c(0)  = ', F12.3, &
                          /,1X,' c(1)  = ', F12.3, &
                          /,1X,' c(2)  = ', F12.3, &
                          /,1X,' nvals = ', I12 )
          ELSE
             WRITE (*,"(' Error from lsq_fit_2: ', I6 )") error
          END IF fit_error
       END IF toobig

   ELSE fileopen

       ! Else file open failed. Tell user.
       WRITE (*,1030) istat
       1030 FORMAT (1X, 'File open failed—status = ', I6)

   END IF fileopen
END PROGRAM
```

To properly test subroutine `lsq_fit_2`, we need to call it with three different data sets:

1. A valid data set with a known answer.
2. An invalid data set that produces a singular set of equations.
3. An invalid data set with too few input data points.

The program must be able to correctly handle all three cases. For the first data set, let's place five points exactly fitting the equation $y(x) = 1 + x + \dfrac{1}{2} x^2$ into a file called LSQFT21:

-1.0	0.5
0.0	1.0
1.0	2.5

```
                              3.0          8.5
                              2.0          5.0
```

If we call program `test_lsq_fit_2` with this data set, the results are

```
C>test_lsq_fit_2
This program performs a least-squares fit of an
input data set to a parabola. Enter the name
of the file containing the input (x,y) pairs:
lsqft21

Regression coefficients for the least-squares fit parabola:
  c(0)  =        1.000
  c(1)  =        1.000
  c(2)  =         .500
  nvals =            5
```

For the second data set, let's place three points in a file LSQFT22 but make two of them duplicates of each other. In this case there will be three input points, but they will represent only two distinct locations along the parabola. Since a minimum of three independent variables are required to solve a set of three equations in three unknowns, this data set should produce a singular set of equations:

```
                              1.1          4.4
                              1.1          4.4
                              3.0          4.0
```

If we call program `test_lsq_fit_2` with this data set, the results are

```
C>test_lsq_fit_2
This program performs a least-squares fit of an
input data set to a parabola. Enter the name
of the file containing the input (x,y) pairs:
LSQFT22
Error returned from lsq_ft_2:          1
```

Finally, let place two points in the LSQFT23. Since there is not enough data to fit the parabola, the program ought to return with the error code set to 2.

```
                              0.0          0.5
                              3.0          1.0
```

If we call program TLSQF2 with this data set, the results are

```
C>test_lsq_fit_2
This program performs a least-squares fit of an
input data set to a parabola. Enter the name
of the file containing the input (x,y) pairs:
LSQFT23
Error returned from lsq_fit_2:          2
```

The program seems to be working correctly for all possible input cases.

We can use this program to fit the time and position data from Table 12–1 to a parabola, which we know from physics should be the proper shape for this data set. If the time and position data in Table 12–1 are placed in file LSQPOS and the program is run, the results are

```
C>test_lsq_fit_2
This program performs a least-squares fit of an
input data set to a parabola. Enter the name
of the file containing the input (x,y) pairs:
LSQPOS

Regression coefficients for the least-squares fit parabola:
     c(0)  =        53.133
     c(1)  =        -5.618
     c(2)  =        -4.189
     nvals =            18
```

This curve is plotted in Figure 12–3c. As you can see, it does fit the data pretty well.

■ 12.2

NUMERICAL APPLICATIONS

In this section we will design a few procedures that have practical engineering and scientific applications. We have already seen a number of such procedures. Chapter 6 included statistics subroutines, sorting subroutines, simultaneous equation solvers, and random number generators; Chapter 7 introduced plotting subroutines; and Chapter 8 included subroutines to take the derivative of a function and to solve larger or ill-conditioned systems of simultaneous equations. Versions of the binary tree developed in Chapter 11 also have many applications in science and engineering.

We will now develop additional procedures that integrate user-specified functions and that find the real roots of equations. These subroutines are straightforward implementations that will solve many practical problems, but the subroutines have significant limitations. More sophisticated procedures for solving these types of problems are available either free or for purchase from many different vendors.

12

12.2.1 Numerical Integration—Finding the Area under a Curve

We learned how to take the numerical derivative of a function in Chapter 8. The derivative of a function is defined by the equation

$$\frac{d}{dx}f(x) = \lim_{\Delta x \to 0} \frac{f(x + \Delta x) - f(x)}{\Delta x} \tag{8–1}$$

The derivative of a function $f(x)$ at a point x_0 may be interpreted as the slope of the function at that point.

In contrast, the definite integral of a function $f(x)$ may be interpreted as the total area under the curve of the function between a starting point and an ending point. Figure 12–6a shows a function $f(x)$ plotted as a function of x. The area under this curve between points x_1 and x_2 is equal to the definite integral of the function $f(x)$ with respect to x between points x_1 and x_2. The calculation of a definite integral by numerical methods is known as *numerical quadrature*. How can we find this area?

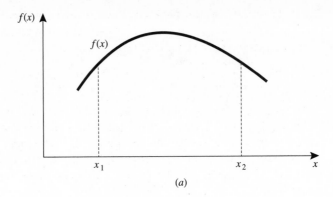

(a)

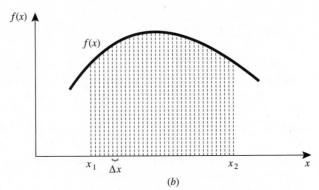

(b)

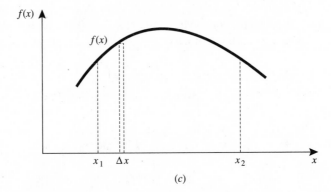

(c)

FIGURE 12–6

(a) A plot of $f(x)$ versus x. The area under this curve between points x_1 and x_2 is equal to $\int_{x_1}^{x_2} f(x)\,dx$. (b) The area under the curve between points x_1 and x_2 divided into many small rectangles. (c) Each rectangle is Δx wide and $f(x_i)$ high, where x_i is the center of rectangle i. The area of the rectangle is $area = f(x_i)\Delta x$.

In general, we do not know the area under a curve of arbitrary shape. However, we *do* know the area of a rectangle. The area of a rectangle is just equal to the length of the rectangle times its width:

$$\text{area} = \text{length} \times \text{width}$$

Suppose that we fill the entire area under the curve between points x_1 and x_2 with a series of small rectangles and then add up the areas of each of the rectangles. If we do so, then we will have an estimate of the area under the curve $f(x)$. Figure 12–6b shows the area under the curve filled with many small rectangles, each of width Δx and length $f(x_i)$, where x_i is the position of the rectangle along the x-axis. Adding up the area in these rectangles gives us an approximate equation for the area under the curve

$$A \approx \sum_{x_1}^{x_2} f(x)\,\Delta x \tag{12–17}$$

The area calculated by Equation (12–17) is only approximate, since the rectangles do not exactly match the shape of the curve that they are approximating. However, the more rectangles that the area under the curve is divided into, the better the resulting fit will be (compare Figure 12–6b with Figure 12–7). If we use an infinite number of infinitely thin rectangles, we could calculate the area under the curve precisely. In fact, that is the definition of integration! An integral is the sum given by equation (12–17) in the limit as Δx gets very small and the number of rectangles gets very large.

$$\int f(x)\,dx = \lim_{\Delta x \to 0} \sum f(x)\,\Delta x \tag{12–18}$$

12

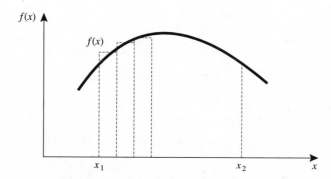

FIGURE 12–7
When the area under the curve is divided into only a few rectangles, the rectangles do not match the shape of the curve as closely as when the area under the curve is divided into many rectangles. Compare this figure to Figure 12–6b.

Example 12–3 Numerical Integration (Numerical Quadrature): Write a subroutine to find the area under a curve $f(x)$ between two points x_1 and x_2, where $x_1 \leq x_2$. (Or expressed in terms of calculus, write a subroutine to calculate the definite integral of the function $f(x)$ between two points x_1 and x_2). The subroutine should allow the user to specify the function to be integrated and the step size Δx as calling arguments.

Solution This subroutine should divide the area under the curve into N rectangles, each of which is Δx wide and $f(x_c)$ tall (where x_c is the value of x at the center of the rectangle). It should then sum up the areas of the rectangles and return the result. The number of rectangles N is given by

$$N = \frac{x_2 - x_1}{\Delta x} \tag{12–19}$$

The value of N should be rounded up to the next whole integer. If N is rounded up, then the last interval will be less than Δx wide.

1. **State the problem.**

   Write a subroutine to find the area under a curve of $f(x)$ [integrate $f(x)$] between two points x_1 and x_2, where $x_1 \leq x_2$, using rectangles to approximate the area under the curve. The subroutine should allow the user to specify the function to be integrated, the step size Δx, and the starting and ending values of the integral as calling arguments.

2. **Determine the inputs and outputs.**

   The inputs to this subroutine are

   a. The function $f(x)$ to integrate.
   b. The step size Δx.
   c. The starting value x_1.
   d. The ending value x_2.

   The outputs from this subroutine are

   a. The area `area` under the curve.
   b. An error flag `error`.

3. **Describe the algorithm.**

   This subroutine can be broken down into three major steps:

   ```
   Check to see that x₁ ≤ x₂
   Calculate the number of rectangles to use
   Add up the area of the rectangles
   ```

   The first step of the program is to check that $x_1 \leq x_2$. If it is not, an error flag should be set and the subroutine should return to the calling program. The second step is to calculate the number of rectangles to use using Equation (12–19). The third step is to calculate the area of each rectangle and to add up all the areas. The detailed pseudocode for these steps is

```
                              IF x1 > x2 Then
                                  error ← 1
                              ELSE
                                  error ← 0.
                                  area ← 0.
                                  n ← INT( (x2-x1) / dx + 1. )
                                  DO for i = 1 to n
                                      xstart ← x1 + REAL(i-1) * dx
                                      width ← MIN (dx, x2 - xstart )
                                      height ← f( xstart + width/2. )
                                      area ← area + width * height
                                  END of DO
                              END of IF
```

Note that the starting position `xstart` of rectangle `i` can be found from the starting position of the integration plus `i-1` steps of `dx` each, since `i-1` rectangles have preceded rectangle `i`. The width of each rectangle is `dx` except for the last one, which may be smaller. (The `MIN` function assures that the last rectangle will have the proper width.) Finally, the height of the rectangle is calculated to be the size of function `f` at the center of the rectangle.

4. **Turn the algorithm into Fortran statements.**

The resulting Fortran subroutine is shown in Figure 12–8.

FIGURE 12–8

Subroutine `integrate`.

```
SUBROUTINE integrate ( f, x1, x2, dx, area, error )
!
!   Purpose:
!     To integrate function f(x) between x1 and x2 using
!     rectangles of width dx to approximate the area
!     under the curve f(x).
!
!   Record of revisions:
!       Date      Programmer        Description of change
!       ====      ==========        =====================
!     02/15/96    S. J. Chapman     Original code
!
IMPLICIT NONE

! Declare calling arguments:
REAL, EXTERNAL :: f               ! Function to integrate
REAL, INTENT(IN) :: x1            ! Starting point for integral
REAL, INTENT(IN) :: x2            ! Ending point for integral
REAL, INTENT(IN) :: dx            ! Step size
REAL, INTENT(OUT) :: area         ! Area under the curve
INTEGER, INTENT(OUT) :: error     ! Error flag:
                                  !   0 = No error
                                  !   1 = x1 > x2

! Declare local variables:
REAL :: height                    ! Height of rectangle
INTEGER :: i                      ! Index variable
INTEGER :: n                      ! Number of rectangles to integrate
REAL :: width                     ! Width of rectangle
```

(continued)

(concluded)

```
REAL :: xstart                    ! Starting position of rectangle

! First, check to make sure that x1 <= x2.
errchk: IF ( x1 > x2 ) THEN
   error = 1
ELSE
   ! Clear error flag and area.
   error = 0
   area = 0

   ! Calculate the number of intervals to use.
   n = INT( (x2-x1) / dx + 1. )

   ! Calculate and sum the areas of each rectangle.
   sum: DO i = 1, n
      xstart = x1 + REAL (i-1) * dx
      width  = MIN ( dx, x2 - xstart )
      height = f( xstart + width/2. )
      area   = area + width * height
   END DO sum
END IF errchk

END SUBROUTINE integrate
```

5. Test the program.

We must develop a test driver program and a test function to integrate in order to test this subroutine. The test function should be something whose integral can be calculated analytically for comparison with the subroutine output. For this case we will integrate the function $f(x) = 3x^2 + 0.5$ from $x_1 = 0$ to $x_2 = 3$. The test driver program and function are shown in Figure 12–9.

FIGURE 12–9
The test driver program for subroutine integrate.

```
PROGRAM test_integrate
!
!  Purpose:
!    To test subroutine integrate, which integrates a function.
!    The function to be integrated is passed to the subroutine
!    as a calling argument. This driver routine will integrate
!    the function with step sizes dx of 1.0, 0.5, 0.1, 0.05,
!    and 0.01.
!
!  Record of revisions:
!      Date        Programmer          Description of change
!      ====        ==========          =====================
!    02/15/96    S. J. Chapman         Original code
!
IMPLICIT NONE

! List of variables:
REAL, DIMENSION(7) :: area       ! Area under the curve
REAL, DIMENSION(7) :: dx         ! Step size
INTEGER :: error                 ! Error flag
```

(continued)

(concluded)

```
INTEGER :: i                    ! Index variable
REAL :: x1 = 0.                 ! Starting point for integral
REAL :: x2 = 3.                 ! Ending point for integral

! Declare the external function being passed to subroutine
! INTEG1.
REAL, EXTERNAL :: test_fun

! Initialize step sizes
dx = (/ 1., 0.5, 0.1, 0.05, 0.01, 0.005, 0.001 /)

! Call subroutine "integrate" with each step size, and print
! out the results.
DO i = 1, 7
   CALL integrate ( test_fun, x1, x2, dx(i), area(i), error )
END DO

! Write out results.
WRITE (*,1000)
1000 FORMAT ('0',' Step Size',5X,'Area',/, &
             ' ',' =========',5X,'====')

DO i = 1, 7
   WRITE (*,'(1X,F9.4,3X,F9.4)') dx(i), area(i)
END DO

END PROGRAM
REAL FUNCTION test_fun(x)
!
!  Purpose:
!     Function to be integrated.
!
IMPLICIT NONE

REAL, INTENT(IN) :: x

! Evaluate function.
test_fun = 3 * x**2 + 0.5

END FUNCTION test_fun
```

The analytic solution to this problem is

$$\int_0^3 (3x^2 + 0.5)\, dx = (x^3 + 0.5x)\Big|_0^3 = 27 + 1.5 = 28.5$$

If we call program test_integrate, the results are

```
C>test_integrate
```

Step Size	Area
=========	====
1.0000	27.7500
.5000	28.3125
.1000	28.4925
.0500	28.4981
.0100	28.4999
.0050	28.5000
.0010	28.5000

Notice that the smaller the step size became, the closer the final answer was to the truth. However, the smaller the step size, the longer it takes to calculate the integral. At some point, a smaller step size no longer makes sense. For example, changing the step size from 0.01 to 0.005 doubled the work required to calculate the answer but only changed the least-significant digit of the number! A step size of 0.01 would probably have been good enough for this function.

Many techniques for determining the area under a curve are more sophisticated than simply dividing the area into rectangles and summing the area of each rectangle. Some of them use different functions to approximate the area under the curve (e.g., trapezoids instead of rectangles). Others have variable step sizes, automatically using large step sizes in regions of the function that do not change rapidly and smaller step sizes in regions of the function that do change rapidly. These more sophisticated integration subroutines are designed to achieve the same accuracy as our subroutine with fewer steps, thus reducing computation time. In addition, some of these techniques also determine the maximum error possible between the actual area and the calculated value. Descriptions of these techniques appear in any numerical-methods textbook.

12.2.2 Finding the Roots of Equations

Computers are often used to find the roots of an equation. The roots of an equation such as

$$f(x) = 0 \qquad (12\text{–}20)$$

are those values of x that satisfy the equation. We can use explicit formulas to find the roots of some simple functions like quadratic equations. However, there is no simple closed-form way to calculate the roots of most equations.

Without a standard closed-form way to calculate the roots of an equation, we must find the roots by searching for them using some trial-and-error method. First, we will pick a trial value for x and evaluate the function $f(x)$ for that x to see how close to zero it is. Then we will pick a new trial value for x based on the results of the first value and repeat the process until we come up with a value for x for which $f(x)$ is acceptably close to zero. This trial-and-error process is known as *iteration*. It is a common technique used to solve many classes of computer problems.

Let's examine a sample function to see how we can apply iteration to find the roots of an equation. Suppose that we want to find the roots to the equation

$$\cos x = x \qquad (12\text{–}21)$$

In other words, we want to find those values for x for which $\cos x = x$. The first step in finding the roots of the equations is to rewrite it in the form $f(x) = 0$ so that solving for the roots becomes a matter of searching for zero in the function $f(x)$.

$$f(x) = \cos x - x = 0 \qquad (12\text{–}22)$$

A plot of the function $f(x) = \cos x - x$ is shown in Figure 12–10. As you can

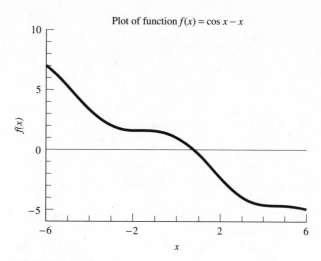

Plot of function $f(x) = \cos x - x$

FIGURE 12–10
Plot of the function $f(x) = \cos x - x$.

see, it has one zero crossing in the range of the function plotted. How can we find that zero crossing with a computer? What clue tells us that a zero crossing has occurred? The answer is simple. If we evaluate a function at one point x_1 and get a positive value, and then evaluate the function at another point x_2 and get a negative value, then a zero crossing must occur somewhere between x_1 and x_2! For example, if we evaluate the function $f(x) = \cos x - x$ at $x = 0$, we find that $f(0) = 1.0$. If we then evaluate the function at $x = 1$, we find that $f(1) = -0.4597$. Since the sign of the function changed between 0 and 1, a zero crossing (and therefore a root of the equation) must occur somewhere between 0 and 1.

Now suppose that we know that a root is located between two values x_1 and x_2. How do we close in on the actual value of the root? A good way to find that value is by the method of *bisection*. In bisection we calculate the value of the function at the point x_m exactly halfway between x_1 and x_2, and compare the sign of $f(x_m)$ with the signs of $f(x_1)$ and $f(x_2)$. The sign of $f(x_m)$ will differ from the sign of one of the other two values, and we will know that the root lies somewhere between x_m and that value. This process repeats (iterates) over and over until we have located the root to the desired accuracy.

For example, consider the function $f(x) = \cos x - x$. We know that $f(0) = 1.0$ and $f(1) = -0.4597$, so a root of this function lies somewhere between 0 and 1. Let's iterate in on it. The first five steps that we take while locating the root follow.

Iteration	x_1	x_m	x_2	$f(x_1)$	$f(x_m)$	$f(x_2)$	Result
1	0.0	0.5	1.0	1.0	0.338	−0.460	$0.5 < x < 1.0$
2	0.5	0.75	1.0	0.338	−0.018	−0.468	$0.5 < x < 0.75$
3	0.5	0.625	0.75	0.338	0.186	−0.018	$0.625 < x < 0.75$

(continued)

(concluded)

Iteration	x_1	x_m	x_2	$f(x_1)$	$f(x_m)$	$f(x_2)$	Result
4	0.625	0.6875	0.75	0.186	0.085	−0.018	$0.6875 < x < 0.75$
5	0.6875	0.71875	0.75	0.085	0.034	−0.018	$0.71875 < x < 0.75$

After five iterations, we know that the root lies somewhere between 0.71875 and 0.7500. If we continue this process, we can find the root to any desired accuracy.

The process of solving for the roots of an equation involves three steps:

1. Express the equation in the form $f(x) = 0$ so that roots of the equation will occur at the zero crossing of the function $f(x)$.
2. Scan the function at a regular spacing until two adjacent samples have a different sign. When that happens, a zero crossing must occur somewhere in between the two samples.
3. Calculate the value of the function at the point halfway through the region in which the zero crossing occurs to determine which half of the region the zero crossing is in. Repeat this process until the location of the zero crossing (root) is known to the desired accuracy.

EXAMPLE 12–4 Finding the Roots of an Equation: Write a subroutine to find a root of a user-supplied equation. The equation must be in the form $f(x) = 0$, where $f(x)$ is a Fortran function passed to the subroutine as a calling argument. The subroutine will work by evaluating the function $f(x)$ starting at a position x_1 and at intervals of Δx thereafter until either position x_2 is reached or the sign of $f(x)$ changes. If the sign of $f(x)$ never changes, no root was found in the interval. If the sign does change, the subroutine will locate the position of the root by repeatedly bisecting the interval where the sign of $f(x)$ changes. The root will be considered correct when it is accurate to five significant digits.

SOLUTION This subroutine has two basic parts. The first part will be a DO loop that goes from x_1 to x_2 in steps of Δx, looking for a point where $f(x)$ changes sign. Once it finds an interval in which $f(x)$ changes sign, it will locate the position of the root by repeatedly bisecting the interval until it is accurate to five significant digits. When it finds the root, it will return to the calling program.

How can we determine when the root is known to five significant digits? Each time that the interval is bisected, we know that the root must lie somewhere in that interval. If the ratio of the length of that interval to the value of the root is less than 10^{-5}, then the root will be known to five significant digits. In equation form, the convergence criterion is

$$\frac{x_b - x_a}{x_m} \leq 10^{-5} \qquad (12\text{--}23)$$

where x_a and x_b are the limits of the interval in which the root lies and x_m, the midpoint of the interval, is the best estimate of the root.

1. **State the problem.**

Write a subroutine to find a root of a user-supplied equation. The equation must be in the form $f(x) = 0$, where $f(x)$ is a Fortran function passed to the subroutine as a calling argument. The subroutine will search for a root between positions x_1 and x_2 in intervals of Δx.

2. **Define the inputs and outputs.**

The inputs to this subroutine are

a. The function $f(x)$ to check for roots.
b. The starting value to search x_1.
c. The ending value to search x_2.
d. The step size Δx.

The outputs from this subroutine are

a. The position of any root found in variable `root`.
b. An error flag `error`.

3. **Describe the algorithm.**

This subroutine can be broken down into three major steps:

```
Check to see that x1 ≤ x2
Scan to find a zero crossing
Bisect the vicinity of the zero crossing until (xb - xa)/xm < epsilon
```

The first step of the program is to check that $x_1 \leq x_2$. If it is not, an error flag should be set and the subroutine should return to the calling program. The second step is to search from x_1 to x_2 in steps of Δx to find a zero crossing. If no zero crossing is found, set the error flag and return. If one is found, then locate the position of the root by repeatedly bisecting the interval until the position is known to five significant digits.

How can we detect a sign change? We will create two logical variables `l_val_a` and `l_val_b`. They will be true when the function values are greater than zero and false otherwise. Then we can test to see if `l_val_a` is equivalent to `l_val_b`. If so, there has been no sign change between points `xa` and `xb`. If not, a sign change has occurred, so we know that a root exists between `xa` and `xb`.

The detailed pseudocode for these steps follows.

```
IF x1 > x2 Then
    error ← 1
    aroot ← 0.
ELSE
    error ←2
    aroot ← 0.

    ! Get number of steps to search
    n ← NINT( (x2-x1) / dx + 1. )

    ! Now search for a zero crossing. Get value
    ! at first step.
    xa ← x1
    val_a ← f(xa)
    l_val_a ← val_a > 0.
    outer: DO for i = 1 to n

        ! Get value at end of interval.
```

```
        xb ← MIN( x1 + REAL(i-1) * dx, x2 )
        val_b ← f(xb)
        l_val_b ← val_b > 0.

        ! Is there a sign change in this interval?
        sign_change: IF l_val_a .NEQV. l_val_b THEN

            ! There was a sign change in the interval. The
            ! root is somewhere between xa and xb. Process
            ! it in a WHILE loop.
            inner: DO
                ! Get value at midpoint.
                xm ← (xa + xb) / 2.
                val_m ← f(xm)
                l_val_m ← val_m > 0.

                ! Test for convergence.
                IF ((xb - xa) / xm) <= epsilon THEN
                    aroot ← xm
                    error ← 0
                    EXIT outer

                ELSE IF l_val_a .EQV. l_val_m THEN
                    ! The sign change was in the 2nd half.
                    xa ← xm
                    val_a ← val_m
                    l_val_a ← l_val_m

                ELSE
                    ! The sign change was in the 1st half.
                    xb ← xm
                    val_b ← val_m
                    l_val_b ← l_val_m
                END of IF
            END of DO inner
        END of IF sign_change

        ! We are still searching for a sign change here.
        ! Set new starting point for next interval.
        xa ← xb
        val_a ← val_b
        l_val_a ← l_val_b
    END of DO outer
END of IF
```

Note that this subroutine returns with the first root that it finds while scanning between x_1 and x_2. If you want to continue searching for more roots, you must call the subroutine again with a new x_1 that is slightly larger than the root discovered in the previous call to the subroutine.

4. **Turn the algorithm into Fortran statements.**

The resulting Fortran subroutine is shown in Figure 12–11.

FIGURE 12–11
Subroutine to locate a real root of a user-supplied function.

```
SUBROUTINE root ( f, x1, x2, dx, aroot, error )
!
! Purpose:
```

(continued)

(continued)

```
!     To find a root of function f(x) between x1 and
!     x2, searching with step sizes of dx.
!
!  Record of revisions:
!     Date        Programmer          Description of change
!     ====        ==========          =====================
!     02/16/96    S. J. Chapman       Original code
!
IMPLICIT NONE

! Declare calling arguments
REAL, EXTERNAL :: f                  ! Function to find roots of
REAL, INTENT(IN) :: x1               ! Starting point for search
REAL, INTENT(IN) :: x2               ! Ending point for search
REAL, INTENT(IN) :: dx               ! Step size
REAL, INTENT(OUT) : arrot            ! Root of function.
INTEGER, INTENT(OUT) :: error        ! Error flag:
                                     ! 0 = No error.
                                     ! 1 = x1 > x2.
                                     ! 2 = No root found

! Declare parameter:
REAL, PARAMETER :: epsilon = 1.0E-5 ! Convergence criterion

! Declare local variables:
LOGICAL :: l_val_a          ! True if f(xa) > 0
LOGICAL :: l_val_b          ! True if f(xb) > 0
LOGICAL :: l_val_m          ! True if f(xm) > 0
INTEGER :: i                ! Index variable
INTEGER :: n                ! Number of steps to search
REAL :: val_a, val_b, val_m ! f(xa), f(xb), f(xm)
REAL :: xa, xb, xm          ! Start, middle, end of interval

! First, check to make sure that the interval to search is valid.
error_chk: IF ( x1 > x2 ) THEN
   error = 1              ! Error—Starting point after end.
   aroot = 0.

ELSE

   ! Initialize error flag to 2, since no root found yet
   error = 2
   aroot = 0.

   ! Get number of steps to search over for sign change.
   n = NINT( (x2-x1) / dx + 1. )

   ! Now search for a zero crossing. Get starting value
   ! at first step.
   xa = x1
   value_a = f(xa)
   l_value_a = value_a > 0.

   ! Search for a sign change between x1 and x2.
   outer: DO i = 1, n

      ! Get value at end of interval.
      xb = MIN( x1 + REAL(i-1) * dx, x2 )
      value_b = f(xb)
      l_value_b = value_b > 0.
```

(continued)

(concluded)

```
                ! Is there a sign change in this interval?
                sign_change: IF ( l_value_a .NEQV. l_value_b ) THEN

                    ! There was a sign change in the interval. The
                    ! root is somewhere between xa and xb. Process
                    ! it in a WHILE loop.
                    inner: DO

                        ! Get value at midpoint.
                        xm = (xa + xb) / 2.
                        value_m = f(xm)
                        l_value_m = value_m > 0.

                        ! Test for convergence.
                        IF (ABS((xb - xa) / xm) <= epsilon) THEN
                            aroot = xm
                            error = 0
                            EXIT outer

                        ELSE IF (l_value_a .EQV. l_value_m) THEN
                            ! The sign change was in the second half.
                            xa = xm
                            value_a = value_m
                            l_value_a = l_value_m

                        ELSE
                            ! The sign change was in the first half.
                            xb = xm
                            value_b = value_m
                            l_value_b = l_value_m
                        END IF
                    END DO inner
                END IF sign_change

                ! We are still searching for a sign change here.
                ! Set new starting point for next interval.
                xa = xb
                value_a = value_b
                l_value_a = l_value_b
        END DO outer
END IF error_chk

END SUBROUTINE root
```

5. Test the program.

We must develop a test driver program and a test function to solve for in order to test this subroutine. The test program is shown in Figure 12–12. Note that the function to be tested must be declared in a separate procedure.

FIGURE 12–12

The test driver program for subroutine `root`.

```
PROGRAM test_root
!
! Purpose:
!    To test subroutine root, which locates the roots of
```

(continued)

(concluded)

```
!   function "fun" that fall between x=x1 and x=x2.
!
!   Record of revisions:
!      Date       Programmer          Description of change
!      ====       ==========          =====================
!    02/16/96    S. J. Chapman        Original code
!
IMPLICIT NONE

! Declare the external function passed to subroutine root.
REAL, EXTERNAL :: fun

! Declare parameter:
REAL, PARAMETER :: epsilon = 1.0E-5 ! Convergence criterion

! List of variables:
REAL :: aroot              ! Root
REAL :: dx = 0.1           ! Step size
INTEGER :: error           ! Error flag
REAL :: x1 = -6.           ! Starting point to search for root.
REAL :: x2 = 6.            ! Ending point to search for root.

! Tell user what we are doing.
WRITE (*,100) x1, x2
100 FORMAT ('0', 'Searching for roots between ',F14.5,' and ',F14.5, '.')

! Begin WHILE loop.
DO
   IF ( x1 > x2 ) EXIT

   ! Call subroutine root with each step size.
   CALL root ( fun, x1, x2, dx, aroot, error )

   ! Write out results.
   IF ( error == 0 ) THEN
      WRITE (*,1010) aroot
      1010 FORMAT (' ', 'There is a root at ',F14.5, '.' )
      x1 = aroot + epsilon * ABS(aroot)
   ELSE IF ( error == 2 ) THEN
      WRITE (*,1020) x1, x2
      1020 FORMAT (' ', 'No root found between ',F14.5, ' and ',F14.5, '.')
      x1 = x2 + epsilon
   END IF
END DO
END PROGRAM
```

We will test this subroutine with several different functions. First, let's use the function in equation (12–22) that we worked with in the previous discussion.

$$f(x) = \cos x - x = 0 \qquad (12–22)$$

The corresponding function subprogram would be

```
REAL FUNCTION fun(x)
!
!   Purpose:
!      Function used to test subroutine root.
!
IMPLICIT NONE
REAL, INTENT(IN) :: x
```

```
fun = COS(x) - x
END FUNCTION fun
```

and the result of running the test driver program with this function would be

```
C>test_root

Searching for roots between          -6.00000 and            6.00000.
There is a root at              .73908.
No root found between           .73909 and          6.00000.
```

This answer is consistent with our hand calculations, when we found that the root was somewhere between 0.71875 and 0.75.

Now let's try a function with more than one root between -6 and 6. The function

$$f(x) = \cos x - \sin 2x = 0 \qquad (12\text{--}24)$$

is periodic and has many roots within the range we are examining. This function is shown in Figure 12–13. When we implement this equation as a function subprogram and call subroutine root with this function, the results are

```
C>test_root

Searching for roots between          -6.00000 and            6.00000.
There is a root at          -5.75959.
There is a root at          -4.71238.
There is a root at          -3.66520.
There is a root at          -1.57080.
There is a root at           0.52360.
There is a root at           1.57079.
There is a root at           2.61799.
```

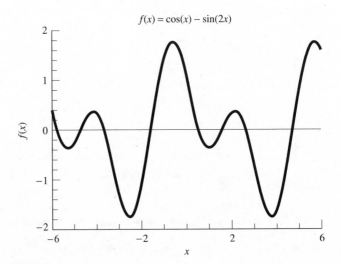

FIGURE 12–13
Plot of the function $f(x) = \cos x - \sin 2x$. This function is used to test subroutine root.

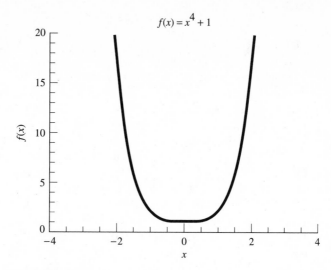

FIGURE 12–14
Plot of the function $f(x) = x^4 + 1$. This function is used to test subroutine `root`.

```
There is a root is at              4.71239.
No root found between              4.71243 and           6.00000.
```

Finally, let's try the function with no roots between -6 and 6. The function

$$f(x) = x^4 + 1 = 0 \qquad (12\text{–}25)$$

has no real roots at all. It is shown in Figure 12–14. When we call subroutine `root` with this function, the results are

```
C>test_root
```

```
Searching for roots between       -6.00000 and           6.00000.
No root found between          -6.00000 and         6.00000.
```

Subroutine `root` appears to be working correctly.

Finding the roots of an equation can be much more complicated than we have shown here. For example, this subroutine would never detect an even number of repeated roots, since if an even number of roots occur at a given location, the sign of the function doesn't change there. In addition, the subroutine could miss roots if two of them are closer together than the step size Δx used in the search. It also cannot find complex roots of an equation.

Many other techniques are available to help solve for the roots of equations. One of these techniques, the Newton-Raphson method, is the subject of exercise 12–12 at the end of this chapter. The details of other root-solving techniques appear in advanced numerical-methods textbooks. Many excellent root-solving techniques that have been developed over the years are available in free and commercial libraries. If you are solving for the roots of an equation in a real problem, it makes sense to use one of these high-quality procedures.

■ 12.3
SUMMARY

Computer calculations are generally not perfect. Because of the finite precision of computer floating-point values, some truncation or round-off error occurs in any sequence of calculations. If the sequence of calculations is long enough, the output from the program can be meaningless, even though every equation in the program is correct. Eventually, the errors will come to dominate the solution.

Some problems are more sensitive to the effects of truncation or round-off errors than others. For example, round-off errors can have a serious effect on the solution of ill-conditioned systems of equations, while having relatively little effect on the solution of well-conditioned systems of equations. In general, problems that involve subtracting two nearly equal numbers are very sensitive to round-off errors. (This effect is the basic problem associated with solving ill-conditioned systems.) If a problem requires you to subtract nearly equal numbers at some point in the solution process, you should consider using double-precision real numbers for the problem.

Another common source of error in computer programs is using an inappropriate model to analyze a particular problem. For example, it makes no sense at all to try to fit a straight line to data that is not straight. Linear regression only makes sense if the process being modeled exhibits linear behavior. If not, modeling should be done with an equation that matches the theoretical behavior of the data.

The study of mathematical methods for use on computers is a branch of mathematics known as numerical analysis. It is normally the subject of one or more separate courses following this course.

Many collections of high-quality algorithms have been developed for solving numerical problems on computers, and they have been collected into libraries of Fortran procedures. Some of these libraries will be discussed in Chapter 13. In writing your own programs, you should use these procedures whenever they are available, instead of trying to rewrite them on your own.

Several subroutines with practical engineering and scientific applications were developed in this chapter. These routines illustrate the thought processes that engineers apply to the design of their applications and also provide some useful subroutines that can serve as building blocks in other programs.

12.3.1 Summary of Good Programming Practice

The following guidelines should be adhered to when working with programs:

1. When adding a large series of numbers, add the smallest numbers first and the larger ones later to minimize truncation and rounding errors.
2. Whenever possible, simplify your expressions to contain as few operations as possible. The fewer the operations that you perform, the smaller the cumulative errors will be and the faster the program will run.
3. Wherever possible, use predeveloped libraries of procedures to solve numerical problems. The procedures in these libraries are usually better tested and more reliable than any that you could create from scratch.

4. Think carefully about what you want to do *before* you start programming. Pay attention to the types of models appropriate to the data that you are working with. Otherwise, garbage in will yield garbage out!

■ 12.4
EXERCISES

12–1 Central Difference Method of Derivatives The derivative of a function $f(x)$ is defined by Equation (8–1).

$$\frac{d}{dx} f(x) = \lim_{\Delta x \to 0} \frac{f(x + \Delta x) - f(x)}{\Delta x} \tag{8–1}$$

It is a way of calculating the slope (or tangent) of a curve at a particular point. In Chapter 8, we calculated the derivative of the function $f(x) = 1/x$ for the location $x_0 = 0.15$ directly from this definition. Figure 12–15 shows the calculation of the derivative of $f(x)$ directly from Equation (8–1).

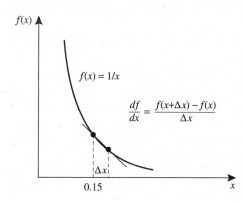

FIGURE 12–15
The calculation of the derivative directly from Equation (8–1). This equation is a forward difference equation; it compares the values at the point being evaluated (x_0) and a point beyond the point being evaluated ($x_0 + \Delta x$) to determine the slope $\frac{df}{dx}$.

If we examine Figure 12–15, we can see that the slope of the expression $\frac{f(x + \Delta x) - f(x)}{\Delta x}$ is significantly different from the actual tangent to the curve at x_0 and will remain so until Δx gets to be very small. This is true because we are looking at the curve $f(x)$ on only one side of the point we are evaluating. If instead we subtract two points at equal distances on either side of x_0, the difference $\frac{f(x + \Delta x/2) - f(x - \Delta x/2)}{\Delta x}$ has a slope that is more nearly equal to the tangent of the curve at the point we are evaluating (see Figure 12–16). Therefore the numerical approximation of the derivative should be better if we express the definition of the derivative as

$$\frac{d}{dx} f(x) = \lim_{\Delta x \to 0} \frac{f(x + \Delta x/2) - f(x - \Delta x/2)}{\Delta x} \tag{12–26}$$

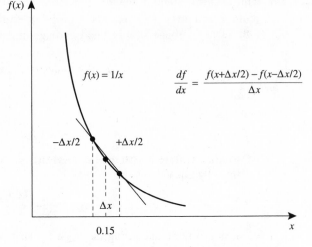

FIGURE 12–16
The calculation of the derivative from Equation (12–26).
This equation is a central difference equation; it compares
the values at two points equal distances before $\left(x_0 - \dfrac{\Delta x}{2}\right)$
and after $\left(x_0 + \dfrac{\Delta x}{2}\right)$ the point being evaluated to determine the slope $\dfrac{df}{dx}$ at x_0.

Write a subroutine to calculate the derivative from Equation (12–26) and then test the
routine by evaluating the function $f(x) = 1/x$ for the location $x_0 = 0.15$. Compare the
results derived from Equations (8–1) and (12–26) for a series of step sizes. How do
the two numbers compare? Which is more accurate? (Equation (8–1) is known as a
forward difference equation, while Equation (12–26) is known as a *central difference*
equation.)

12–2 Create a test data set by calculating points (x_i, y_i) along the curve $y(x) = x^2 - 4x + 3$
for $x_i = 0, 0.1, 0.2, \ldots, 5.0$. Next use the intrinsic subroutine `random_number` to add
random noise to each of the y_i values. Then use subroutine `lsq_fit_2` to try to estimate the coefficients of the original function that generated the data set. Try this when
the added random noise has the following ranges:

a. 0.0 (No added noise)
b. [−0.1, 0.1)
c. [−0.5, 0.5)
d. [−1.0, 1.0)
e. [−1.5, 1.5)
f. [−2.0, 2.0)

How did the quality of the fit change as the amount of noise in the data increased?

12–3 Repeat exercise 12–2 using a data set that contains all the points (x_i, y_i) along the curve $y(x) = x^2 - 4x + 3$ for $x_i = 0, 0.1, 0.2, \ldots, 10.0$. How does the longer data set affect the quality of the fit?

12–4 In this chapter we stated that the coefficients of a linear least-squares fit to the polynomial $y(x) = c_0 + c_1 x$ are the solutions of the following system of equations

$$N c_0 + \left(\sum x\right) c_1 = \sum y \tag{12–15}$$

$$\left(\sum x\right) c_0 + \left(\sum x^2\right) c_1 = \sum xy$$

Prove that the solutions of Equations (12–15) are identical to Equations (4–5) and (4–6) if $c_1 = m$ and $c_0 = b$.

$$m = \frac{\left(\sum xy\right) - \left(\sum x\right)\bar{y}}{\left(\sum x^2\right) - \left(\sum x\right)\bar{x}} \tag{4–5}$$

$$b = \bar{y} - m\bar{x} \tag{4–6}$$

where $\bar{x}$ is the mean (average) of the x values and $\bar{y}$ is the mean (average) of the y values.

12–5 It can be shown that the coefficients of a least-squares fit to the nth-order polynomial $y(x) = c_0 + c_1 x + c_2 x^2 + \cdots + c_n x^n$ are the solutions of the following system of n equations in n unknowns:

$$N c_0 \quad + \left(\sum x\right) c_1 \quad + \left(\sum x^2\right) c_2 \quad + \cdots + \left(\sum x^n\right) c_n \quad = \sum y$$

$$\left(\sum x\right) c_0 + \left(\sum x^2\right) c_1 \quad + \left(\sum x^3\right) c_2 \quad + \cdots + \left(\sum x^{n+1}\right) c_n = \sum xy$$

$$\left(\sum x^2\right) c_0 + \left(\sum x^3\right) c_1 \quad + \left(\sum x^4\right) c_2 \quad + \cdots + \left(\sum x^{n+2}\right) c_n = \sum x^2 y$$

$$\cdots$$

$$\left(\sum x^n\right) c_0 + \left(\sum x^{n+1}\right) c_1 + \left(\sum x^{n+2}\right) c_2 + \cdots + \left(\sum x^{2n}\right) c_n \quad = \sum x^n y$$

Write a subroutine that implements a least squares fit to any polynomial of any order. Use dynamic memory allocation to create arrays of the proper size for the problem being solved. (*Note:* As the order of the polynomial being fitted increases, the size of the system of simultaneous equations to be solved increases and the system of equations becomes progressively less well conditioned. You may wish to use the double-precision subroutine dsimul to solve your system of simultaneous equations!)

12–6 Create a test data set by calculating points (x_i, y_i) along the curve $y(x) = x^6 + x^5 - 3x^4 - 4x^2 + 2x + 3$ for $x_i = 0, 0.1, 0.2, \ldots, 5.0$. Next use the intrinsic subroutine random_number to add random noise to each of the y_i values. Then use the higher-order least-squares fit subroutine created in exercise 12–5 to try to estimate the coefficients of the original function that generated the data set. Try to solve for the coefficients when the added random noise has the following ranges:

a. 0.0 (No added noise)
b. $[-0.1, 0.1)$

12

    c. [−0.5, 5.0)
    d. [−1.0, 1.0)

How did the quality of the fit change as the amount of noise in the data increased? How does the quality of the higher-order fit for a given amount of noise compare to the quality of a quadratic fit (exercise 12–2) for the same amount of noise?

12–7 Integration of Curves Specified by Discrete Points The integration subroutine in Example 12–3 is designed to integrate a user-specified function passed as a calling argument. Sometimes a continuous user-specified function is not available. Instead, we will need to find the area under a curve specified by a series of discrete (x,y) data points. In that case we can determine the area between each pair of (x,y) points by fitting a trapezoid between adjacent pairs of points and adding up the areas of all of the trapezoids (see Figure 12–17). Write a subroutine to calculate the area under a function specified by a series of discrete (x,y) data points. Test your subroutine by creating data sets containing (x,y) pairs from the function $f(x) = \sin^2 x$ from $x_1 = 0$ to $x_2 = 3$ using step sizes Δx of 0.1, 0.05, 0.01, and 0.005 and integrating the data sets with your subroutine.

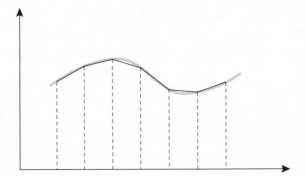

FIGURE 12–17
Filling the area under a curve $f(x)$ with trapezoids.

12–8 Simpson's Rule The integration subroutine in Example 12–3 fitted rectangles of size Δx under the curve to be integrated and then added up the areas of all of the rectangles. While this approach works as long as the step size Δx is small enough, each rectangle is a fairly poor approximation to the smoothly varying curve being integrated. If we can fill in the area under the curve with a shape that more nearly approximates the true curve, then the results of the integration should be better for any given step size. This reasoning led a mathematician named Simpson to try fitting a parabola to sets of three successive points along the curve. Such a parabolic fit is smoothly varying, so it should better approximate a smoothly varying curve. Integration using approximating parabolas is known as Simpson's Rule.

    The equation for the area under a parabola fitting three successive points can be derived as

$$A = \frac{\Delta x}{3}[f(x - 2\Delta x) + 4f(x - \Delta x) + f(x)] \tag{12–27}$$

where Δx is the step size being used. Note that we must have an even number of intervals of size Δx, or there will be a left-over interval at the end that can't be fitted with a parabola.

Write a subroutine that integrates a user-defined function using Simpson's Rule with a specified step size. The function to be integrated will be passed to the subroutine as a calling argument. Note that the subroutine must be smart enough to slightly modify the Δx passed to it so that there will be an exactly even number of intervals between the first and last points to integrate. Compare the performance of this subroutine for a given step size with the performance of the subroutine in Example 12–3 when integrating the function $f(x) = \sin x$ from $x_1 = 0$ to $x_2 = \pi$ using step sizes of 0.5, 0.1, 0.05, and 0.01.

12–9 Try both the rectangular integration subroutine of Example 12–3 and the Simpson's Rule integration subroutine of exercise 12–8 on the following functions over the specified ranges at step sizes of $\Delta x = 0.5$, 0.1, 0.05, 0.01, and 0.005. If you have taken integral calculus, compare the results with the analytical solution. How well do the two subroutines approximate the actual value of the functions?

a. $f(x) = x^4 + 1$ over the range $-2 \leq x \leq 2$.
b. $f(x) = x^5 - 2x^4 - 2x^3 + 4x^2 + x - 2$ over the range $-2 \leq x \leq 2$.
c. $f(x) = \sin^2 x - 1$ over the range $-\pi \leq x \leq \pi$.

12–10 Rejecting "Wild" Points When a data set is analyzed, usually most of the data behaves approximately as expected, but a few really wild points appear in the middle of the data set. These wild points are often so far away from the rest of the data that they obviously are not real. If those data points are left in the data set when it is analyzed, they can distort the results of the analysis. For example, examine Figure 12–18a. Most of the data points in Figure 12–18a appear to lie roughly along a straight line, but two of the points are really far away from the line. Those points are wild points. If a linear least-squares fit is performed on the data with the wild points present, they distort the fit (Figure 12–18b). If the wild points are eliminated from the data set, a least-squares fit produces much better results (Figure 12–18c).

12

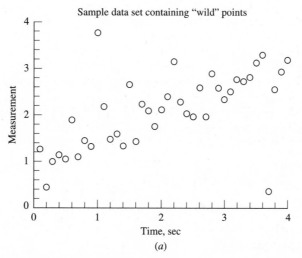

Sample data set containing "wild" points

Measurement / Time, sec

(a)

FIGURE 12–18
(*a*) A sample data set containing "wild" data points. (*b*) A linear least squares fit with wild points included. (*c*) A linear least-squares fit with wild points excluded.

(continued)

(concluded)

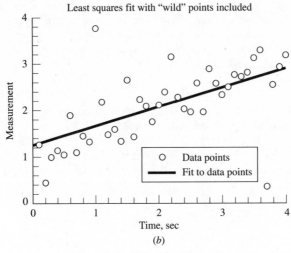

(b)

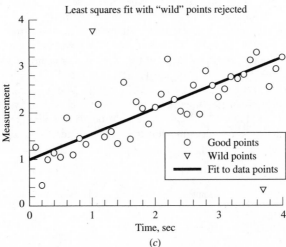

(c)

It is common for an analyst to edit wild points out of a data set as a part of the analysis process. How can wild points be edited out? The most common approach to such editing is to reject points that are more than a certain number of standard deviations away from the rest of the data in the set. One possible procedure is described next:

1. If the data is expected to behave in a linear fashion, perform a linear least-squares fit to the entire data set.
2. Calculate the distance of each data point from the fitted line and determine the standard deviation of the distance of the data points from the line. The distance of a data point (x_i, y_i) from the line may be calculated as follows:

Expected value of y_i $\hat{y}_i = m\,x_i + b$

Distance of point from line: $d = y_i = \hat{y}_i$

where $\hat{y}_i$ is the expected value of y_i, m is the slope of the fitted line, and b is the intercept of the fitted line. Then calculate the standard deviation using the equations presented in earlier chapters.

3. Reject as wild any points that are more than *threshold* standard deviations away from the rest of the data set, where *threshold* is a user-specifiable quantity.

4. Refit the data without the wild points to update the slope and intercept of the line fitted to the data.

Write a subroutine that will perform a least-squares fit to a data set, reject any points more than `threshold` standard deviations away from the rest of the data, and then perform a new fit with the remainder of the data. The quantity `threshold` should be specified by the user in a calling argument, and the number of points actually rejected should be returned in an argument to the calling program unit. When the subroutine is written, test it on the following data set using a rejection threshold of 3.

Time, s	Measurement	Time, s	Measurement
	Table of measurements		
0.1	1.2528	2.1	2.3929
0.2	0.4373	2.2	3.1488
0.3	0.9886	2.3	2.2762
0.4	1.1365	2.4	2.0197
0.5	1.0393	2.5	1.9674
0.6	1.9057	2.6	2.5918
0.7	1.0968	2.7	1.9639
0.8	1.4423	2.8	2.8846
0.9	1.3135	2.9	2.5716
1.0	3.7680	3.0	2.3368
1.1	2.1781	3.1	2.5031
1.2	1.4717	3.2	2.7563
1.3	1.5945	3.3	2.7283
1.4	1.3275	3.4	2.8041
1.5	2.6522	3.5	3.1251
1.6	1.4280	3.6	3.2839
1.7	2.2315	3.7	0.3361
1.8	2.0951	3.8	2.5426
1.9	1.7505	3.9	2.9296
2.0	2.1190	4.0	3.1786

12–11 Find the real roots of the following equations in the range $-10 \le x \le 10$.

a. $\sin^2 x = 0.25$

b. $f(x) = x^4 - 5x^2 + 5 = 0$

    c. $0.1x^3 - 2x^2 + 3x + 3 = 0$

    d. sinc $x = 0.1$ $\left(\textit{Note: } \text{sinc } x = \dfrac{\sin x}{x}\right)$

12–12 Newton-Raphson Method for Finding Roots The Newton-Raphson method is an alternative technique for finding the roots of the equation $f(x) = 0$. In the bisection algorithm that we used in this chapter, we located a zero crossing by calculating the value of $f(x)$ at the midpoint of an interval containing a zero crossing and then repeating the process with the half of the original interval that still contained the zero crossing. The process was repeated until the function $f(x)$ was within an acceptable distance of zero. By contrast, the Newton-Raphson method uses the slope of the curve near the zero crossing of the function to make a more intelligent estimate of the location of the zero crossing. Because each guess made by the Newton-Raphson method is better than each guess made by the bisection method, we can find the zero crossing in fewer iterations.

    To understand the Newton-Raphson method, examine Figure 12–19. The figure shows a function $f(x)$ near a zero crossing (and therefore, near a root of the equation). Suppose that we start at a point on the function $P_1 = (x_1, y_1)$. If we calculate the slope of the function at P_1 and project that slope down to $y = 0$, we will be at point x_2, which is closer to the zero crossing than x_1 is. The value of the function at x_2 is $y_2 = f(x_2)$. If we calculate the slope of the function at $P_2 = (x_2, y_2)$ and project that slope down to $y = 0$, we will be at point x_3, which is even closer to the zero crossing than x_2 is. This process converges to the location of the zero crossing in just a few iterations.

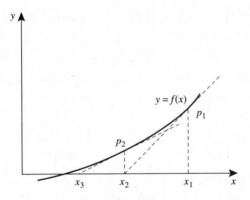

FIGURE 12–19
The Newton-Raphson method for finding the root of an equation.

    How can we find the slope m_1 of the function at point P_1? The slope of a curve at any given point is the derivative of the curve at that point, so we can use our derivative calculating subroutine from exercise 12–2 to get the slope of the function at a point.

    How can we find point x_2 given a knowledge of point $P_1 = (x_1, y_1)$ and the slope of the tangent line m_1? It comes directly from the equation for a straight line $y = m x + b$. Since we know x_1, y_1, and m_1, we can solve for the y-intercept b_1.

$$b_1 = y_1 - m_1 x_1 \qquad (12\text{–}28)$$

Given the slope m_1 and intercept b_1 of the line, we can find the location where the line crosses the x-axis. Since $y_2 = 0$ there, we can calculate a value for x_2.

$$x_2 = \frac{-b_1}{m_1} \qquad (12\text{–}29)$$

Finally, substituting Equation (12–28) into Equation (12–29) yields

$$x_2 = x_1 - \frac{y_1}{m_1} \tag{12–30}$$

Write a subroutine to find a root of a user-supplied equation of the form $f(x) = 0$, where $f(x)$ is a Fortran function passed to the subroutine as a calling argument. The subroutine will search for a root between positions x_1 and x_2 in intervals of Δx and will use the Newton-Raphson method to zero in on the location of the root once it has discovered a zero-crossing interval. Assume that a root has been found when two successive approximations to the root x_{i-1} and x_i satisfy the equation

$$\frac{x_i - x_{i-1}}{x_i} < 10^{-5} \tag{12–31}$$

Test the subroutine on the three equations given in exercise 12–9.

12–13 The bisection method for zeroing in on the location of a root is a repetitive process that lends itself to a recursive implementation. Write a version of the bisection algorithm that uses a recursive subroutine to locate the final position of the root.

12–14 Write a modified version of the bisection subroutine in Example 12–4 that returns the number of iterations required to zero in on the root within a sign-change interval. Also, write a modified version of the Newton-Raphson method subroutine in exercise 12–12 that returns the number of iterations required to zero in on the root within a sign-change interval. Use both modified subroutines to find the root of the function

$$f(x) = \sin x - x^2 = 0$$

between 0.0 and 1.0 with a step size Δx of 0.2. How many iterations were required by each technique to find the root of the function to five significant digits of accuracy?

12–15 The Newton-Raphson method for finding a root of an equation has a potential problem—sometimes it will not converge to a solution no matter how many iterations are performed. This condition typically occurs when the function gets "trapped in a valley" of the function. For example, Figure 12–20 shows a plot of the function $f(x) = x^3 - 5x^2 + 3x + 12$ for the range $-2 \le x \le 5$. It is possible for iterations of the Newton-Raphson method to get trapped in the valley between 2 and 4. No matter how many times we iterate, the estimates of the root will continue to bounce back and forth between about 2.5 and about 3.5, never converging to a correct answer and never escaping the valley. If this condition were to happen to the root-solving subroutine generated in exercise 12–13, the subroutine would run forever without returning to the main program. Modify the Newton-Raphson subroutine to avoid this problem by setting an error flag and returning if an acceptable root is not found within 20 iterations after a sign change is detected.

12–16 Finding Even Numbers of Repeated Roots The root-solving subroutine in Example 12–4 cannot find an even numbers of repeated roots, since no sign change occurs on either side of the location of the roots. For example, the function $f(x) = x^2 - 2x + 1$ has two roots at $x = 1$. If we evaluate this function at $x = 0.9$ and $x = 1.1$, the results are $f(x) = 0.01$ and $f(x) = 0.01$. There is no sign change on either side of the roots! A plot of the function is shown in Figure 12–21.

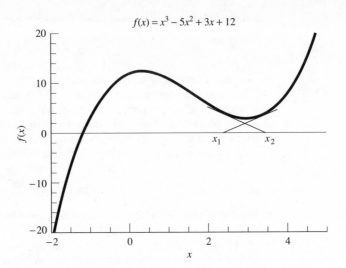

FIGURE 12–20
Plot of the function $f(x) = x^3 - 5x^2 + 3x + 12$.

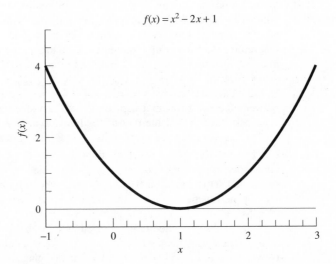

FIGURE 12–21
Plot of the function $f(x) = x^2 - 2x + 1$. Note that the sign of the function does not change at the location of the double roots at $x = 1$.

This problem occurs whenever the function is tangential to the x-axis at the location of the root. In other words, it occurs when the slope of the function (and hence the derivative of the function) is equal to zero at the location of the roots. Note that the slope of the function is negative before the location of the roots, positive after the location of the roots, and exactly zero at the location of the roots.

This fact suggests a strategy for detecting both odd and even numbers of repeated roots. While performing the interval search, we can check the sign of both the function itself and its derivative. If the function $f(x)$ changes sign within an interval, then an odd number of roots are present in that interval and we can search for them using the bisection method as in Example 12–4. If the derivative $\dfrac{d}{dx} f(x)$ changes sign within an interval and the value of $f(x)$ is small at both ends of the interval, then there is probably a repeated root within the interval. If it exists, the repeated root can be located by using the bisection method to locate the point at which the derivative of the function is zero and seeing if $f(x)$ is zero at that point. (Because the derivative can change sign without a root being present, we must check to confirm that $f(x) \approx 0$ in the interval where the derivative changes sign. Also, we must set an error flag and return if a root is not found within an acceptable number of iterations.)

Write a subroutine that accepts a function $f(x)$ as a dummy argument and searches at regular intervals for both sign changes in $f(x)$ and sign changes in $\dfrac{d}{dx} f(x)$ where $f(x)$ is nearly zero. If it finds either case, it should look for the root(s) by bisection and then return an error if a root is not found within 20 iterations. Use the central difference subroutine of exercise 12–1 to calculate the derivatives of the function. Test your subroutine by looking for the roots of the following functions in the range $-10 \le x \le 10$:

a. $f(x) = x^3 - 11x^2 + 39x - 45 = 0$
b. $f(x) = x^3 - 5x^2 + 3x + 12 = 0$
c. $f(x) = \sin x + 1 = 0$
d. $f(x) = x^4 - 4x^3 + 6x^2 - 4x + 1 = 0$
e. $f(x) = x^5 - 2x^4 - 2x^3 + 4x^2 + x - 2 = 0$

12–17 Interpolation   A least-squares fit of order n calculates the nth-order polynomial that best fits an (x,y) data set in a least-squares sense. Once this polynomial has been calculated, it can be used to estimate the expected value y_0 associated with any location x_0 within the data set. This process is called *interpolation*. Write a program that calculates a quadratic least-squares fit to the following data set and then uses that fit to estimate the expected value y_0 at $x_0 = 3.5$.

Noisy measurements

x	y
0.00	−23.22
1.00	−13.54
2.00	−4.14
3.00	−0.04
4.00	3.92
5.00	4.97
6.00	3.96
7.00	−0.07
8.00	−5.67
9.00	−12.29
10.00	−20.25

12

12–18 Extrapolation Once a least-squares fit has been calculated, the resulting polynomial can also be used to estimate the values of the function beyond the limits of the original input data set. This process is called *extrapolation*. Write a program that calculates a linear least-squares fit to the following data set and then uses that fit to estimate the expected value y_0 at $x_0 = 14.0$.

Noisy measurements

x	y
0.00	−14.22
1.00	−10.54
2.00	−5.09
3.00	−3.12
4.00	0.92
5.00	3.79
6.00	6.99
7.00	8.95
8.00	11.33
9.00	14.71
10.00	18.75

12

Fortran Libraries

One of the greatest advantages of Fortran subprograms is that they are *reusable*. Once a procedure has been written to perform a particular task, we can use that procedure over and over again whenever we need to perform that task. For example, in Example 6–1, we wrote a subroutine to sort an array of real values into ascending order. We can now use that subroutine to sort arrays of real values in a totally different program at any time in the future.

A Fortran programmer does not have to constantly reinvent the wheel. Once one programmer has created a working, debugged procedure to perform a particular task, any other programmer can perform the same function simply by invoking that procedure.

Let's suppose that you are a programmer working on a large project, one portion of which requires you to solve a system of simultaneous linear equations. You happen to know that another programmer, Susan Jones, has already written and debugged a subroutine to solve a system of simultaneous linear equations. What can you do? There are at least three possibilities. First, you could write your own subroutine to solve the system of linear equations, but that would be a stupid waste of time. Second, you could get the *source code* to Susan's subroutine and *compile* it together with your own program. This approach would work, but Susan would have to agree to give you her source code, and you would waste time recompiling code that has already been compiled. Finally, you could get the compiled *object file* for her subroutine and *link* it with your code. This option is the best choice, since you will not waste time recompiling her subroutine when it has already been compiled.

To make Fortran procedures available for easy reuse, their object files are often collected into **libraries.** A *library* is a collection of compiled Fortran object files organized into a single disk file, which is indexed for easy recovery. When a Fortran program invokes procedures that are located in a library, the linker searches the library to get the compiled objects for the procedures being invoked and includes them in the final program.

Object libraries are very useful. Procedure objects in a library do not have to be recompiled for use, so it is quicker to compile and link programs using library procedures. In addition, libraries can be distributed in object form only, protecting the source code that someone invested so much time writing.

One way to create a Fortran 90/95 library is to place all the source procedures into a module, to compile the module into an object file, and to distribute that object file for use by programmers (see Figure 13–1a). Fortran modules are an excellent way to distribute libraries, since they also provide an explicit interface to the procedures in the library. The Fortran compiler can automatically check the interfaces at each invocation of a procedure in the library.

However, this approach to creating a library does have a significant disadvantage. When a module is accessed by USE association, many Fortran 90/95 compilers include the entire contents of the module in the resulting executable program. This technique can cause a serious problem if the library is very large, containing hundreds or thousands of procedures. A program may only want to use one procedure from the module, and to get that one procedure it may end up being linked with many megabytes of excess baggage! Some very large libraries partially alleviate this problem by breaking their list of procedures into "chapters" grouped by function and creating a separate module for each chapter. The programmer can then access only the chapters of the library containing the procedures that he or she needs.[1]

Many libraries were written in an earlier version of Fortran or in other languages such as C. These libraries consist of separately compiled procedures whose objects have been collected into a common file by a special program called a **librarian.** The resulting library can be linked with the Fortran program after compilation, and only the procedures actually required by the program will be linked into the final executable program. However, the procedures in the library will *not* have explicit interfaces. It is possible to provide explicit interfaces for these libraries by defining separate interfaces for each of the procedures in the library, collecting them into a module, and compiling the module. That module can be accessed by USE association to define explicit interfaces for all of the procedures in the library without actually linking excess code into the resulting program.[2]

This approach to creating a Fortran library has a major advantage: It provides an explicit interface through the interface module while linking only the required procedures into the final executable program. However, this method also has a major disadvantage. Each procedure now has a separate interface definition, which must match exactly the calling sequence of the procedure itself if the library is to work properly. This requirement can create a configuration control problem, since any time the calling sequence of a procedure in the library is modified, the corresponding interface must also be manually updated.

With libraries, Fortran is almost infinitely extensible. For example, if you are writing programs to perform statistical analyses, you can purchase an off-the-shelf statistical subroutine library that will perform extremely complicated statistical processes with a single subroutine call. The library will make your program easier and quicker to write and debug. The hardest part of the analysis will be performed in the subroutine library, and that portion of the code has already been debugged!

---

[1]The NAG *f*90 Fortran 90 Library, which will be described later in this chapter, adopts this approach to creating a library.

[2]The Digital Visual Fortran 90 version of the IMSL Library, which is described later in this chapter, adopts this approach to creating a library.

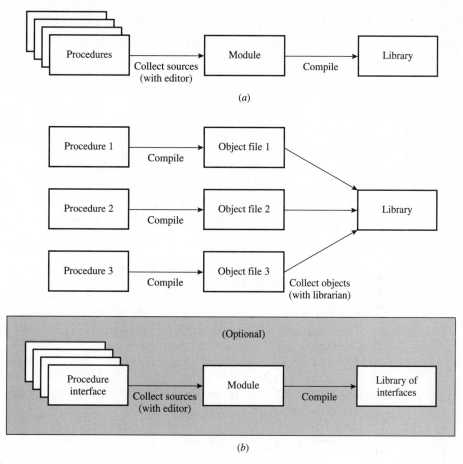

FIGURE 13–1
Two ways to create Fortran libraries: (*a*) Fortran 90/95 procedures can be placed in a module, and that module can be compiled and then accessed by other program units through USE association. This approach has the advantage of automatically providing an explicit interface to all library procedures. (*b*) Older Fortran procedures or procedures in other languages can be separately compiled, and a librarian can gather their object files into a library. Optionally, explicit interfaces can be provided for these procedures by defining the interfaces separately, collecting them into a module, compiling that module, and then accessing the interfaces in other program units through USE association.

Good Programming Practice
Place any procedures that you may wish to reuse into a library. The procedures in a library are easy to keep track of and may be linked quickly into any new programs that you write.

13.1

TYPES OF Fortran LIBRARIES

An enormous inventory of Fortran procedure libraries is available to help you write programs that perform various special functions. For example, you can find specialized libraries for calculating statistical functions, solving mathematical equations, processing signals, plotting data, analyzing seismic data, and many more functions. Whenever you need to write a sophisticated program in some specialized area, you can usually purchase a library package to make the task easier.

Some libraries are provided free by the computer vendors themselves. These libraries usually contain subroutines and functions (called *system utilities*) that permit you to perform simple but useful tasks on the computer. For example, procedures in the library will get the name of the computer on which the program is being run, the amount of memory available, the priority of the program, etc.

Be careful when using procedures from these libraries. Because these procedures differ from processor to processor, using them will make a program less portable. The best way to use such library procedures is to include each one in a special user-written interface procedure and to call the system library procedure through the interface procedure everywhere in the program.

For example, most processors have a mechanism to pass command-line arguments to a program when it is started. This mechanism is implemented as a special procedure in a system library, but it is different for every type of computer. To use such a procedure, a programmer might define an interface subroutine `get_arguments` that gets the command-line arguments from the system library subroutine and returns them to the calling program in a standard format. If the program is moved to another computer, subroutine `get_arguments` would have to be rewritten to use the system library procedure on the new computer, but none of the program units calling `get_arguments` would have to be modified at all! If a program is written in this fashion, then when it is moved between computers, only the interface procedures have to be rewritten.

13

EXAMPLE 13–1 Interface Procedure to Get Command-Line Arguments: Fortran does not have a standard procedure to return command-line arguments to a user. Instead, the information is available from subroutines or functions contained in the system libraries supplied by each computer and/or compiler vendor. The calling sequence of these procedures will probably differ from processor to processor, so using them will make your programs nonportable.

However, sometimes we need to have command-line information. If we do need it, then the call to the system library procedure should be encapsulated inside an interface subroutine with a standard calling sequence; all the program units in the program that need the information should call the interface subroutine. If the program is later moved to another processor, only the interface subroutine will have to be rewritten. The other program units in the program will not have to change, since they call only the interface subroutine, not the system library procedure. The interface subroutine itself may have to be totally rewritten for the new computer, but as long as the calling sequence of the subroutine is un-affected, the change will not affect the rest of the program.

To illustrate this idea, we will now write an interface subroutine `get_argu-ments` that returns the command-line arguments with which the program was started. This example is written for Digital Visual Fortran 90, you should write a version of the interface routine with the same calling sequence on whatever processor you are using to run Fortran programs.

SOLUTION Two system library procedures in Digital Visual Fortran return information about command-line arguments. They are described in the reference manual accompanying the compiler. Function `nargs()` returns the number of arguments on the command line, and subroutine `getarg` returns the arguments themselves one at a time. Function `nargs()` has no calling arguments and returns an integer result. The calling sequence for subroutine `getarg` us

```
CALL getarg ( n, string, status )
```

where the arguments are

Argument	Type	Description
n	INTEGER(KIND=2)	Argument number to retrieve; in the range $0 \leq n < nargs() - 1$.
string	CHARACTER(LEN=*)	String containing the argument.
status	INTEGER(KIND=2)	Number of characters returned; -1 for error

These system library procedures are not the same from processor to processor. We will hide them inside the interface subroutine `get_arguments`.

1. **State the problem.**

Write an interface subroutine `get_arguments` to fetch the command-line arguments when a program is started. The subroutine should return the arguments in a character array and should return a value indicating the number of valid arguments returned. It should also return an error status to the calling program.

2. **Define the inputs and outputs.**

The input to this subroutine is the number of elements in the character array to hold the command-line arguments. The outputs from the subroutine are (1) an integer value containing the number of arguments returned, (2) the character array containing the arguments, and (3) an error status. Two possible errors could be returned from this subroutine: a -1 to indicate that an error occurred in the underlying system subroutine or a positive number to indicate that the character array was too small to hold all the arguments. The positive number will be the number of arguments actually present on the command line. A 0 error status indicates success.

3. **Describe the algorithm.**

This program can be broken down into three major steps:

```
Get the number of arguments
See if they fit into array
Retrieve them and store them in the character array
```

The detailed pseudocode for this subroutine is

```
num_args = nargs ()
IF num_args > num_string THEN
   err = num_args
   num_args = num_string
ELSE
   error = 0
END of IF

DO for i = 0 to num_args-1
   CALL getarg (i, string(i+1), status )
   IF status < 0 then
      error = status
      EXIT
   END of IF
END of DO
```

4. Turn the algorithm into Fortran statements.

The resulting Fortran subroutine is shown in Figure 13–2. It calls subroutine getargs from the Digital Visual Fortran system library. Note that the subroutine has been placed inside a module so that it will have an explicit interface.

FIGURE 13–2
Subroutine get_arguments (version for Digital Visual Fortran).

```
MODULE interfaces
CONTAINS
   SUBROUTINE get_arguments ( num_args, string, num_string, error )

   !  Purpose:
   !    To return the command-line arguments supplied when a
   !    program was started. This version is designed for use
   !    with the Digital Visual Fortran system libraries.
   !
   !  Record of revisions:
   !      Date        Programmer           Description of change
   !      ====        ==========           =====================
   !    03/02/96    S. J. Chapman          Original code
   !
   USE dflib                ! Use the Digital Visual Fortran system lib
   IMPLICIT NONE

   ! List of calling arguments:
   INTEGER,INTENT(OUT) :: num_args       ! No of arguments returned
   INTEGER,INTENT(IN) :: num_string      ! No of strings to hold args
   CHARACTER(len=*),DIMENSION(num_string),INTENT(OUT) :: string
                                         ! Array to hold arguments
   INTEGER, INTENT(OUT) :: error         ! Error flag: 0 = no error
                                         !   -1 = sys library error
                                         !   +num = too many arguments

   ! Define local variables
```

(continued)

(concluded)

```fortran
    INTEGER(KIND=2) :: i                    ! Index variable
    INTEGER(KIND=2) :: status               ! Subroutine status

    ! Get number of arguments
    num_args = nargs()

    ! Check for too many arguments.
    IF ( num_args > num_string ) THEN ! too many
       error = num_args
       num_args = num_string
    ELSE
       error = 0
    END IF

    ! Get arguments.
    DO i = 0, num_args-1
       CALL getarg (i, string(i+1), status )
       IF ( status < 0 ) then
          error = status
          EXIT
       END IF
    END DO
    END SUBROUTINE get_arguments

END MODULE interfaces
```

5. Test the program.

To test this subroutine, we need to write a test driver program. The test driver program will get its command-line arguments using subroutine `get_arguments` and then display the result. The test driver program is shown in Figure 13–3

FIGURE 13–3

The test driver program for subroutine `get_arguments`.

```fortran
PROGRAM test
!
!  Purpose:
!    To test subroutine test_get_arguments. This program
!    examines its command line arguments using subroutine
!    test get arguments.
!
!  Record of revisions:
!     Date        Programmer          Description of change
!     ====        ==========          =====================
!   03/02/96    S. J. Chapman         Original code
!
USE interfaces
IMPLICIT NONE

! List of parameters:
INTEGER, PARAMETER :: num_string = 4 ! No of strings to hold args

! List of local variables:
INTEGER :: i                         ! Loop index
```

(continued)

(concluded)

```
INTEGER :: num_args                    ! Number of arguments returned
CHARACTER(len=30),DIMENSION(num_string) :: string
                                       ! Array to hold arguments
INTEGER :: error                       ! Error flag: 0=no error
                                       !   -1=sys library error
                                       !   +num=too many arguments
! Get the arguments.
CALL get_arguments( num_args, string, num_string, error )

! Display results.
WRITE (*,'(1X,A,I2,A)') 'There are ', num_args, ' arguments.'
DO i = 1, num_args
   WRITE (*,'(1X,A,I2,A,A)') 'Argument ', i, ' is: ', string(i)
END DO
WRITE (*,'(1X,A,I2,A)') 'Error status = ', error

END PROGRAM
```

To test the subroutine, we will start the driver program with no extra arguments, with two arguments, and with five arguments, and see what happens in each case.

```
C>test
There are  1 arguments.
Argument  1 is: C:\BOOK\F90\CHAP13\TEST.EXE
Error status = 0

C>test 1 2
There are 3  arguments.
Argument  1 is: C:\BOOK\F90\CHAP13\TEST.EXE
Argument  2 is: 1
Argument  3 is: 2
Error status = 0

C>test This is another test !
There are  4 arguments.
Argument  1 is: C:\BOOK\F90\CHAP13\TEST.EXE
Argument  2 is: This
Argument  3 is: is
Argument  4 is: another
Error status = 6
```

In the first case, the subroutine returned one argument—the name of the program itself, which was the only thing on the command line. In the second case, the subroutine correctly recovered all the arguments on the command line. In the third case, the subroutine recovered the first four arguments on the command line, which is all that it had room for in array `strings`. Then it set the error flag, indicating that there were actually six arguments to retrieve. The program appears to be working correctly.

> **Good Programming Practice**
> Use interface subroutines and functions to hide calls to processor-dependent system libraries. Restricting processor-dependent calls to a few interface procedures increases the portability of a program.

Many third-party vendors sell procedure libraries to perform specific functions. The disadvantage of using one of these libraries is that you must purchase it first. On the other hand, a company can save programming and debugging effort by purchasing and using the library. Software engineering time is so expensive that a company almost always wins by purchasing off-the-shelf subroutines if they are available. Another major advantage is *host-computer independence.* The vendor of a procedure library usually supports versions of the library on many different processors. If you write a program that uses the library on one computer system and then you need to make it work on another type of computer, all you have to do is to purchase a copy of the library for the new computer. The vendor of the library has done all the hard work of translating the library procedures for you!

A number of excellent general purpose scientific and engineering libraries are available for purchase. Two of the best are the IMSL Library, from Visual Numerics, Inc.,[3] in the United States and the NAG Library, from the Numerical Algorithms Group, Ltd.,[4] in the United Kingdom. Both libraries contain a broad range of procedures to solve many scientific and engineering problems, and both come in Fortran 90 versions complete with explicit interfaces for all procedures. (The special version of the NAG Library for Fortran 90 is known as *fl90*.) Also, both libraries come with extensive on-line documentation to help programmers select the proper procedure to solve a specific problem.

Both the IMSL library and the NAG Library come with an extensive set of procedures to solve linear systems of equations, perform integration and differentiation, perform interpolation and extrapolation, solve differential equations, find the roots of equations, perform statistical analysis, and so on. They are amazingly complete collections of high-quality algorithms that can serve as building blocks to solve almost any scientific or engineering problem. The IMSL Library comes bundled with the Professional Edition of Digital Visual Fortran.

Another source of high-quality algorithms is the book *Numerical Recipes in Fortran: The Art of Scientific Computing.*[5] This book contains a smorgasbord of useful procedures to solve many scientific and engineering problems, and it is available with a companion disk containing the source code for all of the procedures. The number and type of algorithms supported is less than the full IMSL or NAG libraries, but the algorithms in this book have two major advantages: They are much cheaper, and they come with source code so your programs will be more easily portable between processors.

In addition, many free Fortran scientific and mathematical libraries that have been developed over the years at universities and at government research laboratories are available for downloading and use from the Internet. A good source for these libraries is the Netlib collection at URL http://www.netlib.org. An excellent example is LAPACK, the Linear Algebra PACKage. It is a library designed to solve problems based on linear algebra, including linear equations, least-squares fits, and eigenval-

13

[3]Visual Numerics, Inc., 9990 Richmond Avenue, Suite 400, Houston, Texas 77042-4548.
[4]The Numerical Algorithm Group, Ltd., Wilkinson House, Jordan Hill Road, Oxford, OX2 8DR, UK
[5]W. H. Press, B. P. Flannery, S. A. Teukolsky, and W. T. Vetterling, *Numerical Recipes in Fortran: The Art of Scientific Computing* (Cambridge University Press, various).

ues/eigenvectors. The U.S. National Science Foundation (NSF) funded the development of the library, and the NSF and other U.S. government agencies fund its continued maintenance. These high-quality procedures are available free for use, provided that the origins of the routines is acknowledged. (A small subset of LAPACK procedures is included on the disk that accompanies the instructors manual for this book and at the book's Web site.) A Fortran 90-specific version of the LAPACK library should be released by the time this book is published.

You will do much better to use any of the above procedures than to attempt to write your own for a function that is present in one of the libraries. The algorithms in the libraries have been extensively debugged, and they are designed to minimize problems associated with the limitations of computer mathematics.

Procedure libraries also support *device independence.* A properly designed procedure library permits programmers to work with many different types of devices without changing their source code. The best example of this use occurs in plotting graphical data on an output device (e.g., laser printer, plotter, or CRT terminal). The Fortran language contains no standard method for plotting graphics on an output device. The reason is that there are literally hundreds of graphical output devices, each with its own special commands and control codes. It is impossible to build standard support for all possible devices into a general-purpose language.

A number of third-party library vendors have stepped into this breach. They sell libraries that permit a programmer to generate graphics output in a device-independent manner and then to plot it on whatever output device is desired at the moment. These libraries include special interface subroutines that are called by the programmer. The format of the calls is the same regardless of the computer on which the program is running or the output device on which the data is to be plotted. The interface routines produce a device-independent intermediate file (called a *metafile*) containing the graphical data in a standard format. Then a special program is run to translate the device-independent graphical data into the commands required for the particular output device being used. The graphical output from these libraries may be redirected to different types of devices without changing the original computer program. These libraries enable programmers to plot their output interactively on a terminal while a program is being tested and debugged and then to send the output to a hard-copy device when the program is working correctly.

■ 13.2

USING Fortran LIBRARIES

The general principles of how to build and use libraries are the same for all libraries on all computers. However, the specific details differ on different types of computers. This section describes the general principles of library use, and your instructor will provide the information you need to make and use libraries on your particular computer.

13.2.1 Making Libraries and Linking Programs with Libraries

A library may contain any number of procedures. They may all be placed in a single module, or they may be separately compiled. In either case the object files are added to the library using a special program called the librarian. The librarian places all of the objects into a single large file and generates a table of contents describing each procedure in the library and where to find it within the file.

To use procedures from the library in one of your programs, you must include the appropriate subroutine calls in the program and then compile the program with the Fortran compiler. If the procedures are in a module, you must include the module's name in a USE statement in each program unit that invokes the library procedures. Next you must link the program with the *linker* to produce an executable file. You may need to specify the name of your library when you run the linker, if it is not searched by default. The linker will search the table of contents in the library to see if any of the procedures you need are present in the library. If they are, then the linker will extract those procedures from the library and include them in your final executable program.

Remember that the procedures for compiling subprograms, placing them in libraries, and using the libraries vary from processor to processor. You must ask your instructor or a knowledgeable user for the proper procedures on your particular system.

13.2.2 Selecting and Using Library Procedures

Suppose we are working on a programming project and want to use library procedures to make the job easier. How do we identify the proper procedures to use, and how do we apply them properly? A good place to start is with the library's index.

Normally, any Fortran library will come with an index that classifies the procedures in the library by function. If we know what we want to do, it is a simple matter to look into the index to find one or more procedures that are candidates to do the job. Then we can turn to the manual pages describing the procedures to confirm that they do what we want. The manual pages will tell us exactly how to use the subroutines or functions, including the calling sequence, the type and dimension of each calling argument, and the possible error codes, if any.

We will illustrate this process with the small library BOOKLIB that comes with this book. The descriptions for this library may be found at the books Web site (see Preface). As an example, suppose that we want calculate the inverse of a matrix using the procedures in the BOOKLIB library. If we check the library index, we see that subroutine max_inv inverts matrices. Let's turn to the manual page for this procedure.

The manual page for subroutine mat_inv is reproduced in Figure 13–4. From that page we can see that mat_inv is a generic subroutine, consisting of four specific subroutines to invert single-precision real, double-precision real, single-precision complex, and double-precision complex matrices, respectively. Note that the manual page shows the calling sequence required by this subroutine, including the type of each calling argument, the dimension of each array, the direction (input or output) of the argument, and a description of its contents. The arguments passed from the calling program unit must match this list in type and size, or a compilation error will occur if there is an explicit interface between the calling program unit and the subroutine. If there is an implicit interface and the arguments do not match, the results will be unpredictable. The page also includes a description of the algorithm implemented by the subroutine and an example of how to use the subroutine.

FIGURE 13–4

Manual page for subroutine `mat_inv`.

`mat_inv` (single/double/single complex/double complex)

Purpose: To invert an N × N matrix using Gauss-Jordan elimination and the maximum pivot technique.

Usage:
```
USE booklib
CALL mat_inv ( A, B, NDIM, N, ERROR )
```

Arguments:

Name	Type	Dim	I/O	Description
A	R/D/C/Z	NDIM × NDIM	I	Matrix to invert (May be any kind of real or complex.)
B	Same as A	NDIM × NDIM	O	Inverse matrix A^{-1} (Same kind as A.)
NDIM	Int		I	Declared size of matrices.
N	Int		I	No. of rows and columns actually used in A
ERROR	Int		O	Error flag: 0 = No error 1 = No inverse found (pivot too small)

Algorithm:

This subroutine uses Gauss-Jordan elimination and the maximum pivot technique to construct the inverse of an n x n matrix. It initializes matrix B to the identity matrix and then performs Gauss-Jordan elimination on a copy of matrix A, applying exactly the same operations to matrix B that were applied to matrix A. When the operation is over and the copy of A contains the identity matrix, B will contain matrix A^{-1}. These matrix inversion routines suffer from the same conditioning problems as Gaussian elimination routines, so the double-precision version will be required for large and/or ill-conditioned matrices.

Examples:

This example declares two 10 × 10 arrays a and b, initializes array a with a 2 × 2 matrix, and inverts the matrix using subroutine `mat_inv`.

```
USE booklib
IMPLICIT NONE
INTEGER, PARAMETER :: ndim = 10
REAL, DIMENSION(ndim,ndim) :: a, b
INTEGER :: error, i, j, n = 2
a(1,1) = 1.; a(2,1) = 2.; a(1,2) = 3.; a(2,2) = 4.
CALL mat_inv (a, b, ndim, n, error )
WRITE (*,1000) ((b(i,j), j = 1, n), i = 1, n)
1000 FORMAT (1X, 'b = ', /, (4X,F10.4,4X,F10.4))
```

Result:
```
 b  =
      -2.000        1.5000
       1.000        -.5000
```

13

In the argument list for this subroutine, the sizes of the matrices A and B are declared by argument NDIM, while the size of the matrix to invert is declared by argument N. Why is there a distinction between the declared size of the matrices and the size of the matrix to be processed? Matrices A and B may be declared large enough to contain the largest size problems that a particular program will ever need to handle. For example, matrices a and b may be declared as 4 × 4 matrices in order to support problems up to that size, but the current problem may only require 2 × 2 matrices. We must tell the subroutine that the matrices are 4 × 4 so that it will know how to locate a term like a(1,2). Therefore, we pass ndim to the subroutine. On the other hand, we must also tell it that we only want to invert a 2 × 2 portion of the matrix. If we just let the subroutine invert all of the values declared in the matrices, then the operation would fail because of the zeros in the unused portion of the array. For this reason, we also pass N.

Recall from Chapter 5 that arrays are allocated in memory column order. All of column 1 is allocated, and than all of column 2, and so on. Because of this allocation scheme, a subroutine using a rank-2 array must know the number of rows in the

Two-dimensional 4 × 4 array a:

$$a = \begin{bmatrix} a(1,1) & a(1,2) & a(1,3) & a(1,4) \\ a(2,1) & a(2,2) & a(2,3) & a(2,4) \\ a(3,1) & a(3,2) & a(3,3) & a(3,4) \\ a(4,1) & a(4,2) & a(4,3) & a(4,4) \end{bmatrix}$$

FIGURE 13–5
Memory allocation for a 4 × 4 array a.

Memory allocation for the 4 × 4 array a:

a(1,1)
a(2,1)
a(3,1)
a(4,1)
a(1,2)
a(2,2)
a(3,2)
a(4,2)
a(1,3)
a(2,3)
a(3,3)
a(4,3)
a(1,4)
a(2,4)
a(3,4)
a(4,4)

13

array in order to calculate the memory location of any element in that array. If we again consider the 4 × 4 array a, we can see that element a(1,2) is the fifth element in the array, since the entire first column is allocated in memory before the first element in the second column (see Figure 13–5). The subroutine must know that the array has four rows, or it cannot determine the proper element to access.

Example 13–2 Inverting Matrices: Let's illustrate the effect of passing incorrect array sizes to subroutines by inverting a 3 × 3 matrix that is stored in an array of size 4 × 4 with the BOOKLIB library routine mat_inv. We will do this inversion two times:

1. Once with the correct array sizes (4 × 4) and correct number of rows and columns to invert (3 × 3).
2. Once with incorrect array sizes (3 × 3) but with the correct number of rows and columns to invert (3 × 3). (Novice programmers using a library for the first time often make this mistake.)

SOLUTION A program to invert a 3 × 3 matrix a and store the result in matrix b is shown in Figure 13–6. Note that the BOOKLIB library has been included by USE association. Matrices a and b can each hold 4 × 4 values.

FIGURE 13–6
Program to test subroutine mat_inv.

```
PROGRAM test_mat_inv
!
!   Purpose:
!     To illustrate the use of library subroutine mat_inv and
!     also to illustrate the errors caused by passing incorrect
!     array sizes to mat_inv.
!
!   Record of revisions:
!      Date          Programmer          Description of change
!      ====          ==========          =====================
!     03/04/96     S. J. Chapman         Original code
!
USE booklib                              ! Use BOOKLIB library

IMPLICIT NONE

! List of variables:
REAL, DIMENSION(4, 4) :: a      ! Input matrix
REAL, DIMENSION(4, 4) :: b      ! Output matrix
INTEGER :: error                ! Error flag
INTEGER :: i, j                 ! Index variables
INTEGER :: n                    ! Actual size of matrix to invert
INTEGER :: ndim                 ! Declared size of a & b

a = RESHAPE ((/1.,2.,3.,0.,1.,3.,2.,0.,-1.,2.,-3.,0.,0.,0.,0.,0./), &
            (/4,4/))
b = 0.
```

(continued)

(concluded)

```
! Call mat_inv subroutine correctly to invert 3 x 3 matrix a
! and place the result in b.
ndim = 4
n = 3
CALL mat_inv ( a, b, ndim, n, error )

! Print out matrix a.
WRITE (*, '(/1X,A)') 'Matrix a:'
WRITE (*, '(3X,4F10.4)') ((a(i,j), j=1,4), i=1,4)

! Print out matrix b.
WRITE (*,'(/1X,A)') 'Result with matrix sizes declared correctly:'
WRITE (*,'(3X,4F10.4)') ((b(i,j), j=1,4), i=1,4)
WRITE (*,'(1X,A,I2)') 'Error flag = ', error
! Call mat_inv subroutine with all parameters equal to 3.
b = 0.                            ! Clear b
ndim = 3                          ! Error
n = 3
CALL mat_inv ( a, b, ndim, n, error )

! Print out matrix b.
WRITE (*,'(/1X,A)') 'Result with matrix sizes declared incorrectly:'
WRITE (*,'(3X,4F10.4)') ((b(i,j), j=1,4), i=1,4)
WRITE (*,'(1X,A,I2)') 'Error flag = ', error

END PROGRAM
```

When this program is executed, the results are

```
C>test_mat_inv

Matrix a:
      1.0000    1.0000   -1.0000     .0000
      2.0000    3.0000    2.0000     .0000
      3.0000    2.0000   -3.0000     .0000
       .0000     .0000     .0000     .0000

Result with matrix sizes declared correctly:
     -3.2500     .7500    3.7500     .0000
      5.0000     .0000   -1.6667     .0000
      1.0000    -.2000     .2500     .0000
       .0000     .0000     .0000     .0000
Error flag = 0

Result with matrix sizes declared incorrectly:
      -.2000   -1.4000     .2000     .0000
      -.4000   -1.0000     .0000     .0000
      1.0000   -1.2000     .0000     .0000
      3.6000    -.8000     .0000     .0000
Error flag = 0
```

When both the physical sizes of the arrays (ndim) and the number of rows and columns in use (n) are correct, the output from the subroutine is correct, as we can prove by multiplying the 3×3 matrices a and b together. If the size of the arrays were specified incorrectly to be 3×3, then the subroutine will not be able to index into the arrays properly. It will believe that the fourth memory location in array a is a(1,2), when in fact it is a(4,1). This confusion causes the subroutine to invert the matrix $a = \begin{bmatrix} 1. & 0. & 2. \\ 2. & 1. & 0. \\ 3. & 3. & -1. \end{bmatrix}$ and the results are stored in the wrong locations in b. In order to get a correct answer, we must specify correctly both the sizes of the arrays and the portion of those arrays actually in use.

A subroutine does not actually need to know how many columns are in a two-dimensional array in order to access a given array element properly. Therefore, many older library procedures are written using **assumed-size arrays,** and only the number of rows are specified when two-dimensional arrays are passed to the procedures. However, procedures that used assumed-size arrays cannot use array operations. Most newly written Fortran 90/95 library procedures will use either explicit-shape dummy arrays with all dimensions passed to the procedure or **assumed-shape arrays** together with an explicit interface.

Another advantage of using explicit-shape arrays or assumed-shape arrays in library procedures is that it is possible to use the bounds-checking option available with most compilers to help debug new programs. In fact, it is possible to make two libraries with the same procedures: a debugging library and a standard library. The procedures in the debugging library will be compiled with all the checking options turned on. They will run slowly, but they will tell a user if any out-of-bounds references occur. The procedures in the standard library will be compiled with all the checking options turned off. They will run quickly, but the user will not be informed if an error occurs. Normally, a programmer would link with the debugging library while testing a new program to catch any errors in the program. Once the program has been debugged, he or she will link to the standard library so that the program will run faster.

13

Quiz 13–1

This quiz provides a quick check to see if you understand the concepts introduced in sections 13.1 and 13.2. If you have trouble with the quiz, reread the sections, ask your instructor, or discuss the material with a fellow student. The answers to this quiz are found in the back of the book.

1. Determine how to create libraries and place procedures into libraries on your computer.

2. Determine how to link with libraries on your computer.

3. Find a subroutine or function in library BOOKLIB that will take the cross product of two vectors. Write a program that uses that procedure to calculate the cross product of the vectors va = [10. −2. 40.] and vb = [7. −10. −4.]. Compile the program, link it with BOOKLIB, and execute it. What is the result of the program?

■ 13.3
EXAMPLES

The diskette that accompanies the instructor's manual for this book contains a number of the useful procedures that we have developed in the book, as well as some others of general interest. The procedures are also available at the book's Web site. Your instructor will probably have compiled the procedures and generated a `BOOKLIB` library on the computer that you are using with this course. He or she will be able to tell you how to access this library.

The procedures contained in the library are described in the instructor's manual and in documentation available at the book's Web site. The purpose of each procedure is given in the documentation, together with a description of its calling sequence, arguments, and algorithm. The documentation also indicates which module must be included in a `USE` statement in order to access the procedure. To use the library, you should look through the descriptions of the procedures to locate one that performs the function you need and then check to see what its calling sequence is. Once you know which procedure you want to use and how it is called, you can add the appropriate calls to your program. You should be sure to include the proper module in a `USE` statement in the program unit invoking the procedure. Finally, you should search the appropriate library when you are linking the program to create an executable file.

When you go to work in industry, you will probably be using procedures from much larger libraries in your programs. The approach will be exactly the same in that case as it is with our simple library:

1. Search the library documentation for the subroutines or functions to perform the task you need.
2. Check the documentation for the proper calling sequence for the procedures.
3. Insert calls to the procedures in your program.
4. Include appropriate `USE` statements and link the program with the library containing the desired procedures.

The following four examples illustrate the use of routines from the `BOOKLIB` library in the solution of practical problems.

EXAMPLE 13–3 Solving Simultaneous Equations with the LAPACK Library:
Gauss-Jordan elimination was introduced in Chapter 6 as a simple technique for finding the solutions of systems to simultaneous equations. As we saw in Chapter 8, this simple technique can produce poor or meaningless answers for ill-conditioned systems of equations. We got around that problem in Chapter 8 by working harder—we used a double-precision version of the subroutine to solve the ill-conditioned sets of equations.

Another way to attack the problem of ill-conditioned systems of equations is by working smarter. That is, we could investigate algorithms that are less sensitive to cumulative round-off errors for solving the system of equations. The free LAPACK library contains high-quality algorithms that are the cumulation of more than 30 years of research into numerical methods. Naturally, these algorithms should do a better job that the simple Gauss-Jordan elimination technique that we used. We will now see how the algorithms in the library compare to simple single- and double-precision Gauss-Jordan elimination for solving simultaneous equations.

Write a program that solves a system of simultaneous equations three times and compares the results. It should solve the system using single-precision Gauss-Jordan elimination, double-precision Gauss-Jordan elimination, and the single-precision LAPACK simultaneous equation subroutine. The program should check the quality of each solution by substituting it back into the original equations and calculating the resulting residual error.

SOLUTION This program can be based on program `test_dsimul` from Chapter 8, since that program already solve a system of simultaneous equations using both single- and double-precision Gauss-Jordan elimination and checks the quality of its answers by substituting them back into the original equation.

If we check the library documentation, we see that the LAPACK subroutine to solve a single-precision set of simultaneous equations is `sgesv`, which is found in module `lapack_s`. The other procedure that we need is `simul`, which is found in module `booklib`. (Note that `simul` is a generic subroutine that performs both single- and double-precision calculations.) Therefore, the program must include both modules in USE statements. The calling sequences for both procedures are described in the appropriate pages of the library documentation.

The resulting Fortran program appears in Figure 13–7. Note that this program uses the ONLY option on the USE statements to access only subroutines `simul` and `sgesv` from the libraries.

FIGURE 13–7

A program to test LAPACK library subroutine `sgesv`.

```
PROGRAM test_sgesv
!
!   Purpose:
!     To test LAPACK subroutine sgesv, which solves a set of N
!     linear equations in N unknowns.  This test driver also calls
!     subroutine simul to solve the problem in single precision
!     and subroutine dsimul to solve the problem in double precision.
!     The results of the three solutions together with their errors
!     are displayed in a summary table.
!
!   Record of revisions:
!       Date          Programmer        Description of change
!       ====          ==========        =====================
!     12/12/95     S. J. Chapman        Original code
! 1.  04/09/96     S. J. Chapman        Modified from program
!                                           test_dsimul
!
USE booklib, ONLY: simul                 ! Use BOOKLIB library
USE lapack_s, ONLY: sgesv                ! Use LAPACK subset library
IMPLICIT NONE

! Declare parameters
```

(continued)

(continued)

```fortran
INTEGER, PARAMETER :: sgl = SELECTED_REAL_KIND(p=6)    ! Single
INTEGER, PARAMETER :: dbl = SELECTED_REAL_KIND(p=13)   ! Double

! List of local variables
! First, variables for simul solution
REAL(KIND=sgl), ALLOCATABLE, DIMENSION(:,:) :: a
                                ! Single-precision coefficients
REAL(KIND=sgl), ALLOCATABLE, DIMENSION(:):: b
                                ! Single-precision constant values
REAL(KIND=sgl), ALLOCATABLE, DIMENSION(:) :: soln
                                ! Single-precision solution
REAL(KIND=sgl), ALLOCATABLE, DIMENSION(:) :: serror
                                ! Array of single-precision errors
INTEGER :: serror_flag          ! Error flag from simul
REAL(KIND=sgl) :: serror_max    ! Max single-precision error


! Variables for dsimul solution
REAL(KIND=dbl), ALLOCATABLE, DIMENSION(:,:) :: da
                                ! Double-precision coefficients
REAL(KIND=dbl), ALLOCATABLE, DIMENSION(:) :: db
                                ! Double-precision constant values
REAL(KIND=dbl), ALLOCATABLE, DIMENSION(:) :: dsoln
                                ! Double-precision solution
REAL(KIND=dbl), ALLOCATABLE, DIMENSION(:) :: derror
                                ! Array of double-precision errors
INTEGER :: derror_flag          ! Error flag from dsimul
REAL (KIND=dbl) :: derror_max   ! Max double-precision error


! Variables for single-precision LAPACK solution
INTEGER, ALLOCATABLE, DIMENSION(:) :: ipiv
                                ! Pivot indices
REAL(KIND=sgl), ALLOCATABLE, DIMENSION(:,:) :: la
                                ! Single-precision coefficients
REAL(KIND=sgl), ALLOCATABLE, DIMENSION(:) :: lb
                                ! Single-precision constant values
REAL(KIND=sgl), ALLOCATABLE, DIMENSION(:) :: lerror
                                ! Array of single-precision errors
INTEGER :: lerror_flag          ! Error flag from sgesv
REAL(KIND=sgl) :: lerror_max    ! Max single-precision error
INTEGER :: nrhs = 1             ! Number of right-hand sides


! Other variables
INTEGER :: i, j                 ! Loop index
INTEGER :: istat                ! I/O status
INTEGER :: n                    ! Size of system of eqns to solve
CHARACTER(len=20) :: filename   ! Input data file name
! Get the name of the disk file containing the equations.

WRITE (*,*) 'Enter the file name containing the eqns: '
READ (*,'(A20)') filename

! Open input data file. Status is OLD because the input data must
! already exist.
OPEN ( UNIT=1, FILE=filename, STATUS='OLD', ACTION='READ', &
     IOSTAT=istat )
```

(continued)

13

(continued)

```fortran
! Was the OPEN successful?
open_ok: IF ( istat == 0 ) THEN

   ! The file was opened successfully, so read the number of
   ! equations in the system.
   READ (1,*) n

   ! Allocate memory for that number of equations
   ALLOCATE ( a(n,n), b(n), soln(n), serror(n), da(n,n), &
           db(n), dsoln(n), derror(n), ipiv(n), la(n,n), &
           lb(n), lerror(n), STAT=istat )

   ! If the memory is available, read in equations and
   ! process them.
   solve: IF ( istat == 0 ) THEN

      DO i = 1, n
         READ (1,*) (da(i,j), j=1,n), db(i)
      END DO


      ! Copy the coefficients to single precision for the
      ! single-precision solution.
      a  = da
      b  = db
      la = da
      lb = db

      ! Display coefficients.
      WRITE (*,1000)
      1000 FORMAT (/,1X,'Coefficients before calls:')
      DO i = 1, n
         WRITE (*,'(1X,7F11.4)') (a(i,j), j=1,n), b(i)
      END DO

      ! Solve equations.
      CALL simul (a, b, soln, n, n, serror_flag )
      CALL sgesv (n, nrhs, la, n, ipiv, lb, n, lerror_flag )
      CALL simul (da, db, dsoln, n, n, derror_flag )

      ! Display error flags:
      WRITE (*,'(/,A,I6)') ' simul error flag  = ', serror_flag
      WRITE (*,'(A,I6)')   ' sgesv error flag  = ', lerror_flag
      WRITE (*,'(A,I6)')   ' dsimul error flag = ', derror_flag

      ! Check for round off by substituting into the original
      ! equations and calculate the differences.
      serror_max = 0.
      derror_max = 0._dbl
      lerror_max = 0.
      serror = 0.
      lerror_max = 0.
      derror = 0._dbl
      lerror_max = 0.
      DO i = 1, n
         serror(i) = sum ( a(i,:)  * soln(:)  ) - b(i)
         derror(i) = sum ( da(i,:) * dsoln(:) ) - db(i)
         lerror(i) = sum ( a(i,:)  * lb(:)    ) - b(i)
      END DO
      serror_max = MAXVAL ( ABS ( serror ) )
```

(continued)

(concluded)

```
              derror_max = MAXVAL ( ABS ( derror ) )
              lerror_max = MAXVAL ( ABS ( lerror ) )

              ! Tell user about it.
              WRITE (*,1010)
              1010 FORMAT (/1X, ' I   SP X(I)    LP X(I)  DP X(I)        ', &
                     ' SP ERR       LP ERR       DP ERR ')
              WRITE (*,1020)
              1020 FORMAT ( 1X,' === ========   ======== ========        ', &
                     ' ========   ========    ======== ')
              DO i = 1, n
                 WRITE (*,1030) i, soln(i), lb(i), dsoln(i), serror(i), &
                              lerror(i), derror(i)
                 1030 FORMAT (1X, I3, 2X, 3G11.5, 3F13.8)
              END DO

              ! Write maximum errors.
              WRITE (*,1040) serror_max, lerror_max, derror_max
              1040 FORMAT (/,1X,'Max simul single-precision error: ',F15.8,&
                     /,1X,'Max sgesv single-precision error: ',F15.8, &
                     /,1X,'Max dsimul double-precision error:',F15.8)

           END IF solve

           ! Deallocate dynamic memory
           DEALLOCATE ( a, b, soln, serror, da, db, dsoln, derror, &
                        ipiv, la, lb, lerror )

     ELSE open_ok

        ! Else file open failed. Tell user.
        WRITE (*,1050) istat
        1050 FORMAT (1X,'File open failed--status = ', I6)

     END IF open_ok

     END PROGRAM
```

To test this program, we will use the same ill-conditioned 6×6 system of equations that was used in Chapter 8.

$$
\begin{array}{rcr}
-2.0\ x_1 + 5.0\ x_2 + 1.0\ x_3 + 3.0\ x_4 + 4.0\ x_5 - 1.0\ x_6 & = & 0.0 \\
2.0\ x_1 - 1.0\ x_2 - 5.0\ x_3 - 2.0\ x_4 + 6.0\ x_5 + 4.0\ x_6 & = & 1.0 \\
-1.0\ x_1 + 6.0\ x_2 - 4.0\ x_3 - 5.0\ x_4 + 3.0\ x_5 - 1.0\ x_6 & = & -6.0 \\
4.0\ x_1 + 3.0\ x_2 - 6.0\ x_3 - 5.0\ x_4 - 2.0\ x_5 - 2.0\ x_6 & = & 10.0 \\
-3.0\ x_1 + 6.0\ x_2 + 4.0\ x_3 + 2.0\ x_4 - 6.0\ x_5 + 4.0\ x_6 & = & -6.0 \\
2.0\ x_1 - 1.00001\ x_2 - 5.0\ x_3 - 2.0\ x_4 + 6.0\ x_5 + 4.0\ x_6 & = & 1.0001
\end{array}
$$

Placing this system of equations in a file called SYS6.ILL and running program test_sgesv on this file, produces the following results:[6]

---

[6]To reproduce these results with the Lahey Fortran 90 compiler, it is necessary to compile the BOOKLIB library with the −o0 option, which turns off all optimizations. If the optimizer is used, the Lahey compiler stores intermediate single-precision results as double-precision values in CPU registers; the calculation is effectively performed in double precision. This practice makes the single-precision version of procedure simul look misleadingly good.

```
C>test_sgesv
Enter the file name containing the eqns:
sys6.ill

Coefficients before calls:
   -2.0000     5.0000     1.0000     3.0000     4.0000    -1.0000      .0000
    2.0000    -1.0000    -5.0000    -2.0000     6.0000     4.0000     1.0000
   -1.0000     6.0000    -4.0000    -5.0000     3.0000    -1.0000    -6.0000
    4.0000     3.0000    -6.0000    -5.0000    -2.0000    -2.0000    10.0000
   -3.0000     6.0000     4.0000     2.0000    -6.0000     4.0000    -6.0000
    2.0000    -1.0000    -5.0000    -2.0000     6.0000     4.0000     1.0000

simul error flag  =      0
sgesv error flag  =      0
dsimul error flag =      0

   I    SP X(I)    LP X(I)    DP X(I)         SP ERR      LP ERR      DP ERR
  ===  ========   ========   ========       ========    ========    ========
    1   -44.171    -38.867    -38.529       2.83736500  .00000143   .00000000
    2   -11.193    -10.085    -10.000      -3.96770900 -.00000572   .00000000
    3   -52.927    -47.535    -47.155      -2.92594100  .00000525   .00000000
    4    29.878     26.338     26.137      -4.72323000 -.00000858   .00000000
    5   -17.985    -15.977    -15.850       4.52078600 -.00000572   .00000000
    6   -5.6973    -5.1222    -5.0856      -3.96770200 -.00001419   .00000000

Max simul single-precision error:      4.72323000
Max sgesv single-precision error:       .00001419
Max dsimul double-precision error:      .00000000
```

Notice that the single-precision LAPACK subroutine did almost as well as the double-precision Gauss-Jordan subroutine in solving the ill-conditioned set of equations! It pays to take advantage of smart algorithms when they are available.

EXAMPLE 13–4 *Interpolating between Data Points:* When engineers or scientists make measurements in the real world, they usually record the data only at discrete intervals. For example, the voltage in a sensing circuit might be measured and recorded only once a second during an experiment. What happens if, after the experiment, it is necessary to know the voltage at some point *between* the recorded measurements? Then the user must *interpolate* between the measured values to estimate the unknown voltage.

In this example, we will write a program to interpolate a data value at a user-specified point within a data set, using BOOKLIB routines to do the hard work.

SOLUTION The input measurements must be in the form (x,y) pairs, where x is the independent variable (such as the time at which a measurement is made) and y is the dependent variable (the measurement itself). The input measurements will be read from a user-specified input file, where each (x,y) pair occupies a separate line in the file. The data in the file must be ordered in terms of increasing values of x. The program must be able to ask the user for the input file name, to read the measurement data, and then to ask the user for the point x_0 at which to interpolate a value y_0.

If we check the library documentation, we see that BOOKLIB contains two interpolation procedures. One is called interp, it performs a linear interpolation between points in the input data set. The other one is called `spline_int`; it interpolates using smoothed curves between points. In this example we will interpolate points using `interp`. You will be asked to re-solve this problem using the cubic spline subroutines in exercise 13–13 at the end of the chapter.

Subroutine `interp` returns an error if the point to be interpolated is outside the range of the input data set, so the program that we write must handle this situation.

1. State the problem.

Write a program to read an input data set and to interpolate a measured value at a user-specified point within the data set.

2. Define the inputs and outputs.

The inputs to this program are
a. The file name of the file containing the data set.
b. A file containing the data set, organized in (x,y) pairs in order of increasing x, with one (x,y) pair per line.
c. The point x_0 at which to estimate the value y_0.
The output from this program is the value y_0.

3. Describe the algorithm.

This program will read in the input data set and the desired position at which to interpolate the value y_0. It must present the data to subroutine `interp` and display the results. The program will also have to handle error codes returned by `interp`. The pseudocode for this program follows.

```
Prompt user for the input file name "filename"
READ filename
Prompt user for the desired point x0
READ x0
OPEN File filename
IF Open successful THEN
   READ data value from file
   IF Read successful THEN
      CALL interp to interpolate the point y0
      Check for errors in subroutine interp
      IF no errors THEN
         Write out y0
      ELSE
         Tell user of interp failure
      END of IF
   ELSE
      Tell user of read failure
   END of IF
ELSE
   Tell user of open failure
END of IF
```

4. Turn the algorithm into Fortran statements.

The resulting Fortran program is shown in Figure 13–8. This program calls subroutine `interp` from the BOOKLIB library.

FIGURE 13–8
A program to interpolate values in a data set, using BOOKLIB routine interp.

```fortran
PROGRAM interpolate
!
!   Purpose:
!     To interpolate the value y0 at position x0, given a set of
!     (x,y) measurements organized in increasing order of x.
!
!   Record of revisions:
!      Date       Programmer          Description of change
!      ====       ==========          =====================
!    03/04/96   S. J. Chapman         Original code
USE booklib                          ! Use the library
IMPLICIT NONE

! List of parameters:
INTEGER, PARAMETER :: max_size = 1000

! List of variables:
INTEGER :: error                     ! Error flag: 0=no error.
LOGICAL :: exceed = .FALSE.          ! Logical indicating that array
                                     ! limits are exceeded.
CHARACTER(len=20) :: filename        ! Input data file name
INTEGER :: nvals = 0                 ! Number of data values to sort
INTEGER :: status                    ! I/O status: 0 for success
REAL :: temp1, temp2                 ! Temp variables for reading (x,y)
REAL, DIMENSION(max_size) :: x       ! Values of independent var x.
REAL :: x0                           ! Pos at which to interpolate y0.
REAL, DIMENSION(max_size) :: y       ! Values of dependent variable y.
REAL :: y0                           ! Interpolated value.

! Get the name of the file containing the input data.
WRITE (*,*) 'Enter the file name with the (x,y) data: '
READ (*,'(A20)') filename

! Get point x0 at which to interpolate data.
WRITE (*,*) 'Enter point x0 at which to interpolate y0: '
READ (*,*) x0

! Open input data file. Status is OLD because the input data
! must already exist.
OPEN ( UNIT=9, FILE=filename, STATUS='OLD', ACTION='READ', &
       IOSTAT = status )

! Was the OPEN successful?
fileopen: IF ( status == 0 ) THEN        ! Open successful

   ! The file was opened successfully, so read the (x,y) data.
   DO
      READ (9,*,IOSTAT=status) temp1,temp2 ! Get value
      IF ( status /= 0 ) EXIT            ! Exit on end of data
      nvals = nvals + 1                  ! Bump count
      size: IF ( nvals <=  max_size ) THEN ! Too many values?
         x(nvals) = temp1                ! No: Save values
         y(nvals) = temp2                !
      ELSE
         exceed = .TRUE.                 ! Yes: Array overflow
      END IF size
   END DO
```

(continued)

(concluded)

```
        ! Was the array size exceeded? If so, tell user and quit.
     toobig: IF ( exceed ) THEN
           WRITE (*,1000) nvals, max_size
           1000 FORMAT (' Max array size exceeded: ', I6, '>', I6)
        ELSE
           ! Limit not exceeded: interpolate the data.
           CALL interp ( x, y, nvals, x0, y0, error )

           ! Now display results.
           IF ( error  ==  0 ) THEN
              WRITE (*,1010) x0, y0
              1010 FORMAT (' The interpolated value at x = ', ES14.6, &
                          ' is ',ES14.6, '.')
           ELSE
              WRITE (*,1020)
              1020 FORMAT (' ERROR--Point is outside the range of x.')
           END IF
     END IF toobig

ELSE fileopen
     WRITE (*,1030) status
     1030 FORMAT (' Could not open file. status = ', I6)
END IF fileopen

END PROGRAM
```

5. Test the program.

To test this program, we will create an input data file INTDAT containing the following (x,y) data pairs (note that $y = x^2$ for this data set):

.0	.00
.5	.25
1.0	1.00
1.5	2.25
2.0	4.00
2.5	6.25
3.0	9.00
3.5	12.25
4.0	16.00
4.5	20.25
5.0	25.00

We will test the program using the values $x_0 = 3.1$ and $x_0 = 5.5$.

```
C>interpolate
Enter the file name with the (x,y) data:
intdat
Enter point x0 at which to interpolate y0:
3.1
The interpolated value at x =   3.100000E+00 is  9.650000E+00.

C>interpolate
Enter the file name with the (x,y) data:
intdat
Enter point x0 at which to interpolate y0:
5.5
ERROR--Point x0 is outside the range of x.
```

13

The correct value of y_0 for $x_0 = 3.1$ is 9.61. As you can see, the interpolation program came pretty close to the correct answer. Also, the program correctly identified $x_0 = 5.5$ as being outside the range of the input data set.

EXAMPLE 13–5 Generating Noisy Simulated Data: A common practice in engineering or scientific applications is to simulate the operation of a large system (such as an airplane) before it is built. It is much less expensive to find and correct design errors in simulations before a piece of hardware is built than it is to fix the thing afterwards. The simulated system is fed input data typical of data the real system would see, and engineers observe the response of the simulation to the inputs. If an error is found, the simulation is modified. The process is repeated until a successful design has been created.

To make certain that a design works, the simulated input data must be typical of the data that the system would see in the real world. Since all real-world measurements are noisy, some random noise must also corrupt the simulated input data to make the input realistic. These noisy input data sets are often generated by special simulation procedures.

In this example we will develop a subroutine to generate a simulated input signal consisting of a sine wave corrupted by a known amount of noise. The equation for a sinusoidal signal is

$$y(t) = \sqrt{2} \, A \sin 2\pi f t \qquad (13\text{–}1)$$

where A is the root-mean-square (rms) amplitude of the sinusoid, f is the frequency of the sinusoid in hertz, and t is time in seconds. We will generate our test signal by calculating the values of $y(t)$ at specific times separated by Δt seconds. The output values from the test sinusoid will be

$$y_0 = y(0)$$

$$y_1 = y(\Delta t)$$

$$y_2 = y(2\Delta t)$$

$$\cdots$$

$$y_i = y(i\Delta t)$$

If the spacing between each sample of the waveform is Δt seconds, then there will be $1/\Delta t$ samples per second. If the sampling frequency is defined as

$$f_S = \frac{1}{\Delta t} \qquad (13\text{–}2)$$

the expression for the test sinusoid in Equation (13–1) becomes

$$y_i = \sqrt{2} A \sin \left(2\pi \frac{f}{f_S} i \right) \qquad (13\text{–}3)$$

To make our sinusoidal input signal, we will corrupt this sinusoidal with noise. Let's check the BOOKLIB library to see what sort of noise generation routines are available. A quick check of the library documentation reveals three random-number-generating functions: function random_u, which generates a uniform random noise sequence whose amplitude varies between 0.0 and 1.0; function random_n, which generates a Gaussian random noise sequence centered at 0.0 with a standard deviation of 1.0; and function random_r, which generates a Rayleigh random noise sequence with a mean of 1.25 and a standard deviation of about 0.6. The distribution of samples produced by the uniform random noise function random_u is shown in Figure 13–9a. As you can see, there is an equal probability that any number between 0 and 1 will be produced by the function. The distribution of samples produced by the Gaussian random noise function random_n is shown in Figure 13–9b. It is the classic bell-shaped curve that describes so many phenomena in nature (including, probably, the distribution of grades in this class!). The distribution of samples produced by the Rayleigh random noise function random_r is shown in Figure 13–9c. The distribution of samples produced by function random_n is most representative of the types of noise that might corrupt our real signals, so we will use function random_n to simulate the noise on our test signal.

How much noise should be combined with the sinusoid? For some tests, we want to add very little noise to the simulated input signal, while for others, we want to add a lot of noise to the signal. The amount of noise mixed in with the desired signal is specified by a quantity called the *signal-to-noise ratio* (SNR). The SNR is the ratio of the desired signal amplitude to the noise amplitude. It is usually expressed on a logarithmic scale in decibels (dB). The SNR of a signal is given by the equation

$$\text{SNR} = 20 \log_{10}\left(\frac{A_{\text{signal}}}{A_{\text{noise}}}\right) \tag{13–4}$$

where A_{signal} is the rms amplitude of the signal and A_{noise} is the rms amplitude of the noise. For this example we should be able to specify the desired SNR of the test signal, and the program should be able to use Equation (13–4) to add the proper amount of noise to the desired sinusoidal signal.

With this background let's formally state the problem we are trying to solve: *Write a program that will generate a simulated input signal consisting of a sinusoid corrupted by a specified amount of Gaussian noise. The amplitude and frequency of the sinusoid, the sampling frequency f_S, and the SNR of the signal should be under user control. Also, the user should be able to specify the duration of the test signal in seconds. The subroutine that generates the test signal should place the resulting output signal in an array so that it may be easily passed to a system to be tested. The program should also write the test signal to disk.*

We will also plot the output signal generated by this program for several different signal-to-noise ratios. These plots will make obvious the corrupting effect of noise on the simulated input data.

SOLUTION The program must be able to ask the user for the critical information, calculate a sinusoidal signal corrupted by noise, and output the test signal in a user-specified array.

13

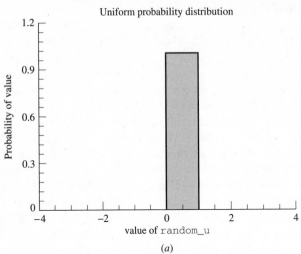

Uniform probability distribution

(a)

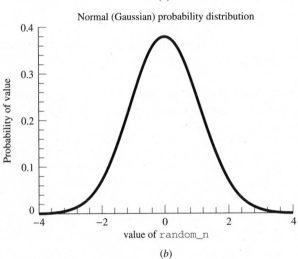

Normal (Gaussian) probability distribution

(b)

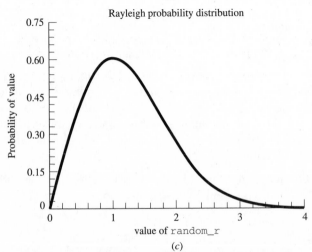

Rayleigh probability distribution

(c)

FIGURE 13–9

(*a*) Probability distribution of values generated by function `random_u`. (*b*) Probability distribution of values generated by function `random_n`. (*c*) Probability distribution of values generated by function `random_r`.

13

1. **State the problem.**

The problem has been succinctly stated above.

2. **Define the inputs and outputs.**

The inputs to this program are

a. The desired rms amplitude A of the sinusoid.
b. The desired frequency f of the sinusoid in hertz (Hz).
c. The desired sampling frequency f_S in Hz.
d. The duration of the signal (`total_length`) in seconds.
e. The desired signal to noise ratio in dB.
f. The name of a file to which the simulated data may be written.

The output from this program is an array containing the desired test signal. Note that the array must be able to hold the entire test signal. Since the length of the signal is `total_length` seconds and there are f_S samples per second, the number of samples required is

$$\text{nsamp} = (\text{total\_length})(f_S) + 1 \qquad (13\text{--}5)$$

where the 1 is for the extra sample at time zero. Therefore the output array must be at least `nsamp` samples long.

3. **Describe the algorithm.**

This program can be broken down into four major steps:

```
Get the input parameters from the user
Calculate the desired signal plus noise
Return the result in the output array
Write the data to disk
```

The first step of the program is to get the desired input parameters from the user. Then the program must calculate the desired signal corrupted by the specific amount of noise. This step belongs in a subroutine, since it is a logically separate function. Furthermore, if we write the test generator as a subroutine, we will be able to include that subroutine directly into the programs written for the system we are trying to test. Finally, we will return the results in the output array and write them out to a disk file so that we can see what we have done.

The detailed pseudocode for the main program follows.

```
Prompt user for the desired rms amplitude
READ amp
Prompt user for the desired frequency
READ freq
Prompt user for the desired sampling frequency
READ fs
Prompt user for the total signal length
READ total_length
Prompt user for the desired SNR
READ snr
Prompt user for filename
READ filename
OPEN File "filename"
```

13

```
IF OPEN successful THEN
    CALL test_signal to calculate signal
    Check for errors in subroutine test_signal
    IF no errors THEN
        WRITE out results to disk
    ELSE
        Tell user of test_signal failure
    END of IF
ELSE
    Tell user of OPEN failure
END of IF
```

Subroutine `test_signal` performs the actual work of calculating the test signal. The user-specified input parameters `amp`, `freq`, `fs`, `total_length`, and `snr` must be passed to the subroutine, as well as an output array to put the results in. The subroutine will calculate the number of samples required in the output signal and determine if enough space is available in the output array. If so, it will calculate the desired signal from Equation (13–3)

$$y_i = \sqrt{2}\, A\, \sin\left(2\pi \frac{f}{f_S} i\right) \tag{13–3}$$

for $i = 0$ to `nsamp` - 1. The required amplitude of the noise may be derived by solving for the noise amplitude in Equation (13–4)

$$A_{\text{noise}} = \frac{A_{\text{signal}}}{10^{(\text{snr}/20)}} \tag{13–6}$$

The detailed pseudocode for subroutine `test_signal` follows.

```
nsamp ← NINT ( total_length / dt ) + 1
amp_noise ← amp / ( 10.**(snr/20.))
IF nsamp > array length
    Set error code
ELSE
    Calculate factor ← 2 * pi * freq / fs
    Calculate peak_amp ← SQRT(2.) * amp
    DO for i = 1 to nsamp
        output(i) ← peak_amp * SIN (factor * REAL(i)) &
                        + amp_noise * g_random1()
    END of DO loop
END of IF
```

4. Turn the algorithm into Fortran statements.

The resulting Fortran program is shown in Figure 13–10. Note that this program calls function `random_n` from the BOOKLIB library.

FIGURE 13–10
Program to generate a sinusoidal signal corrupted by noise.

```
PROGRAM get_signal
!
! Purpose:
!   To generate a test signal consisting of a user-specified
!   sinusoidal signal corrupted by noise.
```

(continued)

(continued)

```
!
!   Record of revisions:
!      Date        Programmer          Description of change
!      ====        ==========          =====================
!    03/19/96    S. J. Chapman         Original code
!
IMPLICIT NONE

! List of parameters:
INTEGER, PARAMETER :: maxlen = 10000 ! Max length of output

! List of local variables:
REAL :: amp                          ! RMS amplitude of sinusoid
INTEGER :: error                     ! Error flag: 0 = No error
CHARACTER(len=32) :: filename        ! Output file name
REAL :: freq                         ! Frequency of sinusoid in Hz
REAL :: fs                           ! Sampling frequency
INTEGER :: i                         ! Index variable
INTEGER :: nsamp                     ! No. of output samples
REAL,DIMENSION(maxlen) :: output     ! Output signal
REAL :: snr                          ! Desired SNR
INTEGER :: status                    ! I/O status flag
REAL :: total_length                 ! Total signal length in secs

! Get sinusoid amplitude.
WRITE (*,*) 'Enter the desired amplitude of the sinusoid: '
READ (*,*) amp

! Get sinusoid frequency.
WRITE (*,*) 'Enter the desired freq of the sinusoid, in Hz: '
READ (*,*) freq

! Get sampling interval.
WRITE (*,*) 'Enter sampling frequency in Hz: '
READ (*,*) fs

! Get total signal length, in seconds.
WRITE (*,*) 'Enter total signal length in seconds: '
READ (*,*) total_length

! Get SNR in dB.
WRITE (*,*) 'Enter desired SNR in dB: '
READ (*,*) snr

! Get output file name.
WRITE (*,*) 'Enter output file name: '
READ (*,'(A)') filename

! Open output file on unit 7.
OPEN ( 7, FILE=filename, STATUS='REPLACE', ACTION='WRITE', &
       IOSTAT=status )

! Was the file open successful?
openok: IF ( status == 0 ) THEN

   ! Yes. Calculate the resulting test data set.
   CALL test_signal ( amp, freq, fs, total_length, snr, &
                      maxlen, output, nsamp, error )
```

(continued)

13

(continued)

```
    ! Check for errors in subroutine test_signal.
    result: IF ( error /= 0 ) THEN
       WRITE (*,*) 'Error in subroutine test_signal: no data.'
    ELSE
       ! Data is OK. Write out results.

       DO i = 1, nsamp
          WRITE (7, '(1X,F14.6,3X,F14.6)') REAL(i-1)/fs, output(i)
       END DO
    END IF result

ELSE openok
   ! A file OPEN error occurred.
   WRITE (*,'(3A,I6)') 'Open error in file ', filename, &
                       ' STATUS = ', status
END IF openok

! Close output file
CLOSE (UNIT=7, STATUS='KEEP')

END PROGRAM

SUBROUTINE test_signal ( amp, freq, fs, total_length, snr, &
                         maxlen, output, nsamp, error )
!
!   Purpose:
!     To generate a test signal consisting of a user-specified
!     sinusoidal signal corrupted by noise.
!
!   Record of revisions:
!      Date          Programmer          Description of change
!      ====          ==========          =====================
!    03/19/96      S. J. Chapman         Original code
!
USE booklib                             ! Use BOOKLIB library
IMPLICIT NONE

! List of parameters:
REAL, PARAMETER :: pi = 3.141593 ! pi

! List of calling arguments:
REAL, INTENT(IN) :: amp                 ! RMS amp of sinusoid
REAL, INTENT(IN) :: freq                ! Frequency of sinusoid, Hz
REAL, INTENT(IN) :: fs                  ! Sampling frequency, Hz
REAL, INTENT(IN) :: total_length        ! Total signal length, sec
REAL, INTENT(IN) :: snr                 ! Desired SNR
INTEGER, INTENT(IN) :: maxlen           ! Length of array "output"
REAL, DIMENSION(maxlen), INTENT(OUT) :: output ! Output signal
INTEGER, INTENT(OUT) :: nsamp           ! No. of output samples
INTEGER, INTENT(OUT) :: error           ! Error flag: 0 = No error

! List of local variables:
REAL :: amp_noise                       ! Noise amplitude
REAL :: factor                          ! 2 * pi * freq / fs
INTEGER :: i                            ! Index variable
REAL :: peak_amp                        ! Peak Signal Amplitude

! Calculate nsamp and noise amplitude
nsamp = NINT ( total_length * fs ) + 1
```

(continued)

(concluded)

```
amp_noise = amp / ( 10.**(snr/20.) )

! Is there enough room to place the data in the output array?
IF ( nsamp > maxlen ) THEN
   ! No--Set error condition and get out.
   error = 1
   nsamp = 0

ELSE

   ! Yes--Calculate the output data array.
   factor = 2. * pi * freq / fs
   peak_amp = SQRT(2.) * amp
   DO i = 1, nsamp
      output(i) = peak_amp * SIN ( factor * REAL(i-1) ) &
                  + amp_noise * random_n()
   END DO
END IF

END SUBROUTINE test_signal
```

5. Test the program.

To test this program, we can run it with the following parameters and plot the output signals:

```
amp           = 10
freq          = 1 Hz
fs            = 100 Hz
total_length  = 2 seconds
snr           = 0, 10, 20, and 30 dB
```

The output from this program is plotted in Figure 13–11. The effect of differing amounts of noise on the test data set are obvious in this plot.

EXAMPLE 13–6 *Detecting Signals in the Presence of Noise*: A common problem faced by engineers throughout the world is the *detection of signals buried in noise*. In a communications system, an engineer might try to extract a transmitted radio signal from a background of random noise. To do so, he or she must process the received signal in some fashion that enhances the desired signal while suppressing the undesired noise that was received at the same time. The detection of signals buried in noise is also important to mechanical engineers. For example, excessive vibrations occurring at certain frequencies in mechanical turbines indicate bearing wear and the need for maintenance. In this case the signal that the engineer wants to detect is the vibration associated with worn bearings, and the noise is all of the other sound produced by the turbine. Sonar systems are another example of the need to detect signals buried in noise. The power systems aboard Russian (and European) ships run at a frequency of 50 Hz, while the power systems aboard U.S. ships run at a frequency of 60 Hz. Therefore, the detection of a 50-Hz sonar signal might indicate the presence of a potential adversary, while the detection of a 60-Hz signal might indicate the presence of a potential friend. In this case the engineer is trying to detect the 50-Hz or 60-Hz tones against the background of the general sea noise.

13

13

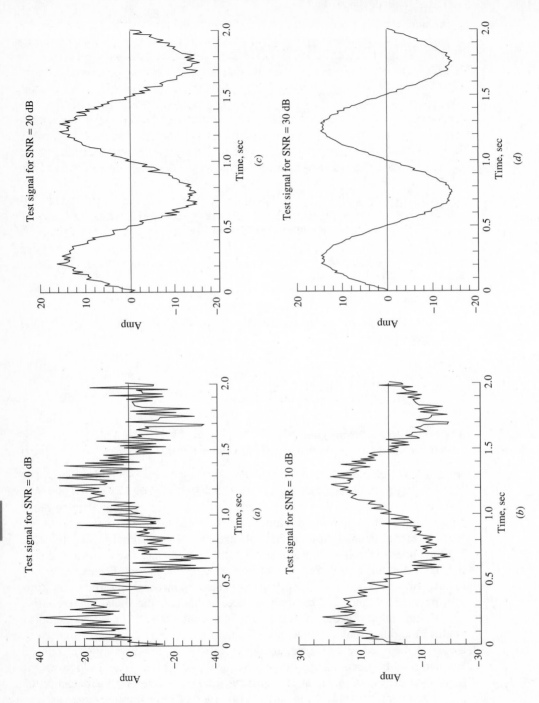

FIGURE 13–11
Sample output from the test_signal subroutine for (a) 0 dB SNR, (b) 10 dB SNR, (c) 20 dB SNR, and (d) 30 dB SNR. For all cases, amp = 10, freq = 1 Hz, dt = 0.01 sec, and total_length = 2 sec.

There are many ways of detecting signals in the presence of noise. One very common approach, which works for *narrowband signals,* is to analyze the frequency content of the received signal plus noise. If a signal is narrowband, then it occupies only a small range of frequencies and all of its energy will be concentrated there. Random noise, on the other hand, is typically *broadband*, occupying a wide range of frequencies. Because the energy of the noise is spread over a large band of frequencies, the energy at any particular frequency will be relatively small. The energy of the narrowband signal is all concentrated at one frequency, so even a relatively weak signal can be stronger than the portion of the noise energy occurring at the same frequency. This comparison can be done by examining the *spectrum* of the signal plus the noise.

This process is illustrated in Figure 13–12. Figure 13–12*a* shows a 10-Hz sinusoid with an rms amplitude of 1 volt (V). Figure 13–12*b* shows a Gaussian random noise with an rms amplitude five times larger than that of the sinusoid. Finally, Figure 13–12*c* shows the sinusoidal signal plus the random noise added together. From Equation (11–4), this waveform has a signal-to-noise ratio of

$$\text{SNR} = 20 \log_{10} \left(\frac{A_{\text{signal}}}{A_{\text{noise}}} \right) = 20 \log_{10} \left(\frac{1}{5} \right) = -14 \text{ dB}$$

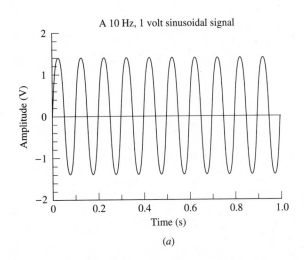

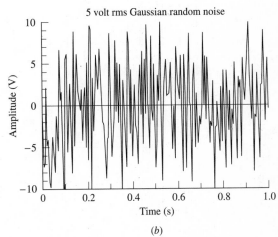

FIGURE 13–12

Detecting a narrowband signal in the presence of noise: (*a*) A 10 Hz sinusoidal signal with an amplitude of 1 volt. (*b*) Gaussian random noise with an rms amplitude of 5 volts. (*c*) The sum of the signal in (*a*) with the noise in (*b*). Note that no trace of the signal is visible to the naked eye. (*d*) The frequency spectrum of the 10 Hz, 1 volt sinusoidal signal. (*e*) The frequency spectrum of the Gaussian random noise. (*f*) The frequency spectrum associated with the signal in (*c*), which contains both the signal and the noise. Note that the 1-volt signal out of a background noise that is five times as strong.

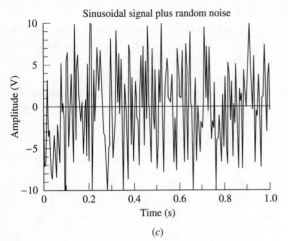

(c)

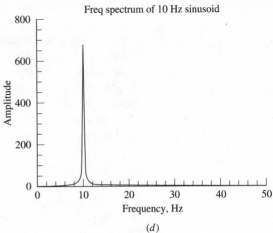

(d)

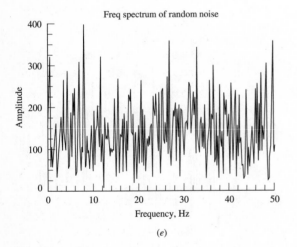

(e)

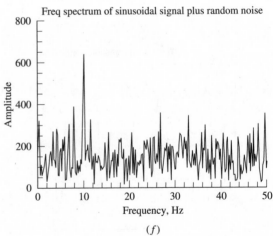

(f)

You can't even see the sinusoidal signal in the presence of all of that noise!

Now, let's look at the frequency spectra of these three signals. The frequency spectrum of the pure sinusoid is shown in Figure 13–12d. Notice that all the energy in the signal is concentrated in a narrow band of frequencies around 10 Hz. The frequency spectrum of the random noise is shown in Figure 13–12e. Notice that the energy in the noise is scattered more or less evenly throughout all frequencies. Finally, the frequency spectrum of the sinusoidal signal plus the noise is shown in Figure 13–12*f*. In this figure the signal can be picked out of the noise even though the rms amplitude of the noise was five times greater than the rms amplitude of the signal!

Examining the frequency spectra of signals is a very good way to detect narrowband signals in the presence of noise. How can we determine the frequency content of a signal? The standard way to determine the frequency content of a time signal is to calculate the *discrete Fourier transform* (DFT) of that signal. The DFT is defined by the equation

$$F_n = \sum_{k=0}^{N-1} t_k e^{2\pi i k n T/f_s} \tag{13–7}$$

where

t_k = the kth time sample of the signal being analyzed.
N = the total number of samples in the signal being analyzed.
T = the duration of the signal being analyzed in seconds.
f_S = the sampling frequency of the signal being analyzed.
F_n = the nth frequency component of the output spectrum (a complex number). There will be N components in the complete output spectrum.

The relationship between the length of the signal being analyzed T, the sampling frequency f_S, and number of samples N is

$$N = f_S T \tag{13–8}$$

The fixed relationship between the sampling frequency f_S and the spacing ΔF between components of the output frequency spectrum is

$$\Delta F = \frac{f_S}{N} = \frac{1}{T} \tag{13–9}$$

Therefore, the longer the signal being analyzed, the greater the density of samples in the resulting spectrum.

The detailed theory of the DFT is far beyond the scope of this book. It is normally discussed during graduate-level digital-signal-processing courses. Fortunately, we don't have to worry about that! The beauty of having a procedure library available is that *someone else* studied the theory and wrote and checked the subroutine implementing the algorithm. All that we users have to know is the calling sequence of the subroutine and just enough theory to use the subroutine intelligently.

The BOOKLIB library included with this book contains an implementation of the DFT known as the *fast Fourier transform* (FFT). The FFT is just a fast implementation of the DFT algorithm given in Equation (13–7). It has the special restriction that the number of samples in the time series being analyzed must be a power of 2 (16, 32, 64, 128, 256, etc.). If the number of samples in the series is not a power of 2, then trailing zeros must be added at the end of the series until the total number of samples is a power of 2. This process is called *zero padding*.

With this background, let's state the problem that we want to solve: *Write a program that can analyze a time sequence to determine if any narrowband sig-*

13

nals are buried within the data. Plot the output frequency spectrum of the time series and determine by inspection whether a signal is present.

SOLUTION Since the times series to be analyzed can be quite long, they should be read from an input disk file. For compatibility with the test data generator created in the previous example, we will assume that the input data file contains two values per line, with the first one being the time of the sample and the second being the value of the sample. (This program does not need the times of each sample, so it will have to be designed to skip over that information.)

The program will need to know the name of the input disk file and also the sampling frequency of the input data set. It will open the input file and read in all the data samples. If necessary, the program will zero pad the end of the data until it is a power of 2 long and then calculate the complex frequency spectrum of the signal by calling BOOKLIB routine fft. The program must then calculate the amplitude of the frequency spectrum. Finally, the amplitude of the spectrum will be displayed with BOOKLIB routine plotxy.

1. **State the problem.**

   The problem has been succinctly stated above.

2. **Define the inputs and outputs.**

   The inputs to this program are
   a. The name of a file containing the input data.
   b. The input data in the file.
   c. The sampling frequency f_S of the data.
   The output from this program is a plot of the amplitude spectrum of the input time series.

3. **Describe the algorithm.**

   This program can be broken down into four major steps:

   ```
   Read the input data
   Calculate the complex amplitude spectrum using "fft"
   Calculate the magnitude of the amplitude spectrum
   Plot the magnitude of the amplitude spectrum
   ```

   The first step of the program is to get the desired input data from the user. The program should open a user-supplied file, containing an unknown number of data points in the form of (time, value) pairs, with one pair per line. The program will read in all of the data, stopping when the end of the file is detected. The detailed pseudocode for this step follows.

   ```
   Prompt user for the input file name "filename"
   READ "filename"
   Prompt user for sampling frequency "fs"
   READ fs
   OPEN file "filename"
   IF OPEN is successful THEN
       WHILE
           READ time, temp (time is a dummy variable-we don't need it.)
           IF READ not successful EXIT
   ```

```
              nvals ← nvals + 1
              IF nvals <= maxsiz THEN
                  data1(i) ← temp
              ELSE
                  exceed ← .true.
              END of IF
          END of WHILE

          IF array size was exceeded THEN
              Tell user and quit
          ELSE
          ...
          ... (Insert processing here)
          ...
          END of IF
      ELSE
          File open failed--tell user and quit.

      END of IF
```

If we examine the description of subroutine fft, we see that the input data must be of type COMPLEX and the length of the array must be a power of 2. Therefore, we must transfer the input data from real array data1 into the complex array cdata1 and then zero pad the length array cdata1 up to the next power of 2 before calling subroutine fft. The next power of 2 can be calculated by subroutine nxtmul, which is also found in BOOKLIB. Subroutine fft can then be called to calculate the complex amplitude spectrum, with the resulting spectrum being returned in array cdata2. The detailed pseudocode for these steps follows.

```
              ! Convert to complex
              cdata1(1:nvals) ← data1(1:nvals)

              ! Zero pad
              CALL nxtmul ( nvals, 2, iexp, fft_size )
              cdata1(nvals+1:fft_size) ← (0.,0.)

              ! Call "fft" to calculate complex spectrum
              CALL fft ( cdata1, cdata2, fft_size, status )
```

Finally, we want to plot the magnitude of the amplitude spectrum of the data. If the spectrum can be presented as a series of (frequency, value) pairs, then we can use BOOKLIB subroutine plotxy to do the plotting. Subroutine plotxy can handle up to a maximum of 65 data bins, so each bin plotted will have many frequency samples. We will plot the maximum value for any frequency sample falling in a given bin. The detailed pseudocode for this step follows.

```
      ! Generate (freq, value) pairs to plot at a spacing of 1 Hz.
      ! Frequency values in each x bin
      DO from i = 0 to NINT(fs)
          xplot(i) ← REAL(i)
      END of DO

      ! Calculate maximum spectral amplitudes in each plotting bin
      DO from i = 1 to fft_size
          ! Calculate frequency of data point to nearest Hz
          ifreq ← NINT ( ( fs / fft_size ) * (i - 1) )
```

13

```
          yplot(ifreq) ← MAX ( yplot(ifreq), CABS(cdata2(i)) )
     END of DO

     ! Plot data.
     CALL plotxy ( xplot, yplot, NINT(fs), plu )
```

4. **Turn the algorithm into Fortran statements.**

The resulting Fortran program is shown in Figure 13–13. Note that this program invokes procedures fft, nxtmul, and plotxy from the BOOKLIB library.

FIGURE 13–13
Program spectrum of Example 13–6.

```
PROGRAM spectrum
!
!   Purpose:
!     To calculate and plot the spectrum of an input data set.
!
!   Record of revisions:
!       Date        Programmer          Description of change
!       ====        ==========          =====================
!     03/20/96    S. J. Chapman         Original code
!
USE booklib                            ! Access BOOKLIB
IMPLICIT NONE

! List of parameters:
INTEGER, PARAMETER :: ilu = 9          ! Input data unit
INTEGER, PARAMETER :: maxsiz = 8192    ! Maximum FFT size
INTEGER, PARAMETER :: plu = 6          ! Output plot unit

! List of variables:
COMPLEX DIMENSION(maxsiz) :: cdata1    ! Complex input data
COMPLEX DIMENSION(maxsiz) :: cdata2    ! Complex spectrum
REAL, DIMENSION(maxsiz) :: data1       ! Real input data
LOGICAL :: exceed = .FALSE.            ! Array size exceeded
CHARACTER(len=32) :: filename          ! Input file name
INTEGER :: fft_size                    ! FFT size (power of 2)
REAL :: fs                             ! Sampling freq (Hz)
INTEGER :: i                           ! Index variable
INTEGER :: iexp                        ! Exp of new pwr of 2
INTEGER :: ifreq                       ! Freq to nearest Hz
INTEGER :: nvals                       ! No of vals to process
INTEGER :: status                      ! I/O status
REAL :: temp                           ! Scratch variable
REAL :: time                           ! Sample time (dummy)
REAL, DIMENSION(0:64) :: xplot         ! Array of freqs to plot
REAL, DIMENSION(0:64) :: yplot         ! Array of spectral values

! Get the name of the file containing the input data.
WRITE (*,*) 'Enter the file name containing the input data: '
READ (*, '(A32)') filename

! Get the sampling frequency of the input data.
WRITE (*,*) 'Enter the sampling frequency of the input data: '
READ (*,*) fs
```

(continued)

(continued)

```
! Open input data file. Status is OLD because the input
! data must already exist.
OPEN ( ilu, FILE=filename, STATUS='OLD', ACTION='READ', &
       IOSTAT=status )

! Was the OPEN successful?
fileopen: IF ( status == 0 ) THEN          ! Open successful

   ! The file was opened successfully, so read the data
   ! into the program.
   DO
      READ (ilu,*,IOSTAT=status) time, temp ! Get value
      IF ( status /= 0 ) EXIT                ! Exit on end
      nvals = nvals + 1                      ! Bump count
      size: IF ( nvals <= maxsiz ) THEN      ! Too many values?
         data1(nvals) = temp                 ! No: Save value
      ELSE
         exceed = .TRUE.                     ! Yes: overflow
      END IF size
   END DO

   ! Was the array size exceeded? If so, tell user and quit.
   toobig: IF ( exceed ) THEN
      WRITE (*,1020) nvals, maxsiz
      1020 FORMAT (' Maximum size exceeded: ', I6, ' > ', I6)
   ELSE

      ! Limit not exceeded. Convert the real input data to
      ! complex form.
      cdata1(1:nvals) = data1(1:nvals)

      ! Zero pad the data.
      CALL nxtmul ( nvals, 2, iexp, fft_size )
      cdata1(nvals+1:fft_size) = (0.,0.)

      ! Call "fft" to calculate complex spectrum.
      CALL fft ( cdata1, cdata2, fft_size, status )
      ! Generate (freq, value) pairs to plot at a frequency
      ! spacing of 1 Hz. First, place the frequency values
      ! in each "x" plotting bin.
      xvals: DO i = 0, NINT(fs)
         xplot(i) = REAL(i)
      END DO xvals

      ! Calculate the maximum spectral amplitudes for each
      ! "y" plotting bin.
      yvals: DO i = 1, fft_size
         ! Calculate the freq of the data point to nearest Hz.
         ifreq = NINT ( (fs / REAL(fft_size)) * REAL(i-1) )
         ! Calculate max spectral amplitude for this freq bin.
         yplot(ifreq) = MAX ( yplot(ifreq), CABS(cdata2(i)) )
      END DO yvals

      ! Plot spectrum.
      CALL plotxy ( xplot, yplot, NINT(fs), plu )
   END IF toobig

ELSE fileopen
```

(continued)

(concluded)

```
    ! If we get here, the open failed.
    WRITE (*,'(1X,A,A)') 'Open failed on file: ', filename
END IF fileopen

END PROGRAM
```

5. Test the program.

To test this program, we will run program get_signal with the following parameters:

```
amp           = 2.
freq          = 12 Hz
fs            = 50 Hz
total_length  = 10 seconds
snr           = −5 dB
filename      = EX13-6. DAT
```

A plot of the output test data from program get_signal is shown in Figure 13–14. Note that the signal is hidden within the random noise. If we now feed the file EX13-6.DAT to program spectrum, the results are

```
C> spectrum
Enter the file name containing the input data:
EX13-6.DAT
Enter the sampling frequency of the input data:
50
         89.3473                                                    672.4326
           +-------------------------------------------------------------+
 0.0000  |    *                                                          |
 0.7656  |      *                                                        |
 1.5313  |                                                               |
 2.2969  |        *                                                      |
 3.0625  |  *                                                            |
 3.8281  |          *                                                    |
 4.5938  |                                                               |
 5.3594  |           *                                                   |
 6.1250  |     *                                                         |
 6.8906  |      *                                                        |
 7.6563  |      *                                                        |
 8.4219  |                                                               |
 9.1875 *|                                                               |
 9.9531  |          *                                                    |
10.7188  |      *                                                        |
11.4844  |                                                               |
12.2500  |                                                              *|
13.0156  |         *                                                     |
13.7813  |          *                                                    |
14.5469  |                                                               |
15.3125  |      *                                                        |
16.0781  |        *                                                      |
16.8438  |             *                                                 |
17.6094  |                                                               |
18.3750  |      *                                                        |
19.1406  |        *                                                      |
19.9063  |     *                                                         |
20.6719  |       *                                                       |
```

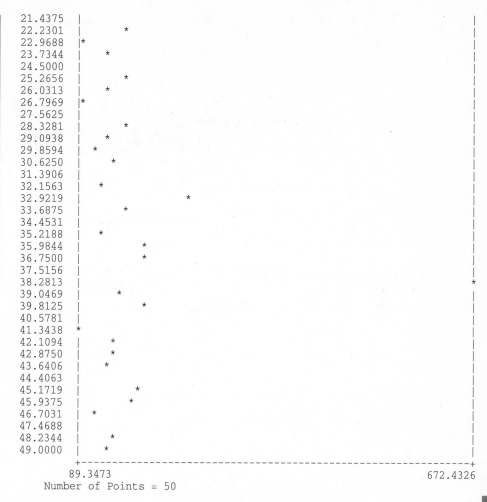

```
    21.4375  |
    22.2301  |           *
    22.9688  |*
    23.7344  |      *
    24.5000  |
    25.2656  |         *
    26.0313  |      *
    26.7969  |*
    27.5625  |
    28.3281  |         *
    29.0938  |     *
    29.8594  |   *
    30.6250  |     *
    31.3906  |
    32.1563  |    *
    32.9219  |                   *
    33.6875  |      *
    34.4531  |
    35.2188  |    *
    35.9844  |           *
    36.7500  |           *
    37.5156  |
    38.2813  |                                                    *
    39.0469  |     *
    39.8125  |          *
    40.5781  |
    41.3438 *
    42.1094  |     *
    42.8750  |     *
    43.6406  |    *
    44.4063  |
    45.1719  |         *
    45.9375  |        *
    46.7031  |   *
    47.4688  |
    48.2344  |      *
    49.0000  |    *
             +-------------------------------------------------------+
             89.3473                                         672.4326
        Number of Points = 50
```

The peak of the spectrum occurs at 12 Hz, so we have properly detected the 12-Hz signal embedded in the noise. A detailed plot of the output spectrum is shown in Figure 13–15. As you can see, the detailed spectrum matches the results of our line printer plot.

Notice that in addition to the signal peak at 12 Hz, another peak occurs at 38 Hz. In fact, the entire spectrum is symmetrical about the 25-Hz point! A point at 25 Hz + Δf has exactly the same amplitude as the point at 25 Hz − Δf. This effect always occurs when working with FFTs and sampled-data systems. In fact, the data below 25 Hz is a valid picture of the frequency content at those frequencies, while the data above 25 Hz is just a mirror image of the data below 25 Hz. The data above 25 Hz is said to be *"aliased"*. *Aliasing* is the effect that causes wagon wheels to appear to be rotating backward in old Western movies.

What is special about 25 Hz in the above data set? The answer is that it is *half of the sampling frequency* f_S. In general, all frequencies greater than half the sampling

Plot of data used to test program "spectrum"

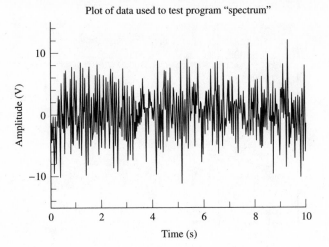

FIGURE 13–14
Plot of test data generated by program `get_signal` and used to test program `spectrum`.

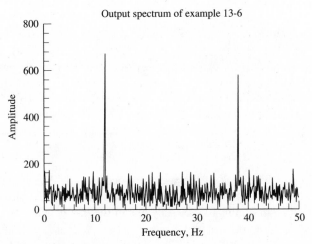

FIGURE 13–15
The output spectrum produced by program `spectrum`.

frequency will be aliased, and all frequencies below that point will be valid. Half of the sampling frequency f_s has a special name: the Nyquist frequency $f_{nyquist}$. If you intend to analyze the frequency content of a data set, you must make certain that the Nyquist frequency of the data set is higher than the highest frequency that you are looking for.

■ 13.4
SUMMARY

Libraries are a convenient mechanism for storing the compiled object files from procedures that you may want to reuse in the future. When a procedure is placed in a library, it is stored in the library's file and an entry is made in the library's table of contents to tell the linker where to find the procedure. One common way to create a Fortran 90/95 library is to place all the desired sources in a module and to compile the module. Another approach is to compile each source file separately and to collect the object files with a librarian. In this approach it is possible to create a separate module containing interfaces to the procedures so that they will have an explicit interface.

Some libraries are available directly from computer vendors. These libraries typically contain utilities to return important system or program information or to interface with specific pieces of hardware attached to the computers. The format of the procedures in these libraries varies from one computer to another, so calling these procedures will make your code nonportable. To keep your code as portable as possible, you should call system library procedures through an *interface subroutine* or *interface function*. If you later want to move the program to another computer, only the interface procedures will need to be rewritten.

Many prebuilt libraries are available from commercial software vendors. These third-party libraries provide procedures to solve problems in specific areas such as engineering, signal processing, plotting, and statistics. Using these libraries can save a great deal of time when you are writing a new program, since many of the hardest functions have already been programmed and debugged for you. They can also improve the portability of your code, since it is possible to buy these libraries for many different computers.

The sample problems in the last section of the chapter illustrate the use of the simple Fortran library BOOKLIB.

13.4.1 Summary of Good Programming Practice

The following guidelines should be adhered to when working with libraries:

1. Use libraries to store and keep track of the subroutines and functions that you may be able to use in more than one program.
2. Purchase and use appropriate third-party libraries to make the development of complex programs in specialized areas easier. Buying an off-the-shelf product to perform a specific function is almost always easier and less expensive than developing and debugging the function for yourself.
3. Always use interface procedures between your code and system libraries supplied by your computer's vendor. All of the machine-specific code in your program will be concentrated in the interface procedures, so only the interface procedures will need to be modified when the program is moved to another computer.

13.5
EXERCISES

13–1 List the advantages of using libraries.

13–2 What are system libraries? Why should they be used with caution? If you are going to use a system library procedure, how should you use it?

13–3 Write a form of the interface subroutine `get_arguments` that works correctly for your compiler and computer.

13–4 **Creating and Using a Library** Build a library called `mylib` and insert subroutines `sort` (Example 6–1) and `random0` (Example 6–7) into it. Do this exercise two times. (*a*) Place both sources into a single module named `mylib` and compile the module. (*b*) Compile the sources separately to create object modules. Then use your computer's librarian to create library `mylib` and to add the two subroutines to it. Finally, create a module containing the interface definitions for `mylib`.

13–5 Write a test program that generates 1000 random numbers between 0 and 10 and then sorts them into ascending order. Use subroutines `random0` and `sort` in the program. Link the program with library `mylib` to access subroutines `random0` and `sort`.

13–6 **Plotting** Use subroutines in the `BOOKLIB` library to calculate and plot the function $sinc(x)$ between -2π and 2π. Then calculate the derivative of $sinc(x)$ with respect to x and plot the derivative between -2π and 2π.

13–7 **Matrix Inversion** Calculate the inverse of the 4×4 arrays a and b using the matrix inverse subroutine in library `BOOKLIB`. Confirm your answers by multiplying a by a^{-1} and b by b^{-1} to show that the result is the identity matrix in each case.

$$a = \begin{bmatrix} 4 & 2 & 8 & -6 \\ 2 & -4 & 3 & -5 \\ 8 & 3 & 1 & -2 \\ -6 & 5 & -2 & 2 \end{bmatrix} \qquad b = \begin{bmatrix} -5 & 7 & 2 & 3 \\ 7 & 4 & 5 & 1 \\ 2 & 5 & -3 & -2 \\ 3 & 1 & -2 & -2 \end{bmatrix}$$

The identity matrix I is a matrix with all zeros except for the diagonal elements, which are all ones. The identity matrix for a 4×4 array is

$$I = \begin{bmatrix} 1 & 0 & 0 & 0 \\ 0 & 1 & 0 & 0 \\ 0 & 0 & 1 & 0 \\ 0 & 0 & 0 & 1 \end{bmatrix}$$

13–8 Explain the distinction between `ndim` and `n` in Example 13–2.

13–9 **Heapsort** The selection sort algorithm that was introduced in Chapter 5 and the insertion sort algorithm that was introduced in Chapter 11 are by no means the only types of sorting algorithms available. One alternate possibility is the *heapsort* algorithm, the description of which is beyond the scope of this book. However, an implementation of the heapsort algorithm is included in `BOOKLIB`.

If you have not done so previously, write a set of elapsed-time subroutines for your computer, as described in exercise 6–31. Generate an array containing 5000 random values. Use the elapsed-time subroutines to compare the time required to sort these 5000 values using the selection sort and the heapsort algorithms. Which algorithm is faster? (*Note:* Be sure that you are sorting the same array each time. The best way to do so is to make a copy of the original array before sorting and then sort the two arrays with the different subroutines.)

13–10 Random Number Distributions   The principal differences among the three BOOK-LIB random-numbers-generating functions random_n, random_r, and random_u is the distribution of the values produced by each of the functions. Generate a 10,000-element array of random numbers produced by each of the random number generators; then use the histogram subroutine built into BOOKLIB to plot a histogram of the noise distributions they produce. How do they compare?

13–11 Higher-Order Least-Squares Fits   The BOOKLIB library contains two subroutines to perform least-squares fits to a polynomial of user-specified order: single- and double-precision versions of lsqfit. Write two programs that read (x,y) values from an input data file and fit a polynomial of user-specified order to the data. To test your programs, generate a file containing 21 (x,y) values from the equation

$$y(x) = 1 + 2x - x^2 + 4x^3 + 8x^4$$

for $x = 0.0, 0.25, 0.50, \ldots, 5.0$.
a. Perform a fourth-order fit to the data set using both versions of lsqfit. How do the resulting coefficients compare to the known values in the equation that generated the data?
b. Perform a ninth-order fit to the data set using both versions of lsqfit. How do the resulting coefficients compare to the known values in the equation coefficients? (In this case the coefficients of x^5, x^6, etc. should all turn out to be zero, since they were not in the equation that generated the input data.)
c. What is the difference between the performance of lsqfit_sgl and lsqfit_dbl on higher-order fits?

13–12   Use a BOOKLIB subroutine to plot the function $y(x) = e^x$ from $x = 0$ to $x = 3$ in steps of 0.1. Next take the derivative of the function $y(x) = e^x$ at $x = 0, 0.1, \ldots, 3.0$, and plot the derivative of the function. Compare the function to its derivative. How do they compare?

13–13 Cubic Spline Interpolation   In Example 13–4, we used the linear interpolation subroutine interp to interpolate a data set from the function $y(x) = x^2$ at the point $x_0 = 3.1$. Use BOOKLIB procedures to perform a cubic spline interpolation of the same data set at the same point. How does the quality of the cubic spline interpolation compare to that of the linear interpolation?

13–14   Create a data set of points from the $y(t) = \cosh t$ for $t = -5, -4.8, \ldots, 4.8, 5.0$. Use BOOKLIB procedures interp and spline_int to interpolate the function at $t = 2.25$ and compare the results of the two interpolation procedures to the true answer. How accurate were the two interpolation procedures?

13

13–15 Comparing DFTs with FFTs The discrete Fourier transform (DFT) is defined in Equation (13–7). The fast Fourier transform (FFT) is a special algorithm for calculating the DFT in cases where the number of data points is a power of 2. Compare the DFT and the FFT in the following steps:

    a. Create a 512-point data set containing the function sin *x* sampled at 1/16 second intervals as follows:

```
COMPLEX:: DIMENSION(512) :: cdata
dt = 1. / 16.
DO i = 1, 512
   cdata(i) = SIN(REAL(i-1)*dt)
END DO
```

    b. Take the DFT of these samples using the routines in BOOKLIB. Time the DFT routine execution with subroutine elapsed_time from exercise 6–31.

    c. Take the FFT of these samples using the routines in BOOKLIB. Time the FFT routine execution with subroutine elapsed_time from exercise 6–31.

    d. How much difference in speed is there between the DFT and FFT algorithms?

13–16 Integrate the function $f(x) = 1 + 4x - 2x^2$ from $x_1 = 0$ to $x_2 = 3$ using a step size of Δx of 0.05.

13–17 Create a data set consisting of 40 (x,y) pairs of values, where $x(t) = \sin t$ and $y(t) = \sin(2t + \pi/6)$ for $t = 0$ to 2π in steps of $\pi/20$. Plot the data set using subroutines in BOOKLIB.

13–18 Derivative Use a BOOKLIB procedure to calculate the derivative of the function $y(x) = \sin x$ between $x = 0$ and $x = 2\pi$ at 101 equally spaced points. Perform this calculation three times with step sizes Δx of 0.1, 0.01, and 0.001, respectively. Compare the answer in each case with the results of the analytic derivative of sin *x*:

$$\frac{d}{dx} \sin x = \cos x$$

13–19 Use a BOOKLIB procedure to calculate the derivative of the function $y(x) = \sin x$ between $x = 0$ and $x = 2\pi$ at 101 equally spaced points. Allow the procedure to calculate its own optimal step size. Compare the answer with the results of the analytic derivative of sin *x* and with the results of the previous exercise.

13–20 Constant False Alarm Rate (CFAR) A simplified radar receiver chain is shown in Figure 13–16*a*. When a signal is received in this receiver, it contains both the desired information (returns from targets) and thermal noise. After the detection step in the receiver, we want to pick out received target returns from the thermal noise background. We can do so by setting a threshold level and then declaring that we see a target whenever the signal crosses that threshold. Unfortunately, the receiver noise can sometimes cross the detection threshold even if no target is present. If that happens, we will declare the noise spike to be a target, creating a *false alarm*. The detection threshold needs to be set as low as possible so that we can detect weak targets; but if it is set too low, we will get many false alarms.

    After video detection, the thermal noise in the receiver has a Rayleigh distribution. Figure 13–16*b* shows 100 samples of a Rayleigh-distributed noise with a mean amplitude of 10 volts. Note that one false alarm would occur even if the detection thresh-

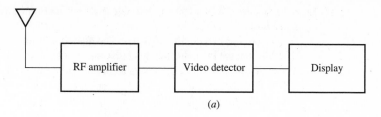

(a)

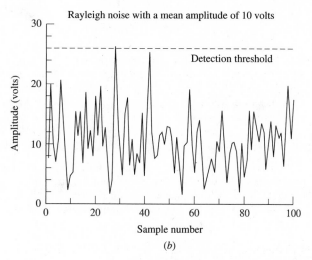

(b)

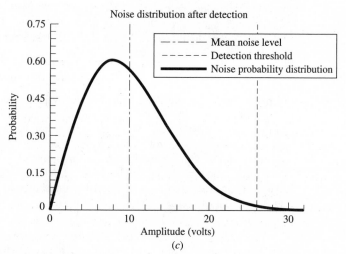

(c)

FIGURE 13–16

(a) A typical radar receiver. (b) Thermal noise with a mean of 10 volts
output from the detector. The noise sometimes crosses the detection
threshold. (c) Probability distribution of the noise out of the detector.

13

old were as high as 26! The probability distribution of these noise samples is shown in Figure 13–16c.

Detection thresholds are usually calculated as a multiple of the mean noise level; if the noise level changes, the detection threshold will change with it to keep false alarms under control. This method of detection is known as *constant false alarm rate* (CFAR) detection. A detection threshold is typically quoted in decibels. The relationship between the threshold in dB and the threshold in volts is

$$\text{Threshold (volts)} = \text{Mean Noise Level (volts)} \times 10^{\frac{dB}{20}} \qquad (13\text{–}10)$$

or

$$dB = 20 \log_{10}\left(\frac{\text{Threshold (volts)}}{\text{Mean Noise Level (volts)}}\right) \qquad (13\text{–}11)$$

The false alarm rate for a given detection threshold is calculated as

$$P_{fa} = \frac{\text{Number of False Alarms}}{\text{Total Number of Samples}} \qquad (13\text{–}12)$$

Write a program that generates 1,000,000 random noise samples with a mean amplitude of 10 volts and a Rayleigh noise distribution. Determine the false alarm rates when the detection threshold is set to 5, 6, 7, 8, 9, 10, 11, 12, and 13 dB above the mean noise level. At what level should the threshold be set to achieve a false alarm rate of 10^{-4}?

13–21 Probability of Detection (P_d) versus Probability of False Alarm (P_{fa}) The signal strength returned by a radar target usually fluctuates over time. The target will be detected if its signal strength exceeds the detection threshold for any given look. The probability that the target will be detected can be calculated as

$$P_d = \frac{\text{Number of Target Detections}}{\text{Total Number of Looks}} \qquad (13\text{–}13)$$

Suppose that a specific radar looks repeatedly in a given direction. On each look the range between 10 km and 20 km is divided into 100 independent range samples. One of these range samples contains a target whose amplitude has a normal distribution with a mean amplitude of 7 volts and a standard deviation of 1 volt. All 100 of the range gates contain system noise with a mean amplitude of 2 volts and a Rayleigh distribution. Determine both the probability of target detection P_d and the probability of a false alarm P_{fa} on any given look for detection thresholds of 8.0, 8.5, 9.0, 9.5, 10.0, 10.5, 11.0, 11.5, and 12.0 dB. What threshold would you use for detection in this radar?

Redundant, Obsolescent, and Deleted Fortran Features

The Fortran language has a number of odds and ends that have not logically fit in our discussions in the previous chapters. These miscellaneous features of the language are described here.

Many of the features we will be describing in this chapter date from the early days of the Fortran language. They are the skeletons in Fortran's closet. For the most part, they are either incompatible with good structured programming or are obsolete and have been replaced by better methods. As such, *you should not use these features in new programs that you write.* However, you may see them in existing programs that you are required to maintain or modify, so you should be familiar with them.

Many of these features are classified as either **obsolescent** or **deleted** in Fortran 95. An *obsolescent* feature is one that has been declared undesirable and that has been replaced in good usage by better methods. It is still supported by all compilers, but it should not be used in any new code. As their use declines, obsolescent features are candidates for deletion in future versions of Fortran. A *deleted* feature is one that has officially been removed from the Fortran language. It may be supported by your Fortran compiler for backward compatibility reasons, but there is no guarantee that it will work with all compilers.

Because the features described in this chapter are generally undesirable, there are no examples or quizzes featuring them. The contents of the chapter may be used as a cross-reference to help you understand (and possibly replace) older features found in existing programs.

14.1

PRE-Fortran 90 CHARACTER RESTRICTIONS

Before Fortran 90, the Fortran character set for naming variables officially included only the uppercase letters A to Z and the digits 0 to 9. The lowercase letters were undefined in the standard but were usually made equivalent to the corresponding up-

752   CHAPTER 14

percase ones if a particular compiler supported them at all. In addition, the underscore character (_) was not legal in a variable name.

All Fortran names (procedure names, variable names, etc.) were restricted to a
maximum of six characters. Because of these restrictions, you may encounter strange
and hard to read names in older programs.

14.2

OBSOLESCENT SOURCE FORM

The fixed-source form dates back to the old 80-column IBM card format. Its limitations were based on the limitations of the IBM card and use of card punches for program and data entry. The fixed-source form has been replaced by the free-source form,
which should be used in all new programs.

It is easy to convert a fixed-source form program into free-source form. A Fortran
program to accomplish this conversion is freely available on the Internet. It was written by Michael Metcalf at CERN in Geneva, and is named `convert.f90`. It is included on the disk accompanying the instructor's manual for this book.

The fixed-source form has been declared obsolescent in Fortran 95, which means
that it is a candidate for deletion in future versions of Fortran. All new programs
should use the free-source form.

14.3

REDUNDANT DATA TYPE

Versions of Fortran before Fortran 90 had two types of real variables: `REAL` and `DOU-
BLE PRECISION`. Double-precision variables were defined as having higher preci-
sion than real variables, but the exact precision and range of each data type varied
from computer to computer. Thus double precision on a VAX computer was a 64-bit
variable, whereas double precision in a Cray supercomputer was a 128-bit variable.
This difference made programs that depended on having variables with a certain minimum range and precision inherently less portable.

These older data types have been replaced by the parameterized real data type in
which it is possible to explicitly specify the range and/or precision required for a given
data item.

The `DOUBLE PRECISION` data type should never be used in new Fortran programs.

14.4

OLDER, OBSOLESCENT AND/OR UNDESIRABLE SPECIFICATION STATEMENTS

The syntax of many specification statements was different before Fortran 90. In addition, the following five obsolete and/or undesirable Fortran statements may appear
in the declaration section of a Fortran program:

1. The `IMPLICIT` statement
2. The `DIMENSION` statement
3. The `EQUIVALENCE` statement
4. The `DATA` statement
5. The `PARAMETER` statement

These statements are described below.

14.4.1 Pre-Fortran 90 Specification Statements

The form of many specification statements was different before Fortran 90. Attributes could not be declared in a type declaration statement, and the double colons (: :) were not used. In addition, variables could not be initialized in a type declaration statement.

The lengths of character variables were declared using an asterisk followed by the length in characters. The asterisk and length could be attached to either the `CHAR-ACTER` statement, in which case it applied to all variables in the statement, or a specific variable name. If it were attached to a specific variable name, the length applied only to that variable.

Pre-Fortran 90 type specification statements took one of the following forms:

```
INTEGER list of integer variables
REAL list of real variables
DOUBLE PRECISION list of double precision variables
COMPLEX list of complex variables
LOGICAL list of logical variables
CHARACTER list of character variables
CHARACTER*<len> list of character variables
```

Examples of some pre-Fortran 90 type specification statements are

```
INTEGER I, J, K
DOUBLE PRECISION BIGVAL
CHARACTER*20 FILNM1, FILNM2, YN*1
```

The `CHARACTER*<len>` form of the character type declaration statement has been declared obsolescent in Fortran 95, which means that it is a candidate for deletion in future versions of Fortran.

14.4.2 The `IMPLICIT` Statement

By default, named constants and variables whose names begin with the letters `I` through `N` are integers, while all other named constants and variables are of type real. The `IMPLICIT` statement permits us to override these defaults.

The general form of the `IMPLICIT` statement is

```
IMPLICIT type1 ( a1, a2, a3, ...), type2 ( b1, b2, b3, ...), ...
```

where `type1`, `type2` and so on are any legal data types: `INTEGER`, `REAL`, `LOGICAL`, `CHARACTER`, `DOUBLE PRECISION`, or `COMPLEX`. The letters `a1`, `a2`, `a3`, and so on are the first letters whose type will be *type1*, and so forth for the other types. If a range of letters is to be declared at the same type, then the range may be indicated by the first and last letters separated by a dash (-). For example, the following statements declare that variables starting with the letters a, b, c, i, and z will be COMPLEX, and variables beginning with the letter d will be DOUBLE PRECISION. Variables beginning with other letters will retain their default types. Finally, the variables i1 and i2 are explicitly declared to be integers, overriding the IMPLICIT statement.

```
IMPLICIT COMPLEX (a-c, i, z), DOUBLE PRECISION d
INTEGER :: i1, i2
```

The IMPLICIT NONE statement was described in Chapter 2 and has been used throughout the book. It cancels all default types. When the IMPLICIT NONE statement is used in a program, every named constant, variable, and function name in the program must be declared explicitly. Since every named constant and variable in your program should be declared explicitly, well-designed program does not need the standard IMPLICIT statement. Only the IMPLICIT NONE statement should be used. However, you must be familiar with the IMPLICIT statement because you will encounter it in older Fortran programs.

Good Programming Practice

The only IMPLICIT statement you should use in your programs is IMPLICIT NONE. All of your programs should include the IMPLICIT NONE statement, and all named constants, variables, and functions in your programs should be explicitly typed.

14.4.3 The DIMENSION Statement

The DIMENSION statement is a declaration statement used to declare the *length* of arrays. The general form of a DIMENSION statement is

```
DIMENSION array ( [i1:]i2, [j1:]j2, ... ), ...
```

where *array* is an array name and *i1, i2, j1, j2*, and so on are the dimensions of the arrays. For example, a six-element array array1 could be declared with the following statement:

```
DIMENSION array1(6)
```

Notice that the DIMENSION statement declares the length of an array, but not its type. If array1 is not included in any type specification statement, then its type will default to real because the name begins with the letter A. To declare both the type and the length of the array, we have to use one of the following sets of statements.

```
REAL, DIMENSION(6) :: array1
```

or

```
REAL :: array1
DIMENSION array1(6)
```

The DIMENSION statement is only needed when we declare the length of an array while using default typing. Since we never use default typing in good Fortran programs, there is no need to ever use this statement. It is a holdover from earlier versions of Fortran.

Good Programming Practice

Do not use DIMENSION statements in your programs. Since all variables and arrays in your program will be explicitly typed, the lengths of the arrays can be declared in the type declaration statements with the DIMENSION attribute. Well-designed programs do not need DIMENSION statements.

 14.4.4 The DATA Statement

Before Fortran 90, it was not possible to initialize variables in a type declaration statement. Instead, the variables were initialized by a separate DATA statement, which took the form

    DATA var_names/values/, var_names/values/, ...

where *var_names* are a list of variable names and *values* are the values to be assigned to those variables. There must be a one-to-one correspondence between the number of variables in the data statements and the number of values to initialize them. A single value could be repeated several times by preceding it with a repeat count followed by an asterisk. For example, the following statement initializes variables a1, b1, and c1 to 1.0, 0.0, and 0.0, respectively:

    DATA a1, b1, c1 / 1.0, 2*0.0 /

Arrays may also be initialized in DATA statements. If an array is mentioned in a DATA statement, then there must be enough data values to initialize all of the elements in the array. The values are assigned to the array elements in column order. The following DATA statement initializes the 2 × 2 array a1:

    REAL a1(2,2)
    DATA a1 / 1., 2., 3., 4. /

Since values are assigned to the array elements in column order, this statement initializes a1(1,1) to 1.0, a1(2,1) to 2.0, a1(1,2) to 3.0, and a1(2,2) to 4.0.

You can change the order in which values are assigned to array elements by using an implied DO loop. Thus the following DATA statement initializes the 2 × 2 array a2:

    REAL a2(2,2)
    DATA ((a2(i,j), j=1,2), i=1,2) / 1., 2., 3., 4. /

This implied DO loop initializes the array elements in the order a2(1,1), a2(1,2), a2(2,1), a2(2,2), so the values become a(1,1) = 1.0, a(1,2) = 2.0, a(2,1) = 3.0, and a(2,2) = 4.0.

The DATA statement is redundant because data initializations can be made directly in type declaration statements. It should not be used in new programs.

Good Programming Practice

Do not use DATA statements in your programs. Instead, initialize your variables in their type declaration statements.

14.4.5 The PARAMETER Statement

The parameter or named constant was introduced in FORTRAN 77. At that time parameters were declared in a PARAMETER statement of the form:

```
INTEGER SIZE
PARAMETER ( SIZE = 1000 )
```

The PARAMETER attribute was introduced in Fortran 90 so that the same parameter can now be declared as

```
INTEGER, PARAMETER :: size = 1000
```

The older PARAMETER statement was retained for backward compatibility, but it should never be used. The syntax of that statement is not consistent with other Fortran statements, and it is simpler to declare a parameter value in its type declaration statement anyway.

Good Programming Practice

Do not use PARAMETER statements in your programs. Instead, use the PARAMETER attribute of a type declaration statement.

14.5

SHARING MEMORY LOCATIONS: COMMON AND EQUIVALENCE

The COMMON statement and the EQUIVALENCE statement permit different variables to physically share the same memory locations, either between program units or within a single program unit. Both of these statements have been replaced by better methods in Fortran 90/95.

14.5.1 COMMON Blocks

We saw in Chapter 6 that modules may be used to share data between program units. If a data item is defined in a module and has the PUBLIC attribute, then any program unit that uses the module can access the data item. This technique is the standard way to share data among program units in Fortran 90/95. However, modules did not exist before Fortran 90, and a totally different mechanism was used to share data.

Before Fortran 90, information was shared among program units through COMMON blocks. A COMMON block is a declaration of a region of computer memory that is accessible to every program unit containing the common block. The structure of a COMMON block is

```
COMMON / name / var1, var2, var3, ...
```

where *name* is the name of the COMMON block and *var1*, *var2*, and so on are variables or arrays allocated in successive memory locations starting at the beginning of the block. Before Fortran 90, a COMMON block could contain any mixture of real, integer, and logical variables and arrays, or it could contain character data, but noncharacter and character data could not be mixed in the same COMMON block. This restriction has been removed in Fortran 90/95.

A procedure can have as many COMMON blocks as the programmer wishes to declare, so it is possible to create separate COMMON blocks for logical groupings of data that need to be shared. Each separate COMMON block must have a unique name. The names have global scope, so they must be unique within the entire program.

When an array appears in a COMMON block, the size of the array may be declared in either the COMMON block or the type declaration statement, but *not* in both places. The following pairs of statements are legal and completely equivalent

```
REAL, DIMENSION(10) :: a       ! Preferred
COMMON / data1 / a


REAL :: a
COMMON / data1 / a(10)
```

whereas the following statements are illegal and will produce an error at compilation time:

```
REAL, DIMENSION(10) :: a
COMMON / data1 / a(10)
```

COMMON blocks permit procedures to share data by sharing a common region of memory. The Fortran compiler allocates all COMMON blocks with the same name in any program unit to the *same region of memory,* so that any data stored there by one procedure may be read and used by any of the other ones. The COMMON blocks with a given name do not all have to be the same length in every procedure, since the Fortran compiler and linker are smart enough to allocate enough memory to hold the largest block declared in any of the procedures.

A sample pair of routines with COMMON blocks is shown in Figure 14–1.

14

FIGURE 14–1

A main program and subroutine sharing data through a COMMON block.

```
PROGRAM main
IMPLICIT NONE
REAL :: a, b
REAL, DIMENSION(5) :: c
INTEGER :: i
COMMON / common1 / a, b, c, i
...
CALL sub11
END PROGRAM

SUBROUTINE sub11
REAL :: x
REAL, DIMENSION(5) :: y
INTEGER :: i, j
COMMON / common1 / x, y, i, j
...
END SUBROUTINE
```

Variables and arrays are allocated in a COMMON block in the order in which they are declared in the COMMON statement. In the main program, variable a occupies the first word in the block, variable b occupies the second word, and so on. In the subroutine, variable x occupies the first word in the block, and array element $y(1)$ occupies the second word, and so on. Therefore, variable a in the main program is really the same as variable x in the subroutine. They are two different ways to refer to the same memory location. Note that the variables in the main program and the subroutine are related by their relative positions in their common blocks. This technique is known as **storage association** because the variables are associated by sharing a single physical storage location.

Both COMMON blocks and modules are convenient ways to share large volumes of data between procedures. However, COMMON blocks must be used carefully to avoid problems, since they are subject to two types of errors that don't affect modules. Both of these errors are illustrated in Figures 14–1 and 14–2. Note that the five-element array c in the main program and the corresponding five-element array y in the subroutine are misaligned because there is one fewer value declared in the block before the array in the subroutine than in the main program. Therefore, $c(1)$ in the main program will be the same variable as $y(2)$ in the subroutine. If arrays c and y are supposed to be the same, this misalignment will cause severe problems. Also, note that real array element $c(5)$ in the main program is identical to integer variable i in the subroutine. It is extremely unlikely that the real variable stored in $c(5)$ will be usable as an integer in subroutine sub1. This type mismatch must also be prevented. Neither the array misalignment nor the type mismatch can occur when using modules to share data between program units, so modules are the best way to share data in all modern Fortran programs.

To properly use a COMMON block, we must ensure that all variables in the block appear *in the same order* and have *the same type and size* in every program unit containing the block. In addition, it is good programming practice to keep the *same names* for each of the variables in every program unit containing the block. The program will be much more understandable if the same names apply to the same variables in all procedures.

Memory address	Program main	Subroutine sub1
0000	a	x
0001	b	y(1)
0002	c(1)	y(2)
0003	c(2)	y(3)
0004	c(3)	y(4)
0005	c(4)	y(5)
0006	c(5)	i
0007	i	j

FIGURE 14–2
Memory allocation in COMMON block /common1/, showing the misalignment between arrays c and y.

> ***Good Programming Practice***
> Use modules rather than COMMON blocks to share data between program units. If you do use COMMON blocks, you should be sure to declare the blocks identically in every procedure containing them so that the variables always have the same name, type, and order in each procedure.

 14.5.2 Initializing Data in COMMON Blocks: The BLOCK DATA Subprogram

The DATA statement was introduced in section 14.4.4. It may be used to initialize the values associated with local variables in a main program or subprogram. However, it may *not* be used in a main program or procedure to initialize variables in COMMON blocks. The following sample program illustrates the reason for this restriction:

```
PROGRAM test
CALL sub1
CALL sub2
END PROGRAM

SUBROUTINE sub1
INTEGER ival1, ival2
COMMON / mydata / ival1, ival2
DATA ival1, ival2 / 1, 2/
...
END SUBROUTINE sub1

SUBROUTINE sub2
```

```
INTEGER ival1, ival2
COMMON / mydata / ival1, ival2
DATA ival1, ival2 / 3, 4/
...

END SUBROUTINE sub2
```

Here COMMON block /mydata/ is exchanged between subroutines sub1 and sub2. Subroutine sub1 attempts to initialize ival1 and ival2 to 1 and 2, respectively, while subroutine sub2 attempts to initialize ival1 and ival2 to 3 and 4, respectively. And yet, they are the same two variables! How could the Fortran compiler possibly make sense of this situation? The simple answer is that it can't.

To guarantee that the variables in a COMMON block have only one set of initial values, the Fortran language prohibits the use of DATA statements with common variables in any Fortran main program or procedure. Instead, it includes a special type of program unit whose only function is to initialize the variables in a COMMON block: the BLOCK DATA subprogram. Since COMMON variables may be initialized in only one place, there is no ambiguity about what values to assign to them.

A BLOCK DATA subprogram begins with a BLOCK DATA statement and may contain any number of type definition statements, COMMON statements, and DATA statements. It must not contain any executable statements. A sample BLOCK DATA subprogram follows.

```
BLOCK DATA initial
INTEGER ival1, ival2
COMMON / mydata / ival1, ival2
DATA ival1, ival2 /1, 2/
END BLOCK DATA
```

The name of this BLOCK DATA subprogram is initial. (BLOCK DATA names are optional; this subprogram would have worked equally well with no name.) The subprogram initializes the variables ival1 and ival2 in COMMON block /mydata/ to 1 and 2, respectively.

14.5.3 The Unlabeled COMMON Statement

An alternative form of the COMMON statement is called the unlabeled COMMON statement. An unlabeled COMMON statement has the form

```
COMMON var1, var2, var3, ...
```

where *var1*, *var2*, and so on are variables or arrays allocated in successive memory locations starting at the beginning of the common block. The unlabeled COMMON statement is exactly the same as an ordinary COMMON block except that this COMMON block has no name.

The unlabeled COMMON statement is a relic left over from earlier versions of Fortran. Before FORTRAN 66, programmers could declare only one COMMON area in any given program. The unlabeled COMMON statement should never be used in any modern Fortran program.

14.5.4 The EQUIVALENCE Statement

In the past, it was sometimes useful to refer to a particular location in computer memory by more than one name. Computer memory was a limited and very expensive resource. Because computer memory was so expensive, it was common for large computer programs to reuse portions of memory for scratch calculations in different procedures within the program. Since dynamic memory allocation did not exist before Fortran 90, a single fixed block of scratch memory would be declared. This block of memory would be large enough for any temporary calculations within the program and would be used over and over whenever scratch memory was needed. Different portions of the program would often refer to the scratch memory by different names, but the same physical memory would be used each time.

To support such applications, Fortran provided a mechanism for assigning two or more names to the same physical memory location: the EQUIVALENCE statement. The EQUIVALENCE statement appears in the declaration section of a program after all type declaration statements and before any DATA statements. The form of the EQUIVALENCE statement is

```
EQUIVALENCE ( var1, var2, var3, ...)
```

where var1, var2, and so on are variables or array elements. Every variable appearing within the parentheses in an EQUIVALENCE statement is assigned to the same memory location by the Fortran compiler. If some of the variables are array elements, then this statement also fixes the relative relationships of all elements within the arrays. Consider the following example:

```
INTEGER, DIMENSION(2,2) :: i1
INTEGER, DIMENSION(5) :: j1
EQUIVALENCE ( i1(2,1), j1(4) )
```

Here i1(2,1) and j1(4) occupy the same memory location. Because of the way arrays are laid out in memory, i1(1,2) and j1(5) will also occupy a single memory location (see Figure 14–3).

EQUIVALENCE statements are inherently quite dangerous. A common problem occurs when we first perform some calculation using an equivalenced array under one name (say, array1) in a program and then perform a different calculation using the same equivalenced array under another name (say, array2) in another part of the program. If we then try to access values in array1, we will find that they have all been destroyed by the operations on array2. This problem is especially troublesome if someone other than the original programmer is modifying the program. Because data in array array1 has been destroyed without array1 ever appearing in an assignment statement, it can be very hard to track down this bug.

Since computer memory has become less expensive and more plentiful over the years, the need for equivalencing arrays has decreased dramatically. You should not equivalence variable names in your programs unless you have a very good reason to do so. If you need to reuse scratch memory arrays in your program, you should use allocatable arrays or pointers to allocate and deallocate the scratch memory dynamically.

14

Memory address	Name 1	Name 2
001		j1(1)
002		j1(2)
003	i1(1,1)	j1(3)
004	i1(2,1)	j1(4)
005	i1(1,2)	j1(5)
006	i1(2,2)	
007		
008		

FIGURE 14–3
The effect of the EQUIVALENCE statement on memory allocation in a Fortran program. Because i1(2,1) and j1(4) must be the same physical location, arrays i1 and j1 will overlap in the computer's memory.

Another use of the EQUIVALENCE statement was to assign the same memory address to variables of *different types* so that the same bit pattern could be examined in different ways. For example, a real variable and an integer variable could be assigned to the same location. When a real variable was stored in that location, the integer variable could be used to examine the bit patterns. If you have any older code that uses EQUIVALENCE statements in this fashion, you can replace it with the TRANSFER intrinsic function. For example, the following code takes the exact bit pattern of real variable value and stores it in integer variable ivalue:

```
INTEGER :: ivalue
REAL :: value
...
ivalue = TRANSFER(value, 0)
```

Finally, note that the EQUIVALENCE statement effectively assigns two or more names to the same memory location. From this statement, it follows that names must be associated with memory locations, or they may not be equivalenced. Names that are not associated with a specific memory location (for example, dummy argument names) may not be used in an EQUIVALENCE statement.

Good Programming Practice
Do not use EQUIVALENCE statements in your programs. If you need to reuse scratch memory arrays in your program, you should allocate and deallocate them dynamically with allocatable arrays or pointers.

■ 14.6

UNDESIRABLE SUBPROGRAM FEATURES

The following subprogram features are undesirable and should never be used in modern Fortran programs:

1. Alternate subroutine returns.
2. Alternate entry points.
3. The statement function.
4. Passing intrinsic functions as arguments.

14.6.1 Alternate Subroutine Returns

When a Fortran program calls a normal subroutine, the subroutine is executed and then control returns to the first executable statement following the subroutine call.

It is sometimes useful to execute different code in the calling procedure depending on the results of the subroutine call. Earlier versions of Fortran supported such operations by providing alternate subroutine returns. Alternate subroutine returns are statement labels passed as calling arguments to the subroutine. When the subroutine executes, it can decide to return control to any of the statement labels specified in the argument list. Alternate subroutine returns are specified in the following manner:

1. The statement labels associated with all possible alternate returns are specified as arguments in the CALL statement by preceding each label with an asterisk:

    ```
    CALL SUB1 (a, b, c, *n1, *n2, *n3)
    ```

    where n1, n2, and n3 are the statement numbers to which execution may be transferred.

2. The alternate returns are specified in the SUBROUTINE statement by asterisks:

    ```
    SUBROUTINE sub1 (a, b, c, *, *, *)
    ```

    where the asterisks correspond to the locations of the alternate returns in the calling statement.

3. The particular alternate return to be executed is specified by a parameter on the RETURN statement:

    ```
    RETURN k
    ```

    where k is the *position* of the alternate return to be executed. In the above example, there are three possible alternate returns, so k could take on a value from 1 to 3.

The example in Figure 14–4 has two possible returns. The first return is for normal completion, and the second one is for error conditions.

14

FIGURE 14–4
A program fragment illustrating the use of alternate subroutine returns.

```
CALL calc ( a1, a2, result, *100, *999 )
! Normal return--continue execution.
100 ...
...
STOP

! Error in subroutine call--process error and stop.
999 WRITE (*,*) 'Error in subroutine calc. Execution aborted.'
STOP 999
END PROGRAM

SUBROUTINE calc ( a1, a2, result, *, * )
REAL a1, a2, result, temp

IF ( a1 * a2 >=  0. ) THEN
   result = SQRT(a1 * a2)
ELSE
   RETURN 2
END IF

RETURN 1
END SUBROUTINE
```

Alternate subroutine returns should *never* be used in modern Fortran code. They make program maintenance and debugging much harder by making it difficult to follow the execution path through the program. They contribute to the spaghetti code so commonly found in older programs. Other, much better ways are available to provide different program execution paths depending on the results of a subroutine call. The simplest and best approach is to include a logical IF construct that tests the subroutine return parameters immediately after the subroutine call and then takes action depending on the status returned by the subroutine.

 Alternate subroutine returns have been declared obsolescent in Fortran 95, which means that this feature is a candidate for deletion in future versions of Fortran.

 Good Programming Practice
Do not use alternate subroutine returns in your programs. They make programming debugging and maintenance much harder, and simple, structured alternatives are available.

 14.6.2 Alternate Entry Points

The normal entry point for a Fortran procedure is the first executable statement in the procedure. However, program execution can start at a different point within the procedure if that point is specified with an ENTRY statement. An ENTRY statement has the form

$$\text{ENTRY } name \ (\ arg1, \ arg2, \ ...)$$

where *name* is the name of the entry point and $arg1$, $arg2$, and so on are the dummy arguments passed to the procedure at the entry point. When a subprogram is invoked by the name specified in the ENTRY statement, execution begins at the first executable statement following the ENTRY statement instead of beginning at the first executable statement in the subprogram.

A common use of the ENTRY statement occurs when a subprogram must be initialized the first time it is used, but not thereafter. In that case the subprogram may include a special initialization entry point. For example, consider the subroutine in Figure 14–5, which evaluates a third-order polynomial for a specific input value x. Before the pzolynomial can be evaluated, the coefficients of the polynomial must be specified. If the coefficients of the polynomial change infrequently, we can specify them in a special ENTRY to the subroutine.

FIGURE 14–5
A subroutine illustrating the use of multiple entry points.

```
PROGRAM test
REAL :: a = 1., b = 2., c = 1., d = 2.
CALL init1 ( a, b, c, d )
DO I = 1, 10
    CALL eval3 ( REAL(i), result )
    WRITE (*,*) 'EVAL3(', i, ') = ', result
END DO
END PROGRAM

SUBROUTINE eval3 ( x, result )
!
!      Evaluates a third-order polynomial of the form:
!         RESULT = A + B*X + C*X**2 + D*X**3
!
!      Declare calling arguments
IMPLICIT NONE
REAL :: a1, b1, c1, d1, x, result

! Declare local variables
REAL, SAVE :: a, b, c, d

! Calculate result
result = a + b**x + c*x**2 + d*x**3

RETURN

! Entry NINTL specifies the values of a, b, c, and d
! to be used when evaluating the polynomial.

ENTRY init1(a1, b1, c1, d1)
a = a1
b = b1
c = c1
d = d1

RETURN
END SUBROUTINE
```

Note from this example that the various entry points in a subroutine do not have to have the same calling sequence. However, we must be sure to call each entry point with the proper argument list for that particular entry point.

The use of entry points should be discouraged. A major disadvantage of ENTRY statements occurs when we need to modify the code of a procedure containing multiple entry points. If the different entry points use common code segments or variables, we can get in serious trouble. In the process of changing the procedure to make one entry point work correctly, we can inadvertently change the operation of another entry point. After a procedure containing multiple entry points is modified, both the entry point being modified and all other entry points must be tested *very* carefully.

The original reason for using multiple entry points in a procedure was to share segments of code for multiple purposes, thus reducing the size of the completed program. This reason no longer makes sense because memory is so inexpensive. There is no good reason to *ever* use an alternate entry point in a modern Fortran program. If you write separate procedures for each function you need, your code will be much more maintainable.

If you need to share data among multiple procedures, the data (and possibly the procedures themselves) should be placed in a module. We can write the subroutine in Figure 14–5 without entry points, as shown in Figure 14–6. Variables a, b, c, and d are made available to both subroutines eval3 and init1 through host association, and the subroutines are made available to the main program through USE association.

FIGURE 14–6
The subroutine in Figure 14–5 without multiple entry points.

```
MODULE evaluate
IMPLICIT NONE
PRIVATE
PUBLIC eval3, init1

! Declare shared data.
REAL, SAVE :: a, b, c, d

! Declare procedures
CONTAINS
   SUBROUTINE eval3 ( x, result )
   !
   !      Evaluates a third-order polynomial of the form:
   !         RESULT = A + B*X + C*X**2 + D*X**3
   !
   ! Declare calling arguments
   REAL, INTENT(IN) :: x
   REAL, INTENT(OUT) :: result

   ! Calculate result
   result = a + b**x + c*x**2 + d*x**3

   END SUBROUTINE eval3
   SUBROUTINE init1 (a1, b1, c1, d1 )
   !
   ! Subroutine INITL specifies the values of a, b, c, and d
   ! to be used when evaluating the polynomial.
   !
   REAL, INTENT(IN) :: a1, b1, c1, d1
   a = a1
   b = b1
```

(continued)

(concluded)

```
      c = c1
      d = d1
      END SUBROUTINE initil
END MODULE

PROGRAM test
USE evaluate
REAL :: a = 1., b = 2., c = 1., d = 2.
CALL initl ( a, b, c, d )
DO i = 1, 10
   CALL eval3 ( REAL(i), result )
   WRITE (*,*), 'EVAL3(', i, ') = ', result
END DO
END PROGRAM
```

Good Programming Practice
Avoid alternate entry points in your programs. There is no good reason to use them in a modern Fortran program.

14.6.3 The Statement Function

An external function (see Chapter 6) is a procedure that returns a single value to the invoking program unit. Its input values are passed via an argument list. An external function is invoked by being named as part of a Fortran expression.

Internal functions (see Chapter 9) are similar to external functions except that internal functions are entirely contained within another program unit and may be invoked only from that program unit.

A third type of Fortran function is the *statement function*. A statement function consists of a single statement. The statement function must be defined in the declaration section of a Fortran program unit before the first executable statement in the program unit. An example of a statement function is shown in Figure 14–7.

FIGURE 14–7
A program using a statement function.

```
PROGRAM polyfn
!
! This program evaluates a third-order polynomial
! of the form:
!    RES = A + B*X + C*X**2 + D*X**3
! using a statement function.

IMPLICIT NONE

! Declare local variables.
REAL :: a, b, c, d, x, y
```

(continued)

14

(concluded)

```
INTEGER :: i

! Declare dummy arguments of the statement function.
REAL :: a1, b1, c1, d1, x1, res

! Declare statement function res.
res(a1,b1,c1,d1,x1) = a1 + b1**x1 + c1*x1**2 + d1*x1**3

! Set up coefficients of polynomial res.
a = 1.
b = 2.
c = 1.
d = 2.

! Evaluate polynomial for x values of 1 through 10.
C
DO i = 1, 10
   x = REAL(i)
   y = res(a,b,c,d,x)
   WRITE (*,*) 'y(',i,') = ', y
END DO
END PROGRAM
```

In this example, real statement function `res` is defined as

$$res(a1,b1,c1,d1,x1) = a1 + b1**x1 + c1*x1**2 + d1*x1**3$$

where `a1`, `b1`, `c1`, `d1`, and `x1` are *dummy arguments*. The types of the function and its dummy arguments must all be declared or defaulted before the function is defined. The dummy arguments are placeholders for the actual values that are used when the function is executed later in the program. The dummy arguments must agree in type and number with the actual arguments that are used when the function is executed. At execution time the value in the first argument of the function will be used instead of `a1` wherever `a1` appears in the statement function, and so forth for all other arguments.

If you take a close look, you will notice that a statement function looks exactly like an assignment statement that assigns a value to an array element. Therefore, all statement functions must be defined in the declaration section of a program, before the first executable statement, so that the Fortran compiler can identify them.

Like internal functions, statement functions can only be used in the program unit in which they are declared. They are limited to functions that can be evaluated in a single expression with no branches or loops. In addition, the calling arguments must be variables, constants, or array elements. Unlike external or internal functions, it is not possible to pass whole arrays to a statement function.

Statement functions are a very old feature of Fortran, dating all the way back to FORTRAN 1 in 1954. They have been replaced by internal functions. Internal functions can do anything a statement function can do, and much more besides. You should never use statement functions in your programs.

 Statement functions have been declared obsolescent in Fortran 95, which means that this feature is a candidate for deletion in future versions of Fortran.

Good Programming Practice

Never use statement functions in your programs. Use internal functions instead.

14.6.4 Passing Intrinsic Functions as Arguments

It is possible to pass a *specific intrinsic function* as a calling argument to another procedure. If the name of a specific intrinsic function is included as an actual argument in a procedure call, then a pointer to that function is passed to the procedure. If the corresponding dummy argument in the procedure is used as a function, then when the procedure is executed, the intrinsic function in the calling argument list will be used in place of the dummy function in the procedure. Generic intrinsic functions may not be used as calling arguments—only specific intrinsic functions may be used.

Before it can be used as a calling argument to a procedure, a specific intrinsic function must be declared in an INTRINSIC statement in the calling program. The INTRINSIC statement is a specification statement of the form

```
INTRINSIC name1, name2, ...
```

It states that *name1*, *name2*, and so on are names of intrinsic functions. The INTRINSIC statement must appear in the declaration section of a procedure, before the first executable statement. The reason that an INTRINSIC statement is required is the same as the reason that an EXTERNAL statement is required: It permits the compiler to distinguish between a variable name and an intrinsic function of the same type.

A sample program illustrating the passing of an specific intrinsic function as an argument is shown in Figure 14–8. This program is a modification of the test driver program in Figure 6–25. It calculates the average value of the intrinsic function SIN(X) over 101 samples in the interval [0,2π], and the result is printed out.

FIGURE 14–8
Program illustrating the passing of an intrinsic function as a calling argument.

```
PROGRAM test_ave_value2
!
!  Purpose:
!    To test function ave_value by calling it with the intrinsic
!    function sin.
!
!  Record of revisions:
!    Date          Programmer          Description of change
!    ====          ==========          =====================
!    10/25/95      S. J. Chapman       Original code
!
IMPLICIT NONE

! Declare functions:
REAL :: ave_value                  ! Average value of function
INTRINSIC sin                      ! Function to evaluate
```

(continued)

14

(concluded)

```
! Declare parameters:
REAL, PARAMETER :: twopi = 6.283185 ! 2 * Pi

! Declare local variables:
REAL :: ave                        ! Average of my_function

! Call function with func=sin.
ave = ave_value ( sin, 0., twopi, 101 )
WRITE (*,1000) 'SIN', ave
1000 FORMAT (1X,'The average value of ',A,' between 0. and twopi is ', &
            F16.6,'.')

END PROGRAM
```

When program `test_ave_value2` is executed, the results are

```
C:\BOOK\F90\CHAP6>test_ave_value2
The average value of SIN between 0. and TWOPI is        .000000.
```

Passing intrinsic functions as calling arguments is very confusing and is only possible for specific intrinsic functions. You should not use this technique in your programs.

▪ 14.7

MISCELLANEOUS EXECUTION CONTROL FEATURES

Fortran has two statements that pause or stop the execution of a program: PAUSE and STOP. However, the PAUSE statement is rarely used in a modern Fortran program because a combination of WRITE and READ statements can perform the same function more flexibly. The STOP statement is more common, but it is often not necessary either, since program execution will terminate when the END statement is reached. However, having multiple stopping points in a program is occasionally useful. In that case each stopping point will need a STOP statement. If a program has multiple STOP statements, each one should be labeled with a unique argument (explained in section 14.7.2) so that the user can tell which STOP statement was executed.

Finally, an older form of the END statement indicates the end of a separately compiled program unit.

14.7.1 The PAUSE Statement

When we write Fortran programs whose results are meant to be viewed from a terminal, we need to pause the program at certain points while the user examines the results displayed on the terminal. Otherwise, the information may scroll off the top of the display before anyone can read it. After the user reads output data on the terminal, he or she can either continue the program or abort it.

Earlier versions of Fortran used the `PAUSE` statement to pause the execution of a program until the user started it again. The general form of the `PAUSE` statement is

PAUSE *prompt*

where *prompt* is an optional value to be displayed when the `PAUSE` statement is executed. The prompt may be either a character constant or an integer between 0 and 99999. When the `PAUSE` statement is executed, the value of *prompt* is displayed on the terminal and execution stops until the user restarts the program. When the program is restarted, execution begins at the statement following the `PAUSE` statement.

The `PAUSE` statement was never particularly common, since `WRITE` and `READ` statements can perform the same function with much more flexibility.

 The `PAUSE` statement has been deleted in Fortran 95, which means that it is no longer an official part of the Fortran language.

14.7.2 Arguments Associated with the `STOP` Statement

Like the `PAUSE` statement just described, it is possible to include an argument with the `STOP` statement. The general form of the `STOP` statement is

STOP *stop_value*

where *stop_value* is an optional value to be displayed when the `STOP` statement is executed. The *stop_value* may be either a character constant or an integer between 0 and 99999. It is mainly used when a program has multiple `STOP` statements. If each `STOP` statement is associated with a separate *stop_value*, then the programmer and user can tell which `STOP` statement was executed when the program quit.

If a program has multiple `STOP` statements, you should use either a separate argument on each one or a separate `WRITE` statement before each one to tell a user which `STOP` a program halted on. An example program with multiple `STOP` statements is shown in Figure 14–9. The first `STOP` occurs if the file specified by the user does not exist. It is clearly marked by the `WRITE` statement that occurs just before it. The second `STOP` statement occurs when the program completes normally. If this stop is executed, the message `'Normal Completion.'` will be printed out when the program terminates.

FIGURE 14–9

A program to illustrate the use of multiple `STOP` statements in a single program unit.

```
PROGRAM stop_test
!
!  Purpose:
!    To illustrate multiple STOP statements in a program.
!
```

(continued)

(concluded)

```
IMPLICIT NONE

! Declare parameters:
INTEGER, PARAMETER :: lu = 12        ! I/O unit

! Declare variables:
INTEGER :: error                     ! Error flag
CHARACTER(len=20) :: filename        ! File name

! Prompt user and get the name of the input file.
WRITE (*,*) 'Enter file name: '
READ (*,'(A)') filename

! Open the input file
OPEN (UNIT=lu, FILE=filename, STATUS='OLD', IOSTAT=error )

! Check to see of the OPEN failed.
IF ( error > 0 ) THEN
   WRITE (*,1020) filename
   1020 FORMAT (1X,'ERROR: File ',A,' does not exist!')
   STOP
END IF

! Normal processing...
...

! Close input file, and quit.
CLOSE (lu)

STOP 'Normal completion.'
END PROGRAM
```

As Fortran has improved over the years, the use of multiple STOP statements has declined. Modern structured techniques usually result in programs with a single starting point and a single stopping point. However, there are still occasions when multiple stopping points might occur in different error paths. If you do have multiple stopping points, be sure that each one is labeled distinctively so that the user can tell them apart.

14.7.3 The END Statement

Before Fortran 90 all program units terminated with an END statement instead of separate END PROGRAM, END SUBROUTINE, END FUNCTION, END MODULE, or END BLOCK DATA statements. The END statement is still accepted for backward compatibility in independently compiled program units such as main programs, external subroutines, and external functions.

However, internal procedures and module procedures *must* end with an END SUBROUTINE or END FUNCTION statement. The older form won't work in these types of procedures that did not exist before Fortran 90.

14.8

OBSOLETE BRANCHING AND LOOPING STRUCTURES

Chapter 3 described the logical `IF` structure and the `CASE` structure, which are the standard ways to implement branches in modern Fortran, and the various forms of the `DO` loop, which are the standard iterative and while loops in modern Fortran. This section describes additional ways to produce branches and older forms of `DO` loops. They are all archaic survivors from earlier versions of Fortran that are still supported for backward compatibility. These features should *never* be used in any new Fortran program. However, you may run into them if you ever have to work with old Fortran programs. They are described here for possible future reference.

14.8.1 The Arithmetic `IF` Statement

The arithmetic `IF` statement goes all the way back to the origins of Fortran in 1954. The structure of an arithmetic `IF` statement is

$$IF\ (arithmetic\_expression)\ label1,\ label2,\ label3$$

where *arithmetic_expression* is any integer, real, or double-precision arithmetic expression and *label1*, *label2*, and *label3* are labels of executable Fortran statements. When the arithmetic `IF` statement is executed, the arithmetic expression is evaluated. If the resulting value is negative, execution transfers to the statement at *label1*. If the value is zero, execution transfers to the statement at *label2*. If the value is positive, execution transfers to the statement at *label3*. An example statement is

```
          IF ( x - y ) 10, 20, 30
    10    (code for negative case)
          . . .
          GO TO 100
    20    (code for zero case)
          . . .
          GO TO 100
    40    (code for positive case)
          . . .
   100    CONTINUE
          . . .
```

The arithmetic `IF` should *never* be used in any modern Fortran program.

The arithmetic `IF` statement has been declared obsolescent in Fortran 95, which means that it is a candidate for deletion in future versions of Fortran.

14

> **Good Programming Practice**
> Never use the arithmetic `IF` statement in your programs. Use the logical `IF` structure instead.

14.8.2 The Unconditional GO TO Statement

The GO TO statement has the form

```
GO TO label
```

where *label* is the label of an executable Fortran statement. When this statement is executed, control jumps unconditionally to the statement with the specified label.

In the past, GO TO statements were often combined with IF statements to create loops and conditional branches. For example, a while loop could be implemented as

```
10 CONTINUE
   ...
   IF ( condition ) GO TO 20
   ...
   GO TO 10
20 ...
```

Modern Fortran has better ways to create loops and branches, so the GO TO statement is now rarely used. The excessive use of GO TO statements tends to lead to spaghetti code, so their use should be discouraged. However, the statement will prove useful on some rare occasions (such as exception handling).

Good Programming Practice
Avoid the use of GO TO statements whenever possible. Use structured loops and branches instead.

14.8.3 The Computed GO TO Statement

The computed GO TO statement has the form

```
GO TO (label1, label2, label3,..., labelk), int_expr
```

where *label1* through *labelk* are labels of executable Fortran statements and the *int_expr* evaluates to an integer between 1 and k. If the integer expression evaluates to 1, then the statement at *label1* is executed. If the integer expression evaluates to 2, then the statement at *label2* is executed, and so forth up to k. If the integer expression is less than 1 or greater than k, an error condition occurs and the behavior of the statement will vary from processor to processor.

In the following example of a computed GO TO statement, the number 2 would be printed out when the program is executed.

```
PROGRAM test
i = 2
GO TO (10, 20), i
10 WRITE (*,*) '1'
GO TO 30
20 WRITE (*,*) '2'
30 STOP
END PROGRAM
```

The computed GO TO should *never* be used in any modern Fortran program. It has been entirely replaced by the CASE structure.

 The computed GO TO statement has been declared obsolescent in Fortran 95, which means that it is a candidate for deletion in future versions of Fortran.

 Good Programming Practice
Never use the computed GO TO statement in your programs. Use the CASE structure instead.

 ### 14.8.4 The Assigned GO TO Statement

The assigned GO TO statement has two possible forms:

    GO TO *integer variable*, (*label1, label2, label3,..., labelk*)

or

                    GO TO *integer variable*

where *integer variable* contains the statement number of the statement to be executed next and *label1* through *labelk* are labels of executable Fortran statements. Before this statement is executed, a statement label must be assigned to the integer variable using the ASSIGN statement.

        ASSIGN *label* TO *integer variable*

When the first form of the assigned GO TO is executed, the program checks the value of the integer variable against the list of statement labels. If the value of the variable is in the list, then execution branches to the statement with that label. If the value of the variable is not in the list, an error occurs.

When the second form of the assigned GO TO is executed, no error checking is done. If the value of the variable is a legal statement label in the program, control branches to the statement with that label. If the value of the variable is not a legal statement label, execution continues with the next executable statement after the assigned GO TO.

In the following example of an assigned GO TO statement, the number 1 would be printed out when the program is executed.

```
PROGRAM test
ASSIGN 10 TO i
GO TO i (10, 20)
10 WRITE (*,*) '1'
GO TO 30
20 WRITE (*,*) '2'
30 END PROGRAM
```

The assigned GO TO should *never* be used in any modern Fortran program.

14

The ASSIGN statement and the assigned GO TO statement have been deleted from Fortran 95, which means that they are no longer an official part of the Fortran language.

Good Programming Practice

Never use the assigned GO TO statement in your programs. Use the logical IF structure instead.

14.8.5 Older Forms of DO Loops

Before Fortran 90, DO loops had a different form than the one taught in this book. Modern counting DO loops have the structure

```
DO i = istart, iend, incr
    . . .
END DO
```

where istart is the starting value of the loop, iend is the ending value of the loop, and incr is the loop increment.

Early FORTRAN DO loops had the structure

```
        DO 100 i = istart, iend, index
        . . .
100     . . .
```

A statement label is included in this form of the loop, and all of the code from the DO statement until the statement containing that statement label is included in the loop. An example of the earlier loop structure is

```
        DO 100 i = 1, 100
        a(i) = REAL(i)
100     b(i) = 2. * REAL(i)
```

Most programmers used this form of the DO loop from the beginning of FORTRAN until about the mid-1970s.

Because the end of this earlier form of the DO loop is so hard to recognize, many programmers developed the habit of always ending DO loops on a CONTINUE statement, which is a statement that does nothing. In addition, they indented all the statements between the DO and the CONTINUE statement. An example of a "good" FORTRAN 77 DO loop is

```
        DO 200 i = 1, 100
           a(i) = REAL(i)
           b(i) = 2. * REAL(i)
200     CONTINUE
```

As you can see, this form of the loop is much easier to understand than the earlier one.

The termination of a DO loop on any statement other than an END DO or a CONTINUE has been declared obsolescent in Fortran 95, meaning that it is a candidate for deletion in future versions of the language.

Another feature of older DO loops was the ability to terminate more than one loop on a single statement. For example, in the following code, two DO loops terminate on a single statement.

```
      DO 10 i = 1, 10
      DO 10 j = 1, 10
10    a(i,j) = REAL(i+j)
```

This sort of structure was terribly confusing, and it should not be used in any modern Fortran program.

The termination of more than one DO loop on a single statement has been declared obsolescent in Fortran 95, meaning that the structure is a candidate for deletion in future versions of the language.

Finally, FORTRAN 77 added the ability to use single-precision or double-precision real numbers as DO loop indices. This was a terrible decision, since the behavior of DO loops with real indices varied from processor to processor (see Chapter 3). Fortran 90 declared the use of real numbers as loop indices to be obsolescent.

The use of single- and double-precision real numbers as DO loop indices has been deleted from Fortran 95, which means that it is no longer an official part of the Fortran language.

Good Programming Practice

Never use any of these older forms of the DO loop in new program.

14.9

REDUNDANT FEATURES OF I/O STATEMENTS

A number of features of I/O statements have become redundant and should not be used in modern Fortran programs. The END= and ERR= clauses in I/O statements have been largely replaced by the IOSTAT= clause. The IOSTAT= clause is more flexible and more compatible with modern structured programming techniques than the older clauses, and only the IOSTAT= clause should be used in new programs.

Similarly, several format descriptors have been made redundant and should no longer be used in modern Fortran programs. The H format descriptor was an old way to specify character strings in a FORMAT statement. It was briefly mentioned in Table 10–1. It has been completely replaced by the use of character strings surrounded by single or double quotes.

 The H format descriptor has been deleted from Fortran 95, which means that it is no longer an official part of the Fortran language.

The P scale factor was used to shift the decimal point in data displayed with the E and F format descriptors. It has been made redundant by the introduction of the ES and EN format descriptors and should never be used in any new programs.

The D format descriptor was used to input and output double-precision numbers in earlier versions of Fortran. It is now identical to the E descriptor except that on output a D instead of an E may appear as the marker of the exponent. There is no need to ever use the D descriptor in a new program.

14

The BN and BZ format descriptors control the way blanks are interpreted when reading fields from card-image files. By default, Fortran 90/95 ignores blanks in input fields. In FORTRAN 66 and earlier, blanks were treated as zeros. These descriptors are provided for backward compatibility with very early versions of Fortran; they should never be needed in any new program.

The S, SP, and SS format descriptors control the display of positive signs in a format descriptor. These descriptors are completely unnecessary and should never be used.

▪ 14.10
SUMMARY

This chapter introduced a variety of miscellaneous Fortran features. Most of these features are redundant, obsolescent, or incompatible with modern structured programming. They are maintained for backward compatibility with older versions of Fortran.

The only feature described here that should be used in any new program is arguments on multiple STOP statements. Since modern programming practices greatly reduce the need for STOP statements, they will not be used very often. However, if you do write a program that contains multiple STOP statements, you should make sure that you use WRITE statements or arguments on STOP statements to identify each of the possible stopping points in the program.

Procedures that must work with older Fortran code may occasionally need COMMON blocks, but completely new programs should use modules for data sharing instead of COMMON blocks.

In addition, the unconditional GO TO statement is useful in rare circumstances, such as for exception handling. Most of the traditional uses of the GO TO statement have been replaced by the modern IF, CASE, and DO constructs, so GO TO statements will be very rare in any modern Fortran program.

Table 14–1 summarizes the features of Fortran that should not be used in new programs and gives suggestions for replacing them if you run into these features in older code.

▪ **TABLE 14–1**
Summary of older Fortran features

Feature	Status	Comment
	Source form	
Fixed-source form	Obsolescent in Fortran 95	Use free form
	Specification statements	
CHARACTER*<len> statement	Obsolescent in Fortran 95	Use CHARACTER(len=<len>) form
COMMON blocks	Redundant	Use modules to exchange data.
DATA statement	Redundant	Use initialization in type declaration statements.

(continued)

(continued)

DIMENSION statement	Redundant	Use dimension attribute in type declaration statements.
EQUIVALENCE statement	Unnecessary and confusing	Use dynamic memory allocation for temporary memory. Use the TRANSFER function to change the type of a particular data value.
IMPLICIT statement	Confusing but legal	*Do not use.* Always use IMPLICIT NONE and explicit type declaration statements.
PARAMETER statement	Redundant; confusing syntax	Use parameter attribute in type declaration statements.
Unlabeled COMMON	Redundant	Use modules to exchange data.

Undesirable subprogram features

Alternate entry points	Unnecessary and confusing	Share data between procedures in modules; do not share code between procedures.
Alternate subroutine returns	Obsolescent in Fortran 95	Use status variable; test status of variable after subroutine call.
Statement function	Obsolescent in Fortran 95	Use internal procedures.

Execution control statement

PAUSE statement	Deleted in Fortran 95	Use a WRITE statement followed by a READ statement.

Branching and looping control statements

Arithmetic IF statement	Obsolescent in Fortran 95	Use logical IF.
Assigned GO TO statement	Deleted in Fortran 95	Use block IF or CASE construct.
Computed GO TO statement	Obsolescent in Fortran 95	Use CASE construct.
GO TO statement	Rarely needed	Largely replaced by IF, CASE, and DO constructs with CYCLE and EXIT statements.
DO 100 ... ... 100 CONTINUE	Redundant	Use DO ... ... END DO
DO loops terminating on executable statement	Obsolescent in Fortran 95	Terminate loops on END DO statements.
Multiple DO loops terminating on same statement	Obsolescent in Fortran 95	Terminate loops on separate statements.

I/O features

H format descriptor	Deleted in Fortran 95	Use single or double quotes to delimit strings.
D format descriptor	Redundant	Use E format descriptor

14

(continued)

(concluded)

P scale factor	Redundant and confusing	Use ES or EN format descriptors.
BN and BZ format descriptors	Unnecessary	Blanks should always be nulls, which is the default case.
S, SP and SS format descriptors	Unnecessary	Processor's default behavior is acceptable.
ERR= clause	Redundant and confusing	Use IOSTAT= clause.
END= clause	Redundant and confusing	Use IOSTAT= clause.

14.10.1 Summary of Fortran Statements and Structures

Arithmetic IF Statement

```
            IF (arithmetic expression) label1, label2, label3
```

Example:

```
        IF (b**2-4.*a*c) 10, 20, 30
```

Description:
   The arithmetic IF statement is an obsolete conditional branching statement. If the arithmetic expression is negative, control will be transferred to the statement with label *label1*. If the arithmetic expression is zero, control will be transferred to the statement with label *label2*, and if the arithmetic expression is positive, control will be transferred to the statement with label *label3*.
   The arithmetic IF statement has been declared obsolescent in Fortran 95.

14

Assigned GO TO Statements

```
            ASSIGN label TO int_var
            GO TO int_var
```

or

```
            GO TO int_var, (label1, label2, ... labelk)
```

Example:

```
            ASSIGN 100 TO i
            ...
            GO TO i
               ...
            100 ... (execution continues here)
```

Description:

The assigned GO TO statement is an obsolete branching structure. A statement label is first assigned to an integer variable using the ASSIGN statement. When the assigned GO TO statement is executed, control branches to the statement whose label was assigned to the integer variable.

The assigned GO TO statement has been deleted in Fortran 95.

COMMON Block

```
            COMMON / name / var1, var2, ...
            COMMON var1, var2, ...
```

Example:

```
            COMMON / shared / a, b, c
            COMMON a, i(-3:3)
```

Description:

This statement defines a COMMON block. The variables declared in the block will be allocated consecutively starting at a specific memory location. They will be accessible to any program unit in which the COMMON block is desired. The COMMON block has been replaced by data values declared in modules.

14

Computed GO TO Statement

                    GO TO (*label1, label2, ..., labelk*), *int_var*

Example:

                    GO TO (100, 200, 300, 400), i

Description:

   The computed GO TO statement is an obsolete branching structure. Control is transferred to one of the statements whose label is listed, depending upon the value of the integer variable. If the variable is 1, then control is transferred to the first statement in the list and so on.

   The computed GO TO statement has been declared obsolescent in Fortran 95.

CONTINUE Statement

                                CONTINUE

Description:

   This statement is a placeholder statement that does nothing. It is sometimes used to terminate DO loops or as a location to attach a statement label.

DIMENSION Statement

                    DIMENSION *array([i1:]i2, [j1:]2, ...), ...*

Example:

                    DIMENSION a1(100), a2(-5:5), i(2)

Description:

   This statement declares the size of an array, but *not* its type. If the type is not declared on a separate type declaration statement, it will be defaulted. DIMENSION statements are not required in well-written code, since type declaration statements will perform the same purpose.

14

DO Loops (old versions)

```
                    DO k index = istart, iend, incr
                       ...
             k      CONTINUE
```

or

```
                    DO k index = istart, iend, incr
                       ...
             k      Executable statement
```

Examples:

```
                    DO 100 index = 1, 10, 3
                       ...
            100     CONTINUE
```

or

```
                    DO 200 i = 1, 10
            200     a(i) = REAL(i**2)
```

Description:

    These forms of the DO loop repeatedly execute the block of code from the statement immediately following the DO up to and including the statement whose label appears in the DO. The loop control parameters are the same in these loops as they are in modern DO constructs.

    Only the versions of the DO loop that end in an END DO statement should be used in new programs. DO loops that terminate in a CONTINUE statement are legal but redundant and should not be used. DO loops that terminate on other statements (such as the one in the second example) have been declared obsolescent in Fortran 95.

ENTRY Statement

```
                    ENTRY name ( arg1, arg2, ...)
```

Example:

```
                    ENTRY sorti ( num, data1 )
```

Description:

    This statement declares an entry point into a Fortran subroutine or function subprogram. The entry point into a Fortran subroutine or function subprogram. The entry point is executed with a CALL statement or function reference. The dummy arguments arg1, arg2, ... are placeholders for the calling arguments passed when the subprogram is executed. This statement should be avoided in modern programs.

14

EQUIVALENCE Statement

$$\text{EQUIVALENCE (} var1, \; var2, \; ...)$$

Example:

$$\text{EQUIVALENCE (} scr1, \; iscr1)$$

Description:

The EQUIVALENCE statement specifies that all the variables in the parentheses occupy the same location in memory.

GO TO Statement

$$\text{GO TO } label$$

Example:

$$\text{GO TO 100}$$

Description:

The GO TO statement transfers control unconditionally to the executable statement that has the specified statement label.

IMPLICIT Statement

$$\text{IMPLICIT } type1 \; (a_1, \; a_2, \; a_3, \; ...), \; type2 \; (b_1, \; b_2, \; b_3, \; ...), \; ...$$

Example:

$$\text{IMPLICIT COMPLEX (c,z), LOGICAL (1)}$$

Description:

The IMPLICIT statement overrides the default typing built into Fortran. It specifies the default type to assume for parameters and variables whose names begin with the specified letters. This statement should never be used in any modern program.

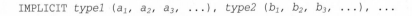

PAUSE Statement

PAUSE *prompt*

Example:

PAUSE 12

Description:

The PAUSE statement is an executable statement that temporarily stops the execution of the Fortran program until the user resumes it. The prompt is either an integer between 0 and 99999 or a character constant. It is displayed when the PAUSE statement is executed.

The PAUSE statement has been deleted in Fortran 95.

Statement Function

name(*arg1, arg2, . . .*) = expression containing *arg1, arg2, ...*

Example:

Definition: quad(a,b,c,x) = a * x**2 + b * x + c
Use: result = 2. * pi * quad(a1,b1,c1,1.5*t)

Description:

The statement function is an older structure that has been replaced by the internal function. It is defined in the declaration section of a program and may be used only within that program. The dummy arguments *arg1, arg2*, and so on are replaced by actual values when the function is used.

Statement functions have has been declared obsolescent in Fortran 95. They should never be used in any modern program.

14

Quick Summary of Common Attributes Used in Type Declaration Statements

Statement	Description (page in text)	Example of usage
ALLOCATABLE	Declares that an array is allocatable (280)	`REAL,ALLOCATABLE,DIMENSION(:) :: a`
DIMENSION	Declares the rank and shape of an array (217)	`REAL,DIMENSION(10,10) :: matrix`
EXTERNAL	Declares that a name is a function external to a program unit (364)	`REAL,EXTERNAL :: fun1`
INTENT	Specifies the intended use of a dummy argument (310)	`INTEGER,INTENT(IN) :: ndim`
OPTIONAL	Declares that a dummy argument is optional (485)	`REAL,OPTIONAL,INTENT(IN) :: maxval`
PARAMETER	Defines named constant (34)	`REAL,PARAMETER :: pi = 3.141593`
POINTER	Declares that a variable is a pointer (589)	`INTEGER,POINTER :: ptr`
PRIVATE	Declares that an object is private to a module (515)	`REAL,PRIVATE :: internal_data`
PUBLIC	Declares that an object in a module is visible outside the module (515)	`REAL,PUBLIC :: pi = 3.141593`
SAVE	Preserves local variables in a procedure between invocations of the procedure (332)	`REAL,SAVE :: sum` `SAVE`
TARGET	Declares that a variable may be pointed to by a pointer (589)	`INTEGER,TARGET :: val1`

ASCII and EBCDIC Coding Systems

Each character in the default Fortran character set is stored in 1 byte of memory, so there are 256 possible values for each character variable. The table shown below contains the characters corresponding to each possible decimal, octal, and hexadecimal value in both the ASCII and the EBCDIC coding systems. Where characters are blank, they either correspond to control characters or are not defined.

Decimal	Octal	Hex	ASCII character	EBCDIC character
0	0	0	NUL	NUL
...	...	...	...	...
32	40	20	space	
33	41	21	!	
34	42	22	"	
35	43	23	#	
36	44	24	$	
37	45	25	%	
38	46	26	&	
39	47	27	'	
40	50	28	(	
41	51	29	)	
42	52	2A	*	
43	53	2B	+	
44	54	2C	,	
45	55	2D	-	
46	56	2E	.	

Decimal	Octal	Hex	ASCII character	EBCDIC character
47	57	2F	/	
48	60	30	0	
49	61	31	1	
50	62	32	2	
51	63	33	3	
52	64	34	4	
53	65	35	5	
54	66	36	6	
55	67	37	7	
56	70	38	8	
57	71	39	9	
58	72	3A	:	
59	73	3B	;	
60	74	3C	<	
61	75	3D	=	
62	76	3E	>	
63	77	3F	?	
64	100	40	@	Blank
65	101	41	A	
66	102	42	B	
67	103	43	C	
68	104	44	D	
69	105	45	E	
70	106	46	F	
71	107	47	G	
72	110	48	H	
73	111	49	I	
74	112	4A	J	¢
75	113	4B	K	.
76	114	4C	L	<
77	115	4D	M	(
78	116	4E	N	+
79	117	4F	O	|
80	120	50	P	&
81	121	51	Q	

A

Decimal	Octal	Hex	ASCII character	EBCDIC character
82	122	52	R	
83	123	53	S	
84	124	54	T	
85	125	55	U	
86	126	56	V	
87	127	57	W	
88	130	58	X	
89	131	59	Y	
90	132	5A	Z	!
91	133	5B	[	$
92	134	5C	\	*
93	135	5D	]	)
94	136	5E	^ (or ↑)	;
95	137	5F	_	¬
96	140	60	`	-
97	141	61	a	/
98	142	62	b	
99	143	63	c	
100	144	64	d	
101	145	65	e	
102	146	66	f	
103	147	67	g	
104	150	68	h	
105	151	69	i	
106	152	6A	j	
107	153	6B	k	,
108	154	6C	l	%
109	155	6D	m	_
110	156	6E	n	>
111	157	6F	o	?
112	160	70	p	
113	161	71	q	
114	162	72	r	
115	163	73	s	
116	164	74	t	

A

Decimal	Octal	Hex	ASCII character	EBCDIC character
117	165	75	u	
118	166	76	v	
119	167	77	w	
120	170	78	x	
121	171	79	y	
122	172	7A	z	:
123	173	7B	{	#
124	174	7C	|	@
125	175	7D	}	'
126	176	7E	~	=
127	177	7F	DEL	"
128	200	80		
129	201	81		a
130	202	82		b
131	203	83		c
132	204	84		d
133	205	85		e
134	206	86		f
135	207	87		g
136	210	88		h
137	211	89		i
...	...	...	...	...
145	221	91		j
146	222	92		k
147	223	93		l
148	224	94		m
149	225	95		n
150	226	96		o
151	227	97		p
152	230	98		q
153	231	99		r
...	...	...	...	...
162	242	A2		s
163	243	A3		t
164	244	A4		u

Decimal	Octal	Hex	ASCII character	EBCDIC character
165	245	A5		v
166	246	A6		w
167	247	A7		x
168	250	A8		y
169	251	A9		z
...	...	...	...	...
192	300	C0		}
193	301	C1		A
194	302	C2		B
195	303	C3		C
196	304	C4		D
197	305	C5		E
198	306	C6		F
199	307	C7		G
200	310	C8		H
201	311	C9		I
...	...	...	...	...
208	320	D0		}
209	321	D1		J
210	322	D2		K
211	323	D3		L
212	324	D4		M
213	325	D5		N
214	326	D6		O
215	327	D7		P
216	330	D8		Q
217	331	D9		R
...	...	...	...	...
224	340	E0		\
225	341	E1		
226	342	E2		S
227	343	E3		T
228	344	E4		U
229	345	E5		V
230	346	E6		W

A

Decimal	Octal	Hex	ASCII character	EBCDIC character
231	347	E7		X
232	350	E8		Y
233	351	E9		Z
...	...	...	...	...
240	360	F0		0
241	361	F1		1
242	362	F2		2
243	363	F3		3
244	364	F4		4
245	365	F5		5
246	366	F6		6
247	367	F7		7
248	370	F8		8
249	371	F9		9
...	...	...	...	...
255	377	FF		

A

Fortran 90/95 Intrinsic Procedures

This appendix describes the intrinsic procedures built into the Fortran 90 and Fortran 95 languages and provides some suggestions for their proper use. All the intrinsic procedures that are present in Fortran 90 are also present in Fortran 95, although some have additional arguments. Procedures that are only in Fortran 95 and procedures that have additional arguments in Fortran 95 are highlighted in the tables and discussions below.

The majority of Fortran intrinsic procedures are functions, although a few are subroutines.

B.1

CLASSES OF INTRINSIC PROCEDURES

Fortran 90/95 intrinsic procedures can be broken into three classes: elemental, inquiry, or transformational. An **elemental function**[1] is one that is specified for scalar arguments, but which may also be applied to array arguments. If the argument of an elemental function is a scalar, then the result of the function will be a scalar. If the argument of the function is an array, then the result of the function will be an array of the same shape as the input argument. If there is more than one input argument, all of the arguments must have the same shape. If an elemental function is applied to an array, the result will be the same as if the function were applied to each element of the array on an element-by-element basis.

An **inquiry function** or **inquiry subroutine** is a procedure whose value depends on the properties of an object being investigated. For example, the function PRESENT(A) is an inquiry function that returns a true value if the optional argument A is present in a procedure call. Other inquiry functions can return properties of the system used to represent real numbers and integers on a particular processor.

---

[1]One intrinsic subroutine is also elemental.

A **transformational function** is a function that has one or more array-valued arguments or an array-valued result. Unlike elemental functions that operate on an element-by-element basis, transformational functions operate on arrays as a whole. The output of a transformational function will often not have the same shape as the input arguments. For example, the function DOT_PRODUCT has two vector input arguments of the same size and produces a scalar output.

▨ B.2
ALPHABETICAL LIST OF INTRINSIC PROCEDURES

Table B–1 contains an alphabetical listing of the intrinsic procedures included in Fortran 90 and Fortran 95. The table is organized into five columns. The first column of the table contains the *generic name* of each procedure and its calling sequence. The calling sequence is represented by the keywords associated with each argument. Mandatory arguments are shown in roman type, and optional arguments are shown in italics. The use of keywords is optional, but they must be supplied for optional arguments if earlier optional arguments in the calling sequence are missing or if the arguments are specified in a nondefault order (see section 9.4). For example, the function SIN has one argument, and the keyword of the argument is X. This function can be invoked either with or without the keyword, so the following two statements are equivalent:

```
result = sin(X = 3.141593)
result = sin(3.141593)
```

Another example is the function MAXVAL. This function has one required argument and two optional arguments.

```
MAXVAL ( ARRAY, DIM, MASK )
```

If all three calling values are specified in that order, then they simply may be included in the argument list without the keywords. However, if the MASK is to be specified without DIM, then keywords must be used.

```
value = MAXVAL ( array, MASK = mask )
```

The types of the most common argument keywords follow (any kind of the specified type may be used).

A	Any
BACK	Logical
DIM	Integer
I	Integer
KIND	Integer
MASK	Logical
STRING	Character
X, Y	Numeric (integer, real, or complex)
Z	Complex

For the types of other keywords, refer to the detailed procedure descriptions in the following sections.

B

The second column contains the *specific name* of an intrinsic function, which is the name by which the function must be called if it is to appear in an INTRINSIC statement and be passed to another procedure as an actual argument. If this column is blank, then the procedure does not have a specific name and so may not be used as a calling argument. The types of arguments used with the specific functions are

c, c1, c2, ...	Default complex
d, d1, d2, ...	Double-precision real
i, i1, i2, ...	Default integer
r, r1, r2, ...	Default real
l, l1, l2, ...	Logical
str1, str2, ...	Character

The third column contains the type of the value returned by the procedure if it is a function. Obviously, intrinsic subroutines do not have a type associated with them. The fourth column is a reference to the section of this appendix in which the procedure is described, and the numbers in the fifth column correspond to notes at the end of the table.

Procedures that are present only in Fortran 95 appear with a shaded background.

TABLE B-1
Specific and generic names for all Fortran 90/95 intrinsic procedures

Generic name, keyword(s), and calling sequence	Specific name	Function type	Section	Notes
ABS(A)		Argument type	B.3	
	ABS(r)	Default real		
	CABS(c)	Default real		2
	DABS(d)	Double precision		
	IABS(i)	Default integer		
ACHAR(I)		Character(1)	B.7	
ACOS(X)		Argument type	B.3	
	ACOS(r)	Default real		
	DACOS(d)	Double precision		
ADJUSTL(STRING)		Character	B.7	
ADJUSTR(STRING)		Character	B.7	
AIMAG(Z)	AIMAG(c)	Real	B.3	
AINT(A,*KIND*)		Argument type	B.3	
	AINT(r)	Default real		
	DINT(d)	Double precision		
ALL(MASK,*DIM*)		Logical	B.8	
ALLOCATED(ARRAY)		Logical	B.9	
ANINT(A,*KIND*)		Argument type	B.3	
	ANINT(r)	Real		
	DNINT(d)	Double precision		
ANY(MASK,*DIM*)		Logical	B.8	

B

■ **TABLE B–1** (*Continued*)

Generic name, keyword(s), and calling sequence	Specific name	Function type	Section	Notes
ASIN(X)	ASIN(r) ASIN(r) DASIN(d)	Argument type Real Double precision		
ASSOCIATED(POINTER,*TARGET*)		Logical	B.9	
ATAN(X)	ATAN(r) DATAN(d)	Argument type Real Double precision	B.3	
ATAN2(Y,X)	ATAN2(r2,r1) DATAN2(d2,d1)	Argument type Real Double precision	B.3	
BIT_SIZE(I)		Integer	B.4	
BTEST(I,POS)		Logical	B.6	
CEILING(A,*KIND*)		Integer	B.3	4
CHAR(I,*KIND*)		Character(1)	B.7	
CMPLX(X,*Y*,*KIND*)		Complex	B.3	
CONGJ(X)	CONJG(c)	Complex	B.3	
COS(X)	CCOS(c) COS(r) DCOS(d)	Argument type Complex Real Double precision	B.3	
COSH(X)	COSH(r) DCOSH(d)	Argument type Real Double precision	B.3	
COUNT(MASK,*DIM*)		Integer	B.8	
CPU_TIME(TIME)		Subroutine	B.5	5
CSHIFT(ARRAY,*SHIFT*,*DIM*)		Array type	B.8	
DATE_AND_TIME(*DATE*,*TIME*,*ZONE*,*VALUES*)		Subroutine	B.5	
DBLE(A)		Double precision	B.3	
DIGITS(X)		Integer	B.4	
DIM(X,Y)	DDIM(d1,d2) DIM(r1,r2) IDIM(i1,i2)	Argument type Double precision Real Integer	B.3	
DOT_PRODUCT(VECTOR_A,VECTOR_B)		Argument type	B.3	
DPROD(X,Y)	DPROD(x1,x2)	Double precision	B.3	
EOSHIFT(ARRAY,SHIFT,*BOUNDARY*,*DIM*)		Array type	B.8	
EPSILON(X)		Real	B.4	

B

TABLE B–1 (*Continued*)

Generic name, keyword(s), and calling sequence	Specific name	Function type	Section	Notes
EXP(X)	CEXP(c) DEXP(d) EXP(r)	Argument type Complex Double precision Real	B.3	
EXPONENT(X)		Integer	B.4	
FLOOR(A,*KIND*)		Integer	B.3	4
FRACTION(X)		Real	B.4	
HUGE(X)		Argument type	B.4	
IACHAR(C)		Integer	B.7	
IAND(I,J)		Integer	B.6	
IBCLR(I,POS)		Argument type	B.6	
IBITS(I,POS,LEN)		Argument type	B.6	
IBSET(I,POS)		Argument type	B.6	
ICHAR(C)		Integer	B.7	
IEOR(I,J)		Argument type	B.6	
INDEX(STRING,SUBSTRING,*BACK*)	INDEX(str1,str2)	Integer	B.7	
INT(A,*KIND*)	IDINT(i) IFIX(r)	Integer Integer Integer	B.3	1 1
IOR(I,J)		Argument type	B.6	
ISHFT(I,SHIFT)		Argument type	B.6	
ISHFTC(I,SHIFT,*SIZE*)		Argument type	B.6	
KIND(X)		Integer	B.4	
LBOUND(ARRAY,*DIM*)		Integer	B.8	
LEN(STRING)	LEN(str)	Integer	B.7	
LEN_TRIM(STRING)		Integer	B.7	
LGE(STRING_A,STRING_B)		Logical	B.7	
LGT(STRING_A,STRING_B)		Logical	B.7	
LLE(STRING_A,STRING_B)		Logical	B.7	
LLT(STRING_A,STRING_B)		Logical	B.7	
LOG(X)	ALOG(r) CLOG(c) DLOG(d)	Argument type Real Complex Double precision	B.3	
LOG10(X)	ALOG10(r) DLOG10(d)	Argument type Real Double precision	B.3	

B

■ **TABLE B–1** (*Continued*)

Generic name, keyword(s), and calling sequence	Specific name	Function type	Section	Notes
LOGICAL(L,*KIND*)		Logical	B.3	
MATMUL(MATRIX_A,MATRIX_B)		Argument type	B.3	
MAX(A1,A2,*A3*,...)		Argument type	B.3	
	AMAX0(i1,i2,...)	Real		1
	AMAX1(r1,r2,...)	Real		1
	DMAX1(d1,d2,...)	Double precision		1
	MAX0(i1,i2,...)	Integer		1
	MAX1(r1,r2,...)	Integer		1
MAXEXPONENT(X)		Integer	B.4	
MAXLOC(ARRAY,*DIM*,*MASK*)		Integer	B.8 6	
MAXVAL(ARRAY,*DIM*,*MASK*)		Argument type	B.8	
MERGE(TSOURCE,FSOURCE,MASK)		Argument type	B.8	
MIN(A1,A2,*A3*,...)		Argument type	B.3	
	AMIN0(i1,i2,...)	Real		1
	AMIN1(r1,r2,...)	Real		1
	DMIN1(d1,d2,...)	Double precision		1
	MIN0(i1,i2,...)	Integer		1
	MIN1(r1,r2,...)	Integer		1
MINEXPONENT(X)		Integer	B.4	
MINLOC(ARRAY,*DIM*,*MASK*)		Integer	B.8 6	
MINVAL(ARRAY,*DIM*,*MASK*)		Argument type	B.8	
MOD(A,P)		Argument type	B.3	
	AMOD(r1,r2)	Real		
	MOD(i,j)	Integer		
	DMOD(d1,d2)	Double precision		
MODULO(A,P)		Argument type	B.3	
MVBITS(FROM,FROMPOS,LEN,TO,TOPOS)		Subroutine	B.6	
NEAREST(X,S)		Real	B.3	
NINT(A,*KIND*)		Integer	B.3	
	IDNINT(i)	Integer		
	NINT(x)	Integer		
NOT(I)		Argument type	B.6	
NULL(*MOLD*)		Pointer	B.8	5
PACK(ARRAY,MASK,*VECTOR*)		Argument type	B.8	
PRECISION(X)		Integer	B.4	
PRESENT(A)		Logical	B.9	
PRODUCT(ARRAY,*DIM*,*MASK*)		Argument type	B.8	
RADIX(X)		Integer	B.4	

B

TABLE B–1 (*Continued*)

Generic name, keyword(s), and calling sequence	Specific name	Function type	Section	Notes
RANDOM_NUMBER(HARVEST)		Subroutine	B.3	
RANDOM_SEED(*SIZE*,*PUT*,*GET*)		Subroutine	B.3	
RANGE(X)		Integer	B.4	
REAL(A,*KIND*)		Real	B.3	
	FLOAT(i)	Real		1
	SNGL(d)	Real		1
REPEAT(STRING, NCOPIES)		Character	B.7	
RESHAPE(SOURCE,SHAPE,*PAD*,*ORDER*)		Argument type	B.8	
RRSPACING(X)		Argument type	B.4	
SCALE(X, I)		Argument type	B.4	
SCAN(STRING, SET, *BACK*)		Integer	B.7	
SELECTED_INT_KIND(R)		Integer	B.4	
SELECTED_REAL_KIND(*P*,*R*)		Integer	B.4	3
SET_EXPONENT(X, I)		Argument type	B.4	
SHAPE(SOURCE)		Integer	B.8	
SIGN(A,B)		Argument type	B.3	
	DSIGN(d1,d2)	Double precision		
	ISIGN(i1,i2)	Integer		
	SIGN(r1,r2)	Real		
SIN(X)		Argument type	B.3	
	CSIN(c)	Complex		
	DSIN(d)	Double precision		
	SIN(r)	Real		
SINH(X)		Argument type	B.3	
	DSINH(d)	Double precision		
	SINH(r)	Real		
SIZE(ARRAY, *DIM*)		Integer	B.8	
SPACING(X)		Argument type	B.4	
SPREAD(SOURCE,DIM,NCOPIES)		Argument type	B.8	
SQRT(X)		Argument type	B.3	
	CSQRT(c)	Complex		
	DSQRT(d)	Double precision		
	SQRT(r)	Real		
SUM(ARRAY,*DIM*,*MASK*)		Argument type	B.8	
SYSTEM_CLOCK(COUNT,COUNT_RATE,COUNT_MAX)		Subroutine	B.5	
TAN(X)		Argument type	B.3	
	DTAN(d)	Double precision		
	TAN(r)	Real		

B

■ **TABLE B–1** (*Concluded*)

Generic name, keyword(s), and calling sequence	Specific name	Function type	Section	Notes
TANH(X)	DTANH(d) TANH(r)	Argument type Double precision Real	B.3	
TINY(X)		Real	B.4	
TRANSFER(SOURCE,MOLD,*SIZE*)		Argument type	B.8	
TRANSPOSE(MATRIX)		Argument type	B.8	
TRIM(STRING)		Character	B.7	
UBOUND(ARRAY,*DIM*)		Integer	B.8	
UNPACK(VECTOR,MASK,FIELD)		Argument type	B.8	
VERIFY(STRING,SET,*BACK*)		Integer	B.7	

1. These intrinsic functions cannot be passed to procedures as calling arguments.
2. The result of function CABS is real with the same kind as the input complex argument.
3. At least one of P and R must be specified in any given call.
4. Argument KIND is available only in Fortran 95 for this function.
5. These procedures are available only in Fortran 95.
6. The argument *DIM* is only available in Fortran 95 version of functions MAXLOC and MINLOC.

These intrinsic procedures are divided into broad categories based on their functions. Refer to Table B–1 to determine which of the following sections will contain a description of any particular function of interest.

The following information applies to all of the intrinsic procedure descriptions:

1. All arguments of all intrinsic functions have INTENT(IN). In other words, all of the functions are pure. The intent of subroutine arguments is specified in the description of each subroutine.
2. Optional arguments are shown in italics in all calling sequences.
3. When a function has an optional KIND dummy argument, then the function result will be of the kind specified in that argument. If the KIND argument is missing, then the result will be of the default kind. If the KIND argument is specified, it must correspond to a legal kind on the specified processor; otherwise, the function will abort. The KIND argument is always an integer.
4. When a procedure is said to have two arguments of the same type, it is understood that they must also be of the same kind. If this condition is not true for a particular procedure, the procedure description will explicitly say so.
5. The lengths of arrays and character strings will be shown by an appended number in parentheses. For example, the expression

   Integer(m)

implies that a particular argument is an integer array containing m values.

◼ B.3

MATHEMATICAL AND TYPE CONVERSION INTRINSIC PROCEDURES

ABS(A)

- Elemental function of the same type and kind as A.
- Returns the absolute value of A, $|A|$.
- If A is complex, the function returns $\sqrt{\text{real}^2 + \text{imag}^2}$.

ACOS(X)

- Elemental function of the same type and kind as X.
- Returns the inverse cosine of X.
- Argument is real of any kind, with $|X| \leq 1.0$, and $0 \leq \text{ACOS}(X) \leq \pi$.

AIMAG(Z)

- Real elemental function of the same kind as Z.
- Returns the imaginary part of complex argument Z.

AINT(A, *KIND*)

- Real elemental function.
- Returns A truncated to a whole number. AINT(A) is the largest integer that is smaller than $|A|$, with the sign of A. For example, AINT(3.7) is 3.0, and AINT(−3.7) is −3.0.
- Argument A is real; optional argument *KIND* is integer.

ANINT(A, *KIND*)

- Real elemental function.
- Returns the nearest whole number to A. For example, ANINT(3.7) is 4.0, and ANINT(−3.7) is −4.0.
- Argument A is real; optional argument *KIND* is integer.

ASIN(X)

- Elemental function of the same type and kind as X.
- Returns the inverse sine of X.
- Argument is real of any kind, with $|X| \leq 1.0$, and $-\pi/2 \leq \text{ASIN}(X) \leq \pi/2$.

ATAN(X)

- Elemental function of the same type and kind as X.
- Returns the inverse tangent of X.
- Argument is real of any kind, with $-\pi/2 \leq \text{ATAN}(X) \leq \pi/2$.

B

`ATAN2(Y,X)`

- Elemental function of the same type and kind as `X`.
- Returns the inverse tangent of `Y/X` in the range $-\pi < \text{ATAN2}(Y,X) \leq \pi$.
- `X,Y` are real of any kind, and must be of same kind.
- Both `X` and `Y` cannot be simultaneously 0.

`CEILING(A,KIND)`

- Integer elemental function.
- Returns the smallest integer $\geq$ `A`. For example, `CEILING(3.7)` is 4, and `CEILING(-3.7)` is -3.
- Argument `A` is real of any kind; optional argument *KIND* is integer.
- Argument *KIND* is only available in Fortran 95.

`CMPLX(X,Y,KIND)`

- Complex elemental function.
- Returns a complex value as follows:

  1. If `X` is complex, then `Y` must not exist and the value of `X` is returned.
  2. If `X` is not complex and `Y` doesn't exist, then the returned value is `(X,0)`.
  3. If `X` is not complex and `Y` exists, then the returned value is `(X,Y)`.

- `X` is complex, real, or integer; `Y` is real or integer; and *KIND* is integer.

`CONJG(Z)`

- Complex elemental function of the same kind as `Z`.
- Returns the complex conjugate of `Z`.
- `Z` is complex.

`COS(X)`

- Elemental function of the same type and kind as `X`.
- Returns the cosine of `X`.
- `X` is real or complex.

`COSH(X)`

- Elemental function of the same type and kind as `X`.
- Returns the hyperbolic cosine of `X`.
- `X` is real.

`DBLE(A)`

- Double-precision real elemental function.
- Converts value of `A` to double-precision real.
- `A` is numeric. If `A` is complex, then only the real part of `A` is converted.

`DIM(X,Y)`

- Elemental function of the same type and kind as `X`.

- Returns X-Y if > 0; otherwise, returns 0.
- X and Y are integer or real; both must be of the same type and kind.

DOT_PRODUCT(VECTOR_A,VECTOR_B)

- Transformational function of the same type as VECTOR_A.
- Returns the dot product of numeric or logical vectors.
- Arguments are numeric or logical vectors. Both vectors must be of the same type, kind, and length.

DPROD(X,Y)

- Double-precision real elemental function.
- Returns the double-precision product of X and Y.
- Arguments X and Y are default real.

EXP(X)

- Elemental function of the same type and kind as X.
- Returns e^x.
- X is real or complex.

FLOOR(A,*KIND*)

- Integer elemental function.
- Returns the largest integer $\leq$ A. For example, FLOOR(3.7) is 3, and FLOOR(-3.7) is -4.
- Argument A is real of any kind; optional argument *KIND* is integer.
- Argument *KIND* is only available in Fortran 95.

INT(A,*KIND*)

- Integer elemental function.
- This function truncates A and converts it into an integer. If A is complex, only the real part is converted. If A is integer, this function changes the kind only.
- A is numeric; optional argument *KIND* is integer.

LOG(X)

- Elemental function of the same type and kind as X.
- Returns $\log_e(x)$.
- X is real or complex. If real, X > 0. If complex, X ≠ 0.

LOG10(X)

- Elemental function of the same type and kind as X.
- Returns $\log_{10}(x)$.
- X is real and positive.

B

`LOGICAL(L,`*`KIND`*`)`

- Logical elemental function.
- Converts the logical value `L` to the specified kind.
- `L` is logical, and *`KIND`* is integer.

`MATMUL(MATRIX_A,MATRIX_B)`

- Transformational function of the same type and kind as `MATRIX_A`.
- Returns the *matrix product* of numeric or logical matrices. The resulting matrix will have the same number of rows as `MATRIX_A` and the same number of columns as `MATRIX_B`.
- Arguments are numeric or logical matrices. Both matrices must be of the same type and kind and of compatible sizes. The following constraints apply:
  1. In general, both matrices are of rank 2.
  2. `MATRIX_A` may be rank-1. If so, `MATRIX_B` must be rank-2 with only one column.
  3. The number of columns in `MATRIX_A` must always be the same as the number of rows in `MATRIX_B`.

`MAX(A1,A2,`*`A3`*`,...)`

- Elemental function of same kind as its arguments.
- Returns the maximum value of `A1`, `A2`, and so on.
- Arguments may be real or integer; all must be of the same type.

`MIN(A1,A2,`*`A3`*`,...)`

- Elemental function of same kind as its arguments.
- Returns the minimum value of `A1`, `A2`, and so on.
- Arguments may be real or integer; all must be of the same type.

`MOD(A1,P)`

- Elemental function of same kind as its arguments.
- Returns the value `MOD(A,P)` $= A - P*INT(A/P)$ if $P \neq 0$. Results are processor dependent if $P = 0$.
- Arguments may be real or integer; they must be of the same type.
- Examples:

Function	Result
`MOD(5,3)`	2
`MOD(-5,3)`	-2
`MOD(5,-3)`	2
`MOD(-5,-3)`	-2

B

MODULO(A1,P)

- Elemental function of same kind as its arguments.
- Returns the modulo of A with respect to P if P ≠ 0. Results are processor dependent if P = 0.
- Arguments may be real or integer; they must be of the same type.
- If P > 0, then the function determines the positive difference between A and the next lowest multiple of P. If P < 0, then the function determines the negative difference between A and the next highest multiple of P.
- Results agree with the MOD function for two positive or two negative arguments; results disagree for arguments of mixed signs.
- Examples:

Function	Result	Explanation
MODULO(5,3)	2	5 is 2 up from 3
MODULO(−5,3)	1	−5 is 1 up from −6
MODULO(5,−3)	−1	5 is 1 down from 6
MODULO(−5,−3)	−2	−5 is 2 down from −3

NEAREST(X,S)

- Real elemental function.
- Returns the nearest machine-representable number different from X in the direction of S. The returned value will be of the same kind as X.
- X and S are real, and S ≠ 0.

NINT(A,*KIND*)

- Integer elemental function.
- Returns the nearest integer to the real value A.
- A is real.

RANDOM_NUMBER(HARVEST)

- Intrinsic subroutine.
- Returns pseudorandom number(s) from a uniform distribution in the range $0 \leq$ HARVEST < 1. HARVEST may be either a scalar or an array. If it is an array, then a separate random number will be returned in each element of the array.
- Arguments:

Argument	Type	Intent	Description
HARVEST	Real	OUT	Holds random numbers. May be scalar or array.

RANDOM_SEED(*SIZE,PUT,GET*)

- Intrinsic subroutine.

- Performs three functions: (1) restarts the pseudorandom number generator used by subroutine RANDOM_NUMBER, (2) gets information about the generator, and (3) puts a new seed into the generator.
- Arguments:

Argument	Type	Intent	Description
SIZE	Integer	OUT	Number of integers used to hold the seed (n).
PUT	Integer(m)	IN	Set the seed to the value in PUT. Note that $m \geq n$.
GET	Integer(m)	OUT	Get the current value of the seed. Note that $m \geq n$.

- SIZE is integer; PUT and GET are integer arrays. All arguments are optional, and at most one can be specified in any given call.
- Functions:

  1. If no argument is specified, the call to RANDOM_SEED restarts the pseudorandom number generator.
  2. If SIZE is specified, then the subroutine returns the number of integers used by the generator to hold the seed.
  3. If GET is specified, then the current random generator seed is returned to the user. The integer array associated with keyword GET must be at least as long as SIZE.
  4. If PUT is specified, then the value in the integer array associated with keyword PUT is set into the generator as a new seed. The integer array associated with keyword PUT must be at least as long as SIZE.

REAL(A, KIND)

- Real elemental function.
- This function converts A into a real value. If A is complex, it converts the real part of A only. If A is real, this function changes the kind only.
- A is numeric; KIND is integer.

SIGN(A, B)

- Elemental function of same kind as its arguments.
- Returns the value of A with the sign of B.
- Arguments may be real or integer; they must be of the same type.

SIN(X)

- Elemental function of the same type and kind as X.
- Returns the sine of X.
- X is real or complex.

SINH(X)

- Elemental function of the same type and kind as X.

- Returns the hyperbolic sine of X.
- X is real.

SQRT(X)

- Elemental function of the same type and kind as X.
- Returns the square root of X.
- X is real or complex.
- If X is real, X must be ≥ 0. If X is complex, then the real part of X must be ≥ 0. If X is purely imaginary, then the imaginary part of X must be ≥ 0.

TAN(X)

- Elemental function of the same type and kind as X.
- Returns the tangent of X.
- X is real.

TANH(X)

- Elemental function of the same type and kind as X.
- Returns the hyperbolic tangent of X.
- X is real.

B.4

KIND AND NUMERIC PROCESSOR INTRINSIC FUNCTIONS

Many of the functions in this section are based on the Fortran models for integer and real data. These models must be understood in order to make sense of the values returned by the functions.

Fortran uses *numeric models* to insulate a programmer from the physical details of how bits are laid out in a particular computer. For example, some computers use two's-complement representations for numbers, while other computers use sign-magnitude representations for numbers. Approximately the same range of numbers can be represented in either case, but the bit patterns are different. The numeric models tell the programmer what range and precision can be represented by a given type and kind of numbers without requiring a knowledge of the physical bit layout on a particular machine.

The Fortran model for an integer i is

$$i = s \times \sum_{k=0}^{q-1} w_k \times r^k \tag{B-1}$$

where r is an integer exceeding 1, q is a positive integer, each w_k is a nonnegative integer less than r, and s is $+1$ or -1. The values of r and q determine the set of model integers for a processor. They are chosen to make the model fit as well as possible to the machine on which the program is executed. Note that this model is independent of the actual bit pattern used to store integers on a particular processor.

The value r in this model is the *radix* or base of the numbering system used to represent integers on a particular computer. Essentially all modern computers use a base 2 numbering system, so r is 2. If r is 2, then the value q is one less than the number of bits used to represent an integer (1 bit is used for the sign of the number). For a typical 32-bit integer on a base 2 computer, the model of an integer becomes

$$i = \pm \sum_{k=0}^{30} w_k \times 2^k \tag{B–2}$$

where each w_k is either 0 or 1.

The Fortran model for a real number x is

$$x = \begin{cases} 0 & \text{or} \\ s \times b^e \times \sum_{k=1}^{p} f_k \times b^{-k} \end{cases} \tag{B–3}$$

where b and p are integers exceeding 1, each f_k is a nonnegative integer less than b (and f_1 must not be 0), s is +1 or −1, and e is an integer that lies between some integer maximum e_{max} and some integer minimum e_{min}. The values of b, p, e_{min}, and e_{max} determine the set of model floating-point numbers. They are chosen to make the model fit as well as possible to the machine on which the program is executed. This model is independent of the actual bit pattern used to store floating-point numbers on a particular processor.

The value b in this model is the radix or base of the numbering system used to represent real numbers on a particular computer. Essentially all modern computers use a base 2 numbering system, so b is 2, and each f_k must be either 0 or 1 (f_1 must be 1).

The bits that make up a real or floating-point number are divided into two separate fields: one for the mantissa (the fractional part of the number) and one for the exponent. For a base 2 system, p is the number of bits in the mantissa, and the value of e is stored in a field that is one less than the number of bits in the exponent.[2] Since the IEEE single-precision standard devotes 24 bits to the mantissa and 8 bits to the exponent, p is 24, $e_{max} = 2^7 = 127$, and $e_{min} = -126$. For a typical 32-bit single-precision real number on a base 2 computer, the model of the number becomes

$$x = \begin{cases} 0 & \text{or} \\ \pm 2^e \times \left(\dfrac{1}{2} + \sum_{k=2}^{24} f_k \times 2^{-k} \right), & -126 \le e \le 127 \end{cases} \tag{B–4}$$

The inquiry functions DIGITS, EPSILON, HUGE, MAXEXPONENT, MINEXPONENT, PRECISION, RANGE, RADIX, and TINY all return values related to the model para-

---

[2]It is one less than the number of bits in the exponent because 1 bit is reserved for the sign of the exponent.

meters for the type and kind associated with the calling arguments. Of these functions, only `PRECISION` and `RANGE` matter to most programmers.

BIT_SIZE(I)

- Integer inquiry function.
- Returns the number of bits in integer `I`.
- `I` must be integer.

DIGITS(X)

- Integer inquiry function.
- Returns the number of significant digits in `X`. This function returns q from the integer model in Equation (B–1) or p from the real model in Equation (B–3).
- `X` must be integer or real.
- **Caution:** This function returns the number of significant digits in the base of the numbering system used on the computer. For most modern computers, this is base 2, so this function returns the number of significant bits. If you want the number of significant decimal digits, use `PRECISION(X)` instead.

EPSILON(X)

- Integer inquiry function of the same type as `X`.
- Returns a positive number that is almost negligible compared to 1.0 of the same type and kind as `X`. The returned value is b^{1-p}, where b and p are defined in Equation (B–3).
- `X` must be real.
- Essentially, `EPSILON(X)` is the number that, when added to 1.0, produces the next number representable by the given `KIND` of real number on a particular processor.

EXPONENT(X)

- Integer inquiry function of the same type as `X`.
- Returns the exponent of `X` in the base of the computer numbering system. This is e from the real number model as defined in Equation (B–3).
- `X` must be real.

FRACTION(X)

- Real elemental function of same kind as `X`.
- Returns the mantissa or the fractional part of the model representation of `X`. This function returns the summation term from Equation (B–3).
- `X` must be real.

HUGE(X)

- Integer inquiry function of the same type as `X`.
- Returns the largest number of the same type and kind as `X`.
- `X` must be integer or real.

B

KIND(X)

- Integer inquiry function.
- Returns the kind value of X.
- X may be any intrinsic type.

MAXEXPONENT(X)

- Integer inquiry function.
- Returns the maximum exponent of the same type and kind as X. The returned value is e_{max} from the model in Equation (B–3).
- X must be real.
- **Caution:** This function returns the maximum exponent in the base of the numbering system used on the computer. For most modern computers, this is base 2, so this function returns the maximum exponent as a base 2 number. If you want the maximum exponent as a decimal value, use RANGE(X) instead.

MINEXPONENT(X)

- Integer inquiry function.
- Returns the minimum exponent of the same type and kind as X. The returned value is e_{min} from the model in Equation (B–3).
- X must be real.

PRECISION(X)

- Integer inquiry function.
- Returns the number of significant *decimal digits* in values of the same type and kind as X.
- X must be real or complex.

RADIX(X)

- Integer inquiry function.
- Returns the base of the mathematical model for the type and kind of X. Since most modern computers work on a base 2 system, this number will almost always be 2. This number is r in Equation (B–1) or b in Equation (B–3).
- X must be integer or real.

RANGE(X)

- Integer inquiry function.
- Returns the *decimal* exponent range for values of the same type and kind as X.
- X must be integer, real, or complex.

RRSPACING(X)

- Elemental function of the same type and kind as X.

- Returns the reciprocal of the relative spacing of the numbers near X. The result has the value $|x \times b^{-e}| \times b^p$, where b, e, and p are defined as in Equation (B–3).
- X must be real.

SCALE(X,I)

- Elemental function of the same type and kind as X.
- Returns the value $x \times b^I$, where b is the base of the model used to represent X. The base b can be found with the RADIX(X) function; it is almost always 2.
- X must be real, and I must be integer.

SELECTED_INT_KIND(R)

- Integer transformational function.
- Returns the kind number for the smallest integer kind that can represent all integers n whose values satisfy the condition ABS(n) < 10**R. If more than one kind satisfies this constraint, then the kind returned will be the one with the smallest decimal range. If no kind satisfies the requirement, the value −1 is returned.
- R must be integer.

SELECTED_REAL_KIND(P,R)

- Integer transformational function.
- Returns the kind number for the smallest real kind that has a decimal precision of at least P digits and an exponent range of at least R powers of 10. If more than one kind satisfies this constraint, then the kind returned will be the one with the smallest decimal precision.
- If no real kind satisfies the requirement, a −1 is returned if the requested precision was not available, a −2 is returned if the requested range was not available, and a −3 is returned if neither was available.
- P and R must be integers.

SET_EXPONENT(X,I)

- Elemental function of the same type as X.
- Returns the number whose fractional part is the fractional part of the number X and whose exponent part is I. If X = 0, then the result is 0.
- X is real, and I is integer.

SPACING(X)

- Elemental function of the same type and kind as X.
- Returns the absolute spacing of the numbers near X in the model used to represent real numbers. If the absolute spacing is out of range, then this function returns the same value as TINY(X). This function returns the value b^{e-p}, where b, e, and p are as defined in Equation (B–3), as long as that value is in range.
- X must be real.

B

- The result of this function is useful for establishing convergence criteria in a processor-independent manner. For example, we might conclude that a root-solving algorithm has converged when the answer gets within 10 times the minimum representable spacing.

TINY(X)

- Elemental function of the same type and kind as X.
- Returns the smallest positive number of the same type and kind as X. The returned value is $b^{e_{\min}-1}$, where b and $e_{\min}$ are as defined in Equation (B–3).
- X must be real.

■ B.5
DATE AND TIME INTRINSIC SUBROUTINES

CPU_TIME(TIME)

- Intrinsic subroutine.
- Returns processor time expended on current program in seconds.
- Arguments:

Argument	Type	Intent	Description
TIME	Real	OUT	Processor time

- The purpose of this subroutine is to time sections of code by comparing the processor time before and after the code is executed.
- The definition of the time returned by this subroutine is processor dependent. On most processors it is the CPU time spent executing the current program.
- On computers with multiple CPUs, TIME may be implemented as an array containing the times associated with each processor.
- Fortran 95 only.

DATE_AND_TME(DATE, TIME, ZONE, VALUE)

- Intrinsic subroutine.
- Returns date and time.
- All arguments are optional, but at least one must be included:

Argument	Type	Intent	Description
DATE	Character(8)	OUT	Returns a string in the form CCYYMMDD, where CC is century, YY is year, MM is month, and DD is day.
TIME	Character(10)	OUT	Returns a string in the form HHMMSS.SSS, where HH is hour, MM is minute, SS is second, and SSS is millisecond.

B

ZONE	Character(5)	OUT	Returns a string in the form ±HHMM, where HHMM is the time difference between local time and Coordinated Universal time (UTC, or GMT).
VALUES	Integer(8)	OUT	See table below for values.

- If a value is not available for *DATE*, *TIME*, or *ZONE*, then the string is blank.
- The information returned in array *VALUES* is

VALUES(1)	Century and year (e.g., 1996).
VALUES(2)	Month (1–12).
VALUES(3)	Day (1–31).
VALUES(4)	Time zone difference from UTC in minutes.
VALUES(5)	Hour (0–23).
VALUES(6)	Minutes (0–59).
VALUES(7)	Seconds (0–60).
VALUES(8)	Milliseconds (0–999).

- If no information is available for one of the elements of array *VALUES*, that element is set to the most negative representable integer (−HUGE(0)).
- Note that the seconds field ranges from 0 to 60. The extra second is included to allow for leap seconds.

SYSTEM_CLOCK(COUNT, COUNT_RATE, COUNT_MAX)

- Intrinsic subroutine.
- Returns raw counts from the processor's real-time clock. The value in COUNT is increased by 1 for each clock count until COUNT_MAX is reached. When COUNT_MAX is reached, the value in COUNT is reset to 0 on the next clock count. Variable COUNT_RATE specifies the number of real-time clock counts per second, so it tells how to interpret the count information.
- Arguments:

Argument	Type	Intent	Description
COUNT	Integer	OUT	Number of counts of the system clock. The starting count is arbitrary.
COUNT_RATE	Integer	OUT	Number of clock counts per second.
COUNT_MAX	Integer	OUT	The maximum value for COUNT.

- If there is no clock, COUNT and COUNT_RATE are set to −HUGE(0) and COUNT_MAX is set to 0.

B

B.6

BIT INTRINSIC PROCEDURES

The layout of bits within an integer varies from processor to processor. For example, some processors place the most significant bit of a value at the bottom of the memory representing that value, while other processors place the least significant bit of a value at the top of the memory representing that value. To insulate programmers from these machine dependencies, Fortran defines a bit to be a binary digit w located at position k of a nonnegative integer based on a model nonnegative integer defined by

$$j = \sum_{k=0}^{z-1} w_k \times 2^k \tag{B-5}$$

where w_k can be either 0 or 1. Thus bit 0 is the coefficient of 2^0, bit 1 is the coefficient of 2^1, and so on. In this model z is the number of bits in the integer, and the bits are numbered 0, 1, . . . , $z - 1$, regardless of the physical layout of the integer. The least significant bit is considered to be at the right of the model, and the most significant bit is considered to be at the left of the model, regardless of the actual physical implementation. Thus shifting a bit left increases its value, and shifting a bit right decreases its value.

Fortran 90/95 includes 10 elemental functions and one elemental subroutine that manipulate bits according to this model. The elemental functions IOR, IAND, NOT, and IEOR perform logical operations on bits. The elemental functions ISHFT and ISHFTC perform shift operations. The elemental function IBITS and the elemental subroutine MVBITS may reference bit subfields. Finally, the elemental functions BTEST, IBSET, and IBCLR perform single-bit processing.

BTEST(I,POS)

- Logical elemental function.
- Returns true if bit POS of I is 1, and false otherwise.
- I and POS must be integers, with $0 \leq$ POS $<$ BIT_SIZE(I).

IAND(I,J)

- Elemental function of the same type and kind as I.
- Returns the bit-by-bit logical AND of I and J.
- I and J must be integers of the same kind.

IBCLR(I,POS)

- Elemental function of the same type and kind as I.
- Returns I with bit POS set to 0.
- I and POS must be integers, with $0 \leq$ POS $<$ BIT_SIZE(I).

IBITS(I,POS,LEN)

- Elemental function of the same type and kind as I.

- Returns a right-adjusted sequence of bits extracted from I of length LEN starting at bit POS. All other bits are 0.
- I, POS, and LEN must be integers, with POS + LEN < BIT_SIZE(I).

IBSET(I,POS)

- Elemental function of the same type and kind as I.
- Returns I with bit POS set to 1.
- I and POS must be integers, with $0 \le$ POS < BIT_SIZE(I).

IEOR(I,J)

- Elemental function of the same type and kind as I.
- Returns the bit-by-bit exclusive OR of I and J.
- I and J must be integers of the same kind.

IOR(I,J)

- Elemental function of the same type and kind as I.
- Returns the bit-by-bit inclusive OR of I and J.
- I and J must be integers of the same kind.

ISHFT(I,SHIFT)

- Elemental function of the same type and kind as I.
- Returns I logically shifted to the left (if SHIFT is positive) or right (if SHIFT is negative). The empty bits are filled with 0's.
- I must be an integer.
- SHIFT must be an integer, with ABS(SHIFT) <= BIT_SIZE(I).
- A shift to the left implies moving the bit in position i to position $i + 1$, and a shift to the right implies moving the bit in position i to position $i - 1$.

ISHFTC(I,SHIFT,*SIZE*)

- Elemental function of the same type and kind as I.
- Returns the value obtained by shifting the *SIZE* right-most bits of I circularly by SHIFT bits. If SHIFT is positive, the bits are shifted left; and if SHIFT is negative, the bits are shifted right. If the optional argument *SIZE* is missing, all BIT_SIZE(I) bits of I are shifted.
- I must be integer.
- SHIFT must be integer, with ABS(SHIFT) <= *SIZE*.
- *SIZE* must be a positive integer, with 0 < SIZE <= BIT_SIZE(I).

MVBITS(FROM,FROMPOS,LEN,TO,TOPOS)

- Elemental subroutine.
- Copies a sequence of bits from integer FROM to integer TO. The subroutine copies a sequence of LEN bits starting at FROMPOS in integer FROM and stores them starting at TOPOS in integer TO. All other bits in integer TO are undisturbed.

B

- Note that FROM and TO can be the same integer.
- Arguments:

Argument	Type	Intent	Description
FROM	Integer	IN	The object from which the bits are to be moved.
FROMPOS	Integer	IN	Starting bit to move; must be ≥ 0.
LEN	Integer	IN	Number of bits to move; FROMPOS + LEN must be $\leq$ BIT_SIZE(FROM).
TO	Integer, same kind as FROM	INOUT	Destination object.
TOPOS	Integer	IN	Starting bit in destination; $0 \leq \text{TOPOS+LEN} \leq \text{BIT\_SIZE(TO)}$.

NOT(I)

- Elemental function of the same type and kind as I.
- Returns the logical complement of the bits in I.
- I must be integer.

B.7

CHARACTER INTRINSIC FUNCTIONS

These functions produce, manipulate, or provide information about character strings.

ACHAR(I)

- Character(1) elemental function.
- Returns the character in position I of the ASCII collating sequence.
- If $0 \leq I \leq 127$, the result is the character in position I of the ASCII collating sequence. If $I \geq 128$, the results are processor dependent.
- I must be integer.
- IACHAR is the inverse function of ACHAR.

ADJUSTL(STRING)

- Character elemental function.
- Returns a character value of the same length as STRING, with the nonblank contents left justified. That is, the leading blanks of STRING are removed, and the same number of trailing blanks are added at the end.
- STRING must be character.

ADJUSTR(STRING)

- Character elemental function.

B

- Returns a character value of the same length as `STRING`, with the nonblank contents right justified. That is, the trailing blanks of `STRING` are removed, and the same number of leading blanks are added at the beginning.
- `STRING` must be character.

CHAR(I, *KIND*)

- Character(1) elemental function.
- Returns the character in position `I` of the processor collating sequence associated with the specified kind.
- `I` must be integer in the range $0 \leq I \leq n - 1$, where n is the number of characters in the processor-dependent collating sequence.
- *KIND* must be an integer whose value is a legal kind of character for the particular computer; if it is absent, the default kind of character is assumed.
- `ICHAR` is the inverse function of `CHAR`.

IACHAR(C)

- Integer elemental function.
- Returns the position of a character in the ASCII collating sequence. A processor-dependent value is returned if `C` is not in the collating sequence.
- `C` must be character(1).
- `ACHAR` is the inverse function of `IACHAR`.

ICHAR(C)

- Integer elemental function.
- Returns the position of a character in the processor collating sequence associated with the kind of the character.
- `C` must be character(1).
- The result is in the range $0 \leq \text{ICHAR}(C) \leq n - 1$, where n is the number of characters in the processor-dependent collating sequence.
- `CHAR` is the inverse function of `ICHAR`.

INDEX(STRING, SUBSTRING, *BACK*)

- Integer elemental function.
- Returns the starting position of a substring within a string.
- `STRING` and `SUBSTRING` must be character values of the same kind, and *BACK* must be logical.
- If the substring is longer than the string, the result is 0. If the length of the substring is 0, then the result is 1. Otherwise, if *BACK* is missing or false, the function returns the starting position of the *first* occurrence of the substring within the string, searching from left to right through the string. If *BACK* is true, the function returns the starting position of the *last* occurrence of the substring within the string.

LEN(STRING)

- Integer inquiry function.

B

- Returns the length of STRING in characters.
- STRING must be character.

LEN_TRIM(STRING)

- Integer inquiry function.
- Returns the length of STRING in characters, less any trailing blanks. If STRING is completely blank, then the result is 0.
- STRING must be character.

LGE(STRING_A, STRING_B)

- Logical elemental function.
- Returns true if STRING_A $\geq$ STRING_B in the ASCII collating sequence.
- STRING_A and STRING_B must be of type default character.
- The comparison process is similar to that used by the $>=$ relational operator except that the comparison always uses the ASCII collating sequence.

LGT(STRING_A, STRING_B)

- Logical elemental function.
- Returns true if STRING_A $>$ STRING_B in the ASCII collating sequence.
- STRING_A and STRING_B must be of type default character.
- The comparison process is similar to that used by the $>$ relational operator except that the comparison always uses the ASCII collating sequence.

LLE(STRING_A, STRING_B)

- Logical elemental function.
- Returns true if STRING_A $\leq$ STRING_B in the ASCII collating sequence.
- STRING_A and STRING_B must be of type default character.
- The comparison process is similar to that used by the $<=$ relational operator except that the comparison always uses the ASCII collating sequence.

LLT(STRING_A, STRING_B)

- Logical elemental function.
- Returns true if STRING_A $<$ STRING_B in the ASCII collating sequence.
- STRING_A and STRING_B must be of type default character.
- The comparison process is similar to that used by the $<$ relational operator except that the comparison always uses the ASCII collating sequence.

REPEAT(STRING, NCOPIES)

B

- Character transformational function.
- Returns a character string formed by concatenating NCOPIES copies of STRING one after another. If STRING is 0 length or if NCOPIES is 0, the function returns a 0-length string.
- STRING must be of type character; NCOPIES must be a nonnegative integer.

SCAN(STRING,SET,*BACK*)

- Integer elemental function.
- Scans STRING for the first occurrence of any one of the characters in SET and returns the position of that occurrence. If no character of STRING is in set, or if either STRING or SET is 0 length, the function returns a 0.
- STRING and SET must be of type character and the same kind, and *BACK* must be of type logical.
- If *BACK* is missing or false, the function returns the position of the *first* occurrence (searching left to right) of any of the characters contained in SET. If *BACK* is true, the function returns the position of the *last* occurrence (searching from right to left) of any of the characters contained in SET.

TRIM(STRING)

- Character transformational function.
- Returns STRING with trailing blanks removed. If STRING is completely blank, then a 0-length string is returned.
- STRING must be of type character.

VERIFY(STRING,SET,*BACK*)

- Integer elemental function.
- Scans STRING for the first occurrence of any one of the characters *not* in SET and returns the position of that occurrence. If all characters of STRING are in SET, or if either STRING or SET is 0 length, the function returns a 0.
- STRING and SET must be of type character and the same kind, and *BACK* must be of type logical.
- If *BACK* is missing or false, the function returns the position of the *first* occurrence (searching left to right) of any of the characters not contained in SET. If *BACK* is true, the function returns the position of the *last* occurrence (searching right to left) of any of the characters not in SET.

▧ B.8

ARRAY AND POINTER INTRINSIC FUNCTIONS

This section describes the 24 standard array and pointer intrinsic functions. Arguments that appear in many of these functions are described in detail before we examine the functions themselves.

1. The rank of an array is defined as the number of dimensions in the array. It is abbreviated as r throughout this section.
2. A scalar is defined to be an array of rank-0.
3. The optional argument *MASK* is used by some functions to select the elements of another argument to operate on. When present, *MASK* must be a logical array of

B

the same size and shape as the target array; if an element of *MASK* is true, then the corresponding element of the target array will be operated on.

4. The optional argument *DIM* is used by some functions to determine the dimension of an array along which to operate. When supplied, *DIM* must be a number in the range $1 \le DIM \le r$.

5. In the functions ALL, ANY, LBOUND, MAXVAL, MINVAL, PRODUCT, SUM, and UBOUND, the optional argument *DIM* affects the type of argument returned by the function. If the argument is absent, then the function returns a scalar result. If the argument is present, then the function returns a vector result. Because the presence or absence of *DIM* affects the type of value returned by the function, the compiler must be able to determine whether the argument is present when the program is compiled. Therefore, *the actual argument corresponding to DIM must not be an optional dummy argument in the calling program unit.* If it were, the compiler would be unable to determine whether DIM is present at compilation time. This restriction does not apply to functions CSHIFT, EOSHIFT, SIZE, and SPREAD, since the argument *DIM* does not affect the type of value returned from these functions.

To illustrate the use of *MASK* and *DIM*, let's apply the function MAXVAL to a 2 × 3 real array array1 ($r = 2$) and two masking arrays mask1 and mask2 defined as follows:

$$array1 = \begin{bmatrix} 1. & 2. & 3. \\ 4. & 5. & 6. \end{bmatrix}$$

$$mask1 = \begin{bmatrix} .TRUE. & .TRUE. & .TRUE. \\ .TRUE. & .TRUE. & .TRUE. \end{bmatrix}$$

$$mask2 = \begin{bmatrix} .TRUE. & .TRUE. & .FALSE. \\ .TRUE. & .TRUE. & .FALSE. \end{bmatrix}$$

The function MAXVAL returns the maximum value(s) along the dimension *DIM* of an array corresponding to the true elements of *MASK*. It has the calling sequence

```
result = MAXVAL(ARRAY,DIM,MASK)
```

If *DIM* is not present, the function returns a scalar equal to the largest value in the array for which *MASK* is true. Therefore, the function

```
result = MAXVAL(array1,MASK=mask1)
```

will produce a value of 6, whereas the function

```
result = MAXVAL(array1,MASK=mask2)
```

will produce a value of 5. If *DIM* is present, then the function will return an array of rank $r - 1$ containing the maximum values along dimension *DIM* for which *MASK* is true. That is, the function will hold the subscript in the specified dimension constant while searching along all other dimensions to find the masked maximum value in that subarray and then repeat the process for every other possible value of the specified dimension. Because each row of the array has three elements, the function

```
result = MAXVAL(array1,DIM=1,MASK=mask1)
```

will search along the *columns* of the array at each row position and will produce the vector [4.   5.   6.], where 4. was the maximum value in column 1, 5. was the maximum value in column 2, and 6. was the maximum value in column 3. Similarly, each column of the array has two elements, so the function

$$\text{result = MAXVAL(array1,DIM=2,MASK=mask1)}$$

will search along the *rows* of the array at each column position and will produce the vector [3.   6.], where 3. was the maximum value in row 1 and 6. was the maximum value in row 2.

ALL(MASK,*DIM*)

- Logical transformational function.
- Returns true if all MASK values are true along dimension *DIM* or if MASK has 0 size. Otherwise, it returns false.
- MASK is a logical array.
- *DIM* is an integer in the range $1 \leq DIM \leq r$. The corresponding actual argument must not be an optional argument in the calling procedure.
- The result is a scalar if *DIM* is absent. It is an array of rank $r - 1$ and shape (d(1),d(2),...,d(DIM-1),d(DIM+1),...,d(r)), where the shape of MASK is (d(1),d(2),...,d(r)). In other words, the shape of the returned vector is the same as the shape of the original mask with dimension *DIM* deleted.

ANY(MASK,*DIM*)

- Logical transformational function.
- Returns true if any MASK value is true along dimension *DIM*. Otherwise, it returns false. If MASK has 0 size, it returns false.
- MASK is a logical array.
  DIM is an integer in the range $1 \leq DIM \leq r$. The corresponding actual argument must not be an optional argument in the calling procedure.
- The result is a scalar if *DIM* is absent. It is an array of rank $r - 1$ and shape (d(1),d(2),...,d(DIM-1),d(DIM+1),...,d(r)), where the shape of MASK is (d(1),d(2),...,d(r)). In other words, the shape of the returned vector is the same as the shape of the original mask with dimension *DIM* deleted.

COUNT(MASK,*DIM*)

- Logical transformational function.
- Returns the number of true elements of MASK along dimension *DIM*, and returns 0 if MASK has 0 size.
- MASK is a logical array.
  DIM is an integer in the range $1 \leq DIM \leq r$. The corresponding actual argument must not be an optional argument in the calling procedure.
- The result is a scalar if *DIM* is absent. It is an array of rank $r - 1$ and shape (d(1),d(2),...,d(DIM-1),d(DIM+1),...,d(r)), where the shape of MASK is (d(1),d(2),...,d(r)). In other words, the shape of the returned vector is the same as the shape of the original mask with dimension *DIM* deleted.

B

`CSHIFT(ARRAY,SHIFT,`*`DIM`*`)`

- Transformational function of the same type as `ARRAY`.
- Performs a circular shift on an array expression of rank-1, or performs circular shifts on all the complete rank-1 sections along a given dimension of an array expression of rank-2 or greater. Elements shifted out at one end of a section are shifted in at the other end. Different sections may be shifted by different amounts and in different directions.
- `ARRAY` may be an array of any type and rank, but not a scalar.
  `SHIFT` is a scalar if `ARRAY` is rank-1. Otherwise, it is an array of rank $r - 1$ and of shape $(d(1),d(2),...,d(DIM-1),d(DIM+1),...,d(r))$, where the shape of `ARRAY` is $d(1),d(2),...,d(r))$.
  `DIM` is an optional integer in the range $1 \le DIM \le r$. If *`DIM`* is missing, the function behaves as though *`DIM`* were present and equal to 1.

`EOSHIFT(ARRAY,SHIFT,`*`DIM`*`)`

- Transformational function of the same type as `ARRAY`.
- Performs an end-off shift of an array expression of rank-1, or performs end-off shifts on all the complex rank-1 sections along a given dimension of an array expression of rank-2 or greater. Elements are shifted off at one end of a section, and copies of a boundary value are shifted in at the other end. Different sections may have different boundary values and may be shifted by different amounts and in different directions.
- `ARRAY` may be an array of any type and rank, but not a scalar.
  `SHIFT` is a scalar if `ARRAY` is rank-1. Otherwise, it is an array of rank $r - 1$ and of shape $(d(1),d(2),...,d(DIM-1),d(DIM+1),...d(r))$, where the shape of `ARRAY` is $(d(1),d(2),...,d(r))$.
  `DIM` is an optional integer in the range $1 \le DIM \le r$. If *`DIM`* is missing, the function behaves as though *`DIM`* were present and equal to 1.

`LBOUND(ARRAY,`*`DIM`*`)`

- Integer inquiry function.
- Returns all the lower bounds or a specified lower bound of `ARRAY`.
- `ARRAY` is an array of any type. It must not be an unassociated pointer or an unallocated allocatable array.
  `DIM` is an integer in the range $1 \le DIM \le r$. The corresponding actual argument must not be an optional argument in the calling procedure.
- If *`DIM`* is present, the result is a scalar. If the actual argument corresponding to AR-RAY is an array section or an array expression, or if dimension *`DIM`* has 0 size, then the function will return 1. Otherwise, it will return the lower bound of that dimension of `ARRAY`. If *`DIM`* is not present, then the function will return an array whose *i*th element is `LBOUND(ARRAY,i)` for i = 1,2, . . . ,*r*.

`MAXLOC(ARRAY,`*`DIM`*`,`*`MASK`*`)`

- Integer transformational function, returning a rank-1 array of size *r*.
- Returns the location of the maximum value of the elements in `ARRAY` along di-

mension DIM (if present) corresponding to the true elements of $MASK$ (if present). If more than one element has the same maximum value, the location of the first one found is returned.

- ARRAY is an array of type integer or real.
  DIM is an integer in the range $1 \le DIM \le r$. The corresponding actual argument must not be an optional argument in the calling procedure.
  $MASK$ is a logical scalar or a logical array conformable with ARRAY.
- If DIM is present and $MASK$ is not present, the result is a rank-1 array containing the subscripts of the first element found in ARRAY having the maximum value. If DIM is not present and $MASK$ is present, the search is restricted to those elements for which $MASK$ is true. If DIM is present, the result is an array of rank $r - 1$ and of shape $(d(1),d(2),...,d(DIM-1),d(DIM+1),...,d(r))$, where the shape of ARRAY is $(d(1),d(2),...,d(r))$. This array contains the subscripts of the largest values found along dimension DIM.
- The optional argument DIM is only present in Fortran 95.
- For example, if

$$ARRAY = \begin{bmatrix} 1 & 3 & -9 \\ 2 & 2 & 6 \end{bmatrix} \text{ and MASK} = \begin{bmatrix} .TRUE. & .FALSE. & .FALSE. \\ .TRUE. & .TRUE. & .FALSE. \end{bmatrix}$$

then the result of the function MAXLOC(ARRAY) is $(/2,3/)$. The result of MAXLOC(ARRAY,MASK) is $(/2,1/)$. The result of MAXLOC(ARRAY,DIM=1) is $(/2,1,2/)$, and the result of MAXLOC(ARRAY,DIM=2) is $(/2,3/)$.

MAXVAL(ARRAY, DIM, $MASK$)

- Transformational function of the same type as ARRAY.
- Returns the maximum value of the elements in ARRAY along dimension DIM (if present) corresponding to the true elements of $MASK$ (if present). If ARRAY has 0 size or if all the elements of $MASK$ are false, then the result is the largest possible negative number of the same type and kind as ARRAY.
- ARRAY is an array of type integer or real.
  DIM is an integer in the range $1 \le DIM \le r$. The corresponding actual argument must not be an optional argument in the calling procedure.
  $MASK$ is a logical scalar or a logical array conformable with ARRAY.
- If DIM is not present, the result is a scalar containing the maximum value found in the elements of ARRAY corresponding to true elements of $MASK$. If $MASK$ is absent, the search is over all of the elements in ARRAY. If DIM is present, the result is an array of rank $r - 1$ and of shape $(d(1),d(2),...,d(DIM-1),d(DIM+1),...,d(r))$, where the shape of ARRAY is $(d(1),d(2),...,d(r))$.
- For example, if

$$ARRAY = \begin{bmatrix} 1 & 3 & -9 \\ 2 & 2 & 6 \end{bmatrix} \text{ and MASK} = \begin{bmatrix} .TRUE. & .FALSE. & .FALSE. \\ .TRUE. & .TRUE. & .FALSE. \end{bmatrix}$$

then the result of the function MAXVAL(ARRAY) is 6. The result of MAXVAL(ARRAY,MASK) is 2. The result of MAXVAL(ARRAY,DIM=1) is $(/2,3,6/)$, and the result of MAXLOC(ARRAY,DIM=2) is $(/3,6/)$.

B

MERGE(TSOURCE,FSOURCE,MASK)

- Elemental function of the same type as TSOURCE.
- Selects one of two alternative values according to MASK. If a given element of MASK is true, then the corresponding element of the result comes from array TSOURCE. If a given element of MASK is false, then the corresponding element of the result comes from array FSOURCE. MASK may also be a scalar in which case either all of TSOURCE or all of FSOURCE is selected.
- TSOURCE is any type of array; FSOURCE is the same type and kind as TSOURCE. MASK is a logical scalar or a logical array conformable with TSOURCE.

MINLOC(ARRAY,*DIM*,*MASK*)

- Integer transformational function, returning a rank-1 array of size r.
- Returns the *location* of the minimum value of the elements in ARRAY along dimension *DIM* (if present) corresponding to the true elements of *MASK* (if present). If more than one element has the same minimum value, the location of the first one found is returned.
- ARRAY is an array of type integer or real.
  DIM is an integer in the range $1 \le DIM \le r$. The corresponding actual argument must not be an optional argument in the calling procedure.
  MASK is a logical scalar or a logical array conformable with ARRAY.
- If *DIM* is not present and *MASK* is not present, the result is a rank-1 array containing the subscripts of the first element found in ARRAY having the minimum value. If *DIM* is not present and *MASK* is present, the search is restricted to those elements for which *MASK* is true. If *DIM* is present, the result is an array of rank $r - 1$ and shape $(d(1),d(2),...,d(DIM-1),d(DIM+1),...,d(r))$, where the shape of ARRAY is $(d(1),d(2),...,d(r))$. This array contains the subscripts of the smallest values found along dimension *DIM*.
- The optional argument *DIM* is only present in Fortran 95.
- For example, if

$$\text{ARRAY} = \begin{bmatrix} 1 & 3 & -9 \\ 2 & 2 & 6 \end{bmatrix} \text{ and MASK} = \begin{bmatrix} \text{.TRUE.} & \text{.FALSE.} & \text{.FALSE.} \\ \text{.TRUE.} & \text{.TRUE.} & \text{.FALSE.} \end{bmatrix}$$

then the result of the function MINLOC(ARRAY) is (/1,3/). The result of MINLOC(ARRAY,MASK) is (/1,1/). The result of MINLOC(ARRAY,DIM=1) is (/1,2,1/), and the result of MINLOC(ARRAY,DIM=2) is (/3,1/).

MINVAL(ARRAY,*DIM*,*MASK*)

- Transformational function of the same type as ARRAY.
- Returns the minimum value of the elements in ARRAY along dimension *DIM* (if present) corresponding to the true elements of *MASK* (if present). If ARRAY has 0 size or if all the elements of *MASK* are false, then the result is the largest possible positive number of the same type and kind as ARRAY.
- ARRAY is an array of type integer or real.
  DIM is an integer in the range $1 \le DIM \le r$. The corresponding actual argument

must not be an optional argument in the calling procedure.

$MASK$ is a logical scalar or a logical array conformable with ARRAY.

- If DIM is not present, the result is a scalar containing the minimum value found in the elements of ARRAY corresponding to true elements of $MASK$. If $MASK$ is absent, the search is over all of the elements in ARRAY. If DIM is present, the result is an array of rank $r - 1$ and of shape $(d(1), d(2), \ldots, d(DIM-1), d(DIM+1), \ldots, d(r))$, where the shape of ARRAY is $(d(1), d(2), \ldots, d(r))$.
- For example, if

$$\text{ARRAY} = \begin{bmatrix} 1 & 3 & -9 \\ 2 & 2 & 6 \end{bmatrix} \text{ and MASK} = \begin{bmatrix} .\text{TRUE.} & .\text{FALSE.} & .\text{FALSE.} \\ .\text{TRUE.} & .\text{TRUE.} & .\text{FALSE.} \end{bmatrix}$$

then the result of the function MINVAL(ARRAY) is -9. The result of MINVAL(ARRAY,MASK) is 1. The result of MINVAL(ARRAY,DIM=1) is $(/1,2,-9/)$, and the result of MINLOC(ARRAY,DIM=2) is $(/-9,2/)$.

NULL(*MOLD*)

- Transformational function.
- Returns a disassociated pointer of the same type as $MOLD$ if present. If $MOLD$ is not present, the pointer type is determined by context. (For example, if NULL() is being used to initialize an integer pointer, the returned value will be a disassociated integer pointer.)
- $MOLD$ is a pointer of any type. Its pointer association status may be undefined, disassociated, or associated.
- This function is useful for initializing the status of a pointer at the time it is declared. It is only available in Fortran 95.

PACK(ARRAY,MASK,*VECTOR*)

- Transformational function of the same type as ARRAY.
- Packs an array into an array of rank-1 under the control of a mask.
- ARRAY is an array of any type.

  MASK is a logical scalar or a logical array conformable with ARRAY.

  $VECTOR$ is a rank-1 array of the same type as ARRAY. It must have at least as many elements as the mask has true values. If MASK is a true scalar with the value true, then it must have at least as many elements as the ARRAY has.
- This function packs the elements of ARRAY into an array of rank-1 under the control of MASK. An element of ARRAY will be packed into the output vector if the corresponding element of MASK is true. If MASK is a true scalar value, then the entire input array will be packed into the output array. The packing is done in column order.
- If argument $VECTOR$ is present, then the length of the function output will be the length of $VECTOR$. This length must be greater than or equal to the number of elements to be packed.
- For example, if

$$\text{ARRAY} = \begin{bmatrix} 1 & -3 \\ 4 & -2 \end{bmatrix} \text{ and MASK} = \begin{bmatrix} .\text{FALSE.} & .\text{TRUE.} \\ .\text{TRUE.} & .\text{TRUE.} \end{bmatrix}$$

B

then the result of the function PACK(ARRAY,MASK) will be [4   −3   −2].

PRODUCT(ARRAY,*DIM*,*MASK*)

- Transformational function of the same type as ARRAY.
- Returns the product of the elements in ARRAY along dimension *DIM* (if present) corresponding to the true elements of *MASK* (if present). If ARRAY has 0 size or if all the elements of *MASK* are false, then the result has the value 1.
- ARRAY is an array of type integer, real, or complex.
  DIM is an integer in the range $1 \leq DIM \leq r$. The corresponding actual argument must not be an optional argument in the calling procedure.
  MASK is a logical scalar or a logical array conformable with ARRAY.
- If *DIM* is not present or if ARRAY has rank-1, the result is a scalar containing the product of all the elements of ARRAY corresponding to true elements of *MASK*. If *MASK* is also absent, the result is the product of all the elements in ARRAY. If *DIM* is present, the result is an array of rank $r - 1$ and of shape (d(1),d(2),..., d(DIM−1),d(DIM+1),...,d(r)), where the shape of ARRAY is (d(1), d(2),...,d(r)).

RESHAPE(SOURCE,SHAPE,*PAD*,*ORDER*)

- Transformational function of the same type as SOURCE.
- Constructs an array of a specified shape from the elements of another array.
- SOURCE is an array of any type.
  SHAPE is a one- to seven-element integer array containing the desired extent of each dimension of the output array.
  PAD is a rank-1 array of the same type as SOURCE. It contains elements to be used as a pad on the end of the output array if SOURCE does not have enough elements.
  ORDER is an integer array of the same shape as SHAPE. It specifies the order in which dimensions are to be filled with elements from SOURCE.
- The result of this function is an array of shape SHAPE constructed from the elements of SOURCE. If SOURCE does not contain enough elements, the elements of *PAD* are used repeatedly to fill out the remainder of the output array. *ORDER* specifies the order in which the dimensions of the output array will be filled; by default they fill in the order $(1, 2, \ldots, n)$ where n is the size of SHAPE.
- For example, if SOURCE = [1   2   3   4   5   6], SHAPE = [2   5], and PAD = [0   0], then

$$\text{RESHAPE(SOURCE,SHAPE,PAD)} = \begin{bmatrix} 1 & 3 & 5 & 0 & 0 \\ 2 & 4 & 6 & 0 & 0 \end{bmatrix}$$

and

$$\text{RESHAPE(SOURCE,SHAPE,PAD,(/2,1/))} = \begin{bmatrix} 1 & 2 & 3 & 4 & 5 \\ 6 & 0 & 0 & 0 & 0 \end{bmatrix}$$

SHAPE(SOURCE)

- Integer inquiry function.

- Returns the shape of SOURCE as a rank-1 array whose size is r and whose elements are the extents of the corresponding dimensions of SOURCE. If SOURCE is a scalar, a rank-1 array of size 0 is returned.
- SOURCE is an array or scalar of any type. It must not be an unassociated pointer or an unallocated allocatable array.

SIZE(ARRAY, *DIM*)

- Integer inquiry function.
- Returns the extent of ARRAY along a particular dimension if *DIM* is present; otherwise, it returns the total number of elements in the array.
- ARRAY is an array of any type. It must not be an unassociated pointer or an unallocated allocatable array.
  DIM is an integer in the range $1 \le DIM \le r$. If ARRAY is an assumed-size array, *DIM* must be present and must have a value less than r.

SPREAD(SOURCE, DIM, NCOPIES)

- Transformational function of the same type as SOURCE.
- Constructs an array of rank $r + 1$ by copying SOURCE along a specified dimension (as in forming a book from copies of a single page).
- SOURCE is an array or scalar of any type. The rank of SOURCE must be less than 7.
  DIM is an integer specifying the dimension over which to copy SOURCE. It must satisfy the condition $1 \le DIM \le r + 1$.
  NCOPIES is the number of copies of SOURCE to make along dimension DIM. If NCOPIES is less than or equal to 0, a 0-sized array is produced.
- If SOURCE is scalar, each element in the result has a value equal to SOURCE. If source is an array, the element in the result with subscripts $(s_1, s_2, \ldots, s_{n+1})$ has the value SOURCE $(s_1, s_2, \ldots, s_{DIM-1}, s_{DIM+1}, \ldots, s_{n+1})$.
- For example, if SOURCE $= [1 \quad 3 \quad 5]$, then the result of function SPREAD(SOURCE,

$$
\text{DIM=1, NCOPIES=3) is the array} \begin{bmatrix} 1 & 3 & 5 \\ 1 & 3 & 5 \\ 1 & 3 & 5 \end{bmatrix}.
$$

SUM(ARRAY, *DIM*, *MASK*)

- Transformational function of the same type as ARRAY.
- Returns the sum of the elements in ARRAY along dimension *DIM* (if present) corresponding to the true elements of *MASK* (if present). If ARRAY has 0 size, or if all the elements of *MASK* are false, then the result has the value 0.
- ARRAY is an array of type integer, real, or complex.
  DIM is an integer in the range $1 \le DIM \le r$. The corresponding actual argument must not be an optional argument in the calling procedure.
  MASK is a logical scalar or a logical array conformable with ARRAY.
- If *DIM* is not present or if ARRAY has rank-1, the result is a scalar containing the sum of all the elements of ARRAY corresponding to true elements of *MASK*. If *MASK*

B

is also absent, the result is the sum of all the elements in ARRAY. If *DIM* is present, the result is an array of rank $r - 1$ and of shape (d(1),d(2),...,d(DIM−1), d(DIM+1),...,d(r)), where the shape of ARRAY is (d(1),d(2),...,d(r)).

TRANSFER(SOURCE,MOLD,*SIZE*)

- Transformational function of the same type as MOLD.
- Returns either a scalar or a rank-1 array with a physical representation identical to that of SOURCE but interpreted with the type and kind of MOLD. Effectively, this function takes the bit patterns in SOURCE and interprets them as though they were of the type and kind of MOLD.
- SOURCE is an array or scalar of any type.
  MOLD is an array or scalar of any type.
  SIZE is a scalar integer value. The corresponding actual argument must not be an optional argument in the calling procedure.
- If MOLD is a scalar and *SIZE* is absent, the result is a scalar. If MOLD is an array and *SIZE* is absent, the result has the smallest possible size that makes use of all the bits in SOURCE. If *SIZE* is present, the result is a rank-1 array of length *SIZE*. If the number of bits in the result and in SOURCE are not the same, then bits will be truncated or extra bits will be added in an undefined, processor-dependent manner.
- Example 1: TRANSFER(4.0,0) has the integer value 1082130432 on a PC using IEEE Standard floating-point numbers because the bit representations of a floating point 4.0 and an integer 1082130432 are identical. The transfer function has caused the bits associated with the floating point 4.0 to be reinterpreted as an integer.
- Example 2: In the function TRANSFER((/1.1,2.2,3.3/),(/(0.,0.)/)), the SOURCE is three real values long. The MOLD is a rank-1 array containing a complex number, which is two real values long. Therefore, the output will be a complex rank-1 array. In order to use all of the bits in SOURCE, the result of the function is a complex rank-1 array with two elements. The first element in the output array is (1.1,2.2), and the second element has a real part of 3.3 together with an unknown imaginary part.
- Example 3: In the function TRANSFER((/1.1,2.2,3.3/),(/(0.,0.)/),1), the SOURCE is three real values long. The MOLD is a rank-1 array containing a complex number, which is two real values long. Therefore, the output will be a complex rank-1 array. Since the *SIZE* is specified to be 1, only one complex value is produced. The result of the function is a complex rank-1 array with one element: (1.1,2.2).

TRANSPOSE(MATRIX)

- Transformational function of the same type as MATRIX.
- Transposes a matrix of rank-2. Element (i,j) of the output has the value of MATRIX(j,i).
- MATRIX is a rank-2 matrix of any type.

B

UBOUND(ARRAY,*DIM*)

- Integer inquiry function.
- Returns all the upper bounds or a specified upper bound of ARRAY.
- ARRAY is an array of any type. It must not be an unassociated pointer or an unallocated allocatable array.
  DIM is an integer in the range $1 \leq DIM \leq r$. The corresponding actual argument must not be an optional argument in the calling procedure.
- If *DIM* is present, the result is a scalar. If the actual argument corresponding to ARRAY is an array section or an array expression, or if dimension *DIM* has 0 size, then the function will return 1. Otherwise, it will return the upper bound of that dimension of ARRAY. If *DIM* is not present, then the function will return an array whose ith element is UBOUND(ARRAY,i) for $i = 1,2,\ldots,r$.

UNPACK(VECTOR,MASK,FIELD)

- Transformational function of the same type as VECTOR.
- Unpacks a rank-1 array into an array under the control of a mask. The result is an array of the same type and type parameters as VECTOR and the same shape as MASK.
- VECTOR is a rank-1 array of any type. It must be at least as large as the number of true elements in MASK.
  MASK is a logical array.
  FIELD is of the same type as VECTOR and conformable with MASK.
- This function produces an array with the shape of MASK. The first element of the VECTOR is placed in the location corresponding to the first true value in MASK, the second element of VECTOR is placed in the location corresponding to the second true value in MASK, and so on. If a location in MASK is false, then the corresponding element from FIELD is placed in the output array. If FIELD is a scalar, the same value is placed in the output array for all false locations.
- This function is the inverse of the PACK function.
- For example, suppose that

$$
\text{V} = [1 \quad 2 \quad 3], \text{M} = \begin{bmatrix} \text{.TRUE.} & \text{.FALSE.} & \text{.FALSE.} \\ \text{.FALSE.} & \text{.FALSE.} & \text{.FALSE.} \\ \text{.TRUE.} & \text{.FALSE.} & \text{.TRUE.} \end{bmatrix}, \text{ and } \text{F} = \begin{bmatrix} 0 & 0 & 0 \\ 1 & 1 & 1 \\ 0 & 0 & 0 \end{bmatrix}.
$$

Then the function UNPACK(V,MASK=M,FIELD=0) would have the value

$$
\begin{bmatrix} 1 & 0 & 0 \\ 0 & 0 & 0 \\ 2 & 0 & 3 \end{bmatrix}, \text{ and the function UNPACK(V,MASK=M,FIELD=F) would have}
$$

the value $\begin{bmatrix} 1 & 0 & 0 \\ 1 & 1 & 1 \\ 2 & 0 & 3 \end{bmatrix}$.

B

▨ B.9

MISCELLANEOUS INQUIRY FUNCTIONS

ALLOCATED(ARRAY)

- Logical inquiry function.
- Returns true if ARRAY is currently allocated; returns false if ARRAY is not currently allocated. The result is undefined if the allocation status of ARRAY is undefined.
- ARRAY is any type of allocatable array.

ASSOCIATED(POINTER, *TARGET*)

- Logical inquiry function.
- There are three possible cases for this function:

  1. If *TARGET* is not present, this function returns true if POINTER is associated, and false otherwise.
  2. If *TARGET* is present and is a target, the result is true if TARGET does not have size 0 and POINTER is currently associated with TARGET. Otherwise, the result is false.
  3. If *TARGET* is present and is a pointer, the result is true if both POINTER and TARGET are currently associated with the same non–0-sized target. Otherwise, the result is false.

- POINTER is any type of pointer whose pointer association status is not undefined. *TARGET* is any type of pointer or target. If it is a pointer, its pointer association status must not be undefined.

PRESENT(A)

- Logical inquiry function.
- Returns true if optional argument A is present, and false otherwise.
- A is any optional argument.

B

Order of Statements in a Fortran 90/95 Program

Fortran programs consist of one or more program units, each of which contains at least two legal Fortran statements. Any number and type of program units may be included in the program, but one and only one main program may be included.

All Fortran statements may be grouped into 1 of 17 possible categories, which are listed below. (Undesirable, obsolescent, or deleted Fortran statements appear in small type.)

1. Initial statements (PROGRAM, SUBROUTINE, FUNCTION, MODULE, and BLOCK DATA).
2. Comments.
3. USE statements.
4. IMPLICIT NONE statement.
5. Other IMPLICIT statements.
6. PARAMETER statements.
7. DATA statements.
8. Derived type definitions.
9. Type declaration statements.
10. Interface blocks.
11. Statement function declarations.
12. Other specification statements (PUBLIC, PRIVATE, SAVE, etc.).
13. FORMAT statements.
14. ENTRY statements.
15. Executable statements and constructs.
16. CONTAINS statement.
17. END statements (END PROGRAM, END FUNCTION, etc.).

The order in which these statements may appear in a program unit is specified in Table C–1. Horizontal lines indicate varieties of statements that may not be mixed; vertical lines indicate types of statements that may be interspersed.

TABLE C–1
Requirements on statement ordering

PROGRAM, FUNCTION, MODULE, SUBROUTINE, or BLOCK DATA statement		
USE statements		
IMPLICIT NONE statement		
FORMAT and ENTRY statements	PARAMETER statements	IMPLICIT statements
	PARAMETER and DATA statements	Derived type definitions Interface blocks Type declaration statements Specification statements Statement function statements
	DATA statements	Executable statements and constructs
CONTAINS statement		
Internal subprograms or module subprograms		
END statement		

Note from this table that nonexecutable statements generally precede executable statements in a program unit. The only nonexecutable statements that may be legally mixed with executable statements are FORMAT statements, ENTRY statements, and DATA statements. (The mixing of DATA statements among executable statements has been declared obsolescent in Fortran 95.)

In addition to the above constraints, not every type of Fortran statement may appear in every type of Fortran scoping unit. Table C–2 shows which types of Fortran statements are allowed in which scoping units.

TABLE C–2
Statements allowed in scoping units

Kind of scoping unit	Main program	Module	Block data	External subprogram	Module subprogram	Internal subprogram	Interface body
USE statement	Yes	Yes	Yes	Yes	Yes	Yes	Yes
ENTRY statement	No	No	No	Yes	Yes	No	No
FORMAT statement	Yes	No	No	Yes	Yes	Yes	No
Miscellaneous declarations (see notes)	Yes	Yes	Yes	Yes	Yes	Yes	Yes
DATA statement	Yes	Yes	Yes	Yes	Yes	Yes	No
Derived type definition	Yes	Yes	Yes	Yes	Yes	Yes	Yes
Interface block	Yes	Yes	No	Yes	Yes	Yes	Yes
Executable statement	Yes	No	No	Yes	Yes	Yes	No
CONTAINS statement	Yes	Yes	No	Yes	Yes	No	No
Statement function statement	Yes	No	No	Yes	Yes	Yes	No

Notes:
1. Miscellaneous declarations are PARAMETER statements, IMPLICIT statements, type declaration statements, and specification statements such as PUBLIC and SAVE.
2. Derived type definitions are also scoping units, but they do not contain any of the above statements and, therefore, are not in the table.
3. The scoping unit of a module does not include any module subprograms that the module contains.

C

Glossary

This appendix contains a glossary of Fortran terms. Many of the definitions here are paraphrased from the definitions of terms in the Fortran 90 and 95 Standards, ISO/IEC 1539:1991, and ISO/IEC 1539:1997.

actual argument An expression, variable, or procedure that is specified in a procedure invocation (a subroutine call or a function reference). It is associated with the dummy argument in the corresponding position of the procedure definition unless keywords are used to change the order of arguments.

algorithm The "formula" or sequence of steps used to solve a specific problem.

allocatable array An array specified as ALLOCATABLE with a certain type and rank. It can later be allocated a certain extent with the ALLOCATE statement. The array cannot be referenced or defined until it has been allocated. When no longer needed, the corresponding storage area can be released with the DEALLOCATE statement.

allocation statement A statement that allocates memory for an allocatable array.

allocation status A logical value indicating whether an allocatable array is currently allocated. It can be examined using the ALLOCATED intrinsic function.

alpha release The first completed version of a large program. The alpha release is normally tested by the programmers themselves and a few colleagues in order to discover the most serious bugs present in the program.

argument A placeholder for a value or variable name that will be passed to a procedure when it is invoked (a dummy argument) or the value or variable name that is actually passed to the procedure when it is invoked (an actual argument). Arguments appear in parentheses after a procedure name both when the procedure is declared and when the procedure is invoked.

argument association The relationship between an actual argument and a dummy argument during the execution of a procedure reference. Argument association is performed either by the relative position of actual and dummy arguments in the procedure reference and the procedure definition or by means of argument keywords.

argument keyword A dummy argument name. It may be used in a procedure reference followed by the equals sign provided the procedure has an explicit interface.

argument list A list of values and variables that are passed to a procedure when it is invoked. Argument lists appear in parentheses after a procedure name both when the procedure is declared and when the procedure is invoked.

array   A set of data items, all of the same type and kind, which are referred to by the same name. Individual elements within an array are accessed by using the array name followed by one or more subscripts.

array constructor   An array-valued constant.

array element   An individual data item within an array.

array element order   The order in which the elements of an array appear to be stored. The physical storage arrangement within a computer's memory may be different than this order, but any reference to the array will make the elements appear to be in this order.

array overflow   An attempt to use an array element with an index outside the valid range for the array; an out-of-bounds reference.

array pointer   A pointer to an array.

array section   A subset of an array, which can be used and manipulated as an array in its own right.

array specification   A means of defining the name, shape, and size of an array in a type declaration statement.

array valued   Having the property of being an array.

array-valued function   A function whose result is an array.

array variable   An array-valued variable.

ASCII   The American Standard Code for Information Interchange (ANSI X3.4 1977), a widely used internal character coding set. This set is also known as ISO 646 (International Reference Version).

ASCII collating sequence   The collating sequence of the ASCII character set.

assignment   Storing the value of an expression into a variable.

assignment operator   The equal (=) sign, which indicates that the value of the expression to the right of the equal sign should be assigned to the variable named on the left of the sign.

assignment statement   A Fortran statement that causes the value of an expression to be stored into a variable. The form of an assignment statement is "variable = expression."

associated   A pointer is associated with a target if it currently points to that target.

association status   A logical value indicating whether a pointer is currently associated with a target. The possible pointer association status values are undefined, associated, and unassociated. The association status can be examined using the ASSOCIATED intrinsic function.

assumed-length character declaration   The declaration of a character dummy argument with an asterisk for its length. The actual length is determined from the corresponding actual argument when the procedure is invoked. For example:

```
CHARACTER(len=*) :: string
```

 assumed-length character function   A character function whose *return length* is specified with an asterisk. This function must have an explicit interface. The function has been declared obsolescent in Fortran 95. In the following example, my_fun is an assumed-length character function

```
FUNCTION my_fun ( str1, str2 )
CHARACTER(len=*), INTENT(IN) :: str1, str2
CHARACTER(len=*) :: my_fun
```

assumed-shape array   A dummy array argument whose bounds in each dimension are represented by colons, with the actual bounds being obtained from the corresponding actual argument when the procedure is invoked. An assumed-shape array has a declared data type

D

and rank, but its size is unknown until the procedure is actually executed. It may be used only in procedures with explicit interfaces. For example:

```
SUBROUTINE test( a, ... )
REAL, DIMENSION(:,:) :: a
```

assumed-size array An older pre–Fortran 90 mechanism for declaring dummy arrays in procedures. In an assumed size array, all the dimensions of a dummy array are explicitly declared except for the last dimension, which is declared with an asterisk. Assumed-size arrays have been superseded by assumed-shape arrays.

attribute A property of a variable or constant that may be declared in a type declaration statement. Examples are PARAMETER, DIMENSION, SAVE, and POINTER.

automatic array An explicit-shape array that is local to a procedure, some or all of whose bounds are provided when the procedure is invoked. The array can have a different size and shape each time the procedure is invoked. When the procedure is invoked, the array is automatically allocated with the proper size, and when the procedure terminates, the array is automatically deallocated. In the following example, scratch is an automatic array:

```
SUBROUTINE my_sub ( a, rows, cols )
INTEGER :: rows, cols
...
REAL, DIMENSION(rows,cols) :: scratch
```

automatic character variable A local character variable in a procedure whose length is specified when the procedure is invoked either by a dummy argument or by a value in a module or COMMON block. When the procedure is invoked, the variable is automatically created with the proper size, and when the procedure terminates, the variable is automatically destroyed. In the following example, temp is an automatic character variable:

```
SUBROUTINE my_sub ( str1, str2, n )
CHARACTER(len=*) :: str1, str2
...
CHARACTER(len=n) :: temp
```

automatic-length character function A character function whose return length is specified when the function is invoked either by a dummy argument or by a value in a module or COMMON block. These functions must have an explicit interface. In the following example, my_fun is an automatic length character function:

```
FUNCTION my_fun ( str1, str2, n )
INTEGER, INTENT(IN) :: n
CHARACTER(len=*), INTENT(IN) :: str1, str2
CHARACTER(len=n) :: my_fun
```

beta release The second completed version of a large program. The beta release is normally given to "friendly" outside users who have a need for the program in their day-to-day jobs. These users exercise the program under many different conditions and with many different input data sets, and they report any bugs they find to the program developers.

binary digit A 0 or 1, the two possible digits in a base 2 system.

binary operator An operator that is written between two operands. Examples include +, -, *, /, >, <, and .AND..

binary tree A tree structure that splits into two branches at each node.

bit A binary digit.

D

block   A sequence of executable statements embedded in an executable construct, bounded by statements that are particular to the construct, and treated as an integral unit. For example, the statements between IF and END IF are a block.

```
IF ( x > 0. ) THEN
    ...
    (code block)
    ...
END IF
```

BLOCK DATA program unit   A program unit that provides initial values for variables in named COMMON blocks.

block IF construct   A program unit in which the execution of one or more blocks of statements is controlled by an IF statement, and optionally by one or more ELSE IF statements and up to one ELSE statement.

bound   An upper bound or a lower bound; the maximum or minimum value permitted for a subscript in an array.

bounds checking   The process of checking each array reference before it is executed to ensure that the specified subscripts are within the declared bounds of the array.

branch   *(a)* A transfer of control within a program, as in an IF or CASE structure. *(b)* A linked structure that forms part of a binary tree.

bug   A programming error that causes a program to behave improperly.

byte   A group of 8 bits.

card identification field   Columns 73–80 of a fixed-source form line. These columns are ignored by the compiler. In the past these columns were used to number the individual cards in a source card deck.

central processing unit (CPU)   The part of the computer that carries out the main data processing functions. It usually consists of one or more *control units* to select the data and the operations to be performed on it and *arithmetic logic units* to perform arithmetic calculations.

character   A letter, digit, or other symbol.

character-constant edit descriptor   An edit descriptor that takes the form of a character constant in an output format. For example, in the statement

```
100 FORMAT (" X = ", x)
```

the "X = " is a character-constant edit descriptor.

character context   Characters that form a part of a character literal constant or a character-constant edit descriptor. Any legal character in a computer's character set may be used in a character context, not just those in the Fortran character set.

character data type   An intrinsic data type used to represent characters.

character-length parameter   The type parameter that specifies the number of characters for an entity of type character.

character operator   An operator that operates on character data.

character set   A collection of letters, numbers, and symbols that may be used in character strings. Two common character sets are ASCII and EBCDIC.

character string   A sequence of one or more characters.

character variable   A variable that can be used to store one or more characters.

close   The process of terminating the link between a file and an input/output unit.

collating sequence   The order in which a particular character set is sorted by relational operators.

combinational operator   An operator whose operand(s) are logical values, and whose result is a logical value. Examples include .AND., .OR., and .NOT..

comment   Text within a program unit that is ignored by a compiler, but provides information for the programmer. In free-source form, comments begin with the first exclamation point (!) on a line that is not in a character context and continue to the end of the line. In fixed-source form, comments begin with a `C` or `*` in column 1 and continue to the end of the line.

`COMMON` block   A block of physical storage that may be accessed by any of the scoping units in a program. The data in the block is identified by its relative position, regardless of the name and type of the variable in that position.

compilation error   An error that is detected by a Fortran compiler during compilation.

compiler   A computer program that translates a program written in a computer language such as Fortran into the machine code used by a particular computer. The compiler usually translates the code into an intermediate form called object code, which is then prepared for execution by a separate linker.

complex   An intrinsic data type used to represent complex numbers.

complex constant   A constant of the complex type, written as an ordered pair of real values enclosd in parentheses. For example, (3.,−4.) is a complex constant.

complex number   A number consisting of a real part and an imaginary part.

component   One of the elements of a derived data type.

component selector   The method of addressing a specific component within a structure. It consists of the structure name and the component name, separated by a percent (%) sign, for example, `student%age`.

computer   A device that stores information (data) and instructions for modifying that information (programs). The computer executes programs to manipulate its data in useful ways.

concatenation   The process of attaching one character string to the end of another one by means of a concatenation operator.

concatenation operator   An operator (`//`) that combines two characters strings to form a single character string.

conformable   Two arrays are conformable if they have the same shape. A scalar is conformable with any array. Intrinsic operations are only defined for conformable data items.

constant   A data object whose value is unchanged throughout the execution of a program. Constants may be named or unnamed.

construct   A sequence of statements starting with a `DO`, `IF`, `SELECT CASE`, `FORALL`, or `WHERE` statement and ending with the corresponding terminal statement.

control character   The first character in an output buffer, which is used to control the vertical spacing for the current line.

control mask   In a `WHERE` statement or construct, an array of type logical whose value determines which elements of an array will be operated on. This definition also applies to the `MASK` argument in many array intrinsic functions.

counting loop   A `DO` loop that executes a specified number of times based on the loop control parameters (also known as an iterative loop).

CPU   *See* central processing unit.

data   Information to be processed by a computer.

data abstraction   The ability to create new data types, together with associated operators, and to hide the internal structure and operations from the user.

data dictionary   A list of the names and definitions of all named variables and constants used in a program unit. The definitions should include both a description of the contents of the item and the units in which it is measured.

data hiding   The idea that some items in a program unit may not be accessible to other program units. Local data items in a procedure are hidden from any program unit that invokes the procedure. Access to the data items and procedures in a module may be controlled using `PUBLIC` and `PRIVATE` statements.

data object   A constant or a variable.

data type   A named category of data that is characterized by a set of values, together with a

D

way to denote these values and a collection of operations that interpret and manipulate the values.

deallocation statement A statement that frees memory previously allocated for an allocatable array or a pointer.

debugging Locating and eliminating bugs from a program.

default character set The set of characters available for use by programs on a particular computer if no special action is taken to select another character set.

default complex The kind of complex value used when no kind type parameter is specified.

default integer The kind of integer value used when no kind type parameter is specified.

default kind The kind type parameter used for a specific data type when no kind is explicitly specified. The default kinds of each data type are known as default integer, default real, default complex, and so on. Default kinds vary from processor to processor.

default real The kind of real value used when no kind type parameter is specified.

default typing The type assigned to a variable when no type declaration statement is present in a program unit, based on the first letter of the variable name.

deferred-shape array An allocatable array or a pointer array. The type and rank of these arrays are declared in type declaration statements, but the shape of the array is not determined until memory is allocated in an `ALLOCATE` statement

defined assignment A user-defined assignment that involves a derived data type. This is done with the `INTERFACE ASSIGNMENT` construct.

defined operation A user-defined operation that either extends an intrinsic operation for use with derived types or defines a new operation for use with either intrinsic types or derived types. This is done with the `INTERFACE OPERATOR` construct.

deleted feature A feature of older versions of Fortran that has been deleted from later versions of the language. An example is the Hollerith (`H`) format descriptor.

dereferencing The process of accessing the corresponding target when a reference to a pointer appears in an operation or assignment statement.

derived type (or **derived data type**) A user-defined data type consisting of components, each of which is either intrinsic type or another derived type.

dimension attribute An attribute of a type declaration statement used to specify the number of subscripts in an array and the characteristics of those subscripts such as their bounds and extent. This information can also be specified in a separate `DIMENSION` statement.

direct access Reading or writing the contents of a file in arbitrary order.

direct access file A form of file in which the individual records can be written and read in any order. Direct access files must have fixed-length records so that the location of any particular record can be quickly calculated.

DO construct A loop that begins with a `DO` statement and ends with an `END DO` statement.

DO loop A loop that is controlled by a `DO` statement.

DO loop index The variable that is used to control the number of times the loop is executed in an iterative `DO` loop.

double precision A method of storing floating-point numbers on a computer that uses twice as much memory as single precision, resulting in more significant digits and (usually) a greater range in the representation of the numbers. Before Fortran 90, double-precision variables were declared with a `DOUBLE PRECISION` type declaration statement. In Fortran 90/95, they are just another kind of the real data type.

dummy argument An argument used in a procedure definition that will be associated with an actual argument when the procedure is invoked.

dynamic memory allocation Allocating memory for variables or arrays at execution time, as opposed to static memory allocation, which occurs at compilation time.

dynamic variable A variable that is created when it is needed during the course of a pro-

D

gram's execution and destroyed when it is no longer needed. Examples are automatic arrays and character variables, allocatable arrays, and allocated pointer targets.

EBCDIC Extended Binary Coded Decimal Interchange Code. This is an internal character-coding scheme used by IBM mainframes.

edit descriptor An item in a format that specifies the conversion between the internal and external representations of a data item. (Identical to format descriptor.)

elemental An adjective applied to an operation, procedure, or assignment that is applied independently to the elements of an array or corresponding elements of a set of conformable arrays and scalars. Elemental operations, procedures, or assignments may be easily partitioned among many processors in a parallel computer.

elemental function A function which is elemental.

elemental intrinsic procedure An intrinsic procedure that is defined for scalar inputs and outputs, but which can accept an array-valued argument or arguments and will deliver an array-valued result obtained by applying the procedure to the corresponding elements of the argument array(s) in turn.

elemental procedure (user defined) A user-defined procedure that is defined with only scalar dummy arguments (no pointers or procedures) and with a scalar result (not a pointer). An elemental function must have no side effects, meaning that all arguments are `INTENT(IN)`. An elemental subroutine must have no side effects except for arguments explicitly specified with `INTENT(OUT)` or `INTENT(INOUT)`. If the procedure is declared with the `ELEMENTAL` prefix, it will be able to accept an array-valued argument or arguments and will deliver an array-valued result obtained by applying the procedure to the corresponding elements of the argument arrays in turn. User-defined elemental procedures are available in Fortran 95 only.

end-of-file condition A condition set when an endfile record is read from a file, which can be detected by an `IOSTAT` clause in a `READ` statement.

endfile record A special record that only occurs at the end of a sequential file. It can be written by an `ENDFILE` statement.

error flag A variable returned from a subroutine to indicate the status of the operation performed by the subroutine.

executable statement A statement that causes the computer to perform some action during the execution of a program.

execution error An error that occurs during the execution of a program (also called a run-time error).

explicit interface A procedure interface that is known to the program unit which will invoke the procedure. An explicit interface to an external procedure may be created by an interface block, or by placing the external procedures in modules and then accessing them by `USE` association. An explicit interface is automatically created for any internal procedures or for recursive procedures referencing themselves. (*Compare* with implicit interface.)

explicit-shape array A named array that is declared with explicit bounds in every dimension.

explicit typing Explicitly declaring the type of a variable in a type declaration statement (as opposed to default typing).

exponent (*a*) In a binary representation, the power of 2 by which the mantissa is multiplied to produce a complete floating-point number. (*b*) In a decimal representation, the power of 10 by which the mantissa is multiplied to produce a complete floating-point number.

exponential notation Representing real or floating-point numbers as a mantissa multiplied by a power of 10.

expression A sequence of operands, operators, and parentheses, where the operands may be variables, constants, or function references.

extent The number of elements in a particular dimension of an array.

D

external file   A file that is stored on some external medium. This file contrasts with an internal file, which is a character variable within a program.

external function   A function that is not an intrinsic function or an internal function.

external procedure   A function subprogram or a subroutine subprogram, which is not a part of any other program unit.

external unit   An i/o unit that can be connected to an external file. External units are represented by numbers in Fortran I/O statements.

field width   The number of characters available for displaying an output formatted value or for reading an input formatted value.

file   A unit of data that is held on some medium outside the memory of the computer. It is organized into records, which can be accessed individually using READ and WRITE statements.

 fixed-source form   An obsolescent method of writing Fortran programs in which fixed columns were reserved for specific purposes. (*Compare* with free-source form.)

floating point   A method of representing numbers in which the memory associated with the number is divided into separate fields for a mantissa (fractional part) and an exponent.

format   A sequence of edit descriptors that determine the interpretation of an input data record or specify the form of an output data record. A format may be found in a FORMAT statement or in a character constant or variable.

format descriptor   An item in a format that specifies the conversion between the internal and external representations of a data item. (Identical to edit descriptor.)

format statement   A labeled statement that defines a format.

formatted file   A file containing data stored as recognizable numbers, characters, and so on.

formatted output statement   A formatted WRITE statement or a PRINT statement.

formatted READ statement   A READ statement that uses format descriptors to specify how to translate the data in the input buffer as it is read.

formatted WRITE statement   A WRITE statement that uses format descriptors to specify how to format the output data as it is displayed.

Fortran character set   The 86 characters that can be used to write a Fortran program.

free format   List-directed I/O statements, which do not require formats for either input or output.

free-source form   The newer and preferred method of writing Fortran programs, in which any character position in a line can be used for any purpose. (*Compare* with fixed-source form.)

function   A procedure that is invoked in an expression and computes a single result that is then used in evaluating the expression.

function reference   The use of a function name in an expression, which invokes (executes) the function to carry out some calculation, and returns the result for use in evaluating the expression. A function is invoked or executed by naming it in an expression.

function subprogram   A program unit that begins with a FUNCTION statement and ends with an END FUNCTION statement.

function value   The value that is returned when the function executes.

generic function   A function that can be called with different types of arguments. For example, the intrinsic function ABS is a generic function, since it can be invoked with integer, real, or complex arguments.

generic interface block   A form of interface block used to define a generic name for a set of procedures.

generic name   A name that is used to identify two or more procedures, with the compiler determining the required procedure at each invocation from the types of the nonoptional ar-

D

guments in the procedure invocation. A generic name is defined for a set of procedures in a generic interface block.

global accessibility   The ability to directly access data and derived type definitions from any program unit. This capability is provided by USE association of modules.

global entity   An entity whose scope is that of the whole program. It may be a program unit, a common block, or an external procedure.

global storage   A block of memory accessible from any program unit—a COMMON block. Global storage in COMMON blocks has largely been replaced by global accessibility through modules.

guard digits   Extra digits in a mathematical calculation that are beyond the precision of the kind of real values used in the calculation. They are used to minimize truncation and round-off errors.

head   The first item in a linked list.

hexadecimal   The base 16 number system in which the legal digits are 0 through 9 and A through F.

host   A main program or subprogram that contains an internal subprogram is called the host of the internal subprogram. A module that contains a module subprogram is called the host of the module subprogram.

host association   The process by which data entities in a host scoping unit are made available to an inner scoping unit.

host scoping unit   A scoping unit that surrounds another scoping unit.

ill-conditioned system   A system of equations whose solution is highly sensitive to small changes in the values of its coefficients or to truncation and round-off errors.

imaginary part   The second of the two numbers that make up a COMPLEX data value.

implicit interface   A procedure interface that is not fully known to the program unit that invokes the procedure. A Fortran program cannot detect type, size, or similar mismatches between actual arguments and dummy arguments when an implicit interface is used, so some programming errors will not be caught by the compiler. All pre-Fortran 90 interfaces were implicit. (*Compare* with explicit interface.)

implicit type declaration   Determining the type of a variable from the first letter of its name. Implicit type declaration should never be used in any modern Fortran program.

implied DO loop   A shorthand loop structure used in input/output statements, array constructors, and DATA statements, which specifies the order in which the elements of an array are used in that statement.

implied DO variable   A variable used to control an implied DO loop.

index array   An array containing indices to other arrays. Index arrays are often used in sorting to avoid swapping large chunks of data.

infinite loop   A loop that never terminates, typically because of a programming error.

initial statement   The first statement of a program unit: a PROGRAM, SUBROUTINE, FUNCTION, MODULE, or BLOCK DATA statement.

initialization expression   A restricted form of constant expression that can appear as an initial value in a declaration statement. For example, the initialization expression in the following type declaration statement initializes pi to 3.141592.

```
REAL :: pi = 3.141592
```

input buffer   A section of memory used to hold a line of input data as it is entered from an input device such as a keyboard. When the entire line has been input, the input buffer is made available for processing by the computer.

input device   A device used to enter data into a computer, for example, a keyboard.

D

input format   A format used in a formatted input statement.

input list   The list of variable, array, and/or array element names in a READ statement into which data is to be read.

input statement   A READ statement.

input/output unit   A number, asterisk, or name in an input/output statement referring to either an external unit or an internal unit. A number is used to refer to an external file unit, which may be connected to a specific file using an OPEN statement and disconnected using a CLOSE statement. An asterisk is used to refer to the standard input and output devices for a processor. A name is used to refer to an internal file unit, which is just a character variable in the program's memory.

inquiry intrinsic function   An intrinsic function whose result depends on properties of the principal argument other than the value of the argument.

integer   An intrinsic data type used to represent whole numbers.

integer arithmetic   Mathematical operations involving only data of the integer data type.

integer division   Division of one integer by another integer. In integer division, the fractional part of the result is lost. Thus the result of dividing an integer 7 by an integer 4 is 1.

interface   The name of a procedure, the names and characteristics of its dummy arguments, and (for functions) the characteristics of the result variable.

interface assignment block   An interface block used to extend the meaning of the assignment operator (=).

interface block   *(a)* A means of making an interface to a procedure explicit. *(b)* A means of defining a generic procedure, operator, or assignment.

interface body   A sequence of statements in an interface block from a FUNCTION or SUBROUTINE statement to the corresponding END statement. The body specifies the calling sequence of the function or subroutine.

interface function   A function used to isolate calls to processor-specific procedures from the main portion of a program.

interface operator block   An interface block used to define a new operator or to extend the meaning of a standard Fortran operator (+,-,*,/,>, etc.).

internal file   A character variable that can be read from and written to by normal formatted READ and WRITE statements.

internal function   An internal procedure that is a function.

internal procedure   A subroutine or function that is contained within another program unit and can only be invoked from within that program unit.

intrinsic data type   One of the predefined data types in Fortran: integer, real, double precision, logical, complex, and character.

intrinsic function   An intrinsic procedure that is a function.

intrinsic procedure   A procedure that is defined as a part of the standard Fortran language (see Appendix B).

intrinsic subroutine   An intrinsic procedure that is a subroutine.

invoke   To CALL a subroutine or to reference a function in an expression.

i/o unit   *See* input/output unit.

iteration count   The number of times that an iterative DO loop is executed.

iterative DO loop   A DO loop that executes a specified number of times based on the loop control parameters (also known as a counting loop)

keyword   A word that has a defined meaning in the Fortran language.

keyword argument   A method of specifying the association between dummy arguments and actual arguments of the form "DUMMY_ARGUMENT=actual_argument". Keyword arguments permit arguments to be specified in any order when a procedure is invoked; they are especially useful with optional arguments. Keyword arguments may be used only in procedures with explicit interfaces. An example of the use of a keyword argument is

$$\text{kind\_value = SELECTED\_REAL\_KIND(r=100)}$$

kind   All intrinsic data types except for DOUBLE PRECISION may have more than one processor-dependent representation. Each representation is known as a different kind of that type and is identified by a processor-dependent integer called a kind type parameter.

kind selector   The means of specifying the kind type parameter of a variable or named constant.

kind type parameter   An integer value used to identify the kind of an intrinsic data type.

language extension   The ability to use the features of a language to extend the language for other purposes. The principal language extension features of Fortran are derived types, user-defined operations, and data hiding.

lexical functions   Intrinsic functions used to compare two character strings in a character-set-independent manner.

librarian   A program that creates and maintains libraries of compiled object files.

library   A collection of procedures that are made available for use by a program. They may be in the form of modules or separately linked object libraries.

line printer   A type of printer used to print Fortran programs and output on large computer systems. The name reflects the fact that large line printers print an entire line at a time.

link   The process of combining object modules produced from program units to form an executable program.

linked list   A data structure in which each element contains a pointer that points to the next element in the structure. (It sometimes contains a pointer to the previous element as well.)

list-directed input   A special type of formatted input in which the format used to interpret the input data is selected by the processor in accordance with the type of the data items in the input list.

list-directed I/O statement   An input or output statement that uses list-directed input or output.

list-directed output   A special type of formatted output in which the processor selects the format used to display the output data in accordance with the type of the data items in the output list.

literal constant   A constant whose value is written directly, as opposed to a named constant. For example, 14.4 is a literal constant.

local entity   An entity defined within a single scoping unit.

local variable   A variable declared within a program unit, which is not also in a COMMON block. Such variables are local to that scoping unit.

logical   A data type that can have only two possible values: TRUE or FALSE.

logical constant   A constant with a logical value: TRUE or FALSE.

logical error   A bug or error in a program caused by a mistake in program design (improper branching, looping, etc.)

logical expression   An expression whose result is either TRUE or FALSE.

logical IF statement   A statement in which a logical expression controls whether the rest of the statement is executed.

logical operator   An operator whose result is a logical value. There are two types of logical operators: combinational (.AND., .OR., .NOT., etc.) and relational (>, <, ==, etc.).

logical variable   A variable of type LOGICAL.

loop   A sequence of statements repeated multiple times and usually controlled by a DO statement.

loop index   An integer variable that is incremented or decremented each time an iterative DO loop is executed.

lower bound   The minimum value permitted for a subscript of an array.

machine language The collection of binary instructions (also called op codes) actually understood and executed by a particular processor.

main memory The computer memory used to store programs that are currently being executed and the data associated with them. Main memory is typically semiconductor memory; it is much faster and also much more expensive than secondary memory.

main program unit A program unit that starts with a PROGRAM statement. Execution begins here when a program is started. A program can have only one main program unit.

mantissa *(a)* In a binary representation, the fractional part of a floating-point number that, when multiplied by a power of 2, produces the complete number. The power of 2 required is known as the exponent of the number. The value of the mantissa is always between 0.5 and 1.0. *(b)* In a decimal representation, the fractional part of a floating-point number that, when multiplied by a power of 10, produces the complete number. The power of 10 required is known as the exponent of the number. The value of the mantissa is always between 0.1 and 1.0.

many-one array section An array section with a vector subscript having two or more elements with the same value. Such an array section cannot appear on the left side of an assignment statement.

mask *(a)* A logical expression that controls assignment of array elements in a masked array assignment (a WHERE statement or a WHERE construct). *(b)* A logical argument in several array intrinsic functions that determines which array elements will be included in the operation.

masked array assignment An array assignment statement whose operation is controlled by a logical MASK that is the same shape as the array. The operation specified in the assignment statement is only applied to those elements of the array corresponding to true elements of the MASK. Masked array assignments are implemented as WHERE statements or WHERE constructs.

matrix A rank-2 array.

mixed-mode expression An arithmetic expression involving operands of different types. For example, the addition of a real value and an integer is a mixed-mode expression.

module A program unit that allows other program units to access constants, variables, derived type definitions, interfaces, and procedures declared within it by USE association.

module procedure A procedure contained within a module.

name A lexical token consisting of a letter followed by up to 30 alphanumeric characters (letters, digits, and underscores). The named entity can be a variable, a named constant, a pointer, or a program unit.

named association Argument association, USE association, or host association.

named constant A constant that has been named by a PARAMETER attribute in a type declaration statement or by a PARAMETER statement.

NAMELIST input/output A form of input or output in which the values in the data are accompanied by the names of the corresponding variables, in the form NAME=*value*. NAMELISTs are defined once in each program unit and can be used repeatedly in many I/O statements. NAMELIST input statements can be used to update only a portion of the variables listed in the NAMELIST.

nested The inclusion of one program construct as a part of another program construct, such as nested DO loops or nested block IF constructs.

node An element in a linked list or binary tree.

nonadvancing input/output A method of formatted I/O in which each READ, WRITE, or PRINT statement does not necessarily begin a new record.

nonexecutable statement A statement used to configure the program environment in which computational actions take place. Examples include the IMPLICIT NONE statement and type declaration statements.

D

numeric type   Integer, real, or complex data type.

object module   The file output by most compilers. Multiple object modules are combined with libraries in a linker to produce the final executable program.

obsolescent feature   A feature from earlier versions of Fortran that is considered to be redundant but that is still in frequent use. Obsolescent features have been replaced by better methods in later versions of Fortran. An example is the fixed-source form, which has been replaced by free form. Obsolescent features are candidates for deletion in future versions of Fortran as their use declines.

octal   The base 8 number system in which the legal digits are 0 through 7.

one-dimensional array   A rank-1 array, or vector.

operand   An expression that precedes or follows an operator.

operation   A computation involving one or two operands.

operator   A character or sequence of characters that defines an operation. Unary operators have one operand; binary operators have two operands.

optional argument   A dummy argument in a procedure that does not need to have a corresponding actual argument every time the procedure is invoked. Optional arguments may exist only in procedures with an explicit interface.

out-of-bounds reference   A reference to an array using a subscript either smaller than the lower bound or larger than the upper bound of the corresponding array dimension.

output buffer   A section of memory used to hold a line of output data before it is sent to an output device.

output device   A device used to output data from a computer, for example, printers and CRT displays.

output format   A format used in a formatted output statement.

output statement   A statement that sends formatted or unformatted data to an output device or file.

parameter attribute   An attribute in a type declaration statement that specifies that the named item is a constant, not a variable.

parameterized variable   A variable whose kind is explicitly specified.

pass-by-reference   A scheme in which arguments are exchanged between procedures by passing the memory locations of the arguments, instead of the values of the arguments.

pointer   A variable that has the POINTER attribute. A pointer may not be referenced or defined unless it is associated with a target. If it is an array, it does not have a shape until it is associated, although it does have a rank. When a pointer is associated with a target, it contains the memory address of the target and thus "points" to it.

pointer array   An array that is declared with the POINTER attribute. Its rank is determined in the type declaration statement, but its shape and size are not known until memory is allocated for the array in an ALLOCATE statement.

pointer assignment statement   A statement that associates a pointer with a target. Pointer assignment statements take the form "pointer => target".

pointer association   The process by which a pointer becomes associated with a target. The ASSOCIATED intrinsic function can check the association status of a pointer.

pointer attribute   An attribute in a type declaration statement that specifies that the named item is a pointer, not a variable.

precision   The number of significant decimal digits that can be represented in a floating-point number.

preconnected   An input or output unit that is automatically connected to the program and does not require an OPEN statement. Examples are the standard input and standard output units.

present   A dummy argument is present in a procedure invocation if it is associated with an actual argument, and the corresponding actual argument is present in the invoking program

D

unit. The presence of a dummy argument can be checked with the PRESENT intrinsic function.

printer control character   The first character of each output buffer. When it is sent to the printer, it controls the vertical movement of the paper before the line is written.

private   An entity in a module that is not accessible outside the module by USE association; declared by a PRIVATE attribute or in a PRIVATE statement.

procedure   A subroutine or function.

procedure interface   The characteristics of a procedure, the name of the procedure, the name of each dummy argument, and the generic identifiers (if any) by which it may be referenced.

processor   A processor is the combination of a specific computer with a specific compiler. Processor-dependent items can vary from computer to computer or from compiler to compiler on the same computer.

program   A sequence of instructions on a computer that causes the computer to carry out some specific function.

program unit   A main program, a subroutine, a function, a module, or a block data subprogram. Each unit is separately compiled.

pseudocode   A set of English statements structured in a Fortran-like manner and used to outline the approach to be taken in solving a problem without getting buried in the details of Fortran syntax.

public   An entity in a module that is accessible outside the module by USE association; declared by a PUBLIC attribute or in a PUBLIC statement. An entity in a module is public by default.

pure procedure   A pure procedure is a procedure without side effects. A pure function must not modify its dummy arguments in any fashion, and all arguments must be INTENT(IN). A pure subroutine must have no side effects except for arguments explicitly specified with INTENT(OUT) or INTENT(INOUT). Such a procedure is declared with a PURE prefix, and pure functions may be used in specification expressions to initialize data in type declaration statements. Note that all elemental procedures are also pure. Pure procedures are available in Fortran 95 only.

random access   Reading or writing the contents of a file in arbitrary order.

random access file   Another name for a direct access file: a form of file in which the individual records can be written and read in any order. Direct access files must have fixed-length records so that the location of any particular record can be quickly calculated.

random access memory (RAM)   The semiconductor memory used to store the programs and data that are actually being executed by a computer at a particular time.

range   The difference between the largest and smallest numbers that can be represented on a computer with a given data type and kind. For example, on most computers a single-precision real number has a range of 10^{-38} to 10^{38}, 0, and -10^{-38} to -10^{38}.

rank   The number of dimensions of an array. The rank of a scalar is zero. The maximum rank of a Fortran array is seven.

rank-1 array   An array having only one dimension, where each array element is addressed with a single subscript.

rank-2 array   An array having two dimensions, where each array element is addressed with two subscripts.

rank-*n* array   An array having n dimensions, where each array element is addressed with n subscripts.

real   An intrinsic data type used to represent numbers with a floating-point representation.

real number   A number of the REAL data value.

real part   The first of the two numbers that make up a COMPLEX data value.

record   A sequence of values or characters that is treated as a unit within a file. (A record is a "line" or unit of data from a file.)

record number   The index number of a record in a direct access (or random access) file.

recursion   The invocation of a procedure by itself, either directly or indirectly. Recursion is only allowed if the procedure is declared with the RECURSIVE keyword.

recursive   Capable of being invoked recursively.

reference   The appearance of a data object name in a context requiring the value at that point during execution; the appearance of a procedure name, its operator symbol, or a defined assignment statement in a context requiring execution of the procedure at that point; or the appearance of a module name in a USE statement. Neither the act of defining a variable nor the appearance of the name of a procedure as an actual argument is regarded as a reference.

relational expression   A logical expression in which a relational operator compares two nonlogical operands to give a logical value for the expressions.

relational operator   An operator that compares two nonlogical operands and returns a TRUE or FALSE result. Examples include >, >=, <, <=, ==, and /=.

repeat count   The number before a format descriptor or a group of format descriptors, which specifies the number of times that they are to be repeated. For example, the descriptor 4F10.4 is used four times.

result variable   The variable that returns the value of a function.

root   (a) The solution to an equation of the form $f(x) = 0$. (b) The node from which a binary tree grows.

round-off error   The cumulative error that occurs during floating-point operations when the result of each calculation is rounded off to the nearest value representable with a particular kind of real value.

run-time error   An error that only manifests itself when a program is executed.

SAVE attribute   An attribute in the type declaration statement of a local variable in a procedure, specifying that the value of the named item is to be preserved between invocations of the procedure. This attribute can also be specified in a separate SAVE statement.

scalar variable   A variable that is not an array variable. The variable name refers to a single item of an intrinsic or derived type, and no subscripts are used with the name.

scope   The part of a program in which a name or entity has a specified interpretation. Fortran has three possible scopes: global scope, local scope, and statement scope.

scoping unit   A scoping unit is a single region of local scope within a Fortran program. All local variables have a single interpretation throughout a scoping unit. The scoping units in Fortran are (1) a derived type definition; (2) an interface body, excluding any derived type definitions and interface bodies within it; or (3) a program unit or subprogram, excluding derived type definitions, interface bodies, and subprograms within it.

scratch file   A temporary file that is used by a program during execution and is automatically deleted when the file is closed. A scratch file may not be given a name.

secondary memory   The computer memory used to store programs that are not currently being executed and the data that is not currently needed. Secondary memory is typically a disk. It is much slower and also much less expensive than main memory.

sequential access   Reading or writing the contents of a file in sequential order.

sequential file   A form of file in which each record is read or written in sequential order. Sequential files do not require a fixed record length. They are the default file type in Fortran.

shape   The rank and extent of an array in each of its dimensions. The shape can be stored in a rank-1 array, with each element of the array containing the extent of one dimension.

side effects   The modification by a function of the variables in its input argument list, variables in modules made available by USE association, or variables in COMMON blocks.

single precision   A method of storing floating-point numbers on a computer that uses less memory than double precision, resulting in fewer significant digits and (usually) a smaller range in the representation of the numbers. Single-precision numbers are the "default real" type, the type of real number that results if no kind is specified.

size   The total number of elements in an array.

source form   The style in which a Fortran program is written—either free form or fixed form.

specific function   A function that must always be called with a single type of argument. For example, the intrinsic function IABS is a specific function, while the intrinsic function ABS is a generic function.

specification expression   A restricted form of scalar integer constant expression that can appear in a type specification statement as a bound in an array declaration or as the length in a character declaration.

specifier   An item in a control list that provides additional information for the input/output statement in which it appears. Examples are the input/output unit number and the format specification for READ and WRITE statements.

statement entity   An entity whose scope is a single statement or part of a statement, such as the index variable in the implied DO loop of an array constructor.

statement label   A number preceding a statement that can be used to refer to that statement.

static memory allocation   Allocating memory for variables or arrays at compilation time, as opposed to dynamic memory allocation, which occurs during program execution.

static variable   A variable allocated a compilation time and remaining in existence throughout the execution of a program.

storage association   A method of associating two or more variables or arrays by aligning their physical storage in a computer's memory. This technique was commonly achieved with COMMON blocks and EQUIVALENCE statements but is not recommended for new programs.

stride   The increment specified in a subscript triplet.

structure   *(a)* An item of a derived data type. *(b)* An organized, standard way to describe an algorithm.

structure component   A part of an object of derived type that may be referenced by a component selector. A component selector consists of the object's name followed by the component's name, separated by a percent sign (%).

structure constructor   An unnamed (or literal) constant of a derived type. It consists of the name of the type followed by the components of the type in parentheses. The components appear in the order in which they were declared in the definition of the derived type. For example the following line declares a constant of type person:

```
john = person('John','R','Jones','323-6439',21,'M','123-45-6789')
```

subroutine   A procedure that is invoked by a CALL statement and that returns its result through its arguments.

subscript   One of the integer values in parentheses following an array name, which are used to identify a particular element of the array. Each dimension of the array has one subscript value.

subscript triplet   A method of specifying one dimension of an array section by means of the initial and final values and a stride. Colons separate the three components of the subscript triplet, and some of them may be defaulted. For example, the following array section contains two subscript triplets: array(1:3:2,2:4).

substring   A contiguous portion of a scalar character string.

substring specification   The specification of a substring of a character string. The specification takes the form char_var(istart:iend), where char_var is the name of a character variable, istart is the first character in char_var to include in the substring, and iend is the first character in char_var to include in the substring.

syntax error   An error in the syntax of a Fortran statement, detected by the compiler during compilation.

tail   The last item in a linked list.

target   A variable that has the TARGET attribute and that can be the destination of a pointer.

test driver program   A small program that is written specifically to invoke a procedure for the purpose of testing it.

top-down design   The process of analyzing a problem by starting with the major steps and successively refining each step until all the small steps are easy to implement in Fortran code.

transformational intrinsic function   An intrinsic function that is neither an elemental function nor an inquiry function. It usually has array arguments and an array result whose elements have values that depend on the values of many of the elements of the arguments.

tree   A form of linked list in which each node points to two or more other nodes. If each node points to two other nodes, the structure is a binary tree.

truncation   *(a)* The process in which the fractional part of a real number is discarded before the number is assigned to an integer variable. *(b)* The process in which excess characters are removed from the right side of a character string before it is assigned to a character variable of shorter length.

truncation error   *(a)* The error caused by terminating a calculation before it is complete. *(b)* The cumulative error that occurs during floating-point operations when the result of each calculation is truncated to the next lower value representable with a particular kind of real value.

truth table   A table showing the result of a combinational logic expression for all possible combinations of operand values.

two-dimensional array   A rank-2 array.

type declaration statement   A statement that specifies the type and optionally the attributes of one or more variables or constants: `INTEGER`, `REAL`, `DOUBLE PRECISION`, `COMPLEX`, `CHARACTER`, `LOGICAL`, or `TYPE` (type name) statement.

type parameter   A parameter of an intrinsic data type. `KIND` and `LEN` are the type parameters.

unary operator   An operator that has only one operand, such as `.NOT.` or the unary minus.

undefined   A data entity that does not have a defined value.

unformatted file   A file containing data stored in a sequence of bit patterns that are a direct copy of a portion of the computer's memory. Unformatted files are processor dependent and can only be produced by unformatted `WRITE` statements and read only by unformatted `READ` statements on the particular type of processor that produced them.

unformatted input statement   An unformatted `READ` statement.

unformatted output statement   An unformatted `WRITE` statement.

unformatted READ statement   A `READ` statement that does not contain a format specifier. Unformatted `READ` statements transfer bit patterns directly from an external device into memory without interpretation.

unformatted record   A record consisting of a sequence of bit patterns that are a direct copy of a portion of the computer's memory. Unformatted records are processor dependent and can only be produced by unformatted `WRITE` statements and read only by unformatted `READ` statements on the particular type of processor that produced them.

unformatted WRITE statement   A `WRITE` statement that does not contain a format specifier. Unformatted `WRITE` statements transfer bit patterns directly from a processor's memory to an external device without interpretation.

unicode   An internal character coding scheme that uses 2 bytes to represent each character. The unicode system can represent 65,536 possible different characters. The first 128 unicode characters are identical to the ASCII character set, and other blocks of characters are devoted to various languages such as Chinese, Japanese, Hebrew, Arabic, and Hindi.

uninitialized array   An array in which some or all of the elements have not be initialized.

uninitialized variable   A variable that has been defined in a type declaration statement, but for which no initial value has been assigned.

unit   An input/output unit.

D

unit specifier   A specifier that specifies the unit on which input or output is to occur.

unit testing   The process of testing individual procedures separately and independently before combining them into a final program.

upper bound   The maximum value permitted for a subscript of an array.

USE association   The manner in which the contents of a module are made available for use in a program unit.

USE statement   A statement that references a module in order to make the contents of the module available for use in the program unit containing it.

value separator   A comma, a space, a slash, or end of record that separates two data values in a list-directed input.

variable   A data object whose value may be changed during program execution.

variable declaration   The declaration of the type and, optionally, the attributes of a variable.

varying string   A form of characer data in which the length is not fixed at the time of the declaration of the character variable but may vary during the execution of the program. Varying strings are not a part of the Fortran 90/95 standard but are included in a Fortran auxiliary standard.

vector   A rank-1 array.

vector subscript   A method of specifying an array section by a rank-1 array containing the subscripts of the elements to include in the array section.

well-conditioned system   A system of equations whose solution is relatively insensitive to small changes in the values of its coefficients, or to truncation and round-off errors.

WHERE construct   The construct used in a masked array assignment.

while loop   A loop that executes indefinitely until some specified condition is satisfied.

whole array   An array that has a name.

word   The fundamental unit of memory on a particular computer. The size of a word varies from processor to processor but is typically 16, 32, or 64 bits.

work array   A temporary array used for the storage of intermediate results. This array can be implemented as an automatic array in Fortran 90/95.

D

Answers to Quizzes

Quiz 1–1

1. (a) 11011_2 (b) 1011_2 (c) 100011_2 (d) 1111111_2
2. (a) 14_{10} (b) 85_{10} (c) 9_{10}
3. (a) 162655_8 or $E5AD_{16}$ (b) 1675_8 or $3BD_{16}$ (c) 113477_8 or $973F_{16}$
4. $131_{10} = 10000011_2$, so the 4th bit is a zero.
5. (a) ASCII: M; EBCDIC: ((b) ASCII: {; EBCDIC: #   (c) ASCII: (unused); EBCDIC: 9
6. (a) -32768 (b) 32767
7. Yes, a 4-byte variable of the real data type can be used to store larger numbers than a 4-byte variable of the integer data type. The 8 bits of exponent in a real variable can represent values as large as 10^{38}. A 4-byte integer can represent values up to 2,147,483,647 (about 10^9). To do this, the real variable is restricted to 6 or 7 decimal digits of precision, while the integer variable has 9 or 10 decimal digits of precision.

Quiz 2–1

1. Valid integer constant.
2. Invalid. Commas not permitted within constants.
3. Invalid. Real constants must have a decimal point. (However, many compilers will accept this form.)
4. Invalid. Single quotes within a character string delimited by single quotes must be doubled. Correct forms are `'That"s ok!'` or `"That's ok!"`.
5. Valid integer constant.
6. Valid real constant.
7. Valid character constant.
8. Valid logical constant.

9. Valid character constant.
10. Invalid. Character constants must be enclosed by single or double quotes.
11. Valid character constant.
12. Valid real constant.
13. Invalid. Logical constants must be surrounded by periods.
14. Invalid. Real exponents are expressed using the E symbol instead of ^.
15. Same.
16. Same.
17. Different.
18. Different.
19. Valid program name.
20. Invalid. Program name must begin with a letter.
21. Valid integer variable.
22. Valid real variable.
23. Invalid. Name must begin with a letter.
24. Valid real variable.
25. Invalid. Name must begin with a letter.
26. Invalid. No double colons (: :) present.
27. Valid.

Quiz 2–2

1. The order is (1) exponentials, working from right to left; (2) multiplications and divisions, working from left to right; (3) additions and subtractions, working from left to right; (4) relational operators (= = , / = , > , > = , < , < =), working from left to right; (5) .NOT. operators; (6) .AND. operators, working from left to right; (7) .OR. operators, working from left to right; (8) .EQV. and .NEQV. operators, working from left to right. Parentheses modify this order—terms in parentheses are evaluated first, starting from the innermost parentheses and working outward.
2. (a) Legal: Result = 12;   (b) Legal: Result = 42;   (c) Legal: Result = 2;   (d) Legal: Result = 2;   (e) Illegal: Division by 0;   (f) Legal: Result = −40.5. Note that this result is legal because exponentiation precedes negation in operator precedence. It is equivalent to the expression: -(3.**(4./2.)) and does *not* involve taking the real power of a negative number.;   (g) Legal: Result = 0.111111;   (h) Illegal: Two adjacent operators.
3. (a) 7;   (b) −21;   (c) 7;   (d) 9
4. (a) Legal: Result = 256;   (b) Legal: Result = 0.25;   (c) Legal: Result = 4;   (d) Illegal: Negative real number raised to a real power
5. The statements are illegal, since they try to assign a value to parameter k.
6. RESULT = 44.16667
7. a = 3.0; n = 3

Quiz 2–3

1. r_eq = r1 + r2 + r3 + r4
2. r_eq = 1./(1./r1 + 1./r2 + 1./r3 + 1./r4)
3. t = 2. * pi * SQRT(1/g)
4. v = v_max * EXP(-alpha*t) * COS(omega*t)
5. $d = \frac{1}{2}at^2 + v_0 t + x_0$
6. $f = \dfrac{1}{2\pi\sqrt{LC}}$
7. $E = \frac{1}{2}L\,i^2$
8. The results are

$$126 \quad 5.000000E-02 \quad T$$

Make sure that you can explain why a is equal to 0.05!

9. (a) Legal: Result = .FALSE.; (b) Illegal: .NOT. only works with logical values; (c) Legal: Result = .TRUE.; (d) Legal: Result = .TRUE.; (e) Legal: Result = .TRUE.; (f) Legal: Result = .TRUE.; (g) Legal: Result = .FALSE.; (h) Illegal: .OR. only works with logical values.
10. (a) Legal: Result = 'bcd'; (b) Legal: Result = 'ABCd'; (c) Legal: Result = .FALSE.; (d) Legal: Result = .TRUE.; (e) Illegal: can't compare strings with numbers (f) Legal: Result = .TRUE.; (g) Legal: Result = .FALSE.
11. The results are shown below. Can you explain why each value was assigned to a given variable by the READ statements?

$$1 \quad 3 \quad 180 \quad 2.000000 \quad 30.000000 \quad 3.489839E-02$$

Quiz 3–1

1.
```
IF ( x >= 0. ) THEN
    sqrt_x = SQRT( x )
    WRITE (*,*) 'The square root of x is ', sqrt_x
ELSE
    WRITE (*,*) 'Error--x < 0!'
    sqrt_x = 0.
END IF
```

2.
```
IF ( ABS(denominator) < 1.0E-10 ) THEN
    WRITE (*,*) 'Divide by zero error!'
ELSE
    fun = numerator / denominator
    WRITE (*,*) 'FUN = ', fun
END IF
```

3.
```
IF ( distance > 300. ) THEN
    cost = 110. + 0.20 * ( distance - 300. )
ELSE IF ( distance > 100. ) THEN
    cost = 50. + 0.30 * ( distance - 100. )
ELSE
    cost = 0.50 * distance
END IF
average_cost = cost / distance
```

4. These statements are incorrect. There is no ELSE in front of IF (VOLTS < 105.).

5. These statements are correct. They will print out the warning because `warn` is true, even though the speed limit is not exceeded.

6. These statements are incorrect, since a real value is used to control the operation of a `CASE` statement.

7. These statements are correct. They will print out the message `'Prepare to stop.'`

8. These statements are technically correct, but they are unlikely to do what the user intended. If the temperature is greater than 100°, then the user probably wants `'Boiling point of water exceeded'` to be printed out. Instead, the message `'Human body temperature exceeded'` will be printed out, since the `IF` structure executes the first true branch that it comes to. If the temperature is greater than 100°, it is also greater than 37°.

Quiz 3–2

1. 4
2. 0
3. 1
4. 7
5. 9
6. 0
7. `ires = 10`
8. `ires = 55`
9. `ires = 10`
10. `ires = 100`
11. `ires = 21`
12. Invalid—These statements redefine `DO` loop index `i` within the loop.
13. Valid
14. Illegal—`DO` loops overlap.

Quiz 4–1

Note: There is more than one way to write each `FORMAT` statement in this quiz. These answers represent one of many possible correct answers to these questions.

1. ```
WRITE (*,100)
100 FORMAT ('1',24X,'This is a test!')
```

2. ```
WRITE (*,110) i, j, data1
100 FORMAT ('0',2I10,F10.2)
```

3. ```
WRITE (*,110) result
110 FORMAT ('1',T13,'The result is ',ES12.4)
```

4.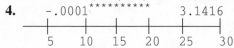
```

5.
```
      .000    .602E+24     3.14159
  +---+---+---+---+---+---+
    5   10  15  20  25  30
```

6.
```
**********6.0200E+23   3.1416
  +---+---+---+---+---+---+
    5   10  15  20  25  30
```

7. 32767
```
    24
  *****
  +---+---+---+---+---+---+
    5   10  15  20  25  30
```

8.
```
   32767 00000024 -1010101
  +---+---+---+---+---+---+
    5   10  15  20  25  30
```

9. ABCDEFGHIJ   12345
```
  +---+---+---+---+---+---+
    5   10  15  20  25  30
```

10.
```
                    ABC12345IJ
  +---+---+---+---+---+---+
    5   10  15  20  25  30
```

11. ABCDE   12345
```
  +---+---+---+---+---+---+
    5   10  15  20  25  30
```

12. Correct. All format descriptors match variable types.

13. Incorrect. Format descriptors do not match variable types for `test` and `ierror`.

14. This program skips to the top of a page and writes the following data.

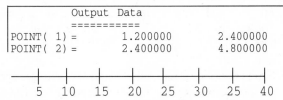

```
            Output Data
            ===========
POINT( 1) =      1.200000      2.400000
POINT( 2) =      2.400000      4.800000


  +---+---+---+---+---+---+---+
    5   10  15  20  25  30  25  40
```

Quiz 4–2

Note: There is more than one way to write each FORMAT statement in this quiz. These answers represent one of many possible correct answers to these questions.

1.
```
READ (*,100) amplitude, count, identity
100 FORMAT (9X,F11.2,T30,I6,T60,A13)
```

2.
```
READ (*,110) title, i1, i2, i3, i5, i5
100 FORMAT (T10,A25,/(4X,I8))
```

E

3. `READ (*,120) string, number`
`120 FORMAT (T11,A10,///,T11,I10)`

4. $a = 1.65 \times 10^{-10}$, $b = 17.$, $c = -11.7$

5. $a = -3.141593$, $b = 2.718282$, $c = 37.55$

6. $i = -35$, $j = 6705$, $k = 3687$

7. `string1 = 'FGHIJ'`, `string2 = 'KLMNOPQRST'`, `string3 =`
`'UVWXYZ0123 '`, `string4 = ' _TEST_ 1'`

8. Correct.

9. Correct. These statements read integer `junk` from columns 60–74 of one line and then read real variable `scratch` from columns 1–15 of the next line.

10. Incorrect. Real variable `elevation` will be read with an `I6` format descriptor.

Quiz 4–3

Note: There is more than one way to write each statement in this quiz. These answers represent one of many possible correct answers to these questions.

1. `OPEN (UNIT = 25, FILE = 'IN052691', ACTION = 'READ', IOSTAT = istat)`
`IF ( istat /= 0 ) THEN`
`   WRITE (*,'(1X,A,I6)') 'Open error on file. IOSTAT = ', istat`
`ELSE`
`   ...`
`END IF`

2. `OPEN (UNIT = 4, FILE = out_name, STATUS = 'NEW', ACTION = 'WRITE', &`
`      IOSTAT = istat)`

3. `CLOSE (UNIT = 24)`

4. `READ (8,*,IOSTAT = istat) first, last`
`IF ( istat < 0 ) THEN`
`   WRITE (*,*) 'End of file encountered on unit 8.'`
`END IF`

5. `DO i = 1, 8`
`   BACKSPACE (UNIT = 13)`
`END DO`

6. Incorrect. File `data1` has been replaced, so there is no data to read.

7. Incorrect. You cannot specify a file name with a scratch file.

8. Incorrect. There is nothing in the scratch file to read, since the file was created when it was opened.

9. Incorrect. You cannot use a real value as an i/o unit number.

10. Correct.

Quiz 5–1

1. 15

2. 256

3. 41

4. Valid. The array will be initialized with the values in the array constructor.

5. Valid. All 10 values in the array will be initialized to 0.

6. Valid. Every 10th value in the array will be initialized to 1000, and all other values will be initialized to zero. The values will then be written out.

7. Invalid. The arrays are not conformable because `array1` is 11 elements long and `array2` is 10 elements long.
8. Valid. Every 10th element of array `in` will initialize to 10, 20, 30, and so on. All other elements will be zero. The 10-element array `sub1` will be initialized to 10, 20, 30, . . . , 100, and the 10-element array `sub2` will be initialized to 1, 2, 3, . . . , 10. The multiplication will work because arrays `sub1` and `sub2` are conformable.
9. Mostly valid. The values in array `error` will be printed out. However, since `error(0)` was never initialized, we don't know what will be printed out, or even whether printing that array element will cause an I/O error.
10. Valid. Array `ivec1` will be initialized to 1, 2, . . . , 10, and array `ivec2` will be initialized to 10, 9, . . . , 1. Array `data1` will be initialized to 1., 4., 9., . . . , 100. The `WRITE` statement will print out 100., 81., 64., . . . , 1. because of the vector subscript.
11. Probably invalid. These statements will compile correctly, but they probably do *not* do what the programmer intended. A 10-element integer array `mydata` will be created. Each `READ` statement reads values into the entire array, so array `mydata` will be initialized 10 times over (using up 100 input values!). The user probably intended for each array element to be initialized only once.

Quiz 5–2

1. 645 elements. The valid range is `data_input(-64,0)` to `data_input(64,4)`.
2. 210 elements. The valid range is `filenm(1,1)` to `filenm(3,70)`.
3. 294 elements. The valid range is `in(-3,-3,1)` to `in(3,3,6)`.
4. Invalid. The array constructor is not conformable with array `dist`.
5. Valid. `dist` will be initialized with the values in the array constructor.
6. Valid. Arrays `data1`, `data2`, and `data_out` are all conformable, so this addition is valid. The first `WRITE` statement prints the five values: 1., 11., 11., 11., 11., and the second `WRITE` statement prints the two values: 11., 11.
7. Valid. These statements initialize the array and then select the subset specified by `list1 = (/1,4,2,2/)`, and `list2 = (/1,2,3/)`. The resulting array section is

$$\texttt{array(list1,list2)} = \begin{bmatrix} \texttt{array(1,1)} & \texttt{array(1,2)} & \texttt{array(1,3)} \\ \texttt{array(4,1)} & \texttt{array(4,2)} & \texttt{array(4,3)} \\ \texttt{array(2,1)} & \texttt{array(2,2)} & \texttt{array(2,3)} \\ \texttt{array(2,1)} & \texttt{array(2,2)} & \texttt{array(2,3)} \end{bmatrix}$$

$$\texttt{array(list1,list2)} = \begin{bmatrix} 11 & 21 & 31 \\ 14 & 24 & 34 \\ 12 & 22 & 32 \\ 12 & 22 & 32 \end{bmatrix}$$

E

8. Invalid. There is a many-one array section of the left side of an assignment statement.

9. The data on the first three lines would be read into array input. However, the data is read in column order, so mydata(1,1) = 11.2, mydata(2,1) = 16.5, mydata(3,1) = 31.3, etc. mydata(2,4) = 15.0.

10. The data on the first three lines would be read into array input. The data is read in column order, so mydata(0,2) = 11.2, mydata(1,2) = 16.5, mydata(2,2) = 31.3, etc. mydata(2,4) = 17.1.

11. The data on the first three lines would be read into array input. This time, the data is read in row order, so mydata(1,1) = 11.2, mydata(1,2) = 16.5, mydata(1,3) = 31.3, etc. mydata(2,4) = 17.1.

12. The data on the first three lines would be read into array input. The data is read in row order, but only the first five values on each line are read by each READ statement. The next READ statement begins with the first value on the next input line. Therefore, mydata(2,4) = 11.0.

13. −9.0

14. The rank of array mydata is 2.

15. The shape of array mydata is 3 × 5.

16. The extent of the first dimension of array data_input is 129.

17. 7

Quiz 5–3

1. LBOUND(values,1) = -3; UBOUND(values,2) = 50; SIZE(values,1) = 7; SIZE(values) = 357; SHAPE(values) = 7,51

2. UBOUND(values,2) = 4; SIZE(values) = 60; SHAPE(values) = 3,4,5

3. MAXVAL(input1) = 9.0; MAXLOC(input1) = 5,5

4. SUM(arr1) = 5.0; PRODUCT(arr1) = 0.0; PRODUCT(arr1, MASK = arr1 / = 0.) = -45.0; ANY(arr1 > 0) = T, ALL(arr1 > 0) = F

5. The values printed out are SUM(arr2, MASK = arr2 > 0.) = 20.0.

6.
```
REAL, DIMENSION(5,5) :: input1
FORALL ( i = 1:5, j = 1:5 )
    input1(i,j) = i + j - 1
END FORALL
WRITE (*,*) MAXVAL(input1)
WRITE (*,*) MAXLOC(input1)
```

7. Invalid. The control mask for the WHERE construct (time > 0.) is not the same shape as the array dist in the body of the WHERE construct.

8. Invalid. Array time must be allocated before it is initialized.

9. Valid. The resulting input array is

$$data1 = \begin{bmatrix} 1 & 0 & 0 & 0 & 0 \\ 0 & 0 & 0 & 0 & 0 \\ 3 & 2 & 1 & 0 & 0 \\ 0 & 0 & 0 & 0 & 0 \\ 5 & 4 & 3 & 2 & 1 \end{bmatrix}$$

10. Valid. Since the array is not allocated, the result of the ALLOCATED function is FALSE, and output of the WRITE statement is F.

Quiz 6–1

1. The call to `ave_sd` is incorrect. The second and third arguments are declared as integers in the calling program, but they are reals within the subroutine.
2. These statements are valid. When the subroutine finishes executing, `string2` contains the mirror image of the characters in `string1`.
3. These statements are incorrect. Subroutine `sub3` uses 30 elements in array `iarray`, but there are only 25 values in the array passed from the calling program. Also, the subroutine uses an assumed-size dummy array, which should not be used in any new programs.

Quiz 6–2

1. The `SAVE` statement or the `SAVE` attribute should be used in any procedure that depends on local data values being unchanged between invocations of the procedure. All local variables that must remain constant between invocations should be declared with the `SAVE` attribute.
2. An automatic array is a local array in a procedure whose extent is specified by variables passed to the procedure when it is invoked. The array is automatically created each time the procedure is invoked and is automatically destroyed each time the procedure exits. Automatic arrays should be used for temporary storage within a procedure. An allocatable array is an array declared with the `ALLOCATABLE` attribute and allocated with an `ALLOCATE` statement. It is more general and flexible than an automatic array, since it may appear in either main programs or procedures. Allocatable arrays can create memory leaks if misused. Allocatable arrays should be used to allocate memory in main programs.
3. If procedures are placed in a module and accessed by `USE` association, then they will have explicit interfaces, allowing the compiler to catch many errors in calling sequence.
4. Assumed-shape dummy arrays have the advantage (compared to assumed-size arrays) that they can be used with whole array operations, array intrinsic functions, and array sections. They are simpler than explicit-shape dummy arrays because the bounds of each array do not have to be passed to the procedure. The only disadvantage associated with them is that they must be used with an explicit interface.
5. This program will work on many processors, but it has two potentially serious problems. First, the value of variable `isum` is never initialized. Second, `isum` is not saved between calls to `sub1`. When it works, it will initialize the values of the array to 1, 2, . . . , 10.
6. There is no error in this program. The main program and the subroutine share data using a module. The output from the program is `a(5) = 5.0`.
7. The calling sequence to subroutine `sub3` is in error, and the error will be caught by the compiler because `sub3` has an explicit interface. The second argument of `sub3` is `INTENT(OUT)`, and the corresponding argument in the calling sequence is a constant.

E

8. This program is invalid. Subroutine `sub4` uses assumed-shape arrays but does not have an explicit interface.

Quiz 6–3

1.
```
REAL FUNCTION f2(x)
IMPLICIT NONE
REAL, INTENT(IN) :: x
f2 = (x - 1.) / (x + 1.)
END FUNCTION
```

2.
```
REAL FUNCTION tanh(x)
IMPLICIT NONE
REAL, INTENT(IN) :: x
tanh = (EXP(x) - EXP(-x)) / (EXP(x) + EXP-(x))
END FUNCTION
```

3.
```
FUNCTION fact(n)
IMPLICIT NONE
INTEGER, INTENT(IN) :: n
INTEGER :: fact
INTEGER :: i
fact = 1.
DO i = n, 1, -1
   fact = fact * i
END DO
END FUNCTION
```

4.
```
LOGICAL FUNCTION compare(x,y)
IMPLICIT NONE
REAL, INTENT(IN) :: x, y
compare = (x**2 + y**2) > 1.0
END FUNCTION
```

5. This function is incorrect because `sum` is never initialized. The sum must be set to zero before the `DO` loop is executed.

6. This function is invalid. Argument `a` is `INTENT(IN)`, but its value is modified in the function.

7. This function is invalid.

Quiz 7–1

1. False for ASCII, and true for EBCDIC.

2. False for both ASCII and EBCDIC.

3. False.

4. These statements are legal.

5. This function is legal, provided that it has an explicit interface. Automatic-length character functions must have an explicit interface.

6. `ipos1` = 17, `ipos2` = 0, `ipos3` = 14, `ipos4` = 37

E

Quiz 7–2

1. Valid. The result is -1234 because buff1(10:10) is 'J', not 'K'.
2. Valid. After these statements outbuf contains
   `'           123        0        -11          '`
3. The statements are valid. ival1 = 456789, ival2 = 234, rval3 = 5678.90.

Quiz 8–1

1. This answer to this question is processor dependent. You must consult the manuals for your particular compiler.
2. (−1.980198E-02, −1.980198E-01)
3.
```
PROGRAM complex_math
!
!  Purpose:
!    To perform the complex calculation:
!       D = ( A + B ) / C
!    where A = ( 1., -1.)
!          B = (-1., -1.)
!          C = (10., 1.)
!    without using the COMPLEX data type.
!
 IMPLICIT NONE
!
REAL :: ar = 1., ai = -1.
REAL :: br = -1., bi = -1.
REAL :: cr = 10., ci = 1.
REAL :: dr, di
REAL :: tempr, tempi

CALL complex_add ( ar, ai, br, bi, tempr, tempi )
CALL complex_divide ( tempr, tempi, cr, ci, dr, di )

WRITE (*,100) dr, di
100 FORMAT (1X, 'D = (',F10.5,',',F10.5,')')

END PROGRAM
SUBROUTINE complex_add ( x1, y1, x2, y2, x3, y3 )
!
!  Purpose:
!    Subroutine to add two complex numbers (x1, y1) and
!    (x2, y2), and store the result in (x3, y3).
!
IMPLICIT NONE

REAL, INTENT(IN) :: x1, y1, x2, y2
REAL, INTENT(OUT) :: x3, y3

x3 = x1 + x2
y3 = y1 + y2

END SUBROUTINE complex_add
SUBROUTINE complex_divide ( x1, y1, x2, y2, x3, y3 )
!
!  Purpose:
```

E

```
!     Subroutine to divide two complex numbers (x1, y1) and
!     (x2, y2), and store the result in (x3, y3).
!
IMPLICIT NONE

REAL, INTENT(IN) :: x1, y1, x2, y2
REAL, INTENT(OUT) :: x3, y3
REAL :: denom

denom = x2**2 + y2**2
x3 = (x1 * x2 + y1 * y2) / denom
y3 = (y1 * x2 - x1 * y2) / denom

END SUBROUTINE complex_divide
```

It is much easier to use the complex data type to solve the problem than it is to use the definitions of complex operations and real numbers.

Quiz 8–2

1.
```
WRITE (*,100) points(7)%plot_time%day, points(7)%plot_time%month, &
              points(7)%plot_time%year, points(7)%plot_time%hour, &
              points(7)%plot_time%minute, points(7)%plot_time%second
100 FORMAT (1X,I2.2,'/',I2.2,'/',I4.4,' ',I2.2,':',I2.2,':',I2.2)
```

2.
```
WRITE (*,110) points(7)%plot_position%x, &
              points(7)%plot_position%y, &
              points(7)%plot_position%z
110 FORMAT (1X,' x = ',F12.4, ' y = ',F12.4, ' z = ',F12.4 )
```

3. To calculate the time difference, we must subtract the times associated with the two points, taking into account the different scales associated with hours, minutes, seconds, and so on. The following code converts the times to seconds before subtracting them and also assumes that both points occur on the same day, month, and year. (It is easy to extend this calculation to handle arbitrary days, months, and years as well, but you must use double-precision real arithmetic for the calculations.) To calculate the position difference, we use the equation

$$dpos = \sqrt{(x_2 - x_1)^2 - (y_2 + y_1)^2 + (z_2 - z_1)^2}$$

```
time1 = points(2)%plot_time%second + 60.*points(2)%plot_time%minute &
      + 3600.*points(2)%plot_time%hour
time2 = points(3)%plot_time%second + 60.*points(3)%plot_time%minute &
      + 3600.*points(3)%plot_time%hour
dtime = time2 - time1
dpos = SQRT ( &
       (points(3)%plot_position%x - points(2)%plot_position%x )**2 &
     + (points(3)%plot_position%y - points(2)%plot_position%y )**2 &
     + (points(3)%plot_position%z - points(2)%plot_position%z )**2 )

rate = dpos / dtime
```

4. Valid. This statement prints out all of the components of the first element of array points.

5. Invalid. The format descriptors do not match the order of the data in `points(4)`.

6. Invalid. Intrinsic operations are not defined for derived data types, and component `plot_position` is a derived data type.

Quiz 9–1

1. An internal subroutine is a subroutine that is contained within a main program or procedure and that is compiled together with that program unit. It is placed after the last executable statement in the program unit and is preceded by a `CONTAINS` statement. The internal subroutine is accessible only from the program unit that contains it. By contrast, an external subroutine is separately compiled and can be called from any program unit.

2. The scope of an object is the portion of a Fortran program over which the object is defined. The three levels of scope are global, local, and statement.

3. Host association is the process by which data entities in a host scoping unit are made available to an inner scoping unit. If variables and constants are defined in a host scoping unit, then those variables and constants are inherited by any inner scoping units *unless* another object with the same name is explicitly defined in the inner scoping unit.

4. When this program is executed $z = 3.666667$. Initially, z is set to 10.0, and then function `fun1(z)` is invoked. The function is an internal function, so it inherits the values of derived type variable `xyz` by host association. Since `xyz%x` $= 1.0$ and `xyz%z` $= 3.0$, the function evaluates to $(10. + 1.)/3. = 3.666667$. This function result is then stored in variable `z`.

5. `i` $= 20$. The first executable statement changes `i` to 27, and the fourth executable statement subtracts 7 from it to produce the final answer. (The `i` in the third statement has statement scope only, and so does not affect the value of `i` in the main program.)

6. These statements are illegal. The program name `abc` must be unique within the program.

7. Recursive procedures are procedures that can call themselves. They are declared using the `RECURSIVE` keyword in `SUBROUTINE` or `FUNCTION` statement. If the recursive procedure is a function, then the `FUNCTION` statement should also include a `RESULT` clause.

8. This function is illegal because it contains a type declaration for the function name `sum_1_n` and no type declaration for the result variable `sum`. When a `RESULT` clause is used, only the type of the result variable should be declared, not the type of the function name.

9. Keyword arguments are calling arguments of the form `KEYWORD = value`, where `KEYWORD` is the name used to declare the dummy argument in the procedure definition and `value` is the value to be passed to that dummy argument when the procedure is invoked. Keyword arguments may only be used if the procedure being invoked has an explicit interface. Keyword arguments may be used to allow calling arguments to be specified in a different order or to specify only certain optional arguments.

E

10. *Optional* arguments do not have to be present when a procedure is invoked, but they will be used if they are present. Optional arguments may be used only if the procedure being invoked has an explicit interface. They may be used for input or output data that is not needed every time a procedure is invoked.

Quiz 9–2

1. An interface block is a way to specify an explicit interface for a separately compiled external procedure. It consists of an INTERFACE statement and an END INTERFACE statement. Between these two statements are statements declaring the calling sequence of the procedure, including the order, type, and intent of each argument. Interface blocks may be placed in the declaration section of an invoking program unit. Otherwise, they may be placed in a module, and that module may be accessed by the invoking program unit via USE association.

2. A programmer might choose to create an interface block for a procedure because the procedure may be written in a language other than Fortran or because the procedure must work with both Fortran 90/95 and older FORTRAN 77 applications.

3. The interface body contains a SUBROUTINE or FUNCTION statement declaring the name of the procedure and its dummy arguments, followed by type declaration statements for each of the dummy arguments. It concludes with an END SUBROUTINE or END FUNCTION statement.

4. This program is valid. The multiple definitions for x1 and x2 do not interfere with each other because they are in different scoping units. When the program is executed, the results are

```
This is a test.        613.000        248.000
```

5. A generic procedure is defined using a named interface block. The name of the generic procedure is specified in the INTERFACE statement, and the calling sequences of all possible specific procedures are specified in the body of the interface block. Each specific procedure must be distinguishable from all other specific procedures by some combination of its nonoptional calling arguments. If the generic interface block appears in a module and the corresponding specific procedures are also defined in the module, then they are specified as being a part of the generic procedure with MODULE PROCEDURE statements.

6. This generic interface is illegal because the number, types, and order of the dummy arguments for the two specific procedures are identical. The two sets of dummy arguments must be different so that the compiler can determine which one to use.

7. A MODULE PROCEDURE statement is used to specify that a specific procedure is a part of a generic procedure (or operator definition) when both the specific procedure and the generic procedure (or operator definition) appear within the same module. This statement is used because any procedure in a module automatically has an explicit interface. Respecifying the interface in a generic interface block would involve declaring the explicit interface of the procedure twice, which is illegal.

8. A user-defined operator is declared using the INTERFACE OPERATOR block, while a user-defined assignment is declared using the INTERFACE ASSIGNMENT block. A user-defined operator is implemented by a one- or two-argument function (for unary and binary operators, respectively). The arguments of the function must have INTENT(IN), and the result of the function is the result of the operation. A user-defined assignment is implemented using a two-argument subroutine. The first argument must be INTENT(OUT) or INTENT(INOUT), and the second argument must be INTENT(IN). The first argument is the result of the assignment operation.

9. Access to the contents of a module may be controlled using PUBLIC and PRIVATE statements or attributes. It might be desirable to restrict access to the internal components of some user-defined data types, or to restrict direct access to procedures used to implement user-defined operators or assignments, so these items can be declared to be PRIVATE.

10. The default type of access for items in a module is PUBLIC.

11. A program unit accessing items in a module by USE association can limit the items in the module that it accesses by using the ONLY clause in the USE statement. A programmer might wish to limit access in this manner to avoid conflicts if a public item in the module has the same name as a local item in the programming unit.

12. A program unit accessing items in a module by USE association can rename the items in the module that it accesses by using the => option in the USE statement. A programmer might wish to rename an item in order to avoid conflicts if an item in the module has the same name as a local item in the programming unit.

Quiz 10–1

1.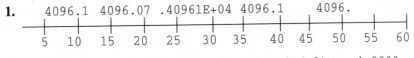
   ```
   4096.1  4096.07  .40961E+04  4096.1      4096.
   ```

2. Data1 (1) = -17.2000,   Data1 (2) =   4.0000,
   Data1 (3) =   4.0000,   Data1 (4) =   .3000,
   Data1 (5) = -2.2200
   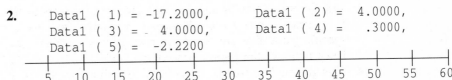

3. 12.200000E-06 12.345600E+06
   1.220000E-05   1.234560E+07
   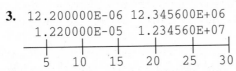

4. i =   -2002 j =   -1001 k =   -3
   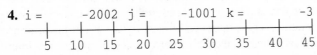

Quiz 10–2

1. A formatted file contains information stored as ASCII or EBCDIC characters. The information in a formatted file can be read with a text editor. By contrast, an unformatted file contains information stored in a form that is an exact copy of the bit patterns in the computer's memory. Its contents cannot be easily examined. Formatted files are portable between processors, but they occupy a relatively large amount of space and require extra processor time to perform the translation on input and output. Unformatted files are more compact and more efficient to read and write, but they are not portable between processors of different types.

2. A direct access file is a file whose records can be read and written in any arbitrary order. A sequential access file is a file whose records must be read and written sequentially. Direct access files are more efficient for accessing data in random order, but every record in a direct access file must be the same length. Sequential access files are efficient for reading and writing data in a sequential order but are very poor for random access. However, the records in a sequential access file may have variable lengths.

3. The INQUIRE statement is used to retrieve information about a file. The information may be retrieved by (1) file name or (2) i/o unit number. The third form of the INQUIRE statement is the IOLENGTH form. It calculates the length of a record in an unformatted direct-access file in processor-dependent units.

4. Invalid. It is illegal to use a file name with a scratch file.

5. Invalid. The RECL = clause must be specified when opening a direct access file.

6. Invalid. By default, direct access files are opened unformatted. Formatted I/O cannot be performed to unformatted files.

7. Invalid. By default, sequential access files are opened formatted. Unformatted I/O cannot be performed to formatted files.

8. Invalid. Either a file name or an i/o unit may be specified in an INQUIRE statement, but not both.

9. The contents of file 'out.dat' will be

```
&LOCAL_DATA
A =    -200.000000    -17.000000    0.000000E + 00    100.000000
30.000000
B =        -37.000000
C =    0.000000E + 00
/
```

Quiz 11–1

1. A pointer is a Fortran variable that contains the *address* of another Fortran variable or array. A target is an ordinary Fortran variable or array that has been declared with the TARGET attribute so that a pointer can point to it. The difference between a pointer and an ordinary variable is that a pointer contains the address of another Fortran variable or array, whereas an ordinary Fortran variable contains data.

2. A pointer assignment statement assigns the address of a target to a pointer. The difference between a pointer assignment statement and an ordinary assignment statement is that a pointer assignment statement assigns the address of a Fortran variable or array to a pointer, whereas an ordinary assignment statement assigns the value of an expression to the target pointed to by the pointer.

```
ptr1 = > var    ! Assigns address of var to ptr1
ptr1 = var      ! Assigns value of var to target of ptr1
```

3. The possible association statuses of a pointer are associated, disassociated, and undefined. When a pointer is first declared, its status is undefined. It may be associated with a target using a pointer assignment statement or an ALLOCATE statement. The pointer may be disassociated from a target by the NULLIFY statement, the DEALLOCATE statement, by assigning a null pointer to it in a pointer assignment statement, or by using the NULL() function (Fortran 95 only).

4. Dereferencing is the process of accessing the corresponding target when a reference to a pointer appears in an operation or assignment statement.

5. Memory may be dynamically allocated with pointers using the ALLOCATE statement. Memory may be deallocated using the DEALLOCATE statement.

6. Invalid. This is an attempt to use ptr2 before it is associated with a target.

7. Valid. This statement assigns the address of the target variable value to pointer ptr2.

8. Invalid. A pointer must be of the same type as its target.

9. Valid. This statement assigns the address of the target array array to pointer ptr4. It illustrates the use of POINTER and TARGET statements.

10. Valid, but with a memory leak. The first WRITE statement will print out an F because pointer ptr is not associated. The second WRITE statement will print out a T followed by the value 137 because a memory location was allocated using the pointer and the value 137 was assigned to that location. The final statement nullifies the pointer, leaving the allocated memory location inaccessible.

11. Invalid. These statements allocate a 10-element array using ptr1 and assign values to it. The address of the array is assigned to ptr2, and then the array is deallocated using ptr1. This step leaves ptr2 pointing to an invalid memory location. When the WRITE statement is executed, the results are unpredictable.

12. Valid. These statements define a derived data type containing a pointer and then declare an array of that derived data type. The pointer contained in each element of the array is then used to allocate an array, and each array is initialized. Finally, the entire array pointed to by the pointer in the fourth element is printed out, and the first element of the array pointed to by the pointer in the seventh element is printed out. The resulting output is

```
31  32  33  34  35  36  37  38  39  40
61
```

E

Quiz 13–1

1. The answer to this question is processor dependent.
2. The answer to this question is processor dependent.
3. An appropriate program follows.

```
PROGRAM cross_product
!
!  Purpose:
!     To take the cross product of two vectors a and b.
!
USE booklib
IMPLICIT NONE

REAL, DIMENSION(3) :: va = (/ 10., -2., 40. /)
REAL, DIMENSION(3) :: vb = (/  7., -10.,-4. /)
REAL, DIMENSION(3) :: vc

! Calculate cross product.
vc = cross_prod (va, vb)
WRITE (*,'(A,3(2X,F10.4))') ' The cross product is ', vc

END PROGRAM
```

The cross product of vectors va and vb is [408.0000 320.0000 -86.0000].

E